THE

FIRST FIFTY YEARS

OF

RELIEF SOCIETY

KEY DOCUMENTS
IN LATTER-DAY SAINT WOMEN'S HISTORY

THE

FIRST FIFTY YEARS

OF

RELIEF SOCIETY

KEY DOCUMENTS
IN LATTER-DAY SAINT WOMEN'S HISTORY

EDITED BY

Jill Mulvay Derr
Carol Cornwall Madsen
Kate Holbrook
Matthew J. Grow

THE CHURCH
HISTORIAN'S
PRESS

THE CHURCH HISTORIAN'S PRESS is an imprint of the Church History Department
of The Church of Jesus Christ of Latter-day Saints, Salt Lake City, Utah,
and a trademark of Intellectual Reserve, Inc.

www.churchhistorianspress.org

Art direction: Richard Erickson.
Cover and jacket design: Riley M. Lorimer and Sheryl Dickert Smith. Interior design: Richard Erickson.
Typography: Riley M. Lorimer.

Jacket image: Provo, Utah, Fourth Ward Relief Society Presidency. Left to right: Mary M. Boyden, Margaret
Watson, Delia Booth, Sara Eggertson Cluff. Photograph by Conkling Photography, Provo, Utah, ca. 1892.
Church History Library, Salt Lake City.

Library of Congress Cataloging-in-Publication Data

The first fifty years of Relief Society: key documents in Latter-day Saint women's history /
edited by Jill Mulvay Derr, Carol Cornwall Madsen, Kate Holbrook, [and] Matthew J. Grow.
pages cm
Includes bibliographical references and index.
ISBN 978-1-62972-150-7 (hardbound : alk. paper)
1. Relief Society (Church of Jesus Christ of Latter-day Saints)—History—19th century. 2. Mormon women—
History—19th century. I. Derr, Jill Mulvay, editor. II. Madsen, Carol Cornwall, 1930– editor.
III. Holbrook, Kate, editor. IV. Grow, Matthew J., editor.

BX8643.R38F57 2016   267'.449332—dc23   2015032416

Printed in the United States of America on acid-free paper.
10 9 8 7 6 5 4 3 2 1

Contents

The First Fifty Years of Relief Society

Reference Material

Detailed Contents

Part 1: 1830, 1842–1845

Part 2: 1854–1866

Part 3: 1867–1879

Part 4: 1880–1892

Illustrations

Textual Illustrations

Contextual Illustrations

Introduction

As Latter-day Saints prepared to leave Nauvoo, Illinois, in the early months of 1846 for their long trek to the West, clerks packed into one small box and one large box stacks of records, including Joseph Smith's journals and history, as well as minutes, ledgers, and letters from the Saints' sojourns in New York, Ohio, Missouri, and Illinois. These early accounts of the church's beginnings accompanied the Saints to their new home in the Mountain West and served as the foundation for the enduring community they established there. At least one important record made the journey outside the inventoried boxes. "A Book of Records. Containing the proceedings of The Female Relief Society of Nauvoo" traveled west with its primary author, Relief Society secretary Eliza R. Snow.[1] This treasured volume was crucial to the reconstitution and expansion of the Relief Society, the organization through which Latter-day Saint women ministered, in the last half of the nineteenth century. It is the foundational document in this collection.

Nineteenth-century Latter-day Saint women understood the significance of their records. Their individual and collective documents evidence a deep faith in the religion that emerged from the visions and revelations of Joseph Smith: The Church of Jesus Christ of Latter-day Saints, formally established in 1830.[2] Its members believed it to be the kingdom of God on earth, and they regarded its doctrine, ordinances, and authority structure as divinely revealed and essential to their spiritual salvation. Church membership was at once intensely personal and essentially communal, a system of belief that affected an individual's entire way of life. This volume examines Latter-day Saint women's temporal and spiritual activities, demonstrating how the church served as the reference point for their marriage and family life, church service, and civic engagement. The private and corporate records created by women illuminate

---

1. See Jill Mulvay Derr and Carol Cornwall Madsen, "Preserving the Record and Memory of the Female Relief Society of Nauvoo, 1842–92," *Journal of Mormon History* 35, no. 3 (Summer 2009): 89–95; Historian's Office Catalogs and Inventories, 1846–1904, CHL.

2. The church was initially known as the Church of Christ and received its current name in 1838. (See "Church of Jesus Christ of Latter Day Saints," in Dean C. Jessee et al., eds., *Journals, Volume 1: 1832–1839*, vol. 1 of the Journals series of *The Joseph Smith Papers*, ed. Dean C. Jessee et al. [Salt Lake City: Church Historian's Press, 2008], 463.)

their belief that the church both ennobled and challenged women, and their conviction that the church enriched their own relationship to the divine.

Church members believed that records established precedent and helped nourish faith. Both the Bible and the Book of Mormon, one of the Latter-day Saints' unique books of scripture, underscored the importance of keeping, preserving, and studying records. Before the formation of the Relief Society in 1842, the church's institutional records were largely created by and focused on the activities of the men who led the church. For example, Joseph Smith's revelations were recorded, edited, and published primarily through the efforts of his male counselors, scribes, and clerks; and official church minute books recorded the deliberations of the all-male presidencies, quorums, and councils that governed the church generally and locally. Latter-day Saint women had occasionally helped create official church records. Emma Smith, Joseph's wife, served as a Book of Mormon scribe and helped preserve the manuscript of the book as well as other important records.[3] Eliza R. Snow recorded epistles for Joseph Smith in a record book called the Book of the Law of the Lord.[4] Of course, women also kept personal records. Lucy Mack Smith, Joseph's mother, wrote a history of her family and church beginnings that is the only record for many of the events it documents,[5] and hundreds of Latter-day Saint women wrote letters, diaries, and reminiscences.

The establishment of the Female Relief Society of Nauvoo in March 1842 and the appointment of Eliza R. Snow as the organization's first secretary marked the beginning of institutional record keeping by and about Latter-day Saint women. The minutes Snow and other women kept of Relief Society meetings from 1842 through 1844 are the single most important document in this volume. In addition to chronicling members' beliefs and contributions, the Nauvoo minutes include sermons Joseph Smith delivered during six of the nine visits he made to the society in 1842. Containing the only recorded words he directed exclusively to the women of the church, the minutes were regarded as a sacred and prophetic record that provided the authorization and pattern for women's temporal and spiritual ministry.[6]

---

3. Linda King Newell and Valeen Tippetts Avery, *Mormon Enigma: Emma Hale Smith,* 2nd ed. (Urbana: University of Illinois Press, 1994), 79; Michael Hubbard MacKay et al., eds., *Documents, Volume 1: July 1828–June 1831,* vol. 1 of the Documents series of *The Joseph Smith Papers,* ed. Dean C. Jessee et al. (Salt Lake City: Church Historian's Press, 2013), xxx–xxxi (hereafter *JSP,* D1).

4. See Andrew H. Hedges et al., eds., *Journals, Volume 2: December 1841–April 1843,* vol. 2 of the Journals series of *The Joseph Smith Papers,* ed. Dean C. Jessee et al. (Salt Lake City: Church Historian's Press, 2011), 8, 131–133, 137–143, 143–150 (hereafter *JSP,* J2).

5. Lucy Mack Smith, History, 1844–1845, 18 books, CHL; Lucy Mack Smith, History, 1845, CHL.

6. See Document 1.2.

Willard Richards, Joseph Smith's clerk, gave Snow a book for keeping minutes of the meetings. Thereafter, she and her assistants kept a record during the two years the society functioned in Nauvoo. These minutes remained in Snow's possession through her tenure as Relief Society president in Utah Territory (1880–1887) and then passed to her successor, Zina D. H. Young (1888–1901), and in turn to her successor, Bathsheba W. Smith (1901–1910). Not until 1911, following Bathsheba Smith's death, did the volume become part of the collection of the church historian, finally joining the historical records boxed up in Nauvoo.[7] The minutes, then, were uniquely a women's record. For nearly seven decades they remained in women's possession. Excerpts were read in Relief Society meetings, celebrated at women's gatherings, and frequently published in the *Woman's Exponent,* a semimonthly newspaper edited by and for Latter-day Saint women from 1872 to 1914.[8] Excerpts were also published, after some revisions, in the official *History of the Church.*[9] Joseph Smith's six sermons to the Relief Society were repeatedly quoted to inspire women and to explain and legitimize their ministry. Snow described the volume as "a Treasure beyond Price."[10] Passages from the minutes have been quoted in numerous historical articles and books, but never before have the minutes been published in their entirety in print.[11]

This foundational record of the Female Relief Society of Nauvoo served as a constitution for the Relief Society, setting forth its purposes, structure, and procedures. In the initial organizational meeting, Joseph Smith stated that "the minutes of your meetings will be precedents for you to act upon— your Constitutio[n] and law."[12] Its role as constitution had particular significance during the reestablishment of the Relief Society in Utah beginning in 1867. Called by Brigham Young to assist in reconstituting the organization, Snow took the record she had preserved for more than two decades, carried it from

---

7. See source note at beginning of Document 1.2.

8. The *Woman's Exponent* published at least fifty articles related to the Nauvoo Relief Society—either extracts from the minutes, a review of its history, or reports of anniversary celebrations. (Derr and Madsen, "Preserving the Record and Memory of the Female Relief Society of Nauvoo," 106; see also Document 3.21.)

9. See Document 2.2.

10. Agnes S. Armstrong, Letter to the Editor, *Woman's Exponent,* Aug. 15, 1875, 4:42–43.

11. Images of the complete minutes were published in DVD format in Richard E. Turley Jr., ed., *Selected Collections from the Archives of the Church of Jesus Christ of Latter-day Saints,* 2 vols., 74 DVDs (Provo, UT: Brigham Young University Press, 2002). Images and a transcript of the complete minutes are also at josephsmithpapers.org.

12. Document 1.2, entry for Mar. 17, 1842.

ward to ward, and read to women and their bishops the account of the March 1842 organizational meeting so they could replicate the recorded pattern.[13]

The Nauvoo minute book also contributed to a record-keeping consciousness and became a model for local minute books in Utah. Title pages of some of the local minute books commenced in the late 1860s display format and wording copied from the title page of the Nauvoo minute book. In some instances, Snow wrote the title page or initial entries, revealing her deep commitment to maintaining the precedent established with the Nauvoo record.[14]

The minute book also taught women the significance of their records. The seriousness with which women kept minute books underscored the sense of permanence and importance they attributed to their Relief Society work as well as the written record of it. For example, the Relief Society minutes for the Salt Lake City Seventh Ward were kept initially in the 1850s in a very long and narrow account book, which was actually a newspaper subscription book. When the Relief Society was reorganized in 1868, the local women started to keep the minutes there again, and then they obtained a new minute book. In this big, thick minute book they recopied some of the previous meetings' minutes and continued to keep records of their meetings well into the 1890s.[15] These women esteemed their Seventh Ward minutes the same way Eliza R. Snow treasured the Nauvoo Relief Society minutes. Official organizations for children and young women, which the Relief Society nurtured, also kept minute books according to the same model. The commitment of women keeping records resulted in hundreds of official Relief Society records that are now preserved in the Church History Library in Salt Lake City, Utah.

In addition to these official minutes, thousands of other extant documents record and shed light on the history of the Relief Society in its first decades. Like the minutes, some of these records were also created in an ecclesiastical setting, such as reports of sermons given by women or men in church conferences, annual reports from local Relief Societies, and official letters from church leaders. Other records are public in nature. Examples include newspaper articles and editorials, political petitions and transcripts of speeches, and published poetry. Still other records are essentially personal, such as private correspondence, diary entries, and reminiscences.

----

13. See Document 3.6.

14. See, for example, Snow's titles pages in Thirteenth Ward, Salt Lake Stake, Thirteenth Ward Relief Society Records, 1854–1857, CHL; and Sixteenth Ward, Riverside Stake, Sixteenth Ward Relief Society Minutes and Records, 1868–1968, CHL.

15. Seventh Ward, Pioneer Stake, Seventh Ward Relief Society Minutes and Records, 1848–1922, CHL; see also Document 3.3.

The collection of documents published in this volume has been selected from among the thousands of available records to illustrate the development of the society across the first fifty years of its existence, beginning with the establishment of the Relief Society in 1842. The organization was suspended from 1845 to the mid-1850s, when attempts were made to organize the Relief Society on a congregational level in some areas of Utah Territory. A more general and permanent reorganization began in 1867, and the Relief Society's roles within the church structure and within women's lives expanded over the succeeding decades.

The seventy-eight documents in this collection thus represent the Relief Society—and through it, some of the broader patterns of the lives of Latter-day Saint women—from 1842 to 1892. The story these records tell is more institutional than personal, more collective than individual. But the public and private often merged in women's lives, so these documents illuminate various aspects of women's experience. The records give insight into the spiritual dimension of their lives, as women sought holiness and cultivated spiritual gifts; their ecclesiastical activities, as they ministered within the church structure through the Relief Society and other organizations; and their political, temporal, and social pursuits, as they sought to build what they viewed as the kingdom of God through actions as diverse as relieving the poor, running cooperative stores, and storing grain.

Seeking Holiness

In his addresses to the Female Relief Society of Nauvoo, Joseph Smith emphasized charity and purity. "Let your hearts expand— let them be enlarged towards others," he implored. At the same time he exhorted personal contrition. "All hearts must repent— be pure and God will regard them and bless them."[16] He entreated society members to become "separate from all the evils of the world, choice, virtuou[s] and holy."[17] Three decades later Eliza R. Snow delivered a similar message to women: "It is the duty of each one of us to be a holy woman."[18] Women's pursuit of holiness is a prominent motif in these documents as they testified and experienced spiritual manifestations and gifts.

---

16. Document 1.2, entry for Apr. 28, 1842.
17. Document 1.2, entry for Mar. 31, 1842.
18. Document 3.23. A broader "holiness movement" had also been spreading among other Christian denominations in the United States since the early 1800s, gaining particular favor among Methodist women. For example, see Phoebe Palmer, *The Way of Holiness, with Notes by the Way; Being a Narrative of Experience Resulting from a Determination to Be a Bible Christian* (New York: Piercy and Reed, 1843).

Women generally preached at Relief Society meetings and other women's gatherings, though on occasion male church leaders did so.[19] Just three months after he officially organized the church, Joseph Smith ordained his wife, Emma, to "expound Scriptures & exhort the Church."[20] As president of the Female Relief Society of Nauvoo, she exhorted women to "watch and pray," to "be ambitious to do good," to "deal frankly with each other," and to avoid "stirring up strife among ourselves and hardness and evil fee[l]ings."[21] Upon the reestablishment of the Relief Society in Utah Territory, Brigham Young appointed Eliza R. Snow to instruct Latter-day Saint women.[22] Many of the hundreds of sermons that Snow delivered between 1868 and her death in 1887 survive in women's local minute books and in the *Woman's Exponent.* These sources also contain counsel from other leading women and dozens of lesser-known women appointed locally as Relief Society officers "to instruct, to exhort, to strengthen, and to build up a holy people unto the Lord."[23]

Women frequently testified in their own meetings as well as in congregational fast meetings, generally held once a month. In an August 1843 meeting, one woman said she "stood a living wittness for Jesus of Nazareth knew he had pourd his Spirit upon her."[24] Latter-day Saints considered faith in and knowledge of Jesus Christ as the redeemer of humankind to be received from the Holy Spirit.[25] Many Latter-day Saint meetings, including Relief Society meetings, became sites for sharing this witness of the Spirit. They often spoke of the latter-day restoration of Jesus Christ's ancient church as one of the most significant blessings in their lives. "We are engaged in a good work, and the Principles that we have embraced are life and Salvation unto us," declared Margaret T.

---

19. Outside of the monthly fast meetings, nineteenth-century Latter-day Saint women rarely addressed mixed congregations. Notable exceptions were the first two women to speak in general conference: Lucy Mack Smith in 1845 and Zina D. H. Young in 1879. Nineteenth-century Latter-day Saint women did participate in missionary work to a limited degree. Married women sometimes accompanied their husbands on missions; the first unmarried women called to full-time missionary service were appointed in 1898. (Ronald W. Walker, "Lucy Mack Smith Speaks to the Nauvoo Saints," *BYU Studies* 32, nos. 1–2 [Winter and Spring 1992]: 276–284; "General Conference," *Deseret Evening News,* Oct. 8, 1879; George Q. Cannon, Apr. 6, 1898, in *Sixty-Eighth Annual Conference of the Church of Jesus Christ of Latter-day Saints* [Salt Lake City: Deseret News, 1898], 7; see also Catherine A. Brekus, *Strangers and Pilgrims: Female Preaching in America, 1740–1845,* Gender and American Culture [Chapel Hill: University of North Carolina Press, 1998].)
20. Document 1.1; see also Doctrine and Covenants 25:7.
21. Document 1.2, entries for Mar. 17 and Aug. 4, 1842.
22. See Document 3.5.
23. Document 4.8.
24. Document 1.2, entry for Aug. 5, 1843.
25. See, for example, Doctrine and Covenants 46:13.

Smoot in Salt Lake City in 1870.[26] The same year, at a Relief Society meeting in Nephi, Utah, President Amelia Goldsbrough "encouraged the sisters to faithfulness said each one must be saved for themselves . . . felt that she would never give up mormonism whatever she might be called to pass through."[27] Such testifying remained a key element of gatherings.

Women also regarded the Holy Spirit as the channel through which they might receive spiritual gifts as described in the New Testament and in Joseph Smith's revelations. In March 1842 Joseph Smith summarized these as "the gift of tongues, prophecy, revelation, visions, healing, interpretation of tongues, and so forth."[28] His April 28, 1842, sermon to Relief Society members, with 1 Corinthians chapters 12 and 13 as his text, addressed women's practice of these charismatic gifts of the Spirit.[29]

With respect to the gift of tongues, which some Saints had practiced since the early 1830s, Joseph Smith expressed both support and caution.[30] "Speak in tongues for your comfort," he advised, but not for doctrinal instruction.[31] During the difficult westward trek, small groups of women found consolation in speaking in and interpreting tongues and thereby set a precedent for later women's gatherings.[32] Latter-day Saint women and men continued to exercise this gift in the succeeding decades. "Several spoke in toungs the interpretat[ion] was splended," Jane Wilkie Hooper Blood wrote in 1883.[33] Yet the practice seems to have diminished as the first generation of Saints gradually died off. Eliza R. Snow mourned in 1880 that "there are many children, to say nothing of older people, who never even heard the gift of tongues."[34]

Nineteenth-century Latter-day Saint women particularly cherished the gift of healing, and it became closely associated with their ministry among the sick

---

26. Document 3.16.

27. Document 3.19.

28. Joseph Smith, "Church History," *Times and Seasons,* Mar. 1, 1842, 3:709, in Karen Lynn Davidson et al., eds., *Histories, Volume 1: Joseph Smith Histories, 1832–1844,* vol. 1 of the Histories series of *The Joseph Smith Papers,* ed. Dean C. Jessee et al. (Salt Lake City: Church Historian's Press, 2012), 500.

29. Document 1.2, entry for Apr. 28, 1842.

30. See Mark Lyman Staker, *Hearken, O Ye People: The Historical Setting of Joseph Smith's Ohio Revelations* (Salt Lake City: Greg Kofford Books, 2009), 175–191.

31. Document 1.2, entry for Apr. 28, 1842.

32. See Maureen Ursenbach Beecher, ed., *The Personal Writings of Eliza Roxcy Snow,* Life Writings of Frontier Women 5 (Logan: Utah State University, 2000), 176–180; Donna Toland Smart, ed., *Mormon Midwife: The 1846–1888 Diaries of Patty Bartlett Sessions,* Life Writings of Frontier Women 2 (Logan: Utah State University Press, 1997), 8, 77–79, 174, 380; and Jill Mulvay Derr et al., *Women of Covenant: The Story of Relief Society* (Salt Lake City: Deseret Book; Provo, UT: Brigham Young University Press, 1992), 13, 45, 68, 90, 429.

33. Document 4.3.

34. Relief Society Record, 1880–1892, CHL, Nov. 3, 1880.

and needy. As with speaking in tongues, healing by faith was practiced among women in evangelical congregations, whence many Latter-day Saint converts came. The fact that Mormon women did not initially agree about whether they should engage in the practice prompted Joseph Smith's April 28, 1842, sermon to the Relief Society on spiritual gifts. After remarking on speaking in tongues, he "offered instruction respecting the propriety of females administering to the sick by the laying on of hands— said it was according to revelation." "If the sisters should have faith to heal the sick," he stated, "let all hold their tongues."[35] A "Mrs. Chase" celebrated Smith's teaching: "If the sisters are faithful, the gifts of the gospel shall be with us, especially the gift of healing," she told members of the Relief Society a few months later.[36]

Latter-day Saints invoked the Bible in claiming healing as a sign that followed believers and as a gift of the Spirit.[37] Joseph Smith emphasized that such signs "should follow all that believe whether male or female."[38] Both men and women performed healing blessings by laying on hands and invoking the name of Jesus Christ. Over time, men who were ordained to priesthood office also increasingly invoked priesthood authority when they administered healing blessings. Women gave blessings of healing in Nauvoo, during the Saints' trek westward, and in Utah. They also gave blessings intended to renew commitment and to bolster flagging spirits in small female gatherings that promoted spirituality and sisterhood.

Joseph Smith's successors as church president, including Brigham Young, John Taylor, and Wilford Woodruff, also encouraged women's use of the gift of healing.[39] In 1880 as John Taylor set apart Zina D. H. Young as first counselor to Eliza R. Snow in the Relief Society general presidency, he assured her, "Thou shalt have the gift to heal the sick."[40] Earlier that year, Emmeline B. Wells in the *Woman's Exponent* described the close connections between the Relief Society and faith healing: "One of the strongest features of this remarkable organization is the cultivation of the gift of faith. That great power has been manifested under the hands of sisters in administering to the sick is a fact to which many can testify; and is not this one positive proof that the Lord

35. Document 1.2, entry for Apr. 28, 1842.
36. Document 1.2, entry for June 23, 1842. For a history of male and female Mormon ritual healings, see Jonathan A. Stapley and Kristine Wright, "The Forms and the Power: The Development of Mormon Ritual Healing to 1847," *Journal of Mormon History* 35, no. 3 (Summer 2009): 42–87; and Jonathan A. Stapley and Kristine Wright, "Female Ritual Healing in Mormonism," *Journal of Mormon History* 37, no. 1 (Winter 2011): 1–85.
37. 1 Corinthians 12:28, 30; Mark 3:14–15; 16:17–18.
38. Document 1.2, entry for Apr. 28, 1842.
39. See Document 4.8.
40. Document 4.5.

recognizes them and approves their labors in this direction? Is there anything more heavenly than to give comfort and relief to the sick and distressed? We think not."⁴¹

In addition to these blessings of health and comfort, Latter-day Saint women ritually washed and anointed one another before childbirth at a time of high maternal and infant mortality and sparse and questionable medical treatment. The practice emerged from women's experiences as midwives, as faith healers, and as officiators in temple ceremonies. Through this ritual, empathetic women pronounced a series of specific blessings upon the body to provide spiritual strength and emotional comfort. Zina D. H. Young told the Cache Valley Relief Society in 1886, "I wish to speak of the great privilege given to us to wash and anoint the sick and suffering of our sex. I would counsel every one who expects to become a mother to have this ordinance administered by some good faithful sister."⁴²

Latter-day Saint women and men believed that the blessings given by women for health and comfort, as well as the washings and anointings before childbirth, were performed by the power of faith. In 1880 the Quorum of the Twelve Apostles composed a circular letter that supported women's healing of the sick and outlined certain parameters. Women might "administer to all the sick or afflicted in their respective families, either by the laying on of hands, or by the anointing with oil in the name of the Lord: but they should administer in these sacred ordinances, not by virtue and authority of the priesthood, but by virtue of their faith in Christ."⁴³ Eliza R. Snow stated three years later, "Women can administer in the name of Jesus but not by virtue of the Priesthood the promise which Jesus made was to all not to either sex."⁴⁴

In the twentieth century, church leaders gradually and then exclusively emphasized the scriptural mandate to "call for the elders of the church" (James 5:14) and instructed members that it was more appropriate for men ordained to priesthood offices to give such blessings of healing or comfort. By the 1930s and 1940s, women's laying on of hands to heal the sick had become a rare rather than a common practice among Latter-day Saint women.⁴⁵

---

41. Document 4.1.

42. Logan Utah Cache Stake, Logan Utah Cache Stake Relief Society Minutes and Records, 1868–1973, CHL, vol. 2, Sept. 11, 1886.

43. Document 4.8.

44. Morgan Utah Stake, Morgan Utah Stake Relief Society Minutes and Records, 1878–1973, CHL, Apr. 28, 1883; see also Document 4.19.

45. Stapley and Wright, "Female Ritual Healing in Mormonism," 75–83.

Ministering with Authority

"The mission of the Latter-day Saints is to reform abuses which have for ages corrupted the world, and to establish an era of peace and righteousness. The Most High is the founder of this mission," Harriet Cook Young told women assembled in the tabernacle in Salt Lake City in 1870.[46] The documents in this collection show that Young and other Latter-day Saints believed Joseph Smith's accounts of divine revelation and heavenly visitations, including the appearances of ancient prophets and apostles who conferred upon him the authority to establish the church and administer ordinances. Saints believed that this ancient sacred authority, or priesthood, was restored to prepare the world for Christ's millennial reign and forward the salvation of humankind. According to their beliefs, this priesthood ordered, authorized, and sanctified the ecclesiastical structure and holy rites through which men and women ministered to their fellow Saints.

Distinct church offices emerged over time, as did an understanding of how the offices related to one another. For example, a circa April 1830 revelation named Joseph Smith an apostle and described the office of apostle, but the ordination of twelve men as apostles and the formation of the Quorum of the Twelve Apostles did not occur until five years later.[47] A July 1830 revelation to Joseph Smith regarding his wife, Emma, designated her "an Elect Lady" to be ordained to "expound Scriptures & exhort the Church."[48] As the twelve-year gap in Part 1 of this collection illustrates, Emma Smith did not fully undertake these roles until 1842, when she became president of the Female Relief Society of Nauvoo.

By organizing the Relief Society "after the pattern of the Church of Jesus Christ of Latter-day Saints," with a president and two counselors, Joseph Smith established the first church offices for women, and he counseled them "to administer in that authority which is confer'd on them."[49] He also provided for other officers to be selected when need arose: "If any Officers are wanted to carry out the designs of the Institution, let them be appointed and set apart, as

---

46. Document 3.13.

47. See Doctrine and Covenants 20; and "Apostle," in *JSP*, D1:495.

48. Document 1.1; see also Doctrine and Covenants 25:7; and Document 1.2, entry for Mar. 17, 1842.

49. Document 1.2, entry for Apr. 28, 1842. Eliza R. Snow wrote in 1868: "'The Female Relief Society of Nauvoo,' was organized after the pattern of the Church of Jesus Christ of Latter-day Saints, with a Presidentess, who chose two Counselors. These were ordained and set apart by the Priesthood, and were to fill those offices so long as they faithfully discharged the trust committed to them. This quorum was fully authorized to appoint such officers, committees and assistants as were requisite from time to time, either to fill permanent offices or to perform any temporary agency that circumstances might demand." (Document 3.6.)

Deacons, Teachers &c. are among us."[50] Previously, only men ordained to priesthood offices had filled leadership positions or associated in councils or quorums.[51]

The 1842 joining together of Latter-day Saint women under the direction of a women's presidency, commissioned to "preside just as the [First] Presidency, preside over the church,"[52] added a new dimension to the church's structure and to women's lives. The small circle of Nauvoo women who had initially laid plans for an independent sewing society set their design aside and embraced Joseph Smith's invitation to be organized "according to the order of God" and "connected with the priesthood."[53] Although the name women selected for their council, Female Relief Society, linked them with the female benevolent movement of the period, they also viewed themselves as "daughters of Zion" who felt "the popular Institutions of the day should not be our guide."[54]

Members of the Relief Society believed that the Melchizedek Priesthood (the higher of two orders of priesthood in the church) authorized and sanctified the offices they held. A revelation to Joseph Smith declared that the Melchizedek Priesthood "holds the right of presidency, and has power and authority over all the offices in the church in all ages of the world, to administer in spiritual things."[55] In 1868 Eliza R. Snow described the Relief Society as "an organization that cannot exist without the Priesthood, from the fact that it derives all its authority and influence from that source."[56] During his lifetime, Joseph Smith was the president of this priesthood, which his revelations also referred to as "the holy order."[57] Order was indeed an essential component, and Smith taught Relief Society women, as he also taught men, "the necessity of every individual acting in the sphere allotted him or her; and filling the several

---

50. Document 1.2, entry for Mar. 17, 1842.

51. *Quorum* became the preferred name for men associated in a priesthood office. These groups were usually composed of a specific number of members. By contrast, membership in the Female Relief Society of Nauvoo was limited to those found worthy but not to a specific number. (See Doctrine and Covenants 107, 124.)

52. Document 1.2, entry for Mar. 17, 1842.

53. Reynolds Cahoon, a member of the Nauvoo temple committee and husband of Relief Society member Thirza Cahoon, remarked to the Nauvoo women, "There are many Benevolent Societies abroad designd to do good but not as this ours is according to the order of God connected with the priesthood according to the same good principals." Sarah M. Kimball later recalled Joseph Smith saying, "I have desired to organise the Sisters in the order of the Priesthood I now have the key by which I can do it. . . . I will organise you in the Order of the Priesthood after the pattern of the church." (Document 1.2, entry for Aug. 13, 1843; Document 4.10.)

54. Document 1.2, entry for Mar. 17, 1842.

55. Doctrine and Covenants 107:8.

56. Document 3.6.

57. Doctrine and Covenants 77:11; 84:18.

offices to which they were appointed."[58] His appointment of Emma Smith as Relief Society president established a pattern for women's ministry in the church.

In 1842, the year Joseph Smith created a place for women in the developing ecclesiastical structure, he introduced sacred rites linked to the temple, or "House of the Lord," under construction on a Nauvoo hillside. A revelation to Joseph Smith in 1841 referred to this temple as "the house of the daughters of Zion."[59] Latter-day Saints saw the temple as a connecting place between heaven and earth where divine power would be bestowed, or endowed, upon the women and men who worshipped there. Temple ordinances, or covenant-making rituals associated with the Melchizedek Priesthood, included the "endowment" and "sealings" or marriages. The endowment consists of four key elements: a preparatory ceremonial washing and anointing, a course of instruction, the making of covenants, and a sense of divine presence.[60] Latter-day Saints believed that the temple rites were the means of fulfilling the mandate to become "a kingdom of priests, and an holy nation."[61] Joseph Smith spoke of this purpose in his March 31, 1842, address to the Relief Society, saying he would "make of this Society a kingdom of priests an [as] in Enoch's day— as in Pauls day."[62] His statement made an impression. Bathsheba W. Smith later recounted that Joseph Smith "wanted to make us, as the women were in Paul's day, 'A kingdom of priestesses.'" She then explained, "We have that ceremony in our endowments as Joseph taught."[63]

In 1843 Emma Smith became the first woman to receive the endowment, and she then administered those elements specifically relating to women to other women who, with their husbands, comprised the small group invited to officiate in temple rites prior to completion of the temple.[64] When the Nauvoo temple was ready for ordinance work in December 1845, more than a year after Joseph Smith's death, some of these endowed women, who were also members of the Relief Society, served among the first temple officiators who assisted in giving the ordinances to more than two thousand women before the exodus from Nauvoo in 1846. Sarah Pea Rich, one of these officiators, recalled

---

58. Document 1.2, entry for Apr. 28, 1842; see also Doctrine and Covenants 84:109.

59. Doctrine and Covenants 124:11.

60. Alma P. Burton, "Endowment," in *Encyclopedia of Mormonism,* ed. Daniel H. Ludlow, 5 vols. (New York: Macmillan, 1992), 2:454–456.

61. Exodus 19:6.

62. Document 1.2, entry for Mar. 31, 1842.

63. "Pioneer Stake," *Woman's Exponent,* July and Aug. 1905, 34:14.

64. See Volume Introduction to Nauvoo Journals, 1 May 1843–22 June 1844, in Andrew H. Hedges et al., eds., *Journals, Volume 3: May 1843–June 1844,* vol. 3 of the Journals series of *The Joseph Smith Papers,* ed. Ronald K. Esplin and Matthew J. Grow (Salt Lake City: Church Historian's Press, 2015), xxi.

how "we were to be there at 7 in the morning and remain untill work was done at ten or twelve o clock at night if necessary." She expressed gratitude for "the faith and knowledge that was bestowed upon us in that temple by the influence and help of the Spirit of the Lord."[65]

Only rarely do documents in this collection explicitly refer to the meaning of temple promises to women. Church members believed these ordinances were sacred and should not be exposed to the world. Yet women's profound connection to the temple pervaded their institutional and private lives. Temple ordinances sanctified their marriages and opened new opportunities for women to minister to one another.

Joseph Smith taught that the temple sealing united a husband and wife into the eternities and that this "new and everlasting covenant" of marriage was an "order of the priesthood."[66] Smith's associate, Newel K. Whitney, spoke of this when he addressed members of the Relief Society in May 1842, a few days after he received the endowment ordinance. Whitney stated: "In the beginning God created man male and female and bestow'd upon man certain blessings peculiar to a man of God, of which woman partook, so that without the female all things cannot be restor'd to the earth it takes all to restore the Priesthood."[67] A revelation to Smith promised faithful husbands and wives sealed in marriage an inheritance of heavenly "thrones, kingdoms, principalities, and powers, dominions," and "exaltation and glory in all things," including "a continuation of the seeds forever and ever."[68] Latter-day Saints believed that the temple sealing established earthly patriarchs and matriarchs who could not only engender life physically, but who could give life in a spiritual sense by teaching righteous principles and administering ordinances of salvation to others.[69] Records that speak of women sharing the priesthood with their husbands appear to refer to temple sealings.[70] Phebe Woodruff labeled this union as the "Patriarchal order of marriage": "We are sealed to our husbands for time and eternity, that we may dwell with them and our children in

---

65. Sarah P. Rich, Autobiography, 1885, CHL, 65–66.

66. Doctrine and Covenants 131:2.

67. Document 1.2, entry for May 27, 1842; Joseph Smith, Journal, May 4, 1842, in *JSP*, J2:53–54.

68. Doctrine and Covenants 132:19.

69. See Kathleen Flake, "The Emotional and Priestly Logic of Plural Marriage," *Leonard J. Arrington Mormon History Lecture Series,* no. 15 (Logan: Utah State University Press, 2010), 14; see also Carol Cornwall Madsen, "Mothers in Israel: Sarah's Legacy," in *Women of Wisdom and Knowledge: Talks Selected from the BYU Women's Conferences,* ed. Marie Cornwall and Susan Howe (Salt Lake City: Deseret Book, 1990), 179–201.

70. For example, Lucy Meserve Smith recalled casting out evil spirits "by virtue of the Holy Priesthood conferred upon me in common with my companion in the Temple of our God." (Document 2.4; see also Edward Hunter, in "Grain Meeting," *Woman's Exponent,* Dec. 1, 1877, 6:102.)

the world to come, which guarantees unto us the greatest blessing for which we are created."[71]

Latter-day Saints of that day also believed that sealings could include plural marriages, or the marriage of a man to more than one woman. During the era covered by this volume, Latter-day Saints practiced plural marriage. Indeed, polygamy, as it was commonly known, became a distinguishing characteristic of nineteenth-century Latter-day Saints, and particularly Latter-day Saint women. Plural marriage is nearly omnipresent in women's records because it forged their extended and overlapping family relationships and because it was central to the way they understood themselves as "a chosen generation, a royal priesthood, an holy nation, a peculiar people."[72]

The documents in this volume shed light on the development of plural marriage and its ramifications for women's collective experience. In Nauvoo, stating that he was acting upon revelation, Joseph Smith introduced the practice of plural marriage quietly among some of his trusted associates, including some members of the Relief Society.[73] Knowing the practice would be controversial and would create a stark distance between the Latter-day Saints and the rest of American society, Smith required confidentiality of participants. Plural marriage, known to many by rumor only, created significant divisions among the Saints in Nauvoo: those who engaged in plural marriage, and those who did not; those who supported it, and those who did not. Distrust and dissension within the church and opposition from outside critics fueled events leading to the 1844 mob murder of Joseph Smith. The Relief Society may have been a forum for expressing objections to plural marriage, a possibility that likely contributed to the cessation of Relief Society meetings following Joseph Smith's death.[74] In the West, plural marriage played a different role. Especially after the formal announcement of the practice in 1852, plural marriages were public knowledge with no attempt at secrecy. These marriages facilitated women's networks, and extended family connections became a framework onto which the Relief Society organization could be at least partially overlaid.

The Relief Society was also linked to Latter-day Saint temple ordinances in two ways that reinforced women's authority to minister. First, the temple rites that sealed husband and wife in marriage, monogamous or polygamous, often influenced the ecclesiastical relationship between women and men. For example, Emma Smith, as Joseph's wife, was the first president of the Relief Society.

---

71. Document 3.13.
72. 1 Peter 2:9.
73. See *JSP*, J2:xxiv–xxvii.
74. See Document 1.13.

In Utah, Eliza R. Snow, a widow of Joseph Smith who then married church president Brigham Young, became the next general Relief Society president. On a local level, a bishop sometimes operated in connection with his wife who had been appointed to serve as Relief Society president. (Protestant ministers and their wives often followed a similar pattern.) Ecclesiastical relationships based on this marriage model assumed that partners filled complementary roles. While Relief Society women accepted the authority of male church leaders and agreed not to "overstep the counsel"[75] of the bishop or stake president, they often operated in a somewhat separate sphere and could rely on informal family ties as well as the formal church organization to resolve problems. The move away from this husband-wife model by the late nineteenth century meant that these relationships between female and male church leaders became more hierarchical and more often defined by formal policies.

A second connection between the Relief Society and temple ordinances stemmed from Emma Smith's position as the first female officiator of temple rites, a position that prefigured the close temple association of her successors as Relief Society president, Eliza R. Snow, Zina D. H. Young, and Bathsheba W. Smith. Each of these women, like Emma Smith, served concurrently as Relief Society president and head of female temple officiators: Snow in the Endowment House (precursor to the temple) in Salt Lake City, and Zina Young and Bathsheba Smith in the Salt Lake temple. In these women, the ecclesiastical authority of the Relief Society president was coupled with the ritual authority of the leading female temple officiator. Snow was known by her contemporaries both as "a Priestess in the House of the Lord"[76] and as "President of all the Relief Societies in the Church."[77]

Various documents in this volume demonstrate how women and men negotiated issues of institutional authority within the framework of their belief in divine revelation and the sanctifying power of priesthood order and ordinances. From the time Joseph Smith extended church offices and temple privileges to women, questions emerged regarding the possibilities and limitations of their authority. Were women authorized to heal the sick? Were women intruding on the bishop's role as they assisted the poor?

---

75. Document 3.6.

76. "Pen Sketch of an Illustrious Woman," *Woman's Exponent,* Feb. 1, 1881, 9:131.

77. Weber Stake, Weber Stake Relief Society Minutes and Records, 1867–1968, CHL, vol. 6, p. 6. In the new pattern formalized in the 1920s, a husband and wife were called as temple president and temple matron, each appointed to lead male or female officiators in their specific temple. The Relief Society continued to have responsibility for distributing temple clothing until 1981. (Derr et al., *Women of Covenant,* 197–198, 248–249, 501n24.)

For instance, the 1880 appointment of a general presidency for the Relief Society[78] both permanently expanded women's offices and altered the relationship between the Relief Society and the organizations for young women and children. Emma Smith had served as the only Relief Society president in Nauvoo, but in reestablishing the Relief Society in Utah, Brigham Young called for individual ward Relief Societies with ward presidencies. In 1877, in connection with Young's broad effort to standardize the organization of wards and stakes, he appointed the first stake Relief Society presidency in Ogden to coordinate the work of the several ward societies.[79] Young's successor, John Taylor, worked with Eliza R. Snow to call stake-level Relief Society presidencies in other locales and to organize similar stake-level presidencies for the Young Ladies' Mutual Improvement and Primary Associations. These changes reflected church leaders' commitment to regularizing the stake and ward ecclesiastical structure throughout the church. As part of this movement toward greater formalization, members of the Quorum of the Twelve Apostles who had been serving as stake presidents were released to resume their duties in ministering to the general church rather than in a specific locale. Within this context, in 1880 John Taylor appointed three new presidencies at the general or churchwide level for the Relief Society, the Young Ladies' Mutual Improvement Association, and the Primary Association.[80]

With the establishment of these general presidencies, the three women-led organizations had leadership at all three ecclesiastical levels (ward, stake, and general) of church governance. The change also separated these organizations into distinct entities that operated less interdependently than before. The Relief Society had long exercised leadership over the affiliated organizations it had nurtured for younger women and children. Indeed, Relief Society presidents had often appointed and set apart the officers for these organizations. A letter issued by the church's First Presidency in 1880 indicated that this practice should not continue: "All ladies selected as presidents, should be blessed and set apart, by the President of the Stake, or by the Bishop of the Ward, wherein the branch society is organized."[81] This new standardized structure for women more fully integrated them with ward and stake priesthood councils. It gradually replaced the matriarchal network (with leaders such as "Aunt Eliza," "Aunt Zina," and "Aunt Emmeline") that had held the Relief Society and the

---

78. See Documents 4.4 and 4.5.

79. See Document 3.26; and William G. Hartley, "The Priesthood Reorganization of 1877: Brigham Young's Last Achievement," *BYU Studies* 20, no. 1 (Fall 1979): 3–38.

80. Document 4.4.

81. Document 4.8.

organizations for younger women and children together in a wide-reaching web forged by both formal and familial relationships.

In this setting of multiplying women's presidencies, the First Presidency and other church leaders emphasized that women's offices were not priesthood offices. John Taylor told those in attendance at the 1880 meeting during which he set apart Eliza R. Snow and her counselors as the Relief Society's general presidency that he had been present at the Nauvoo Relief Society organizational meeting and participated in the laying on of hands to ordain the Nauvoo officers. "The ordination then given did not mean the confering of the Priesthood upon those sisters yet the sisters hold a portion of the Priesthood in connection with their husbands," Taylor explained. Snow and Bathsheba Smith then "stated that they so understood it in Nauvoo and have always looked upon it in that light."[82] For much of the century, the words "ordain" and "set apart" were often used interchangeably (and sometimes together) in connection with women being appointed to offices in the Relief Society. For instance, when Taylor laid his hands on Snow at the 1880 meeting, he stated, "I set thee apart to preside over the Relief Societies . . . and I confer on thee this power and authority and ordain thee to this office."[83] Over time, the term "ordain" came to be associated only with the laying on of hands to ordain a man to a priesthood office. Setting apart, on the other hand, was associated with other church offices, including women's offices.

As seen in this reestablishment of a Relief Society general presidency in 1880, the documents in this collection provide glimpses of the development of the increasingly formal ecclesiastical structure that became the church's mode of operation in the late nineteenth and, especially, the twentieth centuries. The hierarchy of presidencies, councils, and offices, previously interwoven with extended familial networks, gradually largely supplanted those networks. This transition was well under way when, following a decade of intense antipolygamy legislation and prosecution, the church announced in 1890 its intention to end the practice of plural marriage, which had played a major role in forging and reinforcing familial networks. A functional formal ecclesiastical structure aided the slow and difficult move away from plural marriage and also facilitated church growth and more friendly relations with people and institutions outside the church. Indeed, in the fall of 1892 the Relief Society became a legally incorporated entity, in part to support its new connection with the national and international councils of women, while still maintaining its place as part of the church structure. Latter-day Saint women "administer[ed] in that

---

82. Document 4.5.

83. Document 4.5.

authority which is confer'd on them"[84] in the church's ecclesiastical structure and in the sacred ordinances performed in temples, though the parameters of their authority changed over time. As these documents attest, women both initiated and accommodated such changes. They created organizations for young women and children, and they developed programs to provide charitable relief and other service within their communities and the church. Women also adapted to the ecclesiastical formalization that modified some past practices. They viewed themselves not as an independent sisterhood but as part of a larger kingdom, grounded in prophetic revelation and priesthood authority. "In the Church and Kingdom of God," Eliza R. Snow emphasized, "the interests of men and women are the same; man has no interests separate from that of women, however it may be in the outside world, our interests are all united."[85]

Building the Kingdom

Joseph Smith charged the Relief Society in Nauvoo not only with a spiritual ministry, "to save souls," but also with a temporal one, to "relieve the poor."[86] Latter-day Saints, though, saw this distinction between spiritual and temporal as a false dichotomy; temporal actions that contributed to the building of the kingdom of God, they believed, were essentially spiritual. In their view, braiding straw, spinning silk, and operating the cash register at a Relief Society store were all spiritual activities. Records in this volume show the diversity of women's contributions. In the early years of the Relief Society in Nauvoo and territorial Utah, members provided charitable relief for impoverished Latter-day Saints and recent immigrants, as well as for American Indian women and children. After the reestablishment of the Relief Society in 1867, women's efforts became increasingly elaborate, including grain storage, silk production, medical training, and the establishment of a hospital.

Relief Society women in Utah considered the home industries that Brigham Young assigned them, particularly in the 1860s and 1870s, to be an extension of Joseph Smith's charge to assist in the spiritual and economic well-being of the community.[87] Under the direction of Eliza R. Snow and ward Relief Society presidents, the organization implemented programs to help the Saints avoid dependence on outside manufacturers and merchants and enable the Saints to become self-sustaining. Beginning with the Fifteenth Ward in

---

84. Document 1.2, entry for Apr. 28, 1842.

85. "R.S. Reports," *Woman's Exponent*, June 1, 1875, 4:2.

86. Document 1.2, entry for June 9, 1842.

87. See, for example, remarks by Zina D. H. Young, Minutes, June 18, 1875, *Woman's Exponent*, July 15, 1875, 4:27.

1868, many Relief Societies built meeting halls, some of which included stores. As with many of the structures, the design of the Fifteenth Ward Hall was patterned after that of Joseph Smith's red brick store in Nauvoo, where the Relief Society was first organized, with a store on the main level and a meeting or work room upstairs. For those who had lived in Nauvoo, this design emphasized the link between Relief Society and mercantile activity.[88] The stores sold a variety of goods, including religious books, tailored and ready-made clothing, woolen goods, bedspreads, rag carpets, hats, and medicines. Mormon women and girls themselves crafted many of the materials they sold. They braided straw hats, baskets, and rugs; produced silk for fine apparel and decorative items; and sold some of their home-crafted articles on commission. Brigham Young wanted Relief Society women to run the stores and to use the profits to benefit various programs within the church.[89] For instance, funds raised by the Weber County Relief Society supported immigration of converts, missions, the construction of the Logan and Manti temples, and the Relief Society's hospital.[90]

In the view of Relief Society members, the charge to build the kingdom included establishing organizations for young women and for children. The Young Ladies' Mutual Improvement Association began with the strong encouragement of Brigham Young, who worried about outside moral influences and an increase in imported products that would impact the Saints with the completion of the transcontinental railroad in 1869. Initially, he encouraged his older daughters to meet in his home and gain instruction from more experienced women like Eliza R. Snow and Mary Isabella Horne. At the same time, he called for a churchwide retrenchment in which well-to-do members were to simplify their habits, particularly in food and dress. He encouraged lighter meals with fewer courses and more practical clothing with fewer adornments. The Young Ladies' Mutual Improvement Association began in 1870 as part of the women's Retrenchment Association and then developed into a separate organization.[91]

Aurelia Spencer Rogers initiated the idea of an organization for children nearly a decade later in 1878. Rogers thought young boys were behaving poorly and wanted, for the sake of both the community and the girls destined to

---

88. Jennifer Reeder, "'To Do Something Extraordinary': Mormon Women and the Creation of a Usable Past" (PhD diss., George Mason University, 2013), 150–157.

89. Brigham Young, Apr. 6, 1869, in *Journal of Discourses,* 26 vols. (Liverpool: Various publishers, 1855–1886), 12:374–375; see also Leonard J. Arrington, *Great Basin Kingdom: An Economic History of the Latter-day Saints, 1830–1900* (Cambridge, MA: Harvard University Press, 1958), 305–306.

90. History of the Relief Society in Weber County, 1887, Richards Family Collection, 1837–1961, CHL.

91. See Documents 3.15, 3.16, and 3.18.

marry those boys, to train them up to be more respectful and responsible. After learning of the idea from Rogers, Eliza R. Snow obtained the support of the church's First Presidency, named the organization "Primary," and went about establishing the new organization throughout the church.[92]

Records also demonstrate the way Relief Society members reacted to threats against the church. The nineteenth-century Relief Society operated in a world where women were assuming an expanded public role. In 1842, when the Relief Society was organized, American women were active in early abolition and reform efforts in the United States. The Seneca Falls Convention six years later is often seen as the beginning of an organized women's rights movement. During the last half of the nineteenth century, American women were increasingly active politically at local, state, and national levels. At the same time, Relief Society women expanded the public aspects of their work, particularly after the reestablishment of the Relief Society in Utah. Female Latter-day Saints took a more active role in public speaking and writing, which significantly increased their visibility and political influence. When the Utah territorial legislature granted women suffrage in 1870, women obtained a new channel for pursuing their work. Beginning that year, the Relief Society mobilized women in mass meetings to protest proposed antipolygamy legislation that threatened Latter-day Saint domestic life and that would eventually target woman suffrage in Utah. Hundreds of women enthusiastically embraced the opportunity to represent themselves and their opinions. When protesting these laws, Relief Society members worked to transform the national image of Latter-day Saint women from downtrodden and abused to proactive and empowered. Besides the mass meetings, the *Woman's Exponent* provided the central forum for this expression.

During this period, as part of their suffrage efforts, Latter-day Saint women forged connections with the broader women's movement. Beginning in the mid-1870s, Latter-day Saint women corresponded with leaders of the national movement for woman suffrage, supported suffrage petitions, and sent representatives to the East to create and maintain connections with the suffrage movement. While the controversy over plural marriage often made Latter-day Saint women less welcome in some national women's organizations, the National Woman Suffrage Association always supported their voting

---

92. See Document 3.30.

rights.⁹³ *Exponent* articles appeared in national women's newspapers, and the *Exponent* reprinted articles from those papers as well.⁹⁴

During this formative period, as women sewed clothing, tended the sick, gathered wheat, expanded their organizations, published a newspaper, and fought legal battles, they believed they were doing their part toward establishing God's kingdom, and they referred often to the Nauvoo minutes to help define their work and their identity as female saints of the latter days.

———— ⸘ ————

This book is divided into four parts, each with a historical introduction and a group of documents demonstrating the activities of the Relief Society during a particular historical era. Part 1 contains the 1830 revelation to Emma Smith and thirteen documents related to the Relief Society from 1842 to 1845, particularly the Nauvoo Relief Society minutes. Part 2 features six documents exploring the tentative reestablishment of Relief Society organizations at a local level in Utah during the 1850s and 1860s. Part 3 contains thirty documents from 1867, when Brigham Young called for the reorganization of the Relief Society, through the late 1870s. The final section includes twenty-eight documents from 1880, when Eliza R. Snow was appointed as the first general Relief Society president since Emma Smith, through the fiftieth anniversary of the organization in 1892. Each document includes a bibliographic note, a historical introduction, and a transcript of the text that has been carefully verified three times. In addition, footnotes explaining the historical context and any textual issues accompany each document.

The first documents in this book—the 1830 revelation to Emma Smith and the Nauvoo minutes—and the final document, an account of the Relief Society's Jubilee celebration in 1892, serve as bookends for the collection and demonstrate how the Relief Society's collective memory of its history defined the organization throughout the nineteenth century. The Jubilee featured Sarah M. Kimball, Emmeline B. Wells, Bathsheba W. Smith, and Mary Isabella Horne sharing their memories from across the prior fifty years and providing a sense for what was most important to them.⁹⁵ Sometimes, their

93. See Joan Iverson, "The Mormon-Suffrage Relationship: Personal and Political Quandaries," *Frontiers: A Journal of Women Studies* 11, nos. 2–3 (1990): 8–16; and Lola Van Wagenen, "Sister-Wives and Suffragists: Polygamy and the Politics of Woman Suffrage, 1870–1896" (PhD diss., New York University, 1994).

94. See Carol Cornwall Madsen, "'Remember the Women of Zion': A Study of the Editorial Content of the *Woman's Exponent,* A Mormon Woman's Journal" (master's thesis, University of Utah, 1977), 8–10, 26; and Document 3.21.

95. See Document 4.28.

facts were not quite right. For example, Wells gave the wrong date for Eliza R. Snow's reorganization of the Relief Societies. In addition, the history they presented left out episodes of disconnection and conflict. Instead they emphasized strength, harmony, and continuity. Theirs was a sacred worldview and their narrative of women's efforts told of the hand of God in their achievements. Although the following documents sometimes complicate the narrative of harmony and continuity, they also illuminate how this sacred worldview informed Mormon women's lives in diverse times and places.

By the time of the Jubilee, the Relief Society was on a secure enough foundation to celebrate a half-century of growth and achievement. The grand Jubilee commemorative exercises were held in the tabernacle in Salt Lake City on March 17, the date of the society's organization in Nauvoo. The tabernacle was adorned with flags, banners, flowers, portraits of the first three Relief Society presidents, and a representation of the key that Joseph Smith said he had turned to the women fifty years before. Seven of the central presidency and board members in 1892 had been part of the society in Nauvoo. Male church leaders joined the celebration. Several of them, along with Relief Society leaders, addressed the audience, lauding the work of the past and anticipating the promise of the future. Participants read both the revelation given to Emma Smith in 1830 and portions of the Nauvoo Relief Society minutes. These foundational documents continued to affirm women's authority and stewardship within the church's ecclesiastical structure as well as its most sacred ordinances. "This momentous event for woman," wrote the Relief Society general presidency, "causes us to view with wonder the past, with gratitude the present and with faith the future."[96] The Jubilee made a public statement that whatever changes or expansion the Relief Society would face to remain viable in an ever-changing world, it would retain its unbreakable ties with the past in some form or another.

For nearly thirty more years that link would be clearly visible. The first five presidents of the Relief Society, concluding with Emmeline Wells, had known Joseph Smith and had participated in the Nauvoo experience. Not only in their presence but in their programs and pronouncements they evoked the spirit and ideals of that first Relief Society. As these living links with Nauvoo gradually left the scene, a new generation of women, whose experience and vision were rooted firmly in the twentieth century, took their place. Their vision was to the future, not the past. For them, Nauvoo was history, not memory. At the passing of Wells in 1921, Susa Young Gates, one of the younger board members,

---

96. Zina D. H. Young, Jane S. Richards, and Bathsheba W. Smith, "Letter of Greeting," *Woman's Exponent,* Jan. 15 and Feb. 1, 1892, 20:108.

noted that with her death Nauvoo faded quietly into history, "dear, but very distant."[97] For later generations of Latter-day Saint women the story of the founding of the Relief Society became iconic, and the ubiquitous March 17 anniversary celebrations featured only brief extracts from the minutes, if any.[98]

The Nauvoo record itself has remained largely unseen and unread for nearly a century. The continuing story of the nineteenth-century Relief Society, recorded in hundreds of local minute books by thorough and conscientious secretaries and in thousands of other documents, is likewise largely undiscovered and untold. Together, the Nauvoo minutes and the other documents in this selection demonstrate how Joseph Smith and other Latter-day Saints envisioned new possibilities for women within Latter-day Saint organization, belief, and practice, and how women made meaning and helped create permanence for their collective ministry.

---

97. Susa Young Gates, "Our President Emeritus, Emmeline B. Wells," *Relief Society Magazine* 8, no. 7 (July 1921): 417.

98. Derr and Madsen, "Preserving the Record and Memory of the Female Relief Society of Nauvoo," 113–114.

Editorial Method

This volume presents verbatim transcripts of seventy-eight documents that were selected from among thousands of available records to illustrate the development of the Relief Society across the first fifty years of its existence. These transcripts were prepared largely according to the editorial procedures developed by the Joseph Smith Papers Project.

Version Selection

For many of the documents included in this volume, multiple early versions exist. For example, the report of a discourse may have been published in both the daily and the weekly editions of the *Deseret News.* The editors have usually selected the earliest known extant version for inclusion in this volume, without necessarily mentioning other available versions. Annotation in this volume points out exceptions to this general practice as well as significant variations between relevant early versions.

In cases where an original document contains material not relevant to a study of the Relief Society for this period (such as a sermon or a personal memoir covering a variety of subjects), the relevant material is presented herein as an excerpt. In all such cases, the transcript is clearly identified as an excerpt and ellipsis points are employed to show where material was omitted. Otherwise, the transcripts in this volume are unabridged.

The documents are arranged in chronological order by creation date, except that the handful of reminiscent accounts are placed where their content is most relevant.

Rules of Transcription

To ensure accuracy in representing the texts, transcripts were verified three times against either the original documents or copies, each time by a different reader or pair of readers.

The approach to transcription employed in this volume is a conservative style of what is known as "expanded transcription." The transcripts render most words letter by letter as accurately as possible, preserving the exact spelling of the originals. This includes incomplete words, variant spellings of personal names, repeated words, and idiosyncratic grammatical constructions. The transcripts also preserve substantive revisions made by the original scribes.

Canceled words are typographically rendered with the strikethrough bar, while inserted words are enclosed within angle brackets. Cancellations and insertions are also transcribed letter by letter when an original word was changed to a new word simply by canceling or inserting letters at the beginning or end of the word—such as "sparingly" or "attend⟨ed⟩". However, for cases in which an original word was changed to a new word by canceling or inserting letters in the middle of the word, to improve readability the original word is presented stricken in its entirety, followed by the revised word in its entirety. For example, if a scribe revised "falling" to "failing" by canceling the first "l" and inserting an "i", the revision would be transcribed as "~~falling~~ ⟨failing⟩" instead of "fal⟨i⟩ling". Insubstantial cancellations and insertions—those used only to correct spelling and punctuation—are silently emended, and only the final spelling and punctuation are reproduced.

The transcription of punctuation differs from the original in a few other respects. Dashes of various lengths are standardized to a consistent pattern. Where a scribe used short vertical marks to identify superscript letters, the letters are rendered as superscript but the marks are not reproduced. In some cases of repetitive punctuation, only the final mark or final intention is transcribed while any other characters are silently omitted. Flourishes and other decorative inscriptions are not reproduced or noted. When the original document sets off a quotation by using quotation marks at the beginning of each line that contains quoted matter, the quotation is formatted as a block quote and the original quotation marks are not reproduced. Punctuation is never added silently.

Incorrect dates and other errors of fact are left to stand. The intrusive *sic,* sometimes used to affirm original misspelling, is never employed, although where words or phrases are especially difficult to understand, editorial clarifications or corrections are inserted in brackets. Correct spellings of personal names are supplied in brackets the first time each incorrect name appears in a document (unless the correct name cannot be determined). Where a personal name is incomplete in the original document, enough additional information is supplied in brackets to allow the reader to find the full name in the biographical directories that accompany this volume (see additional discussion under "Annotation Conventions" below).

Some handwriting in the documents is difficult to decipher. Where capitalization, spelling, or punctuation is ambiguous, deference is given to the scribe's usual practice. Where that is ambiguous, modern convention is favored.

Formatting is standardized. Original paragraphing is retained, except that in journal and minute entries the first paragraph of the entry is run in with the original dateline. Standardized editorial datelines—typographically distinguishable from the text—have been added before entries in minute books and other multiple-entry documents. All paragraphs are given in a standard format, with indention regularized and with empty lines between paragraphs omitted. Extra space between words or sentences is not captured unless it appears the scribe left a blank space as a place holder to be filled in later. Block quotations of letters, minutes, and other similar items within the texts are set apart with block indentions, even when such items are not set off in the original. Horizontal rules and other separating devices inscribed or printed in the original are not reproduced. Line ends are neither typographically reproduced nor symbolically represented. End-of-line hyphens are not transcribed, and there is no effort to note or keep a record of such hyphens. This leaves open the possibility that the hyphen of an ambiguously hyphenated compound escaped transcription or that a compound word correctly broken across a line ending without a hyphen is mistakenly transcribed as two words. As many end-of-line hyphens have been editorially introduced in the transcripts, a hyphen appearing at the end of a line may or may not be original to the document.

In transcripts of printed sources, typeface, type size, and spacing have been standardized. Characters set upside down are silently corrected. Printers sometimes made changes to the text, such as to correct spelling mistakes or replace damaged type, after printing had already begun, meaning that the first copies to come off the press may differ from later copies in the same print run. No attempt has been made to analyze more than one copy of the printed texts transcribed here, aside from sometimes consulting another copy when the one used for transcription is indeterminable or ambiguous.

Except where explicitly noted in annotation, redactions and other changes made on a document after the original production of the text are not transcribed, nor are labeling and other forms of archival marking.

Transcription Symbols

The following symbols are used to transcribe and expand the text:

[roman]   Brackets enclose editorial insertions that expand, correct, or clarify the text. This convention is frequently applied to the abbreviated or incorrect spelling of a personal name, such as L. [Louisa] G. Richards. Obsolete or ambiguous abbreviations are expanded with br[acket]s. Bracketed editorial insertions also provide reasonable reconstructions of badly miss[p]elled worsd [words]. Missing or illegible words may be supplied within brackets when the supplied word is based on textual or contextual evidence. Bracketed punctuation is added only when necessary to follow complex wording. All brackets in this volume were supplied by the editors of this volume, unless otherwise noted.

[roman?]	A question mark is added to conjectured editorial insertions, such as where an entire word was [accidentally?] omitted and where it is difficult to maintain the sense of a sentence without some editorial insertion.
[*illegible*]	An illegible word is represented by the italicized word [*illegible*] enclosed in brackets.
◊	An illegible letter or other character within a partially legible word is rendered with a diamond. Repeated diamonds represent the approximate number of illegible characters (for example: sto◊◊◊◊s).
[p. x]	Bracketed editorial insertions indicate the end of an originally numbered page, regardless of the location of the page number on the original page. No page indicator is given for the last page of a document if the document was transcribed from a multiple-entry source (such as an article from a newspaper or a minute entry from a minute book) and if there is text following the featured document on that same page.
[p. [x]]	Bracketing of the page number itself indicates that the page was not originally numbered and that the number of the page is editorially supplied.
underlined	Underlining is typographically reproduced. <u>Individually</u> <u>underlined</u> <u>words</u> are distinguished from <u>passages underlined with one continuous line</u>.
superscript	Superscription is typographically reproduc^{ed}.
~~canceled~~	A single horizontal strikethrough bar is used to indicate any method of cancellation: strikethrough, cross-out, wipe erasure, knife erasure, overwriting, or other methods. ~~Individually~~ ~~canceled~~ ~~words~~ are distinguished from ~~passages eliminated with a single cancellation~~. Characters individual~~ly~~ canceled at the begin~~ning~~ or end of a word are distinguished from ~~words canceled in their entirety~~.
⟨inserted⟩	Insertions in the text—whether interlinear, intralinear, or marginal—are enclosed in angle brackets. Letter⟨s⟩ and other characters individual⟨ly⟩ insert⟨ed⟩ at the beginning or end of a word are distinguished from ⟨words⟩ inserted in ⟨their⟩ entirety.
TEXT	The word TEXT begins textual footnotes describing significant details not comprehended by this scheme of symbolic transcription.
		A line break artificially imposed in an original document is rendered as a vertical line in textual notes.

Annotation Conventions

The documents in this volume do not present a unified narrative. Annotations—including historical introductions and footnotes—supply background and context to help readers better understand and use the documents. The aim of the annotation is to serve scholars and students of Mormon history, women's history, and American religious history generally, whose familiarity with these fields may vary widely. Each document receives its own introduction, which is intended to establish the historical context. While these introductions may include cross-references to information found elsewhere in the volume, they are intended to serve as stand-alone explanations, meaning that a certain amount of repetition occurs throughout the various introductions.

Sources are cited in full the first time they appear in a document, after which a short citation form is generally used within the notes in that particular document. Citations to the Book of Mormon and other Latter-day Saint scriptures are usually referenced to modern editions. The names of two frequently cited repositories are abbreviated in citations: Church History Library, The Church of Jesus Christ of Latter-day Saints, Salt Lake City (CHL); and Family History Library, The Church of Jesus Christ of Latter-day Saints, Salt Lake City (FHL). As each document herein is numbered, document numbers rather than document names are used in internal cross-references.

Naturally, many terms with specialized meaning in this period of Mormon history appear in the texts and annotation. While some of these terms may be explained or defined in this volume, a working familiarity with the terminology has been assumed. Researchers seeking additional information on Mormon terminology may especially benefit by consulting the glossary on josephsmithpapers.org and the *Encyclopedia of Mormonism,* online at eom.byu.edu.

The names of more than two thousand individuals appear in these documents. Most of them have been identified through extensive research. Roughly four hundred women and men who play more prominent roles in the documents receive a short biography included in the back of this volume. The sources for these biographical sketches are available in the biographical directory published online at churchhistorianspress.org. The online directory also provides brief biographical information—typically full name, birth place and date, names of parents, and death place and date—for almost all the other individuals named in the documents in this volume.

The back matter of this volume also includes a chart identifying the women who served as general officers of the Relief Society, Young Ladies' Mutual Improvement Association, and Primary Association during the time period covered by this volume.

THE FIRST FIFTY YEARS
OF RELIEF SOCIETY

KEY DOCUMENTS
IN LATTER-DAY SAINT WOMEN'S HISTORY

PART 1: 1830, 1842–1845

Women and men who embraced Latter-day Saint theology sought to become a "pure people," "a kingdom of priests," and a "holy nation" worthy to build a literal city of Zion where Jesus Christ would rule after his Second Coming.[1] Alone and in families, these Latter-day Saints gathered together in communities in upstate New York, and later in Ohio, Missouri, and Illinois. Devout brothers and sisters opened their homes for meetings and donated their means and land to the emerging church. Joseph Smith gradually elaborated the church's organizational structure and ordinances, a process that culminated during the early 1840s when Saints settled in and around the city of Nauvoo, located on the banks of the Mississippi River in western Illinois.

In Nauvoo, women acquired new organizational responsibilities through the establishment of the Relief Society and participated with men in temple ordinances, the faith's highest rituals. These women believed that their full integration into "the priviliges & blessings & gifts of the priesthood," as Joseph Smith told the Relief Society, was essential to the complete restoration of the primitive gospel as taught by Jesus Christ and his apostles.[2] In Nauvoo in the 1840s and in succeeding decades, they built upon the foundation of Smith's revelations to envision and understand their sacred labors in Zion. Part 1 contains early documents that proved formative to this process.

Strong, supportive women surrounded Joseph Smith in his family, including his mother, Lucy Mack Smith, and his wife, Emma Hale Smith, who served as his first scribe when he translated the Book of Mormon. In July 1830 Joseph dictated a revelation addressed to Emma about her role in the fledgling church (Document 1.1). The revelation, canonized in 1833 as part of the Book

---

1. Doctrine and Covenants 100:16; Exodus 19:6; Doctrine and Covenants 124:118; Articles of Faith 1:10; 1 Peter 2:9; see also A. D. Sorensen, "Zion," in *Encyclopedia of Mormonism,* ed. Daniel H. Ludlow, 5 vols. (New York: Macmillan, 1992), 4:1624–1626.

2. Joseph Smith, Journal, Apr. 28, 1842, in Andrew H. Hedges et al., eds., *Journals, Volume 2: December 1841–April 1843,* vol. 2 of the Journals series of *The Joseph Smith Papers,* ed. Dean C. Jessee et al. (Salt Lake City: Church Historian's Press, 2011), 52 (hereafter *JSP,* J2).

of Commandments—the first published collection of Joseph Smith's revelations—recognized Emma's gifts, gave her specific assignments, and promised that she would be ordained "to expound Scriptures & exhort the Church." It is the only one of Joseph's canonized revelations directed specifically to an individual woman.

Twelve years later, in 1842, the Female Relief Society of Nauvoo was organized. Joseph Smith's remarks at six of their meetings were included in the society's minutes, formally titled "A Book of Records. Containing the proceedings of The Female Relief Society of Nauvoo" (Document 1.2). At the group's first meeting, when Emma Smith was elected president of the society by the women, Joseph invoked the July 1830 revelation as the mandate for assigning her new responsibilities. He stated that her new position would be the means of fulfilling promises pronounced in the 1830 revelation, including that "not she alone, but others, may attain to the same blessings."[3] Thus, these two records—the 1830 revelation for Emma Smith and the Relief Society "Book of Records," or Nauvoo Relief Society Minute Book—became permanently linked as complementary and foundational documents. Both address women's relationship to God as well as their spiritual and temporal responsibilities to their families and the religious community. The twelve other documents in Part 1, dating from 1842 to 1845, demonstrate how a new degree of institutional inclusion for women introduced new possibilities as well as new tensions in the 1840s.

The years between the 1830 revelation for Emma Smith and the 1842 establishment of the Relief Society were a defining period for the church. Moving from its New York beginnings to Ohio in early 1831, the church then pressed into Missouri in summer 1831 while retaining a core in Ohio; after pressure for most members to leave Ohio in early 1838 and then a violent expulsion by Missouri militia in winter 1838–1839, the church reassembled most of its members in western Illinois. Church membership grew from a few hundred at the end of 1830 to an estimated fifteen thousand by the end of 1845. About a third of those members lived outside Nauvoo and its surrounding communities.[4] During these years, Joseph Smith's revelations established the form and officers of the church organization, the areas of authority of its leaders and workers, and a foundation of church doctrine, and emphasized the need for unity and harmony among the members.

---

3. Document 1.2, entry for Mar. 17, 1842.

4. Dean May, "A Demographic Portrait of the Mormons, 1830–1980," in *The New Mormon History: Revisionist Essays on the Past,* ed. D. Michael Quinn (Salt Lake City: Signature Books, 1992), 121–124.

Women actively contributed to the Latter-day Saint community as it expanded and relocated. They fed and sheltered new arrivals; some wives accompanied their husbands on missions.[5] In Kirtland, Ohio, where the first temple was built, women sewed and mended clothing for those who constructed it, and they made carpets and curtains for the interior of the temple or "House of the Lord."[6] Mary Fielding wrote in 1837 that on the occasion of one of many spiritual outpourings in that edifice, "the Bretheren as well as the Sisters were all melted down and we wept and praised God together."[7] When ritual washings and anointings were introduced in the temple at Kirtland, only men participated. These ordinances prepared potential missionaries and church leaders to fulfill offices and other assignments, and some women were angry about their exclusion from the ceremonies.[8] Though women voted in general church assemblies or conferences from at least 1835 onward, they did not receive ecclesiastical offices and other formal leadership or missionary assignments, as men did.[9] Lay men ordained to priesthood offices gradually assembled according to office in groups known as quorums, which provided men opportunities for collective learning and service.[10]

The organization of the Relief Society in 1842 gave women their own organization, in some ways analogous to a priesthood quorum, in which they could receive collective doctrinal instruction and have new opportunities for service. Years later, one member of the Nauvoo Relief Society compared the women's group to the School of the Prophets, in which church elders assembled in the 1830s to receive ecclesiastical instruction and prepare for temple rituals.[11] In

5. For example, Mercy Fielding Thompson and Phebe Woodruff accompanied their husbands on missions in the early church. (Mercy Fielding Thompson, Autobiographical Sketch, 1880, CHL, 2–4; Thomas G. Alexander, *Things in Heaven and Earth: The Life and Times of Wilford Woodruff, a Mormon Prophet* [Salt Lake City: Signature Books, 1991], 60–61, 122–123.)

6. "Extracts from Heber C. Kimball's Journal," *Times and Seasons,* Apr. 15, 1845, 6:867; "R. S. Reports," *Woman's Exponent,* Sept. 1, 1876, 5:50; Edward W. Tullidge, *The Women of Mormondom* (New York: Tullidge and Crandall, 1877), 76.

7. Mary Fielding Smith to Mercy Fielding Thompson, July 8, 1837, Mary Fielding Smith Collection, ca. 1832–1848, CHL.

8. George A. Smith, Mar. 18, 1855, in *Journal of Discourses,* 26 vols. (Liverpool: Various publishers, 1855–1886), 2:215.

9. For women's participation in early church conferences, see Ileen Ann Waspe, "The Status of Woman in the Philosophy of Mormonism from 1830 to 1845" (master's thesis, Brigham Young University, 1942), 63–71, 86–111, 138–167.

10. See "Ecclesiastical Organizational Charts," in Dean C. Jessee et al., eds., *Journals, Volume 1: 1832–1839,* vol. 1 of the Journals series of *The Joseph Smith Papers,* ed. Dean C. Jessee et al. (Salt Lake City: Church Historian's Press, 2008), 452–460 (hereafter *JSP,* J1); and Gregory A. Prince, *Power from on High: The Development of Mormon Priesthood* (Salt Lake City: Signature Books, 1995), 26–31.

11. Phebe Woodruff, in Fourteenth Ward, Salt Lake Stake, Fourteenth Ward Relief Society Minutes and Records, 1864–1957, CHL, Feb. 16, 1869, p. 16; see also "School of the Prophets," in *JSP,* J1:471.

Nauvoo, women and men were thus organized or ordered "according to the law of Heaven," both within the church structure and the temple.[12] Indeed, in contrast to the rituals of the temple in Kirtland, both men and women participated in the temple ordinances introduced in Nauvoo. Women long remembered Joseph Smith teaching that "the organization of the Church of Christ was never perfect until the women were organized."[13]

Early Relief Society Meetings in Nauvoo

Though Latter-day Saints saw themselves as a chosen people set apart from the world, the early activities of the Relief Society reflected broader trends in the religious and cultural life of the United States. Following the eighteenth-century Great Awakening, and particularly throughout the religious revivals of the early nineteenth century, tens of thousands of women converted to various denominations and began organizing prayer, missionary, moral reform, and benevolent societies. A national conversation concerning women's social roles emerged as women became evangelical preachers and activists in antislavery societies, and new academies and seminaries for women flourished.[14] These developments were familiar to Latter-day Saint women, many of whom came from communities in the eastern and southern United States where activist women had established their own organizations. The efforts of a small group of Mormon women to formally unite their labors to sew clothing for temple workmen in the spring of 1842 prompted Joseph Smith to invite them to become part of a new organization intended to diverge from the models then thriving among their contemporaries.

Though the founding cluster of Mormon women initially intended to establish their organization upon a constitution similar to those of other democratically spirited women's groups, Joseph Smith invited them to be organized "after the pattern, or order, of the priesthood," that is, with a president and two

---

12. John Taylor, in Document 1.2, entry for Mar. 17, 1842.

13. Sarah M. Kimball, "Early Relief Society Reminiscence," Mar. 17, 1882, Relief Society Record, 1880–1892, CHL. Minutes of the Nauvoo Relief Society do not contain such a statement by Joseph Smith but do record two of his close associates expressing a similar idea. (Document 1.2, entries for May 27, 1842; Aug. 13, 1843; see also Documents 3.6, 3.29, and 4.28.)

14. Hundreds of women's societies for benevolence, moral reform, and temperance existed in the United States during this era. Some of them had been organized before 1800, and many of them were affiliated with churches. The topic has been studied widely by such scholars as Lori D. Ginzberg, *Women and the Work of Benevolence: Morality, Politics, and Class in the Nineteenth-Century United States* (New Haven, CT: Yale University Press, 1990); Keith E. Melder, *Beginnings of Sisterhood: The American Woman's Rights Movement, 1800–1850* (New York: Schocken Books, 1977), 42–43; and Mary Kelley, *Learning to Stand and Speak: Women, Education, and Public Life in America's Republic* (Chapel Hill: University of North Carolina Press, 2006).

counselors, ordained by the laying on of hands.[15] The new presidency would make decisions and set precedents that would serve as the society's constitution, and they would also expound the scriptures and exhort the members to righteousness and good works.[16] The minutes of the Relief Society in Nauvoo reveal both similarities and differences between this and other women's organizations. Commonalities included leadership by women; use of parliamentary procedure and petitions; the recording of proceedings and reporting of work; and goals of charitable community service, moral reform, and personal piety. The Relief Society served, as did other early women's voluntary associations, as a means by which women continued their expansion to public roles.

The Nauvoo Relief Society minutes and other documents in Part 1 reflect the interweaving of women's concerns and broader church issues from 1842 to 1845. Women's collective charity succored those in need and increased women's public visibility. Accusations from Missouri officials against Joseph Smith, opposition from Illinois citizens outside of Nauvoo, and internal dissent within the church presented challenges to the Saints' civic and political influence that eroded community peace and stirred women's political action. The building of the temple in Nauvoo and the inauguration of temple ordinances strengthened and ordered family ties, but Joseph Smith's introduction of plural marriage to a small group of confidants divided the female community and threatened to fracture the church. At the same time, new roles for women in church organization and their participation in temple ordinances brought forth questions about women's religious authority. Many of these issues would shape Latterday Saint women's experience for the rest of the century.

Charity and Civic Action

One of the Relief Society's imperatives was "searching after objects of charity, and . . . administering to their wants."[17] The prolonged poverty of refugees from Missouri and the influx of convert immigrants from the British Isles necessitated an expanded ministry to the poor. The minutes of the Nauvoo Relief Society vividly demonstrate charitable activities as members reported

---

15. "First Organisation," n.d., ca. July 1880, Relief Society Record, p. 5; see also Document 1.2, entries for Mar. 31 and Apr. 28, 1842.

16. By contrast, many other contemporary women's groups published and distributed their constitutions, including the Female Cent Institution of the New Hampshire Missionary Society, the Providence Female Domestic Missionary Society, and the Concord Female Benevolent Association. (William Henry Allison, *Inventory of Unpublished Material for American Religious History in Protestant Church Archives and Other Repositories* [Washington DC: Carnegie Institution of Washington, 1910], 208.)

17. Joseph Smith, in Document 1.2, entry for Mar. 17, 1842.

specific needs and discussed how to meet them. The Saints' Nauvoo newspaper, *Times and Seasons,* announced in 1842 the society's philanthropic mission both in an editorial likely written by Elder John Taylor of the Quorum of the Twelve Apostles (Document 1.3) and in a poem by society secretary Eliza R. Snow (Document 1.4). The *Nauvoo Neighbor,* the Saints' secular newspaper at this time, published Snow's report of the society's first-year operations, including donations received, in July 1843 (Document 1.8).

In spring 1843, because of an ever-increasing membership, the Relief Society was divided into four units, corresponding to the four municipal wards. Visiting committees were appointed in each unit "to search out the poor and suffering" and to "call on the rich" for donations, a practice common in many contemporaneous women's societies and one that set the precedent for collecting and disbursing charitable funds in future Relief Societies. Women visited families to discover want and contributed such items as onions and shawls, soap and thread, blankets and pennies. They labored, as one woman said, as though "our Salvation depended on our Liberality to the poor."[18]

Emma Smith, often sick, frequently traveling, and wrestling with the introduction of plural marriage, did not attend any of the Relief Society's 1843 meetings. However, neither her absence nor that of her counselor, Sarah Cleveland, who moved from Nauvoo in 1843 (see Document 1.7), deterred the Relief Society from pursuing its mandate to succor the poor and aid the families of the men constructing the temple. To further the same imperatives, "auxiliary societies" of women seem to have been organized in at least two settlements near Nauvoo.[19]

Independent of the Female Relief Society of Nauvoo but reflecting similar impulses, Latter-day Saint women created sewing societies in Boston and Lowell, Massachusetts, in part to raise money for the Nauvoo temple (see Document 1.12). The collective humanitarian efforts of women far exceeded unorganized individual aid in scope and regularity, and the Relief Society became the primary conduit of the church's social welfare efforts during the two years of its presence in Nauvoo. An April 1844 letter from Ellen Briggs Douglas shows the gratitude of a British immigrant who received Relief Society assistance (Document 1.11).

In addition to charitable work, Latter-day Saint women in Nauvoo took their first collective political action. Even as log houses were giving way to

---

18. Document 1.2, entry for July 28, 1843. Several contemporaneous benevolent societies also organized committees to visit the poor and ascertain their needs—for example, the Society for the Relief of Women and Children, the Female Hebrew Benevolent Society of Philadelphia, and the Ladies' Christian Association.

19. Document 1.2, entries for Mar. 24 and July 14, 1842; Sept. 2, 1843.

handsome brick buildings, as educational and social facilities were being constructed, and as the temple was beginning to take shape, the social climate in Nauvoo was plagued with lingering effects of the Missouri expulsion and rumblings of hostility in Illinois. Joseph Smith fought extradition orders to Missouri for allegations of treason and of complicity in an 1842 murder attempt on former Missouri governor Lilburn W. Boggs. These threats led about a thousand Relief Society members to sign a petition to Illinois governor Thomas Carlin in July 1842, proclaiming Joseph Smith's innocence (Document 1.5).[20] In addition, between 1839 and 1842 some women submitted individual redress petitions to the federal government for Missouri losses, and others signed a petition for redress prepared late in 1843 and presented to Congress in 1844.[21]

Temple Ordinances

While publicly the Relief Society was primarily a charitable organization and secondarily an influence for social reform, the organization also arose within the context of the introduction of temple ordinances in Nauvoo. A revelation Joseph Smith dictated in January 1841 commanded the building of a temple for "your anointings, and your washings, and your baptisms for the dead" and for other ordinances yet to be revealed.[22] In his addresses to the Relief Society in 1842, Smith anticipated the completion of this temple and exhorted women to prepare to "move according to the ancient Priesthood."[23] An entry in his journal had earlier stated that a restoration of the "ancient order of [God's] Kingdom" would prepare "the earth for the return of [Jehovah's] glory, even a celestial glory; and a kingdom of Priests & Kings to God & the Lamb forever. on Mount Zion."[24] Smith told the women he intended "to make of this Society a kingdom of priests an [as] in Enoch's day— as in Pauls day."[25] These intentions would be realized in the temple rituals in which both women and men would participate.

Recognizing that completing the temple would require years of work, Joseph Smith introduced the temple ritual known as the "endowment" to nine men in May 1842 in the upper room of his Nauvoo store.[26] On September 28,

---

20. Document 1.2, entry for Aug. 31, 1842.

21. Clark V. Johnson, ed., *Mormon Redress Petitions: Documents of the 1833–1838 Missouri Conflict*, Religious Studies Center Monograph Series 16 (Provo, UT: Religious Studies Center, Brigham Young University, 1992).

22. Doctrine and Covenants 124:39, 28.

23. Document 1.2, entry for Mar. 31, 1842.

24. Joseph Smith, Journal, Jan. 6, 1842, in *JSP*, J2:26.

25. Document 1.2, entry for Mar. 31, 1842; see also Exodus 19:6.

26. Joseph Smith, Journal, May 4–5, 1842, in *JSP*, J2:53–54; Historian's Office, Joseph Smith History,

1843, Emma Smith became the first woman to receive the endowment.[27] Joseph's promise that Relief Society members would see "the blessings of the endowment rolling on"[28] was confirmed as Emma began to help administer the ordinance to other women.[29] The "endowed" men and women (most of the latter of whom were Relief Society members) formed a special group—referred to in Joseph Smith's journal as a "council," "quorum," or "prayer meeting" and later known as the "anointed quorum"—that became thoroughly acquainted with all the temple rites.[30] When the temple was completed after the death of Joseph Smith, members of this vanguard administered ordinances to the broader church membership, beginning in December 1845. More than five thousand Latter-day Saints participated in these ordinances before departing Nauvoo in February 1846.[31]

Joseph Smith taught that unity, charity, and purity were all elements in the Saints' mandate to build Zion, and all were emphasized in temple rituals, as well as in the instructions Emma and Joseph Smith delivered to the Relief Society. Both Presidents Smith charged members to ferret out iniquity and disloyalty in the female community, promote reform, and cultivate forgiveness. Because the Relief Society was intended, in part, to prepare members for the temple, worthiness in this "select Society of the virtuous" was an issue. By the society's third meeting, Joseph Smith advised that members "go into a close examination of every candidate."[32] Similar to the practice used with men when they entered priesthood quorums, potential members were scrutinized for worthiness and loyalty. Women petitioned for the privilege of membership, as evidenced in the application of Susan Cuthbertson (Document 1.9).

Plural Marriage

As hundreds of converts moved into Nauvoo, and as new doctrines were introduced to the Saints about the nature of God and the role of temples,

---

Draft Notes, ca. 1839–1856, CHL, May 4, 1842.

27. Joseph Smith, Journal, May 4–5, 1842, in *JSP*, J2:53–54; Joseph Smith, Journal, Sept. 28, 1843, in Andrew H. Hedges et al., eds., *Journals, Volume 3: May 1843–June 1844,* vol. 3 of the Journals series of *The Joseph Smith Papers,* ed. Ronald K. Esplin and Matthew J. Grow (Salt Lake City: Church Historian's Press, 2015), 104 (hereafter *JSP,* J3).

28. Document 1.2, entry for Aug. 31, 1842.

29. Joseph Smith, Journal, Sept. 28, 1843, in *JSP,* J3:104.

30. See Volume Introduction to Nauvoo Journals, 1 May 1843–22 June 1844; and "The Quorum," in *JSP,* J3:xx–xxi, 487.

31. Glen M. Leonard, *Nauvoo: A Place of Peace, a People of Promise* (Salt Lake City: Deseret Book; Provo, UT: Brigham Young University Press, 2002), 261.

32. Document 1.2, entry for Mar. 31, 1842.

maintaining the unity of the Saints became an increasing challenge. The marriage of husband and wife for eternity, with the promise of eternal family increase—"a continuation of the seeds forever and ever"—was solemnized through an ordinance associated with and eventually reserved for the temple.[33] Saints came to understand this ordinance of celestial or eternal marriage—performed under priesthood authority and "sealed" or sanctioned by God—to be essential to the exaltation of both women and men.[34] The Joseph Smith revelation that expounded this doctrine also included the principle of plural marriage and the requirement that this Old Testament practice be instituted as part of the "restitution of all things."[35]

While Smith did not teach plural marriage publicly in Relief Society meetings or to the membership at large, in 1841 he began privately introducing the principle of plural marriage to trusted associates.[36] Even many of these individuals found it difficult to accept. Speaking for himself and fellow apostles Brigham Young and Heber C. Kimball, John Taylor later declared they had "been glad if it hadn't come in our day but that somebody else had something to do with it instead of us." Still, they committed to the practice, believing it "was substantiated by scripture and made manifest also by revelation."[37] Smith privately taught the concept to several members of the Relief Society, many of whom stated that they received their own spiritual affirmation that this principle was of God. Some of these women subsequently married Smith or other church leaders as plural wives.[38] These marriages, or "sealings," performed by authorized officiators with witnesses present, instituted relationships that the participants considered to be divinely sanctioned and permanent.[39]

Wide differences in church members' knowledge and acceptance of the new marriages fueled grave misunderstanding, speculation, and accusations that threatened the unity of the church and ultimately estranged many Saints. Though these marital innovations were not discussed in public meetings, they

---

33. Doctrine and Covenants 132:19.

34. Doctrine and Covenants 132:7; 124:28.

35. Doctrine and Covenants 132:40, 45; Acts 3:21.

36. Some of these participants later signed affidavits affirming their involvement. (Joseph F. Smith, Affidavits about Celestial Marriage, 1869–1915, CHL; Volume Introduction to Nauvoo Journals, Dec. 1841–Apr. 1843, in *JSP,* J2:xxiv–xxx.)

37. John Taylor, "Sermon in Honor of Martyrdom," June 27, 1854, George D. Watt, Papers, ca. 1846–1865, CHL, as transcribed by LaJean Purcell Carruth, 7–8.

38. See, for example, Mary Elizabeth Lightner, Address at Brigham Young University, Apr. 14, 1905, transcript, Mary E. Lightner Papers, 1865–1914, 20th Century Western and Mormon Manuscripts, L. Tom Perry Special Collections, Harold B. Lee Library, Brigham Young University, Provo, UT; and Emily Dow Partridge Young, Diary and Reminiscences, Feb. 1874–Nov. 1883, CHL, 1–3.

39. Joseph F. Smith, Affidavits about Celestial Marriage, 1869–1915, CHL; Volume Introduction to Nauvoo Journals, Dec. 1841–Apr. 1843, in *JSP,* J2:xxiv–xxv.

were widely rumored. Reports regarding holy and unholy liaisons in Nauvoo surfaced in the women's meetings, spurring both unequivocal condemnations of immorality and efforts to quell rumors. Some men, including Nauvoo mayor and church official John C. Bennett, "got an inkling of these things" and appropriated the doctrine as a pretext for seducing women.[40] Joseph Smith had not authorized Bennett to marry plural wives or perform marriages, and Bennett, soon estranged from Smith, sought to expose Smith's secret marriages.[41]

As tales of immoral acts flew among curious church members, many of them new to the faith, those who had not received Smith's private instruction regarding authorized plural marriage were confused and disturbed. Rumors incriminated Joseph and Emma Smith and other respected men and women. The Relief Society assumed a role in defending the reputation not only of the Smiths but of the women of Nauvoo generally.[42]

Public attempts to warn women against seduction and help them distinguish plural marriage from imitative liaisons only exacerbated the confusion because church leaders did not acknowledge or explain the practice in a public setting.[43] Those who practiced plural marriage considered their unions to be pure and holy, recorded and permanent. They unequivocally condemned adultery and fornication, and they did not view their marriages as bigamy or polygamy, though the latter was a term Utah Saints later accepted. Another contingent of church members saw no difference between authorized and counterfeit plural marriage, equated any plural marriage with adultery, and explicitly condemned both.

On two occasions, once in 1842 and again in 1844, Relief Society members publicly denounced every form of licentiousness, including the "Spiritual Wife System" and polygamy (Documents 1.6 and 1.10). The second of these statements, a document labeled "The Voice of Innocence from Nauvoo," was drafted by William W. Phelps, a clerk for Joseph Smith, and read to a large congregation of Saints in early March 1844. Emma Smith read the document and Relief Society members unanimously endorsed it at each of the society's last four recorded meetings in March 1844.[44] In response to public accusations

---

40. These men "corrupted their own bodies and sought to destroy others and they succeeded in great measure with many." (Taylor, "Sermon in Honor of Martyrdom," 8.)

41. Leonard, *Nauvoo,* 343, 349–356; Volume Introduction to Nauvoo Journals, Dec. 1841–Apr. 1843, in *JSP,* J2:xxvii–xxxi.

42. See, for example, Document 1.2, entry for Mar. 24, 1842.

43. For published statements, see Samuel Bennett et al., "On Marriage," *Times and Seasons,* Oct. 1, 1842, 3:939–940; and "John C. Bennett," *Times and Seasons,* Aug. 1, 1842, 3:868–869.

44. Document 1.2, entries for Mar. 9 and 16, 1844.

of immorality, the document declared the virtue of the women of Nauvoo and denounced slanderers, seducers, and any unchaste conduct. To those who rejected plural marriage, the "Voice of Innocence" and other public condemnations of adultery and bigamy seemed hypocritical if they did not represent a serious intention to stop the practice of plural marriage. The women's published statements had potentially different meanings to those with different understandings of and feelings about the marriages Joseph Smith was sanctioning.[45] Emma Smith's vacillating approval of and disdain for plural marriage further complicated the situation.[46]

Final Relief Society Meetings in Nauvoo

The dearth of contemporaneous references to the "Voice of Innocence" or to activities of the Relief Society in 1844 make it difficult to assess precisely what happened at the society's last recorded meetings in March 1844, or in their wake. The minutes of the meetings are enigmatic, but clearly Emma Smith tried to win women's full support for "put[t]ing down iniquity," and she seems to have mounted an intensified effort at what she considered moral reform, with the intent to halt all plural marriage, including the practice authorized by her husband.[47]

During the last four recorded meetings, two each on March 9 and March 16, 1844, Emma Smith presided. She spoke explicitly of her own authority—presumably referring to the 1830 revelation naming her "Elect Lady," her ordination by her husband "to expound Scriptures & exhort the Church," and her position as Relief Society president whose decisions, made in connection with her two counselors, were to "be considered law" for the society.[48] The small circle of women who had received the endowment through her administration and joined with her in the anointed quorum would also have understood her authoritative role in women's temple ordinances. Apart from these official roles, Emma, as Joseph Smith's wife of seventeen years, was the church's first lady and was much loved by church members, many of whom had been the beneficiaries of her compassion. Relief Society women who crowded into the four nearly identical March 1844 meetings voted to endorse the "Voice of

---

45. See Document 1.6.

46. For Emma Smith's views on plural marriage, see Brian C. Hales, *Joseph Smith's Polygamy*, 3 vols. (Salt Lake City: Greg Kofford Books, 2013), 2:33–138; Linda King Newell and Valeen Tippetts Avery, *Mormon Enigma: Emma Hale Smith*, 2nd ed. (Urbana: University of Illinois Press, 1994), 106–182; and Richard Lyman Bushman, *Joseph Smith: Rough Stone Rolling* (New York: Knopf, 2005), 490–499.

47. Document 1.2, entries for Mar. 9 and 16, 1844.

48. Document 1.1; Document 1.2, entry for Mar. 17, 1842.

Innocence" and heard their "Presidentess" authoritatively agitate for a significant change in moral behavior, "a reformation in boath men & woman."[49]

On May 26, 1844, Joseph Smith seemed to blame the "Voice of Innocence" for the mounting fury he faced from dissidents that spring, asserting that he "never had any fuss with these men until that Female Relief Society brought out the paper against adulterers and adulteresses," though he had himself announced its writing and presentation.[50] Even though a direct relationship between Relief Society activities and the fomentation of the dissidents cannot be further documented, a tenuous connection seems to have lingered in the public mind. Eliza R. Snow remarked in 1868: "It has been said that the Society in Nauvoo did more harm than good, but it was not So."[51] In the early 1880s, when both the practice of plural marriage and the reconstituted Relief Society were well established, John Taylor, who became president of the church in October 1880, recalled that in Nauvoo "much disturbance arose among the Sisters." According to Taylor, "Sister Emma . . . made use of the position she held to try to pervert the minds of the sisters" and "taught the Sisters that the principle of Celestial Marriage [plural marriage] as taught and practiced by Joseph Smith the prophet was not of God." This, Taylor commented, was "the reason why the Relief Society did not continue."[52]

In early June 1844 a group of disaffected Saints published one issue of the *Nauvoo Expositor,* a newspaper intended to expose Joseph Smith's practice of plural marriage, his teachings regarding the nature of God, and the melding of civil and religious authority in Nauvoo. Destruction of the paper and its press by Nauvoo officials—including Joseph Smith, who was then serving as mayor—outraged neighbors who were already alienated by rumors of polygamy as well as by Smith's political activities, including his candidacy for U.S. president in 1844. Escalating conflicts culminated in the mob murder of Joseph Smith and his brother Hyrum at Carthage, Illinois, on June 27, 1844.[53]

The tensions surrounding plural marriage seem to have led some church leaders to lose confidence in the Relief Society sometime in the spring or

---

49. Document 1.2, entry for Mar. 16, 1844.

50. Joseph Smith, Discourse, May 26, 1844, Joseph Smith, Collection, 1827–1846, CHL; Document 1.10; Joseph Smith, Journal, Mar. 7, 1844, in *JSP,* J3:194, 198; Joseph Smith, Discourse, Mar. 7, 1844, Joseph Smith Collection, CHL.

51. Snow continued with an interpretation of the end of the Nauvoo Relief Society, saying that "Emma Smith . . . gave it up so as not to lead the society in Erro[r]." (West Jordan Ward, West Jordan Utah South Stake, West Jordan Ward Relief Society Minutes and Records, 1868–1973, CHL, Minute Book A, Sept. 7, 1868.)

52. "Relief Society Report," Relief Society Record, July 17, 1880; "R.S. Reports," 53–54; Harrisville Ward, Farr West Stake, General Minutes, 1850–1977, CHL, vol. 14, June 29, 1881.

53. Bushman, *Rough Stone Rolling,* 514–517, 539–550.

summer of 1844. Neither the minutes nor other sources document additional Relief Society meetings during 1844, and by spring 1845 the society was defunct.[54] In the aftermath of Joseph Smith's death, the majority of Saints in Nauvoo voted in August 1844 to sustain the Quorum of the Twelve Apostles as the governing council of the church. In March 1845, when women may have anticipated beginning another season of Relief Society meetings, Brigham Young, president of the Quorum of the Twelve, announced his decision to "stay" Relief Society proceedings (Document 1.13), and subsequently "the labors of the Society ceased." Asserting his presiding authority amidst the challenge of alternate claims, including from the Smith family, Young unequivocally foreclosed the possibility of female church members officially gathering or of Emma Smith presiding.

There is no evidence of remonstrance from the women who followed Young and the Quorum of the Twelve, the same women who would later reestablish the society in the Rocky Mountains while Emma Smith remained in the Midwest.[55] Indeed, shortly after Young's announcement one member of the disbanded society wrote in her diary of the church as a whole, "There appears to be the most union that has ever ben," and noted that "the Temple prospers."[56] Completion of the Nauvoo temple, so prominent in Joseph Smith's instruction to the Relief Society, became a primary concern. Women in Nauvoo and elsewhere continued to pool resources to speed work on the temple (see Document 1.12). Throughout the fall of 1845 Saints prepared for the westward exodus, and in December the first of thousands of women began to

---

54. A few sources make reference to scattered gatherings of women, although these meetings are not recorded in the Nauvoo Relief Society minutes. For example, when Joseph Smith returned from a May 1844 trial where he was found not guilty, he went to the home of Hezekiah Peck, "where a number of Mormon women had assembled . . . for the purpose of praying for the deliverance of the prophet." Peck's wife, Martha, was an early member of the Relief Society.[a] Zina Huntington Jacobs recorded that she "went to the Masonic hall with the sisters" on June 18, 1844.[b] Hosea Stout wrote that on March 13, 1845, he organized women into an association to promote home industry and manufacture, based on "the order which was instituted in Nauvoo."[c] (a. "Some of the Remarks of John S. Reed," *Times and Seasons,* June 1, 1844, 5:551; Document 1.2, entry for Apr. 14, 1842. b. Zina D. H. Young, Diary, 1844–1845, CHL, June 18, 1844. c. Juanita Brooks, ed., *On the Mormon Frontier: The Diary of Hosea Stout, 1844–1889,* 2 vols., reprint [Salt Lake City: University of Utah Press, 2009], 1:27.)

55. Emma Smith and some other Relief Society members did not endorse leadership of the church by Brigham Young and the Quorum of the Twelve Apostles. Sarah Scott Hall, a resident of Nauvoo who did not join or refer to the Relief Society, recorded her dissenting views regarding plural marriage and other matters in letters to her parents in Massachusetts, published in George F. Partridge, ed., "The Death of a Mormon Dictator: Letters of Massachusetts Mormons, 1843–1848," *New England Quarterly* 9 (Dec. 1936): 583–617.

56. Young, Diary, Mar. 10, 1845.

receive temple ordinances through the ministrations of men and women "endowed" earlier under Smith's direction.

The issue of gender and authority in the Church of Jesus Christ of Latter-day Saints was brought to the fore by the organization and suspension of the Female Relief Society of Nauvoo. Documents in Part 1 show that Saints wrestled with such questions as whether women should be engaged in the structured charity work that had been the responsibility of bishops, whether women might speak in tongues and heal, the circumstances under which women could exhort the church, and the relationship between male and female church leaders. As is illustrated by Eliza R. Snow's 1845 hymn, "My Father in Heaven," with its references to a Mother in Heaven (Document 1.14), the effort of Joseph and Emma Smith and their fellow Saints to answer these questions carved out new spaces for women in both Latter-day Saint experience and theology. Unresolved in Nauvoo, these questions run not only through but well beyond the discourse of this era.

1.1 Revelation, July 1830 (Doctrine and Covenants 25)

Revelation to Emma Smith, [July] 1830. Featured version, titled "27ᵗʰ Commandment AD 1830," copied [ca. Mar. 1831] in Revelation Book 1, pp. 34–35, in Michael Hubbard MacKay et al., eds., Documents, Volume 1: July 1828–June 1831, vol. 1 of the Documents series of The Joseph Smith Papers, ed. Dean C. Jessee et al. (Salt Lake City: Church Historian's Press, 2013), 161–164.[57]

Emma Hale married Joseph Smith on January 18, 1827, at South Bainbridge, New York.[58] According to Joseph's mother, Lucy Mack Smith, Emma accompanied her husband that fall to an upstate New York hill and waited in a wagon while he retrieved the metal plates from which he would translate the Book of Mormon.[59] Emma assisted as a scribe in the early translation work.[60] The couple first lived with Joseph's family at Manchester, New York, until late 1827, when they moved to Harmony in northeastern Pennsylvania to live with Emma's parents.[61] There, in 1828, Joseph and Emma buried their first child, a son who "died the same hour" he was born.[62] Over the next two years, as the couple tried to evade threats to the work of translation, they moved several times between Harmony and upstate New York. From these early years onward, Emma experienced the force of opposition to Joseph's revelations through recurring verbal, physical, and legal attacks against him.

Joseph dictated the following revelation to Emma in early July 1830, a few months after the Church of Christ was officially organized on April 6, 1830.[63] On June 28, 1830, Oliver Cowdery, the church's "second elder," baptized Emma at Colesville, New York.[64] With others baptized that morning, Emma anticipated her confirmation that evening,[65] but her

---

57. In *Documents, Volume 1,* this revelation is labeled "Revelation, July 1830–C [D&C 25]." The use of the letter "C" after the date distinguishes this revelation from two other July 1830 revelations.

58. For biographical information on Emma Smith, see, for example, Linda King Newell and Valeen Tippetts Avery, *Mormon Enigma: Emma Hale Smith,* 2nd ed. (Urbana: University of Illinois Press, 1994); and Mark L. Staker, "'A Comfort unto My Servant, Joseph': Emma Hale Smith (1804–1879)," in *Women of Faith in the Latter Days,* vol. 1, *1775–1820,* ed. Richard E. Turley Jr. and Brittany A. Chapman (Salt Lake City: Deseret Book, 2011), 343–362.

59. Lucy Mack Smith, History, 1844–1845, 18 books, CHL, bks. 5, 6–7.

60. Lucy Mack Smith, History, 1844–1845, bks. 7, 11; Edmund C. Briggs, "A Visit to Nauvoo in 1856," *Journal of History* 9, no. 4 (Oct. 1916): 454; Joseph Smith III, "Last Testimony of Sister Emma," *Saints' Herald,* Oct. 1, 1879, 289–290.

61. Joseph Smith et al., History, 1838–1856, vols. A-1–F-1 (original), A-2–E-2 (fair copy), CHL, vol. A-1, 8–9 (hereafter JS History).

62. Karen Lynn Davidson et al., eds., *Histories, Volume 1: Joseph Smith Histories, 1832–1844,* vol. 1 of the Histories series of *The Joseph Smith Papers,* ed. Dean C. Jessee et al. (Salt Lake City: Church Historian's Press, 2012), 28.

63. For more detail on the dating of this revelation, see the introduction to this document in Michael Hubbard MacKay et al., eds., *Documents, Volume 1: July 1828–June 1831,* vol. 1 of the Documents series of *The Joseph Smith Papers,* ed. Dean C. Jessee et al. (Salt Lake City: Church Historian's Press, 2013), 161 (hereafter *JSP,* D1).

64. JS History, vol. A-1, 30, 43.

65. After baptism, converts were confirmed members of the church "by the laying on of hands for the baptism of fire and the Holy Ghost." (JS History, vol. A-1, 44; Doctrine and Covenants 20:41.)

Emma Hale Smith. 1842. A July 1830 revelation to Joseph Smith addressed his wife, Emma, by name, called her an "Elect Lady," and instructed her to "expound Scriptures & exhort the Church." She became the first president of the Relief Society twelve years later, around the time she posed for this portrait. Portrait by David Rogers. (Courtesy Community of Christ Library-Archives, Independence, MO.)

husband's arrest disrupted the meeting. Charged with "being a disorderly person; of setting the country in an uproar by preaching the Book of Mormon," Joseph was tried and acquitted in one county, immediately arrested a second time, and then tried and discharged in a neighboring county.[66] After several days in custody and court, Joseph rejoined Emma, who—while "awaiting with much anxiety the issue of those ungodly proceedings"—had gathered with other women to pray for his deliverance.[67]

This revelation was one of three Joseph Smith dictated in early July 1830 at Harmony after this period of harassment.[68] Each of these three revelations (now known in Latter-day Saint scripture as Doctrine and Covenants sections 24, 25, and 26, respectively) included instructions to specific individuals regarding prayer, learning, and the call to expound scriptures or to preach. The revelation directed to Emma Smith called her "my daughter in Zion" and an "Elect Lady," and addressed both her domestic and public responsibilities.

It is uncertain how widely known or distributed this revelation was among the church membership in the early 1830s. In one of his denunciatory letters written to an Ohio newspaper in the fall of 1831, Ezra Booth claimed to have a copy of the "27th commandment to Emma my daughter in Zion" in his possession. Additionally, Eber D. Howe included the revelation in its entirety in his 1834 critique of the church, *Mormonism Unvailed*.[69] The revelation was first published by the church in the Book of Commandments (1833) and subsequently in the Doctrine and Covenants (1835).[70] Church historian John Whitmer copied the revelation into an official manuscript book known as Revelation Book 1 in about March 1831; as his is the earliest recorded version of the revelation, Whitmer's text appears below, as it was published in *Documents, Volume 1*, of *The Joseph Smith Papers.*

Through the 1830s, as the community of Saints grew and moved from New York to Ohio, Missouri, and Illinois, Emma Smith ministered to her husband, their children, the extended Smith family, and sick and needy Saints. Her surviving letters to Joseph reveal her affection for him as well as her involvement in his private business concerns.[71] In 1835, as directed in this revelation, she completed the church's first hymnal, published early the next year as *A Collection of Sacred Hymns, for the Church of the Latter Day Saints.*[72] In 1842, at the founding meeting of the Female Relief Society of Nauvoo, Joseph Smith read this

---

66. JS History, vol. A-1, 43–48; *JSP,* D1:115.

67. JS History, vol. A-1, 48; "Some of the Remarks of John S. Reed," *Times and Seasons,* June 1, 1844, 5:551.

68. See *JSP,* D1:156–161.

69. Ezra Booth, "Mormonism—No. II," *Ohio Star* (Ravenna), Oct. 20, 1831, [3]; Eber D. Howe, *Mormonism Unvailed* (Painesville, OH: By the author, 1834), 101–102.

70. *A Book of Commandments, for the Government of the Church of Christ, Organized according to Law, on the 6th of April, 1830* (Zion [Independence, MO]: W. W. Phelps, 1833), 58–59; *Doctrine and Covenants of the Church of the Latter Day Saints,* comp. Joseph Smith Jr. et al. (Kirtland, OH: F. G. Williams, 1835), 178–179.

71. For example, see Emma Smith to Joseph Smith, Apr. 25, 1837; May 3, 1837; Mar. 7, 1839; and Dec. 6, 1839, all in the Documents series at josephsmithpapers.org.

72. *A Collection of Sacred Hymns, for the Church of the Latter Day Saints,* ed. Emma Smith (Kirtland, OH: F. G. Williams, 1835). Emma Smith compiled the hymns in collaboration with William W. Phelps, who edited and published the hymnal. See also Michael Hicks, *Mormonism and Music: A History* (Urbana: University of Illinois Press, 1989), 10–23.

1830 revelation to the twenty women assembled. He also read 2 John 1:1, a verse that references an "elect lady," in order to "show that respect was then had to the same thing; and that why she [Emma] was called an Elect lady is because, [she was] elected to preside." Emma Smith, elected as president at the meeting, was not ordained to the new office because, Joseph Smith stated, she had been "ordain'd at the time, the [1830] Revelation was given."[73]

——— ❧ ———

27[th.] Commandment AD 1830

A Revelation to Emma [Smith] given at Harmony Susquehan[na] County state of Pennsylvania giving her a command to select Hymns &c

A Revelation I give unto you concerning my will Behold thy sins are for given thee & thou art an Elect Lady[74] whom I have called murmer not because of the things which thou hast not seen for they are withheld from thee & the World which is wisdom in me in a time to come[75] & the office of thy calling shall be for a comfort unto my Servent Joseph thy husband in his afflictions with consoleing words in the spirit of meekness & thou shalt go with him at the time of his going & be unto him a Scribe that I may send Oliver [Cowdery] whithersoever I will & thou shalt be ordained under his hand to expound Scriptures & exhort the Church[76] according as it shall be given thee by my spirit for he shall lay his hands upon the[e] & thou shalt receive the Holy Ghost & thy time shall be [p. 34] Given to writings & to Learning & thou needest not fear for thy husband shall support thee from the Church for unto them is ~~thy~~ his calling that all things might be revealed unto them whatsoever I will according to their faith & verily I say unto ~~you~~ thee that thou shalt lay

---

73. Document 1.2, entry for Mar. 17, 1842.

74. See 2 John 1:1; and Document 1.2, entry for Mar. 17, 1842.

75. "Things which thou has not seen" may be a reference to the gold plates from which Joseph Smith translated the Book of Mormon. Eleven men, including several who had served as Joseph Smith's scribes, stated that they saw the plates. Emma Smith, although she also acted as scribe, did not see the plates but later recalled, "The plates often lay on the table without any attempt at concealment, wrapped in a small linen table cloth, which I had given [Joseph] to fold them in. I once felt of the plates, as they thus lay on the table, tracing their outline and shape. They seemed to be pliable like thick paper, and would rustle with a metalic sound when the edges were moved by the thumb, as one does sometimes thumb the edges of a book." (Testimony of Three Witnesses, Late June 1829; Testimony of Eight Witnesses, Late June 1829, in *JSP*, D1:378–387; Joseph Smith III, "Last Testimony of Sister Emma," *Saints' Herald*, Oct. 1, 1879, 290; see also Newell and Avery, *Mormon Enigma*, 25.)

76. In contemporary American Protestant denominations, women sometimes served as teachers and exhorters in informal meetings, though they were generally not allowed to preach in formal worship services. No records indicate that Emma Smith functioned as an exhorter or a teacher until the establishment of the Relief Society in 1842. (See Catherine A. Brekus, *Strangers and Pilgrims: Female Preaching in America, 1740–1845*, Gender and American Culture [Chapel Hill: University of North Carolina Press, 1998], chap. 3.)

aside the things of this world & seek for the things of a better & it shall be given thee also to make a selection of Sacred Hymns as it shall be given thee which is pleasing unto me to be had in my Church for my Soul delighteth in the song of the heart yea the song of the ~~heart~~ righteous is a prayer unto me & it shall be answered with a blessing upon their heads wherefore lift up thy heart & rejoice & cleave unto the covenants which thou hast made continue in the spirit of meekness & beware of Pride let thy soul delight in thy husband & the glory which shall come upon him keep my commandments continually & a crown of righteousness thou shalt receive & except thou do this where I am ~~thou~~ ye cannot come & verily I say unto you that this is my voice unto all even so amen

Nauvoo Relief Society Minute Book. This substantial volume contains the minutes of the Female Relief Society of Nauvoo from its founding on March 17, 1842, through its final meeting on March 16, 1844. Eliza R. Snow, secretary of the Nauvoo society, later carried the book to Utah and used it frequently in instructing local Relief Society leaders and members. (Church History Library, Salt Lake City.)

1.2 Nauvoo Relief Society Minute Book

Nauvoo Relief Society, "A Book of Records. Containing the proceedings of The Female Relief Society of Nauvoo," Minute Book, Mar. 17, 1842–Mar. 16, 1844; handwriting of Eliza R. Snow, Phebe M. Bartholomew Wheeler, Hannah M. Ells, and an unidentified scribe; 123 pages; CHL (MS 3424). Includes redactions and archival marking.

This record is a bound ledger book measuring 12⅜ × 8⅛ × 1 inches (31 × 21 × 3 cm). The book has a tight-back case binding sewn on vellum tapes and a brown suede leather cover with tooling around the edges. Tooled lines on the spine correspond with the vellum tapes. The spine also has a red leather label with "LEDGER" in gold lettering. The paper, which is ruled with thirty-four blue horizontal lines, one red double horizontal line, and five red vertical lines (one of them double), measures 12⅛ × 7¾ inches (31 × 20 cm). The book originally contained fifteen gatherings of eight leaves each, a twelve-leaf gathering of tabbed index pages at the front, and flyleaves in the front and back; the front flyleaves are missing. The first gathering after the index pages currently contains only five leaves. Two leaves were apparently removed from this gathering before the book was used. At some point, an unknown scribe paginated the book up to page 26, beginning with the verso of the last index page. The leaf that would have been paginated 2 and 3 is also now missing. This leaf was presumably removed before the book was used as a minute book for the Relief Society, as page 1 shows ink transfer from the title page (numbered page 4).

The index pages are ruled with thirty-six blue horizontal lines and are blank with three exceptions. The recto of the "A–B" leaf includes a note about provenance, described below. The verso of the "A–B" leaf has an inscription in Eliza R. Snow's hand reading "Jane Easton commenc'd work August 9th 1852." The recto of the "L–M" leaf has an index entry for "Mc.Intire Geo. 2" in an unknown hand. As page 2 is missing from the volume, this entry possibly indicates that the book was originally going to be used as a ledger before being presented to the Relief Society to record the minutes of their meetings. Before Willard Richards presented the book to the Relief Society, he may have removed the leaf with the notations for George McIntire.[77]

The Relief Society minute book fills 123 pages after the index pages. Page 5 is blank other than the page number. Pages [27]–[127] are paginated in graphite, possibly inscribed when other redactions and notations in graphite were made. The remainder of the pages are blank, except for the verso of the last flyleaf in the back, which is inscribed in Eliza R. Snow's handwriting: "Commenc'd in C.H. | July 7ᵗʰ this week two days | "12ᵗʰ two days— 9 | "12ᵗʰ 14— 7 | "21–23ᵈ— 13 | health | "26ᵗʰ 28ᵗʰ— 14 | Aug 1st. July 31ˢᵗ— 5— 1 | Aug. 2ᵈ mo. 0— 1 | "4ᵗʰ w. 5— 2".

Eliza R. Snow's handwriting also appears on pages 4 and 6–[96]; she used blue ink on pages 4 and 6–[79], and brown ink on pages [80]–[96]. Phebe M. Wheeler took over as scribe for pages [97]–[122], except for page [119], which was inscribed by an unidentified scribe in brown ink. Wheeler's writing is in black ink except for the minutes of the meeting reported on pages [116]–[118], which are in blue ink. Hannah M. Ells's handwriting appears on pages [123]–[127] in brown ink.

Graphite redactions and marginal notations appear throughout the volume, usually on pages where sermons were recorded. These notations are not included in the transcript. A pink ribbon bookmark stamped "WILLES-HORNE DRUG Co. PRESCRIPTION DRUGGISTS DESERET NEWS B'LDG." was inserted at some point between pages [91] and [92]. A brown cotton chemise (possibly from dress lining material) was created for this volume, either in Nauvoo or in Utah. No conservation work has been done on this volume, except that two pieces of cellophane tape were added to the volume sometime after 1930 (the year cellophane tape was invented). One of these pieces of tape, which taped pages 13 and 14 together along the

---

77. In January 1842 Joseph Smith signed two promissory notes to George McIntire. (Joseph Smith to George McIntire, Promissory Notes, Nauvoo, IL, Jan. 17 and 20, 1842, Joseph Smith Collection, 1827–1846, CHL.)

bottom of the gutter, has fallen off, leaving residue on the page; the other piece, repairing a tear at the bottom of page 14, remains.

The title page of the minute book indicates that Willard Richards presented this volume to the Relief Society on March 17, 1842, the date of the first meeting of the Relief Society. It is unlikely the volume was used as the original record of the minutes, as there are few editing marks. There are some copy errors, indicating that the minutes were probably recorded on loose pages and then later copied into this volume.

As noted in the historical introduction to this document and in the introduction to this publication, Eliza R. Snow had possession of this record in Utah Territory and read from it publicly on many occasions. At Snow's death the book passed to her successor as Relief Society general president, Zina D. H. Young. When Young died in 1901 the book passed to her successor, Bathsheba W. Smith, who died in 1910. A provenance note in the beginning of the Nauvoo Relief Society Minute Book reads: "This record was obtained from Bathsheba Merrill who received it in the effects of her mother Sister Bathsheba W. Smith after her death, and was filed in the Historian's Office July 3, 1911. | Joseph F. Smith Jr."

This record of thirty-three meetings of the Female Relief Society of Nauvoo commences with the founding meeting on March 17, 1842. A few weeks earlier Sarah M. Granger Kimball, a wealthy young matron in Nauvoo, proposed forming a "Ladies' Society" to provide clothing for workers constructing the temple in the city. Church leaders had recently assigned more than two hundred missionaries to hasten work on the stone structure finally emerging from its foundation.[78] Women's sewing and benevolent associations flourishing in other U.S. cities probably informed Kimball's idea to formally unite women to clothe missionary-workers.[79] Eliza R. Snow, well-known Mormon poet and former secretary to her county commissioner father, drafted a constitution for Kimball's proposed society. When Snow presented her constitution and bylaws to Joseph Smith, he praised the documents but asked the women to forego their "Ladies' Society" in favor of "something better."[80]

Twenty women responded to Smith's invitation to gather in the large assembly room above the dry goods store he had recently opened on Water Street in Nauvoo. The red brick store's offices and upper story provided space for church and city administration and for public and private gatherings.[81] For example, the Nauvoo Masonic Lodge established its lodge in the store's upper room on March 15 and conducted rites there on March 16. The lodge also met in the upper room on the evening of Thursday, March 17, after the women's meeting was concluded. Joseph Smith, who had joined the fraternal order and advanced to

---

78. Document 4.10. Church leaders asked members to supply provisions to the builders: "Beds and bedding, socks, mittens, shoes, clothing of every description, and store goods are needed for the comfort of the laborers this winter." (Brigham Young et al., "Baptism for the Dead," *Times and Seasons,* Dec. 15, 1841, 3:625–627.)

79. For the broader context, see, for example, Nancy F. Cott, *The Bonds of Womanhood: "Woman's Sphere" in New England, 1780–1835* (New Haven, CT: Yale University Press, 1997), 126–159; and Lori D. Ginzberg, *Women and the Work of Benevolence: Morality, Politics, and Class in the Nineteenth-Century United States* (New Haven, CT: Yale University Press, 1990).

80. Document 4.10.

81. The store opened for business January 5, 1842. The upper story was often used for meetings by the Nauvoo City Council, the Nauvoo Masonic Lodge, the Female Relief Society of Nauvoo, and other organizations. ("Store," in Andrew H. Hedges et al., eds., *Journals, Volume 2: December 1841–April 1843,* vol. 2 of the Journals series of *The Joseph Smith Papers,* ed. Dean C. Jessee et al. [Salt Lake City: Church Historian's Press, 2011], 424–425 [hereafter *JSP,* J2].)

the degree of Master Mason the day before the organization of the Relief Society, occasionally made references to Masonry when he addressed Relief Society women in 1842.[82] More frequently, he referred to the Saints' rising temple and the priesthood order and blessings connected with it.

Organized "after the pattern, or order, of the priesthood," as Sarah Kimball recalled Joseph Smith saying, the women formally elected a president, Emma Smith, who in turn appointed two counselors, Sarah M. Kingsley Cleveland and Elizabeth Ann Smith Whitney.[83] Joseph explained that Emma had been "ordain'd at the time" of a July 1830 revelation, which told her "to expound the scriptures to all; and to teach the female part of community." Apostle John Taylor ordained Emma's counselors and blessed Emma.[84] The women's presidency thus followed the pattern of the three-member presidencies of men's priesthood quorums.

Eliza Snow and other scribes recorded minutes for seventeen meetings of the Female Relief Society of Nauvoo in 1842, twelve meetings in 1843, and four meetings in 1844.[85] At nearly every meeting, donations were listed and the names of those nominated for membership were submitted for a yea or nay vote. By the end of 1844, approximately 1,336 women had been admitted as members of the Relief Society. The number of participants and the place, timing, and character of the meetings varied during the three years. In May 1842, attendance having outgrown the small "Lodge Room" above Joseph Smith's store, Relief Society women began meeting outdoors in a grove near the rising temple.[86]

The election of Emma Smith as the society's president and the frequent attendance of and counsel from her husband probably helped speed the growth of the women's organization during its first year. Emma Smith encouraged women in their new enterprise, provided spiritual counsel, and coordinated assistance to the poor. The minutes indicate that Joseph Smith attended nine of the meetings held in 1842 and addressed members on March 17 and 31, April 28, May 26, June 9, and August 31.[87] The minutes are the only contemporaneous record of teachings that Joseph Smith directed specifically to women as a group. A letter that Joseph Smith and others wrote to the Relief Society on March 31, 1842, was also copied into the minutes following the September 28, 1842, entry.

---

82. Nauvoo Masonic Lodge Minute Book, 1841–1846, CHL, Mar. 15–16, 1842; Joseph Smith, Journal, Mar. 15–16, 1842, in *JSP*, J2:45.

83. Relief Society Record, "First Organisation," n.d., ca. June 1880, p. 5, Relief Society Record, 1880–1892, CHL; see also Document 4.10.

84. Document 1.2, entry for Mar. 17, 1842; Joseph Smith, Journal, Mar. 17, 1842, in *JSP*, J2:45.

85. For 1842, the record references eighteen meetings but contains no minutes for the seventeenth meeting. For 1843, the record notes fourteen meetings but contains minutes for only twelve (the ninth meeting was canceled because of bad weather and there appear to be two different versions of the September 15 meeting, one of which was dated August 15). In 1844, four meetings were held, two each on March 9 and March 16.

86. The Latter-day Saints frequently held public meetings in three groves near the temple site in Nauvoo: one to the west of the site, which was the most common meeting place and likely the site of the Relief Society meetings; one to the south; and one to the northeast. The groves each had a stand for speaking. ("Grove," in *JSP*, J2:416.)

87. The meetings Joseph Smith attended without delivering extended remarks were on March 24, May 12, and May 27, 1842.

The Relief Society did not assemble in the winter. When it resumed meeting in June 1843, more than one thousand women had enrolled as members. The group soon divided into four sections or wards that met separately in rotation. Because Sarah Cleveland, first counselor in the women's presidency, had moved from Nauvoo, second counselor Elizabeth Ann Whitney presided in the absence of President Emma Smith, who battled sickness, traveled to purchase goods and visit family, and wrestled with Joseph Smith's practice of plural marriage.[88] Following the first two meetings in the summer of 1843, society secretary Eliza R. Snow moved to Morley Settlement, twenty-five miles south of Nauvoo, and assistant secretary Phebe M. Bartholomew Wheeler recorded minutes and donations.[89] Relief Society visiting committees, appointed in each ward in July 1843,[90] began to report needs of Nauvoo families and collect contributions for the poor and destitute, particularly new immigrants. From 1840 through 1845, nearly forty-seven hundred immigrants came from the British Isles, some three-quarters of them from 1841 through 1843.[91] After a second winter hiatus, the Female Relief Society of Nauvoo reconvened on March 9, 1844, with Hannah M. Ells serving as secretary. Minutes for the last meeting on March 16, 1844, indicate an adjournment sine die, and no extant record suggests that further meetings took place.

At some point before the Latter-day Saints' trek to the West from Nauvoo, which began in February 1846, Eliza R. Snow again took possession of the Relief Society minute book. When the Relief Society was reestablished in territorial Utah, Snow often used the minute book in local meetings and as a guide for the organization. She and other Relief Society leaders in Utah not only preserved the record as an artifact but also referenced it in their speeches and publications to perpetuate the memory and meaning of the Relief Society's beginnings in Nauvoo.[92]

———— ❧ ————

[93]A
Book of Records.
Containing
the proceedings
of
The Female Relief Society of Nauvoo.

---

88. On Cleveland's move, see Document 1.7; on Emma Smith's activities in this period, see Linda King Newell and Valeen Tippetts Avery, *Mormon Enigma: Emma Hale Smith,* 2nd ed. (Urbana: University of Illinois Press, 1994), 155–168.

89. "Morley's Settlement," *Nauvoo Journal* 11, no. 1 (Spring 1999): 153–155. Snow moved back to Nauvoo in April 1844. (Eliza R. Snow, Journal, 1842–1882, CHL, July 21, 1843, and Apr. 14, 1844.)

90. Document 1.2, entry for July 28, 1843.

91. See Richard L. Jensen, "Transplanted to Zion: The Impact of British Latter-day Saint Immigration upon Nauvoo," *BYU Studies* 31, no. 1 (Winter 1991): 77–87.

92. Jill Mulvay Derr and Carol Cornwall Madsen, "Preserving the Record and Memory of the Female Relief Society of Nauvoo, 1842–92," *Journal of Mormon History* 35, no. 3 (Summer 2009): 88–117.

93. TEXT: Eliza R. Snow handwriting begins.

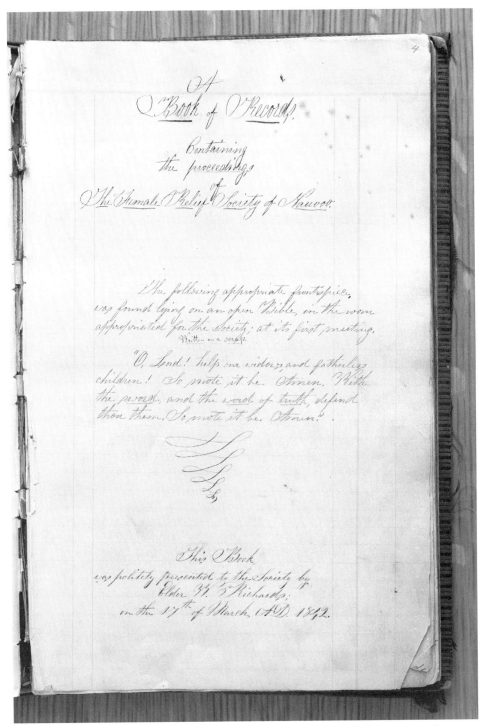

4

A
Book of Records.

Containing
the proceedings
of
The Female Relief Society of Nauvoo.

The following appropriate frontispiece,
was found lying on an open Bible, in the room
appropriated for the Society; at its first meeting.
Written on a scrap.

"O, Lord! help our widows, and fatherless
children.! So mote it be. Amen. With
the sword, and the word of truth, defend
thou them. So mote it be. Amen."

This Book
was politely presented to the Society by
Elder W. Richards;
on the 17th of March, A.D. 1842.

Title page. Eliza R. Snow, appointed secretary of the Female Relief Society of Nauvoo at its first meeting, inscribed this title page in the organization's minute book. (Church History Library, Salt Lake City. Photograph by Welden C. Andersen.)

The following appropriate frontispiece, was found lying on an open Bible, in the room appropriated for the Society; at its first meeting.

⟨Written on a scrap.⟩

"O, Lord! help our widows, and fatherless children! So mote it be. Amen. With the sword, and the word of truth, defend thou them. So mote it be. Amen."[94]

This Book,
was politely presented to the Society by
Elder W. [Willard] Richards;
on the 17th of March, AD. 1842. [p. 4]

[page 5 blank]

March 17, 1842 • Thursday

A Record of the
Organization, and Proceedings of
The Female Relief Society of Nauvoo.

Nauvoo Lodge Room
March 17th 1842.

Present— President Joseph Smith, John Taylor, Willard Richards, Emma Smith and others.[95]

Elder John Taylor was call'd to the chair by Prest. Smith, and elder W. Richards appointed Secretary,

Meeting commenced by singing "The spirit of God like a fire is burning" &c.—[96] Prayer by elder Taylor.

---

94. This was likely a prayer used at the opening of the Nauvoo Masonic Lodge. Masonic ritual customarily used the phrase "so mote it be" ("mote" is the archaic form of "might"), often reminded participants of their duties to widows and orphans, and sometimes used sword imagery. During the initiation of a Masonic lodge, an open Bible is placed on an altar. (Cornelius Moore, comp., *The Craftsman, and Freemason's Guide* [Cincinnati: Jacob Ernst, 1854], 66, 113–114, 152, 192–193.)

95. Taylor and Richards were members of the Quorum of the Twelve Apostles. Richards, who was also Joseph Smith's clerk, recorded minutes of this organizational meeting, presumably on loose paper, until Eliza R. Snow was elected secretary partway through the meeting. Following that point, Snow recorded minutes for the remainder of the first meeting, as well as for subsequent meetings. Sometime after the first meeting, Snow copied Richards's minutes and her own minutes of the first meeting into the record book presented to the society by Richards. The record book has few strikeovers and insertions, suggesting Snow kept minutes on loose paper that she later copied into the official record book. Richards made a separate summary of the meeting in his March 17, 1842, entry in Joseph Smith's journal. (Joseph Smith, Journal, Mar. 17, 1842, in *JSP*, J2:45.)

96. Hymn 90, *A Collection of Sacred Hymns, for the Church of the Latter Day Saints,* ed. Emma Smith (Kirtland, OH: F. G. Williams, 1835), 120; and Hymn 252, *A Collection of Sacred Hymns for the Church of Jesus Christ of Latter Day Saints,* ed. Emma Smith (Nauvoo, IL: E. Robinson, 1841), 274. This hymn was written by William W. Phelps and sung at the dedication of the Kirtland temple in March

Joseph Smith's red brick store. Circa 1885–1886. The founding meeting of the Female Relief Society of Nauvoo took place March 17, 1842, on the second floor of this dry goods store. Several groups met in the upper room, including priesthood quorums, the Masonic lodge, the temple committee, and others. As membership blossomed, the Relief Society had to move their meetings outdoors to a grove near the temple. Photograph taken or obtained by Brigham H. Roberts. (Church History Library, Salt Lake City.)

When it was mov'd by Pres^t· Smith and seconded by Mrs. [Sarah] Cleveland, that a vote be taken to know if all are satisfied with each female present; and are willing to acknowledge them in full fellowship, and admit them to the privileges of the Institution about to be formed.

The names of those present were then taken as follows

Mrs Emma Smith

Mrs. Sarah M. Cleveland	Bathsheba W. Smith
Phebe Ann Hawkes	Phebe M. Wheeler
Elizabeth Jones	Elvira A. Co[w]les
Sophia Packard	Margaret A [Norris] Cook
Philinda Merrick	Athalia Robinson
Martha Knights	Sarah M. Kimball
Desdemona Fulmer	Eliza R. Snow
Elizabeth Ann Whitney	Sophia Robinson
Leonora Taylor	Nancy Rigdon[97]

Sophia R. Marks

Pres^t· Smith, & Elders Taylor and Richa◊ds[98] [p. 6] withdrew while the females went into an investigation of the motion, and decided that all present, be admitted according to the motion, and that

Mrs. Sarah [Ward] Higbee

Thirza Cahoon

Kezia A. Morrison

Miranda N. Hyde

Abigail Allred

Mary Snider

Sarah [Stiles] Granger

[*4 lines blank*]

should be admitted;[99] whose names were presented by Pres^t· Smith.

1836. (Minutes, *LDS Messenger and Advocate*, Mar. 1836, 2:280–281; Karen Lynn Davidson, *Our Latter-day Hymns: The Stories and the Messages* [Salt Lake City: Deseret Book, 1988], 30–31.)

97. The names of Athalia Robinson and Nancy Rigdon are stricken out in a different ink. Both women were daughters of Sidney Rigdon, who at this time was a counselor in the church's First Presidency. Rigdon was excommunicated in 1844 and thereafter established himself as the leader of a schismatic branch of the church in Pennsylvania; the names of his two daughters were presumably stricken out at or after that time.*ᵃ* This practice followed the scriptural injunction that the names of apostates should be "blotted out" from church records.*ᵇ* Consequently, Athalia Robinson and Nancy Rigdon do not appear in many early Relief Society histories, which officially list eighteen rather than twenty founding members.*ᶜ* (*a.* See Richard S. Van Wagoner, *Sidney Rigdon: A Portrait of Religious Excess* [Salt Lake City: Signature Books, 1994], 352–360. *b.* See, for example, Exodus 32:33; and Mosiah 26:32, 36. *c.* For example, see Document 4.28.)

98. TEXT: "Richa[*page torn*]ds".

99. TEXT: "should be admitted;" possibly inserted.

Pres.^t Smith, & Elders Taylor & Richards return'd and the meeting was address'd by Pres.^t Smith, to illustrate the object of the Society— that the Society of Sisters might provoke the brethren to good works in looking to the wants of the poor— searching after objects of charity, and in administering to their wants— to assist; by correcting the morals and strengthening the virtues of the female community, and save the Elders the trouble of rebuking; that they may give their time to other duties &c. in their public teaching.[100]

Pres.^t Smith further remark'd that an organization to show them how to go to work would be sufficient. He propos'd that the Sisters elect a presiding officer to preside over them, and let that presiding officer choose two Counsellors to assist in the duties of her Office— that he would ordain them to preside over the Society— and let them preside just as the Presidency, preside over the church;[101] and if [p. 7] they need his instruction— ask him, he will give it from time to time.

Let this Presidency serve as a constitution— all their decisions be considered law; and acted upon as such.

If any Officers are wanted to carry out the designs of the Institution, let them be appointed and set apart, as Deacons, Teachers &c. are among us.[102]

The minutes of your meetings will be precedents for you to act upon— your Constitutio[n] and law.[103]

He then suggested the propriety of electing a Presidency to continue in office during good behavior, or so long as they shall continue to fill the office with dignity &c. like the first Presidency of the church.—[104]

---

100. The duties of elders of the church included "to teach, expound, exhort, baptize, and watch over the church." (Doctrine and Covenants 20:42; see also 2 Timothy 4:2.)

101. The First Presidency, the presiding body of the church, consisted of a president and at least two counselors or assistant presidents. A church presidency was first organized in March 1832. In 1842 the First Presidency included Joseph Smith as president, with Hyrum Smith as associate president and Sidney Rigdon and William Law as counselors. In November 1831 Joseph Smith dictated a revelation instructing that "the duty of the president of the office of the High Priesthood is to preside over the whole church." ("First Presidency," in Dean C. Jessee et al., eds., *Journals, Volume 1: 1832–1839,* vol. 1 of the Journals series of *The Joseph Smith Papers,* ed. Dean C. Jessee et al. [Salt Lake City: Church Historian's Press, 2008], 466 [hereafter *JSP,* J1]; Revelation, 11 Nov. 1831–B, in Matthew C. Godfrey et al., eds., *Documents, Volume 2: July 1831–January 1833,* vol. 2 of the Documents series of *The Joseph Smith Papers,* ed. Dean C. Jessee et al. [Salt Lake City: Church Historian's Press, 2013], 135.)

102. Deacon and teacher were offices in the Aaronic Priesthood. For information on their duties, see Doctrine and Covenants 20:53–59.

103. Smith's designation of the presidency and minutes as the new group's "constitution" underscored the distinction between this organization and its short-lived precursor, the sewing society initiated by Sarah M. Kimball, for which Eliza R. Snow composed a constitution and bylaws. (See Document 4.10.)

104. Members of the First Presidency and the Quorum of the Twelve Apostles served for life or "during good behavior." Of the men who served in the general church presidency during Joseph Smith's

Motioned by Sister Whitney and seconded by Sister Packard that Mrs. Emma Smith be chosen President— passed unanimously—[105]

Mov'd by Pres.^t Smith, that Mrs. Smith proceed to choose her Counsellors, that they may be ordain'd to preside over this Society, in taking care of the poor— administering to their wants, and attending to the various affairs of this Institution.

The Presidentess Elect, then made choice of Mrs. Sarah M. Cleveland and Mrs. Elizabeth Ann Whitney for Counsellors—

President Smith read the Revelation to Emma Smith,[106] from the book of Doctrine and Covenants; and stated that she was ordain'd at the time, the Revelation was given, to expound the scriptures to all; and to teach the female part of community; and that not she alone, but others, may attain to the same blessings.— [p. 8]

The 2.^d Epistle of John, 1st verse, was then read to show that respect was then had to the same thing; and that why she was called an Elect lady is because, elected to preside.[107]

Elder Taylor was then appointed to ordain the Counsellors— he laid his hands on the head of Mrs Cleveland and ordain'd her to be a Counsellor to the Elect Lady, even Mrs. Emma Smith, to counsel, and assist her in all things pertaining to her office &c.

Elder T. then laid his hands on the head of Mrs. Whitney and ordain'd her to be a Counsellor to Mrs. Smith, the Pres.^t of the Institutio[n]— with all the privileges pertaining to the office &c.

He then laid his hands on the head of Mrs. Smith and blessed her, and confirm'd upon her all the blessings which have been confer'd on her, that she might be a mother in Israel[108] and look to the wants of the needy, and be a

---

lifetime, only two, Joseph Smith and Hyrum Smith, died while in office. For a variety of reasons, the remainder ceased functioning in their roles in the presidency before their deaths. (For further information, see "Ecclesiastical Organization Charts," in *JSP,* J1:455–459; and "Ecclesiastical Officers and Church Appointees," in *JSP,* J2:505–508.)

105. Forty years later, Sarah M. Kimball recalled that when Joseph Smith invited women to attend the March 17, 1842, organization meeting, he stated: "I wish Emma to be nominated and elected President of the organisation in fulfilment of the revelation in the Doctrine and Covenants which Says She is an Elect Lady." (Document 4.10.)

106. Document 1.1.

107. The March 17, 1842, entry in Joseph Smith's journal, written by scribe Willard Richards, reads: "Assisted in organizing 'The Female Relief Society of Nauvoo' . . . gave much instru[c]tion. read in the New Testament & Book of Doctrine & Covenants. concer[n]ing the Elect Lady. & Shewed that <u>Elect</u> meant to be <u>Elected</u> to a <u>certain</u> <u>work</u> &c, & that the revelation was then fulfilled by Sister Emma's Election to the Presidency of the Society, she having previously been ordained to expound the Scriptures." (Joseph Smith, Journal, Mar. 17, 1842, in *JSP,* J2:45, underlining in original.)

108. See Judges 5:7; and 2 Samuel 20:19. On the historical use of the phrase "Mother in Israel," see

pattern of virtue; and possess all the qualifications necessary for her to stand and preside and dignify her Office, to teach the females those principles requisite for their future usefulness.

Pres^t· Smith then resumed his remarks and gave instruction how to govern themselves in their meetings— when one wishes to speak, address the chair— and the chairman responds to the address.[109]

Should two speak at once, the Chair shall decide who speaks first, if any one is dissatisfied, she appeals to the house—

When one has the floor, occupies as long as she pleases.

Proper manner of address is Mrs. Chairman [p. 9] or President and not Mr. Chairman &c.

A question can never be put until it has a second

When the subject for discussion has been fairly investigated; the Chairman will say, are you ready for the question? &c.

Whatever the majority of the house decide upon becomes a law to the Society.

Pres^t· Smith proceeded to give counsel— do not injure the character of any one— if members of the Society shall conduct improperly, deal with them, and keep all your doings within your own bosoms, and hold all characters sacred—

It was then propos'd that Elder Taylor vacate the chair.

Pres^t· Emma Smith and her Counsellors took the chair, and

Elder Taylor mov'd— sec^d by Pres^t· J. Smith that we go into an investigation respecting what this Society shall be call'd— which was

carried unanimously

Carol Cornwall Madsen, "Mothers in Israel: Sarah's Legacy," in *Women of Wisdom and Knowledge: Talks Selected from the BYU Women's Conferences,* ed. Marie Cornwall and Susan Howe (Salt Lake City: Deseret Book, 1990), 179–201. About six weeks before the organization of the Relief Society, on February 6, 1842, Emma Smith gave birth to a son who did not survive. This was the sixth of Joseph and Emma Smith's children (five natural, one adopted) to die in infancy. The three sons and one adopted daughter living in March 1842 lived to adulthood, along with the last son born in 1844. ("Joseph Smith Pedigree Chart," The Joseph Smith Papers, accessed Apr. 6, 2015, http://www.josephsmithpapers.org.)

109. In recommending the use of parliamentary procedure, Joseph Smith may have drawn either from local traditions or from Thomas Jefferson's *Manual of Parliamentary Practice,* published in 1801, with second and third editions in 1812 and 1822. On this particular point, Jefferson's manual states, "When any member means to speak, he is to stand up in his place, uncovered, and to address himself, not to the House, or any particular member, but to the Speaker, who calls him by his name, that the House may take notice who it is that speaks." (Thomas Jefferson, *A Manual of Parliamentary Practice: Composed Originally for the Use of the Senate of the United States* [Philadelphia: Hogan and Thompson, 1840], 38; Don H. Doyle, "Rules of Order: Henry Martyn Robert and the Popularization of American Parliamentary Law," *American Quarterly* 32, no. 1 [Spring 1980]: 4–5.)

Pres.^{t.} Smith continued instructions to the Chair to suggest to the members anything the chair might wish, and which it might not be proper for the chair to put, or move &c.

Mov'd by Counsellor Cleveland, and secon'd by Counsellor Whitney, that this Society be called <u>The</u> <u>Nauvoo</u> <u>Female</u> <u>Relief</u> Society.

Elder Taylor offered an amendment, that it be called <u>The</u> <u>Nauvoo</u> <u>Female</u> <u>Benevolent</u> <u>Society</u> which would give a more definite and extended idea of the Institution— that Relief be struck out and Benevolent inserted.

Pres.^{t.} Smith offer'd instruction on votes— [p. 10]

The motion was seconded by Counsellor Cleveland and unanimously carried, on the amendment by Elder Taylor.

The Pres.^{t.} then suggested that she would like an argument with Elder Taylor on the words Relief and Benevolence.

Pres.^{t.} J. Smith mov'd that the vote for amendment, be rescinded, which was carried—

Motion for adjournment by Elder Richards and objected by Pres.^{t.} J. Smith.—

Pres.^{t.} J. Smith— Benevolent is a popular term— and the term <u>Relief</u> is not known among popular Societies— <u>Relief</u> is more extended in its signification than <u>Benevolent</u> and might extend to the liberation of the culprit— and might be wrongly construed by our enemies to say that the Society was to relieve criminals from punishment &c. &c— to relieve a murderer, which would not be a benevolent act—

Pres.^{t.} Emma Smith, said the <u>popularity</u> of the word benevolent is one great objection— no person can think of the word as associated with public Institutions, without thinking of the Washingtonian Benevolent Society which was one of the most corrupt Institutions of the day— do not wish to have it call'd after other Societies in the world—[110]

Pres.^{t.} J. Smith arose to state that he had no objection to the word <u>Relief</u>— that on question they ought to deliberate candidly and investigate all subjects.

Counsellor Cleveland arose to remark concerning the question before the house, that we should not regard [p. 11] the idle speech of our enemies—

---

110. Allied with the broader Washingtonian Temperance Society, founded in 1840, Martha Washingtonian societies were composed of working- and lower-middle-class women who sought to reform inebriates and succor their families. According to historian Ruth M. Alexander, "As early as 1842, the Washingtonian movement showed signs of weakening as it was beset with internal disputes over its inexperienced leaders, lack of organization, alienation of elite temperance and religious leaders, and 'low-class' social affairs." (Ruth M. Alexander, "'We Are Engaged as a Band of Sisters': Class and Domesticity in the Washingtonian Temperance Movement, 1840–1850," *Journal of American History* 75, no. 3 [Dec. 1988]: 775; Lori D. Ginzberg, *Women and the Work of Benevolence: Morality, Politics, and Class in the Nineteenth-Century United States* [New Haven, CT: Yale University Press, 1990], 202–204.)

we design to act in the name of the Lord— to relieve the wants of the distressed, and do all the good we can.—

Eliza R. Snow arose and said that she felt to concur with the President, with regard to the word Benevolent, that many Societies with which it had been associated, were corrupt,— that the popular Institutions of the day should not be our guide— that as daughters of Zion, we should set an example for all the world, rather than confine ourselves to the course which had been heretofore pursued— one objection to the word <u>Relief</u> is, that the idea associated with it is that of some great calamity— that we intend appropriating on some extraordinary occasions instead of meeting the common occurrences—

Pres^{t.} Emma Smith remark'd— we are going to do something <u>extraordinary</u>— when a boat is stuck on the rapids[111] with a multitude of Mormons on board we shall consider <u>that</u> a loud call for <u>relief</u>— we expect extraordinary occasions and pressing calls—

Elder Taylor arose and said— I shall have to concede the point— your arguments are so potent I cannot stand before them— I shall have to give way—

Pres^{t.} J. S. said I also shall have to concede the point, all I shall have to give to the poor, I shall give to this Society—

Counsellor Whitney mov'd, that this Society be call'd <u>The</u> <u>Nauvoo</u> <u>Female</u> <u>Relief</u> <u>Society</u>— secon^{d.} by Counsellor Cleveland—

E. R. Snow offer'd an amendment by way of transposition of words, instead of The <u>Nauvoo</u> <u>Female</u> <u>Relief</u> <u>Society</u>, it shall be call'd The <u>Female</u> <u>Relief</u> <u>Society</u> of Nauvoo— Seconded by Pres^{t.} J. Smith and carried— [p. 12]

The previous question was then put— Shall this Society be call'd <u>The</u> <u>Female</u> <u>Relief</u> <u>Society</u> of <u>Nauvoo</u>?— carried unanimously.—

Pres^{t.} J. Smith— I now declare this Society organiz'd with President and Counsellors &c. according to Parliamentary usages— and all who shall hereafter be admitted into this Society must be free from censure and receiv'd by vote—

Pres^{t.} J. Smith offered . . . .$5.00 in gold piece to commence the funds of the Institution.

Pres^{t.} Emma Smith requested that the gentlemen withdraw before they proceed to the choice of Secretary and Treasurer, as was mov'd by Pres^{t.} J. Smith—

<u>Willard</u> <u>Richards.</u> Sec^{ty.}

---

111. The "rapids" refers to the Des Moines or Lower Rapids, an eleven-mile stretch of the Mississippi River just north of Keokuk, Iowa, where the river dropped about twenty-two feet. These rapids were impassable for steamboats during months of low water and potentially treacherous during many other months. (Louis C. Hunter, *Steamboats on the Western Rivers: An Economic and Technological History* [New York: Dover, 1993], 188.)

The gentlemen withdrew when it was Motioned and secon^d. and unanimously pass'd that Eliza R. Snow be appointed Secretary, and Phebe M. Wheeler, Assistant Secretary——

Motioned, secon^d. and carried unanim^ly. that Elvira A. Coles be appointed Treasurer—

Pres^t. E. Smith then arose and proceeded to make appropriate remarks on the object of the Society— its duties to others also its relative duties to each other Viz. to seek out and relieve the distressed— that each member should be ambitious to do good— that the members should deal frankly with each other— to watch over the morals— and be very careful ⟨of⟩ the character and reputation— of the members of the Institution &c.

P. A. Hawkes— Question— What shall we reply to interrogatories relative to the object of this Society?

Pres^t. E. Smith replied— for charitable purposes. [p. 13]

Mov'd and pass'd that Cynthia Ann Eldridge be admitted as a member of this Society—

Cou^lr. Sarah M. Cleveland donated to the fund of the Society $12½
Sarah M. Kimball do [ditto]. 1.00
Pres^t. Emma Smith do 1.00
Coun^lr. E. A. Whitney do. 50

Pres^t. E. Smith said that Mrs. Merrick is a widow— is industrious— performs her work well, therefore recommend her to the patronage of such as wish to hire needlework— those who hire widows must be prompt to pay and inasmuch as some have defrauded the laboring widow of her wages, we must be upright and deal justly—

The business of the Society concluded— the gentlemen before mentioned return'd—,

Elder Richards appropriated to the fund of the Society, the sum of . $1,00
Elder Taylor do. 2.00

Elder T. then arose and address'd the Society by saying that he is much gratified in seeing a meeting of this kind in Nauvoo— his heart rejoices when he sees the most distinguished characters, stepping forth in such a cause, which is calculated to bring into exercise every virtue and give scope to the benevolent feelings of the female heart— he rejoices to see this Institution organiz'd according to the law of Heaven— according to a revelation previously given to Mrs E. Smith appointing her to this important calling— and to see all things moving forward in such a glorious manner— his prayer is that the blessings of God and the peace of heaven may rest on this Institution henceforth——

The Choir then sang "Come let us rejoice in the [p. 14] day of salvation["] &c.[112]

Motion'd, that this meeting adjourn to next week, thursday, ten o'clock—A M.

The meeting then arose and was dismiss'd by prayer by Elder Taylor.—

March 24, 1842 • Thursday
Minutes of the proceedings
of the
Second Meeting of the
Society.

Lodge Room
March 24th 1842.

Meeting open'd with singing "How pleas'd and blest was I" &c.—[113] Prayer by Pres[t.] Emma Smith.

Pres[t.] E. Smith then rose and said that measures to promote union in this Society must be carefully attended to— that every member should be held in full fellowship— as a society, hop'd they would divest themselves of every jealousy and evil feeling toward each other, if any such existed— that we should bring our conduct into respectability, here & eveery where else— said she rejoic'd in the prospect before her——.

Pres[t.] E. Smith continued by saying, that those wishing to join the Society could have the privilege—

Mov'd, seconded & unanimously carried that the following persons be receiv'd as members of this Society— to wit.

K [blank] [Catherine] Walker,	Jane Law [p. 15]
Elizabeth Eldridge	Mary Woolley
Cirinda Murrill	Agnes Smith
Sarah Hillman	Sarah Brown
Sarah Roberts	Fanny F. [Maria] Huntington
Mercy Thompson	Sarah Ann Higbee
Eunice Wilber [Wilbur]	Elizabeth [Davis] Durfee
Louisa Beman	Elizabeth Hills
Diantha Billings	Emeline Corlin [Carling]
Vilote Kimlall [Vilate Kimball]	Lucy [Mack] Smith

112. This hymn, which actually begins, "Now let us rejoice in the day of salvation," was written by William W. Phelps and was sung at the dedication of the Kirtland temple in March 1836. (Hymn 263, *Collection of Sacred Hymns* [1841], 286; Minutes, *LDS Messenger and Advocate,* Mar. 1836, 2:276; Davidson, *Our Latter-day Hymns,* 31–32.)

113. Hymn 13, *Collection of Sacred Hymns* [1841], 20.

Eliza Ann Mills
Sophia F. Wilber
Julia Ann Sessions
~~Ma◊◊ Smith~~ Lucy A. Munjar
Mary Smith
Martha [Patty] Sessions
Elizabeth C. Lee
[Mrs.] A [*blank*] P. Rockwood
[Nancy Rockwood]
Hannah Mark[h]am
Cynthia Baggs
Loisa Follett
Mary Jane Warner
Sarah Moon
Abigail Leonard

Lucy Millican [Millikin]
Zina Jacobs
Sally Davis
Sabra Gribble
Kezia A. Morrison
Caroline Ballard
Melissa Dodge

Katharine Wilkie
Elizabeth Allred
Cyrena Murrill [Merrill]
Sylva Lyons
Sarah Brown
Soloma Chapman
Abigail Kelsey

Mrs. Mary Smith then rose and said the Instututution had her hearty concurrence— that nothing was more laudable than feeding the hungry, clothing the naked &c.— that she desired to aid in accomplishing objects so generous.

Mrs. Vilote Kimball said she had not fully understood what were the objects of the Institution but desired to be found aiding in every benevolent cause [p. 16]

Pres^t. E. Smith said, no one need feel delicate in reference to inquiries about this Society— there is nothing private— its objects are purely benevolent.

Mother Lucy Smith arose and said she rejoic'd in view of what was doing—[114] as she came in and look'd upon the sisters, it gave her feelings of deep interest— Wept— said she was advanc'd in years and could not stay long—[115] hop'd the Lord would bless and aid the Society in feeding the hungry, clothing the naked— that her work was nearly done— felt to pray that the blessings of heaven might rest upon the Society.

Pres^t. E. Smith rose and read from the Book of records, the proceedings of the first meeting of the Society— She then proceeded to read to the honorable body, a report, wherein Clarissa Marvel was accus'd of scandalous falsehoods

---

114. Lucy Mack Smith was the mother of Joseph Smith and his ten siblings and a matriarchal figure in the early years of the church; her participation in and benediction upon the Relief Society were of singular significance. For a discussion of the leading role "Mother Smith" filled in the early church, see "Editor's Introduction: The Domestic Spirituality of Lucy Mack Smith," in Lavina Fielding Anderson, ed., *Lucy's Book: A Critical Edition of Lucy Mack Smith's Family Memoir* (Salt Lake City: Signature Books, 2001), 11–65.

115. Lucy Mack Smith was sixty-six years old.

on the character of Pres.̇ Joseph Smith, without the least provocation, praying that they would in wisdom adopt some plan to bring her to repentance— said she presum'd that most of the Society knew more about Clarissa Marvel than herself——

Mrs. Agnes Smith said Clarissa Marvel had liv'd with her nearly a year— she had seen nothing amiss of her—

Councillor [Elizabeth Ann] Whitney propos'd that some one be appointed to go and labor with her and if possible reform her——

Mov'd and carried that Mrs. Markam be one to go and converse with C. Marvel.

Mrs. Markam objected on the ground that she was unacquainted with the circumstances. [p. 17]

Pres.̇ Smith said that would make no difference— she could attend to it— that it should be be done in a private manner, with great prudence—

Mrs. Pres.̇ continued, by saying that we intend to look into the morals of each other and watch over each other— that she intended to walk circumspectly and to shun the appearance of evil— all are required to be very careful in their words and actions at all times— said she believed Clarissa Marvel might be reform'd.[116]

Mrs. Billings inquired if C. M. had parents.

Pres.̇ Smith said she has no parents— she is under our care and observation— she needs friends——

Mrs. [Elizabeth] Jones enquired if the proceedings of this Society should be divulged out of the Society

Pres.̇ Smith said all proceedings that regard difficulties should be kept among the members— as to the Institution, its objects are charitable— none

---

116. Marvel was later cleared of the accusation of slander against Joseph Smith. The September 28, 1842, entry in the Nauvoo minute book is followed by a copy of Marvel's signed statement that she had never seen or reported "any thing improper or unvirtuous in the conduct or conversation of either President Smith or Mrs. Agnes Smith." Agnes Moulton Smith was the widow of Joseph's deceased brother Don Carlos Smith (1816–1841). By this time, she had likely married Joseph Smith as a plural wife. On January 6, 1842, Brigham Young wrote a journal entry in Masonic code, stating, "J Smith was Agness." The "was" may be an abbreviation for "wedded and sealed to." In addition, in 1892 Mary Ann West, who lived with Agnes in Nauvoo and was a plural wife of Joseph Smith's brother William, stated in a deposition that Agnes had told her she had become a plural wife of Joseph Smith following the death of her husband, Don Carlos, because it had been "the wish of her husband." (Document 1.2, entries for Mar. 31 and Apr. 14, 1842; Brigham Young, Journal, July 1837–Apr. 1845, Brigham Young Office Files, 1832–1878, CHL, Jan. 6, 1842; Mary Ann West, Testimony, Salt Lake City, Utah Territory, ca. Mar. 22, 1892, pp. 499–500, questions 141–144; pp. 521–522, questions 676–687, 696–699, Reorganized Church of Jesus Christ of Latter Day Saints v. Church of Christ Independence, MO, et al. [C.C.W.D. Mo. 1894], typescript, Testimonies and Depositions, 1892, CHL.)

can object to telling the good— the evil withhold— hoped all would feel themselves bound to observe this rule.

Councillor Whitney said she felt deeply interested— thought we could not take too much pains in this matter— to avoid all evil— We must avoid the appearance of evil— we must pray much for each other that we may succeed in the work before us and have wisdom given us in all our pursuits.——

Mother Lucy Smith said— this Institution is a good one— we must watch over ourselves— that she came into the church of Jesus Christ of Latter-day Saints, to do good— to get good, and to get into the celestial kingdom. She said we must [p. 18] cherish one another, watch over one another, comfort one another and gain instruction, that we may all sit down in heaven together.

Mrs. Hillman rose and said she was contemplating the blessings with which we were surrounded— the privileges of this Society— said she desir'd to be watch'd over and aided in the better performance of her duty.—

Prest. Smith said all who wish'd should have informatio[n] respecting this Society; as they would be published.—[117] She hinted the propriety of having Auxiliary Societies form'd in other parts of the City— any one who felt dispos'd might send in a request to this effect— said it was the duty of every person to inquire into the condition of the poor and represent their true state.[118]

Councillor Whitney call'd on the members to contribute to the fund

The following appropriations were made to the fund of the Society——

	$.
Mary Jane Warner	.. 25
Martha Sessions	.. 25
Sylva Lyons	1.00
Jane Law	1.00
Sophia Robinson	.. 25
Louisa Beman	.. 50
Sarah Brown	.. 25
Mary Woolley	.. 25

Mrs. [Phebe Ann] Hawkes arose to represent Mrs. Drury as an object of charity, being sick and destitute of food. [p. 19]

Mrs. Wooley corroborated the testimony of Mrs Hawkes—

117. On April 1, 1842, the church newspaper in Nauvoo, the *Times and Seasons,* published an article announcing the establishment and explaining the purposes of the Relief Society. (Document 1.3.)

118. No auxiliary societies were formed at this time, though some Latter-day Saint women at La Harpe, Illinois (about twenty-five miles east of Nauvoo), and at Lima, Illinois (about thirty miles south of Nauvoo), sent contributions or met to make quilts for the Nauvoo society. (See Document 1.2, entries for July 14, 1842; Sept. 2, 1843.)

Motioned and seconded that the board direct the Treasurer to give an order on the Store— carried unanim^sly.

Motioned that 2 dollars be appropriated to Mrs. Drury—

Pres^t. Smith said we want the names of those widows who want work—

Mrs. Agnes Smith solicited the patronage of the Society as a Milliner and Dressmaker.

Pres^t. Smith said we should assist each other in this way— said Mrs. Solome Chapman was in want of work, knitting, sewing &c.

Mrs Jones represented Mrs. Baggs as needing assistance—

Mrs. Thompson enquired whether anything except money would be received into the Treasury; such as jewelry, clothing &c. &c.

Mrs. Warner said her means were limited but would give provisions.

Pres^t. Smith hinted the propriety of placing such provisions as should be donated, into the hands of the Treasurer—

Mrs. Higbee suggested the propriety of having an Auxiliary Society—

Councillor remark'd that as many were present who were not at the previous meeting; it was necessary to refer to the order established at the organization of the Society. Viz. that of addressing the Chair.[119]

Mrs. Mary Smith suggested the propriety of procuring Palm leaves[120] for the benefit of individuals [p. 20] spoke of sister Daviss as soliciting that work—

Pres^t. Smith said the object was to supply the poor with money— provisions, cloathes, old cloathes &c. that it was wisdom to keep all the money we could, for the purchase of materials to do with.

Mrs. Velote Kimball represented widow More, as needy and deserving charity— said she would work; understood the business of braiding Palm leaves———

Mrs. Hillman corroborates Mrs. Kimball's statement———

Mrs Markam exprest her satisfaction in being in a situation to bring her abilities into action— said it was her aim to walk humbly before God. desired the prayers of the Society that she might be enabled to do whatever the Lord should require at her hands—

Pres^t. Smith suggested the propriety of appointing at the next meeting; persons who may wait on those who represent the poor—

Motioned that the meeting adjourn until next thursday, 2. o'clock—

---

119. At the organizational meeting of the Relief Society on March 17, 1842, Joseph Smith instructed, "When one wishes to speak, address the chair." (Document 1.2, entry for Mar. 17, 1842.)

120. Braided palm leaves were used to make hats. Palm leaves may have been shipped up the Mississippi River from New Orleans. (See Thomas Dublin, "Women's Work and the Family Economy: Textiles and Palm Leaf Hatmaking in New England, 1830–1850," *Tocqueville Review* 5, no. 2 [1983]: 297–316.)

Mov'd, seconded & pass'd that Pres.ᵗ Joseph Smith be call'd in, to close the meeting.

Pres.ᵗ J. Smith and Elders B. [Brigham] Young, H. [Heber] Kimball, W. [Willard] Richards & J. [John] Snider entered— The choir sung—

Prayer by Elder Brigham Young. [p. 21]

March 31, 1842 • Thursday

Minutes of the Proceedings
of the
Third Meeting of the Society[121]—

Lodge Room March 30ᵗʰ [31st] 1842.[122]

Meeting opened with Singing—

Prayer by Pres.ᵗ Joseph Smith—

The house full to overflowing.

Prest. J. Smith arose— spoke of the organization of the Society— said he was deeply interested that it might be built up to the Most High in an acceptable manner— that its rules must be observed— that none should be received into the Society but those who were worthy— propos'd that the Society go into a close examination of every candidate— that they were going too fast—[123] that the Society should grow up by degrees— should commence with a few individuals— thus have a select Society of the virtuous and those who will walk circumspectly— commended them for their zeal but said sometimes their zeal was not according to knowledge—[124] One principal object of the Institution, was to purge out iniquity— said they must be extremely careful in all their examinations or the consequences would be serious

Said all difficulties which might & would cross our way must be surmounted, though the soul be <u>tried</u>, the heart faint, and hands hang down— must not retrace our steps— that there must be decision of character aside from sympathy— that when instructed we must obey that voice, observe the

---

121. TEXT: Double underline in original.

122. The date should read March 31, 1842. That date aligns with Thursday, when Relief Society meetings were generally held during this period. Joseph Smith's journal records that he spoke to the Relief Society in the afternoon of Thursday, March 31. Extracts from the minutes of this meeting were published with significant modifications in the *Deseret News,* September 5, 1855. (Joseph Smith, Journal, Mar. 31, 1842, in *JSP,* J2:48; Document 2.2.)

123. In addition to the twenty charter members at the March 17, 1842, founding meeting, seven other women joined that first day and forty-eight more women joined on March 24, 1842. No new members were admitted at this March 31 meeting. At Joseph Smith's request, twenty new names were held over and presented at the next meeting on April 14, 1842.

124. See Romans 10:2.

Constitution[125] that the blessings of heaven may rest down upon us— all must act in concert or nothing can be done— that the Society should move according to the ancient Priesthood, hence there should be a select Society separate from all the evils of the world, choice, virtuou[s] and holy— Said he was going to make of this Society a kingdom of priests an in Enoch's day— as in Pauls day—[126] that it is the privilege of each member to live long [p. 22] and enjoy health— Pres.^t Smith propos'd that the ladies [gentlemen] withdraw, that the Society might proceed to business— that those wishing to join should have their names presented at the next meeting.——

Pres.^t J. Smith withdrew—

Pres.^t E. [Emma] Smith rose & said she would like to hear from those appointed to enquire into the case of Clarissa M. [Marvel][127]

Mrs. [Diantha] Billings said— we visited her, questioned her closely— she appear'd like an innocent girl—

---

125. Joseph Smith stated that the society's presidency should "serve as a constitution" and that the society's minutes "will be precedents for you to act upon— your Constitutio[n] and law." (Document 1.2, entry for Mar. 17, 1842.)

126. See Exodus 19:6; and Revelation 1:6. Joseph Smith's remarks at this meeting associate women with the "ancient Priesthood." The January 6, 1842, entry in Joseph Smith's journal, apparently dictated by Smith, stated that God was initiating the restoration of "the ancient order of his Kingdom," which would prepare "the earth for the return of his glory . . . and a kingdom of Priests & Kings to God & the Lamb forever. on Mount Zion."^a Most early Latter-day Saints understood this connection between priesthood and women as a part of temple worship. For example, Bathsheba W. Smith, a founding member of the Relief Society and one of the small vanguard of men and women who received temple ordinances from Joseph Smith prior to the completion of the temple at Nauvoo, recalled in a 1905 address that Joseph Smith "wanted to make us, as the women were in Paul's day, 'A kingdom of priestesses.'" She then explained, "We have that ceremony in our [temple] endowments as Joseph taught."^b At the August 13, 1843, Relief Society meeting, Nauvoo temple building committee member Reynolds Cahoon explicitly tied the women's organization to the temple, saying, "This Society is raisd by the Lord to prepare us for the great blessings which are for us in the House of the Lord."^c Eliza R. Snow, who had long ministered to women in temple rituals, also taught of the connection between Relief Society, priesthood restoration, and heavenly destiny in an 1875 address in which she appealed to women to join the Relief Society "for your own cultivation, to elevate to prepare you to become queens and priestesses, to prepare you to become suitable companions to your husbands, to become as anciently, holy women of God."^d Elsewhere, Snow promised faithful women they would "become Queens of Queens, and Priestesses unto the Most High God."^e On May 4, 1842, five weeks after this March 31 Relief Society meeting, Joseph Smith introduced temple ceremonies to nine trusted male associates gathered in the assembly room above his store.^f (a. Joseph Smith, Journal, Jan. 6, 1842, in *JSP*, J2:26. b. "Pioneer Stake," *Woman's Exponent,* July and Aug. 1905, 34:14. c. Document 1.2, entry for Aug. 13, 1843. d. Gunnison Ward, Gunnison Stake, Gunnison Ward Relief Society Minutes and Records, 1872–1949, CHL, June 28, 1875, p. 27. e. Eliza R. Snow, "An Address," *Woman's Exponent,* Sept. 15, 1873, 2:63. f. Joseph Smith, Journal, May 4, 1842, in *JSP*, J2:53; Historian's Office, Joseph Smith History, Draft Notes, ca. 1839–1856, CHL, May 4, 1842.)

127. At the prior meeting of the Relief Society, Marvel had been accused of slander against Joseph Smith. (Document 1.2, entry for Mar. 24, 1842.)

Mrs Markam [Hannah Markham] corroborated the statement of Mrs. Billings.

Pres^t· E. S. said, We are call'd upon to find the origin of the report—

Mrs. Billings refer'd to Mrs. Winchester, with whom C. M. had resided—

Mrs. W. Had heard C. M. speak of Pres^t· J. Smith & family in the most respectful manner.

Councillor [Sarah] Cleveland propos'd that the rumor be trac'd out— and the innocent clear'd—

Mrs. Gribble said Laura Jones & Hannah Burgess have reported against C. M.

Councillor [Elizabeth Ann] Whitney motion'd that 2 persons be appointed to see L. Jones & H. B. carried unan^ly·

Councillor C. motioned that Mrs. Allred and Mrs. [Elizabeth Davis] Durfee be appointed to see them and cite them to appear at the next meeting.

Mrs. Durfee objected.

Pres^t· E. S. said we were going to learn new things— our way was straight— said we wanted none in this society but those who could and would walk straight and were determined to do good and not evil— said that Mrs. Durfee must serve unless she could provide [p. 23] a better person to officiate in her stead—

Councillor Cleveland remark'd that they had put their shoulder to the wheel and exhorted them to do with their might— we have entered into this work in the name of the Lord let us boldly go forward——

After appropriate remarks Pres^t· E. Smith, said she had an Article to read which would test the ability of the members in keeping secrets; as it was for the benefit of the Society, and that alone——

Read the Article.—[128] Then gave strictures on female propriety and dignity &c. &c.

Mother [Lucy Mack] Smith rose and said she was glad the time had come that iniquity could be detected and reproach thrown off from the heads of the church— We come into the church to be sav'd— that we may live in peace and sit down in the kingdom of heaven— If we listen to, and circulate every

---

128. The March 31, 1842, entry in the journal of Joseph Smith, as recorded by his clerk Willard Richards, notes with respect to this article or epistle: "In council at his office with. Elders [Brigham] Young. [John] Taylor &^c. & wrote an Epistle to the Female Relief Soci[e]ty and spake to the Socity in the afternoon." This epistle is recorded in the Nauvoo Relief Society Minute Book following the minutes for September 28, 1842. It warns women against unnamed men who claim authority from Joseph Smith or other church leaders to "deceive and debauch the innocent." On April 10, 1842, Joseph Smith publicly denounced such deceptions: "Preached in the grove after Elder Wm Law. had spoken. a[nd] pronounced a curse upon all Adulterers & fornicators & unvirtuous persons. & those who had made use of his name to carry on their iniquitous designs." (Joseph Smith, Journal, Mar. 31 and Apr. 10, 1842, in *JSP*, J2:48, 50.)

evil report we shall idly spend the time which should be appropriated to the reading the Scriptures, the Book of Mormon— we must remember the words of Alma— pray much at morning, noon and night—[129] feed the poor &c.—[130] She said she was <u>old</u>— could not meet with the Society but few times more— and wish'd to leave her testimony that the Book of Mormon is the book of God— that Joseph is a man of God, a prophet of the Lord set apart to lead the people— If we observe his words it will be well with us; if we live righteously on earth, it will be well with us in Eternity——

Councillor Cleveland arose and address'd mother Smith, returning thanks for her testimony, and counsel— express'd many good wishes; that she [p. 24] might receive much comfort and consolation in this Society— that the Lord would lengthen her days— that she may cheer the Society with her presence, aid it by her counsels and prayrs long before she shall take her departure to sit down by the side of her beloved Partner.[131]

Mrs. [Mercy] Thompson made mention of a lone widow with one child, late from England, without friends, in want of a home.

Mrs. [Sarah] Brown proposed to take her in

Mrs. [Elizabeth] Jones laid before the Society her expectations of soon journeying to Ohio, to visit friends who were moving in the higher classes of Society; and requested the prayers of this Society that her testimony may be instrumental of good. &c.

Motioned by Councillor Cleveland and seconded by the President, that Mrs. Jones have a recommend from this Society— carried unanim^{ly.}.

Upon Motion of Councillor Cleveland, the meeting adjourn'd to thursday, ~~15th~~ 14th of April 2. o.clock.

The following is a copy of the <u>recommend</u>, ~~to~~ for Mrs. Jones

The <u>Female</u> <u>Relief</u> <u>Society</u> of <u>Nauvoo</u>, recommends Mrs. Elizabeth Jones, as a member of said Society, in good standing;— and she is <u>hereby</u> <u>Authorized</u> to receive all such <u>donations</u> as friends abroad shall feel disposed to put into her hands, to be appropriated to the Fund of the Institution; for the benefit of the poor, the widow, and the fatherless.[132]

---

129. See Alma 37:37.

130. See Mosiah 4:26.

131. Joseph Smith Sr. (1771–1840), husband of Lucy Mack Smith and father of Joseph Smith. ("Joseph Smith Pedigree Chart," The Joseph Smith Papers, accessed Apr. 6, 2015, http://www.josephsmith-papers.org.)

132. A recommend or certificate such as this was evidence that the bearer had the authority to solicit

By Order of the Board.[133]
Eliza R. Snow, Secretary. [p. 25]

April 14, 1842 • Thursday

Minutes of the Proceedings
of the
<u>Fourth</u> Meeting of the Society.

Lodge Room, April 14,[th] 1842.

Meeting opened with singing "How pleasant 'tis to see" &c.[134]

Prayer by Pres[t.] Emma Smith— after which Councillor [Sarah] Cleveland arose and address'd the meeting, informing them that the case of Clarissa M. [Marvel] had been satisfactorily settled she having testified in her own hand writing that she had said no wrong &c.[135] Mrs. C. continued by cautioning the Society against speaking evil of Pres[t.] J. Smith and his companion— that it would not be a light thing in the sight of God— that they had prov'd themselves; and the case of C. M. should be a warning, how we hear and how we speak— express'd her fears that the Lord would cut off those who will not take counsel &c.

Motioned by Councillor Cleveland, seconded by Councillor [Elizabeth Ann] Whitney, that the following persons be received into this Society—— passed unanimously,

Clarissa Wilcox	~~Lydia Anderson~~[136]
Phebe Knights [Knight]	Catharine Mellon [Malin]
[*blank*] Wight	Hannah Pierce
Lydia Huntington	Betsey Roundy
Phebe Miller	Phebe Chase
Phebe Angell	Nancy H. Rockwood
Drusilla Hendricks	Nancy Winchester
Polly [Knight] Stringham	Martha Peck
Asenath Sherman	Cornelia J. Fisher
Lydia Anderson	Electa E. Whiteside

---

funds on behalf of an organization. A photograph of an original Relief Society certificate appears in "An Interesting Old Document," *Relief Society Magazine* 23, no. 6 (June 1936).

133. This is very likely a reference to the Relief Society presidency, as no other board existed within the Relief Society at this time.

134. Hymn 251, *Collection of Sacred Hymns* [1841], 273.

135. Marvel's statement was recorded later in the minutes, following the account of the September 28, 1842, meeting.

136. TEXT: This name was knife-erased, presumably because it had already been written in the first column.

Charlotte Hawes

Pres^{t.} E. Smith arose and address'd the meeting by saying that the disagreeable busines of searching out those that were iniquitous, seem'd to fall on her— [p. 26] said it was an unpleasant task, but her desire was to do good— wish'd all the members of this Society to assist her— said it was necessary to begin at home— to eradicate all evil from our[137] own hearts— and warn those who wish to join, with us, to come calculating to divest themselves of every thing wrong and unite to expose iniquity, to search it out and put it away— She said the Society had other duties to attend to than seeing to the wants of the poor. Exhorted the members so to conduct as to have the honor of commencing a good work and of carrying it out— enforc'd the necessity of walking in a manner that would be approbated of God.

While the Officers of the Board were examining petitions of various persons who applied for membership Mrs. Pres^{t.} call'd on the Society to occupy the time; which was spent much to the edification of those present, by Mother [Lucy Mack] Smith and others, by way of exhortation, admonition, encouragement &c. &c.

After passing examination on the various petitions presented; the following names were presented to the Society, and the persons received as members, to wit.

Mercy Ann Bruce	Sarah Head
Nancy N. Tracy	Sarah Davis
Olive Farr	Sophronia Norris
Susannah Be[ckel]hymer	Mary Sloan
Julia Stone	Delia Curtis
Emily Whitmark [Whitmarsh]	Catharine Wood
Charlotte Curtis	Mary Munjar
Jane Allen	Mary C. Coray
Elizabeth Johnson	Caroline Kingsbury
Loisa [Louisa] M. Lyman	Jane Ann Green
Mary E. Lightner	Amy Clothier [p. [27]]
Magdalene Moesser	Mary H. Felshaw
Ruth Sayers	Eliza Grant
Caroline M. Bullard	Susan Younger
Mary Ann Bullard	Asenath Sherman
Mary Smith	~~Cornelia J. Fisher~~[138]

---

137. TEXT: Possibly "one".

138. TEXT: This name was knife-erased, presumably because it had already been included in a list of new members two pages earlier.

Mahitable Calkins
Kuhamath B. Derby
Eveline Rollin
Huldah Harmon
Eliza M. Green[e]
Elizabeth Bills
Ruth Williams
Hannah Marsh
Marcia Allen

Electa G. [Eleanor] Whiteside
Jane A. Young
Rebecca Reed
Sarah Ann Waitt
Amanda M. Pierce
Hannah Smith
Anna Partridge
Elizabeth Fory[139]
Sarah Noe

Pres.ᵗ Smith then call'd on those, if any present who knew of cases of the poor to be represented.

Mrs. [Phebe Ann] Hawkes spoke of the Drury family— still sick needing our prayers— if nothing more—[140]

Mary Smith said her husband had given her the privilege of donating weekly one bushel of corn meal for the poor— wish'd to know where it should be deposited.— also mentioned the case of a motherless child needing a home— whereupon,

It was decided that for the present it should remain in the care of Mrs. Eldridge— decided also that the meal offered by Mrs. Smith as well as all other provisions, should be put into the care of the Treas. where the needy may apply for the same——

The following donations in money were made, to wit,
Caroline Kingsbury 25
Sylva Lyons [Sylvia Lyon] 50
[p. [28]]
Athalia Robinson 25
Charlotte Hawes 1.25
Vilate Kimball 50
Catharine Wilkie   2.00
                                                                      4.75

The meeting adjourn'd to thursday, the 28ᵗʰ of April, at 2 o.clock, P.M.[141]

Donations • March 31 and 29, 1842

The following donations were made at the <u>Third</u> meeting of the Society; inadvertently omitted in the proper place of insertion.

139. TEXT: Possibly "Foory".
140. During the Relief Society meeting on March 24, 1842, "Mrs. Hawkes arose to represent Mrs. Drury as an object of charity, being sick and destitute of food." (Document 1.2, entry for Mar. 24, 1842.)
141. As recorded in the minutes that follow, a "special meeting" of the Relief Society was held on April 19, 1842, before the next regularly scheduled meeting was held on April 28.

to wit.

Eliza Mills	.. 37½
Martha Knights	1.00
Mercy R. Thompson.	1.25
Lucy Millican [Millikin]	.. 25
Elizabeth Jones.	1.00
Mary Wool[l]ey	.. 25
Margaret A. [Norris] Cook.	.. 25
Abigail Kelsey	3.00
Abigail Leonard	1.12½
Phebe Hawkes	.. 37½
Kezia Ann Morrison.	.. 50
	9.37½

The following is a
List of Articles
given to the <u>Female</u> <u>Relief</u> <u>Society</u> of Nauvoo,
by <u>Dr.</u> <u>Willard</u> <u>Richards.</u>

March 29th	2 Quilt covers—	4.50	9...
	1 Gown	. . . .	6...
	1 Bonnett	. . . .	1.25
	16 Skeins of Silk—	6¼	1
[p. [29]]			
	1 Basket		.. 50
	1 Gold Ring		87
	1 pr Wristlets.		2[.]25

April 19, 1842 • Tuesday

Minutes of the Proceedings of the
Fifth Meeting
of the
<u>Female</u> <u>Relief</u> <u>Society.</u>

Lodge Room, April 19th.

A special meeting of the Society being conven'd agreeably to previous appointment; Prest. Emma Smith not being present, Councillor [Sarah] Cleveland presided—

The meeting was opened with singing— prayer by Councillor Cleveland.— singing by the choir—

The names of the following persons, were then read— no objections offered, they were unanimously received—

C[ouncillor] Clnd [Cleveland] then [arose and addressed] the meeting by [sa]ying that as this meeting[142]

Judith T. Haven	Mary Ann Fulmer
Nancy Lyons	Temperance Mack
Dulcina Sherman	Almira Corey [Covey]
Mary Nobles	Priscinda Buel [Presendia Buell]
Mary M. Smith	Jane Benbow
Eliza Partridge	Fanny M. Redfield
Sarah Ripley	

Councillor Cleveland then arose and address'd the meeting by saying, that inasmuch as the [p. [30]] meeting was specially called for the admission of Mrs. Buel who resided at a distance— was deprived of the privileges enjoyed by the sisters in Nauvoo, and wished to become a member of this Society; there was not much business to be attended to, therefore we might spend the time in religious exercises before the Lord— spoke of the happiness she felt in the present association of females, and made very appropriate remarks respecting the duties & prospects of the Society— that it was organiz'd after the order of heav'n &c. &c.

Councillor [Elizabeth Ann] Whitney also made many interesting remarks and invited all present to speak their sentiments freely—

Mrs. Buel arose and said that she rejoiced in the opportunity— that she considered it a great privilege she felt that the spirit of the Lord was with the Society, and rejoic'd to become a member altho' residing at a distance and could not attend the meetings.[143]

Mother [Lucy Mack] Smith spoke very pathetically of her lonely situation, and the feelings she had as she reflected on the care which father Smith [Joseph Smith Sr.] always felt for the sisters when in life he presided over the meetings.[144]

Mrs. [Elizabeth Davis] Durfee bore testimony to the great blessing she received when administered to, after the close of the last meeting, by Pres^t. E. Smith & Councillors Cleveland and Whitney. she said she never realized

---

142. TEXT: This text was copied by Eliza R. Snow, then knife-erased before the list of names was written here. Snow then recopied this text below the list of names.

143. Buell lived in Lima, Illinois, about thirty miles south of Nauvoo. (Presendia Lathrop Huntington Kimball, Reminiscences, 1881, CHL, Apr. 16, 1881.)

144. Joseph Smith Sr. was ordained as the church's first patriarch in December 1834. Patriarch is "an office in the Melchizedek Priesthood with the authority and responsibility to give inspired blessings similar to those given by the Old Testament patriarchs." Small groups gathered in blessing meetings to receive "patriarchal blessings" from Joseph Smith Sr. ("Patriarch," in *JSP*, J1:469.)

more benefit thro' any administration— that she was heal'd, and thought the sisters had more faith than the brethren.

Miss [Eliza R.] Snow after making observations with regard to the Society— the importance of acting in wisdom & walking humbly before God &c. said she had a blessing for Mrs. Buel, that inasmuch as she had become a member of [p. [31]] this Society, as the spirit of a person pervades every member of the body, so shall the Spirit of the Lord which pervades this Society be with her—[145] she shall feel it and rejoice— she shall be blest wherever she is, and the Lord shall open the way and she shall be instrumental in doing much,— thro' her own exertions by the instrumentality of others, she shall be enabled to contribute much to the fund of the Society— she shall warm up the hearts of those who are cold and dormant, and shall be instrumental in doing much good—

Mrs. [Abigail] Leonard, Councillor W. and Councillor C. bore testimony to the truth of what Miss Snow had said to Mrs. Buel—

Councillor Cleveland stated that she many times felt in her heart, what she could not express it in our own language, and as the Prophet had given us liberty to improve the gifts of the gospel in our meetings, and feelings the power resting upon, desired to speak in the gift of tongues; which she did in a powerful manner.[146]

Mrs. Sessions arose and gave the interpretation of what Councillor C. had spoken in an unknown tongue, and said that God was well pleas'd with this

---

145. TEXT: "her" written over an erased word, possibly "me".

146. No explicit statement by Joseph Smith about women exercising "gifts of the gospel" was recorded in minutes for the four earlier Relief Society meetings. Glossolalia, or speaking in unrecognizable tongues or language, had been part of the Latter-day Saint religious experience since the early 1830s, though not without controversy.[a] According to the Bible, speaking "with new tongues" signaled both belief in Jesus Christ and the presence of the Holy Spirit.[b] A March 1831 Joseph Smith revelation confirmed the importance of "tongues" and other gifts of the spirit listed by Paul in 1 Corinthians 12:4–11.[c] Latter-day Saint women and men experienced the gift of tongues in their informal and formal gatherings, where it seems to have served primarily as a source of comfort and inspiration and was sometimes combined with the gift of prophecy. At the Relief Society meeting held on April 28, 1842, Joseph Smith instructed the Relief Society to "not indulge too much in the gift of tongues" but said that the women could "speak in tongues for your comfort."[d] For specific examples of women speaking in tongues, as well as changes in the practice over time, see Maureen Ursenbach Beecher, ed., *The Personal Writings of Eliza Roxcy Snow,* Life Writings of Frontier Women 5 (Logan: Utah State University Press, 2000), 176–180; Donna Toland Smart, ed., *Mormon Midwife: The 1846–1888 Diaries of Patty Bartlett Sessions,* Life Writings of Frontier Women 2 (Logan: Utah State University Press, 1997), 7–8, 77–79; and Jill Mulvay Derr et al., *Women of Covenant: The Story of Relief Society* (Salt Lake City: Deseret Book; Provo, UT: Brigham Young University Press, 1992), 13, 45, 68, 90, 429. (*a.* See Mark Lyman Staker, *Hearken, O Ye People: The Historical Setting of Joseph Smith's Ohio Revelations* [Salt Lake City: Greg Kofford Books, 2009], 119–191. *b.* See Mark 16:17; and Acts 2:1–4. *c.* See Doctrine and Covenants 46:8–26. *d.* Document 1.2, entry for Apr. 28, 1842.)

Society, that if we would be humble and faithful the Lord would pour out upon the members generally the gift of prophecy—[147] that when the speaker laid her hand on the head of Sister Snow, she said that not only she should have the spirit but that all should have it also— that the speaker then address'd herself to Mother Smith saying that the prayers of father Smith were now answered upon the members of the Society— that the days of Mother S. should be prolong'd and she should meet many times with the Society, should enjoy much in the society of the [p. [32]] sisters & shall hereafter be crown'd a mother of those that shall prove faithful &c.

The meeting was very interesting, nearly all present arose & spoke, and the spirit of the Lord like a purifying stream, refreshed every heart.

Mrs. Mary Smith recommended Elizabeth Eaton to the patronage of the Society, as a person skilful in needlework—[148]

The meeting clos'd with prayer by Mother Smith and singing by the choir— after which

Mrs. Leonard was administered to for the restoration of health, by Councillors Cleveland & Whitney.

Donations by	$
Mary Snider	94
Elizabeth Durfee	25
Fanny Huntington	25
Cynthie Eldridge	50
W. [Willard] Richards	20.87
Martha Sessions	75
Desdemona Fulmer	1.25

[p. [33]]

April 28, 1842 • Thursday

Minutes of the Proceedings
of the
~~Fifth~~ Sixth Meeting of the Society.[149]

Lodge Room, April 28,[th] 1842.

The Meeting ~~meet~~ met according to adjournment, present Pres[t.] Joseph Smith and Elder W. [Willard] Richards—

---

147. See Doctrine and Covenants 46:22.

148. Eaton was admitted to the Relief Society at the following meeting, April 28, 1842.

149. Extracts from the minutes of this meeting were published with significant modifications in the September 19, 1855, issue of the *Deseret News*. (See Document 2.2.)

President Smith arose and said that the purport of his being present on the occasion was, to make observations respecting the Priesthood, and give instructions for the benefit of the Society[150] That as his instructions were intended only for the Society; he requested that a vote should be taken on those present who were not members, to ascertain whether they should be admitted— he exhorted the meeting to act honestly and uprightly in all their proceedings— inasmuch as they would be call'd to give an account to Jehovah. All hearts must repent— be pure and God will regard them and bless them in a manner that they could not be bless'd in any other way—

A vote was then taken on the following names, to wit,

Hannah Dibble	aye	Elizabeth Sprague	ay
Sally Angell	ay	Mary MᶜCarle [McCarroll]	"
Mary Ann Man[s]field	do [ditto]	Marianne Chase	"
Lydia A. Taylor	do	Elizabeth Music	"
Harriet P. Decker	no	Olive Chase	"
Sarah D. Rich	ay	Phebe Woodruff	"
Philote Pack	"	Abigail Tippetts	"
Julia Pack	"	Catharine Petty	"
Sarah Foster	"	Charity Stoddard	"
Sarah Boyce [Boice]	"	Elizabeth Rolfe	"
Catharine Head	"	Jane Judd	"
Lury[151] [Lucy] Scovill	"	Emerett L. Randall	"
Emily Partridge	"	Emily Spencer	"
Louisa Knight	"	Anna Cleveland	"

[p. [34]]

Tryphena Crandall—	aye	Rachel Drollinger—	aye
C [blank] Wood	No	Mary H. Palmer—	"
Elizabeth H. Barlow	aye	Lucinda A Hartwell	"
Charlotte Higbee	"	Amida [Amanda Barnes] Smith	"
Lucinda A. Hartwell	"	Elizabeth Edwards	"
Caroline Butler	"	Roxena Repsher	"

---

150. The April 28, 1842, entry in Joseph Smith's 1841–1842 journal, written by his scribe Willard Richards, reads: "at Two o'clock after-noon met the members of the 'Female relief Society' and after presiding at the admission of many new members. Gave a lecture on the pries[t]hood shewing how the Sisters would come in possession of the priviliges & blesings & gifts of the priesthood— & that the signs should follow them. such as healing the sick casting out devils &c. & that they might attain unto. these blessings. by a virtuous life & conversation & diligence in keeping all the commandments." (Joseph Smith, Journal, Apr. 28, 1842, in *JSP*, J2:52.)

151. TEXT: Possibly "Lucy".

Mary Ann Badlam	"	Ruth Curtis	"
Maria Gribble—	"	Lydia Knights [Knight]	"
Ann Montague	"	A [*blank*] Clements	"
Sarah Ann Whitney	"	Susan McArthur	"
Almeda Snider [Snyder]	"	Angeline E. Robinson	no

A Committee was then appointed to inquire into the cases of those persons to whom objections were made

Councillors [Elizabeth Ann] Whitney and [Sarah] Cleveland, Mrs. Allred, [Elizabeth Davis] Durfee [Vilate] Kimball and [Charlotte] Hawes to be the committee.

Committee retir'd— and Prest. J. Smith arose and call'd the attention of the meeting to the 12th Chap. of 1st Cor. "Now concerning spiritual gifts" &c.— Said that the passage which reads "no man can <u>say</u> that Jesus is the the ~~Christ~~ ⟨Lord⟩ but by the holy ghost," should be translated, no man can <u>know</u> &c[152]

He continued to read the Chap. and give instructions respecting the different offices, and the necessity of every individual acting in the sphere allotted him or her; and filling the several offices to which they were appointed—[153] Spoke of the disposition of man, to consider the lower offices in the church dishonorable and to look with jealous eyes upon the standing of others— that it was the nonsense of the human heart, for a person to be aspiring to other stations than appointed of God— that it was better for individuals to magnify their respective callings, and wait patiently till God shall say to them come up higher. He said the reason of these remarks being made, was, that some little thing was circulating in the Society, that some persons [p. [35]] were not going right in laying hands on the sick &c.[154] Said if he had common sympathies, would rejoice that the sick could be heal'd: that the time had not been before, that these things could be in their proper order— that the church is not now organiz'd in its proper order, and cannot be until the Temple is completed[155]——— Pres^{t.} Smith continued the subject by adverting to the commission

---

152. 1 Corinthians 12:3. Joseph Smith had not altered this verse as part of his earlier revision of the King James Bible. (See Scott H. Faulring et al., eds., *Joseph Smith's New Translation of the Bible: Original Manuscripts* [Provo, UT: Religious Studies Center, Brigham Young University, 2004], 507.)

153. Joseph Smith's 1832 revelation on priesthood included similar instructions: "Therefore, let every man stand in his own office, and labor in his own calling." (Doctrine and Covenants 84:109.)

154. At the April 19, 1842, meeting of the society, "Mrs. Leonard was administered to for the restoration of health," and Mrs. Durfee "bore testimony to the great blessing" of healing she had received when Emma Smith and her counselors administered to her at a previous meeting. (Document 1.2, entry for Apr. 19, 1842.)

155. See Doctrine and Covenants 124:28, 39. At a Relief Society meeting on August 13, 1843, Nauvoo temple building committee member Reynolds Cahoon said: "there are many Benevolent Societies abroad

given to the ancient apostles "Go ye into all the world" &c.— no matter who believeth; these signs, such as healing the sick, casting out devils &c. should follow all that believe whether male or female.[156] He ask'd the Society if they could not see by this sweeping stroke, that wherein they are ordaind, it is the privilege of those set apart to administer in that authority which is confer'd on them—[157] and if the sisters should have faith to heal the sick, let all hold their tongues, and let every thing roll on.

He said, if God has appointed him, and chosen him as an instrument to lead the church, why not let him lead it through? Why stand in the way, when he is appointed to do a thing? Who knows the mind of God? Does he not reveal things differently from what we expect?— He remark'd that he was continually rising— altho' he had every thing bearing him down— standing in his way and opposing— after all he always comes out right in the end.

Respecting the female laying on hands, he further remark'd, there could be no devil in it if God gave his sanction by healing— that there could be no more sin in any female laying hands on the sick than in wetting the face with water— that it is no sin for any body to do it that has faith, or if the sick has faith to be heal'd by the administration.

He reprov'd those that were dispos'd to find fault with the management of concerns— saying if he undertook to lead the church he would lead it right— that he calculates to organize the church in proper order &c. [p. [36]]

President Smith continued by speaking of the difficulties he had to surmount ever since the commencement of the work in consequence of aspiring men, "great big Elders" as he call'd them, who had caused him much trouble, whom he had taught in the private counsel; and they would go forth into the world and ploclaim [proclaim] the things he had taught them; as their own revelations— said the same aspiring disposition will be in this Society, and

---

designd to do good but not as this ours is according to the order of God connected with the priesthood according to the same good principals & knowledge will grow out of it . . . you kneed not doubt but this Society is raisd by the Lord to prepare us for the great blessings which are for us in the House of the Lord in the Temple." (Document 1.2, entry for Aug. 13, 1843.)

156. Mark 16:17, 18. Joseph Smith's 1832 revelation on priesthood emphasized that "every soul who believeth on your words, and is baptized by water for the remission of sins, shall receive the Holy Ghost," with signs and "many wonderful works" following "them that believe." Latter-day Saint women had begun performing healing blessings in the 1830s. (Doctrine and Covenants 84:64–66; Jonathan A. Stapley and Kristine Wright, "Female Ritual Healing in Mormonism," *Journal of Mormon History* 37, no. 1 [Winter 2011]: 1–11.)

157. Counselor Elizabeth Ann Whitney remembered that she was "ordained and set apart under the hand of Joseph Smith the Prophet to administer to the sick and comfort the sorrowful." Diantha Morley Billings, who joined the Relief Society on March 24, 1842, "was blessed and set apart to administer to the sick." (Elizabeth Ann Whitney, "A Leaf from an Autobiography," *Woman's Exponent,* Nov. 15, 1878, 7:91; "In Memoriam," *Woman's Exponent,* June 1, 1879, 8:251.)

must be guarded against— that every person should stand and act in the place appointed, and thus sanctify the Society and get it pure—

He said he had been trampled underfoot by aspiring Elders, for all were infected with that spirit, for instance P. [Parley] Pratt O. [Orson] Pratt, O. [Orson] Hyde and J. [John] Page had been aspiring— they could not be exalted but must run away as tho' the care and authority of the church were vested with them—[158] he said we had a subtle devil to deal with, and could only curb him by being humble.

He said as he had this opportunity, he was going to instruct the Society and point out the way for them to conduct, that they might act according to the will of God— that he did not know as he should have many opportunities of teaching them— that they were going to be left to themselves,— they would not long have him to instruct them— that the church would not have his instruction long, and the world would not be troubled with him a great while, and would not have his teachings— He spoke of delivering the keys to this Society and to the church— that according to his prayers God had appointed him elsewhere[159]

---

158. Joseph Smith appears to be criticizing Parley P. Pratt (1807–1857), Orson Pratt (1811–1881), Orson Hyde (1805–1878), and John E. Page (1799–1867), all members of the Quorum of the Twelve Apostles, for two issues: for earlier public conflicts between each man and Smith; and for publicly teaching things Smith had shared privately. In 1837, financial disputes—precipitated by the national panic of 1837 and the local failure of the Kirtland Safety Society, a banking institution of which Joseph Smith was president—led to the temporary disaffection of the Pratt brothers. Orson Hyde publicly criticized Smith's leadership the following year during conflict between Mormons and Missourians and was disfellowshipped from the church and removed from the apostolic quorum; he was restored to fellowship within the church and the Quorum of the Twelve Apostles in 1839. Page failed to fill a mission with other members of the Twelve to England in 1839, as well as a mission to accompany Orson Hyde to Jerusalem in 1841. Smith chided Page at the April 1842 church conference. It is more difficult to pinpoint instances when, without Smith's authorization, these apostles publicly preached information that Smith had taught them in private. By this time, Parley Pratt was a prolific writer who had published some theological ideas, such as the doctrine of theosis (humanity's potential for divinization), that Smith did not teach publicly until later. (Terryl L. Givens and Matthew J. Grow, *Parley P. Pratt: The Apostle Paul of Mormonism* [New York: Oxford University Press, 2011], 96–102, 125–126; Wilford Woodruff, Journals, 1833–1898, Wilford Woodruff, Journals and Papers, 1828–1898, CHL, May 29 and June 27, 1839; *JSP,* J1:343n38; "Conference Minutes," *Times and Seasons,* Apr. 15, 1842, 3:762; John Quist, "John E. Page: An Apostle of Uncertainty," *Journal of Mormon History* 12 [1985]: 53–56.)

159. On many occasions between 1838 and 1844, Joseph Smith expressed premonitions of his death. While imprisoned in Liberty, Missouri, in 1838 and 1839, Smith told Lyman Wight that "he should not live to see forty years, but told him [Wight] not to reveal it untill he was dead." In addition, at a young boy's funeral on April 9, 1842, Joseph Smith stated, "Some has supposed that Br Joseph could not die but this is a mistake it is true their has been times when I have had the promise of my life to accomplish such & such things, but having accomplish those things I have not at present any lease of my life & am as liable to die as other men." (Woodruff, Journal, Apr. 9, 1842, and July 28, 1844.)

He exhorted the sisters always to concentrate their faith and prayers for, and place confidence, in those whom God has appointed to honor, whom God has plac'd at the head to lead— that we should arm them with our prayers.— [p. [37]] that the keys of the kingdom are about to be given to them, that they may be able to detect every thing false— as well as to the Elders[160]

He said if one member becomes corrupt and you know it; you must immediately put it away. The sympathies of the heads of the church have induc'd them to bear with those that were corrupt; in consequence of which all become contaminated— you must put down iniquity and by your good example provoke the Elders to good works— if you do right, no danger of going too fast: he said he did not care how fast we run in the path of virtue. Resist evil and there is no danger. God, men, angels, and devils can't condemn those that resist every thing that is evil— as well might the devil seek to dethrone Jehovah, as that soul that resists every thing that is evil.

The charitable Society— this is according to your natures— it is natural for females to have feelings of charity— you are now plac'd in a situatio[n] where you can act according to those sympathies which God has planted in your bosoms. If you live up to these principles how great and glorious!— if you live up to your privilege, the angels cannot be restrain'd from being your associates— females, if they are pure and innocent can come into the presence of God;[161] for what is more pleasing to God than innocence; you must be innocent

---

160. The term "keys" had multiple meanings for Latter-day Saints in the 1840s. On May 1, 1842, three days after this address to the Relief Society, Joseph Smith preached in a public gathering in Nauvoo "on the keys of the kingdom" and stated, "The keys are certain signs & words by which false spirits & personages may be detected from true.— which cannot be revealed to the Elders till the Temple is completed."*a* On other occasions, Smith employed the terms "keys" and "keys of the kingdom" with reference to both knowledge and authority. Scriptural passages refer to "the key of knowledge" or "the key of the knowledge of God," which Latter-day Saints associate with the ordinances of the Melchizedek Priesthood, including temple ordinances.*b* For Latter-day Saints, as for Catholics, keys also denote the authority of ecclesiastical office.*c* Both ancient and modern scriptures assign the governing and sealing "keys of the kingdom" to the apostles or "the Presidency of the High Priesthood."*d* (*a.* Joseph Smith, Journal, May 1, 1842, in *JSP*, J2:53. *b.* See Luke 11:52; and Doctrine and Covenants 84:19–23. *c.* "Keys," in *The Oxford English Dictionary,* ed. J. A. Simpson and E. S. C. Weiner, 2nd ed., 20 vols. [Oxford: Clarendon, 1989], 8:405. *d.* See Matthew 16:19; and Doctrine and Covenants 27:12–13; 81:2; see also "Keys," in *JSP*, J1:468; Doctrine and Covenants 107:18–19; 124:95, 97; and Jared Lindquist, "'Unlocking the Door of the Gospel': The Concept of 'Keys' in Mormonism and Early American Culture," *Archive of Restoration Culture: Summer Fellows' Papers, 1997–1999* [Provo, UT: Joseph Fielding Smith Institute for Latter-day Saint History, 2000], 29–41.)

161. Joseph Smith's 1832 revelation on priesthood states that the "power of godliness" cannot be manifest to mankind without priesthood authority and ordinances. It also explains that Moses taught this and "sought diligently to sanctify his people that they might behold the face of God." The Book of Mormon refers to the righteous coming into or dwelling in the presence of God. (Doctrine and Covenants 84:19–23; see also 2 Nephi 2:8; and Mormon 7:7; 9:13.)

or you cannot come up before God. If ~~ye~~ ⟨we⟩ would come before God let us be pure ourselves. The devil has great power— he will so transform things[162] as to make one gape at those who are doing the will of God— You need not be tearing men for their deeds, but let the weight of innocence be felt; which is more mighty than a millstone hung about the neck. Not war, not jangle, not contradiction, but meekness, love, purity, these are the things that should magnify us.— Achan[163] must be brought to light— iniquity must be purged out— <u>then</u> the vail will be rent and the blessings of heaven will flow down [p. [38]]— they will roll down like the Missisippi river. This Society shall have power to command Queens in their midst— I now deliver it as a prophecy that before ten years shall roll round, the queens of the earth shall come and pay their respects to this Society— they shall come with their millions and shall contribute of their abundance for the relief of the poor— If you will be pure, nothing can hinder.

After this instruction, you will be responsible for your own sins. It is an honor to save ~~yourself~~ yourselves— all are responsible to save themselves.

Pres.^t Smith, after reading from the above mentioned Chapter, continued to give instruction respecting the order of God, as established in the church; saying every one should aspire only to magnify his own office &c.——

He then commenc'd reading the 13th chapter, "Though I speak with the tongues of men" &c; and said don't be limited in your views with regard to your neighbors' virtues, but be limited towards your own virtues; and not think yourselves more righteous than others; you must enlarge your souls toward others if yould [you would?] do like Jesus, and carry your fellow creatures to Abram's bosom.

He said he had manifested long suffering and we must do so too—— Pres^t. Smith then read, "Though I have the gift of prophecy" &c. He then said, though one should become mighty— do great things— overturn mountains &c and should then turn to eat and drink with the drunken; all former deeds would not save him— but he would go to destruction!

As you increase in innocence and virtue, as you increase in goodness, let your hearts expand— let them be enlarged towards others— you must be longsuff'ring and bear with the faults and errors of mankind. How precious are the souls of men!— The female part of community are apt to be [p. [39]] contracted in their views. You must not be contracted, but you must be liberal in your feelings.

---

162. TEXT: "things" written over a knife-erased illegible word.
163. Joshua 7 recounts Achan's disobedience and deception.

Let this Society teach how to act towards husbands to treat them with mildness and affection. When a man is borne down with trouble— when he is perplex'd; if he can meet a smile, an argument— if he can meet with mildness, it will calm down his soul and soothe his feelings. When the mind is going to despair, it needs a solace.

This Society is to get instruction thro' the order which God has established— thro' the medium of those appointed to lead— and I now turn the key to you in the name of God and this Society shall rejoice and knowledge and intelligence shall flow down from this time—[164] this is the beginning of better days, to this Society

When you go home never give a cross word, but let kindness, charity and love, crown your works henceforward. Don't envy sinners— have mercy on them, God will destroy them.— Let your labors be confin'd mostly to those around you in your own circle; as far as knowledge is concerned, it may extend to all the world, but your administrations, should be confin'd to the circle of your immediate acquaintance, and more especially to the members of the Society.

Those ordain'd to lead the Society, are authoriz'd to appoint to different offices as the circumstances shall require.

If any have a matter to reveal, let it be in your own tongue. Do not indulge too much in the gift of tongues, or the devil will take advantage of the innocent. You may speak in tongues for your comfort but I lay this down for a rule that if any thing is [p. [40]] is taught by the gift of tongues, it is not to be received for doctrine.[165]

Prest. S. then offered instruction respecting the propriety of females administering to the sick by the laying on of hands— said it was according to revelation &c. said he never was plac'd in similar circumstances, and never had given the same instruction.

He clos'd his instructions by expressing his satisfaction in improving the opportunity.

---

164. Joseph Smith used similar wording on February 6, 1836, when, with reference to missionary work, he declared to the Kirtland elders quorum: "this night the key is turned to the nations." Parallel language appears in a published letter from Hyrum Smith inviting the Saints to come to Nauvoo to build the temple "in this place, wherein their dead may be redeemed, and the key of knowledge that unfolds the dispensation of the fullness of times may be turned, and the mysteries of God be unfolded." (Kirtland Elders Quorum, "A Record of the First Quorumum of Elders Belonging to the Church of Christ: In Kirtland Geauga Co. Ohio," 1836–1838, 1840–1841, Community of Christ Library-Archives, Independence, MO, Feb. 6, 1836; Letter from Hyrum Smith, *Times and Seasons,* Nov. 1, 1841, 3:589; see also Woodruff, Journal, June 27, 1839.)

165. At the April 19, 1842, meeting of the society, Sarah M. Cleveland spoke "in the gift of tongues" and Mrs. Sessions "gave the interpretation." (Document 1.2, entry for Apr. 19, 1842.)

contrasted in their views. You must not be contrasted, but you must be liberal in your feelings.

Let this Society teach how to act towards husbands, to treat them with mildness and affection. When a man is borne down with trouble—when he is perplex'd, if he can meet a smile, not an argument—if he can meet with mildness, it will calm down his soul and soothe his feelings. When the mind is going to despair it needs a solace.

This Society is to get instruction thro' the order which God has established—thro' the medium of those appointed to lead—and I now turn the key to you in the name of God and this Society shall rejoice and knowledge and intelligence shall flow down from this time—this is the beginning of better days to this Society.

When you go home never give a cross word, but let kindness, charity and love, crown your works henceforward. Don't envy sinners—have mercy on them, God will destroy them—Let your labors be confin'd mostly to those around you in your own circle; as far as knowledge is concern'd, it may extend to all the world, but your administrations, should be confin'd to the circle of your immediate acquaintance, and more especially to the members of the Society.

Those ordain'd to lead the Society, are authoriz'd to appoint to different offices as the circumstances shall require.

If any have a matter to reveal, let it be in your own tongue. Do not indulge too much in the gift of tongues, or the devil will take advantage of the innocent. You may speak in tongues for your comfort but I lay this down for a rule that if any thing is

Record of Joseph Smith sermon. The minutes of the Nauvoo Relief Society record six addresses by Joseph Smith, all in 1842. The page shown here reports part of Smith's April 28 address, in which he told the members, "I now turn the key to you in the name of God and this Society shall rejoice and knowledge and intelligence shall flow down from this time." The handwriting on this page is that of Eliza R. Snow. (Church History Library, Salt Lake City. Photograph by Welden C. Andersen.)

The spirit of the Lord was pour'd out in a very powerful manner, never to be forgotten by those present on that interesting occasion.

The Committee appointed to investigate into the cases of individuals, returned & reported that the objections against A. E. Robi[n]son were remov'd; and accordingly she was received by a unanimous vote.

The following ~~persons~~ ⟨names⟩ were also read and voted as follows

Lydia Knight	aye	Hannah A. Dibble	aye
Rebecca Reed	aye	Polly Sherwood	"
Amy Clothier	no	Mary C. Miller	"
Mary Smith	aye	Laura Russ	"
Aphia Yale	"	Jane Miller	"
Anna Jones	~~aye~~ no	Hannah Whitlock	"
Elizabeth Eaton	aye	Eliza Moses[166]	"
Lydia M. Smith	aye	Abigail Works	"
Rosetta L. Snow	"	[*blank*] Johnson	"
Nancy King	"		

The gentlemen withdrew and the sisters proceeded to business, concerning the poor &c. [p. [41]]

Councillor Whitney call'd on those who could represent the poor, to do so.

The family by the name of Drury was represented as being very needy.

Pres^t E. Smith said there was some provision in the treasury— and call'd for a vote whether some should be appropriated for the above object.

Carried in the affirmative.

Mrs. Nighman [Jane Neyman] was represented as being destitute

Pres^t. S. recommended that the widow Nighman should be visited to inquire if she was dispos'd to reform the order of her house.[167]

After several exhortations by individuals and many comforting words &c., it was motioned, secon[d]ed and carried that we adjourn until next thursday, 2 o.clock.

The meeting arose and was dismiss'd by Councillor Whitney.

The following donations were made[168]

to wit.

$

Sally Angell 18¾

166. TEXT: Possibly "Mores".

167. The moral conduct of the daughters of "the widow Nighman" prompted the question regarding the "order of her house." (See Nauvoo High Council Minutes, 1839–1845, CHL, May 24 and 25, 1842; and "Chauncey L. Higbee," *Nauvoo Neighbor*, May 29, 1844, [3]; see also 67n175 herein.)

168. TEXT: Six pinholes in paper, as if something was attached at one point.

Lydia Anderson	25
Elizabeth Allred	50
Abigail Leonard	25
Eliza Green[e]	62½
—— [Melissa] Bird	25
Nancy Winchester	50
Olive Farr	50
Kuhamath Derby—	1.00
[*blank*] Wight— appropriates	5.00

2 dollars of which to the schooling of widow [Prudence] Barkdall's children and 3, to widow [Cynthia] Baggs' for schooling her children

Magdalene Moesser donates pr. week out of the store .. 25
[p. [42]]

May 12, 1842 • Thursday

Minutes of the Proceedings
of the
Seventh Meeting of the Society.

Lodge Room, May 13th. [12th][169]

The meeting opened with singing, "Thy mercy my God is the theme of my song." &c.[170]

Pray'r by Prest. Joseph Smith.

The following names were then presented to the Society and were unanimously receiv'd— to wit.

Eunice R. [Bagg] Shurtliff	Adoline Roundy
Phebe Woodworth	Elizabeth [Harris] Henderson
Dorotha [Duritha] Lewis	Hannah Lytle
Elizabeth Malam [Milam]	Abigail Goldsmith
Jane A. Moore	Harriet Rice
Malinda Lewis	Esther S.[171] Morrill
Hannah Drolinger	Maria Haven
Caroline Tippets	Sarah Mellin
Electa Peck	Eliza Ann Mellin [Malin]
Fanny Hartshorn	Eliza Rolfe
Jane Twist	Fanny Lytz [Litz]

169. Joseph Smith's journal indicates that he attended a Relief Society meeting on May 12, 1842. (Joseph Smith, Journal, May 12, 1842, in *JSP*, J2:55–56.)
170. Hymn 271, *Collection of Sacred Hymns* [1841], 297.
171. TEXT: Possibly "L."

Elmena [Elmira] Miller
Nancy M. Cahoon
Martha B. [Paine] Thomas
Hannah Annis
Jane Olmstead
Elizabeth King
Mary King
Elizabeth Lee
Nancy B. [Daniels] Andrews
Lucy Foot [Lucia Foote]
Sarah Peck
Henrietta Rich
Margaret Dany [Dana]
Mary Kelsey
Kezia Burk
Lois Sherman
Phebe Merrill
Barbara Evans
Mary Ann Hyde
Elizabeth Matthews
Elizabeth Balla[r]d
Mary Ann Ivings [Ivins]
Irona H. Cowles
Betsey Ann Eldridge
Caroline Tomlinson
Betsey Tomlinson
Annis Roberts
Sibyl Stephens [Stevens]
Huldah Butler
Lucy McOlney
Lydia Carter
Pamela [Permelia] Drury
Ruth Drury
Sarah Harmon
Sarah Mackley
Lucinda Baggs
Betsey Baggs
Mary Clapp
Margaret Clapp
Elizabeth Coolage

Selina [Sabina] Adams
Eunice Baldwin
Eunice Holbrook
Elizabeth Gillett
Maria Ferry
Arminta Graham
Dorcas Dykes
Mary Younger
Mary Mayberry
Nancy Alexander
Deonicia [Dionitia] Plumb
Polly Gaylord
Betsey Green [p. [43]]
Alvira Alexander
Harriet Stratten
Abigail Jackson
Margaretta Wilcox
Esther Franklin
Olive B. Hale
Julia A. Jencks
Elizabeth Whiteside
Emily [Emelia] Parks
Christiana Winn
Susannah Parish
Aurelia Harmon
Eliza Hill
Sarah Brown
Sally King
Mary B. King
Mercy Jones
Jane Nelson
Mary Duke
Anna Potter
Huldah Nickerson
Huldah A. Barrus
Mary Ann Nickerson
Louisa Pratt
Clarinda Phillips
Nancy Gardner
Loisa Leavitt

Lucinda Turner
Loisa Hildreth
Lois Cutler
Lomira Cutler
Sarah Hayle
Dorothy Hoyt
Caroline Weeks
Margaret Ault
Polly Perry
Adoline L West
Sally M. Anderson
Nancy Johnson
Abigail Hawes
Nancy Bagley
Hannah Carter
Anna Wight
Jemima Peck
Sarah Ann Billings
Clarissa Chase
Sarah Lincoln
Julia Ann Hale
Sophia Billings
Selina Chase
Alice Wal[l]work
Lucy Clemons [Clements]
Lucretia Marsh
Margaret Fosset [Fausett]
Catharine Hendricks
Nancy Booth
[*blank*] Fordham
[*blank*] Spencer
Harriet Decker
Margaret Hurr [Herr]
Amarellar [Avarillar] Casper
Elmira Daily [Almira Daley]
Elizabeth A. Hall
Sophia Reels [Reals]

Aurelia Curtiss [Curtis]
Elizabeth J. Burnes
Maria Thompson
Elizabeth Brady
Kezia Hendricks[on]
Sarah Roberts
Hannah Carroll [p. [44]]
Olivia Evans
Margaret Hulet
Amelia C. [Caroline Amelia] Webb
Betsey Carrico
Margaret Stuart [Stewart]
Anna Harmon
Sophronia M. Harmon
Amanda Rogers
Eda Rogers
Annis Thompson
Abigail Bingham
Anna Landers
Betsey Clough [Cluff]
Rhoda Bentley
Elizabeth Owens
Lucy Ann Alldred [Allred]
Julia McMurtin [McMurdie]
Julia Ann Allred
Abigail Allred
Deborah Blakeman [Blackman]
Harriet Finch
Sabra Morrison
Olive Farr
Sally Foster
Luena Luce
L. [*blank*] Newman
Abigail Thornd [Thorn]
Mary Southworth
Huldah Teeples
Sabra Vooheers

The cases of the poor were then represented

Pres.ᵗ J. Smith said that in his opinion, all men now considered in good standing, ~~holding notes~~ [p. [45]] against ⟨whom⟩ widows, hold notes; if they will not pay them, ought to be discountenanc'd by the <u>Relief</u> <u>Society</u>—

Sister Chapman's case was represented—

Mov'd & carried that Sister Chapman's garden should be plowed.

Kezia Morrison said if some one would plow said garden, she would pay from the store

Sist. Matthews propos'd to send a man to plow it.

Motion'd & carried that those persons who refuse to pay poor widows what is due them, be forever discountenanc'd by this Society.

Mov'd & carried that those men who refuse to pay sister Hillman, what she holds in notes against them, be complain'd of at the Masonic Lodge.[172]

The following donations were then received

		$
Amanda [Barnes] Smith—	donated	1.00
Martha Sessions—	do [ditto]	.. 62
Catharine Wilkie		2.00
Percinda Ball		.62
Mary J. Warner		75
Susan McArthur		25
Elizabeth Rolfe		50
Adah Coleman		12½
Sarah Higbee	children's clothes	~~25~~
Hannah Marsh		~~12½~~ 25
Mary A. Hyde		12½
Emeline Carlin[g]	Gold Pin	
Nancy King		25
Annis Thompson		62½
Caroline Tomlinson		1.75
Sabra Gribble	1 Bed Quilt	2.00

After singing by the choir & pray'r by Pres.ᵗ J. Smith, the meeting adjourn'd at 6 o.clock [p. [46]]

May 19, 1842 • Thursday

Minutes of the Proceedings

of the

---

172. Masons who did not keep moral obligations could be censured by their lodge. For instance, John C. Bennett was disciplined for sexual immorality by both the Pickaway, Illinois, lodge and the Nauvoo lodge. (*JSP*, J2:65n255, 67n268.)

Eighth Meeting of the Society.

Lodge Room, May 19th.

Meeting open'd with prayer by Councillor [Elizabeth Ann] Whitney

Singing by the choir—

The following names were then receiv'd, to wit.

Caroline Angell	Sybil Jacobs
Eleanor Daviss	Eliza Wilber
Pamela [Permelia] Dayton	Ruth Tyler
Anna Buck	Betsey Motley
Charity Butler	Caroline Ha[r]mon
Hannah Huntsman	Ann Abbott
Irena E. Lincoln	Martha B[o]yington
Elizabeth Dana	Rebecca More
Catharine C. Brush	Elizabeth Romney
Martha A. Hovey	Sally Ann Chamberl[a]in
Abiah Porter	Julia Fish
Delia DeVol	Jane Bolentine [Ballantyne]
Mary Abbot	Lucy Groves
Lovina Johnson	Polly Sweat
Mary Littlefield	Sarah Roberts
Lettice Bent	Ruth Tyler

Councillor Whitney then rose and said, she was burthened in mind in thinking of existing evils in the church— was desirous that this Society become more obedient to the gospel in keeping all the commandments— exhorted them to humility and watchfulness— said the more she had heard and seen of corrupt members, the more she was stimulated to faithfulness— that the gifts and blessings of the gospel were ours, if found faithful and pure before God &c.

Mrs. Pres.ᵗ said this day was an evil day— that [p. [47]] there is as much evil in this as in any other place—[173] said she would that this Society were pure before God— that she was afraid that under existing circumstances, the sisters were not careful enough to expose iniquity— the time had been when charity

---

173. One example of the concern for public morality occurred five days before this Relief Society meeting, on May 14, 1842, when at a meeting of the Nauvoo City Council, Joseph Smith "advocated strongly the necessity of some active measures being taken to suppress. houses & acts of infamy in the city." At that meeting, a city ordinance was passed that stated, "All brothels or houses of ill fame, erected or being in the City of Nauvoo, be and the same hereby are henceforth prohibited and by law declared public nuisances." (Joseph Smith, Journal, May 14, 1842, in *JSP*, J2:56; "An Ordinance concerning Brothels and Disorderly Characters," *Wasp*, May 14, 1842, [3].)

had covered a multitude of sins—[174] but now it is necessary that sin should be expos'd— that heinous sins were among us— that much of this iniquity was practiced by some in authority, pretending to be sanction'd by Prest. Smith.[175]

Mrs. Prest· continued by exhorting all who had err'd to repent and forsake their sins— said that satan's forces were against this church— that every saint should be at the post

Councillor [Sarah] Cleveland said the same stratagems were now employ'd, as anciently in Balaam's time, when he was required to curse Israel and could not—[176] yet they were drawn into sin thro' the propensities of their natures— so with this people the gentiles cannot curse them— but can draw them into iniquity.

Motion'd, seconded and carried that Lucy Ann Munjar be suspended for a time—

The following donations were then receiv'd— to wit

	$
Mary Snider	·· 94
Sally [Polly] Angell	2,18
Lydia Anderson	.25
Elizabeth Allred	50
Abigail Leonard	25
Eliza Green[e]	62
Mrs. [Melissa] Bird	25

---

174. See 1 Peter 4:8.

175. This comment reflected the furor in Nauvoo regarding several men who had seduced or attempted to seduce women by claiming that Joseph Smith had authorized them to engage in extramarital affairs. On April 10, 1842, Joseph Smith "Preached in the grove after Elder Wᵐ Law. had spoken. a[nd] pronounced a curse upon all Adulterers & fornicators & unvirtuous persons. & those who had made use of his name to carry on their iniquitous designs." Smith likely referred to John C. Bennett and Chauncey L. Higbee, among others. On May 11 Smith and other leaders withdrew "the hand of fellowship" from Bennett. Two weeks later, at the Nauvoo Masonic Lodge on May 26, Bennett "confessed the charges preferred again[s]t him concerning. females in Nauvoo." At the lodge meeting, Smith and others "established beyond the possibility of contradiction" that Bennett had "seduced certain females whose characters previously was unsullied." On May 24 and 25, 1842, three witnesses testified before the Nauvoo high council that each had been seduced in Nauvoo by Higbee, who taught them that it was "right to have free intercourse with women if it was kept secret" and that "Joseph Smith therised [authorized] him to practice these things." That week, four women (Margaret J. Nyman, Matilda J. Nyman, Sarah Miller, and Catherine Warren), three of whom were presumably the three aforementioned witnesses, signed affidavits that Higbee had seduced them "most clandestinely, with wicked lies . . . by using the name of Joseph Smith." (Joseph Smith, Journal, Apr. 10 and May 26, 1842, in *JSP*, J2:50, 63; Joseph Smith et al., "Notice," May 11, 1842, Joseph Smith Collection, CHL; Lodge to Abraham Jonas, June 21, 1842, Letters Pertaining to Freemasonry in Nauvoo, 1842, CHL; Nauvoo High Council Minutes, May [21], 24, and 25, 1842; "Chauncey L. Higbee," *Nauvoo Neighbor*, May 29, 1844, [3].)

176. Numbers 22–24.

Nancy Winchester	50
Olive Hurr	50
Kuhamah [Ruhamah] Derby	1,00
Anna Wight	5,00
[*blank*]	25

[p. [48]]

Sis. [Cynthia] Baggs was represented as in want of shoes

A Scotch family destitute of food.

Nehemiah Harmon's family represented destitute of clothing, sheets, pillow cases &c

Sister Anderson gives to br. Whitlock an order on Pres^t· Joseph Smith's Store.   .. 25—

The meeting adjourn'd at 6 o'clock—[p. [49]]

May 26, 1842 • Thursday

Minutes of the Proceedings
of the
Ninth Meeting of the Society.

Lodge Room May 26th·

Meeting opened with singing "How firm a foundation" &c.—[177] Prayar by Coun. [Sarah] Cleveland— Mrs. Prest. not present— House full to overflowing.[178]

Coun. [Elizabeth Ann] Whitney arose and propos'd that the necessities be considered and donations received— that all other business be defer'd on account of the absence of the Prest.— She also propos'd that a few of the congregation retire to sister [Mercy] Thompson's and engage in prayer.

The following Donations receiv'd.

	$
Sylvia Lyons [Lyon]	.. 50
Mary Snider	.. 50
Margaret Hurr [Herr]	.. 25
Sarah Granger	1.00
Mary M. Smith	2.00
Sarah Davis	.. 62½
Mrs. [Hannah] Whitlock	.. 50

---

177. Hymn 102, *Collection of Sacred Hymns* [1841], 110.

178. Joseph Smith's journal entry for May 26, 1842, as recorded by Willard Richards, notes: "Female Releif Soceity.— so full that many could get no admittance." (Joseph Smith, Journal, May 26, 1842, in *JSP,* J2:63.)

Lydia Anderson		1.51
Nancy Rockwood		.. 50
Nancy King		.. 25
Martha [Patty] Sessions		12[.]00
Sylva Lyons	in clothing	2,00
Nancy Cahoon		.. 35
Thirza Cahoon	children's clothes	
Eliza Mills	bed Quilt	3.00

Councillor Whitney gave an exhortation to humility and watchfulness &c.— rejoic'd at the numbers present who were uniting their faith with their works, alluding to Donations just receiv'd. [p. [50]]

Prest. J. Smith & wife then entered.

Prest. J. Smith rose, read the 14ᵗʰ Chap. of Ezekiel— said the Lord had declar'd by the prophet that the people should each one stand for himself and depend on no man or men in that state of corruption of the Jewish church— that righteous persons could only deliver their own souls— app[l]ied it to the present state of the church of Latter-Day Saints— said if the people departed from the Lord, they must fall— that they were depending on the prophet hence were darkened in their minds from neglect of themselves— envious toward the innocent, while they afflict the virtuous with their shafts of envy.

There is another error which opens a door for the adversary to enter. As females possess refin'd feelings and sensitivenes[s], they are also subject to an overmuch zeal which must ever prove dangerous, and cause them to be rigid in a religious capacity— should be arm'd with mercy notwithstanding the iniquity among us. Said he had been instrumental in bringing it to light— melancholy and awful that so many are under the condemnation of the devil & going to perdition.[179]

With deep feeling said that they are our fellows— we lov'd them once. Shall we not encourage them to reformation?

We have not forgivn them seventy times—[180] perhaps we have not forgiven them once. There is now a day of salvation to such as repent and reform— they

---

179. Joseph Smith's comment likely referenced the controversy surrounding John C. Bennett. The entry in Joseph Smith's journal for this day notes: "Masonic Lodge in the A.M. Dʳ John C. Bennet[t] confessed the charges preferred again[s]t him concerning. females in Nauvoo. & was forgiven Joseph plead in his behalf.— Dr Bennet was notified the day previous that the first Presidency. Twelve & Bishops had withdrawn fellowship from him & were about to publish him. but on his humbling himself & requesting it the withdrawal was withheld from the paper." The previous day Catherine Warren confessed before the Nauvoo high council to unchaste conduct with Bennett and was also forgiven. (Joseph Smith, Journal, May 26, 1842, in *JSP*, J2:63; Nauvoo High Council Minutes, May 25, 1842.)

180. See Matthew 18:22; and Doctrine and Covenants 98:40.

should be cast out from this Society, yet we should woo them to return to God lest they escape not the damnation of hell!

When there is a mountain top there also is a vally— we should act in all things an a proper medium— to every immortal spirit. Notwithstanding the unworthy are among us, the virtuous should not from self-importance grieve and oppress needlessly those unfortunate ones, even [p. [51]] these should be encourag'd to hereafter live to be honored by this Society who are the best portions of community. Said he had two things to recommend to the Society, to put a double watch over the tongue. No organiz'd body can exist without this at all. All organiz'd bodies have their peculiar evils, weaknesses and difficulties— the object is to make those not so good, equal with the good and ever hold the keys of pow'r which will influence to virtue and goodness. Should chasten and reprove and keep in it all in silence, not even mention them again, then you will be established in power, virtue and holiness and the wrath of God will be turn'd away. One request to the Prest. and Society, that you search yourselves— the tongue is an unruly member—[181] hold your tongues about things of no moment,— a little tale will set the world on fire. At this time the truth on the guilty should not be told openly— Strange as this may seem, yet this is policy.[182] We must use precaution in bringing sinners to justice lest in exposing these heinous sins, we draw the indignation of a gentile world upon us (and to their imaginatio[n] justly too)

It is necessary to hold an influence in the world and thus spare ourselves an extermination; and also accomplish our end in spreading the gospel or holiness in the earth.

If we were brought to desolation, the disobedient would find no help. There are some who are obedient yet men cannot steady the ark— my arm can not do it— God must steady it.[183] To the iniquitous show yourselves merciful. I am advis'd by some of the heads of the church to tell the Relief Society to be virtuous— but to save the church from desolation and the sword beware, be still, be prudent. Repent, reform but do it in a way to not destroy all around you. I do not want to cloak iniquity— all things contrary to the will [p. [52]] of God, should be cast from us, but dont do more hurt than good with your tongues— be pure in heart— Jesus designs to save the people out of their sins.

---

181. See James 3:8.
182. At several other Relief Society meetings, Relief Society members received counsel to keep society business confidential. (See Document 1.2, entries for Mar. 24 and May 27, 1842; see also the letter copied into the minutes following the Sept. 28, 1842, entry.)
183. See 1 Samuel 6:6–7; and 1 Chronicles 13:9–10.

Said Jesus ye shall do the work which ye see me do—[184] These are the grand key words for the Society to act upon.

If I were not in your midst to aid and council you, the devil would overcome you. I want the innocent to go free— rather spare ten iniquitous among you than than condemn one innocent one. "Fret not thyself because of evil doers."[185] God will see to it.

Mrs. Prest. rose and said all idle rumor and idle talk must be laid aside yet sin must not be covered, especially those sins which are against the law of God and the laws of the country— all who walk disorderly must reform, and any knowing of heinous sins against the law of God, and refuse to expose them, becomes the offender— said she wanted none in this Society who had violated the laws of virtue.

The following persons were receiv'd, to wit.

Sarah Ann Spears	Fidelia Cotten [Colton]
Mary M. Sawyer	Evaline Carter
Mary A. Peck	Disly [Disey] Allen
Margaret Brush	Judith Benjamin
Ruth Rob[e]y	Matilda Fausett
Sophia Claridge	Mary Holt
Rachel Allen	Nancy Drysdale
Electa Murdock	Elizabeth Pierce
Sylva Beecher	Harriet Pinkam
Mary E. Beecher	Jane Sherwood
Polly Chittendon	Mary Lowry
Jane F. Pea	Mary Dewell
Sarah Sweat	Lydia Bair
Mary Reed	Rucinda Hurr [Horr] [p. [53]]
Fanny Crosby	Mary Newberry
Mary Albridge	Lucretia Young
Sarah Van [Van Blaracom]	Eliza Ann Cheny
Mary A. Pearce [Pierce]	Prudena Oaks [Prudence Oakes]
Rebecca Hoop[es]	Sally M. Clark
Ferra Dana	Beulah Hoyt
Polly J. Younger	Priscilla Chase
Mary Ann Hadfield	Eliza Douglas
Mary D. Guimore	Adaline Perry
Lucinda Dudley	Betsey Pedigrue [Pettigrew]

---

184. See John 14:12; see also Joseph Smith Translation, Mark 3:23.
185. Psalm 37:1; Proverbs 24:19.

Elizabeth Rosin [Rawson]   Elizabeth Taylor
Meeting adjourn'd to meet in the Grove on the following day.

May 27, 1842 • Friday
Minutes of the Proceedings of the
<u>Tenth</u> Meeting of the Society.

May 27th.

Meeting in the Grove— open'd with singing— prayer by Prest E. Smith.

Prest. E. Smith arose and address'd the congregation, said all must have grace for themselves &c.— that the first business is to finish the business commenc'd yesterday— requested if any were present who came to make ridicule of the Society, that they would withdraw.

The following persons were receiv'd. to wit.

Nancy Flemming	Almena Haskins
Sophia A. [Bundy] Packard	Sarah Powers
Elizabeth Barnum	Sarah Lyons
Marcia A. Root	Mary Ann Bigler
Elizabeth Bullard [Ballard]	Sally Hawley
Eliza Odercark [Odekirk]	Asenath Janes[186] [p. [54]]
Lillis Barney	Sarah Ames
Eliza Kelley [Kelly]	Sarah Dodley [Dudley]
Mary Jinkins [Jenkins]	Lovina Dodge
Anna M. Hulett	Dorcas Averett
Mary Pearsons [Parsons]	Catharine Raymond
Mary C. Rawson	Mary Asherley [Ashley]
Martha Murdock	Loisa Stout
Eliza Pace	Mary Wilson
Jane V. Lee	Almira [Lucy Alvira] Atwood
Lydia Stewart	Violette O. Harding
Celinda Hoyt	Thomazin Downing
Sally McArthur	Sarah Brinton
Mary Ann Call	Lucy Ann W. Cutler
Hannah Ames	Clarinda Cutler
Elizabeth Ames	Amanda Babcock
Betsey Arnold	Asenath Babcock
Nancy M. [Case] Winchester	Sarah Morrison
Patience Johnson	Eunice Warnuth [Warmouth]
Clarissa J. More	Nancy Wilson

---

186. TEXT: Possibly "Jones".

Dolly Wightman
Rebecca Reed
Elizabeth Pilkington
Caroline Partridge
Eliza Delany
Charlotte Allen
Rachel M[c]Call
Lydia M. Brown
Desdemona Gleason
Sylvia Vanfleet
Esther Russell
Nancy Baldwin
Mary Ann Dimick
Sarah Hadfield
Phebe Curtiss [Curtis]
Ann Powers
Susanna C. Perry
Christianna Lytle
Deborah Houghton
Mary M. Carpenter
Mary Houghton
Charity Riley
Mary Hardman
Abigail Bentley
Mary Winnegar [Winegar]
Isabel Strickland
Melissa J. Bigler
Margaret Moon
Mary Okey
Ann Birch
Eliza A Allen
Julia Ann Chapman
Elizabeth Ann Dort
Sarah Wild
Abigail Abbott
Anna Gifford
Lucy Parker
Maria Empey
Mary Ann Empey
Ellen Parker

Sally Baker
Phebe Harding
Eliza Harvey
Frances Humphrey
Betsey Rhodabank
Frances Kelley [Kelly]
Sophrona Daviss [Davis]
Mary Johnson
Juliet Johnson
Beulah A. Clark
Margaret Carn [Garn]
Esther Huse
Mary Lower
Polly Ann Butler
Jemima Johnson [p. [55]]
Sarah L. Hoyt
Caroline Butterfield
Olive Newell
Sarah Strong
Elizabeth Walker
Katharine Huntsman
Julia Ann Shumway
Sarah Burket
Lavinia Clough [Lavina Cluff]
Martha Nelson
Rhoda Nelson
Betsey Stephen
Susannah Cummings
Mabel Sharp
Mary Parsons
Mary Wilcox
Mary Aldridge
Hannah Henderson
Mary Ann Dixon [Dickson]
Levina W. Murphy
Polly M. Colton
Albina Merrill
Caroline E. Grover
Nancy Timmon
Sophronia Drake

Lorena Barrows
Hannah B. Merriam
Rebecca Hodge
Delecta Clark
Huldah M. Clark
Elizabeth H. Hyde
Prudence Miles
Lucy [Turner] Atwood
Terissa Judd
Cynthia Clyde
Abigail Dow
Rebecca Holman
Nancy Green[e]
Ellen Rockwood
Sarah M'Gill [McGill]
Mary Newberry
Clarissa C. Cutler
Nancy Gilbert
Tanor [Tamer] Washburn
Susanna Rigby
Polly McLellin [McClellan]
Maria Sc[h]oles
Melissa Bird
Eliza Ann Haven
Ann Parry
Sarah Dodge
Sarah Ann Wood
Julia E. Stone
Sally Ann Reed
Elizabeth Hugh
Amanda Higbee
Margaret Shirts
Celinda Fuller
Mary Jones
Caroline Huntington
Harriet Clark
Rhoda Pearson
Hester Myers
Phebe Madison
Elizabeth Pool

Flora Drake
Dolly [Polly] Daniels
Sarah Earl
Mary Ann Coons
Polly Vaughn
Elizabeth Stewart
Melinda Stewart
Rebecca W. Holman
Ann Bosley [p. [56]]
Rebecca Wight
Rachel Worthington
Rebecca Warner
Sarah Lytle
Sarah Higgins
Phebe Leavitt
Mary Peck
Mrs. John [Harriet] Luce

Amelia Green

Mrs. President said the case of L. A. [Lucy Ann] Munjar was put over— read a certificate and spoke [p. [57]] of dropping the subject.[187] She impress'd the necessity of being united in doing good to the poor— said she had hired a poor man to plough ⟨and fence⟩ father Knights [Joseph Knight Sr.'s] lot at $.22,60, and solicited the Society in behalf of the payment which might be made in provision, clothing and furniture.

Prest. J. Smith and Bishop [Newel K.] Whitney then came upon the stand.

Bishop Whitney arose and after some preliminary remarks, proceeded to address the congregation by saying that he rejoic'd and did rejoice at the for- mation of the Society that we might improve upon our talents and to prepare for those blessings which God is soon to bestow upon us.[188]

In the beginning God created man male and female and bestow'd upon man certain blessings peculiar to a man of God, of which woman partook, so that without the female all things cannot be restor'd to the earth it takes all to

---

187. Munjar was admitted as a member March 24, 1842, and suspended as a member May 19, 1842. (Document 1.2, entries for Mar. 24 and May 19, 1842.)

188. Whitney almost certainly was referring to blessings associated with temple rites in which he had recently participated. On May 4 and 5, 1842, Whitney and eight other men met with Joseph Smith in the upper room of Smith's red brick store. Willard Richards participated in these events and made both a brief entry in Smith's journal as well as a more extended description that later became part of Joseph Smith's multivolume manuscript history. Richards recorded that Smith spent the day "instructing them in the principles and order of the Priesthood, attending to washings, anointings, endowments and the communication of Keys pertaining to the Aaronic Priesthood, and so on to the highest order of the Melchisedec Priesthood. . . . In this Council was instituted the Ancient order of things for the first time in these last days." This marked the introduction of temple ceremonies often collectively termed "the endowment." Because the temple in Nauvoo was still under construction, the upper room of Smith's store was specially arranged for the ceremonies. The circle of those who received the endowment through Joseph Smith in May 1842 expanded gradually after September 1843 and became known variously as the quorum, the temple quorum, the anointed quorum, and the Holy Order. Emma Smith received her en- dowment September 28, 1843, the first woman to enter this temple quorum. Approximately sixty-five men and women received the endowment before Joseph Smith's death in 1844. Whitney and other May 1842 initiates were aware that "there was nothing made known to these men but what will be made known to all Saints, of the last days, so soon as they are prepared to receive, and a proper place is prepared to com- municate them." (Historian's Office, Joseph Smith History, Draft Notes, ca. 1839–1856, CHL, May 4, 1842; Joseph Smith, Journal, May 4 and 5, 1842, in *JSP*, J2:53, 54n198; Joseph Smith et al., History, 1838– 1856, vols. A-1–F-1 [original], A-2–E-2 [fair copy], CHL, vol. C-1, 1328–1329 [hereafter JS History]; Joseph Smith, Journal, Sept. 28, 1843, in Andrew H. Hedges et al., eds., *Journals, Volume 3: May 1843–June 1844,* vol. 3 of the Journals series of *The Joseph Smith Papers,* ed. Ronald K. Esplin and Matthew J. Grow [Salt Lake City: Church Historian's Press, 2015], 104 [hereafter *JSP,* J3]; Andrew F. Ehat, "Joseph Smith's Introduction of Temple Ordinances and the 1844 Mormon Succession Question" [master's thesis, Brigham Young University, 1982], 25–45; Carol Cornwall Madsen, "Mormon Women and the Temple: Toward a New Understanding," in Maureen Ursenbach Beecher and Lavina Fielding Anderson, eds., *Sisters in Spirit: Mormon Women in Historical and Cultural Perspective* [Urbana: University of Illinois Press, 1987], 84–86.)

restore the Priesthood.[189] It is the intent of the Society, by humility and faithfulness; in connexion with those husbands that are found worthy. Rejoice while contemplating the blessings which will be pour'd out on the heads of the saints. God has many precious things to bestow, even to our astonishment if we are faithful. I say again I rejoice in the prospect of what lays before. It becomes us to prepare by striving for union one with another, that we may be prepar'd for the day of choosing— man will not choose but God will say who <u>is</u> and who is <u>not</u> worthy.

We must humble ourselves and live by the rule given for our practice— we must lose sight of vain things and remember that the eye of God is upon us. If we are striving to do right, altho' we may err in judgment many times yet we are justified in the sight of God if we do the best we can according to our judgment. We need not go astray [p. [58]] if we will strive in all the energy of our souls to do right.

I rejoice that God has given us means whereby we may get intelligence and instruction. It is our privilege to stand in an attitude to get testimony for ourselves— it is as much our privilege as that of the ancients saints. We must prove all things and hold fast that which is good.[190] There are blessings lying before which are worth striving to obtain. It is our duty to humble ourselves— it is our most reasonable service to do it— must proceed to receive grace for grace, light and intelligence—[191] if we have intelligence we have pow'r— knowledge is power: if we understand all things we shall not be barren or unfruitful in the knowledge of God.[192] I desire all evil things may be done away; but far as possible throw the vail of charity over failings— when we see one out of the way, we ought in humility to go to, and counsel, and strive to bring back those who have stray'd from the holy principles— we must do as we would wish to be done by, this is the way to win souls and bring them back. There are many things to be taken into consideration. Far be it from me to harbor iniquity and outbreaking sins. We may have different views of things, still there is some criterion which all may come to, and by bringing our minds and wills into subjection to the law of the Lord, may come to unity.

It is impossible while finding fault with one another to be united. Would to God I had pow'r to bridle my tongue— We are ⟨am⟩ too apt when I hear anything, to make remarks, but of late have decreed to set a double watch on

---

189. For a discussion of early Mormon marriage rituals and Newel K. Whitney's understanding of the divine authority he and his wife possessed, see Kathleen Flake, "The Development of Early Latter-day Saint Marriage Rites, 1831–53," *Journal of Mormon History* 41, no. 1 (Jan. 2015): 77–102.

190. See 1 Thessalonians 5:21.

191. See Doctrine and Covenants 93:12, 13, 20, 36.

192. See 2 Peter 1:8.

my tongue and not offend one of the little ones. I wish nobody harm— wish it were in my pow'r to save all within the reach of mercy— would glory in it. Perhaps some would say from my past life that I had not been so faithful as I might have heen, or my voice would [p. [59]] oftener have been heard in the congregation of the saints, but I rejoice in God that it is as well with me as it is. I assure you there are great blessings before, that would astonish you if you could behold them.[193] I came here for the purpose of hearing Prest. Smith and of being instructed by him.[194] I wish to encourage you to persevere in the ways of righteousness. I tell you there are blessings before to be confer'd as soon as our hearts are prepar'd to receive them.— you have my heart's desire for the prosperity of the Society and pray my heav'nly Father that you may go on and glorify your profession.

The meeting then adjourn'd. [p. [60]]

June 9, 1842 • Thursday

Minutes of the Proceedings
of the
Eleventh Meeting of the Society.

Grove, June 9[th.]

Prest J. Smith opened the meeting by pray'r and proceeded to address the congregation on the design of the Institution— said it is no matter how fast the Society increases if all are virtuous— that we must be as particular with regard to the character of members, as when the Society first started— that sometimes persons wish to put themselves into a Society of this kind, when they do not intend to pursue the ways of purity and righteousness, as if the Society would be a shelter to them in their iniquity.

Prest. S. said that henceforth no person shall be admitted but by presenting regular petition signed by two or three members in good standing in the Society— whoever comes in must be of good report.[195]

---

193. Heber C. Kimball, one of the nine men who received the endowment through Joseph Smith on May 4 and 5, 1842, expressed a similar sentiment in a letter to fellow apostle Parley P. Pratt: "We have recieved some pressious things through the Prophet on the preasthood that would caus your Soul to rejoice." (Heber C. Kimball to Parley P. Pratt, June 17, 1842, Parley P. Pratt, Correspondence, 1842–1855, CHL.)

194. Though Joseph Smith attended the meeting, he was apparently ill. His journal entry for May 27, 1842, as recorded by Willard Richards, notes: "A billious attack. at home taking medicine." (Joseph Smith, Journal, May 27, 1842, in *JSP*, J2:64.)

195. The question of vetting potential members had arisen earlier. Eliza R. Snow later wrote, "The Society soon became so popular that even those of doubtful character in several instances applied for admission, and to prevent imposition by extending membership to such ones inadvertently, stricter rules were adopted than seemed requisite at first. Each one wishing to join the Society was required to present

Harriet Luce and Mary Luce were receiv'd into the Society by recommend.

Objections previously made against Mahala Overton were remov'd— after which Prest Smith continued his address— said he was going to preach mercy Supposing that Jesus Christ and angels should object to us on frivolous things, what would become of us? We must be merciful and overlook small things.

Respecting the reception of Sis. Overton, Prest. Smith It grieves me that there is no fuller fellowship— if one member suffer all feel it— by union of feeling we obtain pow'r with God. Christ said he came to call sinners to repentance and save them. Christ was condemn'd by the righteous jews because he took sinners into his society— he took them ⟨up⟩on the principle that they [p. [61]] repented of their sins.[196] It is the object of this Society to reform persons, not to take those that are corrupt, but if they repent we are bound to take them and by kindness sanctify and cleanse from all unrighteousness, by our influence in watching over them— nothing will have such influence over people, as the fear of being disfellowship'd by so goodly a Society as this. Then take Sis. O. as Jesus received sinners into his bosom.

Sis. O. In the name of the Lord I now make you free, and from this hour if any thing should be found against you

Nothing is so much calculated to lead people to forsake sin as to take them by the hand and watch over them with tenderness. When persons manifest the least kindness and love to me, O what pow'r it has over my mind, while the opposite course has a tendency to harrow up all the harsh feelings and depress the human mind.

It is one evidence that men are unacquainted with the principle of godliness, to behold the contraction of feeling and lack of charity. The pow'r and glory of Godliness is spread out on a broad principle to throw out the mantle of charity. God does not look on sin with allowance, but when men have sin'd there must be allowance made for them.[197]

All the religious world is boasting of righteousness— tis the doctrine of the devil to retard the human mind and retard our progress, by filling us with selfrighteousness— The nearer we get to our heavenly Father, the more are we dispos'd to look with compassion on perishing souls— to take them upon our shoulders and cast their sins behind our back. [*blank*] I am going to talk to all

a certificate of her good moral character, signed by two or more responsible persons." (Document 1.2, entry for Mar. 31, 1842; Eliza R. Snow, "The Female Relief Society," *Woman's Exponent,* June 15, 1872, 1:9; for an example of an application for membership, see Document 1.9.)

196. See Mark 2:16–17.

197. See Alma 45:16; and Doctrine and Covenants 1:31.

this Society— if you would have God have mercy on you, have mercy on one another.[198]

Prest. S. then refer'd them to the conduct of the Savior when he was taken and crucified &c.[199]

He then made a promise in the name of the [p. [62]] Lord saying, that soul that has righteousness enough to ask God in the secret place for life, every day of their lives shall live to three score years & ten— We must walk uprightly all day long— How glorious are the principles of righteousness! We are full of selfishness— the devil flatters us that we are very righteous, while we are feeding on the faults of others— We can only live by worshipping our God— all must do it for themselves— none can do it for another. How mild the Savior dealt with Peter, saying "when thou art converted, strengthen thy brethren"—[200] at an other time he said to him "lovest thou me? "Feed my sheep".—[201] If the sisters love the Lord let them feed the sheep and not destroy them. How oft have wise men & women sought to dictate br. Joseph by saying "O if I were br. Joseph I would do this and that." But if they were in br. Joseph's shoes, they would find that men could not be compel'd into the kingdom of God, but must be dealt with in long suff'ring— and at last we shall save them. The way to keep all the saints together and keep the work rolling, is to wait with all long suff'ring till God shall bring such character to justice. There should be no license for sin, but mercy should go hand in hand with reproof.

Sisters of this Society, shall there be strife among you? I will not have it— you must repent and get the love of God. Away with selfrighteousness. The best measure or principle to bring the poor to repentance is to administer to their wants— the Society is not only to relieve the poor, but to save souls.

Prest. S. then said that he would give a lot of land to the Society by deeding it to the Treasurer, that the Society may build houses for the poor. He also said he would give a house— frame not finished— said that br. [p. [63]] [Reynolds] Cahoon will move it on to the aforesaid lot, and the Society can pay him by giving Orders on the Store— that it was a good plan to set those to work who are owing widows and thus make an offsett &c. &c.[202]

---

198. See Matthew 6:14; and Doctrine and Covenants 82:1.

199. See Luke 23:34.

200. Luke 22:32.

201. John 21:15–17.

202. Eliza R. Snow later recalled that plans to build "comfortable houses for homes for the homeless, sick and destitute" and to furnish labor "adapted to the strength and capacities of such as were able to work" were abandoned. "The sudden death of the Prophet, and subsequent expulsion from Nauvoo, blasted all these fond anticipations," she wrote. (Document 3.6.)

The following names were receiv'd.

Violetta Burgess
Rosanna Lyman
Sarah Fisher
Elizabeth Edwards
Mary Moore
Sabra Prior
Marina Prior
Elizabeth Crafton
Flavilla L. Leavitt
Roxana Huntsman
Lucinda E. Cole
Persis Stiles
Sarah W. Gibbs
~~Sophia Coots~~ Catharine Pope
Phebe Rannals [Reynolds]
Rhoda A. Fulmer
Martisha Smith
Nancy Houghton
Mary I. Horne
Catharine Nicolson
Eliza Canfield
Anna Demill
Elizabeth Maudsley[203]
Nancy Henderson
Margaret Avery
Elizabeth ~~Avery~~ Gates
Lydia Badger
Mary J. Melks
Betsey Bidwell
Lydia Edwards
Eleanor Edwards
Phebe McNall
Araminta Vorth [North]
Eunice Cone
Sarah Rawlins
Julia Owens
Nancy Stewart

Ann Bowberry [Rowberry]
Mary Bowberry [Rowberry]
Charlotte Jenkins
Zilpha Jacobs
Charity Bickmore
Mary R. Maxton
Mary Ann Stevens
Betsey Foot
Jane Jenkins
Wealthy Pratt
Agnes Moss
Mary Moss
Sarah Zundal
Mary Ann Greenwell
Mary Ann Green
Margaret Smoot
Sarah Bullard
Elizabeth Mittwell [Withnell]
Harriet Little
Lucy Seel[e]y
Elizabeth Lemon
Lydia Hadlock
Martha J. Powers
Maria Clark
Nancy Simpson
Elizabeth Browett
Margaret Stow
Maria Hodson
Ann Slater [p. [64]]
Mary H. Hoyg
Mary Winterbotton
Mary Ann Allen
Eda Sweat
Mary Henderson
Naomi C. Price
Mary Wilson
Amanda Wilson

---

203. TEXT: Possibly "Mandsley".

Agnes Wilson
Philinda Stanley
Elizabeth Hendricks
Mahala Dudley
Mary Ann Maxton
Catharina Wilson
Nancy Karr [Kerr]
Tirzah Chase
Eliza Chase
Nancy Chase
Diana Chase
Sarah Buthrick [Bathrick]
Polly Leach
Diana Camp
Elizabeth Merrills
Abigail Bradley
Mary Hustin [Houston]
Lydia F. [Ann] Gibbs
Candace Evans
Jane Judd
Mary Ives
Mary Jane Morris
Mahala Morris
Mary Blake
Lodemia Barnet
Elizabeth Helm
Mary McIlwrick
Clarissa Smith
Mary Smith
Caroline Smith
Louisa Camfield [Canfield]
Charity Shepherd
Lucinda Kinyun
Jane Jones
Mary Carter
Mary Tytle[204] [Lytle]
Mary Owen
Mrs. Gay

Elizabeth Scott
Lydia M. Luce
Esther Wood
Sarah Meeks
Susanna Adams
Mary Thompson
Elizabeth Wilson
Emily Wilson
Mary Wilson
Margaret Wilkinson
[Nancy] Ann Smithies
Sarah A. Murply [Murphy]
Mary Owins
Chara Owens [Owen]
Mary Mitchell
Abigail Burbank
Susanna Wakefield
Huldah Judd
Susanna C. Boyce
Elizabeth C. Allen
Nancy M. Murphy
Talitha C. Garlick
Sarah K. Taylor
Catharine Minnerly
Catharine Mulliner
Margaret Myers [p. [65]]
Martha H. [Kelley] Wilson
Sarah I. [Jane] Weeks
Margaret Willis
Lavina Boren
Alice El[l]ison
Hannah A. Che[e]sebrough
Alice Martin
Eliza Jenkins
Mary Richardson
Ann Vowles
Mary Davis
Ruth Stoddard

204. TEXT: Possibly "Teytle".

Mrs. [Sarah] Winter
Sarah Marsden
Ann Delany
Mrs. Worthington
Mary Stilly
Mrs. Williams
Mrs. Richards
Jane Gandolf
Jane Roberts
Mary Evans

Susan Wallace
Margaret Butterfield
Harriet Roberts
Elizabeth Frampton
Sarah Cox
Margaret Empey
Jane A. Foot
Mary Allred
Nancy W. Allred
Orissa A. Allred
Sarah L. Taylor
Mary C. Egbert
Eliza Ann Dusette
Abi Salina Burk
Jane Tidwell
Susan Strong
Mary Mayberry
Sophia Anderson
Sarah H. Head [Sarah Head Bracken]
Mary Head
Mary Wall
Elizabeth Wilson

Malinda Chipman
Charlotte Chase
Esther Gleason
Ann E. Hoskinson
Abigail Woolsey
Polly Woolsey
Elmira Meacham
Polly Meacham [Mecham]
Mary Jane Butterfield
Betey A. [Elizabeth Ann] Burkett
Sarah J. Burkett
Catharine Skinner
Eleanor Taylor
Mary Burkett
Jane Burkett
Mary Ann Bracken
Elsey Ann Curtiss [Curtis]
Lydia M. Luce
Hannah M. Swasey
Louis Judd
Charity Sharp
Mavy [Mary] Roles [p. [66]]
Abigail D. Hovey
Sarah Rockwell
Sarah Remington
Katharine [Catherine] Walker
Cyntha Yeamans
Deborah Leithead
Eliza J. Wilber

The following donations were then receiv'd, to wit—

	$
Lucinda E. Cole	.. 50
Mrs. Chase	.. 75
Elizabeth Romley [Romney]	.. 75
Mary Rollins	1,00
Roxana Repsher	2,25

Mrs. Curtis	1,,50
Maria C. Perry	.. 50
Maria Scholes	1,87
Cyrena Merrills [Merrill]	.. 31
Albina Merrills [Merrill]	.. 25
Rhoda Bentley	.. 50
Lodemia Barnet	.. 25
Mary Ann Peck	.. 25
Mary Greenwell	.. 25
Amanda Rogers	1,00
Diantha Billings	.. 25
Sophronia Drake	.. 37
Hannah Smith	.. 50
Sarah Head	.. 75
Loisa Pratt	.. 50
Hannah Pierce	1,00
Mary Woolley	.. 50

[p. [67]]

	$
Elmira Miller	1,25
Unknown—	.. 25
do [ditto]	.. 50
Philena Stanley	1,50
Jemima Newcomb	4,00
Julius Guinand	2.00
Mrs. [Mary] Felshaw	1,00
Hannah Ells	1,00
Mary Smith	1,87
Ann Bosley	1,50

June 23, 1842 • Thursday

Minutes of the Proceedings
of the
Twelfth meeting of the Society.

Grove, June 23[d.]

Meeting commenc'd with singing "Awake ye saints of God awake" &c.—[205] Pray'r by Councillor [Sarah] Cleveland

---

205. Hymn 113, *Collection of Sacred Hymns* [1841], 121.

Mrs. Pres.^t propos'd that the Society place funds in the hands of the Treasurer, for the purpose of preparing the house in contemplation for the poor.

On motion of Councillor Cleveland, resolved that all applying to the Treasurer for relief, without a recommend, shall be aided at the discretion of the President.

Coun. C. said the time had come that all must live by faith alone— the pow'rs of darkness were array'd against us, but said she fear'd nothing.

Coun. W. [Elizabeth Ann Whitney] rose— encourag'd the sisters to look for long life to do good— spoke of the glory to come &c. [p. [68]]

Mrs. President said she was rejoic'd to see the increasing union of the Society— hop'd we should live right before God, among ourselves and before the world.

Coun. C. said we should be extremely careful in handling character— be merciful and not oppress any especially those persons objected to by some, yet considered virtuous, such should be held in their place— should not feel themselves numbered with the vile— said we would have none among us who would speak against the prophet of the Lord, or the authorities of the church &c——

Mrs. President propos'd that a Circular go forth from this Society, expressive of our feeling in reference to Dr. [John C.] Bennett's character— requested all who could wield the pen, to write and send in their productions, out of which, a selection should be made— said Dr. B. had proclaim'd that the Relief Society would be the means of a mob forth-coming—[206] said she could not be afraid of mobs— desired the objects of the Society— the true situatio◊◊ of

---

206. Emma Smith's call for a circular may have resulted in a statement on marriage published in the October 1, 1842, edition of the *Times and Seasons*. Bennett was excommunicated from the church and resigned as mayor of Nauvoo in May 1842; he left Nauvoo on June 21, 1842. About a month later, approximately one thousand women signed a petition to Governor Thomas Carlin from the Female Relief Society, prepared on July 22, 1842. The petition called Bennett "an unvirtuous man & a most consummate scoundrel a stirrer up of sedition & a vile wretch unworthy the attention or notice of any virtuous man." On June 24, 1842, the day following this Relief Society meeting, Joseph Smith sent a letter to Carlin describing Bennett's serial adultery, manipulation of Joseph Smith's teachings, and hostility toward the Latter-day Saints. Smith reported to Carlin, "It is rumored, and strong evidence exists that Bennett and David and Edward Kilbourn[e] have posted Bills in Galena calling upon the people to hold meetings and have themselves in readiness at a moments warning to assemble and come here and mob us out of the place and try to kidnap me." Bennett soon began printed attacks against the Latter-day Saints; for his 1842 attack on the Relief Society, see John C. Bennett, *The History of the Saints; or, An Exposé of Joe Smith and Mormonism* (Boston: Leland and Whiting, 1842), 220–225. (Documents 1.5 and 1.6; Joseph Smith et al., "Notice," May 11, 1842, Joseph Smith Collection, CHL; Joseph Smith, Journal, May 19, 1842, in *JSP*, J2:58, 67n269; Joseph Smith to Thomas Carlin, June 24, 1842, in Joseph Smith, "Copies of Letters, &c. &c.," 1839–1843, Joseph Smith Collection, CHL, 233–235.)

matters might be represented— said we had nothing to do but to fear God and keep the commandments, and in doing so we shall prosper.

Mrs. Chase prophesied that henceforth, if the sisters are faithful, the gifts of the gospel shall be with us, especially the gift of healing— &c. &c.

The following persons were then receiv'd by petition and recommend.

Nancy H. Davidson
Mary Kempton
Maria Champlin
Olive Cathcart
Mary J. [Isabella] Horne
Susan Stillson
Louisa Butterfield
Betsey Ogden
P. [Patience] D. Palmer
Hannah Driggs
Sarah Gibbons
Sally Allred

Abigail Hovey
Polly Meckand [Meacham?]
Mary Ann Hubbard
Lovina Thayre [Thayer]
Esther Briarly
Eleanor Simmons [Helenora Symons]
Sarah Sagers
Martha Rogers
Margaret McCall
Amanda Simmons
Barbara Study
Mary Ann Russell
Eliza Hough
Leah Childs
Patience Childs

Mary Edgar [Eager]
A. [blank] Parker
Mary C. McCall
Lucinda Harmon [p. [69]]
Mary Ann Hales
Sally Killien [Killian]
Adah Phippen
Ann McCaslin
Susan[nah] McCaslin [McCauslin]
Eliza Mitchell
Milly Knight
Phebe Cole [Phoebe Van Alstyne Cole]
Mary Brown
Mary Ann Lumereaux [Lamoreaux]
Cynthia McLellin
Harriet Ellis
Lucinda Page
Polly Vanansdale [Van Ausdall]
Lucina Snow
Amy A. Smith
Mary Ann Nickerson
Polly Leach
Martha Helsen [Helsor]
Rhoda Smith
Emily J. Burke
Christiana Wood

Objections were remov'd against the following persons, to wit.

Elizabeth Garlick
Mary Garlick

Hannah Garlick
Talithacuma Garlick [p. [70]]

Donations.

	$
Hannah Huntsman	.. 50
Emma Smith	14,00

Elizabeth [Davis] Durfee	14 00
Margaret Dana	.. 50
Sarah Lincoln	1.00
Sarah Foster	71.00
Martha Sessions	.. 25
Catharine Wilkie	4,00
Mary Abbott	6,00
Susan McArthur	6,00
Irene H. Cowles	1,50
Sarah Higbee	2.00
Bulah Hoyt	25
Mary Ann Hadfield	2,00
Emma Smith	1,00
Elizabeth Corey	1,25
Eunice Holbrook	25
Matilda Case	1,75
Catharine Spencer	1,25
Lucy Foot	.. 50
Lydia Huntington	.. 25
Mary Greenwell	.. 25
Nancy Winchester	.. 50
Sophia Aldridge	. .6
Ruth C—	.. 12
Louisa Knight	.. 12
Loisa Pratt	.. 50
Catharine Spencer	.. 50
Sybil Jacobs	.. 12
Susannah Cummins	.. 50
Abigail Bradford	12
Elizabeth Matthews	.. 50
[p. [71]]	
Catharine Raymond	.. 80
Mary Wooley	1,00
Philinda Stanley	.. 12
Mary Wooley	1,25
Rebecca Hodge	.. 62
Amanda [Barnes] Smith	1,00
Emeline Carlin[g]	2.50
Nancy King	.. 12
Drusilla Hendricks	.. 12

Thirza [Stiles] Cahoon	1.00
Rachel Allen	.. 31
— Chase	.. 25
E. [Elizabeth] Maudsley	.. 20
Elizabeth Burn[e]s	.. 20
Melinda Lewis	2[.] 33
Susan A. Chapman	.. 12

[p. [72]]

July 7, 1842 • Thursday

Minutes of the
Thirteenth Meeting of the
Society.

Grove July 7ᵗʰ

Meeting opened by singing "When I survey the wondrous cross" &c.²⁰⁷
Pray'r by sister [Sophia] Packard.

Mrs. President not present,²⁰⁸ the busines of the Society was defer'd, and the time spent in exhortation and speaking, singing and prayer, much to the comfort and edification of those present.

The following Donations were made to wit.

$

Mary Akerly	.. 50
Catharine Spencer	.. 20
Sophia Packard appropriated to Mrs. Birch	20 lbs. flour
Mrs. D[e]uel appropriated to Mrs. Birch	27 do [ditto]
Mrs. Winchester appropriated for Mrs. Hawkes.	25 do

Prayer for the children earnestly recommended by Councillors [Sarah] Cleveland, [Elizabeth Ann] Whitney and others.

Meeting adjourn'd to next week. [p. [73]]

July 14, 1842 • Thursday

Fourteenth
Meeting of the Society——

---

207. Hymn 249, *Collection of Sacred Hymns* [1841], 272.

208. The entry in Joseph Smith's journal for the day before this meeting records, "Rode out to La Harpe [Illinois] with sister Emma and others." (Joseph Smith, Journal, July 6, 1842, in *JSP*, J2:74.)

Grove, July 14th.

Meeting opened by pray'r by Councillor [Sarah] Cleveland
The following persons receiv'd as members of the Society, to wit.

Rebecca Shirtliff	Patty Gates
Susan Thornton	Harriet Scovill
Ann Wormsley [Wamsley]	Lucetta Murdock
Sarah Dunn	Sarah M. Chaffin
Louisa Clark	Jane Barber
Nancy Hamer	Sally S. [Briggs] Alvord
Eliza Ells	Amanda Sanders
Frances Campion	Abigail Shelton
Elizabeth Boice [Boyce]	Roxcy Keller
Nancy Jackson	Caroline McCaslin
Elizabeth Cox	Mary Ann Case
Elizabeth Hardy	Dorothy Fry
Lucinda Bingham	Elizabeth Sumner
Mariah Sirine	Elizabeth Blackhurst
Mary Ann Dunn	Tamina Miner
Angeline Holden	Elizabeth King
Lydia Gates	Polly King
Matilda Case	Maria Lane
Celestia Baken [Bacon]	Laura McGeer [Laura M. Geer]
Mary Ames	Johanna Bennett
Nancy A. Co[u]lson	Cynthia Durphy
Elizabeth Corey	Almira J. Cairns
Louisa McCarty	Mary Whittle
Sophia Lanyon	Ronana [Roxana] Freeman
Rosetta Glazier	Mary Baldwin
Adaline Bonn[e]y	Olive Baldwin [p. [74]]
Rene Baldwin	Mary Stoddard
Mehitable Duty	Mary Ann Price
Julyanna Fenswith [Julia Ann Farnsworth]	A. [Aggatha] A. Lee
Mary Clark	Almeda Stringham
Mary Rogers	Betsey Ann N. Pettigrew
Amy Porter	Caroline K. Pettigrew
Sylvia Carter	Lucinda S. Knights [Knight]
Lucinda G. Pace	Eliza Harrower [Harrover]
Ruth Luce	Martha Wilcox
Abigail Whaley	Mary Henderson
Jane Mills	Martha T. Workman

Esther S. Tyler
Eliza Robberd [Roberts]
Maria Hendricks
Mary Barton
Susan Brown
Caroline Crosby
Jane Hanks
Polly [Dolly] Brown
Nancy Brown
Rebecca Tryon
Eunice Eaton
[Elizabeth] Matilda King
Caroline H. Robinson
Olive Martin
Ellen Carter
Evaline Palmer
Elizabeth Outhouse
Anna Downey
Susanna H[o]uston
Nancy Porter
Elizabeth Bullard
Kezia Hunter
Charlotte E. Magary [McGary]
Jemima Brace
Verona G. [Jemima] Brace
Sally Fowler
Lucretia C. Bartholomew
Lucy Hawkes
Lydia Fido

Lovica Butler
Susanna Butler
Mary Middleton
Sarah C. Ellsworth
Martha Jane Garrett
Mary Ann Cole
Phebe A. [Amanda] Cole
Sally Fisher
Sarah Ellsworth
Mary Lance
Sarah Thompson
Mary Ann Deming
Polly [Knight] Stringham
Mary Ann Munghar
Jennett Kelsey
Diana Kelsey
Mary H[o]uston
Anna H[o]uston
Ellen Neibaur
Betsey Ames
Mary Hawley
Abigail Abbott
Peggy Patten [p. [75]]
Delana Parker
Mary M. Hoyt
Susanna Green
Sarah Ann Wilcox
Sarah Mᶜ[C]Lure [Killian]

The case of Sis. Brown was then laid before the meeting— sis. [Sophia] Packard objected— After many very pointed remarks concerning the necessity of acting upon the principle of forgiveness, the case was again presented upon the consideration that sis. Brown had manifested deep repentance for whatever imprudence she had been guilty of, and solicited forgiveness of the Society. Sis. A. Smith objected to her reception, on the ground that former objectors had not been satisfied—

The case of sis. Nighman [Jane Neyman],²⁰⁹ wishing admittance, was als[o] presented and objected.

209. This matter was discussed earlier at the April 28, 1842, Relief Society meeting. (Document 1.2,

Mrs. President said she could not urge fellowship where the sisters could not feel to fellowship— but where we cannot fellowship as a christian, we must not let the persons suffer in our midst. She then recommended old sis. [Prudence] Oakes[210] [211]to the charity and the watch care of the Society.

Meeting adjourn'd—

Donations.	$
Rebecca Shirtliff.	1,00
Ann Wurmsley [Wamsley]	25,
Sarah Dunn	2,25
Louisa Clark	75
Eliza Ells	4,00
Frances Campion	3,00
Elizabeth Boice	25
Elizabeth Cox	50
Elizabeth Hardy	25

[p. [76]]

	$
Lucinda Bingham	3,00
Mary Ann Dunn	.. 50
Angeline Holden	.. 37
Lydia Gates	1,62
Matilda Case	1,75
Celestia Baken	.. 37
Elizabeth Corey	1,25
Sophia Lanyon	11,00
Patty Gates	1,00
Harriet Scovil	1,25
Lucetta Murdock	.. 75

The above contributions were received from the Laharpe sisters, by Mrs Jones.[212]

August 4, 1842 • Thursday

Fifteenth Meeting
of the Society.

Grove, August 4th, 1842.

---

entry for Apr. 28, 1842.)

210. TEXT: Possibly "Oaks".

211. TEXT: Ink changes to darker blue ink.

212. La Harpe, Illinois, was located about twenty-five miles east of Nauvoo. Latter-day Saint women at Lima, Illinois, also sent contributions. (Document 1.2, entry for Sept. 2, 1843.)

Meeting open'd with singing.

Pray'r by Prest. Emma Smith.

Mrs. Prest. arose and address'd the Society upon the necessity of being united among ourselves— said we shall have sufficient difficulty from abroad without stirring up strife among ourselves and hardness and evil fee[l]ings, one towards another &c.

The following persons were then receiv'd,

Charity Taylor	Abigail Andrews
Margaret M. Rainey	Diana Bloxham [p. [77]]
Mary Pitt	Christiana Allaman
Caroline Pitt	Mary J. Drake
Sarah Hickeson	Sarah Jolly
Evelina Boggs	Almira Higgins
Betsey Mackley	Elizabeth C. Allen
[213]Mary Ann Mackley	Amanda C. Clift
Harriet Stevens	Elizabeth Bracken
Eliza Deuel	Lucretia C. Maxwell
Mary S. Chapman	Ruth B. Kimball
Fanny Herryman	Harriet Knowlton
Hannah Flint	Elizabeth Meeds [Meeks]
Mary Call	Martha Outhouse
Hannah Webb	Frances Green
Lucretia Lindsey	Elizabeth Hinson
Rosannah Forge[u]s	Sarah Wixom
Hannah Fish	Sally Levett [Leavitt]
Sarah Fish	Lucina Meehum [Mecham]
Mercy Baker	Susan Daniels
Louisa Sessions	Sarah Daniels
Phidelia [Elizabeth Fidelia] King	Electa C. Williams
Mary Wood	Roxcinda White [Rosina Wight]
Susanna Merrill	Susan L. Merrill

The case of sister Brown was presented to the Society— many voted in the affirmative— an objection made, when Mrs. Prest. call'd for an expression of the meeting, to ascertain how many think best for sis. Brown to see her objectors, as had been propos'd by some individuals.[214]

---

213. TEXT: Ink changes back to previous blue ink.

214. Objections to Brown's admittance to the Relief Society had been raised at the prior meeting. (Document 1.2, entry for July 14, 1842.)

Vote pass'd in the affirmative. Mrs. [Catharine] Wilkie requested the privilege of being present at an interview between Sis. Brown and a Sister who had told scandalous tales on Sis. B. in company with Coun. C. [Sarah Cleveland]— said now her obj's were greater against that person than [p. [78]] sis. B.

Mrs Prest. said she could have the privilege as she was one that had obj.ᵗ

Mrs. Prest. then proceeded to make observations respecting her visit to Quincy— that she was prosper'd— was cordially rec'd by the Governor who assured us of his protection &c.²¹⁵ She said we could govern this generati[o]n in one way if not another— if not by the mighty arm of power, we can do it by faith & prayer. If we will try to live uprightly, said she believed we should not be driven.

Mrs. Pres.ᵗ continued by Saying God knows we have a work to do in this place— we have got to watch and pray and be careful not to excite feelings— not make enemies of one another &c.

Mrs. [Roxsena] Repsher motion'd a vote of thanks to Pres.ᵗ E. Smith

Mrs. Pres.ᵗ said she does not want the thanks but the prayers of the Society.

Mrs. Durfee recommended to the sister to sustain by their diligence and faithfulness, that character before the world, which our Pres.ᵗ has represented abroad.

Mrs. Parker was requested to state the result of her visit to sis. Miller's

Reported that sis. M. was glad to have the Society watch over her— acknowledg'd she had done wrong and determin'd to do better.

Meeting adjourn'd. [p. [79]]

August 31, 1842 • Wednesday

²¹⁶Sixteenth Meeting
of the
Society.

Grove, August 31.ˢᵗ·

Pres.ᵗ Joseph Smith opened the meeting by addressing the Society.²¹⁷ He commenced by expressing his happiness and thankfulness for the privilege of being present on the occasion. He said that great exertions had been made on the part of our enemies, but they had not accomplished their purpose— God had enabled him to keep out of their hands— he had war'd a good warfare

---

215. On July 28, 1842, Emma Smith, Eliza R. Snow, and Amanda Barnes Smith delivered a petition from the Nauvoo Relief Society to Governor Thomas Carlin in Quincy, Illinois. (Document 1.5.)

216. TEXT: Ink changes from blue to brown ink.

217. The entry in Joseph Smith's journal for this date, as recorded by Willard Richards, states, "In the P.M rode up to the Grove with his lady to attend the Female Relief Society's meeting." (Joseph Smith, Journal, Aug. 31, 1842, in *JSP*, J2:124.)

inasmuch as he had whip'd out all of [John C.] Bennett's host— his feelings at the present time were, that inasmuch as the Lord Almighty had preserv'd him today. He said it reminded him of the Savior, when he said to the pharisees, "Go ye and tell that fox, Behold I cast out devils, and I do cures today and tomorrow, and the third day I shall be perfected." &c.[218]

He said he expected the heavenly Father had decreed that the Missourians shall not get him— if they do, it will be because he does not keep out of the way.

Pres[t.] S. continued by saying, I shall triumph over my enemies— I have begun to triumph over them at home and I shall do it abroad— all those that rise up against me will feel the weight of their iniquity upon their own heads— those that speak evil are abominable characters— and full of iniquity— All the fuss and all the stir against me, is like the jack in the lantern, it cannot be found. Altho' I do wrong, I do not the wrongs that I am charg'd with doing— the wrong that I do is thro' the frailty of human nature like other men. No man lives without fault. Do you think that even Jesus, if he were here would be without fault in your eyes? Th[e]y said all manner of [p. [80]] evil against him— they all watch'd for iniquity.

How easy it was for Jesus to call out all the iniquity of the hearts of those whom he was among? The servants of the Lord are required to guard against those thing[s] that are calculated to do the most evil— the little foxes spoil the vines—[219] little evils do the most injury to the church. If you have evil feelings and speak of them to one an other, it has a tendency to do mischief— these things result in those evils which are calculated to cut the throats of the heads of the church.

When I do the best I can— when I am accomplishing the greatest good, then the most evils are got up against me. I would to God that you would be wise. I now counsel you, if you know any thing, hold your tongues, and the least harm will be done.

The Female Relief Society has taken the the most active part in my welfare— against my enemies— in petitioning to the Governor—[220] These measures were all necessary— Do you not see that I foresaw what was coming beforehand, by the spirit of prophesy?— All had an influence in my redemption from the hand of my enemies.

If these measures had not been taken, more serious consequences would have resulted.

---

218. Luke 13:32.
219. See Song of Solomon 2:15.
220. See Document 1.5.

I have come here to bless you. The Society has done well— their principles are to practice holiness— God loves you and your prayers in my behalf shall avail much— Let them not cease to ascend to God in my behalf. The enemy will never get weary— I expect he will array every thing against me— I expect a tremendous warfare. He that will war the christian warfare will have the angels of devils and all the infernal powers of darkness continually array'd against [p. [81]] him. When wicked and corrupt men oppose, it is a criterion to judge if a man is warring the christian warfare. When all men speak evil of you, blessed are ye &c.[221] Shall a man be considered bad, when men speak evil of him? No: If a man stands and opposes the world of sin, he may expect all things array'd against him.

But it will be but a little season and all these afflictions will be turn'd away from us inasmuch as we are faithful and are not overcome by these evils. By seeing the blessings of the endowment rolling on, and the kingdom increasing and spreading from sea to sea; we will rejoice that we were not overcome by these foolish things.

Prest. S. then remark'd that a few things had been manifested to him in his absence, respecting the baptisms for the dead, which he should communicate next sabbath if nothing should occur to prevent.[222]

Pres[t.] S. then address'd the throne of Grace.[223]

---

221. See Matthew 5:11.

222. Joseph Smith first publicly discussed vicarious baptism for the dead during a funeral sermon in August 1840. The first baptisms for the dead were performed by September 1840 in the Mississippi River near Nauvoo. In December 1840 Smith elaborated on the doctrine to members of the Quorum of the Twelve Apostles serving missions in England: "This was certainly practiced by the ancient churches and St. Paul endeavours to prove the doctrine of the resurrection from the same, and says, 'else what shall they do which are baptized for the dead.'" Smith further remarked, "The Saints have the privilege of being baptized for those of their relatives who are dead, who they feel to believe would have embraced the gospel if they had been priviledged with hearing it, and who have received the gospel in the spirit through the instrumentality of those who may have been commissioned to preach to them while in prison." Though Joseph Smith remarked at this August 31 Relief Society meeting that he would address the topic the following Sunday, which was September 4, he was unable to preach that day because he was in hiding to avoid arrest and extradition to Missouri. However, in early September, Smith wrote two letters to the Saints (now found in sections 127 and 128 of the Doctrine and Covenants) giving instructions on baptism for the dead. (Simon Baker, "15 Aug. 1840 Minutes of Recollection of Joseph Smith's Sermon," Joseph Smith Collection, CHL; Joseph Smith to "the Twelve," Dec. 15, 1840, Joseph Smith Collection, CHL; Joseph Smith to "all the saints in Nauvoo," Sept. 1, 1842, in *JSP*, J2:131–133; Joseph Smith to "the Church of Jesus Christ," Sept. [7], 1842, in *JSP*, J2:143–150; Jane Neymon and Vienna Jacques, Statement, Nov. 29, 1854, Historian's Office, Joseph Smith History Documents, ca. 1839–1880, CHL; see also Glen M. Leonard, *Nauvoo: A Place of Peace, a People of Promise* [Salt Lake City: Deseret Book; Provo, UT: Brigham Young University Press, 2002], 238–239.)

223. See Hebrews 4:16.

Pres^t· Emma Smith then rose and presented the following names, which were unanimously receiv'd

to wit.

Lucy Stevens	Jane Manhard
Rachel Page	Mary Chipman
Cherrizade Averett	Mary Wilsey
Polly W. Hyde	Hannah York
Eunice S. Hyde	Nancy Walker
Martha Stafford	Sally [Sarah Waterman] Phelps
Hannah Price	Sarah Phelps
Catharine Harwood	Jane Melling
Margaret Copeland	Elizabeth J. [Jane] Henderson
Mary Hoover	Emily Morgan
Sabina A. Harrison	Laura Kelly
Susannah Bigler	Mary E. [Mc]Mullin [p. [82]]
Mary Goff	Mary M. Dodge
Sarah Stewart	Esther Ann Gheen
Catharine Head	Elizabeth Study
Nancy Dickson	Ann Green
Loisa Eager	Martha J. Corey [Coray]

The prayers of Society requested in behalf of Mrs. [Roxsena] Repshar.

Pres^t· J. S. remark'd that sis. Repshar had long since been advised to return to her husband— has been ascertain'd by good evidence that she left her husband without cause— that he is a moral man and a gentleman— she has got into a way of having revelations, but not the rev. of God— if she will go home we will pray for her, but if not our prayers will do no good.

Pres^t· S. said he had one remark to make respecting the baptism for the dead— to suffice for the time being, until he has opportunity to discuss the subject to greater length— that is, all persons baptiz'd for the dead must have a Recorder present, that he may be an eye-witness to testify of it.[224] It will be necessary in the grand Council, that these things be testified— let it be attended to from this time, but if there is any lack it may be at the expense of our friends— they may not come forth &c.

---

224. The day following this Relief Society meeting, Joseph Smith wrote a letter to the Saints calling for proxy baptisms for the dead to be witnessed by a recorder. The letter was published in the *Times and Seasons* on September 15, 1842, and canonized as section 105 in the 1844 edition of the Doctrine and Covenants (section 127 in the modern Latter-day Saint edition). (Joseph Smith to "all the saints in Nauvoo," Sept. 1, 1842, in *JSP*, J2:131–133; "Tidings," *Times and Seasons*, Sept. 15, 1842, 3:919–920; *The Doctrine and Covenants of the Church of Jesus Christ of Latter Day Saints; Carefully Selected from the Revelations of God*, comp. Joseph Smith, 2nd ed. [Nauvoo, IL: John Taylor, 1844], section 105.)

Prayer by br. [Erastus] Derby.
Meeting adjourn'd

Donations

	$
Mrs. Winnegar [Mary Winegar]	1,00
Delany Parker	.. 12½
[blank] Newell	1,25
Polly T. Hyde	1,00
E. Modsley [Elizabeth Maudsley]	6
Anna Smith	50

[p. [83]]

	$
Agnes Marsh	.. 12½
Myrza Alexander	12½
[blank] Chapman	37
[blank] Green	50
Hannah Ann Dibble	
Susanna Be[ckel]hymer	1,50
[blank]	50
Eliza Hills	2,50

[p. [84]]

September 28, 1842 • Wednesday

Eighteenth Meeting[225]
of the
Society.

Grove, Sept. 28th.

Mrs. President not present.[226] Councillors [Sarah] Cleveland and [Elizabeth Ann] Whitney presided— the following persons were received into the Society— to wit.

Jerusha Dalyrimple	Caroline L. Curtiss
Margaret Dunn	Margaret West
Adaline Dunn	Polly Meecham [Meacham]

---

225. This minute book numbers Relief Society meetings in sequence for each of the three years it covers. For 1842, the minutes have no record for the seventeenth meeting, which would have been held at some point between August 31 and September 28. It is also possible that there was no additional meeting and that the scribe accidentally skipped from sixteen to eighteen in numbering the meetings.

226. In the entry he made in Joseph Smith's journal for the day following this meeting, scribe Willard Richards recorded, "This day Sister Emma began to be sick with fever; consequently president Joseph kept in the house and with her all day." Joseph and Emma were both sick for the next week. (Joseph Smith, Journal, Sept. 29–Oct. 7, 1842, in *JSP*, J2:159–162.)

Clarissa Herriman
Jennette C. Russell
Melvina C. Snow
Susan Hervey [Harvey]
Sally G. Canfield
Sarah Mowerry
Elizabeth Robbins
Harriet Marsh
Sally Peacock
Julia Daniels
Elizabeth Mount
Lodema Winnegar [Winegar]
Susanna Yocom
Lucy J. Leonard

Ann F. Kinsey
Surviah Taylor
Maryette Coray
Permelia M. Dayton
Mary Vanansdall [Van Ausdall]
Anne Vanansdall [Anna Van Ausdall]
Maria Harris
Naomi Kellogg
Elizabeth Packer
Catharine Mikesell
Hannah Page
Saria Garner
Catharine E. Crouse
Mary Fose

Meeting adjourn'd <u>Sine</u> <u>Die</u>. [p. [85]]

Copied Documents • March 31 and April 2, 1842

The following Epistle was read before the Society, early after its organization— but was not forwarded to be recorded; the Secretary not being present at the time of its reading; else it would have appear'd in its proper place.[227]

To the Hon., the President of the Female Relief Society of Nauvoo, Greeting:

Can the "Female Relief Society of Nauvoo" be trusted with some important matters that ought actually to belong to them to see to, which men have been under the necessity of seeing to, to their chagrin & mortification, in order to prevent iniquitous characters from carrying their iniquity into effect; such, as for instance, a man who may be aspiring after power and authority, and yet without principle,— regardless of God, man, or the devil, or the interest or welfare of man, or the virtue or innocence of woman?

Shall the credulity, good faith, and stedfast feelings of our sisters, for the cause of God or truth, be impos'd upon by believing such men, because they say they have authority from Joseph, or the First Presidency, or any other Presidency of the Church; and thus, with a lie in their mouth, deceive and debauch the innocent, under the

---

227. Emma Smith read this letter at the March 31, 1842, meeting of the Relief Society. She said it would "test the ability of the members in keeping secrets; as it was for the benefit of the Society, and that alone." (Document 1.2, entry for Mar. 31, 1842.)

assumption that they are authoriz'd from these sources? <u>May</u> <u>God</u> <u>Forbid</u>!

A knowledge of some such things having come to our ears, we improve this [p. [86]] favorable opportunity, wherein so goodly a number of you may be inform'd that no such authority ever has, ever can, or ever will be given to any man, and if any man has been guilty of any such thing, let him be treated with utter contempt, and let the curse of God fall on his head, and let him be turned out of Society as unworthy of a place among men, & denounced as the blackest & the most unprincipled wretch; and finally let him be damned!

We have been informed that some unprincipled men, whose names we will not mention at present, have been guilty of such crimes.[228] We do not mention their names, not knowing but what there may be some among you who are not sufficiently skill'd in Masonry as to keep a secret, therefore, suffice it to say, there are those, and we therefore warn you, & forewarn you, in the name of the Lord, to check & destroy any faith that any innocent person may have in any such character; for we do not want any one to believe <u>any</u> <u>thing</u> as coming from us, contrary to the old established morals & virtues & scriptural laws, regulating the habits, customs & conduct of society; and all persons pretending to be authoriz'd by us, or having any permit, or sanction from us, are & will be <u>liars</u> & <u>base</u> <u>impostors</u>, & you are authoriz'd on the very first intimation of the kind, to denounce them as such, & shun them as the flying fiery serpent, whether they are prophets, Seers, or revelators; Patriarchs, twelve Apostles, Elders, Priests, Mayers, Generals, City Councillors, Aldermen, Marshalls, Police, Lord Mayors or the Devil, are alike culpable & shall be damned for such evil practices; and if you yourselves adhere to anything [p. [87]] of the kind, you also shall be damned.

Now beloved Sisters, do not believe for a moment, that we wish to impose upon you, we actually do know that such things have existed in the church, and are sorry to say that we are obliged to make mention of any such thing, and we want a stop put to them, and we desire you to do your part, and we will do ours, for we wish to keep the commandments of God in all things, as given directly from heav'n to us, living by every word that proceedeth out of the mouth of the Lord.

---

228. John C. Bennett, Chauncey Higbee, and other men had been seducing young women by telling them they had God's sanction through Joseph Smith to do so. (See 67n175 herein; Documents 1.5 and 1.6; and Part 1 introduction.)

May God add his blessing upon your heads and lead you in all the paths of virtue, piety & peace, that you may be an ornament unto those to whom you belong, and rise up and crown them with honors, & by so doing, you shall be crown'd with honor in heav'n and shall sit upon thrones, judging those over whom you are plac'd in authority, and shall be judg'd of God for all the responsibilities that we confer'd upon you.

At a more convenient and appropriate season, we will give you further information upon this subject.

Let this Epistle be had as a private matter in your Society, and then we shall learn whether you are good <u>masons</u>.

We are your humble Servants in the Bonds of the New & Everlasting Covenant."—[229] Signed by

Hyrum Smith	Joseph Smith, President of
Heber C. Kimball	the church of Jesus Christ
Willard Richards	of Latter Day Saints
Vinson Knights[230]	Brigham Young, Prest. of
	the Quorum of the Twelve

P.S. If the Lord be God, serve him; but if baal, then <u>serve him.</u>[231]

[p. [88]]

Copy of a Certificate, which was also read before the Society, at the same time that the preceding Epistle was presented.

Nauvoo, April 2th 1842.

This is to certify that I never have at any time or place, seen or heard any thing improper or unvirtuous in the conduct or conversation of either President Smith or Mrs. Agnes Smith.

I also certify that I never have reported any thing derogatory to the characters of either of them.

Signed, Clarissa Marvel

X

her mark.[232]

---

229. The phrase "new and everlasting covenant" appeared in Joseph Smith's revelations "as synonymous with the 'fulness of [the] gospel'—the sum total of the church's message—or with individual elements of it." ("New and everlasting covenant," in *JSP,* J1:469.)

230. Hyrum Smith was the associate president of the church, Heber C. Kimball and Willard Richards were apostles, and Vinson Knight was a bishop in Nauvoo. ("Vinson Knight" and "Ecclesiastical Officers and Church Appointees," in *JSP,* J2:470, 506–509.)

231. See 1 Kings 18:24.

232. At the Relief Society meeting on April 14, 1842, Sarah Cleveland stated that the "case of

The foregoing, closes the record of the proceedings of the Female Relief Society during the first year of its organization.

Recorded by

Eliza R. Snow, Secretary. [p. [89]]

June 16, 1843 • Friday

The Female Relief Society of Nauvoo, resumed its meetings— June 16th 1843.

Minutes of the Proceedings

of the

First Meeting of the Society.

June 16th 1843.

Meeting convened according to previous instructions of Prest. Emma Smith, who not being present, Councillor [Elizabeth Ann] Whitney presided.[233]

Meeting opened by singing "Let Zion in her beauty rise" &c—[234] Prayer by Mrs. Chase.

Councillor Whitney rose and address'd the meeting by saying that she felt alone in consequence of the absence of the President, from whom she had received instructions that we might not only relieve the wants of the poor but also cast in our mites to assist the brethren in building the Lord's House— said she had felt a deep interest on the subject since last sabbath hearing Prest. Smith's remarks—[235] wished the sisters to express their feelings— our Prest., Mrs. Smith said we might speak to the Temple Com., and whatever they wished and we could, we might do—[236] Coun. W. then presented the case of

Clarissa M. had been satisfactorily settled she having testified in her own hand writing that she had said no wrong," a reference to this certificate. There appears to be a discrepancy in the dating of this document. The minutes state that it was read before the Relief Society at the same time as the preceding epistle, which was presented on March 31, 1842, but this document is dated April 2, 1842. (Document 1.2, entry for Apr. 14, 1842.)

233. Sarah Cleveland, the other counselor, was not present because she had recently moved from Nauvoo. (See Document 1.7.)

234. Hymn 134, *Collection of Sacred Hymns* [1841], 144.

235. On Sunday, June 11, 1843, Joseph Smith delivered a sermon at the temple grounds. According to Wilford Woodruff, he "asked what was the object of Gathering the Jews together or the people of God in any age of the world, the main object was to build unto the Lord an house whereby he could reveal unto his people the ordinances of his house and glories of his kingdom & teach the peopl the ways of salvation for their are certain ordinances & principles that when they are taught and practized, must be done in a place or house built for that purpose." The Saints were thus building "unto the Lord an house to prepare them for the ordinances & endowment washings & anointings &c.," including the ordinances of vicarious baptism for the dead. (Joseph Smith, Journal, June 11, 1843, in *JSP*, J3:31–35; Woodruff, Journal, June 11, 1843.)

236. In October 1840 a three-member temple committee—Reynolds Cahoon, Elias Higbee, and Alpheus Cutler—was charged with overseeing the building of the temple at Nauvoo and managing

Mrs. Mills whom several of the sis. in company with mother Smith, visited in the morning.

Sec. E. A. [Elvira Annie Cowles] Holmes, then rose— said she was not altogether prepared to give a full and correct statement of the Receipts and Expenditure of the Society but would make a statement so soon as she could see Mrs. Smith and adjust some unsettled accounts— suffice it to say about 500 dollars have been rec$^{d.}$ and nearly 400 expended during the first year of the Society— much good had been [p. [90]] done and the hearts of many made to rejoice.[237]

The sisters express'd their feelings one by one an unanimous sentiment seem'd to pervade the hearts of all present, to wit, a desire to assist in forwarding the Temple and in aiding the cause of Zion.

Sis. Jones said she would be willing to go about and solicit material, if counsel'd so to do— she also offered to board one to work on the Temple.

Mrs. Durfee said if the heads of the Society wished, she is willing to go abroad with a wagon & collect wool &c. for the purpose of forwarding the work.

Mrs. Smith suggested that merchant's wives donate material that others may be employ'd.

Miss [Phebe M.] Wheeler— said she is willing to give any portion, or all of her time—

Mrs. Granger willing to do anything, knit, sew, or wait on the sick, as might be most useful.

Miss [Hannah] Ells said she had felt willing to go out and solicit donations &c.

Mrs. Angell said she was willing to repair old clothes if necessary when new material cannot be obtain'd.

Mrs. Smith propos'd getting wool and furnish old ladies with yarn to knit socks to supply the workme[n] on the Temple next winter.

Sis. [Polly Knight] Stringham offered to make men's clothes and take work on the Temple.

Sis. [Mary] Felshaw proposes to give some soap.

Coun. Whitney arose and corroborated the testimony of Sis Chase respecting the glorious manifestation in behalf of Sis. Mills.

---

finances and construction. Higbee died on June 8, 1843, and was replaced by Hyrum Smith on the committee. ("Ecclesiastical Officers and Church Appointees," in *JSP*, J2:509; Joseph Smith, Journal, June 8 and Oct. 10, 1843, in *JSP*, J3:30, 110.)

237. The first official annual report of the Relief Society, dated June 30, 1843, was printed in the *Nauvoo Neighbor* on July 12, 1843. (Document 1.8.)

Mrs. Chase then spoke in a very animated strain, by way of encouragement to the sisters, saying the angels are rejoicing over you &c. [p. [91]]

Sis. [Philinda] Stanley proposed giving every tenth pound of flax, also one qt. milk per day

Miss [Louisa] Beman will make clothes

Sis Smith propos'd getting muslin &c. from merchants not belonging to the church, who were friendly— proposed calling on Mr. Orr.

Coun. Whitney then address'd the Society on the subject of Mothers' discharging their duties towards their daughters, in teaching them to be sober as cultivate a realizing sense of the necessity of conducting with propriety in the Lord's House,— exhorted to instruct them in love &c.

Sis. Geen [Esther Gheen] offered to donate thread of her own spinning— requested prayers for a paralytic daughter—

Pray'r by Mrs. Smith— Meeting adjourned without day. [p. [92]]

July 7, 1843 • Friday

Second Meeting of Society.
Meeting of the
First Ward.

In consequence of having no room sufficiently commodious for the whole Society, it was recommended by the President that the Society be divided for the purpose of meeting, according to the 4 City Wards,[238] and meet by rotation, one Ward at a time, that all might have equal privileges: Accordingly notice was given at the Grove on sunday the 2^d of July that the members residing in the first City Ward, would convene at the room occupied as a Masonic Hall,[239] on the friday following, at 2. o,clock.

Agreeably with the before mentioned appointmment, the members of the Society residing in the 1st Ward, and a few individuals of other Wards, who had not understood the recent arrangement; convened in the room under the Hall, the Hall being occupied by the Masonic Fraternity.

Friday July 7th 1843.

---

238. In March 1841 the Nauvoo City Council divided the city into four municipal wards to facilitate, as in other towns and cities in the United States, the transaction of local public business. Church leaders also divided the city into ecclesiastical wards. In December 1842 Nauvoo was divided into ten tithing wards in the city and three tithing wards in the adjacent rural areas. Under the direction of bishops, the wards helped facilitate the organization of work parties for the temple and the care of the poor. (See Leonard, *Nauvoo*, 177–178; and "An Ordinance Dividing the City into Wards," *Times and Seasons*, Mar. 1, 1841, 2:337–338.)

239. This room was the assembly room on the second floor of Joseph Smith's red brick store in Nauvoo. ("Store [JS's red brick store]," in *JSP*, J2:424.)

93

Second Meeting of Society.

Meeting of the
First Ward.

In consequence of having no room sufficiently commodious for the whole Society, it was recommended by the President that the Society be divided for the purpose of meeting, according to the 4 City Wards, and meet by rotation, one Ward at a time, that all might have equal privilege; Accordingly notice was given at the Grove on sunday the 2 of July that the members residing in the first City Ward, would convene at the room occupied as a Masonic Hall, on the friday following, at 2. o, clock.

Agreeably with the before mentioned appointment, the members of the Society residing in the 1st Ward, and a few individuals of other Wards, who had not understood the recent arrangement, convened in the room under the Hall, the Hall being occupied by the Masonic Fraternity.

Friday July 7th 1843.
Present Councillor Whitney, Mrs. Billings &c.
Meeting opened by singing "Redeemer of Israel" &c.
Pray'r by Coun. Whitney.
Coun. Whitney then arose and after expressing her regret that we were not favored with the presence of our Pres. on this occasion, and after many appropriate remarks, requested the sisters to speak and express to each other their feelings as the members of one family.

Mrs. Pratt mentioned the needy circumstances of br. Henderson, a widower with nine children — she recommended him as an industrious, and worthy person &c.

Mrs. Durfee presented the case of Sister Rockwell

Meeting minutes, July 7, 1843. In their second meeting in the year 1843, women of the Nauvoo Relief Society began assembling in four separate ward groups "in consequence of having no room sufficiently commodious for the whole Society." The four groups later combined back into one that fall. The July 7, 1843, entry is the last one in the minute book inscribed by Eliza R. Snow, who moved south of Nauvoo not long after this meeting. (Church History Library, Salt Lake City. Photograph by Welden C. Andersen.)

Present Councillor [Elizabeth Ann] Whitney, Mrs. Billings &c.

Meeting opened by singing "Redeemer of Israel" &c.[240]

Pray'r by Coun. Whitney.

Coun. Whitney then arose and after expressing her regret that we were not favored with the presence of our Pres.t on this occasion, and after many appropriate remarks, requested the sisters to speak and express to each other their feelings as the members of one family.

Mrs. Pratt mentioned the needy circumstances of br. Henderson, a widower with nine children— she recommended him as an industrious, and worthy person &c.

Mrs Durfee presented the case of [Orrin] Porter Rockwell [p. [93]]— express'd much feeling of sympathy awakened in her heart by recent recitals of his sufferings— recommended the sisters to unite like the ancient saints in faith & pray'r for his deliverance.[241]

Mrs. Sessions mentioned the case of a man whose name she did not know, who had been fo[r] some length of time begging— had heard he had plenty of money— She described his dress.— Mrs. Pratt said she knew him— that his appearance bespoke deep poverty.

Mrs. Sessions spoke of some articles of clothing, to wit. 2 pr. pantaloons and 1 shirt, which she designed either to donate to the Society or to the Temple, as Society shall think proper.

Sis. Pratt recommended an English family, mostly females, who wished the influence of the Society in supplying them with work— can do millinery— fine washing &c.

Mrs. Pratt proposed taking the responsibility of overseeing the cutting & making of clothes, being herself a tailoress.

Sis. [Anna] Downey wishes to take sewing & knitting for Society.

Sis. Abbott wishes the same

Sis. Wooley [Mary Woolley] said she has red yarn which she purpos'd for a carpet, but thinks it will do more good in mittens, & will contribute it for the sisters to knit.

Sis. Geene [Esther Gheen] said she has some coarse linnen which will do for pantaloons, which she will donate, also thread to make it.

---

240. Hymn 119, *Collection of Sacred Hymns* [1841], 127.

241. On March 4, 1843, Rockwell was arrested on a charge of assault with intent to kill former Missouri governor Lilburn W. Boggs. Rockwell was incarcerated in Missouri in the Jefferson City jail from March until August, when he was transported to the Liberty jail and later to the Independence jail, where he remained until his acquittal and release on December 13, 1843. (See Document 1.5; and JS History, vol. E-1, 1827–1829.)

Coun. Whitney spoke of a young man from England, who had been sick for a year— now at her house— he came from Mr. Ivan's, who said he had sooner pay his board than keep him. Mrs. W. said she wished to do all in her power, but her family being large, thought perhaps he might be better accommodated at another place. She said bishop W. [Newel K. Whitney] was soliciting means for his support.

Sis Jones said she is willing to take the sick man [p. [94]] to her house if it is thought wisdom— that her house is not so still as desirable for a sick person.

Sis. Markham said— has been requested by a sister of La Harpe to ask of the Society for a girl from 12 to fourteen to live with her till of age.— recommended the sis. as a suitable person for the charge of such a girl.

Sis. Allen recommended a daughter of br. Parks, who wants to get situations for 2, who are now in Mo.

Sis. Lyons said when the poor come to sis. W. and sis. [Elvira Cowles] Holmes, if they cannot supply them, send them with orders to her.

Coun. W. said it is the counsel of Pres.ᵗ E. Smith to keep accounts of small donations, when the sisters are call'd upon at their homes to assist from time to time; and bring such accounts to the Treasurer.

Sis. Snow said she will do knitting & sewing

Sis. Granger is willing to do any thing that is needed

Sis. [Olive] Farr has flax which she will contribute

Sis. Kelsey proposes to spin said flax upon shares.

Sis. Farr has tow more than she needs.²⁴²

Sis. Smith proposes to spin said tow, which the sisters think advisable to make into pantaloon cloth.

Sis. Lyons will give one Bunch cotton yarn and Sis. Wooley one do [ditto], to fill the tow on, for s.ᵈ cloth,

Sis. [Mahala] Overton will weave said cloth as a donation.

Sis. Geen will give some flax and

Sis. Chase will spin it.

Sis [Lucinda] Turner will donate in work when needed.

Sis. Jones said Miss Fulmer [Desdemona Fullmer] wished needlework and proposed giving to Society one third of the price of making pr. pantaloons which Sis. Jones furnished her to make.

---

242. Tow is the "coarse and broken part of flax or hemp, separated from the finer part by the hatchel or swingle [instruments used to clean flax]." ("Tow," in *An American Dictionary of the English Language,* ed. Noah Webster [New York: Harper and Brothers, 1845], 847; see also "Swingle," in *American Dictionary* [1845], 818.)

	cts
Sis. Esther Smith donated	12½

[p. [95]]

	cts
Sis. Sarah Kimball do	50

A union of feeling prevail'd through the meeting, all present manifested a disposition to do all in their power towards assisting the poor and in forwarding the building of the Temple.

Meeting closed with prayer by Sis. [Sophia] Packard.

E. R. Snow, Sec.ʸ [p. [96]]

July 15, 1843 • Saturday

²⁴³Third Meeting of Society
Meeting of the
Second Ward

July 15 1843

Meeting conven'd according to previous appontmt [appointment] presᵗ· Emma Smith being detaind Councillor [Elizabeth Ann] Whitney p[r]esided

Meeting opend by singing "come thou fount of every blessing"²⁴⁴ prayer by Coun Whitney

Councillor Whitney then rose, said she rejoiced that we could enjoy the pr[i]vilege of associating together to converse on things of th[e] Kingdom to comfort and edify each other while passing through this vale of tears, made many appropriate remarks said could we abide a celestial baw [law?] and be made meet for the celestial kingdom how glorious will it be requested the sisters present to free their minds as the spirit of the Lord should direct that all should make known the wants of the ⟨poor⟩ said that though prest Emma Smith was absent yet that she requested the society to do all the good in their power regretted her abscence &c

The sisters expessd [expressed] their minds one by one a union of sentiment seemed to prevail among them all (viz) in forwarding the Temple and in relieving the wants of the want of the poor

Sis King said she would knit or sew half th[e] time

Sis Duel [Mary Deuel] said she would do sewing she also represented an English ~~Sister~~ Br who is suffer[i]ng extreme poverty

Sis Gribble donates $1 per month to the poor

---

243. TEXT: Eliza R. Snow handwriting ends; Phebe M. Wheeler begins.
244. Hymn 76, *Collection of Sacred Hymns* [1841], 85.

Coun Whitny again said— it is the council of ~~E Smith~~ prest E Smith to keep accounts of small donations given at their homes from time to time [p. [97]] and bring such accounts to the Treasurer

Sis James [Drusilla] Hendricks spoke in a pathetic manner upon the subject of the ⟨temple⟩ refered to the revelation concerning it— that if we faild in keeping the commandment the consequences would be serious[245]

Coun W again remarked appropriately spoke of the blessings in reserve for us if faithful in keeping the commandment concring [concerning] these Houses to be built &c

Sister King called to mind the past suffering of the Saints when they were driven from <u>Mo</u>— (all wept) and greatly desir'd that we might avoid the inevitable consequenses of disobedience[246]

Mrs Whitney continued said that prayer and faith together withe our efforts must agree proposed that some should pray to this effect

One of the sister's p[r]ayed

	$	
Sister Malissa King donated calico ap[r]on	25	
Sister Boice ⟨will give⟩ a pr linnen pantelloons		
Sister Orson [Catherine] Spencer donates 4 yds bleach, a cotton cloth and vest pattern	1 75	
Sister Barrass [Huldah Barrus] will give shingles		
Sister Nickerson will give 4 lb candles and 1000 shingles—		

Sister Husted rose wept said She had nothing to give spoke of her trouble in <u>Mo</u> the Death of her Husband &c

Counsellor Whitney seaid it was not her duty to give not even her mite but rather— she should be helped then reccommended her to the charity

Sister King said Sister Husted kneeded help

Sis Elisabeeth [Elizabeth] King will give Sister Husted flowr

~~◊ another sister~~ Sis [Philinda] Stanly offerd a bushel of corn

---

245. On January 19, 1841, Joseph Smith dictated a revelation declaring that a "holy house" should be built unto the Lord's "holy name" so that "all things pertaining to this house, and the priesthood thereof" might be revealed. The revelation promised blessings to those faithful in meeting this requirement and "cursings, wrath, indignation, and judgment" to those who "do not do the things" required. This revelation (section 124 in the modern Latter-day Saint Doctrine and Covenants) was first published as "Extracts from a Revelation Given to Joseph Smith, Jr., Jan. 19th 1841," *Times and Seasons*, June 1, 1841, 2:424–429.

246. Joseph Smith's revelations are replete with warnings to the Saints about the consequences of disobedience to the laws and teachings of the gospel. An 1834 revelation, for example, told the Saints that "were it not for the transgressions of my people . . . they might have been redeemed" from their enemies and avoided the difficulties that confronted them while in Missouri. (Doctrine and Covenants 105:2; see also Doctrine and Covenants 97:26; 103:8, 63, 71.)

Sister P[hebe] M Wheeler a calico dress [p. [98]]

Sister [Mahala] Overton said she would color or weave for the Society

Sister Corrol[247] [Hannah Carroll] said she would weave for the Society

Meeting closed— prayer by sister Wheeler

P M Wheeler assistant Sec[y]

July 21, 1843 • Friday

Meeting of the
Third ward[248]

July 21st 1843

Meeting conven'd Mrs President not present Mrs [Elizabeth Ann] Whitney & Mrs Billing's present

Sister Whitney rose Spoke[249] of the Privilege of the Sisters Hoped we should be one and ⟨feel⟩ a freedom to speak of things that mostly concerned us and realise the wants of the Poor

Sis Miller named that she would do any thing that she could do—

There was a case of Widow Warner living at Br Jonathan Taylor's with 5 small children that kneeded assistance verry much

The case of Mother Smith was then mentiond that she was in the decline of life and that she requested the prayers of the Society that she might yet be ennabled to prove a Blessing to those who may enquire of the things of the Kingdom

Sister Durfee said she would give some rolls for the Society[250]

Sister Wolly [Mary Woolley] namd that she would spin 2 lb

Sister Lee said she would spin 2 lbs—

Sis Rhoda Ann Bentley will donate a counterpain[251] to be appropriated as the Society shall direct [p. [99]]

Sister Abagail Wollsey [Woolsey] said she would knit what 2 lb would make

Sister Stewart will give a pr socks

Sister Whitney then rose and remark'd appropriately on the privileges of the kingdom said we should be up an⟨d⟩ doing.

---

247. TEXT: Possibly "Carrol".

248. The sequence in which other 1843 meetings are numbered in this minute book indicates that this meeting was the fourth meeting of the Relief Society held that year.

249. TEXT: Possibly "Spake".

250. The rolls mentioned were probably carded wool rolled in preparation for hand-spinning. (See "Roll," in *American Dictionary* [1845], 709.)

251. A counterpane, or counterpoint, is a coverlet or cover for a bed, stitched or woven in squares. ("Counterpane," and "Counterpoint," in *American Dictionary* [1845], 199.)

$

Sister Lee donat'd cash   31

Nancy Wilson will donate pr panteloons and babes petticoat

Sister [Rebecca] Hodges will donate Table cloth to the Society [*blank*]
closed by prayer

July 28, 1843 • Friday

Fifth Meeting of Society

Meeting of the

Fourth ward

July 28 1843

Meeting commenced with singing "This Earth was once a garden place"[252]
Prayer by Sister J [Sarah] Smith

Councillor [Elizabeth Ann] Whitney requested the sisters to improve the
time to advantage regretted that so few were met hoped the meetings might
not be discontinu[e]d Suggested the propriety of having the separate wards
meet togather said she was sorry that the Prest Emma Smith was not here to
preside— and cheer us Said we had her approbation that she would have the
Society be active & persevering in doing good &c

Sister Billings made some verry appropriate remarks desired we might
remember the poor in particular represented the case of Sister Harmons whose
family is sick

Sis Joshua [Sarah] Smith said as it is a sickly time we are called to the alle-
viation of the poor and suffering many are suffering at this presant time said
that [p. [100]] Sister Modley [Elizabeth Maudsley] and Sister [Mary] Mc Ewen
were sick & distress'd in want of help

Donations $

Sister Lyons [Sylvia Lyon]   50

Selinda Simpson   8 yds calico   2 00

Clarrissa Eastman   1 pr Shoes   1 25

Dolly Markum [Dorothy Meacham] said she would spin 2 or 3 pounds
wool said she had givn all her Jewelry for the Temple was willing to do any
thing she could

Sister Meecum said our Salvation depended on our Liberality to the poor &c

Mrs Whitney continued the subject refered to one of the revelations "said
"by this shall ye know that ye are my deciples["][253] The Lord confirms it again
& again he is delighted with our acts of charity &c

---

252. Hymn 250, *Collection of Sacred Hymns* [1841], 272.

253. John 13:35.

Sis Joshua Smith requested widow Meecum [Lucina Mecham] to open her heart to the society as she had been sick Sis Meecum wept

Sister Meecum said she could sustain herself if the Society could furnish her work would like Spinning

Sister Lyons donates patent Wheel head—   75

Sister Jones— 100 lb pounds of wool can can be procur'd on condition that half of it can be returnd in cloth to the owner

C Whitney suggested the necessity of having a committee so appointed to search out the poor and suffring— To call on the rich for aid and thus as far as possible relieve the wants of all

Accordingly appointed a Comittee (to wit)

First ward

Lydia Granger	Harriet Marcum
Sophia Packard	Elizabeth Jones

Second ward

Mrs James [Drusilla] Hendricks	Ms [Rebecca] Hodge [p. [101]]
Miss P[hebe] M Wheeler	Mrs Orson [Catherine] Spencer

Third— ward

Selinda Simpson—	Sister Peck
Sister Winchester—	Sister Rice

Fourth ward—

Sister Allred	Siste[r] Joshua Smith
Sister Stephen Meecum [Dorothy Meacham] Sister Billings	

Councllor Whitney then rose, said when you go to those who have means tell them you are appointed to releave the needy— call on them— the Spirit of the Lord will bless you in it and stimulate the hearts of the rich— provoke them to good works— Let us try to do it

Donations		$
Sister [Mahala] Overton	a Bed Spread	1 00
Elisabeth Allred	Soap	00 50
Sister [Abigail] Forges—	Cash	12½
	2 small dresses	62½

Sister [illegible] Widow Meecum will spin 50 lb Wool for the society and thake [take] her pay in provisions of th[e] Society

Meeting then ajournd [p. [102]]

August 5, 1843 • Saturday

Sixth meeting of Society
Meeting of the
Fourth ⟨First⟩ Ward

August 5th 1843

Meeting commenced with singing "Thou Lord through every changing scene"[254]

Prayer by Sister Joshua [Sarah] Smith

Agreeably with a prior appointment the Members of the Society residing in the first ward and a few Individuals belonging to other wards conven'd at the dwelling house of Sister [Elizabeth] Jones

The House full

Mrs prest and her Councillors absent

Mrs Holms [Elvira Cowles Holmes] Treasurer absent

But deeming it important to hear the report of the Committee who were appointed at the Meeting of the 4th ward to search out the <u>poor</u>, <u>sick</u>, and <u>distress'd</u> and to alleviate them also to receive the donations of th[e] first ward the Society proceeded to attend to most important business omitting all that could be omitted to a future time

Committee of the 4 ward reports as follows

Sister Joshua Smith found many sick in the 4 ward & some destitute in want of things to eat and to use went and visited Sister [Mary] McEwen and Sis Modley [Elizabeth Maudsley] found them and their families in suffering want they kneed attendance every day

Sister Meecum visited Nehemiah Harmons found them poor sick & distressd and no bedding nothing comfortable entirely destitute

Sister Meecum and Sister Billings solicited Donations for the same

		$	
Sis Anderson	gave 1 pr stockings	00	25

[p. [103]]

		$	
Sister Far [Olive Farr]	a calico Dress and cape		
Sister B Ammer	a peck of onions 1 lb sugar		
Sister Clayton	14 lb flowr	$	52
Lydia Moon	one Shirt	00	50
Margaret Moon	one Shawl		
Sarah Mendanhall	a pr of pillow slips	00	25
	one toweel one Shirt	00	50

Ester Ann Geen [Esther Ann Gheen] 3 pillow slips bolster slip 2 little shirts 2 mens shirts one dress 2 small dresses 2 aprons tape and thead   2 50

Abagail Forges	2 lb sugar—	00	14

Report of the committee of the first ward

---

254. Hymn 58, *Collection of Sacred Hymns* [1841], 65.

Sister [Elizabeth] Jones— Sister [Harriet] Marcum and myself have visited our ward went to eve[r]y house found many sick but more comfortable than we expected found ~~and~~ Sister Miller and old Lady sick with bed or bedding no changes of cloothing found Sister Broomley very sick nothing at all to eat calld on Sister Morrisson who gave things for her relief

Sister Marcum— reports to corroborate with Sister Jones said they found few suffering ones

Sister [Lydia] Granger reports that there were 2 families by the river sick & no thing to eat nothing but one cup of coffee A Mrs Holt & Child are great sufferers

The Comittee of the ~~first~~ Second and third ward not prepad [prepared] to report

Sister Jane Michael representd a Br who had been sick some months

Sister Angel rose said she had lately found a sister late from England destitute a widow of late soon expecting to be confind who had just been to prest Hyram Smiths [Hyrum Smith's] for help said she had no home had had 6 children lost several of them; her husband just before she [p. [104]] left England and one child on the water

Sister [Jane] Olmsted will give soap 50 worth & wash McEwen ⟨family⟩ for Sister Jones will take her in and take care of her

	$
Mrs Woolly [Mary Woolley] will give 1 yd fine Muslin	
a flannel petticoat pinning blanket	00 60
Rosanna Lyman quarter lb tea	00 25

Sister Sweat will 50 cents worth soap

Sister German [Rachel Jerman] will give a suit of cloaths to old Mrs Miller 4 yds bleach'd muslin 3 yds Canton flannel 2 Spools cotton thr[ea]d   1 00

Sister Pratt representd Br Hendersons as destitute for cloathing offerd to cut and make old garments for them

Philinda Simpson cotton flannel & sugar	00 75
Catharine Miller 2 lb sugar	14
Delinda Parker Pair cotton stockings	25
Salvina Adams 3 yds cotton drilling	75
Martha Thomas soap & provisions	1 00

Sister Charles rich [Sarah Rich] then rose and reqestd requested a reccommend from the Soci[e]ty as she was soon to leave for Ottoway a vote was calld expressive of thei[r] minds and carried in her favo[r][255]

---

255. A photograph of the recommend made out to Sarah D. Rich and dated August 5, 1843, was published in the June 1936 issue of the *Relief Society Magazine*. Similar to the recommend for Elizabeth Jones that is recorded in the Relief Society minutes for March 31, 1842, it reads: "Nauvoo Ill August 5 1843

Sister Chase then rose and spoke on the necessity of prayer and faith exhorted the Sisters to faithfulness to be much in prayer said she stood a living wittness for Jesus of Nazereth knew he had pourd his Spirit upon her Inasmuch as we visit the sick we shall be blesst I mean to do all that I can to releave their necessities we must be humble and and overcome the powers of darkness & live by faith

Meeting adjourned [p. [105]]

August 13, 1843 • Sunday

Minuets of proceedings of the
Seventh Meeting of Society
Second Ward

At the House formerly occupied by Father Snow[256]

August 13 1843—

Present Councillor [Elizabeth Ann] Whitney and Mrs Billings

Meeting opend withe Singing

Prayer by Sister Chase

Coun— Whitney said she had hoped the Prest would be present this afternoon desird the Sisters would remember her in th[e]ir preyers that she was pleasd with our last Meeting (viz of the First ward then address'd the Society on the priviliges and blessings of this Kingdom

Sister Billings rose said I can say with Sis Whitney we are called to rejoice notwithstanding the trials Sickness and death thro which we have been calld to pass thro in Missouri I am thankful we have lived it through and now it becomes us to be faithful and to walk humbly befor God I feel my unworthiness desire that I may war a good warfare and at last be receivd into the Kingdom of God exhorted the sisters to be bold not timid or fearful in bearing their testimony

---

| The 'female relief society' of Nauvoo recommends, Mrs Sarah D Rich— as a member of said society in good standing:— and she is hereby authoriz'd to recover all such donations as friends abroad shall feel dispos'd to put into her hands to be appropriated to the fund of the Institution for the Benefit of the poor the Widow and the Fatherless | By Order of the Board [signed] E R Snow Secretary | P M Wheeler assistant secretary." ("An Interesting Old Document," *Relief Society Magazine* 23, no. 6 [June 1936]; Document 1.2, entry for Mar. 31, 1842.)

256. The house was likely that occupied until June 1842 by Eliza R. and Lorenzo Snow's father, Oliver Snow, who was sometimes referred to as "Father Snow." The house stood on the corner of Knight and Partridge Streets, on the southwest corner of block 79, two blocks west of the temple site. ("List of Property in the City of Nauvoo," 1841, Nauvoo, IL, Records, 1841–1845, CHL; "A Record of the Names of the Members of the Church of Jesus Christ of Latterday Saints, as Taken by the Lesser Priesthood, in the Spring of 1842," after 1844–after 1846, in Far West and Nauvoo Elders' Certificates, 1837–1838, 1840–1846, CHL, [16].)

Sister Orson [Catherine] Spencer rose said she had been appontd [appointed] as one of Comm^ttee— of the 2d city ward was willing to do all in her power for the relief of the poor sick and distressd but that her health was delicate ⟨&⟩ could not do much said she had thought we were taking the Bishops place in looking after the poor & solicitting donations²⁵⁷ &c said as the wards were extensive felt she was not adequate to the burthen desird some on[e] might be appointed in her place reportd a sick family which she had visited and hand[e]d in her donations [p. [106]]

P. [Phebe] M. Wheeler of the 2d city ward reports as follows I visited some few families some were sick, some not Sick found one family Br. Chatmans—; verry poor and destitute would represent them to the charity of the relief society Br Chatman is constantly employd on the walls of th[e] Temple he has 4 small children not quite 5 nearly destitute for cloathing also would reccommend to the charity of of this society Sis Francis Lew Law who is sick & without a home an aged widow Lady at present destitute of money

Sister Reed offerd to take her and Nurse her if some one would provide her board

Sis [Drusilla] Hendricks then rose said she had understood that she was one of the Comm^tee. appointed to look after the poor but said she had a great burthen uppon her, did not know what she could d do felt that as her family was situated she could not do much desird that some one might be appointed in her place

Coun Whitney verry feelingly remarked that they were only directed to ⟨do⟩ the little that they could without Injury to themselves &c

Sister Billings said none were ◊requird to go beyond their strength

Sister [Elizabeth] Jones of Comm^ttee of the first city ward reports that many were sick and suffering the necessarry Comforts of life and receivd Donations as follows

		$
Sister Wolly [Mary Woolley]	11 lb flowr.	oo 28
Sister [Margaret] Smoot	6 lb flour	oo 15
Sis German [Rachel Jerman]	1¾ lb butter	—8
Sister Chase donated a Calico dress to Sis Miller		1 50
Sis Rice gave 4 lb butter loaf bread 5 lb flour		oo 40

---

257. From the appointment of the first Latter-day Saint bishop in February 1831, stewardship over the temporal affairs of the church—particularly care of the poor—was a primary aspect of the bishop's role and responsibilities. (Doctrine and Covenants 42:31; 84:112; 107:68; 119; and 120.)

said as Committee of the 3d city ward she meant [p. [107]] to go forward in this benevolent work said she had found the people as far as she had gone generly comfortable

Sis Olive Frost represented a a sick family whom the Com^ttee had overlooked a Br Burgess & family

Eliza Duel	donates 2 lb Sugar	12½	
Sis Jones	a Chicken to Sister Longden	00	6
Sis Simpson	1 lb butter	00	8
	and Sundry articles	00	40
~~Sister Wolly~~	~~10 lb flowr~~	00	25
~~Sis Smoot~~	~~6 lb flowr~~	00	15
Mrs Dan	gave several small articles for	00	
	a child	00	30
Mrs Coolage [Elizabeth Coolidge]	3 yds Shirting	00	37
Widow Nights [Martha Knight]—	cash	00	15
Mrs Cowls	crackers	00	25
Mrs Mc entile	8 lb flowr	00	20
Mrs [Catherine] Orr	sundry articles for the sick	00	31
	also 3 y^ds. cotton cloth	00	30
Mrs Orson Spencr	sundry articles for the sick	00	51

The following names were then presented to the Society and the persons receivd as Members

Eunice S Baxter	Belinda Newel
Mary Stewart	Louisa Sangers
Maria Ferry	Phebe Groves[258] [Graves]
Sarah L Mendenhall	Eliza A Groves[259] [Graves]
Thirsa McNoll	Elizabeth Thompson

Elder [Reynolds] Cahoon[260] who had been invited to attend rose and said that he felt a delicacy in rising to address the society but was rejoiced to see their Benevolent exertions said he was as perfectly satisfied withe the order of this society as that of the gospel on the commencement of this Church of Jesus Christ of Latter day Saints [p. [108]] said there are many Benevolent Societies abroad designd to do good but not as this ours is according to the order of God connected with the priesthood according to the same good principals & knowledge will grow out of it reproved the Sisters for their fearfulness said they were not acting in the Bishop's place nor intruding upon them in their calling

---

258. TEXT: Possibly "Graves".
259. TEXT: Possibly "Graves".
260. Cahoon was a member of the temple committee. ("Church Appointees," in *JSP*, J2:509.)

That the ◊eelief Society was organised according to the mind of God that Emma had directed to the appointment of this Com^tee that Joseph had appointed Emma to direct—; the society had covenanted to follow Joseph that they had nothing to do but to move forward said the objects and principles of this society are vast not fully understood a most important part of the Church to look after the sick without— Notwithstanding th[e] Bishops there would be a lack in the Church the Order of th[e] Priesthood is not complete without it; let every one act in their place, then all will move on most gloriously the purposes of God will be accomplished chided the Committee who had expressed fears of acting out of their place— In the Bishop's place sa[i]d they were in their place and those who would act perseveringly in their place— Should be bless'd with great blessings more than they could conceive The organisation of this Society & the Church is similar according to the mind & order of God in it every want may be suppli[e]d every place filled— take couredge and use every exertion within your power Every on[e] has their duty and place you may do much good in cheering the hearts of the pilgrim Saints who come to Zion as stran[g]ers a word of consolation may ennable them to rise up in the Spirit of God with cheerfulness How long will it be before a this society will want a store house to store the[i]r goods I am far from thinking the Bishop will have th[e] only [p. [109]] Storehouse²⁶¹ The time will come when all persons will find reliefe thro this Society— Why should not this prospect buoy you up above the difficulties which may cross your way I am unable to express my feelings on this vast subject The Lord has set his hand to accomplish this very object Then act with all cheerfulness I contend you have a perfect right to relieve the poor in the name of the Lord to claim assistance of each other for this object without any hesitation This is the design in the almighty in forming it you kneed not doubt but this Society is raisd by the Lord to prepare us for the great blessings which are for us in the House of the Lord in the Temple be faithful and comfort and edify one annothe [another] in all things be faithful in reporting the sick that each may know and do their duty in all things That; that, Can be Shaken will be shaken hereafter²⁶² we shall have enough to try every power of our Souls here is the use of the word of Comfort

    I have no more to say

—————————————

261. Joseph Smith's revelations exhorted church members to "remember the poor, and consecrate of thy properties for their support." The monies, goods, and properties accumulated were to be kept in a "storehouse, to administer to the poor and the needy." The bishop was appointed to distribute this "residue," and the storehouse became known as the "bishop's storehouse." (Doctrine and Covenants 42:30, 34; see also Doctrine and Covenants 51:13; 58:24; and R. Quinn Gardner, "Bishop's Storehouse," in *Encyclopedia of Mormonism,* ed. Daniel H. Ludlow, 5 vols. [New York: Macmillan, 1992], 1:123–125.)

262. See Hebrews 12:27.

The committee then rose (namely) sister O Spencer Sister Hendricks and P M Wheeler said they had not understood clearly what was expected of the Committee but would do what they could most cheerfully P M Wheeler presented case of Sister Lew to the Society Siste[r] [Harriet] Marcum said she had no more; ~~to~~ no more objections to make in doing her duty as a com[mit]tee

The Com^ttee all seemd to have gaind new courage desird to remain in their places and do with their might all they could do—

Meeting closed

Prayer by Elder Cahoon [p. [110]]

Undated Meeting • August 1843

Meeting of the female Relef Society
of the third Ward[263]

commenced Singing "the Glorious day is rolling on"[264] Prayer by Sister Peck—
The following names as members were receiv'd by unanimous vote

Jane Rawlins

Ann Hunter	Mary Graham
Margaret P. Downing	Sarah Wellfery
Almira Palmer	Mary Knowlton
Polly A Sabins [Mary Ann Sabin]	Lucinda Cunningham
Julia A [Foster] Hampton	Hannah Smith
Abagail C Owens	Leah Rawlins
Elisa Evans	Susan Winegar
Polly Canklin [Conklin]	Ester Moraletile [Esther Maleta Johnson]
Clarrissa Miller	Emily Worton
Martha Akes	Lavinia Haze [Lovina Hayes]
Penina Frost	Elizabeth Welker
Maria Vansal [Vancil]	Jane Stocker
Darinda Kimball	Asennath [Asenath] Burt

Counsellor [Elizabeth Ann] Whitney Spoke of the disappointment on account of Sister Emmas Sickness

Mrs Billings Spoke of the case of a little girl who lived with Mrs Sheour

Miss Frost spoke of the sick said Mrs Burgess & family were disstressd

Mrs Pratt gave Sugar & coffee

---

263. The sequence in which other 1843 meetings are numbered in this minute book indicates that this meeting was the eighth meeting of the Relief Society held that year.

264. Hymn 11, *Collection of Sacred Hymns* [1835], 17; Hymn 135, *Collection of Sacred Hymns* [1841], 146.

Mrs J [Sarah] Smith said many of the sick were suffring and some were getting better

Mrs Meecum said she had been sick had not been able to attend to her duty but said Mrs Charles [Elizabeth] Ivins would assist from time to time when calld upon Spoke of a Mrs Nickerson Who had no home [p. [111]]

Mrs Webb said she would take her in

Sistr— [Lydia] Granger of the first ward said she had visited the sick in her ward many were suffering some getting better

Mrs Heaps donated one dollar order on Mr Law

Mrs Lyon	one Wheel head	$ 75
Dr [Robert] Foster	do [ditto]	8 00

Which was given to Steers mentiond by sister Simpson

Sistr— Peck reported Mr Cuyes and family as sick and destitute administerd to th[e]ir relief

Eunice Holbrook gave 2 lbs sugar	00 20

Mrs Sessions said that Mr [Joseph] Dobson was sick & destitute had 3 chairs which he wanted to sell for provisions

Mrs [Elizabeth] Jones said a little girl was brought to her as an object of charity

Mrs Hunter gave calico for a dress for her

Mrs Jones said she had obtain 40 lb of wool as a donation to the Temple by Mrs Elvira Saxon Who wishes to become a member of the female Relief Soc[i]ety Sister Saxon was received by unanimous vote

Mrs Aldridge said she had visited the sick in the 4th ward and administerd to their wants

Mrs Kimball stated a Mr [John] Charleston & family were sick his wife very low & in great need of a nurse said she had assisted them

Mrs [Rebecca] Hodge gave on[e] pr of pillow slips and table cloth—	2 50

a Hymn then sung "Mortals awake with angels join"[265]

Prayer by Mrs Whitney

Meeting closed [p. [112]]

September 2, 1843 • Saturday

Tenth meeting of the Society
~~of the~~ First Ward

Snow House[266]   Sep 2d 1843

---

265. Hymn 12, *Collection of Sacred Hymns* [1841], 19.
266. On the Snow house, see 113n256 herein.

The fourth ward were prevented meeting at the Lodge room from the rain[267]

Meeting opend by prayer and singing

prayer by Sister Joshua [Sarah] Smith

In compliance with Councillor Whitneys [Elizabeth Ann Whitney's] request proceeded to business

Prest Emma Smith absent also he[r]— Counsellors

Mrs [Elvira Cowles] Holmes the Treasurer not presant

~~Sister Granger reported~~

The Committee then proceeded to report as follows

Sister [Lydia] Granger & Sister [Elizabeth] Jones of the first ward found that many were sick and suffer[in]g said there were some imposters Spoke of Hannah Jones who is late from England a widow and ⟨had⟩ applied to this society for help had found her to be a corrupt ⟨person⟩ as they had enquird into her Character and knew it to be corrupt

Sister Meecum Sister Joshua Smith of th[e] 4th ward report that about 20 families are very sick and others getting sick Br Law and the Bishops have supplied some so that they are mostly supplied with meal[268] & flowr at present

Sister ⟨Granger⟩ spoke of Sister Broomley as destitute of dresses $

said she would donate one of her own 1 00

also one shirt 00 50

She also represented a family of Holts as ~~of~~ objects of charity

Sister Joshua Smith mentiond the case of N Nicholson [p. [113]]

P[hebe] M Wheeler represented Siste[r] Reed as an object of charity to the society

$

Sister Lyons donated 00 50

to Siste[r] Reed for a dress

Sister Reed desird to get work of the Society

Siste[r] Jones rose said she had an orphan boy on her hands James Bayley who had been with her 3 weeks and now inclining to drepsey [dropsy] could eat nothing but crackers and was in need of medicine which she could not get without money solicited help for him

Sister Packerd [Sophia Packard] spoke of Mrs [Clarissa] Merrifield as poor & needy Spoke of annother family and destitute and ⟨had had⟩ no thing but

---

267. This minute book numbers Relief Society meetings in sequence for each of the three years it covers. For 1843, the minutes have no record for the ninth meeting, which would have been a meeting of the Fourth Ward Relief Society. As noted here, what would have been the ninth meeting was evidently canceled because of bad weather.

268. TEXT: Possibly "meat".

potatoes and roasted corn in 4 days has money due him but cant get it Sister Packard said she desird to do her duty and magnify her calling faithfully

Sister Fordham representd a family near her in extreme want Also a Br Willcox with a large family in extreme want ⟨near to⟩ ~~and~~ Jeremiah Curtiss, North East from the Temple

Sister Granger spoke of a family of Wights the Man very sick nothing to eat

Sister Jones suggested the propriety of of taking measures to detect imposters said that Siste[r] Emma had a counciled all to report to whom donations were given

		$
Sister Chase rose & said that she was willing to do all she could for the sick herself and sis Geene [Esther Gheen] had Given		1 00
to Sister Miller		

Said she had had a family dependant on her hands who were poor and needy

Sis Packard said that Martha Thomas will donate of provision   00 50

[p. [114]]

Donations		$	
Sister Warner	12 lbs flowr—	00	30
Sister [Mary] Snider	3 lb sugar—	00	36
Sister Risen [Sophia Riser]	12 lb flowr	00	30
Sister [Mary Ann] Oakley	3 yds Shirting 3 yds calico	00	75
Sister Simmons	8 lb flowr	00	20
Sarah Bayley [Bailey]	1 lb sugar 1 lb of coffee	00	25
Mary Yearsley	1 pr sheets & cash 31 cents	1	37½
Hannah Pierse one Quilt one shirt pr pillow slips and sundries 12½ cents		2	50
Sister Chandler Rodgers [Amanda Rogers] 15 [k]nots of white Stocking yarn		00	50
Sister [Sylvia] Lyon Sundry articles for th[e] sick and distress'd handed ov[e]r to Sister Longdon [Sarah Langdon]			
Sis Riley Sis [Sarah] dobson and the blind brother		4	81½
Thirsa McNol	flowr & Meat	00	20
Charity Stoddard	in tin ware	1	00
Irena Cowley [Cowles]	1 lb rice	6 00 00[269]	
Sister Brosier [Sarah Brazier]	cash	~~12½~~ 00	12½
Sister Dan	12 apples	00	6

---

269. TEXT: It appears that the scribe accidentally noted this amount as six dollars, then corrected the amount to six cents. The scribe made a similar mistake on the next line.

Martha Thomas	meat	oo	10
Mrs Ferry	meat	oo	8
Mrs Nickerson	bread & butter	oo	6
Ruth Williams	flowr & meat	oo	75
Sophia Packard	bread and meat	oo	18
Mrs [Mary] McKenzie	1 lb sugar—	oo	12
Sis Husted	8 lb pork	oo	12
Anothe[r] Sister	8 lb flowr	oo	20
Siste[r] Brewster	4 lb flowr	oo	10
Sister [Keziah] Morrison	cash	oo	25
Mr [John] Finch Merchant	2 lb rice	oo	12
Sister Daniel [Maria] Hendricks	1 lb candles		12

[p. [115]]

Sister [Philinda] Stanley said the flax which she had given to the Society is spun and ready for weaving

Sister Lyons said the cotton was ready for the loom

Sister Joshua Smith then rose and ~~said~~ proposd that we as a society get to gather materials for for the Saints for bedding that many may not suffer as they did last wintr

Sister Lyons thought so too said in Lima the Sisters were now at work making quilts for this Society

Sister Green said she would give Siste[r] Reed a bed quilt also her daughter a Mantaumaker[270] should cut and help make her dress

Sister Prusia [Persis] Johnson will give a cotton and woollen skirt to Siste[r] Reed

Sister Simpson 5 lb flowr & soap for Br Hooms

a hymn was then sung

Prayer by Sister Packerd

Meeting Ajournd

Undated Meeting • September 1843

[271]Eleventh meeting of the
Society
Second Ward

Meeting opend with singing and prayer

Prayer by Sister Jones

---

270. A mantuamaker is a dressmaker. "Mantua," a corrupted form of the French "manteau," is a lady's gown. ("Mantua," and "Mantuamaker," in *American Dictionary* [1845], 516.)

271. TEXT: Ink changes from brown to blue ink.

P[hebe] M Wheeler rose and said that as the prest and councillors were not present and yet necessa[r]y that the Society proceed to business Councillor [Elizabeth Ann] Whitney having requested her to attend and do the best she could She desird [p. [116]] that some one might be appointed by the voice of the society to act for the present time for the Society

It was motion'd and seconded by sister Orson [Catherine] Spencer and unanimously carried thas [that] sister M. Peck act for the Society for this pressent time

The following names were receiv'd by vote

Margaret McDougall	Agnes Hill
Mahala D More	Nancy Bradly
Artemisia Wiscom [Wixom]	

Sister Peck rose said we would like to hear from the sicke poor— that our sympathies may be awaken'd for them that they may be relievd and comforted

Sister [Lydia] Granger said she had only visited a few families

Sister Huntsman said Br Levi Stalts [Stilts] family were in a suffering condition— living in the 2ᵈ Ward on La Harpe road

Sis King said she had visited the sick of 2ᵈ ward found but few suffring families

Sister Granger said the sick of th[e] 4ᵗʰ ward were no better their sufferings verry great

Sis Wheeler spoke of the situation of Sistr [Francis] Lew Law Who is late from New York left her funds there $300 which is due her this present season said she desired to get to New Orleans and from thence to N. York it being the voice of the first ward that Sister Emma should be cunsulted Sister [Sophia] Packard was appointed to see her

Sister Packerd rose said that she had laid her case before ~~Sistr Emma~~ the Prest that as she ⟨Mrs Lew Law⟩ was now in reduced circumstances and had money due her it was her council that the Society help her to N Orleans

Sister Sessions said she would give her   00 50

[p. [117]]

	$
Sister Simpson	00 25
Sister Orson Spencer	00 25
Phebe M Wheeler	00 25
Sister Hunter	1 ~~25~~ 00[272]
The Society	1 00

---

272. TEXT: "25" (cents) was overwritten by "1 00".

Society	Cash	00 50
Donations receiv'd		
Millicent Parks		00 18
Mrs Hovey		00 25
Mrs Leathhead [Deborah Leithead]		00 06
Fanny Parks		00 1 ~~12½~~ 00²⁷³
Mrs Jolly [Sarah Jolley]		00 12½
Sis Sarah Brown	3 lb pork	00 81
Sis Maria Barnum	7 lb flowr	00 14
[*illegible*] ◊◊ched [*illegible*]		
Mrs Elizabeth Huntsman	2 fowls	00 20
Sister [Lydia] Granger—		00 12½

Mrs Ann Hunter 29½ yds of unbleachd cotton cloth 11 ⟨cents⟩ yd and 17 yds of calico 12½ cents yd — 5 24

Susan Hunter — 1 00

Sister [Sophia] Packard rose said she had a great burthen on her mind it was the situation of the sick and bereav'd Mentiond a family or 9 children late orphans Sister Sessions spoke most tenderly of Sister Emma our Prest said She was verry sick and desird that the Society would unite in faith and prayer for her that she may be heal'd

Prayer was made in her behalf

A hymn sung

Prayer by Sister Sessions

P M Wheeler Assistant Secʸ [p. [118]]

September 15, 1843 • Friday • First of Two Entries

²⁷⁴Minutes of the

Twelfth Meeting

of the F R Society

Sept 23ᵈ 15ᵗʰ.

Meeting commenced with singing and and prayer by Sister [Elizabeth Ann] Whitney

The following members were received into the Society

Juliet Balis [Bayles]	Cinthia Weston
Christiana Riser	Sarah Meekam [Mecam]
Alvira Meekam [Elvira Mecham]	Mary Devenport [Davenport]
Mary Pugh	Eliza Elvira Allred

---

273. TEXT: "00 12½" was overwritten by "1 00".

274. TEXT: Phebe M. Wheeler handwriting ends; unidentified begins.

The minutes of the last meeting read Sister Whitney spoke very feelingly exhorting to unity & trust in the Lord and have faith that our sick may be healed & our lives prolonged &[275] to remember Sister Emma that her life be spared that she might be with us

Mrs Smith rose said, she had visited the sick said they were getting better she had carried Tonic & pills 3 dollars worth she could not go on foot to gather donations & distribute to the poor but would go when she could [p. [119]]

September 15, 1843 • Friday • Second of Two Entries

[276]Minuts of the
Thirteenth Meeting of the Society

August [September] 15[277]

Meeting commenced with singing prayer by Sister [Elizabeth Ann] Whitney

The following persons receivd into the Society to wit

Juliet Balis [Bayles]	Christiana Riser
Cynthia Weston	Sarah Meecum [Mecam]
Mary Devenport [Davenport]	Alvira Meecum [Elvira Mecham]
Mary Pugh	Elisa Alvera Alred [Eliza Elvira Allred]

The minuets of the last meeting read Sister Whitney spoke verry feelingly to the Society upon the necessity of being united in faith that sickness may be turnd aside lives prolonged desird the Society to pray for Siste[r] Emma Sister Joshua [Sarah] Smith said she had visited the sick found them better but had carried them tonicks and pills 3ˢ worth spoke of her inabilaty to visit the[m] as She had done as her strength was failing said that Sister [Elizabeth] Jones had

---

275. TEXT: "&" possibly wipe-erased.

276. TEXT: Unidentified handwriting ends; Phebe M. Wheeler begins.

277. As indicated here, the record book gives the date of this meeting as August 15 and describes it as the thirteenth meeting of the society. However, both the date and the meeting number are very likely scribal errors, as this meeting appears to be the same meeting described in the immediately preceding entry dated September 15 and called the twelfth meeting. The minutes for the September 15 meeting, recorded by an unidentified scribe, and for this "August 15" meeting, recorded by Phebe Wheeler, contain the same contents, including the speakers and the eight women admitted as members of the society, except that the minutes for the preceding September 15 entry end abruptly and appear incomplete. Given the placement of this entry in the record book, the correct date for this meeting appears to be September 15, rather than August 15. Two other factors make it highly unlikely that the meeting being described could have occurred on August 15 or even any time in August: first, the seventh meeting of the society was held August 13, making it improbable that there was another meeting held two days later; and second, this meeting records a vote in favor of recombining the four wards into one for Relief Society meetings, a vote that almost certainly did not occur in August, because the minutes of two early September meetings show the society still meeting separately in wards.

to[o] hard a task desird some one would take the young man who was sick on her hands Br Willcox family was represented as extreme⟨ly⟩ poor Sister Pack proposed that Sis [Mary] Woolley & Siste[r] Geene [Esther Gheen] be added to th[e] Committee to look after the poor also that the 1⁰ 2ᵈ 3ᵈ & 4ᵗʰ ward be join'd as one and all meet togather which was carried—

Donations		$
Sarah Meeks	sundry articles	1 00
Sister [Lucy] Hatfield	to²⁷⁸ flowr	00 90
Sister Price	sundry articles	00 50
Sis Lyons	sundries	00 50
Br Heaps [Thomas Heap]	1 pint wine	00 25
Sister Ivins	flour	00 50
Sister Smith for keeping Sister Nickeson two weeks		3 00

[p. [120]]

It was proposd that the comittee go forwa[r]d and do all the good they can A union of feeling prevaild in behalf of the poor and afflicted

Donations	$
To Sundries given by Br felshaw [William Felshaw] for poor	00 50
Sundry articles by Sis [Susanna] Yocum	2 00
To Sundry articles & attendance on Sister [Elizabeth] Dobson	2 25
To attendance on Sister [Phebe] Emmet	1 25
To sundry articles persons names unknown	00 75

Meeting ajournd
Prayer by Siste[r] J Smithe [Sarah Smith]

October 14, 1843 • Saturday

Fourteenth Meeting
of Society

Oct 14 1843²⁷⁹

Lodge Room

Comenced with singing with singing "Come Holy Spirit Heavenly dove"²⁸⁰
Prayer by Sis J [Sarah] Smith
persons receivd as members of society
Catharine Clawson
Susan Culbertson [Cuthbertson]²⁸¹   Elizeabeth Carbey

---

278. TEXT: Possibly "10".
279. TEXT: Dashed underline under "1843".
280. Hymn 39, *Collection of Sacred Hymns* [1841], 47.
281. See Cuthbertson's application for admission in Document 1.9.

Prest Emma Smith abs[e]nt Coun [Elizabeth Ann] Whitney rose said she was happy to again meet the Society but sory the Emma is not present Spoke of th[e] blessings that awated the Saints exhortd <u>all</u> to faithfulness and humility that we may be prepard for th[e] trials & temptations which surroung [surround] us [p. [121]]

desird the Committee to report

Sister J Smith said many of the sick which had been better were getting worse with ague and were destitute for of food said she felt deeply interested for th[e] Temple sa[i]d O that we might rouse to action and thus call down th[e] blessings of God upon us

Sister Peck said that this Society had done a great good in relieving the distressd we have not said "be ye warmd and cloathed["] without trying to do it[282]

Siste[r] Pratt represented th[e] situation of Sis Jones Siste[r] Ann Jones who is in extreme want

Siste[r] M— Dougall [Margaret McDougall] offers to work for widow Nights [Martha Knight] desird pray[er]s for Sister Hormans[283] who is sick has long been sick some 8 months

Siste[r] Smith mentiond Sister Langdons[284] family sick and without food

P[hebe] M Wheeler proposd the the Society that a sew[i]ng Society be appointd that garments and bed coveri[n]g may be mad[e] and given to such as are suffer[i]ng cold and nakedness

Movd secon[de]d and unanimously carried that the sisters meet on Thursday afternoon of nex[t] week at 1. o clock to comfort th[e] poor

Donations omited

Meeting ajournd

P M Wheeler assistent sec[ry] [p. [122]]

March 9, 1844 • Saturday

[285]The Female Relief Society of Nauvoo resumed its Meetings— March 9[th] 1844

Mienetes [Minutes] of the ~~First~~ Procidings of the
First Meeting of the Society

Room over Brick Store
March 9 1844

---

282. See James 2:16.
283. TEXT: Possibly "Harmons".
284. TEXT: Possibly "Longdons".
285. TEXT: Phebe M. Wheeler handwriting ends; Hannah M. Ells begins.

Meeting conveind— Presedent E. [Emma] Smith. Proceeded to Open the Meeting— appointed— H. [Hannah] Ells, <u>Sectary</u>

Stated the object of the Meeting, read an Epistle called the <u>Voice</u> of <u>Innocence</u>— adressed the Meeting on the late Slander, of Hiram [Hyrum] Smith &c by O F Bostic [Orsamus F. Bostwick] w[h]ich calld forth— the ⟨of reading of⟩ above Epistle—[286] it was then asertaned by vote, who would be willing to receeve the princples of vurtue, keep the commandments of God, and uphold the Pres^tss in puting ⟨down⟩ iniquity— was received by unanimous voice— Pres^t E. S. Said her determination was to do her Duty Effectully— in puting down transgresion

Counslor Witney [Elizabeth Ann Whitney]— requested the Sisters to Pray that Sister Emma might be supported, to teach us the princples of Righteousness expressed her fears, that Jugement would bgin at the house of God— Pres^t S. said it was high time for Mothers to wach over their Daughters & exhort them to keep the path of virtue— the present Meeting then ajourned in order to make room for those who could not get admitance in the fore part of the day—

12 o c A M— th[e] following Persons were then received by vote—

Rachel Foster	Clarsesa Labanno [Clarissa LeBaron]
Mary Ann Shefflin	Nancy [*blank*]
Mary All[e]y	Mary S. Nelson
Hannah [*blank*]	Mary Stuart
Catharine Tuttle	Harriet Carter
Sarah Har	Susan Ashby [p. [123]]
	Brick Store Affternoon

1 oclock Meeting Called to order by

Prest— Emma S— again staded the object of the ⟨Meeting⟩ that it was on account of the Slander of P. Hiram Smith by a vile man— Bostwic— wich had ex[c]ited th[e] indignation; of the Breatheren against him; and called forth the present remarks; the [']Voice of Inocence' was then read and approved— continued firther by exhorting all to take heed to their ways; and follow the teachings of Broather Joseph; and when he Preacheas against vice to take heed to it; and said; he meant what he said; concludid her remarks by requ[e]sting all to use theire common senses; and they would teach us right princples if we

---

286. Bostwick's accusations against Hyrum Smith and Nauvoo women triggered a court case against Bostwick for slander and precipitated Joseph Smith's request that William W. Phelps write a document in defense of the women of Nauvoo, the "epistle" referred to here and titled "The Voice of Innocence from Nauvoo." Under the heading "Virtue Will Triumph," the document was published in the *Nauvoo Neighbor* on March 20, 1844. (Document 1.10.)

123

The Female Relief Society of Nauvoo
resumed its meetings — March 9th 1844

Minutes of the Proceedings of the

First Meeting of the Society
Room over Brick Store
March 9 1844

Meeting Convened — President E. Smith. Proceeded
to open the Meeting — appointed — H. Ells Secretary
Stated the object of the Meeting, read an Epistle called
the voice of Innocence — addressed the Meeting on
the late Slander, of Hiram Smith &c by 6 Brethren
which called forth the reading above Epistle — it was then ascertained
by vote, who should be willing to Receive the principles of
virtue, keep the commandments of God, and uphold
the Pres't in putting down iniquity — was received by
unanimous voice — Pres't E. S. said her determination
was to do her duty Effectually — in putting down transgression
Counselor Whitney — requested the Sisters to Pray that Sister
Emma might be supported, to teach us the principles
of Righteousness expressed her fears, that judgement would
begin at the house of God — Pres't S. said it was high time
for Mothers to watch over their daughters & exhort
them to keep the path of virtue — the present meeting
then adjourned in order to make Room for those who
could not get admittance in the fore part of the day —
12 oc A M — the following persons were then received
by vote —

Rachel Carter   Clarissa Lebanna
Mary Ann Shefflin   Nancy
Mary Alley   Mary P. Nelson
Hannah   Mary Stuart
Catharine res Tuttle   Harriet Carter
Sarah Hear   Susan Ashby

Meeting minutes, March 9, 1844. The Nauvoo Relief Society met four times in 1844, twice on March 9 and twice on March 16. In the two March 9 meetings, Emma Smith read a document titled "Voice of Innocence," which William W. Phelps had written and Smith had somewhat revised (see Document 1.10). Hannah M. Ells took minutes of the 1844 meetings. (Church History Library, Salt Lake City. Photograph by Welden C. Andersen.)

would adheare to them— further that we must be willing to forgive ⟨what has past⟩ in consideration of repentance & reformation— Meeting— adjoured to meet again Next Sat^y 10 OClock[287]

H. M. Ells Sec^d

Abigal Gray	Elisabeth Moss
Eliza Gray	Emly Jacobs
Catharine A. Curtis	Rachel Swaner
Jane S Richards	Elisabeth Miles
Mary Cole	Emily Merrell
Susanah Cambill	Mary Guinomd [Guinand]
Ann Cotten [Cottam]	Sophia Pollard
Sarah Littlewood	Catherine Jameion [Jemeion]
Mary Bundys	Dolly Duncon [Duncan]
Isabela Willby [Isabella Wilkie]	Alice Robinson
Ann Bushby [Busby]	Sarah Gibbs
Lidia Savery [Lydia Severy]	Sally Pollard
Mary Bedford	Sarah Stuart
Dellia [Amelia Delilah] Mikesell	Mehaatable Chase
Ester McMin [Esther McMeans]	Rebeca Romand [Rebecca Raymond]
Elizabeth Clark	Ennice Leffinwell [Eunice Leffingwell]
	Amy [*blank*] [p. [124]]

March 16, 1844 • Saturday

Minutes of Preceedings of Se[c]ond
Meeting of the Society
Room over Brick Store March 16th ⟨1844⟩
10 oClock A.M

Meeting Opend with singing.

Prayer by Prest Emma Smith.

Mrs Prest— the⟨n⟩ arose and adress'd the Meeting upon the Nec[e]ssity of being united amoung ourselves and Strenthing [strengthening] each others hands in ordor that we may be able to do much good amoung the poor— [*blank*] again read the Epistle in Defence of the virtues Female part of the community of Nauvoo[288] exhorted them to cleanse thier hearts and Ears and said the time had come when we must ~~through~~ throw the Mantle of Charity

---

287. The entry in Joseph Smith's journal for this date, as recorded by scribe Willard Richards, reads, "The Female Relief Society, Met twice in the assembly room and sanctind [sanctioned] the voice of Innocen[ce] from Nauvo[o].— & adjued [adjourned] 1 week to accommodate members who could not get in." (Joseph Smith, Journal, Mar. 9, 1844, in *JSP*, J3:199–200.)

288. Document 1.10.

round to shield those who will <u>repent</u> and <u>do</u> so <u>no more</u> Spoke of J. C. Bennets [John C. Bennett's] Spiritual Wife system, theat some taught it as the Doctrene of B Joseph—[289] She advised all to abide the Book of Mormon— Dr Coven'ts [Doctrine and Covenants] &c[290] then read that Epistle of Presedent J. Smiths; rewritten in this Book of Record—[291] Meeting then closed to reopen— 12 OClock—

One OClock Meeting calld to order Pres Emma Smith again adresse[d.] the Society Read Boath the former Epistles;— Desired none shluld [should] lift their hand or voice; to adopt the princples unless they where willing to maintain their integrity through time & Eternity Said thease contain the princples, the Society started upon; but was sorry to have to say [p. [125]] all had adhe

all had not adhere'd to them—

again exhorted— to follow the teachings of Presede[t] J Smith— from the Stand— said their could not not be stronnger Language used than that just read— and that was these are ⟨the⟩ words of B. Joseph her Husband— &c Said she wanted to see a reformation in boath men & woman— also exhorted— to

---

289. Following Bennett's excommunication in May 1842, Relief Society members publicly condemned his conduct and teachings. Likewise, church leaders emphatically disclaimed any connection between "spiritual wifery" and plural marriage, as Parley P. Pratt explained a year later in the *Prophet*. Pratt stated that Bennett's "Spiritual Wife Doctrine" was "another name for whoredom, wicked and unlawful connection, and every kind of confusion, corruption, and abomination" and was "as foreign from the real principles of the Church as the devil is from God." (Joseph Smith et al., "Notice," May 11, 1842, Joseph Smith Collection, CHL; Document 1.2, entry for June 23, 1842; Parley P. Pratt, "This Number Closes the First Volume of the 'Prophet,'" *Prophet*, May 24, 1845, [2]; see also Documents 1.5 and 1.6.)

290. The Book of Mormon forbids the taking of more than one wife, with one exception: "For if I will, saith the Lord of Hosts, raise up seed unto me, I will command my people." Otherwise, "there shall not any man among you have save it be one wife." The 1835 edition of the Doctrine and Covenants also defines marriage as a union between one woman and one man: "We declare that we believe, that one man should have one wife; and one woman, but one husband, except in case of death, when either is at liberty to marry again." Joseph Smith's revelation concerning eternal and plural marriage, recorded in 1843 (Doctrine and Covenants 132 in the modern Latter-day Saint canon), was first included in the 1876 edition of the Doctrine and Covenants. (Jacob 2:27–30; "Marriage," ca. Aug. 1835, in *Doctrine and Covenants of the Church of the Latter Day Saints*, comp. Joseph Smith et al. [Kirtland, OH: F. G. Williams, 1835], section 101; Revelation, July 12, 1843, in Revelations Collection, 1831–ca. 1844, 1847, 1861, ca. 1876, CHL; *The Doctrine and Covenants, of the Church of Jesus Christ of Latter-day Saints, Containing the Revelations Given to Joseph Smith, Jun., the Prophet, for the Building Up of the Kingdom of God in the Last Days* [Salt Lake City: Deseret News, 1876], section 132.)

291. Emma Smith read "The Voice of Innocence" (the "Epistle in Defence of the virtues" mentioned earlier in the paragraph) and the March 1842 letter to Relief Society members (the "Epistle of Presedent J. Smiths" mentioned in this line) because both warned women against seducers. The latter document, addressed "To the Hon., the President of the Female Relief Society of Nauvoo" and signed by Joseph Smith, Brigham Young, and other church leaders, appears following the minutes for the Relief Society meeting of September 28, 1842, but was read at the March 31, 1842, meeting of the society. (Document 1.10; Document 1.2, entry for Mar. 31, 1842, and letter copied into the minutes following the Sept. 28, 1842, entry.)

look affter the poor— also to examin the conduct of their Leaders of this Society— that you may sit in judgement on their heads— and said if thier ever was any authourity on the Earth she had it— and had yet— Prest. E. S. closed her remarks by say[i]ng she should like to have <u>all</u> the Society present to geather— she said it was her intention to present the Officers of the Society for fellowship— when a place can be obtaind that all can be present— [*blank*] Meeting ajou [adjourned] until a suitable place can be obtaind—

H. [Hannah] M. Ells
<u>Secy</u>

the followig names were rece'd
Sophia, M. Burgess
Hareet Hamilton
Sarah Gabbit

Mary C Allen
Jane Roadiback [Rodeback]

Ammy Chase
Sarah M Jhonson [Johnson]
Chastina Hollylike [Hadlock]
Maria M [Emmoliza] Green
Lucy Merrill
Cyantha [Cynthia] Osborn
Maryann Greenhouch
Diana Cole
Mary Cole
Rosana Marks
Adelia Cole
Charlott Portor [Potter]
Mary Oldige [Aldridge]
[*blank*] [Suritta] Colum
Mary A Preist
Lavina Willson [Lovina Wilson]
Martha L More
Elisebeth Kelting
Ellen Hartly
Alice Willding
Elisebeth White
Sarah M Noris
Mary Travis

Seliana [Silence] Ward
Rushton Margrett [Margaret Rushton]
Eliza Odercark [Odekirk]
C Elmira Babitt [Almira Babbitt]
Adelia Bently
Clarrisia Hught [Haight]
Mary Grove
Cathrine Harty
Harriet Pixson
Mary Robins
Orpha Davies [p. [126]]
Mary A. Rilands [Roylance]
Eliza Booth
Sarah Sheffild
Ann Pine
Mary A Yearsly
Ann Miles
Susana Slater
Larata [Floretta] Green
Mary Parker
Mary A Powers
Emely Davis
Mary Rus[s]ell
E◊mira Prentic [Almira Prentiss]
Caroline Parsons
Maria M Green
Cidny [Sidney] Jones [p. [127]]

1.3 "Ladies' Relief Society," April 1, 1842

"Ladies' Relief Society," Times and Seasons *(Nauvoo, IL), Apr. 1, 1842, vol. 3, no. 11, p. 743.*

Two weeks after the organization of the Female Relief Society of Nauvoo on March 17, 1842, the *Times and Seasons,* the church newspaper in Nauvoo, published this editorial. The author both described the intended activities of the Relief Society for an audience that would have known little or nothing about it and offered an endorsement of the society. Though the editorial misstated the name of the organization and the date of its founding, this enthusiastic report may have contributed to the Relief Society's rapid growth.

The *Times and Seasons* began publication in November 1839 and by this time was a semimonthly publication.[292] In January 1842 Joseph Smith dictated a revelation that instructed the Quorum of the Twelve Apostles to "take in hand the Editorial department of the Times and Seasons."[293] The quorum appointed John Taylor and Wilford Woodruff to edit the newspaper and "take charge of the whole establishment under the direction of Joseph the Seer." Smith thus served as the newspaper's editor, while Taylor did much of the writing and Woodruff assisted with the business aspects.[294] Though this article on the Relief Society was attributed to the editor, Joseph Smith, it was likely authored primarily by Taylor who, along with Smith, had been present at the inaugural meeting of the Relief Society. Taylor's wife, Leonora, was one of the society's founding members.[295]

Most of this article was later copied into the Manuscript History of the Church and then published in the early twentieth century as part of the *History of the Church,* establishing it as a traditional account of the beginning of the Relief Society.[296] The transcript below is taken from the original *Times and Seasons* publication.

———— ৵ৎ ————

LADIES' RELIEF SOCIETY.

A society has lately been formed by the ladies of Nauvoo for the relief of the poor, the destitute, the widow and the orphan; and for the exercise of all benevolent purposes. The society is known by the name of the "Ladies' Relief

---

292. Peter Crawley, *A Descriptive Bibliography of the Mormon Church,* 3 vols. (Provo, UT: Religious Studies Center, Brigham Young University, 1997), 1:20–21.

293. Joseph Smith, Journal, Jan. 28, 1842, in Andrew H. Hedges et al., eds., *Journals, Volume 2: December 1841–April 1843,* vol. 2 of the Journals series of *The Joseph Smith Papers,* ed. Dean C. Jessee et al. (Salt Lake City: Church Historian's Press, 2011), 38 (hereafter *JSP,* J2).

294. Wilford Woodruff, Journal, 1833–1898, Wilford Woodruff, Journals and Papers, 1828–1898, CHL, Feb. 3, 1842; Joseph Smith, Journal, Mar. 2, 1842, in *JSP,* J2:39.

295. Document 1.2, entry for Mar. 17, 1842.

296. Joseph Smith et al., History, 1838–1856, vols. A-1–F-1 (original), A-2–E-2 (fair copy), CHL, vol. C-1, 1302; Joseph Smith et al., *History of the Church of Jesus Christ of Latter-day Saints,* ed. B. H. Roberts (Salt Lake City: Deseret News, 1902–1912 [vols. 1–6], 1932 [vol. 7]), 4:567–568.

Society of the City of Nauvoo;" and was organized on Thursday the 24th of March A. D. 1842.[297]

The society is duly organized with a Presidentess or Chairwoman, and two Councillors, chosen by herself; a Treasurer and Secretary. Mrs. Emma Smith takes the Presidential chair, Mrs. Elizabeth Ann Whitney, and Mrs. Sarah M. Cleveland are her Councillors; Miss Elvira Cole [Cowles] is Treasuress, and our well known and talented poetess, Miss E[l]iza[298] R. Snow Secretary.

There was a very numerous attendance at the organization of the society and also at their subsequent meetings of some of our most intelligent, humane, philanthropic, and respectable ladies; and we are well assured from a knowledge of those pure principles of benevolence that flow spontaneously from their humane, and philanthrophic bosoms, that with the resources they will have at command they will fly to the relief of the stranger, they will pour in oil and wine to the wounded heart of the distressed;[299] they will dry up the tear of the orphan, and make the widow's heart to rejoice.

Our Ladies have always been signalized for their acts of benevolence and kindness; but the cruel usage that they have received from the barbarians of Missouri, has hitherto prevented their extending the hand of charity in a conspicuous manner; yet in the midst of their persecutions, when the bread has been torn from their helpless offsprings by their cruel oppressors, they have always been ready to open their doors to the weary traveller, to divide their scanty pittance with the hungry; and from their robbed and impoverished wardrobes, to divide with the more needy and destitute; and now that they are living in a more genial soil, and among a less barbarous people, and possess facilities that they have not heretofore enjoyed, we feel convinced that with their concentrated efforts the condition of the sufferring poor, of the stranger and the fatherless will be ameliorated.

We had the privelege of being present at their organization, and were much pleased with their *modus operandi*, and the good order that prevailed; they are strictly parliamentary in their proceedings; and we believe that they will make pretty good democrats.[300]—ED.

---

297. The article misstates the society's name (the Female Relief Society of Nauvoo) and date of organization (March 17, 1842). (See Document 1.2, entry for Mar. 17, 1842.)

298. TEXT: In the copy used for transcription, there is a blank space between the *E* and the *i*.

299. See Luke 10:34.

300. On the use of parliamentary procedure in the Relief Society's meetings, see 33n109 herein.

1.4 Eliza R. Snow, "The Female Relief Society of Nauvoo," July 1, 1842

Eliza R. Snow, "The Female Relief Society of Nauvoo. What Is It?" Times and Seasons *(Nauvoo, IL), July 1, 1842, vol. 3, no. 17, p. 846.*

Eliza R. Snow was elected secretary of the Female Relief Society of Nauvoo at its first meeting on March 17, 1842.[301] Her poem describing the new organization appeared fifteen weeks later in the church's semimonthly *Times and Seasons.* It marked the first published comment by a woman regarding the Relief Society.

By this time, Snow was well known as a poet in Nauvoo. Two of her hymns had been published in 1835 in the first Latter-day Saint hymnal, compiled by Emma Smith and William W. Phelps. Between 1839 and 1841, the Illinois *Quincy Whig* published twenty of Snow's poems, many of them pleading for justice for the thousands of Saints driven from their homes in northwestern Missouri. During the same period, she regularly contributed poetry to the *Times and Seasons.* In the spring of 1841, her epic poem "Time and Change" was printed in Nauvoo as a pamphlet.[302]

In addition to having skill as a poet, Snow was experienced as a transcriber and a recorder, having served as secretary for her father, Oliver Snow, a justice of the peace and county commissioner in Ohio.[303] As Relief Society secretary, she fastidiously recorded in the Relief Society "Book of Records," or minutes, the names of members and donors, as well as remarks made in meetings. Her precision and persistence in this task indicate her belief that she was constructing a significant, enduring record. Likewise, the following poem reflects Snow's sense of the significance of the newly established society. Though membership grew rapidly between March and June 1842, some women may have expressed doubts regarding the organization. When Emma Smith addressed those gathered on May 27, 1842, she "requested if any were present who came to make ridicule of the Society, that they would withdraw."[304] Snow's six stanzas clarify the society's purposes by distilling ideas and sometimes drawing phrases from her minutes of the first twelve meetings.[305]

---

301. Document 1.2, entry for Mar. 17, 1842.

302. "Great Is the Lord: 'Tis Good to Praise" and "The Glorious Day Is Rolling On" are Hymns 70 and 71 in *A Collection of Sacred Hymns, for the Church of the Latter Day Saints,* ed. Emma Smith (Kirtland, OH: F. G. Williams, 1835), 92–94. Snow's poems in the *Quincy Whig* appeared between May 4, 1839, and June 26, 1841. The pamphlet is *Time and Change: A Poem in Blank Verse. Also Two Odes, One for the Sons of Liberty, the Other for the Fourth of July. By Miss Eliza R. Snow* (Nauvoo, IL: E. Robinson, 1841). Snow published most of these poems in her *Poems: Religious, Historical, and Political,* 2 vols. (Liverpool: F. D. Richards, 1856; Salt Lake City: Latter-day Saints' Printing and Publishing Establishment, 1877). All are reproduced in Jill Mulvay Derr and Karen Lynn Davidson, eds., *Eliza R. Snow: The Complete Poetry* (Provo, UT: Brigham Young University Press; Salt Lake City: University of Utah Press, 2009).

303. Eliza R. Snow, "Sketch of My Life," n.d., Bancroft Library, University of California, Berkeley, 1; Maureen Ursenbach Beecher, ed., *The Personal Writings of Eliza Roxcy Snow,* Life Writings of Frontier Women 5 (Logan: Utah State University Press, 2000), 257.

304. Document 1.2, entry for May 27, 1842.

305. For example, the phrases "The poor, the widow, and the fatherless," "paths of virtue," "To give

THE FEMALE RELIEF SOCIETY OF NAUVOO.

—

WHAT IS IT?

It is an Institution form'd to bless
The poor, the widow, and the fatherless—
To clothe the naked and the hungry feed,
And in the holy paths of virtue, lead.

To seek out sorrow, grief and mute despair,
And light the lamp of hope eternal there—
To try the strength of consolation's art
By breathing comfort to the mourning heart.

To chase the clouds that shade the aspect, where
Distress presides; and wake up pleasures there—
With open heart extend the friendly hand
To hail the stranger, from a distant land.

To stamp a vetoing impress on each move
That Virtue's present dictates disapprove—
To put the tattler's coinage, scandal, down,
And make corruption feel its with'ring frown.

To give instruction, where instruction's voice
Will guide the feet and make the heart rejoice—
To turn the wayward from their recklessness,
And lead them in the ways of happiness.

It is an *Order*, fitted and design'd
To meet the wants of body, and of mind—
To seek the wretched, in their long abode—
Supply their wants, and raise their hearts to God.

E. R. SNOW

---

instruction," and "heart rejoice" are quotations from Snow's minutes. (Document 1.2, entries for Mar. 17, Mar. 31, and Apr. 28, 1842.)

1.5 Nauvoo Female Relief Society, Petition to Thomas Carlin, circa July 22, 1842

Nauvoo Female Relief Society, Petition, to Thomas Carlin, [ca. July 22, 1842]; eight pages; CHL (MS 15535).

In late July 1842 members of the Female Relief Society petitioned Illinois governor Thomas Carlin not to extradite Joseph Smith to Missouri for trial. More than two months earlier, on May 6, 1842, Lilburn W. Boggs, a former governor of Missouri, was shot and seriously wounded at his home in Independence, Missouri. In October 1838 Boggs had sanctioned the expulsion of the Latter-day Saints from Missouri in his "extermination order." Suspicion for the attack on Boggs quickly centered on the Mormons. On May 21, for instance, the Illinois *Quincy Whig* suggested that Joseph Smith and the Latter-day Saints were responsible for the attack.[306] In July the *Sangamo Journal,* a newspaper in Springfield, Illinois, began publishing explosive letters from John C. Bennett, who had been both mayor of Nauvoo and assistant president of the church before his excommunication for adultery in May 1842. In one of his letters, published on July 15, Bennett accused Smith of ordering Orrin Porter Rockwell, a Latter-day Saint who was in Independence at the time of the attack, to shoot Boggs.[307] Five days after the publication of Bennett's letter, Boggs made a sworn statement that Joseph Smith "was Accessary before the fact" in the assassination attempt and requested that Governor Thomas Reynolds of Missouri seek the extradition of Smith from Illinois to stand trial.[308] Reynolds officially requested the extradition two days later.[309]

The threat of Smith's potential extradition led church members and other citizens of Nauvoo to write three petitions to Governor Carlin. First, on July 22, the Nauvoo City Council appointed John Taylor, William Law, and Brigham Young as a committee, assisted by city recorder James Sloan, "to prepare a Petition to lay before the Governor of this State, praying that he will protect Lieu^t Genl Joseph Smith from arrest under any Writ from Missouri, and the Inhabitants of this City and its vicinity from the intrigues of evil designing Men."[310] About eight hundred men signed the petition.[311] A second petition, the Relief

306. "Assassination of Ex-Governor Boggs of Missouri," *Quincy (IL) Whig,* May 21, 1842, [3].

307. "Further Mormon Developments!! 2d Letter from Gen. Bennett," *Sangamo Journal* (Springfield, IL), July 15, 1842, [2].

308. Lilburn W. Boggs, Affidavit, July 20, 1842, Joseph Smith Extradition Records, 1839–1843, Abraham Lincoln Presidential Library, in Andrew H. Hedges et al., eds., *Journals, Volume 2: December 1841–April 1843,* vol. 2 of the Journals series of *The Joseph Smith Papers,* ed. Dean C. Jessee et al. (Salt Lake City: Church Historian's Press, 2011), 380 (hereafter *JSP,* J2).

309. Thomas Reynolds, Requisition to Thomas Carlin, July 22, 1842, Joseph Smith Extradition Records, 1839–1843, Abraham Lincoln Presidential Library, Springfield, IL, in *JSP,* J2:380.

310. Nauvoo City Council, "A Record of the Proceedings of the City Council of the City of Nauvoo Handcock County, State of Illinois, Commencing A.D. 1841," ca. 1841–1845, CHL, July 22, 1842, 95–97 (hereafter Nauvoo City Council Minute Book).

311. Joseph Smith et al., History, 1838–1856, vols. A-1–F-1 (original), A-2–E-2 (fair copy), CHL, vol. C-1, 1359 (hereafter JS History).

Society petition featured here, was prepared that same day and was at some point thereafter copied and "signed by about one thousand Ladies."[312] Finally, a "petition was also drawn up by many Citizens in, and near Nauvoo, who were not Mormons, setting forth the same things" as the first and second petitions.[313]

The Relief Society petition's affirmation of female decorum and its emotional appeal for protection parallel contemporaneous women's petitions to local, state, and federal officials.[314] The draft of the petition is in John Taylor's handwriting, and both Taylor and James Sloan made corrections; the extent of Relief Society leaders' input on the document is unclear. Because Carlin's copy of the petition is apparently not extant, the unsigned draft of the petition is reproduced below. Since both Taylor and Sloan had also been involved in preparing the city council petition, the city council and Relief Society petitions highlight many of the same themes.

Emma Smith, Eliza R. Snow, and Amanda Barnes Smith delivered the Relief Society petition to Governor Carlin in Quincy on July 28.[315] Snow recorded that Carlin "received us with cordiality, and as much affability and politeness as his Excellency is master of, assuring us of his protection, by saying that the laws and Constitution of our country shall be his polar star in case of any difficulty. He manifested much friendship, and it remains for time and circumstance to prove the sincerity of his professions."[316] Much later, Snow recalled that, notwithstanding Carlin's acknowledgment of Smith's "innocence," "soon after our return, we learned that at the time of our visit, and while making protestations of friendship, the wily Governor was secretly conniving with the basest of men to destroy our leaders."[317]

Indeed, Governor Carlin issued a writ for Joseph Smith's arrest on August 2. Though Smith was arrested on August 8, he petitioned for a writ of habeas corpus, which the Nauvoo Municipal Court granted. The arresting officer then returned to Quincy to receive instructions from the governor, and Joseph Smith went into hiding for most of the time until January 1843.[318] Between August 16 and September 7, Emma Smith and Carlin exchanged four letters. She argued for her husband's innocence and asked Carlin not to

---

312. JS History, vol. C-1, 1359. In the published *History of the Church,* the petition is misdated as September 5, 1842, likely because a clerk wrote on the back of the petition draft, "Ladies Releif Society to Gov. Carlin Sept. 5th 1842." A biographical sketch of Amanda Barnes Smith states, "The petition was signed by every member of the Relief Society." (Joseph Smith et al., *History of the Church of Jesus Christ of Latter-day Saints,* ed. B. H. Roberts [Salt Lake City: Deseret News, 1902–1912 (vols. 1–6), 1932 (vol. 7)], 5:146; "Amanda Smith," *Woman's Exponent,* June 15, 1881, 10:2, 13.)

313. JS History, vol. C-1, 1359.

314. See Alisse Theodore Portnoy, "'Female Petitioners Can Lawfully Be Heard': Negotiating Female Decorum, United States Politics, and Political Agency, 1829–1831," *Journal of the Early Republic* 23, no. 4 (Winter 2003): 573–610.

315. A biographical sketch of Amanda Barnes Smith states, "President Joseph Smith wished the ladies to make the effort themselves, and himself named the sisters who were to be the bearers of the petition." ("Amanda Smith," *Woman's Exponent,* June 15, 1881, 10:13.)

316. Eliza R. Snow, Journal, 1842–1882, CHL, July 29, 1842.

317. Eliza R. Snow, "Sketch of My Life," n.d., Bancroft Library, University of California, Berkeley, 14.

318. Joseph Smith, Journal, Aug. 8, 1842; Volume Introduction to Nauvoo Journals, Dec. 1841–Apr. 1843, in *JSP,* J2:xxxi, 81.

Petition to Governor Thomas Carlin. One thousand Nauvoo Relief Society members signed a petition requesting that Illinois governor Thomas Carlin not extradite Joseph Smith to Missouri for trial. Emma Smith, Eliza R. Snow, and Amanda Barnes Smith delivered the petition to Carlin at Quincy, Illinois, on July 28, 1842. The version shown here is a draft in the handwriting of John Taylor, with revisions by Taylor and James Sloan. (Church History Library, Salt Lake City.)

extradite him; Carlin responded that he was bound by law to accede to Missouri's extradition orders.[319]

On August 31 Joseph Smith attended a Relief Society meeting and thanked the women for their petition, commenting, "The Female Relief Society has taken the the most active part in my welfare— against my enemies— in petitioning to the Governor— These measures were all necessary. . . . If these measures had not been taken, more serious consequences would have resulted." He also told the women that "God had enabled him to keep out of" the hands of his enemies, and he "had war'd a good warfare inasmuch as he had whip'd out all of [John C.] Bennett's host."[320] Smith's legal battle continued over the next several months, until a federal judge in January 1843 ruled that Boggs's affidavit (and thus Reynolds's requisition based on that affidavit) was legally flawed, ending this particular attempt to extradite Smith to Missouri.[321]

To his Excellency Thomas Carlin Gov. of the State of Ill.

We the undersigned members of the Nauvoo Releif Society & Ladies of Nauvoo hearing many reports concerning; mobs threats of extermination & other excitement set on foot by John C. Bennet calculated to disturb the peace happiness & well being of this community, have taken the liberty to ~~lay before~~ ⟨petition⟩[322] your excellency ~~the following statements~~ ⟨for protection⟩

It may be considered irrelevant for Ladies to petition your excellen[cy] on the above named subject & may be thought by you sir to be officious [p. 1][323] & that it would be more becoming for our husbands ~~our~~ Fathers ~~our~~ brothers & sons to engage in this work & in our defence; this sir we will admit in ordinary cases is right & that it would be more consistent with the delicacy of the female character to be silent but on occasions like the present that our desires for the peace of society the happiness of our freinds, The desire to save the lives of our husbands our our fathers our brothers our children & our own lives will be a sufficient palliation in the estimation of your excellency for the step we

---

319. Emma Smith to Thomas Carlin, Aug. 16, 1842; Thomas Carlin to Emma Smith, Aug. 24, 1842; Emma Smith to Thomas Carlin, Aug. 27, 1842; Thomas Carlin to Emma Smith, Sept. 7, 1842, in *JSP,* J2:111–114, 126–130; see also Andrew H. Hedges and Alex D. Smith, "The Lady and the Governor: Emma Hale Smith's and Thomas Carlin's 1842 Correspondence," *Mormon Historical Studies* 9 (Fall 2008): 139–152.

320. Document 1.2, entry for Aug. 31, 1842.

321. For a summary of the legal maneuverings, with supporting documentation, see "Appendix 1: Missouri Extradition Attempt, 1842–1843, Selected Documents," in *JSP,* J2:377–402.

322. TEXT: Insertions in this document are in the handwriting of John Taylor unless otherwise noted.

323. TEXT: All page numbers were inserted by James Sloan.

have taken in presenting this petition in support of the one already sent your [p. 2] Excellency by the male inhabitants of this city.—³²⁴

We would respectfully represent to your Excellency that we have not yet forgot the scenes of grief misery & woe that we had to experience from the hands of ruthles & bloodthirsty mob⟨s⟩³²⁵ in the state of Mo. ◊◊en ~~tyranny & oppression ruled~~³²⁶— the cup of misery was prepared by ~~the~~ Lying slander & misrepresentation it was ⟨wrung out &⟩ filled by tyranny & oppression, & by a ruthless in human mob. We had to drink it to the dregs. Your ecellency will bear with us if we remind you of the cold blooded atrocities that we w◊◊◊ witnessed in that state our ~~heart thrills~~ ⟨bosoms heave⟩ with horror [p. 3] ⟨our eyes are dim;⟩ our knees tremble; our hearts are faint when we think of their horrid deeds ~~of~~ & if the petitions of our husbands brothers fathers & sons will not avail with your Excellency we beseech you to remember ⟨that of⟩ their wives mothers ⟨sisters⟩ & daughters.— let the voice of injured innocence in Mo speak; let the blood of our fathers our Brothers our sons & daughters speak let the tears of the widows the orphans the maimed the impoverished speak & let the injuries sustained by fifteen thousand innocent robbed ⟨spoiled⟩ persecuted & injured people speak let the tale of our woe be told ⟨let it be told without varnish ~~or~~ prejudice or colour⟩ & we are perswaided that there is no heart but will be softened no feelings but will be affected [p. 4] & no person but what will flee to our side.³²⁷

Far be it from us to accuse your excellency of obduracy or injustice we believe you to be a human feeling benevolent & patriotic man & therefore we appeal to you.—

Concerning John C Bennet who is trying ⟨with other political Demagogues⟩³²⁸ to disturb our peace we believe him to be ⟨an unvirtuous man &⟩ a most consummate scoundrel a stirrer up of sedition & a vile wretch unworthy the attention or notice of any virtuous man & his published statements concerning Joseph Smith are barefaced unblushing [p. 5] falsehoods.³²⁹

---

324. Nauvoo City Council Minute Book, July 22, 1842, 95–97.

325. TEXT: The *s* was inserted by James Sloan.

326. TEXT: John Taylor crossed out the first portion of this cancellation; James Sloan crossed out "sion ruled".

327. The petition prepared by the Nauvoo City Council on the same day likewise emphasized the persecutions of the Latter-day Saints in Missouri: "we had to suffer banishment, exile, the confiscation of our Properties, & have diseases, distress, & misery entailed upon us & our Children, the effects of which we bear about in our Bodies, & are indelibly engraven on our Minds." (Nauvoo City Council Minute Book, July 22, 1842, 95.)

328. TEXT: Insertion by James Sloan.

329. The petition prepared by the city council similarly stated, "Your Excellency must be acquainted with the false statements & seditious designs of John Cook Bennett with other political Demagogues,

We would farther represent to your excellency concerning Joseph Smith that we have the utmost confidence in him ⟨as being a man of⟩ virtue integrity honesty truth & patriotism, we have never either in public or private heard him teach any principles but the principles of virtue & righteousness & so we have knowledge we know him to be a pure chaste virtuous & godly man.—

Under these circumstances we would petition your excellency to excert your priviledges in an official capacity & not to suffer him should he be demanded to go into the state of Mo. for we know that if he is ⟨should⟩ it would be the delivering up the innocent to be murdered he would reprent [represent?] to your excellencey [p. 6] that we are a law abiding people a virtuous people & we would respectfully refer your Excelleny to the official document⟨s⟩[330] of this state during our three years residen[c]e ⟨in⟩ it⟨,⟩ in proof of this. if we transgress laws we are willing to be tried by those laws but we dread mobs we dread illegal process we dread fermentation calumny & lies knowing that our difficulties in Mo first commenced with these thing ⟨x⟩[331] & we therefore appeal to the honor philanthrophy justice benevolence justice & patriotism of your excellency to afford us all legal protection & to grant us our request & we as are duty bound will ever pray [p. 7]

⟨x see foregoing Page where this Comes in.⟩[332]

We pray that we may not be delivered into the hands of mob or illegal proceedings of the malitia but that we may have the priviledg of self defence in case of attack without having to contend with legalized mobs as in Mo

⟨have a knowledge of the political⟩[333] [p. [8]]

---

pertaining to us as a People, we presume Sir, that you are acquainted with the infamous Character of that individual, from certain statements made to us by yourself. . . . Concerning those statements made by him against Joseph Smith, we know that they are false; Joseph Smith has our entire confidence, we know that he has violated no Law, nor has he in any wise promoted sedition, or rebellion." The Latter-day Saints' view of Bennett's character was not unique; Thomas Ford, who succeeded Carlin as governor of Illinois, called Bennett "probably the greatest scamp in the western country." (Nauvoo City Council Minute Book, July 22, 1842, 96; Thomas Ford, *A History of Illinois, from Its Commencement as a State in 1818 to 1847* [Chicago: S. C. Griggs; New York: Ivison and Phinney, 1854], 263.)

330. TEXT: The *s* was inserted by James Sloan. All other emendations on this manuscript page were made by Sloan.

331. TEXT: At this point, James Sloan inserted an "x" in the margin of the text, indicating that the document's final paragraph should be transferred to this point.

332. TEXT: This note by James Sloan indicates that the following paragraph should be transferred to the point in the preceding paragraph where Sloan made an "x."

333. TEXT: James Sloan inserted these words and then crossed them out.

1.6 Emma Smith and Others, Statement, October 1, 1842

Emma Smith, Elizabeth Ann Whitney, Sarah M. Cleveland, Eliza R. Snow, Mary C. Miller, Lois Cutler, Thirza Cahoon, Ann Hunter, Jane Law, Sophia R. Marks, Polly Z. Johnson, Abigail Works, Catharine Petty, Sarah Higbee, Phebe Woodruff, Leonora Taylor, Sarah Hillman, Rosannah Marks, and Angeline Robinson, Statement, Times and Seasons *(Nauvoo, IL), Oct. 1, 1842, vol. 3, no. 23, p. 940.*

The statement on marriage featured below was part of an effort by Latter-day Saints to counteract the growing influence of John C. Bennett in late 1842. Bennett, who joined the church in 1840, served as mayor of Nauvoo and as a member of the church's First Presidency during 1841 and into 1842. He was excommunicated from the church in May 1842 on the charge of adultery.[334] As John Taylor recalled, Bennett and others "got an inkling" of Joseph Smith's private teachings on plural marriage and "made use of some of those principles to corrupt to destroy not only himself but others."[335]

Bennett, in turn, accused Joseph Smith of fraud, murder, and liaisons with "*clandestine wives.*" In July 1842, not long after the *Times and Seasons* published notice of Bennett's excommunication—and reprinted affidavits regarding his deceptions and immoral activities[336]—Bennett's first attacks on Smith and the church began appearing in the Springfield, Illinois–based *Sangamo Journal.* By the autumn of 1842, his "disclosures" had been widely published in newspapers in the United States. With a book-length exposé at press, Bennett also began delivering lectures on "The Secret Wife System at Nauvoo."[337]

Refuting Bennett's assertions regarding "secret wives" presented those church members who knew about Joseph Smith's plural marriage in Nauvoo, including some Relief Society members, with a dilemma: how to openly refute Bennett's false claims without acknowledging or explaining the practice of plural marriage in a public setting. Bennett's highly visible lectures in New York and the pending publication of his exposé made a public refutation imperative.[338] Even before Bennett's public attacks began, Emma Smith had proposed to the Relief Society on June 23 that "a Circular go forth from this Society, expressive

---

334. Joseph Smith et al., "Notice," May 11, 1842, Joseph Smith Collection, 1827–1846, CHL; Joseph Smith et al., "Notice," *Times and Seasons,* June 15, 1842, 3:830.

335. LaJean Purcell Carruth and Mark Lyman Staker, "John Taylor's June 27, 1854, Account of the Martyrdom," *BYU Studies* 50, no. 3 (2011): 43.

336. Bennett's excommunication was announced in Joseph Smith et al., "Notice," *Times and Seasons,* June 15, 1842, 3:830. A full disclosure about Bennett's history, supported by documents, was published in Joseph Smith, "To the Church of Jesus Christ of Latter Day Saints, and to All the Honorable Part of Community," *Wasp,* June 25, 1842, [3]; that article was reprinted in the *Times and Seasons* on July 1, 1842.

337. Andrew H. Hedges et al., eds., *Journals, Volume 2: December 1841–April 1843,* vol. 2 of the Journals series of *The Joseph Smith Papers,* ed. Dean C. Jessee et al. (Salt Lake City: Church Historian's Press, 2011), xxvii–xxx (hereafter *JSP,* J2); see also Andrew F. Smith, *The Saintly Scoundrel: The Life and Times of Dr. John Cook Bennett* (Urbana: University of Illinois Press, 1997), 98–141.

338. Latter-day Saints in Nauvoo knew about Bennett's forthcoming book by early September. (James Arlington Bennet to Joseph Smith, Aug. 16, 1842, in *JSP,* J2:133–136.)

of our feeling in reference to Dr. Bennett's character."[339] Latter-day Saints answered Bennett's accusations through a variety of channels, including petitions to the Illinois governor[340] and missionaries sent out specifically to counter Bennett's influence.[341]

In addition, church members responded in the October 1, 1842, edition of the *Times and Seasons*. The newspaper printed a copy of a statement on marriage from the 1835 edition of the Doctrine and Covenants: "We declare that we believe, that one man should have one wife; and one woman, but one husband, except in case of death, when either is at liberty to marry again."[342] This was followed by a statement signed by leading Mormon men that refuted Bennett's claims as "foul and infamous slander upon an innocent people."[343]

The same issue of the *Times and Seasons* also published a similar statement signed by nineteen prominent members of the Nauvoo Relief Society, perhaps related to Emma Smith's earlier call for such a statement, in which the women distanced themselves from Bennett's activities and accusations. This document, which is reproduced below, illustrates the complex situation in refuting Bennett's claims, in that at least three of the undersigned women had firsthand experience with plural marriage: Eliza R. Snow was sealed to Joseph Smith on June 29, 1842, in the presence of Sarah M. Cleveland, and Elizabeth Ann Whitney was present on July 27, 1842, when her daughter Sarah Ann Whitney was sealed to Smith.[344] It is unclear when Emma Smith learned of the plural wives Joseph Smith married in Nauvoo, though she knew of some of them by spring 1843.[345]

In signing the statement on marriage, these women who knew about plural marriage likely differentiated in their minds between what they saw as an inspired system of marriage, commanded by God, and Bennett's practice of unlicensed bigamy or polygamy, which they believed manipulated innocent women to serve men's baser desires.[346] Eliza R.

---

339. Document 1.2, entry for June 23, 1842.

340. See Document 1.5.

341. See *JSP*, J2:75n303.

342. "On Marriage," *Times and Seasons*, Oct. 1, 1842, 3:939; see "Marriage," ca. Aug. 1835, in Doctrine and Covenants 101, 1835 ed., in Robin Scott Jensen et al., eds., *Revelations and Translations, Volume 2: Published Revelations*, vol. 2 of the Revelations and Translations series of *The Joseph Smith Papers*, ed. Dean C. Jessee et al. (Salt Lake City: Church Historian's Press, 2011), 561 (hereafter *JSP*, R2).

343. The men's petition stated: "We have given the above rule of marriage as the only one practiced in this church, to show that Dr. J. C. Bennett's 'secret wife system' is a matter of his own manufacture; and further to disabuse the public ear, and shew that the said Bennett and his misanthropic friend Origen Bachelor, are perpetrating a foul and infamous slander upon an innocent people, and need but be known to be hated and despised." The rest of the petition was very similar to the women's reproduced below. ("On Marriage," *Times and Seasons*, Oct. 1, 1842, 3:939.)

344. Joseph F. Smith, Affidavits about Celestial Marriage, 1869–1915, CHL, Eliza R. Snow, Affidavit, Salt Lake Co., Utah Territory, June 7, 1869, 1:25; and Sarah Ann Whitney Kimball, Affidavit, Salt Lake Co., Utah Territory, June 19, 1869, 1:36.

345. Brian C. Hales, *Joseph Smith's Polygamy*, 3 vols. (Salt Lake City: Greg Kofford Books, 2013), 2:33–61.

346. For a similar differentiation, before the public announcement of Latter-day Saint plural marriage in 1852, between the "spiritual wife doctrine" and the "holy and sacred ordinances" of sealing (including sealings between men and plural wives), see Parley P. Pratt, "This Number Closes the First Volume of the 'Prophet,'" *Prophet*, May 24, 1845, [2]; see also "A Special Conference of the Elders," *Deseret News*, Extra, Sept. 14, 1852, 14–22.

Snow later wrote, "At the time the sisters of the Relief Society signed our article, I was married to the prophet— we made no allusion to any other system of marriage than Bennett's— his was prostitution, and it was truly <u>his</u>, and he succeeded in pandering his course on the credulity of the unsuspecting by making them believe that he was thus authorized by the Prophet. In those articles there is no reference to divine plural marriage. We aimed to put down its opposite."[347]

——— ❧ ———

We the undersigned members of the ladies' relief society, and married females do certify and declare that we know of no system of marriage being practised in the church of Jesus Christ of Latter Day Saints save the one contained in the Book of Doctrine and Covenants,[348] and we give this certificate to the public to show that J. C. Bennett's "secret wife system" is a disclosure of his own make.

Emma Smith, President,
Elizabeth Ann Whitney, Counsellor,
Sarah M. Cleveland, Counsellor,
Eliza R. Snow, Secretary,

Mary C. Miller,
Lois Cutler,
Thirza Cahoon,
Ann Hunter,
Jane Law,
Sophia R. Marks,
Polly Z. Johnson,
Abigail Works.

Catharine Pettey [Petty],
Sarah Higbee,
Phebe Woodruff,
Leonora Taylor,
Sarah Hillman,
Rosannah Marks,
Angeline Robinson,

---

347. Eliza R. Snow to Joseph F. Smith, n.d., Joseph F. Smith, Papers, 1854–1918, CHL, underlining in original.

348. "Marriage," ca. Aug. 1835, in Doctrine and Covenants 101, 1835 ed., in *JSP*, R2:561.

1.7 Sarah M. Cleveland, Letter to the Nauvoo Female Relief Society, May 1, 1843

Sarah M. Cleveland, "To the Presidency, and Ladies of the Female Relief Society of Nauvoo," Times and Seasons *(Nauvoo, IL), May 1, 1843, vol. 4, no. 12, p. 187.*

After having served as first counselor in the Relief Society presidency during the organization's first year, fifty-four-year-old Sarah M. Kingsley Cleveland wrote the following letter to bid farewell to her "sisters and friends" in the society. Cleveland and her husband, John, a merchant who never joined the church, planned to leave Nauvoo to find work. As the oldest of the twenty charter members of the Relief Society, Cleveland was a devoted and charismatic participant. She suggested the name for the society, conducted meetings when Emma Smith was absent, often spoke to the group, gave healing blessings to other women, and spoke in tongues.[349]

Even before the establishment of the Relief Society, Cleveland was a friend to Emma Smith. When Smith and her children fled Missouri in 1839, the Clevelands housed them in Quincy, Illinois, for three months; Joseph Smith joined them for an additional three weeks following his escape from jail.[350] After Joseph and Emma Smith moved to Nauvoo, they encouraged the Clevelands to relocate there as well; the Smiths selected a lot across from their own home for them, "in the orchard according to the desire of Sister Cleveland and also one on the river, adapted to Mʳ Clevelands trade."[351] In June 1842 Sarah Cleveland was present at the marriage of Joseph Smith and Eliza R. Snow; at some point, she herself may have been sealed to Joseph Smith as a plural wife.[352] Sarah is not mentioned further in the Nauvoo Relief Society minutes.[353]

---

349. See Document 1.2. On Sarah Cleveland, see Todd Compton, *In Sacred Loneliness: The Plural Wives of Joseph Smith* (Salt Lake City: Signature Books, 2001), 271–287.

350. Emma Smith to Joseph Smith, Mar. 7, 1839, in Joseph Smith, "Copies of Letters, &c. &c.," 1839–1843, Joseph Smith Collection, 1827–1846, CHL, 37 (hereafter Joseph Smith Letterbook 2); Joseph Smith to Emma Smith, Mar. 21, 1839, Joseph Smith Collection, CHL; Joseph Smith, Journal, Apr. 16, 1839–May 10, 1839, in Dean C. Jessee et al., eds., *Journals, Volume 1: 1832–1839,* vol. 1 of the Journals series of *The Joseph Smith Papers,* ed. Dean C. Jessee et al. (Salt Lake City: Church Historian's Press, 2008), 336–338.

351. Joseph and Emma Smith to John and Sarah Cleveland, May 24, 1839, Joseph Smith Letterbook 2, p. 12.

352. Joseph F. Smith, Affidavits about Celestial Marriage, 1869–1915, CHL, Eliza R. Snow, Affidavit, Salt Lake Co., Utah Territory, June 7, 1869, 1:25. For Cleveland's possible sealing to Joseph Smith, see Church of Jesus Christ of Latter-day Saints, Nauvoo Temple, Nauvoo, Hancock Co., IL, Sealings and Adoptions of the Living, 1846–1857, vol. A, pp. 503–504, microfilm 183,374, U.S. and Canada Record Collection, FHL; and "Plural Marriage," in *The Historical Record, a Monthly Periodical, Devoted Exclusively to Historical, Biographical, Chronological and Statistical Matters* (Salt Lake City, 1882–1890), May 1887, 6:234.

353. The Clevelands returned to Nauvoo by 1845. John Lyman Smith married Augusta Cleveland, the daughter of Sarah and John Cleveland, in Nauvoo on July 9, 1845. (John L. Smith, Autobiography and Diaries, 1846–1895, CHL, July 9, 1845.)

Cleveland's undated letter to the Relief Society was published in the *Times and Seasons* on May 1, 1843, before the first Relief Society meetings of that year were held.

———— ?& ————

TO THE PRESIDENCY, AND LADIES OF THE FEMALE RELIEF SOCIETY OF NAUVOO.

Beloved sisters and friends—As I shall necessarily be absent from your pleasant society, for a season, my husband not having succeeded in business in Nauvoo as he anticipated, I could not take my leave without soliciting your kind wishes and prayers for the time being, that we find it necessary to locate ourselves elsewhere, until a more favorable door is opened, for our residence with the church.

I wish also to acknowledge my grateful sense, of the much kindness, and good feelings, which has been manifested toward me, during my visit amongst you; and in return you have my sincere prayers, that the best of heaven's blessings may rest upon you: and may the cause of *humanity, benevolence,* and *mercy,* flourish in your midst, under the benign auspices of an approving heaven, and the smiles of the Holy one of Israel. And may the heart of the widow, the fatherless, the poor, and the destitute, for whose benefit the society was organized, be made to rejoice through the means of your benevolent exertions. And feel assured, that while this is made the grand rallying point, for the active energies of your minds, no power, however desirous it may be to vilify, and call in question your good name, will be able to tarnish the lustre of your good deeds, or pluck from your standard, the laurels which will be woven by the hand of gratitude as a shining trophy to your name, to all eternity.

With respect and affection, I am yours in the bands of the gospel,

SARAH M. CLEVELAND.

1.8 Nauvoo Female Relief Society, Report, June 30, 1843

Nauvoo Female Relief Society, Report, June 30, 1843, in "Female Relief Society," Nauvoo Neighbor *(Nauvoo, IL), July 12, 1843, vol. 1, no. 11, p. 2.*

This first annual report of the Female Relief Society of Nauvoo, dated June 30, 1843, established the organization's pattern of systematic reporting on its donations, expenditures, and activities. Reform organizations of the time, including women's groups, often issued similar annual reports of their activities and finances.[354] At the organizational meeting on March 17, 1842, Eliza R. Snow was elected secretary and Elvira A. Cowles was elected treasurer. Joseph Smith gave "$5.00 in gold piece" at the inaugural meeting "to commence the funds of the Institution."[355] On March 24, in response to a question, Emma Smith suggested that in-kind contributions, "such as jewelry, clothing &c.," could be donated to the society and placed "into the hands of the Treasurer."[356]

The minutes of the Nauvoo Relief Society record many of the donations and expenditures in charitable causes during the organization's first year. In a June 16, 1843, meeting of the Relief Society, treasurer Elvira Cowles Holmes reported "she was not altogether prepared to give a full and correct statement of the Receipts and Expenditure of the Society but would make a statement so soon as she could see Mrs. Smith and adjust some unsettled accounts— suffice it to say about 500 dollars have been rec.d and nearly 400 expended during the first year of the Society— much good had been done and the hearts of many made to rejoice."[357] Two weeks later, Snow wrote this report of the Relief Society's first year of activities, including an account of donations received and expenditures, for the *Nauvoo Neighbor* and the *Times and Seasons*. The versions appear to be identical to one another, including in the typesetting; the *Neighbor* version was the first published and is therefore featured here.

———— ❧ ————

FEMALE RELIEF SOCIETY.

The first annual report of the Female Relief Society of Nauvoo; being a correct statement of the receipts and disbursements of the society, from its organization, March 16th [17th] 1842 to March 16th 1843, to wit.

Received in donations of money, clothing, prov[i]sions[358] &c. &c. $507,00
Expended in appropriations for the relief of the poor. $306,48
Leaving at the time aforesaid, a balance of $200.52

---

354. See, for instance, the "Annual Report of the American Female Moral Reform Society," *Advocate of Moral Reform* (New York City), June 1, 1841, 7:81–83.

355. Document 1.2, entry for Mar. 17, 1842.

356. Document 1.2, entry for Mar. 24, 1842.

357. Document 1.2, entry for June 16, 1843.

358. TEXT: In the copy used for transcription, there is a blank space between the *v* and the *s*.

as follows, to wit.

Cash	$, 29,00
Share in the Nauvoo House[359]	50,00
Note of hand by J. [James] Emmett	12[,]oo
[360]Orders	19,00
Cow, the use of which is appropriated to widow H.	14,00
Shingles	7,50
various articles of clothing, provision &c &c	77,02
	$200,52

An apology is due to the members of the Society for our delay in presenting this report. We would only say, it was unavoidable in consequence of circumstances beyond the control of the Treasurer, Mrs. E. A. Holmes, which rendered it impossible for her to make satisfactory returns at an earlier period.

We hope the Ladies of the Society will feel encouraged to renew their exertions, knowing that the blessings of the poor are resting upon them: We feel assured from what has passed under our personal observation, that many during the inclemency of the winter, were not only relieved, but preserved from famishing, through their instrumentality. More has been accomplished than our most sanguine anticipations predicted, and through the assistance and blessing of God, what may we not hope for the future?

By Order of the President.[361]

ELIZA R. SNOW, Secretary.

Nauvoo June 30th 1843.

---

359. In January 1841 Joseph Smith dictated a revelation that commanded the building of a home for himself and his family, which would also serve as a "house for boarding, a house that strangers may come from afar to lodge therein; therefore let it be a good house, worthy of all acceptation, that the weary traveler may find health and safety while he shall contemplate the word of the Lord." The revelation named the building as the Nauvoo House and specified that funds should be raised for its construction by selling shares for fifty dollars. In August 1842 Hyrum Smith encouraged the purchase of stock, as "it is important that the Nauvoo House should be finished that we may have a suitable house wherein to entertain the great ones of the earth and teach them the truth." (Doctrine and Covenants 124:23, 60, 64–66; Joseph Smith, Journal, Aug. 29, 1842, in Andrew H. Hedges et al., eds., *Journals, Volume 2: December 1841–April 1843,* vol. 2 of the Journals series of *The Joseph Smith Papers,* ed. Dean C. Jessee et al. [Salt Lake City: Church Historian's Press, 2011], 121.)

360. TEXT: In the copy used for transcription, this line and the next line are obscured by a fold in the page. Obscured text supplied from "Female Relief Society," *Times and Seasons,* Aug. 1, 1843, 4:287, which appears to share identical typesetting with the *Nauvoo Neighbor* version.

361. Emma Smith.

1.9 Susan Cuthbertson, Application to Nauvoo Female Relief Society, circa September 1843

Susan Cuthbertson, Application, [ca. Sept.] 1843; one page; Beinecke Rare Book and Manuscript Library, Yale University, New Haven, CT (WA MSS S-1644 F349).

At the third meeting of the Female Relief Society of Nauvoo, on March 31, 1842, Joseph Smith expressed concern that the society was growing "too fast" and advised "that none should be received into the Society but those who were worthy— propos'd that the Society go into a close examination of every candidate."[362] On June 9, 1842, he suggested a formal process for application: "henceforth no person shall be admitted but by presenting regular petition signed by two or three members in good standing in the Society— whoever comes in must be of good report."[363] As Eliza R. Snow later explained, "The Society soon became so popular that even those of doubtful character in several instances applied for admission, and to prevent imposition by extending membership to such ones inadvertently, stricter rules were adopted than seemed requisite at first. Each one wishing to join the Society was required to present a certificate of her good moral character, signed by two or more responsible persons."[364]

Following this pattern, Susan McGee Cuthbertson (or Cuthbert) applied for admission to the Relief Society circa September 1843 and was accepted as a new member on October 14, 1843.[365] A native of Ireland, she emigrated to the United States likely between 1841 and early 1843 and then married Edward Cuthbertson (or Cuthbert) on July 21, 1843, in Nauvoo.[366] Cuthbertson's application was signed by Rebecca Reed and her daughter Lydia R. Reed. The application was apparently retained for some time by Phebe M. Bartholomew Wheeler, the assistant secretary of the Relief Society.[367]

---

362. Document 1.2, entry for Mar. 31, 1842.

363. Document 1.2, entry for June 9, 1842.

364. Eliza R. Snow, "The Female Relief Society," *Woman's Exponent,* June 15, 1872, 1:10. In addition, Snow stated, a "commission was appointed to go and inquire into the character of all applicants" who desired to live righteously and prepare themselves to become "holy women." (Gunnison Ward, Gunnison Stake, Relief Society Minutes and Records, 1872–1949, Sept. 30, 1872, vol. 1, p. 27.)

365. Document 1.2, entry for Oct. 14, 1843.

366. She was living with her parents and three women in Lanarkshire, Ireland, in 1841. (1841 Scotland Census, Lanarkshire, Barony Middle Carlton, 14, p. 9.)

367. Wheeler's second husband, Oliver Olney (whom she married in October 1843), evidently later made various inscriptions on the same sheet on which Cuthbertson had written her application.

Navoo the 21 [*illegible*] 1843
Ladies
I Susan Cuthbertson Desires to Join the friendly famel [female] Society in Navoo if it meets your minds

Misses Rabaca Reed
Miss Lady [Lydia] R Reed[368]

---

368. TEXT: The second signature appears to be in the same handwriting as the first signature.

1.10 William W. Phelps with Emma Smith Revisions, "The Voice of Innocence from Nauvoo," February–March 1844

William W. Phelps, "The Voice of Innocence from Nauvoo," [ca. Feb. 1844]; copy featured below made [Mar. 1844] by Thomas Bullock, with revisions thereafter made by Emma Smith, [Mar. 1844]; three pages; CHL (MS 15540).

Joseph Smith and the small group of his trusted associates who had privately entered into plural marriages considered their relationships to be holy matrimony, sealed or confirmed by divine authority and approval. Joseph Smith's 1843 revelation regarding plural marriage specified that he was the sole possessor of the authority for the performance of such marriages.[369] However, as knowledge of the practice of plural marriage spread, it prompted counterfeit practices and abuse, such as John C. Bennett's notion of "spiritual wifery."[370] Publicly addressing these dangers posed a significant challenge for Relief Society leaders in Nauvoo.

From the Relief Society's first meeting, President Emma Smith emphasized the group's responsibility "to watch over the morals— and be very careful of the character and reputation— of the members of the Institution."[371] As the practice of plural marriage slowly expanded, the Relief Society was drawn into disputes involving the gap between public pronouncements against "spiritual wifery" and the private practice of authorized plural marriage. In 1842 nineteen Relief Society members published a statement refuting Bennett's claims that the church promoted a "secret wife system."[372] Over the next two years, more rumors of polygamy and "spiritual wifery" buzzed through Nauvoo and the surrounding area.

On February 26, 1844, a man named Orsamus F. Bostwick was brought before the mayor's court in Nauvoo and fined for slander. Bostwick had claimed that Hyrum Smith had spiritual wives and that many women in Nauvoo were involved with "spiritual wifery," promiscuity, and prostitution.[373] Two days later, William W. Phelps, a printer who sometimes

---

369. Revelation, July 12, 1843, Kingsbury copy, in Revelations Collection, CHL (Doctrine and Covenants 132).

370. See Document 1.5; see also Andrew H. Hedges et al., eds., *Journals, Volume 2: December 1841– April 1843,* vol. 2 of the Journals series of *The Joseph Smith Papers,* ed. Dean C. Jessee et al. (Salt Lake City: Church Historian's Press, 2011), xxviii n64.

371. Document 1.2, entry for Mar. 17, 1842.

372. Document 1.6.

373. John Scott, Testimony, Nauvoo, IL, Feb. 26, 1844, Nauvoo, IL, Records, 1841–1845, CHL. An entry in Joseph Smith's journal reads: "P.M. held Court at the Mansion. City of Nauvoo. vs. O[rsamus] F. Bostwick. on complaint of Hyrum Smith for slanderous Language conering [concerning] Hyrum and certain f[e]males— of Nauvoo fined Bostwick— $50.00 & costs." Bostwick's attorney, Francis M. Higbee, threatened to appeal the case to the municipal court and then the county circuit court in Carthage, an act that Joseph Smith feared would only "stir up the mob— & bring them upon us." An affidavit of Luman H. Calkins dated June 22, 1844, noted that Calkins had met William Nesbit on a steamboat traveling from St. Louis to Nauvoo and learned that Nesbit had outlined a "conspiracy in Nauvoo to kill Joseph, and Hyrum, and all that believed on them" and that he "had made arrangements

acted as Joseph Smith's clerk and ghostwriter—and who also served as city clerk and assisted in keeping the church history—was "writing on O[rsamus] F Bostwick for women."[374] Whether "for women" means *at the request of women* or *on behalf of women* is not clear. Phelps's document, titled "The Voice of Innocence from Nauvoo," was then copied by Thomas Bullock, a clerk for Joseph Smith. "Voice of Innocence" gave Relief Society women a means for responding to insulting rumors and the allegations of Bostwick and others.

On March 7, in a public meeting at the Nauvoo temple before an audience of about eight thousand church members, Joseph Smith denounced Bostwick and asked the large assembly "to speak out. say whether such men should be. tolerated. and supported in our midst." At this meeting, Phelps read aloud the "Voice of Innocence," to which the assembly responded by saying "Amen" twice. During an afternoon continuation of that meeting, "notice was given for th[e] relief society to meet" the following Saturday to adopt the statement written by Phelps.[375]

At some point Emma Smith made some alterations to Bullock's copy of the "Voice of Innocence"; that edited copy is used below as the featured text. On March 9, 1844, Smith read her slightly amended version at the first meeting of the Relief Society held that year. She spoke on the Bostwick controversy, and the assembled members of the Relief Society unanimously voted that they were "willing to receeve the princples of vurtue, keep the commandments of God, and uphold the Pres[ss] in puting down iniquity." Smith further expressed that her "determination was to do her Duty Effectully— in puting down transgresion."[376]

Since the meeting room could not accommodate all the members of the Relief Society who wished to attend, Emma Smith presided over three more meetings—one on the afternoon of March 9 and two on March 16—that all approved the "Voice of Innocence." On March 16 Smith denounced "J. C. Bennets [John C. Bennett's] Spiritual Wife system" and exhorted Relief Society members to "cleanse thier hearts and Ears" and "throw the Mantle of Charity round to shield those who will <u>repent</u> and <u>do</u> so <u>no more</u>." She called for a "reformation in boath men & woman." By this point, Emma Smith opposed plural marriage as practiced by her husband and others in Nauvoo.[377] She thus encouraged Relief Society members to follow the published statements of Joseph Smith and the church, as well as her

---

with M[r.] Bostwick of S[t.] Louis— to send him a brace of the best pistols for the purpose of being ready when he wanted them" for the murder of Joseph and Hyrum Smith. (Joseph Smith, Journal, Feb. 26, 1844, in Andrew H. Hedges et al., eds., *Journals, Volume 3: May 1843–June 1844,* vol. 3 of the Journals series of *The Joseph Smith Papers,* ed. Ronald K. Esplin and Matthew J. Grow [Salt Lake City: Church Historian's Press, 2015], 183–184 [hereafter *JSP,* J3]; Jill Mulvay Derr et al., *Women of Covenant: The Story of Relief Society* [Salt Lake City: Deseret Book; Provo, UT: Brigham Young University Press, 1992], 61; Luman H. Calkins, Affidavit, June 22, 1844, Joseph Smith Office Papers, 1835–1844, CHL.)

374. Joseph Smith, Journal, Feb. 28, 1844, in *JSP,* J3:184; for more on Phelps as a writer and clerk, see Samuel Brown, "The Translator and the Ghostwriter: Joseph Smith and W. W. Phelps," *Journal of Mormon History* 34, no. 1 (Winter 2008): 26–62.

375. Joseph Smith, Journal, Mar. 7, 1844, in *JSP,* J3:191, 194, 198; Joseph Smith, Discourse, Nauvoo, IL, Mar. 7, 1844, Joseph Smith Collection, 1827–1846, CHL.

376. Document 1.2, entry for Mar. 9, 1844.

377. Volume Introduction to Nauvoo Journals, 1 May 1843–22 June 1844, in *JSP,* J3:xix; see also Document 4.5.

husband's teachings "from the Stand," implying that they should abide by his public remarks against spiritual wifery rather than any private teachings regarding plural marriage.[378]

The version of "Voice of Innocence" amended by Emma Smith and read to the Relief Society was then published in the *Nauvoo Neighbor* on March 20, 1844, above the names of Emma Smith and Hannah M. Ells (secretary pro tem of the Relief Society). The article included a brief introduction that explained, "At *four* overflowing meetings of the Ladies of Nauvoo, Members of the Female Relief Society, (each meeting being composed of different members that all might have the opportunity of expressing their feelings) held at Gen Smith's large assembly room on Saturdays the 9th and 16th of March 1844. The following preamble and resolutions were read and *unanimously adopted* at each meeting."[379]

Publication of "The Voice of Innocence" possibly fanned the flames of the swelling firestorm over plural marriage in Nauvoo. Joseph Smith continued to be the subject of accusations from critics within and outside the church, some threatening legal action against him. On May 26, 1844, he addressed the Saints in a long sermon describing the hypocrisy of his traducers and noted that he "never had any fuss with these men until that Female Relief Society brought out the paper against adulterers and adulteresses."[380]

The Voice of Innocence
From Nauvoo.

The corruption of wickedness which manifested itself in such horrible deformity on the trial of Orsemus F. Bostwick last week, for slandering President Hyrum Smith and the Widows of the City of Nauvoo, has awakened all the kindly feelings of female benevolence, compassion and pity, for the softer sex to spread forth the mantle of charity to shield the characters of the virtuous mothers, wives and daughters of Nauvoo, from the <u>blasting breath</u> and <u>poisonous touch</u> of debauchees, vagabonds, and rakes, who have jammed themselves into our city to offer <u>strange fire</u> at the shrines of infamy, disgrace and degradation; as they and their kindred spirits have done in all the great cities throughout the world: corrupting their way: on the earth, and bringing woman, poor defenceless woman, to wretchedness and ruin.

As such ignoble blood now begins to stain the peaceable habitations of the Saints, and taint the pure air of the only City in the world that pretends, to work righteousness in Union, as the <u>sine</u> <u>qua</u> <u>non</u>, for happiness, glory and salvation: and, as such ungodly wretches, burning or smarting with the sting of their own shame, have doubtless, transported with them; some of the miserable dupes of their licentiousness, for the purpose of defiling the fame of this goodly city: mildewing the honesty of our mothers: blasting the chastity of widows

378. Document 1.2, entries for Mar. 9 and 16, 1844, underlining in original.

379. "Virtue Will Triumph," *Nauvoo Neighbor*, Mar. 20, 1844, [2], italics in original.

380. Joseph Smith, Discourse, Nauvoo, IL, May 26, 1844, Joseph Smith Collection, CHL.

and wives, and corrupting the virtue of our unsuspecting daughters, it becomes US in defence of our rights, for the glory of our ~~mothers~~[381] fathers; for the honor of our Mothers; for the happiness of our husbands; and for the well fare of our dear children, to rebuke such an outrage upon the sanctity of Society; to thwart such a death blow at the hallowed marriage covenant: and to ward off such poisoned daggers from the hearts of our innocent daughters, ~~for blast them of~~ ⟨for the honor of⟩ Nauvoo; and write ~~in~~ ⟨with⟩ indellible Ink, upon every such villain: <u>Vitare perditoris!</u>[382] Beware of the Wretch! and, so put in every virtuous woman's hand a rod, to scourge such tormentors of domestic felicity, with vengeance through~~out~~ the world: Curse the man that preys upon female virtue! Curse the man that slanders a woman: Let the righteous indignation of insulted innocence, and virtue spurn him from society; Let the dignity of the Mother's of Israel kick the blood thirsty pimp from the pale of social communion. Let the widows and wives who tread in the foot steps of their queenly mother Eve, drive such fag ends of creation, as was Cain, to the Land of Nod,[383] and let the timid daughters of Nauvoo, dread such [p. [1]] <u>Canker worms</u>[384] more than the pestilence that walketh in darkness, and ~~spurn~~ ⟨shun⟩ them as the serpent on the land and the shark in the Sea. My God! My God! is there not female virtue and valor enough in this City to let such mean men die of the rot:— that the Sexton may carry their putrid bodies beyond the limits of the City for food, for Vultures and Eagles? Refuse them female courtesy: deny them the pleasure of family correspondence and family intercourse: curse the Woman that speaks to such rotten flesh ⟨if she knows who they are⟩: Curse the man that will harbor them; and Curse the Lawyer that will stoop from the dignity of his profession, to plead for them: <u>The Apologer is as mean as the Murderer!</u>

Female virtue is a pearl of great price,[385] and should glitter in the abodes of men; as in the Mansions of bliss for the glory and honor of him, whose image she bears and whose help meet she is, and every attempt of man to seduce that virtue, is, next to murder, a robbery that cannot be restored. If woman swerves from the rules of righteousness:

"Ruin ensues, reproach and shame;
And one false step bedims her fame.

---

381. TEXT: Deletion by Thomas Bullock. Except for this deletion and two additional emendations noted below, all emendations in this document appear to have been made by Emma Smith.
382. Latin for "avoid the destroyer." Phelps often used phrases from Latin and other languages in his writing. (See Brown, "The Translator and the Ghostwriter," 50.)
383. See Genesis 4:16; and Moses 5:41.
384. TEXT: Double underline in original.
385. See Matthew 13:45–46.

In vain the loss she may deplore
In vain review her life before;"
With tears she must in anguish be
Till God says, "Set that captive free".[386]

Many of the distinguished females of Nauvoo, have waded to their present habitations through persecution, sorrow, and death, robbed and ~~ravished~~ ⟨insulted⟩, and bereaved of husbands and children by the combined powers, of priests and spiritual wickedness in high places,[387] but none of these piercing calamities of man touch the heart of woman with such severe poignancy, as the envenomed Slander of O. F. Bostwick. that "he could take a half bushel of meal ⟨obtain his vile purposes⟩ and get what accommodation he wanted[388] with almost any woman in the City"[389]

Wo to the Wretch that can thus follow the blood stained Mobbers of Missouri, in their hellish career, and ~~dreul~~ ⟨deal⟩ his slander about the streets of Nauvoo, as he may imagine with impunity! Wo to the Man, or Lawyer, that filthifies himself by (~~licking that dreul as he attempts to~~) advocate⟨ing⟩ such ⟨the⟩ a rotten hearted raven's rights, ⟨or recommend him to the Sympathies of any being but Satan⟩[390] to the sympathies of any being but Satan! [p. [2]]

Has any man a Mother in this City? honor says, clear such rubbish from her door:

Has any man a Wife? benevolence whispers trap such beasts of the field that they may not wrong the flock, nor kill the lambs. Has any Man a Widowed Mother? humanity seems to caution him—thy Mother is in danger, protect her, from the Stench of such Carrion! Has any Man, Daughters? the voice of reason compels him to exclaim: There is a Wolf in the path, Beware! Has any Man, Sisters? the blood of his kindred says, evil be to him that evil thinks:[391] and Let the whole virtuous female population of the City, with one

---

386. The first four lines of this poem are an excerpt from a long passage spoken by Jane Shore, the title character in Nicholas Rowe's *The Tragedy of Jane Shore*, a play written in the style of Shakespeare and produced in London in 1714. (Nicholas Rowe, *The Tragedy of Jane Shore* [London: Bernard Lintot, 1736], 12; Brett Wilson, "Jane Shore and the Jacobites: Nicholas Rowe, the Pretender, and the National She-Tragedy," *ELH* 72 [Winter 2005]: 827.)

387. See Ephesians 6:12.

388. TEXT: "accommodation he wanted" double underlined in original.

389. John Scott testified in the Nauvoo mayor's court on February 26, 1844, that Bostwick had told him "he could take half a bushel of meal, and get what accommodation he wantd with almost any woman in the city." (John Scott, Testimony, Nauvoo, IL, Feb. 26, 1844, Nauvoo, IL, Records, 1841–1845, CHL.)

390. TEXT: When Emma Smith made the preceding insertion, she apparently intended that it would replace the following phrase ("to the sympathies of any being but Satan!").

391. The phrase "evil to him who evil thinks" is translated from the medieval French phrase used as the motto of the Order of the Garter, begun in the fourteenth century by King Edward III of England.

voice, declare that the Seducer of female Chastity, the Slanderer of Female Character, or the Defamer of the Character of the Heads of the Church or the canker worms of our husband's ~~heaven,~~ ⟨peace;⟩[392] the prostitute, or their pimps, whether in the character, of elites lawyer, doctor, or c̲i̲s̲i̲s̲b̲e̲o̲,[393] shall have no place in our houses, in our affections, or in our Society.

Wherefore,

Resolved unanimously that Joseph Smith, the Mayor of the City, be tendered our thanks for the able and manly manner in which he defended injured innocence in the late trial of O.F. Bostwick for slandering president Hyrum Smith "and almost all the women of the City."

Resolved unanimously that we view with unqualified disapprobation and scorn the conduct of any man or woman, whether in word or deed, that reflects dishonor, upon the poor persecuted mothers, widows, wives and daughters of the Saints of Nauvoo: they have borne aspersions, slanders and hardships enough: forbearance has ceased to be a virtue, and retaliation, like the "dagger or the bowl"[394] ought to close the lips of such cowardly ~~aspersions~~ ⟨assassins⟩—[395]

Resolved unanimously that while we render credence to the doctrines of Paul, that n̲e̲i̲t̲h̲e̲r̲ ̲t̲h̲e̲ ̲m̲a̲n̲ ̲i̲s̲ ̲w̲i̲t̲h̲o̲u̲t̲ ̲t̲h̲e̲[396] woman; n̲e̲i̲t̲h̲e̲r̲ ̲i̲s̲ ̲w̲o̲m̲a̲n̲ w̲i̲t̲h̲o̲u̲t̲ t̲h̲e̲ ̲m̲a̲n̲ i̲n̲ ̲t̲h̲e̲ ̲L̲o̲r̲d̲,[397] yet we raise our voices and hands against John C. Bennett's "Spiritual Wife System," as a scheme of profligates to seduce women; and they that harp upon it, wish to make it popular for the convenience of their own cupidity: wherefore, while the marriage bed, undefiled is honorable, let polygamy, bigamy, fornication, adultery, and prostitution, be frowned out of the hearts of honest men to drop in the gulf of fallen nature, ⟨"⟩where the worm dieth not, and the fire is not quenched!⟨"⟩[398] and ⟨let⟩ all the Saints say

Amen! [p. [3]]

(George Frederick Beltz, *Memorials of the Most Noble Order of the Garter, from Its Foundation to the Present Time* [London: William Pickering, 1841], xcviii.)

392. TEXT: Emendation by Thomas Bullock.

393. This Italian word should be spelled "cicisbeo." The term was used to refer to a recognized "gallant" (lover or suitor) of a married woman. ("Cicisbeo," in *The Oxford English Dictionary*, ed. James A. H. Murray et al., 12 vols., 1933, reprint [Oxford: Oxford University Press, 1970], 2:414.)

394. This expression is a reference to violent death, either homicidal or suicidal, and implied a certain inevitability to the act. (See, for example, Lord Byron to Thomas Moore, Sept. 19, 1818, in Thomas Moore, *Letters and Journals of Lord Byron: With Notices of His Life*, 2 vols. [London: John Murray, 1830], 2:199.)

395. TEXT: Emendation probably by Thomas Bullock.

396. TEXT: "the" double underlined in original.

397. See 1 Corinthians 11:11.

398. See Mark 9:44–48.

1.11 Ellen Briggs Douglas, Letter to Family Members, April 14, 1844

Ellen Briggs Douglas, Letter to "Fathers and Mothers and Sisters and Brothers," Apr. 14, 1844; typescript; five pages; Ellen W. Parker, Letters, 1842–1851, CHL (MS 5539 8).

The first Latter-day Saint missionaries to the British Isles arrived in Liverpool in 1837. The following year, Heber C. Kimball, an apostle, baptized George and Ellen Briggs Douglas in Lancashire. As the number of church members in England rose in the early 1840s—a result of a more concerted missionary effort led by several apostles—leaders encouraged converts to emigrate to Nauvoo.[399] Along with their three sons and four daughters, George and Ellen Douglas emigrated, arriving in Nauvoo in early 1842. Living conditions were difficult for the Douglases and many other English immigrants, as Ellen explained in a letter to her parents: "We rented a house at 5 shilings a month. . . . Our house is not such a fine one, but there are many that are much worse, and I prayed that we might have one to ourselves for there is 3 or 4 families in one room, and many have to pitch their tents in the woods, or any where where they can."[400]

Ellen Douglas soon became involved with the Female Relief Society in Nauvoo. "There is now in this city a female Charity Society, of which I am a member," Douglas wrote to her parents in June 1842. "We are in number 8 or 9 hundred. Jo Smith's wife is the head of our society and we meet on a Thursday at 1 o'clock, where we receive instructions both temporary [temporally] and spiritually."[401] In July 1842 George Douglas died, leaving Ellen a widow with eight children. Several months after George's death, Ellen expressed the view that "we can get our living without troubling anyone if we have our health and we have enjoyed good health as ever we did in England."[402]

By 1844, however, Ellen Douglas's circumstances had changed in Nauvoo's unhealthy environment. A daughter later stated that following George's death, her mother suffered both from poverty and "the fever and ague."[403] Unable to work during an extended illness, Douglas applied to the Relief Society for assistance and received a generous supply of clothing for herself and her children. In the following April 14, 1844, letter to family members in England, Douglas recounted her illness, described her joy at living among the Saints, and shared news about her children and many other English immigrants in Nauvoo from the same region of Downham, Lancashire, England. As originals of the letter are not known to be extant, the following transcript is reproduced from a typescript made circa 1939 by James H. Douglas, a grandson of Ellen Briggs Douglas.[404]

---

399. On the beginnings of the church in England, see James B. Allen et al., *Men with a Mission, 1837–1841: The Quorum of the Twelve Apostles in the British Isles* (Salt Lake City: Deseret Book, 1992).

400. George and Ellen Douglas to Father and Mother, June 2, 1842, typescript, CHL.

401. George and Ellen Douglas to Father and Mother, June 2, 1842, typescript, CHL.

402. Ellen Douglas to Family, Feb. 1, 1843, typescript, Ellen W. Parker, Letters, 1842–1851, CHL.

403. Alice Parker Isom, "Memoirs of Alice Parker Isom," ca. 1885, CHL, 2. Ague was the colloquial term for malaria.

404. James Douglas transcribed six letters between Ellen Douglas and her family in England, which

Nauvoo,
April, 14, 1844.

Dear Fathers and Mothers and Sisters and Brothers:—[405]

I know [now] take up my pen to write a few lines to you to let you know that we received your kind letter dated No. 19th, on the 9th day of March. How it came here we know not. We are all in good state of health and spirits at present, for which I feel thankful. We have had some sickness in our family since we wrote last, Ralph[406] and his uncle[407] went up the River about 10 miles to work on a brick yard. They hired each for one month. They came home every week and Ralph when he had done his time came home in good health, but the next day was taken very ill. This was about the middle of August. He was very ill the first 9 days, not able to git up while I made the bed. After that he began to have the ague and fever, which is ⟨a⟩ very common complaint in this land. He was about 10 weeks before he could work much, and before he got well I was taken very ill with the same complaint, but a great deal worse. I was four or five weeks very ill; indeed not able to do any thing. Ralph got me some medicine to throw it off and I begun to get a little better, so I thought I would try to wash a few clothese, and it just brought me down again. I was just 13 weeks and never washed but that one time. Sometimes I thought I should die and then I thought of my poor children. I prayed for their sakes that I might live. I didn't pray alone, but a many of the brothers and sisters prayed likewise and our prayers were answered, and I now am living in good state of health at present, for which I feel to praise my Heavenly Father.

Richard has been very healthy ever since we came to this land and he looks as well as ever you saw him.[408] Ann and all the rest of the children but Isabelle have had very good health.[409] Isabelle has been ill two or three times two or three weeks at a time. She looks about the same she did when we left you. After I begun [p. [1]] to get well I went down into the city on a visit to where

---

he stated were "written from Nauvoo and Saint Louis between the years of 1842 and 1852." James, who received the letters from his father, Richard Douglas, wrote in February 1939, "The letters to me are price-less and I am taking this means of preserving them in bookform [that is, transcribing them] and I hope my posterity and future family generations may read them with the same interest and pleasure that I have read them." (James H. Douglas, Feb. 2, 1939, Ellen W. Parker, Letters, 1842–1851, CHL.)

405. Douglas wrote this letter to her mother, Isabella Briggs, and her stepfather, Robert Douglas, who married in 1821. Ellen Douglas and her mother had married brothers, George and Robert Douglas. (William Bennett Price, ed., *The Register of the Parish Church of St. Leonard, Downham, 1605–1837* [Leyland, England: Lancashire Parish Register Society, 1979], 80, 88, 156, 158.)

406. Douglas's son Ralph Briggs Douglas.

407. Probably James Douglas.

408. Douglas's son Richard Douglas.

409. Douglas's daughters Ann Douglas and Isabella Douglas.

Ann lived, and I stayed two nights and I had a horse to ride home on. The woman where Ann lived would have me make application to the female Relief Society for some clothing which I needed for myself and family. I refused to do so, but she said I needed something and that I had been so long sick and if I would not do it myself she would do it for me. I agreed and we went to one of the sisters and she asked me what I needed most. I told her that I needed a many things. While I was sick my children were out their clothes because I could not men[d] them, so she said she would do the best she could for me. Ann came over in a few days and they brought the wagon and fetched me such a present as I never received before from no place in the world. I suppose the things they sent were worth as much as 30 shillings.

I wrote before and told you that I expected that I should have a house of my own before now by the assistance of the Church, but I have not got one yet. We was sick so long. Ralph and James[410] got a cow up the River and we have kept her all winter without giving any milk, but we expect her to have a calf every day. She has had one calf and is but three years old. She cost 9 dollars in work. She is a very pretty cow. We live where we did when we first came here and expect to do till we get a place of our own. We raised about 35 chickens. We keep them for our own use. How long do you think we might have stayed in England before we could have had a cow?

Ralph and James is detching [ditching] on the prarie and Richard is sawing in a saw pit close by where we live. I have told you before that money was scarce. We can buy good strong cotton here now at 5 pence and 6 pence per yard, a yard wide, good print at 6 pence, thread and pots are the dearest of anything here. [p. 2]

You also want us to give you some account of Margaret Wilkinson. I expect you have heard of her death before now.[411] She lived at a place called Happanooce.[412] She had a very good place. She was sick about 10 days and died. James was with her when she died. It was at the time that Ralph and James was working up the River, and he came down to let us know that she was dead, and James Spencer and me went and brought her down to Nauvoo and had her buried close by my husband. They was very nice to her and thought a great deal of her. They said she was a good girl. She came to Nauvoo on the 4th day of July on a visit and stopped one week. She was one

---

410. Probably James Douglas, the uncle to Douglas's children mentioned earlier in the letter.

411. Wilkinson was buried at Nauvoo, August 14, 1843. (William D. Huntington, *Cemetery Records, 1839–1845*, CHL, [7].)

412. This is likely a reference to Appanoose, an area in southern Iowa. (L. L. Taylor, ed., *Past and Present of Appanoose County, Iowa: A Record of Settlement, Organization, Progress and Achievement*, 2 vols. [Chicago: S. J. Clarke Publishing, 1913], 1:87.)

night at my house and we went the next day to Old John Parker's[413] and Nancy Smithe's[414] and Jane Hall was there also. We had a very happy day all together and did not think it was the last time we should meet on earth, but you see that in the midst of life we are in death.[415] She died firm in the faith that she professed. There is a letter at James Smitheses that she wrote herself and wished them to send a long with one of their own, but they have never had the opportunity, but they will send it and then her friends will know how she enjoyed herself.

You also wanted to know something about James Spencer. He is well and he is got married about two months since, and I was very glad of it because he is old and needed a home so that he could be comfortable in his old age, and I think he has acted wisely in choosing a companion, I mean near his age. She had a house and a cow and 2 horses and 2 mules, and she was a widow.[416] Her husband died about the time that Isabelle died. She is a American, no children.

Dear parents, there are many things which I could like to mention which would do you good, but I have not room. Ralph wants William[417] to come to Nauvoo and I say that he would do better here than in England. We should be glad to see any of you. I never in my life [p. 3] enjoyed myself better than I do now. We had a Conference here which begun on the 6th day of April and lasted four or 5 days. I attended it 4 days and it is supposed that there was from 15 to 20 thousand present, and the teaching which we heard made our hearts rejoice.[418] I for one feel to rejoice and to praise my God that he ever sent the Elders of Israel to England and that he ever gave me a heart to believe them. I

---

413. This is likely John Parker Sr., an English immigrant who arrived in 1840; in March 1846 Douglas married his son John Parker Jr. In an earlier letter to her parents, Douglas wrote, "Old John and Ellen Parker are both in good health and spirits." (George and Ellen Douglas to Father and Mother, June 2, 1842, typescript, CHL.)

414. This is likely a reference to Nancy Ann Knowles Smithies, the wife of James Smithies. In an earlier letter to her parents, Douglas had stated, "James Smithes and his family are all in good health." (George and Ellen Douglas to Father and Mother, June 2, 1842, typescript, CHL.)

415. This phrase was included, among other places, as part of the burial ceremony in the Church of England's *Book of Common Prayer*. (*The Book of Common Prayer, and Administration of the Sacraments, and Other Rites and Ceremonies of the Church* [Oxford: Clarendon, 1825], 182.)

416. Spencer married Mary Mitchell on February 12, 1844, in Nauvoo. (Nauvoo, IL, Recorder, Marriage Record, Feb. 1842–Dec. 1845, CHL, 21.)

417. Likely a reference to William Douglas, the son of Robert and Isabella Douglas. William was both cousin and uncle to Ralph.

418. The church held a general conference on April 6–8, 1844. On the afternoon of April 7, Joseph Smith delivered what became known as the King Follett discourse. For accounts of this sermon, see the respective reports of Willard Richards, Wilford Woodruff, Thomas Bullock, and William Clayton at josephsmithpapers.org. (See Historian's Office, General Church Minutes, 1839–1877, CHL, Apr. 6–7, 1844; "Conference Minutes," *Times and Seasons,* May 1, 1844, 5:522–524.)

want to know whether you believe my testimony or not concerning the Prophet of the Most High God, because the day will come when you will know that I have told you the truth.[419]

I want you to send us some berry trees and a few choice plum stones. You may put them in a firkin and send them the first opportunity. I will pay anyone for the trouble of them. I should also be glad of a ball of twist. You may send them with Cottoms at Wadinton[420] if they come. I hope you will forgive all my mistakes.

I remain, Your affectionate daughter,
Ellen Douglas.

James Hawworth landed here on the 5th d day of April and is at Cottoms.[421] He brought Jo Boothman[422] a letter and I read it and I found that William's child was dead. My very best respects to you all, fathers, mothers, sisters and brothers, uncles and aunts and cousins and to Ann Wiglesworth, and tell her I still mean to fulfill my promise if ever it lies in my power, and my very best respects to all the Saints and to all enquiring friends.

Ellen Douglas [p. 4]

Dear Mother, my girls wishes you to send them a lock of your hair and they want some of you to send them every one of them a doll. There is no dolls to sell here. There is almost anything here now. There is 1 or 2 hundred shops in this city now and when we came here there was not more than 2 or 3. William Tomson said he would buy Vilate Ellen[423] another when she had done her other, so now is the time. George[424] wants his grandfather to come. While I have been writing he has asked me more than a half dozen times if I had sent

---

419. In an earlier letter to her parents, Douglas wrote, "I must say something about the Prophet the Lord has raised up in those last day. I feel to rejoice that I have been permitted to hear his voice for I know that this is the work of the Lord and all the powers of earth or hell can not gainsay it. The time is not far hence when all will know that this is the work of the Lord and not of men." (See George and Ellen Douglas to Father and Mother, June 2, 1842, typescript, CHL.)

420. In an earlier letter to her family, Douglas stated that Thomas and Ann Cottam, as well as several other immigrants from "Waddington," were "well." (Ellen Douglas to Family, Feb. 1, 1843, typescript, Ellen W. Parker, Letters, 1842–1851, CHL.)

421. This may be a reference to the Thomas Cottam family mentioned in the preceding footnote.

422. In a later letter, Douglas wrote that Joseph Boothman was living near her family in St. Louis and that he had recently married Mary Smith. (Ellen Parker to Mother, July 30, 1851, typescript, Ellen W. Parker, Letters, 1842–1851, CHL.)

423. Douglas's daughter Vilate Ellen Douglas.

424. Douglas's son George Douglas.

for him. My children will join in sending their kind love to you all. V. Ellen wants uncle Robert.[425]

> I remain, yours affectionately,
> Ellen Douglas. [p. 5]

---

425. Robert Douglas, Ellen Douglas's stepfather and the brother of Ellen Douglas's deceased husband, George Douglas.

1.12 Boston Female Penny and Sewing Society, Minutes, January 28, 1845

Boston Female Penny and Sewing Society, Minutes, Jan. 28, 1845, in "Boston Female Penny and Sewing Society," Prophet *(New York, NY), Feb. 8, 1845, vol. 1, no. 38, p. [2].*

In 1843 women in Nauvoo, led by sisters Mercy Fielding Thompson and Mary Fielding Smith, organized a fund-raising effort for the construction of the Nauvoo temple. In her autobiography, Mercy recalled that while pondering how she could contribute to the temple, she received spiritual inspiration: "Try to get the Sisters to subscribe one cent per week for the purpose of buying glass and nails for the Temple." Joseph Smith endorsed the plan and Hyrum Smith, a member of the temple building committee and husband of Mary Fielding Smith, "was much plea[s]ed and did all in his power to encourage and help by speaking to the Sisters on the subject in private and public promising them that they should receive their blessings in that Temple."[426] While the penny subscription effort was not an official project of the Relief Society in Nauvoo, it primarily involved Relief Society members and is an example of the public efforts of women in Nauvoo.

Besides promoting the penny subscription effort in Nauvoo, Mercy Thompson and Mary Smith wrote a letter to the "Sisters of the Church of Jesus Christ in England," announcing that one thousand women had already joined their effort.[427] The church periodical in England, the *Latter-day Saints' Millennial Star,* published the letter in June 1844 along with an endorsement of the "Ladies Subscription for the Temple" by Hyrum Smith on behalf of the First Presidency. The *Millennial Star* urged its readers, "We feel much to encourage this plan, and trust that the sisters in England will manifest that they will not be behind the sisters in Nauvoo in this laudable work."[428]

Church members in Boston also learned about the penny subscription drive and organized the Boston Female Penny and Sewing Society on July 16, 1844.[429] A letter that described the society in the *Prophet,* a Latter-day Saint newspaper in New York City, stated, "The ladies of the Boston branch are determined not to be behind hand in assisting the rolling on of the cause of Christ." The officers, all women, included Mary McAllester as president, two vice presidents, a secretary, a treasurer, and six members of a Committee of Arrangement. The society announced that it would lend its "aid in the purchase of glass, nails, &c, for the Temple of God, now being erected in Nauvoo." Members of the society

---

426. Mercy Rachel Fielding Thompson, Autobiographical Sketch, 1880, CHL, 8. In a sermon at the April 1844 church conference, Hyrum Smith provided a different version of the origins of the penny subscription effort: "No member of the Female Relief Society got it up; I am the man that did it; they ought not to infringe upon it; I am not a member of the Female Relief Society; I am one of the committee of the Lord's House." ("Conference Minutes," *Times and Seasons,* Aug. 1, 1844, 5:596.)

427. Mary Fielding Smith and Mercy Rachel Fielding Thompson, "To the Sisters of the Church of Jesus Christ in England," *LDS Millennial Star,* June 1844, 5:15.

428. Hyrum Smith, "The Ladies Subscription for the Temple," *LDS Millennial Star,* June 1844, 5:15.

429. The initial name of the organization was the "Boston Latter day Saint's Sewing and penny Society." (A Mc. A. to Mr. Editor, July 25, [1844], *Prophet,* Aug. 3, 1844, [2].)

Nauvoo temple sampler. This cross-stitch by Ann Eckford circa 1846 celebrates the completed Nauvoo temple, built in part with contributions from individual Relief Society members and groups such as the Boston Female Penny and Sewing Society. The border stitching contains the names of members of the Quorum of the Twelve. (Church History Museum, Salt Lake City.)

planned to meet one day a month to sew; each member was also to donate one penny per week.[430]

One day after the Boston society formed, Latter-day Saint women in Lowell, Massachusetts, formed the "'Lowell Latter Day Saints' Benevolent Sewing Society,' for the purpose of purchasing material and making same into clothing, for such travelling Elders as may stand in need."[431] Organized similarly to the popular sewing and charitable societies of the time, these societies did not act as official branches of the Nauvoo Female Relief Society. Nevertheless, with their similar goals and strategies, they may have functioned like satellite Relief Societies in purpose.

The minutes of the second quarterly meeting of the Boston society, reproduced below, were published first in the *Prophet* and then in the Nauvoo *Times and Seasons*.[432] The months between the organization of this society—which occurred roughly three weeks after Joseph Smith's death—and the time of this conference were tumultuous ones for Latter-day Saints in the eastern states. The questions of succession and plural marriage that plagued the Saints in Nauvoo also created divisions within the branches of the church in Boston and other eastern cities.[433] Nevertheless, Parley P. Pratt, who at the time of this meeting had recently arrived in the East to supervise church affairs, noted, "The saints in Boston are not only increasing in number by additions almost daily, but they are increasing in faith, in confidence, in union, and in an understanding of the kingdom and government of God."[434] Separately from the penny subscription effort, eastern Latter-day Saints were also encouraged by church leaders to pay tithing, through designated church agents, for the temple's construction.[435] The church in Boston numbered between three hundred and four hundred members during this era.[436]

As demonstrated by these minutes, the Boston Female Penny and Sewing Society remained active in 1845. Efforts continued among women in Nauvoo as well during 1845. A month after the publication of these minutes, Mary Smith and Mercy Thompson stated in the *Times and Seasons* that the penny subscription effort had already raised one thousand

430. A Mc. A. to Mr. Editor, July 25, [1844], *Prophet,* Aug. 3, 1844, [2]; see also A. McAllister to Mr. Editor, Oct. 15, 1844, *Prophet,* Oct. 19, 1844, [2].

431. Abby E. Switzer et al. to Mr. Editor, *Prophet,* Aug. 17, 1844, [2]; see also "Constitution of the Lowell Latter-day Saints Benevolent Sewing Society," *Prophet,* Sept. 14, 1844, [3]. The *Prophet* urged others to "go and do likewise" in forming similar societies. ("To the Sisters," *Prophet,* Sept. 14, 1844, [2].)

432. "Boston Female Penny and Sewing Society," *Times and Seasons,* Mar. 1, 1845, 6:820. The *Prophet* was published between May 18, 1844, and May 24, 1845 (when it was given the new title *New-York Messenger*). In February 1845, when this article was published, Samuel Brannan was editing the paper with the frequent assistance and oversight of Parley P. Pratt. (Peter Crawley, *A Descriptive Bibliography of the Mormon Church,* 3 vols. [Provo, UT: Religious Studies Center, Brigham Young University, 1997–2012], 1:254–257.)

433. Terryl L. Givens and Matthew J. Grow, *Parley P. Pratt: The Apostle Paul of Mormonism* (New York: Oxford University Press, 2011), 230–235.

434. Parley P. Pratt to Mr. Editor, Jan. 11, [1845], *Prophet,* Jan. 18, 1845, [3].

435. See Parley P. Pratt, "Proclamation," *Prophet,* Jan. 4, 1845, [2]; and "Receipt of Tithing," *Prophet,* Feb. 8, 1845, [2].

436. Jedediah M. Grant to Wilford Woodruff, July 13, 1845, Wilford Woodruff, Journals and Papers, 1828–1898, CHL.

dollars and that most of the participants "seem inclined to continue paying their cent a week until the temple is finished."[437] The fund-raising effort, centered in Nauvoo but reaching into the eastern states and even England, raised approximately two thousand dollars before the completion of the Nauvoo temple in late 1845.[438]

——— ❧ ———

Boston Female Penny and Sewing Society.

At the second quarterly meeting of the Female Penny and Sewing Society, held at Sister M. MacAllster's 296 Washington street Boston, on Tuesday evening Jan. 28th, 1845.

M. MAC ALLISTER. Prest.
MARY G. ALLEN, Sec.
ELVIRA BALDWIN. Tres.

Meeting opened by prayer.

Moved and seconded that the treasurer report the receipts for the last six months, (carried.)

Report,—Received from the members of the Society.	$15,44
Donations from Brethren,	3,50
Work,	10,72
For the constitution,	,37
Making in all monies received,	$30,03
Money paid out for sundry articles,	8,76
Leaving in all,	21,27

Moved and seconded, that the above report be accepted, (carried.) that the above money be paid to Br. Benson,[439] and have it forwarded for the use of the Temple, (carried unanimous.)

Sister Baldwin resigns the office of treasurer moved and seconded that Sister Clarisa Devenport be appointed treasurer, (carried.)

---

437. Mary Smith and Mercy R. Thompson, "Notice," *Times and Seasons*, Mar. 15, 1845, 6:847. Some of the money raised also went to the liquidation of church debts. (See Brigham Young to Mary Smith and Mercy R. Thompson, Dec. 5, 1844, Mary Fielding Smith Collection, ca. 1832–1848, CHL; and Matthew McBride, *A House for the Most High: The Story of the Original Nauvoo Temple* [Salt Lake City: Greg Kofford Books, 2006], 167–168.)

438. For an overview of the effort, see McBride, *A House for the Most High*, 163–168.

439. In January 1845 Ezra T. Benson was serving as president of the Boston conference and as a tithing agent. (Elden J. Watson, *Manuscript History of Brigham Young, 1846–1847* [Salt Lake City: By the author, 1971], 256.)

Moved and seconded that the minutes of this meeting be published in the Prophet, Nauvoo Neighbor[440] and Times and Seasons.[441]

Moved and seconded that the Sisters of the Boston branch of the Church of Jesus Christ of Latter Day Saints have a Levee,[442] and that the proceedings of the same be applied for the building of the Temple.

MARY MACALLISTR, Pres't.

MARY G. ALLEN, Sec'y.

---

440. These minutes were not published in the *Nauvoo Neighbor.* The *Nauvoo Neighbor* served as the Latter-day Saints' secular newspaper from 1843 through 1845. The *Times and Seasons* was the *Nauvoo Neighbor*'s religious counterpart.

441. "Boston Female Penny and Sewing Society," *Times and Seasons,* Mar. 1, 1845, 6:820.

442. The women were likely planning a fund-raising ball. Webster's 1828 dictionary defines a "levee" as a "concourse of persons who visit a prince or great personage in the morning." It also defines "drawing-room" as a place where "distinguished personages hold levees, or private persons receive parties." ("Levee," and "Drawing-room," in *An American Dictionary of the English Language,* ed. Noah Webster [New York: S. Converse, 1828].)

1.13 Brigham Young, Discourses, March 9, 1845 (Excerpts)

Brigham Young, Discourse, Mar. 9, 1845 (excerpt); three pages in excerpt; Nauvoo High Priests Quorum Record, 1841–1845, CHL (CR 1000 1).

Brigham Young, Discourse, Mar. 9, 1845 (excerpt); Record of Seventies, Book B, 1844–1848, pp. 77–78, First Council of the Seventy Records, CHL (CR 3 51).

When Brigham Young met with two groups of Latter-day Saint men in March 1845, he foreclosed any possibility that Relief Society meetings might recommence that spring, as had been the pattern in previous years. Young was adamantly opposed to women resuming their meetings after a hiatus of nearly a year. Young's reasons can partially be surmised from his remarks to the men, featured in these excerpts from the minutes of the Nauvoo high priests quorum and the Nauvoo seventies quorums.

Following the mob murders of Joseph and Hyrum Smith on June 27, 1844, Latter-day Saints in Nauvoo experienced intense community turmoil. Through that summer until early 1846, when the majority of Saints departed Nauvoo to migrate westward, members of the church grappled with questions over church leadership, finances, and doctrine. A majority of members supported leadership by the Quorum of the Twelve Apostles, with Young at its head. This presiding quorum, deemed second in authority to the First Presidency and closely associated with Joseph Smith and the doctrines he introduced in Nauvoo, assumed leadership at a church conference in early August 1844. As the Twelve worked to unite the membership, complete the Nauvoo temple, and cope with hostile outsiders, dissenting church members repeatedly contested their authority.[443] The movement toward organizational stability was tortuous, and what role if any the Female Relief Society might play in the developing structure was unclear.

Tensions between Brigham Young and Emma Smith, Joseph Smith's widow and president of the Relief Society, likely fueled Young's concern about Relief Society meetings. Their differences centered on the working out of Joseph Smith's temporal and spiritual legacy, including the settlement of his estate, succession to church leadership, and the role of plural marriage in the church. In July 1844 William Clayton, Joseph Smith's clerk, wrote that the intermingling between church property and personal Smith family property made the settlement of the estate a challenge. He explained that "the property is chiefly in the name of the Trustee in Trust [Joseph Smith] while the obligations are considered personal."[444] As the mother of five fatherless children, Emma Smith necessarily focused on her family's needs, whereas Young and the Twelve sought the broader interests of the church.[445] Complicating these differences was Emma Smith's support of leadership of the church by those who opposed the Quorum of the Twelve. Soon after Joseph's death,

---

443. Leonard J. Arrington, *Brigham Young: American Moses* (New York: Alfred A. Knopf, 1985), 113–119.

444. William Clayton, Journal, 1842–1845, CHL, July 4, 1844. The trustee-in-trust, a position established in December 1841 and initially held by Joseph Smith, oversaw church properties. (Arrington, *Brigham Young: American Moses,* 117–118.)

445. Arrington, *Brigham Young: American Moses,* 118. At the time of Joseph Smith's death, Emma

Emma suggested Nauvoo Stake president William Marks should serve as a trustee for the church and as its president.[446]

Emma Smith's opposition to the practice of plural marriage as introduced by Joseph Smith and supported by the Quorum of the Twelve was another element in the schism in her relationship with Young and the apostles. She at one time gave her permission for her husband to marry additional wives, but she then vacillated and at length conclusively voiced her opposition both privately and publicly.[447] Personal hurt was one dimension of Emma Smith's stand against plural marriage; another was the responsibility given to the Relief Society by Joseph Smith for "correcting the morals and strengthening the virtues of the female community."[448] In her role as president of the Relief Society, Emma Smith may have attempted to unite women in opposing plural marriage because she rejected the view that it was a divinely revealed principle and she believed it to be morally wrong. John Taylor later reported, "Sister Emma got severely tried in her mind about the doctrine of Plural Marriage and she made use of the position she held to try to pervert the minds of the sisters in relation to that doctrine."[449] Emma Smith expressed her opposition to plural marriage in her calls for a reformation in morals at the Relief Society meetings on March 9 and March 16, 1844, in which the society endorsed "The Voice of Innocence from Nauvoo."[450] Brigham Young believed that Emma Smith's efforts to thwart the practice of plural marriage contributed to the furor against Joseph and Hyrum Smith and helped lead to their deaths.[451]

Less than a year after their deaths, on Sunday, March 9, 1845, Young addressed the topic of Relief Society in two meetings of men assembled as quorums of the higher or Melchizedek priesthood. A quorum of men ordained to the office of high priest met in the Masonic Hall.[452] In addition, the Nauvoo seventies quorums assembled that day in three sessions—morning, afternoon, and evening—in the recently dedicated Seventies Hall. In Nauvoo, nearly "all elders under the age of thirty-five" were ordained as seventies.[453] Young spoke first to the high priests and later to the seventies. Near the end of his remarks to the

---

Smith had four living children and was pregnant with her last child, David Hyrum Smith. (Richard Lyman Bushman, *Joseph Smith: Rough Stone Rolling* [New York: Alfred A. Knopf, 2005], xvii, 554.)

446. Clayton, Journal, July 4, 1844; James M. Monroe, Journal, 1841–1842, 1845, CHL, Apr. 24, 1845.

447. For a discussion of the sources indicating Emma Smith's positions on plural marriage, see Brian C. Hales, *Joseph Smith's Polygamy*, 3 vols. (Salt Lake City: Greg Kofford Books, 2013), 2:33–138.

448. Document 1.2, entry for Mar. 17, 1842.

449. Relief Society Record, 1880–1892, CHL, July 17, 1880, 11. Eliza R. Snow later stated, evidently in reference to Emma Smith's role as the president of the Nauvoo Relief Society, that Emma Smith "gave it up so as not to lead the society in erro[r]." (West Jordan Ward, West Jordan Utah South Stake, Relief Society Minutes and Records, 1868–1973, CHL, Sept. 7, 1868.)

450. See Document 1.10; and Document 1.2, entries for Mar. 9 and 16, 1844.

451. Historian's Office, General Church Minutes, 1839–1877, CHL, Feb. 25, 1855.

452. The March 9 minutes stated that the high priests met "at the usual place." Other entries, including those dated December 22, 1844–January 26, 1845, and March 16, 1845, identified the location as the Masonic Hall. (High Priests Quorum Record, 1841–1845, CHL, Dec. 22, 1844–Jan. 26, 1845; Mar. 9 and 16, 1845.)

453. Alan K. Parrish, "Seventy," in *Encyclopedia of Mormonism,* ed. Daniel H. Ludlow, 5 vols. (New York: Macmillan, 1992), 3:1301.

high priests, he said that "he had preached the caps all off his pistols, and the buttons off his coat."[454] In both meetings, with just such energy, Young expressed his opposition to further Relief Society meetings.

When Young addressed these meetings, the atmosphere in Nauvoo was still highly charged. A little over a month earlier, Young and other leaders expressed their concern that Nauvoo was "infested by mobocrats."[455] Not wanting to add fuel to opposition fires, Young counseled, "Let every man stay at home and mind his own business."[456] George Miller, president of the high priests quorum, declared on March 2, "Our worst foes are those who have been in our midst, and pretended to be one with us." They were "always aiming to destroy the head, of this church— They begun with Joseph— and will endeavor to destroy all the rest."[457]

In addition, Young was concerned about the continuing challenges to his authority by Sidney Rigdon, a former counselor in the First Presidency who asserted his claim to lead the church as its guardian. In his comments to the seventies on March 9, Young addressed the disunity the Latter-day Saints continued to experience from the succession crisis and "Mr. Rigdon['s] cause." Young declared that he had "a right to speak for I am a man having authority & not as the Scribe." He stated that "whenever I see Men striving to divide this people I will rise up by the power of Israel God" to rebuke them.[458] On March 9 Miller attempted to raise "means to support a police about the houses of the twelve— & elsewhere."[459] A week later, on March 16, one of the high priests "illustrated our present situation by alluding to a boat in the Niagara river just above the falls— we must make an effort, and stem the rapids, until we get into still waters above."[460]

Most of Brigham Young's recorded addresses date to the Utah period. They show that his rhetoric was colorful, expressive, and sometimes coarse, a reflection of his frontier upbringing. After arriving in Utah, Young edited many of his talks before they were published. "In printing my remarks," he said, "I often omit the sharp words, though they are perfectly understood and applicable here, for I do not wish to spoil the good I desire to do. Let my remarks go to the world in a way the prejudices of the people can bear."[461] He did not have the benefit of editing the clerks' notes of his remarks delivered on March 9, 1845.

Young's rejection of the Female Relief Society of Nauvoo ended formally organized women's meetings. The suspension was long-standing but ultimately temporary. In 1854, in Utah Territory, separated from the conflicts that assailed the church in Nauvoo, Young supported the formal calling of women leaders and the recommencement of Relief Society meetings (see Part 2).

———— ❧ ————

454. High Priests Quorum Record, Mar. 9, 1845.

455. Historian's Office, General Church Minutes, Jan. 30, 1845.

456. High Priests Quorum Record, Jan. 26, 1845.

457. High Priests Quorum Record, Mar. 2, 1845.

458. First Council of Seventy, "General Record of the Seventies Book B. Commencing Nauvoo 1844," 1844–1848, Book B, in First Council of the Seventy, Records, 1837–1885, CHL, Mar. 9, 1845.

459. High Priests Quorum Record, Mar. 9, 1845.

460. Orson Spencer, High Priests Quorum Record, Mar. 16, 1845.

461. Brigham Young, "Remarks," *Deseret News,* Aug. 12, 1857, 180.

Discourse to High Priests Quorum

Nauvoo. Sunday, March 9th 1845. . . . [p. [1]][462] . . .

Pres. [Brigham] Young spoke . . . [p. [4]] . . .

Reli[e]f society— going to meet again— I say I will curse ev[e]ry man that lets his wife or daughters meet again— until I tell them— What are relief societies for? To relieve us of our best men— They relieved us of Joseph and Hyrum— that is what they will lead to— I dont ⟨want⟩ the advice or counsel of any woman— they would lead us down to hell—

There is no woman on the face of the earth that ⟨can⟩ save herself— but if she ever comes into the Celestial Kingdom, she must be led in by some man— God knew what Eve was. He was acquainted with woman thousands and millions of years before—

He made a few remarks in relation to the revival of the Female Relief Society, and disapprobated it. [p. [5]] . . .[463]

Discourse to Seventies Quorums

City of Nauvoo Sunday Evening March 9th 1845. . . . [p. 77] . . .

President Brigham Young, arose & said he would make remarks relative to thing in which many of or our Sister have been engaged they have no right to meddle in the affairs of the kingdom of God outside the pale of this they have a right to meddle because many of them are more sagacious & shrewd & more competent to attend to things of the financial affairs. the never can hold the keys of the Priesthood apart from their husband. When I want Sisters or the Wives of the members of this church to get up Relief Society I will summon them to my aid but until that time let them stay at home & if you see Females huddling together veto the concern and if they say Joseph started it tell them it is a damned lie for I know he never encouraged it but I know where the Chit[464] was laid but I am determined to stay these proceedings for by it our best men have been taken from us. One ounce of prevent⟨ive⟩ is better than one pound cure. . . . [p. 78] . . .

---

462. TEXT: The original record book is not paginated at this point, so pagination supplied here will be for the March 9, 1845, entry rather than for the record book. The ellipsis points in these two excerpts have been supplied by the editors of this volume to indicate omissions from the original documents.

463. Brigham Young continued his speech on other subjects, including treatment of wives. On that topic, he said, "If you want to make a queen of your wife, make her a queen, not a lackey."

464. Webster's 1828 dictionary defines "chit" as "a shoot or sprout; the first shooting or germination of a seed or plant." ("Chit," in *An American Dictionary of the English Language,* ed. Noah Webster [New York: S. Converse, 1828].)

BACK NUMBERS.

The back numbers of the Times and Seasons, for September and October, were not printed in their time, but the publication will *continue* until the volume is full.

CORRECTION.

In the Times and Seasons of August 15, the History says, "Brother Rich was called in question for transgressing the word of wisdom," &c. It should have read *Leonard Rich*.

NOTICE.

Robert Reid, James Riley, and Charles Pemberton of St. Louis, have this day been cut off from the church by the council of the Twelve.

W. RICHARDS, Clerk.

Nov. 1845.

NOTICE.

Elder Nelson Bates of the New Hampshire presidency, from whom the hand of fellowship was withdrawn, and published in the Messenger, is now restored to the full fellowship and confidence of the church.

W. RICHARDS, Clerk.

P. S. It was not our intention that Br. Bates should have been published.

POETRY.

For the Times and Seasons.

MY FATHER IN HEAVEN;

BY MISS ELIZA R. SNOW.

O my Father, thou that dwellest
In the high and glorious place;
When shall I regain thy presence,
And again behold thy face?
In thy holy habitation
Did my spirit once reside?
In my *first* primeval childhood
Was I nurtur'd near thy side?

For a wise and glorious purpose
Thou hast plac'd me here on earth,
And withheld the recollection
Of my former friends and birth:
Yet oft times a secret something
Whispered you're a stranger here;
And I felt that I had wandered
From a more exalted sphere.

I had learn'd to call thee father,
Through thy spirit from on high;
But until the key of knowledge
Was restor'd, I knew not why.
In the heav'ns are parents single?
No, the thought makes reason stare;
Truth is reason—truth eternal
Tells me I've a mother there.

When I leave this frail existence—
When I lay this mortal by,
Father, mother, may I meet you
In your royal court on high?
Then, at length, when I've completed
All you sent me forth to do,
With your mutual approbation
Let me come and dwell with you.

City of Joseph, Oct. 1845.

The Times and Seasons,

Is Printed and Published about the first and fifteenth of every month, on the corner of Main and Kimball Streets, Nauvoo, Hancock County, Illinois, by

JOHN TAYLOR,

EDITOR AND PROPRIETOR

TERMS.—Two Dollars per annum, payable in all cases in advance. Any person securing five new subscribers, and forwarding us Ten Dollars current money, shall receive one volume gratis All letters must be addressed to John Taylor, editor, POST PAID, or they will not receive attention.

Eliza R. Snow poem. Eliza Snow's best-known hymn text, later titled "O My Father," was first published in the church newspaper *Times and Seasons*. Frequently sung in church meetings, it became a particular staple at Relief Society gatherings. (Church History Library, Salt Lake City.)

1.14 Eliza R. Snow, "My Father in Heaven," October 1845

Eliza R. Snow, "My Father in Heaven," Oct. 1845, Times and Seasons *(Nauvoo, IL), Nov. 15, 1845, vol. 6, no. 17, p. 1039.*

Eliza R. Snow, who served as secretary of the Female Relief Society of Nauvoo from 1842 to 1844 and married Joseph Smith on June 29, 1842, completed the following poem, initially titled "My Father in Heaven," a little over a year after the death of her husband and within a short time after the death of her father, Oliver Snow.[465] Since her marriage, Snow had lived with Sarah Cleveland, Joseph and Emma Smith, Jonathan and Elvira Cowles Holmes, Leonora Snow Leavitt Morley, and Stephen and Hannah Markham.[466] Her marriage was a secret, and wherever she lived in Nauvoo, Snow was always a guest. She composed the poem while living in the Markhams' attic, where she moved on April 14, 1844, in a room where the ceiling was "so low that she could almost reach the rafters as she lay in bed."[467]

By 1845 Snow was well known for her poetry; she had published numerous poems prior to her baptism in 1835 and since then had written dozens of poems and published many in both Latter-day Saint and other newspapers. "My Father in Heaven" was the last poem Snow wrote in Nauvoo; it appeared in the November 15, 1845, issue of the *Times and Seasons,* with the subscript "City of Joseph, Oct. 1845." Rootedness is one of its major themes, as it speaks of place, habitation, residing, and dwelling while describing the entire Latter-day Saint conception of the plan of salvation: spirit life in a premortal state, the veil of forgetting, the purpose of life, and return after death to a loving Father. Snow's poem also speaks of the Latter-day Saint belief in Mother in Heaven. The extant writings and discourses of Joseph Smith include no mention of a Mother in Heaven, but later accounts indicate that he taught this doctrine to Snow and others in private.[468]

---

465. It is unknown how long it took news of her father's death to reach Snow, but he died at Walnut Grove, Illinois, approximately ninety miles from Nauvoo, on October 17, 1845. For the biographical and cultural context of this poem, see Jill Mulvay Derr, "The Significance of 'O My Father' in the Personal Journey of Eliza R. Snow," *BYU Studies* 36, no. 1 (1996–1997): 85–126.

466. Eliza R. Snow, Journal, 1842–1882, CHL, June 29, 1842; Aug. 14 and 17–18, 1842; Feb. 11, 1843; July 21, 1843; Apr. 14, 1844.

467. Bathsheba W. Smith, "An Item of History," *Woman's Exponent,* June 1901, 30:3; Snow, Journal, Apr. 14, 1844.

468. Zina D. H. Young recalled asking Joseph Smith whether she would see her mother again following her mother's death in July 1839. Smith replied affirmatively and added, "More than that, you will meet and become acquainted with your eternal Mother, the wife of your Father in Heaven." Further, David McKay (father of David O. McKay) reported a conversation he had with Snow while driving her from Huntsville to Eden, Utah. He asked whether Snow learned of a Mother in Heaven by revelation from God. She responded, "No," and explained that her inspiration had come from Joseph Smith's teachings.

References to a Mother in Heaven appear in Nauvoo publications following the death of Joseph Smith and before Eliza Snow's "My Father in Heaven." In late 1844 those gathered to dedicate the Seventies Hall sang a hymn that contained the couplet "Come to me; here's the myst'ry that man hath not

The poem was first published explicitly as a hymn in 1851.[469] In 1855 the *Deseret News* called it Brigham Young's favorite hymn.[470] Snow's first printed compilation of poems, *Poems: Religious, Historical, and Political,* features this poem on the first page.[471]

———— ❧ ————

POETRY,
For the Times and Seasons.
MY FATHER IN HEAVEN,[472]
BY MISS ELIZA R. SNOW

O my Father, thou that dwellest
    In the high and glorious place;
When shall I regain thy presence,
    And again behold thy face?
In thy holy habitation
    Did my spirit once reside?
In my *first* primeval childhood
    Was I nurtur'd near thy side?

For a wise and glorious purpose
    Thou hast plac'd me here on earth,
And withheld the recolleection
    Of my former friends and birth:
Yet oft times a secret something
    Whispered you're a stranger here;

---

seen; / Here's our Father in heaven, and Mother, the Queen." Phelps also wrote about a Mother in Heaven in "Paracletes," his fictional series that contextualized the earth's history within a grander cosmic scheme. (Susa Young Gates, *History of the Young Ladies' Mutual Improvement Association of the Church of Jesus Christ of Latter-day Saints* [Salt Lake City: Deseret News, 1911], 15–16; David McKay to Mrs. James Hood, Mar. 16, 1916, copy, CHL; William W. Phelps, "Come to Me," *Times and Seasons,* Jan. 15, 1845, 6:783; Joseph's Speckled Bird [William W. Phelps], "Paracletes," *Times and Seasons,* May 1, 1845, 6:891–892; June 1, 1845, 6:917–918; Samuel Brown, "William Phelps's Paracletes, an Early Witness to Joseph Smith's Divine Anthropology," *International Journal of Mormon Studies* 2 [Spring 2009]: 62–82; Derr, "The Significance of 'O My Father'"; see also David L. Paulsen and Martin Pulido, "'A Mother There': A Survey of Historical Teachings about Mother in Heaven," *BYU Studies* 50, no. 1 [2011]: 70–97.)

469. *Sacred Hymns and Spiritual Songs, for the Church of Jesus Christ of Latter-day Saints, in Europe* (Liverpool: F. D. Richards, 1851), 143.

470. "Deseret Theological Institute," *Deseret News,* June 20, 1855, 120.

471. Eliza R. Snow, *Poems: Religious, Historical, and Political,* 2 vols. (Liverpool: F. D. Richards, 1856; Salt Lake City: Latter-day Saints' Printing and Publishing Establishment, 1877), 1:1.

472. By 1856 "My Father in Heaven" was also known as "O My Father." In her first published volume of poems, Snow titled the work "Invocation, or the Eternal Father and Mother." (Derr, "The Significance of 'O My Father,'" 105; Snow, *Poems,* 1:1.)

And I felt that I had wandered
  From a more exalted sphere.

I had learn'd to call thee father
  Through thy spirit from on high;
But until the key of knowledge[473]
  Was restor'd, I knew not why.
In the heav'ns are parents single?
  No, the thought makes reason stare;
Truth is reason—truth eternal
  Tells me I've a mother there.

When I leave this frail existence—
  When I lay this mortal by,
Father, mother, may I meet you
  In your royal court on high?
Then, at length, when I've completed
  All you sent me forth to do,
With your mutual approbation
  Let me come and dwell with you.
City of Joseph,[474] Oct. 1845.

---

473. For "key of knowledge," see Doctrine and Covenants 84:19; 128:14.

474. "City of Joseph" was a name the Latter-day Saints gave to Nauvoo after the Nauvoo city charter was repealed by the Illinois state legislature in January 1845. (Glen M. Leonard, *Nauvoo: A Place of Peace, a People of Promise* [Salt Lake City: Deseret Book; Provo, UT: Brigham Young University Press, 2002], 464–472.)

PART 2: 1854–1866

In April 1857 a group of nineteen women assembled ten miles north of Salt Lake City and defined the work they proposed to do "under the name of the Female Relief Society of the City Bountiful." Their charter read: "We . . . whose names shall hereafter be attached . . . ever feeling a lively duty in our Redeemer's Kingdom, and for the general welfare of Zion's cause, Do mutually unite ourselves together for the benefit of the poor and all other Charitable purposes wherein we can prove ourselves useful to our fellow creatures."[1] The statement, with its emphasis on charity and usefulness, suggests the purpose and variety of work undertaken by many of the first Latter-day Saint Relief Societies in the West. Largely isolated within local wards or congregations, most of the Relief Societies organized during this period functioned for four years or less, and sometimes discontinuously. Notwithstanding the earnest intentions of its members, the 1857 "Female Relief Society of the City Bountiful" operated for only six months.[2] Early Utah Relief Societies lacked the centralized leadership, organizational procedures, and expanded responsibilities that strengthened and invigorated those permanently reestablished after 1867. Yet as pioneer women labored collectively in their new frontier environment, they repeatedly eked out of their scarcity something to benefit those in need—Indian women and children, Saints confronting poverty and sickness, and impoverished immigrants.

New Beginnings in the West

A hiatus of ten years and thirteen hundred miles separated the Female Relief Society of Nauvoo, Illinois, from the Relief Society established in Utah

---

1. "Relief Society," in East Bountiful Ward, Davis Stake, Manuscript History and Historical Reports, 1877–1897, CHL.

2. A history of this Relief Society indicated that it "was discontinued November 1857" after "just a little more than 6 months duration" because of the tumult in Utah Territory caused by the Utah War. ("History of the Bountiful First Ward Relief Society Beginning 24 April 1857 to 5 February 1961" [unpublished typescript, 1961], copy at CHL, 1.)

Territory in 1854. The last recorded meeting of the Nauvoo Relief Society took place in March 1844.[3] Between February and September 1846, thousands of Latter-day Saints followed Brigham Young and the Quorum of the Twelve Apostles in a mass exodus from Nauvoo. Seeking a new and uncontested home in the Rocky Mountains, the Saints trekked across the Great Plains to the Great Basin, with the first company arriving in the Valley of the Great Salt Lake in July 1847. By that fall, more than two thousand Saints had gathered in their new mountain home. The 1850 census numbered their ranks at 11,380.[4]

As Latter-day Saint women journeyed westward, generally in family groups—some of which were extended by plural marriage—they clustered informally to pray, sing, testify, prophesy, and bless, and they continued such gatherings in their new home. Shared privations forged close connections that facilitated women's nursing of the sick and aid to the poor. But the formal reorganization of women as a cooperative component of church government according to the pattern established by the Female Relief Society of Nauvoo was not accomplished for several years. In Illinois in 1845, in the wake of the murders of Joseph and Hyrum Smith, Brigham Young had halted operations of the Female Relief Society, declaring he would "get up Relief Society" again when he decided to "summon them [the women] to my aid."[5] When Young called for the reestablishment of the Relief Society in the 1850s, he did so in a very different context than that which had given rise to the Female Relief Society of Nauvoo.

The remote mountain desert environment of the Great Basin posed new challenges for the Saints, not the least of which was association with the native peoples who had long occupied the area. In addition, a new and persistently conflicted connection between the church and the U.S. government began with the establishment of Utah Territory in 1850; that conflict intensified in subsequent years. Finally, as church leaders encouraged the immigration of thousands of converts from throughout the United States, Great Britain, and Europe, population in the Great Basin increased and Mormon colonization expanded to scattered areas of the territory, necessitating a more elaborate order of church governance and aid to those impoverished by immigration and resettlement. These realities shaped the form of Latter-day Saint women's first Relief Societies in the West.

---

3. See Document 1.2, entry for Mar. 16, 1844.

4. James B. Allen and Glen M. Leonard, *The Story of the Latter-day Saints* (Salt Lake City: Deseret Book, 1976), 220–225, 234–238, 241–247.

5. Document 1.13.

Female Council of Health and "Indian Relief Societies"

The hardships of the westward trek and isolated frontier settlement brought health concerns, including distinctly female concerns, to the forefront. Midwives and other women began attending meetings of the Council of Health with male practitioners when the group was formed in 1849.[6] Some women, however, were uncomfortable discussing medical matters in the Council of Health, which caused "a slackness of attendence of the females, which was suposed to be caused by there being present male members." As a result, the Female Council of Health was organized by July 1851.[7] Midwife Phoebe Angell, mother of Brigham Young's wife Mary Ann Angell, was designated president of the women's council, and she chose two midwives as counselors. The women's council met about twice a month, initially in Angell's home. As membership expanded, the group later held some meetings in the newly erected tabernacle on the south end of the temple block.[8] On November 13, 1852, the council selected one woman each from most of the city's nineteen wards "to look after the poor."[9] After Angell died in November 1854, her counselor Martha "Patty" Sessions became president of the Female Council of Health, though by then Sessions was also serving as president of the newly organized Relief Society of Salt Lake City's Sixteenth Ward.[10]

Beginning in the fall of 1853, Brigham Young and other church leaders sought to improve the Saints' relations with American Indians, who resented a steadily increasing Mormon presence in the lands they inhabited. The close of 1853 had seen the waning of the Walker War, a series of bloody skirmishes between Utes (headed by Chief Wakara, known to Latter-day Saints as Walker) and settlers. Hoping to heal the fractured relationship, at the October 1853 general conference Young announced the assignment of two dozen missionaries to labor among local Indians; their task would be "to civilize them, teach them to work, and improve their condition by your utmost faith and

---

6. Priddy Meeks, Reminiscences, 1879, typescript, CHL, 60–62; Historical Department, Journal History of the Church, 1896–, CHL, Jan. 21 and Mar. 21, 1849; Patty Bartlett Sessions, Diary, May 8, 1850, in Donna Toland Smart, ed., *Mormon Midwife: The 1846–1888 Diaries of Patty Bartlett Sessions,* Life Writings of Frontier Women 2 (Logan: Utah State University Press, 1997), 146.

7. Female Council of Health, Minutes, Aug. 14, 1852, CHL; Sessions, Diary, July 8, 1851, in Smart, *Mormon Midwife,* 166.

8. Sessions, Diary, Sept. 17, 1851; Mar. 24 and May 12, 1852, in Smart, *Mormon Midwife,* 168, 174, 176; Female Council of Health, Minutes, Aug. 14, 1852, CHL; Richard L. Jensen, "Forgotten Relief Societies, 1844–67," *Dialogue: A Journal of Mormon Thought* 16, no. 1 (Spring 1983): 107.

9. Sessions, Diary, Nov. 13, 1852, in Smart, *Mormon Midwife,* 182.

10. Sessions, Diary, June 10 and Nov. 16, 1854, in Smart, *Mormon Midwife,* 205, 210.

1

August 14th 1852.

Females Counsel of health met in the Tabernacle.
Meeting opened by singing and prayer by Sister Patty Perry.

Elder G. D. Watts was Voted in unanimously as Clerk to that counsel.

Sister Angel came in After the Appointment of the Clerk, on being made acquainted with the appointment she expressed her entire satisfaction.

Bro Sprague spoke, that as he had to open the door, and take charge of the house he wished to know if his being present would be an intrusion if he came into the Counsel at any time.

A vote was taken which was unanimous in favour of his coming and going as he pleased.

Sister Patty Perry told the reason of this seperate counsel, which was in consequence of a slackness of attendance of the females, which was supposed to be caused by there being present Male Members. This meeting is for all females, whether they are members or not. The other for the Counsel of health only.

Sister Angel spoke, exhorting the Counsel, not to trust in the knowlege which is obtained from Books, or to trust in herbs altogether. but seek to the Lord for wisdom. She refered to a circumstance in Nauvoo when much Chill and fever was among the people she cried to the Lord that he would show her some thing to do them good. In the night she received the following receipt as though a voice spoke to her. "Take Lobelia one handful, connect such a portion, put it in one pint of vinegar, let it stand over night, and administer it to the sick when the Chill comes on, A table spoon full once every hour. She bore testimony of the great good this receipt did. She used one Bushel of Lobelia that Summer.

Sister Gibbs gave a receipt for Piles. Pearl oil.
Docter Sprague give a receipt for a bite of an Cut, or the Third preperation of Lobelia

Female Council of Health minutes. This women's organization in early Utah was a precursor of the Relief Societies that were formally reinstated in 1854. This minute entry for August 14, 1852, demonstrates women's collaboration in addressing community needs through visits. (Church History Library, Salt Lake City.)

diligence."[11] The effort to "civilize" the American Indians included instruction about agriculture and the adoption of Latter-day Saint religious beliefs and cultural practices, including in relationship to clothing. At the same conference, Parley P. Pratt of the Quorum of the Twelve spoke of redeeming "the children of Nephi and Laman," Book of Mormon figures from whom, Saints believed, the American Indians descended. Further, Pratt called for assistance in clothing Indian women and children.[12]

A group of seventeen women in Salt Lake City responded to Pratt's call in February 1854 when they independently organized a "Socity of females for the purpose of making clothing for Indian women and Children" (see Document 2.1). They met weekly in various homes through the spring. In May, Young and other church leaders negotiated peace with Wakara and other chiefs in central Utah. Shortly thereafter, Young, in company with Pratt and other church leaders and their wives, toured the southern settlements and preached rapprochement with the Indians. When the company reached Harmony, Washington County, one of the newly arrived missionaries wrote, at Pratt's suggestion, to the *Deseret News:* "We are much in want of old clothing, especially shirts, to help cover the nakedness of the Indians, especially of the women. What will the Salt Lake Saints do about it?"[13]

On June 4, 1854, less than a week after his return to the Salt Lake Valley, Young officially proposed to "the Sisters . . . to form themselves into societys to relieve the poor b[reth]ren" and "to clothe the Lamanite children and women and cover their nakedness." He advised women to "meet in their own wards and it will do them good."[14] The response was immediate. On June 6, women in the Fourteenth Ward met with their bishop "to be organised into a society."[15] On June 10 Patty Sessions recorded that in the Sixteenth Ward "the sisters organised a benevolent society to clothe the Indians & squa[w]s I was put in Presidentes."[16] On June 13 the independent group of seventeen women disbanded and "each member joined the scociety in their own wards," their president Matilda Dudley becoming president of the Thirteenth Ward Female Indian Relief Society (see Document 2.1). Brigham Young's financial records

11. Brigham Young, Discourse, Oct. 9, 1854, in *Deseret News,* Nov. 24, 1853, [2]; see also Brigham Young, Heber C. Kimball, and Willard Richards, "Tenth General Epistle," *Deseret News,* Oct. 15, 1853, [3].

12. Parley P. Pratt, Remarks, Oct. 9, 1853, in "Minutes of the General Conference," *Deseret News,* Oct. 15, 1853, [3].

13. T. D. Brown, May 19, 1854, Letter to the Editor, *Deseret News,* June 22, 1854, [2].

14. Brigham Young, Remarks, June 4, 1854, in Historian's Office, General Church Minutes, 1839–1877, CHL; Edyth Jenkins Romney, Thomas Bullock Minutes (Loose Papers), 1848–1856, Brigham Young Office Files Transcriptions, 1974–1978, CHL.

15. Eliza Maria Partridge Lyman, Journal, 1846–1885, CHL, June 6, 1854.

16. Sessions, Diary, June 10, 1854, in Smart, *Mormon Midwife,* 205.

list women's contributions by ward, often under the designation "Indian Relief Society." Societies in at least seventeen wards in the Salt Lake Valley donated clothing and bedding at a total value of $1,540, along with $44 in cash, to the church's Indian relief effort in 1854 and 1855.[17]

Relief Society Expansion

As the urgent call for Indian relief subsided, some ward Relief Societies stopped meeting or were reconstituted to meet other needs. The Fourteenth Ward Female Relief Society, for example, was organized a second time "by Bishop [Abraham] Hoagland (agreeable to the request of President Brigham Young) on the seventeenth day of September 1856," and Phebe Carter Woodruff was appointed president (see Document 2.3). She had been a member of the Female Relief Society of Nauvoo. Indeed, scattered through these early Relief Societies were women who had been associated with the Nauvoo Relief Society.[18] Though many of the Saints in Utah had not been acquainted with the Nauvoo Relief Society, the simple organizational pattern inaugurated in Nauvoo was replicated within each ward: a president and two counselors, set apart by priesthood leaders, and committees to visit the ward by block to assess needs and collect donations for aiding the poor. Woodruff immediately established such committees in the Fourteenth Ward. There, as in other wards, meetings began with singing and prayer, followed sometimes by an address by a bishop or encouragement from the president or her counselors. Women gathered primarily to work together, often for a full day at a time. They might card or spin wool or sew quilts. Typically, they sewed carpet rags: stitching scraps of fabric together into long strips that could be rolled into manageable balls and then braided or woven on a loom to make carpet for the floors of a meetinghouse or home.

The Relief Societies helped fund immigration through the Perpetual Emigrating Fund, a system under which immigrants borrowed the costs of their travel to Utah and agreed to eventually repay the loans so that other converts could similarly benefit. In addition, Relief Society women also assisted arriving immigrants, including those who began to arrive in 1856 with the use

---

17. Financial Journal, July 1853–Nov. 1854, Brigham Young Office Files, 1832–1878, CHL; Jensen, "Forgotten Relief Societies," 114–115.

18. Many other women appointed as ward Relief Society presidents in the 1850s had been members of the Female Relief Society of Nauvoo, including, in Salt Lake City, Lydia Goldthwaite Knight (First Ward), Amanda Barnes Smith (Twelfth Ward), Lydia Granger (Fifteenth Ward), Sarah Granger Kimball (Fifteenth Ward), and Patty Sessions (Sixteenth Ward); in Bountiful, Elizabeth Haven Barlow; in Ogden, Patience Delila Pierce Palmer; in Willard, Mary Ann Hubbard; and in Spanish Fork, Lucretia Gay.

of low-cost handcarts pulled by converts who walked across the plains. Lucy Meserve Smith, president of a Relief Society in Provo, forty miles south of Salt Lake City, recalled how in 1856 she and her associates gathered bedding and clothing for members of the Martin and Willie handcart companies stranded by early snows in the mountains of present-day Wyoming (see Document 2.4).

As Smith's Provo group demonstrates, Female Relief Societies spread to Latter-day Saint settlements beyond the Salt Lake Valley. To the north, Relief Societies were organized in Bountiful, Ogden, and Willard. To the south, at least two Provo wards formed Relief Societies, as did wards farther south in Spanish Fork, Ephraim, and Manti. Cedar City, in Iron County, 250 miles south of Salt Lake City, established a Female Benevolent Society on November 20, 1856 (see Document 2.6). Documentation exists for some twenty-five ward Relief Societies in the 1850s, though there were almost certainly more.[19] Producing an exact tally is difficult because sometimes women from several wards in an area met together as a single Relief Society, and sometimes a single ward formed multiple districts, with a president and counselors heading each district.

When Brigham Young called in June 1854 for the organization of Relief Societies, he advised they be formed within local wards, and he anticipated they would operate under the direction of the ward bishop who presided over the local congregation. Joseph Smith had maintained a close relationship with the Female Relief Society of Nauvoo, at least during its first year when he gave lengthy addresses at six of its meetings.[20] The involvement of male priesthood leaders varied from ward to ward in the 1850s. In Cedar City, priesthood leaders often addressed the women's meetings.[21] In the Salt Lake City Seventh Ward, a new bishopric sought in March 1857 to "resurrect" a defunct Relief Society and then assigned the group such tasks as operating "directly to the assistance of the Bishop" in caring for the poor, providing assistance for converts arriving with "the Great Emigration," and making a cushion for "the seat in the Stand."[22] Women in Willard, in northern Utah, initiated ad hoc committees to assist immigrants. Later they asked the bishop to formally organize them because "the need of a Relief Society was felt by the sisters who had

19. Jill Mulvay Derr, "The Relief Society, 1854–1881," in *Mapping Mormonism: An Atlas of Latter-day Saint History,* ed. Brandon S. Plewe (Provo, UT: Brigham Young University Press, 2012), 102; Jensen, "Forgotten Relief Societies," 113, 119; "History of the Bountiful First Ward Relief Society," 1.

20. See Document 1.2, entries for Mar. 17, Mar. 31, Apr. 28, May 26, June 9, and Aug. 31, 1842.

21. See Cedar City Ward, Parowan Stake, Cedar City Ward Relief Society Minute Book, 1856–1875, CHL.

22. Seventh Ward Relief Society, Minutes, Mar. 24, 1857, Seventh Ward, Salt Lake Stake, Relief Society Records, 1858–1875, CHL.

belonged to the one organized by the Prophet Joseph Smith in Nauvoo."²³ In the Salt Lake City Fourteenth Ward, women independently drafted organizational bylaws and designated officers and committees beyond the traditional presidency and visiting committees (see Document 2.3).

The relationship between Relief Society leaders and priesthood leaders had become a question in Nauvoo, though following the death of Joseph Smith it was quickly overshadowed by the larger question of who had authority to preside as his successor, a question that deeply divided the church.²⁴ The largest segment of members followed Brigham Young and the Quorum of the Twelve Apostles in the move westward, seeking in the isolation of the Great Basin to establish on a firmer footing the church and kingdom of God that Smith had envisioned. Through the 1850s church leaders moved beyond the exigencies of survival to establish civil and religious authority. Brigham Young and the First Presidency in Salt Lake City provided central direction as settlements spread north and south; members of the Quorum of the Twelve often presided in new areas. For example, George A. Smith, husband of Lucy Meserve Smith, presided over villages first in Iron County and then in Utah County (see Document 2.4). Generally, villages became wards, headed by bishops who worked under presiding authorities such as George A. Smith. Church leaders usually directed both civic and church affairs.

Though women were not part of the ecclesiastical priesthood structure of the church, the establishment of Relief Societies provided them a new collective presence in community-building during a period when cooperative labor was imperative. The name church leaders chose for their newly settled land— Deseret, interpreted in the Book of Mormon as "a honey bee"²⁵— signaled the people's commitment to and the necessity of communal industry. Some resources in the territory, including water and public lands, were managed under intertwined ecclesiastical and civil direction. Mormon men donated a portion of their time to public works projects such as constructing canals, fences, and the temple. Women gave of their time and means to aid in such projects as providing carpet for buildings used for both religious and civil purposes. The women's organization worked largely independently, but not without the direction and approval of local priesthood leaders. The lack of total autonomy in this hierarchical system occasionally chafed women as well as men, and dissent was not unknown. Yet committed Latter-day Saints viewed

---

23. Relief Society History, not before 1915, p. 1, inserted in Relief Society Minutes and Records, vol. 14, Brigham City First Ward, Box Elder Stake, Brigham City First Ward Relief Society Minutes and Records, 1878–1982, CHL.

24. See introduction to Document 1.13.

25. Ether 2:3.

unity and harmony as requirements for a latter-day Zion and felt keenly the imperative to become a people "of one heart and one mind."[26]

Temples, such as those Saints had constructed earlier in Ohio and Illinois, played an essential role in the Saints' experience. Though the first temple in the West was not completed until 1877, as early as 1851 church leaders set apart men and women to administer the rituals of the temple in other consecrated spaces.[27] Families that had been established through temple marriage sealings, many of them polygamous families, were another manifestation of priesthood order. Church leaders taught that husbands and fathers presided in the family and that women, through temple ordinances, received priesthood keys "in connection with their husbands."[28] Church leaders' sermons during this period emphasized the importance of the hierarchical priesthood order, as manifest in both ecclesiastical offices and the family.

In 1855 Joseph Smith's addresses to the Nauvoo Relief Society appeared as part of the "History of Joseph Smith" series in the church's Salt Lake City newspaper, the *Deseret News* (see Document 2.2). The printed versions of these discourses included changes approved by Brigham Young, church historian George A. Smith, and other leaders that, among other things, emphasized priesthood authority and order. There is no evidence that the publication changed the actual operation of local Relief Societies; they were already working under the direction of bishops. Perhaps the 1854 reestablishment of the Relief Society in the local units raised some of the same concerns that had surfaced in Nauvoo about the relationship between women of the Relief Society and the ecclesiastical priesthood structure governing the church.[29]

Principles of order and obedience received particular emphasis in 1856 and 1857 in a period that became known as the "Reformation." Concerned about spiritual complacency, church leaders preached sermons throughout the territory, calling on Latter-day Saints to recommit to the faith.[30] Lucy Meserve Smith explained, "The saints were called upon to confess our sins, renew our covenants, and all must be rebaptized for a remission of our sins, and strive to live more perfectly than ever before" (Document 2.4). The movement is particularly evident in minutes of the Cedar City Relief Society (see Document 2.6),

---

26. Moses 7:18.

27. The temple rituals were performed in the Council House beginning in 1851 and in the Endowment House following its May 1855 dedication. (See Lisle G. Brown, "'Temple pro Tempore': The Salt Lake City Endowment House," *Journal of Mormon History* 34, no. 4 [Fall 2008]: 4–8.)

28. See revised version of Joseph Smith's April 28, 1842, address to the Relief Society, in Document 2.2.

29. See Document 1.2, entry for Mar. 16, 1844; Document 1.13; and introduction to Part 1.

30. Paul H. Peterson, "The Mormon Reformation of 1856–1857: The Rhetoric and the Reality," *Journal of Mormon History* 15 (1989): 59–87.

where male and female leaders repeatedly emphasized obedience and ortho-doxy. A member of the stake presidency exhorted Relief Society women in December 1856: "Let us stir ourselves and see if we cannot make a reformation in our houses, right in Cedar City,"[31] a theme that women echoed as they vis-ited women individually in their homes.

Impact of the Utah War

The Utah War, the 1857–1858 threat of armed conflict between Latter-day Saints and the U.S. government, enraged and terrified the residents of Utah and significantly disrupted ward Relief Society operations. In 1847, when Latter-day Saints first settled in the Salt Lake Valley, they had moved into Mexican territory. Then, at the close of the Mexican-American War in 1848, Mexico ceded its northern territories to the United States, including the Great Basin lands where the Saints had settled. Congress organized Utah Territory in 1850, and federal appointees began to play a major role in territorial governance. President Millard Fillmore balanced the selection of non-Mormon officials with Latter-day Saints, including Brigham Young as the first governor. The outside officials generally distrusted the Saints' beliefs and practices, particu-larly plural marriage and the meshing of religious and civil authority. Mounting misunderstandings culminated in 1857 when President James Buchanan sent a large contingent of federal troops to Utah to quash a rumored "Mormon rebellion" and install a new governor to replace Young. Fearing the same violence the Saints had experienced in Missouri and Illinois, Young declared martial law and stationed militias in the mountains to prevent the entry of U.S. troops into the valleys the Saints had settled. In the fall of 1857, Relief Society women knitted woolen stockings, mittens, and other winter clothing for the Saints' army.

The following spring, Young directed residents in the Salt Lake Valley and other northern settlements to evacuate their homes and prepare private and public buildings for burning in the event the troops should enter the valley. Thousands of Saints migrated southward, many of them insufficiently prepared for the trek. Records kept by the Salt Lake City Seventh Ward Relief Society noted that members provided "to a woman from the North as she was moving South One pair of shoes some linsey for her children & a pease of carpet for a bedspread."[32] Emmeline B. Wells wrote that "the regularity of the [Relief

---

31. Cedar City Ward, Parowan Stake, Cedar City Ward Relief Society Minute Book, Dec. 3, 1856.
32. Seventh Ward Relief Society, bk. A, Sept. 24, 1858, p. 31, Seventh Ward, Pioneer Stake, Relief Society Minutes and Records, 1848–1922, CHL.

Society] work was interrupted in 1858 by the entire people moving south. . . . All the money then on hand was expended for food and clothing for the poor."[33] In 1858 Patience Palmer was the Relief Society president in Ogden, forty miles north of Salt Lake City. Her son later recalled that his mother's "Relief Society distributed the carpet the rag carpet for wagon covers, and the woolen carpet for skirts for the women and shirts for men and children. . . . One could see trains of families by the hundreds leaving their homes, their gardens, their fields and everything." The Palmers went to Spanish Fork, where they lived "all summer in a willow shack."[34]

By July 1858 displaced Latter-day Saints had begun returning to their homes after a compromise was reached between Latter-day Saint leaders and the new Utah governor, and the federal troops had established Camp Floyd forty-five miles southwest of Salt Lake City.[35] The "move south," however, had profoundly disrupted their lives and their local congregations. Edwin D. Woolley, bishop of Salt Lake City's Thirteenth Ward, complained that, following church members' return, it was "impossible to get up meetings." The Relief Society had already disbanded, and the ward only rarely met for Sunday worship meetings over the next year.[36]

Nearly all Relief Societies, whether those in wards that moved south or in wards that received evacuees, seemed to vanish after 1858, not to reappear for a decade. There were exceptions such as in Spanish Fork, where Priscilla Merriman Evans left a record of Relief Society operations continuing until and beyond 1867 (Document 2.5). Brigham Young called again for the reestablishment of Relief Societies churchwide in 1867.[37] Having experienced two substantial interruptions in Relief Society operations—from 1844 to 1854 and from 1858 to 1867—women now would find ways to make it a permanent part of church structure.

---

33. Emmeline B. Wells, ed., *Charities and Philanthropies: Woman's Work in Utah* (Salt Lake City: George Q. Cannon and Sons, 1893), 12.

34. William Moroni Palmer, "A Sketch of the Life of Patience Delila Pierce Palmer," ca. 1927, CHL.

35. On the Utah War, see William P. MacKinnon, ed., *At Sword's Point, Part 1: A Documentary History of the Utah War to 1858*, Kingdom in the West, the Mormons and the American Frontier 10 (Norman, OK: Arthur H. Clark, 2008); and Matthew J. Grow, *"Liberty to the Downtrodden": Thomas L. Kane, Romantic Reformer* (New Haven, CT: Yale University Press, 2009), 149–206.

36. Ronald W. Walker, "'Going to Meeting' in Salt Lake City's Thirteenth Ward, 1849–1881: A Microanalysis," in *New Views of Mormon History: A Collection of Essays in Honor of Leonard J. Arrington*, ed. Davis Bitton and Maureen Ursenbach Beecher (Salt Lake City: University of Utah Press, 1987), 147.

37. See Document 3.1.

2.1 Great Salt Lake City Relief Society, Minutes, January–June 1854

Great Salt Lake City Relief Society, "Record of the Female Relief Socity Organized on the 9th of Feb,y in the City of Great Salt Lake 1854 Utah Territory" (Minutes), Jan. 24–June 13, 1854; seventeen pages; L. Tom Perry Special Collections, Harold B. Lee Library, Brigham Young University, Provo, UT (MSS SC 23).

In the early months of 1854, a cluster of women in Salt Lake City organized "a Socity of females for the purpose of making clothing for Indian women and Children." They acted in response to church leaders' renewed emphasis on proselytizing and ministering among the American Indian tribes that had been squeezed by the expansion of Mormon settlements. Following a series of skirmishes between the Ute tribe and the Mormons in 1853, Brigham Young worked to secure peace with the native peoples he considered to be "a remnant of the House of Israel."[38] Parley P. Pratt of the Quorum of the Twelve Apostles stated in the church's October 1853 conference that the Utah Saints, having become sufficiently settled and supplied, were now "able to feed and clothe the Indians, or at least, the women and children."[39]

With the apparent intention of advancing Pratt's proposal, seventeen women assembled in Salt Lake City on February 9, 1854, and resolved to raise means, purchase materials, and make clothing for Indian women and children. They elected a president, two counselors, a secretary and assistant secretary, and a treasurer—following the pattern established by the Female Relief Society of Nauvoo. At least one of the seventeen women, assistant secretary Amanda Barnes Smith, had been a Relief Society member in Nauvoo.[40] Newly elected president Matilda M. Dudley, a thirty-five-year-old single mother and convert from Pennsylvania, hosted the initial meeting in her home in Salt Lake City. The new society comprised women from different ward congregations, and during the next four months the women utilized various members' homes for their long work meetings. Two extant records contain the minutes of the meetings: one kept by secretary Louisa R. Taylor and one by assistant secretary Amanda Barnes Smith.[41] Because the two records are so similar, it appears one was probably copied from the other or that both were copied from the same source. Taylor's record is reproduced below, while footnotes indicate significant differences found in Smith's record.

The small society disbanded in June 1854 after Brigham Young returned from his tour of southern Utah and urged women to "meet in their own wards" and "form themselves into societys," both to relieve the poor and to clothe neighboring American Indians.[42] The

---

38. Brigham Young, Discourse, Oct. 9, 1853, in "Synopsis," *Deseret News,* Nov. 24, 1853, [2].

39. Parley P. Pratt, Remarks, Oct. 9, 1853, in "Minutes of the General Conference," *Deseret News,* Oct. 15, 1853, [3].

40. See Document 1.2, entry for Apr. 28, 1842.

41. Amanda Barnes Smith, Notebook, 1854–1866, CHL.

42. Brigham Young, Remarks, June 4, 1854, in Historian's Office, General Church Minutes, 1839–1877, CHL; Edyth Jenkins Romney, Thomas Bullock Minutes (Loose Papers), 1848–1856, in Brigham Young Office Files Transcriptions, 1974–1978, CHL.

Great Salt Lake City July 10th 1854

Sep. 400 Indian Goods. dr. to Indian relief Society
Shadrack Roundy 16th Ward

For	1 Hickory dress Plaid sleeves	2.—	
"	1 Yellow & Blue homespun dress (new)	2,50	
"	1 do do (old)	1,50	
"	1 blue check cotton gown	2.—	
"	1 White twilled Shirt & sack	2.—	
"	1 Dark green dress homemade	2,50	
"	1 do do	2,50	
"	1 Fustian dress for child	1.—	
"	1 Second hd white cotton shirt	1.—	
"	1 Old merino dress for Child	.50	
"	1 Large plaid homespun dress	2.—	
"	1 New cotton Shift	1,50	
"	1 Old — for child	.20	
"	1 cotton Apron	.75	
"	1 Small Shirt	.25	
"	1 Cotton shift	.50	
"	1 do do New	.60	
"	1 Dark green dress for child	1,50	
"	1 woollen Petticoat purple (old)	1,50	
"	1 Cotton handkerchief	.25	
"	1 Dark calico Apron for Child	.25	
"	1 do do Shirt	.50	
"	1 white Apron	.38	
"	1 Small yellow dress old	.50	
"	1 pair Satinett pants for	2.—	
"	1 Second hand vest	1.—	
"	1 do do hood	.50	
"	1 white woollen Blanket, blue stripe on each side	4.—	
"	1 Sleeve apron	.50	36 08

293 313 House Expenses. dr. to John Shipley
For 2 mo. 3 days labor @ $15.—   31 71

112 352 Wm Sims dr. to Flour a/c
For 32 pounds @ 6   1 92   1 92

69 71

Ledger of Indian Relief Society account. Clothing and other items made and donated by local Relief Societies on behalf of Indian women and children were recorded in Brigham Young's account books. The ledger credits each branch of the Relief Society separately. This entry from July 10, 1854, shows items contributed by members of the Salt Lake City Sixteenth Ward. Most of the donations were received between June and September 1854. (Church History Library, Salt Lake City.)

forerunner group of women dispersed to join newly forming ward Female Relief Societies. Matilda Dudley and Amanda Barnes Smith each became president of a ward society, Dudley in the Thirteenth Ward and Smith in the Twelfth Ward.[43]

———— ⅈ ————

~~Record~~ Record of the
Female Relief Socity Organized on the 9th of Feb,y in the City of Great Salt Lake 1854

Utah Teritory. [p. [1]][44]

January 24, 1854 • Tuesday

Great. Salt Lake City Jan, 24 1854 Sister's Dudly, [Mary] Hawkins, [Mary] Bird and Smith and others met on the 24 ~~of~~ ⟨inst⟩ to take into consideration the Importance of oganizeing a Socity of females for the purpose of making clothing for Indian women and Children after Consultation on the Subject they resolved to Organize Said Socity prayed and adjourned untill the 9 of Febu,y. [p. [2]]

February 9, 1854 • Thursday

Feb. 9st The Sisters met at the house of Matilda Dudly at 9 A.M. and was organized by the ilection of the following officers and ⟨members⟩

President	Matilda Dudly
Councelers	Mary Hawkins
	Mary Bird,
Treasurer	Matilda Dudly
Secretary	Louisa R. Taylor
Ass,istant, Sec,	Amanda Smith

Members

Mary Crowther	Lucia Miller
Mary Kisor [Keysor]	Rebecca, Miller [p. [3]]
Ann, Willis [Willes]	Susan Moore
Sarah J. Thompson	Elizabeth A Capener
Susan E Ludington	Elizabeth Vance
Sarah Capener	Delight Decker

On the motioin of the President the following resolutions were offerd and adopted

---

43. Thirteenth Ward, Salt Lake Stake, Thirteenth Ward Relief Society Records, 1854–1857, CHL; Smith, Notebook, June 10 and 13, 1854.

44. TEXT: Except for the preceding title page on page [1] and a false start on page [7], this record is inscribed on recto pages and the versos are blank.

1   Resolution Resolved that every person that join the Socity should pay 25 ^{cts}

2.   Resolution Resolved that all meetings are to be opened and Closed by Prayer.

3   Resolution Resolved that the Society should ⟨meet⟩ at 9. A.M. and Close at 4 P.M. on the days appointed

4   Resolution Resolved that the Society should make a rag Carpet and dispose of it [p. [4]] to raise means to purchase material to make clothing for Indian women and children

appointed the next meeting at Sister Hawkins[.] Sister. Smith prayed and adjourned untill 16 <u>inst</u>

Sect, Louisa R. Taylor

February 16, 1854 • Thursday

G.S.L. City Feb, 16 <u>inst</u> The Sisters met at the house of Sis, Hawkins at 9 A.M. sewed untill 4 P.M. appointed the next meeting at Sister Bird's house prayer by Sister Hawkins and adjourned utill the 23 <u>inst</u>

Sec., Louisa R. Taylor

February 23, 1854 • Thursday

Feb 23 G.S.L. City. the Sisters met at the house of Sister Bird's sewed untill four P.M. prayer by Bro, [James] Bird[45] appointed the next meeting [p. [5]] at Sister Ludington's house it was resolved on the motion of the President that all the names of those that met on the days appointed should be taken so that it might be known who met and who did not meet with us those that were there was

Sister   Dudly
Si, "   Bird
"   Hawkins
"   Kisor [Keysor]
"   Crowther
"   L. R. Taylor
"   Vance

Sister N. [Nancy] Kennedy name was taken as a member. Sister Bird[46] closed by Prayer

45. Amanda Barnes Smith's record strikes out "prayer by Brother Bird."
46. Amanda Barnes Smith's record states that the closing prayer was offered by "Brother Bird."

Sec, Louisa R. Taylor [p. [6]]

at Sister[47] [p. [7]]

March 2, 1854 • Thursday

S.L. City Mar. 2 <u>inst</u> the meeting was adjourned untill the next week. as that day was fast day to held at the same house.

Sec, Louisa R. Taylor.

March 9, 1854 • Thursday

S.L. City Mar. 9<u>th</u> the sisters met at the house of Sister Ludington ~~they~~ there were present

Sister   Dudly
"   Moore
"   R. Miller
"   C. [Caroline] Hardy

adjourned untill 16 <u>inst</u> appointed the next meeting at Sis, C. Hardy

Sec, L R. Taylor

March 16, 1854 • Thursday

G.S.L. City Mar, 16 <u>inst</u> the sisters met at the house of Caroline Hardys those that were presant were,

Sister   Hawkins [p. [8]]
Sister   Smith
"   C. Hardy
"   E. [Elizabeth] Hardy
"   Taylor
"   Moore
"   R. Miller
"   L. Miller

appointed the next meeting at Sister Smith's Sister Hawkin's Closed by Prayer.

Sec, Louisa R. Taylor

March 23, 1854 • Thursday

Mar, 23, <u>inst</u> G S.L. City Sisters met at the house of sister Smith. those Presant were.

---

47. TEXT: These two words are not canceled in the original, but they are evidently a false start, as they are the only two words on an otherwise blank page. Page [6] (the immediately preceding page) begins with the same two words.

Sister	Dudly
"	Bird
"	Kisor [Keysor]
"	Crowther
"	[Clarissa] Homiston [p. [9]]
Sister	L. Miller
"	R. Miller[48]
"	Moore

appointed the next meeting at Sis, Hawkins house on motion of the President the day of meeting was changed from thursday to Wednsday[49] Sister Bird closed by Prayer,[50]

Sec, L. R. Taylor

March 29, 1854 • Wednesday

G.S.L. City Mar. 2.9[inst] the sisters met at the house of Sister Hawkins those presant were

Sister	Dudly
"	Bird
"	Taylor
"	Hawkins
"	Smith[51]

appointed the next meeting at the house of ⟨C Hardy⟩ Sister Dudly closed by prayer

Sec. L. R. Taylor [p. [10]]

April 14, 1854 • Friday

Aprl, 14th The Sisters met at the house of Sister C. Hardy those Presant were

Sister	Dudly
"	Bird
"	R. Miller
"	C.[52] Homiston
"	E Hardy

---

48. Rather than indicating that both Sisters L. Miller and R. Miller were present, Amanda Barnes Smith's record lists "Sister R. or Sister L. Miller."

49. Amanda Barnes Smith's record adds: "as fast day came on thursday and hinderd them from meeting."

50. Amanda Barnes Smith's notebook records: "Sister Bird opened by prayer Sister Dudly closed by prayer."

51. Amanda Barnes Smith's record adds: "Sis. Hawkins read the 254 hymn."

52. TEXT: The original has only a portion of a letter here, possibly the upper fragment of a "C".

"   Smith
"   N Kennedy[53]
appointed the next meeting at the house of Birds[54] prayer by Sister Homiston

                                                    Sec, L. R. Taylor

April 20, 1854 • Thursday

G L.C. April. 20, the Sisters met at the house of Sister Bird, those Presant were

Sister Dudley   Sister Vance
"   Bird   "   Kennedy
"   Hawkins [p. [11]]

Sister Bird opened by prayer and Sister Hawkins closed by prayer appointed the next meeting at the same place.

                                                    Sec,, L. R. Taylor.

April 27, 1854 • Thursday

G.S.L. City April, 27[inst] The Sisters met at the house of Sister Bird those presant were

Sister   Dudly
"   Bird
"   Crowther
"   Vance

appointed the next meeting at Sister Caroline Hard'ys, Sister Dudly opened by prayer Sister Vance closed by prayer

                                                    Sec, Louisa R. Taylor [p. [12]]

May 3, 1854 • Wednesday

G.S.L. City May 3rd met at the house of Sister C. Hardy's those presant were

Sister Dudy   Sister Homiston
Sister C Hardy   "   Ludington

appointed the next meeting at the same place Sister Dudly closed by prayer

                                                    Sec, Louisa R. Taylor

---

53. Amanda Barnes Smith's record identifies "N Kennedy" as Nancy L. Kennedy and adds "L. R. Taylor" to the list of women present.
54. Amanda Barnes Smith's record adds: "Sung the Redeemer of Israel."

May 10, 1854 • Wednesday

G.S.L. City May 10th the Sisters met at the house of Sister C Hardy those presant were

Sister Dudly	Sister Homiston
" Hawkins	" E. A. Hardy
" C Hardy	" Smith
" Willis	" Ludington
" Kennidy	

Sister Kennidy opened by prayer appointed the next meeting at Sister Hawkins Closed by Sister [p. [13]] Hawkins praying and singing[55]

Sec. L. R. Taylor

May 11, 1854 • Thursday

G.S.L. City May 11th Sisters met at the house of Sister Hawkins prayer by sister Vance singing and prayer by sister Hawkins.

Sec, Louisa R. Taylor

May 20, 1854 • Saturday

G.S. Lake City May 20th Sisters met at the house of sister Hawkins adjourned to meet at the house of sister Henifer [Rebecca Hennefer] closed by singing and prayer

Sec, Louisa R. Taylor

May 28, 1854 • Sunday

G.S.L. City [May] 28,th Sisters met at the house of sister Henipher opened by sister Smith those presant were

Sister Dudly	Sister Bird
" Hawkins	" Crowther
" Vance	" Henipher
" Smith and others	

had a good time[56] [p. [14]]

singing and prayer by Sister Dudly adjourned untill the fourth of June. at the house sister Homiston[57] Rebecca Henipher [c]losed by prayer

Ass, Sec, Amanda Smith

recorded member Eliza Decker,

---

55. Amanda Barnes Smith's record adds: "song Come all ye Sons of God."

56. Amanda Barnes Smith's record adds: "and union of the Spirit."

57. Amanda Barnes Smith's record indicates the next meeting was to be held at the home of Sister Henipher.

Donations	Elezor [Eleazer] Miller[58]	95.	cts
	Jacob, Workman	50	"
	Stephen Mott,	30	"
	Lucia Miller	20	"
	Harriet [Amelia Decker Little] Hanks	25	
	John Hawkens	500	"
	Matilda Dudly	100	"
	Rebecca, Henipher	25	"

Ass, Sec,. Amanda Smith

June 7, 1854 • Wednesday

June 7th the sisters met at the House of Sistr Henipher opened by prayer by sister Dudly, present

Sister M. Dudly.
"   M. Hawkins [p. [15]]

Sister Bird		Sister Crowther	
Sister Smith		" "	Kisor [Keysor]
"	Henipher	"	C. Hardy
"	Ludington	"	Miller
"	J. Copener [Jane Capener][59]		

had a good time. song[60] by sister [Camilla] Cobb,[61] adjourned untill tuesday the 13th at ten[62] O'Clock at the houes of Sister Henipher

Ass, Secr, Amanda Smith.

June 13, 1854 • Tuesday

G.S.L. City June 13th met at the house of sister Henipher sister Bird opened by prayer, finished the cutting of the Carpet rags,[63] singing voted, and carried that the book be kept ~~by~~ in the Scosity meeting closed by sister Dudly

Sec, Amanda Smith

June 13 those presant were[64]

Sister Dudly		Sister Taylor	
"	Bird	"	Smith [p. [16]]

---

58. Husband of Rebecca Van Zant Miller. (See 1850 U.S. Census, Great Salt Lake, Utah Territory, 131.)

59. Amanda Barnes Smith's record identifies "J. Copener" as Jane.

60. Amanda Barnes Smith's record identifies the name of the song as "O stop and tel m[e] red man."

61. Amanda Barnes Smith's record adds: "foloed by sis Dudly."

62. Amanda Barnes Smith's record has "one" rather than "ten."

63. Amanda Barnes Smith's record adds: "the spirit of the Lord was with us and union prevailed sung wake o wake the world fro[m] slepimg [sleeping]."

64. Amanda Barnes Smith's record inserts the word "Omitted" prior to this list of names.

Sister	Hardy	sister	Mary Hardy[65]
"	Ludington	"	R. Miller
"	Sarah Copener [Capener][66]	"	Homiston
"	E.[67] Copener [Capener]	"	Vance
"	Crowther	"	R. Henipher

Sister Homiston paid fifty cents for lot[68] time sister Dudly paid 75[cts] [69] in salerutus[70] this was the last meeting of the Scociety as Brother Brigham Young Counceled the organizeing of Relief Scoceity is in all the Wards of the City and each member joined the scociety in their own wards and our President was called to preside in her own Ward the 13th by Bishop Wolley [Edwin D. Woolley]

Sec. Louisa R. Taylor [p. [17]]

---

65. Amanda Barnes Smith's record lists Mary Hardy but does not use the title "Sister" before her name.

66. Amanda Barnes Smith's record has "sis Copener an Elizabeth." Mary Hardy and Elizabeth Capener were daughters who apparently accompanied their mothers to the meetings.

67. Amanda Barnes Smith's record identifies "E. Copener" as Elizabeth.

68. Amanda Barnes Smith's record has "last."

69. Amanda Barnes Smith's record uses the term "six bits" (which was equal to seventy-five cents).

70. Saleratus is sodium or potassium bicarbonate. Priscilla Merriman Evans described its production in early Utah County: "The saleratus was gatherd on top of the ground in the bottom land. It became quite a comodity later. Women and children would take old brooms, sweep it up and sack it, and haul it over to Provo, and trade for anything they could use in the family. They had some kind of a factory where the saluratus was purified into a sort of soda, to use in bread making." (Priscilla Merriman Evans, Autobiography, ca. 1907, Emma Priscilla Evans Little, Papers, 1870–1941, L. Tom Perry Special Collections, Harold B. Lee Library, Brigham Young University, Provo, UT, 49.)

2.2 Joseph Smith, Discourses to Nauvoo Female Relief Society, March 31 and April 28, 1842, as Revised for "History of Joseph Smith," September 5 and 19, 1855

Joseph Smith, Discourse, Mar. 31, 1842, in "History of Joseph Smith," Deseret News (Salt Lake City, UT), Sept. 5, 1855, vol. 5, no. 26, p. [201].

Joseph Smith, Discourse, Apr. 28, 1842, in "History of Joseph Smith," Deseret News, Sept. 19, 1855, vol. 5, no. 28, pp. [217]–218.

Joseph Smith made several attempts at creating a history of the church. In April 1838 he began his most successful effort, the compilation of what became a multivolume history of himself and the church. By the time the Latter-day Saints left Nauvoo in February 1846, scribes had completed the Manuscript History of the Church of Jesus Christ of Latter-day Saints, as it is often known, to March 1843. Then the history remained essentially dormant until the appointment of George A. Smith as church historian in April 1854. With the assistance of several scribes, Smith completed the history in August 1856.[71]

As part of this process of compiling the Manuscript History, George A. Smith and scribes Thomas Bullock, Leo Hawkins, and Jonathan Grimshaw copied and then edited several discourses Joseph Smith delivered to the Nauvoo Relief Society. In a similar manner, those compiling the history edited many other documents, including other Joseph Smith sermons, before they included them in the Manuscript History. This editing reflected nineteenth-century approaches to texts in which historians often altered original texts when they prepared them for publication. For instance, Jared Sparks, a leading scholar who later became president of Harvard, published twelve volumes of the *Writings of George Washington* in the 1830s in which he substantially revised the original manuscripts before publication both for literary purposes and to present Washington in a more positive light.[72] Similarly, Brigham Young's sermons were often revised before publication by scribe George D. Watt, and the extent of Young's approval of these alterations is unclear.[73]

In late March 1855 Smith and Bullock visited Brigham Young "to read to him Josephs sermon to the Female Relief Society [of] Nauvoo." Young referred them to Eliza R. Snow, "who delivered them the original Sermon in the Female R S Record," meaning the Nauvoo Relief Society Minute Book.[74] Smith, Bullock, Hawkins, and Grimshaw remained in the Historian's Office until ten o'clock that night, and they continued their work on the history

---

71. Dean C. Jessee, "The Writing of Joseph Smith's History," *BYU Studies* 11, no. 4 (Summer 1971): 439–473; "Joseph Smith's Historical Enterprise," in Karen Lynn Davidson et al., eds., *Histories, Volume 1: Joseph Smith Histories, 1832–1844*, vol. 1 of the Histories series of *The Joseph Smith Papers*, ed. Dean C. Jessee et al. (Salt Lake City: Church Historian's Press, 2012), xxii–xxxii.

72. Dean C. Jessee, "The Reliability of Joseph Smith's History," *Journal of Mormon History* 3 (1976): 24–25.

73. Gerrit J. Dirkmaat and LaJean Purcell Carruth, "The Prophets Have Spoken, but What Did They Say? Examining the Differences between George D. Watt's Original Shorthand Notes and the Sermons Published in the *Journal of Discourses*," *BYU Studies* (forthcoming).

74. See Document 1.2.

the following day. Hawkins and Grimshaw copied the sermons, while Bullock (likely with Smith's assistance) edited them.[75] When Heber C. Kimball stopped by in the evening, he "heard Joseph's sermon Read, liked it better as revised."[76] Young likewise stated that he "was much pleased with them."[77] After the sermons were copied, the Nauvoo minute book was returned to Snow.

The revised excerpts from the Nauvoo Relief Society minutes, with particular focus on Joseph Smith's sermons, appeared in several issues of the *Deseret News* in 1855 as part of a serial publication of the Manuscript History titled "History of Joseph Smith." Even before the publication of these Joseph Smith sermons in the *Deseret News,* church leaders recognized their importance. In 1844 Wilford Woodruff asked John McEwan to copy the April 28, 1842, sermon into Woodruff's journal, which McEwan did from Snow's minutes.[78] On June 27, 1849, on the fifth anniversary of Joseph Smith's death, Snow "read Joseph's lectures to a circle of ladies," likely a reference to these sermons in the minute book in Snow's possession.[79]

The sermon of April 28, 1842, with Joseph Smith's endorsement of women's ritual healing, was often reprinted and remained a significant document for nineteenth-century Latter-day Saints. In 1888, for instance, the *Woman's Exponent,* in an editorial note likely written by Emmeline B. Wells, stated that a recent address by apostle Franklin D. Richards to a commemorative meeting of the Relief Society in Ogden had been "predicated" upon Joseph Smith's April 28, 1842, sermon. The *Exponent* noted six reprintings of that sermon in Utah newspapers and periodicals within the previous six years.[80] Over the years, some of the published versions of the April 28, 1842, sermon reflected the original wording in the Nauvoo Relief Society minutes, while other versions reflected the revisions as published in the *Deseret News.*[81] Many women copied that sermon into their journals, using one of the published versions as their source.[82] The revised excerpts featured below served as the basis

---

75. Historian's Office, Journal, 1844–1997, CHL, Mar. 29–30, 1855. Copies of Joseph Smith's March 31 and May 26, 1842, sermons, in the writing of Hawkins and Grimshaw and with Bullock's editing, are now in the Joseph Smith Collection, 1827–1846, CHL.

76. Historian's Office, Journal, Mar. 30, 1855. In a poem composed in March 1855 titled "The Will," Eliza R. Snow possibly reflected on the editing of the sermons she had recorded. (Jill Mulvay Derr and Karen Lynn Davidson, eds., *Eliza R. Snow: The Complete Poetry* [Provo, UT: Brigham Young University Press; Salt Lake City: University of Utah Press, 2009], 500–502.)

77. Historian's Office, Journal, Aug. 8, 1855.

78. "Instructions Delivered by Pres[t] Joseph Smith before the Female Relief Society of Nauvoo. Ap 28, 1842," in back of Wilford Woodruff, Journal, 1841–1842, Wilford Woodruff, Journals and Papers, 1828–1898, CHL.

79. Eliza R. Snow, Diaries, 1847–1849, Henry E. Huntington Library, San Marino, CA, June 27, 1849.

80. "Editorial Note," *Woman's Exponent,* Sept. 1, 1888, 17:52; see also Jonathan A. Stapley and Kristine Wright, "Female Ritual Healing in Mormonism," *Journal of Mormon History* 37, no. 1 (Winter 2011): 16–17, 20; and Jill Mulvay Derr and Carol Cornwall Madsen, "Preserving the Record and Memory of the Female Relief Society of Nauvoo, 1842–92," *Journal of Mormon History* 35, no. 3 (Summer 2009): 107–108. The 1888 Richards address is transcribed as Document 4.20 in this volume.

81. For an example of the use of the original minutes in summarizing the April 28, 1842, sermon, see "The Relief Society. (Copied from the Original Record.), Eliza R. Snow, Secretary," *Woman's Exponent,* Feb. 1911, 39:49–50.

82. See, for example, Hannah Adeline Hatch Savage, *Record of Hannah Adeline Savage, Woodruff,*

for a treatment of the Relief Society in volume 4 of the *History of the Church of Jesus Christ of Latter-day Saints,* published in 1908 after further light editing by B. H. Roberts.[83]

George A. Smith and the scribes left no record of the reasons for their changes. Many of the revisions are minor alterations of wording. Other changes take the sermons from their immediate context of the 1842 Nauvoo Relief Society—and the imminent introduction of temple ordinances—and apply them more broadly to the church as a whole. These edits appear to be an attempt by church leaders to emphasize priesthood authority and order. For instance, the original minutes state that Joseph Smith "said he was going to make of this Society a kingdom of priests an [as] in Enoch's day— as in Pauls day."[84] The revised version reads, "The Lord was going to make of the Church of Jesus Christ a kingdom of priests, a holy people, a chosen generation, as in Enoch's day."

Printed below are two revised Joseph Smith sermons, those of March 31, 1842, and April 28, 1842, as published in two issues of the *Deseret News* in September 1855. Significant differences between the original minutes and the revised versions are noted.

Discourse, March 31, 1842, from *Deseret News,* September 5, 1855

Sunday, 30 [Thursday, March 31, 1842].[85]—I met with the Female Relief Society, and gave them some instructions, of which the following brief sketch was reported by Miss E. R. Snow:—[86]

"President Joseph Smith arose. Spoke of the organization of the Female Relief Society; said he was deeply interested that it might be built up to the Most High in an acceptable manner; that its rules must be observed; that none should be received into it but those who were worthy; proposed a close examination of every candidate; that the society was going too fast. It should grow up by degrees; should commence with a few individuals, thus have a select society of the virtuous, and those who would walk circumspectly: commended them for their zeal, but said sometimes their zeal was not according to knowledge.

Arizona, and Journal, photoreproduction of original manuscript record and journal (Pinedale, AZ: Petersen, 1976), 113–120; see also Pamela Elizabeth Barlow Thompson, Papers, ca. 1875–1891, CHL.

83. Joseph Smith et al., *History of the Church of Jesus Christ of Latter-day Saints,* ed. B. H. Roberts (Salt Lake City: Deseret News, 1902–1912 [vols. 1–6], 1932 [vol. 7]), 4:570, 602–607.

84. Document 1.2, entry for Mar. 31, 1842.

85. As noted in Document 1.2, this meeting was held March 31, 1842, a Thursday.

86. This sentence does not appear in the original Nauvoo Relief Society Minute Book (hereafter referenced as "the original minutes" that are featured in this volume as Document 1.2). In the entry he made in Joseph Smith's journal for March 31, 1842, scribe Willard Richards noted: "Thursday 31 [March 1842] In council at his office with. Elders [Brigham] Young. [John] Taylor &ᶜ. & wrote an Epistle to the Female Relief Socity and spake to the Socity in the afternoon." (Document 1.2, entry for Mar. 31, 1842; Joseph Smith, Journal, Mar. 31, 1842, in Andrew H. Hedges et al., eds., *Journals, Volume 2: December 1841–April 1843,* vol. 2 of the Journals series of *The Joseph Smith Papers,* ed. Dean C. Jessee et al. [Salt Lake City: Church Historian's Press, 2011], 48 [hereafter *JSP,* J2].)

One principal object of the institution was to purge out iniquity: said they must be extremely careful in all their examinations, or the consequences would be serious.

All difficulties which might and would cross our way must be surmounted, though the soul be *tried*, the heart faint, and hands hang down. Must not retrace our steps; there must be decision of character, aside from sympathy. When instructed, we must obey that voice, observe the laws of the kingdom of God,[87] that the blessing of Heaven may rest down upon us. All must act in concert, or nothing can be done, and should move according to the ancient priesthood; hence the saints should be a select people,[88] separate from all the evils of the world—choice, virtuous, and holy. The Lord was going to make of the Church of Jesus Christ a kingdom of priests, a holy people, a chosen generation, as in Enoch's day, having all the gifts as illustrated to the church in Paul's epistles and teachings to the churches in his day[89]—that it is the privilege of each member to live long and enjoy health. He then blessed the saints."[90]

Discourse, April 28, 1842, from *Deseret News,* September 19, 1855

[April] 28 [1842].—At two o'clock. p.m., I met the members of the "Female Relief Society," and after presiding at the admission of many new members, gave a lecture on the Priesthood, showing how the sisters would come in possession of the privileges, blessings, and gifts of the priesthood, and that the signs should follow them, such as healing the sick, casting out devils, &c., and that they might attain unto these blessings by a virtuous life, and conversation, and diligence in keeping all the commandments;[91] a synopsis of which was reported by Miss E. R. Snow.

"Prest. Joseph Smith arose and called the attention of the meeting to the 12th chapter 1st Corinthians. "Now concerning spiritual gifts, I would not have you ignorant."[92] Said that the passage in the 3rd verse, which reads, "No man [p. [217]] can *say* that Jesus is the Lord, but by the Holy Ghost," should be translated "no man can *know* that Jesus is the Lord, but by the Holy Ghost."[93]

---

87. The original minutes read, "observe the Constitution."

88. The original minutes read, "hence there should be a select Society."

89. The original minutes read, "Said he was going to make of this Society a kingdom of priests an [as] in Enoch's day— as in Pauls day."

90. This final sentence does not appear in the original minutes. Rather, Joseph Smith asked that the men "withdraw, that the Society might proceed to business— that those wishing to join should have their names presented at the next meeting."

91. Up to this point, this paragraph was copied with minor changes from Joseph Smith, Journal, Apr. 28, 1842, in *JSP*, J2:52.

92. The phrase "I would not have you ignorant" replaces "&c." in the original minutes.

93. The phrase "that Jesus is the Lord, but by the Holy Ghost" replaces "&c" in the original minutes.

He continued to read the chapter, and give instructions respecting the different offices, and the necessity of every individual acting in the sphere allotted him or her, and filling the several offices to which they were appointed.

Spoke of the disposition of many men[94] to consider the lower offices in the church dishonorable, and to look with jealous eyes upon the standing of others who are called to preside over them.[95] That it was the folly and[96] nonsense of the human heart for a person to be aspiring to other stations than those to which they are appointed of God for them to occupy;[97] that it was better for individuals to magnify their respective callings, and wait patiently till God shall say to them, "come up higher."

He said the reason of these remarks being made was, that some little foolish things were[98] circulating in the society, against some sisters[99] not doing right in laying hands on the sick.[100] Said if the people had common sympathies they would rejoice[101] that the sick could be healed; that the time had not been before that these things could be in their proper order; that the church is not fully[102] organized, in its proper order, and cannot be, until the Temple is completed, where places will be provided for the administration of the ordinances of the priesthood.[103]

President Smith continued the subject, by quoting[104] the commission given to the ancient apostles in Mark, 16th chapter, 15, 16, 17, 18 verses,[105] "Go ye into all the world, and preach the gospel to every creature. He that believeth and is baptized, shall be saved; but he that believeth not shall be damned. And these signs shall follow them that believe: in my name shall they cast out devils; they shall speak with new tongues; they shall take up serpents; and if they drink any deadly thing, it shall not hurt them; they shall lay hands on the sick, and they shall recover."[106]

No matter who believeth, these signs, such as healing the sick, casting out devils, &c., should follow all that believe, whether male or female. He asked

---

94. The original minutes have "man" rather than "many men."
95. The original minutes do not contain the phrase "who are called to preside over them."
96. The words "folly and" do not appear in the original minutes.
97. The original minutes read, "aspiring to other stations than appointed of God."
98. The original minutes read, "some little thing was."
99. The original minutes have "that some persons were" instead of "against some sisters."
100. The original minutes add "&c."
101. The original minutes read, "Said if he had common sympathies, would rejoice."
102. The original minutes have "now" rather than "fully."
103. The original minutes do not contain the phrase "where places will be provided for the administration of the ordinances of the priesthood."
104. The original minutes have "adverting to" rather than "quoting."
105. The scriptural citation does not appear in the original minutes.
106. The original minutes contain only the phrase "'Go ye into all the world' &c."

the Society if they could not see by this sweeping promise,[107] that wherein they are ordained, it is the privilege of those set apart to administer in that authority, which is conferred on them; and if the sisters should have faith to heal the sick, let all hold their tongues, and let everything roll on.

He said, if God has appointed him, and chosen him as an instrument to lead the church, why not let him lead it through? Why stand in the way when he is appointed to do a thing? Who knows the mind of God? Does he not reveal things differently from what we expect? He remarked that he was continually rising, although he had everything bearing him down, standing in his way, and opposing; notwithstanding all this opposition,[108] he always comes out right in the end.

Respecting females administering for the healing of the sick,[109] he further remarked, there could be no devil in it, if God gave his sanction by healing; that there could be no more sin in any female laying hands on and praying for[110] the sick, than in wetting the face with water: it is no sin for any body to administer[111] that has faith, or if the sick have faith to be healed by their administration.

He reproved those that were disposed to find fault with the management of the concerns of the church,[112] saying God had called him to lead the church, and he would lead it right;[113] those that undertake to interfere will be ashamed when their own folly is made manifest;[114] that he calculates to organ[i]ze[115] the church in its proper order as soon as the Temple is completed.[116]

President Smith continued by speaking of the difficulties he had to surmount ever since the commencement of the work, in consequence of aspiring men. "Great big elders," as he called them, who had caused him much trouble; to whom he had taught the things of the kingdom[117] in private councils, they would then go forth into the world and proclaim the things he had taught them, as their own revelations; said the same aspiring disposition will be in this society, and must be guarded against; that every person should stand, and act

107. The original minutes have "stroke" rather than "promise."
108. The original minutes have "after all" rather than "notwithstanding all this opposition."
109. The original minutes read, "Respecting the female laying on hands."
110. The original minutes do not contain the phrase "and praying for."
111. The original minutes have "do it" rather than "administer."
112. The original minutes do not contain the phrase "of the church."
113. The original minutes read, "saying if he undertook to lead the church he would lead it right."
114. The original minutes do not contain the phrase "those that undertake to interfere will be ashamed when their own folly is made manifest."
115. TEXT: In the copy used for transcription, there is a blank space between the *n* and the *z*.
116. The original minutes read, "that he calculates to organize the church in proper order &c."
117. The original minutes do not contain the phrase "the things of the kingdom."

in the place appointed, and thus sanctify the Society and get it pure. He said he had been trampled under foot by aspiring elders, for all were infected with that spirit; for instance, John E. Page and others had been aspiring;[118] they could not be exalted, but must run away as though the care and authority of the church were vested with them. He said he[119] had a subtle devil to deal with, and could only curb him by being humble.

As he had this opportunity, he was going to instruct the ladies of this Society,[120] and point out the way for them to conduct themselves, that they might act according to the will of God; that he did not know that he should have many opportunities of teaching them, as they were going to be left to themselves; they would not long have him to instruct them; that the church would not have his instructions long, and the world would not be troubled with him a great while, and would not have his teachings.

He spoke of delivering the keys of the Priesthood to the church, and said that the faithful members of the Relief Society should receive them in connection with their husbands, that the Saints whose integrity has been tried and proved faithful, might know how to ask the Lord and receive an answer; for according to his prayers, God had appointed him elsewhere.[121]

He exhorted the sisters always to concentrate their faith and prayers for, and place confidence in their husbands, whom God has appointed for them to honor, and in those faithful men whom God has placed at the head of the Church to lead his people;[122] that we should arm and sustain[123] them with our prayers; for the keys of the kingdom are about to be given to them, and they may be able to detect everything false; as well as to all[124] the elders who shall prove their integrity in due season.[125]

---

118. The original minutes read, "for instance P. Pratt[,] O. Pratt, O. Hyde and J. Page had been aspiring."

119. The original minutes have "we" rather than "he."

120. The original minutes have "the Society" rather than "the ladies of this Society."

121. In the original minutes this paragraph reads, "He spoke of delivering the keys to this Society and to the church— that according to his prayers God had appointed him elsewhere." The additions and revisions here in part reflected Brigham Young's teaching that women "never can hold the keys of the Priesthood apart from their husband." (Document 1.13.)

122. The original minutes read, "He exhorted the sisters always to concentrate their faith and prayers for, and place confidence, in those whom God has appointed to honor, whom God has plac'd at the head to lead."

123. The original minutes do not contain the phrase "and sustain."

124. The original minutes do not contain the word "all."

125. The original minutes do not contain the phrase "who shall prove their integrity in due season."

He said if one member becomes corrupt, and you know it, you must immediately put it away, or it will either injure or destroy the whole body.[126] The sympathies of the heads of the church have induced them to bear a long time with those who were corrupt until they are obliged to cut them off, lest all become contaminated;[127] you must put down iniquity, and by your good examples, stimulate[128] the elders to good works; if you do right, there is no danger of your going too fast.

He said he did not care how fast we run in the path of virtue; resist evil, and there is no danger; God, men, and angels will not condemn those that resist everything that is evil, and devils cannot;[129] as well might the devil seek to dethrone Jehovah, as overthrow an innocent soul[130] that resists everything which is evil.

This is a charitable Society, and according to your natures; it is natural for females to have feelings of charity and benevolence.[131] You are now placed in a situation in which you can act according to those sympathies which God has planted in your bosoms.

If you live up to these principles, how great and glorious will be your reward in the celestial kingdom!![132] If you live up to your privileges, the angels cannot be restrained from being your associates. Females, if they are pure and innocent, can come into the presence of God; for what is more pleasing to God than innocence; you must be innocent, or you cannot come up before God; if we would come before God, we must keep ourselves pure, as he is pure.[133]

The devil has great power to deceive;[134] he will so transform things as to make one gape at those who are doing the will of God. You need not be teazing your husbands[135] because of their deeds, but let the weight of your innocence, kindness and affections[136] be felt, which is more mighty than a millstone hung

---

126. The original minutes do not contain the phrase "or it will either injure or destroy the whole body."

127. The original minutes read, "The sympathies of the heads of the church have induc'd them to bear with those that were corrupt; in consequence of which all become contaminated."

128. The original minutes have "provoke" rather than "stimulate."

129. The original minutes read, "God, men, angels, and devils can't condemn those that resist every thing that is evil."

130. The original minutes read, "dethrone Jehovah, as that soul."

131. The original minutes do not contain the phrase "and benevolence."

132. The original minutes do not contain the phrase "will be your reward in the celestial kingdom!!"

133. The original minutes read, "If we would come before God let us be pure ourselves."

134. The original minutes do not contain the phrase "to deceive."

135. The original minutes have "tearing men" rather than "teazing your husbands."

136. The original minutes do not contain the phrase "kindness and affections."

about the neck; not war, not jangle, not contradiction, or dispute,[137] but meek-ness, love, purity—these are the things that should magnify you in the eyes of all good men.[138] Achan must be brought to light, iniquity must be purged out from the midst of the Saints;[139] then the veil will be rent, and the blessings of heaven will flow down—they will roll down like the Mississippi river.

If this Society listen to the council of the Almighty, through the heads of the church, they shall have power to command queens in their midst.[140]

I now deliver it as a prophecy, if the inhabitants of this state, with the people of the surrounding country, will turn unto the Lord with all their hearts, ten years will not roll round before the kings and queens of the earth will come unto Zion, and pay their respects to the leaders of this people: they shall come with their millions, and shall contribute of their abundance for the relief of the poor, and the building up and beautifying of Zion.[141]

After this instruction, you will be responsible for your own sins; it is a desirable honor that you should so walk before our Heavenly Father as to save yourselves; we are all responsible to God for the manner we improve the light and wisdom given by our Lord to enable us to save ourselves.[142]

President Smith continued reading from the above mentioned chapter, and[143] to give instructions respecting the order of God, as established in the church, saying every one should aspire only to magnify his own office and calling.[144]

He then commenced reading the 13th chapter. "Though I speak with the tongues of men and angels, and have not charity, I am become as sounding brass, or a tinkling cymbal;["][145] and said, don't be limited in your views with regard to your neighbor's virtues, but beware of self-righteousness,[146] and be limited in the estimate of your own virtues, and not think yourselves more righteous than others; you must enlarge your souls towards each other, if you

---

137. The original minutes do not contain the phrase "or dispute."
138. The original minutes read, "these are the things that should magnify us."
139. The original minutes do not contain the phrase "from the midst of the Saints."
140. The original minutes read, "This Society shall have power to command Queens in their midst."
141. In the original minutes this paragraph reads, "I now deliver it as a prophecy that before ten years shall roll round, the queens of the earth shall come and pay their respects to this Society— they shall come with their millions and shall contribute of their abundance for the relief of the poor— If you will be pure, nothing can hinder."
142. In the original minutes this paragraph reads, "After this instruction, you will be responsible for your own sins. It is an honor to save yourselves— all are responsible to save themselves."
143. The original minutes begin this paragraph with the words, "Pres.ᵗ Smith, after reading from the above mentioned Chapter, continued."
144. The original minutes have "&c." rather than "and calling."
145. The original minutes contain only the phrase "'Though I speak with the tongues of men' &c."
146. The original minutes do not contain the phrase "but beware of self-righteousness."

would do like Jesus, and carry your fellow-creatures to Abraham's bosom. He said he had manifested long-suffering, forbearance and patience towards the church, and also to his enemies; and we must bear with each others' failings, as an indulgent parent bears with the foibles of his children.[147]

President Smith then read the 2nd verse. "Though I have the gift of prophecy, and understand all mysteries, and all knowledge; and though I have all faith, so that I could remove mountains, and have not charity, I am nothing.["][148] He then said, though a man[149] should become mighty, do great things, overturn mountains, perform mighty works,[150] and should then turn from his high station to do evil,[151] to eat and drink with the drunken, all his former deeds would not save him, but he would go to destruction! As you increase in innocence and virtue, as you increase in goodness, let your hearts expand, let them be enlarged towards others; you must be long-suffering, and bear with the faults and errors of mankind.

How precious are the souls of men! The female part of the community are apt to be contracted in their views. You must not be contracted, but you must be liberal in your feelings. Let this Society teach women how to behave towards their husbands, to treat them with mildness and affection. When a man is borne down with trouble, when he is perplexed with care and difficulty,[152] if he can meet a smile instead of an argument or a murmur[153]—if he can meet with mildness, it will calm down his soul and soothe his feelings; when the mind is going to despair, it needs a solace of affection and kindness.[154]

You will receive instruction through the order of the Priesthood which God has established, through the medium of those appointed to lead, guide, and direct the affairs of the church in this last dispensation;[155] and I now turn the key in your behalf in the name of the Lord,[156] and this Society shall rejoice, and knowledge and intelligence shall flow down from this time henceforth;

---

147. In the original minutes this sentence reads, "He said he had manifested long suffering and we must do so too."

148. The original minutes read, "Prest. Smith then read, 'Though I have the gift of prophecy' &c."

149. The original minutes have "one" rather than "a man."

150. The original minutes have "&c" rather than "perform mighty works."

151. The original minutes do not contain the phrase "from his high station to do evil."

152. The phrase "with care and difficulty" does not appear in the original minutes.

153. The phrase "or a murmur" does not appear in the original minutes.

154. The phrase "of affection and kindness" does not appear in the original minutes.

155. The original minutes read, "This Society is to get instruction thro' the order which God has established— thro' the medium of those appointed to lead."

156. The original minutes read, "and I now turn the key to you in the name of God."

this is the beginning of better days to the poor and needy, who shall be made to rejoice and pour forth blessings on your heads.[157]

When you go home, never give a cross or unkind word to your husbands,[158] but let kindness, charity, and love crown your works henceforward; don't envy the finery and fleeting show of sinners, for they are in a miserable situation; but as far as you can, have mercy on them, for in a short time God will destroy them, if they will not repent and turn unto him.[159]

Let your labors be mostly confined to those around you, in the circle of your own acquaintance,[160] as far as knowledge is concerned, it may extend to all the world; but your administrations should be confined to the circle of your immediate acquaintance, and more especially to the members of the Relief Society. Those ordained to preside over and[161] lead you, are authorized to appoint the different officers, as the circumstances shall require.

If any have a matter to reveal, let it be in your own tongue; do not indulge too much in the exercise of[162] the gift of tongues, or the devil will take advantage of the innocent and unwary.[163] You may speak in tongues for your own comfort, but I lay this down for a rule, that if anything is taught by the gift of tongues, it is not to be received for doctrine.

President Smith then gave instruction respecting the propriety of females administering to the sick by the prayer of faith, the laying on of hands, or the anointing with oil; and said it was according to revelation that the sick should be nursed with herbs and mild food, and not by the hand of an enemy. Who are better qualified to administer than our faithful and zealous sisters, whose hearts are full of faith, tenderness, sympathy, and compassion? No one.[164] Said he was never placed in similar circumstances before, and never had given the same instruction; and closed his instructions by expressing his heartfelt[165] satisfaction in improving this opportunity.

The Spirit of the Lord was poured out in a very powerful manner, never to be forgotten by those present on this interesting occasion.

---

157. The original minutes read, "this is the beginning of better days, to this Society."
158. The original minutes read, "When you go home never give a cross word."
159. The original minutes read, "Don't envy sinners— have mercy on them, God will destroy them."
160. The original minutes read, "in your own circle."
161. The original minutes do not contain the phrase "preside over and."
162. The original minutes do not contain the phrase "the exercise of."
163. The phrase "and unwary" does not appear in the original minutes.
164. The original minutes read, "Prest. S. then offered instruction respecting the propriety of females administering to the sick by the laying on of hands— said it was according to revelation &c."
165. The original minutes do not include the word "heartfelt."

2.3 Salt Lake City Fourteenth Ward Relief Society, Report, 1856–1858, as Published in "Relief Society in the Early Days," July 1, 1895

Salt Lake City Fourteenth Ward Relief Society, "Relief Society in the Early Days" (Report), Woman's Exponent *(Salt Lake City, UT), July 1, 1895, vol. 24, no. 3, p. 21.*

The Female Relief Society of the Salt Lake City Fourteenth Ward functioned at two different times in the 1850s—in 1854 and possibly into 1855 and again between 1856 and 1858. This record of the second iteration, taken from an 1895 *Woman's Exponent* article, covers the eighteen months between September 1856 and March 1858. The article reproduces names of members and officers, resolutions, and a summary of disbursements, but apparently the original documents have not survived. As is evident from the roster of names, several of the church's leading families lived in the Fourteenth Ward, which was located in the center of Salt Lake City and included the blocks between South Temple Street and 300 South Street and between present-day 300 West Street and Main Street.

Eliza Partridge Lyman referred in her journal to the first iteration of the Fourteenth Ward Relief Society, established June 6, 1854, immediately following Brigham Young's announcement that ward Relief Societies should be formed to assist with Indian relief. Lyman wrote: "The sisters in the fourteenth ward (of which I was a resident) met at the school house with their Bishop Abraham Hoagland, to be organised into a society for the purpose of carrying out more thoroughly the instructions of Pres^{nt} Young. Sister Lydia Partridge was appointed President and Phebe Pratt Secretary. Others were appointed to visit the sisters of the Ward and ascertain what they were willing to give toward clothing the poor Indians." Lyman recorded making "a small gift to the society for the Lamanites," some "5 yds of factory cloth, but I hope to be able to give more soon." On June 17, when secretary Pratt resigned, Lyman became secretary and served in connection with her mother, President Lydia Clisbee Partridge.[166] The group apparently disbanded during 1854 or 1855, after the immediate need for clothing Indian women and children had been met.

In September 1856 Bishop Hoagland reestablished the Female Relief Society in the Fourteenth Ward, this time with Phebe Carter Woodruff as president. Two counselors, a secretary, a treasurer, a visiting committee, other officers, and a total of 127 members made a substantial organization. Woodruff's husband, Wilford, a member of the Quorum of the Twelve Apostles, noted in his diary that he attended the women's meeting on June 17, 1857: "In the afternoon I attended the 14 ward female relief society at my House with Robert Campbell we both addressed the meeting there were about 50 prese[n]t sewing knitting sewing carpet rags making quilts &c it is a laudable undertak[i]ng all the females in the ward meet at my house each wednesday afternoon they open & close with prayer Mrs Phebe W Woodruff is President & Mrs Pratt Secretary they clothe all the poor in the ward

---

166. Eliza Maria Partridge Lyman, Journal, 1846–1885, CHL, June 6, 9, and 17, 1854.

& during the last quarter they made a Donation to the perpetual Emigrating fund of $126. I wish all go & do like wise."[167]

———— ❧ ————

RELIEF SOCIETY IN THE EARLY DAYS.

THE Fourteenth Ward Female Relief, Society, organized by Bishop Hoagland (agreeable to the request of President Brigham Young) on the seventeenth day of September 1856, with a President and two counselors, a secretary and treasurer; with power to elect other such officers as might be needed, for the carrying out and management of said society.[168]

We therefore deemed it necessary to elect a visiting committee of nine persons, one to each block to collect subscriptions and enquire into the circumstances and necessities of the poor and report the same to the President of the Society.[169]

We have also an Appraiser Committee of three persons. Together with a superintendence of work Committee of three persons, likewise.[170]

Our meetings are opened and closed by singing and prayer, and occasionally with remarks by Bishop Hoagland, and other brethren of the Priesthood, who may occasionally call in. Also by the President of the Society.

Members are received or expelled by vote according to our rules and By Laws.

P. [PHEBE] W. WOODRUFF, Prest.

Phebe Woodruff, President; Mary I. Horne and Lucinda Southworth, Counselors; Kezia D. Pratt, Secretary; Agnes Hoagland Treasurer; afterwards P. W. Woodruff Treasurer.

---

167. Wilford Woodruff, Journals, 1833–1898, Wilford Woodruff, Journals and Papers, 1828–1898, CHL, June 17, 1857; for more on the Fourteenth Ward society, see "The Female Relief Society," *Deseret News,* Jan. 28, 1857, 372; "The 14th Ward Female Relief Society," *Deseret News,* May 20, 1857, 85; and "The 14th Ward Female Relief Society," *Deseret News,* Aug. 8, 1857, 176.

168. Joseph Smith stated at the initial meeting of the Female Relief Society, "If any Officers are wanted to carry out the designs of the Institution, let them be appointed and set apart, as Deacons, Teachers &c. are among us." (Document 1.2, entry for Mar. 17, 1842.)

169. The Female Relief Society of Nauvoo appointed women's committees to visit those in need within each municipal ward. The committees also collected donations and supervised distribution of goods to the needy. The visitors later became known as teachers or visiting teachers. (Document 1.2, entry for July 28, 1843; Documents 2.5 and 3.9.)

170. Appraisers placed an approximate dollar value on "in kind" donations such as food and clothing. The work overseen by superintendents generally included sewing fabric scraps or rags into strips to be woven into carpet, making quilts, and sometimes carding and spinning wool or other animal hair. Similar names for officers were later adopted in the adjacent Salt Lake City Fifteenth Ward. (See Document 3.9.)

Salt Lake City Fourteenth Ward album quilt. The Fourteenth Ward Relief Society left a tangible record of its members in an album quilt produced in 1857, composed of dozens of colorful blocks created and signed by individual members. Album quilts were created to be keepsakes, and this quilt was divided into two pieces so that more than one family could maintain a connection to the legacy. (Courtesy Carol H. Nielson.)

Visiting Committee: Lavinia [Lovina] Taylor, Grace Richardson, Ellen [Douglas] Parker, Rhoda H. Richards, Elizabeth Pixton, Matilda Wardsworth [Wadsworth], N. [Nancy] A. Stevenson, L. Southworth, Agnes Hoagland.

Appraiser Committee: Phebe Woodruff, Mary I. Horne, Lucinda Southworth.

Superintendence of Work Committee: Lucy L. Van Cott, Sarah B. Foss, Agnes Hoagland.

NAMES OF MEMBERS.

Phebe Woodruff, Mary I. Horne, Lucinda Southworth, Kezia D. Pratt, Agnes Hoagland, Leonora Taylor, Sarah M. Pratt, Emma Standish, Elizabeth Pixton, Sarah B. Phelps, N. A. Stevenson, Ann Longstroff [Longstroth], [Aura] Anetta A. Cummings, Lydia Sharp, Elizabeth K. Stevenson, Rhoda H. Richards, Fanny Spilsbury, Susan [Bayliss] Richards, Sophia Taylor, Esther Ann Hoagland, Jane Taylor, Mary Oakey [Okey], Matilda Wardsworth, Sarah Brown, Ann Jackson, Rachel Middleton, Elizabeth Pratt, Sarah B. Foss, Susan Cornelia Woodruff, Ph[o]ebe Amelia Woodruff, Mary C. Stephen, Susan Pratt, Belinda Pratt, Elizabeth T. Blair, Sarah Church, Mary Ann Taylor, Agnes Taylor, Sarah Lishman [Leishman], Mary Ann Brown, Ann Clewly, Elizabeth [Knight] Johnson, Emily Shelton, Hannah C. Mumford, Lucy L. Van Cott, Mary Ann Taysom, Rebecca Hoagland, Hannah Bird, [Sarah Mariah] Texana Blair, Sarah Jane Blair, Sarah S. Turpin, Maria L. Twinball [Turnbow], Lovina Taylor, Elizabeth [Hillyard] Thompson, Jane C. Romney, Elizabeth M. [Gaskell] Romney, Mary Hall, Sophronia Turnball [Turnbow], Harriet [Utley] Carter, Margaret Hoagland, Isabel Lamoreaux, Annetta Rhodes, Mary Rhodes, Susanna [Liptrot] Richards, Sarah Ann Heyes [Hayes], Ann Agatha Pratt, Mary Campbell, Susan S. Richards, Charlotte F. Richards, Clarissa Snyder, Jesse S. Eddings [Jessie Ann Eddins], Hannah B. Morley, Mary Richards, Alice Watt, Mary S. [Augusta] Snow, Sarah Woodruff, Emma Woodruff, Sarah Morris, Jane Watt, Elizabeth Foss, Olivia C. Foss, Deborah Ann Twinbull [Turnbow], Jane C. Richardson, Celestia L. Pratt, Sarah Richards, Nannie Richards, Caroline Simms [Sims], Mary C. Taylor, Elizabeth Rich, Jane Taylor, Helen [Ellen Benbow] Carter, Alice Thompson, Georgian A. Clements, Martha Robins [Robbins], S. [Sarah] G. Richards, S. S. Richards, Martha T. [Martha Ann Ball Johnson] Blair, Phebe Pratt, Martha T. [Jackson] Darger, Sarah Ivins, Sarah Ann Ballo, Jane E. Richards, Jane Jennings, Helen [Ellen] Winder, Helen Kay, Wilmirth East, Annie Latimer, Mary Perrin, Ellen C. Blair, Martha Price, L. [Lovina] Van Cott, Mary Ann Hooper, Catherine Mulliner, Adelaide Smith, Betsy Standish, Maria Riley, M. A. [Margaret Ann] Foster, M. [Matilda] Rhodes, [Hannah] Victoria Blair,

Sarah Ann Remmington, Fanny Snalam, Rhoda Richards, Grace Richardson, Mary Jane Merrill, Kate Gardener, M. E. [Mary Ellen] France, Margaret Hill, Harriet Phelps, Mary W. Pratt.

BY LAWS.

1.—The name of the society shall be called the Fourteenth Ward Female Relief Society.

2.—It shall be controlled by a president and two counselors, a secretary and treasurer, chosen by the members who shall choose such officers as may be deemed necessary.

3.—The object shall be the relief of the destitute—unemployed, and all whom it may have power to relieve or do good unto, in unison, with the councils of the Church, of Jesus Christ of Latter-day Saints.

4.—Those wishing to become members may be admitted on the recommend of any member. by a vote of any meeting regularly called.

5.—Members will be expelled from the society for unchristianlike conduct, by a majority of votes of any regularly organized meeting.

6.—These, by laws, may be increased, amended, annulled, or added to at any time considered necessary by a majority of the members.

FIRST REPORT.

Fourteenth Ward Female Relief Society, organized on the 17th day of September, 1856. Commenced and carried on our operations in a time of scarcity and under trying circumstances until, the 28th day of March, 1858, about one year and six months, during which time we received from members of the society in the form of contributions of money, wearing apparel, Provisions, etc, amounting to $346.05

Quilts on hand and for Sale, ... 100.00

Overplus for work and Propt 101.12

547.17

By paid out to poor in the Ward, ... $213.77

By paid to our brethren of the army[171] 43.75

By donated to H. C. [handcart] Company, ... 63.65

By donated to P. E. [Perpetual Emigrating] Fund, ... 126.00

By donated quilts to a Temple, ... 100.00

547.17

---

171. This refers to the Utah militia, known as the Nauvoo Legion at the time of the Utah War of 1857–1858.

2.4 Lucy Meserve Smith, Account of Relief Society in 1856, as Recorded in "Historical Sketches," June 12, 1889 (Excerpt)

Lucy Meserve Smith, "Historical Sketches of My Great Grandfathers," June 12, 1889, pp. 1, 51–56 (excerpt); microfilm; Lucy Meserve Smith, Papers, 1848–1892, CHL (MS 8270).

In 1889, at the age of seventy-two, Lucy Meserve Smith composed a historical narrative describing her ancestry and life experiences, including her labors during the 1850s as president of a ward Relief Society in Provo, Utah. A native of Newry, Maine, Lucy Smith was baptized a Latter-day Saint in 1837 and then worked in a cotton mill to fund her move to the Saints' gathering place in Nauvoo. Her skill with a handloom secured her income. In Nauvoo in 1844, at the age of twenty-seven, she became the second wife of George A. Smith; she arrived in the Salt Lake Valley with him and his other wives in 1849.[172]

A member of the Quorum of the Twelve Apostles, George A. Smith was appointed to preside over church affairs in two of the original seven counties in Utah. After overseeing settlement of Iron County in 1851, he began to preside over settlements in Utah County in July 1852.[173] At that time, Lucy and another of her husband's plural wives, Hannah Maria Libby Smith, moved with their husband to Provo, Utah County. There, according to Lucy, the women worked to "provid for the ne[ces]sitie of our family," which included Hannah's young son, Charles Warren, and John Henry, the son of Sarah Ann Libby Smith. Sarah, a wife of George A. Smith, had died in July 1851. Lucy taught school, and she and Hannah "took in spinning and weaving." Lucy wrote, "I did all in my power to ease up the burden of my husband as he was President of Utah County for years."[174] By the time Lucy served as Relief Society president in one of five wards in the Provo Stake, her husband had returned to Salt Lake City to assume the duties of church historian.

Lucy Meserve Smith's account describes the role local Relief Societies played in 1856 in providing aid to two companies of handcart immigrants who straggled into Utah after being devastated in present-day Wyoming by early snows. Smith also reported on a large-scale effort that Relief Societies participated in the following year, during the Utah War. Fearful of the intentions of federal troops sent by U.S. president James Buchanan to Utah in 1857, Brigham Young posted Mormon militia in the mountains east of Salt Lake City, charging them to resist, if events required, the coming army.[175] Smith's was one of many branches of the Relief Society that helped provision these Mormon forces.

---

172. George A. Smith married Bathsheba Wilson Bigler in 1841; following his marriage to Lucy Meserve Smith, he married Nancy Clements, Zilpha Stark, Sarah Ann Libby, and Hannah Maria Libby before immigrating to Utah. In 1857 he married his final wife, Susan Elizabeth West. (See Zora Smith Jarvis, comp., *Ancestry, Biography, and Family of George A. Smith* [Provo, UT: Brigham Young University Press, 1962], 266–307.)

173. See George A. Smith, Journals, 1839–1875, George A. Smith, Papers, 1834–1877, CHL, Apr.–Aug. 1851 and July–Oct. 1852; Historian's Office, Journal, 1844–1997, CHL, July 17, 1852.

174. Lucy Meserve Smith, "Historical Sketches of My Great Grandfathers," 1889, Lucy Meserve Smith, Papers, 1848–1892, microfilm, CHL, 51, 58, 59.

175. See William P. MacKinnon, ed., *At Sword's Point, Part 1: A Documentary History of the Utah*

Salt Lake City June 12ᵗʰ, 1889.

Historical sketches of my Great Grandfathers from the time they landed at Plymmouth Rock . . .¹⁷⁶ [p. 1] . . .

In 1856. the saints were called upon to confess our sins, renew our covenants, and all must be rebaptized for a remission of our sins, and strive to live more perfectly than ever before,¹⁷⁷ Then we had greater manifestations of the power of the evil one. I fasted two days to obtain a testimony from the Holy Spirit that I was accepted of my Heavenly Father, at the same time I kept at work in my loom both days without breaking my fast. One evening after the rest of the family had retired I knelt down to pray, and I was grasped by the wrist very tightly and it seemed as though there was something [p. 51] held over my face so it was very difficult for me to breath or utter a word, Said I old fellow you can figure away, but you've got the wrong pig by the ear this time, I kept praying every breath I could draw which came very hard and loud, but I did not hurry nor I could not be frightened. I went to bed when I got ready, but they followed me still trying to smother me, and after I got into bed I was struck on the shoulder quite hard. The Holy Spirit said to me they can do no harm where the name of Jesus is used with authority. I immediately rebuked them in the name of the Lord Jesus Christ, and by virtue of the Holy Priesthood conferred upon me in common with my companion in the Temple of our God.¹⁷⁸ All that evil sensation left me immediately, I soon fell asleep and was troubled no more at that time, but those wicked spirits seem to go from house to house annoying the saints after that, as they commenced their operations on me first I knew not why.

I was then chosen set apart and blessed to preside over the Relief Society with sister Rua Angeline Holden for my first, and Sister Nancy Bigler Flemming

---

War to 1858, Kingdom in the West: The Mormons and the American Frontier 10 (Norman, OK: Arthur H. Clark, 2008).

176. TEXT: The ellipsis points in this excerpt have been supplied by the editors of this volume to indicate omissions from the original document.

177. Smith is here describing the "Reformation" that took place among the Saints in 1856–1857. Rebaptism, a nineteenth-century practice indicating recommitment, was an essential part of this Reformation movement. (See Paul H. Peterson, "The Mormon Reformation of 1856–1857: The Rhetoric and the Reality," *Journal of Mormon History* 15 [1989]: 59–87.)

178. In an address to the Female Relief Society of Nauvoo, Joseph Smith cited Mark 16:17 and then endorsed women's exercise of spiritual gifts: "'Go ye into all the world' &c.— no matter who believeth; these signs, such as healing the sick, casting out devils &c. should follow all that believe whether male or female." A revised version of the same address published in the *Deseret News* in 1855 included a statement regarding priesthood similar to that here made by Lucy Smith: "He [Joseph Smith] spoke of delivering the keys of the Priesthood to the church, and said that the faithful members of the Relief Society should receive them in connection with their husbands." (Document 1.2, entry for Apr. 28, 1842; Document 2.2.)

Lucy Meserve Smith. Circa 1870. Lucy Meserve Smith wrote in 1889 a reminiscence describing her 1850s Relief Society work in Provo, Utah. Photograph likely by Edward Martin. (Church History Library, Salt Lake City.)

for my second councelors. Sister Sarah Jane Goff Blackburn Sec'y, and Treasurer. [p. 52]

We did all we could, with the aid of the good brethren and sisters, to comfort the needy as they came in with HandCarts late in the Fall[179] they got their hands and feet badly frosted. Br. Stephen Nixon and wife[180] nursed/ and took care of them til they were better we favoured them br. & Sis. N. by quilting a quilt very nicely for them, as our Society was short of funds then we ~~could~~ could not do much, but the four Bishops could hardly carry the bedding and other clothing we got together the first time we met. We did not cease our exersions til all were made comfortable. When the Hand Cart Companies arived, the Desks of the Seminary were loaded with provisions for them.[181] Just at the session of our Oct. Conference news came where these Hand Cart Co's were. President Young and others were excited and anxious for fear those Co's would be caught in the snow in the mountains they could not go on with the Confernce. The Pres't called for men teams clothing, and provisions, and they were soon on the way to meet the Companies with Pres't Young himself til he got into the Canon there he took sick and was oblige to turn back.[182] The sisters stripped off their Peticoats stockings and every thing they could spare, right there in the Tabernacle and piled into the wagons to send to the saints in the mountains.[183] [p. 53] The Snow was fast falling. and the saints were just piling down in a heap with the idea that they must all perish when to their great joy they discovered a light at a distance, then they took new courge and they had everything for their comfort.[184]

I never took more satisfaction and I might say pleasure in any labour I ever performed in my life, such a unimmity [unanimity] of feeling prevailed, I only

179. In 1856 two handcart companies, led by James G. Willie and Edward Martin, left Florence, Nebraska, late in the season and met early snowstorms in present-day Wyoming in October. Brigham Young, hearing of their distress, immediately asked the Saints to gather clothing, food, and other supplies to help bring the stranded Saints into the valley and sent wagons of goods to the relief of the handcart companies. (Brigham Young, Remarks, Oct. 5, 1856, in "Remarks," *Deseret News,* Oct. 15, 1856, 252.)

180. Eliza Hamson Nixon.

181. The seminary was built in 1854 as a school and meetinghouse. ("History of Provo City," *Tullidge's Quarterly Magazine* 3, no. 3 [July 1884]: 245.)

182. See Brigham Young, Remarks, Oct. 5, 1856, in "Remarks," *Deseret News,* Oct. 15, 1856, 252. For Brigham Young's attempt to participate in the rescue, see President's Office, Journals, 1852–1863, Brigham Young Office Files, 1832–1878, CHL, Oct. 13–15, 1856.

183. The "old" tabernacle and adjacent bowery were located at the current site of the Assembly Hall on Temple Square in Salt Lake City.

184. For information on the handcart rescue, see Andrew D. Olsen, *The Price We Paid: The Extraordinary Story of the Willie and Martin Handcart Pioneers* (Salt Lake City: Deseret Book, 2006), 114–176.

had to go into a store and make my wants known, if it was cloth it was measured off without charge.

My councilors and I wallowed through the snow until our clothes were wet a foot high to get things together, give out noticeses &c. We peaced blocks carded bats quilted and got together I think 27. Quilts, besides a great amount of other clothing. in one winter for the needy.

What comes next for willing hands to do? The brethren are called to go into the mountains to stand guard to keep the enemy at bay.[185] They want bedding, socks mittens &c. so we sat up nights and knitted all that was needed til we made out a big load with the Quilts and Blankets which we sent out into the mountains to the brethren. What next: The Provo Brass Band want a nice Flag, they chose a committee and send [p. 54] To me desiring me to boss the concern. I said to the sisters less [let's] go to the fields glean Wheat and pick ground Cherries to pay for material and make the Band a Flag. No sooner said than done we paid br. Henry Maibin part dried Ground-Cherries and the banance [balance] in money for the Gilding, part of the silk was donated the rest we paid for in Wheat, which we had gleaned

The middle of the Flag was white Lutestring Silk[186] with an edge of changable Blue and Green let in the shape of saw teeth and a silk fring around the edge of that and sister Eliza Terrill embroidered the corners with with a hive and bees, butterflies, roses &c.

The gilding was imitation of two Sacks horns [saxhorns] crossed in the middle or centre and gold letters across the top of the Flag (Presented by the Ladies of Provo.)

Provo brass Band

sacks X horns

United we stand[187]

We had a handsone Staff with a beautiful bunch of ribbons on the top and a streamer on the oposite corner. The whole not counting our time or labour cost $76.

I wished to make a speech in behalf of the Ladies of Provo and. Present the Flag to the Standard Bearer and have him make a Speech back to me in behalf

---

185. Brigham Young declared martial law in the territory on September 15, 1857, and through the fall and winter Mormon militia guarded mountain passes to forestall the entry of federal troops into the Salt Lake Valley. (MacKinnon, *At Sword's Point*, 285–288, 339–369.)

186. Lutestring is glossy silk fabric. ("Lutestring," in *The Oxford English Dictionary*, ed. J. A. Simpson and E. S. C. Weiner, 2nd ed., 20 vols. [Oxford: Clarendon, 1989], 9:125.)

187. TEXT: The first and third of these three lines are bowed up and down, respectively, so that the three lines together form an oval shape.

of the Provo Brass Band, but our President James C. Snow put his foot on it. [p. 55]

So we had a Grand Pic Nic Party when I returned from from the City with the beautiful Flag.

We had a nice supper and finished up with a dance Our Flag took the prize in the big teritorial Fair[188]

The next thing we must manufacture Carpets for our Provo New Meeting-House, we soon had them made and in position.[189] . . . [p. 56] . . .

188. The first Deseret State Fair was in Salt Lake City in 1856. At the 1858 fair, a prize was awarded to Henry Maiben for "Flag Painting on Silk." Perhaps this was the flag of the Provo brass band. ("The First Deseret State Fair," *Deseret News,* Oct. 8, 1856, 245; "List of Prizes," *Deseret News,* Oct. 20, 1858, 144.)

189. Construction on the Provo meetinghouse was commenced in 1856, but the building was not dedicated until 1867. Among the items blessed in the dedicatory prayer by John Taylor were the carpets. ("The President's Trip to Utah County," *Deseret News,* Sept. 4, 1867, 282.)

2.5 Priscilla Merriman Evans, Account of Relief Society in 1856–1870, as Recorded in Autobiography, circa 1907 (Excerpt)

Priscilla Merriman Evans, Autobiography, [ca. 1907], pp. 42, 48, 51–54 (excerpt); Emma Priscilla Evans Little, Papers, 1870–1941, L. Tom Perry Special Collections, Harold B. Lee Library, Brigham Young University, Provo, UT (MSS 357).

Priscilla Merriman Evans preserved a record of Relief Society activities in Spanish Fork, Utah, by including in her dictated autobiography excerpts from the no longer extant "old Book" of minutes and accounts she had kept as the organization's secretary. Priscilla Merriman, born at Mounton, Wales, was baptized in 1852 at the age of seventeen. She married Thomas D. Evans, a Welsh missionary, in 1856—two weeks before the couple set sail from Liverpool for Boston. They traveled by cattle car to Iowa City, where they joined a group of Welsh converts walking with handcarts to the Salt Lake Valley. The Evanses settled in Spanish Fork, where over the next two decades they raised twelve children.[190]

In 1850 Latter-day Saint settlers began to cultivate land about sixty miles south of Salt Lake City in the river bottoms of the Spanish Fork River. Settlers erected a fort in 1854, and a year later the territorial legislature granted Spanish Fork a city charter.[191]

Priscilla Evans had lived in the city nearly a year when, in 1857, visiting patriarch John Young met with about forty women to organize a Relief Society, naming Rhoda Snell as president. "Because of the scattered settlement and in order to do more efficient work," one account explains, the ward was divided into districts (first three and later four) to facilitate women's visiting in order to assess needs and collect donations. Each district had a Relief Society presidency and kept its own accounts.[192]

Evans served as secretary in the second district (her account speaks of the Second Ward, but Spanish Fork was not divided into four wards until 1891). Evans served as Relief Society secretary until 1875, when her husband was called on a mission to Europe and she asked for a release. "At that time I already had 10 children," she wrote. "In all those years since the Organization of the Female Relief Society, of Spanish Fork, in 1857 I had done the secretary work, kept all Books and accounts, for the Society. I always attended my meetings when able."[193]

Reading from her old record as her daughter Emma Priscilla Evans Little took down the dictation, Evans noted changes in officers, donations made, and a few of the names of those who contributed goods, time and labor, or money. While most individual ward Relief Societies north of Provo disbanded when the Saints moved south to Provo in 1857, the

---

190. Priscilla Merriman Evans, Autobiography, ca. 1907, Emma Priscilla Evans Little, Papers, 1870–1941, L. Tom Perry Special Collections, Harold B. Lee Library, Brigham Young University, Provo, UT, 42, 44–46, 58.

191. "Descriptive," and "History," entries for 1854 and 1855, in Spanish Fork Ward, Utah Stake, Manuscript History and Historical Reports, 1851–1900, CHL.

192. "Relief Society," in Spanish Fork Ward, Utah Stake, Manuscript History and Historical Reports, 1851–1900, CHL.

193. Evans, Autobiography, 57.

district Relief Societies farther south in Spanish Fork continued to function. In 1871, as part of the movement to reestablish the Relief Society in every ward, Eliza R. Snow, Margaret T. Smoot, and Elizabeth A. Howard visited Spanish Fork and assisted in reorganizing the city's four Relief Societies into two, and, as Evans recorded, "encouraged the Officers and members to do their duties and live up to their responsibilities."[194]

———— ❧ ————

Priscilla Merriman Evans
Dictated by herself and written by her daughter, Emma P. Evans Little. . . . [p. 42] . . .[195]

We reached Salt Lake City. Oct 2—1856.[196] Tired, sick foot sore and weary Wm R. Jones[197] met us at the public Square[198] Salt Lake City, and took us down to his home 60 miles distant, to Spanish Fork in Utah Co. We stayed with him about one month then went to live in the family of Stephen Markham. His family consisted of himself, three wives, seven children, when he took in I and my husband. They lived in a "Dug out"—It was a very large room built half under ground, with a fireplace in one end, and a dirt floor. Lumber was very scarce and three bedsteads were constructed from poles, and rawhide, cut in strips and laced back and forth making a nice springy bed. For the children they had "Trundle" beds with little wooden rollers on, and in the day time those little beds could be rolled under, their mothers bedsteads to utelize space. The dear generous big hearted Stephen Markham took us in to his large family and made us feel like one of them. Mr Markham had been one of the Prophet Joseph's body guard, and went all thru the drivings and persecutions of the Saints, and his great heart was ever open to the wants of those less fortunate than himself.[199] . . . [p. 48] . . .

194. Evans, Autobiography, 54; see also Part 3 herein.

195. TEXT: The ellipsis points in this excerpt have been supplied by the editors of this volume to indicate omissions from the original document.

196. Evans and her husband were members of the third handcart company of 1856, captained by Edward Bunker. It numbered 320 immigrants, nearly all Welsh. The journey to Salt Lake City from Iowa City lasted from June to October. ("Immigration to Utah," *Deseret News,* Oct. 15, 1856, 254; "Foreign Correspondence: Iowa," *Latter-day Saints' Millennial Star,* Aug. 2, 1856, 18:489; Edward Bunker, Autobiography, 1894, CHL, 22–23.)

197. Jones was an 1854 immigrant from Wales. Evans's husband likely knew Jones from the branch in Merthyr Tydfil. (Emigration Book C, 1854–1855, Manifest for Ship *Golconda,* 15, European Mission, Emigration Records, 1849–1925, CHL; Evans, Autobiography, 44–45.)

198. The public square was known at the time as Union Square. The site, located between present-day 200 and 300 North Streets and 300 and 400 West Streets in Salt Lake City, was occupied by the University of Deseret (now the University of Utah) in 1884 and by West High School beginning in 1901.

199. Markham traveled to Utah in the original pioneer company of 1847. He served as bishop of the Palmyra Ward, seven miles south of Provo, from 1853 until 1856, when the settlement was abandoned and Spanish Fork was established on higher ground. (Andrew Jenson, *Latter-day Saint Biographical*

Perhaps this would be an appropriate place to insert some of my Relief Society work.

The very first Organization, of the Four Wards of the relief Society Was Organized by "Uncle John Young" in the "Old Bowery."[200]

as I have to deal with what was the Seccond Ward I will begin with my work.

1ˢᵗ Journal of meetings of the Female Relief Society of Spanish Fork City Utah Co, Utah. Sept 16ᵗʰ, 1857.

The sisters met with a few of the Bretheren at the home of Charles A. Davis.

Meeting opend by singing. Prayer by Bishop John L. Butler.

After singing some instructions were given by Bishop John L. Butler. in regard to moving out as a Female Relief Society. (By the way, Bishop John L. Butler was the first bishop of Spanish Fork. Utah.[201] [p. 51]

The following Officers, were selected and and unanimously Sustained.

President	Lucretia Gay.
1ˢᵗ Councilor	Armelia Berry
2ⁿᵈ "	Letetia Davis
Tressurer	Ruth Davis
Secretary	Priscilla Evans.

Mrs [Hannah] Beck was nominated Secty first, but as she could neither read or write. they Sent for me I was sustained as Sec'ty. altho I had come in with the Hand Cart Co, and had a young babe.[202]

Priscilla Evans.[203]

The Teachers were also selected and sustained, and the names of 40 members enrolled. The above is a copy taken from my old book of the First Organization, of the 2ⁿᵈ Ward. Female Relief Society of Spanish Fork City Utah Co Utah Sept. 16ᵗʰ 1857.

Encyclopedia: A Compilation of Biographical Sketches of Prominent Men and Women in the Church of Jesus Christ of Latter-day Saints, 4 vols. [Salt Lake City: Andrew Jenson History Co., 1901–1936], 3:676–677.)

200. The Spanish Fork Relief Society was organized September 14, 1857, by Patriarch John Young, brother of Brigham Young, widely known as "Uncle John." The bowery was located in the city's public square. ("Relief Society," in Spanish Fork Ward, Utah Stake, Spanish Fork Ward Manuscript History and Historical Reports, 1851–1900, CHL; Elisha Warner, *The History of Spanish Fork* [Spanish Fork, UT: Press Publishing, 1930], 75.)

201. Butler served as bishop of the Spanish Fork Ward from 1856 until his death in 1860. Priscilla Evans incorrectly identified him as the "first bishop of Spanish Fork." The first bishop was William Pace, who served from 1851 to 1856. Butler succeeded Pace when the latter was appointed to serve a mission in England. ("Diagram of the Bishopric of the Spanish Fork Ward," and "History," entry for 1856, in Spanish Fork Ward, Utah Stake, Manuscript History and Historical Reports, 1851–1900, CHL.)

202. The "young babe" is daughter Emma Priscilla Evans, born December 31, 1856. (Evans, Autobiography, 48.)

203. TEXT: This note appears next to the list of officers and is inscribed sideways running up the page.

Thomas D. Evans and Priscilla Merriman Evans. Circa 1901. Handcart pioneers Thomas and Priscilla Evans had lived in Spanish Fork, Utah, for about a year when Priscilla began keeping the minute book for one of the districts in the newly established Spanish Fork Relief Society (1857). Photograph by George Edward Anderson. (Courtesy L. Tom Perry Special Collections, Harold B. Lee Library, Brigham Young University, Provo, UT.)

There are pages of donations, For the Poor, for the Emmigration fund,[204] Temple donations, Flour and all kinds of food gather'd to pay for work done such as Temple clothing and aprons. Carpenter work &c a Sample of donations in early days are as follows. Mary Thomas 3 nails calico,[205] Lydia Markham 1 Pr of wool socks $125. Thirza Thurber, 1/4 yd calico. Adeline Allan [Sarah Adeline Allen] 3 nails calico. Priscilla Evans calico 15 cts Lucy Allen 1 skein of thread 15 cts Wool was 40 cts pr lb. Thread 15 cts skein. Calico 40 cts pr yd. Hickory shirting 40 cts when you could get it.

Here is a little coppied from the "old Book" while Mrs Gay was Pres. Feb 12th 1858. an account of work done to fit out the bretheren who went to Echo Canyon to meet Johnsons Army. in defence of Zion.[206]

Lucretia Gay worked 10 days carding and spinning wool for shirts. she furnished half lb of wool. worked four days carding & and spinning "hair" for Lariets. for the bretheren[207] she worked one day, and donated cloth for one pr of garments $2.40 she also helped to make a pr of Pants and she made, one pr. of mittens. Armelia Berry worked six days knitting. and donated one wool shirt $5.00. Ruth Davis worked five days at sewing and donated 3/4 yard of cloth for sleeves of shirt. Lydia Markham worked 1½ days carding hair. one day quilting, one and half day making garments. She also donated one wool blanket $7.50. Some of the bretheren who were disabled and could not go, sent their clothes [p. 52] Thomas D. Evans let Harrison Beck take his over coat, and another man took his boots. Martha Davis [David] worked two days carding hair, and donated two skeins of wool yarn. Hariet Simmonds [Simmons] donated 1/4 yd calico, and three knots of wool yarn.[208] The above is a sample of the workings of the Female relief Society only of course many donations for different purposes. They made quilts, and all kinds of clothing It was all done

---

204. The Perpetual Emigrating Fund.

205. "Nails" refers to a measurement of fabric. One nail equaled one-sixteenth of a yard or two and a quarter inches. ("Nail," in *An American Dictionary of the English Language,* ed. Noah Webster [New York: S. Converse, 1828].)

206. In 1857 President James Buchanan sent a federal army to Utah in response to reports of a Mormon rebellion and to accompany a new governor who had been appointed to replace Brigham Young in that office. Led by Albert Sidney Johnston, the expedition was often referred to by Latter-day Saints as "Johnston's Army." On the Utah War, see William P. MacKinnon, ed., *At Sword's Point, Part 1: A Documentary History of the Utah War to 1858,* Kingdom in the West: The Mormons and the American Frontier 10 (Norman, OK: Arthur H. Clark, 2008).

207. The women likely spun animal fibers into strands to be woven into ropes. These ropes were then used as lariats to lasso horses or cattle.

208. A "knot" of yarn measured 2,960 inches (82.222 yards), and ten knots made a skein. (Nancy Dick Bogdonoff, *Handwoven Textiles of Early New England: The Legacy of a Rural People, 1640–1880* [Harrisburg, PA: Stackpole Books, 1975], 36.)

by hand as there were no sewing machines. Some of the old Nauvoo Sisters[209] have sheared the sheep washed, carded, and spun, and wove the cloth, and made it up in to clothing by hand. for their husbands and families This kind of work was done to fit out the bretheren who went to meet Johnsons Army. Sister Gay and her councilers Presided nine years when they ⟨she⟩ wished to be released owing to ill health and old age

The reorganization of the Second Ward Female Relief Society.

The seccond Ward Female Relief Society, met in the little white "School House" Feb 14ᵗʰ 1866.[210] Bishop [Albert] Thurber was filling a mission in England and Geo A Wilkins [George Washington Wilkins] Presided.[211]

The following officers were set apart for their various offices by Pres. Geo A. Wilkins, Pres of Teachers Thomas D. Evans and Teacher Andrew Ferguson. Feb 14ᵗʰ 1866.

"The Officers were chosen as follows.

President	Letetia Ann Davis
1ˢᵗ Coun.	Hariet Simmons.
2ⁿᵈ "	Sarah Brockbank.
Treasurer.	Thirza Thurber.
Secretary	Priscilla Evans.

Eight Teachers more were nominated and sustained and the names of more members enrolled. The history of the next four yrs. is about like the past nine yrs. There are pages and pages in the old book of meetings, with a record of work done and credit, for scraps for quilts, wool, thread, yarn, flour, food, and evry thing that could be used. They paid $10.65 to get a box made for scraps and records. they donated and bought silk worm Eggs. and set out Mulbery trees, as counciled by the presiding sisters, The silk industry was a failure here.[212] They made a great many quilts and they ranged in price from $8.00 to $15. cradle quilts four dollars. [p. 53]

---

209. Lucretia Gay (mentioned earlier in this paragraph) may be the "Mrs. Gay" listed as affiliating with the Female Relief Society of Nauvoo on June 9, 1842. (Document 1.2, entry for June 9, 1842.)

210. Schoolhouses were often the first buildings built in a new community and served multiple uses. The "little white school house" was built in 1865 near the public square. (Warner, *History of Spanish Fork,* 91.)

211. Thurber was bishop of the Spanish Fork Ward beginning in 1863, but he served a mission to Britain in 1865–1866. After returning, he again served as bishop until 1874. Wilkins served as a counselor to Bishop Thurber and presided over the ward in Thurber's absence. ("History," entries for 1863, 1865, 1867, 1874, in Spanish Fork Ward, Utah Stake, Manuscript History and Historical Reports, 1851–1900, CHL; William G. Hartley, *Another Kind of Gold: The Life of Albert King Thurber, a Utah Pioneer, Explorer and Community Builder* [Troy, ID: C. L. Dalton, 2011], 477.)

212. Latter-day Saint attempts at sericulture in early Utah date to the late 1850s. Brigham Young, who planted his own mulberry trees in 1866, invited women in an April 8, 1868, conference to pursue silk-raising as part of the Saints' movement for economic self-sufficiency. Relief Society leaders supported the

When the Militia was organized in Spanish Fork, the R. S. made their tents for them by hand.[213] On training days, they looked like an Army. They would take turns meeting in diferent places, from the settlements around. In Spanish Fork when the Visitors would come, they would pitch their Tents, South of town across the river and camp. They would train and have sham battles, and all kinds of interesting skirmishing. There would be hundreds of people there to view them. Government put a stop to the Training in Utah.[214] I suppose they were affraid they would get to be too efficient. in fighting. Letetia A Davis Presided four years. when she was released on account of failing health. She died Jan 26ᵗʰ 1872. . . . [p. 54] . . .

---

venture, which persisted into the 1890s but ultimately did not succeed. (Document 3.4; Chris Rigby Arrington, "The Finest of Fabrics: Mormon Women and the Silk Industry in Early Utah," *Utah Historical Quarterly* 46, no. 4 [Fall 1978]: 376–396.)

213. The militia's Second Division was organized in May 1866 in response to the Black Hawk War, a series of conflicts in central Utah between Indian tribes and settlers. Bishop Albert K. Thurber was elected commander of the Second Brigade. (Hamilton Gardner, "The Utah Territorial Militia," unpublished typescript, [not after 1959], copy at CHL, 545–546.)

214. In September 1870 Utah governor J. Wilson Shaffer issued a proclamation forbidding all musters, drills, and similar activities. (Gardner, "Utah Territorial Militia," 597–598.)

2.6 Cedar City Ward Relief Society, Minutes, September 10 and December 10, 1857, and March 11, 1858

Cedar City Ward Relief Society, Minutes, Sept. 10 and Dec. 10, 1857, and Mar. 11, 1858; Cedar City Ward, Parowan Stake, Relief Society Minute Book, 1856–1875 and 1892, pp. [18]–[19], [21]–[22], [24]–[26], CHL (LR 1514 22).

On November 20, 1856, ninety-five women assembled in the local "tabernacle" as stake president Isaac C. Haight organized the Cedar City, Utah, Relief Society. At that meeting, with "most of the ladies of Cedar" present, Lydia Hopkins was voted president. Hopkins chose Annabella Sinclair Macfarlane Haight, a plural wife of the stake president, as her first counselor; Rachel Taylor Whittaker as her second counselor; and Ellen Whittaker Lunt, Whittaker's daughter, as secretary.[215] Following four weekly meetings, the group met monthly, usually on Thursday afternoons, from January 8, 1857, until April 14, 1859. The society was reorganized in 1868 under a new presidency; Lunt continued as secretary, a position she held until 1879.[216]

In November 1851, four months before Henry Lunt married Ellen Whittaker, he led the first company of Latter-day Saints in founding Cedar City. Located 250 miles south of Salt Lake City, the settlement was part of the Latter-day Saints' "Iron Mission," a project conceived by church leaders in the spring of 1850 to establish agricultural outposts and an iron works in the red rock desert along the anticipated line of Mormon settlements between Salt Lake City and San Diego.[217] Reserves of iron ore, close proximity to beds of coal, and the selection of English, Irish, Scottish, and Welsh miners and iron workers as colonists initially lent promise to the enterprise, but ultimately it produced little quality iron. Suspension of the iron works in October 1858 followed years of hard winters and famine from drought and insects.[218] As a result of these circumstances and the shadow cast by the 1857 massacre at nearby Mountain Meadows—in which settlers, along with American Indians they recruited, slaughtered approximately 120 members of a wagon train traveling from Arkansas to California—many colonists abandoned Cedar City for more attractive settlements.[219] This may help explain the end of recorded Relief Society meetings in 1859.

---

215. Cedar City Ward, Parowan Stake, Cedar City Ward Relief Society Minute Book, 1856–1875, CHL, Nov. 20, 1856, p. 3.

216. "A Brief History of the Relief Society of Cedar City," Mar. 17, 1892, in Cedar City Ward, Parowan Stake, Relief Society Minute Book.

217. For more on the settlement of Cedar City and the Iron Mission, see Morris A. Shirts and Kathryn H. Shirts, *A Trial Furnace: Southern Utah's Iron Mission,* Studies in Latter-day Saint History (Provo, UT: Brigham Young University Press, 2001), chaps. 6–7.

218. See Brigham Young to Isaac C. Haight, Oct. 8, 1858, Brigham Young Letterbook, vol. 4, pp. 432–435, in Brigham Young Office Files, 1832–1878, CHL; Shirts and Shirts, *Trial Furnace,* chap. 14.

219. For more on the Mountain Meadows Massacre, see Ronald W. Walker et al., *Massacre at Mountain Meadows: An American Tragedy* (New York: Oxford University Press, 2008). Cedar City resident Martin Slack stated in a December 1859 letter to the *Deseret News:* "Two years ago there were about 150 families residing in this place; but through various causes, such as a scarcity of water, poor land and the suspension of the iron works—some have removed to other parts of the Territory, and a few more

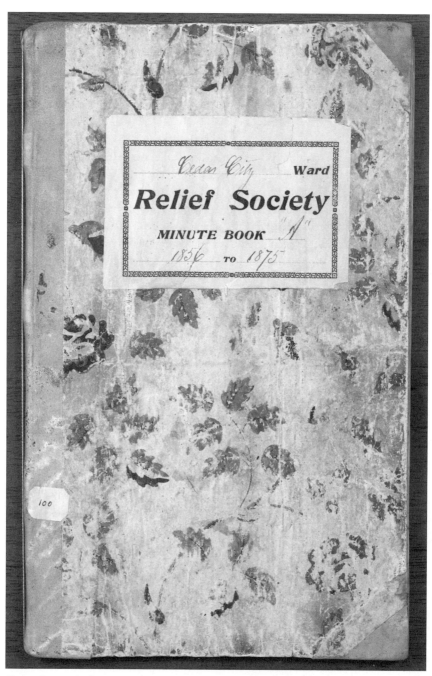

Cedar City Relief Society Minute Book. Ellen Lunt recorded minutes of the Cedar City, Utah, Relief Society from 1856 to 1875. Invited at the December 3, 1856, meeting to donate "a little writing paper" for the secretary's minutes, members contributed sheets of various sizes. Lunt then collated the sheets to fit between pieces of pasteboard that she covered with floral wallpaper she had brought from England. She made a binding for the spine and corners from cured buckskin. The archival labels seen here on the front cover were added later. (Church History Library, Salt Lake City.)

Ellen Lunt's minutes of three Cedar City Relief Society meetings—out of a total of about two dozen recorded between 1856 and 1859—are featured here. The first featured meeting occurred on September 10, 1857, a day before the Mountain Meadows Massacre and while the emigrant company was already under siege. While the situation is not explicitly addressed, the minutes refer to the tension and to the militiamen from Cedar City who were "out acting in our defence." The other two meetings included here are dated December 10, 1857, and March 11, 1858.

As the Cedar City Relief Society Minute Book is one of the few surviving Relief Society minute books from the 1850s, these selected minutes are featured to demonstrate some of the operations and concerns of a local society. The organization of the Cedar City society reflected that of the Nauvoo Relief Society, with a presidency, secretary, and treasurer, and a corps of teachers charged with visiting the poor to ascertain their needs. The teachers also reported their instructions to women regarding obedience, orthodoxy, chastity, cleanliness, and prayer—some of the key principles emphasized during the 1856–1857 Mormon Reformation.

September 10, 1857 • *Thursday*

Met according to appointment 2, 0, clock P.M. Thursday Sep[r] 10th 1857. Opened the meeting by singing, Prayer by Sister Lunt, Singing ⟨Minutes read and approved⟩ Sister Hopkins called for the teachers report Sister Pugmire and sister [Alice] Randle said that the sisters manifested a good spirit and seemed to be improving, that they encouraged them to live their religion, and to continue to improve. Sister Liston said that she with sister [Mary] Mc Connell had visited the north line,[220] and that they ~~they~~ found the sisters doing pretty well, that they instructed them in cleanliness economy &c. felt highly pleased with the sisters as a general thing Sister Willis and Sister Haight said that they found things generally to their satisfaction taught them the necessity of being obedient to their husbands &c—[221] and not to be fearful in these troublesome

---

families anticipate removing next spring." (Martin Slack, Dec. 19, 1859, Letter to the Editor, *Deseret News*, Feb. 15, 1860, 394.)

220. The Relief Society presidency had earlier designated teachers for different portions of the city: the west line, the north line, the middle line and the "new city," the east line, and the south line. The Cedar City fort, built 1853–1854, enclosed the northeast half of the surveyed city. The survey showed a central public square or temple block, with north–south and east–west lines dividing 4 × 20 rod lots for individual families. The "new city" was located outside the fort wall. According to a ward history, "As late as 1857, about half the people lived inside the fort wall. The rest had already built on their lots on the new city survey. The distance from the fort to the second location across the creek was half a mile." (Cedar City Ward, Parowan Stake, Relief Society Minute Book, June 11, 1857; "History," entries for 1852 and 1853, in Cedar Ward, Parowan Stake, Manuscript History and Historical Reports, 1851–1900, CHL.)

221. At the organizational meeting of the Cedar City Relief Society, November 20, 1856, stake president Isaac C. Haight spoke at length on the topic of wives obeying their husbands. General church leaders at this time also emphasized this concept. At an earlier meeting of the Cedar City Relief Society, two

times but to be prayerful and attend to their duties. Mother Whittaker and Sister Annabella found the sisters generally enjoying a good spirit, that they felt to rejoice in visiting the sisters & that they felt the sisters were improveing in all things Sister Haight said that the sisters enjoyed a better spirit than they did eight or nine months ago,— said that these were squally times, and we ought to attend to secret prayer in behalf of our husbands, sons, fathers, & brothers. instructed the sisters to teach their sons & daughters the principles of righteousness, and to implant a desire in their hearts to avenge the blood of the Prophets.[222] Sister Hopkins said that she with sister White had visited the sisters in the middle lines, that they felt well and manifested a good spirit, and was desirous to do well, and to improve,— advised them to attend strictly to secret prayer in behalf of the brethren that are out acting in our defence.—[223]

---

teachers reported that they "had met with a little opposition in regards to obedience to husbands, though those that were willing to live their religion, were also willing to give heed unto that principle." (Cedar City Ward, Parowan Stake, Relief Society Minute Book, Nov. 20, 1856, and June 11, 1857; see also, for example, Heber C. Kimball, July 12, 1857, in *Journal of Discourses*, 26 vols. [Liverpool: Various publishers, 1855–1886], 5:28–30; and Brigham Young, Sept. 21, 1856, in *Journal of Discourses*, 4:56–57.)

222. The phrase "blood of the prophets," which is used in the Bible and the Book of Mormon, was used by Latter-day Saints in this era to refer to the deaths of Joseph and Hyrum Smith, who were murdered by a mob at Carthage, Illinois, in 1844. In 1857 Mormons in Utah, including Brigham Young and other church leaders, were using heated rhetoric against outsiders, including references to the deaths of the Smiths, in the context of the Reformation and the Utah War. Some of the emigrants in the Arkansas wagon company with their cattle passed through Cedar City on September 3, 1857, and some individuals apparently threatened local residents. A later story that circulated in southern Utah about the emigrants was "that one boasted of having a gun that killed Joseph Smith." The three historians who have written the most in-depth study of the massacre state, "If an emigrant in fact made such a boast, it was probably just part of the venting that went on in Cedar City. None of the identified victims of the massacre is known to have had anything to do with the Smith brothers' deaths." (See 2 Kings 9:7; Matthew 23:29–33; Luke 11:50; Revelation 16:6; 18:24; 3 Nephi 9:5–11; and Walker et al., *Massacre at Mountain Meadows*, 67–73, 93–94, 98–100, 132–135.)

223. The Arkansas company passed through territorial Utah when tensions between Mormons and outsiders were high, partly as a result of reports that the U.S. government had sent a federal army to quell a reported Mormon rebellion. Mormons were instructed to not sell grain or other supplies to the wagon train as a wartime measure; in addition, the emigrants had clashed verbally with Mormons regarding where they could graze their cattle. Verbal clashes between members of the Arkansas company and local residents occurred in Cedar City on September 3, and local officials hoped to imprison some of the emigrants. In early September 1857, the wagon train camped at Mountain Meadows, about forty miles southwest of Cedar City. Some local Mormon leaders recruited Paiute Indians to join them in an attack on the train on September 7 that was apparently intended to exact vengeance upon the emigrants and to frighten them. Though the attack was to have appeared as if perpetrated solely by the Paiutes, things did not go as planned and the local Mormons recognized that the emigrants knew that local white men had been involved. On September 9 local ecclesiastical and military leaders conspired to order additional men to the site to preclude any possibility that reports of the initial Mormon violence should reach California. At midday on September 10, shortly before the women's Relief Society meeting, about one-fifth of the Cedar City militia left for Mountain Meadows, where the wagon train emigrants remained under siege. The following day, September 11, the emigrants agreed to leave their circled wagons when Mormon militiamen

The Presidency gave some good instructions to the sisters, which if adhered to, would tend greatly to their benefit.— Sister Liston & Sister Mc-Connell were appointed to visit the East line. Sister Pugmire and Sister Randle the Middle lines, Sister [Mary Ann] Harrison and Sister White the South line. Sister Mc-Murdy [Mary Ann McCurdie] ⟨& Sister [Barbara] Morris⟩ the West line. The Presidency would take the North line. Sister Eliza Ann Haight & Sister Willis the Iron works & the new City.— Sung—Oh how glorious will be the morning &c.—[224] Sister [Celestia] Durfee, Sister Wilden, Mother [Barbara] Morris, Sister [Terressa] Chamberlain, Sister Randle & Sister Jane Bosnell bore their [p. [18]] testimony and felt to rejoice that the time of our redemption was drawing nigh. It was moved and carried, that Margaret Bateman Hannah K Smith [Klingen-smith], Hannah Micholston [Ane Mickelsen] become members of this Society. Sister Hopkins said the bell would be rung half an hour before meeting time for the future.[225] Singing. Benediction by Sister Mary Willis. Adjourned till 2 o clock P.M. Thursday Octr 8th 1857. Ellen Lunt—Secretary . . . [p. [19]] . . .[226]

December 10, 1857 • *Thursday*

Met Pursuant to adjournment 2 o clock P.M. Thursday Dec 10th 1857. Present, Bishop Smith [Phillip Klingensmith], & Elder Henry Lunt. Opened the meeting by Singing Prayer by the Bishop. Singing. Minutes read & accepted. Sister Haight called for a report from the teachers. Sister Pugmire & Sister Randle reported the Sisters on the South line as enjoying a good spirit and doing the best they could. they didn't feel to find any fault with them but felt well with improvement some of them had made, Sister White and Sister Mary-Ann Harrison spent a pleasant day in visiting the sisters on the West line, who were enjoying a good spirit and felt content with their lot, and desirous to live their religion. Sister Liston said, through circumstances unavoidable they didn't visit the Sisters this month, but she felt desirous to do right & to do her duty in all things. Sister Morris said they found the sisters on the north line, doing well and enjoying a good spirit. Sister Eliza Ann Haight said that

---

presented a false flag of truce. The militiamen, aided by Paiutes, then slaughtered approximately 120 men, women, and children, sparing only small children believed to be too young to talk about what they had witnessed. (See Walker et al., *Massacre at Mountain Meadows,* chaps. 10–13.)

224. *Songs of Zion* (n.p., [1853]), in John Freeman, Songbook, ca. 1849, CHL; see also Crawley, *A Descriptive Bibliography of the Mormon Church,* 3 vols. (Provo, UT: Religious Studies Center, Brigham Young University, 2012), 3:118.

225. The Deseret Iron Company cast a large bell in 1855 that was used to call townspeople to assemble for various gatherings. (Shirts and Shirts, *Trial Furnace,* 362–363.)

226. TEXT: The texts of the three minute entries selected for publication in this document have been reproduced in full, without abridgment. The ellipsis points in this document have been supplied by the editors of this volume to represent material omitted between the selected entries.

like Sister Liston they had been prevented from visiting the sisters through circumstances &c. Mother Whittaker & Sister Annabella found the sisters on the East line glad to see them they were enjoying a good spirit but like the rest of the sisters on the other lines as the teachers had reported, were destitute of clothing, they advised the Sisters who had plenty, to cultivate a liberal spirit and administer to the poor, also for those who didn't know how to learn and manufacture their own clothing. Bishop Smith then said, it was some time since he was here before but he thought he would come to day said he was well pleased with this Society and the reports given, and that the sisters felt about right. Spoke on being destitute of clothing, said that it was quite right, and that it was good for us, but there was always a way opened when it was most needed.— Spoke considerable on home manufacture etc. Bro Lunt then arose, and made some very appropriate remarks, spoke on cleanliness, and a many other principles of the Kingdom and said that the sisters would do well to adhere unto the counsel given by the Bishop.— Sister A Haight felt to rejoice in what the brethren had said & exhorted the sisters to listen to the teachings and act thereupon. appointed the teachers to visit the same lines this month as they did the last. but if it was bad weather they needn't go round and it was expected the sisters would do their duty whether the teachers went round or not [p. [21]] It was moved and seconded that Mary-Ann Lunt, Agnes Easton[,] Catherine Whittaker, & Louisa Hunt become members of this Society, carried unanimously. The Bishop again arose, and acquiesced in what Sister Haight had said and encouraged the Sisters to go on in the good work Sister Randle spoke on the wants of the treasury. closed the meeting by singing Benediction by Elder Lunt. Adjourned till 2 o clock P.M. Thursday January 14$^{\underline{th}}$ 1858

Ellen Lunt—Secretary . . . [p. [22]] . . .

March 11, 1858 • Thursday

Met again at the appointed time & place, 2. o. clock P.M. Thursday, March 11$^{\underline{th}}$ 1858. ⟨Sister Hopkins, Presided.⟩ Opened the meeting by singing. Prayer by Sister Ann White. Singing.— [p. [24]] The president called for the teachers report. Sister Pugmire and sister Randle reported the Sisters on the west line feeling well, and manifested a good spirit, and were trying to do the best they could. Sister Harrison & Sister Lund found the sisters on the north line endeavouring to live their religion and most of their habitations were nice and clean. Sister Morris reported the sisters in the middle lines, doing well, with few exceptions, had no fault to find with them. Sister White and sister Mc-Connell found the sisters on the East line enjoying a good spirit, and they believed the sisters were improving Sister Haight & Sister Willis found the sisters in the new City enjoying the good spirit of the Lord, but she didn't find them so well supplied in clothing. Sister Hopkins with sister A Haight & Mother Whittaker enjoyed their visit to the sisters on the south line very much. found them enjoying a good spirit generally, and trying to live their religion. counselled the mothers to instruct their children in every good thing. Sister Haight said she would like for those who understood home manufacture to teach those that didn't.[227] Spoke on bringing some patches to the treasury that there might be some covers made for the benefit of the poor that she wouldn't like to be a whit behind any other society in the mountains. Spoke considerable for the benefit of the sisters. Mother Whittaker said it was rejoicing to her to see the progress the sisters were making in this Society. counselled the sisters to be cautious how they spoke one of another. The President then gave the sisters the privilege to speak their minds. Sister [Roxsena] Patten said she wished to be one with us and whilst sitting down she had been reflecting on the scenes she had witnessed in Nauvoo. Said that she had long been deprived of the privilege that we now enjoyed.[228] Sung Come Come ye Saints &c.—[229] Sister Annabella said that if any of the sisters thought of any thing that would tend to the further advancement of this society she would like to hear it. counselled them to speak their feelings and not be backward. Mother Morris bore her testimony also Sister Lynn. Said they desired to do the will of God, and to keep his commandments. Mother Willis & sister William [Ann] Haslam also bore their testimony Sister Hopkins said she would like to hear the sisters speak that had lately come in if there were any present. Sister Corey [Margaret Corry], Mother [Mary] Hunter, Mother [Ellen] Muir, Mother [Cynthia] Benson, Mother [Margaret] Bateman, & Mother [Ann] White bore their testimony and felt glad and thankful that they were here Mother Simpkins also bore her testimony and spoke in tongues. Sister Hopkins then called on sister Lily [Margaret Lillywhite] [p. [25]] who bore her testimony & expressed her thankfulness that she was gathered to the valleys of the mountains. It was moved and seconded that the

---

227. Home manufacture was an essential element of the Latter-day Saint concern with economic self-sufficiency, a concept that took on renewed importance as U.S. Army troops approached Utah. John Taylor summarized the idea: "We cannot be independent until we can make our own shoes, dresses, shawls, bonnets, pantaloons, hats, and all such things as we need. When we can do these things, raise our own food, manufacture everything we need among ourselves, then we shall be independent of other people." (John Taylor, Jan. 17, 1858, in *Journal of Discourses,* 26 vols. [Liverpool: Various publishers, 1855–1886], 6:168.)

228. Roxsena Higby Repshar (who later in this same meeting was admitted a member of the Cedar City Relief Society) became a member of the Female Relief Society of Nauvoo on April 28, 1842. She married Andrew V. Patten in 1850. (Document 1.2, entry for Apr. 28, 1842; Daughters of the American Revolution, Springfield Chapter, Sangamon Co., IL, Marriage Records, 1822–1870, vol. 3, p. 149, Mar. 22, 1850, microfilm 848,654, U.S. and Canada Record Collection, FHL.)

229. See *Songs of Zion.*

following sisters become members of this Society. Sarah Urie, Elizabeth Haight, [*blank*] [Margaret] Keys, Roxsena R Patten, Margaret Lily, Emma Walker, Mary Lapworth. unanimously carried. Sister A Haight exhorted the sisters to not forget home manufacture. Sister Patten again spoke and expressed her feelings regarding this. Sister Hopkins informed the sisters where the treasury was and said if they had any patches or anything else to spare to take them there. Singing. Benediction by Sister Annabella Haight.

Ellen Lunt—Secretary [p. [26]]

PART 3: 1867–1879

In 1877, near summer's end, Eliza R. Snow sent to twenty-one-year-old Susa Young Dunford [Gates] an invitation. "My Dear Susie," she wrote, "The Book entitled 'The Women of Mormondom' is now out and on sale—pronounced very interesting. We are thinking of sending a few staunch sisters to the States to canvass for the sale of it." Snow hoped Dunford, a daughter of Brigham Young, might go.[1] The new book, edited and narrated by a Mormon man, Edward Tullidge, was esteemed "a woman's book" because it described the stories and beliefs of Mormon women, incorporating autobiographical narratives to do so. "The book has been published by the women of Utah," wrote one reviewer, although the title page showed New York as the place of publication and listed Tullidge and Crandall as the publisher. *The Women of Mormondom* was sold by subscription, a common practice of the era, and had potential to generate income for the women's Relief Society and a new sister organization for younger women such as Dunford (see Document 3.18). "It is three dollars well spent," wrote S. M. Dell after she purchased and perused the book. "To say I am pleased would not half express my feelings."[2]

Women of Mormondom was a product of a collaboration between Tullidge and the Relief Society,[3] reestablished beginning in 1867 and mobilized by 1880 in nearly three hundred branches throughout Utah Territory.[4] During this iteration of the Relief Society, Latter-day Saint women collectively entered the public sphere and gradually increased their ecclesiastical, economic, and political presence. They represented themselves in new ways, both within the church

---

1. Susa Young Gates, *History of the Young Ladies' Mutual Improvement Association of the Church of Jesus Christ of Latter-day Saints, from November 1869 to June 1910* (Salt Lake City: Deseret News, 1911), 121; Eliza R. Snow to Susa Young Dunford [Gates], Aug. 8, 1877, Susa Young Gates, Papers, ca. 1870–1933, CHL. Snow and Dunford were then in Utah Territory; "the States" refers to the eastern United States.

2. Edward W. Tullidge, *The Women of Mormondom* (New York: Tullidge and Crandall, 1877); "The Women of Mormondom," *Woman's Exponent,* Jan. 1, 1878, 6:119; S. M. Dell, in "Notes on 'The Women of Mormondom,'" *Woman's Exponent,* Oct. 1, 1877, 6:69.

3. On the writing of *Women of Mormondom,* see Claudia L. Bushman, "Edward W. Tullidge and *The Women of Mormondom,*" *Dialogue: A Journal of Mormon Thought* 33, no. 4 (Winter 2000): 15–26.

4. "R.S. Reports," *Woman's Exponent,* Sept. 1, 1880, 9:[53]; see also Document 3.1.

organization and within the broader public debate regarding the church. Stereotypes of subjugated Mormon women had existed in the public mind since the 1850s, when the Saints first publicly acknowledged their practice of plural marriage.[5] *Women of Mormondom* was one attempt to correct that image. "The women of Utah," wrote one reviewer of the book, "have undertaken to place themselves in a proper light before the world. They are voluntary disciples of Mormonism and esteem their relationship thereto as wives, mothers and saints, above all else on earth. This is their position and they do not wish the world to be misled in regard to it."[6] *Women of Mormondom* represented a new era during which the Relief Society achieved greater cohesiveness, visibility, and permanence.

The Reestablishment of the Relief Society

During the winter of 1867–1868, Latter-day Saint women in Utah Territory reestablished the Relief Society. Nearly ten years had passed since the Utah War had interrupted ward Relief Society operations. In 1858, thousands of Latter-day Saints in Utah's northern settlements had moved southward en masse as federal troops approached Salt Lake City. Saints returned to their homes after three months, but the effects of the temporary dislocation took years to overcome. Sarah M. Kimball recalled that on January 2, 1868, in the Salt Lake City Fifteenth Ward, "after the lapse of ten years lacking three months, [Relief] Society was reorganized by Bishop [Robert] Burton, with a majority of the former officers." She continued: "We came together renewed our acquaintance, and sought to renew our efforts to do good to the human family, especially the sick and the poor of this Ward."[7] Virtually every ward where the Relief Society had operated in the 1850s had a similar story (see Document 3.7).

---

5. Orson Pratt, Aug. 29, 1852, in *Journal of Discourses,* 26 vols. (Liverpool: Various publishers, 1855–1886), 1:53–66.

6. "The Women of Mormondom," *Woman's Exponent,* Jan. 1, 1878, 6:119. *Women of Mormondom* may have been published in part to offset dissident Fanny Stenhouse's negative portrayal of Mormon women, one of a growing number of critiques of Latter-day Saints and their practice of plural marriage. *Women of Mormondom* also came on the heels of another book by a prominent female dissident. (See Mrs. T. B. H. Stenhouse, *"Tell It All": The Story of a Life's Experience in Mormonism* [Hartford, CT: A. D. Worthington, 1875]; and Ann Eliza Young, *Wife No. 19; or, The Story of a Life in Bondage, Being a Complete Exposé of Mormonism, and Revealing the Sorrows, Sacrifices and Sufferings of Women in Polygamy* [Hartford, CT: Dustin, Gilman, 1876].)

7. Sarah M. Kimball, "Pres. Mrs Kimball's Anual Message for Jan 1st 1873," in Fifteenth Ward, Salt Lake Stake, Fifteenth Ward Relief Society Annual Message, 1873, CHL, 2.

Reestablishing the Relief Society in 1867 marked a significant point of departure for Latter-day Saint women. Not only was their dormant organization resuscitated, but its local operations were standardized and expanded. Connections among wards and between generations and forums for communication developed solidarity and enabled public activism.

Why it took ten years for the organization to reemerge is unclear, but certainly a combination of new circumstances favored the reestablishment of the Relief Society in 1867 and propelled its rapid growth. After the end of the Civil War, church leaders refocused their attention on long-term strategies to strengthen church members temporally and spiritually, reviving and creating institutions to facilitate economic self-sufficiency and to train up the rising generation. The Relief Society fit logically into this expanding organizational structure and assumed a leading role in the movements for home industry and youth development. At the same time, federal officials in Utah Territory and Washington DC attempted through a variety of legislative and judicial means to end plural marriage and curb the church's political and economic power. Latter-day Saint women organized to oppose such measures, becoming highly visible defenders of the doctrine and opponents of federal legislation. Finally, Latter-day Saint women's new public roles were informed at least in part by the women's movement in the United States that gained momentum following the Civil War.

In calling for the reorganization of ward Relief Societies in December 1867, Brigham Young urged women to work with local bishops in assisting the poor (see Documents 3.1 and 3.2). Women immediately organized Relief Society visiting committees in numerous congregations, including the Salt Lake City Seventh Ward, to pursue that directive (see Document 3.3). For Latter-day Saints, the Christian imperative to care for the poor was a central aspect of establishing a Zion-like community—a people of one heart and one mind dwelling in righteousness with no poor among them.[8]

Saints gathered together geographically to separate themselves from the world and strive to become such a people. The isolation they achieved by relocating to the West in the late 1840s had eroded during the next two decades, in part because of the presence of federal territorial officials and army troops and the influx of other non-Mormon outsiders, whom the Saints called "Gentiles." Church leaders cautioned members to resist encroaching worldly

---

8. See Moses 7:18. This verse of scripture defines "Zion" as the title given to the city of Enoch, whose righteous inhabitants were taken up into heaven. Brigham Young taught in 1869: "We have come here to build up Zion. How shall we do it? . . . We have got to be united in our efforts. We should go to work with a united faith like the heart of one man; and whatever we do should be performed in the name of the Lord." (Genesis 5:24; "Remarks," *Deseret News* [weekly], Nov. 24, 1869, 496.)

influences. They exhorted Saints to maintain their identity as a people apart—
"a kingdom of priests, and an holy nation"[9] commissioned by God to bring the
gospel to the world in preparation for the millennial coming of Jesus Christ.
Latter-day Saint women and men believed that through priesthood rites, particularly temple ordinances, they had been "called with a holy calling."[10]

For the Saints, as for many other Americans, the upheaval of the Civil War
stirred millennial anticipation regarding end-times and "the glory of the coming of the Lord."[11] Living far from eastern battlefields, Latter-day Saints
mourned the war's catastrophic losses and gravely contemplated the possible
destruction of the nation. They condemned corrupt government officials and
asserted that the Saints had a divinely mandated role as guardians of the
nation's inspired founding principles. After the war ended, Mormons maintained two intertwined identities. On the one hand, they were part of the
reunited nation: they sent delegates to Congress and assisted with the completion of the transcontinental railroad. At the same time, they remained a people
apart: they sought to become a religious commonwealth through increased
righteousness, sustained economic independence, and a greater measure of
political self-rule. They advanced their separatist agenda during the late 1860s
by reviving and creating institutions such as the Relief Society.

On December 2, 1867, less than a week before Brigham Young called for the
reorganization of ward Relief Societies, he reinstituted an organization for
men: the School of the Prophets.[12] Joseph Smith had established schools with
that name in the 1830s in Kirtland, Ohio, and Jackson County, Missouri,[13]
providing a forum for men who had been ordained to priesthood offices to
assemble and receive instruction and discuss doctrinal and practical matters
that would prepare them to fulfill the duties of those offices.[14] Instigated anew
by Young, multiple Schools of the Prophets functioned in the West from 1867
through 1874, with over nine hundred members eventually meeting in Salt

---

9. Exodus 19:6.

10. Alma 13:8; 2 Timothy 1:9.

11. For example, the millennial fervor of the times is clear in Julia Ward Howe, "Battle Hymn of the
Republic," *Atlantic Monthly* 9 (Feb. 1862): 10.

12. Wilford Woodruff, Journals, 1838–1898, Wilford Woodruff, Journals and Papers, 1828–1898, CHL,
Dec. 2, 1867; "To the Public," in "Local Items," *Deseret Evening News,* Nov. 30, 1867, [3]; "School of the
Prophets," in "Local Items," *Deseret Evening News,* Dec. 2, 1867, [3].

13. See "School of the Prophets," in Dean C. Jessee et al., eds., *Journals, Volume 1: 1832–1839,* vol. 1 of
the Journals series of *The Joseph Smith Papers,* ed. Dean C. Jessee et al. (Salt Lake City: Church Historian's
Press, 2008), 471.

14. A few women were also known to have attended lectures under the auspices of the School of the
Prophets in Kirtland; one was a teenage Sarah M. Granger (Kimball), who later drew upon that experi-
ence while serving in the Relief Society. (Fifteenth Ward, Riverside Stake, Relief Society Minutes and
Records, 1868–1968, CHL, vol. 5, Apr. 11, 1894.)

Lake City and an additional five thousand members in branch schools formed in other towns.[15] As did ward Relief Societies, these schools promoted egalitarian economics, home industry, theological instruction, and unity of thought and action. Fillmore Stake president Thomas Callister saw a parallel relationship between the two, telling Relief Society women in 1869: "This society reminds me of the school of the Prophets and we might almost call you a school of Prophetesses."[16] Through local branches of the Relief Society and Schools of the Prophets, church leaders mobilized a significant portion of the population.

Other organizational innovations supported the younger generation, most of whom had not experienced the church as their parents had known it. First-generation Saints forsook home and family for their new religion and made the arduous trek to the West. Some of them endured persecutions in Ohio, Missouri, and Illinois. Repeated sacrifices secured the faith of these early believers. Without encountering similar challenges, many wondered, how could a second or third generation of Saints become grounded in the religious tradition of their mothers and fathers? Spiritual nurture seemed to be the answer. In addition to the rituals in which young Saints had participated or would participate—including baptism, the weekly sacrament (the Lord's Supper), and temple ordinances—they needed instruction. Sunday schools for children, first introduced in Utah in 1849, reappeared in local congregations beginning in 1866.[17] Relief Society responsibilities expanded to include in 1870 guidance of teenage and young adult women (see Document 3.18), and in 1878 creation of a weekday program for children (see Document 3.30). These institutions and a new association for young men all functioned at the village or ward level. Incorporating women into the ward organizational structure and instituting programs for youth and children also fostered the assimilation of immigrant converts who continued to flow into Utah Territory and bordering areas, the space Latter-day Saints defined as "Zion."

The reconstituted Relief Society played a central role in the movement to preserve Latter-day Saint religious identity and autonomy. Most of the core of women leaders who worked to reestablish the organization had been members of the Female Relief Society of Nauvoo. First among these women was Eliza R. Snow, who had served as secretary of the Nauvoo society and was appointed by

---

15. Leonard J. Arrington, *Great Basin Kingdom: An Economic History of the Latter-day Saints, 1830–1900* (Cambridge, MA: Harvard University Press, 1958), 245–246.

16. Fillmore Ward, Millard Stake, Fillmore Ward Relief Society Minutes and Records, 1868–1947, CHL, vol. 1, Apr. 27, 1869. For more on the Relief Society in Fillmore, see Document 3.8.

17. *Jubilee History of Latter-day Saints Sunday Schools, 1849–1899* (Salt Lake City: Deseret Sunday School Union, 1900), 9–15.

Brigham Young in 1868 to assist bishops in reorganizing the Relief Society in each ward (see Documents 3.5 and 3.6). Snow had in her possession the record book containing the minutes of the Nauvoo Relief Society,[18] which served the organization as its "Constitutio[n] and law."[19] In her newspaper articles and letters and her visits to wards throughout the territory, Snow drew from the minute book to introduce the Relief Society to bishops and church members unfamiliar with its history and workings (see Documents 3.6 and 3.8). She assisted local leaders, such as Sarah M. Kimball in the Salt Lake City Fifteenth Ward, in replicating the organizational pattern initiated in Nauvoo (see Document 3.9). Even the format of the Nauvoo minutes became a template for a new generation of local Relief Society records. Snow personally inscribed title pages and founding minutes in some ward Relief Society records.[20] Efforts to tie the reconstituted Relief Society to its Nauvoo predecessor not only provided a sense of continuity but standardized organizational form and procedure. Kimball, for instance, continued the tradition begun in Nauvoo of writing an annual report (Document 3.10). Thus grounded, local Relief Societies became versatile in undertaking a variety of public projects.

Relief Society and Economic Self-Sufficiency

Many new Relief Society responsibilities stemmed from the Saints' intensified emphasis on economic self-sufficiency. Charitable ministrations remained a fundamental Relief Society obligation. Indeed, money or goods contributed for and dispensed to the poor, many of them immigrants, are reported in virtually every Relief Society record (see Documents 3.19 and 3.22). Nonetheless, women's collective engagement in home industry became one of the most visible aspects of their work and formed an important part of the Saints' countermove against the growing economic strength and capitalist forms of non-Mormon miners and merchants in Utah, which threatened to undermine Latter-day Saint self-sufficiency and their ideals of a Zion community. Federal troops, appointed to guard the western section of the overland mail route during the Civil War, arrived in Utah in October 1862 and erected Camp Douglas in the foothills east of Salt Lake City. These California and Nevada Volunteers, many of them experienced prospectors, successfully pursued silver and gold in the surrounding Oquirrh and Wasatch Mountains. During the 1850s and 1860s church leaders directed various efforts to mine iron ore, lead, coal, and silver,

---

18. See Document 1.2.

19. Document 1.2, entry for Mar. 17, 1842.

20. For example, see Thirteenth Ward, Ensign Stake, Thirteenth Ward Relief Society Minutes and Records, 1868–1906, CHL, vol. 1.

but they feared the rush of outsiders that large-scale mining might precipitate. Generally, they invested their faith and resources in agriculture.[21]

In the 1860s Brigham Young appointed groups of church members to settle in the warmer southern reaches of the territory—some to raise and manufacture cotton, some to produce molasses, some to raise figs, grapes, and other fruits. The Relief Society played an important role in this comprehensive program for reinforcing Mormon economic self-sufficiency. During 1867 and 1868, as the transcontinental railroad drew steadily closer to completion, church leaders accelerated immigration of British and European Saints to further expand colonization and secure land for Mormon agriculture and manufacturing.[22] At the same time the leaders promoted mercantile and manufacturing cooperatives, aiming to dampen the influence of existing and incoming non-Mormon merchants.

Nearly all ward Relief Societies throughout the territory promoted silk production, but projects varied. "Council together and deliberately decide what branch or branches of business will be most likely to succeed in your particular Ward or Settlement, and promptly adopt measures for its promotion," Eliza R. Snow instructed in 1875, noting as examples straw braiding and knitting.[23] By the end of that year Snow was soliciting specimens of women's handiwork for display at the 1876 Philadelphia Centennial Exposition, in connection with which she composed a short history of the Relief Society and its expanding responsibilities (Document 3.24). In 1876 ward societies added to their work the task of storing grain and building granaries (see Document 3.25). These multiplying duties all fell under the rubric of supporting Mormon economic self-sufficiency.

A year before he officially called for the reorganization of the Relief Society, Brigham Young spoke of its potential for boosting home industry. Addressing the First Presidency and the Quorum of the Twelve on December 26, 1866, with respect to "our Temporal Position," Young said that "if we could get up Female releif Socities & they would use their influence to get the Sisters to make their own bonnetts & make & wear their own Home made Clothing it would do much good."[24] In 1868 and 1869, as Young addressed newly reestablished Relief

---

21. For more information on Utah mining in this period, see Richard W. Sadler, "The Impact of Mining on Salt Lake City," *Utah Historical Quarterly* 47, no. 3 (Summer 1979): 236–253.

22. For more on Mormon colonization, see Leonard J. Arrington, *Brigham Young: American Moses* (New York: Alfred A. Knopf, 1985), 167–191, 265–267.

23. Eliza R. Snow, "Talk Number One," *Woman's Exponent*, Apr. 1, 1875, 3:164–165.

24. Wilford Woodruff, Journals, 1833–1898, Wilford Woodruff, Journals and Papers, 1828–1898, CHL, Dec. 26, 1866.

Societies, he emphasized the importance of women's individual and collective involvement in home manufacture (see Documents 3.4 and 3.11).

As the predominant managers of household food and clothing, women understood the importance of home-manufactured goods, an essential of frontier survival. Bathsheba W. Smith wrote of the orchards she and her sister wives (her husband's other wives) planted and maintained and the cloth they wove, indicating that "[we] have done all we could to encourage Home manufactury."[25] But as the Saints became less isolated and possibilities multiplied for purchasing imported ready-made goods, home-manufactured products became a matter of choice, not necessity, for the individual household. In response, a movement for retrenchment among older and younger women centered on simplified meals and clothing and on consuming locally produced instead of imported goods (see Documents 3.15, 3.16, and 3.18).

Efforts toward Political Autonomy

Although Latter-day Saints achieved some degree of economic independence, the political autonomy they hoped for was far more elusive. The decision of the U.S. Congress in 1850 to organize Utah as a territory imposed a longstanding interdependence with federal officials that quickly became distasteful to both sides. Plural marriage figured prominently in the escalating antipathy, and legislative and judicial attempts to end the practice provoked Mormon women to publicly defend their convictions and their marriages. The church first officially acknowledged its doctrine and practice of plural marriage in 1852, triggering a continual barrage of criticism and ridicule from pulpits and presses in America and abroad. The 1856 Republican Party platform denounced slavery and polygamy as the "twin relics of barbarism," and in 1862 the U.S. Congress passed the Morrill Anti-Bigamy Act, intended "to punish and prevent the Practice of Polygamy in the Territories of the United States." The act restricted the amount of property that churches could own in U.S. territories and annulled "certain Acts of the Legislative Assembly of the Territory of Utah" that supported plural marriage.[26] Unfunded and unenforced, the

---

25. Bathsheba W. Smith, Autobiography, ca. 1875–1906, CHL, 42–43.

26. For the Republican platform, see *Proceedings of the First Three Republican National Conventions of 1856, 1860 and 1864* (Minneapolis, MN: Charles W. Johnson, 1893), 43. The Morrill Anti-Bigamy Act was approved in the Thirty-Seventh U.S. Congress, second session. (An Act to Punish and Prevent the Practice of Polygamy in the Territories of the United States and Other Places, and Disapproving and Annulling Certain Acts of the Legislative Assembly of the Territory of Utah [July 1, 1862], *The Statutes at Large, Treaties, and Proclamations, of the United States of America. From December 5, 1859, to March 3, 1863,* vol. 12, ed. George P. Sanger [Boston: Little, Brown, 1863], 37th Cong., 2nd Sess., ch. 126, p. 501.)

Morrill Act had little initial impact. Following the Civil War, however, as federal lawmakers passed Reconstruction legislation for the southern states, they renewed their attempts to reconstruct the social, economic, and political makeup of the Territory of Utah.

Latter-day Saints were outraged by three successive bills proposed (but never passed) to reinforce and implement the Morrill Act—the Wade Bill (1866), the Cragin Bill (1867, 1869), and the Cullom Bill (1869, 1870).[27] The bill authored by Illinois representative Shelby Cullom, chair of the U.S. House Committee on Territories, included such extreme provisions as denying citizenship to those who practiced plural marriage. In response, Mormon women staged a series of protests in the early months of 1870 (see Documents 3.12 and 3.13). Their mass meetings of indignation marked a pivotal moment of politicization for the Relief Society and for Mormon women.[28] They broke the silence they had largely maintained in the public debate over polygamy, but they did not denounce it, as critics had long anticipated they would. Rather, they publicly spoke in support of plural marriage, representing themselves as strong, decisive, and free women, fully committed to their religious beliefs. Their new visibility demonstrated a reality different from the pervasive stereotypes of Mormon women as subjugated and deluded. Reporting on speeches he had heard at the "indignation" meeting in Salt Lake City, a correspondent to the *New York Herald* wrote, "In logic and in rhetoric, the so-called degraded ladies of Mormondom are quite equal to the women's rights women of the East."[29]

Women's defense of plural marriage became an integral part of their presence in the public sphere in the late nineteenth century, a presence facilitated by the recently reestablished Relief Society. The more than one hundred local Relief Societies operating throughout Utah in 1870 provided a new and stable structure for mobilizing women en masse.[30] In local or ward societies women honed their organizational skills and public speaking abilities, and as these units acted collectively Latter-day Saint women exercised new political influence. However, their activism did not halt further federal legislation to curtail the practice of plural marriage. The Poland Act, passed in 1874, transferred

27. See Carol Cornwall Madsen, ed., *Battle for the Ballot: Essays on Woman Suffrage in Utah, 1870–1896* (Logan: Utah State University Press, 1997).

28. See Lola Van Wagenen, "In Their Own Behalf: The Politicization of Mormon Women and the 1870 Franchise," *Dialogue: A Journal of Mormon Thought* 24, no. 4 (Winter 1991): 31–36.

29. "Mormon Women in Council," *New York Herald,* Jan. 23, 1870, 6; see also "Mormon Women in Council," Feb. 16, 1870, 23; and "Polygamy," *New York Herald,* Jan. 23, 1870, [4].

30. A. Milton Musser to Brigham Young, Apr. 10, 1869, Brigham Young Office Files, 1832–1878, CHL. Musser, who was serving as a traveling bishop throughout the Territory of Utah, reported "102 Female Relief Societies" functioning during 1868 and 1869; local records show additional units in operation. ("A. Milton Musser Called by Death," *Deseret Evening News,* Sept. 25, 1909, 5.)

responsibility for civil and criminal cases in Utah from local probate courts to federal district courts, where polygamists would be prosecuted. Relying on the First Amendment clause protecting the free exercise of religion, Latter-day Saints maintained they could not be legally prosecuted for practicing plural marriage, a religious tenet. But an 1879 ruling by the U.S. Supreme Court contradicted that argument and opened the way for more severe congressional legislation in the 1880s, culminating with the 1887 Edmunds-Tucker Act, which included measures for fully enforcing the twenty-five-year-old Morrill Act.[31]

The women's 1870 mass meetings had been pivotal, however, and in their wake Latter-day Saint women maintained a political voice. Their familiarity with and interest in the mounting movement for women's rights fueled their nascent activism. At the first mass protest meeting in 1870, Bathsheba W. Smith "moved that we demand of the Gov the right of Franchise" and Lucy W. Kimball "moved that we be represented at Washington."[32] Between 1867 and 1869, the U.S. House of Representatives and Senate had discussed but not passed bills for extending suffrage to women in the U.S. territories as a test case, or in Utah specifically, with the assumption that women would vote to end polygamy. Utah's territorial legislature acted more decisively, and "An Act Conferring upon Women the Elective Franchise" was passed by the territorial legislature and signed by the acting territorial governor on February 12, 1870. The local *Deseret News,* which had supported the reestablishment of the Relief Society and the entry of women into trades and professions, enthusiastically endorsed the measure (see Document 3.14). Utah Territory thus became only the second territory or state in the nation to extend suffrage to women.[33] Latter-day Saint women delivered to the acting governor a formal expression of thanks for signing the bill (Document 3.17).

If Mormon women were interested in the larger movement for women's rights, some of the movement's most vocal national leaders likewise took interest in the newly enfranchised women of Utah. While traveling in the West, Susan B. Anthony and Elizabeth Cady Stanton visited Salt Lake City early in July 1871. They came at the invitation of the Godbeites, dissenting critics of

31. Sarah Barringer Gordon, *The Mormon Question: Polygamy and Constitutional Conflict in Nineteenth-Century America,* Studies in Legal History (Chapel Hill and London: University of North Carolina Press, 2002), 273–274; see also Document 4.15.

32. "Minutes of a Ladies' Mass Meeting," *Deseret News,* Jan. 12, 1870, 580; Document 3.12.

33. The Territory of Wyoming had passed a similar bill two months earlier, in December 1869. (See Beverly Beeton, *Women Vote in the West: The Woman Suffrage Movement, 1869–1896,* American Legal and Constitutional History [New York: Garland, 1986], 1–22.)

Brigham Young's economic and religious leadership,[34] but the suffrage leaders also addressed a general gathering of women in the "old" tabernacle. According to Stanton's account, the meeting lasted five hours. Stanton took full advantage of the unique opportunity "to speak to Mormon women alone" and lectured on the history of marriage and the dissatisfaction of all women "with their position as inferiors." Though Stanton saw Latter-day Saint women gaining "practical political experience," she could not endorse their religious beliefs, nor could they sanction her radical concepts.[35] During the last week of July an address written by Eliza R. Snow was read to a vast audience at a community celebration (Document 3.20). Snow sought to differentiate Latter-day Saint women's efforts for women's advancement from the work of activists such as Anthony and Stanton who often opposed traditional familial and religious institutions. Ironically, the conservative wing of the suffrage movement in the United States shunned Latter-day Saint women because they viewed Mormonism as a threat to traditional familial and religious institutions. Thus, despite their pronounced differences, Mormon women and radical suffragists formed an amicable alliance that lasted until the end of the century.[36]

Women's New Collective Presence

Latter-day Saint women were not of a single mind regarding women's rights and woman's sphere. They could speak and act collectively, but they also had individual ideas and experiences that increasingly found expression on the pages of the *Woman's Exponent.* The semimonthly periodical established in June 1872 was edited first by Louisa (Lula) Greene Richards and then by Emmeline B. Wells (see Document 3.21). Part of a new generation of American women's newspapers focused on social issues, the *Exponent* had much in common with such publications as the *Woman's Journal,* begun in 1870 in Boston and edited by activist Lucy Stone and her husband Henry Blackwell, and the *New Northwest,* a Portland, Oregon, paper launched by Abigail Scott Duniway in 1871. Although the *Exponent* occasionally republished articles from these

---

34. See Document 3.20; Ronald W. Walker, *Wayward Saints: The Godbeites and Brigham Young* (Urbana: University of Illinois Press, 1998); and Beverly Beeton, "A Feminist among the Mormons: Charlotte Ives Cobb Godbe Kirby," *Utah Historical Quarterly* 59, no. 1 (Winter 1991): 22–31.

35. Elizabeth Cady Stanton, *Eighty Years and More (1815–1897): Reminiscences of Elizabeth Cady Stanton* (New York City: European Publishing, 1898), 283–284, 287.

36. For more about the relationship Mormon women had with national women's organizations, see Documents 4.1 and 4.27; see also Joan Iverson, "The Mormon-Suffrage Relationship: Personal and Political Quandaries," *Frontiers: A Journal of Women Studies* 11, nos. 2–3 (1990): 8–16; Lola Van Wagenen, "Sister-Wives and Suffragists: Polygamy and the Politics of Woman Suffrage, 1870–1896" (PhD diss., New York University, 1994); and Beeton, *Women Vote in the West.*

and other papers and carried suffrage news and editorials on women's rights, it was intended as a forum for Latter-day Saint women. Through the *Exponent,* Mormon women represented themselves to one another and to the broader culture. The paper, which was typeset by women, published women's poems and essays, featured editorials supporting church leaders and plural marriage, and posted minutes of the meetings of local Relief Societies (see Document 3.22) and of its affiliated organizations for young women and children.

The *Woman's Exponent* was a semiofficial Relief Society publication, and its pages charted the society's growth and changes. Over the years local branches of the society multiplied as new settlements were established in Utah Territory and the surrounding area. Continuing immigration increased population and necessitated the division of some wards or congregations. Several branches of the Relief Society were often organized in a single village or town. Eliza R. Snow continued to exercise a leading role, though she was not officially set apart as general president of the Relief Society until 1880.[37] Initially, she and a team of ward Relief Society presidents and other leading women counseled together in meetings of the Senior and Junior Cooperative Retrenchment Association, also known as General Retrenchment, which served essentially as the Relief Society's directing board or council (see Documents 3.15 and 3.16). This council also helped establish and direct emerging ward organizations for younger (junior) women, known first as Retrenchment Associations and later as Mutual Improvement Associations (see Document 3.18).

This governance pattern began to change in July 1877 when Brigham Young, in connection with a massive push toward refining and regularizing church structure, established the first Relief Society organization at a stake level in Weber County.[38] The new Weber Stake Relief Society presidency, under the direction of Jane S. Richards, would oversee and coordinate Relief Society work in various wards in that stake (see Documents 3.26 and 3.28). Similar presidencies were soon appointed in Salt Lake City and other areas (see Document 3.29). Official recognition that the Relief Society must be part of a complete stake or ward organizational structure demonstrated church leaders' full endorsement of the reestablished women's organization. John Taylor, who, as president of the Quorum of the Twelve, assumed leadership of the church following the death of Brigham Young in August 1877, praised the work of the Relief Society and emphasized the importance of women and men working together collaboratively to establish God's kingdom on the earth (see Document 3.27).

---

37. See Document 4.4. Emma Hale Smith, the first Relief Society president, died on April 30, 1879.
38. A stake is a geographically defined ecclesiastical unit usually made up of several wards.

The Relief Society reemerged in the 1860s and 1870s as a cohesive, visible, and permanent organization. Under its auspices, women assumed new ecclesiastical, economic, and political roles in the expanding Mormon community. Religious faith remained at the heart of their multiplying activities, from straw weaving to suffrage. "We shall have elevated aims, if we are holy women," Eliza R. Snow taught the women she addressed as sisters. "We shall feel that we are called to perform important duties. No one is exempt from them. There is no sister so isolated, and her sphere so narrow but what she can do a great deal towards establishing the Kingdom of God upon the earth" (Document 3.23). The same perspective permeated the *Woman's Exponent* and the *Women of Mormondom.* To be sure, neither the disenchanted who left the Latter-day Saint community nor the outside critics who attacked it saw the experience of Latter-day Saint women through the same lens. But this sacred worldview informed and sustained the Relief Society and guaranteed its continuation.

3.1 Brigham Young, Discourse, December 8, 1867 (Excerpt)

Brigham Young, Discourse, Dec. 8, 1867, in "Remarks by President Brigham Young, Made in the Old Tabernacle, G. S. L. City, Sunday, December 8th, 1867," Deseret Evening News (Salt Lake City, UT), Dec. 14, 1867, vol. 1, no. 21, pp. [1]–[3] (excerpt).

With this discourse delivered in the "old" tabernacle in Salt Lake City on December 8, 1867, President Brigham Young initiated the reestablishment of ward Relief Societies, most of which had been dormant for nearly a decade. Two important events occurred in the week before his discourse that may suggest why the time was ripe for reestablishment of the women's organization. On December 2, 1867, Young reorganized the School of the Prophets, a forum where selected priesthood leaders discussed spiritual and temporal concerns.[39] Three days later he proposed in a meeting of local bishops that the responsibility of caring for the poor, who had been receiving weekly allowances from the General Tithing Office in Salt Lake City, be transferred to the bishops, a move that would free up sparse tithing funds for construction of the Salt Lake City temple.[40] Thus, local bishops would be shouldering a larger responsibility for the poor, a development of particular importance since 1868 was rightly projected to be a year of unusually high immigration.

Against this backdrop, Young, in his discourse of December 8, announced that the Relief Society would be revived. Under the auspices of their ward Relief Societies, women would both meet together regularly to discuss spiritual and temporal concerns (paralleling in some ways the School of the Prophets) and work collectively in conjunction with their bishops to relieve the poor. Young spoke about the establishment of both the School of the Prophets and the Relief Society as part of a larger theme of the responsibility of the Latter-day Saints to "establish the Zion of our God upon the earth," including caring for the poor.[41]

The *Deseret Evening News* summarized Young's discourse in its December 9 issue[42] and published the first full report of the discourse on December 14. The following transcript is excerpted from the December 14 report made by Edward L. Sloan.

———— ❧ ————

REMARKS
By President Brigham Young, made in the Old Tabernacle, G. S. L. City, Sunday, December 8th, 1867.

---

39. "School of the Prophets," *Deseret News*, Dec. 4, 1867, 337; Leonard J. Arrington, *Great Basin Kingdom: An Economic History of the Latter-day Saints, 1830–1900* (Cambridge, MA: Harvard University Press, 1958), 245–251.

40. Presiding Bishopric, Bishops Meeting Minutes, 1851–1884, CHL, Dec. 5, 1867; see also Document 3.2.

41. "Remarks," *Deseret Evening News*, Dec. 14, 1867, [1].

42. "Local Items," *Deseret Evening News*, Dec. 9, 1867, [3].

I am now going to preach you a short sermon concerning our temporal duties. My sermon is to the poor, and to those who are not poor. As a people, we are not poor; and we wish to say to the Bishops, not only in this city, but through the country, "Bishops, take care of your poor."[44] The poor in this city do not number a great many. I think there are a few over seventy who draw sustenance from the General Tithing Office. They come to the Tithing Office, or somebody comes for them, to draw their sustenance.[45] If some of our clever arithmeticians will sit down and make a calculation of the hours lost in coming from the various parts of the city to the Tithing Office, and in waiting around there; and then value those hours, if occupied in some useful employment, at twelve and a half cents each, every eight of them making a dollar, it will be found that the number of dollars thus lost by these seventy odd persons in a week would go far towards sustaining them. We have among us some brethren and sisters who are not strong, nor healthy, and they must be supported. We wish to adopt the most economical plan of taking care of them; and we say to you, Bishops, take care of them. You may ask the question, "Shall we take the tithing that should go to the Tithing Office to support them, or shall we ask the brethren to donate for that purpose?" If you will take the time consumed in obtaining the rations drawn by them out of the General Tithing Office,—for every person who is not able to come, must send some one for them—and have that time profitably employed, there will be but little more to seek for their sustenance. Get a house in your Ward, and if you have two sisters, or two brethren, put them in it, make them comfortable, find them food and clothing, and fuel; and direct the time now spent coming to this Tithing Office wisely in profitable labor. Furnish the sisters with needles and thread to work at sewing, and find something for them to do. Take those little girls who have been coming to the Tithing Office, and have them taught to knit edging, and tidies,[46] and other kinds of knitting and make lace, and sell the products of their labor. Those little girls have nimble fingers, and it will only take a little capital to start them at such kinds of work. Where you have

---

43. TEXT: The ellipsis points in this excerpt have been supplied by the editors of this volume to indicate omissions from the original document.

44. A Joseph Smith revelation dated February 9, 1831, defined the responsibility of the bishop "to administer to the poor and the needy." (Doctrine and Covenants 42:30–34.)

45. Located on South Temple Street immediately east of the temple block, the General Tithing Office yard consisted of barns, corrals, and other areas for storing goods donated by church members as tithing. (Arrington, *Great Basin Kingdom*, 133, 362.)

46. Ornamental loose coverings for the arms or headrest of a chair. ("Tidy," in *The Oxford English Dictionary,* ed. J. A. Simpson and E. S. C. Weiner, 2nd ed., 20 vols. [Oxford: Clarendon, 1989], 18:69.)

Brigham Young. 1866. In 1867 church president Brigham
Young called for the reestablishment of the Relief Society in
local wards, later appointing his plural wife Eliza R. Snow to
oversee that effort. He had suspended Relief Society meetings
in 1845 in the aftermath of Joseph Smith's death, then called
for their reinstatement in 1854. The movement to reorganize
came nearly a decade after these early Utah Relief Societies
had faded out, and resulted in a permanent reestablishment of
the organization. Photograph by the studio of Savage and
Ottinger. (Church History Library, Salt Lake City.)

brethren who are not strong enough to saw and split wood, or do some kind of out-door labor, agree with some chairmakers to have his chairs bottomed, and get rushes and set the brethren to bottoming the chairs. If you cannot get that for them to do, procure some flags or rushes, and let them make foot-mats, and sell them, but do not ask too high a price for them, do not ask a dollar or two dollars each for them, for one can be made in an hour or two. And if the market should get stocked with them, get some willows and have willow baskets made, and you can scarcely stock the market with them, for they wear out almost as fast as they can be made. In the Spring have these brethren sow some broomcorn,—they will enjoy working a little out of doors in the nice spring weather; and then in the Fall they can make brooms with the corn. By pursuing this course a Bishop will soon be able to say, "I have accomplished a good work; the brethren and sisters whom I had to help are now in a condition to help themselves." And in a short time, if their labor and time are wisely employed, you can build for them the finest house in the ward. You may call it a poor-house if you choose, though it should be the best house in the ward; and there its inmates can enjoy themselves, the younger ones can be taught music and thus a source of enjoyment be created, as well as being taught in various kinds of profitable employment; and the lives of all be made a blessing to themselves, they being in the enjoyment of happiness and comfort. You may think that I am painting a fancy sketch, but it is practicable, and those are places I intend to visit by and by.

Now, Bishops, you have smart women for wives, many of you; let them organize Female Relief Societies in the various wards. We have many talented woman among us, and we wish their help in this matter. Some may think this is a trifling thing, but it is not; and you will find that the sisters will be the mainspring of the movement. Give them the benefit of your wisdom and experience, give them your influence, guide and direct them wisely and well, and they will find rooms for the poor, and obtain the means for supporting them ten times quicker than even the Bishop could. If he should go or send to a man for a donation, and if the person thus visited should happen to be cross or out of temper for some cause, the likelihood is that while in that state of feeling he would refuse to give anything; and so a variety of causes would operate to render the mission an unsuccessful one. But let a sister appeal for the relief of suffering and poverty, and she is almost sure to be successful, especially if she appeals to those of her own sex. If you take this course you will relieve the wants of the poor a great deal better than they are now dealt by. We recommend these Female Relief Societies to be organized immediately.

. . . Let it be sent forth to the people, that on the first Thursday of each month, the fast day, all that would be eaten by husbands and wives and children and servants, should be put in the hands of the Bishop for the sustenance of the poor.[47] I am willing to do my share as well as the rest, and if there are no poor in my ward, I am willing to divide with those wards where there are poor. If the sisters will look out for rooms for those sisters who need to be taken care of, and see them provided for, you will find that we will possess more [p. [2]] comfort and more peace in our hearts, and our spirits will be buoyant and light, full of joy and peace. The Bishops should, through their teachers, see that every family in their wards, who is able should donate what they would naturally consume on the fast day to the poor.

You have read, probably, that we are starting the school of the prophets. . . . We will start this school of the prophets to increase in knowledge.[48] Brother [David O.] Calder commences to-morrow to teach our youth and those of middle age the art of book-keeping and impart to them a good mercantile education. We expect soon to have our sisters join in the class and mingle with the brethren in their studies, for why should not a lady be capable of taking charge of her husband's business affairs when he goes into the grave? We have sisters now engaged in several of our telegraph offices; and we wish them to learn not only to act as operators but to keep the books of our offices, and let sturdy men go to work at some employment for which by their strength they are adapted; and we hope eventually to see every store in Zion attended by ladies. . . .[49]

---

47. Preceding this statement regarding donations "for the sustenance of the poor" as part of the regular first Thursday "fast day," Young provided a summary of Joseph Smith's introduction of Latter-day Saint "fast meetings" in Kirtland, Ohio, in the 1830s. For more on Kirtland fast meetings, see Mark Lyman Staker, *Hearken, O Ye People: The Historical Setting of Joseph Smith's Ohio Revelations* (Salt Lake City: Greg Kofford Books, 2009), 244–245.

48. Joseph Smith and other church leaders established a School of the Prophets in Kirtland, Ohio, in January 1833 to "prepare elders of the church for their ministry." Participants were instructed in doctrinal and secular topics. Similar group meetings in 1834 were known as the "Elders school" or "school for the Elders." ("School of the Prophets," The Joseph Smith Papers, accessed Apr. 6, 2015, http://www.josephsmithpapers.org.)

49. Another issue of the weekly edition of the *Deseret News* that reported Young's address (December 18, 1867) also included a republication of the editorial "Female Relief Societies" that had first run December 10 (Document 3.2) and, on the same page, a republication of a December 9 editorial that advocated educating women as bookkeepers, typesetters, clerks, and surgeons, noting eleven "female operators" in offices of the Deseret Telegraph Line. ("Female Relief Societies," "Employments for Females," and "Remarks," *Deseret News* [weekly], Dec. 18, 1867, 354, 358; "Employment for Females," *Deseret Evening News,* Dec. 9, 1867, [2].)

3.2 "Female Relief Societies," December 10, 1867 (Excerpt)

"Female Relief Societies," Deseret News *[semi-weekly] (Salt Lake City, UT), Dec. 10, 1867, vol. 2, no. 88, p. [4] (excerpt).*

Two days after President Brigham Young publicly invited bishops to organize Relief Societies in their respective wards,[50] *Deseret News* editor George Q. Cannon, a member of the Quorum of the Twelve Apostles, published in the semiweekly edition of the *News* the following editorial encouraging bishops and female Saints to follow Young's counsel.[51] He republished the editorial eight days later in the weekly edition of the *Deseret News,* which also carried Young's discourse in its entirety.[52] The "Female Relief Societies" editorial emphasized not only the importance of helping the poor but also the opportunity presented to women to step forward and undertake a more active role within the church organization.

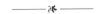

FEMALE RELIEF SOCIETIES.

[53] . . . Our land is a cold one in Winter; but for the number of our population, and the large proportion of laboring people there are here, we have comparatively few who are destitute. Hundreds of poor people have been brought here yearly, most of them entirely ignorant of the modes of obtaining a living in a new country, and in many instances they have had to adopt new employments.[54] But, through the guidance and example of experienced men, they have been enabled to live, and, not unfrequently, surround themselves with the comforts and even the luxuries of life. The success which has attended the labors of the people is truly wonderful. But though prosperity generally prevails throughout our settlements, there are some helpless persons in every Ward who are dependent upon the Bishops for the necessaries of life. The care of the

---

50. See Document 3.1.

51. Cannon had become *Deseret News* editor a month earlier, in November 1867. He had already demonstrated an interest in women's issues with the editorial "Employments for Females"; the same article was republished alongside "Female Relief Societies" in the weekly edition of the *Deseret News* on December 18. Under Cannon's editorship, the *Deseret News* published a significant number of articles concerning women's employment, education, and suffrage, especially from 1868 to 1870. ("Employments for Females," *Deseret Evening News,* Dec. 9, 1867, [2]; *Deseret News* [weekly], Dec. 18, 1867, 354; Kami Wilson, "Substance versus Superficiality: Women's Prescribed Roles in Early Territorial Utah, 1850–70," *Journal of Mormon History* 32, no. 2 [Summer 2006]: 164–169.)

52. "Female Relief Societies," *Deseret News* [weekly], Dec. 18, 1867, 354.

53. TEXT: The ellipsis points in this excerpt have been supplied by the editors of this volume to indicate an omission from the original document.

54. More than 20,000 immigrants arrived in Utah during the 1860s. Immigration in 1866 numbered 3,294; in 1867, 502; and in 1868, 3,187. (Conway B. Sonne, *Saints on the Seas: A Maritime History of Mormon Migration, 1830–1890* [Salt Lake City: University of Utah Press, 1983], 81, 153–154.)

indigent at this season of the year forms no small portion of a Bishop's labors and responsibilities. As a people we should be sensitively careful of our poor. Their prayers and cries ascend to the Lord, and the people whose hands are open to relieve their wants, are blessed of Him.

There is really no necessity for any person to suffer in this community for want of the necessaries of life. Our people believe too firmly in the Scripture that "he that hath pity upon the poor, lendeth to the Lord,"[55] to knowingly permit any person to go destitute while they have anything to share with them. The Bishops have so many cares devolving upon them, so many duties to attend to, that it would not be surprising if, occasionally, some persons, who need assistance should escape their attention. If proper measures, however, were taken in the various Wards, the wants of all might be duly attended to. Many of the poor have heretofore, been dependent upon the Tithing Office for their support. It is now desirable that that Department should be relieved from their calls, that the work of cutting stone, &c., for the Temple may be prosecuted. The care of the poor, therefore, now devolves upon the Bishops.

President Young has suggested a plan which, if rightly carried out, can not fail to relieve the Bishops from the care which they otherwise will be likely to have in providing for the poor. He suggests the organization of Female Relief Societies in the various Wards, whose duty it will be to visit the sick and the helpless and the needy, and learn their wants, and, under their Bishops, collect the means necessary to relieve them.[56] This suggestion must strike every one, who reflects upon the subject, as admirably adapted to meet the wants of the case. These duties would be accepted readily, we believe, by our sisters, if they were satisfied that it was the wish of their Bishops for them to attend to them. There are very many who, we feel assured, would take especial pleasure in the vocation. It would present a field of usefulness to them that they would gladly enter upon. Though women are precluded by their sex from going abroad as missionaries, and from performing many labors which fall to the lot of man, they are not, therefore, devoid of interest in the progress of the Work, or destitute of the desire to contribute, to the full extent of their ability, to the accomplishment of God's purposes.[57] In the sphere which the President proposes they should occupy, there is room for extended usefulness. Woman is peculiarly

---

55. Proverbs 19:17.

56. See Document 3.1.

57. While women sometimes accompanied their husbands on their missions, single female missionaries were not appointed or called until 1898. (See the remarks of George Q. Cannon, on April 6, 1898, in *Sixty-Eighth Annual Conference of the Church of Jesus Christ of Latter-day Saints, Held in the Tabernacle, Salt Lake City, April 6th, 7th, 8th and 10th, 1898, with a Full Report of the Discourses* [Salt Lake City: Deseret News Publishing Co., 1898], 7.)

adapted to fill it. She is, by nature, kind and sympathetic, and the sight of suffering awakens the kindliest emotions within her breast, and until that suffering is alleviated she cannot rest.

Man has his calling—there are duties for which he is peculiarly fitted. But for this class of duties to which we allude he has not the adaptability possessed by woman. They seem to come particularly within her province, and we have no doubt, if the Bishops will act upon the suggestion of the President, and organize these societies, and call the sisters to their aid, they will find that they have an auxiliary force on which they can rely, and one, too, that will relieve them from duties which sometimes press heavily upon them. It is President Young's wish that the Bishops take this suggestion into consideration, and that in the Wards of this City, and in the country Wards where such Societies can find employment, they will take early steps to organize them.

Salt Lake City Seventh Ward minutes, January 4, 1868.
The minute book entry for this reorganization meeting in the
Seventh Ward shows how quickly—in less than a month—
the ward responded to Brigham Young's call to reestablish
the Relief Society. The same book had been used for Seventh
Ward Relief Society minutes during the 1850s. The book had
unusual dimensions; pages were 15½ inches high by 6⅛
inches wide. (Church History Library, Salt Lake City.)

3.3 Salt Lake City Seventh Ward Relief Society, Minutes, January 4 and 28, 1868

Salt Lake City Seventh Ward Relief Society, Minutes, Jan. 4 and 28, 1868; Seventh Ward, Pioneer Stake, Relief Society Minutes and Records, 1848–1922, vol. 1, 1848–1869, pp. 35–37, 42–43, CHL (LR 12586 14).

By mid-January 1868, eleven Salt Lake City wards, including the Seventh Ward, had already heeded Brigham Young's December 1867 counsel to organize Female Relief Societies.[58] From 1854 until at least 1860, a Relief Society had functioned in the Seventh Ward with Elizabeth Campbell Vance serving as its president during most of that time. In fall 1861 Vance and her husband, John, were appointed by church leaders to settle in southern Utah; in parting she left the bishop a final tally of Relief Society donations and expenditures that shows a dearth of resources.[59]

At the first two meetings of the reorganized Seventh Ward Relief Society in January 1868, ward bishop Thomas McLelland, his two counselors, and other ward priesthood leaders addressed the women and proposed leaders and teachers to be sustained by vote of the women present. Elizabeth McLelland, wife of the bishop, was selected as president of the ward Relief Society, a pattern of husband-wife leadership followed in many wards. Subsequent meetings were under the direction of the women. In most wards priesthood leaders continued to address Relief Society meetings from time to time.

The Seventh Ward was a square of nine ten-acre blocks located between 300 South Street and 600 South Street and between present-day 300 West Street and Main Street. Several wealthy non-Mormon merchants resided within these boundaries, and Independence Hall, erected in this section in 1865, initially housed services for other religious groups, including Congregationalists, Catholics, and Episcopalians.[60] Bishop McLelland told women who would be collecting donations for the poor that "Jew and gentile bond and free would all help if called upon."

The following minutes of the Seventh Ward Relief Society's January 4, 1868, reorganization meeting and of its January 28 meeting to appoint teachers were recorded by unidentified scribes in a ward Relief Society minute book first used in 1854, which is labeled

---

58. The eleven wards were the First, Second, Third, Fourth, Fifth/Sixth, Seventh, Eighth, Tenth, Eleventh, Twelfth, and Fourteenth Wards. Membership of the Fifth Ward had been incorporated into the Sixth Ward in July 1860, and the two wards functioned as one unit until around 1877. The Fifth Ward Relief Society was organized September 4, 1877. (Presiding Bishopric, Bishops Meeting Minutes, 1851–1884, CHL, "Bishops' Record from Feb. 1862 to Nov. 1879," Jan. 16, 1868; "History of the Salt Lake City Fifth Ward," comp. Andrew Jenson, in Fifth Ward, Temple View Stake, Manuscript History and Historical Reports, 1849–1964, CHL.)

59. Seventh Ward, Pioneer Stake, Relief Society Minutes and Records, 1848–1922, 5 vols., CHL, vol. 1, Sept. 24, 1858, and Sept. 1, 1861.

60. On Independence Hall, see Brigham Young to Brigham Young Jr., Nov. 17, 1865, Brigham Young Letterbook, vol. 7, p. 831, in Brigham Young Office Files, Brigham Young, Papers, 1832–1878, CHL. See also Thomas Edgar Lyon, "Evangelical Protestant Missionary Activities in Mormon Dominated Areas, 1865–1900" (PhD diss., University of Utah, 1962).

Book A. Later, these and other minutes of meetings held in 1868 were copied with some revisions into a new Seventh Ward Relief Society record, Book B, by various scribes, including Eliza R. Snow.[61] The following transcript comes from Book A; significant revisions made in Book B are described in footnotes.

———— ⳤ ————

January 4, 1868 • Saturday

Minutes of Meeting held in Seventh Ward School room[62] Saturday 4ᵗʰ January 1868. For the purpose of organizing anew The Female Relief Society in Said Ward Meeting opened by Singing. Prayer by Charles W. Hyde. Present Bishop [Thomas] MͨLelland & Councellor's [William] Thorne & [Moses] Thurston

Bishop MͨLelland said we had met according to appointment to organize The Female Relief Society. Sister Vance formerly was President of this Society when organized under Bishop Willy [James Willie] and acted as such until she moved South. Said this Society was designed by the Almighty to be of great benefit to the poor and finding out those in the ward who were really needy and destitute.[63] He would have liked to have seen the house full of the good Sisters of the ward, Sisters full of faith and good works, so that when called upon they would be ready to act under this organization and by the direction of the Holy Spirit Had no fault to find with the labours of those who acted formerly. but wanted to reorganize so that the people might receive the benefits.

Bro Thorne said he was glad this Society was revived again. Many of the Sisters would think they had not much time to attend to this matter but it was necessary that the Sisters should have the privilege of developing the abilities God had given them and show to the people what they were competent to do. In visiting the people they must seek for the Spirit of the Lord that they may have wisdom to comfort and bless and cheer the Spirits of those that are downcast. Said that the hearts of the rich were made glad that they had the means to help the poor, the poor also were made glad by receiving the assistance they needed. Bro Thurston said he was a little disappointed in not seeing more of the Sisters present—thought the people would have been interested enough to attend this meeting and assist in [p. 35] in organizing this Society. it mattered not to him who was appointed President and Teachers but prayed that they

---

61. See "Book B, a Book of Record Containing Minutes of the Doings of the Female Relief Society of the Seventh Ward, Salt Lake City," pp. [i]–3, in Seventh Ward, Pioneer Stake, Relief Society Minutes and Records, 1848–1922, CHL.

62. The later version of these minutes (Book B) identifies the meeting place as "School House."

63. The later version of these minutes (Book B) adds, "and afflicted."

would just be such as the Lord should select. Bro [Frederick] Andrew said he felt this Society would be a great Blessing to the people and would do what he could to sustain it. Brother Hyde said the Female Relief Society was capable of doing a great deal of good and would unite the people together. Said that the Lord had in store for the people Great Blessings if they would only do right The Lord had blessed him abundantly in revealing many things to him to comfort him in his affliction.

Bro [William] McLachlan said that in this country[64] the sisters had a great deal to do and often thought that it kept them from gossiping and talking so much about one another and felt that this was all right. We did not know what we could accomplish until we were put to it and instead of labours decreasing they would continue to increase according to our faithfulness[65] in keeping the commandments of the Lord. that they would be sustained by the Priesthood of God in performing their duty in this matter. Bro [James] Crowther said this Society was a good institution and felt like throwing in his mite to sustain the organization. Bro [James] Howell said he came here to learn something and was glad that this Society was about to be organized again. and that it was necessary we should be united in order that all the members of the Body be cared for that none may suffer[.] Bishop McLelland said the Sisters were rather backward[66] he would like to hear some of them talk. Hee had looked over the Ward and could see many that would fill the Bill. But one at a time only was needed to preside and proposed Sister Elizabeth McLelland [p. 36] for President secconded by Bro Thorne and carried unanimously by all present He proposed Margaret Harrington for First and Elizabeth Huffaker for Seccond Counseller's secconded by Bro Thurston and carried unanimously and that Mary Allice Lambert be Clerk[67] for said organization secconde & carried.[68] Sister McLelland[69] said she felt it was a great responsibility that was laid upon her but would try to do her best in accomplishing the work required of her that if we were united a great deal of good could be done. Several of the sisters expressed their willingness to do any thing that they might be required to do. Bishop McLelland Said they would proceed no further with the organizing at present,

---

64. The later version of these minutes (Book B) replaces "country" with "Church."

65. The later version of these minutes (Book B) reads, "our faith and faithfulness."

66. Unwilling, reluctant, or hesitating. ("Backward," in *An American Dictionary of the English Language,* ed. Noah Webster [New York: Harper and Brothers, 1845], 67.)

67. The later version of these minutes (Book B) uses the term "secretary" for Lambert's position.

68. The later version of these minutes (Book B) inserts "Mrs. Maria Thorne was appointed Treasurer by unanimous vote" at this point, although (as seen below) the original minutes in Book A show the vote taking place at the second meeting on January 28.

69. The later version of these minutes (Book B) instead refers to McLelland as "Mrs. President."

But at another meeting they would assist the President & Council in appointing assistants on the various Blocks. after a few remarks upon the principle of union meeting was dismissed Benediction By

Bro. Thorne

January 28, 1868 • Tuesday

Minutes of Meeting

Female Releif Society Tuesday evening Jan. 28ᵗʰ 1868/ 7ᵗʰ Ward School house opened by prayer by Charles Lambert[70] present Bishop MᶜLelland & councilor Thorn

Minutes of last meeting read and aproved

Bishop Said inasmuch as Sister⟨s⟩ Harrington Huffaker and Lambert were not present at our last meeting he would like them to express their feelings in relation to their appointments, they all expressed their willingness to act and do their best

Bishop said he was satisfied with what the Sisters had said and thought it would be also be necessary to appoint a Treasurer and would propose Sister Maria Thorne sconded, & carried un[animously] [p. 37][71]

Bishop MᶜLelland Councilor Thorne and Bʳ Charles Lambert then proceeded to Ordain The President Council and Clerk

Sister Elizabeth MᶜLelland for President

Sister Margaret Harrington first Councilor

Sister Elizabeth Huffaker for Second

and Sister Mary Alice Lambert for Clerk

The Bishop said the next buiseness was to appoint Teachers on the Various blocks, the following was Named

First	Block	Sisters	
	Block	Sisters	[Mary] Crowther & [Frances] Morgan[72]
2	Dᵒ[73]	Dᵒ	[Eliza] Homer & [Elizabeth] Rose
3	Dᵒ	Dᵒ	[Eliza] Cram & [Catherine] Woodbury
4	Dᵒ	Dᵒ	[Martha] Twigg[s] & [Elizabeth] Cowley
5	Dᵒ	Dᵒ	[Jane] Rigby & [Margaret] Stewart[74]
6	Dᵒ	Dᵒ	[Fanny] Hunter & [Caroline] MᶜLachlan

---

70. The later version of these minutes (Book B) reads, "Meeting Opened with Singing | Prayer by Charles Lambert."

71. TEXT: At this point two leaves (pages 38–41) are missing from the original, having been torn out. The missing pages were evidently numbered before they were removed.

72. The later version of these minutes (Book B) gives her name as "Fanney Morgan."

73. "Dᵒ" is an abbreviation for "ditto."

74. There were two Stewart families living in the Seventh Ward during this time period. Book B clarifies that this reference is to Margaret McCullough Carpenter Gheen Stewart.

7	Dᵒ	Dᵒ	[Elizabeth] Andrew & Vanschoonhover [Mary Van Schoonhoven]
8	Dᵒ	Dᵒ	Whittaker [Elizabeth Whitaker] & [Eliza] Croxall
9	Dᵒ	Dᵒ	[Elizabeth] Cooper & [Elizabeth Henderson] Worley

all were unanimously sustained in their appointments. The Bishop said they would be assisted by the Spirit of the Lord in their labours and be a means of enriching the Ward and bless the poor and do a great ammount of good. he wished them to remember the School house and assist in adorning that when ready. Spoke of the great number of childeren that needed Education.[75] The 7ᵗʰ Ward alone could run 3 good schools and wished their Mothers to train them aright that they might rightly apriaciate their labors Bʳ Thorne said he could bear testimony to the truth of the remarks of the Bishop his instructions were good and calculated to bless. The Lord would never ask any of us to do what we are un able to perform the Sisters would realize to some extent the responsibility resting upon the Priesthoo[d] in the discharge of their duties wished the Sisters to be faithful in calling

Spoke of the great work that could be done if people were united. Our meeting house could be built the next season and prepaired for Meeting next fall. The Privelege of the Sisters were as good as those of the Bretheren

Bʳ Lambert said he was pleased with the remarks of the bretheren and was confident that this Society would do A [p. 42] great deal of good in helping to build up the kingdom of God and releive the wants of the Poor

Bishop MᶜLelland . . . Sisters cease to ask your Husbands for those things you do not realy need . . .[76] told them to seek for wisdom and use all the Economy possible these things were impressed upon his mind and felt like laying them before the Sisters. Made A few remarks upon the good that could be done by this Society that Jew and gentile bond and free would all help if called upon

Bʳ Thorn. There were A great many ~~sick~~ childeren arround and much Sickness wished the Sisters that had a knowledge how to treat the Sick to comunicate this to their sisters so as to remove it from our midst

Benedictation by Wᵐ McLauchlan

---

75. The later version of these minutes (Book B) reads, "Spoke of the necessity of educating the children."

76. TEXT: These ellipsis points and the ones earlier in this paragraph are in the original.

3.4 Brigham Young, Discourse, April 8, 1868 (Excerpt)

Brigham Young, Discourse, Apr. 8, 1868, in "Remarks by President Brigham Young, in the New Tabernacle, Afternoon, April 8, 1868," Deseret News [weekly] (Salt Lake City, UT), May 13, 1868, vol. 17, no. 14, pp. 106–107 (excerpt).

When Latter-day Saints convened in the newly built tabernacle for general conference in April 1868, Brigham Young called a second time for the organization of ward Relief Societies. Only a dozen or so wards had responded to the initial call he had issued four months earlier.[77] This second appeal and the commission of Eliza R. Snow to help establish Relief Societies provided the necessary momentum for wards to organize.[78]

In the 1850s charity was the main emphasis of the Relief Society. Now President Young tied the Relief Society to home industry and the movement for economic cooperation among the Latter-day Saints by inviting women to place themselves "in a condition to administer to the poor" by living frugally and more diligently pursuing cottage or home industries. The manufacture and sale of local goods kept what scarce cash there was in the territory, while excessive expenditures on imports threatened Latter-day Saint economic strength and independence.[79] More imports would inevitably come to Utah with the impending completion of the transcontinental railroad. In this discourse Young emphasized the importance of women's economic contributions and recommended, among other measures, that women cultivate and produce silk locally rather than import it. Through the 1860s Young had encouraged local silk production. A *Deseret News* editorial, "Culture of Silk," published two weeks before Young gave this discourse, noted that Young "has an abundance of mulberry trees, which he has raised from seed imported by him, at considerable expense, from Italy and the South of France. These he has offered for sale; . . . there is, without doubt, great wealth to be derived from their judicious cultivation."[80] Young's April 8 discourse, like so many he delivered, was filled with a wide range of what he termed "practical teachings," including on marriage, fashion, women's and children's health, and farming.[81]

The following transcript is excerpted from the report of Young's April 8 discourse made by George D. Watt for the weekly edition of the *Deseret News,* May 13, 1868.

———— ❧ ————

REMARKS
By President BRIGHAM YOUNG, in the New Tabernacle, afternoon,

---

77. See Documents 3.1 and 3.3.

78. See Documents 3.5 and 3.6.

79. See Leonard J. Arrington, *Great Basin Kingdom: An Economic History of the Latter-day Saints, 1830–1900* (Cambridge, MA: Harvard University Press, 1958), 195–231.

80. "Culture of Silk," *Deseret News* [weekly], Mar. 25, 1868, 52. See Chris Rigby Arrington, "The Finest of Fabrics: Mormon Women and the Silk Industry in Early Utah," *Utah Historical Quarterly* 46, no. 4 (Fall 1978): 376–396.

81. "Remarks," *Deseret News* [weekly], May 13, 1868, 107.

April 8, 1868.

REPORTED BY G. D. WATT

[82]. . . I have a short sermon for my sisters. I wish you, under the direction of your bishops and wise men, to establish your relief societies, and organize yourselves under the direction of the brethren, and establish yourselves for doing business, gathering up your little amounts of means that would otherwise go to waste, and put them to usury, and make more of them, and thus keep gathering in. Let this be commenced forthwith. . . . Let the sisters take care of themselves, and make themselves beautiful, and if any of you are so superstitious and ignorant as to say that this is pride, I can say that you are not informed as to the and pride which is sinful before the Lord, you are also ignorant as to the excellency of the heavens, and of the beauty which dwells in the society of the Gods. Were you to see an angel, you would see a beautiful and lovely creature. Make yourselves like angels in goodness and beauty. Let the mothers in Israel make their sons and daughters [p. 106] healthy and beautiful, by cleanliness and a proper diet. Whether you have much or little clothing for your children, it can be kept clean and healthy, and be made to fit their persons neatly. Make your children lovely and fair that you may delight in them. Cease to send out your children to herd sheep with their skins exposed to the hot sun, until their hands and faces appear as though they lived in an ash heap. I call upon my sisters to lead out in these things, and create your own fashions, and make your clothing to please yourselves independent of outside influences; and make your hats and bonnets to shade you. I wish you, sisters, to listen to these counsels, and place yourselves in a condition to administer to the poor. Get your husbands to provide you with a little of this and a little of that of which you can make something by addoing your own labor. I do not mean that you shall apply to them for five dollars and ten dollars to spend for that which is of no profit, but manufacture something that will be useful as well as beautiful and comely.

You ought to enter into the cultivation of silk. Our bench lands are well adapted to the growth of the mulberry tree, the leaves of which produce the natural food for the silk worm. There is no better land nor climate in the world than we have for this branch of business. We can make ourselves independently rich at this business alone if it is properly pursued. There ought to be a plot of land in each ward devoted to the cultivation of silk, and a cocoonery built in the centre of it, and in the season thereof let the children of the wards who have nothing to do, and aged people, gather the leaves and feed the

---

82. TEXT: The ellipsis points in this excerpt have been supplied by the editors of this volume to indicate omissions from the original document.

worms. The work is light and interesting, while the sales of wound silk, for which there is always a market to be found, will do much towards feeding and clothing poor persons that would otherwise be entirely dependent. . . .

Now, sisters, go to forthwith and get you an acre of land, and get the Bishops and the brethren to fence it, and prepare it for the reception of the trees, and go and help them; but be sure to wear a wide brimmed hat while doing it, so as not to get tanned with the sun and the wind. Go to and raise silk. You can do it, and those who cannot set themselves to work we will set them to work gathering straw, and making straw hats and straw bonnets; we will set others to work gathering willows, and others to making baskets; we will set others to gathering flags and rushes, and to making mats, and bottoming chairs, and making carpets. . . . I wish the sisters to lead out in the fashions. It is very little difference what fashion you produce. I would just as soon see you wear hats with wide brims as not, if you have that fashion that will give comfort and convenience and produce health and longevity. We wish to promote the longevity of the people. Tell your husbands to get you a heifer calf or two and some chickens, and you will feed them, and take care of them, instead of feeding pigs, and if your husbands have springs on their land, get them to clean them out and dam them up a little, and introduce the spawn of the best fish we have in these mountains, and collect all the information that has been printed, and which comes within your reach on the subject of raising fish. And raise your potatoes and parsnips and carrots to feed them with, adding a little corn meal, or a little oatmeal. We can raise fish here, and the cost will be one fourth less per pound than other meats. You may think that fowls are injurious to the garden; but they are not. They will pick up grubs and cut worms, and other destructive insects and the good they do in this respect will far over-balance any trifling injury they may do to young plants. They will keep your gardens clean of these pests, and fatten, giving you plenty of eggs to eat. Take care of them, and get a little patch of lucerne[83] planted to give to your young heifer, and rear her until she gives you her increase. . . .

. . . Brethren, learn. You have learned a good deal it is true; but learn more; learn to sustain yourselves; lay up grain and flour, and save it against a day of scarcity. Sisters, do not ask your husbands to sell the last bushel of grain you have to buy something for you out of the stores, but aid your husbands in storing it up against a day of want, and always have a year or two's provision on hand. A great abundance of fruit can be dried. There are but few families in

83. A plant cultivated as forage for animals; also known as alfalfa in parts of the United States. ("Lucerne," and "Alfalfa," in *The Oxford English Dictionary*, ed. J. A. Simpson and E. S. C. Weiner, 2nd ed., 20 vols. [Oxford: Clarendon, 1989], 9:80; 1:310.)

this city who do not have the privilege of drying and laying up fruit. Yet the majority of families in this community, instead of using fruit that was dried last fall but one are using fruit dried last year when the grasshoppers were here.[84] A year's supply should be kept ahead, so that families would not be compelled to eat fruit that had been injured by grasshoppers and other insects. We should accumulate all kinds of nutritive substances, and preserve them from worms, which can easily be done. If we do not take care of ourselves, we shall have a very poor chance to be taken care of. If we will hearken to the counsel that is given to us we shall know how to sustain ourselves in every particular. Mothers in Israel, sisters, ask your husbands to take care of the sheep they have got, and not wilfully waste them; but multiply them and bring your wool to the factories to be manufactured, or trade it for yarn and cloth. The woolen mills which we now have in the country will work up a great deal of wool if they can get it.[85] Who is there in our community that raises flax? Is there any attention paid to this culture? I think not, but it is, "Husband, sell your wheat, sell your oats to buy me the linen I want." We shall in the future have flax machines here to make the finest of linen; and we can make the cotton and silk in abundance. I would urge the brethren of the southern country to plant cotton sufficient to supply the wants of the factories that are now in the country, and let us continue our labors until we can manufacture everything we want. All this is embraced in our religion, every good word and work, all things temporal, and all things spiritual, things in heaven, things on earth, and things that are under the earth are circumscribed by our religion. We are in the fastnesses of the mountains, and if we do these things, and delight in doing right, our feet will be made fast and immovable like the bases of these everlasting hills. We ought not to desire anything only on righteous principles, and if we want right, let us then deal it out to others, being kind and full of love and charity to all. My brethren and sisters, I have occupied considerable time; but I have not spoken one tenth of what I wish to say to you. By the authority that the Lord has granted to me, I bless you in the name of Jesus Christ. Amen.

---

84. Grasshoppers were a persistent problem for Utah settlers. In 1867 the *Deseret News* noted that "every cloudless day, when the sun is high in the heavens, they [grasshoppers] can be seen on the wing in myriads." Brigham Young warned settlers that summer to store food as "according to present appearances, next year we may expect grasshoppers to eat up nearly all our crops." ("Still Going South," *Deseret News* [weekly], Aug. 21, 1867, 269; "Remarks," *Deseret News* [weekly], Dec. 25, 1867, 362; see also Davis Bitton and Linda P. Wilcox, "Pestiferous Ironclads: The Grasshopper Problem in Pioneer Utah," *Utah Historical Quarterly* 46, no. 4 [Fall 1978]: 336–355.)

85. In 1863 Brigham Young established a woolen factory, with carding and spinning machinery, on Big Kanyon Creek in what is now Parley's Canyon. ("New Woollen Factory," *Deseret News,* Sept. 9, 1863, 56; "Woollen Factory," and "Cotton Factory," *Deseret News,* Sept. 23, 1863, 74.)

3.5 Eliza R. Snow, Account of 1868 Commission, as Recorded in "Sketch of My Life," April 13, 1885 (Excerpt)

Eliza R. Snow, "Sketch of My Life," Apr. 13, 1885, pp. [1], [36]–[37] (excerpt); Bancroft Library, University of California, Berkeley (BANC MSS P-F 57 v.1).

In the spring of 1868 Brigham Young commissioned Eliza R. Snow to assist in reestablishing local Relief Societies. The following excerpt from her handwritten autobiographical account titled "Sketch of My Life" is the only surviving reference from Snow to that appointment.[86] Snow penned "Sketch of My Life" in 1885 for historian Hubert Howe Bancroft, who was then collecting information for his *History of Utah.*[87] Snow does not date the commission, but it seems to be closely tied to the April 1868 general conference, when Young repeated his call for the organization of ward Relief Societies.[88]

Young likely chose Snow, one of his plural wives who lived with the majority of his other wives and children in the Lion House in Salt Lake City, for this assignment in part because of her familiarity with the Nauvoo Relief Society minutes. As Snow noted in this life sketch, she had served as secretary of the Female Relief Society of Nauvoo (1842–1844). Snow's participation in the 1854–1858 Relief Society meetings appears to have been limited, at least in part, because of her assignment from Young to administer women's temple ordinances in the Endowment House on the temple block in Salt Lake City. Nevertheless, minutes for a September 1855 church meeting in the Eighteenth Ward note "an Exho[r]tation to the Sisters by Sister Eliza R Snow also remarks by the Bishop in regard to organizing a society to make up clothing for the Poor."[89]

---

86. The complete document is published in Maureen Ursenbach Beecher, ed., *The Personal Writings of Eliza Roxcy Snow,* Writings of Frontier Women 5 (Logan: Utah State University Press, 2000), 3, 6–45. Beecher notes that this sketch was likely a revised draft of the memoir Snow wrote for Edward Tullidge's *Women of Mormondom,* published in 1877. Tullidge quoted extensively from Snow's memoir, but his volume does not include Snow's Relief Society recollections excerpted here. (Edward W. Tullidge, *The Women of Mormondom* [New York: Tullidge and Crandall, 1877].)

87. Hubert Howe Bancroft, *History of Utah, 1540–1886,* Works of Hubert Howe Bancroft 26 (San Francisco: History Company, 1889). A footnote in Bancroft (719n97) references information from Snow's autobiography, and she is also mentioned as vice president of the Deseret Silk Association in 1880 (726n23). Bancroft's history makes no mention of the Relief Society or Snow's leadership of women. For more information on manuscripts collected by Bancroft, see two articles by George Ellsworth: "Hubert Howe Bancroft and the History of Utah," *Utah Historical Quarterly* 22, no. 2 (Apr. 1954): 99–124; and "A Guide to the Manuscripts in the Bancroft Library Relating to the History of Utah," *Utah Historical Quarterly* 22, no. 3 (July 1954): 197–248.

88. See Document 3.4.

89. Eighteenth Ward, Salt Lake Stake, General Minutes, 1854–1976, CHL, vol. 5, Sept. 6, 1855. The Eighteenth Ward bishop at that time was Lorenzo Dow Young, brother of Brigham Young.

Eliza R. Snow. 1866. Celebrated poet Eliza R. Snow posed for this photo two years before her husband, Brigham Young, commissioned her to assist in organizing local branches of the Relief Society. As Snow worked closely with other women leaders, the Relief Society became the platform for organizing what would become the Young Women and Primary organizations. Snow was set apart as general president of the Relief Society in 1880 and continued to oversee Relief Society work until her death in 1887. Latter-day Saints honored her as the president of all of the women's organizations. Photograph by the studio of Savage and Ottinger. (Church History Library, Salt Lake City.)

Sketch of my Life[90] . . . [p. [1]] . . .

The "Female Relief Society" was organized by Joseph Smith in Nauvoo on the 17th of March, 1842. It was organized after the pattern of the Church of Jesus Christ of Latter-day-Saints, with President and Counselors, and accomplished much good in administering to the sick, relieving the wants of the poor, etc. The prophet had donated to the Society a Lot, and the frame of a house, as a commencement for establishing a home for the homeless, but the ruthless hand of persecution thwarted this benevolent purpose—the Prophet was massacred and the Saints driven from their homes.

From the time of the expulsion from Nauvoo, the Female Relief Society remained in status quo until it was reorganized under the direction of Pres. B. Young in the year 1855, commencing in the Fifteenth Ward, S.L. City.[91]

As I had been intimately associated with, and had officiated as Secretary for the first organization, Pres. Young commissioned me to assist the Bishops in organizing Branches of the Society in their respective Wards; for, at that time, the Bishops had not acquainted themselves with the movement, and did not know how to proceed. To me it was quite a mission, and I took much pleasure in its performance. I felt quite honored and much at home in my associations with the Bishops, and they appreciated my assistance. Each Branch of the Society, although constituting a self-governing body, and empowered to create committees and whatever officers may be needed from time ⟨to time,⟩ in accomplishing its many and increasing labors, is under the direction of its respective Bishop or presiding officer of the Ward.[92]

Not long after the re-organization of the Relief Society, Pres. Young told me he was going to give me a ⟨another⟩ mission. Without the least intimation of what the mission consisted, I replied, "I shall endeavor to fulfil it." He said, "I want you to instruct the sisters."[93] Altho' my heart went "pit a pat" for the time being, I did not, and could not then form an adequate estimate of the

---

90. TEXT: Title triple underlined in original. The ellipsis points in this excerpt have been supplied by the editors of this volume to indicate omissions from the original document.

91. Brigham Young called for the organization of ward Relief Societies in June 1854, primarily for the purpose of making clothing for Indian women and children; these groups were sometimes known as Indian Relief Societies. Snow may have differentiated the short-term task of those societies, which ended early in 1855, from the more extended work of caring for the poor. Lydia Granger was appointed president of the Fifteenth Ward Relief Society in 1855, but no Fifteenth Ward Relief Society records are extant for this period. (See introduction to Part 2; Document 2.1; and History, n.d., in Fifteenth Ward, Salt Lake Stake, Relief Society Annual Message, 1873, CHL.)

92. For Snow's elaboration on the Relief Society's organizational structure and relationship to priesthood leaders, see Document 3.6.

93. At the founding meeting of the Relief Society, Joseph Smith "read the Revelation to Emma Smith, from the book of Doctrine and Covenants; and stated that she was ordain'd at the time, the Revelation was given, to expound the scriptures to all; and to teach the female part of community; and that not she

magnitude of the work before me. To carry into effect the President's requisition, I saw, at once, involved public meetings and public speaking—also travel abroad, [p. [36]] as the Branches of the Society of the sisterhood extended at that time, through several Counties in Utah, and ultimately, all the vallies of the mountains—numbering, at present date, nearly three hundred; besides other Branches in the U.S., Europe, Asia, Islands of the sea, wherever the "Church of Jesus Christ of Latter-day-Saints" has established its Branches.[94] Some years ago, by mutual consent, the word female was dropped, and the Society called "Relief Society."[95]

Its first duty is to look after and relieve the wants of the poor, to accomplish which committees are appointed to visit each family residing in their respective districts, at least, ⟨once⟩ every month, and report to the presiding officers. The cultivation of the members of the Society (which is composed of aged and middle-aged women) physically, mentally, morally, and spiritually, is another prominent feature of the institution, which has proved very beneficial. At the time of its organization in Salt Lake City, the Saints were very poor, and the funds of the Society were raised by contributions of carpet rags, pieces for patchwork <u>etc.</u>, which were converted into carpets, quilts—wool carded, spun, and knitted into socks and stockings, by the industry of the members, who met together, sometimes weekly, at others, once in two weeks, to work the crude material into wearing and saleable articles. . . . [p. [37]] . . .

---

alone, but others, may attain to the same blessings." (Document 1.2, entry for Mar. 17, 1842; see also Document 1.1.)

94. The phrase "Numbers 300 branches, July 24, 1880" was inscribed with other words and images on a white silk banner that accompanied three carriages transporting Relief Society leaders in the 1880 Pioneer Day Jubilee procession in Salt Lake City. The banner is preserved in the Church History Museum in Salt Lake City. ("Year of Jubilee," *Woman's Exponent,* Aug. 1, 1880, 9:36; see also p. 436 herein.)

95. In the fall of 1872, Eliza Snow proposed "the omission of the word 'Female,' and the calling of these associations merely 'Relief Societies.'" Since the name had been established by vote (in the original Female Relief Society of Nauvoo), Snow said, the modification would be "done legally" only if it were approved by vote "from a majority of those interested." Consequently, local Relief Societies reported the voting in their individual wards. ("F. R. Society Reports," *Woman's Exponent,* Oct. 15, 1872, 1:74; see, for example, "F. R. Society Reports" in *Woman's Exponent,* Nov. 15, 1872, 1:90; and Dec. 1, 1872, 1:98.)

3.6 Eliza R. Snow, "Female Relief Society," April 18 and 20, 1868

Eliza R. Snow, "Female Relief Society," Deseret Evening News *(Salt Lake City, UT), Apr. 18, 1868, vol. 1, no. 127, p. [2]; Apr. 20, 1868, vol. 1, no. 128, p. [2].*

Building on Brigham Young's April 8, 1868, general conference remarks regarding the Relief Society, Eliza R. Snow wrote the following article for the *Deseret Evening News*. Published in two installments on April 18 and 20, 1868, and republished in the paper's semi-weekly and weekly editions,[96] it became a singularly important reference for wards she had already visited and those awaiting her visit. Drawing from the minutes of the Female Relief Society of Nauvoo, which she had penned and preserved as secretary, Snow explained the Relief Society's basic organizational patterns and objectives.[97] Her article tied the Relief Society to its Nauvoo beginnings under the direction of Joseph Smith, to the New Testament church, and to the priesthood. It also referred to her private conversations with Joseph Smith regarding the society.

In December 1867, when President Young issued his first public call for the reorganization of local Relief Societies, many Latter-day Saints were unfamiliar with the organization. Young assigned Snow "to assist the Bishops in organizing Branches of the Society in their respective Wards,"[98] a responsibility that apparently included a mandate to provide women and their bishops essential information about the organization's structure and purposes. Snow thus met with many local Relief Societies and wrote letters to others explaining the structure and purposes of the organization.[99] Beginning in 1868, as she traveled from ward to ward to establish the Relief Society, she carried the original Nauvoo minute book with her and often read from it to emphasize the organization's foundations and to provide guidance regarding how it should be organized and what it might accomplish.

———— ❧ ————

FEMALE RELIEF SOCIETY.
(BY ELIZA R. SNOW.)

---

96. "Female Relief Society," *Deseret News* [semi-weekly], Apr. 21, 1868, [3], [8]; "Female Relief Society," *Deseret News* [weekly], Apr. 22, 1868, 81.

97. See Document 3.5; see also Document 1.2.

98. Document 3.5.

99. For example, Snow visited the Eighth Ward in Salt Lake City on May 12, 1868, at a special meeting called to "more fully" organize the ward's Relief Society. During Snow's remarks, she noted that she "had been present when Joseph Smith first spoke of organizing such a Society," read from the Nauvoo minutes, and reminded those present that the Relief Society "was no trifling thing, but an organization after the order of Heaven." In addition, on October 27 Snow attended the formal organization of the Lehi Ward Relief Society (which had been functioning as a "temporary one"). She "read the Records of the organization of the first female Releif Society at Nauvoo," after which ward leaders organized the ward society "legally and properly." (Eighth Ward, Liberty Stake, Relief Society Minutes and Records, 1867–1969, CHL, vol. 1, May 12, 1868; Lehi Ward, Alpine Stake, Relief Society Minutes and Records, 1868–1892, CHL, vol. 1, Oct. 27, 1868; for an example of instruction Snow provided by letter, see Document 3.8.)

This is the name of a Society which was organized in Nauvoo, on the 17th of March, 1842, by President Joseph Smith, assisted by Elders Willard Richards and John Taylor. Although the name may be of modern date, the institution is of ancient origin. We were told by our martyred prophet, that the same organization existed in the church anciently, allusions to which are made in some of the epistles recorded in the New Testament, making use of the title, "elect lady."[100]

This is an organization that cannot exist without the Priesthood, from the fact that it derives all its authority and influence from that source. When the Priesthood was taken from the earth, this institution as well as every other appendage to the true order of the church of Jesus Christ on the earth, became extinct, and had never been restored until the time referred to above.

Last winter President Young instructed the Bishops to organize Female Relief Societies in their various Wards,[101] and at our last Conference repeated the requisition,[102] extending it to all the settlements, calling upon the sisters to enter into organizations, not only for the relief of the poor, but for the accomplishment of every good and noble work. He urged upon them the manufacture of articles made of straw—the cultivation of silk, and the establishing of fashions that would be becoming—such as would be worthy the patronage of sensible, refined and intelligent women who stand, as we in reality do, at the head of the world.

Having been present at the organization of the "Female Relief Society of Nauvoo," and having now in my possession the minutes of the organization and the records of that Society, which is a sample for all others, and also having had considerable experience in that association, perhaps I may communicate a few hints that will assist the daughters of Zion in stepping forth in this very important position, which is replete with new and multiplied responsibilities. If any of the daughters and mothers in Israel are feeling in the least circumscribed in their present spheres, they will now find ample scope for every power and capability for doing good with which they are most liberally endowed.

"The Female Relief Society of Nauvoo," was organized after the pattern of the Church of Jesus Christ of Latter-day Saints, with a Presidentess, who chose two Counselors. These were ordained and set apart by the Priesthood, and were to fill those offices so long as they faithfully discharged the trust committed to them. This quorum was fully authorized to appoint such officers, committees and assistants as were requisite from time to time, either to fill

---

100. See 2 John 1:1; Document 1.1; and Document 1.2, entry for Mar. 17, 1842.
101. See Document 3.1.
102. See Document 3.4.

permanent offices or to perform any temporary agency that circumstances might demand. But, to make these appointments legal they had to be sanctioned by vote of the majority of the meeting when such appointments were made.[103]

In organizing Societies, it is necessary to have a competent Secretary and Treasurer—these and all other officers must be nominated, and the nomination must be seconded, and then a vote of the House called, with opportunity for any to object, if they should feel disposed.

President Joseph Smith told the sisters that he not only wanted them to learn to do business, but he wanted them to learn to do it correctly and in a business-like manner. He *set* the example, and kindly proffered his instructions, not only through the Presidentess, but often met with the Society and gave much wise counsel and precious instruction and encouragement—copies of which are carefully preserved.[104]

Confidence being the key to union, and union the soul of successful concentrated action, he instructed the Society to be very careful in admitting members, that none be received but those of strictly virtuous character—those who could be received with confidence, and full fellowship; and then they should sustain, and hold each other's characters sacred. In dealing with members, when they sit in judgment on those whose conduct was called in question, they could not be too cautious lest they should falsely condemn—they must imitate the example of Jesus, and like him be forbearing, merciful and forgiving.[105]

Through the authority which President Young has conferred upon the Bishops, they now stand in the same relation with the Societies which have been, and are now about to be organized in the wards and settlements, as President Joseph Smith did with the one in Nauvoo. No Society can overstep the counsel of its Bishop—his word is law, to which, all its doings are amenable.

Should the question arise in the mind, of any, What is the object of the Female Relief Society? I would reply—*to do good*—to bring into requisition every capacity we possess for doing good, not only in relieving the poor but in

---

103. See Document 1.2, entry for Mar. 17, 1842.

104. Joseph Smith spoke at length to the Female Relief Society of Nauvoo on March 17 and 31, April 28, May 26, June 9, and August 31, 1842. He also attended meetings on March 24, May 12, and May 27, 1842. A letter that Joseph Smith and others wrote to the Relief Society was also copied into the minutes following the September 28, 1842, entry. (See Document 1.2.)

105. See Document 1.2, entries for Mar. 17, Mar. 31, Apr. 28, and June 9, 1842. The minutes of the June 9 meeting include Smith's extensive remarks on charity.

saving souls.[106] United effort will accomplish incalculably more than can be accomplished by the most effective individual energies.

(*To be continued.*)[107]

FEMALE RELIEF SOCIETY.
(BY ELIZA R. SNOW.)
(*Concluded.*)

As its name indicates, the first grand object of the Society is to seek out, and relieve the wants of the poor. President Smith, in giving instruction to the Society in Nauvoo, said that the sisters could much better look into, and understand the circumstances of destitute families, than the brethren; and as they were more sympathetic in their natures, they could better enter into the feelings of the afflicted, and administer aid and consolation.[108]

Relieving the poor, in most of instances, requires something beyond administering to present necessities. When giving, encourages people in idleness, it has a demoralizing tendency. The sick must be provided for: but to those who have strength to labor, it is far more charitable to give employment and so direct their energies that they can earn what they need, and thus realize the fruits of their own labors. President Joseph Smith proposed deeding a city lot to the Society in Nauvoo, on which we purposed building comfortable houses for homes for the homeless, sick and destitute, and furnish such varieties of remunerative labor as would be adapted to the strength and capacities of such as were able to work.[109] But the sudden death of the Prophet, and subsequent expulsion from Nauvoo, blasted all these fond anticipations, and instead of the generous pleasure of providing and superintending homes for others, we were ourselves homeless until we found an abiding place in the lone wilderness. Although the existence of the Society was short, it accomplished much. During one extremely severe winter, in particular, it was instrumental, through the

---

106. Emma Smith, Lucy Mack Smith, and others exhorted Nauvoo Relief Society members "to do good." Joseph Smith declared that "the Society is not only to relieve the poor, but to save souls." (Document 1.2, entries for Mar. 17, Mar. 24, Mar. 31, June 9, and June 23, 1842.)

107. This marks the end of the April 18, 1868, installment of the two-part article. The second and final installment, dated April 20, 1868, follows.

108. The Nauvoo minutes record Joseph Smith saying, "The charitable Society— this is according to your natures— it is natural for females to have feelings of charity— you are now plac'd in a situatio[n] where you can act according to those sympathies which God has planted in your bosoms." (Document 1.2, entry for Apr. 28, 1842.)

109. "Prest. S. then said that he would give a lot of land to the Society by deeding it to the Treasurer, that the Society may build houses for the poor. He also said he would give a house— frame not finished— said that br. Cahoon will move it on to the aforesaid lot, and the Society can pay him by giving Orders on the Store." (Document 1.2, entry for June 9, 1842.)

blessing of God, in preserving the lives of many who, otherwise, must have perished.[110]

The climate of Nauvoo was a very sickly one, it was a climate in which none but a people of faith and righteousness could prosper. The location was beautiful and very desirable, but, in consequence of its unhealthfulness it had been abandoned, by those who had from time to time tried the experiment, as a place that could not be built up. We had been expelled from Missouri, and in our transit subjected to great hardships and exposures, and our systems were more predisposed to sickness than they would have been under more favorable circumstances, and with all the faith we could exercise, we experienced much sickness.[111] In consequence of this, in connexion with other adverse circumstances, many were unable to obtain those comforts that nature required.

Previous to the organization of the Relief Society, President Smith said that the sisters, by relieving the Bishops and Elders of the care of the poor, would perform a very important work, and be instrumental in doing much good by liberating their hands so that they might devote their time and energies to other labors; he said that such an organization belonged to, and should exist in the Church—that he had long had it on his mind, but had been too much crowded with other duties to attend to it.

The care of the poor was a prominent item in the teachings of the Savior, and it always stands prominently forth among the requirements of our holy religion; and the business of caring for, and attending to the wants of the poor, was a heavy tax on the time as well as on the means of the authorities of the Church, in addition to all the cares and labors incident on commencing settlements in new locations.

In administering to the poor, the Female Relief Society has other duties to perform than merely relieving bodily wants. Poverty of mind and sickness of heart, also demand attention; and many times a kind expression—a few words of counsel, or even a warm and affectionate shake of the hand will do more good and be better appreciated than a purse of gold.

"Evil communications corrupt good manners."[112] Many have apostatized through the influence of bad associations—they come here without the experience that is necessary to know how to estimate character, and forgetting that

---

110. See last paragraph of Document 1.8.

111. Malaria was endemic to the Mississippi River Valley, and early Nauvoo residents were susceptible to the high incidence of disease along the river. Nauvoo Relief Society minutes include many reports of families suffering with "sickness and death." (See Robert Bruce Flanders, *Nauvoo: Kingdom on the Mississippi* [Urbana: University of Illinois Press, 1965], 40, 53–54; and Document 1.2, entries for Aug. 5 and 13, 1843; undated Aug. 1843 entry.)

112. 1 Corinthians 15:33.

"the net which is cast into the sea gathers of every kind,"[113] they are often deceived by fair appearances and oily tongues. When the Saints gather from abroad, strangers to everybody, and subject to be led astray by those who lie in wait to deceive, the F. R. Society should be prompt in looking after the stranger sisters, and introduce them into the society that will refine and elevate, and above all strengthen them in the faith of the Gospel, and in so doing, may be instrumental in saving many.

It would require volumes in which to define the duties, privileges and responsibilities that come within the purview of the Society. President Young has turned the key to a wide and extensive sphere of action and usefulness.[114] But, says one, Where are the means? The means will accumulate. Do not refuse anything that may be donated, from a shoestring, or patch, or a carpet rag, to an elegant house and lot with all the appurtenances thereof. Go at it (under the direction of your bishop) coolly, deliberately, energetically, unitedly and prayerfully, and God will crown your efforts with success.

---

113. See Matthew 13:47.

114. Snow was likely hearkening back to a statement made by Joseph Smith at the sixth meeting of the Nauvoo Relief Society: "I now turn the key to you in the name of God and this Society shall rejoice and knowledge and intelligence shall flow down from this time— this is the beginning of better days, to this Society." In the December 1867 sermon in which Brigham Young called for the organization of individual ward Relief Societies, he also spoke of "the oracles of God, the priesthood and the keys of eternal life," noting, "We are in possession of those keys, and, consequently, we are under greater obligations, as individuals and as a community, to work righteousness." (Document 1.2, entry for Apr. 28, 1842; "Remarks," *Deseret Evening News,* Dec. 14, 1867, [1]; see also Document 3.1.)

3.7 Salt Lake City Thirteenth Ward Relief Society, Minutes, April 18, 1868

Salt Lake City Thirteenth Ward Relief Society, Minutes, Apr. 18, 1868; Thirteenth Ward, Ensign Stake, Relief Society Minutes and Records, 1868–1906, vol. 1, 1868–1898, pp. 1–3, CHL (LR 6133 14).

Rachel Ridgeway Ivins Grant, a forty-seven-year-old widow, was set apart as president of the Salt Lake City Thirteenth Ward Female Relief Society on Saturday, April 18, 1868, only ten days after Brigham Young's conference address emphasizing the importance of organizing Relief Societies.[115] These handwritten minutes from the organizational meeting of the Thirteenth Ward Relief Society provide an example of a bishop appointing a Relief Society presidency in response to Young's request.

Grant served in her position for thirty-five years, joining with a core contingent of ward presidents who worked closely with Eliza R. Snow in forwarding the Relief Society movement. As president, Grant canvassed the Thirteenth Ward for cash and other donations with which to help the needy, while in her sermons she espoused virtues such as obedience and toil. She also traveled throughout the territory to speak and advise other women. "Aunt Rachel," as she was often called, became recognized as a leading woman in the church and an embodiment of Victorian ideals and morals.[116]

When Grant was appointed Relief Society president, the women of the Thirteenth Ward had gathered at their bishop's home to be organized under his direction. Edwin D. Woolley had served as bishop since 1854 and had visited some of the ward's 1855–1857 weekly Relief Society meetings, "mostly devoted to sewing, such as making Quilts, sewing Carpet-Rags, towards making a Carpet for the Old Tabernacle, Braiding Straw for Bonnets &c."[117] Described by one historian as a "kindly but blunt and contrary-minded merchant," Woolley enthusiastically supported the April 1867 organization of a substantial ward Sunday school in which twenty-one women served as teachers.[118] By his own admission, however, he moved more cautiously in organizing a ward Relief Society.

The Thirteenth Ward occupied nine blocks in the heart of Salt Lake City adjacent to Brigham Young's office and family residence. This congregation, the largest in Salt Lake City, included many prominent church and civic leaders, including Eliza R. Snow. Though

---

115. See Document 3.4.

116. Ronald W. Walker, "Rachel R. Grant: The Continuing Legacy of the Feminine Ideal," in *Supporting Saints: Life Stories of Nineteenth-Century Mormons,* ed. Donald Q. Cannon and David J. Whittaker (Provo, UT: Religious Studies Center, Brigham Young University, 1985), 18, 31–36.

117. Ronald W. Walker, "'Going to Meeting' in Salt Lake City's Thirteenth Ward, 1849–1881: A Microanalysis," in *New Views of Mormon History: A Collection of Essays in Honor of Leonard J. Arrington,* ed. Davis Bitton and Maureen Ursenbach Beecher (Salt Lake City: University of Utah Press, 1987), 139; Thirteenth Ward, Ensign Stake, Thirteenth Ward Relief Society Minutes and Records, 1868–1906, CHL, "Historical Sketch of the 13th Ward Relief Society," vol. 1, pp. 646–649.

118. See Walker, "'Going to Meeting,'" 139, 149–150.

Salt Lake City Thirteenth Ward Relief Society presidency. Circa 1872. Top row, left to right: Emmeline B. Wells, assistant secretary; Elizabeth H. Goddard, secretary; Mary W. Musser, treasurer. Bottom row: Margaret T. Mitchell, second counselor; Rachel Ivins Grant, president; Bathsheba W. Smith, first counselor. Photograph by Charles R. Savage studio. (Church History Library, Salt Lake City.)

Snow delivered only brief remarks at this meeting, she was a member of the ward Relief Society and often attended meetings and spoke at length.[119]

———— ❧ ————

Record of the Organization
of the
Female Relief Society of the 13th Ward, Salt Lake City
Bishop Wooley's Residence
April 18th 1868.

Present Bishop Edwin D. Wooley and his Councillors W. [William] S. Godbe and F. [Frederick] A. Mitchell.

Meeting opened by prayer by the Bishop after which the Bishop took the Chair and Br W.S. Godbe was appointed Secretary pro tem.

The Bishop made some very interesting remarks, relative to the organization about to be formed.——— Said he had been slow with regard to the Society—that he had not felt the spirit of it until he had heard the remarks of President Young expressed at the last Conference—that it was not his habit to be in a hurry in his movements—did ⟨not⟩ wish the Sisters to rush in their movements, but ⟨be⟩ cool and deliberate. He said in the organization he wished to select such Sisters for Officers, as would listen to his counsel, and carry out such ⟨measures⟩ as he should suggest from time to time.

The Bishop continued by saying that if the Sisters needed assistance the Brethren would be on hand to help—that he did not wish [p. 1] them to perform heavy and laborious duties, such as would tax their strength &c—he wished them to go to work—to make their own clothing and establish such fashions for dress as would be becoming for the Saints and not subject themselves to imitate fashions which are invented and worn by dishonorable women of the world &c &c

The Bishop then suggested that the meeting proceed to organise the Society, and moved that Mrs Rachael R. Grant be chosen Presidentess which was seconded and carried unanimously.

He then moved that Mrs Grant proceed to choose her Councillors.

Mrs Grant then made choice of Mrs Annie Godbe for her first Councillor, and Mrs Margaret Mitchell for her second Councillor, which was carried unanimously.

The Bishop and his Councillors laid their hands upon the head of Mrs Grant, and blessed, and ordained, her and set her apart to be a Presidentess

---

119. See Walker, "'Going to Meeting,'" 139; see also Thirteenth Ward Relief Society Minutes and Records, vol. 1, Apr. 30 and Aug. 7, 1868.

over the Female Relief Society of the 13,ᵗʰ Ward &c the Bishop officiating as spokesman.

They then proceeded to ordain Mrs Godbe and set her apart to act as first Councillor to the Presidentess—Bro Godbe officiating ~~in~~ in the same manner[.] they ordained Mrs Mitchell to act as second Councillor to Mrs Grant, and with Mrs Godbe to assist her in all the various duties of her office &c—Br Mitchell officiating as spokesman. [p. 2]

It was then moved that Mrs Elizabeth H. Goddard be chosen to act as Secretary, and Mrs Ann L. Musser as Treasurer, seconded and carried unanimously.

The following persons were then appointed to act as Teachers in the Ward, to wit.

Mʳˢ.	Clarissa Schofield [Scofield]	Mʳˢ.	Mary Musser
"	Rosina Godbe	"	Catharine Horricks [Catherine Horrocks]
"	Abbie [Abigail] Rumell	"	Martha Stringam
"	Martha Wells	"	Bathsheba Smith
"	Emily P. Young	"	Phebe Maiben
"	Louisa Spencer	"	Elizabeth Maiben
"	Agnes Parks [Park]	"	Isabelle Anderson

The Bishop then invited Miss E R Snow to make remarks, when she arose and addressed the Sisters present, by saying that this Society has much for its encouragement in the kind remarks of the Bishop and also in combining a great amount of ability—that inasmuch as the Sisters keep humble, and united, there is nothing to prevent their doing much good, and becoming truly a model Society, as suggested by the Bishop &c.

Very appropriate and instructive remarks were then made by Elders Godbe and Mitchell.

The meeting was then adjourned to April 30, at Mʳˢ. Mary Godbe's residence—at 2 P.M.

William S. Godbe, Secretary, pro tem. [p. 3]

3.8 Eliza R. Snow, Letter to Augusta B. Smith, circa May 7, 1868

Eliza R. Snow, Letter to Augusta B. Smith, ca. May 7, 1868; Fillmore Ward, Millard Stake, Relief Society Minutes and Records, 1868–1947, vol. 1, 1868–1877, June 16, 1868, pp. 5–8, CHL (LR 2858 14).

The city of Fillmore was established approximately 150 miles south of Salt Lake City in the fall of 1851, following the legislature's decision to locate the territorial capital there. Legislators named the proposed capital city Fillmore and the new county in which it was located Millard, a double honor for U.S. president Millard Fillmore, who had appointed Brigham Young as first territorial governor of Utah. In 1858 the territorial capital was moved to Salt Lake City, though Fillmore and the surrounding fertile Pahvant Valley continued to attract residents.[120]

The Fillmore Relief Society was organized in the city schoolhouse on May 7, 1868, by Bishop Thomas Callister. The meeting opened with one of his counselors reading Eliza R. Snow's recent April 1868 *Deseret News* article titled "Female Relief Society,"[121] and Callister "remarked that he did not think it necessary to say a great deal of the subject as it was now so well understood." He underscored the importance of "making our own hats and bonnets" as well as administering "to the wants of the poor and needy." After Callister presented the name of Eunice Dunning Holbrook as "presidentess," she was unanimously sustained by those present with two counselors, a secretary, a treasurer, and twenty-one teachers—the "Visiting Committee." These officers were sustained again three weeks later after nearly 140 women were received as additional members, some of them from adjacent settlements.[122]

However, Bishop Callister had misjudged how "well understood" the concept of Relief Society was. Although Holbrook had been a member of the Female Relief Society of Nauvoo, she and other officers soon floundered in a "disorganized state," lamenting the absence of the bishop when he did not attend their meetings.[123] Three weeks after the organization of the local society, Callister himself remarked that "in consequence of his not having had the privilege of meeting with the Saints in Nauvoo, he did not understand as fully as he would like about the organization of such Societies" and hoped to "inform himself as soon as possible" with regard to the organization.[124] At some point—either before or shortly after the organization of the Fillmore Relief Society—Augusta Bowen Cleveland Smith, a member of the visiting committee, wrote to Eliza R. Snow for information on how to operate the society. Smith, an acquaintance of Snow, was a daughter of Sarah M.

---

120. See Edward Leo Lyman and Linda King Newell, *A History of Millard County* (Salt Lake City: Utah State Historical Society, 1999), 40–41, 93.

121. See Document 3.6.

122. Fillmore Ward, Millard Stake, Fillmore Ward Relief Society Minutes and Records, 1868–1947, CHL, vol. 1, May 7 and 28, 1868.

123. Fillmore Ward, Millard Stake, Relief Society Minutes and Records, May 14 and May 21, 1868; Document 1.2, entry for May 12, 1842.

124. Fillmore Ward, Millard Stake, Relief Society Minutes and Records, May 28, 1868.

Cleveland, a friend of Snow who had served as first counselor to President Emma Smith in the Female Relief Society of Nauvoo.[125]

Smith's letter is not extant, but Snow's response, apparently dated May 7, 1868, is reproduced here as it was copied into the Fillmore Relief Society Minute Book. Some evidence indicates that Snow's letter may have been misdated, perhaps when it was copied into the minute book. In her letter, Snow mentioned that she had recently attended a meeting of the Relief Society in Farmington, Utah. That society was organized on May 7 and no mention is made of Snow in its minutes until June 3, when she spoke at a meeting.[126] She may have composed the letter regarding the Fillmore society shortly after her return from that visit, meaning the letter would be dated early June rather than early May.

In any case, on June 16, 1868, the Fillmore society met again "for the purpose of reorganizing or organizing the Society more properly than it had at first been done." They took as a guide Snow's letter, which was copied into the minutes as part of the June 16 entry by secretary Eliza Partridge Lyman. Bishop Callister was absent, and his two counselors directed the meeting. After the reading of Snow's letter, the bishop's counselors made a few remarks and "then withdrew saying they thought the sisters could get along well without them." Eunice Holbrook then spoke briefly about a needy member, donations were recorded, and the meeting adjourned, following the pattern of Snow's instructions.[127]

Two years later, on July 26, 1870, Snow's letter was again read aloud when the Relief Society was reorganized with a new presidency.[128] And the influence of her letter was longer lasting still: Belinda Marden Pratt, appointed Relief Society president in the Fillmore First Ward in October 1877, made a copy of Snow's letter in her personal diary.[129]

———— ❧ ————

Salt Lake City, May 7th 1868

My Dear Sister Smith

I received your letter just as I was starting to go to Farmington to visit the F.R. Society in that place. Since my return I have had so much to attend to, that this is my earliest opportunity for writing to you. I was glad to hear from you, and will with pleasure communicate what I can. I will in the first place answer your question with regard to the necessity of having the Brethren present at your meetings. No. The object of the Society is to relieve the Brethren. It is the business of the Bishop and Counselors, or whoever he may appoint to organize the Sisters. It is expected that he will suggest who to choose for Pres^t and Counselors, although it is the privilege of the Pres^t to choose her own Counselors, or at least they must be those that she has confidence in; but, of

125. On Sarah Cleveland, see Document 1.7.
126. Farmington Ward, Davis Stake, Farmington Ward Relief Society Minutes and Records, 1868–1951, CHL, May 7 and June 3, 1868.
127. Fillmore Ward, Millard Stake, Relief Society Minutes and Records, June 16, 1868.
128. Fillmore Ward, Millard Stake, Relief Society Minutes and Records, July 26, 1870.
129. Belinda M. Pratt, Diary, 1877–1885, Parley P. Pratt Family Papers, 1846–1886, CHL, 54–56.

course, the Bishop has more wisdom in selecting them than she can have,—
The Pres^t and Counselors are to be ordained and set apart, just as Brethren are
set apart for [p. 5] offices. These officers should preside just as the first Presidency preside over the church.[130] The next officer is the Secretary—whose business it is to be present at each meeting and take minutes of all that is said and
done that is worthy of being recorded— the minutes of one meeting must be
read at the next, and then they must be put to vote of the House, and if
accepted, she will record them in the Book (which should be no inferior thing)
of Records, which will be a history of the Society. At each meeting, she will
take the names in full of all the members as they are admitted, and put them
on record. She will also take the names of all who donate, with the names and
prices of all articles donated

to wit, Mrs Ellen Sandford one pr socks prized	$1,00
" Jane Morris one half worn dress	1,50

It is a great ornament to the Society to have a Secretary who will keep the
History, and Record the minutes in a neat and orderly manner. The next officer is the Treasurer—she takes charge of all property donated to the Society,
and holds it subject to the demand of the Presidency. She merely keeps account
of all receipts and disbursements, which should be kept separately— When the
Quarterly report is to be made she adds up all the disbursements, and hands
the account to the Secretary who makes out the report, by adding up all the
receipts, then by deducting the disbursements, she has what remains in
the Treasury, which furnishes the material for Report.[131] When the Report has
been presented and read before the Society—put to vote and accepted, the
secretary puts it on the Record— In admitting members, they should be voted
in separately so that objections can be made—and each one before being put
to vote should be recommended by one or more good Sisters. Three Sisters who
understand business who are familiar with the prices of home manufacture
and of imported goods should be appointed, to constitute a Board of
Appraisers—they should be at the meetings so as to prize the articles when
they are brought forward to be minuted by the Sec,y and Treasurer. It is cus-
tomary to appoint two Teachers (or Visiting Committee) to each Ward or
district. This is a very important calling, and needs Sisters of Wisdom and

---

130. At the first meeting of the Female Relief Society of Nauvoo on March 17, 1842, Joseph Smith
"propos'd that the Sisters elect a presiding officer to preside over them, and let that presiding officer
choose two Counsellors to assist in the duties of her Office— that he would ordain them to preside over
the Society— and let them preside just as the Presidency, preside over the church." (Document 1.2, entry
for Mar. 17, 1842.)

131. The first annual report of the Female Relief Society of Nauvoo set the precedent for such reports. (Document 1.8.)

experience [p. 6] but we have to work with such tools as we can get. If you can place one Sister who is young, with one who is experienced and filled with the Spirit of God, so as to lead the young into the Spirit of it, it will do well. They are not only to go around to solicit donations—they are to understand the circumstances of all both Spiritually and temporally—to speak words of comfort—to warm the cold hearted—to counsel &c &c. I think a month often enough for them to visit. The Presidency with the vote of the House, can appoint any Officers or Committee that may be needed from time to time. Now I will say something about the order of meetings— I will take it for granted that yourself is Presidentess— It would be well for you to appoint one of the Sisters to take lead in singing, and take the responsibility of looking after the Choir— Open your meeting by singing— Prayer— Singing. Secretary reads the minutes of the last meeting (you call on her to do so) in an audible voice in a standing position. You (if they are correct) say, (but you must stand up) I move that the Minutes be accepted— One of Councillors says I second the motion— you say it has been moved and seconded that the minutes be accepted, all in favor of the motion manifest it by the uplifted hand— This is the order to be observed in taking in members after they are recommended— If your meeting is not designed for working, it is well to proceed immediately to business— if there are donations let them be brought forward in order commencing with first District and having the Appraisers on hand, seated near the Pres^tss and Counselors, Sec'y and Treas'r (who should be together) and go all through ⟨with⟩ this District or Ward before you call up another, Observe order so that the Spirit of God will be with you, and learn to do business as orderly and as dignifiedly as men. After the business is done, arise and express your feelings—give instruction &c, call on your Counselors to speak, and if possible get all to speak, if it is no more than five words, in this way you will overcome embarrassment and learn to speak words of wisdom and comfort, and the Holy Spirit will rest upon you, but discourage all enthusiasm.[132] When ready to dismiss, Motion an adjournment— Seconded— All in favor &c. You can act according to circumstances from time to time. In some societies they do all their work at home—others do most of it together— Some meet once in two weeks for work, and once in two weeks without work, just according to circumstances. I had forgotten to say after the vote for adjournment— Singing— Dismiss by [p. 7] Prayer— Well, I do not know whether I have written what you wished to know, If you had asked any other questions

132. Snow presumably intended to discourage "ill-regulated or misdirected religious emotion" or "extravagance of religious speculation." (See "Enthusiasm," in *The Oxford English Dictionary,* ed. James A. H. Murray et al., 12 vols., 1933, reprint [Oxford: Oxford University Press, 1970], 3:216.)

I should have answered them. Volumes might be written and the half not be told—the subject is one of endless varieties— It is a portion of the Order of Heaven.[133]

Yours with love

Eliza R. Snow

PS

I think the F.R. Societies will have a great tendency to check the habit of idle talk by presenting topics of usefulness and interest, for it is calculated to bring into exercise all the powers of reflection, every species of ingenuity and calculation—for it embraces every means of doing good both temporally and spiritually. It is calculated to very much elevate the Female character. Each one should strive to make the meetings useful, interesting and attractive, and so managed that it will be an honor to any one to become a member— it is not a thing of a moment— it need not be rushed forward, yet much energy of character is requisite not only at the commencement, but all the time, Indeed no great good can ever be attained to when energy is wanting. I am glad your feelings are so much engaged in this great, good work, I have no doubt your influence will do a great amount of good.

God bless you and yours forever

E, R, Snow

---

133. On April 19, 1842, Sarah M. Cleveland, a counselor in the presidency of the Female Relief Society of Nauvoo, stated in her "remarks respecting the duties & prospects of the Society— that it was organiz'd after the order of heav'n." On March 17, 1842, Elder John Taylor described the Nauvoo Relief Society as an institution "organiz'd according to the law of Heaven." (Document 1.2.)

3.9 Sarah M. Kimball and Eliza R. Snow, "Duty of Officers of F R Society," circa May 1868

Sarah M. Kimball and Eliza R. Snow, "Duty of Officers of F R Society," [ca. May 1868]; Fifteenth Ward, Salt Lake Stake, Relief Society Minutes, Mar. 1868–May 1869, undated entry, pp. 36–39, CHL (LR 2848 32).

Sarah M. Granger Kimball was a founding member of the Female Relief Society of Nauvoo and of its predecessor, the nascent sewing society that precipitated Joseph Smith's official organization of Latter-day Saint women in 1842.[134] Kimball was "essentially an organizer," wrote an early historian of the Relief Society who had known Kimball. "Many Relief Society enterprises were conceived by her fertile brain and afterwards adopted by that wise leader, Eliza R. Snow." A Relief Society had functioned in the Salt Lake City Fifteenth Ward from 1855 to 1858, and Kimball served as its president for about one year until spring 1858, when operations halted because of the massive evacuation of northern Utah settlements during the Utah War.[135] She was called again as president when the Fifteenth Ward Relief Society reorganized in January 1868 and served in that capacity until her death in 1898.[136] Kimball recommended her labors by noting "she had had some experience in the Practical Workings of the F[emale] R[elief] S[ociety] and felt that considerable good had been accomplished through it and she had been Blessed in Labouring in connection with the Society."[137]

Kimball composed the document featured below with Snow, her longtime friend, in the early months of 1868. Though the title of the featured document indicates it was written by Kimball and revised by Snow, this version has no substantive revisions, meaning an earlier draft must have once existed.

"Duty of Officers," a description of Relief Society officers and their responsibilities, includes offices established in the first meeting of the Female Relief Society of Nauvoo: president and two counselors, secretary, assistant secretary, and treasurer. Joseph Smith further had invited the members of the society to create additional offices as needed: "If any Officers are wanted to carry out the designs of the Institution, let them be appointed and set apart, as Deacons, Teachers &c. are among us."[138] Nauvoo women added additional officers when they set up the first Relief Society visiting committees in July 1843.[139] In this

---

134. See Document 4.10.

135. Susa Young Gates, "Relief Society Beginnings in Utah," *Relief Society Magazine*, Apr. 1922, 187–188. For more on the impact of the Utah War on Relief Society operations, see the introduction to Part 2.

136. The society was reorganized by Bishop Robert T. Burton on January 2, 1868; Kimball and some of the former officers resumed their previous positions. (Fifteenth Ward, Salt Lake Stake, Fifteenth Ward Relief Society Annual Message, 1873, CHL.)

137. Fifteenth Ward, Riverside Stake, Fifteenth Ward Relief Society Minutes and Records, 1868–1968, CHL, vol. 1, Jan. 2, 1868.

138. Document 1.2, entry for Mar. 17, 1842.

139. Document 1.2, entry for July 28, 1843.

Duty of Officers of F R Society.
Written by S M Kimball, revised by E R Snow.

1st

It is the duty of the Presidentess to have the
general oversight of the affairs and interest of
the Society—it is her duty to preside and instruct.

2nd   Counsellors,

It is their duty to counsel with the Pres. and
to seek to sustain and assist her.—It is also
their duty to preside and transact business
in her absence,

3rd   Secretary.

It is the Secretary's duty to take minutes of
all general meetings, and a synopsis of all
Committee reports—To furnish the Pres. with
Orders and receipts, to make out bills of
Merchandise and consignment. To conduct
business correspondence, &c &c. Her book
must contain the general record and
history of the Society,

4th

                    Treasurer,

It is her duty to hold the funds of the Society

Duties of Relief Society officers. Eliza R. Snow and Sarah M. Kimball composed this document to expand the structure of the Salt Lake City Fifteenth Ward Relief Society. They created additional offices to meet the increasing scope of Relief Society endeavors. In Nauvoo, Joseph Smith had invited the Relief Society presidency to appoint officers as needed to "carry out the designs of the Institution." Snow drew upon "Duty of Officers" as she visited and corresponded with local Relief Societies throughout the church. (Church History Library, Salt Lake City.)

document Kimball and Snow gave individual members of the visiting committees the enduring title of teacher, and they further expanded the organizational structure by designating other officers. "Duty of Officers," which exists today as a bound gathering of pages, was copied probably in May 1868 with revisions into the Fifteenth Ward Relief Society's bound minute book, and a number of additional revisions were then marked on that document under Kimball's direction.[140] Significant differences between the featured document and the later copy are identified in footnotes below.

The Fifteenth Ward boundaries ran from South Temple Street on the north to 300 South Street and from present-day 300 West Street to as far west as the Jordan River.[141]

Duty of Officers of F R Society.[142]
Written by S M Kimball, revised by E R Snow.[143]

1st It is the duty of the Presidentess[144] to have the general oversight of the affairs and interest of the Society—it is her duty to preside and instruct.

2nd   Councellors.

It is their duty to counsel with the Pres. and to seek to sustain and assist her—It is also their duty to preside and transact business in her absence.

3rd   Secretary.

It is the Secretarys duty to take minutes of all general meetings. and a synopsis of all Committee reports—to furnish the Pres. with orders and receipts,[145] to make out bills of Merchandise and consignment. To conduct business correspondence, &c &c. Her book must contain the general record and history of the Society.[146]

---

140. Fifteenth Ward, Riverside Stake, Relief Society Minutes and Records, "Relief Society Duties," vol. 1, pp. 42–43. An inserted slip of paper in the volume outlines duties for two additional officers, auditor and historian; see 289n157 herein.

141. Brandon S. Plewe, "The Emergence of Modern Stakes and Wards," in *Mapping Mormonism: An Atlas of Latter-day Saint History,* ed. Brandon S. Plewe (Provo, UT: Brigham Young University Press, 2012), 102.

142. In the later revised version in the bound record book in the Fifteenth Ward Minutes (hereafter "later version"), the title is struck through and replaced with "Relief Society duties."

143. In the later version, the phrase about Snow having revised the document is struck through.

144. The use of the "-ess" suffix to form distinctively female nouns, such as "presidentess" (here) and "deaconess" and "merchantess" (below), underscored the gender of the officers, though these forms were not used universally.

145. In the later version, "furnish the Pres." is struck through and then written back in, "such" is added before "orders," and "as required" is added after "receipts,".

146. In the later version, the final sentence of this paragraph is crossed out and a new sentence is added: "A corresponding sec. may be Elected."

4th   Treasurer.

It is her duty to hold the funds of the Society [p. [36]] Subject to the orders of the Pres—to minute all receipts and disbursements and to report when required.[147]

5th   Presidentess and counsil of Teachers.[148]

It is their duty to preserve order—to preside and instruct in the meetings of that quorum and to see that each teacher[149] performs the duties of her office properly.

Secretary of Teachers quorum should take minutes of their meetings and hand a copy to the Secretary of Society.

6th   Teachers.[150]

It is the duty of Teachers[151] to visit their respective blocks once a month. to inquire after the prosperity and happiness of the members, It is their duty to speak words of wisdom of consolation and peace. It is also their duty to know that the sick are properly taken care of, and if any are in need of assistance from the society—it is the Teachers duty to report to the Pres of their quorum. It is also their duty to receive donations in behalf of the Society, and bring the same to the general meetings, &c &c. [p. [37]][152]

7th   Deaconesses.[153]

It is their duty to open the Hall—adjust seats and to see that the room is in proper order to receive the members—to provide fresh[154] water if necessary—to attend to lights and fire—in short to make everything as pleasant and agreeable as possible for the meetings,

---

147. In the later version, an additional sentence is added at this point: "She should furnish coppy to Auditor of Accts."

148. In the later version, "Teachers" is struck through and replaced by "Committee."

149. In the later version, "teacher" is struck through and "member of committee" inserted.

150. In the later version, "Teachers" is overwritten by "Committee."

151. In the later version, this line reads, "It is their duty to visit the members on their respective blocks . . .".

152. In the later version, the phrase after "Society," is revised to read as follows: "and deposite the same with the Treasurer &c &c."

153. In the later version, "Deaconesses" is replaced by "Deacons." Teacher (an office mentioned earlier in the document) and deacon are offices in the Aaronic Priesthood. No records show the conferral of the Aaronic Priesthood upon women, including women who served in the Relief Society offices of teacher and deaconess (or deacon). The term "deaconess" was never widely adopted, but "teacher" continued as the title for society members assigned to visit women living in specific sections or districts of their wards. (See, for example, Doctrine and Covenants 84:30; for an example of the interchangeable use of "teacher" and "visiting teacher," see *Handbook of the Relief Society of the Church of Jesus Christ of Latter-day Saints* [Salt Lake City: General Board of the Relief Society, 1931], 148–149.)

154. The word "fresh" is not included in the later version.

8th   Messengers.

It is their duty to do such errands as the business of the meetings may require.

9th   Superintendents of work.

They attend to arranging, distributing and putting up the work with all the etc thereunto belonging.[155]

10th   Board of Apprezers.

It is their duty to prize articles and see that they are properly labelled.

11th   Commission Merchantess.[156]

She receives such articles as are to be sold or exchanged and is Subject to such rules as govern commission business. [p. [38]]

12th   Duty of all

It is the duty if all to uphold the Pres·ss and officers, to sustain the reputation of the Society, and to hold each others characters sacred—To be just and truthful in all their sayings and doings—To do all in their power to promote happiness at home. and to use every laudible means to extend the influence of the Society [p. [39]][157]

---

155. In the later version, "thereunto belonging" is struck through.

156. The later version has "Merchant."

157. Two scraps of paper, pinned together and inserted into the bound volume in which the later version is copied, include information about two additional offices: "Auditor's work to examine and attest Society accounts" and "Society Historian Should survey the past and present condition of the Society and make a faithful record that will be worthy of preservation and useful for reference."

3.10 Sarah M. Kimball, Annual Message, circa December 1868

Sarah M. Kimball, Annual message, [ca. Dec. 1868]; microfilm; three pages; Fifteenth Ward, Salt Lake Stake, Relief Society Minutes and Records, 1868–1968, vol. 5, 1874–1894, CHL (LR 2848 14).

In late 1868 or early 1869, Sarah M. Kimball, president of the Salt Lake City Fifteenth Ward Relief Society, summarized her organization's labors of the prior year in an annual message. Kimball had resumed her position as president when the ward Relief Society was reorganized in January 1868 following a ten-year hiatus.[158] Her annual message, inscribed by ward Relief Society secretary Sarah Eliza (Sallie) Russell on loose pages later inserted into the Fifteenth Ward minutes, is an example of the annual reports and messages that ward Relief Societies often used to report on their yearly progress.[159]

One of the Fifteenth Ward Relief Society's significant accomplishments during the year was beginning construction of a "storehouse." In summer 1868 the ward society purchased a lot located within ward boundaries on which to construct a building to be used as a store.[160] Construction of a two-story frame building commenced following a cornerstone-laying ceremony held November 12, 1868.[161] The ground floor housed a cooperative store devoted "to commerce and trade" that opened for business in April 1869. The upper level, completed in July 1869, was used as an assembly hall "dedicated to worship, to Art and to Science" where Relief Society meetings and other public functions were held. The building was officially dedicated August 5, 1869.[162] The Fifteenth Ward Relief Society hall was the first of its kind in the church.[163]

———— ⋆ ————

The first anniversary of the organization of this society has not yet arrived,[164] whether our efforts have been a success or a failure we leave those

---

158. For more information on Kimball and the Fifteenth Ward Relief Society, see Document 3.9.

159. The source document is three loose pages, undated and unsigned, inserted into volume 5 of the Fifteenth Ward Relief Society minutes next to the minutes for April 30, 1885. The document is available only in the microfilm version of these minutes. Textual clues date it to late 1868 or the first days of 1869. Russell, who often transcribed Kimball's addresses, served as secretary of the Fifteenth Ward Relief Society from May 21, 1868, to January 6, 1876.

160. Fifteenth Ward, Riverside Stake, Fifteenth Ward Relief Society Minutes and Records, 1868–1968, CHL, vol. 1, July 16, 1868.

161. Fifteenth Ward Relief Society Minutes and Records, vol. 1, Nov. 12, 1868; Document 3.24.

162. "Co-operation," *Deseret Evening News,* Apr. 29, 1869, [3]; Fifteenth Ward Relief Society Minutes and Records, vol. 1, Nov. 12, 1868, and Aug. 5, 1869; "Dedication," *Deseret News* [weekly], Aug. 11, 1869, 317; see also "Secretary's Annual Report," in Fifteenth Ward Relief Society Minutes and Records, vol. 1, Feb. 4, 1869.

163. Jennifer Reeder, "'To Do Something Extraordinary': Mormon Women and the Creation of a Usable Past" (PhD diss., George Mason University, 2013), 155–157, 168–170.

164. The Salt Lake City Fifteenth Ward Relief Society had resumed operations in January 1868 following a ten-year hiatus. (See Document 3.9.)

Salt Lake City Fifteenth Ward Relief Society hall. Construction of this first Relief Society hall was already under way when President Sarah M. Kimball reported on the labors of her ward society's first year at the close of 1868. Echoing the design of Joseph Smith's red brick store in Nauvoo, the hall had a cooperative store on the main floor and an assembly room—dedicated to art, science, and worship— upstairs. A report of the August 5, 1869, dedicatory ceremony appears in Document 3.24. Later hall designs primarily accommodated church meetings and social events. The photograph comes from Emmeline B. Wells, ed., *Charities and Philanthropies: Woman's Work in Utah* (Salt Lake City: George Q. Cannon and Sons, 1893), copy at Church History Library, Salt Lake City.

who are acquainted with our works and the means we have had in our hands to judge. We know there is a strong prejudice existing in the minds of many against female organizations, and we regret to acknowledge there is cause for their prejudice. We have had to meet and contend with it and we hope with the aid of our Father and God to be able to live it down.[165]

The class of women who haven [have given?] rise to this feeling are those who have rushed from the extreme of inactivity and helplessness to the opposite one and now call for a place in the senate and all public offices and responeibilities neglecting her first and highest duty, that of making home happy.[166]

We thought much upon this subject upon the pain of having our best feeling and endeavors misunderstood and centured [censured] perhaps by those whose judgement and good will we prized the most, the thoughts of all this and of our inability to fight the battle and gain the victory. [p. [1]]

Then the doom of the unprofitable servant arose before us,[167] and with a prayer for strength and wisdom we entered the list of female laborers for the cause of universal good, under the protecting banner of the holy priesthood, armed with such delegated powers and aided by such helps as we are proud to acknowledge from the Gentlemen of the ward, should we fail to accomplish much, we should prove ourselves unworthy of the trust you have confided to our care.

When we think upon the magnitude of the work before the little handfull of men and women here in the mountains, we sometimes tremble for the result. We are so slow to understand the ways of God and to obey his commandments.

In relation to the storehouse being erected, the echo has reached our ears that the society wished, the brethren to do the work, and for them to have the credit of it. We do not know where the sound originated, but we wish to inform all present that it is entirely a mistake.

---

165. At one early Fifteenth Ward Relief Society meeting in 1868, one ward priesthood leader, a Brother Bywater, made "some lengthy remarks upon the Good and Evil that would result from Female gatherings and believed that the good that will result from the Female R.S. would overbalance the evil." Another leader, Brother Pollard, noted that "he had been opposed to Female gatherings untill he met with the Sisters at the Reorganization of the Society, but his Prejudices were now removed and he felt confident it would result in good." (Fifteenth Ward Relief Society Minutes and Records, vol. 1, Jan. 2 and 4, 1868.)

166. The question of the extent to which women's engagement in politics would disrupt family life was a perennial point of debate in the movement for women's rights. More conservative suffragists underscored the importance of home and church as manifest in an 1873 resolution of the American Woman Suffrage Association: "*Resolved, That a government of the people must be a government composed equally of men and women, inasmuch as the equal co-operation of the sexes is essential alike to a happy home, a refined society, a Christian church, and a Republican State.*" ("Of Course We Will," *Deseret News* [weekly], Nov. 12, 1873, 648, italics in original.)

167. See Matthew 25:14–30.

We feel to give much credit to all who have aided us both with means and words of encouragement, and <u>we feel to strike out the word female and call this the Relief Society</u>[168] [p. [2]] for we do not wish to be exclusive but to go hand in hand with you in the accomplishment of all that is good true and noble.[169]

To our sisters who have met with us both in sunshine and storm, and to all whose hearts are with us in this cause we feel that the blessings of heaven are upon you. You know by the feelings of peace and joy that you have experienced after performing some act of kindness that it is "more blessed to give and to do good than it is to receive.["][170] We would encourage you to continue in well doing, and ⟨we⟩ extend an invitation to all the Sisters of the ward who can come to meet with us,[171] we know that we are benefitted by meeting together and that you would be likewise.

With feelings of good will for all we wish you a happy New Year. [p. [3]]

---

168. The omission of the word "female" from the name of the society was a question resolved less than four years later, in the fall of 1872, when Eliza R. Snow formally proposed the change, which was then ratified by local Relief Societies. ("F. R. Society Reports," *Woman's Exponent,* Oct. 15, 1872, 1:74; Nov. 15, 1872, 1:90; Dec. 1, 1872, 1:98; see also Document 3.5.)

169. Kimball frequently emphasized the importance of partnership between the sexes. For example, in her annual Relief Society message for year-end 1872, she praised the men of the ward for treating the women of the Relief Society as "what we think we should be, coworkers with them in this labor of love and duty." (Sarah M. Kimball, "Pres. Mʳˢ Kimball's Annual Message for Jan 1ˢᵗ 1873," in Fifteenth Ward, Salt Lake Stake, Fifteenth Ward Relief Society Annual Message, 1873, CHL; see also, for example, "Greeting," *Woman's Exponent,* Feb. 15, 1890, 18:139.)

170. See Acts 20:35.

171. The Fifteenth Ward Relief Society secretary's annual report for the year 1868 noted that although the membership list included 182 names, "only a comparatively few answer regularly at Roll call, our weekly meetings do not average near that number." ("Secretary's Annual Report," in Fifteenth Ward Relief Society Minutes and Records, vol. 1, Feb. 4, 1869.)

3.11 Brigham Young, Discourse, February 4, 1869

Brigham Young, Discourse, Feb. 4, 1869, in "An Address to the Female Relief Society, Delivered by President Brigham Young, in the 15th Ward Meeting House, Feb. 4, 1869," Deseret News *[weekly] (Salt Lake City, UT), Feb. 24, 1869, vol. 18, no. 3, pp. 31–32.*

Early in 1869 Brigham Young was invited to "meet with, and give instruction to" the Relief Society of the Salt Lake City Fifteenth Ward; he accepted the invitation and requested that Relief Society officers from other local wards "and adjoining settlements" also be invited.[172] The invited group assembled in the Fifteenth Ward meetinghouse in Salt Lake City on the afternoon of February 4, 1869, to hear from Young and other dignitaries, including Eliza R. Snow, Joseph Young, and Franklin D. Richards.[173] The occasion was noteworthy since Young spoke specifically to women rather than to the usual mixed congregation.

In his address Young particularly underscored the need for women's contributions to Latter-day Saint economic self-sufficiency. Since his April 1868 discourse emphasizing home industry and frugality,[174] a significant economic change had taken place in the Salt Lake Valley with the establishment of Zion's Cooperative Mercantile Institution (ZCMI) in October 1868.[175] ZCMI was a church-sponsored wholesale association created by Latter-day Saints who were frustrated by the high prices they were often required to pay to non-Mormon merchants. Individual merchants, ward retail stores, and cooperative enterprises affiliated with the parent institution.[176] According to Young, who was the president of ZCMI, the institution had been formed by "a number of our merchants and leading men" in order to "fill up the gap caused by our refraining to deal with those who are not of us, and . . . [to] supply the retail dealers and consumers with the goods they need at reasonable rates."[177]

Young's February 4 address was summarized in the Fifteenth Ward Relief Society minutes and in the *Deseret Evening News* the same day.[178] A complete report was provided by David W. Evans for the weekly edition of the *Deseret News,* February 24, 1869. The latter version is reproduced below.

---

172. "Invitation," *Deseret Evening News,* Jan. 28, 1869, [3]; Fifteenth Ward, Riverside Stake, Fifteenth Ward Relief Society Minutes and Records, 1868–1968, CHL, vol. 1, Jan. 28, 1869.

173. Fifteenth Ward, Riverside Stake, vol. 1, Feb. 4, 1869; "Fifteenth Ward Female Relief Society," *Deseret Evening News,* Feb. 4, 1869, [3].

174. See Document 3.4.

175. Zion's Cooperative Mercantile Institution, Zion's Cooperative Mercantile Institution Minutes, Oct. 1868–May 1973, CHL, Oct. 16, 1868, pp. 15–19.

176. See Leonard J. Arrington, *Great Basin Kingdom: An Economic History of the Latter-day Saints, 1830–1900* (Cambridge, MA: Harvard University Press, 1958), 293–302; and Martha Sonntag Bradley, *ZCMI: America's First Department Store* (Salt Lake City: ZCMI, 1991), 9–19.

177. Brigham Young to Albert Carrington, Oct. 21, 1868, Brigham Young Letterbook, vol. 11, pp. 95–98, in Brigham Young Office Files, 1832–1878, CHL.

178. Fifteenth Ward, Riverside Stake, Relief Society Minutes and Records, vol. 1, Feb. 4, 1869; "Fifteenth Ward Female Relief Society," *Deseret Evening News,* Feb. 4, 1869, [3].

AN ADDRESS to the Female Relief Society, delivered by PRESIDENT BRIGHAM YOUNG, in the 15th Ward Meeting House, Feb. 4, 1869.

REPORTED BY DAVID W. EVANS.

I am happy to have the privilege of meeting with you, my sisters, on this occasion. It is gratifying to me to see such marked signs of a lively action among those who profess to be Latter-day Saints, and who are capable of doing so much good as the female portion of the Church of Jesus Christ of Latter-day Saints. "Female Relief Society" is a very marked expression, and full of meaning, and brings more to my mind in contemplating the sex, than almost any other expression that could be used.

As the sisters are here from the Relief Societies in the various wards in the city, and perhaps some from a distance, I wish, in my remarks, to lay before them what I, as an individual, consider to be the duty of this portion of our community. Not that I expect to go into the full details; but to touch upon a few points in regard to their duties.

Before me I see a house full of Eves. What a crowd of reflections the word Eve is calculated to bring up! Eve was a name or title conferred upon our first mother, because she was actually to be the mother of all the human beings who should live upon this earth. I am looking upon a congregation designed to be just such beings.[179]

This life, that we now possess, is just as good, and fraught with as great interests, as any life that any being possesses in all the kingdoms that are, consequently I shall commence by saying to these, my sisters, it is their imperative duty before God, their families and their brethren to exercise themselves in the capacity in which they are placed, according to their ability, in order that they may magnify, promote and honor the life they now possess. Permit me, sisters, to say, that we are endowed with a capacity to enjoy and to suffer and to be delighted. Are we delighted with that which is obnoxious? No; but with that which is beautiful and good. Will we promote this? Yes. In the first stages of life we should know how to promote that which we desire, and which would

---

179. Young articulated the Latter-day Saint belief that "Eve" was a title meaning "the mother of all living."[a] Similarly, "Adam" was a title signifying "first father." Mormons viewed Adam and Eve both as mortal parents of humankind and as exemplars of the process by which individuals move through mortality to exaltation, that is, to a glory which "shall be a fulness and a continuation of the seeds forever and ever. Then shall they be gods, because they have no end; therefore shall they be from everlasting to everlasting, because they continue."[b] An 1855 poem by Eliza R. Snow references this belief: "Life's ultimatum unto those that live / As saints of God, and all my pow'rs receive, / Is still the onward, upward course to tread— / To stand as Adam and as Eve, the head / Of an inheritance, a new-formed earth, / And to a spirit race give mortal birth."[c] (*a.* Genesis 3:20; Moses 4:26; Abraham 1:3. *b.* Doctrine and Covenants 132:19–20. *c.* Eliza R. Snow, "Instructions of the Priesthood," *Deseret News,* Feb. 20, 1856, 394.)

cheer and comfort the hearts of individuals, communities or nations. To effect this should be the first consideration of all.

Here are young, middle-aged and aged women who all have experience according to that which they have passed through. On this point I reflect very much and talk but little. Let a young woman start out in life and magnify her existence by helping to fill the world with her posterity as mother Eve was commanded to do,[180] and she should know, in the first place, how to conceive and bring forth that which she would delight in, and which would be a comfort, consolation and pleasure to her in her meditations. This is a matter that people think little about, and upon which but little is said, though there is a great deal yet to be said in regard to this particular point to the mothers and daughters in Israel. The inquiry arises how shall we do this? I can say, truly, we must possess the spirit of meekness, kindness and longsuffering; we must possess patience, that in patience we may possess our souls.[181] We must seek to enjoy the spirit of intelligence that comes directly from Heaven. We should govern and control every evil passion, and order our lives so that we may enjoy the meek and humble spirit of the Lord Jesus. You know how apt we are, in certain cases, to be passionate, and how apt mothers are to be full of extreme desire; it seems as though every feeling of the soul was wrought up. I have known mothers actually ruin their posterity through giving way to the inordinate desires of their own hearts. You see some children who are naturally fond of strong drink, or who are addicted to swearing, lying and stealing. Mothers entail these things in a great measure upon their offspring, and although they may not realize it, yet it is so.[182] My sisters will pardon me when I say there are portions of our community, who actually believe it is no harm to lie; others will steal, and their hands would have to be cut off to prevent their taking that which is not their own, for, just as sure as they come to something that they can secrete, they will do it. I attribute a great deal of this, to the lack of wisdom in fathers and mothers. You may think this is strange doctrine, and may believe that we have control of ourselves in every particular, but it is not so. We do have that power in a measure, and th[r]ough grace and fervency we can gain

---

180. Eve with Adam was commanded to "be fruitful, and multiply, and replenish the earth." (Genesis 1:28; see also Moses 2:28; and Abraham 4:28.)

181. See Luke 21:19; and Doctrine and Covenants 101:38.

182. During the Victorian period (1837–1901), many Christian clergymen and reformers emphasized that children's destinies were unalterably affected by maternal nurturing. For example, one mother warned that "our natural power of leading our children is so great that if *we* do not lead them in the right way, it is hardly too much to say that *no one else* can." (See Christian Women's Association, *A Handbook for Wives and Mothers of the Working Classes* [Glasgow: J. McGeachy, 1873], 29–30; and "Happiness in Childhood," *Domestic Economist and Advisor in Every Branch of the Family Establishment,* Mar. 14, 1850, 1:126, italics in original.)

control over ourselves; but we have not this power naturally. With regard to traits of character we see marked difference, among children of the same family. We see one child with whom it is as natural to lie as it is to breathe; while with others of the same family it is quite different, and you may depend upon anything they say as being strictly true. I see some with whom it is natural to pilfer, and with others of the same family it is just the reverse. These differences in character among members of the same family have come under my observation, and your experience confirms the truth of these remarks.

Now for mothers to do their duty, for these matters depend far more upon the mothers than upon fathers,—they should be filled with patience and kindness, and should seek continually to sanctify themselves and to overcome their weaknesses. Some women have a longing desire for ardent spirits, yet by faith, and the close application of that faith in their prayers to God, they [p. 31] may so far overcome that desire that it will never affect their posterity. Others are given to evil in language, in deeds or in thoughts, which should be overcome in order that the ends of their being may be answered and a righteous posterity raised. For us to start correctly we should know how to produce our own spices [species] so that they may enjoy all the blessings that are in store for the faithful without their having such an immense struggle to overcome the sin that is within them.

If the mothers in Israel could bring forth their children so that they would never have an inbred desire to swear, or do a deed that they should not do, how much more easy and satisfactory it would be for such children to pass through the ordeal of life, than to be tried and tempted, often beyond their strength. I shall leave these points with you for your consideration, being satisfied that a word to the wise is sufficient.

I shall now say a few words to you, as mothers in Israel in a temporal point of view, in regard to your children and the sickness, and disease in general, to which they too often fall victims. Upon matters of this kind every mother should be well posted. Our bodies, especially in infancy, are liable to be filled with pain and distress; and our children often waste away and go into the grave through ignorance. I see many mothers who never take thought or care with regard to these things. A child will run out and play in the wet, get cold and, perhaps, in an hour or two is in a high fever. The mother is very sorry and pets and kisses the child, but does nothing to help it. Perhaps a child is taken sick in the night with the croup,—a disease which comes on suddenly, and which is quick in its operations. In great alarm the mother gets out of bed and lights the candle, and cries "Oh dear! oh dear! what shall I do?" and immediately sends for a neighbor or a friend who, she thinks knows what course to take in such an emergency. How much better it would be if the mother, herself, knew what to do to save her child! It is a mother's duty and business to know how to treat such diseases. They may seem small matters to some; but they are great in their results: for if not met promptly, they carry our children to the grave. In many instances mothers lose their beloved ones through neglecting duties of this kind, when with proper care and attention their children might have been preserved and their neighbors would never have known that they had been sick. These matters should receive the special attention of our sisters, and I anticipate that I am talking to ladies who will pay attention and try to carry out these counsels; if they do, they will realize great benefits therefrom. I urge upon the sisters the necessity of paying some attention to the various diseases of childhood. The people around are afraid the small pox will be here soon; but if they knew what to do, they need not be afraid of it. The same may be said of the measles and the whooping cough. Not but that there are cases of these diseases occasionally, through the weakness of the system, that our common medicines will not touch; but such cases are rare, and if the counsels given are followed, many of the diseases incident to this community, and others as well, would be overcome.[183]

Now, my sisters, I will take up the subject of schools. I will commence by advising this congregation to pay attention to the education of their children.[184] Some may think, "Oh we have our Selectmen appointed, our districts set off and every preparation made, necessary to carry on the education of our children, and we need not give ourselves any further trouble about it."[185] I will say that if the mothers and daughters in Israel will give their attention to this matter they will accomplish a good deal more in the same time than the men will.

---

183. The city sexton's report for 1869 noted 292 children's deaths but identified cause of death in only a few instances, none of which correspond with the diseases mentioned in Young's speech. ("Salt Lake City Sexton's Report for Year, 1869," *Deseret News* [weekly], Jan. 12, 1870, 574.)

184. The provisional government of the State of Deseret chartered the University of Deseret on February 28, 1850, calling for the establishment of common schools under the direction of the university's board of regents. That charter was ratified by the new Utah territorial legislature on October 4, 1851, and the territorial legislature continued to refine laws concerning schools. The original charter of Great Salt Lake City, approved January 9, 1851, included a section empowering the city council to "establish, support, and regulate common schools." (Orson F. Whitney, *History of Utah,* 4 vols. [Salt Lake City: George Q. Cannon and Sons, 1892], 1:434–441, 479; An Act Providing for the Establishment and Support of Common Schools, in *Annual Report of the Territorial Superintendent of Common Schools for the Year 1868* [Salt Lake City: George Q. Cannon, 1869], 10–16.)

185. By 1868, county courts had been authorized to designate school districts, and districts elected trustees to provide oversight for the building of schoolhouses and the hiring and payment of teachers. The territorial school superintendent's annual report for 1868 (submitted February 16, 1869) showed 147 districts reporting for 219 schools, 12,516 students enrolled, and 39 percent of the "school population actually attending school." (*Annual Report of the Territorial Superintendent of Common Schools for the Year 1868,* 3–11.)

I advise the Female Relief Society of this ward to look after the education of their children, and I recommend the introduction, into their schools, of the Deseret Alphabet; not that the old method may be thrown away or discarded, but as a means of facilitating the progress of the children in their studies.[186] If mothers will take this matter in hand, and will take measures to encourage their children and create an interest in their minds in relation to education, they will accomplish much more than the fathers can do. The fathers must be called upon to foot the bill, but it is the mother's business to see that they are schooled.

Extending my remarks upon this subject I should say that the education of females ought to be more thorough and practical than it generally is. For instance, wherever our school mistresses find a natural turn in their female pupils for the study of mathematics, or of any particular branch of learning, a class ought to be formed for the special study of that branch of education. You will find but few, females especially, who have a natural inclination for the study of mathematics; but where it does exist, such a woman, when properly trained, is just as capable of keeping a set of books and occupying a seat in a countinghouse as a man; and the labor is not too arduous. To see a great, fat, lubberly-looking man, who ought to be conducting a railway train or using the pick and spade, sitting continually at a desk is disgusting to me. The females should learn book-keeping, then they would be able to attend to our mercantile operations. I recommend the ladies of the 15th Ward to commence this branch of study. If they commence first, they will have the credit for so doing; and if they progress faster than others they will have the credit of it, for a record of the doings of all these Female Relief Societies will be kept, and it will be known who were fervent and faithful in carrying out the counsels given them in order to enable them to magnify their high callings here on the earth.

We see the necessity of these things every day. Suppose a man, owning a little property, is taken away from his family, and his wife knows nothing about his business or books, or whether she has a dollar or ten thousand; her position would be much more advantageous if she had an acquaintance with book-keeping, for then, without the help of any other person, she could settle up the business of her deceased husband, call in his debts, pay them off, square up his accounts and possess what was left.

186. The Deseret Alphabet was an attempt to devise a phonetic way of writing the English language in hopes of more readily assimilating Latter-day Saint immigrants who were not native English-speakers. A primer using this alphabet had recently been published. ([The Deseret First Book by the Regents of the Deseret University] [Salt Lake City: Deseret University, 1868].)

These things are neglected here and in the world too. See in the fashionable world, the education given to a young lady! It consists mainly of how to bow and curtsey, how to meet a gentleman, how to be graceful in a ball room, how to get into and out of a carriage, how to walk on the streets,—how high her clothes should be lifted or how many feet they should drag behind her; and in addition to this to thrum on the piano and have a smattering of French or Italian.[187] These are what should be called female loafers; they are no good to themselves or anybody else. They cannot knit their stockings, make their dresses or underclothing or do anything useful.

It is quite right for the females of this community to know enough of the etiquette of the day to present themselves with propriety to their brethren, sisters and friends, and to strangers; but beyond what is required of etiquette for this is unnecessary and vain. In this respect many of our sisters are deficient; they manifest too great freedom frequently. A little of this reserve and etiquette is necessary, that we may be able to meet with and act with propriety and decorum among our brethren and sisters, and when we meet with and mingle among strangers. We have to meet with strangers, we are under the necessity of doing so, and we can not grow up and live and die in this ignorant innocence. Our sisters should know enough of etiquette to enable them to deport themselves like ladies in society, and besides that their education should be of that practical and useful character that they would be able to keep books, knit their stockings and to make every particle of clothing they need to wear.

You will see the same variety of taste and character among the female portions of the community as among the males. Among the latter you will find some with a taste for the various branches of mechanics, while others have a taste for being artists, naturalists, &c. It is just so with the sisters. One says, I would like to be a milliner, another a book keeper, another a telegraph operator,

---

187. The nineteenth century carried over a tradition of educating genteel young women in "accomplishments" of the kind referred to here. However, the century also witnessed dramatic developments in women's higher education. While in 1800 no colleges or high schools for women existed, and grammar schools preferred boys over girls, by 1900 a third of all the college students in the United States were women, a result of the opening of coeducational colleges and women's colleges. Additionally, professional education opened to women in fields such as theology, law, medicine, dentistry, pharmacy, veterinary science, technology, and agriculture. Significantly, the frontier colleges preceded the conservative eastern colleges in educating females alongside males; the University of Deseret (later the University of Utah) was the first of the western state universities to admit women, starting with its second term in 1851. (Alice Freeman Palmer, "Women's Education in the Nineteenth Century," in George Herbert Palmer and Alice Freeman Palmer, *The Teacher: Essays and Addresses on Education* [Boston: Houghton Mifflin, 1908], 342, 345, 349–350; Elizabeth Cady Stanton, *Eighty Years and More [1815–1897]: Reminiscences of Elizabeth Cady Stanton* [New York: European Publishing, 1898], 35; "University of Deseret," in *Encyclopedia of Mormonism,* ed. Daniel H. Ludlow, 5 vols. [New York: Macmillan, 1992], 4:1498–1499.)

another a musician, &c.[188] We never ought to employ a man to work as a telegraph operator, but we are under the necessity of doing so, for although we have taught a sufficient number of girls to work our entire line through the Territory,[189] we are still compelled to employ men, for the simple reason that women are brought up in such ignorance that they know nothing about their duty; they do not seem to know but that it is perfectly right, without leave of absence, to run off to a party, or visit here and there for two or three days together. Their mothers do not teach them anything. They are like a plant in a garden that is allowed to grow without cultivation. Just as many branches as the main stem will send forth may grow, bud, blossom or die as they please, the tree is never trimmed or trained in the least. This is too much the way with the female portion of our community. It should not be so.

Why not the mothers of the 15th Ward commence and teach their girls what their duty is, and train them so that they will be a profit to themselves? There is one point in connection with this upon which I would give a word of caution, that is, never urge a child in its studies beyond its ability. This should be watched very closely. It is quite common in our day to put children to their studies and to hold them to them until they become mere machines, actually losing the balance and strength of their minds to that degree that they know nothing but what they read; their natural ability seems to be used up, or benumbed, so that it is useless. Parents and teachers should be careful to avoid this, and never urge a child beyond the power of its mental organization. Without doing this in the least our girls may be taught how to keep books and how to be good telegraph operators. How I should delight to see a wire stretched from here to my office, so that the presidentess of this society might make inquiries upon any topic connected with the welfare of this society without having the trouble to run after it. And then from this Ward to every other

---

188. In early 1868 Young and his counselors in the First Presidency had written about the women's department of the newly reopened University of Deseret: "We are much pleased that ladies are privileged with admission to this school, for, in addition to a knowledge of the elementary branches of education and a thorough understanding of housewifery, we wish the sisters, so far as their inclinations and circumstances may permit, to learn book-keeping, telegraphy, reporting, typesetting, clerking in stores and banks, and every branch of knowledge and kind of employment suited to their sex and according with their several tastes and capacities, that they may be competent to participate in and promote every interest within their power. . . . Thus trained, all, without distinction of sex, will have an open field, without jostling and oppression, for acquiring all the knowledge and doing all the good their physical and mental capacities and surrounding circumstances will permit." (First Presidency, General Epistle [ca. Jan.–Feb. 1868], p. 26, General Epistles, 1841–1868, Brigham Young Office Files, 1832–1878, CHL.)

189. Late in 1867 the *Deseret Evening News* noted that eleven offices of the Deseret Telegraph Line employed "female operators," with many more young women in training for that position. ("Employments for Females," *Deseret Evening News,* Dec. 9, 1867, [2].)

in the city, so that they could do business with each other without running through the mud.[190]

I streneously recommend this society to adopt this counsel. Then you might extend your business operations beyond telegraphy and book keeping. I do not see the least harm in the world in women learning to do any kind of light work that is lawful to do, such as knitting, for instance. We are importing knitting machines, and why not this Ward establish the business of knitting stockings to supply its members? The Ward, no doubt, contains men, women and children who are not well supplied with these useful articles of apparel; and some of them, not being able to knit them, are obliged, perhaps, to go without them unless they can obtain the privilege of working in somebody's garden for them. Now, with a business of this kind started in the Ward, it would be a comparatively easy matter for all of its inhabitants, who wish to do so, to supply themselves.

Another branch of business that might be started with advantage is that of millinery. The ladies of the Ward ought never to go beyond its limits for any article in this line, and if the ladies of the Female Relief Society will take it in hand they will accomplish something useful. By establishing these branches of business you will be of great use and servise to your husbands, sons and brothers.

If you were to make men's clothes there would be no harm in it. It is quite common for women to do this. And sewing machines can be obtained that will sew any kind of cloth, and if you had four, six or eight women associated together in this Ward in making men's clothing, it could, if properly conducted, be made very profitable.

During the past season there has been great demand for clothing by men working on the railroad, and there never is a time but what it is in demand. Now suppose you had capital, and could make clothing, and were to keep a clothing store in this ward, you would find plenty of customers. Then if a man wanted a coat, or a suit of clothes or a pair of boots, he could be immediately accommodated, for you could ea[s]ily change some of your clothing for boots, and keep a supply of them on hand as well as clothing. If you had your telegraph wire you could send your orders into the city to the shoemaker, or other

---

190. After the transcontinental telegraph line connecting the eastern to the western United States was completed through Salt Lake City in October 1861, Brigham Young immediately planned to construct a north–south line throughout Utah Territory. Construction of the territorial line began in 1866; telegraphic communication between Logan and St. George was opened by January 1867. Under the direction of the Deseret Telegraph Company, lines continued to expand to outlying settlements. (Leonard J. Arrington, "The Deseret Telegraph—A Church-Owned Public Utility," *Journal of Economic History* 11 [Spring 1951]: 118–119, 126–127.)

parties, and have them filled without delay, and be able to accommodate either saint or stranger with what they needed. Only get such movements started systematically, and you can make you abilities adapt themselves to the capacities and wants of the ward.

Another branch of business, in which children and aged people might be profitably employed, is that of making baskets[.] Basket willows could [be] planted and raised round the springs in this and other neighborhoods, and with them every kind of basket required by the ladies to market or visit with could be manufactured. You have, most likely, sisters in the ward who, while they are in the enjoyment of tolerable bodily health, are yet so far advanced in years, that they are unable to earn the necessaries of life by active labor; but their time might be used to profit in light labors of this kind. The same may be said of the aged brethren, and if a plan of this kind be adopted, you will find there are but very few who can not do something if you know how to set them to work.

The children, too, after school hours, can be employed to better advantage than running the streets. They can be taught to braid, and with kind words they would as soon sit down and braid a couple of yards of nice, fine, five, seven, nine or eleven strand braid after school for the day is over, as to spend the whole of their time in romping and playing. This would lay the foundation of the manufacture of straw hats and bonnets.

If the ladies of the Female Relief Society, and the sisters of this ward generally, will unitedly and systematically enter upon the paths here indicated, they will not only be able to supply the wants of this ward, but will actually call in capital from other wards. Some may say "How can this be if all the wards adopt a similar course?" In reply, I will say the wards will grow so fast that it will be a long time before we can supply ourselves.

After having referred to the various branches of business—including book-keeping, telegraphing, music, knitting, clothing, milinery, basket and foot-mat making,—which, if systematically conducted might be made advantageous and profitable by the sisters in this and other wards, I will now come to another branch of business I see that in this ward you have already a building reared for the sale of goods,[191] which, I understand, you anticipate will be ready for occupation sometime in April. Suppose you start with $200 worth of goods,

---

191. Young was referencing a two-story frame building then being constructed in the Fifteenth Ward boundaries, which was to have a store on the ground level and an assembly room on the upper level. Sarah E. Russell, secretary of the Fifteenth Ward Relief Society, had spoken about this building earlier in the same meeting. (See Document 3.10; and Fifteenth Ward, Riverside Stake, Minutes and Records, "Secretary's Annual Report," vol. 1, Feb. 4, 1869.)

consisting of a variety of articles, such as the necessities of the ward demand,[192] and you sell that stock daily and realize only five per cent on it, which is a very heavy per centage cheaper than goods have ever been sold in this city; in a week you get thirty per cent and in a short time one hundred per cent, which is a much higher rate of interest than is generally paid for money. If you will start this store, and will permit me to put in capital and take the same percentage that you get, I will furnish you five hundred or a thousand dollars to begin with immediately.

Take up the branches of business I have referred to, conduct them systematically, and use the means I have pointed out, and you will soon find it advantageous and profitable, and you will also find that the wants of the poor will be all supplied, and that they will produce more than they consume, for if they are looked after and cared for, they can probably be set at some labor by which they can sustain themselves.

In conclusion, I will say, if I have not gone sufficiently into details in regard to the business of this society, if you call on me at any time I will add to what I have already said, and give you any counsel you need.[193] I feel now like concluding my conversation. God bless you, Amen.

---

192. The store opened on April 27, 1869, with a stock of goods worth about $2,000 and with "two of the ladies of the society acting as clerks." Among the items listed in a November 1871 inventory of this store were carpet rags, dried apples and peaches, straw for braiding, hickory shirts, soap, school books, coffee, garden seeds, moccasins, cloth for a "Temple Suit," and Valentine's Day cards. ("Co-operation," *Deseret Evening News,* Apr. 29, 1869, [3]; see Fifteenth Ward, Riverside Stake, Relief Society Minutes and Records, "Acct. of Goods on Hand up to Date," vol. 2, Nov. 9, 1871.)

193. At the next Fifteenth Ward Relief Society meeting, President Sarah M. Kimball, reflecting on Young's instruction, remarked that he "had laid out more work than could be accomplished in a century." But, she also told the women, she "felt it to be our duty to do all we would to carry out his council," noting that "it was time we were preparing ourselves for the positions we would have to occupy." (Fifteenth Ward, Riverside Stake, Relief Society Minutes and Records, vol. 1, Feb. 11, 1869.)

3.12 Minutes of "Ladies Mass Meeting," January 6, 1870

"Minutes of a Ladies Mass Meeting," Jan. 6, 1870; Fifteenth Ward, Salt Lake Stake, Relief Society Minutes and Records, 1868–1968, vol. 1, 1868–1873, pp. 139–142, CHL (LR 2848 14).

Women of the Salt Lake City Fifteenth Ward held a mass meeting on January 6, 1870, to plan an organized response to legislation recently introduced in the U.S. House of Representatives by Illinois Republican Shelby Cullom, chair of the House Committee on Territories.[194] The Cullom Bill was the third attempt since the end of the Civil War to pass federal legislation to punish polygamists and curtail the economic and political power of The Church of Jesus Christ of Latter-day Saints. The Wade Bill (1866), the Cragin Bill (1867, 1869), and the Cullom Bill all proposed legal means for enforcing the 1862 Morrill Anti-Bigamy Act, which banned bigamy and restricted the church's ownership of property but did not designate officers or funds for enforcement.[195]

The Cullom Bill stipulated, among other things, that "no one living in or practicing bigamy, polygamy, or concubinage, shall be admitted to citizenship of the United States; nor shall any such person hold any office of trust or profit in said Territory, vote at any election therein, or be entitled to the benefits of the homestead or pre-emption laws of the United States."[196] A copy of the bill reached church leaders on January 3, 1870, and was published in the *Deseret Evening News* on January 4. A clerk in the Church Historian's Office noted that the bill proposed "taking away evry right of the people of Utah, who beleive in or practices, the principles of Celestial [plural] Marriage."[197]

Under the direction of Relief Society president Sarah M. Kimball, Fifteenth Ward women met two days after the bill was published in the *Deseret Evening News* to express their outrage at the bill's drastic measures. Minutes of the January 6 women's meeting, including the resultant resolutions, were recorded in the Fifteenth Ward records and first published in the January 10 issue of the *Deseret Evening News* with some revisions and clarifications.[198] Two proposals made at the end of the meeting—that women demand of the

---

194. *Biographical Directory of the United States Congress, 1774–2005: The Continental Congress September 5, 1774, to October 21, 1788, and the Congress of the United States from the First through the One Hundred Eighth Congresses March 4, 1789, to January 3, 2005, Inclusive,* ed. Andrew R. Dodge and Betty K. Koed (Washington DC: Government Printing Office, 2005), 903.

195. The Morrill Anti-Bigamy Act was approved in the Thirty-Seventh U.S. Congress, second session. (An Act to Punish and Prevent the Practice of Polygamy in the Territories of the United States and Other Places, and Disapproving and Annulling Certain Acts of the Legislative Assembly of the Territory of Utah [July 1, 1862], *The Statutes at Large, Treaties, and Proclamations, of the United States of America. From December 5, 1859, to March 3, 1863,* vol. 12, ed. George P. Sanger [Boston: Little, Brown, 1863], 37th Cong., 2nd Sess., ch. 126, p. 501; Leonard J. Arrington, *Great Basin Kingdom: An Economic History of the Latter-day Saints, 1830–1900* [Cambridge, MA: Harvard University Press, 1958], 356–357.)

196. A Bill in Aid of the Execution of the Laws in the Territory of Utah, and for Other Purposes, H.R. 696, 41st Cong., 2nd Sess. [1870].

197. Historian's Office Journal, Jan. 3, 1870, vol. 31, in Church History Department, Historical Department Office Journal, 1844–2012, 102 vols., CHL; "A Bill," *Deseret Evening News,* Jan. 4, 1870, [2].

198. "Minutes of a Ladies' Mass Meeting," *Deseret Evening News,* Jan. 10, 1870, [2]; see also reprinted

territorial governor the right to vote and that two representative women be sent to Washington DC—were not included in the published minutes. The possibility of extending the franchise to Utah women, with the assumption that they would vote against polygamy and church leaders, had been floated in the U.S. Congress during 1867 and 1868.[199] Publicity regarding the January 6 meeting in the Fifteenth Ward helped spur a similar and much larger "indignation" meeting held the next week in the Salt Lake City tabernacle.[200]

The following transcript is reproduced from the original minutes of the Fifteenth Ward Relief Society. Footnotes identify the most significant differences between the original minutes and the version published January 10 in the *Deseret Evening News*.

——— ⅇ ———

Minutes of a Ladies Mass Meeting.
Held in Society Hall, 15 Ward Salt Lake City[201]
Jan. 6' 1870.

Meeting was opened with prayer by Mrs. Rebecca Jones.

Upon motion of Mrs Mary Moriss Mrs S M Kimball was elected to the chair, and Miss S[arah] E Russell Sec':

Pres Mrs Kimball said we had met to express our feelings in relation to the Cullum bill, now before Congress. She spoke of the part our forefathers had taken in the Struggle for freedom, how they had suffered and bled for the principals of civil and religious liberty, and she felt that we would be unworthy of the names we bear and of the Blood in our vains, should we longer remain silent, while such an infamous bill was before the House, a bill whose object if attained would make of our men menial serfs, and if they make serfs of them what do they make of us.[202] She then called for the vote of all who were in favor of entering a protest against said bill.

The Vote was unanimous.

Mrs M[aria] Burton, Mrs Eliz[th] Duncanson and Mrs Eliza Binder were elected as Committe to frame resolutions.

The Committe retired for this purpose.

Several of the Sisters expressed their feeling in relation to the subject before the House and a determination not tamely to submit to such injustice as our enemies were endeavoring to heap upon us.[203]

---

version in *Deseret News* [weekly], Jan. 12, 1870, 580.

199. See Document 3.14.

200. See Document 3.13.

201. The *Deseret Evening News* report supplies four o'clock in the afternoon as the meeting time.

202. The *Deseret Evening News* version states that the object of the bill, if attained, "would reduce our husbands, sons and brothers to menial serfs &c." but does not include the phrase "and if they make serfs of them what do they make of us."

203. In the *Deseret Evening News* version, this and the prior paragraph are combined in a single

The Resolutions were presented and read by Mrs M S Burton.[204]

[205]At 5 Sisters [Eliza R.] Snow [Lucy] Kimball and [Bathsheba W.] Smith arrived. [p. 139] Sister Snow said we had her hearty concurrence in the measures that had been taken, felt that the Ladies of Utah had too long remained silent while they were being so falsely represented to the world, felt it was high time that we should rise up in the Dignity of our calling and speak for ourselves, that the world thought we were in the bonds of servitude, which we had no power to break, felt it to be right and due to our brethren that we express our feelings and not remain silent beneath such a flood of falsehood.[206]

The world does not know us and truth and justice to our brethren and to ourselves demands us to speak.

Spoke of the Relief Societies said Pres Young was urging the Sisters forward to be more useful and to take a wider sphere of action, and still to honor and fill nobly the position of wife, &c.[207] We are not inferior to the Ladies of the World and we do not want to appear so. Was pleased that this movement had been made and wished to see it extend throughout the Territory.

---

paragraph that reads: "The Committee retired to prepare resolutions; and in the meantime several ladies expressed their views and feelings of indignation and disgust with regard to the Bill, also their determination to resist such gross injustice, &c."

204. The *Deseret Evening News* version lists here the four resolutions (included at the end of the original minutes) and adds: "The foregoing resolutions were received with warm and enthusiastic applause by all present."

205. From this point to the end of the document, the *Deseret Evening News* version reads as follows: "Miss E. [Eliza] R. Snow, Mrs. L. W. [Lucy Walker] Kimball and Mrs. B. [Bathsheba] Smith made a few very appropriate remarks, expressing their hearty concurrence in the movement and in the measures adopted by the meeting. Before closing her remarks, Miss E. R. Snow suggested the propriety of the ladies of Salt Lake City assembling in a general mass meeting, to give expression to their feelings on the subject before us, and also that the example of this Ward be followed by the sisterhood throughout the Territory. Meeting adjourned *sine die*."

206. Outside observers nearly always portrayed Mormon women in negative terms. For example, journalist Samuel Bowles wrote that polygamy "means only the degradation of woman. By it and under it, she becomes simply the servant and serf, not the companion and equal of man." Nevada congressman John Cradlebaugh, who had served as a federally appointed associate justice for the district of Utah, informed his colleagues in the U.S. House of Representatives that Latter-day Saint women were "downtrodden and undone" and that polygamy was "organized, systematic, enforced degradation and prostitution" and "a system of enslaving the women, and of enforcing their subjection." (Samuel Bowles, *Across the Continent: A Summer's Journey to the Rocky Mountains, the Mormons, and the Pacific States, with Speaker Colfax* [Springfield, MA: Samuel Bowles; New York: Hurd and Houghton, 1865], 107; *Biographical Directory of the United States Congress, 1774–2005*, 885; John Cradlebaugh, "Utah and the Mormons," in John C. Rives, *Appendix to the Congressional Globe: Containing Speeches, Important State Papers, and the Laws of the Third Session Thirty-Seventh Congress* [Washington DC: Congressional Globe, 1863], 119–125.)

207. The reestablishment of the Relief Society and encouragement to women to enter trades and professions were integral to the "wider sphere of action" Young recommended. For addresses representative of Young's approach, see Documents 3.4 and 3.11.

Sister Smith said she was pleased with what had been done, and moved that we demand of the Gov the right of Franchise, Vote called and carried.[208]

Mrs Lucy Kimball said she felt that we had borne in silence, as long as it was our duty to bear, and moved that we be represented at Washington Sisters Snow and Kimball was elected as representatives.[209]

Sister Snow said she had seen the day When she was proud of our Country and flag but the Executors of the Gov had disgraced themselves and the Country which had boasted of being a [p. 140] shelter to the world was trying to make slaves of a portion of her citizens, Thought that many of our people did not realize the extent of the degredation, the Bill if passed would bring us to.

Meeting adj. at 6' PM

Bene' by Sister Pollard.

Resolutions adopted.

1st Resolved that we the Ladies of the 15 Ward S L City, in Mass Meeting assembled do solemly protest against the Bill now before Congress (Known as the Cullum Bill) becoming a law on the Statute Book of the United States Government of America,

2nd Resolved that we use all the moral influence vested in us to prevent the national disgrace, that would accrue to our country were such an infamous bill to receive the approval of both Houses of Congress,

3rd Resolved that the passage of the aforesaid Bill would stamp disgrace one the Ensignia of our glorious Republic and that we disapprove each and every attempt made by those intrusted with the Reigns of Government to destroy the Sacred Constitution bequeathed to us by our forefathers,[210] [p. 141]

---

208. There is no record that these women took such formal action, but the Utah territorial legislature actively debated woman suffrage between January 27 and February 10, 1870, when the House unanimously passed a bill enfranchising the women of Utah. Acting governor Stephen A. Mann signed the suffrage bill into law on February 12, 1870, giving the franchise to some forty-three thousand Utah women. (Thomas G. Alexander, "An Experiment in Progressive Legislation: The Granting of Woman Suffrage in 1870," *Utah Historical Quarterly* 38, no. 1 [Winter 1970]: 25–26; Lola Van Wagenen, "In Their Own Behalf: The Politicization of Mormon Women and the 1870 Franchise," *Dialogue: A Journal of Mormon Thought* 24, no. 4 [Winter 1991]: 31–43; Document 3.17; Beverly Beeton, "Woman Suffrage in Territorial Utah," *Utah Historical Quarterly* 46, no. 2 [Spring 1978]: 101–102.)

209. Neither Snow nor Kimball traveled to Washington DC for this purpose. It was not until January 1879 that Emmeline B. Wells and Zina Young Williams officially represented Utah and Mormon women at a convention of the National Woman Suffrage Association in Washington DC; while there they also met with President Rutherford B. Hayes to plead their cause. ("Notes and News," *Woman's Exponent*, Jan. 15, 1879, 7:128; "Woman's Rights Convention," and "American," *Deseret News* [weekly], Jan. 22, 1879, 806, 810; "Over the Hills and Far Away," *Woman's Exponent*, Feb. 1, 1879, 7:186.)

210. TEXT: Near the bottom of this page, the scribe wrote "over".

[shelter to the world, was trying to make slaves of a portion of her citizens, though that many of our people did not realize the extent of the degradation, the Bill if passed would bring us to.]

Meeting adj at 6 P m

Bene by Sister Pollard.

Resolutions adopted,

1st Resolved that we the Ladies of the 15 ward S L City, in mass meeting assembled do solemly protest against the Bill now before Congress (known as the Cullom Bill,) becoming a law on the Statute Book of the United States Government of America,

2nd Resolved that we use all the moral influence vested in us to prevent the national disgrace, that would accrue to our country, were such an infamous bill to receive the approval of both Houses of Congress,

3rd Resolved that the passage of the aforesaid Bill would stamp disgrace one the Ensignia of our glorious Republic and that we disapprove each and every attempt made by those intrusted with the Reigns of Government to destroy the Sacred Constitution bequeathed to us by our forefathers,

over.

Resolutions adopted at protest meeting, January 6, 1870. Two days after provisions of the Cullom Bill appeared in the *Deseret Evening News,* members of the Salt Lake City Fifteenth Ward Relief Society met to express their outrage at the bill's drastic measures. Attendees resolved to protest against what they saw as an unconstitutional bill. The Cullom Bill attempted to curtail the practice of plural marriage and the church's political and economic influence. (Church History Library, Salt Lake City.)

4th   Resolved, that we express our indignation against the originators of the Bill, which is calculated in its nature, to uproot every vestige of civil and religious liberty; destroy the rights of conscience; and reduce our Fathers, husbands, and brethers to the lowest degree of menial Servitude.

3.13 Minutes of "Great Indignation Meeting," January 13, 1870

Minutes of "Great Indignation Meeting," Jan. 13, 1870, in "Great Indignation Meeting of the Ladies of Salt Lake City, to Protest against the Passage of Cullom's Bill," Deseret Evening News *(Salt Lake City, UT), Jan. 14, 1870, vol. 3, no. 44, p. [2]; Jan. 15, 1870, vol. 3, no. 45, p. [2].*

The following minutes include speeches by twelve women given in Salt Lake City in a gathering known as the "Great Indignation Meeting." Between January and March 1870, thousands of Latter-day Saint women assembled in mass "indignation" meetings to protest federal legislation that proposed to deny U.S. citizenship to anyone practicing plural marriage.[211] On January 13, 1870, between five and six thousand Latter-day Saint women congregated in the Salt Lake City tabernacle. Apparently, no men were present except for reporters.[212] Speaking from the pulpit in the "old" tabernacle, women affirmed that they had become plural wives by their own choice and articulated their vehement objections to the antipolygamy legislation pending in Congress. They declared their rights and appealed for the rights of their husbands, fathers, and brothers.

Public defense of plural marriage by women was potentially the most persuasive form of public relations available to the Saints because it answered the key objection: that plural marriage oppressed women. Latter-day Saints first officially acknowledged their practice of plural marriage in 1852, more than a decade after the first plural marriages were contracted in Nauvoo under the direction of Joseph Smith.[213] After that public announcement, Latter-day Saint women began to defend plural marriage publicly as well as privately.[214] For example, Belinda Marden Pratt, a plural wife of apostle Parley P. Pratt, justified the practice by drawing on historical and biblical precedent in *Defence of Polygamy, by a Lady of Utah, in a Letter to Her Sister in New Hampshire,* the first published defense of plural marriage written by a woman.[215] In January 1868, when Republican senator Aaron H. Cragin of New Hampshire introduced antipolygamy legislation in the U.S. Senate, some Mormon women voiced their objections in a letter to the editor of Salt Lake City's *Deseret News.* They stated: "We, the 'Mormon' ladies of Utah, would offer an expression of indignation towards Senator Cragin and his despicable Bill, did we not consider those subjects too preposterously degrading to merit our contempt." The letter was signed: "'Mormon' First Wives, and all other 'Mormon' Wives."[216] However, two years later, when additional

---

211. See Document 3.12.

212. Mary Ann Weston Maughan, Journal, 1817–1901, 3 vols., typescript (Logan: Library of the Utah State Agricultural College, 1955), bk. 1, Feb. 1, 1870, pp. 20–21.

213. David J. Whittaker, "The Bone in the Throat: Orson Pratt and the Public Announcement of Plural Marriage," *Western Historical Quarterly* 18, no. 3 (July 1987): 301–302.

214. For example, Eliza R. Snow defended plural marriage in letters to Dr. Martin L. Holbrook, editor of the New York–based *Herald of Health and Journal of Physical Culture.* (See 368n365 herein; and Jill Mulvay Derr and Matthew J. Grow, "Letters on Mormon Polygamy and Progeny: Eliza R. Snow and Martin Luther Holbrook, 1866–1869," *BYU Studies* 48, no. 2 [2009]: 139–164.)

215. Belinda Marden Pratt, *Defence of Polygamy, by a Lady of Utah, in a Letter to Her Sister in New Hampshire* (Salt Lake City: n.p., 1854).

216. "Correspondence," *Deseret News* [weekly], Jan. 15, 1868, 389.

antipolygamy legislation was proposed in the form of the Cullom Bill in the U.S. House of Representatives, Latter-day Saint women mounted a dramatically different defense of plural marriage: personal and collective indignation expressed publicly through a series of mass meetings.[217]

Women in Salt Lake City first held a protest meeting on January 6, 1870, to organize against the Cullom Bill.[218] The bill declared marriage in Utah Territory to be a "civil contract" and modified the territory's judicial structure in order to prosecute, fine, and imprison any man cohabiting "with more than one woman as husband and wife."[219] The Cullom Bill did not become law, though some of its provisions were incorporated into subsequent federal legislation: the 1874 Poland Act, the 1882 Edmunds Act, and the 1887 Edmunds-Tucker Act.[220]

At the close of the January 6 meeting, Eliza R. Snow suggested "assembling in a general mass meeting" with similar meetings to be held throughout the territory.[221] The January 13 meeting described in the following minutes was the first of these general protest meetings. By March 1870 the *Deseret News* estimated that twenty-five thousand women had taken part in such meetings in over fifty settlements throughout the territory.[222]

Ultimately, these protests served a number of purposes. Mormon women had a chance to show the outside world that they were articulate and willing to defend their beliefs. Through indignation meetings held in local communities, Latter-day Saint women made a dramatic entry into public life and simultaneously quenched any concern of church leaders that the reorganization of the Relief Societies might promote opposition to plural marriage.[223]

Minutes of the January 13 meeting were first published in two installments in the *Deseret Evening News,* January 14 and 15, 1870. Those published minutes are reproduced here.

GREAT INDIGNATION MEETING
Of the Ladies of Salt Lake City, to protest against the passage of CUllom's Bill.

217. See Document 3.12.

218. See Document 3.12. The bill was introduced in the U.S. House of Representatives by Illinois Republican Shelby M. Cullom, chair of the House Committee on Territories.

219. A Bill in Aid of the Execution of the Laws in the Territory of Utah, and for Other Purposes, H.R. 696, 41st Cong., 2nd Sess. [1870].

220. See Sarah Barringer Gordon, *The Mormon Question: Polygamy and Constitutional Conflict in Nineteenth-Century America,* Studies in Legal History (Chapel Hill and London: University of North Carolina Press, 2002), 273–274.

221. "Minutes of a Ladies' Mass Meeting," *Deseret Evening News,* Jan. 10, 1870, [2].

222. "The Ladies' Mass Meetings—Their True Significance," *Deseret News* [weekly], Mar. 9, 1870, 49.

223. At a Lehi Ward Relief Society meeting on October 27, 1869, Eliza R. Snow said, "I was mortified last Conferance to hear president Young say, he was afraid to Call A vote to see if the sisters would sustain polygamy, I told him he had not faith in the sisters and if he had Called the vote he would have found that the sisters would have sustained that principle." (Lehi Ward, Alpine Stake, Lehi Ward Relief Society Minutes and Records, 1868–1892, CHL, vol. 1, Oct. 27, 1869.)

Notwithstanding the inclemency of the weather, the Tabernacle was densely packed with ladies of all ages—old, young and middle aged.

On the motion of Sister Eliza R. Snow, Mrs. Sarah N. [M.] Kimball (President of the Female Relief Society of the 15th ward) was elected president of the meeting.

Mrs. Lydia Alder was appointed secretary of the meeting.

The following ladies were proposed, and unanimously sustained, as a committee to draft resolutions:

Mrs.	M. [Margaret] T. Smoot,	prest.	20th w'd [ward]	F. M. S.[224]
"	M. [Marinda] N. Hyde,	"	17	"
"	Isabella Horn[e],	"	14	"
"	Mary Leaver,	"	8	"
"	Prisc. [Priscilla] Staines,	"	12	"
"	Rachel Grant,	"	13	"

Mrs. Kimball, in rising to address the meeting, said she desired the prayers of all present, that she might be enabled to express herself in a comprehensive manner. They were there to speak in relation to the Government and institutions under which they lived, and she would ask: Have we transgressed any law of the United States? [Loud "No"—from the audience.][225] Then why are we here to-day? We have been driven from place to place, and why? Simply for believing in and practicing the counsels of God as contained in the Gospel of Heaven. The object of that meeting was to consider the justice of a bill now before the Congress of the United States. She said: "We are not here to advocate woman's rights, but man's rights." The bill in question would not only deprive our fathers, husbands and brothers of enjoying the privileges bequeathed to citizens of the United States, but it would also deprive us, as women, of the privilege of selecting our husbands, and against this we most unqualifiedly protest.[226]

While the Committee on resolutions were absent speeches were made by various ladies, the first, as follows, being delivered by

BATHSHEBA W. SMITH.

Beloved Sisters and Friends:—It is with no ordinary feelings that I meet with you on the present occasion. From my early youth I have been identified

---

224. "F. M. S." is an error; this should read "F. R. S.," for "Female Relief Society."

225. TEXT: Brackets in original.

226. In this passage, Sarah Kimball, likely informed by the heightening post–Civil War discussions of women's rights, spoke of marriage as a right. An 1871 Eliza R. Snow poem refers to "holy, honorable wedlock" as "the heav'n taught principle of woman's right— / The universal right—not of a few / More favor'd ones; but sacred right of all." ("How '70 Leaves Us and How '71 Finds Us," *Deseret News* [weekly], Jan. 11, 1871, 580.)

with the Latter-day Saints; hence I have been an eye and ear witness to many of the scenes that have been inflicted upon our people by a spirit of intolerant persecution.

I watched by the bedside of the first Apostle, David W. Patten, who fell a martyr in the Church. He was a noble soul. He was shot by a mob while defending the Saints in the State of Missouri, Ray County, on the 25th of October, 1838. As Bro. Patten's life blood oozed away, I stood by and heard his dying testimony to the truth of our holy religion, declaring himself to be a friend to all mankind: he sacrificed his life freely to defend the innocent. He had no feelings of hostility to his race, but labored to exalt them. His last words, addressed to his wife, were: "Whatever you do, oh! do not deny the faith." This circumstance made a lasting impression upon my youthful mind.[227] In Missouri, mobs were burning houses and killing the Saints, when an army was sent by Governor [Lilburn W.] Boggs, which we supposed had come to protect us; but, alas! time proved that it came to continue the same dreadful work—reducing the whole people from competence to extreme poverty, sending them forth, under an exterminating order, in mid-winter, 200 miles across bleak prairies, among strangers in a strange State, leaving their homes and property to be possessed by their persecutors.[228]

227. David W. Patten, appointed in 1835 as one of the original members of the Quorum of the Twelve Apostles, was mortally wounded in October 1838 in the Battle of Crooked River in Ray County, Missouri. Smith (then Bathsheba Bigler), sixteen years old at the time of Patten's death, later described the scene in her autobiography: "Cap. David W. Patten, who was one of the Twelve Apostels, was braught wounded in to the house where we were. I heard him bear testimony to the truth of Mormonism. He exorted his wife and all present to abide in the faith. His wife asked him if he had anything against her. He answered he had nothing against any one. Elder Heber C. Kimball asked him if he would remember him when he got home. He said he would. Soon after he died without a struggle." (Bathsheba W. Smith, Autobiography, ca. 1875–1906, CHL, 5; see also "A History, of the Persecution, of the Church of Jesus Christ, of Latter Day Saints in Missouri," *Times and Seasons,* June 1840, 1:114, in Karen Lynn Davidson et al., eds., *Histories, Volume 2: Assigned Historical Writings, 1831–1847,* vol. 2 of the Histories series of *The Joseph Smith Papers,* ed. Dean C. Jessee et al. [Salt Lake City: Church Historian's Press, 2012], 246–247.)

228. The Missouri governor's "exterminating order" in 1838 followed months of escalating violence between established Missourians and Latter-day Saints who had been moving into a cluster of northwestern Missouri counties since 1831. Between January and April 1839, at least eight thousand Latter-day Saints fled Missouri and made their way to Quincy, Illinois. The "extermination order," as it is generally known, read in part: "The Mormons must be treated as enemies and must be exterminated or driven from the state if necessary for the public peace." (Parley P. Pratt, *History of the Late Persecution Inflicted by the State of Missouri upon the Mormons* [Detroit: Dawson and Bates, 1839], 59; Joseph Smith, "Church History," *Times and Seasons,* Mar. 1, 1842, 3:708–709, in Karen Lynn Davidson et al., eds., *Histories, Volume 1: Joseph Smith Histories, 1832–1844,* vol. 1 of the Histories series of *The Joseph Smith Papers,* ed. Dean C. Jessee et al. [Salt Lake City: Church Historian's Press, 2012], 497–498, 498n25; Lilburn W. Boggs to John B. Clark, Oct. 27, 1838, copy, Mormon War Papers, 1838–1841, Missouri State Archives, Jefferson City.)

I was intimately acquainted with the life and ministry of our beloved Prophet and Patriarch, Joseph and Hyrum Smith. I know that they were pure men, who labored for the redemption of the human family. For six years I heard their public and private teachings. It was from their lips that I heard taught the principle of celestial marriage,[229] and when I saw their mangled forms cold in death, having been slain for the testimony of Jesus by the hands of cruel bigots, in defence of law, justice and Executive pledges, and although this was a scene of barbarous cruelty, which can never be erased from those who witnessed the heart-rending cries of widows and orphans, and mingled their tears with those of thousands of witnesses of the mournful occasion, the memories of which I hardly feel willing to awaken, yet I realized that they had sealed their ministry with their blood and that their testimony was in force.[230]

On the 9th day of February, 1846—the middle of a cold and bleak winter—my husband, just rising from a bed of sickness, and I, in company with thousands of Saints, were driven again from our comfortable home, the accumulation of six years' industry and prudence, and, with two little children, commenced a long and weary journey through a wilderness, over prairies, deserts and mountains, to seek another home, for a wicked mob had decreed we must leave. Governor [Thomas] Ford, of Illinois, said the laws were powerless to protect us. Exposed to the cold of winter and the storms of spring, we continued our journey amid want and exposure, burying by the way side a dear mother, a son and many kind friends and relatives.[231]

We reached the Missouri River in July.[232] Here our country thought proper to make a requisition upon us for a battalion to defend our national flag in the

---

229. Smith later wrote: "I heard the Prophet give instructions concerning plural marriage; he counselled the sisters not to trouble themselves in consequence of it, that all would be right, and the result would be for their glory and exaltation. . . . Being thoroughly convinced, as well as my husband, that the doctrine of Plurality of wives was from God; and having a fixed determination to attain to Celestial glory, I felt to embrace the whole Gospel, and that it was for my husband's exaltation that he should obey the Revelation on Celestial Marriage, that he might attain to Kingdoms, thrones, Principalities and powers, firmly believing that I should participate with him in all his blessings, glory and honor." (Smith, Autobiography, 11, 13.)

230. Joseph and Hyrum Smith were murdered by a mob at Carthage, Illinois, on June 27, 1844. A public viewing of the bodies took place in Nauvoo, Illinois, on June 28. ("Awful Assassination of Joseph and Hyrum Smith!" *Times and Seasons,* July 1, 1844, 5:560; Joseph Smith et al., History, 1838–1856, vols. A-1–F-1 [original], A-2–E-2 [fair copy], CHL, vol. F-1, 188–189.)

231. Over seven hundred Latter-day Saints died during the June 1846 to May 1847 encampment along the Missouri River in Iowa and what is now the state of Nebraska. Bathsheba Smith later wrote: "Our own family were not exempt. Nancy Clement one of my husbands wives died, also her child, Nancy Adelia. . . . My dear mother died on the 11th of March 1847. . . . On the 4th of April 1847 I had a son born who lived but four hours, we named him John." (Richard E. Bennett, *Mormons at the Missouri Winter Quarters, 1846–1852* [Norman: University of Oklahoma Press, 2004], 140–141; Smith, Autobiography, 17.)

232. The Mormon Trail started on the Missouri River at the encampment the Saints named Winter

war pending with Mexico. We responded promptly, many of my kindred stepping forward and performing a journey characterized by their commanding
officer as "unparalelled in history."[233] With the most of our youth and middle-
aged men gone, we could not proceed, hence we were compelled to make
another home, which, though humble, approaching winter made very desirable. In 1847–8, all who were able, through selling their surplus property,
proceeded; we, who remained, were told, by an unfeeling Indian Department,
we must vacate our houses and re-cross the Missouri River, as the laws would
not permit us to remain on Indian lands![234] We obeyed, and again made a new
home, though only a few miles distant. The latter home we abandoned in 1849,
for the purpose of joining our co-religionists in the then far off region, denom-
inated on the maps, "The Great Desert," and by some later geographers as
"Eastern Upper California."

In this isolated country we made new homes, and, for a time, contended
with the crickets for a scanty subsistence. The rude, ignorant and almost nude
Indians were a heavy tax upon us,[235] while struggling again to make comfortable homes and improvements; yet we bore it all without complaint, for we
were buoyed up with the happy reflections that we were so distant, and had
found an asylum in such an undesirable country, as to strengthen us in the
hope that our homes would not be coveted, and that should we, through the
blessing of God, succeed in planting our own vine and fig tree,[236] no one could

---

Quarters (near present-day Omaha, Nebraska). The trail followed the Platte and Sweetwater Rivers
through what became Nebraska and Wyoming, crossed the Rocky Mountains, and led to the Valley of
the Great Salt Lake. (Brandon S. Plewe, ed., *Mapping Mormonism: An Atlas of Latter-day Saint History*
[Provo, UT: Brigham Young University Press, 2012], 74–77, 80–81.)

233. Following lobbying by Jesse C. Little, a Latter-day Saint leader, and Thomas L. Kane, a social
reformer interested in assisting the Saints, President James K. Polk commissioned a battalion of Mormon
soldiers for the Mexican-American War. U.S. Army officers recruited approximately five hundred men
from the Mormon camps along the Missouri River in July 1846. The departure of so many able-bodied
men was a hardship, but the wages and clothing from the government provided much-needed assistance
for the Saints' westward trek. Roughly eighty women and children traveled along with the Mormon
Battalion. Though all military confrontations were avoided, the battalion blazed a trail through the
Southwest from Santa Fe to San Diego. (For an early account, see Daniel Tyler, *A Concise History of the
Mormon Battalion in the Mexican War, 1846–1847* [Salt Lake City: n.p., 1881].)

234. In 1846 an agreement was made with the local Omaha and Oto tribes to allow the Mormons to
settle the area for at least two years. (Bennett, *Mormons at the Missouri Winter Quarters,* 70–72.)

235. Latter-day Saints both befriended and fought with the American Indians who inhabited the
Great Basin area, including Utes, Shoshones, and Paiutes. Historical interpretations of those relationships
have varied. (See Ronald W. Walker, "Toward a Reconstruction of Mormon and Indian Relations, 1847–
1877," *BYU Studies* 29, no. 4 [Fall 1989]: 23–42; and Sondra Jones, "Saints or Sinners? The Evolving
Perceptions of Mormon-Indian Relations in Utah Historiography," *Utah Historical Quarterly* 72, no. 1
[Winter 2004], 19–46.)

236. "Vine and fig tree" is a common pairing in Old Testament imagery, signifying prosperity and
peace; see Micah 4:4, for example.

feel heartless enough to withhold from us that religious liberty which we had sought in vain amongst our former neighbors.

Without recapitulating our recent history—the development of a people whose industry and morality have extracted eulogy from their most bitter traducers—I cannot but express my surprise, mingled with regret and indignation at the recent proceedings of ignorant, bigoted, and unfeeling men, headed by the Vice-President, to aid intolerant sectarians and reckless speculators, who seek for proscription and plunder, and who feel willing to rob the inhabitants of these valleys of their hard earned possessions, and what is dearer, the constitutional boon of religious liberty.[237]

The following is a verbatim report of the remarks of the next speaker:

MRS. LEVI [REBECCA] RITER.

In rising before this vast assembly my heart is filled with feelings that words cannot express. We have not met here, my beloved sisters, as women of other States and Territories meet, to complain of the wrongs and abuses inflicted upon us by our husbands, fathers and sons; but we are happy and proud to state that we have no such afflictions and abuses to complain of. Neither do we ask for the right of franchise; nor do we ask for more law, more liberty or more rights and freedom from our husbands and brothers; for there is no spot on this wide earth where kindness and affection are more bestowed upon woman, and her rights so sacredly defended as in Utah. We are here to express our love for each other, and to exhibit to the world our devotion to God our Heavenly Father; and to show our willingness to comply with the requirements of the gospel; and the law of Celestial Marriage is one of its requirements that we are resolved to honor, teach and practise, which may God grant us strength to do ("Amen," from the audience). And that we may have a

---

237. Vice President Schuyler Colfax Jr., with his wife and several friends, visited Utah "in a strictly private capacity" in early October 1869. Though Colfax attended few public events, he delivered an impromptu speech in which he both praised Latter-day Saint industry and "alluded in pointed terms to the fact that a law of Congress [the 1862 Morrill Anti-Bigamy Act] was, by the people here, violated." Colfax stated: "Our country is governed by law and no assumed revelation justifies any one in trampling on the law. . . . I do not concede that the institution you have established here [plural marriage], and which is condemned by the law, is a question of religion." Colfax's speech, which cited a passage from the Book of Mormon (Jacob 2:27) to condemn polygamy, was published in the widely read *Republican* (Springfield, Massachusetts) by editor Samuel Bowles, one of Colfax's traveling companions. Publication of the speech drew a lengthy response from John Taylor, of the Quorum of the Twelve Apostles, then stationed in Boston. Other newspaper editors employed Colfax's observations in the press's campaign against Latter-day Saints' practice of plural marriage. ("Arrival of Vice-President Colfax," *Deseret Evening News,* Oct. 4, 1869, [3]; "Serenade of Vice-President Colfax," and "Colfax on Polygamy," *Salt Lake Daily Telegraph,* Oct. 6, 1869, [2]; John Taylor, Letter to the Editor, *Deseret News* [weekly], Nov. 10, 1869, 471; see "The Mormon Question," *Deseret News* [weekly], July 8, 1868, 176.)

continuation of liberty I ask in the name of Jesus Christ! ("Amen," again by the audience).

The resolutions drafted by the Committee were then presented, and carried unanimously, being greeted with loud cheers. They were as follows:

Resolved.—That we, the Ladies of Salt Lake City, in mass meeting assembled, do manifest our indignation and protest against the Bill before Congress, known as the Cullom Bilt, also the one known as the Cragin Bill, and all similar Bills, expressions and manifestos.[238]

Resolved.—That we consider the above named Bills foul blots on our national escutcheon—absurd documents—atrocious insults to the Honorable Executive of the United States Government, and malicious attempts to subvert the rights of civil and religious liberty.

Resolved.—That we do hold sacred the Constitution bequeathed us by our forefathers, and ignore, with laudable womanly jealousy, every act of those men to whom the responsibilities of government have been entrusted, which is calculated to destroy its efficacy.

Resolved.—That we unitedly exercise every moral power and every right which we inherit as the daughters of American citizens, to prevent the passage of such bills; knowing that they would inevitably cast a stigma on our Republican Government by jeopardizing the liberty and lives of its most loyal and peaceable citizens.

Resolved.—That, in our candid opinion, the presentation of the aforesaid bills indicates a manifest degeneracy of the great men of our nation; and their adoption would presage a speedy downfall and ultimate extinction of the glorious pedestal of Freedom, Protection and Equal Rights established by our noble ancestors.

Resolved.—That we acknowledge the Institutions of the Church of Jesus Christ of Latter-day Saints as the only reliable safeguard of female virtue and innocence; and the only sure protection against the fearful sin of prostitution and its attendant evils, now prevalent abroad, and, as such, we *are* and *shall be* united with our brethren in sustaining them against each and every encroachment.

---

238. A bill introduced to the U.S. Senate by Republican senator Aaron H. Cragin of New Hampshire made it unlawful for the church or any of its officers or members to perform marriages, and declared that "criminal cases" arising under the 1862 Morrill Anti-Bigamy Act "shall be heard, tried and determined by the district courts of said Territory of Utah, *without a jury.*" The bill gave Utah's territorial governor the right to appoint all territorial officers and forbade the territorial legislature to assemble, assigning its powers to the territorial governor. The bill did not pass. ("Mr. Cragin's Bill Again," *Deseret News* [weekly], Jan. 8, 1868, 380, italics in original.)

Resolved.—That we consider the originators of the aforesaid bills disloyal to the Constitution, and unworthy of any position of trust in any office which involves the interests of our nation.

Resolved.—That, in case the Bills in question should pass both houses of Congress and become a law by which we shall be disfranchised as a Territory, we, the ladies of Salt Lake City, shall exert all our power and influence to aid in the support of our own State Government.[239]

The meeting was addressed, by several other speakers, whose remarks are given below in the order in which they were delivered:

MRS. [AMANDA BARNES] SMITH,

Relict of Elder Warren Smith, who was murdered at Haun's Mill, then spoke:

Sisters, as I sat upon my seat listening, it seemed as though if I held my peace the stones of the streets would cry out. With your prayers aiding me I will try and make a few remarks.

I obeyed the gospel on the first day of April, 1831, almost thirty-nine years ago; and I have been in the midst of this people ever since. I have seen their travels, their sorrows, their afflictions. I have seen the mourning and sorrow of this people in their calamities, and many is the time my heart has been pained at the scenes of distress I have witnessed. I moved to Kirtland with my husband, a good man and a faithful elder in Israel. He moved his family to Kirtland and bought a beautiful place, but he could not live on it. Our persecutors said we must not stay there. We sold our beautiful home for a song, and we had to sing it ourselves. We traveled all summer to Missouri, our teams poor, and with hardly enough to keep body and soul together. We landed in Caldwell County, near Haun's Mill, nine wagons of us in company. Two days before we landed there we were taken prisoners by an armed mob that demanded every bit of ammunition and every weapon we had. We surrendered them; gave up all. They knew it, for they searched our wagons. A few miles more brought us to Haun's Mill where that awful scene of murder was enacted. My husband pitched his tent by a blacksmith's shop. If I mistake not Bro. David Evans had made a treaty with the mob that they would not molest us. He came in and called the company together, and they knelt in prayer. I sat in my tent, and looking out saw the mob coming, the same that took away our weapons. They came like so many demons or wild Indians. Before I could get to the blacksmith's shop door to tell them, the bullets were whistling amongst

---

239. Many of these resolutions are similar to those passed in the initial mass protest meeting, January 6, 1870. (Document 3.12.)

them. Among those who fell were my husband and a son, and one beautiful boy, now here, a man, in your midst, was wounded worse than death. I was obliged to stay on that awful ground all that night to take care of my poor children. Another sister who had a son wounded, stayed there all night with me. The scene was terrible beyond description. One poor brother was lying in the shop and could not be moved; and the moans of the dying and wounded were heart-rending. Our enemies were not far off and we did not know but they would return. Next morning Brother Joseph Young came to see what could be done. He inquired what should be done with the dead, as there was not time to bury them, for the mob was coming on us, and there were not men to dig the graves. I said anything but leaving their bodies to the fiends that had killed them. There was a deep, dry well close by, and into this the bodies had to be hurried, seventeen in number, some head downwards and some feet downwards.[240]

And this was in America! In the land of liberty and freedom, that boasts of the rights guaranteed to its citizens! We are here to-day to say if such scenes shall be again enacted in our midst. I say to you, my sisters, you are American citizens; let us stand by the truth if we die for it (applause).

MRS. WILMARTH EAST.

It is with feelings of pleasure, mingled with indignation and disgust, that I appear before you my sisters, to express my feelings in regard to the Cullom Bill now before the Congress of this once happy and Republican government. The Constitution for which our forefathers fought and bled and died, bequeathes to us the right of religious liberty,—the right to worship God according to the dictates of our own consciences! Does the Cullom Bill give us this right? Compare it with the Constitution if you please, and see what a disgrace has come upon this once happy and Republican government! Where, O, where is that liberty, bequeathed to us by our forefathers, the richest boon ever given to man or woman, except eternal life or the gospel of the Son of God? I am an American citizen by birthright and, having lived above the laws of the

---

240. On October 30, 1838, amidst escalating tensions between Latter-day Saint settlers and Missourians, about two hundred members of a Missouri militia attacked about thirty Mormon families living near Jacob Hawn's mill on Shoal Creek in Caldwell County. The militia killed seventeen Mormons, some of them children, and wounded another fourteen Mormons. Smith recounted the story of the Hawn's Mill massacre many times. The May 1839 affidavit she swore out at Adams County, Illinois, as part of the Mormon redress effort is included in her autobiography. Her Missouri recollections were published in 1877. (Alexander L. Baugh, *A Call to Arms: The 1838 Mormon Defense of Northern Missouri,* Dissertations in Latter-day Saint History [Provo, UT: Joseph Fielding Smith Institute for Latter-day Saint History; BYU Studies, 2000], 115–127, 213–216; Amanda Barnes Smith, Autobiography, 1858, CHL, 4–7; Edward W. Tullidge, *The Women of Mormondom* [New York: Tullidge and Crandall, 1877], 121–132.)

land I claim the right to worsoip God according to the dictates of my own conscience and the commandments that God shall give unto me. Our Constitution guarantees "Life liberty and the pursuit of happiness to all who live beneath it." What is life to me if I see the galling yoke of oppression placed upon the necks of my husband, sons and brothers as Mr. Cullom would haev it! I am proud to say to you that I am not only a citizen of the United States of America, but a citizen of the kingdom of God, and the laws of this kingdom I am willing to sustain and defend both by example and precept. I am thankful to-day that I have the privilege of living the religion of Jesus our Savior. I am thankful to-day that I have the honored privilege of being the happy recipient of one of the greatest principles ever revealed to man for his redemption and exaltation in the kingdom of God, namely plurality of wives; and I am thankful to-day that I know God is at the helm and will defend his people.

MRS. KIMBALL

Felt thankful to be numbered with this people. We feel to honor God and the gospel communicated to us. She was sorry that Congress is engaged in framing measures for the overthrow of the Latter-day Saints. She prayed that the spirit and feelings of that audience might be felt in the Congress of the United States and that any measures that are calculated to bring evil upon this community, might be thwarted; and that Congress will be made to see the injustice of such measures as those contemplated by the Cullom bill, against good, honest, virtuous and loyal citizens, such as are the people of Utah.

MRS. [MARY] MCMINN

Could not refrain from expressing herself in unison with her sisters, and her indignation at the bill. She was an American citizen. Her father had fought through the revolution with General Washington, and she claimed the exercise of the liberty for which he had fought. She was proud of being a Latter-day Saint.

In answer to an inquiry she stated that she was nearly eighty-five years of age.

E. R. SNOW.

My sisters:—In addressing you at this time I realize that the occasion is a peculiar and an interesting one. We are living in a land of freedom—under a Constitution that guarantees civil and religious liberty to all; black and white, Christians, Jews, Mahometans and Pagans; and how strange it is that such considerations should exist as those which have called us together this afternoon.

Under the proud banner which now waves from ocean to ocean, strange as it may seem, we, who have ever been loyal citizens, have been persecuted from time to time and driven from place to place, until at last, beyond the bounds of civilization, under the guidance of President Young, we found an asylum of peace in the midst of these mountains.

There are, at times, small and apparently trivial events in the lives of individuals with which every other event naturally associates. There are circumstances in the history of nations, which serve as centres, around which everything else revolves.

The entrance of our brave pioneers and the settlement of the Latter-day Saints in these mountain vales, which then were only barren, savage wilds, are incidents with which, not only our own future, but the future of the whole world is deeply associated.

Here they struggled with more than mortal energy, for their hearts and hands were nerved by the spirit of the Most High, and through His blessing they succeeded in drawing sustenance from the arid soil; and here they erected the standard on which the Star Spangled Banner waved its salutations of welcome to the nations of the earth; and, although it had been stained with the blood of innocence,[241] here it has been rescued from the withering touch of tyranny and oppression—here it has been honored and respected, and here it will be bequeathed unsullied to future generations. Yes, that "dear old Flag," which in my girlhood I always contemplated with joyous pride, and to which the patriotic strains of my earliest muse were chanted, here floats triumphantly on the mountain breeze.[242]

Our numbers, small at first, have increased, until now we number one hundred and fifty thousand, and yet, we are allowed only a Territorial Government. Year after year we have petitioned Congress, for what it was our inalienable right to claim,—a State Government; and year after year our petitions have been treated with contempt. Such treatment as we have received from our rulers, has no precedent in the annals of history.

And now, instead of granting us our rights as American citizens, bills are being presented to Congress which are a disgrace to men in responsible stations, professing the least claim to honor and magnanimity—bills, which, if carried into effect, would utterly annihilate us as a people. But this will never

---

241. In one of many references to the June 27, 1844, mob murder of Joseph and Hyrum Smith, Snow wrote in 1854: "Then law-abiding men were slain! / Columbia's Banner wears the stain!" (Eliza R. Snow, "Revolutionary Song," *Deseret News,* July 13, 1854, [2].)

242. As a young woman in her twenties, Snow published patriotic poems in Portage County, Ohio, newspapers, including "Adams and Jefferson" [signed Narcissa], *Western Courier* (Ravenna, OH), Aug. 5, 1826, and "Ode for the Fourth of July" [signed Tullia], June 30, 1830. "Adams and Jefferson" is included in Jill Mulvay Derr and Karen Lynn Davidson, eds., *Eliza R. Snow: The Complete Poetry* (Provo, UT: Brigham Young University Press; Salt Lake City: University of Utah Press, 2009).

be. There is too much virtue yet existing in the nation, and above all, there is a God in heaven, whose protecting care is over us, and who takes cognizance of the acts of the children of men.

My sisters, we have met to-day to manifest our views and feelings concerning the oppressive policy exercised towards us by our Republican Government. Aside from all local and personal feelings, to me it is a source of deep regret that the standard of American liberty should have so far swayed from its original towering position as to have given rise to circumstances which not only rendered such a meeting opportune but absolutely necessary.

Heretofore, while detraction and ridicule have been poured forth in almost every form that malice could invent—while we have been misrepresented by speech and press, and exhibited in every shade but our true light, the ladies of Utah, as a general thing, have remained silent. Had not our aims been of the most noble and exalted character, and had we not known that we occupied a standpoint far above our traducers, we might have returned volley for volley; but we have, all the time, realized that to contradict such egregious absurdities, would be a great stoop of condescension—far beneath the dignity of those who profess to be Saints of the living God; and we very unassumingly applied to ourselves a saying of an ancient apostle in writing to the Corinthians, "*Ye suffer fools, gladly, seeing that yourselves are wise.*"[243]

But there is a point at which silence is no longer a virtue. In my humble opinion we have arrived at this point. Shall we—ought we to be silent when every right of citizenship—every vestige of civil and religious liberty is at stake? When our husbands and sons—our fathers and brothers are threatened, being either restrained in their obedience to the commands of God, or incarcerated year after year in the dreary confines of a prison, will it be thought presumptuous for us to speak? Are not our interests one with our brethren? Ladies, this subject as deeply interests us as them. In the Kingdom of God, woman has no interests separate from those of man—all are mutual.

Our enemies pretend that in Utah, woman is held in a state of vassalage—that she does not act from choice, but by coercion—that we would even prefer life elsewhere, were it possible for us to make our escape. What nonsense! We all know that if we wished, we could leave at any time—either to go singly or we could rise *en masse*, and there is no power here that could or would ever wish to prevent us.

I will now ask this intelligent assembly of ladies: Do you know of any place on the face of the earth, where woman has more liberty, and where she enjoys such high and glorious privileges as she does here, as a Latter-day Saint? "No!"

---

243. 2 Corinthians 11:19.

The very idea of women here in a state of slavery is a burlesque on good common sense. The history of this people, with a very little reflection, would instruct outsiders on this point, it would show at once that the part which woman has acted in it, could never have been performed against her will. Amid the many distressing scenes through which we have passed, the privations and hardships consequent on our expulsion from State to State, and our location in an isolated, barren wilderness, the women in this Church have performed and suffered what could never have been borne and accomplished by slaves.

And now, after all that has transpired, can our opponents expect us to look on with silent indifference and see every vestige of that liberty, for which many of our patriotic grandsires fought and bled, that they might bequeath to us, their children, the precious boon of national freedom, wrested from our grasp? If so, they will learn their mistake, we are ready to inform them. They must be very dull in estimating the energy of female character, who can persuade themselves that women, who, for the sake of their religion, left their homes, crossed the plains with handcarts, or, as many had previously done, drove ox, mule and horse teams from Nauvoo and from other points when their husbands and sons went at their country's call, to fight her battles in Mexico; yes, that very country which had refused us protection and from which we were then struggling to make our escape I say, those who think that such women and the daughters of such women do not possess too much energy of character to remain passive and mute under existing circumstances are "reckoning bills without their host."[244] To suppose that we should not be aroused when our brethren are threatened with fines and imprisonment for their faith in and obedience to the laws of God, is an insult to our womanly natures.

Were we the stupid, degraded, heartbroken beings that we have been represented, silence might better become us; but, as women of God,—women filling high and responsible positions—performing sacred duties—women who stand not as dictators, but as counselors to their husbands, and who, in the purest, noblest sense of refined womanhood, being truly their helpmates; we not only speak because we have the right, but justice and humanity demand that we should.

Instead of being lorded over by tyrannical husbands, we, the ladies of Utah, are already in possession of a privilege which many intelligent and high

---

244. "To reckon without one's host" is a proverbial saying meaning "to calculate one's bill or score without consulting one's host or landlord; to come to conclusions without taking into consideration some important circumstance of the case." ("Host," in *The Oxford English Dictionary,* ed. James A. H. Murray et al., 12 vols., 1933, reprint [Oxford: Oxford University Press, 1970], 5:408.)

aiming ladies in the States are earnestly seeking i. e., *the right to vote*. Although as yet we have not been admitted to the common ballot box, to us the right of suffrage is extended in matters of far greater importance.[245] This we say truthfully not boastingly; and we may say farther, that if those sensitive persons who profess to pity the condition of the women of Utah, will secure unto us those rights and privileges which a just and equitable administration of the laws of the Constitution of the United States guarantees to every loyal citizen, they may reserve their sympathy for objects more appreciative.

My sisters, let us, inasmuch as we are free to do all that love and duty prompt, be brave and unfaltering in sustaining our brethren. Woman's faith can accomplish wonders. Let us, like the devout and steadfast Miriam, assist our brothers in upholding the hands of Moses.[246] Like the loving Josephine, whose firm and gentle influence both animated and soothed the heart of Napoleon, we will encourage and assist the servants of God in establishing righteousness; but, unlike Josephine, never will political inducements, threats or persecutions prevail on us to relinquish our matrimonial ties—they were performed by the authority of the holy priesthood, the efficacy of which extends into eternity.

But, to the law and to the testimony. Those obnoxious, fratricidal Bills—I feel indignant at the thought, that such documents should disgrace our National Capital. The same spirit that prompted Herod to seek the life of Jesus—the same that drove our Pilgrim Fathers to this Continent, and the same that urged the English Government to the system of unrepresented taxation, which resulted in the independence of the American Colonies, is conspicuous in those Bills. If such measures are persisted in, they will produce similar results. They not only threaten extirpation to us, but they augur destruction to the Government. The authors of those Bills would tear the Constitution to shreds. They are sapping the foundation of American freedom—they would obliterate every vestige of the dearest right of man—liberty of conscience, and reduce our once happy country to a state of anarchy.

---

245. Procedures instituted by Joseph Smith in 1830 required that the vote of the church precede any person's ordination to church office and that "all things shall be done by common consent in the church." Women voted in church assemblies from at least 1837, either apart from the male priesthood quorums or together with them. (Doctrine and Covenants 20:65; 26:2; 28:13; Ileen Ann Waspe, "The Status of Woman in the Philosophy of Mormonism from 1830 to 1845" [master's thesis, Brigham Young University, 1942], 116–117.)

246. Aaron and Hur held up the hands of Moses during Israel's battle at Rephidim. Moses's sister Miriam, identified as "the prophetess," led women in a hymn of praise to the Lord following the defeat of Egypt at the Red Sea. (Exodus 15:20–21; 17:12.)

Our trust is in God. He that led Israel from the land of Egypt—who preserved Shadrach, Meshach and Abednego in the fiery furnace; who rescued Daniel from the jaws of hungry lions, and who directed Brigham Young to these mountain vales, lives and overrules the destinies of men and nations. He will make the wrath of man praise Him;[247] and His kingdom will move steadily forward, until wickedness shall be swept from the earth, and truth, love and righteousness reign triumphantly.

The remainder of the proceedings will be printed in to-morrow's issue.[248]

GREAT INDIGNATION MEETING
Of the Ladies of Salt Lake City, to protest against the passage of CUllom's Bill.
(*Continued.*)

HARRIET COOK YOUNG.

In rising to address this meeting, delicacy prompts me to explain the chief motives which have dictated our present action. We, the ladies of Salt Lake City, have assembled here to-day—not for the purpose of assuming any particular political power, nor to claim any special prerogative which may, or may not belong to our sex; but to express our indignation at the unhallowed efforts of men, who, regardless of every principle of manhood, justice and constitutional liberty, would force upon a religious community, by a direct issue, either the curse of apostasy, or the bitter alternative of fire and sword. Surely the instinct of self-preservation, the love of liberty and happiness and the right to worship God are dear to our sex as well as to the other, and when these most sacred of all rights are thus wickedly assailed, it becomes absolutely our duty to defend them.

The mission of the Latter-day Saints is to reform abuses which have for ages corrupted the world, and to establish an era of peace and righteousness. The Most High is the founder of this mission, and in order to its establishment, His providences have so shaped the world's history, that, on this continent, blest above all other lands, a free and enlightened Government has been instituted, guaranteeing to all, social, political and religious liberty. The Constitution of our country is therefore hallowed to us, and we view with a jealous eye every infringement upon its great principles, and demand, in the sacred name of liberty, that the miscreant, who would trample it under his feet, by depriving a hundred thousand American citizens of every vestige of liberty,

---

247. See Psalm 76:10.

248. This marks the end of the January 14, 1870, installment of the two-part article. The second and final installment, dated January 15, 1870, follows.

should be anathematized throughout the length and breadth of the land as a traitor to God and his country.

It is not strange that among the bigoted and the corrupt such a man and such a measure should have originated; but it will be strange indeed, if such a measure find favor with the honorable and high minded men who wield the destinies of the nation. Let this seal of ruin be attached to the archives of our country and terrible must be the results. Woe will wait upon her steps, and sorrow and desolation will stalk through the land; peace and liberty will seek another clime, while anarchy, lawlessness and bloody strife hold high carnival amid the general wreck. God forbid that wicked men be permitted to force such an issue upon the nation!

It is true that a corrupt press, and an equally corrupt priestcraft are leagued against us—that they have pandered to the ignorance of the masses and vilified our institutions to that degree, that it has become popular to believe that the Latter-day Saints are unworthy to live; but it is also true that there are many, very many, right thinking men who are not without influence in the nation, and to such do we now solemnly and earnestly appeal. Let the United voice of this assembly give the lie to the popular clamour that the women of Utah are oppressed and held in bondage. Let the world know that the women of Utah prefer virtue to vice, and the home of an honorable wife to the gilded pageantry of fashionable temples of sin. Transitory allurements, glaring to the senses, as the flame is to the moth, but short lived and cruel in their results possess no charms for us. Every woman in Utah may have her husband, the husband of her choice. Here we are taught, not to destroy our children, but to preserve them, for they, reared in the path of virtue and trained to righteousness, constitute our true glory.

It is with no wish to accuse our sisters who are not of our faith, but we are dealing with facts as they exist. Wherever monogamy reigns, adultery, prostitution, free-love and foeticide,[249] directly or indirectly, are its concomitants. It is not enough to say that the virtuous and the high-minded frown upon these evils, we believe they do, but frowning does not cure them, it does not even check their rapid growth; either the remedy is too weak, or the disease is too strong. The women of Utah comprehend this and they see in the principle of a plurality of wives, the only safeguard, against adultery, prostitution, free-love and the reckless waste of pre-natal life practised throughout the land.

It is as co-workers in the great mission of universal reform, not only in our own behalf, but also, by precept and example, to aid in the emancipation of

249. Intentional destruction of a fetus (foetus); abortion. ("Foeticide," in *Oxford English Dictionary,* 4:379.)

our sex generally, that we accept in our heart of hearts, what we know to be a divine commandment; and here, and now, boldly and publicly we do assert our right, not only to believe in this holy commandment, but to practise what we believe.

While these are our views, every attempt to force that obnoxious measure upon us, must of necessity, be an attempt to coerce us in our religious and moral convictions, against which did we not most solemnly protest, we would be unworthy the name of American women.

MRS. H. [HANNAH] T. KING.

My Dear Sisters:—I wish I had the language I feel to need at the present moment, to truly represent the indignant feelings of my heart and brain on reading last evening a string of thirty "Sections" headed by the words "A Bill in aid of the execution of the laws in the Territory of Utah, and other purposes."! The "other purposes" contain the pith of the matter, and the adamantine chains the compilers of the said "Bill" seek to bind this people with, exceed any thing the feudal times of England, or the serfdom of Russia ever laid upon human beings. My Sisters! are we really in America the world renowned land of liberty, freedom, and equal rights? the land of which I dreamed in my youth as almost an earthly elysium, where freedom of thought and religious liberty were open to all? The land that Columbus wore his noble life out to discover? the land that God Himself helped him to exhume, and that Isabella, a queen— a woman, declared she would pawn her jewels and crown of Castile to give him the outfit which he needed? The land of Washington, "The Father of his Country"—and of a host of noble spirits too numerous to mention? the land to which "The Mayflower" bore the Pilgrim Fathers, who rose up and left their homes, and bade their native land "good night", simply that they might worship God by a purer and holier faith in a land of freedom and liberty, of which America has long been synonymous? Yes, my sisters, this *is* America; but oh! how are the mighty fallen! Who or what is the creature who framed this incomparable document? Is he an Esquimaux or a Chimpanzee, or what isolated land's end spot produced him? What ideas he must have of women! Had he ever a mother, a wife, or a sister? In what academy was he tutored, or to what school does he belong, that he should so coolly and systematically *command* the *women* of this people to turn traitors to their husbands, their brothers, and their sons! Short-sighted man of sections and *the* Bill! Let *us* the women of this people—the sisterhood of Utah, rise *en masse* and tell this nondescript to defer "the Bill" until he has studied the character of *woman* such as *God* intended she should be, *then* he will discover that *devotion, veneration,* and faithfulness are her peculiar attributes; that *God* is her refuge—and *His* servants her oracles, and that especially the women of Utah have paid too high a price for their present position, their present light and knowledge—and their noble *future* to succumb to so mean and foul a thing as the Baskin, Cullum & Co's Bill.[250] Let him learn that they are *one* heart, hand and brain, with the brotherhood of Utah—that God is their Father and their Friend—that into His hands they commit their cause—and on their pure and simple banner they have emblazoned their motto—

"God and my right."

PHOEBE WOODRUFF.

Ladies of Utah, as I have been called upon to express my views upon the important subject, which has called us together this day, I will say that I am happy to be one of your number in this association. I am proud that I am a citizen of Utah, and a member of the Church of Jesus Christ of Latter-day Saints. I have been a member of this Church for thirty-six years, and had the privilege of living in the days of the Prophet Joseph and heard his teachings for many years. He ever counseled us to honor, obey, and maintain the principles of our noble Constitution, for which our fathers fought, and many of them sacrificed their lives to establish. President Brigham Young has always taught the same principle. This glorious legacy of our fathers, the Constitution of the United States, guarantees unto all the citizens of this great Republic the right to worship God according to the dictates of their own consciences, as it expressly says, "Congress shall make no laws respecting an establishment of religion or prohibiting the free exercise thereof." Cullom's bill is in direct violation of this declaration of the Constitution, and, I think it is our duty to do all in our power by our voices and influence to thwart the passage of this bill, which commits a violent outrage upon our rights, and the rights of our fathers, husband and sons; and whatever may be the final result of the action of Congress in passing or enforcing oppressive laws for the sake of our religion, upon the noble men who have subdued these deserts, it is our duty to stand by them and support them by our faith, prayers and works through every dark hour unto the end, and trust in the God of Abraham, Isaac, and Jacob to

---

250. Salt Lake City attorney Robert Newton Baskin stated: "I presented a draft of the [Cullom] bill in 1869 at Washington city to Senator Cullom, who was chairman of the House Committee on Territories." In 1871 the *Deseret News* described Baskin as "the author of what is called in Congress the 'Cullom Bill,' . . . a lawyer of shrewdness and coolness, and inflamed against Mormonism." Baskin became mayor of Salt Lake City in 1892 and associate justice of the Utah Supreme Court in 1899. (Robert N. Baskin, *Reminiscences of Early Utah with Reply to Certain Statements by O. F. Whitney* [Salt Lake City: Signature Books, 2006], 30; "The Great Crusade," *Deseret News* [weekly], Nov. 15, 1871, 478; John Gary Maxwell, *Robert Newton Baskin and the Making of Modern Utah* [Norman: University of Oklahoma Press, 2013], 228, 284.)

defend us, and all who are called to suffer for keeping the commandments of God. Shall we as wives and mothers sit still and see our husbands, and sons, whom we know are obeying the highest behest of heaven, suffer for their religion without exerting ourselves to the extent of our power for their deliverance? No! verily, no!! God has revealed unto us the law of the Patriarchal order of marriage, and commanded us to obey it. We are sealed to our husbands for time and eternity, that we may dwell with them and our children in the world to come, which guarantees unto us the greatest blessing for which we are created. If the rulers of our nation will so far depart from the spirit and the letter of our glorious Constitution as to deprive our Prophets, Apostles and Elders of citizenship, and imprison them for obeying this law, let them grant us this our last request, to make their prisons large enough to hold their wives, for where they go we will go also.

MRS. [MARY ISABELLA] HORNE

Had been connected with the Church since 1835, and spoke her indignation at the bill. She is one of the so called oppressed women of Utah; is the wife of a man who practices plurality of wives and expects always to sustain him. Whether the bill is passed or not, it will be all right, if the Saints only are faithful and true to their God and themselves. She thought if the bill was passed, it would fill up the cup of the iniquity of the nation.

MRS. ELEANOR M. PRATT

Said she was born in America, and thought she was free to teach that which came from God. It is many years since three men in rags came to her home in Mississippi, and by the Bible she held, they proved to her Joseph Smith was a prophet of God. Eleven years after, she heard the same principles in California and received them. For so doing she was turned out of doors, her children were taken from her twice, and innocent blood was shed.[251] She longed

---

251. Eleanor McComb McLean was baptized at San Francisco in May 1854. Her husband, Hector McLean, became opposed to her participation in church meetings. According to Eleanor, the McLeans' marriage unraveled because of her husband's alcoholism, abuse, and religious bigotry. Church apostle Parley P. Pratt, then in San Francisco, unsuccessfully attempted to mediate between the couple. In February 1855, without Eleanor McLean's knowledge, Hector McLean sent their three children to live with her parents in New Orleans. She then traveled to New Orleans but was unsuccessful in her attempts to regain her children. She then journeyed to Utah, where she became Pratt's twelfth wife in November 1855. During fall 1856 she traveled along with Pratt to the eastern United States. While Parley Pratt served a mission, Eleanor Pratt went to New Orleans, told her parents she had renounced the church, and under subterfuge left with two of her children (the third was at a boarding school). Her father notified Hector McLean of her actions, and McLean began a hunt for both Parley and Eleanor Pratt. He found them separately in Indian Territory (now Oklahoma), where he convinced a U.S. marshal to arrest them. Judge John B. Ogden dismissed the charges against both; fearing McLean's violent intent, Ogden secretly released Parley Pratt. McLean and two associates caught up with Pratt about twelve miles from Van

to see the women of Utah rise and express themselves concerning their rights. When she saw innocent blood shed like as in a slaughter house she did not fear as much as to-day. God gave her strength, and the officers and the soldiers trembled at the power God gave her. Fear falls on the enemies of the Saints because the women of Utah do not fear death; and she was willing to let her blood be shed for the principles of truth, but not for any ignoble purpose.

ELIZA R. SNOW.

My Sisters, My remarks in conclusion will be brief. I heard the prophet Joseph Smith say if the people rose up and mobbed us and the authorities countenanced it, they would have mobs to their hearts' content. I heard him say that the time would come when this nation would so far depart from its original purity, its glory, and its love for freedom and its protection of civil and religious rights, that the Constitution of our country would hang as it were by a thread,. He said, also, that this people, the sons of Zion, would rise up and save the Constitution and bear it off triumphantly.[252]

I wish to say to my sisters, to the mothers in Israel and to the daughters, cultivate in your bosoms the spirit of freedom and liberty which has been bequeathed unto us by our fathers, or grandfathers I should say. My grandfather fought in the Revolution and was taken prisoner. He lay in a filthy prison, with a companion who was taken with him, and fed on such a scanty allowance as would scarcely support life.

His companion died, and for the sake of having his allowance of food he covered him up in the bed and kept him just as long as he dare to stay with a decaying body.[253] And the spirit of freedom and liberty is what we should always cultivate, and what mothers should cultivate in the breasts of their sons, that they may grow up brave and noble, and defenders of that glorious Constitution which has been bequeathed unto us. Let mothers cultivate that spirit in their own bosoms. Let them manifest their own bravery and cherish a

---

Buren, Arkansas, and murdered him on May 13, 1857. Eleanor Pratt then made her way back to Utah. (Terryl L. Givens and Matthew J. Grow, *Parley P. Pratt: The Apostle Paul of Mormonism* [New York: Oxford University Press, 2011], 361–391; Eleanor J. McComb Pratt, Reminiscence, ca. 1857, in Eleanor J. McComb Pratt, Papers, ca. 1857, CHL.)

252. In Nauvoo in 1840, Joseph Smith publicly preached: "Even this Nation will, be on the very verge of crumbling to peices and tumbling to the ground and when the constitution is upon the brink of ruin this people will be the Staff up[on] which the Nation shall lean and they shall bear the constitution away from the very verge of destruction." In 1843 Smith spoke "upon the constitution and government of the United States stating that the time would come when the Constitution and Government would hang by a brittle thread and would be ready to fall into other hands but this people the Latterday saints will step forth and save it." (Martha Jane Coray, Notebook, n.d., CHL, July 19, 1840; James Burgess, Journal, Oct. 1841–Dec. 1848, vol. 2, CHL, May 1843.)

253. Snow retold the story in recollections published in Tullidge, *Women of Mormondom*, 30–31.

spirit of encountering difficulties, because they have to be met more or less in every situation of life. If fortitude and nobility of soul be cultivated in your own bosoms, you will transmit them to your children, your sons will grow up noble defenders of truth and righteousness, and heralds of salvation to the nations of the earth. They will be prepared to fill high and responsible situations in religious, judicial, civil and executive positions. I consider it most important, my sisters, that we should struggle to preserve the sacred Constitution of our country, one of the blessings of the Almighty; for the same spirit that inspired the Prophet Joseph Smith inspired the framers of the Constitution, and we should ever hold it sacred and bear it of triumphantly.

My sisters, I am happy to meet with you, although this is not the occasion that we could have desired to meet together; at least the circumstance which has led to the occasion, is one not to be so regarded. Yet I am happy to meet with you; and my desire is that we may as mothers and sisters in Israel defend truth and righteousness, and sustain those who preach it. Every sister in this church should be a preacher of righteousness; and I think we all are; I believe it is our aim to be such. Let us be more energetic to improve our minds, and develop that strength of moral character which cannot be surpassed on the face of the earth. We should do this. The circumstances in which we are placed and our positions in life demand this of us, because we have greater and higher privileges than any other females upon the face of the earth.

Having said so much I will close by saying, God bless you and help us all to keep His holy commandments and be valiant for the truth, that whether life or death, in life and in death, we may triumph over evil and return to the presence of the Holy One, pure, having kept the faith and finished our course, that the crown laid up for us may be presented to us in the kingdom of our God in the eternal world. Amen. (amen from the audience).

Mrs. Zinah D. Young then moved that the meeting adjourn *sine die*, which was carried; and Mrs. Phebe Woodruff offered the closing benediction.

The old Tabernacle was crowded with ladies at this meeting, and as it will comfortably seat five thousand persons, there could not have been fewer than between five and six thousand present on the occasion.

3.14 "Female Suffrage in Utah," February 8, 1870

"Female Suffrage in Utah," Deseret Evening News *(Salt Lake City, UT), Feb. 8, 1870, vol. 3, no. 65, p. [2].*

After the Civil War, vigorous discussions over woman suffrage took place across the United States in the context of the debate over the expansion of voting rights to African Americans. In February 1869 the U.S. Congress passed the Fifteenth Amendment, which prohibited states from denying a citizen the right to vote based on "race, color, or previous condition of servitude." Following ratification by a sufficient number of states, the amendment became part of the Constitution in March 1870. The failure of many advocates of black suffrage to support woman suffrage created deep fissures within the women's movement.[254]

Some suffragists proposed that experimenting with woman suffrage in Utah might prove the desirability of suffrage elsewhere.[255] In 1867 and 1868 Congressman George W. Julian, a Republican from Indiana, proposed three bills, one granting the vote to women in Utah and two extending the franchise to women in all territories. Julian and others mistakenly believed that giving the women an official political voice would relieve the nation of the stain of polygamy as the women would surely vote to relieve themselves of the burden.[256] The *New York Times* opined that women's numerical superiority in Utah rendered it the ideal location for an experiment in woman suffrage: "Perhaps it would result in casting out polygamy and Mormonism in general. . . . Here would be a capital field for women suffrage to make a start, and we presume nobody would object to the experiment."[257] Ignoring these arguments, Latter-day Saint leaders endorsed the proposal. The *Deseret News* stated in March 1869, "Utah is giving examples to the world on many points, and if the wish is to try the experiment of giving females the right to vote in the Republic, we know of no place where the experiment can be so safely tried as in this Territory. Our ladies can prove to the world that in a society where men are worthy of the name, women can be enfranchised without running wild or becoming unsexed."[258] Congress abandoned Julian's bill after

---

254. U.S. Constitution, art. 15, sec. 1. For additional context, see Faye E. Dudden, *Fighting Chance: The Struggle over Woman Suffrage and Black Suffrage in Reconstruction America* (New York: Oxford University Press, 2011).

255. "A New Plan," "Female Suffrage in Utah," and "Female Suffrage—Ends to Be Gained by It," *Deseret News* [weekly], Mar. 24, 1869, 78.

256. Sarah Barringer Gordon, "The Liberty of Self-Degradation: Polygamy, Woman Suffrage, and Consent in Nineteenth-Century America," *Journal of American History* 83, no. 3 (Dec. 1996): 825.

257. "Minor Topics," *New York Times,* Dec. 17, 1867, 4. By 1869 the *Times* editorials were more circumspect, conceding that "we are not over-sanguine as to the result so confidently expected to take place. . . . We are afraid . . . that the female vote in favor of polygamy would, *at first,* be nearly as strong as the male. At all events, powerful as the lever of woman suffrage might be, we doubt whether it could cast out polygamy from Utah." ("The Women of Utah," *New York Times,* Mar. 5, 1869, 6–7.)

258. "Female Suffrage in Utah," *Deseret News* [weekly], Mar. 24, 1869, 78.

finding that both the Mormon press and Utah territorial representative William Hooper supported it.[259]

In December 1869 the Territory of Wyoming was the first territory or state to grant suffrage to women.[260] Utah was not far behind. At the January 6, 1870, Relief Society mass meeting held to protest the federal Cullom Bill, Bathsheba Smith motioned that "we demand of the Gov the right of Franchise." A vote was called on Smith's motion and it carried.[261] Following effective public demonstrations organized and staged by Utah women in protest of national legislation, the territorial legislature began discussion of female suffrage. Latter-day Saint leaders responded favorably to the idea, as did the national press.

On January 27 the territorial legislature formally commenced its consideration of possible woman suffrage legislation. The House's Committee on Elections deliberated between January 27 and February 2, when it issued a report recommending the extension of voting rights to women; three days later, the House unanimously passed such legislation and the Council (the higher chamber of the legislature) took up the bill. As the Council prepared to vote on the measure, the *Deseret Evening News,* under the leadership of editor George Q. Cannon, an avid supporter of female suffrage, printed the following editorial on February 8, 1870. The Council passed the bill the following day, with some amendments that the House rejected. On February 10 a conference committee accepted the House bill and both chambers unanimously passed the legislation. The final bill provided "that every woman of the age of twenty-one years who has resided in this Territory six months next preceding any general or special election, born or naturalized in the United States, or who is the wife, widow or the daughter of a native-born or naturalized citizen of the United States, shall be entitled to vote at any election in this Territory."[262]

FEMALE SUFFRAGE IN UTAH.

THE female suffrage question is now fairly before the nation; its advocates are as earnest in their labors as if the salvation of the world depended upon their success, and the triumph of the movement, we believe, is only a question of time. The agitation of the question has reached the Rocky Mountains. In our neighboring Territory, Wyoming, the cause has triumphed; in Colorado

---

259. Lola Van Wagenen, "Sister-Wives and Suffragists: Polygamy and the Politics of Woman Suffrage, 1870–1896" (PhD diss., New York University, 1994), 7, 7n21.

260. Michael A. Massie, "Reform Is Where You Find It: The Roots of Woman Suffrage in Wyoming," *Annals of Wyoming* 62 (Spring 1990): 3.

261. See Document 3.12.

262. Utah Territory Legislative Assembly Papers, 1851–1872, CHL, Minutes, 19th Sess., Jan. 27–Feb. 10, 1870; An Act Conferring upon Women the Elective Franchise [Feb. 12, 1870], *Acts, Resolutions and Memorials, Passed and Adopted during the Nineteenth Annual Session of the Legislative Assembly of the Territory of Utah* (Salt Lake City: Joseph Bull, 1870), 8; Thomas G. Alexander, "An Experiment in Progressive Legislation: The Granting of Woman Suffrage in Utah in 1870," *Utah Historical Quarterly* 38, no. 1 (Winter 1970): 25–26; see also Document 3.17.

the ladies are petitioning to have female suffrage legalized there.[263] But success by piecemeal will not satisfy those who are acknowledged as the national leaders of the movement; nothing short of an amendment to Constitution of the United States to this effect will do for them, and this is now being eagerly sought; and as Congressmen are noted, among other things, for their gallantry and their susceptibility to female charms, the adoption of such an amendment is not at all improbable.

We believe in the right of suffrage being enjoyed by all who can exercise it intelligently; but our lawmakers, in conferring this great power upon the recently emancipated black race, do not seem to regard intelligence as an indispensible pre-requisite; and we think the suffrage might be conferred with much greater propriety upon intelligent white women than upon ignorant blacks.[264]

The idea of female suffrage is regarded by many as peculiar to and having originated in these last days; but history tells us that a similar movement existed in ancient Greece when that nation was in the meridian of her splendor.[265] If the right of suffrage was granted to the ladies then it certainly did not bring about the reforms considered necessary to preserve that nation from decadence, and whether it would in this is extremely doubtful. However, that is no reason that it should be withheld. We are a decided advocate of the rights of women as well as of men, and believe that the two are so intimately related that they cannot be enjoyed, to the fullest extent compatible with happiness

263. On the successful woman suffrage movement in Wyoming, see Massie, "Reform Is Where You Find It," 2–21. In Colorado, support for suffrage emerged between 1868 and 1870, though suffrage was not granted until 1893. (See Carolyn Stefano, "Networking on the Frontier: The Colorado Women's Suffrage Movement, 1876–1893," in *The Women's West,* ed. Susan Armitage and Elizabeth Jameson [Norman: University of Oklahoma Press, 1987], 265–276.)

264. Many proponents of suffrage agreed with Cannon on this point. Elizabeth Cady Stanton was vehemently opposed to the idea of "the foreign element, the dregs of China, Germany, England, Ireland, and Africa" making laws for "the nobler types of American womanhood who have taught our presidents, senators, and congressmen the rudiments of all they know." Eliza R. Snow later stated, "Congress cannot be acting consistently with itself to withhold suffrage from woman after having conferred it on the negro, the recent subject of abject slavery." (Elizabeth Cady Stanton et al., eds., *History of Woman Suffrage,* 3 vols., 1881–1886, reprint [Rochester, NY: Susan B. Anthony, Charles Mann, 1887], 2:353; Document 3.20.)

265. Cannon's allusion here is unclear. He may have been referring to a Socratic thought experiment proposed in Plato's *Republic,* which suggested that the ideal society may benefit from women sharing the education and employments of men. But women in ancient Greece did not vote or hold political office. One version of the Athenian foundation myth—in which Athena and Poseidon famously compete to determine who would become patron deity of the new city—credits the local female citizens for casting the deciding votes in Athena's favor; when Poseidon objected by flooding the kingdom, he was appeased only by the subsequent disenfranchisement of Athenian women. (See Plato, *Republic,* 451c–457e; and Marilyn A. Katz, "Women and Democracy in Ancient Greece," and Froma I. Zeitlin, "Utopia and Myth in Aristophanes' *Ecclesiazousae,*" in *Contextualizing Classics: Ideology, Performance, Dialogue,* ed. Thomas M. Falkner et al. [Lanham, MD: Rowman and Littlefield, 1999], 41–68, 69–88.)

and well-being, by either sex while the other labors under disability, however limited.

Universal white male suffrage has been more thoroughly tested in this country than in any other; but venality abounds, and thousands of votes are sold to the highest bidders, hence the results of the system are not so satisfactory as could be wished. Female suffrage might have a tendency to promote purity of elections, and its introduction at the ballot box be attended with results as satisfactory as the amalgamation of certain races in the growth and development of powerful nationalities. We believe it would, and we also think it probable that the power this would place in the hands of women would be used for the benefit of their sex, and would be followed in time by legislation of such a character as would tend more to diminish prostitution and the various social evils which overwhelm society than anything hitherto devised under universal male suffrage.

The degraded condition of the women in this Territory is a very fruitful theme among our friends outside; in this respect as well as in many others they seem unmindful of, or callous to, the real evils around themselves, but very sensitive to imaginary ones at a distance. They are like the fabled worthy who, through admiring the splendor of the stars, became, or feigned to be, totally ignorant of the dirt, squalor and wretchedness of earth. This class, while mourning and sighing over the "degradation" of the ladies of Utah, and have suggested a plan for their emancipation from all "thralldom," polygamy included, and that remedy is the suffrage. The subject has been brought before the attention of Congress, and Senator Pomeroy, we believe, a short time ago introduced a bill to confer the suffrage on the ladies of Utah.[266]

It may be gratifying to all outside who are anxious, to learn that the advisability of extending the suffrage to the ladies of Utah has been discussed considerably during the present session of the Territorial Legislature. In the House a few days ago, after an animated discussion on the subject, a committee was appointed to inquire into the propriety of its establishment in this Territory; on the 2nd instant the committee gave in their report, which was quite favorable,

---

266. Senator Samuel C. Pomeroy, a Kansas Republican who served in the Senate from 1861 to 1873, introduced a constitutional amendment in December 1868 that would grant suffrage to both women and African Americans, but his amendment failed in favor of the more restrictive Fifteenth Amendment (ratified February 3, 1870), which extended suffrage along racial but not gender lines. (*Biographical Directory of the United States Congress, 1774–2005: The Continental Congress September 5, 1774, to October 21, 1788, and the Congress of the United States from the First through the One Hundred Eighth Congresses March 4, 1789, to January 3, 2005, Inclusive,* ed. Andrew R. Dodge and Betty K. Koed [Washington DC: Government Printing Office, 2005], 162–184; Dudden, *Fighting Chance,* 164–165; Stanton et al., *History of Woman Suffrage,* 2:324–325.)

and on the 5th the House passed a bill to this effect, hence it is very probable that before the present session of the Legislature closes, female suffrage wil be *un fait accompli* in this Territory; then if, as our friends outside affirm, its exercise will "emancipate" the ladies of Utah, they will be masters, or rather mistresses of the situation. As for ourselves, we have no doubt as to the result, and are satisfied that it will strengthen the cause of Zion, polygamy included. In all matters pertaining to church government the sisters have always had the same right to vote as the brethren; but in civil matters they, here as elsewhere, have had no say; but if this bill passes they will be their equals in that respect too. We are satisfied that the result will be exactly opposite to what our enemies anticipate. On the plural marriage question we are as firmly convinced as we are of our own existence that were its continuance or abolition put to the vote of the female portion of our population to-day it would be sustained by a nine-tenths majority; and upon this score, which has enlisted the mock sympathy of so many, no disadvantage to Zion's cause will ensue. In every other it cannot but result also in good. We have many *friends* around whose constant effort is to out-vote the "Mormons" at their municipal elections so that the discordant elements so overwhelmingly developed in municipal rule everywhere but in Zion might be introduced here. Many of our co[n]temporaries boast that this consummation will soon be brought about now that direct rail communication exists between the cities of Utah and the East and West. We do not anticipate such a result; nevertheless the hopes of our enemies in this respect may be realized. We do not believe, however, that the existence of our most cherished institutions depends on such a frail tenure as the possession of power by the female members of the Church to vote them down. If such be the case, we believe the ladies should have the power to exercise their agency, hence we desire to see the matter tested; and we hope that the bill passed by the House of Representatives of the Territorial Legislature, on Saturday, will be passed by the Council, believing that the result will be an additional proof to the world, that even with this power in their hands the ladies of Utah will remain true to their integrity, and then, as now, will sustain the priesthood, whether acting in a religious or civil capacity, in promoting the cause of Zion and the behests of Heaven.

3.15 Ladies' Cooperative Retrenchment Meeting, Minutes, February 10, 1870

Ladies' Cooperative Retrenchment Society, Minutes, Feb. 10, 1870, in "Minutes of Ladies' Co-operative Retrenchment Meeting," Deseret Evening News (Salt Lake City, UT), Feb. 16, 1870, vol. 3, no. 72, p. [2].

In fall 1869 Brigham Young invited Mary Isabella Hales Horne, president of the Salt Lake City Fourteenth Ward Relief Society, to lead Latter-day Saint women in an effort to simplify meal preparation and their apparel. Young extended the invitation in early November in Gunnison, Utah Territory, where he was visiting as part of an eleven-day tour of twenty settlements in southern Utah and where Horne was visiting some of her family.[267] Young had become frustrated on his trip over the "multitudinous dishes" his various hosts had provided.[268]

When Young returned from the tour, he used the occasion of a Sunday afternoon address to describe the invitation he had given to Horne and to call for reform. Speaking in the Salt Lake City tabernacle on November 14, Young said: "If the people would like something by way of a change, I will propose something to them, as I did to sister Horne, the President of the Female Relief Society in the 14th Ward, who was at Gunnison, about 130 miles south of this place, when we were there. I invited her, when she returned, to call the sisters of the Relief Society together, and ask them to begin a reform in eating and housekeeping. I told her I wished to get up a society whose members would agree to have a light, nice breakfast in the morning, for themselves and children, without cooking something less than forty different kinds of food, making slaves of themselves and requiring three or four hired girls to wash dishes."

In his address Young mocked dinner tables piled with "roast meat, boiled meat and baked meat, fat mutton, beef and pork; and in addition to this two or three kinds of pies and cakes." He denounced the encouragement to family members "to eat and gorge themselves till they are so full that when night comes they will want a doctor." Further emphasizing a return to plain living and self-reliance, Young reiterated his longtime priority of home industry. He advised, "If you want another revolution, let us go to and say we will wear nothing but what we make; and that which we do not make we will not have."[269]

---

267. Young visited Gunnison, Sanpete County, on November 3 and 4, 1869. Joseph Smith Horne, son of Joseph and Mary Isabella Horne, had been serving as bishop of the Gunnison Ward since December 1868. His wife, Lydia Ann Weiler, gave birth to their first child on October 13, 1869; this was likely the event that prompted Mary Isabella Horne's visit to Gunnison from her home in Salt Lake City. ("Local and Other Matters," *Deseret Evening News,* Nov. 4, 1869, [3]; "Remarks," *Deseret News* [weekly], Nov. 24, 1869, 495–496; "Gunnison. History," in Gunnison Ward, Gunnison Stake, Gunnison Ward Manuscript History and Historical Reports, 1861–1949, CHL, Oct. 25 and Dec. 22, 1868; Joseph Smith Horne, Autobiographical Sketch, ca. 1931, CHL; Susa Young Gates, *History of the Young Ladies' Mutual Improvement Association of the Church of Jesus Christ of Latter-day Saints from November 1869 to June 1910* [Salt Lake City: Deseret News, 1911], 31.)
268. "Remarks," *Deseret News* [weekly], Nov. 24, 1869, 495–496.
269. "Remarks," *Deseret News* [weekly], Nov. 24, 1869, 495–496.

Mary Isabella Hales Horne. Circa 1885. While serving as president of the Salt Lake City Fourteenth Ward Relief Society, and at Brigham Young's urging, Mary Isabella Horne called together a dozen presidents of local ward Relief Societies to form a Ladies' Cooperative Retrenchment Society. The retrenchment movement encouraged women to spend less time on superfluous domestic concerns and devote more attention to spiritual and intellectual development. Until women's presidencies were organized at a stake level, the semimonthly retrenchment meeting served as a central governing board for the Relief Society and Young Ladies' organizations. Horne was president throughout the retrenchment society's thirty-four years. Photograph by Charles R. Savage. (Church History Library, Salt Lake City.)

Young's call for reform spawned a movement among women to simplify their eating and apparel, though public signs of the new movement did not appear until February. The "Great Indignation Meeting" held January 13, 1870, in Salt Lake City[270] may have contributed to the delay, though another factor may have been Horne's reluctance to carry out Young's assignment. Horne later recalled, "It was some time before I could gain sufficient courage to perform this labor, but Sister [Eliza R.] Snow urged me to do my duty, so with fear and trembling I endeavored to do so."[271]

On Thursday, February 10, 1870, Horne convened the first reform meeting at her home with "about twelve presidents of branches of the Relief Society."[272] At this gathering, the women decided to title their efforts "retrenchment" rather than "reform" and included in their name the word "co-operative," presumably to indicate their new cooperation across ward boundaries as they sought, according to Horne, "to lighten the labors of the women and give them more time to devote to mental and spiritual culture."[273] The following minutes of this first Ladies' Cooperative Retrenchment Meeting were published in the *Deseret Evening News,* February 16, 1870.

———— ❧ ————

MINUTES OF LADIES' CO-OPERATIVE RETRENCHMENT MEETING,
Held at the residence of Brother Joseph Horne, 14th Ward, Feb. 10th, 1870.

A representative from most of the Wards of the city was present. Mrs. Mary Isabella Horne was appointed President and Mrs. Sarah M. Kimball Secretary.

Meeting opened by singing; prayer by E. R. Snow.

President Horne stated the object of the meeting. All present expressed their sentiments upon the subject under consideration, and the following persons were appointed a committee to draft resolutions expressive of the feelings of the meeting:

E. R. Snow,
M. [Margaret] T. Smoot,
S. M. Kimball.

The committee proceeded to prepare resolutions, which were read before the meeting and unanimously accepted, of which the following is a copy:

Resolved:—That we, realizing the many evils growing out of the excess and extravagance which our present customs require in the great varieties of dishes demanded in table entertainments, do mutually agree to unite our efforts in sustaining by our examples Table Retrenchment in all of our visiting associations and social parties.

---

270. See Document 3.13.
271. "Address of Mrs. M. Isabella Horne," in Document 4.28.
272. "Address of Mrs. M. Isabella Horne," in Document 4.28.
273. "Address of Mrs. M. Isabella Horne," in Document 4.28.

Resolved:—That, as health is the main-spring of happiness, and economy the way-mark to prosperity, we recommend a careful consideration of the results of our present mode of fashionable table serving.

Resolved:—That by carrying out the principles of retrenchment, the time, strength and means, redeemed from useless labor and waste, shall be devoted to noble purposes—such as instructing each other and the rising generation in the principles of physical and intellectual improvement, dietetics, &c.

Resolved:—That inasmuch as many of our good and worthy citizens are deterred from inviting company by the consideration that they cannot compete with their more affluent neighbors, and are thereby deprived of many rich and profitable interviews, we say that henceforth any table neatly spread, with no matter how plain, but wholesome, food, *shall be considered fashionable.*

Resolved:—That, as women of God, we feel it a duty incumbent on us, not only to manifest our "diligence in all good works,"[274] but to unitedly exert all our power and influence to annihilate degenerating habits and customs, and in establishing such as will benefit future generations.

Resolved:—That we invite all good women to co-operate with us, by their influence and example to aid in this important enterprize.

On motion the meeting was adjourned till the 19th inst., in the Society Hall, 19th Ward.[275]

Dismissed by prayer by Mrs. Z. [Zina] D. Young.

After which Mrs. Horn carried out the theory of the meeting by seating the entire company at a neatly spread Retrenchment Table, the meal consisting of good bread and butter, with stewed dried apples, one kind of cake, blancmange,[276] with cream and preserves, and cold water, where, with unclogged

---

274. This quotation, perhaps a paraphrase of similar New Testament verses, appears as a part of ordination ceremonies in Roman Catholic, Anglican, and Episcopal orders, and in a variety of nineteenth-century Christian devotional writings. (See 2 Corinthians 8:7; Hebrews 6:11; 2 Peter 1:5, 10; Richard Challoner, *Considerations upon Christian Truths and Christian Duties; Digested into Meditations for Every Day in the Year,* part 3 [London: J. P. Coghlan, 1784], 45; *The Works of Thomas Goodwin, D.D.,* vol. 5, in *Nichol's Series of Standard Divines: Puritan Period,* ed. Rev. Thomas Smith, 12 vols. [Edinburgh: James Nichol, 1863], 391; and Leonard Bacon, "Harriet A. Tucker," *The Home Missionary* 49 [Apr. 1877]: 281; see also *The Thirty Ninth Report of the American Home Missionary Society. Presented by the Executive Committee at the Anniversary Meeting, May 10, 1865* [New York: John A. Gray and Green, 1865], 71–72.)

275. This second meeting actually took place in the Fifteenth Ward Relief Society hall. (See Document 3.16.)

276. An opaque white jelly made from milk boiled with gelatin or corn flour and usually sweetened and flavored. ("Blancmange," in *The Oxford English Dictionary,* ed. James A. H. Murray et al., 12 vols., 1933, reprint [Oxford: Oxford University Press, 1970], 1:900.)

stomachs and unclouded minds, each enjoyed "a feast of reason and a flow of soul."[277]

Mrs. Mary I. Horne, Pres.,
Mrs. Sarah M. Kimball, Sec.

---

277. Alexander Pope, "The First Satire of the Second Book of Horace," *The Poetical Works of Alexander Pope,* 3 vols. (London: William Pickering, 1835), 3:25.

3.16 Ladies' Cooperative Retrenchment Meeting, Minutes, February 19, 1870

Ladies' Cooperative Retrenchment Society, "Minutes of the 2ⁿᵈ Meeting of the Ladies Co-operative Retrenchment Society," Feb. 19, 1870; Fifteenth Ward, Salt Lake Stake, Relief Society Minutes and Records, 1868–1968, vol. 1, 1868–1873, pp. 151–157, CHL (LR 2848 14).

During the nine-day interim between the first meeting of the Ladies' Cooperative Retrenchment Society[278] and this second meeting held on February 19, 1870, Utah's acting territorial governor, Stephen A. Mann, signed into law a woman suffrage bill.[279] When women from various ward Relief Societies gathered for their second retrenchment meeting, they discussed the developing movement for table retrenchment formally initiated nine days earlier. Additionally, they shared a range of opinions regarding their newly granted right to vote and women's rights generally. The varied nature of the discussion suggests that by the second time these Latter-day Saint women assembled as the Ladies' Cooperative Retrenchment Society, they had some sense that this interward gathering could serve as a forum for sharing, vetting, and directing their expanding collective responsibilities.

Mary Isabella Horne, appointed by Brigham Young to bring women from various wards together, had presided at the first cooperative retrenchment meeting; Eliza R. Snow presided at this second meeting. The group was publicly organized at its ninth meeting, in the Fourteenth Ward assembly hall, on May 28, 1870. Horne was "unanimously accepted" as president at the May 28 meeting, as were her nominees of four counselors: Eliza R. Snow, Zina D. H. Young, Margaret T. Smoot, and Sarah M. Kimball. Bathsheba W. Smith and Phebe C. Woodruff were accepted as additional counselors during the June 25, 1870, meeting. The leadership of the society's "Young Ladies' Department," formed on May 27, 1870, was also publicly recognized at the May 28 meeting.[280]

For a time the name of the group was the Senior and Junior Cooperative Retrenchment Association. It was later called General Retrenchment and eventually Ladies' Semi-Monthly Meeting because it met twice monthly until it disbanded early in 1904. Horne served as its president for its entire thirty-four-year existence.[281] In 1870 Relief Societies were organized only at a ward level, but the Cooperative or General Retrenchment meetings began to function as a governing council for the ward organizations. That role is apparent in the following minutes of the February 19, 1870, meeting as the society, working by parliamentary procedure, appointed both individuals and committees to carry out specific

---

278. See Document 3.15.

279. See Document 3.17.

280. See Document 3.18; Susa Young Gates, *History of the Young Ladies' Mutual Improvement Association of the Church of Jesus Christ of Latter-day Saints, from November 1869 to June 1910* (Salt Lake City: Deseret News, 1911), 33–35, 37; and "Minutes of the Ninth Meeting of the Ladys Cooperative Retrenchment Association," May 28, 1870, Zina D. Young Papers, in Zina Card Brown Family Collection, 1806–1972, CHL.

281. See Document 3.18; and "General Retrenchment Meetings," *Woman's Exponent,* July 1904, 33:15.

assignments. This transcript is reproduced from the original minutes of the Fifteenth Ward Relief Society.

———— 〰 ————

Minutes of the 2ⁿᵈ Meeting of the Ladies Cooperative Retrenchment Society.
Held in the Society Hall 15 Ward

Saturday Feb. 19, 1870.

Most of the Wards of the City were represented Miss E R Snow was elected president, and Mrs L[ydia] D Alder Secretary,

Meeting opened with singing. Prayer by Mrs Har[r]iet Young.

Pres E R Snow arose and said

It is our duty to perform all that comes within the province of woman. There is a great diference of opinion in regard to her sphere, but retrenchment is certainly within her sphere, and as Pres Young has given our beloved Sister Horn the mission,[282] to retrench the table in company and social gatherings I feel that we should all assist her, with heart and hand, it will save the sisters straining every nerve and also be a saving in means.

Pres Young has preached against it for years and now Sister Horn has stepped forward and formed a nucleus, the effects of which will reach to Eternity, and the Sisters will follow in her footsteps. I have said enough. the mark that has been made will be felt in future generations.

Mrs S M Kimball the sec' of the previous meeting, read the minutes before the meeting, also Mrs M I Horn's address on that occasion.[283]

Miss E R Snow arose and ~~said~~ stated thos meetings had been held in some of the Wards and requested the sec'ys' present to read the minutes of said meetings.

Mrs Precinda L Kimball sec'y of the 16ᵗʰ ward read the minutes of the Retrenchment meeting held in that ward. Minutes of the meeting in the 15 Ward read by Mrs S M Kimball, [p. 151] of the 20 by Mrs E[liza] S Dunford, of the 7 Ward read by Mrs. M[ary] A Lambert, of the 11 Ward by Mrs Colum [Ann Coulam], of the 13ᵗʰ Ward read by Mrs E[lizabeth] Goddard.[284]

Miss E R Snow, said in explanation, these were only examples, that we should not be confined to any ro[u]tine, but set on our tables that which is wholesome and convenient, and would like to hear from any of the sisters present in regard to the movement on the topic.

---

282. See Document 3.15.

283. See Document 3.15.

284. Minutes of the ward-level retrenchment meetings mentioned here have not been located except those of the Seventh Ward. (Seventh Ward, Salt Lake Stake, Seventh Ward Relief Society Records, 1858–1875, CHL, Feb. 18, 1870.)

Mrs M I Horn,

Expressed her satisfaction, at the willingness of the sisters in aiding her in what was required at her hands. Said pride must be conquered, and we must reform our tables when we have company, let the food be well cooked plain and palatable, said she believed this to be the starting point of the salvation of the People, and now that we have said let us retrench let us do it, so that we will not leave the ground to go over again, spoke of the case of Martha and Mary in the days of Jesus[285] and exhorted all to be faithful and receive the Blessing of God.

Miss E R Snow,

Arose and said to encourage the sisters on in good works she would read an account of our Indignation Meeting, as it appeared in the Sacrament[o] Union,[286] which account she thought a very fair one, she also stated, that an expression of gratitude was due acting Gov Mann for signing the Document of Woman Suffrage in Utah,[287] for, she said we could not have had the right without his sanction, said that other states had passed bills of this kind over the Gov' head, but we could not do this.[288]

The following named persons were elected by unanimous vote to be a Com' for said purpose, E R Snow, Bashaby [Bathsheba] Smith, S M Kimball

---

285. See Luke 10:38–42.

286. See Document 3.13. The *Sacramento Daily Union* published a correspondent's account of the January 13, 1870, "Great Indignation Meeting" held to protest congressional antipolygamy legislation. The account read in part: "Salt Lake City to-day has been the scene of one of the most remarkable assemblages that probably has ever gathered on this continent. . . . [An indignant sisterhood] denounced the bills as unconstitutional, tyrannical, unprecedented in republicanism, unjust, and worthy only of reprobation, while the authors of them were impaled—figuratively, of course—with numerous sharp-pointed utterances. They defended polygamy, and claimed for it divine sanction and command; maintained it was a part of their religion, and as such they were guaranteed protection in its practice by the Constitution. . . . Altogether the meeting was a most astonishing one, and offers another phase of the Mormon problem for consideration; for there was no mistaking the earnestness and determination of purpose of most who were present." ("Letter from Salt Lake," *Sacramento Daily Union,* Jan. 18, 1870, [1].)

287. Utah territorial secretary and acting governor Stephen A. Mann signed the woman suffrage bill into law on February 12, 1870. (See Document 3.17.)

288. In her statement about passage of suffrage bills in other states, Snow may have relied on an inaccurate statement published three days earlier in the *Deseret News.* Praising Mann for signing the woman suffrage bill, the *Deseret News* inaccurately declared him to be "the first Executive to attach the approving signature to such a measure, for the Governor of Wyoming vetoed the bill in that Territory and it was passed over the veto." In fact, when Governor John A. Campbell signed the Wyoming suffrage act on December 10, 1869, he did so without hesitation—rather to the surprise of the territorial legislature, who were expecting his veto. ("The Woman Suffrage Bill," *Deseret News* [weekly], Feb. 16, 1870, 18; Michael A. Massie, "Reform Is Where You Find It: The Roots of Woman Suffrage in Wyoming," *Annals of Wyoming* 62 [Spring 1990]: 2–21; E. A. Thomas, "Female Suffrage in Wyoming," *Potter's American Monthly* 18 [May 1882]: 492–495; Beverly Beeton, *Women Vote in the West: The Woman Suffrage Movement, 1869–1896,* American Legal and Constitutional History [New York: Garland, 1986], 4.)

M T Smoot, H C Young, Z D Young, Phoebe Woodruff M I Horn M N Hide [Marinda Nancy Hyde], Eliz[th] Cannon, Rachel Grant Amanda Smith. [p. 152]

Mrs S M Kimball,

Said that she had waited patiently a long time, and now that we were granted the right of suffrage, she would openly declare herself a womans rights woman, and called upon those who would to back her up, whereupon many manifested their approval. Said her experience in life had been different to that of many, had moved in all grades of Society, had been both rich and poor, had always seen much good and inteligence in woman, the interests of man and woman cannot be seperated, for the man is not without the woman or the woman without the man in the Lord.[289] She spoke of the foolish custom which deprived the mother of having control over her sons at a certain age. Said she saw the foreshadowing of a brighter day in this respect in the future, said she had entertained ideas that appeared wild that she thought would yet be considered woman's rights. Spoke of the remarks made by bro. Rockwood lately,[290] who said women would have as much prejudice to overcome in occupying certain positions as the men would in letting them, said he considered a woman a helpmate in every department of life.

Mrs Phoebe Woodruff,

Said she was pleased with the Reform and was heart and hand with her sisters, was thankful for the privilage that had been granted to women, but thought we must act in wisdom, and not go too fast, had looked for this day for years. God has opened the way for us, we have borne in patience but the yoke on woman is removed, now that God has moved upon our brethren to grant us this privilege, let us lay it by and wait 'til the time comes to use it, and not run headlong and abuse the privilege Great and blessed things are ahead. All is right and will come out right and woman will receive her reward, in blessings and honor. May God grant us strength to do right in his sight. [p. 153]

Mrs Bashaby Smith,

Said she felt pleased, had no objections to anything that had been said has felt to be heart and hand with all, said she never felt better, nor ever felt weaker and the necessity of greater wisdom and light, but felt determined to do the

---

289. See 1 Corinthians 11:11.

290. Albert P. Rockwood, a longtime member of the Utah territorial legislature, may have spoken during the legislative discussion of the woman suffrage bill. During that process, "a number of ladies, for whom seats had been provided, graced the debate with their presence, and listened with much interest." (Dean C. Jessee and David J. Whittaker, "The Last Months of Mormonism in Missouri: The Albert Perry Rockwood Journal," *BYU Studies* 28, no. 1 [Winter 1988]: 5; "Mormon Suffrage," *Deseret Evening News,* Feb. 10, 1870, [3].)

best she could, felt that woman was coming up in the world. should be encouraged, for there is nothing required of us that we cannot perform.

Mrs Pricinda Kimball,

I feel comforted and blessed this day am glad to be numbered, in moving forward in this reform, feel to exercise double diligence, and try to accomplish what is required at our hands, we must all put our shoulders to the wheel and go a head, I am glad to see our daughters elevated with man and the time come when our votes will assist our leaders and redeem ourselves. But be humble, never fail and triumph will be our's, The day is approaching when woman shall be redeemed from the curse placed upon Eve, and I have often thought that our daughters who are in poligamy will be the first redeemed.[291] Then let us keep the Commandments, and attain a fulness, and always bear in mind that our children born in the Priesthood will be saviors on Mount Zion.[292]

Mrs E. Cannon,

Said she had never taken any active part in any of the late moves, was pleased with everything that was said and done, done the best she could with the rest of the sisters, and ask God to bless us all, and help us to carry out the councils we receive from time to time.

Mrs Z D Young,

Said she was glad to look upon such an assemblage of bright and happy faces, and was gratified to be numbered with the Spirits who had taken tabernacles[293] in this dispensation, [p. 154] and know that we are associated with kings and priests of God, thought we do not realize our privillege. Be meek and humble and do not move one step aside that will incur chastisement, but gain power over ourselves, angels will visit the Earth and are we as hand maids

---

291. Snow frequently wrote and spoke of the curse pronounced upon Eve and woman's ultimate restoration to primordial full equality with man. She viewed the practice of plural marriage as "necessary in the elevation and salvation of the human family—in redeeming woman from the curse, and the world from corruptions." George Q. Cannon, a member of the Quorum of the Twelve Apostles, said that plural marriage was "a principle which, if practiced in purity and virtue, as it should be, will result in the exaltation and benefit of the human family; and that it will exalt woman until she is redeemed from the effects of the Fall, and from that curse pronounced upon her in the beginning." (Genesis 3:16; Eliza R. Snow, "Sketch of My Life," n.d., Bancroft Library, University of California, Berkeley, 13; "Discourse," *Deseret News* [weekly], Nov. 3, 1869, 459.)

292. For "saviors on Mount Zion," see Obadiah 1:21; and Doctrine and Covenants 103:9–10. "Born in the priesthood" (also commonly phrased as being "born in the covenant" or being a "child of the covenant") means a child is heir to spiritual blessings as a result of his or her parents being sealed in a temple marriage ceremony. (Brigham Young, Mar. 29, 1868, in *Journal of Discourses,* 26 vols. [Liverpool: Various publishers, 1855–1886], 12:174; Brigham Young, June 23, 1874, in *Journal of Discourses,* 18:249.)

293. That is, human bodies. (See 2 Peter 1:13–14; Moroni 9:6; and Doctrine and Covenants 93:35.)

of the Lord prepared to meet them.[294] We live in the day that has been looked down upon with great anxiety since the morning of Creation. Do we appreciate this? The Brethren have borne with us in our weakness, now let us put our shoulder to the wheel and help them, strengthen them in their duties and live in Joy, peace and union. God help us to be worthy at his coming.

Mrs M T Smoot,

Said she was thankful to be in our midst and was one with the Brethren and sisters in adopting all the principles that are advanced, we are engaged in a good work, and the Principles that we have embraced are life and Salvation unto us. Many principles are advanced on which we are slow to act, but there are many more yet to be advanced. Womans rights have been spoken of. I have never had any desire for more rights than I have. I have always considered these things beneath the sphere of woman. But as things progress I feel it is right that we should vote. I consider the Path frought with great difficulties. I have always sought to vote at conference,[295] and then I felt I had done all I desired to do I have had a voice in my husband taking more wives, for this I am thankful.[296] I have taken pleasure in practicing this pure principle, although I have been tried in it, yet since the birth of our first child by the second wife, I have never felt to dissolve ties thus formed. "Out of the abundance of the Heart the mouth speaketh . . ."[297] Sister Smoot continued at length in speaking on Poligamy and the Duties growing out of it, and exhorted the sisters to be true women of God, to improve and be faithful to the end. [p. 155]

Pres E R Snow moved to add two more to the Committe. Passed.

Mrs [Harriet] Amelia Young and Mrs Pricinda Kimball were added by unanimous vote.

Mrs [Wilmirth] East

Said she would bear testimony to what had been said, she had found by experience "that obedience was better than sacrifice"[298] felt to be on the safe

---

294. See Joel 2:29; and Luke 1:30.

295. See 325n245 herein.

296. The first wife was to have "a voice" by giving her consent before her husband married other wives, a principle that was generally but not universally applied. Smoot later reflected: "In 1845 and 6 my Husband entered into Plural Marriage, by having other women sealed to him in the [Nauvoo] Temple to which I was perfectly willing, and gave my fullest & freeest consent, believing and receiving it as a part of my religion from which I have never faltered or swerved, and I bear my testimony that my Husband and his wives are virtious, chaste and honorable to their marriage vows, and their children are legitamate, and heirs to the Priesthood of God." (Doctrine and Covenants 132:34, 61; Genesis 16:1–2; Margaret T. Smoot, Autobiographical Sketch, 1881, photocopy, CHL, 2.)

297. TEXT: Ellipsis points in original. See Luke 6:45.

298. See 1 Samuel 15:22.

side and sustain those above us, I cannot quite agree with sister Smoot in regard to womans rights, I have never felt that woman had her privileges, I always wanted a voice in the Politics of the Nation, as well as rear a family, I was much impressed when I read the Poem composed by Mrs. Emily Woodmansee, Who cares to win a womans thoughts, I then thought <u>I</u> care to win a woman's thoughts.[299] My sisters this is a bright day, but we need more wisdom and humility than ever before. I am glad to be associated with you those who have borne the heat and burden of the day, and I ask God to pour blessings on their heads continually.

Mrs. [Johanna] Ballon

Expressed herself pleased, and felt that much time spent now in cooking could be used to better advantage, she desired to live humble and be saved in the Kingdom.

Pres E R Snow,

Said there was another business item she wished to present to the meeting and motioned that Sister B Smith be appointed the mission to preach retrenchment all through the South,[300] and womans rights if she wished to—Passed, Sr Snow suggested that the sisters in the wards where they had not held retrenchment meetings to do so and set the example. Sister Horn has not stepped forward a day too soon the hearts of all are prepared for it. I wish you all to lead out that every good woman may join us if she will. [p. 156]

The meeting was adjourned, until Friday March 4th 2 o'clock at the 14th Ward Assembly Room

Singing "Redeemer of Israel,"[301]

Prayer by Mrs M N Hide. [p. 157]

---

299. The referenced poem has not been located. For an example of protest poetry by Emily Hill Woodmansee, see "Give the 'Mormons' Their Rights" in Document 4.15.

300. Bathsheba W. Smith accompanied her husband, George A. Smith, on an extended tour of southern Utah Territory; after their return, he reported having traveled "more than 1,000 miles among the settlements" and visited "perhaps 30,000 people." On at least one occasion during that trip, Bathsheba Smith presided at a retrenchment meeting (in St. George), noting that she had been "appointed to teach table retrenchment." ("Remarks," *Deseret Evening News,* Apr. 30, 1870, [2]; "Minutes of Ladies Cooperative Retrenchment Meeting," Mar. 26, 1870, Bathsheba W. Smith Collection, 1842–1948, CHL.)

301. Hymn 119, *A Collection of Sacred Hymns for the Church of Jesus Christ of Latter Day Saints,* ed. Emma Smith (Nauvoo, IL: E. Robinson, 1841), 127.

3.17 Eliza R. Snow and Others, Letter to Stephen A. Mann, and Stephen A. Mann Reply, February 19, 1870

Eliza R. Snow, Bathsheba W. Smith, Sarah M. Kimball, Margaret T. Smoot, Harriet C. Young, Zina D. H. Young, Mary Isabella Horne, Marinda N. Hyde, Phebe C. Woodruff, Elizabeth H. Cannon, Rachel I. Grant, Amanda Barnes Smith, Harriet Amelia F. Young, and Presendia H. Kimball, "To His Excellency, the Acting Governor of the Territory of Utah, S. A. Mann," Feb. 19, 1870; and Stephen A. Mann, "To Eliza R. Snow, Bathsheba W. Smith, Marinda N. Hyde, Phebe C. Woodruff, Amelia F. Young and Others," Feb. 19, 1870, Deseret News *[weekly] (Salt Lake City, UT), Mar. 2, 1870, vol. 19, no. 4, p. 1.*

The Utah territorial legislature debated whether to extend voting rights to women from January 27, 1870, until February 10, when both chambers of the legislature (the House and the Council) unanimously passed an act conferring woman suffrage.[302] Territorial secretary and acting governor Stephen A. Mann signed the bill two days later.[303] A native of Vermont, Mann became acting governor in December 1869 when Governor Charles Durkee, at the end of his term, returned to Wisconsin. Mann served four months before the arrival of John Wilson Shaffer, who was appointed governor by President Ulysses S. Grant on January 17, 1870, and arrived in Utah two months later.[304] Mann favorably impressed Latter-day Saint leaders. George A. Smith wrote to territorial delegate William H. Hooper, "We have come to the conclusion that the Governor is really A Man, and instead of being influenced by the ring of hungry agitators, he has exercised his own Judgement, in his relations with the Legislative Assembly, and no Session has gone off more pleasantly since Governor Youngs administration terminated."[305]

The female suffrage bill's unanimous passage by the legislature convinced Mann to sign it into law, even though he wrote to the legislature that he had "very grave and serious doubts of the wisdom and soundness of that political economy which makes the act a law of this Territory, and that there are many reasons which, in my judgment, are opposed to the legislation." On February 14, two days after Mann signed the bill, women voted in a municipal election in Salt Lake City, and women voted at the regular election that August.[306]

On February 19 the Ladies' Cooperative Retrenchment Society met in the hall of the Fifteenth Ward, with representatives from most Salt Lake City wards present. Eliza R. Snow, who presided over the meeting, suggested that the women write "an expression of gratitude" to Governor Mann "for signing the Document of Woman Suffrage in Utah, for,

---

302. See Document 3.14.

303. Thomas G. Alexander, "An Experiment in Progressive Legislation: The Granting of Woman Suffrage in Utah in 1870," *Utah Historical Quarterly* 38, no. 1 (Winter 1970): 26.

304. Thomas A. McMullin and David Walker, *Biographical Directory of American Territorial Governors* (Westport, CT: Meckler, 1984), 300.

305. George A. Smith to William H. Hooper, Feb. 19, 1870, Historian's Office, Letterpress Copybooks, 1854–1879, 1885–1886, CHL.

306. Steven A. Mann to Orson Pratt, Feb. 12, 1870, in "The Woman Suffrage Bill," *Deseret News* [weekly], Feb. 16, 1870, 18–19; Alexander, "An Experiment in Progressive Legislation," 27.

she said we could not have had the right without his sanction."³⁰⁷ The group then selected a committee to write a letter to Mann, which wrote the letter and delivered it to Mann that same day, February 19. George A. Smith commented, "The Ladies said they thought the Governor was about as much embarrass'd as they were."³⁰⁸ On March 2 the weekly edition of the *Deseret News* published the letter to Mann along with his reply, also dated February 19. Both letters are featured below. On the same page where the letters appeared, the *Deseret News* also published a joint resolution of the territorial legislature, praising Mann for "wa[i]ving his personal objections and submitting his Executive prerogative in favor of the unanimous decision and undivided wishes of the Legislative body" in regard to female suffrage.³⁰⁹

——— ❧ ———

Letter to Stephen A. Mann, February 19, 1870

To his Excellency, the Acting Governor of the Territory of Utah, S. A. Mann.

Honored Sir.—In a large and highly respectable assemblage of ladies now convened in the Fifteenth Ward Society Hall—being unanimously chosen committee, we, in conformity with the appointment, for ourselves, and in behalf of the ladies of this Territory, do most respectfully tender you our sincere thanks and grateful acknowledgements for the honor you have conferred on our Honorable Legislature and on the ladies of Utah, by the noble liberality and gentlemanly kindness manifested in signing the Bill entitled "An Act conferring upon women the Elective Franchise."

We beg you to accept this humble expression as a testimonial of our appreciation.

ELIZA R. SNOW,
BATHSHEBA W. SMITH,
SARAH M. KIMBALL,
MARGARET T. SMOOT,
HARRIET C. YOUNG,
ZINA D. YOUNG,
MARY I. HORNE,
MARINDA N. HYDE,
PHEBE C. WOODRUFF,
ELIZABETH H. CANNON,
RACHEL I. GRANT,
AMANDA SMITH,

307. Document 3.16.
308. George A. Smith to William H. Hooper, Feb. 19, 1870, Historian's Office, Letterpress Copybooks.
309. "Joint Resolution of Respect," *Deseret News* [weekly], Mar. 2, 1870, 37.

[Harriet] Amelia F. Young;
Prescendia H. Kimball.

"Society Hall," Salt Lake City,
Feb. 19th, 1870.

Stephen A. Mann Reply, February 19, 1870

Executive Office, U.T.
February 19th, 1870.

To Eliza R. Snow, Bathsheba W. Smith, Marinda N. Hyde, Phebe C. Woodruff, Amelia F. Young and others:

Ladies:—Permit me to say, in reply to your communication of this day, containing the "expressions of a meeting held at Society Hall" as well as on behalf of the ladies of the Territory, of the grateful acknowledgments and appreciations of my official conduct in approving an act entitled: "An Act conferring upon women the elective franchise." It is at all times a source of satisfaction to receive assurances of approval and encouragement in the performance of an official duty, more especially is this the case when the act performed is out of the usual channels and one to which we cannot apply the tests of experience. It is unnecessary for me to state, that this is a new and untrod field of legislation. The subject has been much agitated and we may naturally expect that its practical application, wherever adopted, will be watched with profound interest, for upon its consistent and harmonious working depends, in a great measure, its universal adoption in this Republic. Under a government like ours there is no question of so great importance as that of suffrage. It is the basis upon which the whole superstructure rests, and upon the quality of which depends its advancement, stability and duration. The Constitution, the laws passed in pursuance therewith, the officers elected thereunder all depend for their character upon the intelligent use of the ballot.

Thanking you for the compliment, I will close by expressing the confident hope, that the ladies of this Territory will so exercise the right conferred as to approve the wisdom of the legislation.

I have the honor to be, very respectfully yours,

S. A. Mann.
Acting Governor.

3.18 Young Ladies' Department of the Ladies' Cooperative Retrenchment Association, Resolutions, May 27, 1870

Young Ladies' Department of the Ladies' Cooperative Retrenchment Association, Resolutions, May 27, 1870, in "Resolutions Adopted by the First Young Ladies' Department of the Ladies' Co-operative Retrenchment Association, S.L. City, Organized May 27, 1870," Deseret Evening News *(Salt Lake City, UT), June 20, 1870, vol. 3, no. 178, p. [2].*

During 1869 and 1870, Latter-day Saint women developed a distinct organization for young women, the first such organization in the church's history.[310] This organization, the Young Ladies' Department of the Ladies' Cooperative Retrenchment Association, was initiated in response to Brigham Young's call for simplification in meal preparation, housekeeping, and clothing.[311] The Young Ladies' Department operated both in connection with and separately from the Relief Society.

The first young ladies' organization consisted of Brigham Young's adolescent and young adult daughters (ranging in age from fourteen to twenty-two), both married and unmarried. According to Maria Young Dougall and her sister Susa Young Gates, their father frequently spoke of the importance of organizing his daughters so that his family might "set an example to the daughters of Zion that would be worthy of imitation." Indeed, for several months before the organization, Brigham Young had articulated the concern for reform to members of his large family, particularly to those who gathered for evening prayers at their Salt Lake City residence, the Lion House. Both Dougall and Gates recalled that the initial organization meeting for the Young daughters occurred on Sunday evening, November 28, 1869, two weeks after Young publicly called for reform in the Salt Lake tabernacle.[312] This is traditionally considered the founding date, though the exact events of that evening are unclear; the daughters' memories of the November 28 gathering seem to have been conflated with a similar Lion House gathering six months later. Notes in the Historian's Office Journal for May 25, 1870, recorded that "at prayer time" Young assembled "quite a large number of his family together" along with church historian George A. Smith and his wife, Bathsheba W. Smith. Following prayer, Young told his family that "the eyes of the world were upon them also the eyes of the Saints. . . . He wished his wives and

---

310. An earlier organization that included both single men and women under the age of thirty—a "Young Gentlemen and Ladies Relief Society of Nauvoo"—had been established in 1843 to organize charitable activities. (Glen M. Leonard, *Nauvoo: A Place of Peace, a People of Promise* [Salt Lake City: Deseret Book; Provo, UT: Brigham Young University Press, 2002], 226–227; "A Short Sketch of the Rise of the Young Gentlemen and Ladies Relief Society of Nauvoo," *Times and Seasons*, Apr. 1, 1843, 4:154–157.)

311. See Documents 3.15 and 3.16.

312. Maria Young Dougall, "Reminiscences," *Young Woman's Journal* 30, no. 11 (Nov. 1919): 594; Susa Young Gates, *History of the Young Ladies' Mutual Improvement Association of the Church of Jesus Christ of Latter-day Saints, from November 1869 to June 1910* (Salt Lake City: Deseret News, 1911), 5–12; "Remarks," *Deseret News* [weekly], Nov. 24, 1869, 495–496.

daughters always to adopt their own fashions and to set an example and as far as possible to manufacture what they wore."[313]

On May 27, 1870, which should be considered the formal founding date of the young ladies' organization, Young's daughters organized themselves as the First Young Ladies' Department of the Ladies' Cooperative Retrenchment Association and adopted resolutions composed by Eliza R. Snow,[314] one of Young's plural wives and an avid proponent of reform.[315] The resolutions, as published in the *Deseret Evening News* the following month, are reproduced below.[316] Dougall recalled subsequent meetings where the Young daughters received instructions from older women, including Snow, then assisting with the organization of ward Relief Societies, and Mary Isabella Horne, newly elected president of the Ladies' Cooperative Retrenchment Association.[317] "We were to have resolutions and by-laws," Dougall remembered, "and we were to retrench in our clothing."[318] Four days later, on May 31, the Second Young Ladies' Department of the Ladies' Cooperative Retrenchment Association was organized by another group of young women.[319] Thereafter Retrenchment Associations were organized in various Salt Lake City wards and other settlements, following the pattern set here whereby older women encouraged and directed younger women. In Salt Lake City, the first "young ladies' departments" both met on their own and joined with older women twice monthly in the Senior and Junior Ladies' Cooperative Retrenchment Association. The young ladies' departments soon became known as the Young Ladies'

313. Church History Department, Historical Department Office Journal, 1844–2012, 102 vols., CHL, 31:71. According to an account written by Susa Young Gates several decades later, the November 28, 1869, meeting included George A. and Bathsheba Smith and resulted in the resolutions featured in this document. However, the Church Historian's Office journal indicates that George A. Smith was away from Salt Lake City from November 26 to 30, 1869, and the journal's November 28 entry notes no Lion House meeting. Gates's account, apparently drawn from her own memory and from recollections Bathsheba Smith shared privately with Gates, evidently conflates the initial November 28, 1869, meeting with the May 25, 1870, gathering in the Lion House. (See Gates, *History of the Young Ladies' Mutual Improvement Association,* 5–12; Church History Department, Office Journal, 30:363–365; and Maria Young Dougall, "Reminiscences," *Young Woman's Journal* 30, no. 11 [Nov. 1919]: 594–595.)

314. A manuscript copy of the resolutions made about nine years later includes this note: "We record as belonging to the history of the Y.L.M.I. Association, the following copy of the original 'Resolutions,' as written by the hand of its author, Miss E. R. Snow." (Salt Lake Stake, Young Women's Mutual Improvement Association Minutes and Records, 1871–1973, 5 vols., CHL, vol. 1, 5–7.)

315. For more on Snow's influence in the early young women's organization, see Thirteenth Ward, Ensign Stake, Relief Society Minutes and Records, 1868–1906, CHL, vol. 1, June 2, 1870; Maria Young Dougall, "Reminiscences," *Young Woman's Journal* 30, no. 11 (Nov. 1919): 595; and Clarissa Young Spencer and Mabel Harmer, *Brigham Young at Home* (Salt Lake City: Deseret Book, 1940), 82–86.

316. A handwritten version of these resolutions produced around this same time is extant in the Zina D. Young Papers. As compared to the *Deseret Evening News* version reproduced below, the copy included in Young's papers displays multiple textual variants. The relationship between the *Deseret Evening News* and handwritten versions is unclear. (See "Articles Subscribed to and Adopted by the Young Ladies Department of the Ladies Co-operative Retrenchment Association," n.d., Zina D. Young Papers, Zina Card Brown Family Collection, 1806–1972, CHL.)

317. See Document 3.16.

318. Maria Young Dougall, "Reminiscences," *Young Woman's Journal* 30, no. 11 (Nov. 1919): 594–595.

319. "Resolutions," *Deseret News* [weekly], June 29, 1870, 249.

Retrenchment Association; in 1877 the organization was officially renamed the Young Ladies' Mutual Improvement Association, often abbreviated Y.L.M.I.A.[320]

———— ❧ ————

RESOLUTIONS
Adopted by the First Young Ladies' Department of the Ladies' Co-operative Retrenchment Association, S.L. City, organized May 27, 1870.

Resolved.—That, realizing ourselves to be wives and daughters of Apostles, Prophets and Elders of Israel, and, as such, that high responsibilities rest upon us, and that we shall be held accountable to God, not only for the privileges we inherit from our fathers, but also for the blessings we enjoy as Latter-day Saints, we feel to unite and co-operate with, and do mutually pledge ourselves that we will uphold and sustain each other in doing good.

Resolved.—That, inasmuch as the Saints have been commanded to gather out from Babylon and "n[o]t[321] partake of her sins, that they receive not of her plagues,"[322] we feel that we should not condescend to imitate the pride, folly and fashions of the world; and inasmuch as the church of Jesus Christ is likened unto a city set on a hill to be a beacon of light to all nations, it is our duty to set examples for others, instead of seeking to pattern after them.

Resolved.—That we will respect ancient and modern apostolic instructions. St. Paul exhorted Timothy to teach "the women to adorn themselves in modest apparel—not with braided hair, or gold or pearls, or costly array; but which becometh women pro[f]essing godliness, with good works."[323] Peter, also, in his first epi[s]tle,[324] in speaking of women, says, "Whose adorning, let it not be that outward adorning of plaiting the hair, and wearing of gold, or of putting on apprrel; but let it be the hidden man of the heart, in that which is not corruptible, even the ornament of a meek and quiet spirit, which is in the sight of God, of great price: for after this manner in old time, the holy women also, who trusted in God, adorned themselves."[325] In a revelation given to the Latter-day Saints in 1831, the Lord said, "Thou shalt not be proud in thy heart; let all thy garments be plain, and their beauty, the beauty of the work of thine own

---

320. On the name change, see Brigham Young to Don Carlos and Feramorz Little Young, Aug. 6, 1877, in Brigham Young Office Files, 1832–1878, CHL; and "Home Affairs," *Woman's Exponent,* Oct. 1, 1877, 6:68.

321. TEXT: In the copy used for transcription, there is a blank space between the *n* and the *t*.

322. Revelation 18:4.

323. 1 Timothy 2:9–10.

324. TEXT: In the copy used for transcription, there is a blank space between the *i* and the *t*.

325. 1 Peter 3:3–5.

hands."[326] All of which, we accept as true principle, and such as should be fully illustrated in our practice.

Resolved.—That, with a firm and settled determination to honor the foregoing requirements, and being deeply sensible of the sinful ambition and vanity in dress among the daughters of Zion, which are calculated to foster the pride of the world, and shut out the spirit of God from the heart, we mutually agree to exert our influence, both by precept and by example, to suppress, and to eventually eradicate these evils.

Resolved.—That, admitting variety has its charms, we know that real beauty appears to greater advantage in a plain dress than when bedizened with finery, and while we disapprobate extravagance and waste, we would not, like the Quakers, recommend a uniform, but would have each one to choose the style best adapted to her own taste and person:[327] at the same time we shall avoid, and ignore as obsolete with us, all extremes which are opposed to good sense, or repulsive to modesty.

Resolved.—That, inasmuch as cleanliness is a characteristic of a Saint, and an imperative duty, we shall discard the dragging skirts, and, for decency's sake, those disgustingly short ones, extending no lower than the boot tops. We also regard "paniers," and whatever approximates in appearance toward the "Grecian Bend," a burlesque on the natural beauty and dignity of the human female form, and will not disgrace our persons by wearing them.[328] And, also,

---

326. Doctrine and Covenants 42:40.

327. George Fox, founder of the Religious Society of Friends (or Quakers), recommended simplicity and plainness in dressing as a precaution against vanity and pride, but clothing was not confined to uniform colors or designs. (See Thomas Clarkson, *A Portraiture of Quakerism. Taken from a View of the Education and Discipline, Social Manners, Civil and Political Economy, Religious Principles and Character, of the Society of Friends,* 3 vols. [New York: Samuel Stansbury, 1806], 1:241–267; Mary Anne Caton, "The Aesthetics of Absence: Quaker Women's Plain Dress in the Delaware Valley, 1790–1900," in *Quaker Aesthetics: Reflections on a Quaker Ethic in American Design and Consumption,* ed. Emma Jones Lapsansky and Anne A. Verplanck [Philadelphia: University of Pennsylvania Press, 2003], 246–271.)

328. A "panier" was a "frame of whalebone, wire or other material, used to distend the skirt of a woman's dress at the hips," or "a bunched up part of a skirt forming a protuberance behind." The "Grecian bend" was originally a term applied to a bent posture: "An affected carriage of the body, in which it is bent forward from the hips." At this time, the "Grecian bend" referred to the silhouette achieved when a dress skirt was straight at the front and sides with extreme fullness at the back. A *Deseret News* editorial commented that "fashions have passed from enormous crinolines, which made their wearers look like huge bells, to the long trains which spread out like a peacock's tail, to the present fashion of lank skirts, the short walking costume, the Grecian bend, and the panier." Brigham Young asked Relief Society members to avoid the "Grecian bend," adding that "so far as my taste is concerned I would much rather see a 'Mormon bend' than a 'Grecian bend.'" ("Grecian," and "Pannier," in *The Oxford English Dictionary,* ed. James A. H. Murray et al., 12 vols., 1933, reprint [Oxford: Oxford University Press, 1970], 4:392, 7:425; "Fashions—A Much Needed Reform," *Deseret News* [weekly], June 29, 1870, 246; "Discourse," *Deseret News* [weekly], Aug. 18, 1869, 331–332; see also Carma de Jong Anderson, "Mormon Clothing in Utah, 1847–1900," in *Nearly Everything Imaginable: The Everyday Life of Utah's Mormon Pioneers,* ed. Ronald W.

as fast as it shall be expedient, we shall adopt the wearing of home-made articles, and exercise our united influence in rendering them fashionable.

Mrs. Ella Y. Emp[e]y, Pres.[329]

Mrs. Emily Y. Clawson,

Mrs. Zina Y. Williams,

Mrs. Maria Y. McDougal [Dougall],

Mrs. Caroline Y. Croxall,

Miss Dora [Eudora] Young,

Miss Phebe Young,

Counselors.

Walker and Doris R. Dant, *Studies in Latter-day Saint History* [Provo, UT: Brigham Young University Press, 1999], 175–194; and Ruth Vickers Clayton, "Clothing and the Temporal Kingdom: Mormon Clothing Practices, 1847 to 1887" [PhD diss., Purdue University, 1987], 191.)

329. The version of this document in the Zina Young Papers adds to this list of officers the name of Henrietta L. Southworth—presumably as secretary, although not identified as such. ("Articles Subscribed to and Adopted by the Young Ladies Department of the Ladies Co-operative Retrenchment Association.")

3.19 Nephi Ward Relief Society, Minutes, August–September 1870

Nephi Ward Relief Society, Minutes, Aug. 10–Sept. 1, 1870; five pages; Nephi Ward, Juab Stake, Relief Society Minutes and Records, 1868–1878, vol. 1, 1868–1878, CHL (LR 6002 14).

Latter-day Saints began settling Nephi (originally called Salt Creek) in Juab Valley in 1851; by 1870 the community had nearly thirteen hundred residents.[330] Heeding President Brigham Young's 1867 call to organize branches of the Relief Society throughout Mormon settlements,[331] Nephi Ward bishop Charles H. Bryan held a meeting of women on June 23, 1868, to organize a society and select officers. Bryan appointed Amelia Hallam Goldsbrough as president, Elizabeth Silcox Kendall and Jane Phillips Picton as counselors, Frances Jane Hodson Andrews as treasurer, and Amy Lorette Chase Bigler as secretary. By the end of the first year, the Nephi Relief Society had 144 members, with 30 teachers on the visiting committee and 3 members of a board of appraisers.[332]

Featured below are minutes of three meetings recorded in the Nephi Relief Society Minute Book by secretary Amy Bigler. These selected minutes—for August 10, August 24, and September 1, 1870—suggest that the Nephi women, several of whom had recently visited Salt Lake City, perceived differences between their rural society and the Relief Society units of the more prosperous Salt Lake City wards. Nephi residents had limited access to the manufactured goods available in Salt Lake City. For instance, Salt Lake City offered bakeries and clothing patterns, a situation that partly prompted the calls by Brigham Young and other leaders for Latter-day Saints to retrench and focus more on home manufacture.[333] The Nephi Saints probably had less need for such reminders. As rural Saints, the women of Nephi worked from scratch: they carded, spun, and knitted their own wool; made their own clothes, dresses, and blankets; tended vegetable gardens; and baked their own bread. The detailed donation list included with the minutes of the September 1 meeting gives a glimpse into the lifestyle and economy of the community.

---

330. "History," Andrew Jenson, comp., in Nephi Ward, Juab Stake, Nephi Ward Manuscript History and Historical Reports, 1847–1900, CHL; Francis A. Walker, comp., *Ninth Census–Volume I. The Statistics of the Population of the United States. . . . Compiled, from the Original Returns of the Ninth Census, (June 1, 1870,) under the Direction of the Secretary of the Interior* (Washington DC: Government Printing Office, 1872), 275.

331. See Document 3.1.

332. Nephi Ward, Juab Stake, Nephi Ward Relief Society Minutes and Records, 1868–1878, CHL, June 26, 1869.

333. See Document 3.15. In 1869 Salt Lake City's business listings included five flour mills, five ice cream sellers, six milliners, eight bakeries, eight confectioners, eight hairdressers, nine specialists for gloves and mittens, eleven suppliers of produce and grain, thirteen sources for "fancy goods," seventeen tailors and drapers, seventeen clothing stores, twenty-one dry goods providers, and thirty-two general merchandise stores. (E. L. Sloan, comp., *The Salt Lake City Directory and Business Guide, for 1869* [Salt Lake City: By the author, 1869], 153–171.)

August 10, 1870 • Wednesday

Fifty Sixth Meeting of the Female Relief Society Nephi Social Hall[334] Aug 10, 1870, 1 Oclock PM

Met according to appointment

Called to order by Sister Elizabeth Kendall

Singing And are we yet alive[335]

Prayer by Sister Eliza Bigler

Singing Prayer is the souls sincere desire[336]

Roll called minutes read and accepted

By request Sister A L Bigler related (as far as she could recollect) a conversation had by herself Sister A Goldsbrough and Sister Bathsheba W Smith who is first councellor to the Presidentess of her ward in Salt L City[337]

Remarks by <u>Mrs</u> President said she always felt a diffidence in getting up before the sisters, but felt it a duty

said she was very happy in the society of Sister Smith and that Sister Bigler had given the most of her remarks, said we could see quite a difference in the ~~difference~~ manner of carrying on our meetings to the way they did in the city but presumed we entered into more branches of business than they did have more to do and more to look after, said some might ask what was done with the means that we handled Thought that such people should come and see what was done before they jumped at a conclusion[338] Spoke at some length on the duties of the society and of living faithful before the Lord [p. [1]][339]

---

334. In this period the Nephi Relief Society generally met either in the town's log schoolhouse or in the social hall mentioned here. The Relief Society began construction on a hall, which would be an adobe building located on Main Street, in 1871; the hall was first used on June 24, 1876, at the 208th meeting of the Nephi Relief Society. The building was dedicated November 30, 1881. (Nephi Ward, Juab Stake, Relief Society, Minutes, June 24, 1876; "Relief Society," Andrew Jenson, comp., in Nephi Ward, Juab Stake, Manuscript History and Historical Reports, 1847–1900, CHL.)

335. Hymn 81, *A Collection of Sacred Hymns for the Church of Jesus Christ of Latter Day Saints,* ed. Emma Smith (Nauvoo, IL: E. Robinson, 1841), 90.

336. G. Careless, "Prayer," *Utah Musical Times* 1 (Sept. 1876): 104; see also Karen Lynn Davidson, *Our Latter-day Hymns: The Stories and the Messages* (Salt Lake City: Deseret Book, 1988), 170–171.

337. Amy Bigler and Amelia Goldsbrough had visited with Bathsheba W. Smith in Salt Lake City. Bigler's husband, Jacob G. Bigler, was Smith's brother. Smith, wife of apostle George A. Smith, served as a counselor to Rachel Ivins Grant in the Thirteenth Ward Relief Society. (Thirteenth Ward, Ensign Stake, Thirteenth Ward Relief Society Minutes and Records, 1849–1908, vol. 1, CHL, Nov. 5, 1868.)

338. The next year, when charitable donations were low, counselor Elizabeth Kendall remarked that "she understood that some did not feel like giving any more because they did not know what was done with the means If they would attend meeting they would know But supposed we should always have busy bodies among us." (Nephi Ward, Juab Stake, Relief Society, Minutes, Nov. 30, 1871.)

339. TEXT: The original minute book is not paginated at this point, so pagination supplied here will be for the selected entries presented here, rather than for the minute book.

Sister Frances J Andrews being requested gave a short account of a visit which she made to a meeting of the Female Relief Society in salt Lake City spoke of the manner which they carried on their meeting, spoke of having a chat with sister Eliza Snow

Sister Ann Ashdown and Maria Garret were then presented for membership and ac by unanimous vote Meeting then closed

Singing The day is past and gone[340]

Dismissed by Sister Ruth Hayward to meet again on the 24th of Aug at 1 Oclock PM

A L Bigler Sec

August 24, 1870 • Wednesday

Fifty Seventh Meeting of the Female Relief Society Nephi Social Hall Aug 24 [1870] 1 Oclock PM

Met according to appointment

Called to order by Mrs President

Singing Sweetly may the blessed spirit[341]

Prayer by sister Elizabeth Grace

Singing Once more we come before our God[342]

Roll called minutes read and accepted

The matter of collecting Donations before fast day was spoken of by Sister Goldsbrough and thought best to be attended to at that time according to previous arrangement[343]

Sister Mary Ockey [Okey] was then presented for membership and accepted by unanimous vote also Sister Agnes T Barrowman [Borrowman]

Fold work and close

Singing How will the saints rejoice to tell[344]

Dismissed by sister Jane Foot [Nancy Jane Foote] to meet again on the 7th of Sept at 1 Oclock PM[345]

A L Bigler Sec [p. [2]]

------

340. Hymn 204, *Collection of Sacred Hymns*, 223.

341. Hymn 48, *Sacred Hymns and Spiritual Songs. For the Church of Jesus Christ of Latter-day Saints,* 13th ed. (Liverpool: Albert Carrington; London: L. D. Saints' Book Depot, 1869), 60.

342. Hymn 91, *A Collection of Sacred Hymns, for the Church of Jesus Christ of Latter-day Saints, in Europe,* selected by Brigham Young, Parley P. Pratt, and John Taylor (Manchester: W. R. Thomas, 1840), 105.

343. Following Joseph Smith's pattern of holding a fast day in Kirtland, Ohio, Brigham Young designated the first Thursday of each month as fast day in Utah. During their visiting routes in Nephi, the Relief Society teachers collected fast offerings along with regular donations for the poor. (See Document 3.1.)

344. Hymn 115, *Collection of Sacred Hymns* [1841], 123.

345. Before the planned September 7 meeting of the society was held, a meeting of the board and teachers was held on September 1, 1870.

September 1, 1870 • Thursday

Fifty Eighth Meeting of the Female Relief Society Nephi Social Hall <u>Sept</u> 1ˢᵗ [1870] 2 Oclock PM

according to previous arrangements the Board and teachers met to attend to whatever business might be on hand, to call in the Donation bills[346] and have a testimony meeting Called to order by <u>Mrs</u> President A Goldsbrough

Singing Great God attend while Zion sings[347]

Prayer by sister A Goldsbrough

Singing We thank thee O Lord for a prophet[348]

Donation bills called in as follows

Miss Maria [Mary] Harley by sack making	90
" Harriet Carter by spining 3 skeins of yarn	30
Mrs Mary Brough 1 skein of yarn	35
" Elsie [Mary Elsa] Price 10 lbs of flour	30
" Jerusha Bosnell [Gerusha Boswell] soap	08
" Hannah Foot[e] 10 lbs of flour	30
" Elizabeth Hague 11 lbs of flour	33
" Sarah Cazier rolls[349]	70
" Frances J. Andrews 4 doz of apples	60
" Harriet Broadhead by spining and washing 3 skeins yarn	50
" Maria Love 10 lbs of flour	30
" Sarah Tranter ½ doz eggs	09
" Esther Ockey 3 eggs	04½
" Rebecca Wilson 8 lbs of flour	24
" Ann Andrews rolls	55
" Sarah Baily 1 qt of mulasses	37½
" Eve Riches 1 spool of cotton	10
" Alice Atkinson 1 doz of eggs	18
" Elizabeth Lunt 1 skein of yarn	35
" Susanna Goble 1 doz eggs	18

346. At Relief Society meetings, the teachers turned in "donation bills" indicating what each woman had donated. Since in-kind tithes were stored in the Nephi tithing office, it is likely that the Nephi Relief Society members also stored fast offerings and other donations there, at least until they had their own hall. As cash was scarce, the tithing office functioned as a kind of local bank. (For example, see "Mail Coach," *Deseret News,* May 14, 1853, [4].)

347. Hymn 88, *Collection of Sacred Hymns* [1841], 97.

348. Hymn 152, *Sacred Hymns and Spiritual Songs. For the Church of Jesus Christ of Latter-day Saints,* 12th ed. (Liverpool: George W. Cannon; London: L. D. Saints' Book Depot, 1863), 166.

349. The "rolls" listed among these donations were likely small quantities of carded wool brought from a carding mill ready for spinning. ("Roll," in *The Oxford English Dictionary,* ed. James A. H. Murray et al., 12 vols., 1933, reprint [Oxford: Oxford University Press, 1970], 8:756.)

Fifty Eighth Meeting of the Female Relief Society Nephi social Hall Sept 1st 2 Oclock 1873

According to previous arrangements the Board and teachers met to attend to whatever business might be on hand, to call in the donation bills and have a testimony meeting   Called to order by Mrs President A Goldsbrough

Singing Great God attend while Zion sings

Prayer by sister A Goldsbrough

Singing We thank thee O Lord for a prophet

Donation bills called in as follows

Miss Maria Harley by sack making	90
" Harriet Carter by spining 3 skeins of yarn	30
Mrs Mary Brough 1 skein of yarn	35
" Elsie Price 10 lbs of flour	30
" Jerusha Booknell soap	08
" Hannah Foot 10 lbs of flour	30
" Elizabeth Hague 11 lbs of flour	33
" Sarah Cazier rolls	70
" Frances J Andrews 4 doz of apples	40
" Harriet Broadhead by spining and washing 3 skeins yarn	50
" Maria Love 10 lbs of flour	30
" Sarah Tranter ½ doz eggs	09
" Esther Ockey 3 eggs	04½
" Rebecca Wilson 8 lbs of flour	24
" Ann Andrews rolls	55
" Sarah Baily 1 qt of molasses	37½
" Eve Riches 1 spool of cotton	10
" Alice Atkinson 1 doz of eggs	18
" Elizabeth Lunt 1 skein of yarn	35
" Susanna Goble 1 doz eggs	18
" Emma Beal wool	25
" Sarah Birchall 1 skein of yarn	35
" Elizabeth Miller 1 skein of yarn	35
" Mary Midgley 7½ lbs of flour	22½
" Hannah Jenkins 2½ lbs of flour	07½
" Elizabeth Clark 1 doz of apples	15

List of donations in Nephi minutes. This September 1, 1870, entry in the Nephi, Utah, Relief Society Minute Book lists member donations and gives a glimpse into the lifestyle and economy of the community. The handwriting here is that of Amy L. Bigler, secretary of the Nephi Relief Society at this time. (Church History Library, Salt Lake City.)

" Emma Beal wool	25
" Sarah Berchall [Birchall] 1 skein of yarn	35
" Elizabeth Miller 1 skein of yarn	35
" Mary Midgley 7 ½ lbs of flour	22½
" Hannah Jenkins 2 ½ lbs of flour	07½
" Elizabeth [Ashford] Clark 1 doz of apples	15

[p. [3]]

	$ cts
Mrs Anna Wilkey 1 spool of cotton	10
" Sarah Ann [Hannah] Andrews 2 skeins of linen thread	20
" Charlotte Rollins 1 lb of Butter	15
" Mary Ann Ostler 9 lbs of flour	27
" Harriet Lunt by knitting	25
" Sarah Tolley 2nd 1 spool of cotton	10
Miss Emma Goldsbrough patches	05
Mrs A Goldsbrough sundries	65
" Ellen Goldsbrough carpet rags	05
" Susan Sidwell 1 spool of cotton	10
" Miranda Bryan 2 doz of apples	30
" Elizabeth Grace 7 lbs of flour	21
" Madalene [Mary Madeline] Pyper 1 skein of yarn	35
" Sarah McCune 1 skein of yarn	35
" Elizabeth Godfrey ⟨3 lb⟩ corn meal	09
" Nancy Ann Bigler 1 doz apples	10
" A L Bigler by Indigo[350] and labor	30
" Elizabeth Howles 1 skein of yarn	35

After the bills were disposed of Sister Goldsbrough said the meeting was now open for all to speak that felt to do so

Sister Jane Picton said she felt thankful for a standing in this church and that she was associated with this society Felt that there were many trials to pass through but said the Lord would assist us if we would call upon him Realized he had strengthened her many times and blessed her abundantly hoped that all might prove faithful and gain a place in the Kingdom of heaven

---

350. Indigo bush (*Psorothamnus fremontii* or *Dalea fremontii*) grows natively throughout Utah as a perennial shrub with vivid blue and purple flowers. Indigo bush could be used to make a colored dye and also had a practical medicinal use: the roots could be boiled into a tea to treat gastrointestinal problems or internal hemorrhaging. (Daniel E. Moerman, *Native American Medicinal Plants: An Ethnobotanical Dictionary* [Portland: Timber Press, 2009], 395–396; Raymond M. Turner et al., *Sonoran Desert Plants: An Ecological Atlas* [Tucson: University of Arizona Press, 2005], 335; P. A. Rydberg, *Flora of the Rocky Mountains and Adjacent Plains* [New York: By the author, 1917], 482–483.)

Sisters [Elizabeth] Sowby[,] Hayward[,] Bigler[,] Jones[,] Kendall[,] Wilkey[,] Heinkie [Kienke][,] Broadhead[,] Bryan[,] Wright all bore a faithful testimony to the truth of the latter day work gave a good reports of their wards Felt to rejoice with their sisters in having the privalege of being associated with the Female Relief Society spoke words of comfort and encouragement to all present [p. [4]] exhorted to faithfulness and obedience to those that are placed to guide the affairs of Gods Kingdom here on earth

Sister A Goldsbrough said this meeting was intended for our mutual benefit hoped all would avail themselves of the opportunity offered them of expressing their feelings and speaking of the blessings of God

said she felt thankful for the organization of this society encouraged the sisters to faithfulness said each one must be saved for themselves[351] spoke on predestination and agency felt that she would never give up mormonism whatever she might be called to pass through gave many words of encouragement to the teachers

It being time to close the Choir sung Farewell all earthly honors[352]

Dismissed by sister A L Bigler Sec

---

351. Joseph Smith told the women of the Nauvoo Relief Society, "After this instruction, you will be responsible for your own sins. It is an honor to save yourselves— all are responsible to save themselves." (Document 1.2, entry for Apr. 28, 1842.)

352. Hymn 291, *Collection of Sacred Hymns* [1841], 321.

3.20 Eliza R. Snow, Discourse, July 24, 1871

Eliza R. Snow, Discourse, July 24, 1871, in "Celebration of the Twenty-Fourth at Ogden," Deseret News *[weekly] (Salt Lake City, UT), July 26, 1871, vol. 20, no. 25, pp. 287–288.*

In 1871 a large throng of Latter-day Saints met in Ogden, Utah, to celebrate the Twenty-Fourth of July, the annual commemoration of the 1847 arrival of the pioneer company in the Valley of the Great Salt Lake. Over one thousand people from Salt Lake City took special excursion trains for the occasion, meeting up with Brigham Young and a convoy of church leaders on their return from a tour of Cache County in northern Utah.[353] The festivities began with a grand procession that included the leaders, Mormon Battalion veterans, pioneers, and Relief Society members, followed by a special program at a bowery in the city's Union Square. After an address by Daniel H. Wells and performances by several brass bands and choirs, David McKenzie read this address "prepared for the occasion, by Miss Eliza R. Snow."[354] The weekly edition of the *Deseret News* printed July 26, from which the transcript below is taken, reported that Snow's message "was received by the people with many demonstrations of satisfaction, being frequently and loudly applauded."[355]

Snow's address carefully distinguished between the efforts of Latter-day Saint women to build the kingdom of God and the actions of national women's rights reformers. She was likely responding, at least in part, to the words of Susan B. Anthony and Elizabeth Cady Stanton when they visited Utah a month earlier.[356] They came at the invitation of the anti-authoritarian Godbeite reformers, a group of intellectual dissenters from the Latter-day Saint community,[357] but also met with Mormon women and spoke in the Salt Lake tabernacle. Anthony and Stanton praised the women for receiving the right to vote, but Stanton "did not skim the surface" in one address, voicing her opposition to early marriage and her

---

353. "President Young and Company," *Deseret News* [weekly], July 26, 1871, 281.

354. "Celebration of the Twenty-Fourth at Ogden," *Deseret News* [weekly], July 26, 1871, 286–287. It was not unusual for public addresses to be read by someone other than the writer, especially at outdoor gatherings. For example, at this meeting the address by Daniel Wells was read by George Q. Cannon. Snow's lung capacity and ability to project her voice may have been compromised by her struggle with tuberculosis through the 1850s. Nevertheless, Snow frequently spoke at length at local Relief Society meetings and had addressed the large crowd assembled in the Salt Lake tabernacle for the "indignation" meeting of January 13, 1870. (Susa Young Gates, "Life in the Lion House," pp. 39–40, Susa Young Gates, Papers, 1852–1932, Utah State Historical Society, Salt Lake City; Document 3.13.)

355. "Celebration of the Twenty-Fourth at Ogden," *Deseret News* [weekly], July 26, 1871, 288.

356. During a tour of the West, Anthony and Stanton stopped for a visit in Salt Lake City from June 28 to July 6, 1871. (Lola Van Wagenen, "Sister-Wives and Suffragists: Polygamy and the Politics of Woman Suffrage, 1870–1896" [PhD diss., New York University, 1994], 1–73; Elizabeth Cady Stanton, *Eighty Years and More [1815–1897]: Reminiscences of Elizabeth Cady Stanton* [New York City: European Publishing, 1898], 283–286.)

357. For more on the Godbeites, see Ronald W. Walker, *Wayward Saints: The Godbeites and Brigham Young* (Urbana: University of Illinois Press, 1998). On their hosting of Stanton and Anthony, see "Notes about Women," *Revolution,* June 29, 1871, [5]; Van Wagenen, "Sister-Wives and Suffragists," 1–3; "Miss Anthony's Lecture," *Salt Lake Daily Tribune,* July 3, 1871, [2]; and "Overland Letters," and "The Liberal Party at Salt Lake," *Revolution,* July 20, 1871, [1]–[2], [4].

support for family planning.[358] From Salt Lake City, Stanton wrote a letter criticizing patriarchal religious leaders from Moses to Brigham Young and advocated that women establish "their own constitutions, creeds, and codes, and customs," without priestly male intermediaries, saying that women would not be in their current state of dependence and degradation except "by man's free and fraudulent use of the authoritative 'Thus saith the Lord.'" The continued subjection of Mormon women within a patriarchal religion, Stanton warned, would be their own fault if they did not vote to abolish the practice of plural marriage.[359] In one Utah speech, Anthony remarked that "she had as good a right to receive revelations, direct from God" as did Joseph Smith or Brigham Young, and that "revelations which came exclusively to men would never satisfy her."[360]

Though alarmed by the hostility toward religion of some women's rights reformers and suspicious of portions of the agenda of national women's rights activists, Snow approved of woman suffrage and of the political involvement of Mormon women.[361] She believed that the Latter-day Saint movement would advance the causes of both men and women. "In the Church and Kingdom of God," she emphasized elsewhere, "the interests of men and women are the same; man has no interests separate from that of women, however it may be in the outside world, our interests are all united."[362]

——— ⅇ ———

LATTER-DAY SAINT LADIES OF UTAH:

The day we celebrate is a very important one. Important not only to the Latter-day Saints, as a people, but also highly important to all the nations of the earth.

The arrival of the Pioneers in these valleys, is an event which history will repeat with emphasis to all succeeding generations. It formed the starting point—the commencement of a delightful oasis in the desert wilds of North America—of establishing a midway settlement between Eastern and Western civilization, a connecting overland link, between the rich agricultural products of the Atlantic and the undeveloped mineral treasures of the Pacific. Above all and of consequence of far greater magnitude, it was securing a foothold for the establishment of the Kingdom of God—a government of peace—a home for

358. "Local Items," *Salt Lake Daily Tribune,* July 1, 1871, [3]; "The Woman Awakening," *Revolution,* July 27, 1871, [10].

359. "The City of the Saints," *Revolution,* July 13, 1871, [1]; "Woman Suffrage," *Salt Lake Daily Tribune,* July 1, 1871, [3]. Opposition to patriarchal religion was a common theme among suffrage activists and was included in the "Declaration of Sentiments" adopted by the women's rights convention at Seneca Falls in 1848. (Elizabeth Cady Stanton et al., eds., *History of Woman Suffrage,* 3 vols., 1881–1886, reprint [Rochester, NY: Susan B. Anthony, Charles Mann, 1887], 1:72.)

360. "Local Items," *Salt Lake Daily Tribune,* July 1, 1871, [3]; see also "The Woman Awakening," *Revolution,* July 27, 1871, [10].

361. See, for example, Snow's advocacy of women's petition drives and support of the National Woman Suffrage Association, in "R. S. Reports," *Woman's Exponent,* Jan. 1, 1878, 6:114.

362. "R. S. Reports," *Woman's Exponent,* June 1, 1875, 4:2.

the exiled Saints, and for the oppressed of all nations—a reservoir of freedom and religious toleration, where the glorious flag of liberty now waves triumphantly; and where the sacred Constitution which our noble forefathers were instrumental in forming under the inspiration of the Almighty, shall be cleansed from every stain cast upon it by degenerate Executives, and be preserved inviolate.[363] This in fulfillment of a prediction by the prophet Joseph Smith. Long before political faction had reared its hydra-head in the midst of our Republican Government—long before the intrigues of selfish, disloyal, unscrupulous, speculating, peace-destroying, office-seeking demagogues had attained to their present hideous proportions, I heard the prophet say, "The time will come when the Government of these United States will be so nearly overthrown through its own corruption, that the Constitution will hang, as it were, by a single hair, and the Latter-Day Saints—the Elders of Israel—will step forward to its rescue and save it."[364]

Ladies, please allow me to address you by the more endearing appellation of sisters. We have the privilege of uniting with our brethren in twining a garland with which to decorate the stately brow of this auspicious day. Why should we not? What interests have we that are not in common with theirs, and what have they that are disconnected with ours? We know of none, and we feel assured that they have no more interests involved in the settlement of these valleys than ourselves. Who is better qualified to appreciate the blessings of peace than woman? And where on earth is woman so highly privileged as associated with the Saints in Utah, and where else, on earth, is female virtue held so sacred, and where so bravely defended? Facts answer, NOWHERE!

363. Latter-day Saints considered the U.S. Constitution to be divinely inspired. At the "Great Indignation Meeting" of 1870, many Mormon women based their arguments for religious freedom on the Constitution. Snow's poetry often demonstrated a passionate patriotic idealism, but it also lamented the failure of state and federal governments to protect Saints' property rights and religious freedom. (See Doctrine and Covenants 101:80; 109:54; Document 3.13; and "My Country.—A Lamentation," in Eliza R. Snow, *Poems: Religious, Historical, and Political,* 2 vols. [Liverpool: F. D. Richards, 1856; Salt Lake City: Latter-day Saints' Printing and Publishing Establishment, 1877], 2:119–122.)

364. It is unclear which Joseph Smith discourse Snow is remembering, but records indicate that Smith spoke on this theme on more than one occasion. Martha Jane Knowlton reported that on July 19, 1840, Joseph Smith preached: "Even this Nation will, be on the very verge of crumbling to peices and tumbling to the ground and when the constitution is upon the brink of ruin this people will be the Staff up[on] which the Nation shall lean and they shall bear the constitution away from the very verge of destruction." James Burgess later recollected that on May 6, 1843, Smith spoke "upon the constitution and government of the United States stating that the time would come when the Constitution and Government would hang by a brittle thread and would be ready to fall into other hands but this people the Latterday saints will step forth and save it." These statements became important in Latter-day Saint memory of Smith and were often referenced by Brigham Young and others. (Martha Jane Coray, Notebook, n.d., CHL, July 19, 1840; James Burgess, Journal, Oct. 1841–Dec. 1848, vol. 2, CHL, May 1843; see "Celebration," *Deseret News,* July 13, 1854, [2].)

It is to the Gospel of Jesus Christ that we are indebted for the blessings we enjoy; and how lamentable it is to see women of the world, who, ostensibly aiming to improve society, ignore its divinity and trifle with its sacred truths! Reforms established on such a basis, would, if successful, dissolve every tie and obliterate all that is dear to the heart of a virtuous, high-aiming woman.

The Gospel in its mutilated forms, as now held by the religious sects of the day, has done much towards the elevation of woman; and what will it not do, when fully illustrated in its purity and power, as it was introduced by its great Founder, and as it has been again restored in our day? We should bear in mind that, as yet, its practice is but imperfectly developed. Although perfect principles may be readily enunciated, it is a slow process, and one that requires time, for a people with minds filled with all the false traditions of the age, and with habits commingling the most extreme opposites, to attain to perfection in practice. But this is an event which, although it may be far in the distance, is surely before us, for we know we have the true starting point.[365]

Wiih hearts overflowing with gratitude to God for the blessings of this day, and for the bright prospect of the future before us let us take a retrospective view, and inquire if we were not in concert with our brethren, and with them instrumental in the hand of God in bringing about the interesting event we are now celebrating. Who can calculate the worth of the cheerful submission to privation—the patient endurance of hardships—the heroic fortitude in surmounting difficulties which our sisters manifested, and how much weight they had in encouraging our brethren when under trying circumstances? Who can tell how much influence the unyielding faith and fervent prayers of the mothers, wives and sisters had with Him "who hears the young ravens when they cry,"[366] in strengthening the brave hearts and hands of the noble Pioneers who opened up a path in the trackless desert?

Let us take a glance of reminiscence at the time when, after our expulsion from Nauvoo, and while wending our weary way as outcasts, the United States Government made the most unreasonable and unprecedented requisition known in the annals of history, on our traveling camps, by demanding 500 of

365. In a letter to Dr. Martin L. Holbrook, editor of the New York–based *Herald of Health and Journal of Physical Culture,* Snow wrote that this "correct starting point" was of vital importance to human progress. Only by leaving behind "the corruptions of the world" and gathering in a location "where virtue, purity and innocence can be successfully guarded and defended," Snow said, could the elevation of mankind occur. She employed an analogy to illustrate her view: "It is impossible to purify the water of a muddy stream, while flowing in its own filthy channel, but, if taken out in detach'd portions, it can be cleansed and preserved in purity." Snow felt the Latter-day Saints were in such a position to improve and develop "all the rational and noble faculties of man, physically, morally, mentally and socially." (Eliza R. Snow to Martin L. Holbrook, Nov. 30, 1866, in Eliza R. Snow, Journal, 1842–1882, CHL.)
366. See Psalm 147:9.

our most efficient men—ordering them to march immediately to Mexico, of which this Territory was then the north-eastern part, to assist in the acquisition of territory, and to establish there that dishonored flag, from under the protection of which, we had recently been forced to fly.[367] Some of those noble women yet live, while others have gone to reap the reward of their labors, who, while their husbands, sons and brothers were performing military service and exposing their lives in Mexico, forced by cruel necessity, took the position of teamsters and drove to the mountains. With many similar matter of fact proofs which might be enumerated, who can doubt that "Mormon women" are equal to any and all emergencies? The great questions relative to woman's sphere, etc., which are making some stir in the world abroad, have no influence with us. While we realize that we are called to be co-workers with our brethren in the great work of the last days, we realize that we have no occasion to clamor about equality, or to battle for supremacy. We understand our true position—God has defined the sphere of woman wherever His Priesthood is acknowledged; and although we are not at present living up to all our privileges, and fulfilling all the duties that belong to our sex, the field is open before us, and we are urged to move forward as fast as we can develop and apply our own capabilities. But we never shall be called to officiate in unwomanly positions. Although invested with the right of suffrage, we shall never have occasion to vote for lady legislators or for lady congressmen, from the fact that the kingdom of God, of which we are citizens, will never be deficient in a supply of good and wise men to fill governmental positions, and of brave men for warriors.

How very different our position from that of our sisters in the world at large, and how widely different our feelings and prospects from that class known as "strong-minded," who are strenuously and unflinchingly advocating "woman's rights," and some of them at least, claiming "woman's sovereignty"

---

367. In 1846 the Latter-day Saints successfully lobbied the federal government to commission a battalion of Mormon soldiers for the Mexican War. Known as the Mormon Battalion, this group made the long march to southern California; while all military confrontations were avoided, the battalion blazed a trail through the Southwest. In their recollections about the recruitment of battalion soldiers, most nineteenth-century Latter-day Saints argued that the federal government had imposed an unnecessary hardship on the Saints, even though Mormon leaders at the time had sought for and welcomed the battalion. In 1881 Latter-day Saint leader George Q. Cannon told Thomas L. Kane, a non-Mormon who had used his government connections to assist in lobbying for the battalion, that "probably hundreds of addresses, delivered from the time of the enlistment until the present," had portrayed the government's actions as "heartless and cruel." (George Q. Cannon to Thomas L. Kane, Jan. 29, 1881, Thomas L. Kane and Elizabeth W. Kane Collection, 1762–1982, L. Tom Perry Special Collections, Harold B. Lee Library, Brigham Young University, Provo, UT; for more on the Mormon Battalion, see Daniel Tyler, *A Concise History of the Mormon Battalion in the Mexican War, 1846–1847* [Salt Lake City: n.p., 1881]; see also Matthew J. Grow, *"Liberty to the Downtrodden": Thomas L. Kane, Romantic Reformer* [New Haven, CT: Yale University Press, 2009], 47–92.)

and vainly flattering themselves with the idea that with ingress to the ballot box and access to financial offices, they shall accomplish the elevation of woman-kind. They seem utterly blind and oblivious to an element incorporated with their platform, which, in its nature, is calculated to sap the foundation of all on earth that can impart happines and stability to the domestic and social circles.

We are well aware that society needs purifying but for them to think of bettering its condition by the course and measures they are applying is like the blind leading the blind. [p. 287]

> And all their efforts to remove the curse,
> Are only making matters worse and worse;
> They can as well unlock without a key,
> As change the tide of man's degen'racy.
> Without the Holy Priesthood—'tis at most
> Like reck'ning bills in absence of the host.[368]

Not that we are opposed to woman suffrage. Certainly Congress cannot be acting consistently with itself to withhold suffrage from woman after having conferred it on the negro, the recent subject of abject slavery.[369] But to think of a war of sexes which the woman's rights movement would inevitably inaugurate, entailing domestic feuds and contentions for supremacy, with a corresponding "easy virtue" and dissolution of the marriage tie, creates an involuntary

---

368. These are lines excerpted from Snow's 1855 poem "Woman," first published in the *Mormon*, December 27, 1856. This excerpt demonstrates her ongoing concern with the theological and social import of Eve's transgression and the consequential "curse": "Thy desire shall be to thy husband, and he shall rule over thee." Elizabeth Cady Stanton and other women's rights activists objected to the tradition that "in the covenant of marriage, [woman] is compelled to promise obedience to her husband." Snow taught that this "curse of Eve" would be overcome by obedience to the commandments of God. She closed "Woman" with this couplet: "And thro' obedience woman will obtain / The power of reigning and the right to reign." (Jill Mulvay Derr and Karen Lynn Davidson, eds., *Eliza R. Snow: The Complete Poetry* [Provo, UT: Brigham Young University Press; Salt Lake City: University of Utah Press, 2009], 474–479; Genesis 3:16; Stanton et al., *History of Woman Suffrage*, 1:70; see also Box Elder Stake, Box Elder Stake Relief Society Minutes and Records, 1857–1944, CHL, vol. 1, Nov. 23, 1870; and Bountiful Ward, Davis Stake, Bountiful Ward Relief Society Minutes and Records, 1868–1878, CHL, vol. 1, Nov. 7, 1870.)

369. In February 1869 the U.S. Congress proposed the Fifteenth Amendment, which prohibited the federal government and the states from denying a citizen the right to vote based on "race, color, or previous condition of servitude." It was ratified on February 3, 1870. Women in Utah Territory were granted full suffrage on February 12, 1870. (See Documents 3.14 and 3.17.)

shudder![370] "Order is heaven's first law,"[371] and it is utterly impossible for order to exist without organization, and no organization can be effected without gradation. Our standard is as far above theirs, as the pattern of heavenly things is above the earthly. We have already attained to an elevation in nobility and purity of life, which they can neither reach nor comprehend, and yet they call us "degraded." We cannot descend to their standard; we have a high destiny to fill. It is for us to set the world an example of the highest and most perfect types of womanhood.

Mothers and sisters have grest [great] influence in moulding the characters of the coming men, either for good or evil. All the energies of woman's soul should be brought in to exercise in the important work of cultivating, educating and refining the rising generation. Example is more effectua[l] than precept—both are requisite. In this direction woman has not only acknowledged "rights," but momentous duties, and such as require all the strength of mind and firmness of purpose as have culminated in the epithet, "strongminded." I cannot think that woman was ever endowed with too much strength of mind, if properly directed—it is the perversion of its uses, and misapplication of abilities which have occasioned the odium. It is impossible for either men or women to possess too much knowledge, or be endowed with too much capability, provided they are applied to legitimate purposes. Would any sensible man take pride in announcing that his wife, sister or daughter was weak-minded, silly and effeminate?

According to history, most of the men who have become illustrious as benefactors of mankind, were sons of wise. noble and intelligent mothers. Pres. Young says, "woman is the mainspring and the waymark of society." It was justly remarked, "show me the women of a nation, and I will describe the character of that nation." Admitting so much for woman's influence, what care should be taken in the cultivation of the daughters of Zion as the future mothers of a mighty generation! They shoud be taught to fix their standard of character as far above the level of those of the outside world as is the altitude they inhabit. They should early establish a firmness of integrity surpassing the durability of the impregnable mountains which surround us. Wisely instructed and with proper habits of thought and reflection, they would despise to be seen aping the foolish, extravagant and disgusting fashions of the godless gentile

---

370. Many women's rights reformers, including Elizabeth Cady Stanton and Susan B. Anthony, argued for more liberal divorce laws, which sometimes led to charges that they were advocates of "free love." (Lori D. Ginzberg, *Elizabeth Cady Stanton: An American Life* [New York: Hill and Wang, 2009], 97–101, 144.)

371. Alexander Pope, "An Essay on Man," in *The Poetical Works of Alexander Pope,* vol. 2 (London: William Pickering, 1835), 72.

world. They would scorn to imitate the strange disfiguring of the physical structure which jeopardizes health.[372] A stylish, fashionable lady of the present day, presents more the appearance of a beast of burden, a camel or dromedary heavily laden, than the elegant, dignified, graceful form in which God created woman. Dress is admitted to be an index to the mind. Good taste is much better exhibited in a plain costume than in an extravagant mass of superfluities.

May such high and holy aspirations be kindled in the pure virgin hearts of our young ladies, as will so elevate their thoughts and feelings as to lift them far above the contaminating influences of degenerate civilization. May the young sons of Zion be proof against the deleterious habits which vitiate the taste and undermine the structure of physical strength and perfection—may they become the unwavering champions of truth, freedom and justice, and stand as mighty bulwarks against the aggressors of intolerance and oppression; and may the young daughters of Zion, noble, dignified, loving and graceful— like "polished stones,"[373]—become crowns of excellence and beauty, prepared hereafter to associate with angels and the highest intelligences of the upper world.

---

372. Extreme fashions of the period required tight lacings to slenderize and various wire bustles to add fullness. (Ruth Vickers Clayton, "Clothing and the Temporal Kingdom: Mormon Clothing Practices, 1847 to 1887" [PhD diss., Purdue University, 1987], 256–261.)

373. See Psalm 144:12.

3.21 "Woman's Exponent. A Utah Ladies' Journal," June 1, 1872

"Woman's Exponent. A Utah Ladies' Journal," Woman's Exponent *(Salt Lake City, UT), June 1, 1872, vol. 1, no. 1, p. [8].*

By the time the Latter-day Saints began settling in the West in the late 1840s and 1850s, American women were serving as editors of newspapers and magazines, and a substantial number of women's publications existed across the country.[374] Against this background, Edward L. Sloan, editor of the *Salt Lake Herald,* proposed a women's paper in Utah in 1871 and suggested that twenty-two-year-old Louisa (Lula) Greene, who had written several poems for the *Herald,* be appointed editor. After receiving support from Eliza R. Snow and Brigham Young, her great-uncle, Greene accepted the offer, asking Young to call her to the job as a mission.[375] He did so, and operations began shortly thereafter. Greene moved to Salt Lake City in April 1872 to live and work in the home of another of her great-uncles, Lorenzo Dow Young, the younger brother of Brigham Young. The first issue of the new paper, titled *Woman's Exponent,* was published June 1, 1872. For the first six months of the paper's publication, Greene ran the *Exponent* from a room in the house that contained "a table with writing materials, a few books, magazines, some chairs and a bed."[376] By the fall of 1872, both the *Exponent* and Greene had moved into an office and living quarters that Sloan had constructed not far from the *Herald* offices.[377]

The semimonthly paper, with each issue containing eight pages, included a wide variety of content: news; articles ranging from domestic life to theology to biographies of prominent Mormon women; obituaries of Mormon women; reports and minutes of meetings of women's ecclesiastical and cultural organizations, including the Relief Society, the Primary, young women's groups, and Retrenchment Associations; and poetry and short stories. The Relief Society reports regularly published in the *Exponent* helped unify and connect women of the society across the far-flung Mormon settlements. The paper's circulation was likely between three and four thousand copies, though some articles reached a much broader audience as they were sometimes reprinted in women's magazines throughout the country.

---

374. Frank Luther Mott, *A History of American Magazines,* vol. 2, *1850–1865* (Cambridge, MA: Harvard University Press, 1957), 56; Caroline Garnsey, "Ladies Magazines to 1850," *Bulletin of the New York Public Library* 58 (Feb. 1954): 82; Patricia Okker, *Our Sister Editors: Sarah J. Hale and the Tradition of Nineteenth-Century American Women Editors* (Athens: University of Georgia Press, 1995), 167–220.

375. Lula Greene Richards, "How 'The Exponent' Was Started," *Relief Society Magazine* 14, no. 12 (Dec. 1927): 605–608; Carol Cornwall Madsen, "Voices in Print: The *Woman's Exponent,* 1872–1914," in *Women Steadfast in Christ: Talks Selected from the 1991 Women's Conference Co-Sponsored by Brigham Young University and the Relief Society,* ed. Dawn Hall Anderson and Marie Cornwall (Salt Lake City: Deseret Book, 1991), 69–70; Maureen Ursenbach Beecher, "Eliza R. Snow," in *Mormon Sisters: Women in Early Utah,* ed. Claudia L. Bushman, new ed. (Logan: Utah State University Press, 1997), 25–27.

376. Richards, "How 'The Exponent' Was Started," 607.

377. "Home Affairs," *Woman's Exponent,* Oct. 1, 1872, 1:69; Sherilyn Cox Bennion, "The *Woman's Exponent:* Forty-Two Years of Speaking for Women," *Utah Historical Quarterly* 44, no. 3 (Summer 1976): 228.

Woman's Exponent.

VOL. I.   SALT LAKE CITY, UTAH, JUNE 1, 1872.   No. 1.

NEWS AND VIEWS.

Women are now admitted to fifty American colleges.

Rev. De Witt Talmage is pronounced a success as a sensation preacher.

Theodore Tilton says the best brains in northern New York are wearing white hats. They might wear chapeaux of a more objectionable color.

Daniel W. Voorhees in one day destroyed the political record of a life-time, and that was when he became henchman to a judge with an eclesiastical mission.

An Alabama editor writes "United State," and refuses to write "United States"—a straw to show how Southern sentiment runs. What a state he must be in?

The season of scattering intellectual filth has set in over the country. It occurs quadrennially in the United States, commencing a few months before the Presidential election.

Dr. Newman failed to become a Bishop at the Methodist General Conference, and Dr. Newman mourns this second great defeat. He has remembrances of Salt Lake in connection with the previous one.

Great outcry is raised against the much marrying of the Latter-day Saints. The tendency of the age is to disregard marriage altogether, but there seems no indication of a desire to have the race die out.

The "Alabama" muddle like "confusion worse confounded" becomes worse mixed the more it is stirred. It stretches itself over the path of time, and "like a wounded snake drags its slow length along." The country has become heartily sick of it.

Some Eastern journals head their Utah news with "Deseret." With keen appreciation of the coming and inevitable, they accept the mellifluous name chosen for the region wrested by that industry which "the honey bee" represents, from the barren wilds of nature.

George Francis Train sends us a bundle of Train Ligues. The compliment is appreciated, but the act is like sweetness wasted. We can vote, but not for "the next President of America." Utah has not become Deseret yet, nor can it participate in President making.

The last week of May, 1872, will be memorable in American annals as the first time since the first ordinance of secession was passed in the South, that both houses of Congress had their full list of members. Statesmanship can retain a complete Federal legislature, but the article has grown somewhat scarce.

To pardon the worst class of criminals on condition that they emigrate to the United States, is growing in favor with European monarchies. Germany and Greece so far have done the largest business in this line, the latest batch of villains thus disposed of being the Marathon murderers from Greece. Orders have been forwarded by President Grant to New Orleans, to which port it is understood they have been sent, to prevent their landing. They should be captured, ironed, returned to Athens with Uncle Samuel's compliments, and a bill for direct and "consequential" damages presented.

News comes from France that trailing dresses for street wear are going out of fashion. So many absurd and ridiculous fashions come from Paris that the wonder is thinking American women do not, with honest republican spirit, reject them entirely. This latter one, however, is so sensible that its immediate adoption will be an evidence of good sense wisely directed.

The anti-Mormon bill of Judge Bingham seems to have fared no better in the judiciary committee of the House of Representatives than the one to which Mr. Voorhees stood sponsor. It is gratifying to think that a majority of that committee yet respect the antiquated and once revered instrument still occasionally referred to as the Constitution.

Rev. James Freeman Clark claims "that if it is an advantage to vote, women ought to have it; if a disadvantage men ought not to be obliged to bear it alone." Speaking from experience we feel safe in affirming that the Rev. gentleman is right, and we hope for a time when this immunity may be universally enjoyed by our pure-minded and light-loving sisters. We don't presume that those belonging to the opposite class care anything about it.

Mrs. Carrie F. Young, editor of the "Pacific Journal of Health," has been lecturing in Idaho on Temperance and Woman Suffrage. The editor of the "Idaho World" was not present, but did not regret his absence. He says, "We feel a most decided repugnance to the exhibition of a woman upon the rostrum, advocating such degrading theories as 'woman suffrage' and other cognate subjects." He omits to state whether "Temperance" is one of the "degrading theories" to which he refers.

Force is ever the argument of a bad cause. The principles which cannot be overcome except by the exercise of physical power, present a front that arrests the attention of thinking minds. Where argument fails and force is employed to overcome an opponent, the power of the principles to which opposition is made is admitted. Will those who urge repressive legislation against the people of Utah think of it? Witness the Voorhees bill as an illustration.

A notable event, as a result of the late terrible Franco-German war, is the opening of the German University in Strasbourg, which takes place June 1st—to-day. That famous city on the Rhine, after a siege memorable in the annals of warfare, passed into the hands of the Germans, and now they take the surest means to permanently consolidate their power, by establishing there one of those seats of learning for which Germany has become enviably famous.

Miss Susan B. Anthony, it is said, declared before the Cincinnati Convention met, that if it gave her cause "the cold shoulder," she would go to Philadelphia and pledge the ballots of the women of America to U. S. Grant. As the women of America are yet without ballots, and as it is very questionable, if they had them, whether they would authorize any single individual to pledge them for any candidate, the supposition is fair that Miss Anthony possesses too much good sense to have made any such declaration.

Rev. Mr. Peirce, a Methodist clergyman who has made Salt Lake his headquarters for some time, in lecturing east proposed the extinction of polygamy by the introduction here of vast quantities of expensive millinery goods, and by inducing "Gentile" women to dress in gorgeous style that "Mormon" women might imitate them and run up such heavy dry goods bills that it would be impossible for a man to support more than one wife, if even one. Mr. Peirce, no doubt, preaches modesty and humility occasionally, by way of variety; now he recommends the encouragement of pride, vanity and extravagance to accomplish his "Christian" designs. The course he advises has been largely followed in many places, has tenanted brothels, aided to fill prisons, broken up families, huried women of reputation and position down to degradation and infamy, and has met heavy denunciations from inspired men whom Mr. Peirce professes to revere. He would steal the livery of evil to serve religion in. There is not much of this reverend gentleman, and what little there is must be either very silly or very wicked.

The editor of "The Present Age" has been to a church and heard an orthodox sermon, in which the preacher took occasion to say that all religious "isms," including Mohammedanism, Mormonism and Spiritualism, rested their claims for being true upon miracles." The "Age" is a Spiritualist and denies that his "ism" bases its claims to be true upon miracles. Latter-day Saints deny that Mormonism basis any claim for credence in its miracles; the reverse is the truth. The "Age" defines a miracle to be "the setting aside for the time being of a natural law to meet an unexpected emergency." Had he said a miracle was the bringing into operation of certain natural laws not generally understood or comprehended, he would have been nearer correct. When somebody can tell how a natural law may be or can be set aside, except by the operation of some other natural law, his definition, which is the generally received one, may be entitled to more consideration. We imagine the working of the overland telegraph is as great a miracle to the Cheyenne Indians as any recorded miracle that the "Age" or the orthodox minister can quote.

Mrs. Laura De Force Gordon attended the Cincinnati Convention and claimed a seat as a delegate from California. Her claim was treated with hisses and laughter. She took a position in front of the stand and endeavored to speak, but her voice was drowned by a tumultuous discord. Her persistence in seeking to address an assemblage that treated her claim in such a manner was undignified; while the action of the Convention in receiving her with hisses and uproarious laughter, was disgraceful. The Liberal Republicans assembled in Cincinnati for a general work of purification and reform, evidently stood greatly in need of general reform themselves, in the matter of manners as well as in politics. Mrs. Gordon was as much entitled to a seat in that Convention as Carl Schurz himself, for we have yet to learn that the call for it specified that "male" Republicans only were admissable.

A new periodical in London is called "The Ladies."

First issue of *Woman's Exponent*. Louisa (Lula) Greene edited this first issue of the *Woman's Exponent* (1872–1914), a newspaper produced twice a month by and for Mormon women. The contents included women's personal essays, short stories, poems, reports on the suffrage movement, articles on home and family life, religious doctrine, and minutes of Latter-day Saint women's organizations. The paper fostered a sense of connection among women scattered throughout the Mountain West and abroad. (Church History Library, Salt Lake City.)

The *Exponent* also reprinted articles from various women's publications, particularly suffrage journals.[378]

Louisa Greene Richards (she married Levi Richards in 1873) acted as editor until 1877, followed by Emmeline B. Wells, who served in that position until 1914, when the paper closed and another magazine, officially published by the Relief Society, began as a successor to the privately owned *Exponent*.[379] As editors, Richards and Wells handled the business affairs and wrote not only the editorials but many of the other articles and additional content, including poetry and fiction. During the forty-two years of its publication, the *Exponent* was central to the intellectual, religious, and social lives of many Latter-day Saint women.[380]

The following introductory editorial announced the new journal's mission to accurately represent Mormon women to the world by allowing them a forum to speak for themselves. Indeed, the *Salt Lake Herald*'s April 1872 announcement of the forthcoming paper proclaimed, "The women of Utah are to-day unquestionably more the subject of comment than those of any other portion of the country, or indeed of the world. As they have long exercised the right to think and act for themselves, so they now claim the right to speak for themselves through the potent medium of the types."[381]

WOMAN'S EXPONENT.

A UTAH LADIES' JOURNAL.

The women of Utah to-day occupy a position which attracts the attention of intelligent thinking men and women everywhere. They are engaged in the practical solution of some of the greatest social and moral problems of the age, and a powerful interest is manifested throughout the United States, and, it may be said, the entire civilized world, to learn from reliable sources the views honestly entertained by them on these questions.

They have been grossly misrepresented through the press, by active enemies who permit no opportunity to pass of maligning and slandering them; and with but limited opportunity of appealing to the intelligence and candor of their fellow countrymen and countrywomen in reply.

---

378. Madsen, "Voices in Print," 70–72. Over the years, the *Exponent* referenced and reprinted items from at least thirty-eight different women's publications. The most enduring exchange was with the Boston *Woman's Journal,* the official paper of the American Woman Suffrage Association; it was the only woman's journal to survive longer than the *Exponent*. The *Exponent* also exchanged articles regularly with local papers. (Carol Cornwall Madsen, "'Remember the Women of Zion': A Study of the Editorial Content of the *Woman's Exponent,* A Mormon Woman's Journal" [master's thesis, University of Utah, 1977], 8–10, 26.)

379. Bennion, "*Woman's Exponent,*" 232–234.

380. See Madsen, "Voices in Print," 69–80.

381. "The New Woman's Journal," *Salt Lake Herald,* Apr. 10, 1872, [3].

Who are so well able to speak for the women of Utah as the women of Utah themselves? "It is better to represent ourselves than to be misrepresented by others!"

For these reasons, and that women may help each other by the diffusion of knowledge and information possessed by many and suitable to all, the publication of WOMAN'S EXPONENT, a journal owned by, controlled by and edited by Utah ladies, has been commenced.

The aim of this journal will be to discuss every subject interesting and valuable to women. It will contain a brief and graphic summary of current news local and general, household hints, educational matters, articles on health and dress, correspondence, editorials on leading topics of interest suitable to its columns and miscellaneous reading.

It will aim to defend the right, inculcate sound principles, and disseminate useful knowledge.

Utah, in its Female Relief Societies, has the best organized benevolent institution of the age; yet, but little is known of the self-sacrificing labors of these Societies. In WOMAN'S EXPONENT a department will be devoted to reports of their meetings and other matters of interest connected with their workings; and to this end the Presidents and Secretaries of the various Societies throughout the Territory are requested to furnish communications which will receive due attention.

Miss Eliza R Snow, President of the entire Female Relief Societies, cordially approves of the journal, and will be a contributor to it as she has leisure from her numerous duties.

WOMAN'S EXPONENT will be published semi-monthly, each number containing eight pages, quarto.

The following low rates will place it within the reach of all, and the hope is that it may be made so valuable that it will be found in every family in Utah.

TERMS, Strictly in Advance:

1 Copy [subscription] one year, $2.00[382]   1 Copy six months, $1.00
10 Copies one year,   18.00   10 Copies six months,   9.00

No subscription received for less than six months.

It is earnestly desired that the Bishops, Presidents of Female Relief Societies and others interested in a work of this kind, will interest themselves in getting up clubs; ten copies for the price of nine.

---

382. In 1889 the annual subscription fee was dropped to one dollar, with hopes that the reduced cost would increase circulation and "place this little home publication within the reach of every family in Zion." ("Editorial Notes," *Woman's Exponent*, May 15, 1889, 17:189; "The Woman's Paper," *Woman's Exponent*, June 1, 1889, 18:4.)

Address all communications and subscriptions Publishers WOMAN'S EXPONENT, Salt Lake City, Utah.[383] [p. [8]]

---

383. Over the course of its run, the *Exponent* was housed in a variety of locations in downtown Salt Lake City: Lorenzo Dow Young's home, the "Old Constitution Building," the first floor of the Council House, the Templeton Hotel, the Bishop's Building, and various temporary locations. (Madsen, "'Remember the Women of Zion:' A Study of the Editorial Content of the *Woman's Exponent*," 21–25.)

3.22 Hyrum Ward Relief Society, Report, October 9, 1872

Hyrum Ward Relief Society, Report, Oct. 9, 1872, in "F. R. Society Reports," Woman's Exponent *(Salt Lake City, UT), Nov. 1, 1872, vol. 1, no. 11, p. 82.*

The *Woman's Exponent* regularly published reports from local Relief Societies. The following document, an October 9, 1872, report submitted by Christina Liljenquist and her counselors in the Hyrum, Utah, Relief Society, provides an example of these reports and gives a brief glimpse into the activities and concerns of a rural Relief Society in northern Utah.

In 1856 Latter-day Saints began a concerted effort to establish settlements in Cache Valley in northern Utah and soon established a number of towns, including Logan in 1859 and Hyrum, in the south end of the valley, in 1860.[384] In 1868 Mary Ann Maughan became president of the Relief Society in the Logan First Ward, and Relief Societies were organized in other wards in the valley. Apostle Ezra T. Benson, who also served as stake president of the Cache Valley Stake, instructed that the "Presidentess of the first ward was to preside over the whole, and that when ever she thought proper to call them all to gether it was her privilege."[385] Maughan thus coordinated and supervised the network of Relief Societies in the villages that dotted the valley.[386] This relatively informal arrangement served as a precursor for the establishment of stake Relief Societies.[387]

On May 9, 1868, a Relief Society was first organized in the Hyrum Ward.[388] Two years later, on April 7, 1870, the society was reorganized; Christina Jacobsen Liljenquist, a Swedish immigrant and the wife of ward bishop Ola Nilsson Liljenquist, became the new Relief Society president.[389] A recent visit to Salt Lake City, partly funded by donations from Relief Society members, likely prompted Liljenquist's 1872 letter.[390]

---

384. F. Ross Peterson, *A History of Cache County* (Salt Lake City: Utah State Historical Society, 1997), 25–51.

385. Logan Utah Cache Stake, Logan Utah Cache Stake Relief Society Minutes and Records, 1868–1973, CHL, vol. 1, May 18 and 23, 1868.

386. See Carol Cornwall Madsen, "Creating Female Community: Relief Society in Cache Valley, Utah, 1868–1900," *Journal of Mormon History* 21, no. 2 (Fall 1995): 126–154.

387. See Document 3.26.

388. Hyrum Ward, Hyrum Stake, Hyrum Ward Relief Society Minutes and Records, 1870–1901, CHL, vol. 1, May 9, 1868.

389. Hyrum Ward, Hyrum Stake, Relief Society Minutes and Records, vol. 1, Apr. 7, 1870. For the years 1870–1871, there were approximately 263 members listed as attending Hyrum Relief Society meetings. (See "Attendance of the Hyrum Female Relief Society," in Hyrum Ward, Hyrum Stake, Relief Society Minutes and Records, vol. 1, pp. 2–16.)

390. Hyrum Ward, Hyrum Stake, Relief Society Minutes and Records, vol. 1, Oct. 3 and Nov. 7, 1872.

HYRUM, Cache County, Utah,
October 9th, 1872.

EDITOR WOMAN'S EXPONENT:

The Female Relief Society of this Ward was organized nearly four years ago, and since that time we have accomplished much good. Our Society is in a healthy condition; we have endeavored to do all in our power to comfort and bless the poor, the widow, the fatherless and the sick; thus assisting our Bishop and Teachers in some of their labors. In addition to this we have sent ninety dollars to assist in gathering the poor,[391] and have given forty dollars to aid our Sunday School in purchasing a library and rewards. In connection with this Society there is a Young Ladies' Retrenchment Association. We have a braiding school and make straw hats in Summer.[392]

Although the outside world may number us with the "poor, oppresse[d][393] women of Utah," we experience great pleasure in saying, we have lived in the States and in the old world, but prefer living in, and enjoying the glorious liberties of Utah and her "Mormon" institutions, and in seeking to fill woman's mission as wives, mothers and daughters, aiding suffering humanity wherever found.

> The widow's heart shall share our joy,
> The orphan and oppressed
> Shall see we love the sweet employ
> To succor the distressed,[394]

And thus maintain woman's legitimate rights.[395]

CHRISTINA LILJENQUIST, President,
MARTHA WARD,
LUCY WILSON;   } Counselors.

---

391. Hyrum Relief Society members raised funds for the Perpetual Emigrating Fund throughout 1872. During a July meeting that year, Liljenquist congratulated the women on raising fifty-six dollars "to gather the poor." She "spoke on the emigration, said the sisters had done well and they should recieve their reward she exhorted them to go ahead and do their duty." (Hyrum Ward, Hyrum Stake, Relief Society Minutes and Records, vol. 1, July 11, 1872.)

392. On the braiding school, see Hyrum Ward, Hyrum Stake, Relief Society Minutes and Records, vol. 1, Aug. 1, 1872.

393. TEXT: In the copy used for transcription, a portion of the line is obscured at this point.

394. Hymn 99, *Sacred Hymns and Spiritual Songs. For the Church of Jesus Christ of Latter-day Saints,* 14th ed. (Salt Lake City: George Q. Cannon, 1871), 108–109.

395. Though Liljenquist, with her counselors, here distanced the Hyrum Relief Society members from national women's rights reformers, she supported the extension of suffrage to Utah women. In July 1871 Liljenquist "advised every sister who had a vote to go to the Polls and record the same at the August Elections." (Hyrum Ward, Hyrum Stake, Relief Society Minutes and Records, vol. 1, July 5, 1871.)

3.23 Eliza R. Snow, Discourse, August 14, 1873

Eliza R. Snow, Discourse, Aug. 14, 1873, in "An Address. By Miss Eliza R. Snow. Delivered in the Taberanacle, Ogden, at a Relief Society, Meeting, Thursday Afternoon, August 14th, 1873," Woman's Exponent *(Salt Lake City, UT), Sept. 15, 1873, vol. 2, no. 8, pp. 62–63.*

For nearly nine months, from October 1872 to July 1873, Eliza R. Snow was absent from Utah, traveling broadly in Europe and the Middle East with a delegation of Latter-day Saints. As leader of the Relief Society, she was one of a handful of core members of the tour group, which was headed by George A. Smith, a counselor in the First Presidency, and Snow's brother Lorenzo, a member of the Quorum of the Twelve Apostles. The key destination was Palestine, where the travelers visited "the lands in which the events recorded in the Bible transpired." Most important, at Jerusalem the small group clustered privately to offer a prayer consecrating the land "preparatory to the return of the Jews."[396] Throughout their extensive trip, the "Palestine Tourists," as they were known, sent letters describing their travels to various Utah newspapers. Correspondence with local newspapers was common practice among the throngs of Americans who made the "grand tour" of Europe and the Holy Land during the last half of the nineteenth century.[397] The *Woman's Exponent* published Snow's letters and poems, posting her progress to Relief Society women in wards throughout the territory who had helped fund her expensive journey. Snow later compiled the travelers' letters for publication as *Correspondence of Palestine Tourists* (1875).[398]

This address, delivered by Snow when she visited the Ogden, Utah, Relief Society about six weeks after her return to Utah and reported in the *Woman's Exponent,* contains frequent references to her recent trip abroad and her attempts to correct misinformation regarding the church and particularly Latter-day Saint women. One purpose of the European leg of the tour had been to meet with government and religious leaders to alter the predominantly negative image of the church and ease the way for introducing or reintroducing Latter-day Saint missionaries in various countries.[399] When the delegation met with Adolphe Thiers, president of the French Republic, Snow was excluded since "the presentation being an official one the ladies were not admitted."[400] Likewise, Snow was unable to visit certain religious sites in Rome and the Middle East because she was a woman. Thus, she particularly felt the significance of joining "the brethren" in a ceremonial prayer circle to dedicate "the land of Palestine for the gathering of the Jews and the rebuilding of

---

396. George A. Smith, June 22, 1873, in *Journal of Discourses,* 26 vols. (Liverpool: Various publishers, 1855–1886), 16:88; George A. Smith et al., *Correspondence of Palestine Tourists; Comprising a Series of Letters by George A. Smith, Lorenzo Snow, Paul A. Schettler, and Eliza R. Snow, of Utah. Mostly Written While Traveling in Europe, Asia and Africa, in the Years 1872 and 1873* (Salt Lake City: Deseret News, 1875), 1–2, 259–260, 383–386.

397. See William W. Stowe, *Going Abroad: European Travel in Nineteenth-Century American Culture* (Princeton, NJ: Princeton University Press, 1994).

398. Smith et al., *Correspondence of Palestine Tourists.*

399. See Smith et al., *Correspondence of Palestine Tourists,* 1–2.

400. George A. Smith, Journal, Nov. 1872–June 1873, typescript, CHL, Dec. 17, 1872.

Jerusalem."⁴⁰¹ Snow's speech in Ogden underscored the spiritual and temporal possibilities open to Latter-day Saint women and invited them to pursue new responsibilities, such as medical training. One associate noted that Snow had returned from her long journey abroad "invigorated mentally and physically,"⁴⁰² and the detailed account of her extemporaneous address, recorded by stenographer James Taylor, captures her energy.

———— ❧ ————

AN ADDRESS.
BY MISS ELIZA R. SNOW.
Delivered in the Taberanacle, Ogden, at a Relief Society, meeting, Thursday afternoon, August 14th, 1873.
REPORTED BY JAMES TAYLOR.

[As the first part of the address is of a descriptive nature, in which the speaker delineates the course of travel pursued by President George A. Smith and party, the lately returned tourists, and as the readers of the Exponent have been favored with much the same details through Miss Snow's letters, we merely make a few extracts, giving the latter portion of the address in full.]—Ed.⁴⁰³

* * In Lyons, we saw them weave silk of various descriptions. They weave photograph likenesses and battle scenes, and delineate countenances plainly as if they had been painted.

In the King's Palace in Munich, I was shown window curtains made of glass, in brocade and beautiful colors. Without feeling of them, I should not have thought but that they were silk, but they were glsss.

* * I visited many churches and cathedrals; I visited mosques (a mosque is a Mahamedan place of worship;) saw all I could under the govermnents where we traveled. And the more I saw, the more I felt the necessity of the Lord! having a government on the earth for the sake of the people, and thought, how well off the Saints in Zion were; and what blessings they enjoyed. Blessings and privileges above those of all the nations of the earth. And, we my sisters, we have the privilege of being organized according to the pattern which God has given for the females in the Church of Jesus Christ.⁴⁰⁴ We are privileged above

---

401. Smith et al., *Correspondence of Palestine Tourists,* 260. More than three decades earlier, Orson Hyde, a member of the Quorum of the Twelve Apostles, had journeyed to Palestine and similarly offered a dedicatory prayer. (See Blair G. Van Dyke and Lamar C. Berrett, "In the Footsteps of Orson Hyde: Subsequent Dedications of the Holy Land," *BYU Studies* 47, no. 1 [2008]: 57–73.)

402. Orson F. Whitney, *History of Utah,* 4 vols. (Salt Lake City: George Q. Cannon and Sons, 1904), 4:575.

403. TEXT: This editorial note (including the brackets around it) appears in the original, as do the asterisks in two of the paragraphs that follow, which represent omission of portions of Snow's address by the editor of the *Woman's Exponent.*

404. In 1868 Snow wrote that the Nauvoo Relief Society "was organized after the pattern of the

all other woman-kind on the face of the earth. I thought when I was abroad, I thought before I went, and I have thought much since I returned, how necessary for the Saints of the living God to be more of a distinct people than what they are, to be the Saints of God in very deed—and to be as different from the rest of the world as our privileges are more exalted—we should be a shining light to the nations of the earth.[405] But I often say to myself, are we what we should be?

I was talking with President [Brigham] Young about how we were received abroad.[406] He said that the Saints were growing in influence; and that if they lived up to their privileges,[407] their influence would be far greater than it is now. I told him that I believed that if we were as distinct a people as the Lord wanted us to be our influence would be far greater. He said it would. But instead of that, are we not trying to gain influence by assimulating to the habits and customs, and the spirit of the world?

Now I do not know that this would apply to my sisters in ogden, for they are a live people. Their works exhibit that. And their reputation bespeaks them to be awake to their duties. But still we are never to come to a stand point. We are to be progressing, and growing better. If we have done well to-day, we must do still better to-morrow. We believe in eternal progression. It will not do to say that we have so much to do that we cannot do any more, because the works and duties for women in Zion are constantly increasing. No where on the

---

Church of Jesus Christ of Latter-day Saints, with a Presidentess, who chose two Counselors." The organization and ordination of the first Relief Society presidency is recorded in the Nauvoo Relief Society Minute Book. The First Presidency of the church and other priesthood quorums established the pattern of leadership by a "presidency," that is a president and two counselors or assistant presidents. (Document 3.6; Document 1.2, entry for Mar. 17, 1842; see "Presidency," in Dean C. Jessee et al., eds., *Journals, Volume 1: 1832–1839,* vol. 1 of the Journals series of *The Joseph Smith Papers,* ed. Dean C. Jessee et al. [Salt Lake City: Church Historian's Press, 2008], 469–470.)

405. See Doctrine and Covenants 115:5.

406. The group of Latter-day Saints who went to Palestine hoped to facilitate future missionary work. Brigham Young and Daniel H. Wells, of the First Presidency, instructed George A. Smith to "observe closely what openings now exist, or where they may be effected, for the introduction of the Gospel into the various countries you shall visit." They anticipated Smith would "doubtless be brought in contact with men of position and influence" and hoped that his conversations would assist in "dispelling prejudice, and sowing seeds of righteousness among the people." In one of her first public addresses following her return, Snow told an audience of women, "We did not say so much about our religion as we would had we been sent among them to preach. Whatever we did say to them they received it kindly and many are calculating to visit Salt Lake City. I think our visit will be the means of much good." (Smith et al., *Correspondence of Palestine Tourists,* 1–2; Cooperative Retrenchment Association, Cooperative Retrenchment Association Meeting Minutes, 1871–1874, CHL, July 19, 1873.)

407. On April 28, 1842, Joseph Smith said in his discourse to the Nauvoo Relief Society, "If you live up to these principles how great and glorious!— if you live up to your privilege, the angels cannot be restrain'd from being your associates." (Document 1.2, entry for Apr. 28, 1842.)

earth has woman so broad a sphere of labor and duty, of responsibility and action, as in Utah.

I tried in many instances, to make people believe that women in Utah had more freedom than women had any where else on the earth. But they thought that they knew better than I did. I told them how long I had lived with the people, and that I ought to know better than strangers.

To be sure we have trials; but what are they? I want to ask my sisters now a serious question. When you are filled with the Spirit of God, and the Holy Ghost rests upon you—that comforter which Jesus promised and which takes of the things of God and gives them to us, and shows us things to come, and brings all things to our remembrance[408]—when you are filled with this spirit, do you have any trials? I do not think you do. For that satisfies and fills up every longing of the human heart, and fills up every vacuum. When I am filled with that spirit my soul is satisfied; and I can say in good earnest, that the trifling things of the day do not seem to stand in my way at all. But just let me loose my hold of that spirit and power of the Gospel, and partake of the spirit of the world, in the slightest degree, and trouble comes; there is something wrong. I am tried; and what will comfort me? You cannot impart comfort to me that will satisfy the Immortal mind, but that which comes from the fountain above. And is it not our privilege to so live that we can have this constantly flowing into our souls? To be sure we have many of the crosses of life, but what do we meet them for? Are they for our own good and benefit or do we meet them all as for Zion's sake? Do we let Zion take full possession of our desires, our ambition?

Now my sisters, though I took that tour to Europe and Asia, would I have gone to gratify my own personal selfishness? I felt that it was right for me to go. My sisters sent me.[409] I went believing that good would result from my going. And I have had that belief all the time. I never once regretted starting. I told President [George A.] Smith that I did not think that anything could occur to make me regret that I went. I try never to allow myself to do anything for a selfish gratification. Still we are all frail and weak mortals, of the earth, earthy. But that comforter, which is a legacy that belongs to every Saint of God; and to every one who has been baptized for the remission of sins, will lift our desires to a nobler aim, and we forget all about self. We have self all

---

408. See John 14:26.

409. Local Relief Society minutes record donations to help pay for Snow's journey. For example, in Fillmore, Utah, "Donations for Sister E. R. Snow" totaled $40.80. Snow expressed appreciation to those who contributed in a poem titled "To My Magnanimous Friends." (Fillmore Ward, Millard Stake, Fillmore Ward Relief Society Minutes and Records, 1868–1947, CHL, Nov. 7, 1872; Eliza R. Snow, "Responsive," *Woman's Exponent,* Nov. 1, 1872, 1:83.)

absorbed in the interests of the work of God. We are here to perform duties, and to do our part towards establishing God's Kingdom. We, my sisters, have as much to do as our brethren have. We are to work in union with them. Every woman who fills her position as a wife, honorably, stands as a counselor to her husband. Not a dictator, a counselor. And what a life it is to live my sisters! What a noble life, to live, so as to fill this position, in which we are blessed, and are honorable as women of God.

Paul the Apostle anciently spoke of holy women.[410] It is the duty of each one of us to be a holy woman. We shall have elevated aims, if we are holy women. We shall feel that we are called to perform important duties. No one is exempt from them. There is no sister so isolated, and her sphere so narrow but what she can do a great deal towards establishing the Kingdom of God upon the earth.

I am proud to see so many young ladies associated with the Relief Society in Ogden. There should be an association in every settlement, and in every Ward in Salt Lake City. And wherever there is a Relief Society, the girls and young ladies should have as much to do as other women already in the Retrenchment Association.[411] You need not be startled at the words Retrenchment Association. If you associate together, your minds are improved, you are gaining intelligence, and you are retrenching from ignorance. The Spirit of God will impart instruction to your minds, and you will impart it to each other. I say, God bless you my young sisters. Remember that you are Saints of God; and that you have important works to perform in Zion.

How is it with a great many of our young people? They are baptized when they are eight years old, and have hands laid upon them for the gift of the Holy Ghost.[412] Do they know what the Holy Ghost is? Do they ever minister in the Holy Ghost? Have they ever had the gifts of the Gospel? Look around you and think how many there are, children of the Latter-day Saints, who know no more of the Gospel of Jesus Christ than the heathens do. Why? because they have had nothing to do with it. Their fathers and mothers are good Saints. But they are children of Zion. They can go their own way, and do as they list. They can be full of the spirit of the gentiles, and be so blind that they cannot see the difference between the professions of a gentile and the

---

410. See 1 Peter 3:3–5.

411. The organization of Retrenchment Associations for young women began in the winter of 1869–1870. (See Document 3.18.)

412. Latter-day Saints distinguished between the *power* of the Holy Ghost (the Comforter or Holy Spirit), "which is the gift of God unto all those who diligently seek him," and the *gift* of the Holy Ghost, which an individual receives following baptism "by the laying on of the hands of the elders of the church." (1 Nephi 10:17; Doctrine and Covenants 49:14.)

sincerity of the Saints. They have no light in them. Why is it? Was it so at the beginning of this Church? No it was not. I can bear testimony that in the beginning of the Church, children and young people had the gifts of the Gospel, and prayed and sang. They talked as much as old people. They knew what the Spirit of God was. There was no need of cautioning them about the spirit of the world. They had that monitor within them, the Holy Ghost which showed them things in their true light. I should like to see the effects of it now in our young people. There is some cause why it is not so. And I think it would amount to quite as much, and a little more, to have attention paid to these things in such a manner that it would save the children that are born in Zion, than it would to go to the trouble of raising money, and bringing the Saints from the nations of the earth. Why are there not some steps taken to save the youth?

Now, in Salt Lake City President Young, counseled Sister [Mary Isabella] Horne and myself, and Sister [Margaret] Smoot to organize the Young girls.[413] He wanted his young girls organized first. He dictated who should be president, and she to choose her Counselors, and start out right. But how did it work? There was cold water thrown on the efforts made. It was turned to ridicule by many. They said "what is the use of the girls meeting together, and praying, and talking?" And I would ask what is the use of our brethren meeting together? If the young girls and the boys do not need the Spirit of the Gospel, there does not any person need it. [p. 62] But, I think the state of society in Salt Lake City does need it. You may talk to the young about the follies of the world and the unholy influences of the gentiles till dooms day, and it will make no impression. But you place them in a position where they will get the Holy Ghost, and that will be a sure protection against outside influences. Some will say, "our boys are sent out on missions and then they get the Spirit of God." Some of the boys are sent on missions, and it is necessary to keep them out, that they may retain the Spirit of God, if there is not enough of it at home. Some of our young men who are sent out on missions are obliged to seek to God, but when they come home they are laughed out of it, and perhaps fall into the practices of those who are here! It is not so with all of them to be sure.

In referring again to the organization of the young ladies, I may say we have apostatized in Salt Lake City, but there are so many left as to show what

---

413. The "Young girls" referred to here are the daughters of Brigham Young, rather than young females in general. Snow's remarks here note the assignment she shared with Horne and Smoot in beginning the retrenchment movement for young women during the winter of 1869–1870. The three women were leaders in the older women's retrenchment movement. (See Documents 3.15 and 3.18.)

that organization would have been if carried out as President Young desired it to be. We have organizations of young ladiea in Salt Lake City, who do not need anybody to tell them about the influences and fashions of the world. They have just as much distaste for them as the older folks have. I do think to-day that if that counsel had been carried out among the young girls, and boys, and they had been organized and got the Spirit of God, that our society would have shown a very different character from what it does. Some of the mothers and fathers, who spoke lightly of it, now see the necessity of it, to their sorrow.

"Well, but now, Sister Eliza, are you not scolding folks?" I have to talk so loud, as I want you all to hear, and it may seem like scolding.

There are a great many good things that I could talk about, but I want to talk about things that will produce effects, and effects of salvation. It does not do to fool away our time, thinking that all is well. It is necessary for us to be laying that foundation, which will secure the salvation of the young, as well as of the old, and not leave it to the exigencies of time, nor to the chances of circumstances, but each one of us see to it ourselves, and cultivate those principles that will tend to salvation.

Now, I am thankful that these my young sisters meet together. You will be blest. Sister Richards will be blest for promoting these organizations. I understand you are in connection with the Relief Society. It makes no difference. But I want to say one or two things, that I wish you to remember. It is not only necessary for you to meet together, you should talk to each other, and talk of the Gospel of Jesus Christ. You can talk of your every-day concerns. But accustom yourselves to talking to each other on the principles of the Gospel. It will lay a foundation for your being eminently useful hereafter. That is what you are born for. You might as well have been born in some other nation or dispensation, unless you can feel that you have a mission in Zion. Study the principles of the Gospel, converse on them, understand them, so that you may be able to cope with any of the wisest of the world. They are coming here. They often ask questions of the young, when they would not interrogate the older ones. You want to understand that you are living to be Saints, and never be ashamed to acknowledge yourselves to be Latter-day Saints. It is not enough that you are born in Zion. It is true that the Prophets said it should be an honor to be born in Zion; but it is a dishonor not to live up to the blessings of the Gospel to which you are heirs.

I see the Relief Society here has no house of its own—no house that it can control. I know the sisters are accommodated. But each Society needs a house at its own disposal.[414] And if the sisters in Ogden, with the sanction of the brethren, undertake to build a house, the brethren will help them. It is said that God helps those who help themselves, and the brethren are so god-like that they will help you. Bishop Wooley [Edwin D. Woolley] is now stepping forward to have such a house built in the 13th Ward, in Salt Lake City.[415]

There is another thing I want to mention before I sit down. President Young is requiring the sisters to get students of Medicine. He wants a good many to get a clasical education, and then get a degree for Medicine. So far as getting the degree is concerned, there would be no advantage, but in connection with the degree, the female practitioner stands on the same grounds a man does. Are there here, now, any sisters who have ambition enough, and who realize the necessity of it, for Zion's sake, to take up this study. There are some who are naturally inclined to be nurses; and such ones would do well to study Medicine, if they are inclined to do so. If they cannot meet their own expenses, we have means of doing so. It is proposed that the sisters, instead of expending means to emigrate foreign Saints, spend that means in educating young women.[416] Those who go through this course should be young women. We have, in Salt Lake City, a Mrs. Barker, who proposes to teach.[417] But there are many branches you need to study before going to the expense of being boarded abroad to study. You need to study Physiology, Anatomy, and other kindred branches.

Then, another class of women is wanted more advanced in age, who are natural nurses, and would be willing to study obstetrics; this lady is going to

414. On the building of Relief Society halls, see Jennifer Reeder, "'To Do Something Extraordinary': Mormon Women and the Creation of a Usable Past" (PhD diss., George Mason University, 2013), 150–197.

415. The Thirteenth Ward hall was not built immediately. Relief Society meetings in that ward continued to be held in homes or at the ward assembly rooms until late 1885. The new "Society Hall" was formally dedicated January 21, 1886. (Thirteenth Ward, Ensign Stake, Thirteenth Ward Relief Society Minutes and Records, 1868–1906, CHL, vol. 1, Oct. 28, 1885; Nov. 25, 1885; Jan. 21, 1886, pp. 444–446, 650–651.)

416. Snow's proposal here was heeded. For example, in 1876 a Sister Davis traveled from Salt Lake City to Nephi, Utah, to appeal for such donations: "Sister Davis then gave an account of her mission here which was to gather means to defray the expenses of sister Romania Pratt who was at college studying obstetrics." Pratt studied medicine in New York, Philadelphia, and Boston from 1873 to 1877 and became the first female doctor to practice in Utah. (Nephi Ward, Juab Stake, Nephi Ward Relief Society Minutes and Records, 1868–1878, CHL, vol. 1, Sept. 26, 1876; see also Document 4.11.)

417. Mary Helen Barker, a physician who graduated from Woman's Medical College in Pennsylvania. "A school for ladies, who design studying and becoming conversant with the science of obstetrics, will be opened in this city, in a few days, by Mary H. Barker, M. D. . . . The lady, we understand, is fully competent to give a thorough classical course of that which she undertakes to teach, and is prepared to open a class as soon as books which have been sent for arrive from the East." ("Home Affairs," *Woman's Exponent,* Sept. 1, 1873, 2:53.)

give a series of lectures for their benefit. If some who have natural inclinations for nursing would come and attend these lectures, that would be fulfilling the requirements, so far. We are waiting to get up as large a class as we can. There are some eight or twelve now. President Young said that he wanted one, at least, from every settlement.[418] Of course, so large a city as Ogden, should furnish quite a number; so that we can have our own practitioners, instead of having gentlemen practitioners. In ancient times we know that women officiated in this department, and why should it not be so now? The difficulty is in getting the sisters to feel like undertaking it.

Now if there are any who will attend through all of these classes, their expenses will be met if they are not able to meet them. Several Ogden women should attend this course of lectures, and confine themselves to that particular department.

We have to get up these classes and attend to all these things. Don't you see that our sphere is increasing? Our sphere of action will continually widen, and no woman in Zion need to mourn because her sphere is too narrow.

God bless you, my sisters, and encourage you, that you may be filled with light, and realize that you have no interests but in the welfare of Zion. Let your first business be to perform your duties at home. But inasmuch as you are wise stewards, you will find time for social duties, because these are incumbent upon us as daughte[r]s and mothers in Zion. By seeking to perform every duty you will find that your capacity will increase, and you will be astonished at what you can accomplish. You have been astonished at what duties you have done. The Lord help us. The Lord is with His Saints and helps them to do His will, and He watches over them by night and by day. Inasmuch as we continue faithful, we shall be those that will be crowned in the presence of God and the lamb. You, my sisters, if you are faithful will become Queens of Queens, and Priestesses unto the Most High God. These are your callings. We have only to discharge our duties. By and by our labors will be past, and our names will be crowned with everlasting honor, and be had in everlasting remembrance among the Saints of the Most High God.

---

418. See Document 4.17 for the reminiscence of Emma Anderson Liljenquist, who in the late 1880s came from the "settlements" in Cache County to study obstetrics and nursing in Salt Lake City at the request of her bishop, and then returned home to practice midwifery in Hyrum, Utah.

3.24 Eliza R. Snow, Report to Philadelphia Centennial Exposition, March 1876

Eliza R. Snow, "The Relief Society," Report to the Committee on Charities, Philadelphia Centennial Exposition, [Mar. 1876]; ten pages; Eliza R. Snow, Papers, Special Collections, J. Willard Marriott Library, University of Utah, Salt Lake City (MS 0313).

Eliza R. Snow gathered reports on women's organizations in Utah Territory for the Committee on Charities of the 1876 Philadelphia Centennial Exposition, the first major World's Fair held in the United States. The Committee on Charities, part of the Women's Centennial Executive Committee that built and oversaw the fair's Women's Pavilion, called for reports on women's benevolent societies throughout the nation. As part of this effort, Snow, who served as a member of the Women's Centennial Executive Committee, wrote a ten-page history of the Relief Society, featured below, which she sent to the committee in March 1876.[419] Snow received little response from other Utah women's organizations but did send short reports she had gathered on the Ladies' Benevolent Society of the Congregational Church and the Independent Order of Good Templars, a temperance organization dominated by women.[420] In this history of the Relief Society, Snow emphasized its independence, effective organizational structure, and work on behalf of the poor, as well as the construction of a dedicated Relief Society building in the Salt Lake City Fifteenth Ward.

From May to October 1876, almost ten million people visited the Philadelphia Exposition, which featured exhibits from thirty-six nations. The exposition celebrated the centennial of the Declaration of Independence by highlighting exhibits from throughout the United States and from many foreign nations. In June 1875 a group of women who had helped raise funds for the Centennial Exposition were informed that there would be no room in the exposition's main hall for women's contributions. In response, the women decided to construct a large Women's Pavilion, which occupied forty thousand square feet and highlighted contributions from roughly fifteen hundred women. The Philadelphia exposition thus became the first World's Fair to have a separate building designated to showcase women's contributions to the arts, education, industry, and domestic life.[421]

---

419. Eliza R. Snow to Mrs. A. H. Smith, Mar. 28, 1876; Eliza R. Snow to Mary R. Smith, Mar. 4, 1876, Eliza R. Snow, Papers, Special Collections, J. Willard Marriott Library, University of Utah, Salt Lake City. In her March 28 letter Snow explained that the history was "ready for the Press," as the initial call for reports on women's organizations indicated that the reports would be published in a book. However, print publication was later deemed infeasible, and the reports were instead displayed in the Women's Department. (*Catalogue of Charities Conducted by Women, as Reported to the Women's Centennial Executive Committee of the United States* [Philadelphia: Collins, Printer, 1876], 3–4, 8.)

420. Eliza R. Snow, Papers, 1876, Special Collections, J. Willard Marriott Library, University of Utah, Salt Lake City.

421. Judith Paine, "The Women's Pavilion of 1876," *Feminist Art Journal* 4, no. 4 (Winter 1975–1976): 5–12; Sylvia Yount, "A 'New Century' for Women: Philadelphia's Centennial Exhibition and Domestic Reform," in *Philadelphia's Cultural Landscape: The Sartain Family Legacy,* ed. Katharine Martinez and Page Talbott (Philadelphia: Temple University Press, 2000), 149–160.

In her autobiography, Snow recalled that in November 1875 she was "notified of an appointment" to participate in the Women's Pavilion and not long after was invited to take charge of gathering items from Utah women for exhibition at the fair. Snow quickly organized a twelve-member committee made up primarily of Latter-day Saints and also of representatives from other established faiths in Utah.[422] The committee recognized the women's exhibit as an opportunity to provide a national audience with material evidence that might dispel negative perceptions of Utahns and Mormonism. In late 1875 the committee issued a call for donations of items to be sent to Philadelphia, asking for "all creditable specimens of women's work, both useful & ornamental, from a necklace to a carpet, and all natural curiosities of our own collecting." Those donating items were encouraged to list prices in case individuals at the exposition wished to purchase them.[423] Though only a small sample of the items collected in Utah was sent to Philadelphia as a result of limited funding, Snow's committee organized its own centennial celebration in a territorial fair during the summer of 1876, which Snow remembered as a "grand success."[424]

The Relief Society[425]

Is the principal Charitable Institution in Utah. It is conducted by the women of the Church of Jesus Christ of Latter-Day-Saints,[426] called "Mormons."

The Relief Society is a self-governing body—independent of any written code or instrument, such as Constitution, bye-laws etc.[427] It is organized with President, two Counselors, Secretary, Assistant Secretary, and Treasurer; with power to create, by majority vote of the Society, all officers, both standing and pro-tem, that shall be requisite to carry out the designs of the Institution, from time to time, and under every variety of circumstance: also to fill all vacancies that occur. In addition to the above mentioned, the members of a Visiting Committee, and also those of a Board of Appraisers, hold permanent official positions—all subject to removal through neglect of duty, or abuse of privileges.[428]

---

422. Eliza R. Snow, "Sketch of My Life," n.d., Bancroft Library, University of California, Berkeley, 39.

423. Eliza R. Snow et al., "Circular. To the Relief Societies, Retrenchment Associations, and the Women of Utah, Generally," [1875], International Society Daughters of Utah Pioneers, Pioneer Memorial Museum, Salt Lake City.

424. Snow, "Sketch of My Life," 40; Jill Mulvay Derr et al., *Women of Covenant: The Story of Relief Society* (Salt Lake City: Deseret Book; Provo, UT: Brigham Young University Press, 1992), 83–84.

425. TEXT: All three words triple underlined in original.

426. TEXT: An illegible word is struck through here.

427. In the March 17, 1842, organizational meeting of the Relief Society, Joseph Smith stated, "The minutes of your meetings will be precedents for you to act upon— your Constitutio[n] and law." (Document 1.2, entry for Mar. 17, 1842.)

428. For an earlier statement on Relief Society officers and their roles, see Document 3.9.

This Society was first organized in Nauvoo, Hancock Co. Illinois, where it was instrumental in accomplishing much good. Many of the citizens of that place, had been cruelly and forcibly driven from the State of Missouri by the notorious "<u>exterminating order</u>" of Gov. [Lilburn] Boggs,[429] by which they had been reduced to destitute circumstances, having sacrificed their homes and property to mob violence: and, partly owing to the sickly climate of Nauvoo, and partly from fatigue and exposure on their journey, much sickness prevailed, which occasioned heavy demands on fellow-sympathy, benevolence and kindness. And who so well qualified to officiate in these noble, self-sacrificing duties, as woman! And with her, the constant and large demands were far more generally and satisfactorily met through the united efforts of this effective organization, than otherwise would have been possible. During the extremely severe winter of 1842 and 3, many lives were preserved through its agency.

From the year 1846, the time of the exodus of the Latter-Day-Saints from Nauvoo, the Relief Society was inoperative until 1855, [p. 1] when it was reorganized in Salt Lake City.[430]

It was a hard struggle for a peoples exiled from their homes, with only what provisions they brought in wagons across the trackless plains, and ⟨with⟩ no supplies within the distance of one thousand miles; and ~~with~~ no other capital than brain, bone, and sinew, and unfaltering faith and trust in God, to battle with the elements, and reclaim a sterile desert soil for that support which nature demands. When this was accomplished, and a covenant which had been solemnly made, to assist all of the Nauvoo Saints, who needed assistance, to the valleys of the mountains, was fulfilled, arrangements were entered into, and a "Perpetual Emigrating Fund" established, to assist the suffering saints in Europe to emigrate to Utah. As they arrived by hundreds, and subsequently by thousands, their wants must be supplied, until, through their own efforts, and the kindly aid extended to them, they were enabled to provide for themselves. These circumstances added much to the already onerous labors and responsibilities of the Bishops, who preside as fathers, each over his respective Ward or Settlement.

---

429. The Missouri governor's 1838 "exterminating order" followed months of escalating violence between established Missourians and Latter-day Saints who had been moving into a cluster of northwestern Missouri counties since 1831. The order read in part: "The Mormons must be treated as enemies and must be exterminated or driven from the state if necessary for the public peace." Between January and April 1839, thousands of Latter-day Saints fled Missouri and made their way to Quincy, Illinois. (Lilburn W. Boggs to John B. Clark, Oct. 27, 1838, copy, Mormon War Papers, 1838–1841, Missouri State Archives, Jefferson City; see also William G. Hartley, "Missouri's 1838 Extermination Order and the Mormons' Forced Removal to Illinois," *Mormon Historical Studies* 2, no. 1 [Spring 2001]: 5–27.)

430. See Part 2 in this volume.

The Relief Society came to the relief of the Bishops by administering relief to the poor, in which capacity it has proven to be one of, if not the best organization ever known. Under its auspices, if the needy suffer from want, it must be their own fault, either through unwillingness to accept charity; or concealment of their circumstances; ⟨which⟩ is a very difficult task, for each Branch appoints a sufficient number for Visiting Com. to apportion two to each Block, and these, under ordinary circumstances—in time of general health, visit each family, at least once in each month, and report to the presiding Board; and it is the duty of those visiting women to know precisely the condition of the poor. If any are in want, they are supplied out of the Treasury, and when any are sick, who need assistance, they are specially cared for, and visited as their circumstances demand.

The funds of this Society were commenced, and are now [p. 2] mostly sustained by voluntary donations; however, there are many Branches that have moderate incomes from funds obtained through the various industries of the Society, being the proceeds of labor expended on donated material. Besides stated social and business meetings, each Branch has set days on which to meet and work for the benefit of the poor. Frequently other measures are resorted to for obtaining means, such as getting up Concerts, dances, Fairs &c. &c., the proceeds being devoted to the replenishing of the Treasuries.

Since its first introduction into Salt Lake City, the Society has extended in Branches, from Ward to Ward in the Cities and from settlement to settlement in the country, until it numbers considerably over one hundred Branches; and, as new settlements are constantly being formed, the number is annually increasing. Upwards of one hundred are represented in the Report of Disbursements appended to this sketch—many of them having been recently formed, have only commenced work.

Each Branch adopts measures—makes arrangements—appointments, and directs all of its financial concerns independently—adapting its regulations to whatever may be the peculiarities of its circumstances. Some hold weekly meetings, others semi-monthly, while some, not having accumulated sufficient means to build, have no house at their control, and meet according to convenience. Each organization needs, and as soon as practicable, builds its house, for the transaction of business and for the mutual benefit of its members.

That the Society may be universally effective, and capable of rendering immediate aid in every emergency, it is distributed throughout the Territory in such a manner that no one Branch is very large, consequently the Society Buildings are comparatively small, yet of respectable size, and sufficiently commodious for the purposes required. [p. 3] Utah has no "poor houses." Under the kind, sisterly policy of the Society, the poor feel much less humiliated, and better satisfied by being admitted into hospitable families, ⟨or by having rooms or homes provided for them,⟩ while they are looked after by the Committee, than they would, if immured in a solitary "poor house." Those who are emigrated from foreign countries by the Emigrating Fund, with the exception of the very aged and infirm, very soon, under the wise, fatherly counsels of the Bishops and other authorities of the Church, obtain for themselves comfortable homes, and ⟨are able,⟩ in their turn assist others.

The first industrial meetings of the Society in Salt Lake City, would naturally remind a spectator, of the Israelites in Egypt, making "<u>brick</u> <u>without</u> <u>straw</u>"[431]—the donations consisting of material for patch-work-quilts, rag-carpets, wool to be carded, spun and knitted into ⟨mittens,⟩ socks and stockings (no Machinery had then been imported) old clothes to be made over &c. and, in one instance at least, hair of beeves, was gathered from the slaughtering place, cleansed, carded, spun and knitted. These are things of record, or, probably they would be pronounced fabulous, even by many of the present members of the Society. To the honor of those indefatiguable laborers in the cause of human kindness, love and charity, let their deeds be "<u>engraven</u> <u>in</u> <u>the</u> <u>rock</u> <u>forever</u>."[432] Many of them yet live, and bear verbal testimony of the foregoing.

Those industrial gatherings continue to be very useful—even necessary, and truly interesting: but then, when we were without factories, and minus all kinds of machinery, to witness the strange varieties of work, brought into close fellowship, was a sight not easily forgotten—groups of cheerful faces, young and old, with willing hands—some with scissors, giving form to scraps of prints—some basting work for novices—some sewing—some embroidering—some carding batts for quilts—some spinning (for, on some occasions wheels were brought) for the knitters &c., and all for one common cause, the relief of the poor. Such articles as their condition required were made for the destitute; and, for financial profit, all kinds of useful and [p. 4] ornamental articles, for which suitable material could possibly be obtained, were manufactured. And, be it remembered, these humble, patient workers had not been strangers to the refinements and elegancies of life. Many of them had been reared in the midst of worldly popularity—were well educated, and, in woman's work, artisans of the higher type. For the sake of their religion they had taken "<u>cheerfully</u> <u>the</u> <u>spoiling</u> <u>of</u> <u>their</u> <u>goods</u>"[433]—made their homes in the desert, where they were

---

431. See Exodus 5:4–19.
432. Job 19:24.
433. Hebrews 10:34.

faithfully performing their part, that "<u>the solitary place might be glad for them, and the wilderness become a fruitful field</u>."[434]

These working meetings, as they are called, are always opened and closed by prayer and thanksgiving: the hope of success in these, as well as in every other enterprise, being firmly predicated in a reliance on the blessing of God on the wise and diligent application of those powers and faculties with which He has endowed His children.

The first Society Building was erected in Salt Lake City by the ladies of the 15th Ward. They commenced their labors as above described—their first capital stock being donations of pieces for patch-work, carpet-rags etc and by their indomitable energy and perseverence, they sustained their poor, and in a few years purchased land and built a commodious house, which has been a great convenience for Society purposes, to which the upper story is appropriated, while the lower story is occupied by the Ward Store, which, most of the time, has been conducted by the Society.

The erection of this house constituting a leading movement, the laying of the corner stone was ceremoniously performed. The occasion being an anomaly in the sphere of woman, a large concourse of people assembled on the ground at 2 P.M. of the 12th of Nov. 1868, and the novelty of its being the enterprize of woman ⟨excited⟩ much curiosity as well as interest on that unique occasion.[435] After the usual ceremony of corner-stone-laying, an address was read by Mrs. S. [Sarah] M. Kimball, Pres. of the Society, after which an extempore address was given [p. 5] by Miss E. R. Snow, on woman's relations to the other sex, followed by an encouraging, commendatory speech by R. [Robert] T. Burton, the Bishop of the Ward, and remarks appropriate to the occasion by Mrs. B. [Bathsheba] W. Smith—each speaker occupying the "corner stone," by turns.[436]

[437]<u>Extracts</u> from the <u>Address</u> by <u>Pres.</u> <u>Mrs.</u> <u>Kimball</u>.[438]

<u>Gentlemen</u> and <u>Ladies</u>,

---

434. Isaiah 35:1; 32:15.

435. The hall, located at present-day 340 West 100 South Street, housed a cooperative store on its lower story and an assembly room on the upper floor. Reports of the laying of the hall's cornerstone on November 12, 1868, and of the hall's dedication on August 5, 1869, appear in the record of the Salt Lake City Fifteenth Ward. (Fifteenth Ward, Riverside Stake, Relief Society Minutes and Records, 1868–1968, CHL, vol. 1; see also Document 3.10.)

436. For reports of these addresses, see Fifteenth Ward, Riverside Stake, Relief Society, Minutes, vol. 1, Nov. 12, 1868.

437. In copying Kimball's November 12 address from the Fifteenth Ward Relief Society minutes, Snow edited Kimball's wording. (See Fifteenth Ward, Riverside Stake, Relief Society, Minutes, vol. 1, Nov. 12, 1868.)

438. TEXT: Underlined words in title were double underlined in original.

I appear before you on this interesting occasion in behalf of the Relief Society, to express thanks to Almighty God, that the wheels of progress have been permitted to run until they have brought us to a more extended field of useful labor for female minds and hands.

It will readily be admitted that woman's sphere of labor is not sufficiently extensive and varied to enable her to exercise all of her powers and faculties in the manner best calculated to strengthen, develop and perfect her; nor are her labors sufficiently remunerative to insure her that independence essential to true womanly dignity. . . .[439]

With feelings of humility and gratitude, I contemplate the anticipated result of the completion of our unpretending edifice, the upper story of which will be dedicated to Art and Science[440]—the lower one to Trade and Commerce. I view this as a stepping-stone to similar enterprises, on a grander scale.

The object of the building is to enable the members of the Society more perfectly to combine their labors—their means—their tastes ⟨and⟩ their talents for improvement physically, socially, morally, intellectually and financially, for more extended usefulness.

To those gentlemen who have kindly proffered aid in this enterprise, in behalf of the cause for which we labor, we extend heartfelt thanks.

We feel that our friends who kindly patronize us, will expect much at our hands. We promise you our best endeavors to meet [p. 6] your highest expectations. But we ask you to mercifully remember that the seat of the merchant's counting-room-table is a new one for us to occupy, and, as pioneers for our sex in this department of woman's labor in our Territory, we beg you not to be severe in your criticisms, but show your magnanimity by giving us an approving look and an encouraging word. With such helps, and the continued blessing of God, we have confidence that we shall be enabled to extend needed relief, and make our labors a blessing to the cause of humanity.

---

439. TEXT: The ellipsis is marked in the original with five "x" marks. Snow omitted two paragraphs in which Kimball stated that the "practical part of this theory, unless wisely conducted, may subject us to criticisms and censure" but expressed optimism that their work "in the direction of human progress and universal good" would be recognized. In addition, Kimball recounted her attendance at the cornerstone and dedication ceremonies of the Kirtland, Ohio, temple and the Nauvoo, Illinois, temple, as well as at the cornerstone ceremony of the Salt Lake City temple then under construction. (Fifteenth Ward, Riverside Stake, Relief Society, Minutes, vol. 1, Nov. 12, 1868.)

440. In the original address, Kimball included "worship" among the purposes of the upper story. (Fifteenth Ward, Riverside Stake, Relief Society, Minutes, vol. 1, Nov. 12, 1868.)

At the Dedication of the building, after its completion, the following—composed for the occasion by Miss E. R. Snow, was sung by the Society Choir.[441]

[442]<u>Dedication</u> <u>Hymn</u>[443]

From God, the Source of life and grace,
    Our streams of blessings flow;
This day, His holy name we praise
    And grateful thanks bestow.

Thou God of truth and righteousness,
    For faith we ask of Thee,
Preserve this humble edifice
    From all impurity.

Here let thy holy Spirit rest
    Without a chain to bind:
May all who enter in, be blest
    In body and in mind.

Here may th' influence of thy love,
    Devotion's pulses fire;
And may we strive in every move, [p. 7]
    To lift our natures higher.

May union in this Hall abide
    With Godlike strength and skill:
And Father, let thy wisdom guide,
    And each department fill.

We dedicate this House to Thee,
    As love and labor's bower:
May Zion's welfare ever be
    Its ruling motive power.

And here may thought and speech be free.

441. For a report of the complete dedicatory ceremony, see Fifteenth Ward, Riverside Stake, Relief Society, Minutes, vol. 1, Aug. 5, 1869.

442. See Eliza R. Snow, "Dedication Hymn," in Jill Mulvay Derr and Karen Lynn Davidson, eds., *Eliza R. Snow: The Complete Poetry* (Provo, UT: Brigham Young University Press; Salt Lake City: University of Utah Press, 2009), 795–796.

443. TEXT: Both words triple underlined in original.

Instruction to impart,
Commercial and financially—
　　In science and in art.

In works of mercy, faith and love,
　　To banish want and woe,
The records of this House shall prove
　　We're neither slack nor slow.

Where love and duty mark the way,
　　Improving heart and head,
Onward and upward day by day,
　　We'll move with tireless tread.

O God, our strength—our great reward,
　　Speed Thou, the glorious time
When "Holiness unto the Lord"[444]
　　Shall mark each grand design. [p. 8]

All houses built by the Relief Society, are, on their opening, formally dedicated with appropriate ceremonies.

The foregoing Address and Dedication Hymn are inserted as being expressive of the design of the Institution, which is not merely for the temporal benefit of the poor, although that may properly be termed its first, and one of its constant duties; but what is of still greater importance, it is designed, and has already become a power for good in society, socially, morally, and spiritually—not only in cultivating its members, but also in extending a purifying, elevating and ennobling influence wherever woman's influence can reach.

The other Branches ⟨of the Society⟩ having failed to forward their Reports; the following catalogue, which has been compiled from their Records, is the aggregate of the Disbursements of 110, (one hundred and ten) since the several dates of their organizations.

To wit,

Donations for the relief and support of the poor				$. _60,292,91	
"	for the Emigration of the poor	___	___	5,981,20	
"	for Missions	___ ___	___	___	9,40,43[445]
"	for Sundry Charities	___ ___	___	___	1,917,63
"	for Building purposes	___ ___	___	___	13,465,07

---

444. Exodus 28:36.
445. That is, 940.43.

Total ___ $.__82,397,24[446]

In addition to the above, the Society is doing much, and expending no inconsiderable amount in establishing and promoting various branches of Home Industries.

[447]The <u>Relief Society.—What is it</u>?[448]

It is an Institution formed to bless
The poor, the widow, and the fatherless: [p. 9]
To clothe the naked, and the hungry feed,
And in the holy paths of virtue, lead.

To seek where anguish, grief, and sorrow are,
And light the torch of hope eternal, there:
To prove the strength of consolation's art,
By breathing comfort to the mourner's heart:

To chase the clouds that shade the aspect, where
Sad mis'ry dwells, and waken pleasure there:
With open heart to extend the friendly hand
To welcome strangers from a distant land:

To stamp a withering impress on each move
That virtue's noble self would disapprove:
To put the tattler's coinage, scandal down,
And make corruption feel its scathing frown:

To give instruction, where instruction's voice
Will lead from gross to pure, refining joys:
To turn the wayward from their recklessness,
And guide them in the paths of happiness.

It is an order, fitted and designed
To cultivate and elevate the mind:
To seek the needy, in the lone abode—
Supply their wants, and lead them up to God.

E. R. S.

---

446. In her "Sketch of My Life," Snow recalled this amount as "between ninety 2 and ninety three thousand dollars Disbursed by the Society." (Snow, "Sketch of My Life," 37.)

447. Snow revised this poem for inclusion here; the original version was published in 1842. (See Document 1.4.)

448. TEXT: First three words of this title triple underlined in original. Final three words double underlined in original.

3.25 Committees on the Grain Movement, Minutes, November 17, 1876

Committees on the Grain Movement, Minutes, Nov. 17, 1876, in "General Meeting of Central and Ward Committees, on the Grain Movement," Woman's Exponent *(Salt Lake City, UT), Dec. 1, 1876, vol. 5, no. 13, p. 99.*

At the request of Brigham Young, Emmeline B. Wells published two editorials in the *Woman's Exponent* in fall 1876 urging local Relief Societies to begin a grain storage program and to send in reports on this work. She wrote with the hope that "the subject might be agitated in public and private until every mother and every sister should feel the necessity of immediate action."[449] At a November 11 Retrenchment Society meeting Eliza R. Snow suggested that the women form a central committee to oversee grain storage. At Snow's recommendation, attendees voted to sustain Wells as committee chair; Wells then chose Snow and Bathsheba W. Smith as committee members, who were also voted in unanimously.[450]

The first official meeting of the newly formed Central Grain Committee was held November 17, 1876, in the Salt Lake City Social Hall. Officers of local Relief Societies attended, making this a general meeting of the central committee with the various local ward committees. As evidenced in the published minutes of the meeting transcribed below, the women took their new charge seriously. Likely in part because of their millennial beliefs that calamities would occur before the second coming of Jesus Christ, they anticipated their grain would be needed both by Saints and others during a large-scale famine in the not-too-distant future. They discussed how best to organize the central committee, including how to store the grain and to request cooperation from Relief Societies throughout Utah. Wheat storage would become so closely identified with the work of the Relief Society that two stocks of wheat were later depicted on the official Relief Society emblem.[451]

By 1876 Brigham Young had encouraged the storage of wheat for many years. From 1847 to 1876 the trek west, occasional widespread crop failures, the Utah War, and the Civil War had led Latter-day Saints to be prepared for periodic food shortages. Even after the completion of the transcontinental railroad in 1869 opened the possibility that grain supplies could be acquired from outside Utah rather quickly in time of need, church leaders continued to insist that portions of each grain crop be held over. Voluntary grain-saving, however, had not been collectively successful throughout the territory. The exhortations of church leaders, particularly Brigham Young and Heber C. Kimball, failed to induce the

---

449. "Sisters Be in Earnest," *Woman's Exponent,* Oct. 15, 1876, 5:76; "Be Wise and Hearken to Counsel," *Woman's Exponent,* Nov. 1, 1876, 5:84.

450. "Store Up Grain," *Woman's Exponent,* Nov. 15, 1876, 5:92; "Grain Saving in the Relief Society," *Relief Society Magazine* 2, no. 2 (Feb. 1915): 51–52.

451. Utah artist John Septimus "Jack" Sears created the emblem in a Relief Society–sponsored contest that was held to select an official seal for the 1942 Relief Society centennial celebrations. ("Relief Society Selects Centennial Seal by Jack Sears," *Improvement Era* 44, no. 9 [Sept. 1941]: 542.)

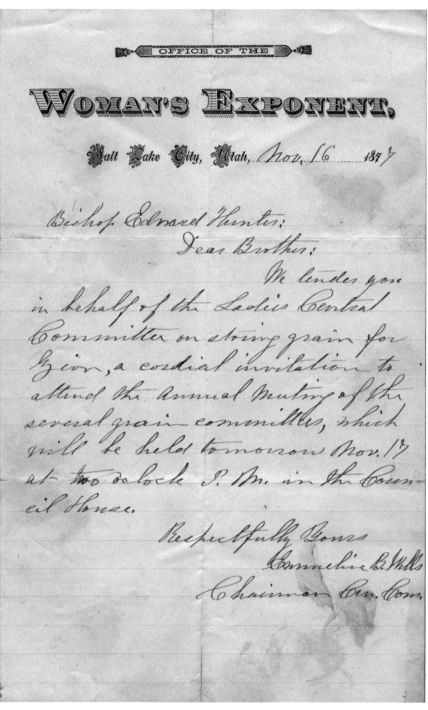

OFFICE OF THE

WOMAN'S EXPONENT,

Salt Lake City, Utah, *Nov. 16* *1877*

Bishop Edward Hunter:

Dear Brother:

We tender you
in behalf of the Ladies Central
Committee on storing grain for
Zion, a cordial invitation to
attend the Annual Meeting of the
several grain committees, which
will be held tomorrow Nov. 17
at two o'clock P. M. in the Council House.

Respectfully Yours

Emmeline B. Wells
Chairman Cen. Com.

Invitation to meeting of grain committees. The second annual meeting of the central and ward grain committees was held November 17, 1877. Emmeline B. Wells, chair of the central committee, invited Edward Hunter, the church's presiding bishop, to the meeting. (Church History Library, Salt Lake City.)

men to forego immediate sale for cash. Finally, Young directed his request to the women.[452]

---- ----

GENERAL MEETING OF CENTRAL AND WARD COMMITTEES,
ON THE GRAIN MOVEMENT.

The meeting was held in the Social Hall on the 17th of November 1876. Called to order, and opened with prayer by Mrs. E. [Elizabeth] Howard. President of Central Committee, Mrs. E. [Emmeline] B. Wells, remarked as follows: "It is very generally understood that this meeting is called to discuss the GRAIN QUESTION, It would be well to let our thoughts and words be concentrated on the subject; we want to make the best use of our time and use all dispatch, that the sisters may get home in good season. We would like the Presidents of Relief Societies to let us know what their ideas are on the subject.["]

Miss E. [Eliza] R. Snow said: It is a very important occasion that has called us together, probably such as never occurred on the earth before. The Lord, through his prophet, has called on the mothers in Israel to prepare for a famine, which makes the subject we are called on to discuss a grave one. We are well assured that the time is fast approaching when the Lord will pour out His indignation on this country,[453] and although we should escape, we will feel the effects of it in a National capacity. Our hearts must be hard indeed, if we will not feel for those who may come to us for help. The Lord showed his servant Joseph that such things would come, and it was of such a nature, and so distressing and revolting to humanity to witness, that he asked the Lord to close it up. We can see, from what has passed, that the predictions of the Servant of God, have been fulfilled to the letter. He has now called on the women of Zion to purchase and take care of wheat, and I hope we may act with wisdom, that the blessing of God may rest upon our labors. We want to decide how to procure the grain and take care of it; and whether we will act in Wards or in a general capacity; we have been told that there is room in the Tithing Office to store it.[454] But perhaps some of the Wards have a good place for storing; if so, and they prefer it, they can do so.

---

452. See E. Cecil McGavin and Albert L. Zobell Jr., "Grain Storage among the Latter-day Saints," *Improvement Era* 44, no. 3 (Mar. 1941): 142–144, 180–186; Emmeline B. Wells, "The Grain Question," *Relief Society Bulletin* 1, no. 9 (Sept. 1914): 1–3; Leonard J. Arrington, "The Economic Role of Pioneer Mormon Women," *Western Humanities Review* 9, no. 2 (Spring 1955): 157–161; and Jessie L. Embry, "Relief Society Grain Storage Program, 1876–1940" (master's thesis, Brigham Young University, 1974).

453. See Psalm 69:24; Zephaniah 3:8; Revelation 14:10; and Doctrine and Covenants 101:11.

454. At the November 11, 1876, retrenchment meeting a few days earlier, Snow repeated Bishop Robert T. Burton's words that wards without suitable grain storage facilities could store grain at the

Mrs. E. B Wells said: Bishop [Edward] Hunter told me we could store the wheat in the Tithing Office, and that the wards could also if they wished, as there was plenty of room unoccupied now; but whatever we do there, we will have to employ help, as the brethren who labor there are all fully employed.

Mrs. S. [Sarah] M. Kimball said: We have appointed a committee to visit in our ward. They report that the feelings of the people have been liberal and good. All we want to know is what steps we are to take in order to push the work forward. I feel that the Lord will bless us in our undertaking.

Mrs. E. B. Wells asked if any of the sisters could inform the meeting where wheat could be purchased.

Mrs. W. [Wilmirth] East: I expect Mrs. [Mary Isabella] Horne can tell us where we can buy wheat, when she returns from the South. I have been told that the brethren residing in the country places, are awakening up, and see the utility of saving grain, and it may not be a very easy matter for the sisters to procure it. We held a meeting in the 14th Ward a short time ago exclusively for this question. The sisters feel the importance of the mission and will do all in their power to accomplish it. We feel that the Lord will open up the way for us to get wheat; and that he will bless us in our efforts.

Mrs. Elizabeth Goddard: I have heard that wheat can be bought for a dollar a bushel; and I think it would be well to take flour also, it can be kept good in sacks for a long time.

Mrs. E. [Elvira] S. Barney: I can report from three counties where they have no grain for sale; Morgan, Summit and Wasatch, were distressed with an early frost, which destroyed nearly all their wheat; but feel sure that we can make this business a success.

Mrs. R. [Rachel] Grant: The 13th Ward intend saving grain. We have had a large bin offered us for that purpose, which we will accept. It has long been preached that the brethren should prepare for a day of famine; it now seems as if the women were to have a hand in it, and I hope the Lord will give us strength to perform our work nobly.

Mrs. Sarah Howard: I feel it is a privilege the Lord has given us, and we will try and be united in it. For my part I will try and do all I can, and I feel that the Lord will open a way whereby we can obtain grain, although it is late in the season. Our Retrenchment Association has commenced a fund for that purpose, we will work in concert with the 20th Ward Relief Society.

General Tithing Office as long as they looked to its maintenance themselves. ("Store Up Grain," *Woman's Exponent*, Nov. 15, 1876, 5:92.)

Mrs. [Annie] Savage said: In the 20th Ward, they intend doing the best they can to help in this work, but just at the present time there are no funds in the Treasury.

Mrs. M. M. [Marinda N.] Hyde, 17th Ward, said: We intend to build a hall for the use of our Society; when we heard of this grain business, we talked the matter over, and think of making the hall smaller, and putting up a bin for wheat in part of it. I would just suggest, that in the States, wheat sometimes spoils, through dampness, but our atmosphere being so dry, I expect it would keep good for some time.

Mrs. E. B. Wells: President Young said the sisters were to solicit help from their husbands and the brethren, for this purpose; by that means we would be able to get funds to purchase the wheat with.

Mrs. [Diana] Reid, of the 16th Ward, said: The sisters of our Ward are willing to do all they can to carry out counsel.

Mrs. L. [Louisa] G. Richards: I think that if we unite our means, and have one energetic sister to buy up the wheat; and by having one, two or three hundred dollars, quite an amount could be procured, and I think would be better than being mixed up in wards.

Miss E. R. Snow said: What I have to give, I intend putting it with the bulk. I know no separate interest. I hope energetic sisters will be appointed to attend to it; one or two in each ward say, or a committee be formed, as may seem necessary.

Mrs. E. B. Wells remarked: I presume all the boards of the Relief Society will co-operate in this work, and I think it will be well for us to unite.

Mrs. Chase of the 1st Ward: I have talked on this subject in our meeting, and we intend to unite with the rest in whatever plan they may suggest. I have a large bin in which a great amount of wheat could be stored; perhaps all we could get this year. We have quite a number of poor, but will be able to help some in all good calls. At one time my husband put up a good deal of wheat but after some time the weevil spoiled it. But I hope we can plan some way to take care of that which the Lord will bless us with.

It was then moved and seconded that a general committee be appointed to purchase, but that will not hinder wards from having ward committees.

The following ladies were elected as a purchasing committee: Mrs. E. S. Barney, Mrs. E. Howard, and Mrs. S. M. Kimball.

Mrs. E. B. Wells said: Let every sister secure and store away every bushel of wheat that it is possible for her to obtain. She also said it will be necessary to have a Treasurer in some central place. Mrs. P. [Priscilla] M. Staines was sustained as Treasurer.

It was proposed that a record be kept of the proceedings in each ward, every name and donation put down in a distinct manner.

It was suggested that we commence at once and have no delay about it. In Manti they have put up 60 or 70 bushels, and we can't be too prompt in this matter. Many of the brethren seem to wish to help us.

Mrs. Mercy Thompson said: Flour that is well sacked and kept in a dry place would keep as well, if not better, than wheat. I have some flour now using, that has been sacked four years, and it is as good, if not better than new flour. I know that the Lord will bless us in our undertaking.

Considerable business was transacted in regard to the Woman's Book about to be published;[455] and the propriety of the sisters making a carpet for the Historian's Office was taken into consideration and the sisters donated liberally for that purpose.

Meeting adjourned until Nov. 24th, at 3 o'clock p. m. Sung "The Spirit of God like a fire is burning."[456] Benediction by Mrs. Rachel Grant.

---

455. The book was Edward W. Tullidge's *The Women of Mormondom* (New York: Tullidge and Crandall, 1877).

456. Hymn 244, *Sacred Hymns and Spiritual Songs for the Church of Jesus Christ of Latter-day Saints,* 15th ed. (Liverpool: Albert Carrington, 1871), 268–270.

3.26 Weber Stake Relief Society, Minutes, July 19, 1877

Weber Stake Relief Society, Minutes, July 19, 1877; Weber Stake, Relief Society Minutes and Records, 1867–1968, vol. 6, 1877–1900, pp. 3–5, CHL (LR 9970 14).

Brigham Young first organized the Relief Society on a stake level at a Relief Society and Young Ladies' meeting in the Ogden tabernacle on July 19, 1877. Ecclesiastical organization was on his mind; he spent the spring and summer of 1877 orchestrating a major reorganization of stakes, wards, and priesthood quorums throughout Utah Territory. At the beginning of the reorganization, there were thirteen stakes in the territory; six of the stakes were presided over by apostles, many stakes were incompletely organized, and leaders of the Salt Lake Stake were perceived to have supervisory authority over the other stakes. During the reorganization, Young and other church leaders created seven new stakes, released the apostles from their stake duties and called many new leaders, and clarified that all stakes were equal to the Salt Lake Stake. For instance, Young reorganized Weber Stake, centered in Ogden, in late May, releasing apostle Franklin D. Richards as stake president.[457] Nevertheless, the decision to appoint a stake Relief Society presidency appears to have been somewhat spontaneous. According to the minutes of the July 19 meeting transcribed below, Young had been discussing the possibility of organizing Relief Society on a stake level with Bathsheba W. Smith and others during the journey to Ogden. After giving a discourse on other topics near the beginning of the meeting, he continued to discuss the idea on the stand while other church leaders addressed the congregation. When Young then arose to give some additional remarks, he turned the new idea into official precedent.

Young appointed Jane Snyder Richards, president of the Ogden Ward Relief Society and the wife of apostle Franklin D. Richards, as the first stake Relief Society president. Since being appointed as a ward president in August 1872, she had already been acting in a supervisory role over other ward Relief Societies in the area, having been blessed with her counselors "under the hands of Apostle Richards and Bp. [Lester J.] Herrick to labor not only in the R. S. of Ogden but also to visit and counsel the societies throughout Weber County."[458] Perhaps as a result of this role, Jane Richards and her counselors, Harriet C. Brown and Sarah G. Herrick, sat on the stand with Brigham Young and other leaders at the July 19, 1877, conference and were referred to in the minutes as the "Presidency of the Stake Relief Societies" at the beginning of the conference. Eliza R. Snow noted that the Weber Stake had "led out in a new direction," a direction that President Young approved and solidified in the July 1877 meeting.[459] Young encouraged the women to hold quarterly stake conferences with reports from each local Relief Society organization, and he promised to return in three months' time to officially open the first conference. Snow summarized the

---

457. See William G. Hartley, "The Priesthood Reorganization of 1877: Brigham Young's Last Achievement," *BYU Studies* 20, no. 1 (Fall 1979): 3–36.

458. History of the Relief Society in Weber County, 1887, in Richards Family Collection, 1837–1961, CHL, 3.

459. Weber Stake, Weber Stake Relief Society Minutes and Records, 1867–1968, CHL, vol. 6, Oct. 30, 1877, p. 28.

event: "At a special meeting of the ladies of Weber Co. President Young had appointed Mrs. Jane S. Richards to preside over the various branches of the Relief Society in that Stake of Zion, and had appointed a meeting to be convened three months from that time, at which he requested they should bring a written report from each society in the county, of their progress and finance from their first organization."[460] Young's sermon was later published, and copies were distributed at the first quarterly conference of the Weber Stake Relief Society.[461]

Following the July 19 meeting, Brigham Young traveled to organize the nearby Box Elder Stake and "required Sister Jane S Richards to leave the bedside of a sick child and go with him. They continued in close conversation during the trip; he instructing her in the varied duties of her presidency and the importance of keeping faithful records of all their doings."[462] Richards recalled, "When President Young first said we were to have Quarterly meetings, I was astonished, it almost made me stagger; the idea of the sisters having a Conference."[463] That summer or fall, "Sister Eliza R. Snow, President of all the Relief Societies in the Church, accompanied Sister Jane S. Richards at a meeting of each ward society in the Weber Stake, and presented her as the president of their Stake organization."[464] Following the Weber example, other stake Relief Society organizations were formed, beginning in December 1877, when Eliza R. Snow organized the Relief Society in the Salt Lake Stake as the second stake Relief Society organization.[465]

The minutes of the July 19 meeting are reproduced below from the Weber Stake Relief Society Minute Book. The textual history of the minutes is somewhat unclear. It appears the minutes as they exist may have been copied into the minute book well after the July meeting and may have been modified to some degree between the time of the meeting and the time they were copied into the minute book.[466] The minutes are also incomplete, as they do not explicitly refer to the selection of Richards as the president of the stake Relief Society. This absence is explained by a note recorded in the minute book directly following the minutes of the July 19 meeting and signed by Franklin and Jane Richards, as well as other leaders: "In the consummate interest felt by the sisters in Pres. Young's visit and discourse, together with the fact of the imperfect organization; and as yet, not fully appreciating the

460. "R. S. Reports," *Woman's Exponent,* Jan. 1, 1878, 6:114; see also Weber Stake Relief Society Minutes and Records, vol. 6, p. 6.

461. See Document 3.28.

462. Weber Stake Relief Society Minutes and Records, vol. 6, p. 5.

463. Salt Lake Stake, Salt Lake Stake Relief Society Record Book, 1868–1903, CHL, June 22, 1878, p. 9.

464. Weber Stake Relief Society Minutes and Records, vol. 6, p. 6.

465. See Document 3.29.

466. In the minute book the minutes are immediately followed by a note (not reproduced in this volume) that is written in the same handwriting and the same ink flow as the minutes, suggesting it was probably inscribed in the minute book at the same time as the minutes. The note refers to events that occurred in fall 1877 and beyond, suggesting the minutes were not copied into the minute book until well after the July meeting. There is also at least one apparent anachronism in the minutes: the minutes refer to Brigham Young's opening discourse as being "famous," an adjective that more likely would have been used in the months after the meeting, when the discourse was published and distributed widely.

importance of records; and as this particular feature of the occasion was omitted in the report of the sermon, it failed of record at the time."[467]

Minutes of a special general Conference, of the Relief Societies and Young Ladies Associations of Weber Stake of Zion, held in the Ogden Tabernacle on Thursday the 19th day of July 1877—

President Brigham Young—(having been invited by Pres. Jane S. Richards, to come to Ogden and talk to the ladies of Weber County,) was present on the stand, also Pres. Daniel H. Wells, and apostles John Taylor, F. D. Richards and Albert Carrington; of the Stake presidency there were present, D. [David] H. Peery—L. J. Herrick and C. [Charles] F. Middleton; of the Presidency of the Stake Relief Societies, Jane S. Richards, Harriet C. Brown and Sarah Herrick;[468] of the Young Ladies Associations, Emily T. Richards, Mary Ann Riley and Mary Ann Ellis.

The Tabernacle was fully occupied, every part being crowded with people of both sexes; as an invitation to attend the meeting, had been extended to all who desired to come.

At 11 o'clock services commenced in the usual manner, by singing and prayer; after which, Pres. Young—being in but feeble health—delivered his famous sermon to the assembled multitude; which is contained in this record, commencing on page 7[469]

467. Weber Stake Relief Society Minutes and Records, vol. 6, pp. 5–6. The note is undersigned by Franklin D. Richards (apostle), David H. Peery (stake president), Charles F. Middleton (counselor in the stake presidency), James Taylor (the reporter of Young's discourse), Zina D. H. Young, Jane S. Richards, Bathsheba W. Smith, Harriet C. Brown, Sarah A. Herrick, and Emily S. Richards (president of the Weber Young Ladies' Association).

468. Brown and Herrick were counselors to Richards in the Ogden Ward Relief Society and later became her counselors in the Weber Stake Relief Society presidency. (Weber Stake Relief Society Minutes and Records, Dec. 16, 1875, vol. 5, p. 5; May 2, 1878, vol. 6, p. 35.)

469. This is a reference to the version of Young's discourse inscribed in volume 6 of the Weber Stake Relief Society Minute Book, beginning on page 7 (following the minutes and a note that follows them). Noting that "these societies are for the improvement of our manners, our dress, our habits and our methods of living," Young focused in his discourse on child-rearing and the roles of mothers; he gave advice on a variety of subjects, including eating a healthy diet, teaching children to avoid contention, training children spiritually, participating in home manufacture, and raising silk. Young also said he had expected to hear reports at the meeting from the Relief Societies in the stake until he was informed that the women had hoped to receive instructions from the brethren. The discourse is also reported in volume 5 of the Weber Stake Relief Society minutes. Since both of these minute book versions are clean copies in longhand, they must have been copied from some other source. Young's discourse was summarized in "Home Affairs," *Woman's Exponent,* Aug. 1, 1877, 6:36–37, and published in full in the October 13, 1877, issue of the *Deseret Evening News;* the October 17, 1877, issue of the weekly edition of the *Deseret News;* and the October 17 and 25, 1877, issues of the *Ogden Junction.* Because Young actually spoke twice at the

Elder Carrington next addressed the meeting. He spoke at some length upon fashion, which to him, he said, was a myth; he asked no odds of Mrs. Grundy;[470] felt that it was beneath the dignity of a saint to follow the fashions of "Babylon"; exhorted the sisters to make their own fashions said that some of the sisters were a head of the brethren in many good things. [p. 3]

Pres. Daniel H. Wells, in the course of his remarks, said he had long conceded woman was a power in the earth; and he hailed these organizations of the sisters, as a harbinger of good results; carrying with it, as it did, an influence more manifest than in times past. Said woman was an indispensible help meet to man, and should occupy that position in all practical work in building up the kingdom of God, as well as in spiritual work and exhaltation. Said that the saints of God should learn to govern and control themselves, according to the laws that govern our being, and the principles of life and salvation.

Elder John Taylor said there were more women present than it was usual to meet; he alluded to woman's faith; referred to the counsel which a woman gave to the rich man, whom the Savior told to go and dip seven times in Jordan; the man felt it was too little a thing, but the woman had faith and intuition; and by listening to her, he was healed, through obedience.[471] Spoke of obeying the laws of life and health, to preserve our lives to the age of a tree;[472] and alluded to the manner in which children are brought up in the aristocratic families of Europe, and said, as saints, we ought to be more particular in the training of our children, than the people of the world are, and pray God ever to help us.[473]

Pres. Young again arose and spoke briefly in regard to a topic, upon which he seemed to be greatly exercised, and of which he had spoken to Sister Bathsheba W. Smith, and others, while on their way to Ogden—namely—that of organizing the Relief Societies so as to require them to hold Quarterly Conferences in each Stake of Zion.

---

meeting—a lengthy discourse at the beginning of the meeting and evidently more brief remarks near the end—it is possible the reports of the opening discourse include information from both of the addresses he gave that day. (Brigham Young, Discourse, July 19, 1877, in Weber Stake Relief Society Minutes and Records, vol. 6, pp. 7–22; vol. 5, pp. 239–256.)

470. "Mrs. Grundy" is an imaginary personage who is "proverbially referred to as a personification of the tyranny of social opinion in matters of conventional propriety." ("Grundy," in *The Oxford English Dictionary*, ed. J. A. Simpson and E. S. C. Weiner, 2nd ed., 20 vols. [Oxford: Clarendon, 1989], 6:906.)

471. See 2 Kings 5:1–14. Elisha directed Naaman to bathe in the Jordan River seven times to be cleansed of leprosy. Naaman had gone to Elisha on the advice of an Israelite slave girl who served Naaman's wife.

472. See Doctrine and Covenants 101:30.

473. The reports given in these minutes for the addresses by Carrington, Wells, and Taylor closely match the reports for their addresses given in the *Woman's Exponent*, indicating the *Exponent* report drew on the minutes or vice versa. ("Home Affairs," *Woman's Exponent*, Aug. 1, 1877, 6:37.)

He had been deliberating with Pres. D. H. Peery, Sister Jane S. Richards and others near him in the stand, upon this subject, while seated during the remarks of Pres. Wells and Apostle Taylor and Carrington; and as a result, proposed that this meeting be adjourned for three months; at which [p. 4] time he would meet with them again; his health permitting. He then instructed the Presidents of the ward Societies, to prepare for that meeting, written reports of the spiritual and financial condition of their several organizations, together with the amount of labor performed by each, since their first organization, and thereafter report their doings at their Quarterly Conferences.[474]

Elder Franklin D. Richards then made a few closing remarks, requesting in behalf of Mrs. Richards, President of Weber County Societies, that the societies prepare reports according to Pres. Young's instructions; to be read at the proposed meeting, three months from that time; to which time, the meeting was then adjourned.

Before closing, a request was made, for all the Sisters, who felt like entering more fully and earnestly into the work of home industries, and helping to become self sustaining, to rise to their feet; to which every one in the room gladly responded.[475]

---

474. For information on how Young's instructions were carried out, see Documents 3.27 and 3.28. The *Exponent* report of the meeting indicates that in his second address at the meeting, Young also gave "practical instructions" concerning sericulture and dress. ("Home Affairs," *Woman's Exponent*, Aug. 1, 1877, 6:37.)

475. The last two paragraphs of these minutes closely match language in the *Woman's Exponent* report, indicating the *Exponent* report drew on the minutes or vice versa. (See "Home Affairs," *Woman's Exponent*, Aug. 1, 1877, 6:37.)

3.27 John Taylor, Discourse, October 21, 1877 (Excerpt)

John Taylor, Discourse, Oct. 21, 1877, in "Discourse Delivered by President John Taylor, in the Ogden Tabernacle, on Sunday Afternoon, October 21, 1877," Deseret News *[semi-weekly] (Salt Lake City, UT), Apr. 16, 1878, vol. 13, no. 23, p. [1] (excerpt).*

John Taylor delivered an address in Ogden, Utah, on October 21, 1877, nine days before the first stake Relief Society conference was held there.[476] Taylor had been present a few months earlier when Brigham Young organized the Weber Stake Relief Society, encouraged the women to hold quarterly conferences with reports from each local Relief Society organization in Weber County, and promised to return in October to open the first conference officially.[477] President Young had died on August 29, 1877. As president of the Quorum of the Twelve Apostles, Taylor was now the church's presiding authority. Taylor had converted to the church in 1836 in Canada and began serving as an apostle in 1838; he was officially sustained as president of the church in October 1880.

The October 20–21, 1877, conference was for the entire Weber Stake (men, women, and children in seventeen wards), and Taylor directed some of his remarks to the Relief Society. His remarks represent one of many times when he expressed his support for the Relief Society and established his own tie to the group by noting that he was one of three priesthood leaders in attendance when the society was first organized in Nauvoo on March 17, 1842. During his administration, Taylor helped make further refinements in the Relief Society organization; the tasks of defining the scope of the general Relief Society presidency, for instance, fell to him.[478]

On Saturday, October 20, Lester J. Herrick, a counselor in the Weber Stake presidency, reported on the success of the stake Relief Society: "They were busy in laying up wheat and he advised the Elders to assist them in this laudable purpose." President Taylor addressed the congregation on Sunday afternoon "on various topics relating to the organization of the priesthood and the duties of all the various departments of the Church."[479] The following transcript is excerpted from the report of Taylor's discourse made by George F. Gibbs for the semiweekly edition of the *Deseret News,* April 16, 1878.

———— ❧ ————

DISCOURSE
DELIVERED BY
PRESIDENT JOHN TAYLOR,
In the Ogden Tabernacle, on Sunday afternoon, October 21, 1877.
REPORTED BY GEORGE F. GIBBS.

---

476. Taylor did not attend the October 30 stake Relief Society conference. (See Document 3.28.)
477. See Document 3.26.
478. See Document 4.5.
479. "Weber Stake Conference," *Deseret News* [weekly], Oct. 24, 1877, 600–601.

[480] . . . Now a few words to the sisters. They have their Relief Societies and Retrenchment Societies, and their Mutual Improvement Societies, all of which are very laudable and praiseworthy. You heard quoted this morning that the man was not without the woman, nor the woman without the man, in the Lord.[481] Or in other words, it takes a woman and a man to make a man. Did you ever think about that, that without a union of the sexes we are not perfect? God has so ordained it. And therefore do we expect to have our wives in the future state? Yes. And do wives expect to have their husbands? Yes. Are we engaged in building up the kingdom of God? Yes. What have we to do? Why our sisters have to learn to manage their household affairs in a proper manner, and to train their daughters in such a manner as will prepare them to become mothers in Israel, competent to attend to the various duties and responsibilities which must sooner or later devolve upon them in the household, and also cultivate their nobler qualities calculated to elevate and exalt women in the estimation of God and man; and not only your daughters, but sons also; begin early to teach them meekness, kindness and gentleness, and withhold not from them such training as will give them an acquaintance with the common branches of education, and if possible afford them a knowledge of science, and of music, and everything that will have a tendency to lead their minds to find enjoyment in the development of the mind, but be sure and have for your base or foundation, the early cultivation of the virtues, and a due regard to their superiors, as well as reverence for God and sacred things. And what next? Teach others who lack the opportunity that your children may possess. Sisters, you are eminently constituted for this work. God has given you both the desire and ability to do it; you can enter into the sympathies of others, and you can better appreciate their feelings than we men can, and you are altogether more competent to minister in such affairs. Hence the prophet Joseph Smith, in his day, organized a Female Relief Society; some of you sisters now before me I remember seeing present on that occasion. Sister Emma Smith was President of that Society, Sister [Elizabeth] Whitney, now of Salt Lake City, was one of her Counselors, Sister [Sarah] Cleveland was the other Counselor, and Sister Eliza Snow was Secretary.[482] This movement, under the auspices of the Relief Societies, was allowed to sleep for a while, but it has again began to awaken, and great good is being accomplished. And what do we want to teach our good sisters? I do not propose to go into details, but will merely say they should be

---

480. TEXT: The ellipsis points in this excerpt have been supplied by the editors of this volume to indicate omissions from the original document.

481. See 1 Corinthians 11:11.

482. See Document 1.2, entry for Mar. 17, 1842.

things most elevating and useful. Teach them to cook aright, to dress aright, and to speak aright; also to govern their feelings and tongues, and unfold unto them the principles of the gospel. Let the elderly ladies teach the younger ones, leading them on in the paths of life, that we may have sisters growing up, whose goodness and praiseworthy principles will make them fit to associate with the angels of God. And if you persevere in this good work God will bless you and your efforts, let male and female operate together in the one great common cause. Sisters, let it be your daily study to make your homes comfortable, more and more pleasant and agreeable, in fact, a little heaven on earth. And brethren, let us treat our wives properly, and prepare proper places for them; be kind to them, and fee[l] to bless them all the day long. Do away with unkind or harsh words, and do not allow hard feelings to exist in your hearts, or find place in your habitations. Love one another, and by each trying to enhance the welfare of the other, that element will characterize the family circle, and your children will partake of the same feeling, and they in turn will imitate your good example, and perpetuate the things they learn at home. . . .

3.28 Weber Stake Relief Society, Minutes, October 30, 1877

Weber Stake Relief Society, Minutes, Oct. 30, 1877; Weber Stake, Relief Society Minutes and Records, 1867–1968, vol. 6, 1877–1900, pp. 23–34, CHL (LR 9970 14).

The first stake Relief Society meeting took place on October 30, 1877, in the Weber Stake. Three months earlier, Brigham Young had appointed Jane S. Richards to preside over the stake Relief Society organization and instructed that the Relief Society should hold its first quarterly conference in October.[483] At the October meeting, Richards presided and Eliza R. Snow called for a vote to sustain Richards as president.[484] Young had hoped to attend the meeting but had died on August 29.

Prominent members of Salt Lake Relief Societies joined the Ogden women that day because this organization of the Relief Society on a stake level was a momentous occasion. Snow, Mary Isabella Horne, Presendia L. Kimball, Emmeline B. Wells, and Sarah M. Kimball each spoke from the pulpit. Richards initially chose Horne and Snow as her counselors, though she later selected women from her own stake as counselors, Harriet C. Brown and Sarah A. Herrick, who had served as her counselors in the Ogden Ward Relief Society presidency.[485] In 1880 Eliza R. Snow became the first official general Relief Society president; as evidenced by her involvement here with the Weber Stake Relief Society, she was already exercising some supervisory authority over all the Relief Societies in the church.[486] The Salt Lake visitors addressed the congregation and expressed their feelings about the church and their vision for the Relief Society. This first quarterly stake Relief Society meeting provided a template for future meetings, which generally offered women a forum to present reports and history, share new information and insights, and feel fellowship. Stake Relief Society conferences brought together women who usually met in their smaller and sometimes isolated ward societies, and also acquainted them with the women from Salt Lake City who provided central Relief Society leadership and oversight.

The minutes of the October 30 conference are reproduced below from the Weber Stake Relief Society Minute Book.

———— ⚹ ————

Minutes of the first Conference
of the Relief Society of Weber Stake.
Held in the Tabernacle, Ogden City—Oct. 30th 1877.
There were present on the stand, Apostle F. [Franklin] D. Richards—Pres. D. [David] H. Peery—Sisters E. [Eliza] R. Snow—Sarah Kimball—M. I.

---

483. See Document 3.26.

484. Richards had already been serving as president since July, but the vote was taken to give members the opportunity to officially sustain her in the office.

485. Weber Stake, Weber Stake Relief Society Minutes and Records, 1867–1968, CHL, May 2, 1878, vol. 6, p. 35; Dec. 16, 1875, vol. 5, p. 5.

486. See Document 4.4.

Horn [Mary Isabella Horne]—E. [Emmeline] B. Wells—L. [Louisa] G. Richards—Zina Y. Williams, of Salt Lake, and Harriet Snow of Brigham City also a number of Bishops— The Tabernacle was well filled, notwithstanding the unfavorable weather— President Jane S. Richards presided.

Meeting opened by singing—'O, my Father'— Prayer by Bish. P. [Pleasant] G. Taylor of Harrisville— Singing—[']How firm a foundation'.[487]

Pres. Jane S. Richards said, Beloved sisters, I am very thankful to see so many here to day. As you are aware, we have met according to the appointment made at the time President Young was with us in July— It was his counsel that the Relief Societies of Weber Co. meet in three months from that time, and report their labors.[488] We will now hear the reports—

Sec. A. [Amelia] M. Frodsham then read the reports of the Relief Societies, and Miss Hattie [Harriet C.] Brown read reports of the Retrenchment Societies.[489]

Sister M. I. Horn then addressed the congregation— She said, My Sisters, I am pleased to stand before you— I have been much interested in the reports— They show what you have been doing, that you are interested in caring for the poor, in assisting to build temples—in advancing silk culture &c.— It has been thought that woman had nothing to do, but attend to her duties at home, [p. 23] to care for and teach her children. But there is more than this. By attending to her public duties, her meetings &c.—She is better qualified to train her children for the great work that devolves upon them. God bless you Sisters. Let us answer to every call that is made upon us, and God will bless us.—

Pres. D. H. Peery said he felt fully paid for coming to meeting, in hearing the reports, and how much the Sisters had done. Was pleased with Sister Horn's remarks— Thought home the place to educate and train the young in honesty and truthfulness. Felt that naturally the sisters had more good in their hearts, than men. Through the influence of his wife he was led to embrace the gospel.[490] Acknowledged God's goodness in His dealings with him. Could see

---

487. Hymns 130 and 237, *Sacred Hymns and Spiritual Songs for the Church of Jesus Christ of Latter-day Saints,* 15th ed. (Liverpool: Albert Carrington, 1871), 143–144, 260–261.

488. See Document 3.26.

489. The Ogden city Relief Society report follows these minutes.

490. David H. Peery married Nancy Campbell (Cambel) Higginbotham, a Latter-day Saint, in 1852, even though he adamantly opposed her religion. A series of family deaths in 1862, including those of his wife and two sons, prompted him to study the religion, and he was baptized later that year. ("Life Story of David Harold Peery," in Autobiographical and Biographical Sketches of Burton, Peery, and Richards Families, n.d., typescript, CHL; Andrew Jenson, *Latter-day Saint Biographical Encyclopedia: A Compilation of Biographical Sketches of Prominent Men and Women in the Church of Jesus Christ of Latter-day Saints,* 4 vols. [Salt Lake City: Andrew Jenson History Co., 1901–1936], 1:756–758.)

a beauty and grandeur in this work— Urged the Sister to lay up wheat—[491] Invoked God's blessing upon all.

Meeting was then adjourned until 2, o'clock— Singing—'Lord dismiss us with thy blessing.'[492] Benediction by Bish. Robert McQuarrie—

Afternoon Session—

Meeting was called to order by Pres. Jane S. Richards— Singing—'God moves in a mysterious way'— Prayer by Apostle F. D. Richards. Singing— 'Arise O glorious Zion'—[493]

Sister Precinda Kimball then addressed the Sisters— She said—I esteem it a great privilege to meet with you— Although we are strangers, we are all sisters— We are blest with the privilege of teaching the yong the principles of eternal life, and of bringing them up in the truth. Your reports are splendid. We are engaged in a great work, and we all desire to be prepared, that when we go behind the vail, we can enjoy the society of the martyrs and others gone before us, Those who have borne the heat and burden of the day, will pass off, and these young ladies will have to take their places. I hope mothers will teach there daughters virtue, and don't cease to pray for them. I pray that peace and prosperity may abound with these my Sisters— Amen. [p. 24]

Sister E. B. Wells next spoke— She said—I must say I feel it a great pleasure to be here. I remember the first time I was here and the good instruction we received from President Young— If he could have heard the reports that have been read to day, and the good things that have been said, he would, no doubt, have been pleased— We have heard a little to day of the work that women can do, and are doing, and if so much good can be accomplished in one County, how very much may be done in all the Stakes of Zion— We have been called upon to store up grain; This is new work for women to engage in, but is an important one, and if we save comparatively little, it will be much better than to have it all carried away and sold—

I rejoice every day in the gospel and in the work of the women of Zion— The Lord has been very kind and good to us. And we ought to be very thankful that we have what thousands of women are denied, that is, the right of Suffrage—[494] The women of the world wonder how we obtained this— I tell them the Lord helped us—

We desire reports of the grain on hand in each County—that we mak[e] a report for our grain meeting, and we would like as many of our sister as can, to

---

491. For more on wheat storage, see Document 3.25.
492. Hymn 97, *Sacred Hymns and Spiritual Songs,* 107–108.
493. Hymns 22 and 23, *Sacred Hymns and Spiritual Songs,* 28–31.
494. For more on woman suffrage in Utah Territory, see Documents 3.14, 3.16, and 3.17.

attend that meeting— We realize there is a vast amount of labor to be done— And we wish to learn the best method of keeping wheat from the moth, mice &c.— The sisters should meet and consult upon these things. There is no limit to the work before us— We want literature of our own, and we should embrace every opportunity for improving ourselves in writing and speaking,—attend to our meetings and keep the spirit of our religion with us— I believe in mothers attending to their homes and teaching their children— We have received very much good instruction— My prayer is that we strived to live by it.

Sister Sarah Kimball said—I am grateful [p. 25] for the privilege of standing before my sisters in this place. I hope I can say something to edify you. I can truly say, this is one of the richest meetings I have ever attended— To the few who are living of those associated with the first organization of this society, how great appears the contrast—[495] Surely, Bro. Joseph, himself, could not fully realize and comprehend the greatness of the structure that would be built upon the foundation he—himself—laid—

When the Nauvoo Temple was about a foot from the ground, there was a great want of means— A few of the sisters thought they would organize themselves into a society of some kind, that they might be better able to assist the brethren in the work of building the temple— We met, drew up a constitution and Sister Snow showed it to Bro. Smith. He said the Lord accepts your offering—but you shall have something better— He then organized us into a Relief Society—Sister Emma Smith being elected president—(The Book of Covenants [Doctrine and Covenants] calls her elect lady, she was then elected.)[496] We were seven in number, but Joseph said we should become a great society.[497] We see his words fulfilled to day.

I remember being here some years ago.— Sister Richards was then sick. Sister Snow washed and annointed her, and told her if she would take charge of the Relief Society in Ogden—she should have health and the Lord would bless her.[498] We can testify that her words have proved true— I ask the Lord to continue his blessing upon her and upon you all.

---

495. In 1842 Kimball called for and hosted the first planning meeting for a charitable "Sewing Society," which led to the organization of the Female Relief Society of Nauvoo. (Documents 1.2 and 4.10.)

496. See Doctrine and Covenants 25:3; and Document 1.1.

497. Because twenty women attended the March 17, 1842, organizational meeting of the Nauvoo Relief Society, Kimball must be referring here to the original planning meeting held in her home some weeks earlier. Kimball recounted the Relief Society's founding story on many occasions but specified the original "seven in number" only here. (See Document 1.2, entry for Mar. 17, 1842; Document 4.10; and Sarah M. Kimball, "Auto-Biography," *Woman's Exponent*, Sept. 1, 1883, 12:51.)

498. Jane Richards "was taken down to her bed with Diptheria and overworking" on November 12, 1870. She wrote, "I was sick for nearly a year and . . . I was so low for months that my life was despaired of. . . . Sister Eliza R. Snow came and visited me and said I must live for there was something for

Sister Eliza R. Snow said—Sister Richards, who is virtually president of this Conference, asks me to speak. I am pleased with the reports, and am thankful to God, for without His assistance our efforts are vain— Union is strength. By unity, our energies, faith and perseverance accomplish much. But it is all by the blessing of God. We have not the wealth of the world, but we have faith [p. 26] bone and sinew. Father Smith[499] said, faith is energy,— and so, also, energy must be faith; for the more energetic a person is, the more faith he has.

We believe that God has endowed us with every faculty that is necessary to enable us to become Goddesses in eternity; but we must also cultivate and improve ourselves. By revelation we know this work is true, and this faith lifts us out of much of the suffering of this life. Still we are inclined to the things of earth. We are gross, we stumble, we live in an atmosphere that is not pure: that weighs us down

I have been thinking what great things grow out of seemingly unimportant events— I consider this meeting a precedent of a great thing. Sister Richards invited President Young to come and talk to the sisters of Weber County. She did not think that Relief Society Conferences would be the result.— He said adjourn your meeting for three months— I think it a key to the Society.—[500] He was with us then, now he has passed behind the vail— Let us carry out his instructions—

Woman stands in a responsible position—every one as counselor to her husband. What wisdom we should have! There is no time to waste, no time to talk over our pains and troubles; the more we dwell upon them, the more we wish to. When we arise and speak by the spirit of God, we give light to those around us— When we meet, let our countenances glow with the spirit, and not give way to sadness. If we acknowledge the hand of God in all things, we find consolation under all circumstances.

I am well aware that a great deal is donated that never reaches the books. President Joseph Smith said this society was organized to save souls.[501] What have the sisters done to win back those who have gone astray?—to warm up

me to do. She said I was the poorest person in flesh that she ever administered to, and I can here say that I was healed by the power of God, and raised up to health and strength." (See Franklin D. Richards, Journals, 1844–1899, Richards Family Collection, 1837–1961, CHL, Nov. 12 and Dec. 25, 1870; Jane S. Richards, Autobiographical Sketch, Mar. 30, 1881, CHL; on female ministration to the sick, see Document 4.19.)

499. Probably a reference to Joseph Smith Sr. (1771–1840) but possibly to his brother John Smith (1781–1854). Both were church patriarchs and well known to Snow.

500. See Document 3.26.

501. See Document 1.2, entry for June 9, 1842.

the hearts of those who have grown cold in the gospel?— Another book is kept of your faith, your kindness, your good works [p. 27] and words. Another record is kept. Nothing is lost. Two years ago I called for reports from all the Relief Societies— From $90 to $100 thousand dollars had been disbursed— and we commenced by saving carpet rags—no other capital.[502]

In regard to laying up grain—it is a very important calling which has been placed upon the women of this Church, and we should be faithful and energetic.— Sister Snow then related some things seen in a vision by a young man, pertaining to laying up grain, the famine &.c.—[503]

Another duty, of great importance, which is required of us, is the culture of silk. Pres. Young told me to teach the sisters how to get rich. Wealth is here; we can draw it from the elements by our own labor and the blessing of God. The cultivation of mulberry trees would be better than green backs, for us, and for future generations. If we had attended to this twenty years ago, we might now be clothed in silk. We have specimens of silk that have been tested—said to be the best from the U.S.— There is wealth in it, if we will only labor and be patient.[504]

Speaking of Sister Richards—I wish to have a vote taken. You have led out in a new direction. This is a new thing. I motion that Sister Jane Richards preside over the Relief Society of this Stake of Zion.—and fill all the offices of an elect lady.[505] The motion was seconded and a vote taken which was unanimous. Sister Snow said, Sister Richards has accepted the position, and has chosen M. I. Horn and E. R. Snow as counsellors. The vote for their acceptance was unanimous.

One thing more to those who have contributed to the "Women of Mormondom"— That work would not have been published, had it not been for the sisters.[506] We must not slacken, but double our diligence, and none of us will lose our reward.

---

502. Snow collected reports to submit to the 1876 Philadelphia Exposition's Committee on Charities and wrote a history of the Relief Society for that event. (Document 3.24.)

503. This may be a reference to Joseph of Egypt. (See Genesis chap. 41.)

504. For more on the silk industry, see Documents 3.4 and 4.3.

505. See Doctrine and Covenants 25:3; and Document 1.1.

506. Snow's reference is to Edward W. Tullidge, *The Women of Mormondom* (New York: Tullidge and Crandall, 1877). The book chronicles the lives of Mormon women from the church's founding through the achievement of suffrage; Mormon women saw it as an opportunity to demonstrate their righteousness and respectability. The *Woman's Exponent* noted, "The book has been published by the women of Utah, and, besides the moral good it will accomplish, it is likely to prove a pecuniary advantage to the Relief and Retrenchment Societies, as a considerable portion of the means derived from its sale is to be applied for the benefit of those organizations." ("The Women of Mormondom," *Woman's Exponent,* Jan. 1, 1878, 6:119.)

Sister Harriet Snow, of Brigham City, Said I am happy to see you all. I rejoice in the principles taught in our society. I love my sisters. Although [p. 28] strangers, we are working to accomplish the same good object. It gives me joy to meet with my sisters. I wonder how those get along that do not attend meeting

It is thought that woman cannot teach woman, but I have a broader view of such things. And I believe that if we cultivate the principles of our religion and take hold with a willing heart, we can accomplish any thing required of us; even the laying up of grain and the cultivation of Silk. Where there is a will; there is a way.

We should make our society as interesting as possible. The Relief Society was first organized by the Prophet Joseph; and we should honor the organization. If we attend our meetings punctually, our hearts will expand, and we shall be the means of doing great good. If we attend to our prayers, God will give us wisdom. I esteem these things, great privileges.

Sister L. G. Richards said—I am an advocate for the principles contained in the Gospel of Christ I feel that we should love them. This meeting is what Sister Snow calls a picnic. I like such meetings; the more baskets opened the better, for I like to hear my sisters. If we were prayerful and energetic, we would have more faith. W[e] should have more faith for our sick; and I feel that we need more patience with our faith.

I would counsel our young sisters to read the Book of Mormon. I have been very much interested in comparing that book with the Bible. We must seek for ourselves to get understanding. I wish to mention the importance of sustaining the Exponent.[507] It goes to nearly all parts of the world, and is doing a great deal of good. I hope the sisters will take it, also lay up grain. I know that Polygamy is a great and glorious principle. I know the Lord orders every thing for the best. I feel to bless you all.

Sister Jane S. Richards then gave out the papers for the different societies, containing President [p. 29] Young's sermon, in this Tabernacle, to the Relief Societies.[508]

A vote was taken to drop the word retrenchment from the name of the Young Ladies Association, and to insert in its place, Mutual Improvement.[509]

---

507. Richards was the founding editor of the *Woman's Exponent.* (See Document 3.21.)

508. This is a reference to Brigham Young's discourse of July 19, 1877, which was first published in the October 13, 1877, issue of the *Deseret Evening News.* It is unclear which published version was distributed. (See Document 3.26.)

509. What were called Young Ladies' Retrenchment Associations at this time had begun as "young ladies' departments" of the Ladies' Cooperative Retrenchment Association. In 1877 the associations were renamed Young Ladies' Mutual Improvement Associations (often abbreviated Y.L.M.I.A.) in order to, as

Sister Zina Young Williams said a few words. Felt to cry out for faith, that she might bring up her children as her beloved father had taught us; knew she could not go too often to the fountain of faith and wisdom; could see that by living our religion, day by day, we are doing a great work. God has given us the way and the means where by we may fit ourselves to be crowned in his kingdom. Asked the blessing of the Lord upon all.

Apostle F. D. Richards felt that he must say a word or two. A little over three months ago, President Young stood where I now stand. You remember how respectfully he asked, 'Will you do these things, sisters'?— One of these things was the raising of silk, I want this society to draw up a memorial, and memorialize your Bishops: put it on your records; let them deny it, if they can[510]

The President talked wheat for twenty years, now the sisters have taken it in hand and are doing something. You should preserve his sermon, which has been printed, and a copy given to each society; and perpetuate his memory by doing the things he taught you. You will be blest in remembering his counsels.

I say, God will bless those sisters who help this work along. I would like to say a word about the Women of Mormondom. That book is going to have a wide circulation. There are calls from England besides those of the Church. It was one of Pres. Youngs last acts to approve of this work.

I pray God to bless you, and that the saints may increase in good works; that we might follow him as he followed Christ.

Moved and carried that this Conference be adjourned to the 31st day of Jan. 1878, in honor of Sister Richards, that being her birthday. [p. 30]

Sister Richards then said, I feel that we have had a good time. It has been a day of rejoicing to me; and of sorrow too; for when this meeting was appointed, we expected our beloved President, Brigham Young, to be here.

Brigham Young explained, "conform in name, as we also wish them to conform in spirit, to the [Young Men's] Mutual Improvement Societies." As these minutes demonstrate, local wards voted to adopt the name change after it had been announced generally. Notwithstanding the name change, young ladies' organizations, mostly in Salt Lake City, continued to meet twice a month with older women in what was first called the Senior and Junior Ladies' Cooperative Retrenchment Association, and later General Retrenchment. This organization continued under the direction of Mary Isabella Horne until the early months of 1904. (Document 3.18; "Home Affairs," *Woman's Exponent,* Oct. 1, 1877, 6:68; Brigham Young to Joseph Don Carlos Young and Feramorz Little Young, Aug. 6, 1877, Brigham Young Letterbook, vol. 15, p. 102, in Brigham Young Office Files, 1832–1878, CHL; "General Retrenchment Meetings," *Woman's Exponent,* July 1904, 33:15.)

510. The Weber County Silk Association was apparently not organized until May 1879, a year and a half after Richards's remarks. Mary Kay was president of the association, with Letitia Peery and Elizabeth Stanford counselors. "All the officers and members of Relief Society and Y. L. M. I. A. were elected members of the Silk Association. Agents were chosen for all the different localities in the county, to see that the mulberry leaves were utilized; and the sisters were urged by Sister Snow to be energetic in promoting the interests of silk culture." ("Relief Society Conference," *Woman's Exponent,* June 1, 1879, 8:253.)

Well, let us try to carry out his counsels. I know my sisters desire to do right. I am proud of them. My desires are, to do the best I can. I feel to say, God bless us all; and bless, especially, the sisters that have come to visit us.

Singing—'May we who know the joyful sound.'[511] Benediction by Bishop John Hart of West Weber.

Mrs. A. M. Frodsham, Sec.

Mrs. Jane S. Richards, Pres.

Report[512]

Prepared and read by Secretary A. M. Frodsham, at the first Relief Society Conference—[513]

The Female Relief Society of Ogden City, was organized Dec. 16th 1867;[514] under the superintendency of Bishop Chauncy West and his counselors; with the following officers—: Sister Mary West President; Sisters Nancy Farr and Harriet C. Brown, Counselors. Sister Mary Ann West, Treasurer, and Sister Louise M. Hopkins, Secretary. Meetings were held monthly.

May 24th 1869, a cooperative mercantile Institution was formed by the Ladies of Weber Co. The officers elected, were, Mrs. Mary West, Pres. Harriet C. Brown Vice Pres.—Miss Rosalthe Canfield Secretary and Treasurer. Also a board of Directors.

A ladies mass meeting was held in the Tabernacle Mar. 17th 1870. Sister Mary West was elected by unanimous vote, to preside over the meeting. She stated the object of the meeting, which was to protest against the Cullom Bill.[515] She expressed [p. 31] her sentiments in regard to unwise legislation, and spoke in defence of Plural Marriage.

June 9th 1870. Meetings of the Relief Society were suspended, on account of the presence of Small Pox in the City.

---

511. Hymn 99, *Sacred Hymns and Spiritual Songs,* 108–109.

512. On July 19, 1877, Franklin D. Richards, in behalf of his wife, Jane, "president of Weber County societies," requested the societies to "prepare a quarterly report of the condition of each society and its financial interests, to be read there three months from that time." The following quarterly report for the Weber County Relief Society was compiled for the October 30, 1877, meeting, where "a statistical report of the finances of the Society was read dating back to the organization of each separate branch of the Society in that county. The condition of each Society in all special respects was also reported in writing. These reports in the aggregate, amount to vast sums that have been gathered in various ways and disbursed to many benevolent purposes." ("Home Affairs," *Woman's Exponent,* Aug. 1, 1877, 6:37; Document 3.26; "Home Affairs," *Woman's Exponent,* Nov. 15, 1877, 6:92.)

513. TEXT: The original record has a faint addition following this line: "Oct 30 1877".

514. The Relief Society in Ogden was organized in 1853, disbanded in 1858 (because of the Utah War), and reorganized in 1867. (History of the Relief Society in Weber County, 1887, in Richards Family Collection, 1.)

515. See Documents 3.12 and 3.13.

On the 27th day of Aug. 1870, our esteemed president, Sister Mary West, was called from mortality, after a brief though severe illness. Her health had been failing for years; but not until the death of her husband,[516] did she really begin to succumb to the hand of disease. The great affliction which his loss occasioned her, seemed never abated to the day of her death; and, no doubt, hastened her final departure. She had filled her offices with honor, and her loss was deeply mourned by her numerous friends.

Oct. 27th 1870 a meeting of the Society was called, and Sister Harriet C. Brown was elected by unanimous vote, to take the place, vacated by the death of our beloved President, Sister Mary West. Sister Rosalthe Canfield was elected Treasurer, and Sister Amelia M. Frodsham Secretary. Subsequently, Sisters Martha Bingham and Sarah Herrick, were chosen Counselors.

Aug. 8th 1872, at a meeting held in the Tabernacle, (Sister Brown wishing to resign,) Sister Jane S. Richards was elected Pres. of the Society by a unanimous vote. She chose Sisters Harriet Brown and Sarah Herrick for her Counselors, and all were set apart for their offices.

Aug. 22nd 1872, it was decided to hold meetings semi monthly.

Oct. 17th 1872, Through the counsel of Sister Eliza R. Snow, and by approval of President Brigham Young, the word Female was dropped from the name of the Society, which was henceforth to be known as the Relief Society.[517]

Dec. 12th, 1872, Sister Rosalthe Canfield resigned as Treasurer, and Sister H. [Huldah] M. Ballantyne [p. 32] was elected to that office. At the same time, the 12th and 13th Districts were dropped from the Society, as they had been organized by themselves. Jan. 30th 1873 a vote was taken that the 14th district be known as the 12th The 3d district was also dropped from the Society, having been organized by itself.[518]

---

516. Her husband, Chauncey W. West, died on January 9, 1870. (Edward W. Tullidge, *Tullidge's Histories, Containing the History of All the Northern, Eastern and Western Counties of Utah,* vol. 2 [Salt Lake City: Juvenile Instructor, 1889], appendix, 67.)

517. The *Woman's Exponent* summarized Snow's explanation for the name change: "'Female Relief Society' was suggested and established by vote when the first organization took place. The question had been agitated for some time, whether the name would not be rendered more appropriate by the omission of the word 'Female,' and the calling of these associations merely 'Relief Societies.' She thought that this modification would improve the application; and others with whom she had communicated on the subject held the same opinion." Accordingly, the various ward and branch Relief Societies voted for the name change; by January 1873, twenty-two ward societies had dropped "Female" from their name. ("F. R. Society Reports," *Woman's Exponent,* Oct. 15, 1872, 1:74; "The Change of Name," *Woman's Exponent,* Jan. 15, 1873, 1:125.)

518. In this period the Ogden Relief Society acted as a single unit, with the city divided into districts. Relief Societies in Ogden began meeting as four individual wards in 1879. (History of the Relief Society in Weber County, 4.)

June 11ᵗʰ 1874, Sister H. M. Ballantyne resigned her office as treasurer and Sister E. [Elizabeth] Y. Stanford was elected to succeed her. Sister Stanford resigned May 27ᵗʰ 1875, and Sister Emily S. Richards was elected to that office.

From Sep. 28ᵗʰ 1876 to Jan. 31ˢᵗ 1877, meetings were again suspended on account of Small Pox.[519] Since that time, by the desires and wishes of the sisters, meetings have been held weekly. All felt to render heart felt gratitude to God for His preserving care that had been over them, and to acknowledge His hand in all things. Many had been called to part with friends that were near and dear unto them, and all felt it a great privilege to be able to meet again and bear testimony to the work we are engaged in, and speak of the Goodness of God.

Much praise is due to the sisters of the society; for their energy and perseverence in assisting our President; also, for their untiring efforts in behalf of the sick and needy. May this energetic and kindly feeling never slacken. But may we ever feel to press onward in the cause we are engaged in, seeking to gain the prize that is for the faithful.

We now come to the financial part of our report. As near as we can estimate, four thousand nine hundred seventy six Dollars and five cents, ($4,976.05) has been received. This amount has been collected by the energy of the teachers and committies, and through the liberality of the saints, also by making rag carpets [p. 33] bed quilts and various other articles; and by giving dancing parties, tea parties, and social entertainments.

The means thus procured has been disbursed in the following manner. Towards building Ladies County Cooperative Store;[520] Emmigration; Missionary purposes; Sending two sisters to the Medical lectures of Doctor Mary Barker, Salt Lake City—[521] Taking care of Sister Peterson when she lost her

519. On October 14 Ogden's mayor issued a proclamation requiring "a yellow flag be raised at each and every house in this city containing any person afflicted with small-pox." The mayor also recommended "that schools and public assemblies of every kind be discontinued until further notice." An agent appointed by the city council reported on October 15 that there were thirty-two cases of smallpox in Ogden, with one fatality. By November 6 the situation seemed to be improving, with only nineteen cases that were either "convalescent" or "of a very mild nature" reported in the city. ("Proclamation," and "Small-Pox Spreading," *Deseret News* [weekly], Oct. 18, 1876, 608; "Our Country Contemporaries," *Deseret News* [weekly], Nov. 15, 1876, 668.)

520. A Ladies Cooperative Mercantile and Millinery Institution of Ogden, sponsored by the Relief Society and led by Mary West, was organized on May 24, 1869, and opened a store on November 22, 1869. Funds to construct a building and begin the cooperative store were raised through the Relief Society; visiting teachers asked for donations and members also raised money "by making rag carpets, bed quilts and various other articles and by giving dancing parties, tea parties and social entertainments." (History of the Relief Society in Weber County, 2, 4; Kate B. Carter, comp., *Heart Throbs of the West: A Unique Volume Treating Definite Subjects of Western History,* 12 vols. [Salt Lake City: Daughters of Utah Pioneers, 1940], 2:477.)

521. See 387n417 herein.

arm, and helping to purchase an artificial one for her. Towards the culture of silk. Building and furnishing the Ogden City Relief Society Straw Store.[522] For the raising of flax. For Endowment clothes used in time of small pox.[523] Two shares for the Woman's Book.[524] Besides constantly donating to the wants of the sick and needy, and for other charitable purposes.

We have still on hand our interest in the Ladies County Cooperative Store. We own the Relief Society Straw Store, and the furniture in it, also some flax. Two shares in the Woman's Book, and a few quilts. The sisters have made some quilts for the Temple, but the money donations they have given to their Bishops.[525] Many sisters responded to the call for the culture of silk. Mulberry trees have been set out and some cocoons have been raised. There is on hand in money and wheat, at the rate of 90 [cts] per bushel, 172½ Bushels.

In holding meetings here today, we remember that we had our Beloved President Brigham Young with us at our last meeting, and in obedience to his counsel these meetings are held. May the Spirit of God rest upon each and every one of us, and help us to carry out his counsels.

Sec.	Jane S. Richards—Pres.
Amela M. Frodsham	Harriet C. Brown ⎫
Treas.	Sarah Herrick ⎭ Coun.
Emily S. Richards [p. 34]	

---

522. The straw store appears to have initially been part of the Ladies Cooperative Mercantile and Millinery Institution of Ogden. Ogden's Relief Society Millinery Store—also known as the Straw Store—was built around 1874. The 1878 Ogden city directory advertised: "Visitors or Residents In Want of Any Kind on Millinery Goods, Hats, Bonnets, Flowers, Trimmings, etc., Plain or Ornamental, Should Call at the Ladies' 'Straw Store' Opposite the City Hall, 5th Street, before making purchases." This store operated until 1882, when it was sold and the proceeds were divided among the four Relief Society organizations in the city. (History of the Relief Society in Weber County, 4; *Directory of Ogden City, and North Utah Record* [Ogden, UT: S. A. Kenner and Thos. Wallace, 1878], x.)

523. Latter-day Saints wore ceremonial clothing as part of the temple endowment; these "endowment clothes" were also used in burials. This may be a reference either to replacing clothes contaminated in the smallpox epidemic or to the use of these clothes in burials of individuals who died from smallpox.

524. Edward W. Tullidge, *The Women of Mormondom* (New York: Tullidge and Crandall, 1877).

525. This refers to donations made for the construction of the Logan temple; the site for the temple had been dedicated on May 18, 1877, and donations were called for from Latter-day Saints living in northern Utah and elsewhere. (See Leonard J. Arrington and Melvin A. Larkin, "The Logan Tabernacle and Temple," *Utah Historical Quarterly* 41, no. 3 [Summer 1973]: 305–306; see also Document 4.20.)

3.29 Mary Isabella Horne and Others, Letter to Salt Lake Stake Relief Society, January 15, 1878

Mary Isabella Horne, Elmina S. Taylor, and Serepta M. Heywood, "To the Presidents and Members of the Relief Society of Salt Lake Stake of Zion, Greeting!" Woman's Exponent *(Salt Lake City, UT), Jan. 15, 1878, vol. 6, no. 16, p. 123.*

Mary Isabella Horne was elected the first president of the Salt Lake Stake Relief Society on December 22, 1877. She had already served for a decade as president of the Salt Lake City Fourteenth Ward Relief Society and was the president of the Ladies' Cooperative Retrenchment Society, an office she continued to hold until 1904.[526] Eliza R. Snow called a special meeting at the Fourteenth Ward assembly rooms to follow the example of the Weber Stake in organizing the Relief Society on a stake level.[527] As chair of the meeting, Snow announced that "President Young had inaugurated a movement previous to his death, which she considered proper to carry out." Snow then nominated Horne as the stake Relief Society president, which was accepted by a unanimous vote of the assembly.[528] This established the second stake Relief Society organization. The actions of the Salt Lake Stake were particularly important given the stake's centrality and large size; it comprised over thirty wards spread throughout Salt Lake County and was by far the largest stake in terms of membership. Within the first year of its organization, the stake Relief Society counted 2,283 officers and members throughout the stake.[529]

In the following letter published in the *Woman's Exponent,* Horne and her counselors, Elmina S. Taylor and Serepta M. Heywood, reviewed the history of the Relief Society and announced that societies would meet quarterly as stakes to report on the activities of the different branches of the organization.[530]

To the Presidents and Members of the Relief Society of Salt Lake Stake of Zion, Greeting!

Beloved Sisters:— Through revelation from God the Prophet Joseph Smith organized the first Society of sisters in this last dispensation, saying to the people that the Priesthood was not firmly established on the earth, without an

---

526. See Document 3.16.

527. See Documents 3.26 and 3.28.

528. Salt Lake Stake, Salt Lake Stake Relief Society Record Book, 1868–1903, CHL, Dec. 22, 1877, p.1.

529. Salt Lake Stake Relief Society Record Book, Sept. 27, 1878, p. 10.

530. The first quarterly meeting of the Salt Lake Stake Relief Society was scheduled for March 23, 1878, in the Fourteenth Ward assembly rooms. Ward Relief Society presidents were asked to prepare reports of "all appropriations, disbursments, and matters of importance." Snow offered to assist women with their compilations by sharing the reports she had received for the 1876 Centennial Exposition. (Salt Lake Stake Relief Society Record Book, Mar. 23, 1878, pp. 5–6; Dec. 22, 1877, p. 2; Document 3.24.)

organization of this kind.[531] He gave the sisters much valuable instruction, and predicted a great future for this organization.[532] In consequence of the exodus from Nauvoo, this Society was broken up. After the Saints were located in these valleys of the mountains, President Brigham Young counseled the organization of branches of this Society, in all the Stakes of Zion;[533] and as the kingdom of God progresses in a more complete organization throughout all the different Stakes of Zion, so by the counsel of our late President are the Relief Societies being organized with a Presidency over the several Stakes of Zion, to meet once in three months and have Reports read from the different branches of the Relief Society through the county. As we have been elected to preside over this county, we feel much need of the Spirit of God to enable us in our weakness to discharge our duties in this position. We feel truly thankful that through the blessing of our Heavenly Father, we, His handmaidens are called to be co-laborers with our brethren in building up the kingdom of God upon the earth, in assisting to build Temples, wherein we can receive blessings for time and eternity. In all the ordinances received in the House of the Lord, woman stands beside the man, both for the living and the dead, showing that the man is not without the woman nor the woman without the man in the Lord.[534] Then what manner of women should we be? Faithful in performing all the duties devolving upon us as daughters of God. Sisters, do we appreciate the privileges we enjoy, and the relationship we sustain to God, to each other, and to His kingdom on the earth? We know there are very many faithful sisters, striving with all their might to do all that is required of them. To all such we say, God bless you, sisters! and give you strength to do all your hearts desire to do in righteousness.

We shall be pleased to visit the different Societies whenever it is convenient to the Societies for us to do so. We would say to the Presidents, Be diligent in laying before the sisters the necessity of doing all they can to promote the interests of Zion, by sustaining our institutions of home-industry, as well as our own literature. We are convinced that there are hundreds of dollars sent out of this country every year for trashy literature in which there is no profit. Sustain our own publications—the WOMAN'S EXPONENT, the only woman's paper published in Zion, our church works, Sister E. R. Snow's poems, and the

---

531. Sarah M. Kimball recalled that in 1842 Joseph Smith said "the organisation of the Church of Christ was never perfect until the women were organised." In August 1843 Reynolds Cahoon told the women of the Nauvoo Relief Society that "the Order of th[e] Priesthood is not complete without it [the Relief Society]." (Document 4.10; Document 1.2, entry for Aug. 13, 1843.)

532. See Document 1.2, entry for Apr. 28, 1842.

533. See Document 3.1.

534. See 1 Corinthians 11:11.

Woman's Book, the Life of Brigham Young[535]—all these works will give the youth a knowledge of what the Saints had to endure while trying to establish the gospel on the earth. Much will be required at the hands of the parents, for the teachings and examples they give their children.

May peace and the blessing of God be in the hearts and habitations of all who are interested in the work of the Lord, is the prayer of

M. Isabella Horne, President,
Elmina S. Taylor,
Serepta M. Heywood, } Counselors.

---

535. For the third quarterly conference of the Salt Lake Stake Relief Society, the minutes report 342 subscriptions to the *Woman's Exponent* held by stake Relief Society members. For more on the *Exponent,* see Document 3.21. The other works referenced are Eliza R. Snow, *Poems: Religious, Historical, and Political,* 2 vols. (Liverpool: F. D. Richards, 1856; Salt Lake City: Latter-day Saints' Printing and Publishing Establishment, 1877); Edward W. Tullidge, *The Women of Mormondom* (New York: Tullidge and Crandall, 1877); and Edward W. Tullidge, *Life of Brigham Young; or, Utah and Her Founders* (New York: Tullidge and Crandall, 1876). In December 1876 Horne had spoken to the Relief Society members in Beaver, Utah, on "sustaining the Exponent" and "assisting in the publication of the Woman's Book." (Salt Lake Stake Relief Society Record Book, Sept. 27, 1878, p. 10; "R. S. Reports," *Woman's Exponent,* Jan. 1, 1877, 5:114, emphasis in original.)

3.30 Aurelia Spencer Rogers, Reminiscences of August 1878, as Published in "History of Primary Work," 1898

Aurelia Spencer Rogers, "Chapter I. History of Primary Work—Letter from E. R. Snow," in Aurelia Spencer Rogers, Life Sketches of Orson Spencer and Others, and History of Primary Work *(Salt Lake City: George Q. Cannon and Sons, 1898), pp. [205]–212.*

Aurelia Spencer Rogers first thought to form an organization for Latter-day Saint children, which became known as the Primary Association (or Primary), in about 1878, a decade and a half before writing the autobiography from which the following passage is taken.[536] Rogers devoted more than a third of her autobiography to Primary history, feeling it "proper to explain to the people and children of the Latter-day Saints, the origin and intent of Primary work." Among other highlights from these foundational years of the Primary, she described Eliza R. Snow's organizing efforts; the appointment of a general Primary president and stake Primary presidencies; Primary fairs held to raise money for temples, hospitals, and the poor; and Primary martial bands that were formed "to encourage in our children a love for music, also a love for all things beautiful."[537]

Concern for the spiritual welfare of children dated back to the early days of the church. According to Eliza R. Snow, "The young took delight in the work, and it was no uncommon thing for the children to speak in tongues, and have the blessings of the Gospel poured upon them. But children get no more than they earn, either of the spirit of the world, or the Spirit of God."[538] In 1861 Brigham Young expressed concern for restless teenagers and encouraged local programs to provide recreation for the youth.[539] The Deseret Sunday School Union, organized in 1867, united efforts to create a system of Sunday schools for youth and adults that focused on both spiritual instruction and basic education.[540] In 1875 Young established the Young Men's Mutual Improvement Association as an organization for young men analogous to the previously established Young Ladies' Retrenchment Associations, which were renamed the Young Ladies' Mutual Improvement Associations in 1877.[541] By 1878 concern shifted to younger children, particularly young

---

536. Rogers completed her manuscript approximately four years before it was published; the delay resulted in part from a national economic depression. (Aurelia Spencer Rogers, *Life Sketches of Orson Spencer and Others, and History of Primary Work* [Salt Lake City: George Q. Cannon and Sons, 1898], 276.)

537. Rogers, *Life Sketches*, i–ii, 229.

538. "R. S. Reports," *Woman's Exponent*, Feb. 15, 1878, 6:138.

539. See Davis Bitton, "Zion's Rowdies: Growing Up on the Mormon Frontier," *Utah Historical Quarterly* 50, no. 2 (Spring 1982): 187.

540. See B. Lloyd Poelman, "Sunday School," in *Encyclopedia of Mormonism*, ed. Daniel H. Ludlow, 5 vols. (New York: Macmillan, 1992), 3:1424–1427. On the differences between the Sunday schools and the Primary, see Carol Cornwall Madsen and Susan Staker Oman, *Sisters and Little Saints: One Hundred Years of Primary* (Salt Lake City: Deseret Book, 1979), 17–19.

541. "History of the General Organization," *Contributor* 1, no. 1 (Oct. 1879): 21; "Home Affairs," *Woman's Exponent*, Oct. 1, 1877, 6:68; see also Document 3.18.

Aurelia Spencer Rogers with Primary general board. Aurelia Spencer Rogers (rear left) first expressed the idea of establishing a church organization for children. Church leaders, Eliza R. Snow in particular, embraced the concept and founded the Primary Association. Rogers became president of the Primary in Farmington, Utah, and a member of the Central Board after a general presidency was appointed in June 1880. She is seen here with (clockwise from Rogers) May Anderson, Josephine R. West, Louie B. Felt, and Lillie T. Freeze. (Courtesy International Society Daughters of Utah Pioneers, Salt Lake City.)

boys with disorderly behavior.[542] In 1880, two years after the Primary was organized, 44 percent of Utah's population was under age fourteen; the need for a children's organization was great.[543]

Rogers was an expert in caring for children. When she was thirteen, she and her fourteen-year-old sister Ellen assumed the care of four younger siblings after their mother died during the flight from Nauvoo in 1846. A few months later, their father, Orson Spencer, began serving a three-year mission, leaving the two oldest children to watch over the others during their journey to and settlement in the Salt Lake Valley. By her eighteenth birthday, she had married Thomas Rogers and given birth to their first son. Over the next two decades, she mothered twelve children, losing five in early childhood. The first Primary was organized in Farmington, Utah, on August 11, 1878, under her leadership. Two weeks later, more than two hundred boys and girls gathered for the first meeting.[544]

At the same time that Rogers was spearheading the Primary organization in Farmington, Snow worked to establish a similar group in the Salt Lake City Eleventh Ward and then throughout the church. Snow consulted with Rogers two years later when it came time to choose a general Primary president—"someone to preside over all the Primary Associations in the Territory." They chose Louie B. Felt, who was president of the Eleventh Ward Primary. In reflecting on her experiences in the period preceding the organization of the Primary in August 1878, Rogers recalled, "While thinking over what was to be done for the best good of the children, I seemed to be carried away in the spirit, or at least I experienced a feeling of untold happiness which lasted three days and nights. During that time nothing could worry or irritate me; if my little ones were fretful, or the work went wrong, I had patience, could control in kindness, and manage my household affairs easily. This was a testimony to me that what was being done was from God."[545]

The following document is a single chapter of Rogers's 1898 autobiography, *Life Sketches of Orson Spencer and Others, and History of Primary Work.* As the title suggests, Rogers divided the volume into two parts, the first focused on her childhood, marriage, and family, especially her father, Orson Spencer; and the second focused on the history of the Primary.

——— ❧ ———

PART SECOND.
CHAPTER I.
HISTORY OF PRIMARY WORK—LETTER FROM E. R. SNOW.

In writing this sketch of the commencement of our Primaries, it is my desire, and shall be my aim to present it in a way that shall be plain to the understanding of all.

---

542. See Bitton, "Zion's Rowdies," 191–195.

543. Madsen and Oman, *Sisters and Little Saints,* xvi.

544. Elizabeth Kohler Ritchie, "Aurelia Read Spencer Rogers: Humble Heroine," in *Sister Saints,* ed. Vicky Burgess-Olson ([Provo, UT]: By the author, 1978), 225–240.

545. Rogers, *Life Sketches,* 212.

In August, 1878, I was called upon to preside over a Primary Association in Farmington. I was always an earnest thinker, and naturally of a religious turn of mind. And for some time previous to the organization of the children, I had reflected seriously upon the necessity of more strict discipline for our little boys.

Many of them were allowed to be out late at night; and certainly some of the larger ones well deserved the undesirable name of "hood[p. [205]]lum." It may seem strange that in a community calling themselves Latter-day Saints, children should be allowed to indulge in anything approaching to rowdyism. But it must be remembered that the age in which we live is one that tends to carelessness in the extreme, not only in regard to religion, but also morality. And not only this, but in many in[s]tances our people have been driven about and persecuted on every hand, until it has seemed to be all they could do to make a living for their children; and an apology might almost be made for negligence in training them up. Yet why should anything be allowed to come before the most sacred duty of parentage, that of looking after the spiritual welfare of the children? was the question which burdened my mind.

Our Bishop must have been similarly impressed, for a meeting of the mothers of our little ones was called by him, at which much good advice and counsel was given.[546]

The subject of training children was thoroughly discussed and the responsibility of guiding their young minds was thrown almost en[p. 206]tirely upon the mothers. I had children of my own, and was just as anxious as a mother could be to have them brought up properly. But what was to be done? It needed the united effort of the parents, and, as is often the case in a community, some of them were careless. A fire seemed to burn within me, and I had a desire at one time to go to the Young Men's Mutual Improvement Association meeting and talk to them; but I did not yield to the impulse, thinking too much, perhaps, of what people might say. The query then arose in my mind could there not be an organization for little boys wherein they could be taught everything good, and how to behave. This was in March; a few weeks later Sister Eliza R. Snow Smith and Sister Emmeline B. Wells, from Salt Lake City, came to Farmington to attend a Relief Society Conference.[547]

After meeting was over, and when on their way to the depot, these sisters in company with Sisters Mary S. Clark, Nancy Clark, and Lorinda [Laurinda]

---

546. Rogers's bishop in Farmington was John W. Hess, whom she described as "zealous in every good cause." (Rogers, *Life Sketches,* 212–213.)

547. This was a quarterly conference of the Davis Stake Relief Society, held in Farmington on July 10, 1878. ("Home Affairs," *Woman's Exponent,* July 15, 1878, 7:29.)

Robinson, stopped at my home for a short call.[548] The topic of our conversation was the [p. 207] young people, and the rough, careless ways many of the young men and boys had at the time. I asked the question, "What will our girls do for good husbands, if this state of things continues?" Sister Eliza seemed deeply impressed with the question; and then I asked.

"Could there not be an organization for little boys, and have them trained to make better men?"

She was silent a few moments, then said there might be such a thing and that she would speak to the First Presidency about it.

The death of President Brigham Young occurred on the 29th of August, 1877: and at the time of the beginning of the Primaries, President John Taylor with his quorum of the Twelve Apostles, presided over the Church.

Sister Eliza consulted with Apostle John Taylor and others of the Twelve, concerning this new move, and it was approved of by them. She accordingly wrote a lettter to Bishop Hess and explained the matter to him. He visited me soon after receiving her letter, and when we had talked awhile on the subject, he asked me [p. 208] if I would be willing to preside over an organization of the children. I felt willing, but very incompetent. From that time my mind was busy thinking how it was to be managed.

Up to this period the girls had not been mentioned; but my mind was that the meeting would not be complete without them; for as singing was necessary,

---

548. Emmeline B. Wells recorded in her diary that, following the conference, she and Eliza R. Snow had dinner at the home of Sarah Harvey Holmes, the stake Relief Society president. While Rogers remembered that the conversation regarding the Primary occurred at her own home, Wells's diary indicates that it occurred in Holmes's home. Wells wrote, "Sister Rogers who was there talked to us about an Association for little boys; she has been much exercised about it and feels that she has some ideas about it. Sister Eliza is greatly interested & thinks it will be a very excellent thing and we all spoke to Bishop [John W.] Hess and he approved & on the way home on the train we decided to go to Br. [John] Taylor and take the matter before him." Eliza R. Snow also gave an account of this meeting with Rogers; she incorrectly dated the conference in Farmington to August 1878 and described it as a "Conference of the Young Ladies." She stated that she and Wells "spent an hour, waiting for the train, with Mrs. Aurelia Rogers." After Rogers stated that "something more could be effected for the cultivation and improvement of the children morally and spiritually than was being done through the influence of day and Sunday-Schools," Snow asked Rogers "if she was willing to take the responsibility and labor on herself of presiding over the children of that settlement, provided the Bishop of the Ward sanctioned the movement." After receiving written approval from Bishop Hess, Snow "informed Mrs. Rogers that she might consider herself authorized to proceed, and organize in Farmington, which she did, and I commenced in the eleventh Ward in Salt Lake City." Snow became a major advocate for the Primary and composed its first curriculum. (Emmeline B. Wells, Diaries, 1844–1920, 46 vols., L. Tom Perry Special Collections, Harold B. Lee Library, Brigham Young University, Provo, UT, vol. 4, July 10, 1878; Eliza R. Snow, "Sketch of My Life," n.d., Bancroft Library, University of California, Berkeley, 38–39; Jill Mulvay Derr and Karen Lynn Davidson, eds., *Eliza R. Snow: The Complete Poetry* [Provo, UT: Brigham Young University Press; Salt Lake City: University of Utah Press, 2009], 959–960.)

it needed the voices of little girls as well as boys to make it sound as well as it should. After some consideration, a letter was sent to Sister Eliza asking her opinion in regard to the little girls taking part.

The following letter was received in answer to mine.

Salt Lake City, Aug. 4, 1878.

My dear sister Rogers: The spirit and contents of your letter pleased me much. I feel assured that the inspiration of heaven is directing you, and that a great and very important movement is being inaugurated for the future of Zion.

Your letter was waiting my return from Provo Valley on Thursday evening—yesterday (Sat.) I read it in our general meeting in the Fourteenth Ward Assembly Rooms.[549] [p. 209]

Soon after my return from Farmington I proposed to Sister Mary J. Thompson to move forward in the Sixteenth Ward and establish a president, requesting her to suggest a whole souled brother who would enter into the spirit of the work; and last evening with her, I called on Brother [John] Perkins, whose feelings were fully enlisted as soon as we informed him of the object in question. He is in daily employment during the week, and although a constant attendant at Sabbath service is willing to devote the afternoon to the benefit of the children, and for the time being deprive himself the enjoyment of the Sacrament. The importance of the movement, and its great necessity is fully acknowledged by all with whom I have conversed on the subject.

President John Taylor fully approbates it, and Joseph F. Smith[550] thinks we might better afford what expense might be incurred in furnishing uniform, musical instruments etc, for the cultivation of the children in Zion, than what we are expending in converting people abroad where elders spend years in converting a very few. [p. 210]

We think that at present, it will be wisdom to not admit any under six years of ago [age], except in some special instances. You are right—

---

549. The reference here is to a General Retrenchment meeting. For a description of this meeting, including Snow's address, see "R. S. Reports," *Woman's Exponent*, Aug. 15, 1878, 7:42. For more on the retrenchment movement, see Document 3.16.

550. Following Brigham Young's death, John Taylor led the church as president of the Quorum of the Twelve Apostles until he was sustained as church president and reorganized the First Presidency in October 1880. Joseph F. Smith, an apostle, had served as a counselor in the First Presidency under Brigham Young since 1866 and became the second counselor when Taylor reorganized the First Presidency.

we must have the girls as well as the boys—they must be trained together.

I think your mind will be directed to a brother who will unite with you in establishing this movement. Brother Perkins thinks that plenty of assistance will be forthcoming as the work progresses. The angels and all holy beings, especially the leaders of Israel on the other side the veil will be deeply interested.

I wish to see and converse with you, but cannot make it convenient at present. Tomorrow is election—on the 6th, if the Lord wills I shall go to Mendon—attend the sisters' Quarterly Conference in Ogden on the 15th and 16th—go to West Porterville on the 17th and return home sometime about the 20th. If I can so arrange will see you on my return.

That God will continue to inspire you in the establishment and development of this great movement, is the earnest prayer of

Your sister and fellow laborer,

E. R. Snow. [p. 211]

Sister Eliza in company with Sister M. Isabella Horne visited me soon after. Sister Snow suggested that the organization be called "Primary."

PART 4: 1880–1892

On July 24, 1880, in Salt Lake City, the annual pioneer parade celebrated the thirty-third anniversary of the entry of the Mormon pioneers into the Salt Lake Valley. Included in the parade were members of the newly organized Central Board of the Relief Society, who rode in carriages behind a large banner they had created for the occasion. Eliza R. Snow, who had been appointed president of the society the month before, had donated the white silk for the banner, which measured more than eight feet tall and four feet wide. Embroidered on the silk were the words "RELIEF SOCIETY | FIRST ORGANIZED BY THE PROPHET JOSEPH SMITH. | Mar. 17th 1842. | NUMBERS 300 BRANCHES | JULY 24th 1880." Also depicted on the banner was a dove bearing in its bill the olive branch of peace. At the top was a representation of the all-seeing eye, and at the lower edge of the banner was a rising star.[1]

The banner was an explicit claim to an inheritance from the organization of the Relief Society in Nauvoo, Illinois, nearly four decades earlier and its reestablishment in the Great Basin under the direction of Brigham Young. The date of its organization by Joseph Smith and statement of its current number of branches announced its Nauvoo origin and its continuing growth in the Mountain West. The olive branch bespoke the Christian virtues of peace and love, symbolizing the society's benevolent mission. The all-seeing eye was a pervasive symbol of faith in an omnipotent God, and the rising star suggested that from the time Joseph Smith "turned the key" to woman in Nauvoo, her star had been ascending.[2] Through the banner, women leaders declared their institutional origins as part of the larger celebration marking the fiftieth anniversary of the church's founding in Fayette, New York, in 1830 (see Document 4.10).

---

1. The banner is located at the Church History Museum, Salt Lake City. See also "Year of Jubilee," *Woman's Exponent,* Aug. 1, 1880, 9:36; and Jill Mulvay Derr et al., *Women of Covenant: The Story of Relief Society* (Salt Lake City: Deseret Book; Provo, UT: Brigham Young University Press, 1992), 124–125.

2. Joseph Smith told the Relief Society women in Nauvoo, "I now turn the key to you in the name of God and this Society shall rejoice and knowledge and intelligence shall flow down from this time— this is the beginning of better days, to this Society." (Document 1.2, entry for Apr. 28, 1842.)

Relief Society banner. The Central Board of the Relief Society rode in carriages behind this white silk banner for the Jubilee Pioneer Day celebration in Salt Lake City in 1880. The banner measures more than eight feet high and four feet wide. (Church History Museum, Salt Lake City.)

Despite the fervent anti-Mormon crusade swirling around them in 1880, Latter-day Saints found much to celebrate. The number of church members had grown from a small houseful to nearly 120,000 in Utah alone.[3] The Saints had colonized additional settlements in Idaho, Nevada, Arizona, Wyoming, New Mexico, and Colorado.[4] By 1880 the church had built its first temple in the West, with two more to be completed before the end of the decade, numerous chapels for Sunday congregational worship, and larger tabernacles (assembly halls) in many communities.

As church membership increased numerically and spread geographically, church leaders standardized organizational forms and procedures to facilitate communication, preserve order, and promote unity (see Document 4.16). These changes helped the church survive escalating legislative attacks on its longtime practice of plural marriage and its dominant political and economic influence in Utah Territory. As a result of this standardization, the Relief Society operated more closely with governing ecclesiastical councils, and at the same time it provided a link between women throughout the growing church. The Relief Society also connected Latter-day Saint women to other advocates for women's rights and advancement. Its representatives became members of the National Woman Suffrage Association and the National Council of Women and began to bridge the chasms that had separated Latter-day Saint women from other women in the United States. This new Mormon participation in a national culture reflected not only a change in the orientation of Mormon women toward the United States, but also the country's expansion in a way that incorporated Utah not as an isolated outpost but as part of a continent-wide nation.[5]

Standardization and Expansion of the Relief Society

When John Taylor installed Eliza R. Snow as general Relief Society president in June 1880, it marked the first time a general Relief Society presidency had governed since the Nauvoo period (see Documents 4.4, 4.5, and 4.6). At the time, Taylor led the church as president of the Quorum of the Twelve

---

3. "Registrars," *Deseret Evening News,* Sept. 1, 1882, [2].

4. Dale F. Beecher, "Colonizer of the West," in *Lion of the Lord: Essays on the Life and Service of Brigham Young,* ed. Susan Easton Black and Larry C. Porter (Salt Lake City: Deseret Book, 1995), 172–208.

5. "In 1889 and 1890 the entire northwestern quarter of the United States—the Dakotas, Montana, Wyoming, Idaho, and Washington—ceased to be territories and became states of the Union. In every state and territory Anglo-Americans and their culture predominated, making a very different region from 1848. The Census Bureau in its introduction to the 1890 census stated that no meaningful frontier line— meaning a Western line of settlement—could be mapped any longer." (Walter Nugent, *Into the West: The Story of Its People* [New York: Alfred A. Knopf, 1999], 97.)

Apostles, Brigham Young having died in 1877; Taylor became the church's third prophet and president a few months later, at the October 1880 conference. His formalizing of Relief Society leadership, together with his appointment of general presidencies for the Primary Association and the Young Ladies' Mutual Improvement Association in June 1880, began a process by which he hoped to promote system, order, and central direction for the organizations and programs of the church.

While Brigham Young had expressed high expectations for women's individual development and progress and had provided numerous opportunities for initiative and leadership in the projects he assigned to the Relief Society, John Taylor defined and systematized those projects. He also sought to define more clearly the relationship of women and their church activities to priesthood leadership by emphasizing a difference between the authority bestowed on women when ordained or set apart for office in their organizations and the transmittal of priesthood authority to men when they were ordained to the various offices in the priesthood. Like his predecessor, Taylor emphasized the importance of the Relief Society to the church and instructed all priesthood leaders to recognize its value in their wards. He frequently spoke of the essential partnership of men and women, individually and collectively, in fulfilling the mission of the church (see Documents 4.4 and 4.5).

Nevertheless, some aspects of women's authority remained ambiguous. Taylor and other church authorities affirmed that through the temple sealing ordinance, women held the priesthood "in connection with their husbands," but what exactly this meant in terms of women's ministry remained unclear (Document 4.20). For example, questions arose surrounding the continuing and common practice of women blessing the sick. In October 1880 Taylor and his counselors in the First Presidency wrote, "It is the privilege of all faithful women and lay members of the Church, who believe in Christ, to administer to all the sick or afflicted in their respective families," but this administration, they explained, should not be "by virtue and authority of the priesthood, but by virtue of their faith in Christ" (Document 4.8). In an 1888 address, apostle Franklin D. Richards answered similar questions, observing that women, though not ordained "to the various orders of the priesthood which were conferred upon us [men]" yet "share with us any and all of the ordinances of the holy anointing, endowments, sealings, sanctifications and blessings that we have been made partakers of." Richards, an assistant church historian, read passages from Joseph Smith's addresses to the Relief Society regarding the privilege of women to heal the sick, and expressed his wish that "all the sisters were so faithful that they were healers of the sick, through the power of God" (Document 4.20; see also Document 4.19).

In harmony with the larger movement for organizational refinement, Eliza R. Snow also worked to standardize the structure of the Relief Society throughout the church. She asked wards and branches to write and gather reports of local activities and to submit periodic reports to the general Relief Society presidency (see Documents 4.9 and 4.12). She also facilitated official formation of general boards for the Primary and the Young Ladies' Mutual Improvement Association (see Document 4.4). Upon Snow's death in 1887, her counselor Zina D. H. Young, who like Snow had been married to both Joseph Smith and Brigham Young, became the general Relief Society president (see Document 4.18). Young, who had been instrumental in establishing silk-farming projects throughout the church (see Document 4.3), presided over the Relief Society's first general conference in 1889 (see Documents 4.23 and 4.24).

The Relief Society also expanded in both membership and geography during this era. Eliza R. Snow reported in the fall of 1880 that the Relief Society had 290 branches in Utah Territory and "more than ten branches" outside Utah.[6] By the close of 1890, the Relief Society reported a membership of 16,741 in 368 branches, including branches in the United States, Canada, England, Scotland, Germany, Switzerland, Norway, Sweden, Denmark, the Sandwich (Hawaiian) and Samoan Islands, Australia, and New Zealand.[7] Most of the foreign branches were small and struggled to survive as faithful members emigrated to Utah. For instance, between 1879 and 1880 the White Chapel (England) Branch lost thirty-three women from emigration,[8] and at the close of 1888 the North London (England) Branch reported that in part because of emigration, "attendance has been very small, the usual number present not exceeding six lately" (Document 4.22). In the Sandwich Islands there were fifteen Relief Society branches by 1883, with a total membership of 345 women (see Document 4.13).

Relief Society organizations in outlying areas in Utah, Idaho, and Arizona Territories, though closer to the headquarters of the church, nonetheless were isolated. For example, the San Juan Stake Relief Society president, who traveled several hundred miles from southeastern Utah to attend the Relief Society conference in Salt Lake City, "spoke of the disadvantages under which the sisters labored in that Stake because of the great distances to be traversed to come together."[9] As missionary work expanded among American Indians in Utah, the church established Relief Societies for American Indian members (see

---

6. "R. S. Reports," *Woman's Exponent,* Sept. 1, 1880, 9:[53].

7. "The Relief Society Report," *Woman's Exponent,* Oct. 15, 1890, 19:68; "The National Council of Women," *Woman's Exponent,* Jan. 1, 1891, 19:109.

8. "R. S., Y. L. M. I. A. and Primary Reports," *Woman's Exponent,* Jan. 1, 1881, 9:118.

9. "Relief Society Conference," *Woman's Exponent,* Oct. 15, 1889, 18:78.

Document 4.7). A binding tie for the women of the Relief Society, whether residing in foreign lands or the harsh climate of Arizona or southern Utah, was the *Woman's Exponent,* which kept women throughout the church informed of Relief Society activities and policies (see Documents 4.14 and 4.21). "It is invalable to us," the women of the London branch wrote of the *Exponent,* "and it is looked for by one and all, we learn so much by it, what our sisters are doing thousands of miles away."[10] Though the *Exponent* was not officially published by the Relief Society, its editor, Emmeline B. Wells (see Document 4.1), was the organization's general secretary during this era and directed the Relief Society's wheat-storage program (see Document 4.2).

During this period, the Relief Society continued earlier efforts to store grain, to manufacture silk, and to improve women's health through better professional care.[11] Church leaders, including Relief Society leaders, recruited some women to leave family and friends to procure medical degrees from schools in the eastern United States.[12] These women made significant sacrifices to complete their training. For instance, when Ellis Reynolds Shipp departed for medical school in Philadelphia, she expressed deep anguish, knowing she would not see her children for more than two years.[13]

When these women returned to Utah as educated physicians, they offered classes in obstetrics and midwifery (see Document 4.17). They also championed the need for a Mormon hospital in Salt Lake City, which led to the construction of the Deseret Hospital, dedicated in July 1882 (see Document 4.11). At the dedication Wilford Woodruff observed that now there was "a place for the treatment of the afflicted, where the Elders could walk in and freely administer the ordinance for the healing of the sick."[14] Women also gave healing blessings in that place.[15]

10. Marion E. Scoles, "Foreign Letter," *Woman's Exponent,* Dec. 1, 1890, 19:93.

11. See Document 3.23.

12. See, for example, Ellis R. Shipp, Journal, 1871–1878, photocopy, CHL, 180; and "The Women of Utah," *Woman's Exponent,* Sept. 1, 1888, 17:49–50.

13. Shipp, Journal, 92.

14. "The Deseret Hospital," *Deseret News* [weekly], July 26, 1882, 430.

15. Hannah Adeline Hatch Savage, *Record of Hannah Adeline Savage, Woodruff, Arizona, and Journal,* photoreproduction of original manuscript record and journal (Pinedale, AZ: Petersen, 1976), 14–15; Christiana D. Pyper, Accounts of Administration to the Sick, 1888 and 1891, George D. Pyper, Papers, 1834–1975, Special Collections, J. Willard Marriott Library, University of Utah, Salt Lake City.

Antipolygamy Legislation and the Manifesto

The greater visibility and responsibility of Latter-day Saint women did little to arrest a vigorous campaign against plural marriage and polygamous families. Both the federal government and organized moral reform associations, mostly associated with evangelical Christianity, increased their attention on Utah during the 1880s, determined to undermine Mormon political and economic authority and to outlaw the practice of plural marriage through federal legislation. Since the territorial legislature had enfranchised Utah women in 1870, federal legislators and opponents of plural marriage had called for a repeal of the statute, hoping to diminish Mormon political control. Though Latter-day Saint women had exercised the franchise for a decade, a significant achievement in the movement for equality, they were nonetheless depicted as oppressed victims of their marital system in the inflammatory novels and lectures that caught the public fancy during this period. The *Woman's Exponent* served as Mormon women's public mouthpiece to refute these derogatory claims.

When the U.S. Supreme Court decided in 1879 that the First Amendment's guarantee of the free exercise of religion was not a defense to an indictment on bigamy charges, Congress had a firmer legal basis for action.[16] The decision validated the 1862 Morrill Act,[17] which outlawed bigamy and provided for sanctions against the practice but had not been rigorously enforced. In 1882 Congress reinforced and amended the Morrill Act in the form of the Edmunds Act, which disenfranchised all present or former polygamists and established a commission to oversee elections in the territory. The Edmunds Act also provided punishment for those convicted of practicing polygamy—or of cohabitation, which was easier for prosecutors to establish.[18]

---

16. United States v. Reynolds, 98 U.S. 145 (1878).

17. An Act to Punish and Prevent the Practice of Polygamy in the Territories of the United States and Other Places, and Disapproving and Annulling Certain Acts of the Legislative Assembly of the Territory of Utah [July 1, 1862], *The Statutes at Large, Treaties, and Proclamations, of the United States of America. From December 5, 1859, to March 3, 1863,* vol. 12, ed. George P. Sanger (Boston: Little, Brown, 1863), 37th Cong., 2nd Sess., ch. 126, p. 501.

18. An Act to Amend Section Fifty-Three Hundred and Fifty-Two of the Revised Statutes of the United States, in Reference to Bigamy, and for Other Purposes [Mar. 22, 1882], *The Statutes at Large of the United States of America, from December, 1881, to March, 1883,* vol. 22 (Washington DC: Government Printing Office, 1883), 47th Cong., 1st Sess., ch. 47, pp. 30–31. For more on the federal government's battle against Mormon polygamy during this period, see Edwin Brown Firmage and Richard Collin Mangrum, *Zion in the Courts: A Legal History of the Church of Jesus Christ of Latter-day Saints, 1830–1900* (Urbana: University of Illinois Press, 1988); and Sarah Barringer Gordon, *The Mormon Question: Polygamy and Constitutional Conflict in Nineteenth-Century America,* Series in Legal History (Chapel Hill and London: University of North Carolina Press, 2002).

Creating the crime of cohabitation meant that women lost the support of their husbands either through sentencing to jail or loss of their presence in the home. After the passage of the Edmunds Act, many Latter-day Saints attempted to align their relationships with their plural families in accordance with the law. This proved difficult, however, as apostle Lorenzo Snow discovered when he was convicted of violating the law for continuing to contact and provide financial support for his plural wives and children, even though "he had not eaten, slept, or lived in the same house with them since the passage of the Edmunds law . . . he lived with one [wife] only." A federal judge in Utah broadly defined what it meant to cohabit: "The offense of cohabitation is complete when a man to all outward appearances is living or associating with two or more women as his wives."[19] Snow served nearly a year in prison on this conviction.[20]

The conviction of husbands under the Edmunds Act placed increased pressure on families. One husband indicted on polygamy charges wrote to his wife, "The malice of ungodly men have rested heavily on me for some years passed, which has caused me to neglect my family and thereby causing you much unhappyness."[21] In Salt Lake City, men accused of practicing polygamy often went into hiding. One Latter-day Saint woman remarked, "The City of the Saints more like the city of Desolation now-a-days as the prosecution that is going on against the polygamists is almost unendurable."[22]

The Edmunds Act had other negative consequences for Mormon families, particularly when prosecutors pressured wives to answer questions before grand juries that might lead to the conviction of their husbands. For instance, Belle Harris—the grandniece of Martin Harris, one of the Three Witnesses to the Book of Mormon, and "a lady with a nursing infant"—was "hauled to the penitentiary" for refusing to testify against her husband.[23] For the same reason, Nellie White was imprisoned in the penitentiary for a little over a month.[24]

---

19. "Another Judicial Outrage," *Deseret News* [weekly], Jan. 6, 1886, 809; "The Snow Case," *Deseret News* [weekly], Feb. 17, 1886, 86.

20. Andrew H. Hedges and Richard Neitzel Holzapfel, eds., *Within These Prison Walls: Lorenzo Snow's Record Book, 1886–1897* (Provo, UT: Religious Studies Center, Brigham Young University, 2010), xlvii–lii.

21. David K. Udall to Eliza Stewart Udall, July 15, 1885, Udall Family Correspondence Collection, 1859–1950, CHL.

22. Martha Hughes Cannon to Barbara Replogle, May 1, 1885, Martha H. Cannon Collection, 1883–1912, CHL.

23. "The Case and Character of Belle Harris," and "Just Compare the Two Cases," *Deseret News* [weekly], May 23, 1883, 277, 280.

24. "Nellie White," *Deseret News* [weekly], July 16, 1884, 401.

As they had in the mass meetings of the 1870s, Mormon women gathered to protest. They protested the Edmunds Act and the increasingly rigorous enforcement of it, including the targeting of plural wives by the legal process. In 1886 a delegation of women presented their grievances to the U.S. president and Congress in Washington (see Document 4.15). Among their grievances, as Dr. Ellen B. Ferguson explained, was their complaint that "young children are brought into court and plied with indecent questions; tender women in delicate health are asked impertinent and insulting questions in court, and many of the leading men and priests of Mormonism are driven into hiding by the exactions of the officials."[25] These protest efforts proved fruitless.

Later, the 1887 Edmunds-Tucker Act, which amended the 1882 Edmunds Act, disenfranchised all Utah women and placed most of the church's property and financial holdings in receivership.[26] While crippling the church financially, these acts also diminished the Mormon electorate and removed Mormons from elected office, allowing non-Mormon residents of Utah to gain political control in both Ogden and Salt Lake City.[27] By 1890 the confiscation of the church's religious property—including the temples—appeared imminent, and even more debilitating legislation was proposed and appeared likely to pass. Church president Wilford Woodruff, after months of deliberation, announced that he had received divine assurance that he should submit to the law of the land. In September 1890 he issued a manifesto suspending further plural marriages, thus ending more than a decade of federal prosecution, constant surveillance, and personal anxiety while paving the way to statehood and economic, political, legal, religious, and social readjustments for Latter-day Saints (see Documents 4.25 and 4.26).[28] Against this tumultuous backdrop, the Relief Society provided stability and a focus for church service and commitment that helped women endure the personal calumny, the fragmentation of their families, and the uncertainties that marked the decade.

25. "At the Capital," *Ogden Daily Herald*, Apr. 20, 1886, [1].

26. An Act to Amend an Act Entitled "An Act to Amend Section Fifty-Three Hundred and Fifty-Two of the Revised Statutes of the United States, in Reference to Bigamy, and for Other Purposes," Approved March Twenty-Second, Eighteen Hundred and Eighty-Two [Mar. 3, 1887], *The Statutes at Large of the United States of America, from December, 1885, to March, 1887*, vol. 24 (Washington DC: Government Printing Office, 1887), 49th Cong., 2nd Sess., ch. 397, pp. 365–641.

27. Firmage and Mangrum, *Zion in the Courts*, 236–237.

28. *Manifesto of the Presidency and Apostles Issued December 12, 1889, Also the Official Declaration or Manifesto by President Wilford Woodruff Prohibiting Further Plural Marriages, and Its Adoption by the General Conference, October 6, 1890* (Salt Lake City: Deseret News, [1890]), 4; Gordon, *The Mormon Question*, 220.

Advocacy for Women's Rights

Travelers, including officers and members of several national women's organizations availing themselves of the transcontinental railroad, came in droves to Salt Lake City to see the Mormons during this era. Many of them left with uncomplimentary accounts of their visit, while others found a unique community of hard-working, dedicated, and unified people. Amidst the growing national sentiment for antipolygamy legislation, the National Woman Suffrage Association and the National Council of Women supported Utah women's efforts to retain their right to vote.

Mormon women affiliated with the National Woman Suffrage Association in January 1879, when Emmeline B. Wells and Zina Young Williams attended the annual convention in Washington DC. They went "in response to official invitation to represent the cause of the women of Mormondom."[29] While in Washington they met with President Rutherford B. Hayes as members of a "committee appointed by the women of the suffrage convention" to solicit his support. During their meeting with President Hayes, Wells and Williams requested that he veto "any bill to enforce the act of 1862," meaning the anti-polygamy Morrill Act.[30] They also prepared a memorial to Congress asking for the Morrill Act to be repealed.[31]

Wells and Williams took an active part in the suffrage convention. Wells served on the committee of resolutions, along with national suffrage leaders Sara A. Spencer and Matilda J. Gage, while Williams was selected a member of the finance committee. Both Wells and Williams were given opportunities to address the convention. In Williams's speech, she "expressed her thanks for the kind manner in which she has been received in Washington, where she expected to meet with prejudice."[32] Though their stay in Washington was brief, both women felt their efforts were beneficial. George Q. Cannon, who was then in Washington as a congressional delegate for Utah Territory, wrote: "Sisters Wells and Williams had done very well here and their visit had been productive of much good. I have said that much in previous letters; but in alluding to their departure home I intended to repeat it. As we are making history, and the trip they have made will doubtless be noticed."[33]

---

29. "For the Capital," *Deseret News* [weekly], Jan. 8, 1879, 769.

30. "American," *Deseret News* [weekly], Jan. 22, 1879, 810.

31. "Women in Politics," *Woman's Exponent,* June 15, 1888, 17:10.

32. "The Utah Ladies in Washington," *Deseret News* [weekly], Jan. 22, 1879, 808.

33. George Q. Cannon to George Reynolds, Feb. 3, 1879, George Q. Cannon, Letterbook, 1871–1879, CHL, 401.

Over the next decade Mormon women continued their involvement in the suffrage movement.[34] The Relief Society and the Young Ladies' Mutual Improvement Association, for instance, participated in the National Council of Women, which suffrage advocates organized on March 31, 1888, at the close of their international convention (see Document 4.27). The purpose of this council was to bring together representatives of women's organizations from all parts of the United States to work together "to the overthrow of all forms of ignorance and injustice, and to the application of the Golden Rule to society, custom and law."[35] Latter-day Saint women addressed this council when it convened in Washington DC in February 1891 and reported the work of the Relief Society and Young Ladies' organizations.[36] Through membership in this organization, Mormon women developed friendships and weakened barriers to misunderstanding. In addition, in the early 1890s, as Utah statehood was fast becoming a reality, Latter-day Saint women took the lead in organizing a campaign to reinstate woman suffrage in Utah. Between 1879 and 1896, the masthead of the *Woman's Exponent* included the motto "The Rights of the Women of Zion, and the Rights of the Women of all Nations."[37]

During the last decade of the nineteenth century, Latter-day Saint women and men increasingly looked beyond the Mountain West valleys where they had initially sought refuge and isolation. The Saints' connection to the United States had proved to be enduring, though painfully conflicted. The decade of the 1880s, with the intense antipolygamy campaign and ultimately President Woodruff's manifesto in 1890, closed as one of the most challenging in the church's brief history.

For the Relief Society, looking back at its beginnings lent strength to moving forward. The society mounted an impressive Jubilee celebration on March 17, 1892, commemorating the fiftieth anniversary of its founding. In introducing the program in the tabernacle in Salt Lake City, Relief Society general president Zina D. H. Young, who three years earlier had told the sisters "there is more difference in our manner of speech, than in the motives of our hearts,"[38] now reiterated that same unifying sentiment, declaring, "O, that my words

---

34. For a detailed discussion of Mormon women's relationship with the suffrage movement, see Lola Van Wagenen, "Sister-Wives and Suffragists: Polygamy and the Politics of Woman Suffrage, 1870–1896" (PhD diss., New York University, 1994), 119–137.

35. "Constitution of the Woman's National Council of the United States," *Woman's Exponent,* Jan. 1, 1891, 19:108.

36. Rachel Foster Avery, ed., *Transactions of the National Council of Women of the United States, Assembled in Washington, D.C., February 22 to 25, 1891* (Philadelphia: Executive Board of the National Council of Women, 1891), 256–260.

37. See *Woman's Exponent* from Nov. 1, 1879, to Dec. 15, 1896.

38. "First General Conference of the Relief Society," *Woman's Exponent,* Apr. 15, 1889, 17:172.

could be heard by all people, not only by you my brethren and sisters in this Tabernacle and throughout Utah, but that they might be heard and understood by all the people of this continent, and not only this continent but the continents of Europe, Asia, Africa and the Islands of the Sea" (Document 4.28). The "grand Jubilee all over the world" proclaimed the Relief Society's divine origin, its tenacious fidelity to Nauvoo roots, and its unity of purpose. With the mingling of male and female voices at the tabernacle pulpit and in the audience, the celebration affirmed the continuing partnership of men and women. As they honored the past, women looked forward to a future with all new challenges and possibilities.

4.1 Emmeline B. Wells, "Women's Organizations," January 15, 1880

Emmeline B. Wells, "Women's Organizations," Woman's Exponent *(Salt Lake City, UT), Jan. 15, 1880, vol. 8, no. 16, p. 122.*

Throughout the 1870s Latter-day Saint women found themselves in a posture of defense, obliged to justify their religious beliefs and practices. The anti-Mormon movement that escalated throughout the decade included the introduction of numerous antipolygamy bills in Congress, a campaign of national women's reform societies against polygamy, a movement to disenfranchise Utah women, and popular lectures and sermons of orators and clergy that inveighed against the church. Mormon women found support and solidarity through their membership in the Relief Society and sought to defend themselves and their religion.[39]

In 1877 Emmeline B. Wells succeeded Louisa Greene Richards as editor of the *Woman's Exponent;* she would also serve as business manager, owner, and publisher.[40] In January 1880, at the beginning of the new decade, Wells published an editorial praising the Relief Society for the important role it played in the church and for being a vehicle of knowledge, growth, influence, and opportunity for its members.

WOMEN'S ORGANIZATIONS.

The organization of the Relief Society in Nauvoo, Ill., in March, 1842, opened perhaps one of the most important eras in the history of woman. It presented the great woman-question to the Latter-day Saints, previous to the woman's rights organizations, which have created such extensive agitation of the subject since, in America, Great Britain and Europe.[41] The question did not present itself in any aggressive form as woman opposed to man, but as a co-worker and helpmeet in all that relates to the well-being and advancement of both, and mutual promoting of the best interests of the community at large. It

---

39. See Documents 3.12, 3.13, and 3.20.

40. Carol Cornwall Madsen, *An Advocate for Women: The Public Life of Emmeline B. Wells, 1870–1920,* Biographies in Latter-day Saint History (Provo, UT: Brigham Young University Press, 2006), 43–45; see also Document 3.21.

41. The meeting generally credited as launching the nineteenth-century women's rights movement took place in Seneca Falls, New York, in July 1848—six years after the organization of the Relief Society. Like many other early Latter-day Saint women, Wells felt that the formation of the Relief Society had benefited women both inside and outside the church: that when Joseph Smith "turn[ed] the key" to women, he initiated a process that would help women achieve their highest potential. (Document 1.2, entry for Apr. 28, 1842; see also Jill Mulvay Derr and Carol Cornwall Madsen, "Preserving the Record and Memory of the Female Relief Society of Nauvoo, 1842–92," *Journal of Mormon History* 35, no. 3 [Summer 2009]: 88–111; "What Hath the Century Wrought," *Woman's Exponent,* Jan. 1, 1901, 29:70–71.)

has given to woman, in its rise and progress, influence on almost all subjects that pertain to her welfare and happiness, and opportunities for expressing her own thoughts, views and opinions; all of which has had a tendency to make her intelligent in regard to matters which before were considered incompatible with "woman's sphere," and unintelligible to her "weaker" mind.

Through these organizations an immense work has been done in developing the faculties and capabilities of woman, that never could have been effected except through some permanent organization, or association, for mutual help, benefit, and interchange of ideas.

The developments and progression made since the commencement of these societies, which exist now throughout the extent of the settlements of the Latter-day Saints, was not dreamed of in the beginning. They are educational in the most general sense; all subjects, religious, moral and mental, in their various bearings, are discussed, and instruction is given on all matters pertaining to life, health and happiness.[42] One of the strongest features of this remarkable organization is the cultivation of the gift of faith. That great power has been manifested under the hands of sisters in administering to the sick is a fact to which many can testify; and is not this one positive proof that the Lord recognizes them and approves their labors in this direction? Is there anything more heavenly than to give comfort and relief to the sick and distressed? We think not.

In reference to this subject it seems appropriate to give the Prophet Joseph's words to the Relief Society in session in Nauvoo, from his own journal:

> I met the members of the Female Relief Society, and after presiding at the admission of many new members, gave a lecture on the priesthood, showing how the sisters would come in possession of the privileges, blessings and gifts of the priesthood, and that the signs should follow them—such as healing the sick, casting out devils, &c., and that they might attain unto these blessings by a virtuous life and conversation, and diligence in keeping all the commandments.[43]

---

42. Nineteenth-century Relief Society lessons were not coordinated churchwide; they were created by local societies and recorded in their records and minutes. General outlines for lessons were first published in the *Woman's Exponent* and later appeared as pamphlets. The first correlated manual of instruction, *Relief Society Guide,* was distributed in January 1914. Lessons for 1915 were published in a new periodical, the *Relief Society Magazine.* (Jill Mulvay Derr et al., *Women of Covenant: The Story of Relief Society* [Salt Lake City: Deseret Book; Provo, UT: Brigham Young University Press, 1992], 186–190.)

43. This excerpt is from the entry made in Joseph Smith's journal after he addressed the Relief Society in Nauvoo on April 28, 1842. Wells here quotes the edited version of this journal entry published in the *Deseret News* in 1855. (Document 2.2; see also the original minutes of the discourse in Document 1.2, entry for Apr. 28, 1842.)

It is gratifying to know that there are sisters still living who listened to the teachings of the Prophet Joseph, and heard him prophesy in regard to the glorious work that would be accomplished through the energy, industry and capability of the sisters, with the blessing of God upon their labors.

Foremost among those connected with the Relief Society of Nauvoo we are proud to mention the name of our aged sister and Mother in Israel, Elizabeth Ann Whitney, who was Counselor to the President of that organization; Sister Eliza R. Snow, who was the able and efficient Secretary, and Sarah M. Kimball, one of its originators and most active and eminent workers. These ladies, with others who are still living, are among the pioneers of this woman movement, or are indeed the very ones who have aided most vigorously in laying the foundation for us who are now engaged in this work. How thankful we are that they still live, and others who took part in those early days, when so little was known of woman's fitness for positions of trust, or her ability to transact business for the public good.

Sisters Mercy R. Thompson, Zina D. Young, Phebe Woodruff, Marinda Hyde, Amanda Smith, Bathsheba W. Smith, Louisa B. Pratt and others whose names are honorable, were members of that Society in its infancy. We honor them as women of God who not only accepted in humility and meekness the additional responsibility placed upon them, but who have continued in the good work from year to year, aiding, assisting and advising, and though they have grown grey in the cause of truth, yet falter not, but maintain with steadfastness and integrity the principles of righteousness, and sustain those who are walking in the same straight and narrow way.

Many of those whose names were enrolled as members of that first organization sleep now in the cold and silent tomb; but think you, my good friends, their glorified spirits are idle? No. They are at work: we know not where nor how, but this we know, that in the economy of heaven there is no inactivity. We are instructed that the spirits of men who pass behind the vail are engaged in preaching to the spirits in prison, as Christ, who went "to preach to the spirits in prison that were sometime disobedient in the days of Noah," &c.[44] If there is specified work for man there is also a place for woman, of this rest assured; and in the good time of the Lord, through the revelations of His holy will, it will be revealed.

Among those who were actively engaged in the work of the Society at a very early period, we ought to make honorable mention of Vilate Murray Kimball, who was well known as an efficient adviser and one of the most benevolent and sympathetic women who ever lived. She was greatly beloved by

---

44. See 1 Peter 3:19–20.

all who knew her, and was a woman of remarkable spiritual endowments. In her experience she had wonderful manifestations of a spiritual nature, which we hope to write up at some future time for the edification of our readers. In speaking of these ladies who have figured conspicuously in the history of this people, we do not depend altogether upon the testimony of others; having been intimately acquainted with all the ladies whose names are mentioned, and with many of the facts interwoven in the incidents which form a portion of the history of the women of this people. That the lives of the women of this age are quite as remarkable as those of any period of the world we feel assured; that great events are about to transpire in which woman will perform an active and important revolutionary part we are not afraid to predict. The great question is, Is she preparing herself for the position she is destined to occupy, and the work which will consequently devolve upon her? This subject opens up a wide field for dissertation.

E. B. W.

4.2 Quorum of the Twelve Apostles, Circular Letter, April 16, 1880 (Excerpt)

Quorum of the Twelve Apostles, "Circular from the Twelve Apostles," Apr. 16, 1880, Deseret Evening News *(Salt Lake City, UT), Apr. 17, 1880, vol. 13, no. 124, p. [2] (excerpt).*

In the ancient Hebrew custom of the Jubilee or fiftieth year, the indebtedness of the poor was absolved, Israelite slaves were freed, and inheritances and lands lost by misfortune or poverty were returned to their natural owners.[45] The Church of Jesus Christ of Latter-day Saints also implemented numerous charitable acts during the 1880 Jubilee celebration of its founding. The church absolved debts Saints had incurred in the past, including half of their tithing commitments and half of their indebtedness to the Perpetual Emigrating Fund.[46] John Taylor, president of the Quorum of the Twelve Apostles,[47] asked banks and businesses to annul debts of the Saints, church members to donate one thousand head of cattle and five thousand sheep to needy Mormon communities, and the Relief Society to donate thirty-four thousand bushels of wheat.[48]

The Relief Society responded to President Taylor's request with a unanimous vote in the affirmative at the April 1880 general conference.[49] Relief Society women had been storing grain for three years at the request of Brigham Young, much of it in their own granaries. They saw this grain as sacred, believing it would be crucial to the survival of church members in the last days. The women, heeding Young's explicit instructions, had earlier decided not to share their wheat with the poor but to preserve it for use during the calamities that would precede Christ's second coming, which many Saints believed was imminent. This attitude toward sharing grain shifted after 1890, but at the time of the Jubilee in 1880, the loaning of grain was a marked departure from current practice.[50]

Responding to the Relief Society's expression of support, Taylor and the Quorum of the Twelve issued the following directive addressed to Emmeline B. Wells, the president of the Relief Society's Central Grain Committee,[51] as well as to presidents of Relief Societies in Salt Lake City and elsewhere who had responsibility for wheat storage.

---

45. See "Jubilee, year of," in *The Anchor Bible Dictionary,* ed. David Noel Freedman, 6 vols. (New York: Doubleday, 1992), 3:1025–1029.

46. On the fund, see Richard L. Jensen, "Steaming Through: Arrangements for Mormon Emigration from Europe, 1869–1887," *Journal of Mormon History* 9 (1982): 3–23.

47. Taylor became president of the church a few months later, in October 1880.

48. "Circular from the Twelve Apostles," *Deseret Evening News,* Apr. 17, 1880, p. [2]; Document 4.8.

49. *The Year of Jubilee. A Full Report of the Proceedings of the Fiftieth Annual Conference of the Church of Jesus Christ of Latter-day Saints, Held in the Large Tabernacle, Salt Lake City, Utah, April 6th, 7th and 8th, A.D. 1880* (Salt Lake City: Deseret News, 1880), 64.

50. Jessie L. Embry, "Relief Society Grain Storage Program, 1876–1940" (master's thesis, Brigham Young University, 1974), 5–8, 16–26; see also Document 3.25.

51. See Document 3.25.

The directive was part of an April 16, 1880, circular letter from the Twelve Apostles published on April 17 in the *Deseret Evening News.* Only the portion of the letter dealing with loaning wheat has been reproduced here.

———— ❧ ————

CIRCULAR FROM THE TWELVE APOSTLES.
SALT LAKE CITY, U. T.
April 16, 1880. . . .[52]

THE LOANING OF RELIEF SOCIETY WHEAT.

To the President of the Central Grain Committee, and Presidents of the various Branches of the Relief Society in Salt Lake City and throughout the Stakes of Zion, having in charge stored Wheat:

In accordance with a unanimous vote of the Sisters present at our late General Conference,[53] we recommend that you loan to your respective Bishops so much wheat as they may consider requisite to meet the necessities of the deserving poor.[54]

We also recommend that the Bishops receipt to you and take receipts from those to whom they distribute, that the wheat loaned may be faithfully returned when circumstances shall permit.

We realize that our Sisters have performed a highly commendable and praiseworthy labor in storing wheat for future emergencies, and we trust that, inasmuch as the wheat [i]s[55] loaned without interest, the Bishops, in carrying out the above measures, will see that they receive a full equivalent for their loans, taking into consideration the losses in changing as well as the difference between old and new wheat as to quality and quantity. The shrinkage is supposed to be about ten per cent. The Bishops should be responsible for the return of the wheat, hence they should loan on good security and to such persons as will return the same according to agreement. It should be loaned

---

52. TEXT: The ellipsis points in this excerpt have been supplied by the editors of this volume to indicate omissions from the original document.

53. At the April 1880 general conference, Taylor told the audience that he had already spoken about the wheat distribution plan with Relief Society general president Eliza R. Snow and received her approval. Conference proceedings report the vote, called by Taylor: "We may as well call a vote on this question now, our sisters are present whom we will ask to vote. All you sisters who are in favor of carrying out this request, hold up your right hand. [A forest of hands went up.] There they go, you see. . . . I think that is the most hearty vote yet." (*Year of Jubilee,* 64, bracketed material in original.)

54. TEXT: In the copy used for transcription, some of the letters in this paragraph are obscured by bold letters bleeding through from the opposite side of the page. These letters have been included without brackets on the likelihood that they were all present in the original.

55. TEXT: Apparent typographical error: capital *I* or lowercase *l* used rather than a lowercase *i.*

mainly for seed. The Tithing Office will in no case be responsible for the return of the whole or any part thereof.[56] . . .

JOHN TAYLOR,
In behalf of the
Council of Apostles.

---

56. The General Tithing Office, located on South Temple Street immediately east of the temple block, included barns, corrals, and other areas for storing goods donated by church members as tithing. (C. Mark Hamilton, *Nineteenth-Century Mormon Architecture and City Planning* [New York: Oxford University Press, 1995], 98–99; see Document 3.1.)

4.3 Jane Wilkie Hooper Blood, Diary Entries for May 1880– September 1883 (Excerpts)

Jane Wilkie Hooper Blood, Diary entries, May 11, 1880–Sept. 30, 1883 (excerpts); microfilm; Jane H. Blood Diaries, 1880–1898, pp. 9–15, 17, 19, 21–23, 25–31, 37–38, 54–55, 68–70, 72–74, 78–79, CHL (MS 8842).

Jane Wilkie Hooper arrived in Kaysville, Utah, as a ten-year-old with her parents in 1855. Young Jane made close friendships in Kaysville that she "hated to leave" when the family relocated to Ogden, about fifteen miles north, in the late 1850s. But her absence was only temporary. After marrying William Blood, she returned to Kaysville, where she became a central figure in the Relief Society for many decades. She noted that on May 14, 1868, "the Female Relief Society was organized in Kaysville. . . . Mary Woolley and I were [visiting] teachers. I worked in the Relief Society as secretary and later as a counselor until 1898."[57] During the era covered by the diary excerpts below, Blood also served as ward Relief Society treasurer. In addition, when Eliza R. Snow organized a Primary Association in Kaysville on September 18, 1879, Blood became Primary president at the bishop's suggestion.[58] These excerpts from her diary give insight into the functioning of the Relief Society and the Primary Association on a local level and the role they played in Blood's life.[59]

The Kaysville Relief Society was organized in the midst of efforts by church leaders to establish the silk industry in Utah, and Blood and other women embraced the enterprise. In the 1850s and 1860s, Brigham Young repeatedly encouraged Latter-day Saints to participate

---

57. Ivy Hooper Blood Hill, ed., *Jane Wilkie Hooper Blood Autobiography and Abridged Diary* (Logan, UT: J. P. Smith, 1966), 14–19.

58. Kaysville Ward, North Davis Stake, Kaysville Ward Primary Association Minutes and Records, 1879–1940, CHL, vol. 1, Sept. 18, 1879; "A Statistical and Financial Report of the Relief Society of Kaysville for the Year Ending Mar 31st 1881," in Kaysville Ward, North Davis Stake, Kaysville Ward Relief Society Minutes and Records, 1878–1937, CHL, 150.

59. These organizations generally met on weekdays. Blood's rare Sunday entries show that she also attended Sunday school with her children and the Saturday and Sunday stake conferences held quarterly. She made no regular note of attending the local Sunday worship service, sacrament meeting, which women with children seem to have attended rather erratically during this period. Latter-day Saints in general did not attend sacrament meetings weekly. "'Going to meeting' clearly was not a popular nineteenth century pastime. Part of the problem lay with economics. Frontier scarcity restricted leisure time and therefore church attendance, especially during crisis years like the period after the move south. Moreover, humdrum meetings contributed to the lack of attendance. During the two- and sometimes three-hour worship services, impromptu speakers often preached interminably, often without the virtue of edifying. . . . Nineteenth-century Mormons simply refused to regard meeting attendance as a serious obligation. While the linking of 'going to a meeting' with religiosity surfaced as early as the 1850s, the idea obviously failed to take hold. Instead of gathering at the chapel, the pioneers declared the faith by adopting a life-style that set them apart from the world and put them to work 'building the kingdom.'" (Ronald W. Walker, "'Going to Meeting' in Salt Lake City's Thirteenth Ward, 1849–1881: A Microanalysis," in *New Views of Mormon History: A Collection of Essays in Honor of Leonard J. Arrington,* ed. Davis Bitton and Maureen Ursenbach Beecher [Salt Lake City: University of Utah Press, 1987], 154–155.)

in silk production,[60] but many Saints remained apathetic. Major progress came in the late 1860s after Young appointed George D. Watt, his shorthand reporter, "to travel throughout the Territory and lecture on Silk culture, and also to organize societies for the cultivation of silk."[61] In 1875 church members organized the Deseret Silk Association with a mix of male and female leadership. Zina D. H. Young was president of the new silk association with Mary Isabella Horne as second vice president; Alexander C. Pyper was superintendent with Anson Call as first vice president. A committee consisting of Eliza R. Snow, Horne, and Elvira Stevens Barney worked to obtain means to procure machinery and other necessities. Zina Young, who believed the silk association would be critical in helping the Saints becoming self-sustaining, visited settlements throughout the territory to encourage silk raising among Relief Society women and other church leaders.[62]

During the April 1877 general conference of the church, an official call to all Latter-day Saint women asked them to actively participate in silk production. Attendees unanimously voted that Relief Societies throughout the church would raise silk as part of their mission and thereby work to clothe themselves and their families.[63] At the same time, membership in the Deseret Silk Association rapidly spread to local Relief Societies. A branch of the association was organized in Davis County, where Jane Blood lived, at a Relief Society meeting in April 1879.[64] Blood's daughter noted, "Mother had an insatiable craving for knowledge, and real creative ability. . . . She was never satisfied after seeing a new kind of handwork until she had learned how to do it. This desire prompted her to go into the silk industry."[65]

———— ❧ ————

May 1880

Tues 11 We Ironed I went to the F R S Meeting[66] . . . [p. 9] . . .[67]

Tue 25 We Ironed I attended F R⟨elief⟩. S⟨ociety⟩. Meeting Sisters [Sarah] Holmes & Clarke [Mary Stevenson Clark] from Farmington Spoke tous [to

---

60. See, for example, "Discourse," *Deseret News*, Jan. 27, 1858, 372–373; and Document 3.4.

61. "Culture of Silk," *Deseret News* [weekly], Mar. 25, 1868, 52; "Society for Cultivating Silk," *Deseret News* [weekly], Nov. 4, 1868, 312.

62. Deseret Silk Association, Minutes, June 1875–Oct. 1878, CHL, June 14 and 21, 1875, and Jan. 3, 1876; "Home Affairs," *Woman's Exponent*, June 15, 1875, 4:13; Mary Ann Hardy, "Minutes of a Meeting," *Woman's Exponent*, July 15, 1875, 4:27.

63. "General Conference at St. George," *Woman's Exponent*, Apr. 15, 1877, 5:172.

64. "Home Affairs," *Woman's Exponent*, May 1, 1879, 7:234. The following year, the Utah Silk Association was organized. The Deseret Silk Association was an undertaking of the church, while the Utah Silk Association was organized as a for-profit business according to the laws of Utah. (R. Simpson, "Utah Silk Association," *Woman's Exponent*, Jan. 15, 1880, 8:126.)

65. Hill, *Jane Wilkie Hooper Blood Autobiography and Abridged Diary*, 27.

66. At this meeting, Blood donated twenty-five cents and a spool of cotton worth seven cents. (Kaysville Ward Relief Society Minutes and Records, vol. 1, May 11, 1880.)

67. TEXT: The ellipsis points in these excerpts have been supplied by the editors of this volume to indicate omissions from the original journal.

us]⁶⁸ I rode with Sister [Mary Ann] Walker down to Annie [Blood Phillips's]
when I got thair Annie had gone up to our house but Wm [William Blood]
brought Her down . . .

Mon 31 William went to town we washed[.] the ⟨baby⟩ was not well Annie
went home I bought 2.00 worth of Silkworms Eggs . . .

June 1880

Tues 8 We irond in the morning I attended F R S Meeting in the after-
noon⁶⁹ went to Elizbeth Bennett in the evening she was sick . . .

Thur 10 Made some wax Flowers

Fri 11   "   "   "   went to Choir practice . . .

Satur 12 I was busey home in the morning went to Meeting in the afternoon Sisters holmes and Clark came both Primary ⟨A⟩sociations [Associations]
held Meeting in the Meeting house⁷⁰ Annie cam[e] [p. 10] . . .

Tue 15 got 50ᶜᵗ Silkworms Egg for I did not think we should have
eneugh . . .

Fri 25 George [Blood] is some better, cleaning out the silkwormes . . .
[p. 11] . . .

July 1880

Thu 8 Working with the silk wormes . . .

Monday 12 We washed[.] Alfred Manning and wife [Rose Manning] came
and Harry [Henry Manning], Maggie [Margaret Manning] and Jane
Manning, Annie [Anna] Parker, Frank Gwilliams, thay were going to Rodes
valley⁷¹ on a visit. William was not well. . . .

Wd 14 I cut out some shirts for William and the boys. I went up to
W[illiam] Smith for mulbery leaves.⁷²

---

68. The Kaysville Ward Relief Society minutes date this meeting to May 24. Holmes and Clark were
local Relief Society leaders. Clark spoke on the importance of Relief Society meetings and of unity with
the Saints. She also "spoke of an old Lamanitish Woman who said she remembered her Grandfather saying, a people would come from the west with a history of their Fathers. Spoke of the purity of some of the
Indian Tribes." Holmes spoke about the importance of acquiring knowledge, raising children to understand the gospel, cultivating silk, and storing grain, commenting, "It is as much a duty to attend to temporal as it is to pray." (Kaysville Ward Relief Society Minutes and Records, vol. 1, May 24, 1880.)

69. At this meeting Blood donated one package of tea worth twenty-five cents. (Kaysville Ward Relief
Society Minutes and Records, vol. 1, June 8, 1880.)

70. For an account of this meeting, see Kaysville Ward Primary Association Minutes and Records,
vol. 1, June 12, 1880.

71. Rhodes (or Rhoades) Valley was the original name of what is today Kamas, Summit County, Utah.
(David Hampshire et al., *A History of Summit County*, Utah Centennial County History Series [Salt Lake
City: Utah State Historical Society, 1998], 73–74.)

72. Silk worms were fed on leaves from mulberry trees, which were imported to Utah for the silk

Jane Wilkie Hooper Blood. Jane Blood served as Relief Society
teacher, counselor, and treasurer and as Primary president in
Kaysville, Utah. Her diary shows how domestic and church activities were interwoven in her daily life. (Courtesy International
Society Daughters of Utah Pioneers, Salt Lake City.)

Thur 15 We picked the red currants Mary Ann [Alice Cannon] Lambert came on a visit I went to Haights Creek for a ride with John [Blood] he went for oak brush for the wormes to spin on . . .

Thurs 22 Ironed Annie [Parker] & Thomas [Phillips] went home, I went to Smiths for leaves I have been every night for a week but most of the ⟨first⟩ silkworms are spinning . . . [p. 12] . . .

Mon 26 I was working with the silk worms . . .

Saturd 31 picked of some of the cocoons attented Primary Meeting[73] . . .

August 1880

Tue 10 we irond Annie came we went to the young Lady's Meeting Sisters Holmes and both Sisters Clarke[74] was to the meeting thay called on me to Speek. . . . [p. 13] . . .

Thur 19 I comenced to teach Mrs [Mary Ann] Lewis and Elizbeth Blaymires to make wax flowers . . .

Wed 25 We finished the boquets of wax flowers and thay took them home. I charged four dollars each for teaching and sold them a glass Shade each for [*blank*] . . . [p. 14] . . .

September 1880

Sat 18 I was working at home in the morning went to meeting in the after noon it is the conferance for the primarys Sisters [Aurelia Spencer] Rogers, [Helena] Hess and Lucy Clark came up we had a good meeting thay cam[e] over to supper Annie came . . . [p. 15] . . .

October 1880

Tue 26 I made the boys over halls [overalls] in the morning went to the sisters Meeting in the afternoon . . .

November 1880

Tue 2 They finished thrashing I had a sewing bee William and I went to vote for the delagate to congress[75] . . . [p. 17] . . .

---

industry. (See Chris Rigby Arrington, "The Finest of Fabrics: Mormon Women and the Silk Industry in Early Utah," *Utah Historical Quarterly* 46, no. 4 [Fall 1978]: 376–396.)

73. Blood spoke at this meeting. (Kaysville Ward Primary Association Minutes and Records, vol. 1, July 31, 1880.)

74. Likely Lucy Augusta Rice Clark and Nancy Areta Porter Stevenson Clark, both of whom were leaders in the local Young Ladies' Mutual Improvement Association in this period.

75. George Q. Cannon won this election for territorial delegate to Congress. ("Territorial Returns," "Allen G. Campbell's Protest," and "The Delegate's Certificate," *Deseret News* [weekly], Dec. 22, 1880, 737, 741, 744.)

December 1880

Sat 4 it is Conferance of this stake the meeting is here Joseph F Smith and John Henry Smith attended . . .

Sun 5 . . . J F [Smith] also spoke to the sisters told them how to live so that thair ⟨children⟩ would grow up to ⟨be⟩ mighty men and wemen told us to teach them the principles of the gosple and to do right from the day thay are born told the men to be good to thair wives and wives to thair husbands and treat all thair famleys good and kind[76] . . .

Mon 6 I bought two Sheep for five dollars. it was money I received for teaching wax flowers. . . . [p. 19] . . .

January 1881

Tue 4 Sewing in the morning I went up to Sister [Mary Ann] Hyde in the afternoon her daughter was sick and she came down for me . . . [p. 21]

Thurs 6 I have been bussy sewing all day this is Maggie [Margaret Ann] Manning weding day. it is the first child Margret [Margaret Galbraith Manning] has had married

Fri 7 I have been bussy working and cooking I made a weding cake for Magie . . .

Fri 21 I have been making burial cloths for little Ray [Renaldo] Mowrey he died with the membraim Croop[77] he had his throte cut and a silver tube put in for him to breath[e] through he suferd dredfull. . . . [p. 22]

Tue 25 sewing on my dress Sister [Louisa] Egbert came to see about me working up my silk

Wed 26 We washed in the morning I went to Egberts in the afternoon

Thur 27 I have been up to Egberts and begun to real my silk

Fri 28 I have been realing silk Annie and ~~me~~ I went to choir practice

Sat 29 We have dismised the meeting for a wile it is such bad wether for the children to come out I have been realing silk . . .

Monday 31. I have been working in the silk we have realed eight skains today I have got got aletter from Margret to tell me Joseph [Manning] is maried . . .

---

76. Two sessions of the stake conference were held this day. Joseph F. Smith wrote in his journal of the morning session, "I then spoke about 45 minutes and enjoyed much of the good spirit." He also spoke "about 45 min." in the afternoon session. (Joseph F. Smith, Journal, in Joseph F. Smith, Papers, 1854–1918, CHL, Dec. 5, 1880.)

77. Mowrey died from diphtheria. (Salt Lake City, Salt Lake Co., UT, Office of Vital Statistics, Death Records of Salt Lake City, Utah, 1848–Sept. 1950, p. 249, microfilm 26,553, U.S. and Canada Record Collection, FHL.)

February 1881

Tue 1 It is Johns [John Blood's] birthday he is fourteen I have been realing silk all day Joseph Manning wife [Josephine Manning] had a son to day

Wed 2 Working withe the silk I got done realing today.

Thu 3 Twisting silk went to a weding at Egberts, Thomas Wriack [Warrick] was maried

Fri 4   "   "   [Twisting silk]
Sat 5   "   "   . . .
Tue 8 Twisting silk . . .
Wed 9   "   "   "
Thur 10   "   "   "

Fri 11 I had to real a little more silk I had eniugh to make it twelve yard of my own raising but I wanted another yd for trimings I bought it from Sister Egbert I paid two dollars for it . . .

Sat 12 I took my silk to farmington to be wove with Sisters Egberts . . . ⟨Joseph Hadfield and wife [Janet Hadfield] weavers.⟩⁷⁸ . . . [p. 23] . . .

March 1881

Tue 15 I have been sewing on a quilt for sister Egbert to pay her for teaching me to real silk . . .

Wed 16 I am still sewing at the quilt

Thu 17 John took Sister Egburt and me to Farmington to see about our silk. ⟨Joseph Hadfield & wife did the weaving⟩⁷⁹

Fri 18 I finished the quilt and took it home. . . .

Tue 22 I have been fixing up my F R. S. Books⁸⁰ to day & think of going to the City to morow. . . .

Tue 29 I began to make my home made silk dress I am very pleased with it because it is my own production

Wed 30 Annie is helping me to make my dress.

thu 31 Sewing Still. . . . [p. 25] . . .

April 1881

Mon 4 I have been Working in the garden planting out cutting of balm of gilierd [Gilead] for shade trees⁸¹ . . . [p. 26] . . .

---

78. TEXT: This sentence was written in a different style, probably at a later time.

79. TEXT: This sentence was written in a different style, probably at a later time.

80. At this time Blood was serving as treasurer of the Kaysville Ward Relief Society. ("A Statistical and Financial Report," in Kaysville Ward Relief Society Minutes and Records, vol. 1, p. 150.)

81. Plants commonly known as "Balm of Gilead" take the name from a balsam tree that produced resin or sap considered to have antiseptic and healing properties. Here the term likely refers to a type of balsam

Friday 22. It is the F R S Conferance here to day and the Pri[m]ary in the afternoon we have had very good meetings here Sisters Emeline Wells & Ellen B. Ferguson came up from the City [Salt Lake City].[82]

Sat 23 We had a splended meeting the Children cam out well.

Sun 24 We went to sunday school there is more ⟨children⟩ coming now than thare has been for some time the parents as a general rule seem to get careless at times about send ing thair children. thay do not know the harm thay are doing by neglicting this duty . . . [p. 27] . . .

May 1881

~~Tue~~ ⟨Mon⟩ 2 It is my birthday we went up in the canyon. Mrs [Eliza] Hooper cam down to see us. my weight is ⟨about 110 lbs⟩ my height is ⟨5 ft 3/8 in⟩ without my shoes[83]

~~Wed~~ ⟨Tue⟩ 3 I have been to Brothers [Edward] Philips Annie [Hannah] Layton baby [Hannah Isabel Layton] is dead and I have been making the cloths and dressing it

Wed 4 I went to the furnial when I came home William was quite sick. my silk wormes are all hatched. . . .

Wed 18 I ironed in the morning & made a cross and started to make the flowers Annie came to help me.

Thu 19 I finished my reath of white flowers, I put on the cross "To the memory of my Mother[84] who died febury 20. 1875. born Febury 18. 1813.["] it looks very nice & I thought it would be good for the children to read and I know if Mother was here she would like it. . . . [p. 28] . . .

Tue 24 We washe and Ironed Maggie Powell [Margaret Annie Powell Cole] helped I went to the woman working meeting in the afternoon. . . . [p. 29] . . .

---

poplar (*Populous candicans*) that was a fast-growing shade tree often planted by early Utah settlers. (See Jeremiah 8:22; "Balm," in *The Oxford English Dictionary,* ed. James A. H. Murray et al., 12 vols., 1933, reprint [Oxford: Oxford University Press, 1970], 1:642; and Emily Anne Brooksby Wheeler, "The Solitary Place Shall Be Glad for Them: Understanding and Treating Mormon Pioneer Gardens as Cultural Landscapes" [master's thesis, Utah State University, 2011], 63, 111.)

82. The minutes date this third annual conference of the Davis Stake Relief Society to April 23, 1881. Wells stated that she "was pleased to see so many brethreen present. It shows their interest. . . . The Elders on missions are proud to have the Exponent to exhibit, it proves that we can work, think & write for ourselves." In the afternoon meeting of the Relief Society, Wells spoke on "industry, home duties, the influence of good books on the mind." (Davis Stake, Davis Stake Relief Society Minutes and Records, 1878–1915, CHL, Apr. 23, 1881.)

83. TEXT: The inserted information reflecting her height and weight was written in a different style.

84. Ann Wilkie Galbraith Hooper (February 18, 1813–February 20, 1875), born at Glasgow, Scotland; died at Hooper, Weber County, Utah. (Hill, *Jane Wilkie Hooper Blood Autobiography and Abridged Diary,* 13, 20; *Pioneer Women of Faith and Fortitude,* 4 vols. [Salt Lake City: Daughters of Utah Pioneers, 1998], 2:1410–1411.)

June 1881

Tue 14 I went to Wm Smiths for leaves & I got some good peach buds I buded some trees, in the afternoon Kate [Henrietta Powell Brown] Annie & I went to meeting Sister Holmes & both Sisters Clarck we had as good a meeting as ever I was at.

Wed 15 we irond & got feed for the wormes. . . .

Fri 17 Kate is took sick with the scarlet feaver I have been coo◊◊◊ing [cooking?] for the men. my wormes started to spin. . . . [p. 30]

Wed 29 we ironed I went with Egberts folks to get osage orange leaves for the silk worms.

Thu 30 we picked of the cocoons Sister [Catherine] Payne, Unice [Mary Eunice] Robins & Annie, came to help us. . . . [p. 31] . . .

September 1881

Wed 7 this morning I went to Brother [Joseph] Egberts to get him to fetch a bit of lumber for a graniary for relief Socity. & the rest of the day working with the peaches. . . .

Sat 10 thair is no Meeting for the Primary to day one of President [Christopher] Layton daughters was burrid I went to the Funial [p. 37] it is Jane Layton she is thirteen years old Bro Alexander Graham died yesterday I have got to make his burial cloths it will take me nearly all night . . . [p. 38] . . .

July 1882

Tue 11 James [Burton] & Eliza Burton came down I went to a[85] Meeting the three Sisters Clarks[86] were here Sister Hyde resigned & Sarah B Layton was apointed President of the Relief Socity[87] . . .

Sat 15 I went to the Primary Meeting this afternoon Jane Manning came on a visit & brought Lawrence [Manning] with her . . .

Tue 18. We washed I went to meeting I was appointed first counciler to Sister Layton[88] . . .

---

85. TEXT: A word—possibly "three"—was written and struck through at this point.

86. Probably Lucy Augusta Rice Clark, Nancy Areta Porter Stevenson Clark, and Mary Stevenson Clark.

87. At this meeting of the Kaysville Ward Relief Society, Bishop Peter Barton read Mary Ann Cowles Hyde's letter of resignation. He "said he did not expect to reorganize today, but thought he may as well put a nomination; he put the name of Sarah B. Layton, it was accepted." Blood kept the minutes of this meeting as secretary pro tem. (Kaysville Ward Relief Society Minutes and Records, vol. 1, July 11, 1882.)

88. The minutes date this meeting to July 17, 1882. After Blood was appointed as first counselor in the ward Relief Society presidency, she resigned her position as treasurer. Blood kept the minutes of this meeting as secretary. (Kaysville Ward Relief Society Minutes and Records, vol. 1, July 17, 1882.)

Fri 21 I attended three meetings & choir practice Sisters E R S [Eliza R. Snow] Smith & Ziny D Young came up to the F. R S meeting we had very good teachings thay told us of our dutys, told the people never to send thare children to outside schooles for it would take them out of the church[89] told the young mothers to try and teach thair young children to love the truth & to keep the commadments of god the Prymary conferance was held in the afternoon sister Eliza asked the children ⟨a⟩ great many good questions & showed them Joseph Smiths watch[90] Ziny D Young spoke well to the little folks I went down to Bp [Peter] Bartons after the third meeting I enjoyed my self well Sisters Eliza & Ziny was thare & sister Layton. [p. 54] . . .

Mon 31 We washed in the morning, I went with Ellin [Beazer] Barton in the afternoon[91] to see her sister Clara [Beazer Burton] she is very sick[92] we washed & anointed her[93] . . .

August 1882

~~Tue 1~~ ⟨Wed 2⟩ We Ironed I went With S[arah] B Layton & Ellen Barton to wash & anoint Clara Barton [Burton] she is very sick . . . [p. 55] . . .

April 1883

Fri 20 . . . I took some of the Primary children to Farmington to the F R S & the P A conferance we had ⟨a⟩ good time I could not take the baby she is not well & she has very sore eyes . . . [p. 68] . . .

---

89. A number of tuition-free parochial schools, staffed by trained teachers from the eastern United States, had been established in Utah. The *Deseret News* also expressed a lack of trust in parochial schools, opining that their "main object" was to "train up youth in opposition to the 'Mormon' religion." ("Begging for Schools," *Deseret News* [weekly], Apr. 26, 1876, 198.)

90. During this period Snow frequently exhibited a gold watch that Joseph Smith had given her, possibly at the organizational meeting of the Nauvoo Relief Society. One of the many accounts of interacting with this watch comes from a recollection of Mary Belnap Lowe, who handled the watch as a child: "One particular instance was in the present Ogden Tabernacle. [Snow] kept it fastened on a long cold [gold] chain about her neck, with the watch in a side pocket. We children were attending a primary convention . . . and Sister Snow told the children to march single file in front of the pulpit where she stood and handle it, so that they would remember that it was Joseph Smith's own watch." (Jennifer Reeder, "Eliza R. Snow and the Prophet's Gold Watch: Time Keeper as Relic," *Journal of Mormon History* 31, no. 1 [Spring 2005]: 119–141; Mary B. Lowe, Statement, May 12, 1941, typescript, CHL.)

91. Barton served as a counselor to Blood in the Kaysville Ward Primary. (Kaysville Ward Primary Association Minutes and Records, vol. 1, Sept. 18, 1879.)

92. Burton died on August 19, 1882. ("Burton, Clara," Utah Department of Heritage and Arts, Cemeteries and Burials Database, accessed Apr. 6, 2015, http://utahdcc.force.com/burials.)

93. See Document 4.19.

May 1883

Tue 22 We washed & I went to meeting Sisters Nancy Clark & Mary Richards were up we had a good Meeting several spoke in toungs the interpretat[ion][94] was splended it told us to prepare to teach the Indians for the time was near when the sisters as well as the Breathers [Brothers] would have to go among them, told us to be faithfull or it would be a great trial to us I wish I could remember all thay said for it was good[95] . . . [p. 69] . . .

June 1883

Sat 9 The children & I went to Meeting I wish my council would attend more regular for it is quite a task to attend alone, but I feel to try & do the best I can for I can see the children need to be taught in the principles of this church, I wish many times I could do more if I had no other dutys I would spend all my time with the young but I have my familey to take care of ⟨I went to practic⟩ . . .

Tue 19. We washed & I went to Meeting I was apointed assistant secretery I have had to take most of the minutes for years . . . [p. 70] . . .

July 1883

Fri 20 We have ⟨had⟩ the harvest men for several days we have been buisey, to day the conferance of the relief society is held here I went in the afternoon I never was at such a meeting,[96] Sisters Eliza R Snow & Zina Young came up from the City thay both spoke well thay spok on celestial Marage told us not to speak against it for it is of god & if we speak evil & try to make mischeif in it we will have to answere for it thay both spoke of the good thay thought would arise from the Prymary Meetings told the mothers to send thair children to the meetings Sister E R Snow felt well felt to bless the people here more

---

94. TEXT: The last part of this word appears to run off the edge of the page.

95. The meeting of the Kaysville Ward Relief Society also included speeches, bearing of testimonies, and singing of hymns. Blood kept the minutes. (Kaysville Ward Relief Society Minutes and Records, vol. 1, May 22, 1883.)

96. The minutes of the Davis Stake Relief Society record the date of this stake Relief Society conference as July 27, 1883. Both Snow and Young spoke in the morning and afternoon sessions of the conference. In the morning, Snow "made interesting remarks concerning the Holy Ghost said we should have it for our constant companion the nearer we draw to God the nearer he condesends to us We should always cultivate and encourage the spirit of God. And if at any time we desire to speak of the goodness of God we should not let any evil influence bind us to our seats Prayed God to bless us all." In the afternoon session, Young addressed the "Primary children that were present related several interesting circumstances where the sick were healed by the power of faith." Snow encouraged the women to "take advantage of the limited privelege we enjoy Politically" and encouraged them to support the *Woman's Exponent,* as it was their only way to "speak through to the world." She "bore a faithful testimony to Plural Marriage gave some good instruction in regard to it related her experience." (Davis Stake Relief Society Minutes and Records, July 27, 1883.)

than she had language to expres she said sisters if you will lift your hearts to god I will bless you in toungues she then blessed us in toungs & Sister Ziny gave the interpretation[97] it was very good meeting dismised with singing we thank the oh god for a prophet[98] by the prymarys that were present benediction by [*blank*] In this evening I visited [p. 72] S B Layton Sisters, Snow & Young were thair Sister Snow said ~~asked~~ sister Layton I would like to hear you speak in toungs a short time she did so & sister snow answered ⟨in tongues⟩[99] her sister Z Young gave the interpretation of both ⟨SBL⟩ said the spiret of god is here with us tonight & we are united spoke of the southers mission & of the trials she had & would have to pass through she bore a faithfull testimony to this work, sister Snow said we have not seen many days like today but we will see many more for the spirit of the lord will be poured out on the sisters foryou have a great work to do among the lamanites[100] & you must be faithfull & prayrfull or you will get discouraged for it is a great work, & even now many of the lamanite woman are having dreams & visions of things that are to come and even know the words you will speak to them when you meet them but we must use wisdom for our enemies would be ready to shed our blood if thay knew what would come to pass among the Indians thay spok many more things that were good prompting us to be faithfull I never spent a better time

97. The minutes record that at the end of the conference, "Sister Snow then blessed us all in tongues the interpretation was given by sister Zina Young." (Davis Stake Relief Society Minutes and Records, July 27, 1883.)

98. Hymn 152, *Sacred Hymns and Spiritual Songs. For the Church of Jesus Christ of Latter-day Saints,* 12th ed. (Liverpool: George Q. Cannon; London: L. D. Saints' Book Depot, 1863), 166.

99. Eliza R. Snow often participated in use of the gift of tongues. In January 1878 she stated, "In the early days of the Church, the young took delight in the work, and it was no uncommon thing for the children to speak in tongues, and have the blessings of the Gospel poured upon them." After President John Taylor set apart Snow and her counselors in the general Relief Society presidency, "Sister [Elizabeth Ann] Whitney than sang one of her sweet songs of Zion in the language which was spoken and sung (the Prophet Joseph Smith said) by our first parents in the Garden of Eden. Sister Snow explained that Joseph Smith told Mother Whitney 'If she would use the gift with wisdom it should remain with her as long as she lived.' Sister Zina then gave the interpretation." ("R.S. Reports," *Woman's Exponent,* Feb. 15, 1878, 6:138; "R. S. Reports," *Woman's Exponent,* Sept. 1, 1880, 9:[53]–54; see also Maureen Ursenbach Beecher, ed., *The Personal Writings of Eliza Roxcy Snow,* Life Writings of Frontier Women 5 [Logan: Utah State University Press, 2000], 151, 178–179, 183–185.)

100. The Book of Mormon spoke of the gospel being preached to the Lamanites: "And the gospel of Jesus Christ shall be declared among them; wherefore, they shall be restored unto the knowledge of their fathers, and also to the knowledge of Jesus Christ." Church members believed that American Indians were descendants of the Lamanites. Many American Indians in Utah Territory had been baptized into the church, and a few began to hold leadership positions in the Relief Society. The Relief Society in Thistle Valley was reorganized in the summer of 1880, and "a native woman . . . was elected second counselor." In May 1883 an Indian woman named Cohn was selected as a counselor in a Relief Society in Box Elder County. (2 Nephi 30:5; "Visit to Sanpete—Notes by the Way," *Woman's Exponent,* Aug. 15, 1880, 9:44–45; "An Interesting Trip," *Woman's Exponent,* July 1, 1883, 12:20–21; see also Document 4.7.)

sister Snow seemes very feeble to day when she blessed us it seemed to me like a farewell I could not help but feel it but if it is the lords will we must be resigned she has done a good work I went to choir practice . . .

Fri 27 I took the team it is the first time I have driv◊◊ [driven?] [p. 73] my colt she went all right, we went to a meeting of the officers of the relief Society . . . [p. 74] . . .

September 1883

Tue 25 I went to meeting some of the sisters felt full of trouble I told them I thought we should feel very thankfull for the blessings of peace & plenty & try & look on the bright side[101] . . .

Sun 30 It is the stake conferance for the young men & wiman here to day we went to

S S & too meetings Brother J F Smith spoke most of the forenoon on parents bringing thair children up right & setting them a good example told us if we had our littl quar[re]ls not to let our children hear us told us if we could not agree on religious points we had better part for our children would not be true to thair religion if thay are brought up in such strife

In the after noon Ziny Young y spoke first on training the young told the mothers to keep the confidence of thair sons & daughter & to keep them in at night told the sisters it is thair privlidge to wash and anoint one another & thair little ones, she told the children in the sunday school that when Brother J F Smith was born his father was in Jail & his mother was taken on a bed & took him to see his father[102] told us Joseph Smith led the church 14 years [p. 78] & presedent Young 33 years

Sister [Anstis Elmina Shepherd] Taylor spoke next told the young ladys to learn to do buisness correctly told them to be virtueous & study the laws of life . . .[103]

---

101. The Kaysville Ward Relief Society minutes record her comments: "Sister J. W. Blood said we should not look on the dark side I hope we will try and over come these feelings. I think we should feel thankful for the Blessings we enjoy." (Kaysville Ward Relief Society Minutes and Records, vol. 1, Sept. 25, 1883.)

102. Joseph F. Smith was born November 13, 1838, shortly after his father and uncle, Hyrum and Joseph Smith, were arrested in Far West, Missouri. On December 1 they were imprisoned in Liberty, Missouri, with other Mormon leaders. (Joseph Fielding Smith, *Life of Joseph F. Smith, Sixth President of the Church of Jesus Christ of Latter-day Saints* [Salt Lake City: Deseret News, 1938], 117, 123–124.)

103. The September 30, 1883, entry continues for two paragraphs after this point.

4.4 Salt Lake Stake Relief Society, Report, June 18 and 19, 1880

Salt Lake Stake Relief Society, Report, June 18 and 19, [1880], in "Salt Lake Stake Relief Society Conference," Woman's Exponent *(Salt Lake City, UT), July 1, 1880, vol. 9, no. 3, pp. 21–22.*

During a quarterly Salt Lake Stake Relief Society conference held in the Assembly Hall on Temple Square in June 1880, the women of the Salt Lake Stake voted to sustain Eliza R. Snow, Zina D. H. Young, and Elizabeth Ann Whitney as the first general presidency of the Relief Society.

Snow, with the assistance of Zina Young, had directed the affairs of the Relief Society as a de facto president since 1868, but Brigham Young had never formally set her apart as president nor officially appointed counselors. Young initiated the large-scale organization of local Relief Societies in December 1867, and early the next year he called on Snow to "assist the Bishops in organizing Branches of the Society in their respective Wards."[104] Ward Relief Societies functioned under local presidents, who received counsel from Snow and her assistants. In 1877 Brigham Young appointed the first stake Relief Society president, in Weber County, after which stake Relief Society organizations were established in Salt Lake City and other communities.[105]

Held in June 1880, this "Sisters' Conference of the Salt Lake Stake of Zion" occupied two days and was both a quarterly meeting of the stake Relief Society and a conference of the stake Primary and Young Ladies' Mutual Improvement Association (Y.L.M.I.A.). In two meetings on Friday, June 18, the women considered Relief Society business. The meeting on Saturday morning focused on the Primary, which had been first organized under the leadership of Aurelia Rogers on a local level in Farmington, Utah, in 1878.[106] During this meeting Eliza R. Snow nominated Louie B. Felt as general Primary superintendent "to preside over all the Primary Associations of all the Stakes of Zion." Felt was sustained along with two counselors, Matilda M. Barratt and Clarissa (Clara) M. Cannon.

President John Taylor then addressed the conference on the responsibilities of the Primary and the Nauvoo founding of the Relief Society. He ended his remarks, "God bless the children and God bless the sisters with Sister Snow at their head." At that point, Mary Isabella Horne, president of the Salt Lake Stake Relief Society, moved that he appoint Eliza R. Snow as president of all the Relief Societies throughout the church. Taylor nominated Snow for the position, and attendees voted to sustain Snow, her chosen counselors, Zina D. H. Young and Elizabeth Ann Whitney, and a secretary and treasurer, Sarah M. Kimball and Mary Isabella Horne. The conference report explained, "These sisters form a central organization for all the Relief Societies of all the Stakes of Zion."

Like the Relief Society, the Y.L.M.I.A. had functioned at the local level without a general presiding board since its founding a decade earlier as the Young Ladies' Department

---

104. See Documents 3.1 and 3.5.
105. See Documents 3.26 and 3.29.
106. See Document 3.30.

of the Ladies' Cooperative Retrenchment Association.[107] Eliza R. Snow and a companion, most often Zina Young or Mary Isabella Horne, assisted individual wards in forming their own branches of the Y.L.M.I.A., although in some cases local authorities organized branches without a visit from Snow.[108] During the Saturday afternoon session of this conference, Snow nominated Elmina S. Taylor as president of the Y.L.M.I.A. central committee. Taylor was sustained, along with Margaret (Maggie) Y. Taylor and Martha (Mattie) J. Horne, counselors; Louise (Louie) M. Wells, secretary; and Fannie Y. Thatcher, treasurer. The newly sustained general officers of the Primary and Y.L.M.I.A., however, did not fully act in their new capacities until after the death of Eliza R. Snow in 1887, who often presided at women's meetings and was honored as the leader of all the women of the church.[109]

The following report of the conference was prepared by Emmeline B. Wells and published in the *Woman's Exponent* on July 1, 1880.

———— ❧ ————

SALT LAKE STAKE RELIEF SOCIETY CONFERENCE.

The Sisters' Conference of the Salt Lake Stake of Zion was held in the Salt Lake Assembly Hall, Friday and Saturday, June 18 and 19 [1880]. The first day was devoted to Relief Society reports, business, etc. Mrs. M. Isabella Horne presiding. Sung, "O, Awake My Slumbering Minstrels." Prayer by Mrs. E. S. Taylor. Singing, "Come, O, thou King of Kings."[110] Minutes of last Conference read by the Stake Secretary, Mrs. E. [Elizabeth] Howard. Reports from the several branches in the county were read, which were very favorable. Pres. Horne made a few remarks relative to the necessity of having correct reports, and said she wanted the sisters to become business women.

Pres. E. R. Snow Smith[111] referred to the good conference in Brigham City, where the young ladies had spoken upon practical principles and were putting

---

107. See Document 3.18.

108. See Augusta Joyce Chrocheron, "Origin of the Y.L.M.I. Association," *Woman's Exponent,* June 15, 1880, 9:10; and Susa Young Gates, *History of the Young Ladies' Mutual Improvement Association of the Church of Jesus Christ of Latter-day Saints, from November 1869 to June 1910* (Salt Lake City: Deseret News, 1911), 13.

109. Consider this statement from the women of Kanab: "We welcome Sisters Eliza and Zina as our Elect Lady and her Counselor, and as Presidents of all the feminine portion of the human race. Although comparatively few recognize their right to this authority. Yet, we know they have been set apart as leading Priestesses of this dispensation. As such we honor them. We welcome them as the honored wives of our revered Prophet Joseph Smith." Augusta Joyce Crocheron referred to Snow as president of the "women's organizations," as did Mary Isabella Horne. ("A Welcome," *Woman's Exponent,* Apr. 1, 1881, 9:165; Augusta Joyce Crocheron, *Representative Women of Deseret, a Book of Biographical Sketches, to Accompany the Picture Bearing the Same Title* [Salt Lake City: J. C. Graham, 1884], 1; Document 4.15; see also "Pen Sketch of an Illustrious Woman," *Woman's Exponent,* July 15, 1881, 10:27.)

110. Hymns 122 and 192, *Sacred Hymns and Spiritual Songs. For the Church of Jesus Christ of Latter-day Saints,* 14th ed. (Salt Lake City: George Q. Cannon, 1871), 133, 209–210.

111. Eliza R. Snow was sealed to Joseph Smith in Nauvoo but did not adopt the use of his family name until after the death of Emma Hale Smith Bidamon in 1879. Snow was formally identified as

them into practice. Said the city council there had donated liberally of land for the purpose of raising mulberry trees to promote sericulture.[112] Spoke of the calamities and judgments that were coming upon the earth and that Zion would be the place of safety.

Meeting closed by singing, "O, Say what is Truth."[113] Benediction by Mrs. S. M. Kimball. 2 p. m.: Meeting opened with singing and prayer by Mrs. E. Howard. After which several of the presidents of Relief Societies gave verbal reports. Mrs. E. B. Wells made a few remarks preceding the reading of an original poem by Bishop O. [Orson] F. Whitney, "The Women of the Everlasting Covenant."[114] She then introduced Dr. Ellen B. Ferguson, who read this grand poem in a smooth, eloquent and effective manner. Pres. Horne then spoke of a committee of two or three sisters being formed in each Relief Society to look after new comers. Joseph Smith had said the mission of the Relief Society was not only to look after the temporal wants of the poor, but to save souls.[115]

"Sister Eliza" explained this subject clearly and definitely and stated that there was a positive necessity for such committee and gave good instruction on the subject. She then asked the sisters to take shares in the Silk Association[116] and to interest themselves in this simple and useful industry, which was now established upon a firm basis.

Bishop [John P.] Johnson, of Provo, heartily endorsed what had been spoken and blessed the sisters in their labors; said he had realized the great help the Relief Society was to the Bishops in many respects. Sang "Lord dismiss us with thy blessing."[117] Prayer by Bishop Johnson.

Eliza R. Snow Smith from 1880 until her death in 1887. (See Jill Mulvay Derr, *Mrs. Smith Goes to Washington: Eliza R. Snow Smith's Visit to Southern Utah,* Juanita Brooks Lecture Series [St. George, UT: Dixie State College, 2004], 1–6; and Davis Stake, Davis Stake Relief Society Minutes and Records, 1878–1915, CHL, vol. 1, July 16, 1880.)

112. For more on silk culture in Utah, see Documents 3.4 and 4.3.

113. Hymn 59, *Sacred Hymns and Spiritual Songs,* 71–72.

114. Whitney's poem, composed in Ohio in 1878, was published in Utah in 1880. (Orson F. Whitney, [Two poems:] *The Women of the Everlasting Covenant* and *The Land of Shinehah* [Salt Lake City: Deseret News, 1880], 1–9.)

115. See Document 1.2, entry for June 9, 1842.

116. Zina D. H. Young, Eliza R. Snow, and Mary Isabella Horne were all members of the board of directors of the Utah Silk Association, incorporated according to territorial laws in January 1880. A share of stock in the association cost ten dollars. (R. Simpson, "Utah Silk Association," *Woman's Exponent,* Jan. 15, 1880, 8:126; Chris Rigby Arrington, "The Finest of Fabrics: Mormon Women and the Silk Industry in Early Utah," *Utah Historical Quarterly* 46, no. 4 [Fall 1978]: 376–396; Utah Silk Association, Stock Certificate, Apr. 11, 1881, CHL.)

117. Hymn 98, *Sacred Hymns and Spiritual Songs,* 107–108.

Saturday morning, June 19th. The middle seats of the Tabernacle were filled with the children of the Primary Associations of the city. President E. R. Snow Smith presiding. Children sang: "Sweet is the work, my God, my King." Mrs. Zina D. Young offered prayer. Children sang: "We thank thee, O God, for a prophet."[118] The first business transacted was to appoint a central committee to preside over the Primary Associations of the Salt Lake Stake of Zion. Mrs. Ellen C. S. Clawson was nominated and sustained as President, Mrs. Camilla Cobb. and Miss Annie Davis as her Counselors. "Sister Eliza" then nominated Mrs. Louie Felt as General Superintendent, to preside over all the Primary Associations of all the Stakes of Zion, which was unanimously carried. Mrs. Matilda M. Barratt and Mrs. Clara M. Cannon were sustained as her Counselors.[119] "Sister Eliza" addressed the children for a few minutes and asked them some questions, which were promptly answered. Mrs. Zina D. Young made a short speech upon obedience, reverence, honesty, truthfulness, etc., adapting her language to the children's comprehension. The children sang by request, "O my Father."[120] "Sister Eliza" announced that President Taylor and President Angus M. Cannon were present, and asked the children who they would like to speak to them; they answered, President John Taylor.

President Taylor said, "I am pleased to have an opportunity of meeting with the children. The ladies of the Relief Societies are doing a good work in teaching the children correct principles, and instructing them that they may grow up to be honorable numbers in the Church of Jesus Christ, and to be honors to the kingdom. I appreciate the efforts of the ladies who are trying to bring the children up in the fear of the Lord; and the Presidents of these Primary Associations. Children you ought to be obedient to your parents and pray morning and night for them and for your presidents, that they may be under the inspiration of the Lord, and God will bless you and give you blessings upon blessings, and he will build up Zion, and these sisters are trying to instruct you in purity and in the laws of God, that your names may be honored in and through eternity; be careful to honor your fathers and mothers. This is one of the ten commandments. We purpose having them written here in this tabernacle, sometime—"Honor thy father and thy mother, etc."[121] Now

---

118. Hymn 50, *A Collection of Sacred Hymns for the Church of Jesus Christ of Latter Day Saints,* ed. Emma Smith (Nauvoo, IL: E. Robinson, 1841), 57–58; Hymn 152, *Sacred Hymns and Spiritual Songs. For the Church of Jesus Christ of Latter-day Saints,* 12th ed. (Liverpool, George Q. Cannon; London: L. D. Saints' Book Depot, 1863), 166.

119. See Aurelia Spencer Rogers, *Life Sketches of Orson Spencer and Others, and History of Primary Work* (Salt Lake City: George Q. Cannon and Sons, 1898), 222–224.

120. See Document 1.14.

121. See Exodus 20:12.

I want to say a word to the Relief Society. You had your meeting yesterday, but as a number of you are here, I will say a few words to you. I consider it a duty for all to do all they possibly can to aid [p. 21] in this work which has been begun in this day. We are peculiarly associated; teaching the juveniles. the young men, and the young women, and the sisters to look after the wants of the poor, the sick, and also to look after the happiness of those they are associated with; it is a great thing to be able to do good, and I have brought along a book here, it is called "The Law of the Lord," and I will have Bro. Nuttall read a little from this book.[122] Joseph Smith organized the Relief society in Nauvoo.

Brother L. John Nuttall then read from the "Law of the Lord" concerning the orgnization of the Relief Society, in the Lodge Room, Nauvoo, March 17, 1842, when Mrs. Emma Smith was appointed President, Elizabeth Ann Whitney and Sarah M. Cleveland, her Counselors.[123]

After Brother N. had finished reading Pres. Taylor made explanatory remarks concerning the organization and the powers and duties it gave to woman. He stated that Emma Smith had been previously ordained to expound the Scriptures, probably by the Prophet Joseph himself, but he did not know, however he (President Taylor) said he was present at that time and was called upon by Joseph to ordain Sisters Whitney and Cleveland, Emma's counselors.[124] Prest. Taylor gave much more instruction to the sisters, and closed his remarks by saying, God bless the children and God bless the sisters with Sister Snow at their head. Mrs. M. I. Horne moved, and Mrs. S. M. Kimball seconded the motion that President Taylor publicly appoint "Sister Eliza" as president of all the Relief Societies. Prest. Taylor stated that Sister Eliza had been secretary of the first organization of Relief Society in Nauvoo. Prest. Taylor then nominated her and she was sustained as president. Sister Eliza then chose Sisters Zina D. Young and Elizabeth Ann Whitney as her counselors, who

---

122. L. John Nuttall was John Taylor's private secretary. "The Book of the Law of the Lord" was the title of a record book that functioned as Joseph Smith's official journal from December 1841 to December 1842. Scribes recorded Smith's revelations and journal entries, as well as donations (in cash and kind) from church members in the form of tithing and contributions toward the construction of the Nauvoo temple. (Andrew H. Hedges et al., eds., *Journals, Volume 2: December 1841–April 1843*, vol. 2 of the Journals series of *The Joseph Smith Papers*, ed. Dean C. Jessee et al. [Salt Lake City: Church Historian's Press, 2011], 3–9 [hereafter *JSP*, J2].)

123. The passage reads: "Thursday 17 Assisted in organizing 'The Female Relief Society of Nauvoo' in the 'Lodge Room' . . . I gave much instru[c]tion. read in the New Testament & Book of Doctrine & Covenants. concer[n]ing the Elect Lady. & Shewed that Elect meant to be Elected to a certain work &c, & that the revelation was then fulfilled by Sister Emma's Election to the Presidency of the Society, she having previously been ordained to expound the Scriptures. her councillors were ordaind by Elder John Taylor. & Emma was Blessed by the same." (Joseph Smith, Journal, Mar. 17, 1842, in *JSP*, J2:45, underlining in original.)

124. See Document 1.2, entry for Mar. 17, 1842.

were then nominated by President Taylor and sustained by the conference; also Sarah M. Kimball as secretary and M. Isabella Horne as treasurer. These sisters form a central organization for all the Relief Societies of all the Stakes of Zion. The children's conference was then adjourned for three months. Sung "Lord dismiss us with thy blessing." Benediction by Prest. Angus M. Cannon.

Saturday afternoon, June 19. The conference of the Y.L.M.I. Associations of the Salt Lake Stake convened. Mrs. M. A. [Mary Ann] Freeze presiding. the remainder of the minutes of this interesting conference will be given in the July 15 number, as we have not space. However, we must notice the appointment of a Territorial Central Committee for the Y.L.M.I.A. On nomination of Mrs. Eliza R. Snow Smith, Mrs. E. S. Taylor was sustained as president of a central committee, and Mrs. Maggie Y. Taylor and Miss Mattie J. Horne [Martha Jane Horne Tingey] as her counselors; Miss Louie Wells, secretary, and Mrs. Fannie Y. Thatcher, treasurer.[125] We regret exceedingly not being able to publish full particulars of this important conference.

E. B. W.

---

125. All of the general officers for the Primary, Relief Society, and Y.L.M.I.A. sustained at this meeting were from Salt Lake City, where roughly 10 percent of all Relief Society branches were located in this period. (1880 U.S. Census, Salt Lake City, Salt Lake Co., Utah Territory, 80B, 93D, 96A, 159C, 201C; "Year of Jubilee," *Woman's Exponent,* Aug. 1, 1880, 9:36; Relief Society Record, 1880–1892, CHL, June 27, 1884.)

4.5 General Relief Society Meeting, Report, July 17, 1880

"Relief Society Report, Seting Apart Officers, &c.," July 17, 1880; Relief Society Record, 1880–1892, pp. 9–14, CHL (CR 11 175).

On July 17, 1880, a month after John Taylor had nominated a new general Relief Society presidency,[126] he attended a general meeting of women held in the Salt Lake City Fourteenth Ward assembly hall to set apart the newly sustained officers. The terms "set apart" and "ordain" were used interchangeably at this time. Taylor used both when setting apart officers on this occasion: "I set thee apart to preside over the Relief Societies in the Church" and "I confer on thee this power and authority and ordain thee to this office."

Eliza R. Snow served seven years in her formal capacity as general president, establishing policies and procedures that would govern the society for years to come. Zina D. H. Young served as first counselor in the presidency until Snow's death in 1887, after which she was appointed Relief Society general president.[127] Second counselor Elizabeth Ann Whitney, who had also been a counselor to Emma Smith, died in 1882, leaving a vacancy in the presidency that was not filled during Snow's administration.[128] Sarah M. Kimball served as general secretary while maintaining her position as president of the Salt Lake City Fifteenth Ward Relief Society.[129] Mary Isabella Horne was named Relief Society treasurer—a position she held until 1901—although she was not set apart on this occasion. Horne served concurrently as general treasurer, president of the Salt Lake Stake Relief Society, and president of the Retrenchment Association.[130]

The following transcript of the July 17 meeting comes from a handwritten report in a general Relief Society record book. A highly similar report of the meeting was published in the *Woman's Exponent* in September 1880, but the *Exponent* report was probably derived from the handwritten report.[131]

———— ❧ ————

126. See Document 4.4.

127. Snow died in the early morning hours of December 5, 1887. ("Eliza Roxie Snow Smith," *Woman's Exponent,* Dec. 15, 1887, 16:108; see also Document 4.18.)

128. See Document 1.2, entry for Mar. 17, 1842; and "Death of Mother Whitney," *Deseret News* [weekly], Feb. 22, 1882, 72.

129. "Seventieth Anniversary," *Woman's Exponent,* Jan. 1, 1889, 17:117. Kimball also served as third counselor, secretary, and vice president during Zina D. H. Young's general presidency.

130. See Susa Young Gates, *History of the Young Ladies' Mutual Improvement Association of the Church of Jesus Christ of Latter-day Saints, from November 1869 to June 1910* (Salt Lake City: Deseret News, 1911), 30–34, 41–45.

131. "R. S. Reports," *Woman's Exponent,* Sept. 1, 1880, 9:[53]–54. The *Exponent* tends to correct punctuation, spelling, and other minor errors in the handwritten report featured here.

Relief Society Report, Seting Apart Officers &c

Minutes of general meeting held in Fourteenth Ward Assembly Hall July 17th 1880 Pres M. Isabella Horne presiding,[132] Choir sang, I'll praise my maker while Ive breath,[133] Prayer by Zina D. Young, Singing, O my Father,[134] Minutes of Young Ladies Mutual Improvment Association of the third Ward read, also of the Primary Associations of the 18th and 11th Wards

Pres. Horne said I am pleased to meet with you and wish to explain that when Conference interferes with our regular semimonthly meetings they stand adjourned until the next regular meeting day. Pres Taylor is expected here this afternoon,

E. R. Snow said, this is our last meeting before the 24th of July, and we have some business to present relating to the celebration.[135] Yesterday Sister Zina and I went to Bountiful and held sweet communion with the Relief Society there.[136] In the afternoon the children assembled and their deportment and attention made an impressive appearence. About three hundred were present, their Conference was called unexpectedly. We were surprised at their ready answers to questions. Sister Roggers [Aurelia Spencer Rogers][137] told us that of those who attended the Association not one had died with Diphtheria or measles which had prevailed there the deaths had all been among those who did not attend the Primary Associtions. If any of the different Ward R. S. have made arrangments to ride in the procession on the approaching 24th they are

---

132. Horne presided here in her capacity either as president of the Salt Lake Stake Relief Society or as president of the Retrenchment Association. (See Documents 3.15 and 3.16.)

133. Hymn 25, *A Collection of Sacred Hymns for the Church of Jesus Christ of Latter Day Saints,* ed. Emma Smith (Nauvoo, IL: E. Robinson, 1841), 35–36.

134. See Document 1.14.

135. The Pioneer Day celebration of July 24, 1880, which coincided with the fiftieth anniversary of the organization of the church in 1830, was celebrated with a "grand procession in the streets" of Salt Lake City. On July 2 Snow and other Relief Society leaders met to discuss the upcoming celebration. It was determined "that the Relief Society be represented in procession with a flag and that room be asked for in the procession for Ten Carriages which were to be occupied by representative ladies." In the Pioneer Day parade, Relief Society representatives rode in three carriages, carrying a decorative white silk banner with the inscription "Relief Society first organized, March 17, 1842." ("Year of Jubilee," *Woman's Exponent,* Aug. 1, 1880, 9:36; Relief Society Record, 1880–1892, CHL, July 2 and 24, 1880.)

136. Snow and Young attended a quarterly conference of the Davis Stake Relief Society, during which "Sister Snow felt to bless the sisters with a new tongue, which she did in a mild & gentle manner Sister Young giving the interpretation by the spirit of God. Many were melted to tears by the softening influence of the Spirit." Snow also organized the Davis Stake Primary Association, with Aurelia Spencer Rogers as president. (Davis Stake, Davis Stake Relief Society Minutes and Records, 1878–1915, CHL, vol. 1, July 16, 1880.)

137. Rogers proposed the idea of a children's organization in 1878 and presided over the Primary Association in Farmington, Utah. (See Document 3.30; Aurelia Spencer Rogers, *Life Sketches of Orson Spencer and Others, and History of Primary Work* [Salt Lake City: George Q. Cannon and Sons, 1898], 205–211.)

requested to report at this meeting Arrangments have been made for Carriages for the Primary and Stake representatives[138]

M̲̲ͬͤ. M. A. [Mary Ann] Freeze Pres. Young Ladies Mutual Improvement Stake organisation, said we will be represented in the procession by central and Stake Committees. We wish to honnor the occasion as it is one of importance and not likely to occur again in less than fifty years[139]

Zina D. Young refered to Home Industries being represented in procession said three carriages would be devoted to the silk department. [p. 9]

Sister Bathsheba Smith said, one carriage is to be adorned with ladies ornamental work and I hope the sisters will contribute of their handy work to make it creditable,

President Taylor having arrived and being invited to address the sisters said, I was not aware til last evening of this meeting, at least I had forgotten it and had arranged to leave this City this afternoon going north to attend meetings at Ogden of the Weber Stake Conference, I understand that one of the objects of this meeting is the ordination of officers of the Relief Society who were elected at your conference held on Saturday June 19ͭͪ at Salt Lake Assembly Hall.[140]

On the occasion of the organization of the Relief Society, by the Prophet Joseph Smith at Nauvoo I was present Sister Emma Smith was elected president and Sister Elizabeth Ann Whitney and Sarah M. Cleveland her Counsellors. The Prophet Joseph then said that Sister Emma was named in the revelation recorded in the Book of Doctrine and Covenants concerning the Elect Lady, and furthermore that she had been ordained to expound the scriptures.[141] By my request my Secretary Elder L. John Nuttall read to you relative to this meeting from the Book of the Law of the Lord at your conference held June 19ͭͪ ult, which explained what was then done.[142]

The ordination then given did not mean the confering of the Priesthood upon those sisters yet the sisters hold a portion of the Priesthood in connection

---

138. In an account of this meeting published in the *Woman's Exponent,* the following information is added at this point: "At our meeting in the Council House I reported 290 Relief Society branches in the Territory. There are more than ten branches outside the Ter. 300 Relief Society Branches is as definite an estimate as we are now able to make, this number will be inscribed on our banner." ("R. S. Reports," *Woman's Exponent,* Sept. 1, 1880, 9:[53].)

139. Young Ladies' Mutual Improvement Association officers occupied three carriages in the parade, bearing a large blue banner inscribed "Improvement our Motto, Perfection our Aim." ("Year of Jubilee," *Woman's Exponent,* Aug. 1, 1880, 9:37.)

140. See Document 4.4.

141. See Document 1.1; and Document 1.2, entry for Mar. 17, 1842.

142. See 471n122 herein.

with their husbands, (Sisters E. R. Snow and Bathsheba Smith, stated that they so understood it in Nauvoo and have always looked upon it in that light)

As I stated, at that meeting, that I was called upon by the Prophet Joseph and I did then ordain Sisters Whitney and Cleveland, and blessed Sister Emma and set her apart. I could not ordain these sisters to anything more, or greater powers than [p. 10] had been confered on Sister Emma who had previously been ordained to expound the scriptures, and Joseph said at that time, that being an Elect Lady had its significance and that the revelation was now fulfilled in Sister Emma being thus elected to preside over the Relief Society.

However after the organization of this society in Nauvoo much disturbance arose among the sisters. I do not want to be personal especially as Sister Emma is dead.[143] But I think that some of those circumstances should be known. Sister Emma got severely tried in her mind about the doctrine of Plural Marriage and she made use of the position she held to try to pervert the minds of the sisters in relation to that doctrine. She tried to influence my first wife to make her believe that the revelation was not correct. Sister [Leonora] Taylor was much troubled thereat and asked me what it meant. Soon after, the Prophet Joseph was in my house, and I spoke to him in my wife's presence, in relation to what Sister Emma had said, and Joseph replied, "Sister Emma would dethrone Jehovah to accomplish her purpose if she could." Some of you sisters are acquainted with what I refer to and the prejudice that then existed.

After the death of the Prophet Joseph Smith, in concequence of the confusion that existed, President B Young thought it best to defer the operations of this organisation and the labors of the Society ceased, until he organised the sisters again ~~here~~ in this City.[144]

Those influences then introduced and then operating were not right, the sisters in the various organisations since have accomplished much good and should not be deprived of their ⟨rights and⟩ privileges because others have done wrong

Pres. Taylor then set apart the Relief Society officers as follows.

Eliza Roxie Snow Smith, I lay my hand upon thy head in the name of Jesus and by authority of the holy priesthood I set thee apart to preside over the Relief Societies in the Church of Jesus Christ of Latter day Saints, and I confer on thee this power and authority and ordain thee to this office that thou [p. 11] mayest have power to expound the scriptures and to bless elevate and strengthen thy sisters. The Lord is well pleased with thee, with thy diligence

---

143. Emma Hale Smith Bidamon died in Nauvoo on April 30, 1879. ("Death of Emma Smith," *Deseret News* [weekly], May 21, 1879, 248.)
144. See Documents 1.13 and 3.1.

fidelity and zeal in the interest of thy sisters. He has blessed thee exceedingly and will continue to bless thee forever and ever; and I bless thee with all thine heart can desire in righteousness and I seal upon thee all former blessings confered upon thee by the holy priesthood, In the name of Jesus Amen.

Zina Diantha Young Smith[145] I lay my hands upon thee in the name of Jesus and by authority of the holy priesthood, and ordain thee to be first counsellor to Eliza R. Snow, Honor thy calling which is an honorable one, sustain and assist thy President and thou shalt have joy in thy labors Thou shall be a wise counsellor the Lord is well pleased with thee and will sustain thee, and no man shall deprive thee of thy blessings thou shalt have the gift to heal the sick and thou shall be blessed in time and in Eternity; in the name of Jesus, Amen.[146]

Elizabeth Ann Smith Whitney, In the name of the Lord Jesus Christ and by virtue of my office and calling, in the holy priesthood, I bless thee and set thee apart to be secend counsillor to Eliza R Snow Smith. Thou hast been tried and found faithful and God has helped thee and thou shalt be blessed in thine old age; and thy name shall be honored through all generations; Thy heart shall be filled with peace and joy and thou shalt be a wise counsellor in thine old age. Thou shall continue to be esteemed as a Mother in Israel, and thou shall continue to be blessed as thou hast been, and when thou hast finished thy labors thou shalt have a place in the Celestial Kingdom of God. with thine husdband. Thou shalt be blessed with all the blessings and privileges pertaining to this office and calling, in the name of Jesus. Amen. [p. 12]

Sarah Melissa Granger Kimball. In the name of the Lord Jesus Christ and by virtue of the Holy Priesthood I set thee apart to the office of Secretary of the Relief Societies in Zion; to record important events and keep a faithful record. Thou shalt be quick to discern and a ready writer. Seek more earnestly for the Spirit of the Lord and thou shalt be blessed more than thou hast ever had power to conceive of. As thou hast been preserved in life, thou shalt continue to be preserved. I Seal upon the thy former blessings and thou shalt be honored in time and in eternity, and have a seat in the Celestial Kingdom of God, in the name of Jesus. Amen.

---

145. Zina Diantha Huntington Jacobs was sealed to Joseph Smith in 1841 and to Brigham Young in 1846.

146. Young was well known for practicing the gift of healing. Between 1889 and 1891, she kept a record of the healing and blessing rituals that she performed, noting the type (washing and anointing, blessing) and purpose of each ritual (health, pregnancy, a broken arm, consolation, and so forth). (Zina D. H. Young, Diary, 1889–1891, in Zina Card Brown Family Collection, 1806–1972, CHL; see also Jonathan A. Stapley and Kristine Wright, "Female Ritual Healing in Mormonism," *Journal of Mormon History* 37, no. 1 [Winter 2011]: 31.)

President Taylor then said, God bless the Treasurer Sister Horne, and bless her with every blessing that her heart desires in righteousness, and Sister Bathsheba Smith,[147] And God bless all the faithful who love Israel and keep God's commandments, do this and every promise heretofore made to you shall be fulfilled and more than has entered into your hearts to conceive of.

The President then took his leave to go by afternoon train to Ogden.

Sister Bathsheba Smith refered to the Prophet Joseph instructing the sisters to conduct their meetings in accordance with parliamentary usages[148]

Sister Whitney then sang one of her sweet songs of Zion in the language which was spoken and sung (the Prophet Joseph said) by our first parents in the Garden of Eden, Sister Snow explained that Joseph Smith told Mother Whitney, If she would use the gift with wisdom it should remain with her as long as she lived. Sister Zina then gave the interpretation. The theme of which was rejoicing and praise to the great Author and Giver of good.

Sister Phebe Woodruff being called on to speak said I am greatly pleased to see [p. 13] my sisters moveing in such order. My heart rejoices in what my eyes have witnessed, and my ears heard this day May we ever be humble and faithful.

Sister Snow called attention to the political Primary Meting to be held the following Wednesday.[149] E. [Emmeline] B. Wells read a call from the central committee (political) and urged the sisters to attend the Primary meetings and feel interested enough in the election to vote. Stake Pres, M. I. Horne followed on the same subject.

Sister Louie Felt gave some instruction to to the Young Ladies relating to the celebration.

Stake Pres, A. [Angus] M. Cannon having come in was invited to speak. Said he was pleased and interested in what he had heard, particularly what was said in relation to voteing. He hoped the sisters would remember that Eterinal vigilence was the price of liberty. The sisters ought not to be unmindful of

---

147. Smith was treasurer of the Salt Lake Stake Relief Society and apparently in charge of a float for the upcoming parade. There may have been a sense that the Salt Lake Stake Relief Society was hosting this meeting since its president, Horne, presided. (See "R.S. Reports," *Woman's Exponent*, May 1, 1880, 8:[182].)

148. See Document 1.2, entry for Mar. 17, 1842.

149. Primary election meetings of the People's Party were held on July 22, 1880. The purpose was to select delegates to attend the "people's convention for Salt Lake County," where they would nominate candidates for the upcoming general election. Emmeline B. Wells and Louie B. Felt were among the delegates representing Salt Lake City's fifth precinct. The election was held August 2, 1880. ("To the Registered Voters of the People's Ticket," *Deseret Evening News*, July 17, 1880, [3]; "The Primaries," *Deseret Evening News*, July 23, 1880, [3]; "General Election," *Deseret Evening News*, July 27, 1880, [2].)

their political duties and privileges even though all seemed calm. If all would vote for those who fear God we would continue to be a free people.

Meeting adjourned for two weeks, Choir sang Doxology Benediction by Pres, A. M. Cannon [p. 14]

4.6 Belinda Marden Pratt, Diary Entry, September 5, 1880

Belinda Marden Pratt, Diary entry, Sept. 5, 1880; Belinda M. Pratt Diary, Oct. 1877–June 1885, p. 69; photocopy; Parley P. Pratt Family Papers, 1846–1886, CHL (MS 2877).

This September 5, 1880, entry from the diary of Belinda Marden Pratt conveyed the joy and satisfaction she felt when she learned about the reorganization of the general Relief Society presidency.[150] Though many Latter-day Saint women had been working in their individual ward Relief Societies for a decade or longer, and some stake officers had been called, the network of ward units was now unified churchwide under a general presidency, as the Relief Society had once been in Nauvoo. Pratt expressed the value to women of this more comprehensive association.

Belinda Marden was born in New Hampshire in 1820 and converted to the church in 1843. She moved to Nauvoo the following year and married Parley P. Pratt, an apostle, in November 1844.[151] She migrated to Utah in 1847 and established a home in Salt Lake City. Her 1854 pamphlet, *Defence of Polygamy, by a Lady of Utah, in a Letter to Her Sister in New Hampshire,* established her as one of the more dedicated female defenders of plural marriage.[152] After her husband's death in 1857, she earned her living by teaching school, sewing, and taking boarders into her home. Pratt served as a teacher in the Salt Lake City Fourteenth Ward Relief Society, as president of the Fillmore Ward Relief Society, and, beginning in 1879, as president of the Millard Stake Relief Society.[153] In her journal Pratt often noted the activities of the local Relief Society and copied a letter from Eliza R. Snow "giving instruction for the benefit of the Relief Society in Fillmore."[154]

———— ❧ ————

1880 Fillmore

Sept 5th—Sunday Morning

In reading "Our Exponent" of the 1st of this month I could only give expression to my feelings in tears. What an age we are living in! How great the responsibilities of the Sisters of the Church. What a work they are accomplishing! And how many there are that do not realize the amount of work before them as helpers in this great dispensation. Others are working with all their might. Teaching their children. Engaged in the Relief Society! Giving of their means

---

150. See Document 4.5.

151. Belinda M. Pratt, Autobiography, 1884, Nephi Pratt Family Papers, 1867–1910, CHL, 2–6.

152. Belinda Marden Pratt, *Defence of Polygamy, by a Lady of Utah, in a Letter to Her Sister in New Hampshire* (Salt Lake City: n.p., 1854).

153. Belinda M. Pratt, Diary, 1877–1885, Parley P. Pratt Family Papers, 1846–1886, CHL, Jan. 18, 1879.

154. Eliza R. Snow to Augusta B. Smith, May 7, 1868, in Pratt, Diary, 54–56; Document 3.8.

Belinda Marden Pratt. Circa 1889. Widowed at the age of thirty-six, Belinda Pratt earned a living taking in boarders and teaching school. Her diary made frequent reference to the developing Relief Society organization; she served as president of the Fillmore, Utah, Ward Relief Society and later of the Millard Stake Relief Society. Photograph by Fox and Symons. (Church History Library, Salt Lake City.)

to the poor. Visiting the Sick Administering comfort and consolation where needed. Engaged in the Starting of Silk Culture Saving up Wheat etc. etc.

Our labors are as great as those of the Brethren and more numerous for the responsibility of training the Young rests almost entirely with the Sisters. In ⟨reading⟩ the Exponent of Sept 1ˢᵗ how my heart rejoiced when, reading of the setting apart of the Presidents over all the Relief Society Sisters [Eliza R.] Snow Smith, Zina D. [Young] and Sister [Elizabeth Ann] Whitney.[155] It seems to me a new impulse is added to us, and my heart rejoices with exceeding great joy. I cannot give utterence to ⟨my⟩ feelings in words But Glory and honor be to them who hath given us so many blessings.

---

155. The September 1, 1880, issue of the *Woman's Exponent* reported that Eliza R. Snow, Zina D. H. Young, Elizabeth Ann Whitney, and Sarah M. Kimball had been set apart as general officers of the Relief Society on July 17, 1880. ("R.S. Reports," *Woman's Exponent,* Sept. 1, 1880, 9:[53]–54; see also Document 4.5.)

4.7 Indianola Ward Relief Society, Minutes, September 16, 1880

Indianola Ward Relief Society, Minutes, Sept. 16, 1880, in "Lamanite Sisters Testify," Woman's *Exponent (Salt Lake City, UT), Oct. 15, 1880, vol. 9, no. 10, pp. 74–75.*

Preaching the gospel to and "gathering" descendants of the house of Israel was a major church objective during the nineteenth century. As Latter-day Saints migrated west and settled in Utah they began proselytizing efforts among the local American Indian tribes. Latter-day Saints believed that American Indians were descendants of the Book of Mormon Lamanites, who in turn were descendants of the Israelites of the Bible; according to Brigham Young, the Indians were "a remnant of the House of Israel, they are of the seed of Abraham, and the Book of Mormon, and all the prophecies concerning that people declare that the gospel shall be preached unto them." When Young sent missionaries to preach to the Indians, he charged them "to civilize them, teach them to work, and improve their condition by your utmost faith and diligence." He urged that "every elder, who is now called unto this work, should immediately commence to learn the Lamanite languages."[156]

Mormon women also engaged in efforts to instruct Indian women. As Relief Societies were organized among groups of Indian converts, the women were not only taught "in their duties as members of the Church" but also received instructions in cooking, washing, and sewing.[157] Other Christian white women in the 1880s had similar priorities for Indian women and came to measure their success "by the degree to which Indian women modeled themselves after middle-class white women and rejected their former practices."[158] The following document—the published minutes of a September 1880 Relief Society meeting organized among Ute Indians in central Utah—reflects similar themes.

In the spring of 1877, Brigham Young authorized John Spencer, an interpreter, missionary, and local branch president, to organize volunteers from the north end of Sanpete County to help the Ute Indians in that area build houses. Young wished the Indians to possess the land in Thistle Valley and to serve as a model for other tribes "how to go to work and sustain themselves."[159] The following year Spencer reported that the Utes "continue to live on their homesteads, in houses from one to three miles apart, and are laboring to improve their claims, looking forward with eagerness to the time when they will receive their [land] patents from Government."[160]

---

156. "Synopsis," *Deseret News,* Nov. 24, 1853, [2]. Young's aspirations here resembled those of other nineteenth-century "assimilationists," who advocated the "progress" of Indians by their acculturation into white American society. (Sherry L. Smith, *Reimagining Indians: Native Americans through Anglo Eyes, 1880–1940* [New York: Oxford University Press, 2000], 6.)

157. "At Casa Grande," *Deseret Weekly,* Apr. 26, 1890, 595; "Visit to Sanpete—Notes by the Way," *Woman's Exponent,* Aug. 15, 1880, 9:44.

158. Louise Michele Newman, *White Women's Rights: The Racial Origins of Feminism in the United States* (New York: Oxford University Press, 1999), 119.

159. Indianola Ward History, 1877, comp. Andrew Jenson, in Indianola Ward, North Sanpete Stake, Indianola Ward Manuscript History and Historical Reports, 1860–1936, CHL, [7]–[9].

160. "Thistle Valley Indians," *Deseret News* [weekly], Nov. 27, 1878, 673.

A report from John Taylor's 1879 trip to Sanpete County noted that the Relief Society in Thistle Valley was made up of white and Indian women "in about equal numbers."[161] The following year, after reorganizing the Relief Society in Thistle Valley, Eliza R. Snow and her traveling party returned to Salt Lake City and reported their experience in the *Woman's Exponent.* They were impressed by the appearance of the Indian women, saying all were "nicely dressed, looking as happy as possible." They also noted the humanitarian efforts the women performed: "The Lamanite sisters have already done some benevolent work, and are very persevering in piecing quilts and other similar labors."[162]

The Indianola Relief Society was evidently the first to include an American Indian woman in the presidency.[163] Spencer baptized ten Indians in August 1879, including a man named Nephi Lehi.[164] Lehi's wife, whose name is recorded in the *Exponent* report as Susan, was appointed second counselor when the Indianola Relief Society was reorganized in August 1880.[165]

———— 𝕡 ————

LAMANITE SISTERS TESTIFY,

At a meeting of the Relief Society of Indianola (Thistle Valley), Sept. 16, 1880, Mrs. [Betsey] Jane Simons, President of the Payson Relief Society, with her counselors and other sisters, were present.[166] Meeting called to order by Pres. Lodisia [Lucy Lodica] Spencer.[167] Singing. Prayer by Pres. Jane Simons. Singing. Roll called, thirteen members present. Minutes of previous meeting read and approved.

Sister Douglas [Agnes Douglass] spoke to the sisters: said she felt glad to have the privilege of meeting with the sisters of Indianola; was glad to see the improvement made by the Lamanite sisters. Also gave some very good instructions, and encouraged them to do right, and the Lord would bless them. Interpreted by Pres. John Spencer, who was present and acted throughout the meeting as interpreter.

Sister Moore said she felt glad to meet with the sisters of Indianola, and that she lived in this day and age of the world, when the Gospel had been

---

161. "Visit to Sanpete," *Deseret News* [weekly], Nov. 26, 1879, 680.

162. "Visit to Sanpete—Notes by the Way," *Woman's Exponent,* Aug. 15, 1880, 9:44.

163. "Visit to Sanpete—Notes by the Way," *Woman's Exponent,* Aug. 15, 1880, 9:44.

164. Indianola Ward, North Sanpete Stake, 1880–1907, in Historian's Office, Record of Members Collection, 1836–1970, CHL, 15.

165. "Visit to Sanpete—Notes by the Way," *Woman's Exponent,* Aug. 15, 1880, 9:44. Her name may actually have been Mary. (See Indianola Ward, North Sanpete Stake, 15; 1880 U.S. Census, Thistle Precinct, Sanpete Co., Utah Territory, 472C; and 1900 U.S. Census, Uintah Valley Indian Reservation, Uintah Co., UT, 76B.)

166. Payson lies near the southern end of Utah Valley. Indianola is twenty miles southeast of Payson (straight across the mountains), which translated, approximately, to a forty-mile distance by wagon.

167. Spencer, president of the Indianola Relief Society, was married to John Spencer.

made known to the human family; and gave some very good instructions. Prayed the Lord to bless them all.

Sister Hancock[168] said she was glad to have the privilege of living in this day. She felt that the Spirit of God was in their midst to-day. Said she could see a great improvement in the Lamanites; also felt well.

Sister Martha Simons spoke to the sisters; said she felt thankful to God for having the privilege of meeting with the Lamanite sisters of Indianola. Said we ought to be faithful and set a good example to the Lamanites, and also teach them to be cleanly and to have faith in God; and gave other good instructions. Prayed that God would bless those who are called to lead the Saints here in Indianola.

Sister Phebe [Onump] (Lamanite) said she felt glad to see the day when the white and the red sis[p. 74]ters could mingle together. Said she knew it was right to keep herself clean; and also encouraged the sisters to diligence.

Sister Mary Tackipo (Lamanite) said she felt glad to meet with the sisters from Payson; had known some of them for a long time. Said she was learning to keep house, and assisting her husband in his labors. Said she liked it better than her former way of doing.

Bro. Joseph [A.] (Lamanite) said he was glad to see the sisters from Payson. Said the Indians with him felt well; felt like doing right, and loved peace.

Sistsr Hannah Moritze (Lamanite) said she felt well in hearing the sisters who had spoken there that day. Was anxious to learn to keep house and to keep herself clean.

Sister Annetta Panawatts (Lamanite) said she felt well and was glad to hear what she had heard. Was willing to learn how to become a good Latter-day Saint, but was rather slow. Said she felt different altogether since she had been baptized.

Sister Jane Simons said she felt well in meeting with the sisters, and of hearing what she had heard from the white women and also the Lamanite sisters. Felt that the Spirit of God was there on that occasion. Gave some good instruction and encouraged the sisters to diligence and to be faithful. Said she was present at the dedication of the Kirtland Temple. Had heard the Prophet

---

168. Likely refers to Phebe Adams Hancock but might instead refer to Amy Experience Hancock. The former served as treasurer when the Payson Relief Society was reorganized. The latter served as counselor at the organization of the original Payson Relief Society and later, after 1885, as vice president of the Payson First Ward Relief Society. She also served as president of the Payson Primary Association. ("In Memoriam," *Woman's Exponent,* May 15, 1897, 25:151; Andrew Jenson, *Latter-day Saint Biographical Encyclopedia: A Compilation of Biographical Sketches of Prominent Men and Women in the Church of Jesus Christ of Latter-day Saints,* 4 vols. [Salt Lake City: Andrew Jenson History Co., 1901–1936], 2:351–352.)

Joseph Smith prophecy in regard to the Lamanites embracing the Gospel in the last days.[169] Related to them a testimony of the laying on of hands.

Sister D, D. [Rebecca] Tanner said she felt well could see a great improvement in the Lamanite's since she came to this valley and in the Relief Society. Prest. John Spencer said he was glad to have the opportunity of meeting with the Relief Society of Indianola and said, I am pleased to see our Sisters who have been with us to-day, said they had an object in view in coming to visit the Lamanite Sisters, described how he found the Lamanites, in their low state some three years previous. Said they are now commencing to gather in, they say the Latter-day Saints are the only friends they have got. President Young told them many years ago that we desired to teach them truth. There is a great labor in teaching them in their temporal as well as their spiritual affairs, also encouraged the sisters in their labors.

Sister Douglas[s] felt glad to see the peace and good order which we have had to-day would like very much to visit the Lamanite sisters at their homes.

Sister [Charlotte] Seely said that she felt glad that the sisters had come to visit and hoped it would not be the last time. Said she felt willing to take hold and assist all she could in teaching the Lamanite sisters, and also the brethren, said they were making great improvements and are willing to learn everything that is taught to them. Brother Joseph's wife was administered to by Brother John Spencer. President Lodisia Spencer spoke, returned her thanks to the visiting sisters said she appreciated the good spirit that had been there that day and was glad her sisters had come from Payson to visit them and hoped it would not be the last time. Singing. Benediction by Bro. Joseph, (Lamanite.)

LODISIA SPENCER Pres.

M. [MORMON] V. SELMAN, CLERK, Protem.

---

169. In the prayer he offered at the dedication of the Kirtland, Ohio, temple on March 27, 1836, Joseph Smith asked that "the remnants of Jacob, who have been cursed and smitten because of their transgression, be converted from their wild and savage condition to the fulness of the everlasting gospel; that they may lay down their weapons of bloodshed, and cease their rebellions. And may all the scattered remnants of Israel, who have been driven to the ends of the earth, come to a knowledge of the truth, believe in the Messiah, and be redeemed from oppression, and rejoice before thee." (Doctrine and Covenants 109:65–67.)

4.8 Quorum of the Twelve Apostles, Draft Circular Letter, October 6, 1880 (Excerpt)

Quorum of the Twelve Apostles, Circular letter (draft), Oct. 6, 1880, pp. [1], [9]–[10] (excerpt); CHL (CR 2 30).

Three months after Eliza R. Snow was set apart as president of all the Relief Societies of the church,[170] the Quorum of the Twelve Apostles composed a circular letter to all priesthood leaders and members of the church on a variety of subjects, including the Relief Society. The portions of this letter having to do with the Relief Society gave important insight into the current thinking on how Relief Society officers should work in connection with local church priesthood leaders and on female church members administering to the sick, reflecting earlier teachings from Joseph Smith and Brigham Young.[171]

The excerpt of the letter below is taken from a thirteen-page handwritten draft located at the Church History Library. The circular might never have been distributed.[172]

Salt Lake City, U. T.
October 6th, 1880.

To all the authorities of the Priesthood, and Latter-day Saints upon the land of Zion, Greeting.

Dear Brethren:—

In the Circular of the First Presidency, published July 11th, 1877, will be found nearly all the great fundamental principles, necessary to the organization and government of the Stakes of Zion.[173] Yet as time passes and the settlements

---

170. See Document 4.5.

171. For example, "It is the privilege of a mother to have faith and to administer to her child; this she can do herself, as well as sending for the Elders to have the benefit of their faith." (Brigham Young, "Remarks," *Deseret News* [weekly], Nov. 24, 1869, 496; see also Joseph Smith, in Historian's Office, General Church Minutes, 1839–1877, CHL, Bullock copy, Apr. 9, 1844; and Brigham Young, Aug. 31, 1875, in *Journal of Discourses,* 26 vols. [Liverpool: Various publishers, 1855–1886], 18:71–72.)

172. This October 6, 1880, draft circular does not appear in the First Presidency Circular Letters, 1855–2013 (CR 1 1) and is not mentioned in the Washing and Anointing Files, 1888, 1903, 1914–1916, 1922, and 1946–1947 (CR 11 304). There is no mention of it in the *Deseret News* for October 1880 or the *Woman's Exponent,* October–December 1880. George Q. Cannon's journal for October 1 and 2, 1880, reports, "Bro Pratt as one of a committee had written a circular which was read and partially approved." Franklin D. Richards's journal entry for October 3, 1880, states, "Council at 10 at Prests. Office J. Taylor W. Woodruff, O. Pratt, CC Rich F.D.R, G.Q.C, J.F.S., A.C., & D.H.W. Considered matter for the circular to be printed. . . . At 2 met same ones in the Endowment House—completed the items offered for Circular." (George Q. Cannon, Journal, 1855–1864, 1872–1901, CHL, Oct. 1 and 2, 1880; Franklin D. Richards, Journals, 1844–1899, in Richards Family Collection, 1837–1961, CHL, Oct. 3, 1880.)

173. First Presidency, *Circular of the First Presidency of the Church of Jesus Christ of Latter-day Saints,* July 11, 1877, copy at CHL.

enlarge, and the inhabitants of Zion spread forth into other territories, new circumstances arise, calling for still further counsel from the general authorities. . . . [p. [1]] . . .[174]

Relief Societies.

Relief Societies have been established in all the Stakes of Zion, according to the pattern originally given by the revelations of the Spirit. These societies are organized among the ladies of Zion,—that they, as well as their brothers, husbands, and fathers, may have a wide and extensive field of usefulness opened before them. The beneficial results, of this benevolent institution, have been most signally manifest, in the laying up of grain against a time of scarcity:[175] some thirty-four thousand bushels of wheat have thus been secured and preserved, which (in consequence of the greatly diminished crops of the preceding year) have proved of incalculable benefit to the industrious poor, in furnishing seed-grain for the present season.[176] These charitable institutions, established in every Stake of Zion, if properly conducted, will comfort the poor, alleviate much suffering, administer consolation and needed help to the widow, the orphan, the sick, the infirm, and the aged.

The general officers of the Society, (who should be experienced ladies,) should travel, more or less, among the Stakes of Zion, organizing new branches of the Society, and instructing those already organized. When visiting any Stake, for this purpose, they should first consult with the President of the Stake and Bishop of the Ward, and by their approbation [p. [9]] and counsel, appoint meetings. All officers selected and appointed in any branch society, should be sanctioned by the majority vote of the ladies present. All ladies selected as presidents, should be blessed and set apart, by the President of the Stake, or by the Bishop of the Ward, wherein the branch society is organized. In blessing and setting apart ladies to perform certain duties in Zion, they should not be ordained to any office in the Priesthood; but they may be appointed as Helps, and Assistants, and Presidents, among their own sex, to instruct, to exhort, to strengthen, and to build up a holy people unto the Lord. In these important duties, God hath given them power; and he will be with them, and greatly bless them, and give them an honorable name which shall not be blotted out,[177] but shall remain for ever

---

174. TEXT: The ellipsis points in this excerpt have been supplied by the editors of this volume to indicate omissions from the original document.

175. For more on the grain storage program, see Document 3.25.

176. Relief Society grain stores had been held in reserve in case of famine. This large donation was made in connection with the church's Jubilee celebrations in 1880. (See Document 4.2.)

177. See Mosiah 26:36; and Alma 1:24; 6:3.

The Sick and Afflicted.

It is the privilege of all faithful women and lay members of the Church, who believe in Christ, to administer to all the sick or afflicted in their respective families, either by the laying on of hands, or by the anointing with oil in the name of the Lord: but they should administer in these sacred ordinances, not by virtue and authority of the priesthood, but by virtue of their faith in Christ, and the promises made to believers: and thus they should do in all their ministrations.[178] [p. [10]] . . .

---

178. Joseph Smith addressed this topic in remarks to the Female Relief Society of Nauvoo: "It is the privilege of those set apart to administer in that authority which is confer'd on them— and if the sisters should have faith to heal the sick, let all hold their tongues, and let every thing roll on." He relied on Mark 16:15–18 as a scriptural foundation for this directive. (Document 1.2, entry for Apr. 28, 1842.)

4.9 Eliza R. Snow, "Instructions to the Secretaries of the Relief Society," January 1882

Eliza R. Snow, "Instructions to the Secretaries of the Relief Society; in Reply to Frequent Inquiries," Jan. 1882, Woman's Exponent *(Salt Lake City, UT), Feb. 15, 1882, vol. 10, no. 18, p. 141.*

At the first meeting of the Female Relief Society of Nauvoo, held March 17, 1842, Joseph Smith told the women, "The minutes of your meetings will be precedents for you to act upon— your Constitutio[n] and law." Eliza R. Snow, who that day was appointed secretary of the new organization, ever after maintained a clear vision of record keeping.[179] When she visited local Relief Societies in later years she often read from the Nauvoo Relief Society minutes.[180]

Sarah M. Kimball, another key figure in the Nauvoo Relief Society, also helped to shape its record-keeping tradition. In the late 1860s, as president of Salt Lake City's Fifteenth Ward Relief Society, and with input from Snow, Kimball outlined the duties of Relief Society officers. The secretary was "to take minutes of all general meetings. and a synopsis of all Committee reports" and to handle business details for the president. The secretary's "book must contain the general record and history of the Society."[181] When the central—or general—Relief Society presidency was formally installed in June 1880, Snow appointed Kimball as secretary.[182]

Meeting minutes became the backbone of the historical record created by local Relief Societies. Extracts of minutes regularly appeared in the *Woman's Exponent*. Though the *Exponent* was not an official organ of the Relief Society, it became the central clearinghouse for news, instructions, and encouragement for the society's far-flung membership.[183] As submissions to the magazine increased, however, coverage of individual societies necessarily decreased. "In regard to publishing Relief Society reports and minutes," the *Exponent* explained in August 1881, "there is not space for anything more than Stake Conference reports, unless it is a new organization or reorganization, or change of some officers. It must be clear to every one that with all the several organizations and their multitude of branches, it is impossible to give them all space for representation."[184] In February 1882 the *Exponent* published the following document, which gave Eliza Snow's response to inquiries from secretaries of local Relief Societies regarding record-keeping practices.

Most stake, ward, and branch Relief Societies retained possession of their original minutes for decades. Beginning in the 1940s church leaders requested that all historical records, including minutes, be sent to the Historian's Office in Salt Lake City for permanent

---

179. Document 1.2, entry for Mar. 17, 1842.
180. Jill Mulvay Derr et al., *Women of Covenant: The Story of Relief Society* (Salt Lake City: Deseret Book; Provo, UT: Brigham Young University Press, 1992), 89; see also Document 3.6.
181. Document 3.9.
182. Document 4.4; see also Document 4.5.
183. See Document 3.21.
184. "Home Affairs," *Woman's Exponent*, Aug. 1, 1881, 10:36.

filing.[185] As a result, the Church History Library currently holds thousands of volumes of Relief Society minutes.

———— ❧ ————

INSTRUCTIONS

TO THE SECRETARIES OF THE RELIEF SOCIETY; IN REPLY TO FREQUENT INQUIRIES.

It is very desirable that a uniformity should exist throughout all the branches of the Relief Society in regard to the Secretaries' Books.

In some business departments of the Relief Society, we are under the necessity of varying, in order to meat [meet] the varied local circumstances of the different branches; but this does not, in any instance, apply to the Secretaries.

In each department we want to learn to do business in the best possible manner, and to adopt the manner in which it can be done with the greatest facility and the least labor.

The Secretaries of the various Branches of the Relief Society are, or should be, historians of their respective Branches. One Book (or when one Book is full another succeeds it) should contain the whole history—all records of the Branch; and those records should comprise everything worthy of preservation, and in as concise a manner as practicable. In this, skill and judgment are requisite, and "practice makes perfect."

In the first place—at the meeting the Secretary should take minutes of all business transactions and whatever is said or done that should be read at the next meeting; all that has been donated to the society since the date of the last meeting, with the name in full of each donor; the amount of each cash donation, and the price of each article donated. These figures properly placed in the margin, are readily footed in making up reports; and all proceedings are readily referred to under their respective dates.

Should the Branch have an organized Board of Teachers (which is unnecessary in small Branches), and that Board a Secretary, a copy of the minutes of each teachers' meeting must be forwarded to the general Secretary in time for her to compile under date whatever is worthy of record, in its proper order in Book.[186]

---

185. "Historian Wants Old Record Books," *LDS Church News,* Mar. 3, 1945, 2; Presiding Bishopric, Salt Lake City, UT, to "All Ward Bishoprics," Apr. 24, 1945, in Presiding Bishopric, Presiding Bishopric Circular Letters, 1875–2013, CHL; Joseph Fielding Smith, Salt Lake City, UT, to Stake Presidents, Bishops, Mission Presidents, and Heads of Auxiliary General Boards, May 2, 1949, in First Presidency, First Presidency General Administration Files, 1923, 1932, 1937–1967, CHL.

186. The active and well-staffed committee of Fifteenth Ward teachers kept detailed minutes of their monthly meetings during this period. From 1868 to 1873 the teacher's committee minutes were included

In making up Quarterly or Annual Reports, the Treasurer will furnish the Secretary with a list of all Disbursements from date of last report, which, after having been read and accepted by the Branch, also read at the Conference for which it was prepared, the Secretary will copy it under date, and thus have in one Book the minutes of each meeting, all the receipts and disbursements, comprising all business matters of the Branch.

The foregoing is in accordance with the original sample Book,[187] which was fully approved by the Prophet Joseph Smith, through whom the revelation was given for the organization of the Relief Society.

E. R. Snow Smith.

S. L. City, January, 1882.

---

in the minute book of the regular ward Relief Society meetings. Two separate minute books devoted exclusively to the teacher's meetings began after 1873: one is labeled "Minutes of 15th Ward RS Committee from Feb 6th 1873 to May 3rd 1883," and the other "Minutes of Committee Meetings from June 7th 1883 to June 7th 1893 15th Ward Relief Society." (Fifteenth Ward, Riverside Stake, Fifteenth Ward Relief Society Minutes and Records, 1868–1968, CHL, vols. 1, 4, and 7.)

187. A reference to the Nauvoo Relief Society Minute Book (Document 1.2 in this volume).

4.10 Sarah M. Kimball, Reminiscence, March 17, 1882

Sarah M. Kimball, "Early Relief Society Reminesence," Mar. 17, 1882; Relief Society Record, 1880– 1892, pp. 29–30, CHL (CR 11 175).

At the fortieth anniversary of the founding of the Relief Society, Sarah M. Kimball gave the following account of the society's origins.[188] Kimball was well qualified to address the subject. As she recalled to a group of men and women gathered to celebrate the anniversary on March 17, 1882, her desire to contribute to the construction of the Nauvoo temple had helped lead to the organization of the Female Relief Society of Nauvoo and she had been one of its charter members. From 1842 to 1882 the Relief Society had remained a vital part of her life,[189] and her years of Relief Society service reflected the organization's accomplishments since its founding. She served for several decades as president of the Fifteenth Ward Relief Society in Salt Lake City, while serving for seven years as secretary of the Central Board under Eliza R. Snow.[190] She was the first ward Relief Society president to have a separate Relief Society hall built for ward members.[191] In 1877 the Fifteenth Ward Relief Society under her direction also completed a grain storage facility for wheat, "built of rock with tin roof, brick floor underlaid with concrete," as part of their grain saving movement.[192]

March 17th <u>1882</u>

Early Relief Society reminesence

Sister Geo. Godard [Elizabeth Goddard] invited a goodly no. of brethren and sisters to their pleasant home in 14th Ward S. L. City to selebrate the 40th (fortieth) Annaversary of the organisation of the Relief Society by the Prophet Joseph Smith.

---

188. Kimball's retelling of the Relief Society origin story was formally recorded on at least four occasions in addition to the March 1882 account presented here: in a Salt Lake Stake Relief Society quarterly conference, June 22, 1878; in an undated (probably circa July 1880) statement in the Salt Lake Stake Relief Society Record Book; in her autobiographical sketch published in the *Woman's Exponent,* September 1, 1883; and as part of the Relief Society's official Jubilee exercises, March 17, 1892. (Salt Lake Stake, Salt Lake Stake Relief Society Record Book, 1868–1903, CHL, June 22, 1878, pp. 7–8; "First Organisation," n.d., ca. July 1880, Relief Society Record, 1880–1892, CHL, 5; "Third Quarterly Conference," *Woman's Exponent,* July 1, 1878, 7:18; Sarah M. Kimball, "Auto-Biography," *Woman's Exponent,* Sept. 1, 1883, 12:51; Document 4.28; see also Janelle M. Higbee, "'President Mrs. Kimball': A Rhetoric of Words and Works" [master's thesis, Brigham Young University, 1998], 58–66.)

189. "President Sarah M. Kimball," *Woman's Exponent,* Dec. 15, 1898, 27:77–78.

190. See Emmeline B. Wells, "Seventieth Anniversary," *Woman's Exponent,* Jan. 1, 1889, 17:117; and Document 4.5.

191. See Document 3.10; see also Sarah M. Kimball, "Auto-Biography," *Woman's Exponent,* Sept. 1, 1883, 12:51.

192. "Home Affairs," *Woman's Exponent,* Oct. 1, 1877, 6:69; see also Document 3.25.

Sarah Melissa Granger Kimball. Sarah Kimball was a prominent presence in Relief Society from its inception in Nauvoo until after its Jubilee celebration. Her bold and innovative leadership of the Salt Lake City Fifteenth Ward Relief Society, for more than forty years, resulted in such pioneering efforts as the first Relief Society hall. (Church History Library, Salt Lake City.)

The following brief account of the origin of the Society was given by Sarah M, Kimball.

March 1, 1842 The Church of Jesus Christ of Latter day Saints was poor in worldly goods and earnest in devotion to the labors required.— The Nauvoo Temple walls were about three feet high, Strong appeals were being made by the President of the Church and others for help to forward the work.

M,<u>iss</u> [Margaret] Cook a maiden lady Seemstress, one day in conversation with me on the subject of a recent appeal for provisions, clothing, beding and general supplies for the workmen and their families, remarked that she would be pleased to contribute needle work if it could be made available. I proffered material for her to make up, and suggested that others might feel as we did. We then agitated the subject of organising a Sewing Society. The object of which should be to aid in the erection of the Temple

About a dozen of the neighboring Sisters by invitation met in my parlor the following Thursday and the subject was further discused, and approved Sister Rigden [Phebe Rigdon] suggested that Sister E. R. Snow be invited to take part and to assist in getting up a Constitution and Bye-laws, the Speaker was delegated to wait on Miss Snow and solicit her aid which was cheerfully and efficiently rendered. A Constitution and bye laws was prepared and submitted to President Joseph Smith. He pronounced it the best constitution that he ever read, then remarked this is not what the sisters want, there is something better for them. I have desired to organise the Sisters in the order of the Priesthood I now have the key by which I can do it[193] [p. 29]

The organisation of the Church of Christ was never perfect until the women were organised. He then said I want you (E. R. Snow) to tell the sisters who delegated you that their offering is accepted of the Lord, and will result in blessing to them. He further said I want the adjourned meeting to meet with me and a few of the brethren in the Masonic Hall on Thursday at 1. P. M. next,[194] And I will organise you in the Order of the Priesthood after the pattern of the church. And I wish Emma to be nominated and elected President of the

---

193. This key appears to be related to the one Joseph Smith noted in the April 28, 1842, Relief Society meeting: "I now turn the key to you in the name of God and this Society shall rejoice and knowledge and intelligence shall flow down from this time." (See Document 1.2, entry for Apr. 28, 1842; and Document 2.2.)

194. The first meeting of the Relief Society was held in a large room on the second floor of Joseph Smith's store in Nauvoo on Thursday, March 17, 1842. The Nauvoo Masonic Lodge sometimes held meetings in that same room. (See Document 1.2.)

Organisation in fulfilment of the revelation in the Doctrine and Covenants which Says She is an Elect Lady.[195] An Elect Lady is one who is elected[196] [p. 30]

---

195. Doctrine and Covenants 25; Document 1.1.

196. Joseph Smith offered an explanation of the term "Elect Lady" at the organizational meeting of the Relief Society in Nauvoo. (Document 1.2, entry for Mar. 17, 1842; Joseph Smith, Journal, Mar. 17, 1842, in Andrew H. Hedges et al., eds., *Journals, Volume 2: December 1841–April 1843,* vol. 2 of the Journals series of *The Joseph Smith Papers,* ed. Dean C. Jessee et al. [Salt Lake City: Church Historian's Press, 2011], 45.)

4.11 Report of Deseret Hospital Dedication, July 17, 1882

"The Deseret Hospital. Dedication Services," Deseret Evening News *(Salt Lake City, UT), July 17, 1882, vol. 15, no. 200, p. [2].*

The featured document is a report of the July 17, 1882, dedicatory proceedings of the Deseret Hospital, which was established by the Relief Society. A movement to establish a hospital in Salt Lake City operated by Latter-day Saints had begun by at least the early 1870s. In 1872 the *Deseret News* asked, "Shall we have an hospital?" The newspaper noted that St. Mark's Hospital, founded earlier that year by the Episcopal Church partly in response to the needs of the mining community, was an excellent facility, but "its capacity is altogether too limited for this large and growing city."[197] Private hospitals also attempted to meet some of the need.[198]

The desire to found a Latter-day Saint hospital corresponded with a growing call for Latter-day Saint women to receive medical training.[199] Some women, such as Romania B. Pratt, attended established medical schools in the eastern United States with support from church leaders and the Relief Society. When Pratt returned to Utah in 1877, she opened an office in Salt Lake City, taught classes in "obstetrics and feminine diseases," and also advocated for the establishment of a local hospital.[200] She argued, "In every growing community there seems to soon develop the need of a hospital devoted more especially to the interest of women and children, and this is now being felt among us."[201]

Eliza R. Snow promoted the establishment of such a hospital as she visited local Relief Societies. At a conference in Spring City, Utah, she "spoke of having a hospital that could be controlled by those of our own faith that there could be a place where the young girls could be taught to administer herbs in faith and become good, efficient nurses and understand the human system."[202] In 1880 a letter to the editor of the *Woman's Exponent* complained that no

---

197. "Shall We Have an Hospital?" *Deseret News* [weekly], Dec. 18, 1872, 699; "Hospitals in the City," *Salt Lake Tribune,* Jan. 1, 1891, 22.

198. See, for example, "Local and Other Matters," *Deseret News* [weekly], July 26, 1871, 281; and "Hospitals in the City," *Salt Lake Tribune,* Jan. 1, 1891, 22. The military hospital at Fort Douglas also served the civilian population. ("A Word of Advice," *Salt Lake Daily Tribune and Mining Gazette,* July 25, 1871, [2].)

199. See Document 3.23; "Minutes of a Special Meeting of the F. R. Societies of Provo," *Woman's Exponent,* Sept. 15, 1872, 1:58; and "R. S. Reports," *Woman's Exponent,* Aug. 1, 1873, 2:35.

200. Early Mormon doctors Romania B. Pratt and Ellis R. Shipp were both graduates of the Women's Medical College in Philadelphia, while Martha Hughes Cannon attended a medical school in Michigan. ("A Biographical Sketch of R. B. Pratt," *Young Woman's Journal* 2, no. 12 [Sept. 1891]: 533–534; "The Women of Utah," *Woman's Exponent,* Sept. 1, 1888, 17:49–50; "Class in Obstetrics," *Deseret News* [weekly], Apr. 30, 1879, 201; "Opened an Office," *Deseret News* [weekly], Nov. 21, 1877, 664; "Class in Obstetrics," *Deseret News* [weekly], Apr. 30, 1879, 201.)

201. "Work for Women," *Woman's Exponent,* Apr. 1, 1879, 7:217.

202. "R. S. Reports," *Woman's Exponent,* Aug. 1, 1879, 8:34; see also "R. S. Reports," *Woman's Exponent,* Oct. 1, 1879, 8:66.

action had yet been taken to found a hospital despite frequent discussions.²⁰³ Latter-day Saint women, including leaders of the Relief Society, soon began making concrete plans along with church leaders to establish a hospital.²⁰⁴ Reflecting later on the work of establishing the hospital, Eliza R. Snow explained, "With the approval of the First Presidency, we commenced the Hospital as no women on earth except Latter-day Saints would have undertaken so gigantic an enterprise—i.e., with nothing. But we had faith in the support and liberality of our brethren and sisters."²⁰⁵

Funding for the hospital came from a variety of sources, including subscriptions, donations from Primary children, and benefit concerts. In-kind contributions provided the hospital with some of the coal, blankets, pillows, quilts, towels, and other materials it needed to operate.²⁰⁶ Circulars were sent to local church leaders soliciting financial assistance to pay expenses. Fundraising was a constant effort for members of the hospital executive board even after the facility opened.²⁰⁷

On July 17, 1882, apostle Franklin D. Richards dedicated the Deseret Hospital.²⁰⁸ By the end of that year, the hospital could accommodate from thirty to thirty-five patients. During its first months of operation the hospital served, on average, between twelve and twenty patients per month.²⁰⁹ Deseret Hospital remained open for twelve years, treating illnesses such as typhoid fever, rheumatism, diphtheritic tonsillitis, and other maladies.²¹⁰ In 1886 the staff treated 334 patients.²¹¹ By 1890 the hospital was showing signs of trouble, as its staff treated just over one hundred patients that year.²¹² By 1894 Deseret Hospital closed its doors.²¹³

———— ❧ ————

203. "Are We to Have a Hospital," *Woman's Exponent,* Mar. 15, 1880, 8:157.

204. See "A Church Hospital," *Deseret Evening News,* Oct. 1, 1880, [3].

205. "The Deseret Hospital," *Deseret News* [weekly], Aug. 1, 1883, 435.

206. "Deseret Hospital," *Woman's Exponent,* Apr. 15, 1883, 11:173; "Home Affairs," *Woman's Exponent,* Aug. 1, 1882, 11:37.

207. See Franklin D. Richards, Journal, 1844–1899, in Richards Family Collection, 1837–1961, CHL, May 22 and Dec. 8–9, 1882; "Deseret Hospital Association," *Deseret News* [weekly], June 14, 1882, 329; and Eliza R. Snow, "The Deseret Hospital," *Woman's Exponent,* July 15, 1883, 12:28.

208. Richards, Journal, July 17, 1882.

209. "Deseret Hospital," *Deseret News* [weekly], Dec. 13, 1882, 737.

210. "Hospitals in the City," *Salt Lake Tribune,* Jan. 1, 1891, 22.

211. "Governor West's Report," *Deseret News* [weekly], Oct. 27, 1886, 642.

212. "Hospitals in the City," *Salt Lake Tribune,* Jan. 1, 1891, 22.

213. Leonard J. Arrington, "The Economic Role of Pioneer Mormon Women," *Western Humanities Review* 9, no. 2 (Spring 1955): 161–163. Arrington attributed the hospital's demise to a number of financial factors, such as that most of the patients were unable to pay for their treatment. The hospital closed in 1893 or 1894. In mid-1895, Romania Pratt announced classes in midwifery to be held in her private office, as the "Deseret Hospital is closed." Extant hospital records seem to indicate that the last year of operation was 1893. (*History of Relief Society, 1842–1966* [Salt Lake City: General Board of Relief Society, 1966], 116; "Class in Midwifery," *Woman's Exponent,* July 15, 1895, 24:32; Deseret Hospital, Patient Accounts, 1886–1893, CHL.)

THE DESERET HOSPITAL.

DEDICATION SERVICES.

THIS morning, at 11 o'clock, a number of ladies and gentlemen interested in the establishment of a hospital for the care and treatment of the sick, under the auspices of the Church of Jesus Christ of Latter-day Saints, assembled at the building on Fifth East Streets, between East Temple and First South,[214] to attend the dedication and the opening of the institution.

Presidents John Taylor and Jos. F. Smith were present, also President W. [Wilford] Woodruff, Apostle F. D. Richards, Prest. of the Stake Angus M. Cannon and Counselor Jos. E. Taylor, Mayor W. [William] Jennings, Elders L. John Nuttall, Joseph Horne and Chas. W. Penrose, the officers of the Institution, physicians, ladies of the Relief Society, etc.

Dr. Seymour B. Young announced the programme of the services.

A select choir led by Prof. C. J. Thomas sung the hymn on page 410.[215]

Prayer was offered by Prest. W. Woodruff.

Choir sang hymn on page 136.[216]

Dr. Seymour B. Young read the circular of the institution as follows:

President—Eliza R. Snow Smith.

Vice-President—Zina D. H. Young.

Executive Board—M. Isabella Horne, Marinda N. Hyde, Phoebe Woodruff, Bathsheba W. Smith, Jane S. Richards, Ellen B. Ferguson, M. D., Romania B Pratt, M. D.,

Secretary—Emeline B. Wells.

Treasurer—Matilda M. Barratt.

Chairman Visiting Committee—Elizabeth Howard.

Finance Committee—Sarah M. Kimball, Priscilla M. Staines, Priscilla Jennings, Annie G. Sharp, Sarah Jane Cannon, Hannah T. King, Elizabeth Groesbeck, Ellen Dinwoodey, Elizabeth H. Goddard, Sophia W. Taylor.

Resident Physician and Surgeon—Dr. Ellen B. Ferguson.

Visiting Board—Dr. Seymour B. Young, Dr. W. [Washington] F. Anderson.

---

214. The mention of "East Temple" street here is probably meant to refer instead to South Temple Street. In modern nomenclature, the hospital was initially located on 500 East, between South Temple and 100 South Streets. (*The Utah Directory, for 1883–84* [Salt Lake City: J. C. Graham, 1883], 65.)

215. Assuming the most recently published church hymnal was used, this was Hymn 342, "This House We Dedicate to Thee." (Hymn 342, *Sacred Hymns and Spiritual Songs. For the Church of Jesus Christ of Latter-day Saints,* 14th ed. [Salt Lake City: George Q. Cannon, 1871], 410.)

216. Hymn 125, "Except the Lord Conduct the Plan," *Sacred Hymns and Spiritual Songs,* 136.

Deseret Hospital board of directors. Circa 1882–1884. The board of the first Latter-day Saint hospital included prominent Relief Society members. Front row, left to right: Jane S. Richards, Emmeline B. Wells. Second row: Phebe Woodruff, Mary Isabella Horne, Eliza R. Snow, Zina D. H. Young, Nancy M. J. Hyde. Back row: Dr. Ellis R. Shipp, Bathsheba W. Smith, Elizabeth A. Howard, Dr. Romania B. Pratt. Photograph by Charles R. Savage. (Church History Library, Salt Lake City.)

Visiting Surgeon—Eye and Ear, Nose and Throat—Dr. Romania B. Pratt.

Clinical Registrar and Dispensary Clerk—Mary F. VanSchoonhoven.

Matron—Mary Ann McLean.

Honorary Committee—The Stake Presidents of the Relief Society are members of the Honorary Committee, each one to represent the interests of the hospital in their respective locality.

ARTICLES OF ASSOCIATION.

ARTICLE 1.—This Association has for it◊ object the e[s]tablishment[217] and management of a Hospital for the sick and injured.

ARTICLE 2—The Executive Board shall have the entire control of the domestic management, shall supervise the expenditures, and make such rules and regulations for the government of the Hospital as shall best promote economy, good order and harmony in all its departments.

ARTICLE 3—The Medical Board shall control the medical and surgical department, and present a report at each meeting of the Executive Board.

ARTICLE 4,—Any lady member of the Church of Jesus Christ of Latter-day Saints, in good standing, may become a member of this Association by the payment of one dollar annually. Such name and amount to be sent to any member of the Board for proposal, and to be voted upon at the next monthly meeting.

APPEAL.

To the Presidents of Stakes, Bishops, Presidents and members of the Relief Society, Superintendents and Presidents Y. L. and Y. M. M. I. Associations.

The urgent necessity which has long existed in our midst, of a place where the sick and suffering, who have a claim upon our sympathy and care, can receive the medical and surgical aid which they require—in connection with the administration of sacred ordinances in their behalf, has impelled those who feel this need most deeply, to an earnest and determined effort in this humane direction, with the sanction and approval of the First Presidency of the Church of Jesus Christ of Latter-day Saints.

We, who have taken upon us the responsibility of inaugurating this

---

217. TEXT: In the copy used for transcription, there is a blank space at the beginning of the word between the *e* and the *t*.

work, make a special appeal to all who are able and willing to aid in securing to those who are the proper subjects for the benefits of this Institution, the medical and surgical care and personal comfort which they require in the period of extreme sickness, and in event of those accidents and emergencies to which all are at any time liable.

In order to assist in meeting the current expenses of the Hospital, it has been suggested that each Relief Society and Mutual Improvement Association subscribe statedly one dollar per month to the Hospital Fund, such amounts to stand as a credit in favor of any member of the Society or Association who may require the benefits of the Institution.

For the furnishing and outfit of the Hospital we appeal to the liberality of our brethren and sisters for donation, of money, provisions, bedding, furniture and domestic utensils.

The Board of Managers expect to establish, in connection with the Hospital, a School, for the purpose of educating midwives and training nurses for the sick;[218] a class whose services will be welcomed both by the public and by the medical profession as efficient aids to the accomplishment of the chief end of all hospital work—the care and cure of the sick.

May the Spirit of Him, to whom the sick and afflicted never appealed for help in vain, influence the hearts of those who are favored with an abundance of this world's goods, to a generous response to this appeal, knowing that such gifts are doubly blessed, blessing both the giver and the receiver.

E. R. Snow Smith, President,
E. B. Wells, Secretary,
E. B. Ferguson, M. D., Res. Surgeon.

RULES AND REGULATIONS.

1. This Hospital is designed for the care and treatment of the sick and injured, more especially among the Latter-day Saints, and for the reception of critical cases of accouchement.

---

218. Several years before the Deseret Hospital opened, Romania Pratt advocated opening a hospital-run training school for nurses. Even after the hospital opened in 1882, it appears that courses offered for training nurses and midwives were privately run, without association with the hospital. The hospital did provide some training programs; an 1885 announcement stated, "A limited number of students will be taken, who will board in the Institution [Deseret Hospital], receive instruction preparatory for future studies, and will be expected in return to devote a certain portion of their time and labor to attendance on the sick and other requirements connected with the Hospital." ("Home Affairs," *Woman's Exponent,* June 1, 1879, 8:251; "Home Affairs," *Woman's Exponent,* Apr. 1, 1883, 11:165; "School in Midwifery," *Deseret News* [weekly], Aug. 29, 1883, 509; "A Card," *Deseret News* [weekly], June 3, 1885, 320.)

2. The price of board and medical attendance, except in the free beds, shall be from $6.00 upwards per week, according to the requirements of the case. All fees to be paid weekly, in advance.

3. The free beds are designed only for those who are unable to pay for services rendered. Persons wishing the benefit of these must have a recommendation signed by the Bishop and President of Relief Society of the Ward in which they reside.

4. All applicants for admission other than accidents, and those persons desiring advice or treatment from the hospital surgeons must present themselves at the Hospital for examamination between the hours of 9 and 11 a.m.

5. No wines, liquors or spirits shall be brought into the Hospital without the consent of the attending surgeon or matron.

6. Patients in free beds shall render, when able, such assistance in nursing as the surgeon in charge may direct.

7. Nurses shall follow implicitly the instructions of the surgeons, matron, and those in authority.

8. No nurse shall leave the patients in her charge at any time without permission from the surgeon or matron.

9. Visitors will be admitted to the Hospital every day from 11 a.m. to 1 p.m., but only one at a time to any patient, unless by special permission.

10. One section, consisting of three ladies of the Visiting Committee, shall be appointed monthly by the Executive Board to visit the Hospital at least twice in every week, to confer with and advise the matron, and shall reporl to the Board at the regular monthly meeting

11. Stated meetings of the Executive and Medical Board shall be held in the Hospital on the first Monday of every month at 11 a. m. Three members and the officers present shall constitute a quorum and their decisions shall be final.

12. Vacancies may be filled by the Board by a majority vote at any regular meeting.

13. At the semi-annual meeting, reports from the Visiting Committee, Medical Board and Finance Committee, of the work of the past half year shall be presented to the Board to be incorporated by the Secretary in the semi-annual report of the Hospital, to be presented to the General Conference of the Church of Jesus Christ of Latter-day Saints.[219]

---

219. Emmeline B. Wells, as secretary to the hospital's executive board, submitted the financial

PRESIDENT JOHN TAYLOR

Said his sympathies were extended to the ladies in their labors of love for the establishment of this hospital, where the sick of the Lord's people could be attended and have the benefit of the ordinances of the Church as well as skillful treatment. Accidents were numerous in these troublous times and sickness was prevalent. It was right that we should have a place where the sick could be efficiently tended. Several of the ladies present had acquired a knowledge of those principles which were needful in proper attention to the sick, which he was pleased to recognize, for it was in accord with our religion to acquire all useful in[f]ormation[220] to deal with disease, and physicians should not be bound by rigid rules, but act as directed by the Lord, because there were so many phases of the same disease and so much difference in the constitutions of mankind. At the same time we were commanded of the Lord to "seek out of the best books words of wisdom," and to seek knowledge by learning.[221] Yet we must not forget to call in the aid of faith, but while we acquire all the intelligence possible to be attained, at the same time we must exercise faith that the blessing of the Lord might be upon our efforts. The officers of the Association and all connected with it, had his best wishes, and he felt that they would have the blessing and favor of God. They should not neglect to avail themselves of all possible sources of knowledge, but seek for it in every direction. He closed by blessing the officers, physicians and attendants, and all connected with the hospital.

PREST. JOSEPH F. SMITH

Endorsed the remarks of President Taylor. This was a step quite necessary to be taken. It was in the interest of the afflicted and the poor. He would have been pleased if the institution could have been started in a better place. It was but a small beginning, yet it was better than none at all, and he expressed the hope that success would attend it, and that perfect union, harmony and good feeling would prevail among all who had the conduct of its affairs, so that the good spirit of the Lord might be with them, and that while they exercised all the skill that was possible, they might be so sensitive to the whisperings of the spirit of the Lord that they would be able to obtain the power of God for the benefit of the sick, and that they might be guided in the channel of the best success. He believed that the Latter-day Saints had the right to obtain the blessing and direction of the Lord in all their affairs, and especially in such

---

reports. (See, for example, "Deseret Hospital," *Woman's Exponent*, Apr. 15, 1883, 11:173.)

220. TEXT: In the copy used for transcription, there is a blank space at the beginning of the word between the *n* and the *o*.

221. Doctrine and Covenants 88:118.

labors as those for the benefit of the afflicted. He invoked the blessing of the Lord upon the efforts of the institution, its officers and all who should receive the benefits thereof.

Apostle F. D. Richards offered the dedicatory prayer,

President W. Woodruff coincided with what had been said, and congratulated the sisters upon the progress of another labor of love connected with the Relief Society. That society, like other features of the Church and Kingdom of God was organized to stay. He endorsed with all his heart the principles enunciated of looking to the Lord. We needed revelation. Men's ideas of medicine changed materially. The course of practice pursued when he was a boy would not be followed now. He related incidents in illustration of this, and showed the necessity of the guidance of the Almighty in the treatment of the sick. He was thankful that we would now have a place for the treatment of the afflicted, where the Elders could walk in and freely administer the ordinance for the healing of the sick, and he felt that this institution would grow and increase and accomplish the purpose desired.

PREST. ANGUS M. CANNON.

Was gratified that the Sisters had been led to take the course which had resulted in the establishment of this hospital. They had been very faithful in their efforts in that Relief Society which was established by the Prophet Joseph Smith. Here was a place where the afflicted of the Lord's people could be watched over in a proper way and could be administered to by the good Samaritans. God had set His hand to establish Zion in its beauty and power, and he felt that this beginning would be looked back to as the germ of something much greater, which would reflect credit upon all engaged in it. He trusted that more extensive grounds would soon be obtained. He related an incident in his experience, showing the necessity and blessing of reliance upon the Lord for the healing of the sick. He hoped that the institution would be sustained by the faith and the means of the people.

MAYOR WM. JENNINGS

Considered that this hospital was much needed in this Territory. The sisters had done a good work. We had become a large community, and people of all classes were among us, also many who were afflicted from various causes. In some of the isolated places of the Territory there was a lack of medical skill, and here was a place to which cases might be brought for treatment which they could not obtain where they lived. Here the sick could be treated in a way that they could not be among persons not of our faith. He hoped the ladies would keep in view, as he believed they would, the fact that this hospital was not for speculation but for relief. He hoped this building would prove large enough for many years to come. It would have his support, both by his faith and his means.

ELDER C. W. PENROSE

Said there was no need for any remarks from him concerning the objects of this institution nor the benefits to follow from it, these had been well set forth by those speakers who had preceded him. He would say, however, that the institution had his sympathy and support, and he believed it would be successful. Some persons might wonder why Latter-day Saints who believed in healing by faith, needed a hospital. He showed that faith and science were not incompatible. That, according to the revelations of God, knowledge was to be obtained by study and also by faith;[222] so with the treatment of the sick; the means ordained of God as remedies should be used and at the same time faith be exercised. They who had sufficient faith could be healed by faith. They who had not faith were to be nourished and treated with proper remedies, and these, it was written, should be used with "prudence and thanksgiving," with judgment and skill, but "not by the hand of an enemy."[223] Therefore skill should be acquired by study. Women had always been recognized as good nurses, but only of recent date as skilled physicians and surgeons. He was glad at the progress of public opinion. He congratulated the ladies on the good work they had accomplished.

Dr. Ellen B. Ferguson was then set apart as resident physician and surgeon under the hands of the brethren, Prest. John Taylor officiating; Dr. Romania B. Pratt was also set apart as visiting physician and surgeon, Prest. Joseph F. Smith pronouncing the blessing; Mrs. Mary Van Schoonhoven was set apart as dispensing clerk, Prest. W. Woodruff being mouth; Mrs. Mary Ann McLean was set apart as matron, Apostle F. D Richards officiating.

The doxology was sung and the Benediction was pronounced by Prest. Joseph E. Taylor.

Mayor Wm. Jennings showed that he was in earnest in his promise of material support by handing a check for $500 to the Treasurer. It is hoped that his liberality will be imitated by other men of means. The institution is in every way worthy of the support of all humane persons and especially of the people called Latter-day Saints.

---

222. See Doctrine and Covenants 88:118.
223. Doctrine and Covenants 89:11; 42:43.

4.12 Eliza R. Snow and Sarah M. Kimball, "The Relief Society," March 1, 1883

Eliza R. Snow and Sarah M. Kimball, "The Relief Society," Woman's Exponent *(Salt Lake City, UT), Mar. 1, 1883, vol. 11, no. 19, pp. 148–149.*

The following document is a March 1883 call from Eliza R. Snow and Sarah M. Kimball for local Relief Societies to send reports twice a year to Kimball as secretary of the Central Board of the Relief Society. Reports of local Relief Societies were already a part of stake Relief Society records.[224] When Brigham Young formally organized the first stake Relief Society in Ogden, Utah, in July 1877, he suggested that the organization hold quarterly meetings.[225] At the women's next meeting on October 30, financial reports were "read dating back to the organization of each separate branch of the Society in that county. The condition of each Society in all special respects was also reported in writing."[226] As other stake Relief Society presidencies were formed, they adopted similar record-keeping practices.[227]

Shortly after Sarah M. Kimball was installed as secretary to the Central Board in 1880, she asked stake secretaries to send her statistical and financial reports of Relief Societies from April 1, 1876, to 1880. Secretaries were also to submit a semiannual report from that time forward.[228] These reports were used by the Central Board to compile a general report of the organization for use in the semiannual general conferences of the church. While it appears these reports were not generally read over the pulpit at the conference, one exception comes from the April 1881 general conference. The Central Board report, read by George Q. Cannon of the First Presidency, noted that the Relief Society had over 12,000 members, 960 of whom subscribed to the *Woman's Exponent.* The societies had donated $3,468 to the poor, $1,214 to temples, $1,617 to other buildings, and $689 to home industries. Assets on hand included $3,342 in cash; property worth $24,099; and 9,859 bushels of wheat. Cannon "passed a high encomium on the neat and comprehensive report the ladies had presented, and also on the labors that the sisters have so zealously performed."[229]

Beginning in 1893, local reports were submitted annually rather than semiannually.[230] Obtaining reports from every ward and branch proved to be a challenge. Mary Isabella Horne, who served as Salt Lake Stake Relief Society president and as treasurer in the general presidency, lamented in 1896 that only twenty-six of fifty Relief Societies in her stake had submitted their reports: "The failure of these wards to send in their reports makes one sorry and angry, for the Salt Lake Stake is looked upon as a pattern."[231] Local Relief

---

224. For more information on Relief Society record-keeping practices, see Document 4.9.
225. See Document 3.26.
226. "Home Affairs," *Woman's Exponent,* Nov. 15, 1877, 6:92; see also Document 3.28.
227. See "R. S. Reports," *Woman's Exponent,* Jan. 1, 1878, 6:114.
228. "Stake Reports Wanted," *Woman's Exponent,* Aug. 1, 1880, 9:35.
229. "Relief Society Report," *Woman's Exponent,* June 1, 1881, 10:5.
230. "Relief Society," *Woman's Exponent,* Oct. 15 and Nov. 1, 1893, 22:53.
231. "Relief Society Conference," *Woman's Exponent,* Oct. 1, 1896, 25:55–56.

Societies continued to submit annual reports to the general Relief Society presidency until at least 1975.[232] General Relief Society reports appeared sporadically in the *Woman's Exponent* and were consistently featured in the *Relief Society Magazine* between 1915 and 1970.[233]

———— ❧ ————

THE RELIEF SOCIETY.

The Relief Society of the Church of Jesus Christ of Latter-day Saints is expected to report semi-annually to the General Conferences in this city, held in April and October, its [p. 148] complete statistical and financial condition. In order to make this report properly, it is necesary to receive particulars of all organizations of the Relief Society in our own and foreign countries. Therefore, when such organizations exist that are not included in the several Stakes of Zion here at home (that report through the Stake Secretary) they should be reported separately in branches to the Secretary of the Central Board, Mrs. Sarah M. Kimball, Salt Lake City, Utah, Box 785, as soon as practicable, now and hereafter twice a year, in time for the general reports. As we are aware there are many of these branches of the Relief Society that have never reported at all, we would suggest that in the first report made they give date of organization and what Elders officiated in organizing; names of officers and such other data as relate thereto; that all may be recorded in perfect order, and in a thorough business-like manner. Hoping that this request may meet with a ready response, and ever praying for those engaged in this great and good work, we are your sisters in the Gospel,

ELIZA R. SNOW SMITH, Pres.,
SARAH M. KIMBALL, Sec.,

Central Board Relief Society.

---

232. See Relief Society, Relief Society Annual Reports, 1913–1973, CHL; Relief Society, Narrative Reports, 1964–1971, 1973–1975, CHL.

233. For examples from the *Relief Society Magazine,* see Amy Brown Lyman, "The April Conference," *Relief Society Magazine* 2, no. 6 (June 1915): 260–265; and Belle S. Spafford, "Report and Official Instructions," *Relief Society Magazine* 57, no. 11 (Nov. 1970): 813–819.

4.13 Sandwich Islands Relief Society, Report, October 5, 1883

Sandwich Islands Relief Society, Report, Oct. 5, 1883, in "Sandwich Islands. Interesting Report," in "R.S., Y.L.M.I.A. and Primary Reports," Woman's Exponent *(Salt Lake City, UT), Nov. 1, 1883, vol. 12, no. 11, p. 86.*

The document featured below is Sarah Partridge's report of an October 1883 Relief Society conference held in the Sandwich Islands (Hawaii). Sarah Lucretia Clayton Partridge had arrived in Honolulu the prior summer with her husband, Edward Partridge Jr., who was the newly appointed president of the Sandwich Islands mission, and some of their children. Missionaries first arrived in Hawaii in December 1850.[234] Edward Partridge served a first mission to the islands in the mid-1850s. In 1856, when he presided over the Kohala, Hawaii, conference, church membership on the islands was reported to be 3,831. Twenty-six years later, when he and Sarah arrived for their mission, they found that church membership had not significantly changed.[235] But there was one noteworthy change from the 1850s: the Relief Society had been officially organized in Hawaii, probably in the early to mid-1870s.[236]

After the Partridges' arrival, Edward immersed himself in the work of supervising the mission, including providing support to the Relief Society branches located on the different islands. On October 7, 1882, he wrote in his journal: "At 4 o clock met with the Relief Societies only 4 represented, organized a first Presidency, as follows, S. L. Partridge President, G. J. Anderson, Kaahanui [Kaleohano] & Nalia [Kekauoha] counsellors, and Kahaole secretary."[237] The following year Sarah Partridge was also appointed to serve as the Primary president.[238] In meeting the demands of these callings, Sarah Partridge was often concerned about her proficiency in the Hawaiian language.[239]

The Relief Society of the church was not the only relief organization the Partridges found on the islands. The king and queen of Hawaii took an interest in assisting the sick

---

234. Edward Partridge Jr., Journals, 1854–1899, CHL, vol. 4, May 27 and June 11, 1882; H. W. Bigler, Letter to the Editor, *Deseret News,* Aug. 22, 1855, 190.

235. "Minutes," *Deseret News,* Aug. 6, 1856, 172. By April 1884 total membership on the islands was reported at 3,549. ("Sandwich Islands Conference," *Deseret News* [weekly], Apr. 30, 1884, 237.)

236. It is somewhat unclear when the Relief Society was first organized in Hawaii. The manuscript history of the Hawaii mission states that on July 6, 1875, "the first Relief Society in Laie (and believed to be the first Relief Society organized in the Hawaiian Mission) was organized by Prest. Frederick A. F. Mitchell with Kapo as president; Kaahanui as first, and Kealohanui as second counselor; Hauhau, secretary and Hanaa treasurer." However, Mitchell had already returned to Utah by this time. Other evidence suggests that the Relief Society was organized prior to 1875. Following her return to Utah, Margaret Mitchell spoke of her experience in Hawaii, reporting that "she had often met with the island sisters in the capacity of a Relief Society." (Hawaii Honolulu Mission, Hawaii Honolulu Mission Manuscript History and Historical Reports, 1850–1967, CHL, vol. 4, July 6, 1875; "Home Affairs," *Woman's Exponent,* Mar. 1, 1875, 3:149; May 1, 1875, 3:181.)

237. Edward Partridge, Journal, vol. 4, Oct. 7, 1882.

238. Sarah C. Partridge, Journals, 1882–1885, CHL, vol. 1, Aug. 19, 1883.

239. See Sarah Partridge, Journal, vol. 1, Mar. 1 and Apr. 19, 1884.

and destitute and founded a "national 'Female Relief Society.'"[240] Various denominations also had organizations analogous to the Relief Society. In December 1876 King Kalakaua visited the Honolulu Branch of the church. His "object in visiting our church was to organize Female Relief Societies, as he is doing in other churches, and after services were through he proceeded to attend to that business. He wished to raise a fund to be applied to the relief of the sick."[241] The following February, Queen Kapiolani visited the church at Laie for the same purpose: "that the wants of the sick and destitute might be administered to, and thereby preserve the lives of many of the nation."[242]

SANDWICH ISLANDS.

INTERESTING REPORT.

A Conference of the Relief Societies of the Sandwich Islands was held at Laie, Oct. 5th, 1883.

On the stand, Mrs. S. L. Partridge, Mrs. [Celestia] Armeda S. Young; native Counselors, Kaahanui and Nalie [Nalia Kekauoha]; also Pres. E. Partridge, J. [James] H Gardner and W. [William] G. Farrell.[243] Meeting was called to order by Pres. Partridge. The Society of Laie having formed themselves into a choir for the occasion, and being dressed in white, arose and sang one of the old songs that used to be sung when Brother George Q. Cannon[244] was on the Islands, and which was composed by Bro. R. Allred.[245] Prayer by

---

240. R. Lanier Britsch, *Unto the Islands of the Sea: A History of the Latter-day Saints in the Pacific* (Salt Lake City: Deseret Book, 1986), 137.

241. Jane E. Molen, "Extracts from a Letter," *Woman's Exponent,* Feb. 15, 1877, 5:139.

242. Jane E. Molen, "Extracts of Letters from Hawaiian Islands," *Woman's Exponent,* June 15, 1877, 6:13. The similarity between the two organizations and the frequent visits of the king and queen to the branches of the church has led to the conclusion that "the king and queen founded a national 'Female Relief Society,' patterned after what they had seen in the LDS Church, to help the poor of the kingdom." (Britsch, *Unto the Islands of the Sea,* 137; see also Joseph H. Spurrier, *The Church of Jesus Christ of Latter-day Saints in the Hawaiian Islands* [Salt Lake City: Hawaii Honolulu Mission, 1978], 18–19; for another firsthand account of the relationship between Queen Kapiolani and the Latter-day Saint Relief Societies, see Henry P. Richards, Diary, 1858–1878, in Henry P. Richards, Papers, 1854–1900, CHL, Sept. 26–27, 1877.)

243. James H. Gardner, of West Jordan, Utah, was set apart for a mission to the Sandwich Islands on November 9, 1880. He returned April 26, 1884. William G. Farrell, of Logan, Utah, was set apart for a mission to the Sandwich Islands on May 25, 1882. He returned February 26, 1885. (Missionary Department, Missionary Department Missionary Record Index, 1830–1971, CHL, "Gardner, James H.," and "Farrell, William G.")

244. George Q. Cannon was among the first missionaries of the church in Hawaii, serving there from December 1850 through July 1854. (H. W. Bigler, "Sandwich Islands Mission," *Deseret News,* Aug. 22, 1855, 190; "Elder's Correspondence," *Deseret News,* Nov. 29, 1851, [1].)

245. Reddin A. Allred and his brother Reddick both served as missionaries on the Sandwich Islands. Reddin reached Honolulu on February 17, 1853. (Reddin A. Allred, "Correspondence," *Deseret News,* Jan. 2, 1856, 344.)

past, present or future existence. Novels are like husks to those who have once feasted on the things of God—the pure bread of life, and have not used to retain that spirit. Satan is manifesting his power, and these spiritual rappings and mediums, which have turned so many people's brain, are only forerunners of the great and more mighty manifestations which are soon to be witnessed from the spirit world. There are millions of the dead looking to this people to attend to this ordinances that will redeem and free them from their prison house, but they will communicate in a more intelligent manner than the present senseless and disgusting mode. We should beware of Satan, and understand that his doctrines are generally the first to be introduced, and we have been warned of his power, which is to be such in the last days that he will be able to deceive almost the very elect. And may God grant that our wisdom, union and faith may increase until Satan can find no foot-hold nor resting place in our midst. Then he will be bound, and can no longer have power to afflict our bodies or spirits.

HELEN MAR WHITNEY.

Oct. 18.b, 1883.

R. S., Y. L. M. I. A. AND PRIMARY REPORTS.

SANDWICH ISLANDS.

INTERESTING REPORT.

A Conference of the Relief Societies of the Sandwich Islands was held at Laie, Oct. 5th, 1883.

On the stand, Mrs. S. L. Partridge, Mrs. Armeda S. Young; native Counselors, Kaahanui and Nalie; also Pres. E. Partridge, J. H Gardner and W. G. Farrell. Meeting was called to order by Pres. Partridge. The Society of Laie having formed themselves into a choir for the occasion, and being dressed in white, arose and sang one of the old songs that used to be sung when Brother George Q. Cannon was on the Islands, and which was composed by Bro. R. Allred. Prayer by Kaahanui. Singing. There are fifteen societies organized on the different Islands at the present time, from all of which written reports were read except one. Verbal reports were also given of nearly all by Presidents or Counselors of the different societies, which reports showed them to be in a flourishing condition. The figures of the condensed reports were as follows: Number of members April 5th, 1883, 332; died, 17; removed, 17; new members, 67; total number of members Oct. 5th 1883, 345; amount of money in the treasury on April 5th, 1883, 330,13; amount donated since April, 272,79¾; given to the poor, 55,20; expended for other purposes, 144,30; amount in the treasury Oct. 5th, 1883, 403, 39¾.

A few remarks were made by Sisters Partridge and Young, and interpreted by President Partridge, who also addressed the meeting a short time, instructing them in their duties and encouraging them in their labors.

Most of the money paid out of the treasury has been donated by the different societies to assist in building a house for the use of the society at Laie; it is considered necessary for them to have such a house, not only for the accomodation of the poor but for other purposes. It would be hard indeed for anyone who has not had the experience to understand the many difficulties to be overcome in trying to introduce and establish these societies among a people so simple in their understandings,and so unaccustomed to anything of the kind, aside from the, to me, almost insurmountable difficulty of learning the native language, it is a labor which requires indefatigable exertions, and patience

without any limit, with a firm reliance upon our Heavenly Father for guidance, strength, and the necessary qualifications to fit us for the duties of the mission. I can see two or three different ways in which I could spend every moment of my time to good advantage, but have to content myself with doing what I can and letting the rest go undone. Our Conference and the visit of the king passed off with an excellent spirit, and in a satisfactory manner in every respect; we all regretted the absence of the queen, who was unavoidably deterred from coming by the serious illness of her sister, the governess of Hawaii, who also intended coming until she was taken sick. I will leave an account of the reception of the king to more interesting correspondents than myself.

A Primary Association was organized by President Partridge, on the 19th of August, Mrs. S. L. Partridge acting as President for the present, and Mrs. Armeda S. Young First Counselor, and Hansa, native woman, Second Counselor, and Victoria Kekauoha, Secretary for the native language, Ernest Partridge in the English, with 39 names enrolled. Here again is the difficulty of trying to teach children without having sufficient knowledge of the language to explain things in clearness and the perfect understanding of the children; however, we can only do our best, trusting that the Lord will bless our efforts. We are very much in need of cards and books, so as to assist us in making our meetings interesting to the children, also to ourselves.

Wishing the EXPONENT every success, I remain your sister in the Gospel,

S. L. PARTRIDGE.

LEWISTON, CACHE COUNTY Y. L. M. I. A.

EDITOR EXPONENT:

A meeting was held for the reorganization of our association on the 29th of June, 1883. The following officers were elected: Mrs Rebecca Rawlins, President; Mrs. Anna E. Funk, First Counselor; Miss Louisa Waddoups, Second Counselor; Mrs. Sarah A. Orchard, Secretary; Miss Emma Kemp, Assistant Secretary; Eliza J. Stephenson, Treasurer and Librarian. We have thirty-four names enrolled; our average attendance is twenty-two; we hold our meetings once in two weeks, and have very good meetings. The young sisters all take a part in helping to make our meetings interesting, and try to do whatever they are called upon. As an association we are trying to improve our minds, and learn the ways of the Lord. Our meetings consist of speaking, recitations, essays, songs readings, etc.

Wishing for the success of the EXPONENT, I remain your sister in the Gospel,

SARAH A. ORCHARD, Secretary.

HYRUM PRIMARY FAIR.

The Primary Association of Hyrum held a Fair in the school house on Tuesday, Oct. 2nd, ult., under the presidency of Lucy Wilson and Georgina Ralph.

This is the first fair held in Hyrum by the Primary. The young ladies also took part, and had a stand for the Y. L. M. I. A. It was a pleasant and enjoyable affair, showing the interest and industry of what little hands can do. The articles exhibited were of the usual kind, tidies, mottoes, wool flowers, pincushions, one skein of home-spun silk by a little girl aged seven. To enumerate them all would be impossible; there was everything, from a miniature parasol to a bed quilt. Every one present expressed their surprise at seeing how much the little ones could do.

On the young ladies' stand were a great many useful and ornamental articles. A crocheted jacket, breakfast shawl and ladies'

hood, by Mrs. Bevans, equal to any imported. A very pretty crocheted petticoat by Miss Rollson. One thing worthy of special notice was a charming bouquet of natural flowers, they were beautifully and artistically arranged, showing great skill and ability, by Georgina Ralph. There was needle work, quilts, carpets and many other things made by the young ladies.

A Primary meeting was held at two p.m. After the usual opening exercises the children took up some time in songs, recitations, etc.

The Association was then divided into three districts. Sister Alice Unsworth to have charge over the first district; Sister Lucy Wilson over the second; and Sister Maria Hansen over the third. The meeting was then addressed by Bishop S. M. Molen, Brother Collins of Bear Lake, Sister Jane E. Molen, Stake President, President Lucy Wilson, and Sister Parkinson, President of the Wellsville Primary. All were well pleased and spoke encouragingly to those present.

Meeting was then dismissed. Benediction by James Unsworth.

Wishing the success of the EXPONENT,

Your sister in the Gospel,

ALICE UNSWORTH, Cor. Sec.

PRIMARY FAIR.

The Primary Association of Lehi City, Utah County, held a very pleasing Fair, beginning Friday, Oct. 19th. In all respects it was a delightful show of the handiwork of the children. Each district held articles of peculiar interest. To enumerate them all would be utterly impossible; it was quite marvelous what they could do in regard to cooking, such as plum puddings, pies, sponge cakes, jelly cakes, rice pudding, cooked chickens, jelly, preserves and different kinds of pickles and beautiful bread and butter.

A very nice show of wool flowers were given on the occasion. One globe of wool flowers was made by the First District to be donated to the Temple; also three very nice quilts made by the First, Second and Third Districts to be presented to the Deseret Hospital. There was some nice plain needle work, such as children's dresses, pillow cases, down to netting and darning. There was a splendid show of rugs, tidies, lily mats, daisy mats, mottoes, paper work in the shape of lanterns, stars, wreaths, chains and pen wipers. Though the girls had a greater display the boys came in for a large share of the praise. There was some splendid carpenter work, and among the rest was a threshing machine, made by a boy 14 years of age, and a cupboard, book case, clock shelf, corner brackets, reel, tool box and saw, made by boys from 12 to 14 years of age. There was a beautiful show of agriculture, such as fine squash, cabbage, potatoes, red peppers, beets, turnips, cucumbers, beans, onions, and a number of other useful things grown by the children of the Primary.

SARAH A. BALL, Secretary.

ITEMS OF A LETTER FROM BELLE M. JOHNSON.

TEMPE, Arizona.

Yesterday a small company came over from Tempe and we all went into the hills to see the ruins of a large town that lies between here and Phoenix. I wish I could describe the loveliness of the scenery around and beyond them. It was late and we did not have time to go over the town, only stopping at two ruins, the first a building seventy or eighty feet square, with a long hall on the south, and the north divided into apartments, and a crumbling rocks showed. But the most imposing is a ruin at least 800 feet long by 150 wide—

Local reports in the *Woman's Exponent.* The *Woman's Exponent* (1872–1914) featured minutes and reports from Relief Societies, Young Ladies' Mutual Improvement Associations, and Primary Associations from diverse locations. Missionary Sarah L. Partridge wrote the October 1883 report of a Sandwich Islands Relief Society conference. (Church History Library, Salt Lake City.)

Kaahanui. Singing. There are fifteen societies organized on the different Islands at the present time, from all of which written reports were read except one. Verbal reports were also given of nearly all by Presidents or Counselors of the different societies, which reports showed them to be in a flourishing condition. The figures of the condensed reports were as follows: Number of members April 5th, 1883, 332; died, 17; removed, 17; new members, 67; total number of members Oct. 5th 1883, 345; amount of money in the treasury on April 5th, 1883, 330,13; amount donated since April, 272,79½; given to the poor, 55,20; expended for other purposes, 144,30; amount in the treasury Oct. 5th 1883, 403,39½.

A few remarks were made by Sisters Partridge and Young, and interpreted by President Partridge, who also addressed the meeting a short time, instructing them in their duties and encouraging them in their labors.

Most of the money paid out of the treasury has been donated by the different societies to assist in building a house for the use of the society at Laie; it is considered necessary for them to have such a house, not only for the accomodation of the poor but for other purposes.[246] It would be hard indeed for anyone who has not had the experience to understand the many difficulties to be overcome in trying to introduce and establish these societies among a people so simple in their understandings, and so unaccustomed to anything of the kind, aside from the, to me, almost insurmountable difficulty of learning the native language, it is a labor which requires indefatigable exertions, and patience without any limit, with a firm reliance upon our Heavenly Father for guidance, strength, and the necessary qualifications to fit us for the duties of the mission. I can see two or three different ways in which I could spend every moment of my time to good advantage, but have to content myself with doing what I can and letting the rest go undone. Our Conference and the visit of the king passed off with an excellent spirit, and in a satisfactory manner in every respect; we all regretted the absence of the queen, who was unavoidable deterred from coming by the serious illness of her sister, the governess of Hawaii, who also

---

246. By the following summer enough money had been collected to purchase lumber for the building, and construction began September 2, 1884. Fundraising continued during construction, with an added urgency supplied by the Partridges, who learned in November 1884 that a new mission president would soon be appointed to replace Edward Partridge. The completed Relief Society house was dedicated by Joseph F. Smith, a counselor in the First Presidency, on March 6, 1885, two days before the Partridges returned home. (Edward Partridge, Journal, vol. 6, Aug. 8, Sept. 2, and Nov. 1, 1884; Jan. 11, Mar. 6, and Mar. 8, 1885; Sarah Partridge, Journal, vol. 2, p. 45.)

intended coming until she was taken sick.[247] I will leave an account of the reception of the king to more interesting correspondents than myself.[248]

A Primary Association was organized by President Partridge, on the 19th of August, Mrs. S. L. Partridge acting as President for the present, and Mrs. Armeda S. Young First Counselor, and Hanaa, native woman, Second Counselor, and Victoria Kekauoha, Secretary for the native language, Ernest Partridge[249] in the English, with 39 names enrolled. Here again is the difficulty of trying to teach children without having sufficient knowledge of the language to explain things in clearness and the perfect understanding of the children; however, we can only do our best, trusting that the Lord will bless our efforts. We are very much in need of cards and books, so as to assist us in making our meetings interesting to the children, also to ourselves.

Wishing the Exponent every success, I remain your sister in the Gospel,

S. L. Partridge.

247. "David Kalakaua was elected king by the Hawaiian legislature on February 12, 1874, and he reigned until 1891." His wife, Kapiolani, "attended Relief Society once in a while." (Britsch, *Unto the Islands of the Sea,* 137.)

248. Sarah Partridge described the occasion in her journal: "the Natives were out in all their glory and made an interesting appearance in their gay colored clothes . . . the Natives were formed in two lines from one Gate to the other the King and Party and escort riding between them, the people cheering as they passed along, at the first gate was the Laie Choir who greeted him as he came up with a Song composed for the ocasion." (Sarah Partridge, Journal, vol. 1, Oct. 6, 1883.)

249. Ernest Partridge was Sarah and Edward Partridge's teenage son. (See Edward Partridge, Journal, vol. 4, May 27, 1882; 1870 U.S. Census, Fillmore, Millard Co., Utah Territory, 335[B]; 1880 U.S. Census, Fillmore, Millard Co., Utah Territory, 464A.)

4.14 Eliza R. Snow, "To the Branches of the Relief Society," September 12, 1884

Eliza R. Snow, "To the Branches of the Relief Society," Sept. 12, 1884, Woman's Exponent *(Salt Lake City, UT), Sept. 15, 1884, vol. 13, no. 8, p. 61.*

Officers and members of different Relief Societies often wrote to general president Eliza R. Snow for guidance. When her responses were delayed or untimely, some women felt hurt. She explained to an impatient correspondent, "There was nothing in the letter in question that specifically demanded an answer, and I have so many letters that <u>must</u> be answered."[250] One solution was to respond through the *Woman's Exponent,* through which she could disseminate information not only to individual inquirers but to Relief Societies throughout the church. In the following *Exponent* article, Snow answered six questions regarding the administration of local Relief Societies.

TO THE BRANCHES OF THE RELIEF SOCIETY.

Being very frequently receiving letters of inquiry relative to duties, practices, privileges, etc., of officers and members of the Relief Society, and being unable to devote sufficient time to answer individually, we gladly accept the privilege extended by Mrs. Wells[251] to respond in general manner through the columns of the Exponent.

"Should a president of teachers be appointed in each branch?"

It is better for small branches not to appoint a president. In those, the teachers should report in the general meetings, and keep no separate minutes. In every branch the president of the organization virtually presides over the teachers; and presidents of teachers are needed only in those branches where there is such accumulation of work as to render it necessary to relieve the presiding board.

"Should the teachers' minutes be read in the general meetings?"

All members who attend meeting should be made acquainted with and have a voice in all business transactions of importance in both departments. No "change has been made" in this respect.[252]

"Is it right for the sisters to raffle?"

---

250. Eliza R. Snow to Wilmirth East, Apr. 23, 1883, Eliza R. Snow, Letters, 1883–1884, CHL, underlining in original.

251. Emmeline B. Wells edited the *Woman's Exponent* from 1877 to 1914. (See Document 3.21.)

252. For information on the history of visiting teaching in early Utah, see Document 3.9; and Jill Mulvay Derr et al., *Women of Covenant: The Story of Relief Society* (Salt Lake City: Deseret Book; Provo, UT: Brigham Young University Press, 1992), 91–92.

We say emphatically, No! Raffle is only a modified name of gamble. President Brigham Young once said to me, "Tell the sisters not to raffle; if the mothers raffle, their children will gamble. Raffling is gambling."

Some say, "What shall we do? We have quilts on hand—we cannot sell them, and we need the means to supply our treasury, which we can obtain by raffling, for the benefit of the poor." Rather let the quilts rot on the shelves than adopt the old adage: "The end will sanctify the means." As Latter-day Saints, we cannot afford to sacrifice moral principle to financial gain.

Let us investigate the subject—Supposing an article, quilt or other property, is put up for raffle: twenty persons donate 25 cents each; all hope to draw the prize, and only one wins, while nineteen who have each contributed as much as the successful one, gain nothing but disappointment, which is almost certain to arouse feelings of jealousy to a greater or less extent.

Why not all donate 25 cents each to replenish the treasury, as well as to run the chances and only one succeed? And then by mutual consent donating the article or articles in question to some charitable purpose, they prevent the cause of jealousy and dissension—the same amount will go to the treasury and no unworthy example and no sacrifice of principle will stain their record.

"Should members of the Relief Society go to the Bishops for counsel?"[253]

The Relief Society is designed to be a self-governing organization: to relieve the Bishops as well as to relieve the poor, to deal with its members, correct abuses, etc. If difficulties arise between members of a branch which they cannot settle between the members themselves, aided by the teachers, instead of troubling the Bishop, the matter should be referred to their president and her counselors. If the branch board cannot decide satisfactorily, an appeal to the stake board is next in order; if that fails to settle the question, the next step brings it before the general board, from which the only resort is to the Priesthood; but, if possible, we should relieve the Bishops instead of adding to their multitudinous labors.

"Is it necessary for sisters to be set apart to officiate in the sacred ordinances of washing anointing, and laying on of hands in administering to the sick?"[254]

---

253. In 1868, when many Relief Societies were being organized, Snow stated, "No Society can overstep the counsel of its Bishop—his word is law, to which, all its doings are amenable." In an 1883 letter she reiterated this position: "But the R.S. is subject to the Bishop of the Ward, we never go in opposition to the Priesthood." (Document 3.6; Eliza R. Snow, Salt Lake City, Utah Territory, to Wilmirth East, Apr. 23, 1883, Eliza R. Snow, Letters, CHL.)

254. This refers both to performing healing blessings and to the practice of blessing pregnant women, or "washing and anointing sisters who are approaching their confinement," not the similarly named temple ordinances. (Document 4.19.)

It certainly is not.[255] Any and all sisters who honor their holy endowments, not only have the right, but should feel it a duty, whenever called upon to administer to our sisters in these ordinances, which God has graciously committed to His daughters as well as to His sons; and we testify that when administered and received in faith and humility they are accompanied with all mighty power.

Inasmuch as God our Eather [Father] has revealed these sacred ordinances and committed them to His Saints, it is not only our privilege but our imperative duty to apply them for the relief of human suffering. We think we may safely say thousands can testify that God has sanctioned the administration of these ordinances by our sisters with the manifestations of His healing influence.[256]

"What age is most suitable for young lady officers?"

The young should fill all official positions in the Young Ladies' branch (ward) Associations. No matter how unequal they feel to the situation, if they possess sufficient energy of character and the true spirit of the Gospel, trust in God, they will be sure to succeed.

E. R. SNOW SMITH.

Salt Lake City, September 12th., 1884.

---

255. On some occasions, church leaders had set apart women to administer to the sick. For instance, on May 5, 1867, Wilford Woodruff recorded, "At the Close of the Meeting Presidet Young with Some of the Twelve laid hands upon the Head of Mother Atwood & blessed her & set her apart to administer to the Sick of her sex." Susanna Smith Adams, a Relief Society leader in Washington County, Utah, "was set apart [in 1854] by Apostle Geo. A. Smith to wait upon her sex in sickness." (Wilford Woodruff, Journals, 1833–1898, Wilford Woodruff, Journals and Papers, 1828–1898, CHL, May 5, 1867; "Death of a Heroine," *Woman's Exponent*, Mar. 1, 1892, 20:127.)

256. The First Presidency apparently did not agree with the position expressed by Snow in these two paragraphs (regarding female administrations) or in response to the prior question (about going to bishops for counsel). Franklin D. Richards's diary entry for September 26, 1884, states, "Prest. Taylor, Cannon, Woodruff, Carrington & myself met with sister Eliza Roxy Snow Smith in Gardo house & corrected her views as contained in W. Exponant of Sept. 15–84, page 91, Questions 4 & 5." (Franklin D. Richards, Journal, 1844–1899, Richards Family Collection, 1837–1961, CHL, Sept. 26, 1884, underlining in original.)

4.15 *"Mormon" Women's Protest*, 1886 (Excerpt)

"Mormon" Women's Protest. An Appeal for Freedom, Justice and Equal Rights. The Ladies of the Church of Jesus Christ of Latter-day Saints Protest against the Tyranny and Indecency of Federal Officials in Utah, and against Their Own Disfranchisement without Cause. Full Account of Proceedings at the Great Mass Meeting, Held in the Theatre, Salt Lake City Utah, Saturday, March 6, 1886 ([Salt Lake City]: Deseret News Co., n.d. [1886]), pp. [ii], 8–10, 17–19, 21–23 (excerpt).

On March 2, 1886, the *Deseret Evening News* announced that a mass meeting would be held four days later in Salt Lake City "for the purpose of making known the grievances of the women of Utah, and protesting against the indignities that have been heaped upon them in the present anti-'Mormon' crusade."[257]

These Latter-day Saint women met to protest the Edmunds Act, a federal statute signed into law in March 1882 that disenfranchised participants in plural marriage, created a new category of crime for "unlawful cohabitation" to make prosecutions for polygamy easier, and provided for fines and imprisonment for participants in plural marriage.[258] Increasingly rigorous federal enforcement of the Edmunds Act caused intense tumult in territorial Utah. As one legal historian explains, "By the mid-1880s the territorial courts were awash in indictments, arraignments, trials, and appeals. The gradually accelerating pace of legal process defined the course of events in Utah, affecting all aspects of life."[259] The women's protest was also directed at the Edmunds-Tucker Bill then pending in Congress, which proposed to take even more drastic measures to end plural marriage than had the Edmunds Act. When this bill became law in 1887, it placed most of the church's property and financial holdings into receivership and disenfranchised all Utah women regardless of church membership or any participation in plural marriage.

On the afternoon of Saturday, March 6, 1886, an estimated two thousand individuals, including some men, assembled for the protest meeting in the Salt Lake Theatre.[260] The meeting consisted primarily of addresses by Latter-day Saint women and the formal adoption of nine resolutions.[261] Among other things, the resolutions objected to the proposed repeal of Utah women's right to vote under the Edmunds-Tucker Bill, the prosecution of antipolygamy laws in the district courts, and the compelling of wives to testify against their husbands. The ninth resolution called upon the women of the United States to "come to our help in resisting these encroachments upon our liberties and these outrages upon our

257. "Mass Meeting," *Deseret Evening News*, Mar. 2, 1886, [3]; "The Ladies' Mass Meeting," *Deseret News* [weekly], Mar. 10, 1886, 119.

258. An Act . . . in Reference to Bigamy, and For Other Purposes [Mar. 22, 1882], *Statutes of the United States of America, Passed at the First Session of the Forty-Seventh Congress, 1881–'82* (Washington DC: Government Printing Office, 1882), 47th Cong., 1st Sess., chap. 47, pp. 30–32.

259. Sarah Barringer Gordon, *The Mormon Question: Polygamy and Constitutional Conflict in Nineteenth-Century America*, Studies in Legal History (Chapel Hill and London: University of North Carolina Press, 2002), 155.

260. For reports of the meeting, see "The Ladies' Mass Meeting," *Woman's Exponent*, Mar. 1, 1886, 14:148–149; and "The Ladies' Mass Meeting," *Woman's Exponent*, Mar. 15, 1886, 14:157–160.

261. *"Mormon" Women's Protest*, iii.

peaceful homes and family relations." A month earlier, the *Woman's Exponent* reprinted a January 1886 article from the *Woman's Journal,* the newspaper of the American Woman Suffrage Association, that similarly urged its readers to oppose a bill then moving its way through Congress which proposed to deprive "the women of Utah of that suffrage which is theirs by long-settled law and practice."[262]

At the end of the protest meeting, a committee formed to compose a memorial for Congress. The memorial included the resolutions adopted in the meeting, cited examples of officers infringing on citizens' rights in their zeal to enforce the Edmunds Act, and ended with an appeal: "We plead for suspension of all measures calculated to deprive us of our political rights and privileges, and to harass, annoy and bring our people into bondage and distress, until a commission, duly and specially authorized to make full inquiry into the affairs of this Territory, have investigated and reported."[263]

Emmeline B. Wells and Ellen B. Ferguson personally delivered the memorial in Washington DC to Congress and President Grover Cleveland. Wells noted, "I walked into the White House . . . where we sat about an hour and a quarter waiting our turn to speak to the President of the United States. Shortly after twelve o'clock we presented to him our credentials and the Memorial of the women of Utah Territory, and had an opportunity of stating to him some facts and incidents relating to the abuses and outrages perpetrated in the name of *law.*"[264] Senator Henry W. Blair, a Republican from New Hampshire, presented the memorial before the Senate on April 6, 1886, asking that it be printed in the *Congressional Record.*[265]

The Utah women also published a ninety-one-page pamphlet, from which excerpts are included below, that printed all of the speeches prepared for the grievance meeting, including some that were not delivered because of lack of time. "The aim of this pamphlet," the compilers wrote, was "to preserve in convenient form, for present use and future reference, the record of the proceedings of that memorable day when the 'Mormon' women, in mass meeting assembled, found it necessary for their own protection and the honor of their sex throughout the world, to memorialize Congress and the President of the United States for relief from insult and oppression at the hands of Federal officials."[266]

———— ❧ ————

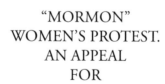

"MORMON"
WOMEN'S PROTEST.
AN APPEAL
FOR

---

262. Hamilton Willcox, "The Utah Women," *Woman's Exponent,* Feb. 15, 1886, 14:138.

263. *"Mormon" Women's Protest,* 47–48, 80–91.

264. "'The Rotunda'—Kirtland—The 'Memorial,'" *Woman's Exponent,* Apr. 15, 1886, 14:169, italics in original.

265. See Emmeline B. Wells, "From a Lady Delegate," *Deseret Evening News,* Apr. 21, 1886; and *Congressional Record: Containing the Proceedings and Debates of the Forty-Ninth Congress, First Session; Also, Special Session of the Senate* (Washington DC: Government Printing Office, 1886), vol. 17, pp. 3137–3138.

266. *"Mormon" Women's Protest,* iv.

FREEDOM, JUSTICE AND EQUAL RIGHTS.

The Ladies of the Church of Jesus Christ of Latter-day Saints protest against the tyranny and indecency of Federal Officials in Utah, and against their own disfranchisement without cause.

Full Account of Proceedings at the Great Mass Meeting, held in the Theatre,

SALT LAKE CITY UTAH,

Saturday, March 6, 1886. [p. [ii]] . . .[267]

PRESIDENT M. ISABELLA HORNE[268]

Made the opening address and stated the object of the meeting. She expressed the regrets of Mrs. Eliza R. Snow Smith, president of the women's organizations of the Latter-day Saints, who was absent from the city and unable to be present, but said that she had received a letter from that lady stating that she was heart and soul in the movement of the hour.[269] The speaker continued:

It is with peculiar feelings that I stand before you this afternoon. To think that, in this boasted land of liberty, there is any need for a meeting of this kind to protest against insult and injury from those who have sworn to administer the law with justice and equity. It has been said by some, "what good will it do to hold a mass meeting?"[270] If it does no other good, it will be a matter of history, to be handed down to our posterity, that their mothers rose up in the dignity of their womanhood to protest against insults and indignities heaped upon them. It will also be written in the archives above, where "angels are silent notes taking,"[271] and will have to be met by those persons who are waging this bitter crusade against us. And why should we, a few people in these valleys of the mountains, be subject to these insults aside from the rest of the commonwealth? Why should we have legislative enactments against us as a people because we obey the laws of God and the first commandment given, "to multiply and replenish

---

267. TEXT: The ellipsis points in this excerpt have been supplied by the editors of this volume to indicate omissions from the original document.

268. Horne was a member of the committee that called the protest meeting and was elected chair of the meeting. (*"Mormon" Women's Protest,* 5, 6.)

269. Snow was quite ill during March and April 1886, as indicated in Weber Stake Primary Association Minutes and Records, 1879–1968, CHL, Minutes, Mar. 20, 1886; and Third Ward, Liberty Stake, Primary Association Minutes and Records, 1879–1966, CHL, Minutes, Apr. 30, 1886.

270. Latter-day Saint women had held several such protest meetings, beginning as early as 1870. (See, for example, Documents 3.12 and 3.13.)

271. Hymn 151, "Do What Is Right," *Sacred Hymns and Spiritual Songs. For the Church of Jesus Christ of Latter-day Saints,* 14th ed. (Salt Lake City: George Q. Cannon, 1871), 165.

the earth."[272] Congress might with more propriety legislate against the priests and nuns of the Catholic church who forbid to marry, for if their practices were universal where would the strength and perpetuity of our nation be?

We as a people do not believe in taking the law in our own hands; it is against the teachings of our Prophet and Seer and our present authorities. The Lord has marked out a course of action for this people. It is written in the book of [p. 8] Doctrine and Covenants that when our enemies persecute and oppress us, we should petition the judges; if they will not hear us, we should petition the governor, and if he will not hear us, we should petition the president.[273] To my own personal knowledge this counsel was obeyed by the Prophet Joseph Smith, who went himself with some of his brethren to the governor of Illinois, Governor Carlin, and the president of the United States, Martin VanBuren, asking that our wrongs of Missouri be redressed. The answer was, "Mr. Smith, your cause is just, but I can do nothing for you."[274] Is it any wonder that the Prophet was led to exclaim, "the glory of American freedom is on the wane."[275] We have been persecuted and driven from our homes a number of times, and submitted without retaliation, for the Lord has said, "vengeance is mine, and I will repay."[276]

Must we, women of the Church of Jesus Christ of Latter-day Saints, still submit to insults and injury without raising our voices against it? And why are we thus persecuted? Because we choose to unite ourselves to honorable, God-fearing men, who, in virtue, honor, integrity and faithfulness to the marriage vow, stand head and shoulders above Federal officials who ply our brethren with questions regarding their future conduct, which is without precedent in the

---

272. Genesis 1:28.

273. Doctrine and Covenants 101:85–89.

274. On November 29, 1839, Joseph Smith and Elias Higbee met with Van Buren seeking redress for Mormon losses in Missouri. According to Smith's history, Van Buren said, "What can I do? I can do nothing for you!— if I do any thing I shall come in contact with the whole state of Missouri." The history adds, "Before we left him, he promised to reconsider what he had said, and observed that he felt to sympathise with us on account of our sufferings." (Joseph Smith et al., History, 1838–1856, vols. A-1–F-1 [original], A-2–E-2 [fair copy], CHL, vol. C-1, 988.)

275. "No honest man can doubt for a moment, but the glory of American liberty, is on the wane; and, that calamity and confusion will sooner or later, destroy the peace of the people." (Joseph Smith, *General Smith's Views of the Powers and Policy of the Government of the United States* [Nauvoo, IL: John Taylor, 1844], 8.)

276. Romans 12:19.

annals of court proceedings.[277] We all feel the insults offered our sisters when brought into court and forced to answer indecent questions by threats of fine and imprisonment.[278] And we do most solemnly protest against further legislative enactments to disfranchise a whole community, who have committed no crime, only for religious belief.

It has been said by the chief executive of the nation, "I wish you could be like us."[279] And what is that? They marry one wife and degrade as many women as they choose. God forbid that we should descend to their level! We believe in the elevation of woman, and live on a higher plane. Our husbands marry wives and honor them and their children by [p. 9] giving them their names and acknowledging them in society. We are not surprised that we are persecuted for obeying the laws of God, for our Savior has said, "it must needs be that offenses come, but woe be to them by whom they come."[280]

At the close of the president's address,[281] a motion was made by Dr. Romania B. Pratt that a committee on resolutions be appointed.

---

277. Following conviction, many Latter-day Saint men continued to state their support for plural marriage. For instance, a federal judge asked Henry Gale, after his conviction for unlawful cohabitation, "whether the defendant had any promises to make as to his future behavior." Gale, an aged resident of Beaver, responded "he had obeyed the word of the Lord, that he therefore, had no promises to make." ("Doings of Deputies," *Salt Lake Herald,* Dec. 19, 1885, 8; see also, for example, Ken Driggs, "The Prosecutions Begin: Defining Cohabitation in 1885," *Dialogue: A Journal of Mormon Thought* 21, no. 1 [Spring 1988]: 117.)

278. For instance, Eliza Shafer and other witnesses were asked if Shafer ever occupied the same bed as her alleged husband, J. W. Snell. Lucy Devereux was asked before a grand jury, "After you went to live at Newsom's house did you not occupy the same bed with him?" (*"Mormon" Women's Protest,* 85; "The Snell Case," *Deseret News* [weekly], Aug. 19, 1885, 489; "The Case of Lucy Devereux," *Deseret News* [weekly], June 17, 1885, 344.)

279. In May 1885 a delegation of Latter-day Saint leaders presented a list of grievances to President Grover Cleveland. In the discussion, Cleveland reportedly said, "I wish you out there could be like the rest of us," a statement that Mormons interpreted as hostile to their practice of plural marriage. ("Report," *Deseret News* [weekly], June 3, 1885, 316–317; see also Erastus Snow, May 31, 1885, in *Journal of Discourses,* 26 vols. [Liverpool: Various publishers, 1855–1886], 26:220–221; and Eliza R. Snow, "That Loathsome Ulcer—What Is It?" *Deseret News* [weekly], July 28, 1886, 435.)

280. See Luke 17:1.

281. As compared to the preceding account of Horne's address, the report published earlier in the *Woman's Exponent* is briefer and has some portions that are differently worded. Horne presumably revised and expanded the address for publication in pamphlet form. The *Exponent* account reads:

"Prest. M. I. Horne expressed the regrets of Mrs. Eliza R. Snow Smith at not being able to be present, but stated that she was heart and soul in the movement.

"Prest. Horne said it was with feelings of sorrow that she contemplated the occasion which called forth the necessity for a protest against the wrongs heaped upon 'Mormon' men and women, because of their obedience to the law of God. The nation could with more consistency legislate against the Catholics for their belief in celibacy than against the 'Mormons' for obeying the first great commandment, 'Be

The motion having prevailed, the following named ladies were appointed as that committee: Romania B. Pratt, Fanny Thatcher and Edna Smith, of Salt Lake City; Jennie Tanner, of Provo, and H. [Harriet] C. Brown, of Ogden. The committee retired to prepare the resolutions. . . . [p. 10] . . .

Here the committee on resolutions re-entered and reported the following, which was read by the secretary, and unanimously and enthusiastically adopted:

PREAMBLE AND RESOLUTIONS OF THE WOMEN OF UTAH IN MASS
MEETING ASSEMBLED.

Whereas, The rights and liberties of women are placed in jeopardy by the present cruel and inhuman proceedings in the Utah courts, and in the contemplated measure in Congress to deprive the women voters in Utah of the elective franchise;[282] and,

Whereas, Womanhood is outraged by the compulsion used in the courts of Utah to force mothers on pain of imprisonment to disclose their personal condition and that of their friends in relation to anticipated maternity, and to give information as to the fathers of their children; and,

Whereas, These violations of decency have now reached the length of compelling legal wives to testify against their husbands without their consent, in violation both of written statutes and the provisions of the common law, therefore, be it [p. 17]

Resolved, By the women of Utah in mass meeting assembled, that the suffrage originally conferred upon us as a political privilege, has

---

fruitful and multiply.' It was a duty of the Saints to appeal to rulers, and if disregarded God would avenge them. President Van Buren had told the Prophet Joseph his cause was just, but the nation could do nothing for his people, and the nation had been vexed ever since. Men were now sent to jail because they would not promise to renounce their wives and children, and the women of the Latter-day Saints could not longer submit in peace to this, and to the insults offered their sisters in the courts. They could not longer go on without protesting against continued adverse legislation. They could not come down to the level of those who degraded women, but would continue in the service of God, and trust in Him." ("The Ladies' Mass Meeting," *Woman's Exponent,* Mar. 1, 1886, 14:148.)

282. Women in territorial Utah received the vote on February 12, 1870. In 1882 the Edmunds Act disenfranchised women that were plural wives. The 1887 Edmunds-Tucker Act stripped the right to vote from all the women of Utah. (Documents 3.14 and 3.17; An Act to Amend Section Fifty-Three Hundred and Fifty-Two of the Revised Statutes of the United States, in Reference to Bigamy, and for Other Purposes [Mar. 22, 1882], *The Statutes at Large of the United States of America, from December, 1881, to March, 1883,* vol. 22 [Washington DC: Government Printing Office, 1883], 47th Cong., 1st Sess., ch. 47, pp. 30–32; An Act to Amend an Act Entitled "An Act . . . in Reference to Bigamy, and For Other Purposes" . . . [Mar. 3, 1887], *Statutes of the United States of America, Passed at the First Session of the Forty-Ninth Congress, 1885–1886* [Washington DC: Government Printing Office, 1886], 49th Cong., 2nd Sess., chap. 397, p. 639, sec. 20.)

become a vested right by possession and usage for fifteen years, and that we protest against being deprived of that right without process of law, and for no other reason than that we do not vote to suit our political opponents.[283]

Resolved, That we emphatically deny the charge that we vote otherwise than according to our own free choice, and point to the fact that the ballot is absolutely secret in Utah as proof that we are protected in voting for whom and what we choose with perfect liberty.

Resolved, That as no wife of a polygamist, legal or plural, is permitted to vote under the laws of the United States, to deprive non-polygamous women of the suffrage is high-handed oppression for which no valid excuse can be offered.

Resolved, That the questions concerning their personal condition, the relationship they bear to men marked down as victims to special law, and the paternity of their born and unborn children, which have been put to women before grand juries and in open courts in Utah, are an insult to pure womanhood, an outrage upon the sensitive feelings of our sex and a disgrace to officers and judges who have propounded and enforced them.[284]

Resolved, That we honor those noble women who, standing upon their rights and refusing to reply to improper and insulting questions, such as no true man nor any court with any regard for propriety would compel them to answer, have gone to prison and suffered punishment without crime,[285] rather than betray the most sacred confidence and yield to the brutal mandates of a little brief authority.

---

283. On February 19, 1886, Vermont senator George F. Edmunds, a prominent sponsor of anti-polygamy legislation, wrote to woman suffragists in New York, "If you and your associates understood the state of things in Utah, I am sure you would support instead of opposing the provision to relieve the women of Utah from the degradation of voting as their Mormon masters require." The Woman Suffrage Party responded that this accusation was incorrect: "Under the effect of political liberty many Mormon women are now beginning to speak out against polygamy." ("Senator Edmunds Scored by a Woman," *Deseret News* [semi-weekly], Mar. 8, 1886, [2].)

284. The actions of federal judges in Utah went too far even for some opponents of polygamy. An editorial in the *Sacramento Daily Record-Union* asked, "Why was it necessary to plunge Belle Harris into prison and refuse her bail, in order to ascertain who is the father of her several children? The woman has exhibited courage in a bad cause, that nevertheless excites respect coupled with pity. We fear our Gentile friends in Utah lack discretion in their zeal." ("The Belle Harris Case," *Sacramento Daily Record-Union*, May 22, 1883, [2].)

285. For instance, Nellie White was imprisoned from May 22 to July 9, 1884, for failure to answer questions put to her by the grand jury. (See "Committed for Contempt," *Deseret News* [weekly], May 28, 1884, 297; "Nellie White," and "Nellie White Is Free," *Deseret News* [weekly], July 16, 1884, 401, 408;

Resolved, That the action of the District Attorney and the Chief Justice of Utah, in compelling a lawful wife to testify for the prosecution in a criminal case involving the liberty of her husband and in face of her own earnest protest, is [p. 18] a violation of laws which those officials have sworn to uphold, is contrary to precedent and usage for many centuries, and is an invasion of family rights and of that union between husband and wife which both law and religion have held sacred from time immemorial.[286]

Resolved, That we express our profound appreciation of the moral courage exhibited by Senators [Wilkinson] Call, [John] Morgan, [Henry] Teller, [Joseph] Brown and others,[287] and also by Mrs. Belva H. [Ann Bennett] Lockwood,[288] who, in the face of almost overwhelming prejudice, have defended the constitutional rights of the people of Utah.

Resolved, That we extend our heartfelt thanks to the ladies of the Woman Suffrage Association assembled in Boston, and unite in praying that God may speed the day when both men and women shall shake from their shoulders the yoke of tyranny.[289]

Resolved, That we call upon the wives and mothers of the United States to come to our help in resisting these encroachments upon our

---

"Mormon" Women's Protest, 85; see also "Just Compare the Two Cases," *Deseret News* [weekly], May 23, 1883, 280.)

286. "The basis for the rule was that the husband and wife were a unity in the eyes of the law, and since the litigant spouse was incompetent to testify because of interest, the other spouse was also considered incompetent." However, for Latter-day Saints to invoke the common law protection would have required establishing the marital relationship, the very thing that the prosecution wanted. ("The Husband-Wife Evidentiary Privilege in Criminal Proceedings," *Journal of Criminal Law and Criminology* 52, no. 1 [May–June 1961]: 74n2.)

287. Wilkinson Call, Democrat from Florida; John Tyler Morgan, Democrat from Alabama; Henry Moore Teller, Republican from Colorado; and Joseph Emerson Brown, Democrat from Georgia. These senators had opposed the pending Edmunds-Tucker Bill. (See remarks of Call, Brown, and Morgan in *Congressional Record: Containing the Proceedings and Debates of the Forty-Eighth Congress, First Session* [Washington DC: Government Printing Office, 1884], vol. 15, pp. 5182–5183, 5190–5191, 5240, 5281–5290; see also "The Attack on Senator Teller," and "Tellers' Defamers," *Deseret News* [weekly], Jan. 27, 1886, 23, 25.)

288. Lockwood, the first female attorney to argue a case before the U.S. Supreme Court, was a committed suffragist and had reservations about the constitutionality of the Edmunds Act of 1882. Lockwood argued that the Edmunds Act was "unjust and inquisitorial" and "a blow at woman suffrage and only a fool or knave would deny it." (See Lola Van Wagenen, "Sister-Wives and Suffragists: Polygamy and the Politics of Woman Suffrage, 1870–1896," Dissertations in Latter-day Saint History [Provo, UT: Joseph Fielding Smith Institute for Latter-day Saint History; BYU Studies, 2003], 120–121.)

289. Probably a reference to the American Woman Suffrage Association, headquartered in Boston. The organization's official newspaper, the *Woman's Journal*, consistently opposed disenfranchisement of Utah women. (See Van Wagenen, "Sister-Wives and Suffragists," 58; see also, for example, Hamilton Willcox, "The Utah Women," *Woman's Exponent*, Feb. 15, 1886, 14:138; Hamilton Willcox, "Amend the Utah Bill," *Woman's Journal*, Feb. 20, 1886, 60; and Editorial, *Woman's Journal*, Mar. 27, 1886, 97.)

liberties and these outrages upon our peaceful homes and family relations, and that a committee be appointed at this meeting to memorialize the President and Congress of the United States in relation to our wrongs, and to take all necessary measures to present our views and feelings to the country.[290] . . . [p. 19] . . .

Miss Nellie Colebrook then read, in a very spirited manner, the following poem, written for the occasion by Emily Hill Woodmansee:

GIVE THE "MORMONS" THEIR RIGHTS.

In behalf of the "Mormons" the following address is respectfully submitted to every lover of freedom and fair play in the United States of America; also to the members of the House of Representatives, and of the Senate, and to all honest hearted people elsewhere.

> Must the "Mormons" be mute, when compassion is weeping?
> And sorrows unnumbered are right at our door?
> Should "the daughter of Zion"[291] be quietly sleeping—
> As if the dark day of her bondage were o'er?
> Our wrongs and our cares—must we welcome as sweet?
> Or walk into snares that are laid for our feet? [p. 21]
>
> Like a whirlwind approaching, vile laws now are pending,
> If passed, all the pillars of freedom will shake;
> "Our cause is most just," yet it claims such defending;
> "The women of Mormondom" needs must awake.
> Thus, we humbly petition Columbia's nation,
> To frown on oppression, and harsh legislation.
>
> Our foes trouble little, or nothing to mention,
> For "poor Mormon women," or "down-trodden wives."
> Were polygamy only the bone of contention,
> The "Mormons" might vote all the rest of their lives.
> Our foes may not count us smart, sensible folks;
> But we see through their purpose—contempt it provokes.
>
> We prize not their pity, whose aim is to plunder
> A people who strictly to peace are inclined;

290. The memorial to be sent to the president and Congress included several accounts of Mormon women's experiences in the district courts of Utah. (*"Mormon" Women's Protest,* 84–88.)

291. See Isaiah 62:11; and Zechariah 9:9.

If the "Mormons" lose patience need any one wonder,
    Who considers our wrongs, by the crafty designed.
Yet they'll harvest disgrace where they hope for renown,
Who for power or place thrust the innocent down.

We appeal to the people in freedom's dominions—
    To the fair-minded millions who love what is right;
Must the "Mormons" be robbed for their faith and opinions—
    Crush'd and ground, 'twixt the millstones of greed and of spite?
Is it needful or lawful to wrest freedom from us
For what we believe, or for what we can't promise?

Our honor is priceless, our rights are all precious,
    Our affections are sacred, our households are dear;
Our husbands are heroes, in spite of the specious
    And wonderful (?) rulings of judges so queer,
Who shift their decisions, around and around,
Till for "Mormons" a verdict of "guilty" is found.

"The world loves its own,"[292] but it "hates us," and fights us,
    Our rights are withheld, and our friends are in prison;
Yet, we never are comfortless, always, the righteous
    "Through much tribulation"[293] to glory have risen.
Let the spirit of fairness, quench bigotry's fire;
Then, the "Mormons" will reap all the praise they desire. [p. 22]

Foretold was our fate, of a truth "men revile us,"[294]
    And the meanest of motives, our foes thus disguise;
Their black-hearted falsehoods will fail to defile us,
    But the masses are misled by plausible lies.
Alas! that such libels so stript of the truth;
Are read more than Bibles, by thousands forsooth.[295]

---

292. John 15:19.

293. Acts 14:22.

294. Matthew 5:11.

295. Both purported exposés of Mormon polygamy and novels about it found large audiences. For instance, J. H. Beadle's *Life in Utah; or, The Mysteries and Crimes of Mormonism. Being an Exposé of the Secret Rites and Ceremonies of the Latter-day Saints, with a Full and Authentic History of Polygamy and the Mormon Sect from Its Origin to the Present Time* (Philadelphia: National, 1870) went through multiple printings, including in German and Russian. An announcement in a publisher's dummy for Beadle's next book claimed that *Life in Utah* had "reached the enormous sale of over 70,000 copies, and was everywhere warmly endorsed by the press and public." Another popular work was Cornelia Paddock's *The Fate of*

If the vex'd "Mormon problem," must have a solution,
    'Tis time something nobler than hate should be tried;
Sure, the "Mormons" have suffer'd enough persecution,
    Yet sustained by their faith, they have lived, they have thrived.
The more they are slander'd, and hunted and driven—
The more they are prosper'd, and favor'd of heaven.

Praise! Surely is due to the stout hearted exiles—
    Who rescu'd from barrenness Utah's broad vales;
Who built all the bridges, and leveled the ridges
    And braved all the hardships such settling entails.
God bless our endeavor; He rescues us ever,
Though ev'ry things fails, shall we doubt Him? No never.

Our homage we yield to the Lord, our defender,
    For manifold mercies, what less can we do?
"To Caesar" the "Mormons" submissively render
    Whatsoever is just, whatsoever is due.[296]
But to those who would crush us or fleece us by law,
We can't for the life of us kneel down in awe.

To statesmen we turn, yea, we ask for protection,
    In the land that with blood, was from tyranny freed;
Must the "Mormons" to-day be the only exception
    To the hosts who can honor their conscience indeed?
Oh ye, whose brave fathers scaled freedom's proud heights
Concede to the "Mormons" their God-given rights. . . . [p. 23] . . .

Madame la Tour: A Tale of Great Salt Lake (New York: Fords, Howard, and Hulbert, 1881). This book was still being printed as late as 1900, with one printing done in Danish. (J. H. Beadle, *The Undeveloped West; or, Five Years in the Territories* [Philadelphia: National, ca. 1873], publisher's dummy, copy at CHL; Chad J. Flake and Larry W. Draper, eds., *A Mormon Bibliography, 1830–1930: Books, Pamphlets, Periodicals, and Broadsides Relating to the First Century of Mormonism,* 2 vols., 2nd ed. [Provo, UT: Religious Studies Center, Brigham Young University, 2004], 1:49–50; 2:47.)
    296. See Matthew 22:17–21.

4.16 Eliza R. Snow, Letter to Salt Lake Stake Relief Society, December 9, 1886

Eliza R. Snow, "To the Officers and Members of the Relief Society of the Salt Lake Stake of Zion, in Conference Assembled; President M. I. Horne Presiding," Dec. [9], 1886; Relief Society General Board Minutes, 1886–1911, vol. 3, 1906–1911, p. 245, CHL (CR 11 182).

As Eliza R. Snow advanced in age, her health declined and her visits to local Relief Society, Young Ladies' Mutual Improvement Association, and Primary Association meetings decreased. She continued to maintain contact with Relief Societies through letters, such as the one below that was read at the quarterly conference of the Salt Lake Stake Relief Society held on December 9, 1886, and then published with the meeting minutes in the *Woman's Exponent*.[297] In her letter Snow encouraged the Relief Society women to "see beyond the dark cloud that rises before us, and rejoice in prospect of the blessing that comes after the tribulation." This was a reference to the antipolygamy crusade that was intensifying against the Latter-day Saints at the time.[298]

The transcript below was reproduced from a handwritten copy of the original letter that is affixed into a volume containing Relief Society general board minutes dated May 1906 to April 1911.

———— ⁊⸱ ————

To the Officers and Members of the Relief Society of the Salt Lake Stake of Zion, in Conference Assembled; President M. [Mary] I. Horne presiding:
Beloved Sisters,

Not anticipating the pleasure of being with you in person to-day, I feel that I shall be with you in spirit, and take the liberty to address you through the medium of pen, ink, and paper—very briefly, being aware that your time is very limited.

I thank our Heavenly Father that I am associated with you, not only in the precious and everlasting bonds of the ~~of the~~ glorious Gospel of the Prince of Peace, but also in the sacred, God-revealed organization of the Relief Society, which places us in position to accomplish more good, both temporally and spiritually than otherwise would be possible. The performing labors of love

---

297. "R. S., Y. L. M. I. A. & P. A. Reports," *Woman's Exponent,* Dec. 15, 1886, 15:110.

298. See Document 4.15. Eliza R. Snow's brother Lorenzo Snow, an apostle, was convicted of unlawful cohabitation in January 1886 and spent eleven months in prison, from March 1886 to February 1887. (See "More from Ogden," *Deseret Evening News,* Jan. 4, 1886, [2]; Franklin D. Richards, Journals, 1844–1899, Richards Family Collection, 1837–1961, CHL, Jan. 15, 1886; and Andrew Jenson, *Latter-day Saint Biographical Encyclopedia: A Compilation of Biographical Sketches of Prominent Men and Women in the Church of Jesus Christ of Latter-day Saints,* 4 vols. [Salt Lake City: Andrew Jenson History Co., 1901–1936], 1:29–30.)

and duty, relieving the wants of the poor—administering to the sick—lifting up those who are bowed down—strengthening the weak—encouraging the desponding—arousing the dormant, <u>etc</u>. <u>etc</u>., is productive of the purest and noblest pleasure enjoyed in mortal life.

May you, my Sisters, in this Conference, realize a copious refreshing from the presence of God. May the spirit of instruction, consolation, love, and union rest on those present—every heart be cheered, and each soul resolve anew to draw closer to God, and lean firmly on Him, that you may see beyond the dark cloud that rises before us, and rejoice in prospect of the blessing that comes after the tribulation. May the Holy Ghost, the Comforter be your constant companion, and you be enabled to acknowledge the hand of God in all things. What He will not overrule for the good of the Saints, He will avert.

Your Sister,

E. R. Snow Smith—

Thursday Morning, Dec. 8th [9th] 1886—[299]

---

299. Thursday fell on December 9. The version of the letter published in the *Exponent* has the correct date, December 9. ("R. S., Y. L. M. I. A. & P. A. Reports," *Woman's Exponent,* Dec. 15, 1886, 15:110.)

4.17 Emma Anderson Liljenquist, Reminiscences of 1887, in "The Story of My Life," circa 1948 (Excerpt)

Emma Anderson Liljenquist, "The Story of My Life," ca. 1948, pp. [1], 14–18 (excerpt); typescript; International Society Daughters of Utah Pioneers, Salt Lake City.

Latter-day Saints in Utah Territory often relied on midwives to treat health problems and deliver babies. As early as the 1850s, church leaders had noted the need for medical training for local midwives; by the 1870s, Brigham Young, Eliza R. Snow, and other church leaders were routinely emphasizing this need and encouraging Latter-day Saint women to obtain medical training.[300] In response, several Utah women attended medical colleges in the eastern United States and then returned to Utah to practice medicine. Many of these newly trained doctors taught courses in Salt Lake City for the benefit of women throughout the territory. Dr. Romania B. Pratt, for example, taught courses "in her office in the Old Constitution Building. The lectures will be given twice a week and the term will continue six months." Dr. Ellis R. Shipp advertised that she was "prepared to give instructions in the art of Midwifery and other branches connected therewith."[301] Midwifery classes were also offered in other settlements.[302]

Emma Anderson Liljenquist, a resident of Hyrum, a town eight miles south of Logan in Cache County, Utah, was in her mid-twenties when her bishop appointed her to study obstetrics and nursing in 1887. She accepted, leaving her husband and three children for six months while she studied in Salt Lake City with Dr. Margaret C. Shipp,[303] a graduate from the Woman's Medical College in Philadelphia. In spring 1885 the *Deseret News* had announced, "Dr. Maggie C. Shipp Will commence a class [in midwifery] on May 11th, at her office. Two lectures will be given every day, Saturdays excepted." Tuition and books were advertised at ten and thirteen dollars, respectively.[304] By the fall of 1888 Shipp had trained nearly forty women, including Emma Liljenquist, to work as nurses and obstetricians.[305] Liljenquist was expecting her fourth child when she graduated.[306]

---

300. See, for example, William France, "Medical," *Deseret News,* Apr. 18, 1855, 44; Document 3.23; and Document 4.11. For information on the Female Council of Health, see the introduction to Part 2.

301. "Class in Obstetrics," *Deseret News* [weekly], Apr. 30, 1879, 201; "Notice," *Deseret News* [weekly], Nov. 9, 1881, 656; "Home Affairs," *Woman's Exponent,* Apr. 1, 1883, 17:164–165; Annie W. Cannon, "The Women of Utah," *Woman's Exponent,* Sept. 1, 1888, 17:49–50.

302. See, for example, "Midwifery!" *Deseret News* [weekly], Nov. 1, 1871, 456.

303. Ellis and Margaret Shipp were both married to the same man and took turns attending medical school. (Gail Farr Casterline, "Ellis R. Shipp," in *Sister Saints,* ed. Vicky Burgess-Olson [Provo, UT: By the author, 1978], 369–372; Claudia L. Bushman, ed., *Mormon Sisters: Women in Early Utah,* new ed. [Logan: Utah State University Press, 1997], 60–61.)

304. "Editorial Notes," *Woman's Exponent,* Apr. 15, 1885, 13:172; "A Class in Midwifery," *Deseret News* [weekly], Apr. 15, 1885, 208.

305. Annie W. Cannon, "The Women of Utah," *Woman's Exponent,* Sept. 1, 1888, 17:49–50.

306. Liljenquist graduated from Shipp's course in March 1888. Clara Margretta Liljenquist was born May 19, 1888. ("Editorial Note," *Woman's Exponent,* Mar. 15, 1888, 16:157.)

Sometime in or after December 1948, Liljenquist completed an autobiography titled "The Story of My Life." The following excerpts from the autobiography give a glimpse into Liljenquist's activities as a Latter-day Saint mother and midwife. These excerpts are taken from a twenty-three-page typed version of the autobiography; little information is available about the creation or provenance of this typescript, but it appears to have been produced in or after 1952 from some earlier version.[307]

THE STORY OF MY LIFE
By
Emma Anderson Liljenquist . . . [p. [1]] . . .[308]

During the period of my 14th, 15th, and the beginning of my 16th years I kept quite steady company with [Olaf] Oscar Liljenquist, son of our Mayor and Bishop, O. [Ola] N. Liljenquist of Hyrum. At the age of 16, on December 25, I consented to be married but, of course, a girl of that age didn't sense the responsibility of married life as I never thought life was anything but a pleasure and so I entered into marriage at an early age never realizing what was ahead of me. . . . [p. 14]

We had been married two years without having any children and we were very concerned over this and decided to make it a thing of prayer and our prayers were answered with a fine son whom we called Oscar Eugene, born September 15, 1880. He was a very good baby and never cried and learned to sing before he could hardly talk. He would sing in all entertainments and was so little they had to stand him on a chair so he could be seen.

We lived and were happy with what little we had. . . .

---

307. On page 22 of the typescript autobiography excerpted here, Liljenquist mentioned an event that occurred in December 1948, thus placing the completion of the document in that month or thereafter. Attached to the autobiography is a final typed page (numbered 24) that gives information about Liljenquist's March 1952 funeral services. Since this final page is numbered in sequence with the autobiography and since the margins, type style and size, and ink density are consistent between the autobiography and this page 24, it seems probable that the typescript version of the autobiography was prepared in or after 1952 from some earlier version. At least three briefer versions of "The Story of My Life" are also extant, one at Utah State University in Logan, Utah, and two at the museum of the International Society Daughters of Utah Pioneers in Salt Lake City. The provenance of these briefer versions is also unclear. The account featured in the present volume has been used because it is more detailed regarding Liljenquist's activities as a midwife. (For the version at Utah State University, see Emma Anderson Liljenquist, "The Story of My Life," typescript, in William Mulder, "Scandinavian Contributions to Cache Valley and Utah," address given to the Cache Valley Historical Society, Apr. 25, 1956, in Papers and Proceedings of the Cache Valley Historical Society, vol. 5, 1955–1956, 5:254–278, Cache Valley Historical Society Papers, 1951–1962, 1983–2008, Special Collections and Archives, Merrill-Cazier Library, Utah State University, Logan.)

308. TEXT: The ellipsis points in this excerpt have been supplied by the editors of this volume to indicate omissions from the original document.

Emma Anderson Liljenquist. Church leaders often set apart midwives for this occupation. Trained and set apart as a midwife, Emma Liljenquist tended to numerous sick patients and estimated she had delivered over a thousand babies in Hyrum, Utah. (Courtesy International Society Daughters of Utah Pioneers, Salt Lake City.)

. . . [M]y second child was born on the 3rd of November 1882 at 12:00 o'clock noon. It was a lovely girl and we named her Mary Agnes. I was all alone when Agnes was born, grandma having taken Eugene and gone to visit the neighbors. Fortunately, my husband came home and he ran for the neighbor lady. Agnes, too, was a very good baby and Aunt Annie [Anna Anderson], father's second wife, would come down and tend the children. She would knit and rock the babies all the time and would make it possible for me to go to choir practice, theater rehearsals, etc. I had a neighbor lady who was such a comfort to me. Her name was Karen Christensen. She would help me make soap, milk the cow, and set the hens, and when it thundered and stormed she would come or I would go to her place. One day in the fall the little boy set fire to the straw stack and it burned it down along with the stable. We salvaged a setting hen and her eggs and all that day little chickens hatched. [p. 15]

On January 1, 1885, New Years Day, on grandma [Anna Christine] Liljenquist and grandma [Maren] Anderson's birthdays, my third child, Hyrum Royal, was born and he weighed 12 pounds. It was during the January thaw and it rained for two weeks. We lived in a log house with a dirt roof and the plaster fell down and made a deep bank of wet mud and plaster. . . .

[Approximately two years pass.]

It was during this period that I was called by the Church to take a course in obstetrics and nursing. I lived in Salt Lake for six months. Dr. Maggie C. Shipp, later married to B. [Brigham] H. Roberts, was the instructor. She lived just [p. 16] east of the Salt Lake Theater[309] on the corner and I lived with a Mrs. [Amelia] Jorgensen on 7th West and every day I walked to the doctor's office, except part time I lived with her. I never once took the street car. I enjoyed the course very much and after being set apart by apostles John Henry Smith and several of the others, I returned home to do my work and being promised by the apostles that if I lived right I should always know what to do in case of any difficulties.

That promise has been fulfilled to the very letter. Many times when one of my patients were seriously ill I have asked my Heavenly Father for assistance and in every case it was given to me. One in particular was a lady who had just given birth to a baby and hemorrhage set in. The husband called the doctor but he did not realize that it was so serious. I placed my hands upon her head and asked the Lord to help us.[310] The hemorrhage ceased and I did the necessary

---

309. The Salt Lake Theatre was located at the northwest corner of present-day State Street and 100 South.

310. On healing blessings given by women, see Document 4.19.

things for her. When the doctor arrived he said he could hardly believe what had happened but said I had done exactly what he would have done. I was so tired and worn out from so many nights out and loss of sleep and trying to maintain my own home. So I went up to Idaho to have a rest and stayed at my son Eugene's home. One day Eugene asked if I would like to ride with him to see his farm. While we were looking over the beautiful fields we saw a man coming toward us on a horse. My son said, "Mother, he is probably coming for you". And sure enough, he was. I went with him to his home where his wife gave birth to twin girls.

I wish that I could tell all of my wonderful experiences during my years as a midwife. Some of them are very touching and others humorous. But I have brought over one thousand babies to Hyrum. Once again I give thanks to my Heavenly Father for His help and the strength the Lord has given me, for without it I could not have rendered this service to my sisters of our community. One of the most touching things about a birth is that the mother's first concern is about her baby; not herself. . . . [p. 17] . . .

It made my heart ache when I had to leave my babies and very often I could hear them crying as I walked down the street, but I had to go with a smile on my face and bring happiness into the sick room for I have never refused anyone who needed my assistance. But my husband and my oldest daughter, Agnes, were very gentle and good to the children. You might ask why I left them, but I had been called by the Church to perform this service and I felt that it was a special calling. . . .

My family was growing[311] but I was still going out taking care of the sick. It was not always maternity cases which I attended. Sometimes an anxious mother called to see if I could treat one of her children, or someone else might have a nervous spell and would ask me if I would just come and sit by their bed and assure them that they were alright and all was well. One blustery January night one of our neighbors, Jonas Nielsen, knocked at our door and asked if I could come and attend to his wife, Augusta, my cousin. She gave birth to a baby boy (Gordon) and after spending the night and part of the next day with her, I came home and gave birth to my fourth little girl and sixth child. She had pretty brown hair and, like the rest, she was very sweet and good. We named her Anna Lillian after one of grandfather's wives [Anna Anderson] who had always been such a great help to me in caring for my children. She had had no children so she loved mine as though they were her own. . . . [p. 18] . . .

---

311. Liljenquist was the mother of nine children, six of whom she bore after she became a midwife.

4.18 Emmeline B. Wells, Letter to Zina D. H. Young, April 24, 1888

Emmeline B. Wells, Letter to Zina D. H. Young, Apr. 24, 1888; five pages; Zina Card Brown Family Collection, 1806–1972, CHL (MS 4780).

When the Relief Society general presidency was formally organized in Utah in 1880, Zina Diantha Huntington Young became the first counselor to President Eliza R. Snow. One history characterized Snow as "the head of the women's work," whereas "Aunt Zina was often said to be its heart."[312] Both women had been married to Joseph Smith and to his successor, Brigham Young.[313] Snow died in her room at the Lion House in Salt Lake City on December 5, 1887. Her funeral was held in the Assembly Hall on the temple block on December 7, 1887, and she was interred in Brigham Young's family cemetery.[314] Following Snow's death, Zina Young was sustained as general president of the Relief Society at the general conference held April 8, 1888.[315] At the conclusion of the conference, Young traveled to Cardston, Alberta, Canada, to be with her pregnant daughter, Zina Young Williams Card.

During this visit, Young received the following letter from Emmeline B. Wells, editor of the *Woman's Exponent.* Wells congratulated Young on her new assignment and assured her that she was also "the choice of the people." Wells also inquired about who had set Young apart as general president of the Relief Society. Young, however, had not been set apart before leaving for Canada. On October 11, soon after Young returned to Salt Lake City, apostles Wilford Woodruff, Joseph F. Smith, and Franklin D. Richards set her apart along with her counselors, Jane S. Richards and Bathsheba W. Smith, and Emmeline Wells as corresponding secretary.[316] Two additional secretaries and a treasurer rounded out the "Central presiding Board."[317] At the time of Young's appointment in 1888, there were twenty-two thousand Relief Society members attending more than four hundred wards and branches.[318]

———— ⁂ ————

312. Jill Mulvay Derr et al., *Women of Covenant: The Story of Relief Society* (Salt Lake City: Deseret Book; Provo, UT: Brigham Young University Press, 1992), 127.

313. Zina Diantha Huntington married Henry Bailey Jacobs on March 7, 1841, in Nauvoo. She was "married or sealed" to Joseph Smith on October 27, 1841. She married Brigham Young in 1846. (See Joseph F. Smith, Affidavits about Celestial Marriage, 1869–1915, CHL, Zina D. H. Young, Affidavit, Salt Lake Co., Utah Territory, May 1, 1869, 1:5.)

314. "Eliza Roxie Snow Smith," *Woman's Exponent,* Dec. 15, 1887, 16:108–110.

315. "April Conference 1888," *Woman's Exponent,* Apr. 15, 1888, 16:172.

316. Franklin D. Richards, Journals, 1844–1899, Richards Family Collection, 1837–1961, CHL, Oct. 11, 1888; "Relief Society Central Board," *Woman's Exponent,* Oct. 15, 1888, 17:76.

317. Sarah M. Kimball, secretary; Romania B. Pratt, assistant secretary; Mary Isabella Horne, treasurer. ("Relief Society Central Board," *Woman's Exponent,* Oct. 15, 1888, 17:76.)

318. Derr et al., *Women of Covenant,* 131.

Office Woman's Exponent
Salt Lake City, Utah
April 24. 1888

President Zina D. H. Young:

My Very Dear Sister:

I regret so much not having seen you again to converse upon generalities, and also to know, who it was that set you apart to the high and holy position of presiding over the Relief Society in all its branches, and in all the Stakes of Zion throughout the Church of Jesus Christ of Latter Day Saints. I suppose it is not a secret, it ought not to be I think; as we are all [p. [1]] interested. I suppose the blessing would be written, or if not in short hand, a synopsis at least.

I feel it is only a very simple tribute to say, that I congratulate ⟨you my beloved sister⟩ on being called, to <u>be</u>, according to the words of Joseph the Prophet, "<u>The</u> <u>Elect</u> <u>Lady</u>"³¹⁹—but one thing I do say, truthfully and feelingly, that you are the choice of the people, I speak advisedly; I mean taken as a whole. Of course you will remember some of the things I said in your biographical sketch published in the Exponent, immediately after the one I wrote for Sister Eliza R. S. S.— I am afraid however that you did not keep a <u>file</u> of them ⟨⟨(the copies)⟩⟩ by you—had I the time I could quote from them, to prove how significant and prophetic [p. [2]] were the sentiments contained therein.³²⁰

May the Heavenly Father watch over and bless you upon your journey, and preserve you from accident, and strengthen you in body and in mind. Do not regret this journey for it will bring you other opportunities of bearing testimony to the truth, and will develop latent faculties that you were not aware of possessing. The Father knows how to fit and prepare his handmaidens—his daughters, for the great callings, whereunto they are and will be called.

We shall miss you here at home in Zion, but you will be making progress, and advancing; becoming acquainted with other lands, and governments, and all the time expanding and broadening the field of [p. [3]] your thoughts and your labors for the <u>women</u> of Zion, and the <u>women</u> of all lands. For the Women of Zion must become <u>leaders</u>, and to be such must not confine themselves to any narrow sphere of thought, or feeling; and travel and association does work wonders, and becomes highly educational in the truest sense to one, who

---

319. A Joseph Smith revelation in July 1830 applied the title "Elect Lady" to his wife, Emma Smith. In remarks to the Nauvoo Relief Society, Joseph Smith explained that Emma Smith was called "an Elect lady" because she was elected to preside. (Document 1.1; Document 1.2, entry for Mar. 17, 1842.)

320. Wells's biographical sketch of Young was published in the *Woman's Exponent* in seven installments between November 15, 1881, and March 15, 1882, under the title "A Distinguished Woman."

Office Woman's Exponent
Salt Lake City, Utah
April 24. 1888

President Zina D. H. Young;

My very Dear Sister:

I regret so much not having seen you again to converse upon generalities, and also to know, who it was that set you apart to the high and holy position of presiding over the Relief Society in all its branches, and in all the Stakes of Zion throughout the Church of Jesus Christ of Latter Day Saints.— I suppose it is not a secret, it ought not to be I think; as we are all

Letter from Emmeline B. Wells to Zina D. H. Young. Emmeline Wells wrote in April 1888 to newly sustained Relief Society president Zina Young to show her support as a friend, editor of the *Woman's Exponent,* and next-door neighbor. Wells would serve as Young's corresponding secretary. (Church History Library, Salt Lake City.)

improves the avenues open to her ⟨or him⟩ for the study of human nature, and various other objects and subjects.

Your sphere has opened wide, and if you grasp with zeal and ardor the advantages of circumstances, and with wisdom crown your experiences, you will be prepared to stand with [p. [4]] Joseph your <u>royal</u> husband and <u>king</u>, side by side, as his loyal queen, without misgivings, knowing you have not hidden your talents in a napkin, but have kept them bright with using, and improving for your own growth in intelligence and knowledge, and for the good of the Zion he loved, and for the establishment of which, with its principles and institutions, he laid down his precious life, and went as a lamb to the slaughter.[321]

Remember me in sincere love to Zina [Card], tell her I pray for her happiness and prosperity, and believe me that I rejoice most cordially in your succession to the office of <u>the</u> high preistess in Zion.

I suppose you will write me occasionally— Very truly your sister

Emmeline B. Wells [p. [5]]

---

321. The last portion of this sentence is a reference to a statement Joseph Smith reportedly made as he prepared to submit himself to arrest in Carthage, Illinois, in June 1844: "When Joseph went to Carthage to deliver himself up to the pretended requirements of the law, two or three days previous to his assassination, he said: 'I am going like a lamb to the slaughter; but I am calm as a summer's morning; I have a conscience void of offense towards God, and towards all men.'" (Doctrine and Covenants 135:4; see also *The Doctrine and Covenants of the Church of Jesus Christ of Latter Day Saints; Carefully Selected from the Revelations of God,* 2nd ed. [Nauvoo, IL: John Taylor, 1844], 444–445.)

4.19 Wilford Woodruff, Letter to Emmeline B. Wells, April 27, 1888

Wilford Woodruff, Letter to Emmeline B. Wells, Apr. 27, 1888; four pages; CHL (MS 5825).

In April 1888 Emmeline B. Wells, corresponding secretary to general Relief Society president Zina D. H. Young, wrote to Wilford Woodruff, president of the Quorum of the Twelve Apostles, asking him to clarify the circumstances in which Latter-day Saint women should wash and anoint other women in preparation for childbirth. The following letter is the response from Woodruff, who had served as the church's presiding officer since the death of President John Taylor in July 1887.

Even before Joseph Smith sanctioned the practice of female healing in 1842,[322] Latter-day Saint women had participated in the practice of ministering to the sick. By 1880 they had formalized a ritual preceding childbirth sometimes called "washing and anointing previous to confinement."[323] In the decades following Smith's statements, both priesthood and Relief Society leaders had addressed the topic of female healing and its relationship to priesthood authority and temple ordinances. Church leaders stated that these women's ministrations were performed through faith rather than priesthood authority.[324]

In a related vein, church members asked whether women needed to be set apart to officiate in female blessings. Priesthood leaders had on occasion set women apart to bless the sick, although this setting apart was not seen as a prerequisite—at least in cases where the ministering woman had been endowed in the temple.[325] Eliza R. Snow explained in 1884, "Any and all sisters who honor their holy endowments, not only have the right, but should feel it a duty, whenever called upon to administer to our sisters in these ordinances, which God has graciously committed to His daughters as well as to His sons."[326] In 1886, Salt Lake Stake Relief Society president Mary Isabella Horne spoke about washing and anointing the sick because some Relief Society members still believed that one had to be specially set apart to minister in these ordinances. Horne "told them that this was an

---

322. "It is the privilege of those set apart to administer in that authority which is confer'd on them— and if the sisters should have faith to heal the sick, let all hold their tongues, and let every thing roll on." (Document 1.2, entry for Apr. 28, 1842.)

323. Jonathan A. Stapley and Kristine Wright, "Female Ritual Healing in Mormonism," *Journal of Mormon History* 37, no. 1 (Winter 2011): 15–16.

324. For example, see Document 4.8.

325. For example, apostle George A. Smith set apart Susanna Smith Adams in 1854 to wait upon women who were ill. On May 5, 1867, Wilford Woodruff recorded, "At the Close of the Meeting President Young with Some of the Twelve laid hands upon the Head of Mother Atwood & blessed her & set her apart to administer to the Sick of her sex." ("Death of a Heroine," *Woman's Exponent,* Mar. 1, 1892, 20:127; Wilford Woodruff, Journals, 1833–1898, Wilford Woodruff, Journals and Papers, 1828–1898, CHL, May 5, 1867.)

326. Document 4.14.

erroneous impression; all good, Latter-day Saints, who had received their blessings, in the house of the Lord might officiate when called upon."³²⁷

In these explanations, both Snow and Horne referred to blessing the sick and washing and anointing as ordinances. When Emmeline Wells asked President Wilford Woodruff for clarification in 1888, she framed her question in similar language: "Are sisters justified in administering the ordinance of washing and anointing previous to confinement to those who received their endowments and have married men outside of the church?" In his response below, Woodruff cautioned that "the <u>ordinance</u> of washing and anointing is one that should only be administered in Temples or other holy places." While he sanctioned the women's practice of "washing and anointing sisters who are approaching their confinement," he also stated that the practice "is not, strictly speaking, an ordinance."

Notwithstanding the clarifications provided by Woodruff's response to Wells, members continued to send questions to the First Presidency concerning women ministering to the sick, and washing and anointing women before childbirth. In 1905 the stake president in Alberta, Canada, wrote, "We would thank you for your opinion on the question of Sisters annointing other sisters who themselves <u>have</u> <u>not</u> been through the Temple." The answer mirrored what Woodruff stated in 1888, "Sisters annointing other sisters for confinement is not a temple ordinance and must not be confounded with it."³²⁸ The Relief Society general presidency turned to Woodruff's response to Wells again in 1909, when they requested and received permission from the First Presidency to distribute copies of Woodruff's letter to stake Relief Society presidents. "The brethren indorsed Pres. Woodruff's letter and approved of letting the stake presidents have a copy."³²⁹

327. "R. S., Y. L. M. I. A. & P. A. Reports," *Woman's Exponent,* Dec. 15, 1886, 15:110. The issue continued to require clarification; see Document 4.20.

328. Edward J. Wood to First Presidency, Nov. 7, 1905, First Presidency, Joseph F. Smith Stake Correspondence, 1901–1918, CHL, underlining in original. As another example, in 1908 Nephi Pratt, a mission president, asked, "In setting Relief Society sisters apart to give them authority to wash and anoint sisters for their confinement is there any particular form of words to be used in doing so? When [women] go to wash, anoint and administer to the sick, in what manner should they proceed." President Joseph F. Smith replied, using language similar to President Woodruff's, "Members of Relief Societies are not set apart and given authority to wash and anoint sisters for their confinement, for the reason that this practice, which has grown up among some of our Relief Societies, is not an ordinance. . . . In thus writing we do not wish it understood that sisters may not wash and anoint for the purpose mentioned, as there is no impropriety whatever in their doing so, inasmuch as they do it in a proper way, that is, in the spirit of faith and prayer." (Joseph F. Smith to Nephi Pratt, Dec. 21, 1908, First Presidency Letterpress Copybooks, 1877–1949, CHL.)

329. Relief Society General Board Minutes, 1886–1911, CHL, Dec. 17, 1909, and Jan. 21, 1910. A shift away from female healing rituals began in the early twentieth century. In 1923 President Heber J. Grant wrote to general Relief Society president Clarissa S. Williams: "In some of the Stakes a practice exists for sisters to wash and anoint with oil for the health of sick sisters, and in some cases they have called in Elders to confirm their anointing. . . . We fail to see the consistency of sisters adminintering [administering] to the sick in the way mentioned and then sending for Elders to confirm their ministrations." Grant's statements on the subject later influenced apostle Joseph Fielding Smith, who wrote to the Relief Society

³³⁰PRESIDENT'S OFFICE
CHURCH OF JESUS CHRIST.
OF LATTER-DAY SAINTS.
³³¹P.O. BOX B.　*Salt Lake City, U.T.*　April 27th *1888.*³³²

Mrs. Emmeline B Wells,

Editor "Woman's Exponent."

Dear Sister:

In a favor which I have received from you, under date of the 24th. inst., you ask,—

"First: Are sisters justified in administering the ordinance of washing and anointing previous to confinements to those who have received their endowments and have married men outside of the Church?"³³³

"Second: Can anyone who has not had their endowments be thus administered to by the sisters if she is a faithful saint in good standing and has not yet had the opportunity of going to [p. [1]] the Temple for the ordinances?"

To begin with I desire to say that the <u>ordinance</u> of washing and anointing is one that should only be administered in Temples or other holy places which are dedicated for the purpose of giving endowments to the Saints. That <u>ordinance</u> ought not to be administered to any one, whether she has received or has not received her endowments, in any other place or under any other circumstances.

But I imagine from your question that you refer to a practice that has grown up among the sisters of washing and anointing sisters who are approaching their confinement. If so, this is not, strictly speaking, an ordinance, unless

---

general presidency in 1946: "While the Authorities of the Church have ruled that it is permissible, under certain conditions and with the approval of the Priesthood, for sisters to wash and anoint other sisters, yet they feel that it is far better for us to follow the plan the Lord has given us and send for the Elders of the Church to come and administer to the sick and afflicted." Smith's letter "became the definitive statement on female ritual administration for the next several decades." (Heber J. Grant, Charles W. Penrose, and A. W. Ivins to Clarissa S. Williams and counselors, Aug. 11, 1923, Liberty Stake Relief Society Scrapbook Selections, 1915–1933, CHL; Joseph Fielding Smith, Letter, July 29, 1946, Relief Society Washing and Anointing Files, 1888, 1903, 1914–1916, 1922, 1946–1947, CHL; Stapley and Wright, "Female Ritual Healing in Mormonism," 81.)

330. TEXT: The top four lines of the document are preprinted letterhead.

331. TEXT: At this point, "<u>E.B. Wells</u>" is written vertically, running up the page.

332. TEXT: The underlining here indicates handwritten portions of this preprinted letterhead.

333. Wells linked healing blessings and temple ordinances in part because, since the days of Joseph Smith, the temple had been a place where both saving ordinances (such as endowments and sealings) and other ceremonies (such as blessings for health) were performed. (See Jonathan A. Stapley and Kristine Wright, "The Forms and the Power: The Development of Mormon Ritual Healing to 1847," *Journal of Mormon History* 35, no. 3 [Summer 2009]: 42–87.)

it be done under the direction of the priesthood and in connection with the ordinance of laying on of hands for the restoration of the sick.

There is no impropriety in sisters washing and anointing their sisters in this way, under the circumstances you describe; but it should be [p. 2] understood that they do this, not as members of the priesthood, but as members of the Church, exercising faith for, and asking the blessings of the Lord upon, their sisters; just as they, and every member of the Church, might do in behalf of the members of their families.

In all these matters, however, care should be taken that wrong ideas be not imbibed and wrong practices be not adopted connected with ordinances of the Gospel.

In reply, therefore, to your two questions, answering you in the above light, I think you are quite justified in doing anything that you can for the benefit of the sisters who are in that condition, who may apply to you, even though they should be married to men outside of the Church; and certainly, as your second question implies, there should be no hesitation about administering to faithful sisters in good standing, though they may not have had the oppor[p. 3]tunity of receiving their endowments, any more than there would be were they to apply to have hands laid upon them by an Elder to rebuke sickness.

As to your third question, "Is it the proper thing for a sister to preside over a Relief Society who has not yet received her endowments?" I would naturally suppose that such a person would be rarely, if ever, called to preside over a Relief Society; because a woman who would be qualified for this, if married, would certainly honor the ordinances of the Lord's house sufficiently to have her marriage solemnized in the Temple, and she could not have this done without receiving her endowments. Other cases, where a person would not have had her endowments, would be that of an unmarried woman, who, I suppose, is rarely called to preside over a Relief Society.

I trust that what I have said on these points will be quite satisfactory to you and will give you the needed information.

I am, with kind regards, Your Brother, W Woodruff [p. [4]]

4.20 Franklin D. Richards, Discourse, July 19, 1888

Franklin D. Richards, Discourse, July 19, 1888, in "Memorial Anniversary. Report of the Relief Soicety Meeting Held in the Ogden Tabernacle, July 19th, 1888, in Commemoration of the Last Public Visit and Instructions of President Brigham Young, on Invitation of President Jane S. Richards, to the Relief Society and Young Ladies' Improvement Associations of the Weber Stake of Zion, Just Eleven Years Ago the 19th Inst.," Woman's Exponent *(Salt Lake City, UT), Sept. 1, 1888, vol. 17, no. 7, pp. 52–54.*

On July 19, 1888, a Relief Society meeting was held in Ogden to commemorate the eleventh anniversary of Brigham Young's appointment of Jane Snyder Richards as the church's first stake Relief Society president.[334] The congregation heard several speeches during the lengthy meeting, including a brief address by Jane Richards and a more extended speech by her husband, Franklin D. Richards, which is featured below. Franklin and Jane Richards, who married in 1842 in Illinois, had moved to Ogden, Weber County, in 1869. Franklin Richards, ordained an apostle in 1849, also served for several years as the president of the Weber Stake. Jane Richards became president of the Ogden Ward Relief Society in 1872 and then president of the Weber Stake Relief Society in 1877.[335] In addition to her stake duties, she was set apart as first counselor to Zina D. H. Young in the general Relief Society presidency on October 11, 1888.[336]

As is evident in the document below, Franklin Richards actively promoted women's advancement, believing benefits would accrue to both women and the church when the women fully engaged in developing their talents. After Franklin Richards accompanied Jane Richards, Eliza R. Snow, and other female leaders to a Relief Society meeting in Ogden in April 1875, he reflected: "These Sisters teach many good things—and in a sphere which the Elders do not seem to occupy. I find it strengthens our hands to encourage them."[337]

During his July 1888 address in Ogden, Franklin Richards read excerpts from an account of Joseph Smith's April 28, 1842, discourse to the Nauvoo Relief Society, in which Smith lectured "on the pries[t]hood shewing how the Sisters would come in possession of the priviliges & blesings & gifts of the priesthood."[338] Richards's explanation of the discourse centered on the blessings of the endowment (a ritual performed in temples), which, he assured the congregation, were accessible to both men and women. On July 30 Richards

---

334. See Document 3.26.

335. Andrew Jenson, *Latter-day Saint Biographical Encyclopedia: A Compilation of Biographical Sketches of Prominent Men and Women in the Church of Jesus Christ of Latter-day Saints,* 4 vols. (Salt Lake City: Andrew Jenson History Co., 1901–1936), 1:117, 120; Document 3.26.

336. "Relief Society Central Board," *Woman's Exponent,* Oct. 15, 1888, 17:76; "Relief Society Central Board," Relief Society Record, 1880–1892, CHL, 63. For evidence that Richards continued in her stake duties, see Weber Stake, Weber Stake Relief Society Conference Minute Book, 1855–1899, CHL.

337. Franklin D. Richards, Journals, 1844–1899, Richards Family Collection, 1837–1961, CHL, Apr. 15, 1875.

338. Joseph Smith, Journal, Apr. 28, 1842, in Andrew H. Hedges et al., eds., *Journals, Volume 2: December 1841–April 1843,* vol. 2 of the Journals series of *The Joseph Smith Papers,* ed. Dean C. Jessee et al. (Salt Lake City: Church Historian's Press, 2011), 52.

Jane Snyder Richards and Franklin D. Richards. Circa 1885. Married in 1842 and longtime residents of Ogden, Utah, Jane and Franklin Richards were strong proponents of both women's rights and the Relief Society organization. He served as a member of the Quorum of the Twelve, and she was the first stake Relief Society president. Photograph by A. J. Hoffman & Co. (Church History Library, Salt Lake City.)

recorded in his journal that he "obtained of Brother John M. Whitaker a large share of Report of the proceedings on the 19th inst at Ogden anniversary meeting and spent much of the day revising and preparing it for Sister E. [Emmeline] B. Wells to publish in the Woman's Exponent."[339] The full proceedings were printed in the *Exponent* in four installments between August 1 and September 15, 1888, with Whittaker identified as the reporter.

—— ❧ ——

MEMORIAL ANNIVERSARY.
REPORT OF THE RELIEF SOICETY MEETING HELD IN THE OGDEN TABERNACLE, JULY 19TH, 1888, IN COMMEMORATION OF THE LAST PUBLIC VISIT AND INSTRUCTIONS OF PRESIDENT BRIGHAM YOUNG, ON INVITATION OF PRESIDENT JANE S. RICHARDS, TO THE RELIEF SOCIETY AND YOUNG LADIES' IMPROVEMENT ASSOCIATIONS OF THE WEBER STAKE OF ZION, JUST ELEVEN YEARS AGO THE 19TH INST.
(REPORTED BY JOHN M WHITTAKER.)

[340]. . . President F. D. Richards spoke as follows:

Being called upon by the sisters to address you for a short time this afternoon, I wish to introduce my remarks by first saying, that Sister [Sarah] Herrick, who has just addressed you, is the Stake Prest. of the Y. L. M. I. A. for Weber County, which, perhaps, I should have stated at the opening of her remarks. She, therefore, spoke in behalf of the Young Ladies of this Stake.

One day this week, it was my privilege to be in company with our beloved President Woodruff, and with some other of the brethren who are associated with him in a state of obscurity, and who do not make their appearance in public assemblies.[341] I made mention of this occasion, with an invitation, if it had been reasonable and consistent for them, to meet with us. And inasmuch as they felt that they could not, he bid me express his love and good wishes to the sisters of the Relief Society and the Young Ladies' Associations, and any and all who might be present who love the work in which we are engaged, and said it would be impossible to attend, though he would like to have done so

---

339. Richards, Journal, July 30, 1888.

340. TEXT: These ellipsis points have been supplied by the editors of this volume. The full report of Richards's sermon, as published in the *Woman's Exponent,* is reproduced here. Material preceding Richards's address in the *Exponent* report has been omitted.

341. Richards recorded that he had spent an hour with Wilford Woodruff, George Q. Cannon, Joseph F. Smith, John Henry Smith, Heber J. Grant, and George Reynolds. Woodruff served as the leader of the church after John Taylor's death in July 1887 and was sustained as church president in April 1889. In the face of federal antipolygamy legislation passed in 1882 and strengthened in 1887, some church leaders limited their public appearances in order to avoid arrest. (Richards, Journal, July 16, 1888, CHL; see also W. Paul Reeve, "Conflict: 1869–1890," in *Mormonism: A Historical Encyclopedia,* ed. W. Paul Reeve and Ardis E. Parshall [Santa Barbara, CA: ABC-CLIO, 2010], 41, 43; Document 4.15.)

exceeding much. He referred to a very interesting party he attended here some [p. 52] years ago, given on the anniversary of Sister Eliza R. Snow Smith's birthday, which many of the Saints present, no doubt, remember. He thought it was the best sister's party he had ever attended.[342]

Our brethren, who are hidden from our society for the present, are always solicitous and anxious for the prosperity of the Church in all its various departments; and they watch over every part of the work of which God has made them overseers, with the deepest solicitude, prayerfulness of heart and with earnestness for its prosperity.

I realize that I am addressing representative ladies of the Weber Stake of Zion, presidents of the Relief Society and associations generally, and many others as well. I always feel anxious when I address my sisters to say something that shall encourage them in their work; because they naturally feel timid and backward and have a reluctance to assume public positions, or public duties, because some think they are making themselves too officious in public, and that ladies have no rights in public duties.

Some of the sisters feel intimidated in their meetings when the brethren are present; while others believe that if the brethren would attend and give them counsel and encouragement, they would be stronger and more able to launch out in the liberty of the spirit and discharge the duties incumbent upon them with a consciousness and heavenly assurance, that would result in the blessings of God upon their labors. It has been so from the beginning of this work that has been laid upon the sisters; it has been looked upon by some of them as being something out of their line and place. Every now and again we hear men speak tauntingly of the sisters and lightly of their public duties. instead of supporting and encouraging them. There are also some who look with jealousy upon the moves of the sisters as though they might come to possess some of the gifts, and are afraid they will get away with some of the blessings of the Gospel, which only men ought to possess. That is the way some look upon woman and her work. They don't like to accord to them anything that will raise them up and make their talents to shine forth as the daughters of Eve and of Sarah. But have feelings of envy and jealousy; and instead of dealing open handedly with them, tell them to go forward and do all the good they can, it

---

342. The party took place on January 21, 1881, Snow's seventy-seventh birthday. Snow did not attend because she and Zina D. H. Young were visiting women's organizations in St. George, where her birthday was also celebrated. Regarding the Ogden celebration, Wilford Woodruff wrote in his journal: "Some 200 sat down to the Table well furnished. . . . Dancing was kept up untill 11 oclok Then Speeches from F. D. Richards & W Woodruff and reading from prose & Poetry on E R Snow untill 12 oclok then dismissed." ("Aunt Eliza's Birthday," *Deseret News* [weekly], Feb. 2, 1881, 833; Wilford Woodruff, Journals, 1833–1898, Wilford Woodruff, Journals and Papers, 1828–1898, CHL, Jan. 21, 1881.)

seems as though they would like to keep them back and not let them do any-thing,—more than is really necessary.

I am sorry to see this feeling. The brethren should understand and see that in so doing they are opposing themselves. Inasmuch as the sisters do not arro-gate authority to themselves I think the brethren, by hindering them, withhold blessings from themselves; if they would work with the sisters they would be more abundantly blessed. The Presidents and Bishops would realize multiplied blessings upon their own heads. Is it not more honorable for a king to rule over a wealthy and noble race, than one reduced to poverty, ignorance and serfdom? Is it not more honorable to preside over a nation that is enlightened, intelligent and enterprising? Is it not much more glorious and honorable to preside over those who are full of faith, who are active in good works, and who are filled with the power of God? Certainly it is. When the sisters have the spirit of their work upon them, they will labor with an honest zeal in the midst of their soci-eties, and it adds blessings thereto. There is no Bishop that encourages and supports an institution of this kind, but who realizes and must acknowledge that these sisters in their different callings, lessen his labors, make easy his call-ing and add to the efficiency of his Stake or ward. The Bishops who do this will be blessed and are blessed at all times.

When I arise to teach the sisters, I am benefitting the teachers and the authorities of the Church in Zion. I do not feel at any time to withhold or be reluctant in instructing or speaking well of them and their labors in the Church. I know that many are afraid to go ahead and do anything without instructions, for fear they may do wrong. And they thus are prevented from doing many things that would materially assist the cause, for fear they may do wrong.

Sisters, do right. Where you desire to launch out and do right, do so, and God will sanctify your labors to the good of your sisters, and also the good of the brethren; and you will make your husbands far more useful wives. You will have more obedient daughters, more dutiful children; children that are more affec-tionate, true, honorable, faithful, and who, in their turn, will make more honor-able husbands and more dutiful wives.

I wish to say to you this afternoon, sisters of the Relief Society and of the Young Ladies' Associations, that while it is expected of you that you will visit the sick, that you shall see to it that none of the brethren and sisters suffer from poverty or for the want of the necessaries of life, while it is your duty and privi-lege to minister to each other and those around you, and even when life has departed, you are to look after them and see that they have proper clothing and burial—I say, while you have these duties continually upon you, you have other privileges and rights, which are known to us and the people in general. It is pleasing to hear the Bishops report to the quarterly conferences the faithfulness of the Relief Society, and the aid they have derived from them, the relief they find by having them to call upon them for aid, and the efficient manner in which they respond to every need.

The Relief Society of Weber Stake raised between $500 and $600, and gave it as a donation to help finish the Logan Temple—a nice little item, which the building committee acknowledged with gratitude, and every name of those who donated was written in the records of the Temple.[343]

In looking over the lists, I find that there is considerable over $500 donated by the Weber societies towards finishing the Manti Temple.[344] The donations from this Stake on the Manti Records, cover eighty pages, and over forty lines to a page, and has on each line the name of the person and the amount paid.

Sisters, tell it to your children at home, that in these records is contained over $100, paid by the little ones of the Primaries; and each boy or girl has their name written there, credited to a nickle, dime or quarter, as the case may be, and it shows who have contributed anything to assist in the completion of that beautiful building. These records will be placed in the Temple at Manti, and will be kept as a perpetual remembrance.

Besides this, the Relief Society of Weber Stake, during the past six years, or there about, since the Deseret Hospital[345] was organized into an association, has contributed, as near as I can recollect, something over one thousand dollars to help maintain and conduct that charitable institution.[346] Some months ago we made application to the Secretary to give us a statement of the number of cases, the kind of affliction, what number got well, what number died, the amount experded [expended], the amount received, etc., etc., in order that it may be known how it stands, what good it has done, and the status of the association at the present time, in order that it may receive the attention and encouragement it should have. I have been told repeatedly what you have a

---

343. The Logan temple was dedicated May 17–19, 1884. Many Relief Societies donated significant amounts of money and other goods toward the construction of the temple. (See, for example, "Statistical and Financial Report of the Relief Society Stakes of Zion for the Half Year Ending April 1ˢᵗ 1883," in Relief Society, Relief Society Stake Financial and Statistical Reports, 1882–1883, CHL; Weber Stake, Weber Stake Relief Society Minutes and Records, 1867–1968, CHL, vol. 8, Jan. 4, 1883; and the October 1877 Ogden Ward Relief Society report included at the end of Document 3.28.)

344. The Manti temple was dedicated May 17, 1888, just two months before Richards's address in Ogden.

345. For more on the Deseret Hospital, see Document 4.11.

346. Some of these donations, which included in-kind donations as well as cash, are reported in local Relief Society records from the period. (See, for example, "Statistical and Financial Report of the Relief Society Stakes of Zion for the Half Year Ending September 15ᵗʰ 1882," in Relief Society Stake Financial and Statistical Reports.)

right to know, that Weber County has been second to none, or only one among the Stakes, who have donated for its support.

In all these lists there is contained in the records concerning the Manti Temple and other things, no less than 3,400 names from this Stake of Zion.

The sisters of the Relief Society at the present time, feel very much the loss of their President Sister Eliza R. Snow Smith. Sister Eliza having passed away, after an illness of more than a year, during which she was unable to attend public meetings. Sister Zina D. Young, her successor, is absent for a short time, but is expected home soon, when she will visit the different branches of the Society, attend to her duties and give advice, as Sister Eliza used to do.[347]

This is a great work. It is a vast auxiliary. It is one of those things spoken of in the Scriptures as "helps" to the government of the kingdom of God. Sisters, be diligent in all things, no matter how the brethren may look upon you. Your organization is just as important as any other in the Church, outside of the priesthood. It has been instituted by the highest authority on earth in this dispensation. It was appointed and established by the Prophet Joseph Smith, in Nauvoo. I am glad that there are some here to-day who were there at that meeting, and who listened to the instructions of the Prophet of God. Sister Eliza was Secretary at the time of the organization. Sister Emma Smith was the presiding officer of that institution, and she was blessed under the hands of Presidents Joseph Smith and John Taylor, to expound the Scriptures and administer to the Saints in this holy office and presidency.

I wish to make a few remarks concerning it and its significance, as it appears to me, for the encouragement of the sisters; and in doing so, I shall refer to some of the sayings of the Prophet Joseph in instituting it. In April, 1842, he made an appointment with the Relief Society in the city of Nauvoo. He attended that meeting and lectured to the sisters himself.[348] There are several present here to-day, who were there and heard him speak, as did also myself. Here are Presendia L. Kimball, Bathsheba W. Smith, Jane S. Richards, and if I could mention them all, there would be quite a number here who were members of that Society.

The Prophet Joseph treated upon the gifts and blessings of the priesthood to be enjoyed by all those who believed, and also upon the character of the work devolved upon its members. And he read, concerning the blessings which

---

347. Snow died on December 5, 1887. Soon after becoming general president of the Relief Society in April 1888, Zina Young traveled to Cardston, Alberta, Canada, to stay with her daughter, Zina Young Card, and assist with the birth of her baby. (See Document 4.18.)

348. Richards is referring to Joseph Smith's April 28, 1842, discourse to the Nauvoo Relief Society, which Eliza R. Snow recorded in the Nauvoo Relief Society Minute Book. (Document 1.2, entry for Apr. 28, 1842.)

he wanted them to understand, were theirs if they would live for them. He read a portion of the 16th chapter of St. Mark, where it says: "Go ye into all the world and preach the Gospel to every creature. He that believeth and is baptized shall be saved; but he that believeth not shall be dammed. And these signs shall follow them that believe: In my name shall they cast out devils; they shall speak with new tongues; they shall take up serpents; and if they drink any deadly thing, it shall not hurt them; they shall lay hands on the sick and they shall recover."[349]

He [Joseph Smith] said, in relation to the females administering to the sick, that there could be no more wrong in it, than in performing any other ordinance of the Church if the Lord gave His sanction by healing the sick under the hands of the sisters.

I will read from the minutes which were taken on that occasion by Sister Eliza:[350]

> He continued to read the chapter, and give instructions respecting the different offices, and the necessity of every individual acting in the sphere allotted him or her, and filling the several offices to which they were appointed.[351]
>
> He said the reason of these remarks being made was, that some little foolish things were circulating in the society, against some sisters not doing right in laying hands on the sick. Said if the people had common sympathies they would rejoice that the sick could be healed; that the time had not been before that these things could be in their proper order; that the Church is not fully organized, in its proper order, and cannot be, until the Temple is completed, where places will be provided for the administration of the ordinances of the Priesthood.

Elder Richards here remarked: [p. 53]

This was just before he commenced giving endowments,[352] and was hastening the work of the Temple to get ready for it; and he says, that

---

349. Mark 16:15–18.

350. Richards read from the minutes as revised for the Manuscript History of the Church and as published in the *Deseret News*, rather than from the original minutes as recorded by Snow. (See Document 2.2; and Document 1.2, entry for Apr. 28, 1842.)

351. At this point, Richards omitted a paragraph of the April 28, 1842, discourse. (See Document 2.2.)

352. The first endowments were given on May 4, 1842, in the upper floor of the red brick store in Nauvoo. Emma Smith received the endowment on September 28, 1843. Members first received the endowment in the Nauvoo temple on December 10, 1845. (Andrew H. Hedges et al., eds., *Journals, Volume 2: December 1841–April 1843*, vol. 2 of the Journals series of *The Joseph Smith Papers*, ed. Dean C. Jessee et al.

as he had this opportunity, he was going to instruct the ladies of this Society, and point out the way for them to conduct themselves, that they might act according to the will of God; that he did not know that he should have many opportunities of teaching them, as they were going to be left to themselves; they would not long have him to instruct them; that the Church would not have his instructions long, and the world would not be troubled with him a great while, and would not have his teachings.

He spoke of *delivering the keys of the Priesthood to the Church, and said that the faithful members of the Relief Society should receive them in connection with their husbands,*[353] that Saints whose integrity has been tried and proved faithful, might know how to ask the Lord and receive an answer; for according to his prayers, God had appointed him elsewhere.

He exhorted the sisters always to concentrate their faith and prayers for, and place confidence in their husbands, whom God had appointed for them to honor, and in those faithful men whom God has placed at the head of the Church to lead His people; that we should arm and sustain them with our prayers; for the keys of the kingdom are about to be given to them, that they may be able to detect everything false; as well as to all the Elders who shall prove their integrity in due season.[354]

President Smith then gave instruction respecting the propriety of females administering to the sick by the prayer of faith, and laying on of hands, or the anointing with oil; and said it was according to revelation that the sick should be nursed with herbs and mild food, and not by the hand of an enemy. Who are better qualified to administer than our faithful and zealous sisters, whose hearts are full of faith, tenderness, sympathy, and compassion? No one. Said he was never placed in similar circumstances before, and never had given the same instruction; and closed his instructions by expressing his heartfelt satisfaction in improving this opportunity.

[Salt Lake City: Church Historian's Press, 2011], 54n198; Joseph Smith, Journal, Sept. 28, 1843, in Andrew H. Hedges et al., eds., *Journals, Volume 3: May 1843–June 1844,* vol. 3 of the Journals series of *The Joseph Smith Papers,* ed. Ronald K. Esplin and Matthew J. Grow [Salt Lake City: Church Historian's Press, 2015], 104; David John Buerger, "The Development of the Mormon Temple Endowment Ceremony," *Dialogue: A Journal of Mormon Thought* 20, no. 4 [Winter 1987]: 47–49.)

353. The version of the discourse from which Richards was reading does not have italics on this passage. (See Document 2.2.)

354. At this point, Richards omitted several paragraphs of the April 28, 1842, discourse. (See Document 2.2.)

The Spirit of the Lord was poured out in a very powerful manner, never to be forgotten by those present on this interesting occasion.

Elder Richards continuing said: I ask any and everybody present who have received their endowments, whether he be a brother Apostle, Bishop, High Priest, Elder, or whatever office he may hold in the Church, "What blessings did you receive, what ordinance, what power, intelligence, sanctification or grace did you receive that your wife did not partake of with you?" I will answer, that there was one thing that our wives were not made special partakers of, and that was the ordination to the various orders of the priesthood which were conferred upon us. Aside from that, our sisters share with us any and all of the ordinances of the holy anointing, endowments, sealings, sanctifications and blessings that we have been made partakers of.

Now, I ask you: Is it possible that we have the holy priesthood and our wives have none of it? Do you not see, by what I have read, that Joseph desired to confer these keys of power upon them in connection with their husbands? I hold that a faithful wife has certain blessings, powers and rights, and is made partaker of certain gifts and blessings and promises with her husband, which she cannot be deprived of, EXCEPT BY TRANSGRESSION of the holy order of God. They shall enjoy what God said they should. And these signs shall follow them if they believe.[355]

Moses said, when some one told him that a certain man was prophesying in the camp, and the people thought he had no right to do so, Moses replied saying: "I would to God that all of the Lord's people were prophets."[356] So I say: I wish all the sisters were so faithful that they were healers of the sick, through the power of God.[357] Then would their children have a foundation to grow up from their youth in the fear and admonition of the Lord and in the power of His might. Sister Eliza R. Snow Smith learned some of these things from the Prophet Joseph Smith; and as he was the organizer of the Church of Christ, so she went through the Territory organizing Relief Societies, and did a wonderful work. She partook of the power of her distinguished husband.

Sisters, may the Lord bless you. Bishops, may the Lord bless us all and give us the spirit of liberality. The more we do for the sisters, the more they will do for us; and so may the Spirit of the Lord bless us all with the feeling of liberality to all, in the name of the Lord Jesus Christ. Amen.[358]

---

355. See Mark 16:17–18; Mormon 9:24; and Doctrine and Covenants 84:65–72.

356. See Numbers 11:26–29.

357. For more on healing blessings given by women, see Document 4.19.

358. TEXT: Following this paragraph, the *Exponent* report concludes with the words "To be Continued," indicating that the report of the July 19 meeting continued into the next installment.

4.21 San Juan Stake Relief Society, Report, November 27, 1888

*San Juan Stake Relief Society, Report, Nov. 27, 1888, in "San Juan Stake," in "R. S., Y. L. M. I. A. &
P. A. Reports,"* Woman's Exponent *(Salt Lake City, UT), Feb. 1, 1889, vol. 17, no. 17, pp. 134–135.*

The following document is a report of the San Juan Stake Relief Society quarterly conference held November 27, 1888. The San Juan Stake, organized in September 1883 in San
Juan County, Utah, was led by pioneers who had reached the area in 1879–1880 as participants in the arduous Hole-in-the-Rock expedition to the far southeast corner of Utah. The
expedition took its name from a cliff that the settlers descended by lowering their wagons
over a very rough road that took them over a month to build. Historian Andrew Jenson
wrote, "These pioneer settlers experienced more hardships than any other colony known in
the history of the Church who have founded settlements in the Rocky Mountains."[359]

Expedition member Jane McKechnie Walton, along with her husband, Charles, and
their three young children, settled in what became Bluff City.[360] She filled a dual role as
president of the Bluff Ward Relief Society and, beginning in 1885, as president of the San
Juan Stake Relief Society.[361] Other members of the pioneer company included Kirsten
Nielson, who served as first counselor in the stake Relief Society presidency and later as
president of the Bluff Ward Relief Society; Eliza Redd, a counselor to Nielson in the Bluff
Ward Relief Society; and Mary N. Jones, who served as a counselor in the San Juan Stake
young women's organization.[362]

The San Juan Stake infrequently entertained visitors from Relief Society headquarters
in Salt Lake City. According to local records, the first member of the Relief Society Central
Board to visit the area was general president Zina D. H. Young, who visited in 1889, four
years after the stake Relief Society was organized.[363] Although Relief Society officers from
Salt Lake City could only occasionally travel to distant Relief Societies, reports of local
proceedings published in the *Woman's Exponent* helped women throughout the church,
particularly in outlying areas, feel connected with each other.

Jane Walton presided over the November 27, 1888, stake Relief Society conference and
received reports from individual ward Relief Societies. The presence of the stake presidency
and three bishops, along with officers of the stake Primary Association and Young Ladies'

---

359. "History of San Juan Stake Relief Society," in San Juan Stake, San Juan Stake Relief Society
Scrapbook, 1885–1968, CHL; David E. Miller, *Hole-in-the-Rock: An Epic in the Colonization of the Great
American West* (Salt Lake City: University of Utah Press, 1966), 143–146; Andrew Jenson, *Encyclopedic
History of the Church of Jesus Christ of Latter-day Saints* (Salt Lake City: Deseret News, 1941), 773.

360. 1880 U.S. Census, Bluff City, San Juan Co., Utah Territory, 345B; "Death of Jane M. Walton,"
Woman's Exponent, Aug. 15, 1891, 20:32.

361. "Death of Jane M. Walton," *Woman's Exponent,* Aug. 15, 1891, 20:32; "History of San Juan Stake
Relief Society," in San Juan Stake Relief Society Scrapbook.

362. San Juan Stake, San Juan Stake Relief Society Minutes and Records, 1885–1973, CHL, Feb. 28,
1887; "History of San Juan Stake Relief Society," in San Juan Stake Relief Society Scrapbook; Miller,
Hole-in-the-Rock, 143–146.

363. "History of San Juan Stake Relief Society," in San Juan Stake Relief Society Scrapbook.

Mutual Improvement Association, reflects the cooperation between male and female leaders in the work of this society. Stake Relief Society secretary Sarah Jane Perkins Rogerson recorded the conference proceedings in the San Juan Stake Relief Society Minute Book[364] and then sent a somewhat revised and abbreviated report to the *Woman's Exponent.* The published report is featured here.

———— ✺ ————

SAN JUAN STAKE.

The Relief Society of the San Juan Stake held their conference at Bluff, Nov. 27th, 1888, Prest. Jane M. Walton presiding. Choir sang, "The Coming Day." Prayer by Prest. [Francis] Hammond. Singing, "Devotional Hymn."[365] A goodly number of the brethren were present, including Prest. F. A. Hammond and Counselors,[366] and the Bishops of the Mancos, Burnham and Bluff Wards,[367] Prest Moiselle M. Halls and Mary N. Jones, of the Stake Presidency of the Y. L. M. I. A.; also Prest. Julia Butt, Stake Prest. of the Primary.

Prest. Walton hoped to be dictated by the right spirit while sho [she] endeavored to address the conference. Considered it a great blessing to have the privilege of holding Relief Society conference. It made her heart feel warm to see the sisters; felt that the Spirit of God had been with us during our conference so far. Knew of a surety that every principle of the Gospel was true; would rather die than deny the truth.

Minutes of the former conference were then read and accepted.[368]

Prest Abigal Stevens of the Burnham Ward, said it gave her pleasure to report her Society. The sisters felt well and united: they held one testimony and two work meetings each month. Desired to continue faithful and true to the end.

---

364. San Juan Stake Relief Society Minutes and Records, vol. 1, Nov. 27, 1888.

365. *Deseret Sunday School Union Music Book, Containing a Large Collection of Choice Pieces for the Use of Sunday Schools* (Salt Lake City: Deseret Sunday School Union, 1884), 29, 74.

366. Hammond was appointed president of the San Juan Stake in 1885, with William Halls and William Adams as counselors. (Jenson, *Encyclopedic History of the Church of Jesus Christ of Latter-day Saints,* 773; San Juan Stake, San Juan Stake Manuscript History and Historical Reports, 1883–1938, CHL, June 21, 1885.)

367. George Halls, bishop of Mancos Ward; Luther C. Burnham, bishop of Burnham Ward; Jens Nielson, bishop of Bluff Ward. The San Juan Stake also included a ward in Moab and a branch in Monticello. (Jenson, *Encyclopedic History of the Church of Jesus Christ of Latter-day Saints,* 74–75, 101, 469, 527–528, 772–773; San Juan Stake Manuscript History and Historical Reports, Sept. 23, 1883; San Juan Stake Relief Society Minutes and Records, Sept. 21, 1885, and May 29, 1886.)

368. The minutes for the August 1888 quarterly conference of the San Juan Stake Relief Society are in San Juan Stake Relief Society Minutes and Records, Aug. 28, 1888. A report of the August conference was printed in "R. S., Y. L. M. I. A. & P. A. Reports," *Woman's Exponent,* Nov. 1, 1888, 17:[87].

Jane McKechnie Walton. Jane and her husband, Charles, were members of the harrowing Hole-in-the-Rock expedition in southeastern Utah. She was Relief Society president of the San Juan Stake. (Courtesy Mike King, via commons.wikimedia.org.)

Sister Neilson reported the Bluff Ward Society. Said the sisters had done as well as could be expected, owing to their few number. "If we will listen to the teachings and instructions of those in authority we will be blest; realized there was a great mission for the sisters to perform.["]

Prest. Walton then resigned her position as Prest of the Bluff Ward, as she had moved from that place.[369] Prest. F. A. Hammond honorably released her, and then made a few needed explanations.

Coun. Moiselle Halls reported the Mancos Society; said the sisters felt more united than at last conference; held testimony and work meetings regularly; were storing up grain. "The teachers are very diligent."

Bishop [Jens] Nielson felt to return Sister Walton a vote of thanks; knew she had done a good work, and had been very kind to the sick.

The Society at Bluff was then organized as follows: Ki[r]sten Nielson, President; Agnes Allen [Allan] and Eliza Redd, Counselors; Jennie Allen [Johanna Allan], Secretary; Ordella Allen [Ardell Allan], Treasurer.[370]

Prest. Hammond moved that Sister Kisten Nielson be honorably released from acting First Counselor to the Stake President. Martha Hammond was then sustained as First and Josephine Wood as Second Counselor to Prest. Jane Walton.

The general and local officers of the Relief [p. 134] Society were sustained. Coun. Martha Hammond spoke a few minutes, giving good counsel.

Coun. Wm. Halls said his advice to the sisters was, to devote themselves to their office and calling. Prayed God to bless all who had been called to fill the different positions.

Prest. Hammond felt to endorse all that had been said by the sisters. Prest Walton adjourned the conference. Choir sang, "Improve the shining moments."[371] Prayer by Bishop Geo. Halls.

SARAH J. ROGERSON, Stake Sec.

---

369. Walton and her husband had been called to settle in nearby Monticello. ("Death of Jane M. Walton," *Woman's Exponent,* Aug. 15, 1891, 20:32.)

370. Rather than naming the secretary and treasurer, the minutes of the meeting state that "the former secretary and treasurer were sustained." In addition, the minutes give the names of four women who were appointed teachers and indicate by whom each newly appointed woman was set apart. (San Juan Relief Society Minutes and Records, Nov. 27, 1888.)

371. *Deseret Sunday School Union Music Book,* 58.

4.22 Marion E. Scoles, Letter to the *Exponent,* circa December 1888

Marion E. Scoles, Letter to the editor of the Woman's Exponent, *[ca. Dec. 1888], in "The North London Ladies' Relief Society,"* Woman's Exponent *(Salt Lake City, UT), Feb. 15, 1889, vol. 17, no. 18, pp. 141–142.*

Marion Eliza Scoles, the second counselor in the Relief Society of the North London Branch, wrote the following letter to the *Woman's Exponent* at the close of 1888, providing a glimpse into the activities of the Relief Society in Great Britain. The North London Branch Relief Society was organized in February 1875. After five years, it had a membership of ten women, who were "energetic and liberal affording very acceptable support to the branch organization in many ways."[372] Minutes from the society's meetings during the 1880s identify the nature of the members' service: visiting the sick, encouraging church members who were not participating regularly, and sharing their means with the less fortunate. Frances Cornell, the first counselor, stated in a meeting that she "was never so happy, as when visiting, and being able to relieve her poorer brethren and sisters."[373] During one visit, Cornell and the branch Relief Society president, Ellen Bradford, found Eliza B. Wonnacott well, but three of her children were "sick with Hooping Cough and Brohnchitis, the baby was very ill indeed, we did that which we thought best and when we left we saw a change for the better." They returned "2 days after and Bro [William] Wonnacott said he knew that we were instruments in the Hands of God in saving his babes life."[374]

Scoles's letter and the local Relief Society minutes from the period also reflect the difficulty that many branches had in keeping their organizations staffed as their members continued to leave England to join the Saints in Utah. At a meeting in 1885, several women expressed their longing to gather to Zion. Sarah Pearce, for instance, "bore a faithful Testimony and declared her knowledge of the work, and expressed a great desire, to be gathered home with Gods people."[375] In her letter to the *Exponent,* Scoles explained the small attendance in part by pointing to the "continued emigration," which had included Frances Cornell in 1887.[376]

———— ❧ ————

372. "R. S., Y. L. M. I. A. and Primary Reports," *Woman's Exponent,* Jan. 1, 1881, 9:118.

373. London North Branch, London England North Stake, North London Branch Relief Society Minutes and Records, 1884–1973, CHL, Nov. 1, 1885; "R. S., Y. L. M. I. A. and Primary Reports," *Woman's Exponent,* Jan. 1, 1881, 9:118.

374. North London Branch Relief Society Minutes and Records, Apr. 4, 1886.

375. North London Branch Relief Society Minutes and Records, Nov. 1, 1885.

376. By the beginning of the twentieth century, members outside the United States were counseled to remain in their own countries and to build the church there. See, for example, Joseph F. Smith, Anthon H. Lund, John Henry Smith, Letter to the Editor of *Evening Times,* Feb. 6, 1911, in First Presidency, Important to the People of the British Isles, CHL.

THE NORTH LONDON LADIES' RELIEF SOCIETY.

EDITOR WOMAN'S EXPONENT:

The President of the above Society has desired me to write you a brief account of the work accomplished by it since its reorganization up till the close of 1888.

The Society was reorganized on March 9th, 1884, with Helen [Ellen] Bradford, President; Frances Cornell and Frances Jennings, Counselors; Caroline Parratt, Secretary; Helen Bradford, Treasurer.

Since that time, however, the First Counselor has emigrated to Utah,[377] and Sister Jennings now holds that position, and Sister M. E. Scoles has been chosen Second Counselor. The Secretary has been succeeded by Elizabeth Bush, who also emigrated to Utah in October last, and that position is at present vacant.

392 visits have been paid, and 62£ 9 shillings and 4½ pence has been given to the poor. The Elders have been assisted to the amount of 25£, 11 shillings and 3½ pence. This is for rent of room and food. The attendance has been very small, the usual number present not exceeding six lately, although we have a number of names on the books. The Saints are scattered, and many too poor to travel, and the means at our command very limited.

The continued emigration and consequent loss [p. 142] of members account for this to some extent, but we are striving to use what we have to the best advantage. We may say though few in number the spirit of unity prevails, and all work harmoniously together, and have great joy in their labors. The Society is doing its best, and there are no hard feelings among us. The Elders meet with the sisters from time to time, and much valuable counsel is given and cherished.

It has been the President's wish, and the sisters have so far carried it out to the best of their ability, that when visiting we should go into the different homes not with a prying curiosity, or a patronizing air, but with true sisterly feelings and sympathy in our hearts for the sufferings and sorrows of others. We have endeavored to carry relief and the precious truths we are in possession of together into the houses of those we visit, and rich is the reward when we hear and see what happiness follows. There is a luxury above all others in this world, and it is the exquisite luxury of doing good to our fellow creatures, although we may be only messengers, only carriers, only instruments in the hands of others, there is one sight seen of us that few others ever see—the grateful look, the eloquent tear, and the fervent "God bless you!" In the first

---

377. Frances Cornell and her husband, Thomas, emigrated to Salt Lake City in 1887. ("The Immigrants," *Deseret News* [weekly], June 8, 1887, 336.)

blush of surprise and thankfulness lies our reward and the reward of the benevolent also.

We desire to go on with this work and lighten many hearts and cheer many homes, and trust that means will ever be in our hands to give to the needy and sick and afflicted, and health to carry on this noble work.

Your sister in the Gospel,

M. E. Scoles, Sec. pro tem.

4.23 Zina D. H. Young, Letter to Eliza Stewart Udall, March 19, 1889, and Eliza Stewart Udall Reply, March 31, 1889

Zina D. H. Young, Letter to Eliza Luella Stewart Udall, Mar. 19, 1889; one page; and Eliza Luella Stewart Udall, Letter to Zina D. H. Young, Mar. 31, 1889; incomplete (unsigned); one page; Relief Society Historical Files, 1888–1984, CHL (CR 11 301).

Eliza Luella Stewart Udall arrived in St. Johns, Arizona, in October 1880 with her husband, David King Udall, who had been appointed as the first bishop of the newly organized St. Johns Ward, and their first child, a three-month-old daughter.[378] At the time of their arrival, church meetings were held "in a bowery (a room built of greasewood and covered with grease wood brush)."[379] Eliza Udall was soon appointed as secretary to fill a vacancy in the ward Relief Society.[380]

Some of the Mormon residents in St. Johns, including Bishop Udall, became embroiled in heated land disputes with original settlers. In 1885 Udall was convicted of perjury in relation to a land claim and sentenced to prison.[381] Eliza Udall encouraged her husband to "be cheerful as possible for I believe you will soon be permitted to return home. If our lives can all be spared to meet again, lets not complain."[382] A month later Eliza Udall wrote to her husband that their baby, Mary, was "quite sick, and has had a very rough time of it. She is reduced as much as a child could be in flesh."[383] Mary died a few days later. David wrote to Eliza: "For you to have to bury one of the sweet little ones, without my presence and support how great the trial you must of indured."[384] In December 1885 David was released from prison.[385]

---

378. David King Udall and Pearl Udall Nelson, *Arizona Pioneer Mormon: David King Udall, His Story and His Family, 1851–1938* (Tucson: Arizona Silhouettes, 1959), 66–67; Andrew Jenson, *Latter-day Saint Biographical Encyclopedia: A Compilation of Biographical Sketches of Prominent Men and Women in the Church of Jesus Christ of Latter-day Saints,* 4 vols. (Salt Lake City: Andrew Jenson History Co., 1901–1936), 1:325.

379. "St. Johns Ward, 1880," in Saint Johns Ward, Saint Johns Stake, Saint Johns Ward Manuscript History and Historical Reports, 1880–1982, CHL.

380. "Historical Sketch of the Relief Society of St. Johns Stake," in Saint Johns Arizona Stake, Saint Johns Arizona Stake Relief Society Minutes and Records, 1887–1973, CHL, 1.

381. C. LeRoy Wilhelm and Mabel R. Wilhelm, *A History of the St. Johns Arizona Stake: The Triumph of Man and His Religion over the Perils of a Raw Frontier* (Orem, UT: Historical Publications, 1982), 29–36, 49–51; "St. Johns Ward, 1885," in Saint Johns Ward Manuscript History and Historical Reports.

382. Eliza L. S. Udall to David K. Udall, Aug. 28, 1885, Udall Family Correspondence Collection, 1859–1950, CHL.

383. Eliza L. S. Udall to David K. Udall, Sept. 23, 1885, Udall Family Correspondence Collection, CHL.

384. David K. Udall to Eliza L. S. Udall, Oct. 5, 1885, Udall Family Correspondence Collection, CHL.

385. David K. Udall to Eliza L. S. Udall, Dec. 20, 1885, Udall Family Correspondence Collection, CHL.

A year and a half later, David Udall was appointed to serve as president of the recently organized St. Johns Stake, and his wife was set apart as president of the St. Johns Stake Relief Society, a capacity in which she served for over thirty years.[386] In March 1889 Eliza Udall received the invitation reproduced below from general Relief Society president Zina D. H. Young to attend a Relief Society conference to be held in conjunction with the church's general conference in Salt Lake City. A similar notice was printed in the *Woman's Exponent:* "It is hoped and expected there will be representative women from all the Stakes of Zion present, and no doubt much needed instruction will be given."[387] Udall declined the invitation but in her reply, also featured below, she gave a brief report of the Relief Society work in St. Johns.[388] The first-ever general Relief Society conference convened at the Assembly Hall in Salt Lake City on April 6, 1889, and included women representing nineteen stakes.[389]

———— ❧ ————

Letter to Eliza Stewart Udall, March 19, 1889

Salt Lake City, Utah
March 19. 1889

Mrs. E. S. L. Uedall
President Relief Society St. John's Stake
Dear Sister:

There will be a General Conference of the Relief Society held in this city sometime during the Annual Conference of the Church in April next. An invitation is hereby most cordially extended to you to be present on that occasion to represent the Relief Society in the Stake over which you have been appointed to preside. If it is not convenient for you to attend, one of your Counselors should be authorized to report in your stead

We are greatly in hopes that each Stake organization of the Relief Society will be represented by the President or one of her Counselors.

All officers and members of the Relief Society are also invited to attend the meeting.

Affectionately Your Sisters in the Gospel
Zina D. H. Young
Pesident
Emmeline B. Wells Cor. Sec'y
Central Board Relief Society

386. Wilhelm and Wilhelm, *History of the St. Johns Arizona Stake,* 351.

387. "Editorial Notes," *Woman's Exponent,* Apr. 1, 1889, 17:164.

388. Udall's husband, the stake president, did attend the conference. (David K. Udall to Eliza L. S. Udall, Apr. 11, 1889, Udall Family Correspondence Collection, CHL.)

389. "First General Conference of the Relief Society," *Woman's Exponent,* Apr. 15, 1889, 17:172–173; see also Document 4.24.

Eliza Stewart Udall Reply, March 31, 1889

[390]Springerville, Apache Co
Arizona March 31st 1889

Prest Zina D. H. Young,

Dear Sister,

Your cordial invitation of 19th ⟨to attend the Gen. Con of R. S.⟩ inst received and am sorry to inform you that it is not practicable for myself or Counsellors to attend owing to the high R. R. [railroad] ~~fare~~ rates & scarcity of Cash in this frontier Country. Our Societies in the St Johns Stake of Zion are in a prosperous condition. Our means is somewhat limited but still I believe we collect sufficiently to provide ⟨for ~~the~~ those who come under our supervision⟩— ~~We feel greatly~~ The sisters are as a rule faithful in attending meetings and are energetic in looking after the poor— We feel like ~~we are~~ ⟨it is a great⟩ ~~deprived~~ privation to live so far from head quarters and not have their kindly & ⟨encourging⟩ visits of our leading sisters & we ~~trust that in the near future we can have the privilege of beholding your dear~~ We will greatly appreciate a visit ~~when~~ ⟨if⟩ the time comes that we can be thus favored. Our sisters ⟨living⟩ in ⟨coming to⟩ this land have many sacrifices to make & it gives me pleasure to state that they nobly do their part in helping to make homes & redeem this barren Country

---

390. The version of Udall's reply transcribed here was probably a draft copy that she retained, as it is unsigned and has several revisions. No other version has been located.

Springerville, Apache Co
Arizona March 31st 1889

Prest Zina D. H. Young,

Dear Sister,

to attend the gen. con of R. S. Your cordial invitation of 19th inst. received and am sorry to inform you that it is not practicable for myself or Counsellors to attend owing to the high R. R. rates & scarcity of Cash in this frontier Country. Our Societies in the St Johns Stake of Zion are in a prosperous condition. Our means is somewhat limited but still I believe we collect sufficiently to provide for those who come under our supervision. The sisters are as a rule faithful in attending meetings and are energetic in looking after the poor. We feel like it is a great deprivation to live so far from head quarters and not have the kindly encouraging visits of our leading sisters & We trust that in the near future we can have the privilege of beholding your dear We will greatly appreciate a visit that we can be thus favored. Our sisters in this land have many sacrifices to make & It gives me Pleasure to state that they nobly do their part in helping

Letter from Eliza Stewart Udall to Zina D. H. Young. Because of the prohibitive cost of travel, St. Johns, Arizona, resident and stake Relief Society president Eliza Udall had to decline the invitation to attend the first Relief Society general conference in Salt Lake City. This document appears to be a draft of that letter that she retained, as it is unsigned and has several revisions. (Church History Library, Salt Lake City.)

4.24 Zina D. H. Young, Discourse, April 6, 1889

Zina D. H. Young, Discourse, Apr. 6, 1889, in "First General Conference of the Relief Society," Woman's Exponent *(Salt Lake City, UT), Apr. 15, 1889, vol. 17, no. 22, pp. 172–173.*

Although Relief Society conferences had been held in many stakes before 1889,[391] that year marked the first annual general Relief Society conference. The conference convened at the Assembly Hall on Temple Square on April 6, 1889, included representatives from nineteen stakes, and was presided over by Zina D. H. Young, who had succeeded Eliza R. Snow as general president after Snow's death in 1887.[392] During the conference Mary Isabella Horne noted "that Sister Eliza's mantle had fallen on Sister Zina just as Elijah's descended upon Elisha."[393]

While Snow had earlier used the semimonthly meetings of the Senior or General Retrenchment Association as a platform to discuss Relief Society matters with the women who attended, the time seemed propitious for Relief Society workers to meet in a general assembly of their own.[394] These general Relief Society conferences, along with visits of general board members to local Relief Societies and the communication network provided by the *Woman's Exponent,* promoted unity and a strong sense of sisterhood among Latter-day Saint women.

Several themes that characterized Young's presidency are evident in the address featured below. She affirmed the close connection of the Relief Society with its Nauvoo beginnings; invoked the memory and example of her predecessor, Eliza R. Snow; and made a fervent appeal for unity and righteous living. Young's address is reproduced here from a report of the conference published in the *Woman's Exponent* the week following the conference.[395] The preliminary remarks Young made as she conducted the meeting are also included in the transcript below.

———— ❧ ————

---

391. For information on the first stake Relief Society conference, held in the Weber Stake in Ogden, Utah, in October 1877, see Document 3.28.

392. "First General Conference of the Relief Society," *Woman's Exponent,* Apr. 15, 1889, 17:172–173; on Snow's death and Young as Snow's successor, see Document 4.18.

393. "First General Conference of the Relief Society," *Woman's Exponent,* Apr. 15, 1889, 17:173.

394. For more on the retrenchment movement and Snow's use of the General Retrenchment meeting as a pro tempore governing board, see Documents 3.16 and 3.18; and Jill Mulvay Derr et al., *Women of Covenant: The Story of Relief Society* (Salt Lake City: Deseret Book; Provo, UT: Brigham Young University Press, 1992), 114–119.

395. A handwritten version of Young's address dated "April 4th 1[8]89" is located in the Zina Card Brown Family Collection, 1806–1972, CHL. The handwritten version covers the same themes as the version featured here, and usually in the same order, but the wording between the two versions is quite different. The handwritten version may be the draft Young spoke from, which would mean the printed version featured here is a heavily edited version of her address; or, Young may have made extemporaneous departures from the draft or spoken from a later draft that has not survived.

FIRST GENERAL CONFERENCE OF THE RELIEF SOCIETY.

The first general conference of the Relief Society was held in the Salt Lake Assembly Hall Saturday evening April 6th, 1889. . . .[396]

Prest. Zina Young said: "My sisters, upon this occasion I hope you will give me your faith and prayers. As I look upon the sisters around me, I realize we miss our beloved Sister Eliza, who on all such occasions was with us. In the providence of the Lord she was taken from us. She mingles with those above; we revere her memory. As this is our first meeting of this kind I hope we can unite our hearts as one that the Lord will bless us in so coming together. May everything be agreeable that takes place here this evening." . . .

PRESIDENT ZINA D. H. YOUNG.

The Relief Society, under whose auspices we have met together here to-night, to receive instruction, and advice in our several duties, was first organized nearly half a century ago, by the Prophet Joseph Smith; after the pattern of the Holy Priesthood,[397] and under its direction, to dispense temporal blessings to the poor and needy: and to give encouragement to the weak, and restrain the erring ones, and for the better development, and exercise of woman's sympathies, and charities, that she might have opportunity to attain spiritual strength, and power for the accomplishment of greater good in the work of the redemption of the human family.

We should be diligent in all the duties of life, as mothers and wives, and as members ot [of] the Church, remembering to attend the meetings of the Saints, including our Fast-day meetings, and pay willing offerings to the poor, and our donations to the Temple; and with whatever belongs, especially to the mothers, observe the law of Tithing that the blessing promised may follow, and that the little children may be taught this important principle by example and educated in the path of duty, which is the path of safety. Teach them to keep the "Word of Wisdom," and to be temperate in all things; avoiding all evil habits and pernicious practises, that they may have strong bodies, and be entitled to the promise that follows obedience to this commandment.[398]

Let us be careful to speak with wisdom before our little ones, avoiding fault-finding, and slang phrases, and cultivate the higher attributes of our

---

396. TEXT: These ellipsis points and those in the next paragraph have been supplied by the editors of this volume. The full report of Young's sermon, as published in the *Woman's Exponent,* is reproduced here. Other material in the *Exponent*'s report of the conference has been omitted.

397. Sarah M. Kimball referenced this relationship between the priesthood and the Relief Society organization nearly a decade earlier. In an undated statement in the Salt Lake Stake Relief Society Record which appears before the volume's July 24, 1880, entry, she wrote: "[Joseph Smith] then declared the Society organized after the pattern, or order, of the priesthood." (Relief Society Record, 1880–1892, CHL, 5.)

398. See Doctrine and Covenants 89.

nature, that will tend to elevate, refine and purify the heart, and make the home the centre of attraction, where the spirit of love, peace and unity will dwell, and that sweet charity that thinketh no evil will ever abide; that we might always be possessed of that heavenly principle embodied in the song "Nay speak no ill."[399]

We should take the utmost pains to teach the children of Zion to be honest, virtuous, upright and punctual in all their duties; also to be industrious and keep the Sabbath day holy; not to be rigid or too severe, but as far as possible make all duties pleasurable. Mothers should never speak a word detrimental to the father's best interest before the children, for they are close observers. Sow good seeds in their young and tender minds, and always prefer principle to policy, thus you will lay up treasures in heaven.

Our sisters who have been called to preside in a Stake capacity, over several branches of the Relief Society, should plead for wisdom from above to direct their efforts, that the greatest possible good may be accomplished. They should visit each branch society in the Stake at least once a year, and oftener if circumstances will permit. Where sisters can do so, it would be desirable and we think profitable, to visit each other's organizations and become acquainted; it will tend to union and harmony, promote confidence, and strengthen the chords that bind us together, for there is more difference in our manner of speech, than in the motives of our hearts.

If the President of the society *cannot* be present to preside, it is her duty to see that one of her counselors attends to take charge of the meeting, for the success of an organization depends very much upon the efficiency and promptitude of its officers. When a vote is required one of the Counselors should make the motion, and after it has received a second, the President should present the motion, and call for the vote. President Joseph Smith's instructions to the Relief Society were, that the meetings should be conducted in a parliamentary manner.[400]

President Young, in great wisdom we believe, established the custom of holding quarterly conferences,[401] for the more perfect unity of interest in the Relief Society, and President Woodruff advises us to continue in this respect as we have been doing in the past. We should also keep correct minutes of our

---

399. The song "Nay, Speak No Ill" had been in circulation among the Latter-day Saints since at least the 1850s. The song first appeared in the official church hymnal in 1948. ("Speak Not Evil of One Another, Brothers," *Deseret News,* Apr. 16, 1853, [1]; *Hymns: Church of Jesus Christ of Latter-day Saints* [(Salt Lake City): Church of Jesus Christ of Latter-day Saints, 1948], 116, 374.)

400. See Document 1.2, entry for Mar. 17, 1842.

401. See Document 3.26.

meetings, that we may have a complete *record*, and then with very little trouble exact reports can be made to the General Conference.

I trust the sisters will not neglect or grow weary in the duty required of them in storing up *wheat*.[402] If it needs changing to preserve it, the Presidency advise, in the case of loaning it, the giving of written security, by the Bishop, for the full amount, and something added to allow for shrinkage, that the loan may be a *safe* business transaction, and that all interested may be satisfied.

When Relief Society Conferences are to be held, the Presidency of the Stake and the Bishops should be informed of the time, and invited to attend the meetings, that harmony and union may exist, and strength and encouragement be given to the diligent sisters, and that others seeing their good works, might be induced to come to meeting, and enjoy the same good spirit and feeling, that pervades the hearts of those who meet often one with another, to be instructed in their duties, and to gain spiritual strength and wisdom for the various vlcissitudies [vicissitudes] of life.

It is the privilege of the sisters, who are faithful in the discharge of their duties, and have received their endowments and blessings in the house of the Lord, to administer to their sisters, and to the little ones, in times of sickness, in meekness and humility, ever being careful to ask in the name of Jesus, and to give God the glory.[403]

Do not find fault with the Providences of God, it will not better our condition and only make our burdens heavier to bear; but rather be patient through all the trials of life, and speak not against the Lord's anointed.

It is our duty to be self-sustaining, and to foster and encourage home industries, and home manufactures, and patronize those institutions that have been established for the best interests of Zion;—to the co-operative stores; and be careful not to use the means we have been blessed with, to build up those, who are seeking to destroy and overthrow the work of God, and to plant discord, strife and dissension in our midst.[404]

The silk culture is one of the branches of home industry, that demands our earnest attention.[405] I have never yet doubted, but, that it would eventually

---

402. For more on the Relief Society's storage of wheat, see Documents 3.25 and 4.2.

403. For more on women's ministrations to the sick, see Document 4.19.

404. For more on the cooperative stores, see Documents 3.24 and 3.28; see also Leonard J. Arrington, *Great Basin Kingdom: An Economic History of the Latter-day Saints, 1830–1900* (Cambridge, MA: Harvard University Press, 1958), 254.

405. For more on the silk industry, see Documents 3.4 and 4.3. Zina Young had been involved in the sericulture movement for many years. When the Utah Silk Association was organized in 1880, Young was a member of the board of directors. (See Mary Ann Hardy, "Minutes of a Meeting of the Relief Society of Payson City," *Woman's Exponent,* July 15, 1875, 4:27; and R. Simpson, "Utah Silk Association," *Woman's Exponent,* Jan. 15, 1880, 8:126.)

become a fruitful source of revenue to this country. In the first sermon that I heard Brigham Young preach in this valley, he remarked "there is silk in these elements,"[406] and I have heard a number of silk weavers say, "Utah silk was the best fib[e]red silk, they had ever seen." Sisters do not be discouraged in any of the duties we have undertaken to perform; I am aware we have many responsibilities resting upon us, and also realize, that we all have great need to be diligent and prayerful. The Deseret Hospital is one of the institutions that needs to be sustained, in order that we may have a place where the sick and the afflicted among our people, may go when it is necessary, and receive the medical and surgical care, nursing and attention suited to their condition; and where they can have the Elders of the Church to administer in the sacred ordinances of the holy priesthood.[407] We should not forget, or neglect our duty to this charitable institution; keep up your monthly donations for the Society, and continue to be members of the Association, and remember "he that giveth to the poor lendeth to the Lord and He will repay."[408]

We should use our influence, too for the establishment and maintenance of educational institutions, in which our children and young people, may be taught the true principles of the everlasting Gospel; and discourage any tendency to outside influences, calculated to lead them into doubt or unbelief.[409] In all things possible, let us endeavor to cultivate our home talent and stimulate our sisters to read, and to write, that they may be intelligent wives and mothers; read good books, especially the Bible, Book of Mormon and Doctrine and Covenants. The Exponent, is at present, the only paper we have where the voice of woman is sent forth especially, to instruct us in our duties, and encourage the brave and determined ones to persevere in the midst of difficulties, and also to give expression to the views and opinions of the women of Zion on subjects of vital importance. And we recommend that the sisters subscribe for it, and read it, that they may be posted upon the condition, growth and progress of the various organizations of the women in Zion, and elsewhere; and become familiar with the efforts being put forth, for the uplifting, and further

---

406. Brigham Young often promoted sericulture. (See, for example, Document 3.4.)

407. On the hospital, see Document 4.11.

408. Proverbs 19:17.

409. Concern about "outside influences" was ongoing. In 1878 a *Deseret News* editorial warned its readers that the ministers of the different religious denominations desired to use education as a means of "leading away 'Mormon' children into the bonds of sectarianism" and "depart from the faith of their fathers." Other denominations—including Episcopal, Congregational, Presbyterian, Methodist, and Catholic—made significant efforts to establish schools in the territory, believing that "the chief instrumentality for gaining a permanent Christian influence [in Utah] must be the education of the children." ("Wolves in Sheep's Clothing," *Deseret News* [weekly], Oct. 2, 1878, 552; J. M. Coyner, comp., *Hand-Book on Mormonism* [Salt Lake City: Hand-Book Publishing, 1882], 78–85.)

advancement of all womankind; and of the changes made from ttme [time] to time in the direction of progress.[410]

Sisters, let us be as one grand phalanx and stand for the right; let us be humble and firm, honor truth, and be valiant in sustaining it, not *presuming*, but trust-worthy in all things. Have we not shouldered the cross of the world's scorn, and braved its anathema with more valor, than the warrior the cannon's fury? Death with him, and then all is over, but we endure to live [p. 172] eternally. Purity, love and integrity, let these virtues live in our hearts; then the sunshine of a loving Father's smile will be ours. Do not doubt the goodness of God or the truth of the work in which we are engaged; but learn obedience, it is better than sacrifice; follow our file leaders and fear not.

May we do a work acceptable to our Heavenly Father, and that will meet the approbation of our brethren, who are called upon to endure for the truth's sake, what the Ancients did, when seeking to establish righteous principles to benefit humanity. May we as women of Zion, ever know and honor our true position, and continue to grow in grace, and abound in good works, until He whose right it is to reign shall come.[411]

---

410. On the *Exponent,* see Document 3.21; and Sherilyn Cox Bennion, "The *Woman's Exponent:* Forty-Two Years of Speaking for Women," *Utah Historical Quarterly* 44, no. 3 (Summer 1976): 222–239.

411. This marks the end of Young's discourse. The *Woman's Exponent* article continues for several more paragraphs, reporting on other proceedings of the conference.

4.25 Emery Stake Relief Society, Report, October 17, 1890

Emery Stake Relief Society, Report, Oct. 17, 1890, in "R. S. Repotr. Emery Stake," Woman's Exponent *(Salt Lake City, UT), Nov. 15, 1890, vol. 19, no. 11, pp. 87–88.*

During the 1880s the church came under intense pressure from the U.S. government to end the practice of plural marriage. In 1882 the Edmunds Act disenfranchised participants in plural marriage.[412] Five years later the Edmunds-Tucker Act disenfranchised all women in Utah Territory and also dissolved the Perpetual Emigrating Fund Company and the Corporation of the Church of Jesus Christ of Latter-day Saints.[413] The proposed Cullom-Struble Bill threatened even more difficulties, while a judicial ruling in 1890 denied U.S. citizenship to future Mormon immigrants, and government agents took other steps that "further reduced the ranks of Mormon voters."[414]

Church president Wilford Woodruff deliberated for many months about how to respond to these increasingly aggressive federal measures before reaching a decision. He wrote in his journal on September 25, 1890: "After Praying to the Lord & feeling inspired by his spirit I have issued the following proclamation." The statement included this critical passage: "Inasmuch as laws have been enacted by Congress forbidding plural marriages which laws have been pronounced constitutional by the court of last resort, I hereby declare my intention to submit to those laws, and to use my influence with the members of the Church over which I preside to have them do likewise."[415]

The Manifesto, as Woodruff's statement was known, was read in the church's general conference on October 6, 1890, "and accepted by a vote of the whole Conference which Act Created a sensation throughout the whole United States."[416] Joseph H. Dean, recently returned from presiding over the Samoan mission, described the reaction of church

---

412. An Act to Amend Section Fifty-Three Hundred and Fifty-Two of the Revised Statutes of the United States, in Reference to Bigamy, and for Other Purposes [Mar. 22, 1882], *The Statutes at Large of the United States of America, from December, 1881, to March, 1883,* vol. 22 (Washington DC: Government Printing Office, 1883), 47th Cong., 1st Sess., ch. 47, pp. 30–32.

413. An Act to Amend an Act Entitled "An Act to Amend Section Fifty-Three Hundred and Fifty-Two of the Revised Statutes of the United States, in Reference to Bigamy, and for Other Purposes," Approved March Twenty-Second, Eighteen Hundred and Eighty-Two [Mar. 3, 1887], *The Statutes at Large of the United States of America, from December, 1885, to March, 1887,* vol. 24 (Washington DC: Government Printing Office, 1887), 49th Cong., 2nd Sess., ch. 397, pp. 365–641; see also Document 4.15.

414. Thomas G. Alexander, "The Odyssey of a Latter-day Prophet: Wilford Woodruff and the Manifesto of 1890," in *In the Whirlpool: The Pre-Manifesto Letters of President Wilford Woodruff to the William Atkin Family, 1885–1890,* ed. Reid L. Neilson, with contributions by Thomas G. Alexander and Jan Shipps (Norman, OK: Arthur H. Clark, 2011), 84; see also introduction to Part 4.

415. Wilford Woodruff, Journals, 1833–1898, Wilford Woodruff, Journals and Papers, 1828–1898, CHL, Sept. 25, 1890.

416. Woodruff, Journal, Oct. 6, 1890; see also *Manifesto of the Presidency and Apostles Issued December 12, 1889, Also the Official Declaration or Manifesto by President Wilford Woodruff Prohibiting Further Plural Marriages, and Its Adoption by the General Conference, October 6, 1890* (Salt Lake City: Deseret News, [1890]); and Official Declaration 1, Doctrine and Covenants.

members in general conference: "Many of the saints seemed stunned and confused and hardly knew how to vote, feeling that if they endorsed it they would be voting against one of the most sacred and important principles of their religion, and yet, as it had been promulgated by the prophet, seer and revelator and the earthly mouthpiece of the Almighty, they felt it must be proper for some reason or other. There were no opposition votes, but many of the saints refrained from voting either way." He further noted, "A great many of the sisters weeped silently, and seemed to feel worse than the brethren."[417]

Church leaders gave little definitive guidance about what the Manifesto meant regarding the status of current plural wives, but several leaders spoke passionately against men deserting their wives and children. Wilford Woodruff, for example, said, "This manifesto only refers to future marriages, and does not affect past conditions. I did not, could not and would not promise that you would desert your wives and children. This you cannot do in honor."[418] Leaders taught that men should support their wives, but cohabitation was supposed to cease. In general, as historian Kathryn Daynes observed, "each family decided for itself how to react to the new situation."[419]

Helen M. Whitney, writing for the *Woman's Exponent,* expressed her faith in church leaders but also in the doctrine that the Saints were laying aside. She reported that she had studied the general conference minutes "with a prayerful heart and desire for the right spirit and understanding to judge of its true source. And the testimony, and spirit that came to me was strong enough to convince me that this step was right." She continued, "Although they have yielded one point to the powers that be, no true saint will *renounce* a truth or a doctrine of this faith for which Joseph Smith and many more have laid down their lives to establish."[420]

Another glimpse into how Mormon women responded to the Manifesto comes from the following report of the Emery Stake Relief Society conference held October 17, 1890, less than two weeks after the Manifesto was read at the general conference. Mormons had settled the Emery area of Castle Valley, in central Utah, in 1877.[421] Ane Ungermann Larsen was appointed president when members organized the Emery Stake Relief Society on August 13, 1882. Larsen selected a first counselor, Josie E. Childs, and a secretary, but roughly two years passed before Ann Beers Pulsipher was appointed as her second counselor.[422] A history of

417. Joseph H. Dean, Journals, 1876–1944, CHL, Oct. 6, 1890. On Dean, see Andrew Jenson, *Latter-day Saint Biographical Encyclopedia: A Compilation of Biographical Sketches of Prominent Men and Women in the Church of Jesus Christ of Latter-day Saints,* 4 vols. (Salt Lake City: Andrew Jenson History Co., 1901–1936), 4:366.

418. Abraham H. Cannon, Diaries, 1879–1895, 20th Century Western and Mormon Manuscripts, L. Tom Perry Special Collections, Harold B. Lee Library, Brigham Young University, Provo, UT, vol. 13, pp. 133–134.

419. Kathryn M. Daynes, *More Wives Than One: Transformation of the Mormon Marriage System, 1840–1910* (Urbana: University of Illinois Press, 2001), 184.

420. Helen M. Whitney, "The Opinion of an American Woman Whose Forefathers Fought for the Liberty That We Are Denied Today," *Woman's Exponent,* Nov. 15, 1890, 19:81–82, italics in original.

421. Stella McElprang, comp., *"Castle Valley": A History of Emery County* (n.p.: Emery County Company of the Daughters of Utah Pioneers, 1949), 17.

422. "Historical Record of the Relief Society of Emery Stake," ca. 1901, in Castle Dale Utah Stake, Castle Dale Utah Stake Relief Society Minutes and Records, 1882–1973, CHL; Edward A. Geary,

the stake Relief Society noted that a "striking feature with these three women [the members of the stake Relief Society presidency] was, they all lived the Plurality of Marriage."[423]

———— ❧ ————

R. S. REPOTR.

EMERY STAKE.

The Semi-annual Conference of the Relief Society of Emery Stake, convened at Orangeville, Oct. 17, 1890. Counselor Annie Pulsifer [Ann Pulsipher] presiding. Choir sang, prayer by Brother E. [Erastus] Curtis,[424] singing, Counselor Pulsifer made a few opening remarks and regreted our beloved President Anna Larsen could not be with us her health would not permit, but desired we would have an interesting time, as she felt the Spirit of the Lord to be with us; the Satistical reports were read and accepted, the Representatives of each ward were called to report. President Robinson [Rhoda Robertson][425] of Orangeville felt well in her labors with her sisters, attended Conference in Salt Lake City and felt amply repaid. The feast of spiritual food she recieved gave her strength to go forward in trying to perform the many duties devolving upon her. Counselor Hannah Seeley [Seely] reported the Castle Dale ward, said the sisters were trying to attend to their duties spiritually and financially the meetings were tolerably well attended (but of course it could be better). Sister Jane Woodward of Huntington said the sisters were on hand and willing to go forward in helping in this great work. We live in an eventful period of time and should be united and help to bear each others burdens, prayed for the Lord to give us strength to do right. Ferron, Molen and Emery wards were not represented. Counselor Pulsifer gave some interesting instructions exhorting the sisters to attend to their spiritual duties spoke of the trials the Saints had gone through and were now passing through, refered to the Manifesto that President Woodruff had issued, spoke very interestingly. Sister Sarah Fullmer also refered to the Manifesto and found it already was trying some people, no matter what men or nations may do, she knew that law was from God. we should stand firm and hold on to the principles of the everlasting Gospel. Sister Jane Peterson of Castle Dale felt pleased to meet with the sisters, had been in

---

A History of Emery County (Salt Lake City: Utah State Historical Society and Emery County Commission, 1996), 118.

423. "Historical Record of the Relief Society of Emery Stake," ca. 1901, in Castle Dale Utah Stake Relief Society Minutes and Records.

424. Probably Erastus Curtis Sr. (1828–1902), but possibly Erastus Curtis Jr. (1858–1941). (See Geary, *History of Emery County,* 66, 69, 76, 78, 124, 140.)

425. Orangeville Ward, Emery Stake, Orangeville Ward Relief Society Minutes and Records, 1882–1967, CHL, vol. 1, pp. 6, 162.

this Church many years; even in Nauvoo with the saints, quoted many sayings of the Prophet Joseph Smith, exhorted the mothers to teach their children the principles of truth and righteousness, spoke very interestingly on other subjects. Sisters J. [Johanna] P. Curtis and J. [Elizabeth Jane] Johnson each bore their testimony and spoke well, Counselor Andrew Anderson of Orangeville addressed the conference a short time. Choir sang "Do what is right."[426] Adjourned until 2 p. m.

Afternoon services. Singing "O God our help." Prayer by Bishop Robinson [Jasper Robertson][427] of Orangeville. Singing "Hark ye mortals."[428] Coun- A Pulsifer spoke very encouragingly to the sisters on different subjects. President [Lodema] Cheney of Y. L. M. I. Association made a few remarks and Bishop Robinson of Orangeville occupied [p. 87] a short time speaking interestingly, thought one great failing we had was ingratitude[.] Paul may plant and Apollus water, but God givith the increase.[429] We were in possession of all truths if we would give them heed, and those truths would lead us to an exaltation in the kingdom of God, if we would only follow the path marked out for us. Sister [Elizabeth] Reid felt to encourage the sisters in this great and good work, had attended Salt Lake City conference and felt greatly built up in her faith and to go forward in every duty. Sister E. Guyman [Elizabeth Guymon] also spoke well and felt encouraged to perform the work required of her, ask an interest in the prayers of all and strive to speak evil of no one. Other sisters spoke and the remainder of the afternoon was given to the W. S. A. [Woman Suffrage Association] to transact some business. President S- Fulmer[430] addressed the meeting in a spirited manner urging the sisters to read and strive to gain all imformation necessary for the advancment of our cause. Several joined and one officer elected. Meettng appointed for Nov. 10th. Conference adjourned for six months.

M. J. [Samantha (Manty) Jane] Shipp, Sec. protem.

Annie U. Larsen, Pres.

---

426. Hymn 151, *Sacred Hymns and Spiritual Songs. For the Church of Jesus Christ of Latter-day Saints,* 14th ed. (Salt Lake City: George Q. Cannon, 1871), 165–166.

427. Jenson, *LDS Biographical Encyclopedia,* 4:463.

428. Hymns 134 and 27, *Sacred Hymns and Spiritual Songs,* 35–36, 147–148.

429. See 1 Corinthians 3:5–6.

430. The prior year Sarah Ann Fullmer had thanked the Orangeville women "for the Honor they had bestowed upon her," possibly referring to her appointment to the suffrage organization. On May 1, 1890, Fullmer "spoke of the Suffrage Association quite Lengthy & wanted the Sisters to get the Spirit [of] Suffrage more than they had." (Orangeville Ward Relief Society Minutes and Records, Oct. 21, 1889, and May 1, 1890; see also Geary, *History of Emery County,* 120.)

4.26 Zina Y. Card, Letter to the *Exponent,* November 20, 1890

Zina Y. Card, Letter to the editor of the Woman's Exponent, *Nov. 20, 1890, in "The Sisters in Canada,"* Woman's Exponent *(Salt Lake City, UT), Dec. 15, 1890, vol. 19, no. 13, p. 101.*

In the aftermath of President Wilford Woodruff's manifesto on plural marriage[431] and her own husband's indictment for illegal cohabitation, Zina Presendia Young Card wrote the following letter from Cardston, Alberta, Canada, to the *Woman's Exponent* in November 1890. Card and her mother, Zina D. H. Young, shared strong convictions about plural marriage. The elder Zina, who had been a plural wife to Joseph Smith and later to Brigham Young, declared in 1878: "It is a principle of the Gods . . . and we want our children to practice it, that through us a race of men and women may grow up possessing sound minds in sound bodies who shall live to the age of a tree."[432] Zina D. H. Young was present at the October 1890 general conference when Woodruff's manifesto on plural marriage was read and approved. She wrote in her diary, "To day the harts of all ware tried but looked to God & submitted . . . we are the same Latterday Saints, but God's true laws they will not allow us to keep sacred."[433]

Card herself entered into plural marriage in 1868; her husband, Thomas Williams, died in 1874, leaving her a widow with two children. A decade later she became a plural wife of Charles O. Card, president of the Cache Stake in northern Utah;[434] in 1887 they moved to Alberta, Canada, to avoid prosecution in the United States.[435] Charles Card reported that once when he and Zina attended a party with several Canadian political leaders, someone "said something about Polygamy to my wife and she fired up in defence and some rather sharp retorts were indulged in."[436]

In March 1890 Charles Card, who had been indicted in Utah for illegal cohabitation, decided to face trial in Utah, hoping he could obtain an acquittal and then perhaps return to his residence in Logan.[437] On November 17, 1890, he gave his "wife & children the parting kiss" and started for Utah to face his indictment. "Whether I go to suffer for keeping

---

431. See Document 4.25.

432. Martha Sonntag Bradley and Mary Brown Firmage Woodward, *4 Zinas: A Story of Mothers and Daughters on the Mormon Frontier* (Salt Lake City: Signature Books, 2000), 348.

433. Zina D. H. Young, Diary, Apr. 1890–Aug. 1897, Zina Card Brown Family Collection, 1806–1972, CHL, Oct. 6, 1890.

434. Bradley and Woodward, *4 Zinas*, 249, 314; Donald G. Godfrey and Brigham Y. Card, eds., *The Diaries of Charles Ora Card: The Canadian Years, 1886–1903* (Salt Lake City: University of Utah Press, 1993), xxxvii.

435. Charles O. Card, Diary, Mar. 21–22, 1887, in Godfrey and Card, *Diaries of Charles Ora Card,* 40–41; Jessie L. Embry, "Exiles for the Principle: LDS Polygamy in Canada," *Dialogue: A Journal of Mormon Thought* 18, no. 3 (Fall 1985): 108–109.

436. Card, Diary, Aug. 28, 1890, in Godfrey and Card, *Diaries of Charles Ora Card,* 149.

437. Charles O. Card to Wilford Woodruff, June 24, 1890, Wilford Woodruff Stake Correspondence Files, 1887–1898, CHL; see also Card, Diary, Mar. 4, 1890, in Godfrey and Card, *Diaries of Charles Ora Card,* 117.

the commands of God in prison or be acquitted the Lord only can tell," he recorded.[438] Three days later, Zina Card wrote this letter.

——— ❧ ———

THE SISTERS IN CANADA.

DEAR EXPONENT:

Our life here seems uneventful compared to yours in "Dear Utah," months have passed since our return, and yet much has happened that was important to us. I am perhaps vain when I fancy it may be of interest to many dear friends in the "land of my birth," to relate some of them.

My dear mother's presence here was the signal for many pleasant gatherings, for spirited and spiritual feasts, when the gifts were ours and she seemed the humble and chosen one to be like a ministering angel to us, giving new courage and patience, by her cheerful precepts and example, but like most of our earthly joys, she has left us, only I trust for a season.[439] Perhaps she has told you of our Fair, held jointly by the R. S., Y. L. M. I. A., and the Primary Association.[440] Like all such affairs it was a big success, we all opened our eyes to see how many useful, pretty and necessary articles were in our possession, how wonderfully smart our little ones are, and what great big delicious, vegetables we have in abundance, a turnip that weighed 23lbs. Eleven potatoes 27lbs. Golden butter, white bread, pies, cakes and tarts all made by the deft little fingers or our dear children. Then the agreeable and genuine surprise given by the Pres. and members of the Relief Society[441] to their beloved President, Sister Zina "Our mother" as they call her.

---

438. Card Diary, Nov. 17 and 21, 1890, in Godfrey and Card, *Diaries of Charles Ora Card,* 158–159. In his December jury trial, Card was found not guilty and allowed to go free. He returned to his family in Cardston in January 1891. The Cards remained in Canada until 1903. (Card, Diary, Dec. 22, 1890, and Jan. 15, 1891, in Godfrey and Card, *Diaries of Charles Ora Card,* 163–164, 168; Bradley and Woodward, *4 Zinas,* 378–380.)

439. Zina D. H. Young arrived in southern Alberta in about early August 1890 and departed for Utah at the end of September 1890. (Zina D. H. Young to Charles O. Card, Aug. 5, 1890, Zina D. Young Correspondence, Zina Card Brown Family Collection, 1806–1972, CHL; Young, Diary, Sept. 29, 1890.)

440. The fair, organized at Card's suggestion, was held September 17, 1890. "Sister Zina Y Card spoke on the subject of our having a fair . . . and use the means that we made towards a bell for the meeting house; thought it [would] benefit our children, it will learn them to try and make themselves useful." (Cardston Ward, Alberta Stake, Cardston Ward Relief Society Minutes and Records, 1887–1911, CHL, bk. A, Aug. 21, 1890; Cardston Ward, Alberta Stake, Cardston Ward Young Women's Mutual Improvement Association Minutes and Records, 1887–1917, CHL, vol. 1, Sept. 17, 1890.)

441. The Cardston Relief Society president was Sarah B. Daines. ("Canada," *Woman's Exponent,* June 1, 1900, 29:4.)

Zina Diantha Huntington Young and daughter Zina Presendia Young Card. This mother and daughter are photographed here circa 1880–1890, in the approximate time period that Zina Young became general president of the Relief Society. They closely supported and advised one another in family and church life. (Church History Library, Salt Lake City.)

We had a charming visit from Prof. Saunders, Gov. Agent for the Experimental Farms, of which there are five.[442] He came to see what progress we were making as agriculturists, expressed himself as surprised and pleased with our progress, and predicted a bright and prosperous future for us.

Mr. Ross, Superentendent and builder of the great Canadian Pacific R. R. gave us a call, he came to look at the country with a view to building a new road from Edmonton some 500 miles north, down through this section of country across the line.[443] The new road will be the highway for coal, coal oil, minerals, timber and the products of the ranchers and farmers of this great land.[444]

The opening of the Canadian and Great Falls Railroad is another important feature here, giving us direct communication by rail within 50 miles, and gives a new impetus to business generally.[445]

Now my dear friends if you want to come and see us, remember it is only 800 miles, will cost you about the same as a trip to San Francisco, or less, and you can get here inside of four days. We do not live in an Eden, nor without hard work, but we have plenty to eat, plenty to wear, can guarantee to keep you cool in Summer and warm in winter.

John T. Caine is elected, some may say, what's that to you?[446] Just let me whisper in your ear, *I was born in Utah*, and every thing that effects her finds

442. William Saunders (1836–1914) was a prominent Canadian scientist and agricultural expert. Charles O. Card met Saunders during an 1888 visit to Ottawa: "We were driven out to the Central Agricultural Farm where we spent a very pleasant & entertaining afternoon listening to Prof. Wm Saunders explain the plans of farm stock, Barnes, offices, Henery [hennery], Cellars, plants, trees, grains, shrubs etc. We found Prof Saunders a regular Encyclopedia of information and with all filled with the milk of human kindness." (Ian M. Stewart, "Saunders, William," *Dictionary of Canadian Biography,* vol. 14, *1911–1920* [Toronto: University of Toronto Press, 1998], 907–908; Card, Diary, Nov. 13, 1888, in Godfrey and Card, *Diaries of Charles Ora Card,* 68.)

443. James Ross (1848–1913) was a railway engineer, contractor, and businessman. The railway line between Calgary and Edmonton was completed in 1891. ("James Ross, Financier, Dies," *New York Times,* Sept. 21, 1913, 15; Theodore D. Regehr, "Ross, James," *Dictionary of Canadian Biography,* vol. 14, *1911–1920,* 896–899.)

444. As was true of the American frontier, the railroads played a significant role in moving "settlers into and wealth out of" western Canada during this period. Contractors and laborers from many areas— including at least one rock and grading crew from Cache Valley, Utah—helped with construction. (Godfrey and Card, *Diaries of Charles Ora Card,* xxiii.)

445. "By 1890 a branch railway connected Lethbridge with Great Falls, Montana, linking this corner of Alberta with American railroads which extended southward to Utah." (Godfrey and Card, *Diaries of Charles Ora Card,* xxiii.)

446. John Thomas Caine (1829–1911), a Mormon convert from the Isle of Man, was Utah Territory's fourth delegate to the U.S. Congress. He served from 1882 to 1893. At the time Card wrote this *Exponent* letter, Caine had just been reelected to his final term in Congress. (Andrew Jenson, *Latter-day Saint Biographical Encyclopedia: A Compilation of Biographical Sketches of Prominent Men and Women in the Church of Jesus Christ of Latter-day Saints,* 4 vols. [Salt Lake City: Andrew Jenson History Co., 1901–1936], 1:726–738; "Voters," *Salt Lake Herald,* Nov. 4, 1890, 4.)

an echo in my heart, do you think any Utah boy or girl could read the rousing speeches from our own faithful sons, fathers and husbands without saying "God bless and help them forever?"

Often my soul is singing:

> O dear Utah I sigh for thee in vain,
> Fain would I die to free thee from the despot's iron chain;
> Once thou coulds't boast of freedom in thy mountains vales and
>   glens,
> O! give me back those good old days, and my dear old home again!

What Jerusalem is to the Jew,—so is Utah to the hearts of her mountain boys and girls, yet I would not, *could* not live there now. Why? because the holy priesthood has said my place was here. So my wings are folded, content in my nest, I sing, no I mean chirp to my little brood, try to be content with all the changes that find me, some unprepared and some otherwise, amongst the former was the "Manifesto," it took my breath away, but it gradually narrowed down from what at first seemed a strange pill to the very draught that was needed in our present state, religiously and politically. It has caused some comment here from various stand points, but we feel our true position is known and appreciated now as it could not be before the issuing of the Manifesto, and the saints here as a whole all feel our leaders are carrying on Christ's work to victory and are *one* with the saints in the land of Zion.

Hum! I fear you will think me tedious so will just add, the health of the saints is excellent, weather delightful. Pres. Card's brief visit filled all with new courage.[447] Our school will begin next week with Sterling Williams as teacher. All our Societies are in excellent running order.

Love to all the dear ones, and hope if any feel that they are neglected they will know they live with truer and more enduring ties in the heart of their absent sister and friend,

ZINA Y. CARD.

Cardston, Alberta Canada, Nov. 20, 1890.

---

447. Presumably a reference to Alberta Stake president Charles O. Card, Zina Card's husband. (Bradley and Woodward, *4 Zinas*, 292.)

4.27 Emmeline B. Wells, "A Glimpse of Washington," March 1, 1891

[Emmeline B. Wells], "A Glimpse of Washington. The Woman's National Council," Woman's Exponent *(Salt Lake City, UT), Mar. 1, 1891, vol. 19, no. 17, pp. 132–133.*

To celebrate the fortieth anniversary of the foundational women's rights convention, held in Seneca Falls, New York, in July 1848, Susan B. Anthony and Elizabeth Cady Stanton, officers of the National Woman Suffrage Association, invited women's associations from around the world to a March 1888 commemorative meeting in Washington DC.[448] The delegates, including three Latter-day Saint women from Utah,[449] agreed to the proposition that an International Council of Women be organized to coordinate the efforts of all the associations dedicated to advancing the status of women politically, economically, socially, and educationally. The delegates were advised to organize national councils in their respective countries, with the United States being the first to do so.[450]

In January 1891, a few weeks before the first triennial convention of the National Council of Women was scheduled to begin, general Relief Society president Zina D. H. Young sent letters to the church's stake Relief Society presidents asking them to collect donations to help cover the costs of sending delegates. Emmeline B. Wells, who was corresponding secretary for the general presidency, immediately thought first counselor Jane S. Richards the best-qualified woman to speak at the convention as a delegate, but Wells consented to attend also.[451] On January 23, Wells, Richards, Sarah M. Kimball, Phebe Y. Beatie, and Caroline S. Thomas were set apart by the church's First Presidency to represent the Relief Society and Young Ladies' Mutual Improvement Association (Y.L.M.I.A.).[452] At this first triennial meeting, which officially opened in Washington DC on February 23, 1891, the Relief Society and Y.L.M.I.A. joined the council as two of the original ten

---

448. Delegates representing fifty-three women's organizations from seven countries attended this congress. (Louise Barnum Robbins, ed., *History and Minutes of the National Council of Women of the United States, Organized in Washington, D. C., March 31, 1888* [Boston: E. B. Stillings, 1898], 3–6.)

449. "The Relief Society, Young Ladies' Society and the Primary organization were respectively represented by Mrs. Margaret Caine, Mrs. Emily Richards and Mrs. Nettie Snell." ("The Women's Council," *Deseret News* [weekly], Apr. 25, 1888, 234.)

450. "The Woman's National Council," *Woman's Exponent,* Mar. 1, 1889, 17:151–152.

451. Emmeline B. Wells, Diaries, 1844–1920, 46 vols., L. Tom Perry Special Collections, Harold B. Lee Library, Brigham Young University, Provo, UT, vol. 14, Jan. 22 and 23, 1891.

452. Wells, Diary, vol. 14, Jan. 23, 1891. Kimball went as president of the Utah Woman Suffrage Association, a position she held from January 1890 to October 1893, when Wells succeeded her. Beatie served on the Relief Society general board. Thomas was an officer of the Y.L.M.I.A. (Carol Cornwall Madsen, *An Advocate for Women: The Public Life of Emmeline B. Wells, 1870–1920,* Biographies in Latter-day Saint History [Provo, UT: Brigham Young University Press, 2006], 270; "Utah W. S. A.," *Woman's Exponent,* Jan. 15, 1890, 18:125; S. M. Kimball, "Greeting," *Woman's Exponent,* Feb. 15, 1890, 18:139; Annie Wells Cannon, "Mrs. Phoebe Young Beatie," *Relief Society Magazine,* Oct. 1931, 562; Young Ladies' Mutual Improvement Association, Certificate of Appointment to Carolina T. Thomas, ca. 1891, CHL.)

Receipt for payment of dues, February 28, 1891. This receipt, issued by M. Louise Thomas, treasurer of the National Council of Women, acknowledges payment of a $100 membership fee by the "Young Woman's Mutual Improvement Association." The Relief Society and the Young Ladies' Mutual Improvement Association were two of the original ten charter member organizations of the council. (Church History Library, Salt Lake City.)

member organizations.[453] By joining the council, the Relief Society moved into a new coop-erative mode with national and international women's organizations.

The following article is Wells's account of this initial meeting as published in the March 1, 1891, issue of the *Woman's Exponent,* of which Wells was the editor.[454] Wells led the delegation that successfully applied for membership in the national council. When the delegation of Mormon women submitted their credentials to the National Council of Women they were uncertain if they would be acknowledged. Susan B. Anthony informed the delegation herself of "the good news that we were admitted without a dissenting vote."[455] The Utah delegates spoke on the last day of the convention, Wednesday, February 25. Thomas read a paper about the Y.L.M.I.A., Richards spoke extemporaneously about the Relief Society, and Wells read prepared remarks about the society.[456]

The strength of the longstanding personal relationships that had developed through two decades of shared work in the national suffrage movement kept Mormon women ac-tive, contributing members to the National Council of Women and the International Council of Women.[457] Both of the Latter-day Saint organizations that joined that year re-tained membership in these councils for more than eighty years.

——— ❧ ———

A GLIMPSE OF WASHINGTON.
THE WOMAN'S NATIONAL COUNCIL.

We had a pleasant journey to this city.[458] Leaving Salt Lake City, Monday, 7 a. m, Feb. 16, and arriving in Washington, Thursday, Feb. 19, at 10 p. m., our train was delayed a short time at Baltimore, or we would have reached here at 8:15 p. m. Mr. and Mrs. F. S. Richards [Franklin S. Richards and Emily Tanner

---

453. For purposes of its membership in the council, the Relief Society called itself the National Woman's Relief Society. "National" was added to the name as a requirement for membership and to emphasize that the society's charitable work was not restricted to Utah. The other eight original member organizations were the National Woman Suffrage Association, National Woman's Christian Temperance Union, Woman's Centenary Association of the Universalists Church, Woman's National Press Association, Wimodaughsis, Illinois Industrial Reform School for Girls, National Free Baptist Woman's Missionary Society, and Sorosis. (Mary Wright Sewall, *Genesis of the International Council of Women and the Story of Its Growth, 1888–1893* [Indianapolis, IN: n.p., 1914], 44.)

454. Though the *Exponent* issue was dated March 1, 1891, the issue was evidently published late, as Wells's article quotes from an article published in another newspaper on March 7, 1891. Wells may have mailed or telegraphed the article from Washington to Utah, or she may have submitted the article in person upon her return. ("Continued Report of the Council," *Woman's Tribune,* Mar. 7, 1891, 75.)

455. Wells, Diary, vol. 14, Feb. 21, 1891; Madsen, *An Advocate for Women,* 266–267.

456. Wells, Diary, vol. 14, Feb. 25, 1891.

457. See Joan Iversen, "The Mormon-Suffrage Relationship: Personal and Political Quandaries," in *Battle for the Ballot: Essays on Woman Suffrage in Utah, 1870–1896,* ed. Carol Cornwall Madsen (Logan: Utah State University Press, 1997), 150–160.

458. Seven delegates traveled from Salt Lake City to Washington DC: Emmeline B. Wells, delegate at large; Jane S. Richards, delegate for the Relief Society; Caroline Thomas, delegate for the Y.L.M.I.A.; her eighteen-year-old daughter, Kate Thomas; Sarah M. Kimball; Electa W. Bullock; and Phebe Y. Beatie. (Wells, Diary, vol. 14, Feb. 16 and 19, 1891.)

Richards][459] met us at the depot and accompanied our party to the Riggs House, where we registered and obtained such rooms as we could get, the house being already pretty well filled. Before we had been in the house an hour we were delighted to meet in the hallway, just for a moment, the *dear friend* of woman, Susan B. Anthony, and she expressed her pleasure at our coming, and gave us two or three good words of welcome and of cheer that we can never forget.

It was arranged before separating for the night that the following morning, Mr. and Mrs. Richards would call (they are at the Randall) and take those who wished to go to the White House and the Capitol Buildings, etc.

The next morning we went first to the White House, then to the War, State and Navy Buildings, and in the afternoon to the Senate and House of Representatives. It is impossible to tell you what we saw and heard, we would want time and space for that, but Mr. Richards told us all he could in the short space of time that we were together, and it was all most interesting, especially so to Mrs. Beattie [Phebe Beatie], Mrs. [Electa] Bullock and Miss Katie Thomas who had never been in Washington before.

During the day Mrs. Richards [Jane Snyder Richards] and the writer, also Mrs. [Caroline] Thomas, succeeded in obtaining an appointment for an interview the next morning at nine a. m. with Mrs. [May] Sewall, the Committee on Credentials for the Council. This was very satisfactory to all concerned, though we were somewhat in doubt as to how the general officers might vote upon our admission to the Council, and here let it be understood that there are certain articles in the Constitution that have to be complied with, etc., and several organizations who came expecting to join the Council are going back without doing so, because of this and that.[460]

On Saturday morning the Utah Delegation presented their *credentials*, and had an interview with Mrs. Sewall, the Cor. Sec'y. of the Woman's National Council as well as Committee on Credentials. Mrs. [Sarah] Kimball and Mrs. E. S. Richards, of Salt Lake City, were also with us. Our interview was satisfactory, as we were then informed exactly what was expected of us.

---

459. Emily Richards, daughter-in-law of delegate Jane S. Richards, was also an active Utah suffragist and often represented Latter-day Saint women at meetings of the National Woman Suffrage Association. ("Editorial Notes," *Woman's Exponent*, July 1, 1888, 17:20–21; "Utah's Lady Delegate," *Woman's Exponent*, Feb. 15, 1889, 17:137–138.)

460. See "Constitution of the National Council of Women of the United States, Organized at Washington, D.C., March 31, 1888," in *Transactions of the National Council of Women of the United States, Assembled in Washington, D.C., February 22 to 25, 1891*, ed. Rachel Foster Avery (Philadelphia: Executive Board of the National Council of Women, 1891), 360–361; and "The National Council of Women," *Woman's Exponent*, Jan. 1, 1891, 19:108–109.

The Executive Committee[461] held a meeting in the afternoon, and after its close we were notified that the Relief Society and Young Ladies' Mutual Improvement Associations were admitted to the Woman's National Council and the delegates entitled to representation.[462]

Saturday evening Mrs. [Jane] Spofford, the hostess here, and a most magnificent woman in heart as well as in appearance, gave a reception to the ladies of the Woman's Council and Convention. Many celebrated ladies were present besides those who live in the house.[463] The large dining room was handsomely decorated with stars and stripes; at one end there was an elevated platform for the musicians, and in a conspicuous place, at the end of the room, there was a large flag hung with one lone star on it representing Wyoming.[464] At the other end of the room stood the ladies who were receiving with Mrs. Spofford; Miss Frances E. Willard, President of the W. N. C.,[465] and N. W. C. Y. U.,[466] she has a lovely face and most genial expression, a smile and pleasant word for everybody. Miss Susan B. Anthony, Vice-President at large, etc., etc., and large she is in every way as well as liberal, she is certainly one of the grandest women of her time, or any other time; Mrs. May Wright Sewall, the Cor. Sec'y. of the W. N. C., and one of the ablest and brightest women of the day. She has excellent executive ability, and is exceedingly helpful with suggestions and ideas in all the work of the two great bodies of women, who are now holding sessions in this city, the Woman's Council and the Suffrage Convention. Mrs. Ella Dietz Clymer, the President of Sorosis,[467] of New York City, was one of the

---

461. A preliminary call for the first triennial meeting of the National Council of Women of the United States, issued on October 6, 1890, explained the organization of the executive board: "So soon as any organization enters the Council its president becomes an acting Vice-President in the Council, and it has also the right to appoint one person to represent it on the Executive Board of the Council. This Board includes the general officers of the Council together with the presidents of all organizations belonging to it, and one delegate besides its president from every organization." The executive board of 1890 included Frances E. Willard, president; Susan B. Anthony, vice president; Mary F. Eastman, recording secretary; M. Louise Thomas, treasurer; and May Wright Sewall, corresponding secretary. (Avery, *Transactions of the National Council of Women of the United States,* 10–11.)

462. See Wells, Diary, vol. 14, Feb. 21, 1891.

463. According to Wells, more than five hundred women were present. (Wells, Diary, vol. 14, Feb. 22, 1891.)

464. In 1869 Wyoming was the first territory or state to grant suffrage to women. The flag at this event "was a large American flag which, instead of the forty-four stars in the Union Jack, had one large lone star with the word 'Wyoming' inscribed under it. Here was the first break in the chain of forty-four States that had denied the right of suffrage to women." ("Women of the Nation," *Woman's Exponent,* Mar. 1, 1891, 19:133.)

465. Woman's National Council, properly titled the National Council of Women.

466. National Woman's Christian Temperance Union, properly abbreviated N.W.C.T.U.

467. Sorosis was an association for professional women, founded in 1868. Clymer explained that Sorosis was intended to promote discussions among "women of literary, artistic, and scientific tastes" and

most attractive women leaders; she is very much complimented in the papers and by the people, not only on account of her beauty, but style and elegance in dress. Mrs. Sara Andrews Spencer was in line with those who were receiving; and the heart of the writer gave a great bound at sight of her intelligent and smiling face, remembering all her help and kindness on our first visit to this wonderful city, and how she had aided us with advice, and who will never be forgotten.[468]

The reception was a brilliant affair, not so much in the way of dress as in the brilliant eyes and faces of the beautiful and celebrated women assembled to greet the hostess and her co-workers. There were, however, some very elegant costumes, some artistic and Parisian. Mrs. Rachel Foster-Avery, whom Miss Anthony declares to be the best cor. sec'y. in the world, wore a very heavy white brocaded silk with an immense train, and she looked charming. She has one of the sweetest faces and most fascinating manners. There are many we would like to mention by name, but cannot do the subject justice, and so will only say there were women lawyers, doctors, ministers, artists, editors, correspondents and reporters.[469]

The ladies (for there were *very* few gentlemen) congregated in groups chatting for a few minutes in a friendly way, and later on a part of the company (for many had already retired) went up to Mrs. Spofford's apartments, and were ushered into a room profusely decorated with flowers, where lunch was served in the most delightful way. Icecream, cakes, dainties and salads, and the most delicious coffee; but the greatest attraction there was the presence of such women as Susan B. Anthony, Isabella Beecher Hooker, Clara Barton and others known to fame, whose noble works are of themselves a living and lasting monument. But we must pass on, and only give them brief recognition now.

---

to promote "principles and facts which promise to exert a salutary influence on women and on society, and the establishment of an order which shall render the female sex helpful to each other. . . . Club life supplies in some degree the place of higher education to those women who have been deprived of the advantages of a college course." (Mrs. J. C. Croly, *The History of the Woman's Club Movement in America* [New York City: Henry G. Allen, 1898], 18–19; Avery, *Transactions of the National Council of Women of the United States,* 296–297.)

468. Spencer, a Washington DC–based suffrage activist and educator, "spoke warmly against the ballot being taken from the women of Utah in the House of Congress. . . . The sisters should not forget her kindness and courage." ("Woman Suffrage and the Coming Convention," *Woman's Exponent,* Dec. 15, 1877, 6:108.)

469. These included the Methodist minister Anna Howard Shaw; journalist Jennie C. Croly (better known by her pseudonym "Jennie June"); M. D. Lincoln ("Bessie Beech"), president of the Woman's National Press Association; Dr. Rachel Brooks Gleason, one of the first female physicians in the United States; Dr. Caroline B. Winslow, moral reformer and editor of the *Alpha* journal; and English temperance activist Florence Balgarnie. ("Women of the Nation," *Woman's Exponent,* Mar. 1, 1891, 19:133–134.)

Sunday there were services in Albaugh's Opera House, as had been previously announced,[470] and in the evening an entertainment was given to raise funds for a Mary Washington monument, although as Miss Anthony said throughout the whole affair, "they never even mentioned that Washington had a mother."

Monday morning the Woman's National Council was formally opened. Miss Willard in the chair, and by her side then and throughout the entire Council, Miss Susan B. Anthony. Mrs. Sewall, the Cor. Sec'y., was the right hand director and manager. She seemed to be the chief person on the staff to assist the President. Rev. Anna Shaw was one of the most efficient helps, and is a most eloquent speaker, as well as being very executive in all her work. She had charge of the bell and was the time-keeper, so much time being allotted to each speaker, and it was her duty to give the signal, even if in the middle of a sentence.

Miss Anthony would almost invariably arise and say in her conciliatory manner, it will all be given in the official report of the Council.

The President's address to the Council was the leading feature of the opening and was immediately printed in pamphlet form and circulated free. It opened with these significant words o[f][471] Elizabeth Cady Stanton's, "A difference of opinion on one question must not prevent us from working unitedly on those on which we can agree."[472]

After Miss Willard's speech, which was a grand one in every sense of the word, came Anna Garlin Spencer, who spoke upon "State Control and Social Care of Dependent Classes;" then "The Care of Defective Children;" Fanny B. Ames [Julia Frances Ames]; "The Need of Women in Public Institutions," Dr. Rose Wright Bryan; "Our Duty to Dependent Races," Alice C. Fletcher; "Women as Police Matrons," Lillie Devereux Blake.[473]

It is not the intention to go into details in this article, but give the opening of the great National Council of Women, to which several great organizations of women have been admitted. Perhaps it will convey but little of the true idea after all, but it shall be the pleasure of the writer to explain and make clear, to

---

470. Frances E. Willard and Anna Howard Shaw spoke. Emmeline B. Wells recorded in her diary, "Today the Council opens with Religious services by women ministers & seats free, I went and many others but we could not get near the door so pressing was the crowd, hundreds outside." (Wells, Diary, vol. 14, Feb. 22, 1891; Avery, *Transactions of the National Council of Women of the United States,* 17–21.)

471. TEXT: In the copy used for transcription, there is a blank space after the *o* where the *f* should be.

472. Willard attributed this statement to Stanton, quoting from her "opening address before the International Council convened in this auditorium three years ago." (See Avery, *Transactions of the National Council of Women of the United States,* 23.)

473. These complete speeches can be found in Avery, *Transactions of the National Council of Women of the United States,* 57–94.

as many as possible, this federation of womens' organizations after her return home.

In regard to the Delegates from the Relief Society and Y. L. M. I. A., in which the members of these organizations are more specially interested, it will perhaps do as well to give you the newspaper reports, until you get it officially from the regular report of the Woman's National Council which is to be published. Here is the statement of the *Washington Post*, the reporter of that paper sitting in the Council during the several sessions of that body:

> Miss Willard then introduced Mrs. Caroline St. Thomas, the delegate from the Young Ladies' National Improvement Association, who read an interesting paper descriptive of the work of the young ladies' organization, which had done a great deal for its members.[474]
>
> Mrs. Jane S. Richards, delegate from the National Women's Relief Society, in a few words expressed the pleasure she had experienced on her attendance on the council.[475] She gave way to Mrs. Emily Wells,[476] of Utah, who told something of the Relief Society, which had its headquarters in New York, and had been in existence over half a century.[477] There were branch societies all over the country and in some foreign lands. It had over 400 branches, 25,000 members, $100,000 worth of real estate, a hospital managed solely by women, and published a paper, the WOMAN'S EXPONENT.
>
> It was an uncompromising enemy of the dram shop,[478] and when

---

474. *Washington Post* error: "St. Thomas" should be Thomas. For Thomas's remarks, see Avery, *Transactions of the National Council of Women of the United States*, 256–258.

475. For Richards's remarks, see Avery, *Transactions of the National Council of Women of the United States*, 258. The following month back in Salt Lake City, Jane S. Richards confessed that she was originally "dreading to go" to Washington but was encouraged by her husband and was thankful she had gone. "The ladies East she said had treated the Delegates from Utah well and were as kind as they could be . . . she had been favored in conversing with many ladies and explaining our position, felt she would like five hundred copies of the manifesto to distribute among them; thought to many of them it would be interesting reading." ("R. S. Reports," *Woman's Exponent*, May 15, 1891, 19:174; see also Emmeline B. Wells to Elmina S. Taylor, Feb. 22, 1891, A. Elmina Shepard Taylor Collection, 1844–1956, CHL.)

476. *Washington Post* error: "Emily" should be Emmeline.

477. *Washington Post* error: Wells actually referred to the Relief Society headquarters in Utah with branches in adjoining states and territories. The Relief Society was organized in 1842. The *Post* error may have been in reference to the church's formal organization in New York in 1830. For Wells's complete remarks, see Avery, *Transactions of the National Council of Women of the United States*, 258–260.

478. Temperance was not an official platform of the National Council of Women, but the organization included temperance activists, and temperance was a popular topic at meetings. (Robbins, *History and Minutes of the National Council of Women of the United States*, 39, 147.)

women had the right of suffrage in Utah,[479] the society furnished a rallying point for the women of the State. The society had done a world of good works of charity, and was one of the most benevolent organizations of women extant.[480]

The Woman's Tribune of Feb. 28, gives, in the report of the Council, the following concerning our delegation:[481]

> Next on the list, The National Improvement Society,[482] was represented by Mrs. Thomas, who spoke briefly on and told in an interesting manner [p. 132] of the benefit young ladies were deriving from it.
>
> The next speaker introduced to the audience was Mrs. Richards, of the National Woman's Relief Society, who began her brief address by saying: "I have the honor to represent Utah. The 25,000 women whom I represent are seeking to have love and peace and goodwill extended to all. On account of the length of the programme I will not speak longer, except to say that I am stopping at the Riggs House, and will be pleased to answer questions there. I will now give way to Mrs. Emmeline B. Wells."
>
> Mrs. Wells is editor of the WOMAN'S EXPONENT, of Salt Lake City, and one of the most interesting women at the Council. She has been chastened and spiritualized by suffering into a sympathy with woman that truly represents the spirit of Him whom those of her faith call Master, as well as those of Christian denominations. Mrs. Wells gave a short account of the Relief Society. Its headquarters are in New York; but it has branch societies all over the country, a hospital managed entirely by women, and has its own organ—The WOMAN'S EXPONENT.

---

479. Utah women voted from 1870 to 1887, when they were disenfranchised by the Edmunds-Tucker Act. (See introduction to Part 4.)

480. The *Woman's Exponent* provided only a small segment of the proceedings of the council, as compared to the coverage given by the *Washington Post*. ("The Woman's Council," *Washington Post,* Feb. 26, 1891, 1–3.)

481. The following quotation comes from the March 7, 1891, issue of the *Woman's Tribune* rather than the February 28 issue. This indicates that the *Woman's Exponent* issue dated March 1, 1891, from which Wells's article is drawn, was published later than March 7, 1891. The *Tribune* was published by the Nebraska Woman Suffrage Association and edited by Clara B. Colby. It was seen as "an important factor in educating the people up to the standard necessary to carry the state [Nebraska] for woman's suffrage." ("Continued Report of the Council," *Woman's Tribune,* Mar. 7, 1891, 75; "Editorial Notes," *Woman's Exponent,* Oct. 15, 1883, 12:77.)

482. Young Ladies' Mutual Improvement Association.

The three days' sessions of the Woman's National Council were of an exceedingly interesting character. In fact so much has been crowded into the minds and hearts of the people who have been listening through these three days that it will take weeks of thought to digest the whole matter, and sufficient material has been furnished to occupy the next four years in developing; the seed which has been planted will surely bring in a rich, a golden and abundant harvest that will bless and comfort the world of humanity.

Grand, noble, yea queenly, are the women who are laboring to unite, in a great band of sisterhood, the several great organizations and bring them in loving unison and fellowship one with another and blessed mutual helpfulness. That the Lord is working through His Holy Spirit upon the women of this nation, and other nations, must be apparent to all who have eyes to see, and ears to hear.[483] That this is woman's era who can longer doubt? Among the foremost of the women of the world, who are actively engaged in the great questions that are being agitated for the benefit of the women of our own and other lands (and what uplifts women, elevates the whole human family), are the very women who have planned and carried into effect this union of organizations, this great federation of associations. One very pleasing and promising feature of the Council is the great number of bright, intelligent, attractive young women that have come forward and taken an active part in the work. This is specially gratifying, for it is and must necessarily be the young women of the present century upon whom the great burden of responsibility will fall and who are to work out the lines of progression that will ensure the victory desired for those who have toiled, lo, these many years.

---

483. Susa Young Gates connected the involvement of Mormon women in these councils with missionary work and gave religious significance to the cause of women's rights: "These . . . delegates who traveled, and still do, so extensively out to the nations of the earth, are constantly carrying the message of Glad Tidings of the Gospel of Jesus Christ, and have and are sowing the seeds of woman's emancipation from the superstition and thralldom of the Middle Ages into her enlarged and glorified sphere." Jane S. Richards's husband, apostle Franklin D. Richards, similarly reflected on "the great good that had been accomplished in sending the Delegates down to Washington . . . thought the association of the sisters among the influential women gathered from the different States would be beneficial, and the knowledge that the Relief Society had branches in many nations would become widely known." He added, "The press throughout the world are talking of the Mormons and wondering what we are going to do; they are anxious to know all they ban [can] about us, we should pursue the course that will help to bring about the time when the Lord will come to reign over all." (Susa Young Gates, "Administration of Bathsheba W. Smith, 1901–1910," typescript, p. 12, History of Women Files, Susa Young Gates, Papers, ca. 1870–1933, CHL; "R. S. Reports," *Woman's Exponent,* May 15, 1891, 19:174.)

4.28 Report of Relief Society Jubilee, March 17, 1892

Report of Relief Society Jubilee, Mar. 17, 1892, in "Relief Society Jubilee. Exercises at the Tabernacle," Woman's Exponent *(Salt Lake City, UT), Apr. 1, 1892, vol. 20, no. 18, pp. 140–144.*

Bathsheba W. Smith, Discourse, Mar. 17, 1892, in "Address of Bathsheba W. Smith," Woman's Exponent, *Apr. 1, 1892, vol. 20, no. 18, p. 139.*

Mary Isabella Horne, Discourse, Mar. 17, 1892, in "Address of Mrs. M. Isabella Horne," Woman's Exponent, *Apr. 1, 1892, vol. 20, no. 18, pp. [137]–138.*

The following *Woman's Exponent* articles provide a report of the Relief Society Jubilee celebration held in the tabernacle in Salt Lake City on March 17, 1892.[484] The celebration, commemorating the fiftieth anniversary of the founding of the Female Relief Society of Nauvoo, was an event of momentous significance to Relief Society women. The *Woman's Exponent* predicted, "The Jubilee to be celebrated this year will crystalize the works and efforts of the women of Zion into something of greater magnitude and more extensive proportions than the Society has hitherto assumed."[485] President Zina D. H. Young, her officers, and the Central Board of the Relief Society planned the event, which was intended to acknowledge the accomplishments of the society in the past and herald the possibilities of its future. All the officers and members of the Central Board except Emmeline B. Wells, corresponding secretary, and Romania B. Pratt, assistant secretary, had been members of the Nauvoo Relief Society, and they invoked the words and promises of Joseph Smith throughout the general celebration in Salt Lake City and in the various ward and stake commemorations throughout the territory.

Displays in the Salt Lake City tabernacle included a floral representation of the key "turned to women" in Nauvoo by Joseph Smith and life-size portraits of Joseph Smith, Eliza R. Snow, and the current president, Zina D. H. Young, all of them hung on the pipes of the great tabernacle organ. Some wondered whether to include a portrait of the first Relief Society president, Emma Smith. Her decision to dissociate herself from the church under Brigham Young's leadership and to remain in Nauvoo when the Saints moved west caused some to doubt the propriety of acknowledging her in the celebration. When asked for his opinion, church president Wilford Woodruff responded that "any one who opposed it must be very narrow minded indeed," and so her life-size portrait appeared with the others.[486]

On March 17, 1892, which fell on Thursday, the same day of the week as the date of organization in 1842, the tabernacle was decorated with flags, bunting, and flowers. Relief Society officers and general church authorities spoke for the program. To unify the celebration between the events in Salt Lake City and celebrations in congregations throughout the

---

484. A report of the Jubilee exercises also appears in a contemporary general Relief Society minute book, but it appears from the handwritten minutes that they were copied from the published *Exponent* report. (Relief Society Record, 1880–1892, CHL, 206–242.)

485. "The Relief Society Jubilee," *Woman's Exponent,* Jan. 15 and Feb. 1, 1892, 20:108.

486. Emmeline B. Wells, Diaries, 1844–1920, 46 vols., L. Tom Perry Special Collections, Harold B. Lee Library, Brigham Young University, Provo, UT, vol. 15, Mar. 15, 1892.

OFFICERS:

ZINA D. M. YOUNG, PRESIDENT,
140 4TH STREET,
SALT LAKE CITY, UTAH.
JANE S. RICHARDS,
2442 LINCOLN AVE.,
OGDEN, UTAH. } COUNSELORS.
BATHSHEBA W. SMITH,
129 N. WEST TEMPLE,
SALT LAKE CITY.
SARAH M. KIMBALL, SECRETARY,
74 S. 2ND WEST,
SALT LAKE CITY, UTAH.
R. B. PRATT, M. D., ASS'T SEC'Y,
206 N. 2ND WEST,
SALT LAKE CITY, UTAH.
M. ISABELLA HORNE, TREASURER,
110 THIRD ST.,
SALT LAKE CITY, UTAH.
EMMELINE B. WELLS, COR. SECRETARY,
25 E. SOUTH TEMPLE ST.,
SALT LAKE CITY, UTAH.

CHURCH OF JESUS CHRIST OF LATTER-DAY SAINTS.

THE RELIEF SOCIETY.

(ORGANIZED MARCH 17, 1842.)

Salt Lake City, Utah, Jan. 21, 1892

LETTER OF GREETING.

TO THE SISTERS OF THE RELIEF SOCIETY THROUGHOUT THE WORLD, WE UNITEDLY EXTEND A HEARTFELT GREETING.

It will be fifty years on Thursday, March 17, 1892, since Joseph Smith the Prophet organized the Relief Society, in Nauvoo, Illinois, by divine inspiration.

Sister Emma Smith was elected President, and Sister Elizabeth Ann Whitney and Sister Sarah M. Cleveland, Counselors. Sister Eliza R. Snow was appointed Secretary, Sister Phebe M. Wheeler, Assistant Secretary, and Sister Elvira A. Cole, Treasurer, after which the ceremony of ordination was performed, and Pres. Joseph Smith declared the Society organized.

This most momentous event for woman, causes us to view with wonder the past, with gratitude the present, and with faith the future, therefore it seems fitting in this our jubilee year, at the close of half a century, that the branches of this Society in all lands, should unite in celebrating this grand anniversary by meeting together in joyful, yet solemn assembly, that this great gathering may mark an important period in the history of this organization for woman.

INSTRUCTIONS.

FIRST: The President and Counselors of each branch of the Relief Society are requested to notify all members of the celebration of the Jubilee.

SECOND: Let the presiding authorities in each locality or ward be consulted, and a cordial invitation extended to them.

THIRD: Let Committees be appointed to assist in making preparations for the day, and to invite those who are to participate in the celebration, that none may be neglected or forgotten.

FOURTH: That all meet promptly at ten o'clock in the morning, rendering such exercises as shall be suitable to this important occasion, including a brief sketch of the history of the Relief Society to be prepared and read by some one selected for the purpose.

FIFTH: At 12 o'clock M. (high noon) let all join in a universal prayer of praise and thanksgiving to God; after which, let each branch arrange an entertainment according to their circumstances, that it may be a time of rejoicing, never to be forgotten.

Zina D. H. Young President.

Jane S. Richards }
Bathsheba W. Smith } Counselors.

Instructions regarding Relief Society Jubilee. In this circular dated January 21, 1892, Zina D. H. Young and her counselors in the Relief Society general presidency instructed Relief Society leaders throughout the church on how to observe the fiftieth anniversary of the society's founding. (Church History Library, Salt Lake City.)

church, each participating congregation offered a commemorative prayer at high noon, corresponding with the prayer Joseph F. Smith, a counselor in the First Presidency, offered in the Salt Lake tabernacle.[487]

Emmeline Wells penned the closing "sentiment" of the Jubilee program. "What does this woman's Jubilee signify? not only that fifty years ago this organization was founded by a Prophet of God, but that woman is becoming emancipated from error and superstition and darkness. That light has come into the world, and the Gospel has made her free, that the key of knowledge has been turned, and she has drank inspiration at the divine fountain." Fifty years after its inception, the Relief Society continued to gain meaning and strength from its Nauvoo roots.

———— ⁊⋆ ————

Report of Jubilee Celebration

RELIEF SOCIETY JUBILEE.

Exercises at the Tabernacle.

The celebration of the fiftieth anniversary of the first organization of the Relief Society March 17, 1842, was held in the Large Tabernacle in Salt Lake City March 17, 1892, and was largely attended by those resident in the City, many strangers and tourists were also present. The stands were handsomely ornamented with flowering plants principally Calla and Easter lilies. The large organ was draped with stars and stripes, the flags extending across and a large oil painting of Joseph the prophet hung high in the centre, below it an immense key made of the most beautiful flowers, underneath which was the picture life-size of Emma Smith the first President of the Relief Society and on her right a picture of Eliza R. Snow the second President, and on her left that of Zina D. H. Young the present President.

Prof. Evan Stephens Musical Director had charge of the Tabernacle Choir, who furnished the singing and Prof. J. [Joseph] J. Daynes accompanied on the organ, the music was specially fine. On the stand was Pres. Joseph F. Smith of the First Presidency, Apostles John Henry Smith and Abraham H. Cannon, President Angus M. Cannon, Dr. James E. Talmage, and of the officers of the Central Board of the Relief Society, President, Zina D. H. Young; Counselor Bathsheba W. Smith; Sarah M. Kimball, Secretary; Romania B. Pratt, Ass't. Secretary; M. Isabella Horne, Treasurer; E. B. Wells Cor. Sec'y.—also Zina Y. W. Card.[488]

---

487. "At 12 o'clock m., (high noon) let all join in a universal prayer of praise and thanksgiving to God." (Zina D. H. Young, Jane S. Richards, and Bathsheba W. Smith, "Letter of Greeting," *Woman's Exponent,* Jan. 15 and Feb. 1, 1892, 20:108; see also "The Relief Society Jubilee," *Deseret Weekly,* Mar. 26, 1892, 483–486.)

488. Zina Young's first counselor, Jane S. Richards, was originally scheduled to speak, but on the

The exercises of this happy occasion opened with the choir singing that Grand Invocation by Eliza R. Snow,

["]O, my Father thou that dwellest."[489]

Prayer was offered by President Angus M Cannon. The choir and congregation joined in singing the hymn,

"How firm a foundation ye saints of the Lord."[490]

A most feeling and eloquent address of greeting and welcome was then delivered by,

PRESIDENT ZINA D. H. YOUNG

My brethren and sisters and friends, I ask an interest in your faith and prayers on this great occasion, so that the spirit of the living God may direct the few words I may utter. I now in the presence of God and before my brethren and sisters, hail this welcome day of Jubilee which has been set apart for us—the sisters of the Relief Society to assemble together. O, that my words could be heard by all people, not only by you my brethren and sisters in this Tabernacle and throughout Utah, but that they might be heard and understood by all the people of this continent, and not only this continent but the continents of Europe, Asia, Africa and the Islands of the Sea.

This day we greet you and all our sisters who are everywhere celebrating this occasion in commemoration of the organization, by the Prophet Joseph Smith, of the Relief Society.

We praise God that our ears have been saluted with the glad tidings of salvation again restored to the earth, through the instrumentality of the Prophet Joseph. We rejoice in the principles of the Gospel revealed from heaven in this age; that the Father and the Son condescended to appear to Joseph, in answer to his fervent prayer for light and knowledge, and that our Heavenly Father pointed to His Son and said "hear ye Him."[491] These things cause us to lift up our hearts to God with thanksgiving and blessing. This is a glorious day in which we live. It is the dispensation of the fulness of times when all things spoken by all the holy prophets will be fulfilled. This is a great day for the sisters of the Relief Society. The daughters of Zion have met here this day, as also wherever they are organized, to celebrate this day, the fiftieth anniversary of our

---

day of the celebration she presided over the Jubilee program held in the Ogden tabernacle. ("The Relief Society," *Woman's Exponent,* Mar. 1, 1892, 20:124; Franklin D. Richards, Journal, Richards Family Collection, 1837–1961, CHL, Mar. 17, 1892.)

489. See Document 1.14.

490. Hymn 237, *Sacred Hymns and Spiritual Songs. For the Church of Jesus Christ of Latter-day Saints,* 14th ed. (Salt Lake City: George Q. Cannon, 1871), 260.

491. See Joseph Smith et al., History, 1838–1856, vols. A-1–F-1 (original), A-2–F-2 (fair copy), CHL, vol. A-1, 3 (hereafter JS History).

organization and to lift our hearts in praise to God. We rejoice at having some of our leading brethren with us today. We anticipate having a good time. The peaceful influence of the spirit of the Lord is with us; it is full of life and joy.

A word as to the duties and labors of the members of these organizations, of the Relief Society is appropriate at this time; as sisters of this organization we have been set apart for the purpose of comforting and consoling the sick and afflicted the poor and distressed, particularly those who love and fear God; to comfort one another in every trial of life, and cheer the depressed in spirit, on all occasions; this is our special mission, therefore keep this in remembrance. If we continue to do these things in the spirit thereof, the Lord, at the time when He comes to make up His jewels, will approve of us.

My sisters everywhere who have humbly embraced the Gospel and are true to it are my sisters. I greet them as such. I pray God to pour out His spirit upon all of you today, and from this time forth. This is a day never to be forgotten because of the goodness of God to us. I hope the Presidents and members of every Relief Society on earth will have such a good time today as will never be forgotten by them. This is my prayer and desire in their behalf. As sisters we have to work out and secure our salvation. Let us honor the Lord for permitting us to live in this dispensation, also honor Him for the glorious principles of truth, light and life which He has revealed to us through His inspired servants.

We pray and ask our Heavenly Father to bless these our sisters, that they may continue to visit the poor and needy and see that none suffer among us. I trust our object will be to improve in good works, that the sisters, in addition to what they have already done, will build houses wherein they can hold their Relief Society meetings and worship the Lord.[492] I hope that the sisters, through the blessings of God will be enabled to do this; that they will continue to sustain the hands of their Bishops, and work unitedly; that they will not neglect their families, nor idle their time away, but look after their home affairs as well as attend to the duties I have named. Let us help our Presidents and each other and stand shoulder to shoulder.

We are blessed with glorious privileges, and have been. The franchise so gloriously given us, and enjoyed so long, has been taken from us without cause. It may be restored to us again; let us hope for this.[493] Let us be pure and upright in our lives and do good continually; be true and humble all our days; may we

---

492. See "Relief Society Halls," in *History of Relief Society, 1842–1966* (Salt Lake City: General Board of Relief Society, 1966), 104–105.

493. Utah women voted from 1870 to 1887, when they were disenfranchised by the Edmunds-Tucker Act. (See introduction to Part 4.)

be guided by the spirit of the Lord day by day. Sisters let us bring up our children in the fear of God. Ask him to give you a portion of His holy spirit to guide you in all things. Do not neglect these matters sisters. See that you perform your duties humbly and faithfully every one of you. If there is one mother present here who does not teach and instruct her children properly, in such a way as the Lord approves of, I plead with you to do so. Call your children around you in the absence of the father, and pray with them. Teach them how to pray and the proper manner in which they should do so, that your prayers and theirs may be heard and answered with blessings upon your heads. Warn the children of the evils that surround us. Lift up your warning voice against temptations now so prevalent in our midst that they may not become a prey to these evils, but grow up in holiness and in purity before the Lord.

Encourage home productions of every kind. Support our paper the WOMAN's EXPONENT by subscribing for it. This paper should be in the family of every Latter-day Saint.

Above all things may we so live as to have the spirit of the Lord dwelling in us continually. Let me say to you sisters be true helpmeets to your husbands. Be one with them in all things in righteousness. Let your desires be to make home what it should be.

When Joseph received his first vision he was told that his name would be spoken of for good or for evil by all men; from that day to the present time, this has been verified.[494] We this day with the saints of God everywhere, honor the name because of his intregrity to God and the principles of light and truth which he was the instrument of restoring to the earth for our salvation, and that of the whole human family if they will but accept the glad message.

May God grant that we may stand firm and faithful to the truth, walking in humility and purity before Him; may His blessing attend this people throughout the world on this great and grand occasion, and henceforth. You mothers and daughters of Israel we greet you and ask the blessings of our Heavenly Father upon you and upon all His people on earth. These are the desires of my heart and may God grant them is my prayer for Jesus sake. Amen.

Mrs. Zina Y. W. Card next read in a very clear and distinct voice the Revelation given to Emma Smith, through Joseph the Seer in Harmony, Penn., July 1830, and published in the Book of Doctrine and Covenants, wherein Sister Emma is called an Elect Lady.[495]

---

494. See JS History, vol. A-1, 5.
495. Doctrine and Covenants 25; see Document 1.1; and Document 1.2, entry for Mar. 17, 1842.

APOSTLE ABRAHAM H. CANNON.

I feel pleased, my brethren and sisters, at having this opportunity of assembling with so worthy an association as the Relief Society. It must be a source of pleasure to our sisters to look back upon the work which has been accomplished since the organization, by the Prophet Joseph, of this Society, and it must fill the hearts of many Latter-day Saints with joy and gratitude to think of the stupendous work which the sisters, connected with these Associations, have done. The great help they have been to the Church of Jesus Christ we poor mortals cannot conceive. But we do know of much that they have [a]ccomplished[496] in [p. 140] their mission. We know many homes to which they have carried comfort and blessing of various kinds; in which they have provided food for the hungry and clothed the naked, and have administered relief to those who were sick and afflicted, God has been with these sisters in their ministrations. By the power of faith and detection which has attended them, a great many marvelous cures have been effected among the people through their prayers and good works. It has been a testimony to those who have witnessed these things that the power of God is in the Church, and is bestowed upon all those who seek Him in faith and in humility.

The work which has already been done by the sisters and the great good accomplished will be almost forgotten in the magnitude of that which the future will develop, for as the Church shall grow and as the honest in heart from the nations of the earth shall be gathered, the field for the exercise of the talents of our sisters will be greatly enlarged, far beyond that of which we can now form a conception, God will put it into the hearts of those who stand at the head of this institution to organize reforms and adopt such measures as shall be of greater benefit to our sisters and to the brethren than in the past. Their hearts and sympathies will become greater in the work of God.

Now, it seems to me, from the opportunities offered our sisters, even in this day they can use an influence and exercise their talents for great good among this people.

We speak of charity, of relief which should be given to the poor, but it is mistaken charity to give to those who are able to earn their own living. Such charity means the encouragement of idleness among this people, who ought to be a nation of workers, and become proficient and industrious in the various occupations of life. Not only young women, young men and middle aged men, but our older sisters also should have some object in life and work for its accomplishment. They should not alone be taught to use their brains but also

---

496. TEXT: In the copy used for transcription, there is a blank space where the *a* should be.

their hands for the accumulation of the material things of life which are essential to our welfare.

I remember when upon my mission to Germany of visiting some of the Industrial Schools which are there established for girls and young women.[497] They were taught therein the art of cooking and other household duties. They received instructions in these things, and were made to understand, to a certain extent at least, the duties which would devolve upon them when they became wives and mothers. In these schools they were also taught to sew and to do all kinds of fancy work to which women's hands should be accustomed. Other institutions are in existence for the good and benefit of the young. It is considered a disgrace by the people there for a young woman to grow up in ignorance of the things pertaining to her life here upon the earth. But how is it with us? Among us today we find there are many growing up with an idea that it is a disgrace to work. Some of our girls seem to think they are gaining great advantages in acquiring the accomplishments which are to be had at schools or home as the case may be, where they receive knowledge of these things, but they forget the duties which will hereafter devolve upon them as wives and mothers in Israel. All such are illy preparing themselves for the great responsibilities which the near future will devolve upon them.

In my estimation it is the duty of our sisters, who have had long experience to impress our daughters with the necessity of acquiring those things which will be a lasting benefit to them. Teach them the use of their hands, in economy, in the management ol [of] those things intrusted to their care, so that when they become wives they may not be such as will cause disunion in the household, neither cause a feeling of disappointment in the hearts of their husbands, but rather be fully capable of performing the duties of wives and mothers, and feel that they have something to live for in this life.

Here is a field, unlimited, for the exercise of the talent of our Relief Society as well as our Church schools. They should draw into their Associations every young woman they can find and teach them to love their fellow creatures here upon earth and administer to their wants. The sisters are capable of entering into the feelings of their sex; of sympathizing with them in their distress, and of providing for them the proper necessities in time of need. They should feel

---

497. Cannon served a mission in Europe from October 1879 to June 1882, with a majority of his time spent in Germany and Switzerland. (Abraham H. Cannon, Diaries, 1879–1895, 20th Century Western and Mormon Manuscripts, L. Tom Perry Special Collections, Harold B. Lee Library, Brigham Young University, Provo, UT; Andrew Jenson, *Latter-day Saint Biographical Encyclopedia: A Compilation of Biographical Sketches of Prominent Men and Women in the Church of Jesus Christ of Latter-day Saints,* 4 vols. [Salt Lake City: Andrew Jenson History Co., 1901–1936], 1:167–168.)

that they have a mission upon earth other than that of appearing well in society and of shining brilliantly, because some others do this.

Brethren and sisters I feel that God is with our sisters in their labors in these societies, I also feel in my heart to ask Him to bless and prosper them, and assist them to do their part in carrying forward His great work in these latter days. Amen.

An historical sketch prepared by Secretary Sarah M. Kimball, taken from the record of the Relief Society was read by Dr. James E. Talmage. The Tabernacle being such a very large building it was thought wise that the reading of written articles should be by young men who could be heard in all parts of the house,[498] although the sketches were *written* by the ladies themselves.

THE RELIEF SOCIETY.[499]

First organization of L. D. S. Relief Society, and instructions given by President Joseph Smith.

By invitation of the President of the Church, a number of sisters convened in the Masonic Lodge room, on the 17th of March 1842, President Joseph Smith, Elders John Taylor and Willard Richards were present.

President Smith stated that the meeting was called for the purpose of making more complete the organization of the Church, by organizing the women in the order of the Priesthood.[500]

John Taylor was called to the chair and Willard Richards acted as secretary. After singing and prayer, a vote was taken to know if all were satisfied with each sister present, and willing to acknowledge them in good fellowship and admit them to all the privileges of the institution about to be organized. All being satisfied, the names of those present were taken as follows:—

Emma Smith, Martha Knight, Elvira A. Cowles, Sarah M. Cleveland, Phebe Ann Hawkes, Margaret A. [Norris] Cook, Desdemona Ful[l]mer, Elizabeth Ann Whitney, Sarah M. Kimball, Elizabeth Jones, Leonora Taylor,

---

498. Talmage was twenty-nine years of age at this time. John Henry Smith, who read an article during the meeting, was forty-three. Abraham H. Cannon, who read several articles during the meeting, was thirty-three.

499. In the following article Sarah M. Kimball summarized portions of the Nauvoo Relief Society Minute Book, focusing primarily on the six discourses Joseph Smith gave to the society in 1842. Kimball's article paraphrases and summarizes extensively, reflecting what she thought important to emphasize at this particular time. (See Document 1.2.)

500. This statement is not found in the Nauvoo Relief Society Minute Book. However, Kimball's 1882 reminiscence of Relief Society beginnings included similar wording. The use of this particular wording eventually proved problematic. (Document 4.10; Jill Mulvay Derr et al., *Women of Covenant: The Story of Relief Society* [Salt Lake City: Deseret Book; Provo, UT: Brigham Young University Press, 1992], 447n88.)

Eliza R. Snow, Sophia Packard, Bathsheba W. Smith, Sophia Robinson, Phillinda Herrick [Merrick], Phebe M. Wheeler, Sophia R. Marks.[501]

Pres. Smith then explained some of the duties that would devolve on members of the Society, said they could provoke the brethren to good works, look after the needs of the poor, and perform charitable acts. Women must assist in correcting the morals and strengthening the virtues of the community. Said it is now in order for the sisters to elect a President to preside over the Society and let her choose two counselors to assist in the duties of her office. He would ordain them, and let them preside just as the Presidency presided over the Church, and if they needed his instruction they could ask and he would be pleased to give it from time to time. Let the Presidency serve as a constitution and their decisions become precedents for you to act upon.

If officers are wanted to carry out the designs of the institution, let them be appointed and set apart, as Teachers, Deacons &c., are among us.

Elizabeth A. Whitney moved, and Sophia Packard seconded the motion, that Emma Smith be elected President of the Society, the vote was put by the chairman and pronounced unanimous. The President Elect, made choice of Sarah M. Cleveland and Elizabeth Ann Whitney as her counselors.

Eliza R. Snow was appointed Secretary and Phebe M. Wheeler assistant Secretary and Elvira A. Cowles Treasurer.[502]

Pres. Joseph Smith read the Revelation to Emma Smith from the book of Doctrine and Covenants, and stated that she was ordained at the time the Revelation was given, to expound the Scriptures, to teach &c.

He then read Scriptures to show that an elect lady is one elected to preside. By request of President Joseph Smith, Apostle John Taylor ordained Sarah M. Cleveland and Elizabeth Ann Whitney, to be counselors to and assist President Emma Smith in the duties of her office, and share in the blessings pertaining thereto.

He then confirmed on Emma Smith her former ordination and blessed her to be a mother in Israel, a pattern of virtue and to possess all the qualifications necessary to enable her to preside with dignity and give such instruction, as may be requisite in her calling as an Elect Lady.

Elder Taylor vacated the chair and Pres. Emma Smith and counselors took the stand.

---

501. Athalia Rigdon Robinson and Nancy Rigdon were both present at the March 17, 1842, meeting, and their names were recorded in the original minutes. Later, their names were struck through. (See Document 1.2, entry for Mar. 17, 1842.)

502. The original minutes indicate that the selection of the secretaries and treasurer occurred later in the meeting, after Joseph Smith had declared the society organized and made a five-dollar donation. (Document 1.2, entry for Mar. 17, 1842.)

A lengthy discussion followed on the question, ["]What shall this Society be called?" Mrs. Cleveland and Whitney advocated the appropriateness of the name Relief Society. John Taylor and Joseph Smith spoke in favor of the word Benevolent, Emma Smith and E. R. Snow argued in favor of Mrs. Cleveland's choice. The gentlemen withdrew their objection and a motion to adopt the name Relief Society was unanimously carried.

Pres. Joseph then said "I now declare this Society organized with the President and counselors. All who shall hereafter be admitted must be free from censure and admitted by vote.["] Pres. Joseph Smith laid down a five dollar gold-piece to commence a Relief Society fund and said "What I do hereafter for charity, I shall do through this society." Sarah M. Cleveland gave 12½ cts. Sarah M. Kimball, $1[.]oo,[503] Emma Smith, $1.oo, Elizabeth Ann Whitney, 50 cts. Willard Richards, $1.oo, John Taylor, $2.oo.

At the 3rd, meeting of the Society, March 30th.[504] President Joseph Smith said, the members of the Society must act in concert, or nothing can be accomplished. To move according to the ancient Priesthood this must be a select Society, separate from the evils of the world.

Sixth meeting April 28th. Pres. Joseph Smith said he was present to speak upon the Priesthood, as his instructions were intended only for members of the Society, he wished those not members to withdraw. After which he called attention to the 12th chapter of Corinthians, "Now concerning Spiritual Gifts &c.," said the passage which reads, "No man can say that Jesus is the Lord but by the Holy Ghost should be translated no man can know &c.,["] continued the reading of the chapter, and gave instructions respecting the different offices and the necessity of every individual, acting in the place allotted to him or her, and filling the office to which they were appointed.

Spoke of the disposition of some to consider the lower offices in the Church dishonorable and to look with jealous eyes on the position of others; said it was the nonsense of the human heart, to aspire to positions not appointed of God, that it was better for individuals to magnify their respective callings and wait patiently till God shall say to them "Come up higher," said it was talked by members of the Society that some were not doing right in laying hands on the sick. If they had common sympathy, they would rejoice that the sick could be healed. The time has not been before when these things could be in their proper order. The Church is not now organized in its proper order and cannot

---

503. TEXT: In the copy used for transcription, there is a blank space where the decimal point should be.

504. The meeting was actually held on March 31, 1842 (the error is in the original minutes). (Document 1.2, entry for Mar. 31, 1842.)

be until the temple is completed. He referred to the commission given [p. 141] to the ancient Apostles, "Go ye into all the world &c.," no matter who believes these signs, such as healing the sick, casting out devils, should follow all that believe, whether male or female.

If the sisters have faith to heal the sick, let them do so, and let the good work roll on. It is no sin for anybody to administer to the sick that has faith, or if the sick have faith to be healed by the administration.

Reproved those that were disposed to find fault, spoke at some length on the difficulties he had had to surmount, ever since the organization of the Church, on account of aspiring men, said the same aspiring disposition will be in this Society, and must be guarded against.

As he had the opportunity he would instruct the Society how to act according to the will of God. He did not know that he should have many opportunities of teaching them, they were going to be left to themselves, they would not long have him to instruct them, the Church would not have his instruction long and the world would not be troubled with him a great while, according to his prayer God had appointed him elsewhere. The congregation was melted to tears.[505]

He exhorted the sisters to sustain with their confidence, their faith, and their prayers, those whom God had appointed to lead. Said the keys are about to be given to you that you may be able to detect anything false, as readily as the Elders. If members of the Society become corrupt, you must deal with them, the sympathies of the heads of the Church have induced them to bear with those that were corrupt, in consequence of which all become contaminated, you must put down iniquity and by your good example provoke the Elders to good works.

If you do right, there is no danger of going too fast, resist evil and there is no danger, neither God, men, angels or devils can condemn those that resist everything that is evil. As well might the devil seek to dethrone Jehovah, as that soul that resists everything evil. You are now placed in a situation where you can act according to those sympathies which God has planted in your bosoms. If you live in accord with your privileges angels cannot be restrained from being your associates.

Women if they are pure and innocent can come into the presence of God. If we would come into the presence of God we must be pure. The devil has great power, his ways are deceptive. Do not be contentious, but let the weight of innocence be felt, which is more mighty than a millstone hung about the neck, meekness, love, purity these are the things that should magnify us.

---

505. This sentence is not found in the original minutes.

Iniquity must be purged out, then the veil will be rent and the blessings of heaven will flow down.

After this instruction you will be more responsible, it is an honor to save yourselves, all are responsible for themselves. Then read the 13th chapter of Cor., "Though I speak with the tongue of men &c.." said do not be limited in your views with regard to your neighbors' virtues, do not think yourselves more righteous than others. You must enlarge your souls towards others, if you would do like Jesus and carry your fellow creatures to Abraham's bosom, He had manifested long suffering and we must do the same.

Said "Though one have the spirit of prophecy &c.," though one should become mighty and do great things, overturn mountains, and then turn to do that which is evil, all former deeds would not save them, but they would go to destruction. As you increase in innocence, virtue and goodness, let your hearts expand, let them be enlarged towards others, you must be long-suffering, and bear with the faults and errors of mankind. How precious the souls of men! The Society is to get instruction through the order which God has established, through the medium of those appointed to lead, and I now turn the key to you in the name of God, and this Society shall rejoice and knowledge and intelligence shall flow down from this time, this is the beginning of better days for you.

When you go home never give a cross word, but let kindness, charity and love crown your works. Do not envy sinners, exercise mercy towards them.

Let your administrations be confined mostly to those around you. As far as knowledge is concerned, it may extend to all the world. But your administrations should be confined to the circle of your acquaintance, and more especially to the members of the Society. Those ordained to lead the Society are authorized to appoint officers as the circumstances shall require.

If any have a matter to reveal, let it be in your own tongue do not indulge too much in the gift of tongues, or the devil will take advantage.

You may speak in tongues for your comfort. But I lay this down as a rule, that if anything is taught by the gift of tongues, it is not to be received for doctrine.

Pres. Smith then gave instruction respecting women administering to the sick by the laying on of hands, said it was according to revelation, he never was placed in similar circumstances, and never had given the same instruction.

At the ninth Relief Society meeting, May 26th, the Prophet read the 14th chapter of Ezekiel, and said the Lord had declared by that prophet that the people should each one stand for themselves and depend on no man or men; in the state of corruption in the Jewish Church, that righteous persons could only deliver their own souls. Applied it to the present condition of the Church of

Latter-day Saints. If the people depart from the Lord, they must fall, they were depending on the Prophet, hence there was darkness in their minds.

He had two things to recommend to the Society. Be guarded in your speech, no organized body can exist without giving heed to this caution. All organized bodies have their peculiar evils, weaknesses and difficulties, the object is to make those not so good equal with the good, and ever hold the keys of power which will influence to virtue and goodness.

When you chasten and reprove, never mention it again, then you will be established in power, virtue and holiness and the wrath of God will be turned away. God designs to save the people out of their sins. Jesus said "Ye shall do the works which ye see me do," these are the grand key-words for the Society to act upon.

The tenth meeting was addressed by Bishop N. [Newel] K. Whitney, Pres. Joseph Smith being present.[506]

Eleventh meeting June 9th. Pres. J. Smith, "It grieves me that there is no fuller fellowship, if one member suffers all feel it, by union of feeling we obtain power with God, Christ said he came to call sinners to repentance and to save them, Christ was condemned by the righteous Jews because he took sinners in to his society, he took them upon the principle that they repent. Nothing is so much calculated to lead people to forsake sin, as to take them by the hand and watch over them with tenderness. The nearer we get to our Heavenly Father, the more we are disposed to look with compassion on perishing souls. I say to this society if you would have God have mercy on you, have mercy on each other. How mild the Savior dealt with Peter saying, "When thou art converted, strengthen thy brethren," at another time he said to him, "Lovest thou me? Feed my sheep." The Society is not only to relieve the poor, but to save souls.

Sixteenth meeting held in the Grove August 31st, 1842. After relating recent difficulties he had encountered while being hunted by his enemies, he said the Relief Society has taken an active part in my welfare in petitioning the Governor in my behalf. These measures were necessary, and your influence helped to bring about my redemption from the hands of my enemies. I have come here to bless you. The Society has done well, their principles are to practice holiness. God loves you and your prayers shall avail much do not cease to let them ascend to God in my behalf. The enemy will never get weary. I expect he will array everything against me, expect a tremendous warfare. He that will

---

506. The tenth meeting was held May 27, 1842. Because Joseph Smith did not give a discourse at the meeting, Kimball only mentions the meeting here without providing a summary. Kimball's account here does not mention that Joseph Smith also attended (but did not give extended remarks at) Relief Society meetings on March 24 and May 12, 1842. (See Document 1.2.)

war the Christian warfare will have the angels and all the powers of darkness continually arrayed against him.

A few things had been manifested to him during his absence, respecting baptism for the dead which he would communicate next Sabbeth i[f][507] nothing should occur to prevent it. He then offered a fervent prayer to God in behalf of the Society. After the transaction of some business in the adjustment of which Pres. Smith offered counsel. Said he had one more remark to make respecting baptism for the dead, which must suffice for the present and until he had lhe [the] opportunity to present the subject at a greater length.

All persons baptized for the dead must have a recorder present, that he may be an eye-witness to testify of it. It will be necessary in the Great Council that these things be testified of. It should be attended to from this time. If there is any lack it may be at the expense of our friends. This was the last R. S. meeting that Pres. Joseph Smith attended.

During the two years administration of Pres. Emma Smith and her associates, visiting sisters were appointed to search out the needy, to find work for the able-bodied to receive contributions and to report conditions.

The labors of the Society were extended to the four wards of the City.

1257 names were enrolled as members. The recorded receipts were $415.24.

An appropriate song composed expressly for the Jubilee by Emily H. Woodmansee, was beautifully rendered by the choir,

"O blest was the day when the Prophet and Seer."[508]

PRAYER OF PRES. JOS. F. SMITH, DELIVERED AT HIGH NOON, MARCH 17, 1892.
[Preliminary Remarks.][509]

I am sorry to announce that in consequence of President Woodruff having a severe cold, he did not feel able to attend this meeting and therefore desires to be excused.[510] He also desires that the people would remember him in their prayers.

Agreeable to the wish of the Presidency of the Relief Society we will unite in prayer. I hope that all the people who are assembled here will lift up their hearts unto God, according to their desires, for blesslngs [blessings] upon the

---

507. TEXT: In the copy used for transcription, there is a blank space after the *i* where the *f* should be.
508. Woodmansee's lyrics were sung to the tune of "The Star-Spangled Banner," and its performance was "a general feature of the proceedings" at Jubilee celebrations throughout Utah. (For complete lyrics see "The Fifth Anniversary," *[Ogden] Standard,* Mar. 22, 1892, 6.)
509. TEXT: Brackets in original.
510. Wilford Woodruff wrote in his journal on March 17, 1892, "I was sick all night but went to the office in the Morning & spent the Day but was nearly sick all Day." (Wilford Woodruff, Journals, 1838–1898, Wilford Woodruff, Journals and Papers, 1828–1898, CHL, Mar. 17, 1892.)

Relief Society throughout all the world, and upon the Church and those who have been called to preside, and to labor for the promulgation of the principles of truth. We will now unite in prayer:

O God, the Eternal Father, in the name of Jesus Christ thy Son, and in humility before thee we thy people have assembled here, on this interesting occasion, we desire to lift up our hearts in prayer and in supplication unto thee, and we desire, Heavenly Father, to draw near unto thee, in spirit and in truth, in humility and in faith, and we pray that thou wilt hear and answer our supplications. We are grateful unto thee O God, the Eternal Father, that we are permitted to celebrate the 50th anniversary of the establishment upon earth of this organization, which is called the Relief Society; and we humbly pray thee that in our hearts this day, we may feel that gratitude which is due to thee, that we have been permitted to pass through a half century, in comparative peace, that we have been preserved by thy powerful arm, from the hands of wicked men, and from those who have sought our destruction and overthrow. We thank thee [p. 142] Heavenly Father that we are permitted to meet unmolested from the powers of evil and from mobs, and from such things as were experienced in the early days of this Church. We thank thee that thou hast planted us safely and firmly in these fertile valleys, and that thou has given us the rich bounties of the earth, and the fatness of the soil for our good, our comfort, our prosperity and our happiness. While we have been surrounded by influences which were not calculated to lead our children in the paths of righteousness and truth, Thou hast preserved us from the designs of the destroyer, and from the powers of darkness. Thou hast given unto us a degree of light which has made our hearts to rejoice and helped us to serve thee. Thou hast given us those blessings we have asked for in righteousness, and power to overcome many of our weaknesses. Thou hast given us a desire to establish righteousness in the midst of the people. Thou hast given us a desire to establish thy Church in the earth, and to seek righteousness. We pray that these desires may continue from this time onward. That we may live with an eye single to thy glory and labor to establish thy work on earth, and bring to pass thy purposes. Wilt thou look upon us with much mercy. We invoke thy blessing at this time upon the aged mothers of the Relief Society. Many have passed away and those that remain who witnessed the establishment of that society by thy servant Joseph Smith, are few, aged, and feeble. Wilt thou continue thy mercies unto them and preserve their lives. Let thy spirit fill their hearts with joy and peace. Sanctify unto them every dispensation of thy providence, cause that their hearts may rejoice in thee and their faith be strengthened in thy promises. May thy word never fail. We pray thee from this time forth to preserve thy saints, and these aged mothers until they are satisfied with life. Wilt thou bless all those who are associated with them throughout the length and breadth of the land. Bless the Presidents, Counselors and members of the Relief Society throughout the earth, in Zion and in foreign lands, upon the islands of the sea, and wherever they are met together this day to celebrate this 50th anniversary. Wilt thou be with them by thy spirit to bless them, to cause their hearts to rejoice before thee. We ask thee to bless the mothers of Israel, and to bless their daughters and bless thy servants and all thy people. We would remember thine aged servant President Woodruff, who is [a]bsent[511] from us on this occasion. Wilt thou cause that he may be restored to perfect health and strength. Continue the vigor of all his faculties; strengthen him in body and mind, and wilt thou make known unto him thy mind and thy will that he may be thy mouth-piece unto thy people and be a father in very deed unto thy Saints; wilt thou bless also with him his counselors and the quorum of the twelve apostles. Cause that the Presidency of thy Church and the twelve apostles shall be one in heart, one in spirit, one in purpose, one in their views for the building up of Zion and the bringing to pass of thy purposes. May thy servants and hand-maidens be devoted to the establishment of the Church in righteousness upon the earth. O God, bless thy people with those mercies that they desire in righteousness. Sustain thy servants and people and preserve them from difficulties and the evils that surround them. May thy spirit direct them and thy power attend them in all they do. May they dedicate their lives unto thee and increase in knowledge. Grant every desire in righteousness unto thy people. Heal the sick, comfort those that mourn; look down in much mercy upon thy people. Have mercy upon the erring ones, call them from the error of their ways and bring them to a knowledge of thy truth that they may devote their lives unto thee. Help us to acknowledge thee in all things. Unite thy people. Bless the elements that surround us; and the soil, that it may be fertile. Bless thy people in their incoming and out-going. Grant, O Heavenly Father, that thy servants whom thou hast chosen to direct thy work may continue steadfast and faithful. Bless thou thy handmaidens who have assembled to commemorate this anniversary. May we understand thy will and keep thy commandments. Bless all thy people and the honorable of the earth everywhere. Fill their hearts with thy peace. Give unto us such things as we most need for we desire only such things as shall bring to pass thy purposes upon the earth. We humbly ask all these blessings in the name of Jesus Christ. Amen.

PRESIDENT JOSEPH F. SMITH.

Following is a synopsis of his remarks:

---

511. TEXT: In the copy used for transcription, there is a blank space where the *a* should be.

"This relief Society, he said, has always had the hearty endorsement and the approval of the First Presidency since its first organization, fifty years ago. It had occurred to the speaker that it would be an excellent thing to erect a building or buildings, as the case might be, where there could be a hall for the Society to meet, and which would be in a measure self-sustaining. He did not know whether this matter had been considered yet. It had already been stated that the Prophet Joseph Smith had presented the Society with a building lot, and he did not see why the plan of building could not yet be carried out. It appeared to him to be an easy matter.[512]

"With regard to the gift of tongues, the speaker said, it was one very much liable to mislead. The adversary can easily take advantage of it. However, where the Spirit of the Lord directs it, it is a good thing. Sometimes, however, persons speak under the influence of a wrong spirit.

"In relation to laying on of hands by sisters, the speaker said it is a proper thing for mothers, who have received their blessings in the house of God to pray for their sick and to rebuke diseases. It is just as much the right of the mother as of the father, although he, holding the Priesthood, can do it by virtue of this, as well as in the name of the Lord. The women are not especially called upon to visit from house to house to administer to the sick, but they can do so properly, if called upon.

"The speaker was thankful for the opportunity of meeting with the Saints, and wished that the Lord might bless the work. He exhorted all to live their religion and do their duties faithfully.["]

After The Days of Nauvoo.
By E. B. Wells.
Read by Apostle A. H. Cannon.

When the Saints left Nauvoo and during their journeyings, the Relief Society meetings were necessarily discontinued, though the sisters never lost sight of the institution, nor the promises made to them by Pres. Jos. Smith, but continued their benevolent work wherever and whenever an opportunity presented itself; they were always ready with willing hands and tender sympathies to perform deeds of love and charity, and many were in need of such kindly acts for those were the days of toil, and of suffering, of scarcity and of hardship.

Among the foremost heroines of that eventful time should be indelibly engraven the names of Vilate Kimball, Mary Ann Young and Elizabeth Ann

---

512. For a description of the immediate challenges that prevented easy construction of a Relief Society building in Nauvoo, see Derr et al., *Women of Covenant,* 174.

Whitney, these Mothers in Israel[513] with kindly deeds and loving words, inspired many a fainting heart with faith and courage, and ministered temporal and spiritual blessings, to hundreds of the daughters of Zion,[514] whose paths were not strewn with roses, but were full of thorns and fiery trials. There were few gifts to bestow, but many lessons of patience and resignation to be learned in the school of experience.

Early in the settlement of the valley in 1851 and in 1852 the sisters had temporary societies in several wards and surrounding places, and though all were comparatively poor, yet they helped those in greater need, and fed and clothed the wandering Indians, whom we have ever thus tried to conciliate.[515] In 1855 when in a more settled condition Pres. Young called upon the Bishops to organize a Relief Society in each ward and gave Sister Eliza R. Snow a mission to assist them in organizing and to take with her Sister Zina D. Young as her Counselor.[516] Of some of these branches we have no record, but Bishop Abraham Hoagland of the 14th Ward in this City, organized a Relief Society Sept. 14, 1856 and appointed Sister Phebe W. Woodruff President; and she chose Sister M. I. Horne, and [Lucinda] Southworth her Counselors.[517] About that time Bishop N. [Nathaniel] V. Jones also organized the 15th, ward and chose Sister Lydia Granger President, the 9th ward was organized with Sister [Harriet] Taft President, etc., other wards followed—but Johnson's army coming here, and the move South, which occurred in 1858[518]—interrupted the regularity of the work of the Society and it was not until after the return of the people to their homes, and when order was again restored that the Sooiety was perfectly organized; to bring about these organizations throughout the several Stakes of Zion Sister Eliza R. Snow, Sister Zina D. Young and other sisters associated with them, traveled and labored assiduously in all kinds of weather,

---

513. See Judges 5:7; and 2 Samuel 20:19. For more on the phrase "Mothers in Israel," see Carol Cornwall Madsen, "Mothers in Israel: Sarah's Legacy," in *Women of Wisdom and Knowledge: Talks Selected from the BYU Women's Conferences,* ed. Marie Cornwall and Susan Howe (Salt Lake City: Deseret Book, 1990), 179–201.

514. See Isaiah 3:16–17; 4:4; Song of Solomon 3:11; and Doctrine and Covenants 124:11.

515. Relief Societies were first organized in Utah in 1854. (See introduction to Part 2.)

516. Relief Societies were reestablished in some Utah wards during the 1850s, but it was not until 1868 that Brigham Young officially charged Eliza R. Snow to help organize them throughout the church. (See Documents 3.1, 3.4, and 3.5; see also Richard L. Jensen, "Forgotten Relief Societies, 1844–67," *Dialogue: A Journal of Mormon Thought* 16, no. 1 [Spring 1983]: 105–125; and Jill Mulvay Derr, "The Relief Society, 1854–1881," in *Mapping Mormonism: An Atlas of Latter-day Saint History,* ed. Brandon S. Plewe [Provo, UT: Brigham Young University Press, 2012], 102–103.)

517. See Document 2.3.

518. On the "move South"—the temporary removal of Salt Lake Valley residents to more southern settlements in anticipation of the arrival of federal troops during the Utah War—see the introduction to Part 2; and Richard D. Poll, "The Move South," *BYU Studies* 29 no. 4 (Fall 1989): 65–88.

and in all sorts of conveyances to assist in making a permanent success of this institution for the women of Zion.

One or two important events bearing upon woman's work transpired during these years that should be mentioned in this connection. The enfranchisement of the women of Utah—which occurred in February 1870—the bill passed the Territorial Legislature and was signed by acting Gov. [Stephen A.] Mann, on the 7th of Feb. two days later the City election took place and the first ballot cast by women here was for Mayor of the City.[519] In June 1872 a Woman's paper was issued for the first time in the Rocky mountain region, the WOMAN'S EXPONENT.[520]

In October 1876—Pres. Young called upon the Sisters to store up grain against a day of famine, and in accordance with that call, fifty thousand bushels of wheat have been deposited in bins and granaries mostly owned by the Relief Society.[521] Undoubtedly this is the first instance in the annals of history of women laying up stores of wheat.

To enumerate all that has been done by the Relief Society would take up too much valuable time; but the works have been those of love and charity and performed in the spirit of meekness and humility.

CENTRAL ORGANIZATION IN UTAH.
By Sarah M. Kimball.
Read by Apostle A. H. Cannon.

A called meeting for the election of the Relief Society Officers was held in the Assembly Hall, Salt Lake City, June 19th, 1880. Pres. John Taylor, Sec. John Nuttal, and Stake Pres. Angus M. Cannon on the stand. On motion Eliza R. Snow was elected to preside over all the branches of the Relief Society in Zion. Zina D. Young and Elizabeth Ann Whitney were elected Counselors, Sarah M Kimball Sec. and M. Isabelle Horne Treas. (Sec. John Nuttal by Pres. Taylor's request read from the Book of the Law of the Lord.)[522]

July 17th Pres. John Taylor met with the Relief Society in the 14th Ward Hall, gave instructions and ordained the President, Counselors and Secretary to their various positions.[523]

July 24th, 1880 the Relief Society took an active part in the grand celebration of Pionee[r] [p. 143] Day in the fiftieth year of the organization of the

---

519. See Document 3.17.
520. See Document 3.21.
521. See Document 3.25.
522. See Document 4.4.
523. See Document 4.5.

Church. Representatives of the Society occupied ten carriages, the first carriage carrying an elegant white silk banner with appropriate inscriptions.[524]

Feb. 1880 the Relief Society Secretary was notified that she was expected to furnish a general semi-annual stastistical and financial report of the Relief Society at the President's Office ten days prior to the 6th of Apr. and Oct. The first general report is dated March 15th, 1881. It cembined [combined] the reports of sixteen stakes, and gave a membership of 12,288, disbursements for six months $3,468,31.[525]

Elizabeth Ann Whitney Counselor to Eliza R. Snow departed this life Feb. 15th, 1882 her honored name crowned with the blessing of Saints.[526]

In June 1882 the Deseret Hospital was established with Eliza R. Snow Pres. of the board of directors.[527] Sept. 1882 Romania B. Pratt was appointed Assistant Secretary.

Jan 21st, 1884 a grand ovation was given in the Social Hall, in honor of the eightieth anniversary of the birth day of Eliza R. Snow.[528]

Apr. 1885 Annual Conference held at Logan Cache Co. Utah, Relief Society report included twenty-two stakes. Total number of members 16,358.[529]

Last general Relief Society report (Oct. 1887) during the administration of Eliza R Snow, members 17,002, branches 302 disbursements to charity for 6 months $7,689,80.[530]

Sister Snow in company with her brother Lorenzo Snow and others, made an extended European tour in 1872 and 3 visited Jerusalem and compiled her interesting book "Correspondence of Palestine Tourists."[531] Her Poems and other writings are much valued.[532]

---

524. The phrase "Numbers 300 branches | July 24th 1880" was inscribed on a white silk banner that accompanied three carriages transporting Relief Society leaders in the Pioneer Day Jubilee procession. The banner is located at the Church History Museum, Salt Lake City. ("Year of Jubilee," *Woman's Exponent,* Aug. 1, 1880, 9:36; introduction to Part 4.)

525. "Report of the Relief Society of Zion for 6 Months Ending General Conference Apr. 6th 1881," Relief Society Record, 1880–1892, CHL, Mar. 15, 1881, pp. 24–25; see also Document 4.12.

526. "Death of Mother Whitney," *Deseret News* [weekly], Feb. 22, 1882, 72–73.

527. See Document 4.11.

528. "An Ovation," *Woman's Exponent,* Feb. 1, 1884, 12:132.

529. "Annual Conference of the Church held at Logan Cache Co Utah," Relief Society Record, Apr. 1885, p. 40; see also "April Conference in Logan," *Woman's Exponent,* Apr. 15, 1885, 22:172.

530. "Last General Relief Society Report during Pres. E. R Snow Smith's Administration," Relief Society Record, Oct. 1887, p. 49.

531. See Document 3.23. The book referenced here is George A. Smith et al., *Correspondence of Palestine Tourists; Comprising a Series of Letters by George A. Smith, Lorenzo Snow, Paul A. Schettler, and Eliza R. Snow, of Utah. Mostly Written While Traveling in Europe, Asia and Africa, in the Years 1872 and 1873* (Salt Lake City: Deseret News, 1875).

532. In 1856 Franklin D. Richards printed a volume of Snow's poetry titled *Poems: Religious, Historical, and Political* (Liverpool: F. D. Richards, 1856). A second volume was printed by the Latter-day

She traveled extensively in the various Stakes of Zion always in the capacity of an instructor, was everywhere received as a loving friend and a wise counselor. As an organizer she was unexcelled. Our beloved Sister and President closed her mortal eyes in the Lion House,[533] Salt Lake City, Utah, Dec. 5th, 1887 aged eighty-three years. Her comparatively long life was eventful beyond that of most women. This Jubilee day March 17th, 1892, the name of Eliza R. Snow will be reverently spoken in various Relief Society branches and in many lands.

Apostle John Henry Smith then read the paper of Mrs. B. W. Smith, and A. H. Cannon read the article of Mrs. M. I. Horne, both of which will be found in another part of the paper.[534]

SENTIMENTS

E. B. Wells.

Read by Apostle A. H. Cannon.

The Relief Society celebrate to-day a Jubilee that reaches around the world. Never before that there is any record of has a woman's Jubilee spread over such an extent of country. Throughout all the wards and settlements, in all the Stakes of Zion is this momentous event being commemorated by meeting and rejoicing together in praise and thanksgiving to God. And not only *here* but in other parts of the United States, North and South, in Canada and Mexico, on the Sandwich and Samoan Islands and New Zealand, in Great Britain, in Holland and the countries of Scandinavia, in Switzerland and Germany, in Asia Minor, Australia and Tasmania. What does this woman's Jubilee signify? not only that fifty years ago this organization was founded by a Prophet of God, but that woman is becoming emancipated from error and superstition and darkness. That light has come into the world, and the Gospel has made her free, that the key of knowledge has been turned, and she has drank inspiration at the divine fountain.[535]

All humanity proclaims this the woman's era. Everything important tends to emphasize the fact; the spirit of *woman's* future destiny rests upon the sisters, and they obey the impulses of the times in which they live! the voice of the

---

Saints' Printing and Publishing Establishment in 1877 in Salt Lake City. (See also Jill Mulvay Derr and Karen Lynn Davidson, eds., *Eliza R. Snow: The Complete Poetry* [Provo, UT: Brigham Young University Press; Salt Lake City: University of Utah Press, 2009].)

533. The Lion House, a residence of Brigham Young and some of his family, was situated on South Temple Street near the center of Salt Lake City.

534. The Bathsheba W. Smith and Mary Isabella Horne articles were published separately in the April 1, 1892, issue of the *Woman's Exponent.* Those articles are reproduced below.

535. On the "key of knowledge," see Document 1.2, entry for Apr. 28, 1842; see also Luke 11:52; and Doctrine and Covenants 84:19; 128:14.

hour! the fulfillment of prophecy! They repeat the hallelujah of woman's redemption; that has been echoed down the ages. The women of Zion in every land lift up their voices to-day in glad Hosannas for the deliverance that has been wrought out for them, and the blessings that have come through this great and grand organization established fifty years ago, and by means of which so much good has been accomplished, not only in works of charity and blessing, but in the development of the higher attributes of the human soul, that tend to purify, exalt snd [and] uplift the world. And while we celebrate this day of days let us cherish in *sacred* remembrance the memory of those who are not with us, but have gone on before; and especially should we all remember the *three* noble pioneer women, who immortalized their names, and reflected honor upon all their sex, by their undaunted courage in traversing the unknown desert plains with the first pioneers to this valley. Let the names of Clara Decker Young, Ellen Sanders Kimball, and Harriet Page Young be handed down to posterity, as the foremost Pilgrim mothers in pioneering Westward of the Rocky Mountains, and remember it was their fidelity to the truth, that gave them the faith and fortitude to endure.[536] And after to-day what new awakening shall come to us who are still in the field of woman's work? The refreshing reminiscences and remembrances of the past should inspire us with renewed zeal and courage for the future; and with a more divine consecration of our labors to the help of all humanity.

The choir then rendered in full voice and strength the celebrated English anthem "Daughter of Zion Awake from thy Sadness."

This grand anniversary Jubilee exercises were closed with a solemn benediction of thanksgiving to God by Apostle John Henry Smith.

---

536. The 1847 Brigham Young Company roster records that 142 men, 3 women, and 2 children were in the company at the Winter Quarters outfitting point. However, some Mississippi Saints joined the company at Fort Laramie and some Mormon Battalion members also joined the company en route. William Clayton's diary entry for April 16, 1847, listed all individuals in the company and stated: "There are 143 men and boys on the list of the pioneer company 3 women and Lorenzo Youngs 2 children. 73 Wagons. O. P. Rockwell has gone back to camp with J. C. Little, Bishop Whitney, Lyman, Wᵐ·, Kimball and J. B. Noble return from here to Winter Quarters." ("Brigham Young Pioneer Company, 1847," *Mormon Pioneer Overland Travel, 1847–1868*, compiled by the Church of Jesus Christ of Latter-day Saints, accessed Apr. 6, 2015, http://history.lds.org/overlandtravels; William Clayton, Diary, 1847, CHL, Apr. 16, 1847.)

Report of Bathsheba W. Smith Address

[537]ADDRESS OF BATHSHEBA W. SMITH

[Read by Apostle John Henry Smith at the Large Tabernacle Salt Lake City March 17, 1892.][538]

MY DEAR BROTHERS AND SISTERS:

I rejoice that I have lived to see this day—the Jubilee of our Relief Society.

Fifty years ago this day our beloved Joseph Smith organized the Relief Society in Nouvoo [Nauvoo].

After the organization was perfected, and the president, Sister Emma Smith, and her Counselors, Sister Whitney and Sister Cleveland, had taken their seats upon the stand, 17 members were admitted.

Hundreds joined the Society within a year.

Bro. Joseph met with us many times and gave us much counsel and valuable instructions; he said "Every virtuous woman should belong to this Society. This Organization is not only for the purpose of administering to the sick and afflicted, the poor and the needy but it is to save souls. If the Sisters come before the Lord in humility and faith and lay hands upon the sick and the Lord heals them, none should find fault. If ye are pure in all things nothing on earth or in heaven can hinder the angels from associating with you."[539]

At one meeting he said, he would not be with us much longer to instruct us.[540] This made us all feel sad. His words soon came to pass and wrung our hearts with sorrow and grief for the great loss we had sustained in losing our dearly beloved Prophet—for a true prophet I know he was.[541]

---

537. As noted in the detailed report above for the proceedings of the Jubilee celebration, the following article by Bathsheba W. Smith was read during the proceedings by John Henry Smith. For unknown reasons, this article was published separately from the fuller Jubilee report in the April 1, 1892, issue of the *Woman's Exponent.*

538. TEXT: Brackets in original.

539. Bathsheba Smith is here recounting in her own words snippets from several discourses Joseph Smith gave to the Nauvoo Relief Society. On March 31, 1842, he said, "The Society should grow up by degrees— should commence with a few individuals— thus have a select Society of the virtuous and those who will walk circumspectly." On April 28, 1842, he said, "If the sisters should have faith to heal the sick, let all hold their tongues, and let every thing roll on," and "If you live up to your privilege, the angels cannot be restrain'd from being your associates." On June 9, 1842, he said, "The Society is not only to relieve the poor, but to save souls." (Document 1.2.)

540. On April 28, 1842, Joseph Smith told the Nauvoo Relief Society women "that he did not know as he should have many opportunities of teaching them— that they were going to be left to themselves,— they would not long have him to instruct them— that the church would not have his instruction long, and the world would not be troubled with him a great while, and would not have his teachings." (Document 1.2.)

541. See "Awful Assassination of Joseph and Hyrum Smith!" *Times and Seasons,* July 1, 1844, 5:560.

It has been a "Labor of Love."[542] The sick and destitute have been blessed, the cast down have been comforted, and the Lord has filled our hearts with joy and peace.

Let us take renewed courage and be more united and earnest in this great work, and if any one has ill feelings towards another, banish them and make this a Jubilee in *very deed*.

May the choicest of Heaven's blessings rest upon all Israel is my prayer in the name of Jesus. Amen.

Report of Mary Isabella Horne Address

[543]ADDRESS OF MRS. M. ISABELLA HORNE

[Read by Apostle Abraham H. Cannon at the Relief Society Jubilee in the Large Tabernacle, Salt Lake City, March 17, 1892.][544]

My Brethren and Sisters:—My heart is filled with praise and gratitude to my Heavenly Father that he has spared my life to meet with you on this important occasion, to celebrate by a grand Jubilee all over the world, the Fiftieth Anniversary of the organization of the Relief Society by the Prophet Joseph Smith in the last dispensation of the fulness of times. I am thankful that I had the privilege of being associated with the first organization and of hearing instructions from the President, Emma Smith.[545] She exhorted us to faithfulness in the discharge of our duties, and especially to humble ourselves and not ask God to humble us, as He might do it in a way that would not be very pleasant to us. These remarks made a lasting impression upon my mind.

After the martyrdom of our beloved Prophet and Patriarch, the Saints were permitted to [p. [137]] remain in Nauvoo till the Temple was completed, and many of us received our endowments in that House of the Lord.[546] Soon after this the people were driven from their homes in the middle of winter during heavy snow storms and severe frost. I with my family crossed the Mississipi

---

542. See 1 Thessalonians 1:3; and Hebrews 6:10.

543. As noted in the detailed report above for the proceedings of the Jubilee celebration, the following article by Mary Isabella Horne was read during the proceedings by Abraham H. Cannon. For unknown reasons, this article was published separately from the fuller Jubilee report in the April 1, 1892, issue of the *Woman's Exponent*.

544. TEXT: Brackets in original.

545. Horne joined the Relief Society in Nauvoo on June 9, 1842. (Document 1.2.)

546. "From early January until the final company left the temple on February 7, endowment groups received the ordinances six days a week, with sessions underway some days from early morning until late at night. More than one hundred Saints were endowed on a typical day, two hundred or more on peak days, and more than five hundred made covenants with the Lord on each of the final two days." (Glen M. Leonard, *Nauvoo: A Place of Peace, a People of Promise* [Salt Lake City: Deseret Book; Provo, UT: Brigham Young University Press, 2002], 568.)

river in the month of February, 1846, and camped with the Saints on Sugar Creek. After that the river froze over and other companies crossed on the ice. Early in the Spring we commenced our weary journey through mud and storm to find a home among the savages in the Rocky Mountains. When we arrived at Council Bluffs a call was made upon Pres. Young by the Government for five hundred of our able-bodied men to go to the Mexican war, which prevented us from continuing our journey and necessitated our going into Winter Quarters, where we were seriously afflicted with that dreadful disease—scurvy. In June, 1847, the saints were organized into companies to follow the Pioneers, and I was with the first company that left Winter Quarters.[547] The trials, hardships and privations that the people of God endured on that long and weary journey were great and can only be understood by those who experienced them.

Children were born on the way before we reached Council Bluffs, myself giving birth to a daughter at Pisgah, the company started forward on the third day after.

When our pilgrimage was over we found ourselves in a barren waste, inhabited by Indians. But we were glad to find a resting place where we could worship God without fearing our enemies were coming upon us. The weather was favorable for building, and the brethren immediately began to saw logs and erect small log houses, into which many of us moved without having either doors windows or floors.

Here again there were many difficulties to overcome. The ground was full of snakes which used to crawl around our houses, but these were soon killed or frightened away. The timber was so full of bugs that it was years before they were entirely subdued. The mice also were very numerous, running over us by day and by night, and destroying considerable clothing, etc., which caused great inconvenience and trouble. We were also obliged to live on short rations, digging roots to add to our store, in order to make our supplies last until something could be raised for food. During that winter many of the Mormon Battalion arrived, and we were under the necessity of sharing our food with them. We could put a little grease into a dish with a rag in it to make a light, and parch a little wheat to make our coffee, but when it came to making soap we were put to our wits' end to get material to make enough to do our washing. I can hardly tell today how we did succeed. But the Lord opened our way and blessed us with cheerful, contented spirits and thankful hearts.

---

547. See Bathsheba Smith's speech in Document 3.13.

I well remember the first harvest home we celebrated. Apostles Parley P. Pratt and John Taylor called upon the sisters to prepare a feast.[548] They prepared what food they could from their meagre store and set a long table in the Fort. Although the food was plain and everything was done in a humble way, our hearts flowed with thanksgiving to our Heavenly Father for the blessings conferred upon us. Our table decorations were sheaves of wheat and other things that had been raised. Although the crops were light we had enough to last us another year, and some to spare to our brethren and sisters that came the following year.

The second year of our being in the valley the crickets threatened to destroy our crops; men, women and children had to fight them, many were driven into the ditches of water and were piled where there was any obstruction, bushels and bushels. The Lord sent the quails to devour them and thus we were saved from starvation.[549]

In the spring of 1849 many of the people left the Fort where we first located and moved to their city lots. During the next few years our numbers rapidly increased, and many poor saints gathered. Pres. Young then found it advisable to again organize a Relief Society. You have heard a sketch read this morning of the organization of the Relief Society in this city both before and after the move, I had the honor of being chosen as First Counselor to our President Phebe Woodruff, and Sister Southworth as Second Counselor, in the first organization of the society in the Fourteenth Ward, where we worked faithfully for the relief of the poor, and made many useful articles of clothing which were given to the poor to make them comfortable for their journey during the Move. We were re-organized in the same ward by Bishop Hoagland in the year 1867, with myself as President, and Sisters Wilmirth East and Susan B. [Conrad] Wilkinson as counselors.[550]

The various branches of the Society have been in good working order from that day till the present, and their labors and the good that has been done cannot be written, and are only known by our Father in heaven.

In the year 1877 the Relief Society was organized in a Stake capacity, and I was selected to fill the office of President of the Salt Lake Stake, with Sisters

548. See Parley P. Pratt, *The Autobiography of Parley Parker Pratt, One of the Twelve Apostles of the Church of Jesus Christ of Latter-day Saints, Embracing His Life, Ministry and Travels, with Extracts, in Prose and Verse, from His Miscellaneous Writings,* ed. Parley P. Pratt Jr. (New York: Russell Brothers, 1874), 406.

549. Horne refers here to the cricket infestation during the spring of 1848. (See William G. Hartley, "Mormons, Crickets, and Gulls: A New Look at an Old Story," *Utah Historical Quarterly* 38, no. 3 [Summer 1970]: 224–239.)

550. See Document 2.3; and Fourteenth Ward, Salt Lake Stake, Fourteenth Ward Relief Society Minutes and Records, 1864–1957, CHL.

Elmina S. Taylor and Sarepta Heywood as Counselors, Elizabeth Howard Sec., and B. W. Smith Treas.[551] Sister Heywood discharged faithfully the duties of her office until her death, when Sister Helen M. Whitney was elected to fill the vacancy.[552] The officers were set apart by Pres. Angus M. Cannon and Counselors. The first Quarterly Conference of the Relief Society of this Stake was held in March, 1878, and have been held regularly up to the present time.[553]

I have been a worker in the Society from the first, and have rejoiced in the work we were called upon to perform in looking after the poor, comforting the sick, watching by their bedsides, and preparing proper clothing for them when they passed away. A great many of our brethren and sisters have been respectably clothed for burial by the members of this society. Thousands of dollars have been collected and given to the poor, besides responding to other calls that have been made upon us. Pres. Young advised the sisters to build houses in which to hold meetings and perform their labors. Many branches have done this, and also built granaries in which to store their wheat, according to the counsel of President Young, who was always interested in the advancement and progress of the sisters.

In 1870 Pres. Young called me to fill an important home mission—that of organizing the sisters into what was then called the Retrenchment Association, its object being to lighten the labors of the women and give them more time to devote to mental and spiritual culture. It was some time before I could gain sufficient courage to perform this labor, but Sister Snow urged me to do my duty, so with fear and trembling I endeavored to do so. In the spring I invited about twelve presidents of branches of the Relief Society to meet with me in my own house. They were all willing to help in the work. We appointed a meeting in the Fifteenth Ward Hall and had a good meeting. It was then that a committee of three ladies, viz:, Mrs. [Harriet] Amelia Folsom Young, Bathsheba W. Smith and Sarah M. Kimball, were appointed to wait upon Acting Governor Mann and thank him for signing the bill giving the elective franchise to women. From that meeting we adjourned to the Fourteenth Ward Hall where an organization was effected with M. Isabella Horne as President,

---

551. See Document 3.29.

552. Heywood died on December 4, 1881. Whitney was elected to succeed her during the semi-annual Relief Society conference of the Salt Lake Stake on March 10, 1882. (Salt Lake Stake, Salt Lake Stake Relief Society Record Book, 1868–1903, CHL, 61, 64; "In Memoriam," *Woman's Exponent*, Dec. 15, 1881, 10:109.)

553. See Salt Lake Stake Relief Society Record Book, Mar. 23, 1878, 5–6; and "Quarterly Conference," *Woman's Exponent*, Apr. 1, 1878, 6:163.

and Eliza R. Snow, Zina D. H. Young, Margaret T. Smoot, Phebe Woodruff, Bathsheba W. Smith and Sarah M. Kimball as her Counselors.[554]

After Sister Smoot moved to Provo, Sister Howard was chosen to fill her place and after Sister Woodruff passed away Sister Minerva W. Snow was chosen to fill the vacancy; since the death of Sister Eliza R. Snow, Sisters Elizabeth T. Webb and Elizabeth Stevenson have been added to our number.

Meetings have been held semi-monthly since that time, and much good instruction has been given, and many of the sisters have obtained a testimony of the truth of the Gospel and the divine mission of Joseph Smith, who had never thought much about religious matters before attending these meetings.

I feel thankful to my Heavenly Father that He inspired the Prophet Joseph to organize the Relief Society and thus open the door for the advancement of woman. May the good work continue. May we appreciate our privileges and go forth faithfully in the discharge of our duties as mothers in Israel is the earnest desire of your co-laborer in the kingdom of God.

---

554. See Documents 3.15, 3.16, and 3.18; and Susa Young Gates, *History of the Young Ladies' Mutual Improvement Association of the Church of Jesus Christ of Latter-day Saints, from November 1869 to June 1910* (Salt Lake City: Deseret News, 1911), 29–40.

REFERENCE MATERIAL

General Presidencies of the Relief Society, Young Ladies' Mutual Improvement Association, and Primary Association, 1842–1892

The following paragraphs identify the officers in the general presidencies of the Relief Society, Young Ladies' Mutual Improvement Association, and Primary Association for the time period covered in this volume.

Relief Society

Emma Smith Presidency

The following women were elected or appointed officers of the Female Relief Society of Nauvoo on March 17, 1842, the day the society was organized:

Emma Smith, President
Sarah M. Cleveland, First Counselor
Elizabeth Ann Whitney, Second Counselor
Eliza R. Snow, Secretary
Phebe M. Wheeler, Assistant Secretary
Elvira A. Cowles, Treasurer

Some of these officers moved from the city and stopped attending meetings, but it does not appear that any of them were formally replaced. Hannah M. Ells served as secretary for the society's meetings on March 9 and 16, 1844. The last meeting of the Nauvoo society was held March 16, 1844. (Document 1.2.)

Eliza R. Snow Presidency

The following women were sustained as the Relief Society general presidency on June 19, 1880, in a quarterly conference of the Salt Lake Stake Relief Society:

Eliza R. Snow, President
Zina D. H. Young, First Counselor
Elizabeth Ann Whitney, Second Counselor
Sarah M. Kimball, Secretary
Mary Isabella Horne, Treasurer

Romania B. Pratt was appointed assistant secretary in September 1882. Elizabeth Ann Whitney died February 15, 1882, and her position was not filled. The remainder of the women served until the death of Eliza R. Snow on December 5, 1887. (Documents 4.4, 4.5, 4.18, and 4.28; Relief Society Record, 1880–1892, CHL, Sept. 1883.)

Zina D. H. Young Presidency

Zina D. H. Young was sustained as Relief Society general president on April 8, 1888, at the general conference of the church. She and the other general officers were set apart six months later. The resulting presidency was as follows:

> Zina D. H. Young, President
> Jane S. Richards, First Counselor
> Bathsheba W. Smith, Second Counselor
> Sarah M. Kimball, Secretary
> Romania B. Pratt, Assistant Secretary
> Mary Isabella Horne, Treasurer
> Emmeline B. Wells, Corresponding Secretary

These women continued to serve in these positions past the year 1892. ("April Conference 1888," *Woman's Exponent,* Apr. 15, 1888, 16:172; "Relief Society Central Board," Relief Society Record, 63; "Relief Society Central Board," *Woman's Exponent,* Oct. 15, 1888, 17:76.)

Young Ladies' Mutual Improvement Association

The first general presidency of the Young Ladies' Mutual Improvement Association was sustained on June 19, 1880, in a quarterly conference of the Salt Lake Stake Relief Society. The initial officers were as follows:

> Elmina S. Taylor, President
> Margaret Young Taylor, First Counselor
> Martha Jane Horne Tingey, Second Counselor
> Louise M. Wells, Secretary
> Fanny Young Thatcher, Treasurer

Maria Y. Dougall replaced Margaret Taylor as first counselor in 1887. Louise Wells died on May 16, 1887, and Mary E. Cook replaced her as secretary. Ann M. Cannon became assistant secretary in April 1891 and replaced Mary Cook as secretary in October of that year. She also became the treasurer after Fanny Thatcher died January 21, 1892. (Document 4.4; Susa Young Gates, *History of the Young Ladies' Mutual Improvement Association of the Church of Jesus Christ of Latter-day Saints from November 1869 to June 1910* [Salt Lake City: Deseret News, 1911], 88–89; "April Conference 1888," *Woman's Exponent,* Apr. 15, 1888, 16:172; Mary E. Cook, "Our Girls," *Young Woman's Journal* 1, no. 8 [May 1890]: 269; Susa Young Gates, "Mrs. Fanny Young Thatcher, Treasurer of the General Board of the Y. L. M. I. A.," *Young Woman's Journal* 3, no. 6 [Mar. 1892]: 242; Ann M. Cannon, "Y. L. M. I. A. Officers' Meeting," *Young Woman's Journal* 2, no. 8 [May 1891]: 385; "First Territorial Conference of the Y. L. M. I. Association," *Young Woman's Journal* 3, no. 2 [Nov. 1891]: 89; Annie M. Cannon, "Y. L. M. I. A. Officers' Meeting," *Young Woman's Journal* 3, no. 8 [May 1892]: 381–382.)

Primary Association

The first general presidency of the Primary Association was sustained on June 19, 1880, in a quarterly conference of the Salt Lake Stake Relief Society. The initial officers were as follows:

> Louie B. Felt, President
> Matilda M. Barratt, First Counselor
> Clara M. Cannon, Second Counselor

Lillie Tuckett Freeze replaced Matilda Barratt as first counselor in 1888. It is unclear when a secretary was first appointed to serve in this presidency, but by 1890 May Anderson is identified in minutes as being the general secretary of the Primary. (Document 4.4; Lillie T. Freeze, "Primary Work from 1880 to 1890," Lillie T. Freeze, Papers, 1886–1928, CHL, 2–3; Primary Association, Primary Association General Board Minutes, 1889–1994, CHL, vol. 1, p. 5.)

Biographical Directory

The names of more than two thousand individuals appear in the documents published in this volume. This register contains brief biographical sketches for roughly four hundred women and men who play more prominent roles in the documents. These include women who attended the first meeting of the Female Relief Society of Nauvoo; held leadership positions in the Relief Society, Young Ladies' Mutual Improvement Association, or Primary Association; contributed in a remarkable way within their ward or community; or participated in national events or were national figures. Also included are biographical sketches for men who held general or local leadership positions in the church or who participated in community or national events. The sources for these biographical sketches are available in the biographical directory published online at churchhistorianspress.org. The online directory also provides brief biographical information for almost all the other women and men named in the documents in this volume. A small number of names are identified in footnotes in the main body of the volume rather than in the biographical directory. Because of research limitations and the imperfect nature of the documents, some names could not be identified.

The biographical entries in this register identify persons by complete name (correctly spelled), birth and death dates, and additional information, such as birthplace and parentage, migrations and places of residence, dates of marriage and names of spouses, number of children, religious and civic positions, and place of death. Any references to baptism denote entry into The Church of Jesus Christ of Latter-day Saints, unless otherwise specified. Locations that are noted include city or town, county, and state, when identified, for the first mention of a locale in each sketch. The counties and states of a handful of well-known cities have been omitted. Parenthetically listed at the end of each biographical entry are the numbers for every document text in which the person's name appears.

Entries for women give all maiden and married names and are generally listed under the surnames by which the women were known at the time they appear in the volume. For example, Ann Atlass Robinson Coulam Doull is listed in this directory as "Coulam Doull, Ann Atlass Robinson" because she was known under the married name Coulam at the time she figures in this volume. For women who were plural wives of Joseph or Hyrum Smith, the surname Smith has not been included; exceptions have been made for women who went by Smith during their lifetimes. Later married names and any alternative spellings that appear in parentheses were disregarded while alphabetizing this register.

In the documents published in this volume, many personal names are given incompletely or are spelled unconventionally. The editors have supplied additional name information in brackets where needed to aid the reader in finding the matching person in the biographical directory. When a name in the text has two or more possible identifications, the name as it appears in the document is listed in this register (or the one online) with a "See" followed by the potential identifications. At times, a name in a document will contain a middle initial that is not present in the person's biographical entry. This omission does not necessarily mean that the middle initial is erroneous; rather, it indicates that researchers were unable to find further documentation that either confirmed or corrected the initial.

Researchers have utilized original sources whenever possible. Readers wishing to conduct further research may consult the documented biographical entries online.

A., Joseph (circa 1855–?). Born in Utah Territory. Baptized at Thistle Creek, Sanpete County, Utah Territory, August 1879. In 1882, accompanied John Spencer and Mormon V. Selman to Strawberry, Duchesne County, Utah Territory, to meet with a group of Uncompahgre Indians waiting to be baptized. Donated to a fund to cover expenses for U.S. Supreme Court case *Cannon v. United States,* 1885. Ordained an elder in the Indianola Ward, North Sanpete Stake, in Indianola, Sanpete County. Attended Sunday school in the Indianola Ward, 1894. Relocated from Indianola to the Uintah and Ouray Indian Reservation, 1896. (4.7)

Alder, Lydia Dunford (July 2, 1846–March 1, 1923). Born at Trowbridge, Wiltshire, England; daughter of Sarah Jones and George Dunford. Baptized, 1867. Immigrated to the United States aboard the *Argo,* 1850. Married George Alfred Alder, 1863; ten children. Migrated to the Salt Lake Valley, 1867. Served as secretary to Marinda N. Hyde and Bathsheba W. Smith in the Salt Lake City Seventeenth Ward Relief Society. Served a mission in England, 1889–1901. Attended the International Congress of Women at London, 1899; at Berlin, 1904; and at Rome, 1914. Died at Salt Lake City. (3.13, 3.16)

Aldridge, Sophia Coleman Stevens (July 14, 1791–December 16, 1860). Born at Shongum (Shawangunk), Ulster County, New York; daughter of Mary Gale and Absalom Coleman. Married first Uzziel Stevens. Married second William Aldridge; sealed to Uzziel Stevens (with William Aldridge acting as proxy), January 26, 1846, in the temple at Nauvoo, Hancock County, Illinois. Migrated to the Salt Lake Valley with the Allen Taylor pioneer company, 1849. Moved to Washington County, Utah Territory, by July 1860. Died at Washington, Washington County. (1.2)

Allan, Agnes McAuslan (November 11, 1821–April 1, 1909). Born at Millcroft, Lanarkshire, Scotland; daughter of Betty Adamson and Peter McAuslan. Married John Allan at Denny, Stirlingshire, Scotland, August 27, 1847. Lived at Grahamston, Renfrewshire, Scotland, 1851. In 1855, migrated to the Salt Lake Valley with help from the Perpetual Emigrating Fund aboard the ship *S. Curling* and with the Charles A. Harper pioneer company. Lived at Coalville, Summit County, Utah Territory, 1870, and at Manassa, Conejos County, Colorado, 1880. Helped settle Bluff, San Juan County, Utah Territory, early 1880s. Appointed counselor in the Bluff Ward Relief Society presidency, 1888. Died at Bluff. (4.21)

Allan, Ardell Holman Stevens (November 3, 1865–April 28, 1937). Born at Holden, Millard County, Utah Territory; daughter of Abigail Holman and Walter Stevens. Lived at Fruitland, San Juan County, New Mexico Territory; at Bluff, San Juan County, Utah Territory; and in Montezuma Valley, Colorado. Married John Allan Jr., 1885; later divorced; two children. Worked as a midwife and nurse. Appointed treasurer of the Bluff Ward Relief Society, 1888. Died at Blanding, San Juan County, Utah Territory. (4.21)

Allan, Johanna (Jenny/Jennie) Amelia Hellstrom (April 20, 1859–October 7, 1891). Born at Motala, Östergötland, Sweden; daughter of Anna Brita Olsson and John Erik

Hellstrom. Married John Allan Jr., December 30, 1885; six children. Moved to Richfield, Sevier County, Utah Territory; to Olio, Rio Arriba County, New Mexico Territory; and to Bluff, San Juan County, Utah Territory. Appointed secretary of the Bluff Ward Relief Society, November 27, 1888. Died at Mancos, Montezuma County, Colorado. (4.21)

Allen Griggs, Mary Geddes (February 8, 1824–?). Born at Boston; daughter of Maria Geddes and John Allen. Paid tithing in Boston, 1842. Participated in the Boston Female Penny and Sewing Society; served as the society's secretary, by January 1845. Married Charles U. Griggs, 1845. Migrated to Nauvoo, Hancock County, Illinois, May/June 1845. Widowed, August 1845, at Nauvoo. (1.12)

Ames, Julia Frances (Fanny) Baker (June 14, 1840–August 21, 1931). Born at Canandaigua, Ontario County, New York; daughter of Julia Canfield and Increase Baker. Married Charles Gordon Ames; four children. Nationally prominent advocate for social welfare and woman suffrage. Instrumental in organizing the Children's Aid Society in Pennsylvania and organized various civic and church charitable organizations in Pennsylvania and Massachusetts. Died at Barnstable, Barnstable County, Massachusetts; buried at Minneapolis. (4.27)

Anderson, Andrew (Anders), Jr. (September 13, 1854–March 10, 1940). Born at Genarp or Häckeberga, Malmöhus, Sweden; son of Anna Christina Olson and Anders (Andrew) Anderson. Immigrated to the United States; migrated to the Salt Lake Valley with the James S. Brown pioneer company, 1859. Settled at Moroni, Sanpete County, Utah Territory, by 1860; later moved to Fountain Green, Sanpete County. Married Diantha Christensen, 1875. Helped settle Castle Dale (later Orangeville), Emery County, Utah Territory, 1878. Served as the first Orangeville Sunday school superintendent, as elders quorum secretary, and in the bishopric. Died at Orangeville. (4.25)

Andrews, Frances Jane Hodson (April 5, 1831–January 2, 1872). Born in Lancashire, England. Immigrated to Utah Territory, 1854. Married John Andrews, 1859. Appointed treasurer of the Relief Society in Nephi, Juab County, Utah Territory, 1868. Died at Nephi. (3.19)

Anthony, Susan Brownell (February 15, 1820–March 13, 1906). Born at Adams, Berkshire County, Massachusetts; daughter of Lucy Read and Daniel Anthony. Taught school, 1839–1849. Involved in contemporary reform efforts; advocated for abolition of slavery, women's right to own property, temperance, and women's labor unions. Helped found the Women's State Temperance Society of New York, 1852. Began publishing the *Revolution* with Elizabeth Cady Stanton, 1868. Elected chair of the executive committee of the National Woman Suffrage Association, 1869. Elected vice president of the National American Woman Suffrage Association (NAWSA), 1890; served as president of NAWSA, 1892–1900. Visited Utah suffragists, 1871 and 1895. Died at Rochester, Monroe County, New York. (4.27)

Avery, Rachel Gordon Foster (December 30, 1858–October 26, 1919). Born at Pittsburgh; daughter of Julia Manuel and J. Heron Foster. Educated in Philadelphia and Europe; studied political economy at the University of Zurich, circa 1885. Married Cyrus Miller Avery, 1888. Served as corresponding secretary of the National American Woman Suffrage Association (NAWSA), 1880–1901; of the International Council of Women, 1888–1893; and of the National Council of Women, 1891–1894. Served as secretary to the International Woman Suffrage Alliance at Berlin, 1904–1909; as first vice president of

NAWSA, 1907–1910; and as president of the Pennsylvania Woman Suffrage Association, 1908–1910. Died at Philadelphia. (4.27)

Baldwin, Elvira Basford (July 14, 1806–July 17, 1891). Born at Livermore, Oxford County, Maine; daughter of Joanna Merrill and Ebenezer Basford. Attended school in Livermore. Lived in the Boston area, circa 1842–1844. Married Daniel Putnam Baldwin, 1844. Served as vice president and treasurer of the Boston Female Penny and Sewing Society, 1844–1845. Sailed to California, 1849; settled at Sacramento, Sacramento County, California, by 1860. Practiced medicine. Participated in civic organizations, including the Sons of Temperance and the International Order of Good Templars. Helped establish orphanages in Sacramento and Vallejo, Solano County, California. Died at Sacramento. (1.12)

Ballantyne, Huldah Meriah Clark. See "Clark Ballantyne, Huldah Meriah."

Barker Bates, Mary Helen (December 17, 1845–August 3, 1924). Born at Hannibel, Oswego County, New York; daughter of Jane Ruth Freeman and Ezra Ferris Barker. Physician and surgeon. Graduated from Woman's Medical College of Pennsylvania, 1873. Opened an obstetrics school for women in Salt Lake City, 1873. Member of the Women's Centennial Executive Committee for Utah. Married George Clinton Bates at Salt Lake City, 1876. Moved to Colorado, circa 1876–1877. Died at Denver. (3.23, 3.28)

Barlow, Elizabeth Haven (December 28, 1811–December 25, 1892). Born at Holliston, Middlesex County, Massachusetts; daughter of Elizabeth Howe and John Haven. Graduated from Bradford Academy and Amherst College; earned teacher's diploma. Baptized, 1837, at Holliston. Married Israel Barlow at Quincy, Adams County, Illinois; eight children. Migrated to the Salt Lake Valley with the Brigham Young pioneer company, arriving mid-September 1848. Appointed president of the Bountiful Ward Relief Society, April 1857, at Bountiful, Davis County, Utah Territory; later served as president of the Bountiful East Ward Relief Society. Died at Bountiful. (1.2)

Barney, Elvira Stevens (March 17, 1832–January 12, 1909). Born at Gerry, Chautauque County, New York; daughter of Minerva Althea Field and Samuel C. Stevens. Baptized, 1844. Migrated to the Salt Lake Valley with the Brigham Young pioneer company, arriving September 20, 1848. Married Royal Barney Jr., 1849. Served a mission to the Sandwich Islands, 1851; returned to Utah Territory, 1856. Attended Wheaton College in Wheaton, DuPage County, Illinois, and Deseret University in Salt Lake City; studied medicine in the eastern United States. Practiced medicine and taught obstetrics in Utah. Died at Salt Lake City. (3.25)

Barratt, Matilda Moorhouse (January 17, 1837–April 14, 1902). Born at Stockport, Cheshire, England; daughter of Mary Clarkson and Samuel Moorhouse. Married John Barratt, 1864; three children. Migrated to Utah Territory, 1876. Served as first counselor in the general Primary presidency, 1880–1888. Served as treasurer of the Deseret Hospital board. Donated funds to build Barratt Hall on the Latter-day Saints' University campus in Salt Lake City; made substantial gifts to the church, to temples, and to funds to build her ward meetinghouse and to support a children's library. Died at Salt Lake City. (4.4, 4.11)

Barton, Clarissa (Clara) Harlowe (December 25, 1821–April 12, 1912). Born at Oxford, Worcester County, Massachusetts; daughter of Sarah (Sally) Stone and Stephen Barton. Taught in and superintended local schools, circa 1836–1854. Moved to Washington DC, 1854; one of the first women to serve as a clerk in the U.S. Patent Office, 1854–1856.

Nursed wounded soldiers on the front lines of the American Civil War and led post-war search efforts for missing soldiers, 1861–1869. Joined International Red Cross relief efforts in Europe during and after the Franco-Prussian War, 1870–1873. Founded the American Red Cross, 1881; directed Red Cross efforts until 1904. Active in contemporary reform efforts, including promoting education, woman suffrage, and civil rights. Died at Glen Echo, Montgomery County, Maryland; buried at Oxford. (4.27)

Beatie, Phebe Young (August 1, 1854–August 22, 1931). Born at Salt Lake City; daughter of Clarissa Ross Chase and Brigham Young. Married Walter J. Beatie at Salt Lake City, January 7, 1872; seven children. Served as an officer in the first Young Ladies' Department of the Ladies' Cooperative Retrenchment Association, 1870. Served on the Relief Society general board. Delegate to the National Council of Women convention, 1891. Served as the executive committee chair of the Utah Woman Suffrage Association, 1891. Attended the executive session of the National Council of Women and reported on Relief Society work, 1904. Vice-regent of the Utah State Society of Daughters of the Revolution; member of the Daughters of the Pioneers. Died at Salt Lake City. (3.18, 4.27)

Beck, Hannah Forsyth (March 4, 1817–November 13, 1872). Born at Reckless, Burlington County, New Jersey; daughter of Margaret Hodson and John Forsyth. Married Joseph Ellison Beck, December 17, 1835; seven children. Migrated to Utah Territory, 1850. Served as secretary of the Spanish Fork Second District Relief Society, at Spanish Fork, Utah County, Utah Territory, September 1857–January 1866. Died at Spanish Fork. (2.5)

Bennett, John Cook (August 3, 1804–August 5, 1867). Born at Fairhaven, Bristol County, Massachusetts; son of Abigail Cook and John Bennett. Moved to Nauvoo, Hancock County, Illinois, 1840. Baptized, September 1840, at Nauvoo. Helped draft Nauvoo Charter, 1840; served as quartermaster general in the Illinois militia, 1840–1842; elected major general and inspector general of the Nauvoo Legion, February 1841. Served as assistant president in the First Presidency, mayor of Nauvoo, chancellor of the University of Nauvoo, and master in chancery of Hancock County, 1841–1842. Excommunicated for adultery, May 11, 1842. Publicly accused Joseph Smith of adultery and the attempted murder of former Missouri governor Lilburn W. Boggs; urged Missouri and Illinois officials to renew charges of treason against Joseph Smith, which resulted in Joseph Smith's arrest in June 1843. Briefly associated with George M. Hinkle's movement, The Church of Jesus Christ, the Bride, the Lamb's Wife, at Moscow, Muscatine County, Iowa Territory, 1843; with Sidney Rigdon, at Nauvoo, 1844; and with James J. Strang's Church of Jesus Christ of Latter Day Saints, at Voree, Racine County, Wisconsin, as general-in-chief, 1846. Excommunicated from the Strangite movement, 1847. Died at Polk City, Polk County, Iowa. (1.2, 1.5, 1.6, 1.10)

Benson, Ezra Taft (February 22, 1811–September 3, 1869). Born at Mendon, Worcester County, Massachusetts; son of Chloe Taft and John Benson. Baptized, July 19, 1840, at Quincy, Adams County, Illinois. Served several missions to the eastern United States. Presided over a church conference at Boston, 1844–1845. Ordained to the Quorum of the Twelve Apostles, July 1846. Migrated to the Salt Lake Valley with the Brigham Young pioneer company, 1847. Presided over the British mission, 1856–1857. Settled in Cache County, Utah Territory, 1857. Served a mission to the Sandwich Islands, 1864. Member of the legislature for the provisional State of Deseret; member of the Utah Territorial House of Representatives for several sessions; elected to the Utah Territorial Council for ten years. Died at Ogden, Weber County, Utah Territory; buried at Logan, Cache County. (1.12)

Berry, Armelia Shanks (January 24, 1804–January 10, 1893). Born at Lebanon, Wilson County, Tennessee; daughter of Armela and William Shanks. Baptized, 1840 or 1841. Married Jesse W. Berry; eleven children. Widowed at Nauvoo, Hancock County, Illinois, 1844. Migrated to the Salt Lake Valley, 1849. Helped settle Spanish Fork, Utah County, Utah Territory. Served as first counselor in the Relief Society presidency at Spanish Fork. Moved to Kanarraville, Iron County, Utah Territory, circa 1862. Died at Richfield, Sevier County, Utah Territory. (2.5)

Bigler, Amy Lorette Chase (November 7, 1822–June 8, 1907). Born at Lincoln, Addison County, Vermont; daughter of Amy Scott and Abner Chase. Married Jacob G. Bigler, June 18, 1844; sealed in the temple at Nauvoo, Hancock County, Illinois, January 31, 1846; ten children. Migrated to the Salt Lake Valley, 1852. Settled at Nephi, Juab County, Utah Territory. Appointed secretary of the Nephi Relief Society at its organization, 1868. Appointed counselor to Mary Pitchforth in the Juab Stake Relief Society presidency, 1883. Died at Nephi. (1.2, 3.19)

Bigler, Eliza Cannon Miller (May 24, 1817–May 1895). Born in County Down, Ireland; daughter of Elizabeth Scott and John Cannon. Married first John Miller, circa 1840. Housed Latter-day Saint missionaries proselytizing in Ireland. Widowed, 1865. Immigrated to the United States and settled at Nephi, Juab County, Utah Territory, by 1867. Married second Jacob G. Bigler as a plural wife, October 10, 1867. Member of the Nephi Relief Society. Died at Nephi. (3.19)

Billings, Diantha Morley (August 23, 1795–May 14, 1879). Born at Montague, Franklin County, Massachusetts; daughter of Edith Marsh and Thomas Morley. Moved to Kirtland, Geauga County, Ohio, 1815. Married Titus Billings, February 16, 1816; nine children. Baptized, 1830; first woman baptized in the Kirtland area. Moved to Jackson County, Missouri; to Clay County, Missouri; to Far West, Caldwell County, Missouri; to Lima, Adams County, Illinois; to Quincy, Adams County; and to Nauvoo, Hancock County, Illinois, by 1840. Joined the Female Relief Society of Nauvoo, March 24, 1842. Appointed a midwife and nurse by Joseph Smith. Endowed in the Nauvoo temple, December 13, 1845. Migrated to the Salt Lake Valley, 1848. Helped settle Manti, Sanpete County, Utah Territory, 1849; served as the only doctor, midwife, or nurse at Manti. Served as the first president of the Manti Ward Relief Society, February 1856–March 1861. Moved to Provo, Utah County, Utah Territory, circa 1864. Died at Provo. (1.2)

Bingham, Martha Ann Lewis (February 20, 1833–November 18, 1898). Born at Franklin, Simpson County, Kentucky; daughter of Joannah Ryan and Benjamin Lewis. Survived the attack at Hawn's Mill settlement on Shoal Creek, Caldwell County, Missouri, 1838. Married Sanford Bingham at Winter Quarters, unorganized U.S. territory, July 18, 1847; twelve children. Migrated to the Salt Lake Valley, 1847. Appointed president of the Riverdale Relief Society, in Weber County, Utah Territory, December 5, 1872. Appointed counselor to Harriet C. Brown in the Weber Stake Relief Society presidency, October 27, 1870. Died at Riverdale; buried at Ogden, Weber County. (3.28)

Bird, James (May 18, 1811–April 20, 1896). Born at Sheringham, Norfolk, England; son of Mary Hagen and William Bird. Immigrated to Utah Territory, 1850. Married

Margaret Montgomery; participated in plural marriage. Lived in the Salt Lake City Fourteenth Ward. Died at Salt Lake City. (2.1)

Bird, Mary Frances Rich (February 10, 1835–?). Born in Missouri. Married James Bird as a plural wife, circa 1850. Migrated to the Salt Lake Valley, 1850. Appointed counselor to Matilda Matey Dudley in the Great Salt Lake City Female Relief Society, February 9, 1854; held meetings at her home. (2.1)

Blackburn, Sarah Jane Goff (March 22, 1831–December 28, 1891). Born in Howard County, Missouri; daughter of Mary Elizabeth Kimbrough and James Goff. Moved to Nauvoo, Hancock County, Illinois, 1840, and to what became Council Bluffs, Pottawattamie County, Iowa, 1846. Married Elias Hicks Blackburn, 1847; seven children. Migrated to the Salt Lake Valley, 1849; settled at Provo, Utah County, Utah Territory. Appointed secretary and treasurer of the Relief Society at Provo, circa 1856. Relocated to Minersville, Beaver County, Utah Territory, before 1870; later moved to Loa, Piute County, Utah Territory. Served as the secretary in the Fremont Ward Relief Society. Died at Loa. (2.4)

Blood, Jane Wilkie Hooper (May 2, 1845–September 7, 1898). Born at Southampton, Hampshire, England; daughter of Ann Wilkie Galbraith and John Hooper. Baptized, May 1853, in Cornwall, England. Emigrated from Liverpool to New Orleans aboard the ship *Golconda;* arrived in the Salt Lake Valley, October 1854. Settled at Kaysville, Davis County, Utah Territory, 1855. Married William Blood, September 9, 1861; ten children. Served as teacher, secretary, treasurer, and counselor in the Kaysville Relief Society; as president of the Kaysville Primary; and as teacher in the Sunday school. Was an active participant in sericulture. Died at Kaysville. (4.3)

Boggs, Lilburn W. (December 14, 1796–March 14, 1860). Born at Lexington, Fayette County, Kentucky; son of Martha Oliver and John M. Boggs. Lived at St. Louis, Franklin, Fort Osage, Harmony Mission, Independence, and Jefferson City, Missouri. Elected Missouri state senator, 1826, 1828, 1842; elected lieutenant governor, 1832. Served as governor of Missouri, 1836–1840. Authorized the "extermination order" expelling Latter-day Saints from Missouri, 1838. Returned to Independence, before 1842. Severely wounded by an assassin, May 6, 1842; accused Joseph Smith of complicity. Migrated to Sonoma, Mexico, 1846; moved to Napa Valley, Napa County, California, 1852. Appointed alcalde of all California north of Sacramento by American military authorities. Died at Napa Valley. (3.13, 3.24)

Bostwick, Orsamus Ferdinand (March 2, 1801–August 9, 1869). Born at Hinesburg, Chittenden County, Vermont; son of Belinda Palmer and Heman Bostwick. Married first Sarah Eddy, 1820; three children. Married second Sarah Bardwell, 1830; four children. Fined for slander against Hyrum Smith, at Nauvoo, Hancock County, Illinois, February 1844. Worked as a blacksmith. Lived at New Orleans and Menard, Randolph County, Illinois. Died at Naples, Scott County, Illinois. (1.10)

Bradford, Ellen Clarke Watkin (April 15, 1850–circa 1936). Born at Barrowden, Rutlandshire, England; daughter of Sarah and William Watkin. Worked as a home care nurse. Married Samuel Bradford, circa 1872. Baptized, April 2, 1882, at Pentonville, Middlesex, England. Appointed president of the North London Branch Relief Society, March 1884. Lived at Tottenham, Middlesex, 1911. Likely died in Middlesex. (4.22)

Broadhead, Harriet Betts (February 19, 1831–March 30, 1927). Born at Coventry, Warwickshire, England; daughter of Elizabeth Bennett and Joseph Betts. Married David

Broadhead, 1850; fourteen children. Immigrated to the United States, 1850. Traveled to the Salt Lake Valley, 1853. Settled at Nephi, Juab County, Utah Territory. Member of the Nephi Relief Society. Died at Nephi. (3.19)

Brockbank, Sarah Brown (November 25, 1819–April 2, 1888). Born at Harefield, Middlesex, England; daughter of Sarah Ford and William Brown. Baptized, May 1851. Immigrated to the United States aboard the *Ellen Maria,* 1852; arrived in the Salt Lake Valley, circa September 1852. Married Isaac Brockbank, October 2, 1852, at Salt Lake City; five children. Settled at Spanish Fork, Utah County, Utah Territory. Appointed second counselor in the Spanish Fork Relief Society presidency, 1866. Died at Spanish Fork. (2.5)

Brown, Harriet Canfield (March 9, 1834–December 27, 1907). Born at Ossian, Allegany County, New York; daughter of Annis Bisbee and Israel Canfield Jr. Baptized, 1851. Married Francis Almon Brown, April 1856; three children. Migrated to the Salt Lake Valley, arriving August 1856. Settled at Ogden, Weber County, Utah Territory. Taught at the Ogden Second Ward school. Appointed counselor and later president of the Ogden City Relief Society presidency, vice president of the Ladies of Weber County Cooperative Mercantile Institution, and counselor in the Weber Stake Relief Society presidency. Died at Ogden. (3.26, 3.28, 4.15)

Buell, Presendia Lathrop Huntington. See "Kimball, Presendia Lathrop Huntington Buell."

Bullock, Electa Wood (July 15, 1834–August 15, 1911). Born at Florence, Huron County, Ohio; daughter of Hannah Daley and Gideon D. Wood. Moved to Far West, Caldwell County, Missouri, 1839, and to Nauvoo, Hancock County, Illinois, 1845. Migrated to the Salt Lake Valley, 1848. Moved to Springville, Utah County, Utah Territory, 1854. Married Isaac Bullock, 1856; nine children. Moved to Provo, Utah County, circa 1857. Active in local amateur theater. Ran the Bullock Hotel in Provo, 1858–1887. President of the Woman Suffrage Association of Utah County, 1891–1911. Chosen as one of seven delegates representing Utah women at the first triennial National Council of Women convention, 1891. Served as one of five managers of the Utah woman's department exhibit at the Chicago World's Fair, 1893. Served as president of the Provo Sixth Ward Relief Society. Died at Provo. (4.27)

Bullock, Thomas (December 23, 1816–February 10, 1885). Born at Leek, Staffordshire, England; son of Mary Hall and Thomas Bullock. Married Henrietta Rushton; participated in plural marriage. Immigrated to the United States, 1843. Served as scribe to Joseph Smith, as deputy city recorder, as clerk to church historian Willard Richards, and as clerk to the Council of Fifty. Migrated to the Salt Lake Valley with the Brigham Young pioneer company, 1847; returned to Winter Quarters, unorganized U.S. territory, and served as clerk with the 1848 Brigham Young company. Served as Salt Lake County recorder and chief clerk of the House of Representatives for the provisional State of Deseret. Served a mission to England, 1856–1858. Worked as chief clerk to Willard Richards and George A. Smith in the Church Historian's Office. Moved to Summit County, Utah Territory, 1862; worked as probate court clerk and county recorder. Died at Coalville, Summit County; buried at Salt Lake City. (1.10, 2.2)

Burton, Maria Susan Haven. See "Haven Burton, Maria Susan."

Burton, Robert Taylor (October 25, 1821–November 11, 1907). Born at Amherstburg, Essex County, Upper Canada; son of Hannah Shipley and Samuel Burton.

Baptized in Upper Canada, 1838. Moved to Nauvoo, Hancock County, Illinois, 1845. Married Maria Susan Haven; participated in plural marriage. Migrated to the Salt Lake Valley with the Brigham Young pioneer company, 1848; settled in the Salt Lake City Fifteenth Ward. Appointed bishop of the Fifteenth Ward, 1867. Served as sheriff, assessor, and collector of Salt Lake County; major general of the Utah militia; a city councilman of Salt Lake City; and a member of the Utah Territorial Council. Presided over the eastern states mission, 1869–1870; served a mission to Europe, 1873–1875. Ordained second counselor in the Presiding Bishopric, 1875. Died at Salt Lake City. (3.24)

Bush, Elizabeth Motts (December 11, 1842–October 21, 1911). Born at Weybread, Suffolk, England; daughter of Martha Godbold and Robert Motts. Moved to the northeast London area to work as a domestic servant, circa 1861. Lived in the St. Pancras area of London with her aunt's family, by 1871. Married her cousin James Bush at Camden Town parish in London, 1873; two children. Served as secretary of the North London Branch Relief Society, 1885–1888. Emigrated from England aboard the ship *Wisconsin,* 1888; settled at Salt Lake City. Died at Salt Lake City. (4.22)

Butler, John Lowe (April 8, 1808–April 10, 1860). Born in Warren County, Kentucky; son of Charity Lowe and James Butler. Married Caroline Farzine Skeen, 1831; participated in plural marriage. Baptized, 1835. Moved to Clay, Caldwell, and Daviess Counties, Missouri. Moved near Quincy, Adams County, Illinois, by 1839; ordained a seventy at Quincy, 1839. Served a mission to Illinois, 1839. Served two missions among the Sioux Indians, 1840–1841. Moved to Nauvoo, Hancock County, Illinois, 1840. Migrated to the Salt Lake Valley, 1852. Settled at Palmyra Fort (later Spanish Fork), Utah County, Utah Territory. Appointed bishop of the Spanish Fork Ward, 1856; served until his death. Died at Spanish Fork. (2.5)

Butt, Julia Ann Mariah Nielson (April 13, 1862–May 6, 1941). Born at Parowan, Iron County, Utah Territory; daughter of Elsie Rasmussen and Jens Nielson. Married Willard G. Butt, 1855, at St. George, Washington County, Utah Territory; four children. Served as president of the San Juan Stake Primary. Died at Provo, Utah County, Utah Territory; buried at Bluff, San Juan County, Utah Territory. (4.21)

Cahoon, Thirza Stiles (October 18, 1789–November 20, 1867). Born at Lansingburgh, Rensselaer County, New York; daughter of Abigail Farrington and Daniel Olds Stiles. Married Reynolds Cahoon, December 1810; eight children. Lived at Harpersfield, Ashtabula County, Ohio, by 1820; moved to Kirtland, Geauga County, Ohio, before 1830. Baptized, November 1830. Moved to Nauvoo, Hancock County, Illinois, by 1841. Charter member of the Female Relief Society of Nauvoo. Migrated to the Salt Lake Valley with the Brigham Young pioneer company, 1848. Settled in the Salt Lake City Thirteenth Ward. Moved to South Cottonwood, Salt Lake County, Utah Territory, circa 1860. Died at South Cottonwood. (1.2, 1.6)

Caine, John Thomas (January 8, 1829–September 20, 1911). Born at Kirk Patrick, Glenfaba, Isle of Man; son of Elinor Cubbon and Thomas Caine. Married Margaret Nightingale, 1850; thirteen children. Immigrated to the United States, 1846; lived at New York City and St. Louis. Baptized in New York, circa 1847–1848. Moved to Salt Lake City, 1852. Served a mission to the Hawaiian Islands. Founder and editor of the *Salt Lake Herald.* Elected to the U.S. House of Representatives, 1882; served six terms, 1882–1893. Elected as a state senator, 1896. Died at Salt Lake City. (4.26)

Calder, David Orson (June 18, 1823–July 3, 1884). Born at Thurso, Caithness, Scotland; son of Ann Johnston and George Calder. Baptized by Orson Pratt, August 1840, at Edinburgh, Midlothian, Scotland; adopted his middle name after Pratt. Married Annie Rogers Mackay, 1848; participated in plural marriage. Immigrated to the United States aboard the *George W. Bourne,* 1851. Migrated to the Salt Lake Valley, 1853. Served as chief clerk and private secretary to Brigham Young, managing director and editor of the *Deseret News,* and treasurer of Zion's Cooperative Mercantile Institution (ZCMI). Helped found Commercial College as part of Deseret University. Began the first music store in the Salt Lake Valley. Died at Lake Point, Tooele County, Utah Territory; buried at Salt Lake City. (3.1)

Canfield, Rosalthe (December 30, 1841–April 7, 1931). Born at Ossian, Allegany County, New York; daughter of Annis Bisbee and Israel Canfield Jr. Migrated to the Salt Lake Valley, 1862. Settled at Ogden, Weber County, Utah Territory. Baptized, June 21, 1863. Taught at the Ogden Second Ward school and helped run the Ladies of Weber County Cooperative Mercantile Institution, both with her sister, Harriet Canfield Brown. Served as teacher and treasurer in the Weber County Relief Society; as treasurer, secretary, and counselor in the Weber Stake Young Ladies' Mutual Improvement Association (Y.L.M.I.A.); as president of the Ogden Fifth Ward Y.L.M.I.A.; and as counselor and president of the Weber Stake Primary board. Served on the Primary general board, 1892–1895. Died at Ogden. (3.28)

Cannon, Abraham Hoagland (March 12, 1859–July 19, 1896). Born at Salt Lake City; son of Elizabeth Hoagland and George Quayle Cannon. Attended Deseret University and practiced architecture. Married Sarah Ann Jenkins, 1878; participated in plural marriage. Served a mission to Europe, 1879–1882. Assumed business control of the *Juvenile Instructor* and associate publications, 1882. Ordained as a president of the Quorum of the Seventy, 1882; ordained to the Quorum of the Twelve Apostles, 1889. Became editor and publisher of the *Contributor,* 1892; became coeditor of the *Deseret News,* October 1892. Died at Salt Lake City. (4.28)

Cannon, Angus Munn (May 17, 1834–June 7, 1915). Born at Liverpool, Lancashire, England; son of Ann Quayle and George Cannon. Baptized, 1844. Immigrated to the United States aboard the *Sidney,* 1842. Migrated to the Salt Lake Valley, 1849. Lived at Parowan, Iron County, Utah Territory, 1850–1851. Participated in plural marriage; married both Sarah Maria Mousley and Ann Amanda Mousley on July 18, 1858. Settled at St. George, Washington County, Utah Territory, 1861–1867; elected first mayor of St. George. Appointed president of the Salt Lake Stake, 1876; served for twenty-eight years. Died at Salt Lake City. (4.4, 4.5, 4.11, 4.28)

Cannon, Clarissa (Clara) Cordelia Moses Mason (April 21, 1839–August 21, 1926). Born at Westfield, Hampton County, Massachusetts; daughter of Lydia Ensign and Ambrose Todd Moses. Sailed to California aboard the *Brooklyn,* 1846. Married first William Henry Mason, 1858 or 1859, at San Francisco; five children. Widowed, 1868. Moved to Salt Lake City, 1872. Married second Angus Munn Cannon as a plural wife, 1875, at Salt Lake City; three children. Served as the first president of the Salt Lake City Fourteenth Ward Primary, as a counselor in the Salt Lake Stake Primary, and as a counselor in the Salt Lake Stake Relief Society. Served as a counselor in the general Primary presidency, 1880–

1895. Moved to Centerville, Davis County, Utah, circa 1916. Died at Centerville; buried at Salt Lake City. (4.4)

Cannon, Elizabeth Hoagland (November 2, 1835–January 25, 1882). Born at Royal Oak, Oakland County, Michigan Territory; daughter of Margaret Quick and Abraham Hoagland. Baptized as a child and moved to Nauvoo, Hancock County, Illinois, with her parents, before 1846. Migrated to the Salt Lake Valley, 1847. Taught school in the Salt Lake City Fourteenth Ward. Married George Q. Cannon, 1854; twelve children. Served missions with her husband in California, the eastern United States, and Europe, 1855–1863. Active in the woman suffrage movement. Died at Salt Lake City. (3.16, 3.17)

Cannon, George Quayle (January 11, 1827–April 12, 1901). Born at Liverpool, Lancashire, England; son of Ann Quayle and George Cannon. Baptized at Liverpool, 1840. Immigrated to the United States aboard the *Sidney,* 1842. Arrived at Nauvoo, Hancock County, Illinois, by April 1843. Apprenticed to his uncle John Taylor at a print shop in Nauvoo. Migrated to the Salt Lake Valley, 1847. Served missions to California, the Sandwich Islands, the eastern and midwestern United States, and Europe, 1849–1864. Helped translate the Book of Mormon into Hawaiian. Married Elizabeth Hoagland, 1854; participated in plural marriage. Involved in publishing the *Western Standard, Latter-day Saints' Millennial Star, Juvenile Instructor,* and *Deseret News.* Ordained to the Quorum of the Twelve Apostles, 1860. Elected as a territorial delegate to U.S. Congress, 1872; served four terms in the House of Representatives, 1873–1881. Incarcerated in the Utah Territorial Penitentiary on charges of unlawful cohabitation, 1888; served five months. Served as counselor to four presidents of the church, 1873–1901. Died at Monterey, Monterey County, California; buried at Salt Lake City. (3.2, 3.14, 4.13)

Cannon, Sarah Jane Jenne (September 11, 1839–May 13, 1928). Born at Camden, Kent County, Upper Canada; daughter of Sarah Comstock Snyder and Benjamin Prince Jenne. Migrated to the Salt Lake Valley, 1848. Baptized, November 1848. Married George Q. Cannon as a plural wife, 1858; seven children. Served on the finance committee for Deseret Hospital. Served on the Relief Society general board. Died at Glendale, Los Angeles County, California. (4.11)

Card, Zina Presendia Young Williams (April 3, 1850–January 31, 1931). Born at Salt Lake City; daughter of Zina Diantha Huntington and Brigham Young. Married first Thomas Child Williams, 1868; two children. Counselor in the first Young Ladies' Department of the Ladies' Cooperative Retrenchment Association, 1870. Widowed, 1874. Moved to Provo, Utah County, Utah Territory, 1878. Attended Brigham Young Academy; headed the academy's domestic science department for seven years. Served as president of the Utah Stake Primary and counselor in the Utah Stake Young Ladies' Mutual Improvement Association (Y.L.M.I.A.). Active in the woman suffrage movement; served as a delegate to the eleventh annual convention of the Woman Suffrage Association in Washington DC, 1879. Married second Charles Ora Card, 1884; three children. Moved to Cardston, Alberta, Canada, 1887. Served as ward and stake president of the Y.L.M.I.A. at Cardston. Moved to Logan, Cache County, Utah, 1903; served as matron of Brigham Young College in Logan. Widowed, 1906, and moved to Salt Lake City. Appointed matron of Latter-day Saint College. Served on the Primary general board. Died at Salt Lake City. (3.18, 3.28, 4.18, 4.26, 4.28)

Carlin, Thomas (July 18, 1789–February 14, 1852). Born in Fayette County, Kentucky; son of Elizabeth Evans and Thomas Carlin. Moved to Missouri, by 1803, and to Illinois, by 1812. Appointed first sheriff of Greene County, Illinois, 1821. Served as an Illinois state senator, 1824–1828. Appointed receiver of public monies by President Andrew Jackson, at Quincy, Adams County, Illinois, 1834. Served as governor of Illinois, 1838–1842. Issued a warrant for Joseph Smith's arrest for alleged involvement in an attempt to kill former Missouri governor Lilburn W. Boggs, 1842. Elected Illinois state representative, 1849. Died near Carrollton, Greene County, Illinois. (1.5, 4.15)

Carrington, Albert (January 8, 1813–September 19, 1889). Born at Royalton, Windsor County, Vermont; son of Isabella Bowman and Daniel Carrington. Graduated from Dartmouth College, 1833. Married Rhoda Maria Woods, 1838; participated in plural marriage. Baptized in Wisconsin Territory, 1841. Moved to Nauvoo, Hancock County, Illinois, 1844. Admitted to the Council of Fifty, 1845. Migrated to the Salt Lake Valley with the Brigham Young pioneer company, 1847. Elected clerk, historian, and postmaster, at Salt Lake City. Chaired the committee that drafted the constitution for the provisional State of Deseret; served as a member of the Utah territorial legislature, until 1868. Edited the *Deseret News,* 1854–1859, 1863–1867. Presided over the European mission, 1871–1873, 1875–1877, 1880–1882. Ordained to the Quorum of the Twelve Apostles, July 3, 1870. Excommunicated, 1885; rebaptized, 1887. Died at Salt Lake City. (3.26)

Chase, Elizabeth Ann Hunt (October 14, 1849–October 13, 1930). Born at New York City; daughter of Margaret Stout Vanderhoof and William Henry Hunt. Baptized, October 14, 1858. Migrated to the Salt Lake Valley, 1860. Married Sisson Almadorus Chase Jr., 1867; twelve children. Settled at Salt Lake City; lived in the Salt Lake City First Ward, by 1870. Died at Salt Lake City. (3.25)

Chase, Miriam Gove (March 22, 1813–November 4, 1909). Born at Lincoln, Addison County, Vermont; daughter of Hannah Chase and Moses Gove. Married Sisson Almadorus Chase, 1832; eight children. Baptized, circa 1840. Migrated to the Salt Lake Valley, 1853. Settled in the Salt Lake City First Ward; appointed president of the First Ward Relief Society, 1870. Died at Payson, Utah County, Utah; buried at Salt Lake City. (3.25)

Chase, Mrs. See "Chase, Elizabeth Ann Hunt," or "Chase, Miriam Gove."

Cheney, Lodema Hutchings (December 3, 1861–October 22, 1918). Born at Springville, Utah County, Utah Territory; daughter of Eliza Ann Pectol and Shepherd Pierce Hutchings. Married David Cheney, 1878; nine children. Lived at Huntington, Emery County, Utah Territory; served as president of the Young Ladies' Mutual Improvement Association (Y.L.M.I.A.) in the Emery Stake, 1890–1893. Moved near Teton, Bingham County, Idaho, before 1900; lived at Archer, Fremont County, Idaho, by 1910. Served as Y.L.M.I.A. president in Idaho, circa 1900–1908. Died in the influenza epidemic of 1918 at Camp Funston, Fort Riley, Geary County, Kansas. (4.25)

Clark Ballantyne, Huldah Meriah (October 26, 1823–April 2, 1883). Born at Genessee, Livingston County, New York; daughter of Delecta Farrar and Gardner Clark. Baptized, 1840. Joined the Female Relief Society of Nauvoo, Hancock County, Illinois, May 27, 1842. Married Richard Ballantyne at Winter Quarters, unorganized U.S. territory, 1847; nine children. Migrated to the Salt Lake Valley with the Brigham Young pioneer company, arriving late September 1848. Settled at Ogden, Weber County, Utah Territory;

served as president of the Ogden Fourth Ward Relief Society, from 1879 until her death. Died at Riverdale, Weber County; buried at Ogden. (1.2, 3.28)

Clark, Lucy Augusta Rice (March 5, 1850–November 13, 1928). Born at Farmington, Davis County, Utah Territory; daughter of Lucy Witter Geer and William Kelsey Rice. Married Timothy Baldwin Clark, 1867; eleven children. Served as president of the first Young Ladies' Mutual Improvement Association at Farmington; served on the Davis Stake Primary board for twenty-six years. Charter member of the Utah Women's Press Club, 1891. Active in the woman suffrage movement. Served as president of the Davis County Woman Suffrage Association and vice president of the state association, as vice president of the Utah State Council of Women, and as a delegate to a national suffrage convention in Washington DC. One of three female candidates for the Utah Senate, 1896. One of the first two women seated at the Republican National Convention, 1908. Died at Salt Lake City; buried at Farmington. (4.3)

Clark, Mary Stevenson (August 29, 1825–November 24, 1911). Born at Gibraltar, Spain; daughter of Elisabeth Stevens and Joseph Stevenson. Moved to Albany, Albany County, New York, 1827, and to Liberty, Clay County, Missouri, 1835. Baptized at Far West, Caldwell County, Missouri, 1837. Married Ezra Thompson Clark, May 18, 1845; eleven children. Migrated to the Salt Lake Valley, 1848. Moved to Farmington, Davis County, Utah Territory, by 1850; lived at Farmington for over sixty years. Served as a counselor in the Davis Stake Relief Society presidency for over twenty years. Died at Farmington. (3.30, 4.3)

Clark, Nancy Areta Porter Stevenson (August 8, 1825–November 13, 1888). Born at Vienna, Trumbull County, Ohio; daughter of Nancy Aretta Warriner and Sanford Porter. Baptized in Jackson County, Missouri, 1833. Married first Edward Stevenson, 1845, at Nauvoo, Hancock County, Illinois; five children. Migrated to the Salt Lake Valley, 1847. Divorced, 1869. Married second Ezra Thompson Clark as a plural wife, July 11, 1870. Served as president of the Davis Stake Young Ladies' Mutual Improvement Association, as president of the Davis Stake Relief Society, and as a temple worker at the Logan temple. Died at Elba, Cassia County, Idaho; buried at Farmington, Davis County, Utah Territory. (2.3, 3.30, 4.3)

Clawson, Ellen Curtis Spencer (November 21, 1832–August 25, 1896). Born at Saybrook, Middlesex County, Connecticut; daughter of Catharine Cannon Curtis and Orson Spencer. Married Hiram Bradley Clawson, 1850; fourteen children. Appointed president of the Salt Lake City Twelfth Ward Primary, 1879, and as president of the Salt Lake Stake Primary, 1880. Died at Salt Lake City. (4.4)

Clawson, Emily Augusta Young (March 1, 1849–March 19, 1926). Born at Salt Lake City; daughter of Emily Dow Partridge and Brigham Young. Attended Brigham Young's schoolhouse; participated in amateur dramatics at the Salt Lake Theatre. Married Hiram Bradley Clawson as a plural wife, 1868; nine children. Served as a counselor in the first Young Ladies' Department of the Ladies' Cooperative Retrenchment Association and as a counselor in the Salt Lake City Twelfth Ward Relief Society. Member of the Utah State Society of the Daughters of the Revolution; served as assistant recording secretary. Died at Salt Lake City. (3.18)

Cleveland, Sarah Marietta Kingsley Howe (October 20, 1788–April 21, 1856). Born at Becket, Berkshire County, Massachusetts; daughter of Sarah Chaplin and Ebenezer

Kingsley. Married first John Howe, 1807; one child. Widowed, 1825. Married second John Alexander Cleveland, 1826; two children. Lived at Nauvoo, Hancock County, Illinois, circa 1842; neighbor of Joseph and Emma Smith. Identified in some sources as a plural wife of Joseph Smith. Joined the Female Relief Society of Nauvoo as a founding member, March 17, 1842; served as a counselor to Emma Smith. Moved from Nauvoo, circa 1843. Died at Plymouth, Hancock County. (1.2, 1.3, 1.6, 1.7, 3.27, 4.4, 4.5, 4.28)

Clymer Glynes, Ella Maria Dietz (January 27, 1847–after 1911). Born at New York City; daughter of Frances Virginia Robinson and William Henry Dietz. Educated at Cottage Hill Seminary in Poughkeepsie, Dutchess County, New York. Married first Edward Myers Clymer, January 27, 1864; one child. Successful Shakespearean actress and dramatic reader in New York City, Paris, and England; author of books, poems, songs, and sonnets. Widowed, 1883. Founder and executive committee member of the professional women's club Sorosis; served as president, 1889–1891. Married second Webster Glynes, 1898. Helped organize the General Federation of Women's Clubs; served as vice president of the New York branch, 1902. Moved to Kensington, London, before 1906. (4.27)

Cobb, Camilla Clara Mieth (May 24, 1843–October 16, 1933). Born at Dresden, Saxony, Germany; daughter of Henrietta Christiana Backhaus and Karl Benjamin Mieth. Among the first church members baptized in Germany, 1855. Emigrated from Germany to England with the Karl G. Maeser family, 1856; sailed to the United States aboard the *Tuscarora,* 1857. Migrated to the Salt Lake Valley, 1860. Assisted Maeser in the Salt Lake City Fifteenth Ward and Twentieth Ward schools. Married James Thornton Cobb, 1864; seven children. Visited relatives in New York and studied kindergarten under the prominent German educator Adolph Douai in New Jersey, summer 1874; returned to Utah and established the territory's first kindergarten. Contributed articles to the *Woman's Exponent* advocating kindergarten education. Appointed counselor in the Salt Lake Stake Primary, 1880; served as president, September 12, 1896–April 20, 1904. Served on the Primary general board, 1898–1917. Died at Salt Lake City. (2.1, 4.4)

Colebrook Rooks Taylor, Ellen (Nellie) Susannah (May 31, 1848–April 2, 1910). Born at Cheltenham, Gloucestershire, England; daughter of Marie Purser and Charles Colebrook. Immigrated to the United States aboard the *Henry Ware,* 1849. Settled in the Salt Lake Valley, circa 1851. Joined the Deseret Dramatic Club at age sixteen at the request of Brigham Young. Married first Charles Rooks; one child. Later divorced. Married second George H. Taylor as a plural wife; one child. Active in the woman suffrage movement; served as vice president and president of the Salt Lake County Woman Suffrage Association. Served as president of the Salt Lake City Fourteenth Ward Young Ladies' Mutual Improvement Association (Y.L.M.I.A.); served as counselor and president of the Salt Lake Stake Y.L.M.I.A., 1898–1904. Served on the Y.L.M.I.A. general board, 1904–1910. Died at Salt Lake City. (4.15)

Cook Blanchard, Margaret Norris (October 21, 1811–June 12, 1874). Born at Churchtown, Lancaster County, Pennsylvania; daughter of Isabella Norris and Stephen Cook. Moved to Nauvoo, Hancock County, Illinois, by 1842. Charter member of the Female Relief Society of Nauvoo. Married John Reid Blanchard, 1844; four children. Endowed in the Nauvoo temple, 1846. Began westward migration, by 1848; lived in Pottawattamie County, Iowa, 1850; migrated to the Salt Lake Valley, by 1854. Lived in Box

Elder County, Utah Territory, 1854. Settled at Farmington, Davis County, Utah Territory, by 1860. Died at Clarkston, Cache County, Utah Territory. (1.2, 4.10, 4.28)

Cornell, Frances Airstup (Aistrup) (May 7, 1844–November 1, 1901). Born at Bourne, Lincolnshire, England; daughter of Mary Lunn and William Aistrup. Baptized in England, 1878. Married Thomas Cornell, 1878; six children. Served as a counselor in the North London Branch Relief Society presidency, 1884. Immigrated to the United States aboard the *Nevada,* 1887. Died at Salt Lake City. (4.22)

Coulam Doull, Ann Atlass Robinson (May 13, 1820–February 13, 1908). Born at Hull, Yorkshire, England; daughter of Martha Taylor and George Atlass. Married first Robert Robinson, circa 1840. Baptized, April 26, 1847. Immigrated to the United States aboard the *Sailor Prince,* 1848. Widowed, 1849. Migrated to the Salt Lake Valley, 1849. Settled in the Salt Lake City Eleventh Ward. Married second John Coulam, by 1850. Served as secretary of the Salt Lake City Eleventh Ward Relief Society, 1869–1870. Widowed, May 1877. Married third George Dunbar Doull. Moved to the Salt Lake City Fifth Ward, by 1900. Died at Salt Lake City. (3.16)

Cowles Holmes, Elvira Annie (November 23, 1813–March 10, 1871). Born at Unadilla, Otsego County, New York; daughter of Phebe Wilbur and Austin Cowles. Moved to Kirtland, Geauga County, Ohio, circa 1836, and to Commerce (later Nauvoo), Hancock County, Illinois, 1839. Helped found the Female Relief Society of Nauvoo and served as treasurer, 1842. Married Jonathan Harriman Holmes, 1842; six children, including one adopted and one from her husband's previous marriage. Later identified herself as a plural wife of Joseph Smith, married on June 1, 1843. Migrated to the Salt Lake Valley, 1847. Taught school. Moved to Farmington, Davis County, Utah Territory, by 1850. Died at Farmington. (1.2, 1.3, 1.8, 4.28)

Crowther, James (October 25, 1816–after 1866). Born at Halifax, Yorkshire, England. Baptized, 1852. Married Mary Cockroft at Salt Lake City, 1855. Lived in the Salt Lake City Seventh Ward. Became a citizen of the United States, 1866. (3.3)

Croxall Cannon, Caroline (Carlie) Partridge Young (February 1, 1851–July 2, 1903). Born at Salt Lake City; daughter of Emily Dow Partridge and Brigham Young. Married first Martin (Mark) Croxall, 1868; eight children, and two children from her husband's previous union. Served as a counselor in the first Young Ladies' Department of the Ladies' Cooperative Retrenchment Association, 1871–1879. Divorced husband. Married second George Q. Cannon as a plural wife, 1884; four children. Joined the Utah State Society of the Daughters of the Revolution; was a charter member of the Daughters of the Pioneers. Served as president of the Cannon Ward Relief Society, 1901–1903. Died at Salt Lake City. (3.18)

Curtis, Erastus, Sr. (May 15, 1828–January 20, 1902). Born at Georgetown, Brown County, Ohio; son of Phoebe Martin and Uriah Curtis. Married Mary Caroline Barton, 1848; participated in plural marriage. Migrated to the Salt Lake Valley, 1852. Early settler of Cottonwood Creek, Emery County, Utah Territory, 1877. Served as the first sheriff of Emery County. Died at Barton, Custer County, Idaho. (4.25)

Curtis, Johanna Price Fullmer (December 13, 1839–November 15, 1913). Born at Murfreesboro, Rutherford County, Tennessee; daughter of Mary Ann Price and John Solomon Fullmer. Migrated to the Salt Lake Valley, 1848. Married Erastus Curtis Sr. as a plural wife, 1860. Member of the Emery Stake Relief Society, in Emery County, Utah Territory. Died at Orangeville, Emery County. (4.26)

Cuthbertson (Cuthbert), Susan McGee (March 18, 1819–March 25, 1860). Born at Tobermore, Kilcronaghan, County Londonderry, Ireland; daughter of Mary and John McGee. Lived near Glasgow, Lanarkshire, Scotland, by 1841. Lived at Nauvoo, Hancock County, Illinois, by 1843. Married Edward Cuthbertson, 1843; seven children. Endowed in the Nauvoo temple, 1846. Family name consistently rendered "Cuthbert" after 1846. Migrated to the Salt Lake Valley, 1848. Settled at Salt Lake City; lived in the Salt Lake City First Ward, by 1856. Died at Salt Lake City. (1.2, 1.9)

Cutler, Lois Lathrop (September 24, 1788–March 23, 1878). Born at Lebanon, Grafton County, New Hampshire; daughter of Lois Huntington and Samuel Lathrop. Married Alpheus Cutler, November 17, 1808, at Lebanon; fourteen children. Lived at Hanover, Chautauque County, New York, by 1830. Baptized, 1832. Lived in Hancock County, Illinois, by 1840. Joined the Female Relief Society of Nauvoo, 1842. Endowed in the Nauvoo temple, 1845. Lived in Pottawattamie County, Iowa, 1850. Husband excommunicated, 1851, and organized the Church of Jesus Christ, 1853. Widowed, 1864. Baptized into the Reorganized Church of Jesus Christ of Latter Day Saints, 1875. Lived in Becker County, Minnesota, 1870. Died at Oak Lake, Audubon Township, Becker County. (1.2, 1.6)

Davis Watson, Annie (November 8, 1844–May 12, 1926). Born at Stockport, Lancashire, England; daughter of Elizabeth Moorehouse and Charles Davis. Immigrated to Utah Territory with her aunt Matilda Moorehouse Barratt, 1876. Settled at Salt Lake City. Served as counselor to Ellen C. S. Clawson in the Salt Lake Stake Primary presidency, 1880–1881. Married Joseph Moralee Watson, 1881. Widowed, 1895. Appointed a worker in the Salt Lake City temple by Lorenzo Snow, 1896. Died at Salt Lake City. (4.4)

Davis, Charles Augustus (October 13, 1810–August 29, 1897). Born at Princeton, Worcester County, Massachusetts; son of Miranda Jones and James Davis. Married Catherine Spring, 1833; participated in plural marriage. Baptized at Nauvoo, Hancock County, Illinois, 1843. Migrated to the Salt Lake Valley, 1850. Settled at Spanish Fork, Utah County, Utah Territory, by 1860. Served as a postmaster at Spanish Fork for twenty-five years. Died at Spanish Fork. (2.5)

Davis, Letitia Ann George (August 2, 1815–January 26, 1872). Born at Haverfordwest, Pembrokeshire, Wales; daughter of Letitia Ann Harris and John George. Married John Tucker Davis in Pembrokeshire, 1839; nine children. Baptized at Liverpool, Lancashire, England, 1842. Migrated to the Salt Lake Valley, 1851. Settled at Spanish Fork, Utah County, Utah Territory, circa 1866. Served as counselor to Lucretia Gay in the Spanish Fork Relief Society; served as president of the Spanish Fork Relief Society for twelve years. Died at Spanish Fork. (2.5)

Davis, Ruth Kennan (October 13, 1821–May 19, 1892). Born at Holden, Worcester County, Massachusetts; daughter of Ruth Parminter and Andrew Kennan Jr. Married Charles Augustus Davis, 1839; twelve children. Migrated to the Salt Lake Valley, 1850. Settled at Spanish Fork, Utah County, Utah Territory, by 1860. Appointed treasurer of the Spanish Fork Relief Society, 1857. Died at Spanish Fork. (2.5)

Decker Young, Harriet Page Wheeler (September 7, 1803–December 22, 1871). Born at Hillsborough, Hillsborough County, New Hampshire; daughter of Hannah Ashby and Oliver Wheeler. Married first Isaac Decker, 1821; six children; later divorced. Baptized, 1834. Lived at Kirtland, Geauga County, Ohio, by 1837; moved to Daviess County, Missouri, 1837; to Far West, Caldwell County, Missouri, 1838; and to Nauvoo, Hancock County, Illinois, 1841. Joined the Female Relief Society of Nauvoo, April 28, 1842. Married second Lorenzo Dow Young as a plural wife, 1843; nine children. Traveled with the Brigham Young pioneer company; one of three women to enter the Salt Lake Valley on July 24, 1847. Died at Salt Lake City. (1.2, 4.28)

Dougall, Clarissa Maria Young (December 10, 1849–April 30, 1935). Born at Salt Lake City; daughter of Clarissa Ross and Brigham Young. Raised by Zina D. H. Young after Ross's death in 1858. Married William B. Dougall, June 1, 1868; five children. Participated in the Young Ladies' Department of the Ladies' Cooperative Retrenchment Association, 1869. Served as counselor in the Salt Lake City Seventeenth Ward Young Ladies' Mutual Improvement Association (Y.L.M.I.A.), 1877–1880, and as president, 1880–1883. Served as counselor to Mary Ann Freeze in the Salt Lake Stake Y.L.M.I.A., 1883–1887. Served as counselor to Anstis Elmina S. Taylor on the Y.L.M.I.A. general board, 1887–1904. Appointed general president of the Y.L.M.I.A., 1905. Active in the woman suffrage movement; served on the executive committee and as an honorary vice president of the Utah Woman Suffrage Association. Served as a delegate to the National American Woman Suffrage Association convention at Washington DC, 1890. Helped found the Daughters of the Utah Pioneers organization. Helped found the Utah chapter of the Daughters of the American Revolution; served as chaplain and vice-regent. Served as a temple worker from 1893 to the time of her death. Died at Salt Lake City. (3.18)

Douglas Parker, Ellen Briggs (November 7, 1806–February 25, 1888). Born at Downham, Lancashire, England; daughter of Isabella (Bella) Briggs. Married first George Douglas, 1827; eight children. Lived at Clitheroe, Lancashire. Baptized in England, 1838. Immigrated to the United States and settled at Nauvoo, Hancock County, Illinois, 1842. Widowed, 1842. Married second John Parker Jr., 1846; two children. Lived at St. Louis, 1846–1852. Migrated to the Salt Lake Valley, 1852; settled at Salt Lake City. Contributed to the Salt Lake City Fourteenth Ward album quilt, 1857. Appointed to settle in southern Utah Territory, 1862; settled at Virgin, Washington County, Utah Territory. Served as president of the Virgin Ward Relief Society. Died at Virgin. (1.11, 2.3)

Douglas, George (February 27, 1838–May 2, 1903). Born at Downham, Lancashire, England; son of Ellen Briggs and George Douglas. Migrated to the Salt Lake Valley, 1852. Married Elizabeth Thompson Davis, 1857. Died at Springfield, Clark County, Ohio; buried at Ogden, Weber County, Utah. (1.11)

Douglas Romney, Vilate Ellen (November 19, 1840–December 9, 1917). Born at Clitheroe, Lancashire, England; daughter of Ellen Briggs and George Douglas. Migrated to the Salt Lake Valley, 1852. Married George Romney, 1857; thirteen children. Died at Salt Lake City. (1.11)

Douglass, Agnes Cross (April 6, 1818–September 5, 1906). Born at Carnmoney, County Antrim, Ireland; daughter of Margaret Sarah McCune and John Cross. Baptized at Campsie, Stirlingshire, Scotland, 1842. Married William Douglass, October 14, 1842, at Belfast, County Antrim; eight children. Immigrated to the United States aboard the *Norfolk,* 1844; settled at Nauvoo, Hancock County, Illinois. Migrated to the Salt Lake

Valley, 1848; settled at Salt Lake City. Joined the Relief Society in Salt Lake City, 1854. Moved to Payson, Utah County, Utah Territory, 1858. Appointed counselor in the Payson Relief Society presidency, 1868. Died at Payson. (4.7)

Dudley Ferguson Paschall Busby, Matilda Matey (March 15, 1818–October 8, 1895). Born at Piketown, Dauphin County, Pennsylvania; daughter of Judith Chase and Lawson Dudley. Baptized, 1849. Married first Henry Stephen Ferguson, 1837; one child. Migrated to the Salt Lake Valley, circa 1851. Settled at Salt Lake City; lived in the Salt Lake City Thirteenth and Twenty-First Wards. Married second Mr. Paschall, circa 1854–1855. Elected president of the Great Salt Lake City Female Relief Society, January 1854. Appointed president and treasurer of the Thirteenth Ward Relief Society, 1855. Married third Joseph Busby, 1856; one child. Worked as a nurse. Died at Salt Lake City. (2.1)

Duncanson, Elizabeth Henderson (February 12, 1819–October 29, 1890). Born at Leith, Midlothian, Scotland; daughter of Margaret Gibb and William Henderson. Married David Martin Duncanson, 1835; one child. Immigrated to the United States aboard the *Berlin,* 1849. Migrated to the Salt Lake Valley, 1855. Settled in the Salt Lake City Fifteenth Ward. Appointed president of the Fifteenth Ward Relief Society teachers committee, 1868. Helped draft resolutions at a mass meeting to protest the Cullom Bill, 1870. Appointed a midwife and nurse by Orson Pratt and George Q. Cannon, 1873. Served as a counselor in the Fifteenth Ward Relief Society presidency. Died at Salt Lake City. (3.12)

Dunford, Eliza Sarah Snow (November 30, 1847–October 5, 1937). Born at Mount Pisgah, Pottawattamie County, Iowa; daughter of Sarah Ann Prichard and Lorenzo Snow. Arrived in the Salt Lake Valley as an infant, 1848. Baptized, June 20, 1857. Married George Dunford, 1869; seven children. Settled at Salt Lake City. Served as secretary of the Salt Lake City Twentieth Ward Relief Society. Died at Holladay, Salt Lake County, Utah; buried at Salt Lake City. (3.16)

Durfee (Durphy) Lott, Elizabeth Davis Goldsmith Brackenbury (March 11, 1791–December 16, 1876). Born at Riverhead, Suffolk County, New York; daughter of Abigail Reeve and Gilbert Davis. Married Gilbert Goldsmith, 1811; two children. Widowed, 1811. Married Joseph Blanchett Brackenbury, circa 1818; five children. Baptized, 1831. Widowed, 1832. Married Jabez Durfee (Durphy), 1834; later separated or divorced. Moved to Far West, Caldwell County, Missouri, circa 1835; to Daviess County, Missouri, December 1837; to Quincy, Adams County, Illinois, 1838; and to Commerce (later Nauvoo), Hancock County, Illinois, 1839. Identified in some sources as a plural wife of Joseph Smith. Joined the Female Relief Society of Nauvoo at its second meeting, 1842. Married Cornelius Lott as a plural wife, 1846. Moved to Salt Lake City, 1855; to De Kalb County, Missouri, 1857; back to Salt Lake City, 1858; to Washington, De Kalb County, by 1860; to Denver, circa 1862; to San Bernardino, San Bernardino County, California, 1865; back to Salt Lake City, 1868; and to White Cloud, Doniphan County, Kansas, by 1870. Baptized into the Reorganized Church of Jesus Christ of Latter Day Saints, 1869. Died at White Cloud. (1.2)

East, Wilmirth Margaret (Matilda) Greer (November 18, 1824–March 31, 1902). Born at Bedford, DeKalb County, Georgia; daughter of Nancy Ann Terry Roberts and Nathaniel Hunt Greer. Married Edward Wallace East, 1839; eleven children. Baptized in Texas, 1853. Migrated to the Salt Lake Valley, 1855; settled in Salt Lake City. Joined the Salt Lake City Fourteenth Ward Relief Society, 1856. Contributed to the Fourteenth Ward album quilt, 1857. Served as counselor to Mary Isabella Horne in the Fourteenth Ward Relief Society presidency, 1867–1878. Active in the woman suffrage movement. Accompanied her husband on a mission to Texas, 1875. Moved to Arizona Territory, circa 1877–1878. Served as president of the Eastern Arizona Stake Relief Society, 1880–1882. Moved to Pima, Graham County, Arizona Territory, 1882. Served as president of the St. Joseph Stake Relief Society, 1883–1898. Died at Pima. (2.3, 3.13, 3.16, 3.25, 4.28)

Ellis Watkins, Mary Ann (March 6, 1857–January 16, 1882). Born at Ogden, Weber County, Utah Territory; daughter of Mary Ann Emmett and John Ellis. Served as counselor to Emily S. Richards in the Ogden City Young Ladies' Mutual Improvement Association. Married Joseph Hyrum Watkins, 1879; one child. Moved to St. Johns, Apache County, Arizona Territory, 1881. Died in childbirth at St. Johns; buried at Ogden. (3.26)

Ells, Hannah M. (March 4, 1808–circa 1845). Born at Newcastle upon Tyne, Northumberland, England; daughter of Hannah Smart and Thomas Ells. Immigrated to the United States aboard the ship *Pocahontas,* 1836; lived at Philadelphia. Moved to Nauvoo, Hancock County, Illinois, circa 1840–1841; worked as a milliner and dressmaker. Joined the Female Relief Society of Nauvoo, 1842. Identified in some sources as a plural wife of Joseph Smith, married 1843 or 1844. Appointed secretary of the Relief Society, 1844. Died at Nauvoo. (1.2, 1.10)

Emmett, James (February 22, 1803–December 28, 1852). Born in Boone County, Kentucky; son of Elizabeth Trowbridge and Silas Emmett. Married Phebe Jane Simpson, 1823. Baptized, 1831. Moved to Nauvoo, Hancock County, Illinois, by December 1843. Admitted to the Council of Fifty, 1844. Led an advance party of Latter-day Saint settlers from Nauvoo to the vicinity of present-day Vermillion, Clay County, South Dakota, 1845–1846. Resided in Tuolumne County, California, by 1850. Died at San Bernardino, Los Angeles County, California. (1.8)

Empey, Ella Elizabeth Young (August 31, 1847–September 7, 1890). Born at Winter Quarters, unorganized U.S. territory; daughter of Emeline Free and Brigham Young. Arrived in the Salt Lake Valley as an infant, 1848. Married Nelson Adam Empey, 1865. Served as the first president of the Young Ladies' Department of the Ladies' Cooperative Retrenchment Association. Died at Salt Lake City. (3.18)

Evans, Priscilla Merriman (May 4, 1835–November 5, 1914). Born at Mounton, Pembrokeshire, Wales; daughter of Ann James and Joseph Merriman. Baptized, 1852. Married Thomas D. Evans, 1856; twelve children. Sailed from Liverpool to Boston aboard the *S. Curling,* 1856; migrated by handcart to the Salt Lake Valley, arriving October 1856. Settled at Spanish Fork, Utah County, Utah Territory. Served as secretary in the Spanish Fork Relief Society, 1857–1875. Served as president and secretary of the Spanish Fork Relief Society teachers committee, circa 1877. Died at Spanish Fork. (2.5)

Farr, Nancy Bailey Chase Kimball (January 27, 1823–September 10, 1892). Born at Bristol, Addison County, Vermont; daughter of Tirzah Wells and Ezra Chase. Baptized in Livingston County, New York, 1838; moved to Commerce (later Nauvoo), Hancock County, Illinois, 1839. Joined the Female Relief Society of Nauvoo, 1842. Married Lorin Farr, January 1, 1845; eleven children. Migrated to the Salt Lake Valley, 1847. Settled at Ogden, Weber County, Utah Territory, 1849. Appointed counselor to Mary Hoagland West in the Ogden Relief Society, 1867. Died at Ogden. (1.2, 3.28)

Farrell, William George (May 24, 1864–October 14, 1945). Born at Logan, Cache County, Utah Territory; son of Maria Charlotte Lundberg and George Lionel Farrell. Baptized, 1874. Served a mission to the Sandwich Islands, 1882–1885. Married Florence Nightingale Caine, 1897. Lived at Salt Lake City. Moved to Los Angeles, circa 1921. Died at Los Angeles. (4.13)

Felt, Sarah Louisa (Louie) Bouton (May 5, 1850–February 12, 1928). Born at Norwalk, Fairfield County, Connecticut; daughter of Mary Barto and Joseph Bouton. Baptized, circa 1858. Migrated to the Salt Lake Valley, 1866. Married Joseph H. Felt at Salt Lake City, 1866. Appointed by Brigham Young to help colonize "the Muddy" (present-day Moapa Valley, Clark County, Nevada), 1867. Returned to Salt Lake City, circa 1870. Appointed the first president of the Salt Lake City Eleventh Ward Primary, 1878. Served as treasurer in the Eleventh Ward Young Ladies' Mutual Improvement Association (Y.L.M.I.A.). Appointed counselor to Mary Ann Freeze in the Salt Lake Stake Y.L.M.I.A., 1879. Served as first general president of the Primary, 1880–1925. Established the publication *Children's Friend,* 1901. Died at Salt Lake City. (4.4, 4.5)

Ferguson, Ellen Brooke (April 1844–March 22, 1920). Born at Cambridge, Cambridgeshire, England; daughter of Eliza and William Lombe Brooke. Married William Ferguson, circa 1857; four children. Immigrated to the United States, circa 1860; lived in Ohio and Illinois. Practiced medicine; published the *Democrat* newspaper with her husband in Eaton, Preble County, Ohio. Moved to Utah Territory, June 1876. Baptized at St. George, Washington County, Utah Territory, July 1, 1876. Lived at St. George and Provo, Utah County, Utah Territory. Moved to Salt Lake City, 1877. Widowed, 1880. Appointed the first resident physician and surgeon for Deseret Hospital, 1882. Participated actively in woman suffrage associations and the Democratic Party both nationally and in Utah. Moved to New York City, circa 1900. Died at Whitestone, Queens, New York. (4.3, 4.4, 4.11)

Fleming, Nancy Bigler (August 6, 1810–July 3, 1886). Born at Shinnston, Harrison County, Virginia (later in West Virginia); daughter of Susannah Ogden and Mark Bigler. Married Josiah Wolcott Fleming, 1828; five children. Baptized in Virginia, 1837. Lived at Nauvoo, Hancock County, Illinois, by 1842. Joined the Female Relief Society of Nauvoo, May 27, 1842. Migrated to the Salt Lake Valley, 1850. Settled at Provo, Utah County, Utah Territory. Appointed counselor to Lucy Meserve Smith in the Relief Society at Provo, 1856. Died at Provo. (2.4)

Foote Allen Miller, Lucia (Lucy) (December 17, 1810–July 22, 1887). Born at Oswegatchie, St. Lawrence County, New York; daughter of Rhoda Hand and Stephen Foote. Joined the Female Relief Society of Nauvoo, Hancock County, Illinois, at its seventh meeting, 1842. Married first Nelson Allen, 1827; widowed, 1846. Married second Eleazer Miller, before 1854; later separated or divorced. Lived at Salt Lake City and in Juab County, Utah Territory. Died at Nephi, Juab County. (1.2, 2.1)

Foss, Sarah Brackett Carter (September 30, 1800–March 4, 1894). Born at Limerick, York County, Maine; daughter of Sarah Fabyan and Ezra Carter. Married Calvin Ira Foss, 1823; seven children. Baptized, 1834. Migrated to the Salt Lake Valley, 1850. Settled at Salt Lake City. Served as a teacher, counselor, and supervisor of the work committee in the Salt Lake City Fourteenth Ward Relief Society, 1856–1885. Died at East Bountiful, Davis County, Utah Territory; buried at Salt Lake City. (2.3)

Freeze, Mary Ann Burnham (October 12, 1845–January 21, 1912). Born at Nauvoo, Hancock County, Illinois; daughter of Mary Ann Huntley and James Lewis Burnham. Migrated to the Salt Lake Valley, 1852. Settled at Bountiful, Davis County, Utah Territory; moved to Richmond, Cache County, Utah Territory, 1861. Married James Perry Freeze, 1863; eight children. Moved to Salt Lake City, 1863. Served as president of the Salt Lake City Eleventh Ward Young Ladies' Mutual Improvement Association (Y.L.M.I.A.), 1871–1886, and of the Salt Lake Stake Y.L.M.I.A., 1878–1898. Appointed to the Y.L.M.I.A. general board, 1898. Died at Salt Lake City. (4.4, 4.5)

Frodsham, Amelia Maria Aldrich Robinson (August 9, 1826–January 24, 1880). Born at Northbridge, Worcester County, Massachusetts; daughter of Amy Cooper and Joseph Aldrich. Baptized in Massachusetts, 1841. Married first James Robinson at Nauvoo, Hancock County, Illinois, circa 1846; two children. Migrated to the Salt Lake Valley, 1852. Married second James Frodsham, 1853; nine children. Settled at Ogden, Weber County, Utah Territory. Served as Relief Society secretary in the Ogden Fourth Ward and the Ogden Stake; served as president of the Primary in the Ogden Fourth Ward. Died at Ogden. (3.28)

Fullmer Benson McLane, Desdemona Catlin Wadsworth (October 6, 1809–February 9, 1886). Born at Huntington, Luzerne County, Pennsylvania; daughter of Susannah Zerfass and Peter Fullmer. Baptized, 1836. Moved to Kirtland, Geauga County, Ohio, by 1837; to Missouri, by 1838; and to Commerce (later Nauvoo), Hancock County, Illinois, circa 1839. Joined the Female Relief Society of Nauvoo at its first meeting, March 17, 1842. Later identified herself as a plural wife of Joseph Smith, married in July 1843. Married second Ezra Taft Benson as a plural wife, 1846; divorced, 1852. Migrated to the Salt Lake Valley, 1848. Married third Harrison Parker McLane, 1853; divorced, 1864; one child. Lived at Salt Lake City and Ogden, Weber County, Utah Territory. Died at Salt Lake City. (1.2, 4.28)

Fullmer, Sarah Ann Stevenson (July 31, 1835–September 7, 1901). Born at Loughborough, Leicestershire, England; daughter of Martha Charles and James Stevenson. Baptized in England, 1848. Immigrated to Philadelphia, 1853; migrated to the Salt Lake Valley, 1857. Married John Solomon Fullmer as a plural wife, 1857; twelve children. Settled in Castle Valley, Emery County, Utah Territory, 1881. Served as a counselor in the Orangeville Ward Relief Society at Orangeville, Emery County. Served as president of the Emery County Woman Suffrage Association. Died at Orangeville. (4.25)

Gardner, James Hamilton (July 29, 1859–January 15, 1952). Born at Mill Creek, Great Salt Lake County, Utah Territory; son of Sarah Hamilton and Archibald Gardner. Baptized, 1868. Served a mission to the Sandwich Islands, 1880–1884; worked in the Laie sugar mill. Married Rhoda Priscilla Huffaker, 1886. Lived in the Snake River Valley, Idaho; moved to Lehi, Utah County, Utah Territory, circa 1890. Worked as general superintendent of the Utah-Idaho Sugar Company. Served as bishop of the Lehi Second Ward. Died at Salt Lake City. (4.13)

Gay, Lucretia Davis (May 21, 1809–March 6, 1886). Born at Princeton, Worcester County, Massachusetts; daughter of Miranda Jones and James Davis. Married Moses Gay, 1830; nine children. Lived at Nauvoo, Hancock County, Illinois, by 1846. Migrated to the Salt Lake Valley, 1852. Settled at Spanish Fork, Utah County, Utah Territory. Served as president of the Spanish Fork Ward Relief Society, 1857–1866. Died at Spanish Fork. (2.5)

Godbe, Ann Thompson (January 31, 1840–January 6, 1928). Born at Alston, Cumberland, England; daughter of Ann Bentley and Ralph Thompson. Migrated to the Salt Lake Valley, 1848. Married William Samuel Godbe, 1855; eight children. Settled at Salt Lake City. Appointed counselor to Rachel Ivins Grant in the Salt Lake City Thirteenth Ward Relief Society, 1868. Associated with the Church of Zion (Godbeites), which was founded by her husband, circa 1869–1880s. Attended the Liberal Institute and the Women's Mutual Improvement Society; active in the woman suffrage movement. Moved to Los Angeles, between 1900 and 1910. Died at Los Angeles. (3.7)

Godbe, William Samuel (June 26, 1833–August 1, 1902). Born at London; son of Sarah LaRiviere and Samuel Godbe. Baptized in England, 1850. Immigrated to the Salt Lake Valley, 1851. Settled at Salt Lake City. Married Ann Thompson, 1855; participated in plural marriage. Served as counselor to Bishop Edwin D. Woolley in the Salt Lake City Thirteenth Ward, circa 1868. Excommunicated, 1869; founded the Church of Zion (Godbeites), circa 1869–1880s. Published the *Utah Magazine* and the *Salt Lake Tribune.* Died at Brighton, Salt Lake County, Utah; buried at Salt Lake City. (3.7)

Goddard, Elizabeth Harrison (March 17, 1817–April 12, 1903). Born at Leicester, Leicestershire, England; daughter of Elizabeth Pipes and John Harrison. Married George Goddard, 1839; thirteen children. Baptized in England, 1851. Immigrated to the United States aboard the *Essex,* 1851; migrated to the Salt Lake Valley, 1852. Settled at Salt Lake City. Served as secretary of the Salt Lake City Second Ward Relief Society, 1853–1855, and as secretary of the Salt Lake City Thirteenth Ward Relief Society, 1855–1900. Died at Salt Lake City. (3.7, 3.16, 3.25, 4.10, 4.11)

Goldsbrough, Amelia Hallam (December 7, 1814–June 11, 1883). Born at Little Common, Yorkshire, England; daughter of Hannah Hallam. Married Henry Goldsbrough, 1845. Baptized in England, 1847. Immigrated to the United States aboard the *Ellen,* 1851; migrated to the Salt Lake Valley, 1857. Settled at Nephi, Juab County, Utah Territory, 1863. Served as president of the Nephi Relief Society, 1868–1878. Served as president of the Juab Stake Relief Society, 1878–1883. Died at Nephi. (3.19)

Grace, Elizabeth Williams (April 29, 1822–February 3, 1899). Born at Liverpool, Lancashire, England; daughter of Ann Jones and John Williams. Married Isaac Grace, 1843; eleven children. Immigrated to the United States aboard the *Ellen,* 1851; migrated to the Salt Lake Valley, 1851. Settled at Nephi, Juab County, Utah Territory. Participated in the Nephi Ward Relief Society. Died at Nephi. (3.19)

Granger, Lydia Dibble (April 5, 1790–September 2, 1861). Born at Granby, Hartford County, Connecticut; daughter of Lydia Granger and Cornish Dibble. Married first Oliver Granger, 1813; eight children. Baptized, circa 1832–1833. Lived at Kirtland, Geauga County, Ohio, and Nauvoo, Hancock County, Illinois. Widowed, 1841. Served as a visiting committee member in the Female Relief Society of Nauvoo. Married second Hyrum Smith as a plural wife, 1843; widowed, 1844. Married third John Taylor as a plural wife, 1846. Migrated to the Salt Lake Valley, 1851; settled at Salt Lake City. Served as the first president of the Salt Lake City Fifteenth Ward Relief Society, 1855–1857. Died at Salt Lake City. (1.2, 4.28)

Grant, Rachel Ridgway Ivins (March 7, 1821–January 27, 1909). Born at Hornestown, Monmouth County, New Jersey; daughter of Edith Ridgeway and Caleb

Ivins. Baptized, circa 1839. Moved to Nauvoo, Hancock County, Illinois, 1842; returned to New Jersey, circa 1844. Migrated to the Salt Lake Valley, 1853. Settled at Salt Lake City. Married Jedediah M. Grant as a plural wife, 1855; one child. Widowed, 1856. Appointed president of the Salt Lake City Thirteenth Ward Relief Society, 1868; served for thirty-five years. Participated in the woman suffrage movement and served on the Central Grain Committee. Died at Salt Lake City. (3.7, 3.13, 3.16, 3.17, 3.25)

Groesbeck, Elizabeth Thompson (August 16, 1820–December 28, 1883). Born at Meadville, Crawford County, Pennsylvania; daughter of Ruth Peterson and John Thompson. Baptized, 1841. Married Nicholas Harmon Groesbeck, 1841; ten children. Migrated to the Salt Lake Valley, 1856; settled at Salt Lake City. Served on the finance committee of the Deseret Hospital Association. Died at Salt Lake City. (4.11)

Guymon, Elizabeth Ann Jones (February 12, 1830–March 2, 1908). Born at Pennsville, Morgan County, Ohio; daughter of Sarah Ann Mallernee and James Naylor Jones. Married Noah Thomas Guymon as a plural wife, 1847; seven children. Migrated to the Salt Lake Valley, 1850; settled in Emery County, Utah Territory, circa 1878–1879. Participated in the Emery Stake Relief Society. Died at Orangeville, Emery County. (4.25)

Haight, Annabella Sinclair Mcfarlane (April 20, 1812–February 10, 1888). Born at Killin, Perthshire, Scotland; daughter of Ann Campbell and Daniel Sinclair. Married first John Mcfarlane, 1833; three children. Widowed, 1846. Baptized in Scotland, 1842. Immigrated to the United States aboard the *Ellen Maria,* 1852; migrated to the Salt Lake Valley, 1853. Married second Isaac Chauncey Haight as a plural wife and settled at Cedar City, Iron County, Utah Territory, 1853. Served as a counselor in the Cedar City Relief Society presidency, beginning in 1856. Died at Cedar City. (2.6)

Halls, George (October 18, 1846–January 3, 1917). Born at Orsett, Essex, England; son of Susanna Selstone and John Halls. Baptized in England, 1855. Immigrated to the United States aboard the *William Tapscott* and migrated to the Salt Lake Valley, 1862. Married Mary Moiselle Hammond, 1876. Moved to Bluff, San Juan County, Utah Territory, 1885. Settled at Mancos, Montezuma County, Colorado, and appointed bishop of the Mancos Ward, 1886. Died at Mancos. (4.21)

Halls, Mary Moiselle Hammond (May 18, 1857–April 29, 1934). Born at Beaver Dams, Washington County, Utah Territory; daughter of Mary Jane Dilworth and Francis A. Hammond. Lived at Ogden, Weber County, Utah Territory, and at Huntsville, Weber County; served as a leader in the Young Ladies' Mutual Improvement Association (Y.L.M.I.A.) and Primary. Married George Halls, 1876; two children. Moved to Bluff, San Juan County, Utah Territory, 1885; settled at Mancos, Montezuma County, Colorado, 1886. Served as president of the San Juan Stake Y.L.M.I.A., circa 1885–1910. Died at Springville, Utah County, Utah Territory. (4.21)

Halls, William (May 25, 1834–June 27, 1920). Born at Orsett, Essex, England; son of Susanna Selstone and John Halls. Baptized in England, 1851. Married Louisa C. Enderby, 1861; participated in plural marriage. Immigrated to the United States aboard the *Underwriter* and migrated to the Salt Lake Valley, 1861. Lived at Huntsville, Weber County, Utah Territory. Moved to Bluff, San Juan County, Utah Territory, 1885; settled at Mancos, Montezuma County, Colorado, 1886. Served as a counselor in the San Juan Stake presidency, circa 1885–1920. Died at Mancos. (4.21)

Hammond, Francis Asbury (November 1, 1822–November 27, 1900). Born at Patchogue, Suffolk County, New York; son of Charity Edwards and Samuel Smith Hammond. Baptized at San Francisco, 1847. Migrated from California to the Salt Lake Valley, 1848. Married Mary Jane Dilworth, 1848; participated in plural marriage. Lived at Huntsville, Weber County, Utah Territory; moved to Bluff, San Juan County, Utah Territory, 1884. Served as president of the San Juan Stake, 1884–1900. Died at Bloomfield, San Juan County, New Mexico Territory; buried at Huntsville. (4.21)

Hammond, Martha Jensina Marcusen Holmes (April 5, 1850–August 23, 1935). Born at Horsens, Skanderborg, Denmark; daughter of Karen Maria Christensen and Rasmus Marcusen. Baptized in Denmark, 1866. Immigrated to the United States aboard the *Manhattan* and migrated to the Salt Lake Valley, 1867. Married first Henry Holmes, 1868. Lived in Weber County, Utah Territory. Widowed, 1876. Married second Francis Asbury Hammond as a plural wife, 1881. Settled at Bluff, San Juan County, Utah Territory, circa 1884. Appointed first counselor in the San Juan Stake Relief Society presidency, 1888; later served as president of the San Juan Stake Relief Society. Moved to Moab, Grand County, Utah, circa 1900. Died at Moab. (4.21)

Hancock, Amy Experience Hancock (May 12, 1835–August 25, 1921). Born at Liberty, Clay County, Missouri; daughter of Experience Wheeler Rudd and Joseph Hancock. Baptized, circa 1846–1847. Migrated to the Salt Lake Valley, 1851. Lived at Provo, Utah County, Utah Territory, and at Payson, Utah County. Married George Washington Hancock, 1852; twelve children. Served as Relief Society counselor and Primary president in the Payson First Ward. Died at Payson. (4.7)

Hancock, Phebe Adams (June 7, 1811–February 4, 1897). Born at Middlesex, Ontario County, New York; daughter of Betsey and Isaac Adams. Baptized, 1836. Married Solomon Hancock, 1836; five children. Served as an officer in the Relief Society at Lima, Adams County, Illinois, circa 1842–1844. Widowed, 1847. Migrated to the Salt Lake Valley, 1849. Settled at Payson, Utah County, Utah Territory, 1852. Served as counselor and treasurer in the Payson Relief Society, beginning in 1856. Died at Payson. (4.7)

Harrington, Margaret Bentley Sanders (February 25, 1805–December 27, 1878). Born at Great Aycliffe, Durham, England; daughter of Ann Wood and Thomas Bentley Jr. Married first John Saunders, 1826; one child. Immigrated to the United States aboard the *Tyrian,* 1841. Settled at Nauvoo, Hancock County, Illinois. Widowed, 1844. Married second Thomas Harrington, circa 1846. Migrated to the Salt Lake Valley, 1848. Settled at Salt Lake City. Appointed counselor to Elizabeth Murphy McLelland in the Salt Lake City Seventh Ward Relief Society, 1868. Died at Salt Lake City. (3.3)

Hart, John Isaac (December 11, 1826–December 20, 1920). Born at Taunton, Somerset, England; son of Nancy Ann McGeorge and Isaac Hart. Married Elizabeth Rice, 1846; participated in plural marriage. Baptized at Bristol, England, 1847. Immigrated to the United States aboard the *Ellen Maria;* migrated to the Salt Lake Valley, 1853. Appointed bishop of the West Weber Ward, 1877. Died at Hooper, Weber County, Utah; buried at Ogden, Weber County. (3.28)

Haven Burton, Maria Susan (April 10, 1826–March 30, 1920). Born at Holliston, Middlesex County, Massachusetts; daughter of Judith Temple and John Haven. Joined the Female Relief Society of Nauvoo, Hancock County, Illinois, May 12, 1842. Married Robert

Taylor Burton, 1845; ten children. Migrated to the Salt Lake Valley with the Brigham Young pioneer company, 1848; settled in the Salt Lake City Fifteenth Ward. Served as treasurer in the Fifteenth Ward Relief Society, 1868–1869. Elected to the committee to frame resolutions protesting antipolygamy legislation; presented resolutions to the audience during the January 1870 mass meeting. Kept an extensive diary, 1875–1919. Died at Salt Lake City. (1.2, 3.12)

Hawkes, Phebe Ann Baldwin Northrop (July 4, 1803–December 1850). Born at Derby, New Haven County, Connecticut; daughter of Esther Sealy and Isaac Baldwin. Married first John B. Northrup, circa 1825; widowed, 1835. Married second Joseph Bryant Hawkes, 1837; four children. Joined the Female Relief Society of Nauvoo, Hancock County, Illinois, at its first meeting, March 17, 1842. Died at Kanesville, Pottawattamie County, Iowa. (1.2, 4.28)

Hawkins, Mary McKee (July 15, 1819–September 19, 1906). Born at Dromore, County Down, Ireland; daughter of Nancy and George McKee. Married John Hawkins, circa 1836; six children. Migrated to the Salt Lake Valley, 1851. Settled in the Salt Lake City Thirteenth Ward. Served as counselor to Matilda M. Dudley in the Great Salt Lake Relief Society presidency, 1854. Left Salt Lake City, 1856; lived in California and Nevada. Joined the Reorganized Church of Jesus Christ of Latter Day Saints, 1871. Died at Genoa, Douglas County, Nevada. (2.1)

Hendricks, Drusilla Dorris (February 8, 1810–May 20, 1881). Born in Summer County, Tennessee; daughter of Catherine Frost and William Dorris. Married James Hendricks, 1827; five children. Baptized, 1835. Moved to Missouri, 1836; lived in Clay County, Missouri, and at Far West, Caldwell County, Missouri. Moved to Nauvoo, Hancock County, Illinois, 1840. Joined the Female Relief Society of Nauvoo, 1842. Migrated to the Salt Lake Valley, 1847; lived at Warm Springs, Salt Lake County, Utah Territory. Moved to Richmond, Cache County, Utah Territory, 1860. Died at Richmond. (1.2)

Hennefer, Rebecca Ann Hays (January 18, 1829–September 25, 1857). Born in New Jersey; daughter of Rebecca Ann Powell and Abraham Hays. Baptized, 1849. Married William Hennefer, 1849; four children. Lived in Pottawattamie County, Iowa, 1850. Migrated to the Salt Lake Valley, 1851. Settled at Salt Lake City; lived in the Salt Lake City Thirteenth Ward. Participated in the first Relief Society organized in Utah, 1854. Died at Salt Lake City. (2.1)

Herrick, Lester James (December 14, 1827–April 18, 1892). Born at Nelson, Portage County, Ohio; son of Sally Judd and Lemuel Herrick. Lived at Kirtland, Geauga County, Ohio; at Jackson County, Missouri; and at Far West, Caldwell County, Missouri. Migrated to the Salt Lake Valley, 1850. Settled at Ogden, Weber County, Utah Territory. Married Sarah Ann Garner, 1851; participated in plural marriage. Served as counselor and bishop of the Ogden Second Ward and as presiding bishop over Weber County; appointed counselor in the Weber Stake presidency, 1877. Died at Ogden. (3.26)

Herrick, Sarah Ann Garner (January 18, 1832–August 12, 1906). Born at Vincennes, Knox County, Indiana; daughter of Mary Hedrick and Philip Garner. Migrated to the Salt Lake Valley, 1849. Settled at Ogden, Weber County, Utah Territory. Married Lester James Herrick, July 13, 1851; two children. Participated in mass meetings to protest the Cullom Bill, 1870. Served as a counselor in the Ogden Ward Relief Society presidency, circa 1870–1877; served as counselor to Jane Snyder Richards in the Weber Stake Relief Society presidency, 1877. Served as president of the Weber Stake Young Ladies' Mutual Improvement Association, 1879–1892. Died at Logan, Cache County, Utah; buried at Ogden. (3.26, 3.28, 4.20)

Hess, John William (August 24, 1824–December 16, 1903). Born at Waynesboro, Franklin County, Pennsylvania; son of Elizabeth Foutz and Jacob Hess. Baptized, 1834. Married Emeline Bigler, 1845; participated in plural marriage. Traveled with the Mormon Battalion, 1847; arrived in the Salt Lake Valley, 1849. Settled at Farmington, Davis County, Utah Territory. Served as bishop of the Farmington Ward, 1855–1882; as counselor in the Davis Stake presidency, 1882–1894; and as president of the Davis Stake, 1894–1903. Died at Farmington. (3.30)

Heywood, Serepta Maria Blodgett (November 22, 1822–December 4, 1881). Born at Monroe, Ashtabula County, Ohio; daughter of Chloe Kiddar and Caleb Blodgett. Married Joseph Leland Heywood, 1841; six children. Baptized, circa 1842. Migrated to the Salt Lake Valley, 1848. Settled at Salt Lake City. Served as counselor to Marinda N. Hyde in the Salt Lake City Seventeenth Ward Relief Society presidency, 1868–1881. Died at Salt Lake City. (3.29, 4.28)

Higbee, Sarah Elizabeth Ward (March 6, 1802–April 1, 1874). Born at Tate Township, Clermont County, Ohio; daughter of Elizabeth Van Etten and James Ward. Married Elias Higbee, 1818; eight children. Baptized, circa 1832. Lived in Jackson, Clay, and Caldwell Counties, Missouri, 1833–1838. Moved to Commerce (later Nauvoo), Hancock County, Illinois, by 1839. Joined the Female Relief Society of Nauvoo as a charter member, March 17, 1842. Widowed, 1843. Moved to Pike County, Illinois, by 1850; moved to Clarence, Shelby County, Missouri, by 1870. Died at Clarence. (1.2, 1.6)

Hillman Coons, Sarah King (August 24, 1798–May 25, 1870). Born at Cambridge, Washington County, New York; daughter of Tahpenas Coy and Jonathan Seymour King. Married first Mayhew Hillman, circa 1818; five children. Baptized, 1832. Lived at Kirtland, Geauga County, Ohio, 1832; at Adam-ondi-Ahman, Daviess County, Missouri, circa 1838; and at Commerce (later Nauvoo), Hancock County, Illinois, by 1839. Widowed, 1839. Joined the Female Relief Society of Nauvoo at its second meeting, March 24, 1842. Married second Lebbeus Thaddeus Coons, 1846. Migrated to the Salt Lake Valley, 1852. Died at Pondtown, Utah County, Utah Territory; buried at Spanish Fork, Utah County. (1.2, 1.6)

Hoagland, Abraham (March 24, 1797–February 14, 1872). Born at Hillsborough, Somerset County, New Jersey; son of Mary Bunn and Lucas Hoagland. Married Margaret Quick, 1825; participated in plural marriage. Baptized in Michigan, 1841. Moved to Nauvoo, Hancock County, Illinois, 1843. Migrated to the Salt Lake Valley, 1847. Settled at Salt Lake City. Served as bishop of the Salt Lake City Fourteenth Ward, 1851–1872. Died at Salt Lake City. (2.3, 4.28)

Hoagland Schwartz, Agnes Taylor Rich (October 2, 1821–December 12, 1911). Born at Hale, Westmorland, England; daughter of Agnes and James Taylor. Immigrated to Canada, where she was baptized, circa 1836. Moved to Hancock County, Illinois. Married first John Rich, 1838; later divorced; four children. Migrated to the Salt Lake Valley, 1847. Married second Abraham Hoagland as a plural wife, 1847; five children. Settled at Salt Lake City. Separated from Hoagland, by 1860; divorced, 1861. Married third Wilhelm

(William) Schwartz, 1862; two children. Served as treasurer and visiting committee member in the Salt Lake City Fourteenth Ward Relief Society upon its organization, 1856; as counselor to Mary Isabella Horne, 1878–1881; and as president of the Fourteenth Ward Relief Society, 1881–1889. Functioned as matron of the Gardo House, official residence of John Taylor (her brother), 1882–1887. Died at Salt Lake City. (2.3)

Holbrook, Eunice Dunning (April 6, 1810–December 30, 1890). Born at Schroon, Essex County, New York; daughter of Susannah Colvin and David Dunning. Married Chandler Holbrook, 1831; seven children. Baptized in New York, 1833. Lived in Clay and Caldwell Counties, Missouri, circa 1836–1839, and at Nauvoo, Hancock County, Illinois, circa 1841–1844. Joined the Female Relief Society of Nauvoo, 1842. Migrated to the Salt Lake Valley, 1848. Settled at Fillmore, Millard County, Utah Territory, before 1856. Served as the first Relief Society president in the Fillmore Ward. Died at Fillmore. (1.2)

Holden, Ruia Angeline Bliss (April 29, 1815–March 27, 1868). Born at Avon, Livingston County, New York; daughter of Lucretia Bishop and John Bliss. Married Edwin Holden, 1833; eight children. Moved to La Harpe, Hancock County, Illinois, 1837. Baptized, 1840, and moved to Nauvoo, Hancock County. Joined the Female Relief Society of Nauvoo, 1842. Migrated to Utah Territory, 1852; settled at Provo, Utah County, Utah Territory. Appointed counselor to Lucy Meserve Smith in the Provo Relief Society, circa 1856. Served as president of the Provo Fourth Ward Relief Society, 1868–1883. Died at Provo. (1.2, 2.4)

Holmes, Sarah Ingersoll Harvey Floyd (September 27, 1816–February 27, 1889). Born at Gloucester, Essex County, Massachusetts; daughter of Dorcas Curtis and Isaac Harvey. Married first Enoch Floyd Jr., 1832; seven children. Baptized, 1842. Migrated to the Salt Lake Valley, 1853. Lived in California, circa 1853–1854; lived in Massachusetts, circa 1854–1862. Widowed, 1855. Returned to the Salt Lake Valley, 1862. Married second Jonathan Harriman Holmes as a plural wife, 1862. Settled at Farmington, Davis County, Utah Territory. Served as president of the Farmington Ward Relief Society and as president of the Davis Stake Relief Society. Moved to St. Charles, Bear Lake County, Idaho Territory; served in the Relief Society and as a counselor in the Bear Lake Stake Primary. Died at St. Charles; buried at Farmington. (4.3)

Hopkins Brown West Moyes, Louise M. (October 29, 1853–October 14, 1931). Born in England or New York; daughter of Louise Butler and William Hopkins. Raised and educated in England and France. Baptized, circa 1859–1863. Settled in Weber County, Utah Territory, circa 1859. Married first Clint Brown, 1861; one child. Later divorced or widowed. Appointed first secretary of the Ogden City Relief Society, 1867. Married second Chauncey West as a plural wife, 1868; one child. Widowed, 1870. Married third Alfred Moyes, 1871; nine children. Moved to Idaho Falls, Oneida County, Idaho Territory, circa 1881; moved to Pocatello, Bingham County, Idaho Territory, 1887. Died at Pocatello. (3.28)

Hopkins, Lydia Okie Van Dyke (June 21, 1803–October 14, 1859). Born at New York City; daughter of Elizabeth Penier and Abraham Okie. Married first Nicholas Van Dyke, 1827; two children. Baptized, 1838. Widowed, 1839. Married second Charles Hopkins, 1840; one child. Migrated to the Salt Lake Valley, 1849. Settled at Dry Creek, Utah County, Utah Territory, 1850; moved to Cedar City, Iron County, Utah Territory, 1856. Served as president of the Cedar City Relief Society, 1856–1859. Died at Cedar City. (2.6)

Horne, Martha (Mattie) Jane. See "Tingey, Martha (Mattie) Jane Horne."

Horne, Mary Isabella Hales (November 20, 1818–August 25, 1905). Born at Rainham, Kent, England; daughter of Mary Ann and Stephen Hales. Immigrated to York, Upper Canada, 1832. Married Joseph Horne, May 9, 1836; fifteen children. Baptized, 1836. Moved to Far West, Caldwell County, Missouri, 1838; to Quincy, Adams County, Illinois, 1839; and to Nauvoo, Hancock County, Illinois, circa 1841. Joined the Female Relief Society of Nauvoo, 1842. Migrated to the Salt Lake Valley, 1847. Settled at Salt Lake City. Served as counselor to Phebe C. Woodruff in the Salt Lake City Fourteenth Ward Relief Society presidency, 1856–1858; served as president of the Fourteenth Ward Relief Society, 1867–1881. Served as president of the Ladies' Cooperative Retrenchment Association, 1870–1904. Served as chairman of the executive committee of Deseret Hospital, 1882–1894. Served as president of the Salt Lake Stake Relief Society, 1877–1903, and as treasurer of the Relief Society general board, 1880–1901. Died at Salt Lake City. (1.2, 2.3, 3.13, 3.15–3.17, 3.23, 3.25, 3.28–3.30, 4.4, 4.5, 4.11, 4.15, 4.16, 4.28)

Horrocks, Catherine MacSwein Dougall (October 8, 1808–August 18, 1892). Born at Dunblane, Perthshire, Scotland; daughter of Jean Douglas and Hugh MacSwein. Married first John Dougall, 1835; three children. Widowed, between 1843 and 1853. Baptized in England, 1853. Immigrated to the United States aboard the *Juventa* and migrated to the Salt Lake Valley, 1855. Settled at Springville, Utah County, Utah Territory. Married second Peter Horrocks, 1860. Lived at Salt Lake City. Served as a teacher in the Salt Lake City Thirteenth Ward Relief Society. Died at Salt Lake City. (3.7)

Howard, Elizabeth Anderson (July 12, 1823–March 12, 1893). Born at Carlow, County Carlow, Ireland; daughter of Lucretia Ward and Robert Anderson. Married William Howard, June 9, 1841; ten children. Baptized, 1851. Immigrated to the Salt Lake Valley, 1853; lived in the Salt Lake City Thirteenth Ward. Moved to Big Cottonwood Canyon, Salt Lake County, Utah Territory; served as secretary of the Big Cottonwood Ward Relief Society, 1867–1868, and as president, circa 1871–1890. Accompanied husband on a mission to England, 1868–1869. Appointed counselor to Mary Isabella Horne in the General Retrenchment Association, 1871. Served on the Central Grain Committee, 1876. Appointed secretary of the Salt Lake Stake Relief Society, 1877. Served as chair of the Deseret Hospital visiting committee, 1882–1884, and as assistant secretary and treasurer, 1884–1893. Served as president of the Salt Lake County Woman Suffrage Association, 1891–1892. Died at Grantsville, Tooele County, Utah Territory; buried at Salt Lake City. (3.25, 4.4, 4.11, 4.28)

Howard, Sarah Langley (April 12, 1820–January 30, 1885). Born at Flackwell Heath, Buckinghamshire, England; daughter of Ann Salter and John Langley. Married Thomas Howard, 1845; seven children. Immigrated to the United States aboard the *Olympus* and migrated to the Salt Lake Valley, 1851. Lived in Salt Lake County, Utah Territory, at Salt Lake City, Mill Creek, and Sugar House. Participated in Central Grain Committee meetings, circa 1876. Died at Salt Lake City. (3.25)

Howell, James (October 20, 1816–November 20, 1893). Born at Childerditch, Essex, England; son of Elizabeth Jay and James Howell. Married Sarah Marshall, 1837. Baptized in England, 1849. Immigrated to the United States aboard the *Chimborazo,* 1855; migrated to the Salt Lake Valley, 1862. Settled at Salt Lake City; lived in the Salt Lake City Seventh Ward. Attended the organization of the Seventh Ward Relief Society, 1868. Lived at

Batesville (later Erda), Tooele County, Utah Territory, by 1880. Died at Erda; buried at Tooele, Tooele County. (3.3)

Huffaker, Elizabeth Melvina Richardson (May 28, 1829–April 26, 1911). Born in Coos County, New Hampshire; daughter of Erepta Melvina Wilder and Stephen Richardson. Lived at Kirtland, Geauga County, Ohio, and at Nauvoo, Hancock County, Illinois, circa 1838–1840. Married Simpson David Huffaker, 1846; fifteen children. Migrated to the Salt Lake Valley, 1847. Settled in Salt Lake City. Appointed second counselor at the organization of the Salt Lake City Seventh Ward Relief Society, 1868. Died at Salt Lake City. (3.3)

Hunter, Ann Standley (February 16, 1808–November 9, 1855). Born at Haverford, Delaware County, Pennsylvania; daughter of Martha Vaughn and Jacob Standley. Married Edward Hunter, 1830; three children. Baptized, 1840. Moved to Nauvoo, Hancock County, Illinois, 1842. Joined the Female Relief Society of Nauvoo, 1843. Migrated to the Salt Lake Valley, 1847. Settled at Salt Lake City; lived in the Salt Lake City Thirteenth Ward. Died at Salt Lake City. (1.2, 1.6)

Hunter, Edward (June 22, 1793–October 16, 1883). Born at Newtown, Delaware County, Pennsylvania; son of Hannah Maris and Edward Hunter. Married Ann Standley, 1830; participated in plural marriage. Baptized in Pennsylvania, 1840. Moved to Nauvoo, Hancock County, Illinois, 1841. Migrated to the Salt Lake Valley, 1847. Settled at Salt Lake City. Served as presiding bishop of the church, 1851–1883. Died at Salt Lake City. (3.25)

Hyde, Charles Walker (July 16, 1814–December 15, 1891). Born at York, Livingston County, New York; son of Polly Wyman Tilton and Heman Hyde. Baptized, 1834. Married Ann Sophia Hansen, circa 1839; participated in plural marriage. Migrated to the Salt Lake Valley, 1848. Settled at Salt Lake City; lived in the Salt Lake City Seventh Ward. Died at Salt Lake City. (3.3)

Hyde, Marinda Nancy Johnson (June 28, 1815–March 24, 1886). Born at Pomfret, Windsor County, Vermont; daughter of Alice (Elsa) Jacobs and John Johnson. Baptized in Ohio, 1832. Moved to Kirtland, Geauga County, Ohio, 1833. Married Orson Hyde, 1834; ten children. Lived in Missouri, 1838–1839; moved to Nauvoo, Hancock County, Illinois. Joined the Female Relief Society of Nauvoo at its first meeting, March 17, 1842. Later identified herself as a plural wife of Joseph Smith, married in 1842 or 1843. Migrated to the Salt Lake Valley, 1852. Settled at Salt Lake City. Divorced Hyde, 1870. Served as president of the Salt Lake City Seventeenth Ward Relief Society, 1868–1886. Served as an executive board member of the Deseret Hospital Association, circa 1882–1886. Died at Salt Lake City. (1.2, 3.13, 3.16, 3.17, 3.25, 4.1, 4.11)

Hyde, Mary Ann Cowles (December 31, 1820–December 1, 1901). Born at Bolivar, Allegany County, New York; daughter of Phebe Wilbur and Austin Cowles. Baptized, 1834. Lived at Kirtland, Geauga County, Ohio, and Commerce (later Nauvoo), Hancock County, Illinois; lived with Joseph Smith's family while working as their maid, circa 1838–1839. Married Rosel Hyde, 1839; twelve children. Joined the Female Relief Society of Nauvoo, May 1842. Migrated to the Salt Lake Valley, 1849. Settled at Kaysville, Davis County, Utah Territory, 1853. Appointed counselor at the organization of the Kaysville Relief Society, 1868; served as president of the Kaysville Relief Society, 1872–1882. Died at Kaysville. (1.2, 4.3)

Jennings, Frances Charlotte Crackles (October 20, 1828–April 20, 1912). Born at Barton, Yorkshire, England; daughter of Sarah Dinsdale and Richard Crackles. Married William Jennings, 1851; twelve children. Baptized at London, 1881. Appointed counselor in the North London Branch Relief Society, 1884. Died at Islington, London. (4.22)

Jennings, William (September 13, 1823–January 15, 1886). Born at Yardley, Worcestershire, England; son of Jane Thornton and Isaac Jennings. Immigrated to the United States, 1847. Married Jane Walker, 1851; participated in plural marriage. Migrated to the Salt Lake Valley, 1852. Baptized in Utah Territory, 1852. Served a mission to Carson Valley, Carson County, Utah Territory, 1856–1857. Served as mayor of Salt Lake City, 1882–1884. Died at Salt Lake City. (4.11)

Johnson, John Peter Rasmus (April 10, 1824–July 9, 1910). Born at Lindved, Sindbjerg, Vejle, Denmark; son of Ane Dorthea Jonasdotter and Johannes Christensen. Married Caroline Marie Tuft, 1845; participated in plural marriage. Baptized in Denmark, circa 1851–1852. Immigrated to the United States and migrated to the Salt Lake Valley, 1854. Settled at Provo, Utah County, Utah Territory, circa 1856. Served as bishop of the Provo First Ward, circa 1864–1902. Died at Provo. (4.4)

Johnson, Polly Zerviah Kelsey (September 14, 1808–June 27, 1850). Born at Killingworth, Middlesex County, Connecticut; daughter of Polly Parmalee and Jonathan Kelsey. Married Aaron Johnson, 1827; four children. Baptized in Connecticut, 1836. Moved to Kirtland, Geauga County, Ohio, 1837; to Far West, Caldwell County, Missouri, 1838; and to Commerce (later Nauvoo), Hancock County, Illinois, 1839. Endowed in the Nauvoo temple, 1845. Accompanied her husband on a mission to the eastern United States, 1848. Began migration to the Salt Lake Valley, June 1850. Died en route to Utah; buried along the Platte River near Fort Kearny, unorganized U.S. territory. (1.6)

Jones, Elizabeth Hughes (March 22, 1803–May 24, 1859). Born at New York City; daughter of Catherine Ivens and John Hughes. Married William C. Jones, 1825; ten children. Joined the Female Relief Society of Nauvoo, Hancock County, Illinois, at its first meeting, March 17, 1842; authorized to collect donations for the Relief Society. Migrated to the Salt Lake Valley, before 1850; lived at Salt Lake City. Died at Sacramento, Sacramento County, California; buried at Fremont, Alameda County, California. (1.2, 4.28)

Jones, Mary Nielson (October 3, 1858–February 28, 1933). Born at Parowan, Iron County, Utah Territory; daughter of Elsie Rasmussen and Jens Nielson. Married Kumen Jones, 1878; two children. Worked as a midwife. Served as a counselor in the San Juan Stake Young Ladies' Mutual Improvement Association. Lived at Bluff, San Juan County, Utah, and Blanding, San Juan County. Died at Blanding. (4.21)

Jones, Nathaniel Vary (October 13, 1822–February 15, 1863). Born at Brighton, Monroe County, New York; son of Lucinda Kingsley and Samuel Jones. Baptized in Wisconsin Territory, 1842. Married Rebecca M. Burton, 1845; participated in plural marriage. Served in the Mormon Battalion, 1846–1847. Migrated to the Salt Lake Valley, 1849. Lived at Salt Lake City. Served as bishop of the Salt Lake City Fifteenth Ward. Died at Salt Lake City. (4.28)

Jones, Rebecca Maria Burton (February 16, 1826–November 19, 1888). Born at Mersea, Essex County, Upper Canada; daughter of Hannah Shipley and Samuel Burton. Baptized in Canada, 1837. Immigrated to the United States and settled at Walnut Grove,

Knox County, Illinois, 1839; moved to Camp Creek, Hancock County, Illinois, 1842, and to Nauvoo, Hancock County, 1844. Married Nathaniel Vary Jones, 1845; eight children. Migrated to the Salt Lake Valley, 1849. Settled in the Salt Lake City Fifteenth Ward. Widowed, 1863. Served as counselor to Sarah M. Kimball in the Fifteenth Ward Relief Society presidency, 1868–1888. Died at Salt Lake City. (3.12)

Kaleohano, Kaahanui (Lilia) (July 2, 1836–September 4, 1885). Lived at Kula, Maui, Hawaii, and at Laie, Oahu, Hawaii. Baptized by George Q. Cannon, July 1851. Married H. K. (Kuakaha) Kaleohano, 1851; at least one child. Served as counselor to Sarah Clayton Partridge in the Relief Society of the Sandwich Islands and as counselor in the Laie Relief Society. Died at Laie. (4.13)

Kekauoha, Nalia Kai-O (circa 1834–April 1905). Born at Koloa, Kauai, Hawaii; daughter of Kahaionakolo and Kai-O. Married Hosea Nahinu Kekauoha, 1851; at least four children. Baptized, 1871. Served as counselor to Sarah Clayton Partridge in the Relief Society of the Sandwich Islands and as counselor in the Relief Society at Laie, Oahu, Hawaii. Died at Laie. (4.13)

Kekauoha Lua, Victoria (May 2, 1868–July 16, 1907). Born at Laie, Oahu, Hawaii; daughter of Nalia Kai-O and Hosea Nahinu Kekauoha. Served as the native-language secretary for the Primary at Laie, 1883. Married Kakelaka Lua, circa 1885; five children. Migrated to Iosepa, Tooele County, Utah Territory, circa 1892–1894. Died at Iosepa. (4.13)

Kendall, Elizabeth Silcox (September 12, 1814–April 30, 1894). Born at Trowbridge, Wiltshire, England; daughter of Patience Bishop and James Silcox. Baptized in England, 1844. Married George Kendall, 1845; five children. Immigrated to the United States aboard the *Ellen Maria* and migrated to the Salt Lake Valley, 1853. Settled at Nephi, Juab County, Utah Territory. Appointed counselor to Amelia Goldsbrough at the organization of the Nephi Relief Society, 1868. Died at Nephi. (3.19)

Kimball, Ellen Sanders (April 11, 1823–November 27, 1871). Born Aagaata Ystensdatter Bake Sondrason at Tinn, Telemark, Norway; daughter of Aase Olsdatter Romersen Bakka and Ysten Sondreson. Immigrated to the United States, circa 1837. Baptized in Illinois, 1842. Moved to Nauvoo, Hancock County, Illinois, 1844. Married Heber C. Kimball as a plural wife, 1846; five children. One of only three women to migrate to the Salt Lake Valley with the Brigham Young pioneer company, 1847. Lived at Salt Lake City and in the Bear River Valley, Rich County, Utah Territory. Died at Salt Lake City. (4.28)

Kimball, Heber Chase (June 14, 1801–June 22, 1868). Born at Sheldon, Franklin County, Vermont; son of Anna Spaulding and Solomon Farnham Kimball. Married Vilate Murray, 1822; participated in plural marriage. Baptized, 1832. Ordained a member of the Quorum of the Twelve Apostles, 1835. Served missions to the British Isles and the eastern United States. Admitted to the Council of Fifty, 1844. Appointed counselor to Brigham Young in the First Presidency, 1847. Migrated to the Salt Lake Valley with the Brigham Young pioneer company, 1847. Elected lieutenant governor for the provisional State of Deseret and served in the Utah territorial legislature. Died at Salt Lake City. (1.2, 1.11, 2.2, 3.25)

Kimball, Lucy Walker (April 30, 1826–October 1, 1910). Born at Peacham, Caledonia County, Vermont; daughter of Lydia Holmes and John Walker. Baptized in New York, 1835. Survived the attack at Hawn's Mill on Shoal Creek, Caldwell County, Missouri, 1838. Moved to Nauvoo, Hancock County, Illinois, by 1840 or 1841. Later identified herself as a plural wife of Joseph Smith, married on May 1, 1843. Married second Heber C. Kimball as a plural wife, 1845; nine children. Migrated to the Salt Lake Valley, 1848. Lived in the Salt Lake City Eighteenth Ward, circa 1848–1868. Moved to Provo, Utah County, Utah Territory, circa 1868; served in the Provo Fourth Ward Relief Society. Moved back to Salt Lake City, before 1900. Died at Salt Lake City. (3.12)

Kimball, Presendia Lathrop Huntington Buell (September 7, 1810–February 1, 1892). Born at Watertown, Jefferson County, New York; daughter of Zina Baker and William Huntington. Married first Norman Buell, 1827; seven children. Moved to Kirtland, Geauga County, Ohio; baptized at Kirtland, 1836. Settled at Lima, Adams County, Illinois, 1840. Later identified herself as a plural wife of Joseph Smith, married on December 11, 1841. Joined the Female Relief Society of Nauvoo, Hancock County, Illinois, at its fifth meeting, 1842. Married third Heber C. Kimball as a plural wife, 1845; two children. Separated from Buell after his disaffection from the church, 1846. Migrated to the Salt Lake Valley, 1848. Lived at Salt Lake City and at Provo, Utah County, Utah Territory; settled in the Salt Lake City Sixteenth Ward, 1862. Appointed secretary of the Sixteenth Ward Relief Society at its founding, 1868. Traveled frequently while engaged in Relief Society work, temple work, and ministering to the sick. Died at Salt Lake City. (1.2, 3.16, 3.17, 3.28, 4.20)

Kimball, Sarah Melissa Granger (December 29, 1818–December 1, 1898). Born at Phelps, Ontario County, New York; daughter of Lydia Dibble and Oliver Granger. Moved to Kirtland, Geauga County, Ohio, 1833. Married Hiram Kimball, 1840; three children. Settled at Nauvoo, Hancock County, Illinois, 1840. Proposed the formation of a charitable society in Nauvoo, 1842; joined the Female Relief Society of Nauvoo as a founding member, March 17, 1842. Migrated to the Salt Lake Valley, 1851. Settled at Salt Lake City. Served as president of the Salt Lake City Fifteenth Ward Relief Society, 1857–1898. Widowed, 1863. Actively participated in leadership roles within the Ladies' Cooperative Retrenchment Society, grain movement, political indignation meetings, and the woman suffrage movement. Appointed secretary to Eliza R. Snow on the Relief Society general board, 1880. Served on the finance committee of the Deseret Hospital Association. Served as president of the Utah Woman Suffrage Association and honorary vice president of the National American Woman Suffrage Association. Elected third vice president of the Relief Society upon its incorporation, 1892. Died at Salt Lake City. (1.2, 3.9, 3.10, 3.12, 3.13, 3.15–3.17, 3.24, 3.25, 3.28, 4.1, 4.4, 4.5, 4.10–4.12, 4.27, 4.28)

Kimball, Vilate Murray (June 1, 1806–October 22, 1867). Born at Florida, Montgomery County, New York; daughter of Susannah Fitch and Roswell Murray. Married Heber C. Kimball, 1822; ten children. Baptized, 1832. Moved to Kirtland, Geauga County, Ohio, 1833; to Far West, Caldwell County, Missouri, 1838–1839; to Atlas and Quincy, Adams County, Illinois, 1839; and to Nauvoo, Hancock County, Illinois, circa 1840. Joined the Female Relief Society of Nauvoo at its second meeting, March 24, 1842. One of the first women to perform ordinances in the Nauvoo temple. Migrated to the Salt Lake Valley, 1848. Settled at Salt Lake City. Died at Salt Lake City. (1.2, 4.1, 4.28)

King, Hannah Tapfield (March 16, 1807–September 25, 1886). Born at Cambridge, Cambridgeshire, England; daughter of Mary Lawson and Peter Tapfield. Married first Thomas Owen King, 1824; ten children. Baptized in England, 1850. Immigrated to the

United States aboard the *Golconda* and migrated to the Salt Lake Valley, 1853. Settled at Salt Lake City. Married second Brigham Young as a plural wife, 1872, but continued to live in marriage with Thomas King. Prolific writer of poetry, essays, and biographies, most published in the *Woman's Exponent*. Appointed president of the Salt Lake City Seventeenth Ward Young Ladies' Mutual Improvement Association, 1880; served as counselor to Marinda N. Hyde in the Seventeenth Ward Relief Society presidency, 1881. Appointed to the finance committee for the Deseret Hospital Association, 1882. Died at Salt Lake City. (3.13, 4.11)

Klingensmith, Phillip (April 3, 1817–circa 1903). Born at Hempfield, Westmoreland County, Pennsylvania; son of Mary Anderson and Phillip Klingensmith. Married Hannah Henry Creemer, 1841; participated in plural marriage. Lived at Cedar City, Iron County, Utah Territory; served as bishop of the Cedar City Ward. (2.6)

Knight Kimball, Martha McBride (March 17, 1805–November 20, 1901). Born at Chester, Washington County, New York; daughter of Abigail Mead and Daniel McBride. Married first Vinson Knight, 1826; seven children. Lived at Perrysburg, Cattaraugus County, New York, by 1830. Baptized in New York, 1834. Moved to Kirtland, Geauga County, Ohio, 1835; to Adam-ondi-Ahman, Daviess County, Missouri, 1838; and to Commerce (later Nauvoo), Hancock County, Illinois, 1839. Joined the Female Relief Society of Nauvoo as a founding member, March 17, 1842. Widowed, July 1842. Later identified herself as a plural wife of Joseph Smith, married in August 1842. Married third Heber C. Kimball as a plural wife, October 1844. Migrated to the Salt Lake Valley, 1850. Settled at Ogden, Weber County, Utah Territory, and at Hooper, Weber County. Appointed counselor in the Weber County Relief Society presidency, 1856. Widowed, 1868. Traveled frequently to southern Utah and made extensive stays to serve in the St. George temple. Died at Hooper; buried at Ogden. (1.2, 4.28)

Knight, Vinson (March 14, 1804–July 31, 1842). Born at Norwich, Hampshire County, Massachusetts; son of Rispah (Rizpah) Lee and Rudolphus Knight. Married Martha McBride, 1826. Baptized, 1834. Moved to Kirtland, Geauga County, Ohio, by June 1835. Lived at Adam-ondi-Ahman, Daviess County, Missouri; appointed acting bishop, 1838. Appointed bishop at Commerce (later Nauvoo), Hancock County, Illinois, May 1839; appointed bishop of Lower Ward at Commerce, October 1839. Appointed presiding bishop of the church, January 19, 1841. Died at Nauvoo. (1.2)

Lambert, Charles (August 30, 1816–May 2, 1892). Born at Kirk Deighton, Yorkshire, England; son of Sarah Greaves and Charles Lambert. Baptized in England, 1843. Immigrated to the United States aboard the *Fanny,* 1844; settled at Nauvoo, Hancock County, Illinois. Married Mary Alice Cannon, 1844; participated in plural marriage. Migrated to the Salt Lake Valley, 1849. Settled at Salt Lake City; served as clerk in the Salt Lake City Seventh Ward. Died at Granger, Salt Lake County, Utah Territory; buried at Salt Lake City. (3.3)

Lambert, Mary Alice Cannon (December 9, 1828–September 7, 1920). Born at Liverpool, Lancashire, England; daughter of Ann Quayle and George Cannon. Baptized in England, 1840. Immigrated to the United States aboard the *Sidney,* 1842. Settled at Nauvoo, Hancock County, Illinois, 1843. Married Charles Lambert, 1844; fourteen children. Migrated to the Salt Lake Valley, 1849. Settled at Salt Lake City; lived in the Salt Lake City

Seventh Ward. Served as secretary in the Seventh Ward Relief Society for fifteen years and as president for twenty-two years. Died at Salt Lake City. (3.3, 3.16, 4.3)

Larsen, Ane (Anna/Annie) Olsen Ungermann (October 1, 1832–May 23, 1913). Born at Aastrup Parish, Maribo, Storstrøm, Denmark; daughter of Maren Jorgensen and Ole Pedersen Ungermann. Baptized in Denmark, 1859. Immigrated to the United States aboard the *Athena* and migrated to the Salt Lake Valley, 1862. Married Christian Grejs Larsen, 1863; one child. Lived at Spring City, Sanpete County, Utah Territory, circa 1863–1880. Moved to Castle Dale, Emery County, Utah Territory, circa 1880. Appointed president of the Emery Stake Relief Society, 1882. Died at Castle Dale. (4.25)

Law, Jane Silverthorn (April 2, 1815–September 8, 1882). Born at York, Upper Canada; daughter of Mary Anderson and Thomas Silverthorn. Married William Law, 1833; eight children. Baptized in Canada, 1836. Migrated to Commerce (later Nauvoo), Hancock County, Illinois, 1839. Joined the Female Relief Society of Nauvoo at its second meeting, March 24, 1842. Left Nauvoo in 1844 after her husband's excommunication from the church. Settled at Shullsburg, Lafayette County, Wisconsin, 1866. Died at Shullsburg. (1.2, 1.6)

Layton, Sarah Barnes (July 6, 1826–September 13, 1906). Born at Sandy, Bedfordshire, England; daughter of Elizabeth Jeffries and William Barnes. Baptized in England, January 1, 1842. Immigrated to the United States aboard the *James Pennel,* 1850. Migrated to the Salt Lake Valley, 1852. Married Christopher Layton as a plural wife, 1852; six children. Settled at Kaysville, Davis County, Utah Territory, 1857. Served as a counselor in the Kaysville Relief Society, 1868–1882, and as president, 1882–1906. Died at Kaysville. (4.3)

Leaver, Mary Ann Hartlett (June 21, 1810–April 4, 1882). Born at Neithrop, Banbury, Oxfordshire, England; daughter of Ann Borscott and Edward Hartlett. Immigrated to the United States, 1830. Married Samuel Leaver Jr., 1831; ten children. Baptized at New York City, 1842. Migrated to the Salt Lake Valley, 1852. Settled at Salt Lake City. Served as president of the Salt Lake City Eighth Ward Relief Society, circa 1868–1882. Died at Salt Lake City. (3.13)

Lehi, Nephi (circa 1842–December 15, 1918). Born in an area that later became part of Utah Territory. Married Mary; seven children. Lived in Thistle Valley, Sanpete County, Utah Territory. Baptized, August 1879. Adopted the surname Lehi, circa 1884. Served as an interpreter, teacher, and elders quorum counselor in the Indianola Ward, in Indianola, Sanpete County. Moved to the Uintah and Ouray Indian Reservation, Utah, 1896. Died at the Uintah and Ouray Reservation. (4.7)

Liljenquist, Anna Christine (Christina) Jacobsen (January 1, 1822–July 5, 1903). Born at Barlose, Svendborg, Denmark; daughter of Johanne Nielsen and Hans Christian Jacobsen. Married Ola Nilsson Liljenquist, 1848; six children. Baptized in Denmark, 1852. Immigrated to the United States aboard the *Westmoreland* and migrated to the Salt Lake Valley, 1857. Lived at Spanish Fork, Utah County, Utah Territory, and at Goshen, Utah County, circa 1858–1862. Settled at Hyrum, Cache County, Utah Territory, 1862. Served as a counselor in the Hyrum Ward Relief Society presidency, 1869–1871; served as president of the Hyrum Ward Relief Society, 1871–1889. Served a mission with her husband at the Logan temple, 1884–1886. Died at Hyrum. (3.22, 4.17)

Liljenquist, Emma Anderson (November 9, 1862–March 2, 1952). Born at Salt Lake City; daughter of Maren Haraldsen and Gustave F. Anderson. Married Olaf Oscar

Liljenquist, 1878; nine children. Graduated from Dr. Margaret C. Shipp's obstetrics course, 1888. Practiced midwifery for many years in Hyrum, Cache County, Utah. Died at Ogden, Weber County, Utah; buried at Hyrum. (4.17)

Liljenquist, Ola Nilsson (September 23, 1825–April 24, 1906). Born at Ignaberga, Kristianstad, Sweden; son of Bingta Larsson and Nils Tykesson. Married Anna Christine Jacobsen, 1848; participated in plural marriage. Baptized in Denmark, 1852. Immigrated to the United States aboard the *Westmoreland* and migrated to the Salt Lake Valley, 1857. Served two missions to Scandinavia, 1859–1862, 1876–1877. Settled at Hyrum, Cache County, Utah Territory, 1862. Served as bishop of the Hyrum Ward, July 1863–1882. Died at Hyrum. (4.17)

Lunt, Ellen Whittaker (June 6, 1830–May 19, 1903). Born at Heywood, Lancashire, England; daughter of Rachel Taylor and James Whittaker. Baptized in England, 1850. Immigrated to the United States aboard the *George W. Bourne* and migrated to the Salt Lake Valley, 1851. Married Henry Lunt, 1852; two children. Lived at Cedar City, Iron County, Utah Territory. Appointed secretary in the Cedar City Relief Society, 1868, and president of the Parowan Stake Relief Society, 1879. Settled at Colonia Pacheco, Chihuahua, Mexico, circa 1890. Died at Corrales, Lopez, Chihuahua; buried at Colonia Pacheco. (2.6)

Maiben, Elizabeth Mary Richards (April 12, 1821–January 11, 1906). Born at Pembroke Dock, Pembrokeshire, Wales; daughter of Eleanor Williams and James William Richards. Baptized, 1853. Immigrated to the United States aboard the *S. Curling* and migrated to the Salt Lake Valley, 1855. Lived at Salt Lake City. Married John Bray Maiben as a plural wife, 1855; three children. Appointed teacher in the Salt Lake City Thirteenth Ward Relief Society, 1868. Settled at Manti, Sanpete County, Utah Territory, 1875. Died at Manti; buried at Salt Lake City. (3.7)

Maiben, Phebe Eleanor Richards (August 13, 1824–January 25, 1906). Born at Pembroke Dock, Pembrokeshire, Wales; daughter of Eleanor Williams and James William Richards. Baptized, 1849. Married John Bray Maiben, 1851; three children. Immigrated to the United States aboard the *S. Curling* and migrated to the Salt Lake Valley, 1855. Appointed teacher in the Salt Lake City Thirteenth Ward Relief Society, 1868. Settled at Manti, Sanpete County, Utah Territory, 1875. Died at Manti; buried at Salt Lake City. (3.7)

Mann, Stephen Allison (August 28, 1837–September 13, 1881). Born in Orange County, Vermont; son of Elizabeth Brackett and Stephen Mann. Graduated from State and National Law School and admitted to the bar in New York. Moved to the Washoe area of Utah Territory (later in Nevada), circa 1859. Appointed Utah territorial secretary, May 1869. Served as acting governor of Utah Territory, December 1869–March 1870. Practiced law in Salt Lake City. Served as clerk and deputy clerk of Washoe City and eastern Nevada. Died at Reno, Washoe County, Nevada. (3.16, 3.17, 4.28)

Marcum, Harriet (?–?). Lived at Nauvoo, Hancock County, Illinois, circa 1843. Participated in the Female Relief Society of Nauvoo; served on the Relief Society visiting committee in the Nauvoo First Ward. (1.2)

Markham Sherman, Hannah Hogaboom (April 1, 1803–January 31, 1892). Born at Manchester, Bennington County, Vermont; daughter of Margaret Darling and John Hogaboom. Married first Stephen Markham, circa 1823; four children. Baptized in Geauga County, Ohio, circa 1837. Moved to Far West, Caldwell County, Missouri, 1838, and to

Nauvoo, Hancock County, Illinois, before 1841. Joined the Female Relief Society of Nauvoo at its second meeting, March 24, 1842; served on the Relief Society visiting committee in the Nauvoo Fourth Ward. Migrated to the Salt Lake Valley, 1850. Settled at Kaysville, Davis County, Utah Territory. Moved to Palmyra, Utah County, Utah Territory, and Spanish Fork, Utah County, 1851. Separated from her husband and moved to California, circa 1852–1856. Married second John Sherman, by 1860. Lived at Newville, Glenn County, California, by 1880. Died at Newville. (1.2)

Markham, Stephen (February 9, 1800–March 10, 1878). Born at Rush, Ontario County, New York; son of Dinah Merry and David Markham. Married Hannah Hogaboom, before 1824; participated in plural marriage. Baptized at Kirtland, Geauga County, Ohio, 1837. Moved to Far West, Caldwell County, Missouri, 1838, and to Nauvoo, Hancock County, Illinois, before 1841. Migrated to the Salt Lake Valley with the Brigham Young pioneer company, 1847; lived in Davis County, Utah Territory, 1850. Helped settle towns of Palmyra, Utah County, Utah Territory, and Spanish Fork, Utah County, circa 1851. Died at Spanish Fork. (2.5)

Marks, Rosannah Robinson (December 6, 1795–October 18, 1862). Born at Pawlet, Rutland County, Vermont; daughter of Mary Upham and Ephraim Robinson. Married William Marks, 1813; eleven children. Baptized in New York, circa 1835. Lived at Kirtland, Geauga County, Ohio, by 1837, and at Nauvoo, Hancock County, Illinois, 1842. Joined the Female Relief Society of Nauvoo, 1844. Affiliated with James J. Strang's Church of Jesus Christ of Latter Day Saints, 1846. Settled at Shabbona, DeKalb County, Illinois, before 1850. Joined the Reorganized Church of Jesus Christ of Latter Day Saints, circa 1859. Died at Shabbona. (1.2, 1.6)

Marks Shaw, Sophia Robinson (March 25, 1827–December 9, 1861). Born at Portage, Livingston County, New York; daughter of Rosannah Robinson and William Marks. Moved to Kirtland, Geauga County, Ohio, by 1837, and to Nauvoo, Hancock County, Illinois, 1842. Joined the Female Relief Society of Nauvoo as a founding member, March 17, 1842. Moved to Shabbona, DeKalb County, Illinois, circa 1846. Married George W. Shaw, 1846; one child. Died at Shabbona. (1.2, 1.6, 4.28)

Matthews Bent, Elizabeth Burgess (August 4, 1788–after 1870). Born at Conway, Franklin County, Massachusetts; daughter of Bathsheba Hatsit and Edward Burgess. Married first Anson Matthews, 1811; ten children. Baptized, 1838. Moved to Hancock County, Illinois, by 1840; lived in the Nauvoo Second Ward, 1842. Joined the Female Relief Society of Nauvoo at its seventh meeting, May 12, 1842. Married second Samuel C. Bent, 1846. Migrated to the Salt Lake Valley, 1848. Settled at Payson, Utah County, Utah Territory, circa 1856. (1.2)

McAllester, Mary Bradley (?–?). Married Ananias McAllester, September 20, 1835, in Bangor, Penobscot County, Maine. Lived at Boston, by 1837. Associated with the Boston Branch of the church. Widowed, 1844. Served as president of the Boston Female Penny and Sewing Society, circa 1844–1845. Worked as a "boys' dressmaker" in Boston, 1845–1846. (1.12)

McLean Ward, Mary Ann (March 7, 1849–October 17, 1924). Born at Sunderland, Durham, England; daughter of Fanny Porter and Francis McLean. Immigrated to the United States, 1851; migrated to the Salt Lake Valley, 1857. Married Joseph Harvey Ward, 1877; one child; divorced, by 1880. Appointed matron of the Deseret Hospital, 1882; also served as first matron of the Utah State Mental Hospital and first matron of the Utah County infirmary. Settled at Provo, Utah County, Utah Territory, 1885. Died at Provo. (4.11)

McLelland, Elizabeth Murphy (August 8, 1824–April 12, 1900). Born at Monaghan, County Monaghan, Ireland; daughter of Mary Summerville and Patrick Murphy. Moved to Scotland, circa 1820. Married Thomas McLelland, 1842; eleven children. Baptized in Scotland, circa 1842. Immigrated to the United States and settled at Nauvoo, Hancock County, Illinois, 1844. Migrated to the Salt Lake Valley, 1848. Settled at Salt Lake City. Appointed president of the Salt Lake City Seventh Ward Relief Society, 1868. Died at Salt Lake City. (3.3)

McLelland, Thomas (March 29, 1819–May 12, 1890). Born at Culmore, County Londonderry, Ireland; son of Mary Lockhart and Edward McLelland. Baptized in Scotland, 1841. Married Elizabeth Murphy, 1842; participated in plural marriage. Immigrated to the United States and settled at Nauvoo, Hancock County, Illinois, 1844. Migrated to the Salt Lake Valley, 1848. Settled at Salt Lake City. Served as bishop of the Salt Lake City Seventh Ward, 1862–1876. Died at Salt Lake City. (3.3)

McMinn, Mary Dull (February 15, 1786–July 12, 1873). Born at Gwynedd, Montgomery County, Pennsylvania; daughter of Elizabeth Dotterer and Christian Dull. Married Robert McMinn, circa 1804; ten children. Lived at Philadelphia; baptized, 1840. Migrated to the Salt Lake Valley, 1850. Lived in the Salt Lake City Seventeenth Ward. Died at Salt Lake City. (3.13)

McQuarrie, Robert (August 17, 1832–November 27, 1917). Born at North Knapdale, Argyleshire, Scotland; son of Agnes Mathieson and Allen McQuarrie. Baptized in Scotland, 1853. Immigrated to the United States aboard the *George Washington* and migrated to the Salt Lake Valley, 1857. Married Hansmine (Mena) Funk, 1860; participated in plural marriage. Settled at Ogden, Weber County, Utah Territory; served as bishop of the Ogden Second Ward, 1877–1917. Died at Ogden. (3.28)

Merrick (Myrick) Knight Keeler, Philinda Clark Eldredge (August 2, 1809–July 9, 1852). Born at Weybridge, Addison County, Vermont; daughter of Frances Goodell and Abner Eldredge. Married first Levi Newton Merrick (Myrick), 1827; four children. Baptized, circa 1833. Widowed during the attack at Hawn's Mill on Shoal Creek, Caldwell County, Missouri, 1838. Settled at Nauvoo, Hancock County, Illinois, circa 1840. Joined the Female Relief Society of Nauvoo as a founding member, March 17, 1842. Married second Vinson Knight as a plural wife, circa 1842; widowed, 1842. Married third Daniel Hutchinson Keeler, 1846; two children. Lived at St. Louis, circa 1847–1852. Began migration to the Salt Lake Valley, 1852; died en route near Fort Laramie, unorganized U.S. territory. (1.2, 4.28)

Miller, Lucia (Lucy) Foote Allen. See "Foote Allen Miller, Lucia (Lucy)."

Miller, Mary Catherine Fry (January 29, 1801–January 31, 1870). Born in Madison County, Virginia; daughter of Catherine Walker and Joshua Fry. Married George Miller, 1822; six children. Moved to Nauvoo, Hancock County, Illinois, 1840. Joined the Female Relief Society of Nauvoo, April 28, 1842. Moved to Lyman Wight's colony in Texas, 1847. Left Texas to join James J. Strang's Church of Jesus Christ of Latter Day Saints, 1848; arrived at Beaver Island, Michigan, 1850. Widowed, 1856. Lived in Burnet County, Texas, by 1860. Baptized into the Reorganized Church of Jesus Christ of Latter Day Saints, 1866. Died at San Bernardino, San Bernardino County, California. (1.2, 1.6)

Mitchell, Frederick Augustus Herman Frank (July 14, 1835–July 26, 1923). Born at Sheffield, Yorkshire, England; son of Sarah Mallinson and Hezekiah Mitchell. Baptized in England, circa 1845. Immigrated to the United States aboard the *Zetland,* 1849. Migrated to the Salt Lake Valley, 1854. Married Margaret Thompson, 1855. Served as counselor to Bishop Edwin D. Woolley in the Salt Lake City Thirteenth Ward. Served a mission to the Sandwich Islands. Settled at Logan, Cache County, Utah. Died at Logan. (3.7)

Mitchell, Margaret Thompson (January 31, 1840–April 6, 1924). Born at Alston Moor, Cumberland, England; daughter of Ann Bentley and Ralph Thompson. Immigrated to the United States aboard the *North America* as an infant, fall 1840. Lived at Nauvoo, Hancock County, Illinois. Baptized, circa 1848. Migrated to the Salt Lake Valley, 1852. Married Frederick Mitchell, 1855; twelve children. Served as second counselor to Rachel Ivins Grant in the Salt Lake City Thirteenth Ward Relief Society. Accompanied her husband on a mission to the Sandwich Islands, 1873. Settled at Logan, Cache County, Utah. Died at Logan. (3.7)

Moore, Clarissa Jane Drollinger (September 12, 1824–January 10, 1905). Born at Springfield, Butler County, Ohio; daughter of Rachel Cook and Samuel Drollinger. Baptized in Clay County, Missouri, 1835. Moved to Nauvoo, Hancock County, Illinois, 1840. Married John Harvey Moore, 1841; ten children. Joined the Female Relief Society of Nauvoo at its tenth meeting, May 27, 1842. Migrated to the Salt Lake Valley, 1852. Settled at Payson, Utah County, Utah Territory. Worked as a midwife in the Payson area. Served as a counselor in the Payson Relief Society presidency. Died at Payson. (4.7)

Moore, Mary Ann Soar (January 22, 1825–September 2, 1885). Born at Beauvale, Nottinghamshire, England; daughter of Edith Burrows and Henry Soar. Married first William Jesse Taylor, 1843; two children. Widowed, 1845. Baptized, 1848. Immigrated to the United States aboard the *Horizon* and migrated to the Salt Lake Valley with the Martin handcart company, 1856. Settled at Payson, Utah County, Utah Territory. Married second John Harvey Moore as a plural wife, 1858. Served as a counselor in the Payson Relief Society presidency and as a counselor to the president of the Payson Silk Association. Died at Payson. (4.7)

Moritze, Hannah (circa 1840–?). Born in an area that later became part of Utah Territory. Married Moritze; one child. Lived in the Thistle Valley, Sanpete County, Utah Territory. Baptized, circa 1879. Participated in the Relief Society at Indianola, Sanpete County. (4.7)

Morrison, Keziah Ann Voorhees (circa 1803–after 1848). Born at Deer Creek Township, Butler County, Pennsylvania; daughter of Sabra Ann Mount and Isaac Voorhees. Married Arthur Morrison Jr., 1825; five children. Lived at Hancock County, Illinois, by 1840; lived in the Nauvoo First Ward. Joined the Female Relief Society of Nauvoo, March 1842. (1.2)

Musser, Ann Leaver (January 6, 1836–April 18, 1871). Born at New York City; daughter of Mary Ann Hartlett and Samuel Leaver. Baptized, 1844. Migrated to the Salt Lake Valley, 1852. Married Amos Milton Musser, 1858; seven children. Appointed treasurer of the Salt Lake City Thirteenth Ward Relief Society, 1868. Died at Salt Lake City. (3.7)

Nielson, Jens (April 26, 1820–April 24, 1906). Born at Tirsted, Maribo, Laaland, Denmark; son of Dorthea Margrethe Thomsen and Niels Jensen. Married Elsie Rasmussen,

1850; participated in plural marriage. Baptized in Denmark, 1854. Immigrated to the United States aboard the *Thornton* and migrated to the Salt Lake Valley with the Willie handcart company, 1856. Settled at Bluff, San Juan County, Utah Territory, 1880. Served as bishop of the Bluff Ward, 1880–1906. Died at Bluff. (4.21)

Nielson, Kirsten Jensen (August 29, 1834–December 19, 1908). Born at Blans, Stokkemarke, Laaland, Denmark; daughter of Kirsten Weaver and Peter Jensen. Baptized in Denmark, 1855. Immigrated to the United States and migrated to the Salt Lake Valley, 1857. Married Jens Nielson as a plural wife, 1858; nine children. Settled at Bluff, San Juan County, Utah Territory, 1880. Appointed counselor in the Bluff Ward Relief Society presidency, 1884; served as president of the Bluff Ward Relief Society, 1888–1908. Died at Bluff. (4.21)

Nixon, Stephen (March 27, 1807–March 5, 1893). Born near Valletta or Vittoriosa, Malta Protectorate, Kingdom of Sicily; son of Margaret Kinsey and William Nixon. Married Harriet Rushton, 1827. Baptized in England, 1841. Immigrated to the United States aboard the *Tremont;* settled at Nauvoo, Hancock County, Illinois, 1842. Migrated to the Salt Lake Valley, 1852. Lived at Provo, Utah County, Utah Territory, 1852–1859. Settled at Wanship, Summit County, Utah Territory, 1859. Died at Willow Creek, Bonneville County, Idaho. (2.4)

Nuttall, Leonard John (July 6, 1834–February 23, 1905). Born at Liverpool, Lancashire, England; son of Mary Langhorn and William Nuttall. Baptized, 1850. Immigrated to the United States and migrated to the Salt Lake Valley, 1852. Married Elizabeth Clarkson, 1856; participated in plural marriage. Lived at Provo, Utah County, Utah Territory, and at Kanab, Kane County, Utah Territory. Served as bishop of the Kanab Ward, 1875–1877, and as president of the Kanab Stake, 1877–1884. Served as private secretary to President John Taylor, 1879–1887, and to President Wilford Woodruff, 1887–1892. Died at Salt Lake City; buried at Provo. (4.4, 4.5, 4.11, 4.28)

Onump, Phebe (circa 1832–March 27, 1897). Born in what later became Utah Territory. Lived in Thistle Valley, Sanpete County, Utah Territory. Married James Onump, a high priest who served as "Head Teacher to the Lamanites" and "assistant Father to the Lamanites" in the Indianola Branch, Sanpete Stake. Participated in the Indianola Relief Society. Died in Thistle Valley. (4.7)

Overton Morris, Mahala Ann Wallace (circa December 1812–February 15, 1844). Born in Bibb County, Alabama; daughter of Prudence Randolph (Turner) and Daniel Wallace. Married first Moses Overton, 1826; widowed, 1834. Lived in the Fourth Ward at Nauvoo, Hancock County, Illinois, by 1842. Joined the Female Relief Society of Nauvoo, 1842. Married second Jacob Morris, 1843. Died at Nauvoo. (1.2)

Packard, Sophia Bundy (June 27, 1800–August 30, 1858). Born at Southampton, Hampshire County, Massachusetts; daughter of Eunice Bartlett and Ephraim Bundy. Married Noah Packard, 1820; seven children. Baptized at Parkman, Geauga County, Ohio, 1832. Lived at Kirtland, Geauga County, 1835–1836, and at Quincy, Adams County, Illinois, 1837–1840. Settled at Nauvoo, Hancock County, Illinois, 1840. Lived in the Nauvoo First Ward. Joined the Female Relief Society of Nauvoo as a founding member, March 17, 1842. Migrated to the Salt Lake Valley, 1850. Settled at Springville, Utah County, Utah Territory, 1851. Died at Springville. (1.2, 4.28)

Panawatts, Annetta (Picklocks) (circa 1845–?). Born in what later became Utah Territory; daughter of Margret and Panawatts. Lived in Thistle Valley, Sanpete County, Utah Territory. Participated in the Relief Society at Indianola, Sanpete County, 1880. Attended Sunday school at the Indianola Branch, 1895–1896. (4.7)

Park, Agnes Steele (April 3, 1827–February 21, 1896). Born at Kilbirnie, Ayrshire, Scotland; daughter of Jenette Alexander and John Steele. Baptized in Scotland, circa 1840. Married Hamilton G. Park, April 1843; ten children. Immigrated to the United States, 1850. Migrated to the Salt Lake Valley, 1852. Settled at Salt Lake City. Appointed a teacher in the Salt Lake City Thirteenth Ward Relief Society, 1868. Died at Salt Lake City. (3.7)

Parker, Ellen Briggs Douglas. See "Douglas Parker, Ellen Briggs."

Parratt Bruce, Caroline Mary (March 25, 1865–?). Born at Shoreditch, Middlesex, England; daughter of Hannah Smith and William Frederick Parratt. Lived at Islington, London, by 1881. Baptized, circa 1884. Served as secretary to Ellen Bradford in the North London Branch Relief Society, 1884–1887. Married Albert Bruce, 1890; at least one child. Lived at Walthamstow, Essex, England, by 1901. (4.22)

Partridge, Edward, Jr. (June 25, 1833–November 17, 1900). Born at Independence, Jackson County, Missouri; son of Lydia Clisbee and Edward Partridge. Baptized near Nauvoo, Hancock County, Illinois, 1841. Migrated to the Salt Lake Valley, 1848. Served a mission to the Sandwich Islands, 1854–1857. Married Sarah Lucretia Clayton, 1858; participated in plural marriage. Served as president of the Sandwich Islands mission, 1882–1885. Settled at Provo, Utah County, Utah Territory; served as president of the Utah Stake, 1895–1900. Died at Provo. (4.13)

Partridge, Emily Dow. See "Young, Emily Dow Partridge."

Partridge, Ernest DeAlton (June 13, 1869–May 2, 1923). Born at Fillmore, Millard County, Utah Territory; son of Sarah Lucretia Clayton and Edward Partridge Jr. Baptized, 1877. Lived in the Sandwich Islands while his father served as mission president, 1882–1885. Served as English-language secretary for the Laie Primary, 1883. Attended Brigham Young Academy and Michigan Agricultural College, 1885–1896. Married Elizabeth Mae Truman, 1896. Taught at Brigham Young University. Died in a railway accident in Emery County, Utah; buried at Provo, Utah County, Utah. (4.13)

Partridge, Sarah Lucretia Clayton (August 1, 1837–January 27, 1919). Born at Farington, Lancashire, England; daughter of Ruth Moon and William Clayton. Immigrated to the United States aboard the *North America,* 1840; settled at Nauvoo, Hancock County, Illinois. Baptized at Nauvoo, 1845. Migrated to the Salt Lake Valley with the Heber C. Kimball pioneer company, arriving late September 1848. Married Edward Partridge Jr., 1858; eight children. Lived in the Sandwich Islands during her husband's service as mission president, 1882–1885. Supervised the mission-wide Relief Society board, organized the mission-wide Primary, and conducted semiannual Relief Society and Primary meetings. Died at Salt Lake City. (4.13)

Peery, David Harold (May 16, 1824–September 17, 1901). Born in Tazewell County, Virginia; son of Eleanor Harman and David Peery. Married first Nancy Campbell Higginbotham, 1852. Widowed, 1862. Baptized, 1862. Migrated to the Salt Lake Valley, 1864. Married second Elizabeth Letitia Higginbotham, 1865. Settled at Ogden, Weber

County, Utah Territory, 1866. Appointed president of the Weber Stake, 1877. Died at Ogden. (3.26, 3.28)

Penrose, Charles William (February 4, 1832–May 16, 1925). Born at Camberwell, London; son of Matilda Sims and Richard Penrose. Baptized, 1850. Married Lucetta Stratford, 1855; participated in plural marriage. Served as a missionary in England and presided over the London conference, circa 1851–1861. Immigrated to the United States on the *Underwriter* and migrated to the Salt Lake Valley, 1861. Ordained to the Fifty-Sixth Quorum of the Seventy, circa 1862–1864. Worked as editor of the *Ogden Junction, Daily Junction* (Ogden), *Deseret News,* and *Salt Lake Herald.* Appointed counselor to Angus M. Cannon in the Salt Lake Stake presidency, 1884. Served as assistant church historian, 1896–1904. Appointed a member of the Quorum of the Twelve Apostles, 1904; counselor to President Joseph Fielding Smith, 1911; and counselor to President Heber J. Grant, 1918. Died at Salt Lake City. (4.11)

Perkins, John Samuel (December 28, 1821–May 20, 1887). Born at Weston Underwood, Buckinghamshire, England; son of Rosanna Kitchener and Samuel Perkins. Baptized in England, circa 1841. Married Sarah Plackett, 1845; participated in plural marriage. Immigrated to the United States aboard the *Minnesota* and migrated to the Salt Lake Valley, 1868. Settled in the Salt Lake City Sixteenth Ward. Worked for the Utah Central Railroad and Union Pacific Railroad; witnessed the driving of the "Golden Spike" at Promontory, Box Elder County, Utah Territory, 1869. Served as a seventy and a Sunday school teacher; became the first president of the Sixteenth Ward Primary, 1878. Died at Salt Lake City. (3.30)

Peterson, Jane Cecilia Roberts Wheeler Snow (June 4, 1836–February 19, 1910). Born at Winchester, Scott County, Illinois; daughter of Harriet McEvers and Horace Roberts. Lived at Nauvoo, Hancock County, Illinois, circa 1844. Baptized, 1847. Migrated to the Salt Lake Valley, 1851. Settled at Provo, Utah County, Utah Territory. Married first Thomas Jefferson Wheeler, 1852; two children. Divorced, 1856. Married second James Chauncy Snow as a plural wife, 1856; eleven children. Lived in Kane and Sanpete Counties, Utah Territory. Widowed, 1884. Married third John Peterson, 1887. Settled at Castle Dale, Emery County, Utah Territory. Served as president of the Relief Society in Castle Dale. Died at Castle Dale. (4.25)

Petty, Catharine Petty (February 7, 1803–August 1, 1877). Born at Dover, Stewart County, Tennessee; daughter of Lydia Harrington and George Petty. Married Albert Petty, 1829; ten children. Baptized by Wilford Woodruff in Tennessee, 1835. Moved to Far West, Caldwell County, Missouri, 1836, and to Nauvoo, Hancock County, Illinois, by 1841. Joined the Female Relief Society of Nauvoo at its sixth meeting, 1842. Participated in Nauvoo temple ordinances, 1845. Migrated to the Salt Lake Valley, 1848. Settled in the Sanpete Valley, 1849. Died at Sterling, Sanpete County, Utah Territory. (1.2, 1.6)

Phelps, William Wines (February 17, 1792–March 7, 1872). Born at Hanover, Morris County, New Jersey; son of Mehitable Goldsmith and Enon Phelps. Baptized, 1831. Appointed church printer, 1831. Became editor of *The Evening and the Morning Star,* published 1832–1833. Published the Book of Commandments. Appointed counselor/assistant president to David Whitmer, president of the church in Missouri, 1834. Helped compile the Doctrine and Covenants and the first Latter-day Saint hymnal, 1835. Acted as clerk to

Joseph Smith and assisted John Taylor in editing the *Times and Seasons* and *Nauvoo Neighbor.* Admitted to the Council of Fifty, 1844. Migrated to the Salt Lake Valley, 1848. Died at Salt Lake City. (1.1, 1.10)

Picton, Jane Phillips (June 9, 1821–September 13, 1890). Born at Moreton Eye, Herefordshire, England; daughter of Eleanor Davies and Thomas Philips. Baptized in England, 1842. Married James Picton, circa 1851–1853; five children. Immigrated to the United States aboard the *Elvira Owen* and migrated to the Salt Lake Valley, 1853. Settled at Nephi, Juab County, Utah Territory. Served as counselor to Amelia Goldsbrough in the Nephi Ward and Juab Stake Relief Society presidencies, 1868–1883. Died at Nephi. (3.19)

Pixton, Elizabeth Cooper (February 8, 1819–March 20, 1904). Born at Chesterfield, Derbyshire, England; daughter of Charlotte Rigley and George Cooper. Married Robert Pixton, 1839; ten children. Immigrated to the United States aboard the *Champion,* 1843; migrated to the Salt Lake Valley, 1848. Lived at Salt Lake City. Served as a visiting committee member in the Salt Lake City Fourteenth Ward Relief Society, 1856; served as president of the Taylorsville Relief Society, after 1878. Died at Taylorsville, Salt Lake County, Utah. (2.3)

Pollard, Mary Ann Bailey (March 1, 1821–November 21, 1895). Born at Lifton, Devon, England; daughter of Mary Brook and James Bailey. Married Joseph Pollard, 1845; nine children. Baptized, circa 1849. Immigrated to the United States aboard the *Clara Wheeler,* 1854–1855; migrated to the Salt Lake Valley, 1857. Settled in the Salt Lake City Fifteenth Ward. Died at Salt Lake City. (3.12)

Pollard, Ruth Ann Allen Reeves (January 23, 1817–February 8, 1881). Born at Pembroke Dock, Pembrokeshire, Wales; daughter of Martha Isaac and John Allen. Baptized in England by John Taylor, 1840. Married first John Edward Reeves, 1846; four children. Immigrated to the United States, 1849; migrated to the Salt Lake Valley, 1861. Married second Joseph Pollard as a plural wife, 1862. Lived in the Salt Lake City Fifteenth Ward. Died at Salt Lake City. (3.12)

Pollard, Sister. See "Pollard, Mary Ann Bailey," or "Pollard, Ruth Ann Allen Reeves."

Pratt, Belinda Marden (December 24, 1820–February 19, 1894). Born at Chichester, Merrimack County, New Hampshire; daughter of Rachel Shaw and John Marden. Married first Benjamin Abbot Hilton, circa 1839; divorced, circa 1844. Baptized, March 1843; moved to Nauvoo, Hancock County, Illinois, 1844. Married second Parley P. Pratt as a plural wife, 1844; five children. Migrated to the Salt Lake Valley, 1847. Settled in the Salt Lake City Fourteenth Ward; served as a Relief Society teacher, 1856–1870. Moved to Fillmore, Millard County, Utah Territory, 1870. Served as counselor and then president of the Fillmore Ward Relief Society; served as the first president of the Millard Stake Relief Society. Died at Salt Lake City. (2.3, 4.6)

Pratt, Eleanor Jane McComb McLean (December 29, 1817–October 24, 1874). Born at Wheeling, Ohio County, Virginia; daughter of Anne Chidester and James McComb. Married first Hector McLean, 1841; three children. Baptized, 1854; separated from McLean soon after. Migrated to the Salt Lake Valley, 1855. Married second Parley P. Pratt as a plural wife, 1855; widowed, 1857. Lived in the Salt Lake City Fourteenth Ward. Died at Salt Lake City. (3.13)

Pratt Penrose, Esther Romania Salina Bunnell (August 8, 1839–November 9, 1932). Born at Washington, Wayne County, Indiana; daughter of Esther Mendenhall and

Luther Ball Bunnell. Lived at Nauvoo, Hancock County, Illinois, circa 1846. Lived in Ohio and Indiana, circa 1847–1855; attended a female seminary at Crawfordsville, Montgomery County, Indiana. Baptized en route to the Salt Lake Valley, 1855. Married first Parley P. Pratt Jr., 1859; seven children. Studied medicine at Bellevue Hospital, New York City, circa 1874–1877; at the Woman's Medical College of Pennsylvania, Philadelphia; at the New England Hospital for Women and Children, Boston; and at the New York Eye and Ear Infirmary, 1881–1882. Taught courses on anatomy, physiology, and obstetrics in Salt Lake City, beginning 1878. Divorced from Pratt, 1880. Married second Charles William Penrose, 1886. Appointed to the Deseret Hospital board of directors, 1882; became a resident physician, 1887. Served as president of the Salt Lake City Twelfth Ward Young Ladies' Retrenchment Association, as treasurer of the Salt Lake Stake Young Ladies' Mutual Improvement Association, and as assistant secretary for the Relief Society Central Board. Retired from active medical practice, 1912. Died at Salt Lake City. (4.11, 4.15, 4.28)

Pratt, Kezia Downes Hill (May 10, 1812–January 11, 1877). Born at Rainow, Cheshire, England; daughter of Elizabeth (Betty) Broadhead and Edward Downes. Married first William Hill, 1834. Baptized in England, 1842. Immigrated to the United States and migrated to the Salt Lake Valley, 1851. Married second Parley P. Pratt as a plural wife, 1853. Settled in the Salt Lake City Fourteenth Ward. Appointed secretary and treasurer to Phebe C. Woodruff in the Fourteenth Ward Relief Society, 1856–1857. Died at Salt Lake City. (2.3)

Pratt, Louisa Barnes (November 10, 1802–September 8, 1880). Born at Warwick, Franklin County, Massachusetts; daughter of Dolly Stephens and Willard Barnes. Married Addison Pratt, 1831; four children. Baptized, 1838. Moved to Nauvoo, Hancock County, Illinois, 1841. Joined the Female Relief Society of Nauvoo, 1842. Migrated to the Salt Lake Valley, 1848. Appointed to accompany Pratt on a mission to the Pacific Islands, 1850–1852; served in Tubuai and Tahiti, French Polynesia. Lived at San Bernardino, San Bernardino County, California, 1852–1858; moved to Beaver, Beaver County, Utah Territory, 1858. Helped organized the first Relief Society in Beaver; served as secretary and counselor in the Beaver Relief Society. Died at Beaver. (1.2, 4.1)

Pratt, Parley Parker (April 12, 1807–May 13, 1857). Born at Burlington, Otsego County, New York; son of Charity Dickinson and Jared Pratt. Married Thankful Halsey, 1827; participated in plural marriage. Baptized, 1830. Ordained a member of the Quorum of the Twelve Apostles, 1835. Admitted to the Council of Fifty, 1844. Migrated to the Salt Lake Valley, 1847. Served missions to Europe, South America, California, and the eastern United States. Murdered at Van Buren, Crawford County, Arkansas. (1.2, 4.28)

Pratt, Romania Salina Bunnell. See "Pratt Penrose, Esther Romania Salina Bunnell."

Pulsipher, Ann Beers (December 25, 1828–May 5, 1912). Born at Banbury, Oxfordshire, England; daughter of Susannah Gazey and William Beers. Baptized, 1844. Immigrated to the United States; migrated to the Salt Lake Valley, 1848. Married Charles Pulsipher, 1849. Settled at Huntington, Emery County, Utah Territory, 1882. Served as counselor to Ane U. Larsen in the Emery Stake Relief Society presidency. Died at Elmo, Emery County; buried at Huntington. (4.25)

Randle, Alice Cattell (November 10, 1818–June 16, 1871). Born at Hartshill, Warwickshire, England; daughter of Elizabeth Dagley and William Cattell. Married

Daniel Randle, 1839. Baptized, 1848. Immigrated to the United States aboard the *Ellen Maria,* 1852. Lived at Cedar City, Iron County, Utah Territory, by 1854. Served as treasurer and teacher in the Cedar City Ward Relief Society, circa 1857–1858. Died at Cedar City. (2.6)

Redd, Eliza Ann Westover (December 17, 1854–March 17, 1938). Born at Salt Lake City; daughter of Eliza Ann Haven and Charles Westover. Moved to Washington, Washington County, Utah Territory, 1862. Baptized, 1863. Married Lemuel H. Redd Jr., 1878; eight children. Settled at Bluff, San Juan County, Utah Territory, 1880. Served as counselor and president of the Bluff Ward Relief Society, and in the San Juan Stake Relief Society presidency. Died at Salt Lake City; buried at Blanding, San Juan County. (4.21)

Reid, Diana Davidson (December 22, 1832–July 19, 1903). Born at Dundee, Scotland; daughter of Maria Armstrong and James Davidson. Baptized in Scotland, 1847. Immigrated to the United States aboard the *S. Curling* and migrated to the Salt Lake Valley, 1855. Married Peter Reid, 1856; seven children. Lived in the Salt Lake City Sixteenth Ward. Served as president of the Sixteenth Ward Relief Society, 1876–1898. Died at La Grande, Union County, Oregon; buried at Salt Lake City. (3.25)

Reid, Elizabeth Jackson (January 17, 1851–March 18, 1934). Born at Manchester, Lancashire, England; daughter of Alice Crompton and Thomas Jackson. Immigrated to the United States and migrated to the Salt Lake Valley, 1855–1856. Lived at Provo, Utah County, Utah Territory, and Payson, Utah County. Married John Kirkwood Reid, 1869; fifteen children. Settled at Castle Dale (later Orangeville), Emery County, Utah Territory, 1879. Served as treasurer and counselor in the Orangeville Ward Relief Society; served as counselor to Ane U. Larsen in the Emery Stake Relief Society presidency. Died at Orangeville. (4.25)

Richards, Emily Sophia Tanner (May 13, 1850–August 19, 1929). Born at South Cottonwood, Great Salt Lake County, Utah Territory; daughter of Rachel Winter Smith and Nathan Tanner. Married Franklin S. Richards, 1868; five children. Lived at Ogden, Weber County, Utah Territory. Served as secretary of the Ogden City Relief Society, assistant secretary of the Weber County Relief Society, president of the Ogden City Retrenchment Association, and first counselor in the Weber Stake Retrenchment Association. Moved to Salt Lake City, 1884. Served on the Relief Society general board, circa 1892–1922. Participated prominently in local and national woman suffrage organizations. Died at Salt Lake City. (3.26, 3.28, 4.27)

Richards, Franklin Dewey (April 2, 1821–December 9, 1899). Born at Richmond, Berkshire County, Massachusetts; son of Wealthy Dewey and Phinehas Richards. Baptized, 1838. Ordained a seventy, 1840. Married Jane Snyder, 1842; participated in plural marriage. Migrated to the Salt Lake Valley, 1848. Ordained to the Quorum of the Twelve Apostles, 1849. Settled at Ogden, Weber County, Utah Territory, 1869; served as president of the Weber Stake, 1869–1877. Served as church historian, 1889–1899. Served as president of the Quorum of the Twelve, 1898–1899. Died at Ogden. (3.26, 3.28, 4.11, 4.20)

Richards, Jane Snyder (January 31, 1823–November 17, 1912). Born at Pamelia, Jefferson County, New York; daughter of Lovisa Comstock and Isaac Snyder. Baptized in Indiana, 1840. Settled at Nauvoo, Hancock County, Illinois, circa 1842. Married Franklin D. Richards, 1842; six children. Joined the Female Relief Society of Nauvoo, 1844. Migrated to the Salt Lake Valley, 1848. Settled in the Salt Lake City Fourteenth Ward. Moved to

Ogden, Weber County, Utah Territory, 1869. Appointed president of the Ogden Relief Society, 1872. As president of the Weber Stake Relief Society, served as the first female stake officer in the church, 1877–1908. Served as first counselor to Zina D. H. Young in the general Relief Society presidency, 1888–1901. Died at Ogden. (1.2, 3.26, 3.28, 4.11, 4.20, 4.27)

Richards, Louisa Lula Greene (April 8, 1849–September 9, 1944). Born at Kanesville, Pottawattamie County, Iowa; daughter of Susan Kent and Evan M. Greene. Migrated to the Salt Lake Valley, 1852. Lived in Utah County, Tooele County, and the Bear Lake Valley, Utah Territory; settled at Smithfield, Cache County, Utah Territory, 1865. Served as secretary of the Smithfield Relief Society. Attended school in Salt Lake City, 1869; began contributing to the *Salt Lake Herald* and *Deseret News*. Founded and edited the *Smithfield Sunday School Gazette,* 1869. First editor of the *Woman's Exponent,* 1872–1877. Married Levi Willard Richards, 1873; seven children. Assisted with the general board of the Young Ladies' Mutual Improvement Association and the Relief Society; member of the Primary general board for twenty-five years. Died at Salt Lake City. (3.23, 3.25, 3.28)

Richards, Mary Thompson (October 21, 1827–September 10, 1905). Born at Alston, Cumberland, England; daughter of Phebe Robson and John Thompson. Immigrated to the United States and settled at Kirtland, Geauga County, Ohio, 1836. Joined the Female Relief Society of Nauvoo, Hancock County, Illinois, 1842. Married first Willard Richards as a plural wife, 1846; two children. Migrated to the Salt Lake Valley, 1848. Widowed, 1854. Participated in the Salt Lake City Fourteenth Ward Relief Society, 1856. Married second Franklin D. Richards as a plural wife, 1857; four children. Settled at Farmington, Davis County, Utah Territory, 1860. Appointed counselor in the Davis Stake Relief Society presidency, 1882. Moved to Logan, Cache County, Utah Territory, 1885; served as matron of the Logan temple. Died at Riverside, Box Elder County, Utah; buried at Farmington. (1.2, 2.3, 4.3)

Richards, Rhoda Harriet Foss (April 19, 1830–November 19, 1881). Born at Saco, York County, Maine; daughter of Sarah Brackett Carter and Calvin Ira Foss. Baptized by her uncle Wilford Woodruff, 1844. Migrated to the Salt Lake Valley, 1850. Married first Willard Richards as a plural wife, 1851; one child. Widowed, 1854. Served on the visiting committee of the Salt Lake City Fourteenth Ward Relief Society, 1856. Married second Franklin D. Richards as a plural wife, 1857; four children. Settled at Farmington, Davis County, Utah Territory, 1858. Served as secretary to Aurelia Spencer Rogers in the first Primary presidency in Farmington. Died at Farmington. (2.3)

Richards, Willard (June 24, 1804–March 11, 1854). Born at Hopkinton, Middlesex County, Massachusetts; son of Rhoda Howe and Joseph Richards. Baptized, 1836. Married Jennetta Richards, 1838; participated in plural marriage. Ordained a member of the Quorum of the Twelve Apostles, 1840. Appointed recorder for the temple in Nauvoo, Hancock County, Illinois, and Joseph Smith's scribe, 1841; church historian, 1842; and church recorder, 1843. Admitted to the Council of Fifty, 1844. With Joseph and Hyrum Smith in the jail in Carthage, Hancock County, Illinois, when the Smiths were murdered. Migrated to the Salt Lake Valley, 1847. Appointed second counselor to Brigham Young in the First Presidency, 1847. Died at Salt Lake City. (1.2, 3.6, 4.28)

Richardson, Grace Rose (January 7, 1827–August 29, 1881). Born at Dundee, Angus, Scotland; daughter of Elspeth and John Rose. Emigrated from Scotland aboard the *John M. Wood* and migrated to the Salt Lake Valley, 1854. Married Darwin Richardson,

1854; three children. Elected to the visiting committee of the Salt Lake City Fourteenth Ward Relief Society, 1856. Died at Salt Lake City. (2.3)

Rigdon Ellis, Nancy (December 8, 1822–November 1, 1887). Born at Pittsburgh; daughter of Phebe Brooks and Sidney Rigdon. Baptized in Ohio, circa 1830. Lived at Kirtland, Geauga County, Ohio, 1831; at Salem, Essex County, Massachusetts, 1836; at Kirtland, 1837; at Far West, Caldwell County, Missouri, 1838; and at Commerce (later Nauvoo), Hancock County, Illinois, 1839. Joined the Female Relief Society of Nauvoo at its first meeting, March 17, 1842. Reportedly rejected a proposal from Joseph Smith during the summer of 1842, leading to public controversy involving Smith, the Rigdon family, and John C. Bennett. Moved to Pittsburgh, 1844. Married Robert Ellis, 1846; nine children. Died at Pittsburgh. (1.2)

Riley, Mary Annie Emmett (December 20, 1853–August 9, 1940). Born at Salt Lake City; daughter of Harriett Emmett and James Riley. Moved to Ogden, Weber County, Utah Territory, circa 1855; settled in the Ogden Second Ward. Served as counselor to Emily Tanner Richards in the first Young Ladies' Mutual Improvement Association presidency organized in Ogden. Died at Ogden. (3.26)

Riter, Rebecca Wollerton Dilworth (August 3, 1815–December 24, 1895). Born at West Chester, Chester County, Pennsylvania; daughter of Eliza Wollerton and Caleb Dilworth. Married Levi Evans Riter, 1830; seven children. Baptized in Pennsylvania, circa 1838–1839. Migrated to the Salt Lake Valley, 1847. Settled at Salt Lake City. Died at Logan, Cache County, Utah Territory; buried at Salt Lake City. (3.13)

Robertson, Jasper (May 8, 1847–January 17, 1916). Born at Walkerville, Green County, Illinois; son of Jane Hunter and Nichols Robertson. Migrated to Utah Territory, 1862; settled at Fountain Green, Sanpete County, Utah Territory, 1863. Married Rhoda Ellen Guymon, 1871. Moved to Orangeville, Emery County, Utah Territory, 1880. Served as the first bishop of the Orangeville Ward, 1882–1906. Died at Orangeville. (4.25)

Robertson, Rhoda Ellen Guymon (April 27, 1853–December 29, 1922). Born at Springville, Utah County, Utah Territory; daughter of Rhoda Ellen Leech and James Guymon. Married Jasper Robertson, 1871; eleven children. Lived at Fountain Green, Sanpete County, Utah Territory. Moved to Orangeville, Emery County, Utah Territory, 1880. Appointed second counselor to Caroline Curtis in the Orangeville Relief Society, 1882; served as president, 1883–circa 1905. Died at Orangeville. (4.25)

Robinson, Angeline Eliza Works (August 22, 1814–April 8, 1880). Born at Aurelius, Cayuga County, New York; daughter of Abigail Marks and Asa D. Works. Baptized, 1835, at Kirtland, Geauga County, Ohio; taught school at Kirtland. Married Ebenezer Robinson, 1835; one child. Migrated to Caldwell County, Missouri, 1837; settled at Commerce (later Nauvoo), Hancock County, Illinois, 1839; lived in the Nauvoo Fourth Ward. Joined the Female Relief Society of Nauvoo, 1842. Followed Sidney Rigdon after the death of Joseph Smith in 1844; affiliated with the Reorganized Church of Jesus Christ of Latter Day Saints, circa 1863. Lived in Pennsylvania and Iowa. Died near Pleasanton, Decatur County, Iowa. (1.2, 1.6)

Robinson, Athalia Rigdon (August 1821–1906). Born at Warren, Trumbull County, Ohio; daughter of Phebe Brooks and Sidney Rigdon. Married George Washington Robinson, 1837; five children. Settled at Nauvoo, Hancock County, Illinois, by 1840; lived in the Nauvoo First Ward. Joined the Female Relief Society of Nauvoo as a founding member, March 17, 1842. Left the church with her husband, circa July 1842; later affiliated with Sidney Rigdon's Church of Christ. Moved to Friendship, Allegany County, New York, 1847. Died at Friendship. (1.2)

Robinson, Laurinda Maria Atwood Pinkham (May 3, 1821–March 1, 1895). Born at Mansfield, Tolland County, Connecticut; daughter of Anna Hartshorn and Elisha Atwood. Lived at Nauvoo, Hancock County, Illinois, by early 1842. Married first Sumner Pinkham, 1842; one child. Married second Joseph Lee Robinson as a plural wife, 1847; eight children. Migrated to the Salt Lake Valley, 1848. Settled at Farmington, Davis County, Utah Territory. Started manufacturing silk, 1876. Appointed president of the Davis Stake Silk Association, 1879. Died at Farmington. (3.30)

Robinson James, Sophia (July 5, 1808–December 26, 1888). Born at Pawlet, Rutland County, Vermont; daughter of Mary Upham and Ephraim Robinson. Lived at Kirtland, Geauga County, Ohio, circa 1836. Joined the Female Relief Society of Nauvoo, Hancock County, Illinois, as a founding member, March 17, 1842. Married Lewis James, 1844; two children. Settled at La Harpe, Hancock County, by 1850. Died at La Harpe. (1.2, 4.28)

Rogers, Aurelia Read Spencer (October 4, 1834–August 19, 1922). Born at Deep River, Middlesex County, Connecticut; daughter of Catherine Curtis and Orson Spencer. Lived at Nauvoo, Hancock County, Illinois, and at Winter Quarters, unorganized U.S. territory. Migrated to the Salt Lake Valley, 1848. Married Thomas Rogers, 1851; twelve children. Settled at Farmington, Davis County, Utah Territory. Served as secretary in the Farmington Relief Society, 1871–1893. Initiated the creation of a church children's organization; served as the president of the newly formed Primary Association, 1878–1880. Appointed president of the Davis Stake Primary, 1880. Served on the Primary general board. Elected as a delegate and attended the Woman Suffrage Convention at Atlanta and the second triennial Congress of the National Council of Women at Washington DC, 1895. Died at Farmington; buried at Salt Lake City. (3.30, 4.3, 4.5)

Rogerson, Sarah Jane Perkins (January 17, 1861–May 3, 1936). Born at Parowan, Iron County, Utah Territory; daughter of Jane Benson and John Perkins. Married John Edward Rogerson, 1878; five children. Settled at Monticello, San Juan County, Utah Territory, 1888. Worked as the first schoolteacher in Monticello. Served as San Juan County clerk for fifteen years and as secretary to the Monticello town board for eighteen years. Served as the secretary of the San Juan Stake Relief Society, 1888–1892. Served as the president of the Monticello Primary and secretary of the Monticello Relief Society for approximately twenty years. Died at Monticello. (4.21)

Russell, Sarah Eliza (August 12, 1840–December 28, 1913). Born at Far West, Caldwell County, Missouri; daughter of Mary Walton and Isaac Russell. Lived at Far West and at Richmond, Ray County, Missouri. Migrated to the Salt Lake Valley, 1861. Served as secretary (1868–1876) and counselor (1876–1883) to Sarah M. Kimball in the Salt Lake City Fifteenth Ward Relief Society presidency. Served as president of the Fifteenth Ward Young Ladies' Retrenchment Association, 1870–1883. Moved to Mesa, Maricopa County, Arizona Territory, circa 1883; served as Primary president in Mesa. Moved to Mexico, 1889; lived at Colonia Juarez and Chuichupa and continued to serve in the Young Ladies' Mutual

Improvement Association and Relief Society. Returned to Arizona Territory, 1911. Died at Mesa. (3.12)

Savage, Annie Fenn Adkins (February 6, 1836–November 30, 1893). Born at Leighton Buzzard, Bedfordshire, England; daughter of Hannah Fenn and Robert Adkins. Immigrated to New York aboard the *Thornton,* 1856. Married Charles Roscoe Savage, 1857; eleven children. Migrated to the Salt Lake Valley, 1860. Settled in the Salt Lake City Twentieth Ward. Served in the Twentieth Ward Relief Society presidency as a counselor to Margaret T. Smoot, 1868–1872, and as president, 1877–1880. Died at Salt Lake City. (3.25)

Scoles Teasdale, Marion Eliza (April 6, 1865–December 17, 1898). Born at Marylebone, London; daughter of Hannah Britten and Matthew Scoles. Baptized at London, 1883. Appointed second counselor in the North London Branch Relief Society presidency, 1887. Immigrated to the United States, 1891; settled at Logan, Cache County, Utah Territory. Taught school and participated in Sunday school, the Young Ladies' Mutual Improvement Association, and the Relief Society. Moved to Nephi, Juab County, Utah Territory, circa 1895. Married George Teasdale, 1897. Died at Nephi. (4.22)

Seely, Charlotte Lenore Reynolds (November 4, 1856–February 18, 1938). Born at Pleasant Grove, Utah County, Utah Territory; daughter of Hannah Johnson and Levi Reynolds. Married William Hazard Seely, 1877; nine children. Settled at Indianola, Sanpete County, Utah Territory, circa 1877. Moved to Birch Creek, Sanpete County, 1898, and to Mount Pleasant, Sanpete County, 1912. Served as an ordinance worker in the Manti temple, 1912–1914. Died at Mount Pleasant. (4.7)

Seely, Hannah Olsson (November 27, 1842–November 27, 1934). Born at Skurup, Malmöhus, Sweden; daughter of Kjerstina Persson and Hans Olsson. Baptized in Sweden, 1855. Immigrated to the United States and traveled to the Salt Lake Valley, 1862. Settled at Mount Pleasant, Sanpete County, Utah Territory. Married Orange Seely, 1863; nine children. Settled at Castle Dale, Emery County, Utah Territory, circa 1879. Owned and operated the first hotel in Castle Dale. Served as first counselor in the first Castle Dale Ward Relief Society presidency. Died at Castle Dale. (4.25)

Selman, Mormon Vernon (July 4, 1855–November 13, 1929). Born at Whitchurch, Glamorgan, Wales; son of Margaret Giles and Isaac Selman. Baptized in Wales, 1864. Immigrated to the United States aboard the *Arkwright* and traveled to the Salt Lake Valley, 1866. Lived at Wellsville, Cache County, Utah Territory; at St. George, Washington County, Utah Territory; and at Payson, Utah County, Utah Territory. Married Louisa Jane Daniels, 1877; participated in plural marriage. Appointed to serve a mission to Indianola, Sanpete County, Utah Territory, 1877; lived there twenty-two years. Moved to Vineyard and Provo, Utah County, by 1900. Died at Provo. (4.7)

Sessions Parry, Martha (Patty) Bartlett (February 4, 1795–December 14, 1892). Born at Newry, York County, Maine; daughter of Martha Anna Hall and Enoch Bartlett. Married David Sessions, 1812; eight children. Baptized in Maine, 1834. Moved to Far West, Caldwell County, Missouri, 1836, and to Nauvoo, Hancock County, Illinois, by 1840. Later identified herself as a plural wife of Joseph Smith, married on March 9, 1842. Joined the Female Relief Society of Nauvoo at its second meeting, March 24, 1842. Migrated to the Salt Lake Valley, 1847. Settled at Salt Lake City. Widowed, 1850. Married John Parry, 1851;

widowed, 1868. Moved to Bountiful, Davis County, Utah Territory, 1872. Delivered thousands of babies as a midwife. Died at Bountiful. (1.2)

Sewall, May Wright Thompson (May 27, 1844–July 22, 1920). Born at Milwaukee; daughter of Mary Weeks Brackett and Philander Montague Wright. Graduated from Northwestern University, 1866. Married first Edward Thompson, circa 1872. Moved to Indianapolis. Widowed, circa 1876. Married second Theodore Lovett Sewall, 1880. Founder and principal of the Girls' Classical School in Indianapolis. Helped found the Indiana Association for Promoting Woman's Suffrage. Served as an officer on the National Council of Women, 1888–1899. Led the World's Congress of Representative Women held at the Chicago World's Fair, 1893. Appointed president of the International Council of Women, 1889. Died at Indianapolis. (4.27)

Shaw, Anna Howard (February 14, 1847–July 2, 1919). Born at Newcastle upon Tyne, Northumberland, England; daughter of Nicolas Stott and Thomas Shaw. Immigrated to the United States, 1851. Lived at Lawrence, Essex County, Massachusetts; moved to Michigan, 1859. Became a licensed Methodist preacher, circa 1870. Studied at Albion College, 1873–1876. Graduated from the Boston University theological school, 1878. Ordained in the Methodist Protestant Church, 1880. Became a lecturer for the Massachusetts State Suffrage Association, 1885. Graduated from Boston University Medical School, 1886. Appointed the superintendent of franchise for the Woman's Christian Temperance Union, 1886. Served as vice president of the National American Woman Suffrage Association, 1892–1904, and as president, 1904–1915. Served as the chair of the woman's committee for the Council of National Defense, 1917–1919; awarded the Distinguished Service Medal. Died at Moylan, Delaware County, Pennsylvania. (4.27)

Shipp Roberts, Margaret (Maggie) Curtis (December 17, 1849–March 13, 1926). Born at St. Louis; daughter of Margaret Morgan and Theodore Curtis. Migrated to the Salt Lake Valley, 1857. Married first Milford Bard Shipp as a plural wife, 1867; nine children. Attended the Woman's Medical College in Philadelphia, 1875–1883. Practiced medicine in Salt Lake City, 1883–1922; taught classes in obstetrics and nursing. Coeditor of and contributing writer to the *Salt Lake Sanitarian,* 1888–1889. Divorced, 1888 or 1892. Married second Brigham Henry Roberts as a plural wife, circa 1890–1894. Helped establish Relief Society nursing classes and school, 1898–1916. Accompanied Roberts on a mission to New York City, 1922. Died at Brooklyn, Kings County, New York; buried at Salt Lake City. (4.17)

Shipp, Samantha (Manty) Jane McDonough Sewell Dotson (May 12, 1844–November 26, 1929). Born at Somerville, Tallahatchie County, Mississippi; daughter of Mary Ann Forrester and Ira McDonough. Married first William Sewell, 1863; two children. Moved to Louisiana, 1866. Widowed, 1869. Baptized, 1870. Lived at Beaver, Beaver County, Utah Territory, by 1870. Married second William Lazarus Hardiman Dotson, 1870; one child. Married third Austin Shipp, 1873; two children. Moved to Castle Dale, Emery County, Utah Territory, 1888; was the first trained midwife at Castle Dale. Participated in the Emery Stake Relief Society. Lived at Driggs, Fremont County, Idaho, by 1910. Died at Phoenix, Maricopa County, Arizona. (4.25)

Simmons, Harriet Bradford (March 30, 1821–March 14, 1891). Born in Jefferson County, Illinois; daughter of Sarah Hood and George Bradford. Married Leven Simmons, 1836; twelve children. Baptized, circa 1842. Migrated to the Salt Lake Valley, 1852. Settled at

Spanish Fork, Utah County, Utah Territory. Served as first counselor to Letitia Ann Davis in the Spanish Fork Second Ward Relief Society presidency. Died at Spanish Fork. (2.5)

Simons, Betsey Jane Tenney Loose (December 1, 1824–January 14, 1904). Born at Hanover, Chautauque County, New York; daughter of Eliza Webb and William Tenney. Baptized, 1834. Moved to Kirtland, Geauga County, Ohio, 1835; to Far West, Caldwell County, Missouri, 1838; and to Quincy, Adams County, Illinois, circa 1839. Married first Robert Loose, 1844; three children. Widowed, 1854. Migrated to the Salt Lake Valley, 1860. Married second Orawell Simons as a plural wife, 1861; two children. Helped settle the Muddy River Valley, Nevada, 1865–1866. Moved to Payson, Utah County, Utah Territory, 1866. Appointed president of the Payson Relief Society, 1868; served for twenty-four years. Died at Payson. (4.7)

Simons, Martha Dixon (June 27, 1825–November 14, 1916). Born at Sackville, Westmorland County, New Brunswick, Canada; daughter of Elizabeth Humphrey and Charles Dixon. Baptized at Kirtland, Geauga County, Ohio, 1837. Married Orawell Simons, 1846; nine children. Migrated to the Salt Lake Valley, 1854. Settled at Payson, Utah County, Utah Territory. Served as a Relief Society teacher, Sunday school teacher, and district superintendent for the Young Ladies' Retrenchment Society; served as president of the Payson First Ward Relief Society, 1892–1901. Died at Salt Lake City. (4.7)

Sloan, Edward Lennox (November 9, 1830–August 2, 1874). Born at Conlig, County Down, Ireland; son of Mary Lennox and John Sloan. Baptized in Ireland, before 1848. Married Mary Elizabeth Wallace, 1851; participated in plural marriage. Immigrated to the United States aboard the *Amazon* and migrated to the Salt Lake Valley, 1863. Journalist and writer associated with the *Latter-day Saints' Millennial Star, Deseret News,* and *Daily Telegraph;* founder and editor of the *Salt Lake Herald.* Encouraged the establishment of the *Woman's Exponent,* founded in 1872. Died at Salt Lake City. (3.1, 3.21)

Smith, Amanda Melissa Barnes Smith (February 22, 1809–June 30, 1886). Born at Becket, Berkshire County, Massachusetts; daughter of Fanny Johnson and Ezekiel Barnes. Married first Warren Smith, 1826; five children. Baptized, 1831. Moved to Kirtland, Geauga County, Ohio, 1837. Survived the attack at the Hawn's Mill settlement on Shoal Creek, Caldwell County, Missouri, 1838; husband and one son were killed. Moved to Quincy, Adams County, Illinois, 1838. Married second Warren Smith (no relation to first husband), 1839; three children. Moved to Nauvoo, Hancock County, Illinois. Joined the Female Relief Society of Nauvoo, 1842. Migrated to the Salt Lake Valley, 1850. Divorced, 1850. Served as assistant secretary in the Great Salt Lake City Relief Society, 1854. Served as counselor to Priscilla Staines in the Salt Lake City Twelfth Ward Relief Society presidency, 1868–1879. Died at Richmond, Cache County, Utah Territory. (1.2, 1.5, 2.1, 3.13, 3.16, 3.17, 4.1)

Smith, Augusta Bowen Cleveland (December 7, 1828–March 27, 1903). Born at Cincinnati; daughter of Sarah Maryette Kingsley and John Alexander Cleveland. Married John Lyman Smith, 1845; eight children. Migrated to the Salt Lake Valley, 1847. Lived at Salt Lake City. Moved to Meadow, Millard County, Utah Territory, by 1868. Served as a member of the visiting committee of the Relief Society in Fillmore, Millard County. Moved to St. George, Washington County, Utah Territory, by 1880. Died at Haden, Fremont County, Idaho. (3.8)

Smith, Bathsheba Wilson Bigler (May 3, 1822–September 20, 1910). Born at Shinnston, Harrison County, Virginia (later in West Virginia); daughter of Susannah Ogden and Mark Bigler. Baptized, 1837. Moved to Far West, Caldwell County, Missouri, 1837; to Quincy, Adams County, Illinois, 1839; and to Nauvoo, Hancock County, Illinois, 1840. Married George Albert Smith, 1841; three children. Joined the Female Relief Society of Nauvoo as a founding member, March 17, 1842. Officiated in the Nauvoo temple, 1845. Migrated to the Salt Lake Valley, 1849. Appointed a teacher in the Salt Lake City Thirteenth Ward Relief Society, 1868. Served on the executive board of the Deseret Hospital Association. Served as treasurer of the Salt Lake Stake Relief Society; as counselor to Rachel Ivins Grant in the Thirteenth Ward Relief Society presidency; as counselor to Mary Isabella Horne in the Senior Retrenchment Association; and as treasurer and president of the Salt Lake City Seventeenth Ward Relief Society. Appointed second counselor to Zina D. H. Young in the general Relief Society presidency, 1888. Served as the fourth general president of the Relief Society, 1901–1910. Died at Salt Lake City. (1.2, 3.7, 3.12, 3.13, 3.16, 3.17, 3.19, 3.24, 3.26, 4.1, 4.5, 4.11, 4.20, 4.28)

Smith Bidamon, Emma Hale (July 10, 1804–April 30, 1879). Born at Willingborough Township, Susquehanna County, Pennsylvania; daughter of Elizabeth Lewis and Isaac Hale. Married first Joseph Smith, 1827; eleven children. Served as a scribe during the translation of the Book of Mormon, 1828. Baptized, 1830. Moved to Kirtland, Geauga County, Ohio, 1831; lived at Hiram, Portage County, Ohio, 1831–1832. Edited *A Collection of Sacred Hymns, for the Church of Jesus Christ of Latter Day Saints,* published at Kirtland, 1835. Lived at Far West, Caldwell County, Missouri, 1838; moved to Commerce (later Nauvoo), Hancock County, Illinois, 1839. Joined the Female Relief Society of Nauvoo as a founding member and appointed its first president, March 17, 1842. Widowed, June 27, 1844. Lived at Fulton, Fulton County, Illinois, 1846–1847; returned to Nauvoo, early 1847. Married second Lewis Crum Bidamon, 1847. Affiliated with the Reorganized Church of Jesus Christ of Latter Day Saints, 1860. Died at Nauvoo. (1.1–1.3, 1.5, 1.6, 1.10, 3.27, 3.28, 4.4, 4.5, 4.10, 4.20, 4.28)

Smith, George Albert (June 26, 1817–September 1, 1875). Born at Potsdam, St. Lawrence County, New York; son of Clarissa Lyman and John Smith. Baptized, 1832. Ordained a member of the Quorum of the Twelve Apostles, 1839, at Far West, Caldwell County, Missouri. Served a mission to England, 1839–1841. Married Bathsheba W. Bigler, 1841; participated in plural marriage. Admitted to the Council of Fifty, 1844. Traveled to the Salt Lake Valley with the Brigham Young pioneer company, 1847. Appointed church historian and recorder, 1854. Appointed first counselor to Brigham Young in the First Presidency, 1868. Died at Salt Lake City. (3.23)

Smith, Hyrum (February 9, 1800–June 27, 1844). Born at Tunbridge, Orange County, Vermont; son of Lucy Mack and Joseph Smith Sr. Married first Jerusha Barden, 1826; participated in plural marriage. Baptized by Joseph Smith, 1829. One of the Eight Witnesses of the Book of Mormon, June 1829. Among the six original members of the church, organized April 6, 1830. Presided over a branch of the church at Colesville, Broome County, New York, 1830–1831. Moved to Kirtland, Geauga County, Ohio, 1831. Ordained a high priest, 1831. Appointed to the Kirtland high council, 1834. Appointed assistant counselor in the presidency of the church, 1837. Widowed, 1837. Appointed counselor in the First

Presidency, 1837. Married second Mary Fielding, 1837. Moved to Far West, Caldwell County, Missouri, 1838. Imprisoned at Liberty, Clay County, Missouri, 1838–1839. Arrived at Quincy, Adams County, Illinois, 1839; moved to Commerce (later Nauvoo), Hancock County, Illinois, 1839. Appointed patriarch of the church, 1840, and a prophet, seer, and revelator in the First Presidency, 1841. Elected to the Nauvoo City Council, 1841. Served as the vice mayor of Nauvoo, 1842–circa 1843, and as a member of the Nauvoo temple committee, 1843. Admitted to the Council of Fifty, 1844. Murdered at Carthage, Hancock County. (1.2, 1.10, 1.13, 3.13)

Smith, John Henry (September 18, 1848–October 13, 1911). Born at Carbunca, Pottawattamie County, Iowa; son of Sarah Ann Libby and George Albert Smith. Migrated to the Salt Lake Valley, 1849. Baptized, 1856. Married Sarah Farr, 1866; participated in plural marriage. Lived at Salt Lake City and Provo, Utah County, Utah Territory. Appointed counselor in the Provo Fourth Ward bishopric, 1867. Served a mission to Europe, 1874–1875. Appointed bishop of the Salt Lake City Seventeenth Ward, 1875. Ordained to the Quorum of the Twelve Apostles by Wilford Woodruff, 1880. Presided over the European mission, 1882–1884. Appointed second counselor to Joseph Fielding Smith in the First Presidency, 1910. Died at Salt Lake City. (4.3, 4.17, 4.28)

Smith, Joseph, Jr. (December 23, 1805–June 27, 1844). Founder and first president of The Church of Jesus Christ of Latter-day Saints, 1830–1844. Born at Sharon, Windsor County, Vermont; son of Lucy Mack and Joseph Smith Sr. Married Emma Hale, 1827. Married other women in plural marriages. Experienced his first vision of Deity, 1820. Published the Book of Mormon and organized the Church of Jesus Christ, 1830. Led followers from New York to Ohio, to Missouri, and to Illinois, 1831–1839. Published the Book of Commandments, 1833; published the Doctrine and Covenants, 1835. Organized the Quorum of the Twelve Apostles, 1835. Dedicated the temple at Kirtland, Geauga County, Ohio, 1836. Assisted in organizing the Female Relief Society of Nauvoo, Hancock County, Illinois, 1842. Served as mayor of Nauvoo, lieutenant general of the Nauvoo Legion, and regent of Nauvoo University. Ran as a candidate for president of the United States, 1844. Murdered at Carthage, Hancock County. (1.1, 1.2, 1.5, 1.10, 1.13, 2.2, 2.5, 3.5, 3.6, 3.13, 3.20, 3.25, 3.27–3.29, 4.1, 4.3–4.5, 4.7, 4.9–4.11, 4.15, 4.18, 4.20, 4.24, 4.25, 4.28)

Smith, Joseph Fielding, Sr. (November 13, 1838–November 19, 1918). Born at Far West, Caldwell County, Missouri; son of Mary Fielding and Hyrum Smith. Migrated to the Salt Lake Valley, 1848. Baptized, 1852. Served a mission to the Sandwich Islands, 1854–1857. Married Levira A. C. Smith, April 4, 1859; participated in plural marriage. Served missions to England, 1860–1863, and Hawaii, 1864; served as president of the European mission, 1874–1875, 1877. Worked in the Church Historian's Office. Ordained to the Quorum of the Twelve Apostles and appointed counselor to the First Presidency, 1866; served with three successive presidents of the church. Served as the sixth president of The Church of Jesus Christ of Latter-day Saints, 1901–1918. Died at Salt Lake City. (3.30, 4.3, 4.11, 4.28)

Smith, Lucy Mack (July 8, 1775–May 14, 1856). Born at Gilsum, Cheshire County, New Hampshire; daughter of Lydia Gates and Solomon Mack Sr. Married Joseph Smith Sr., 1796; eleven children. Baptized, April 6, 1830. Lived at The Kingdom, unincorporated settlement near Waterloo, Seneca County, New York, 1830–1831. Led a company of approximately eighty branch members from Fayette, Seneca County, to Kirtland, Geauga County,

Ohio, 1831. Moved to Far West, Caldwell County, Missouri, 1838; to Quincy, Adams County, Illinois, 1839; and to Commerce (later Nauvoo), Hancock County, Illinois, 1839. Widowed, 1840. Joined the Female Relief Society of Nauvoo at its second meeting, March 24, 1842. Lived at Colchester, McDonough County, Illinois, 1846–1852. Wrote a narrative history of the Smith family, published as *Biographical Sketches of Joseph Smith,* 1853. Died at Nauvoo. (1.2)

Smith, Lucy Meserve Smith (February 9, 1817–October 5, 1892). Born at Newry, Oxford County, Maine; daughter of Lucy Meserve Bean and Josiah Smith. Baptized, 1837. Lived at Nauvoo, Hancock County, Illinois, by 1844; worked for Emma Smith, 1844–1845. Married George Albert Smith as a plural wife, 1844; two children. Moved to Winter Quarters, unorganized U.S. territory, 1846; taught school in Kanesville, Pottawattamie County, Iowa, and at the Pawnee Mission School in Bellevue, Jackson County, Iowa. Migrated to the Salt Lake Valley, 1849. Taught school in the Salt Lake City Seventeenth Ward, 1851. Settled at Provo, Utah County, Utah Territory, 1852. Taught school in Provo. Served as president of the Relief Society in Provo. Died at Salt Lake City. (2.4)

Smith, Mary Fielding (July 21, 1801–September 21, 1852). Born at Honeydon, Bedfordshire, England; daughter of Rachel Ibbotson and John Fielding. Immigrated to Toronto, Upper Canada, 1834. Baptized, 1836. Migrated to Kirtland, Geauga County, Ohio, 1837. Married first Hyrum Smith, 1837; two children. Moved to Far West, Caldwell County, Missouri, 1838; to Quincy, Adams County, Illinois, 1839; and to Commerce (later Nauvoo), Hancock County, Illinois, 1839. Lived in the Nauvoo Fourth Ward. Joined the Female Relief Society of Nauvoo, 1842. Widowed, 1844. Married second Heber C. Kimball as a plural wife, 1844. Migrated to the Salt Lake Valley, 1848. Settled at Salt Lake City. Died at Salt Lake City. (1.2)

Smoot, Margaret Thompson McMeans Adkinson (April 16, 1809–September 1, 1884). Born in Chester County, South Carolina; daughter of Esther Hunter and Anthony McMeans. Married first Charles Adkinson, 1826; one child. Baptized in Tennessee, 1834. Moved to Far West, Caldwell County, Missouri, 1837. Widowed, 1838. Married second Abraham Owen Smoot, 1838. Moved to Nauvoo, Hancock County, Illinois. Joined the Female Relief Society of Nauvoo, 1842. Migrated to the Salt Lake Valley, 1847. Served as president of the Salt Lake City Twentieth Ward Relief Society, 1868–1872. Moved to Provo, Utah County, Utah Territory, 1872. Served as president of the Utah Stake Retrenchment Society, president of the Utah Stake Young Ladies' Mutual Improvement Association, and president of the Utah County Silk Association. Served as president of the Utah Stake Relief Society, 1878–1884. Died at Provo. (1.2, 3.13, 3.15–3.17, 3.23, 4.28)

Snow Smith, Eliza Roxcy (January 21, 1804–December 5, 1887). Born at Becket, Berkshire County, Massachusetts; daughter of Rosetta Leonora Pettibone and Oliver Snow. Moved to Mantua, Trumbull County, Ohio, circa 1806. Baptized in Ohio, 1835. Moved to Kirtland, Geauga County, Ohio, 1837; to Adam-ondi-Ahman, Daviess County, Missouri, 1838; and to Commerce (later Nauvoo), Hancock County, Illinois, 1839. Founding member of the Female Relief Society of Nauvoo, March 17, 1842; served as the organization's first secretary. Later identified herself as a plural wife of Joseph Smith, married on June 29, 1842. Married second Brigham Young as a plural wife, 1844. Migrated to the Salt Lake Valley, 1847. Oversaw the reestablishment and operation of Relief Societies throughout Utah, 1868–1880. Participated in mass meetings protesting antipolygamy legislation. Participated in the Ladies' Cooperative Retrenchment Association. Served a mission to Palestine to witness the rededication of the land for the return of the Jews, 1872–1873. Served as assistant president to Emmeline B. Wells on the Central Grain Committee, circa 1876. Served as the second general president of the Relief Society, 1880–1887. Adopted the surname Smith after 1879. Died at Salt Lake City. (1.2–1.4, 1.6, 1.8, 1.14, 2.2, 3.5–3.9, 3.12, 3.13, 3.15–3.17, 3.19–3.21, 3.23–3.25, 3.27–3.30, 4.1, 4.3–4.6, 4.9–4.12, 4.14–4.16, 4.18, 4.20, 4.24, 4.28)

Snow, Harriet Amelia Prichard Squire (September 13, 1819–May 12, 1890). Born at Aurora, Portage County, Ohio; daughter of Elizabeth Prichard and Aaron Squire. Baptized, 1844. Moved to Nauvoo, Hancock County, Illinois, circa 1846. Married Lorenzo Snow as a plural wife, 1846; five children. Migrated to the Salt Lake Valley, 1848. Moved to Brigham City, Box Elder County, Utah Territory, circa 1856. Served as president of the Brigham City Relief Society. Served as president of the Box Elder Stake Relief Society, 1878–1890. Died at Brigham City. (3.28)

Snow, James Chauncy (January 11, 1817–April 30, 1884). Born at Chesterfield, Cheshire County, New Hampshire; son of Sarah Sawyer Hastings and Gardner Snow. Baptized, 1833. Married Eliza Ann Carter, 1838; participated in plural marriage. Lived at Kirtland, Geauga County, Ohio; at Far West, Caldwell County, Missouri; and at Nauvoo, Hancock County, Illinois. Migrated to the Salt Lake Valley, 1852. Settled at Provo, Utah County, Utah Territory; served as president of the Provo Stake, 1853–1858. Died at Sterling, Sanpete County, Utah Territory; buried at Manti, Sanpete County. (2.4)

Snow, Lorenzo (April 3, 1814–October 10, 1901). Born at Mantua, Portage County, Ohio; son of Rosetta Leonora Pettibone and Oliver Snow. Baptized at Kirtland, Geauga County, Ohio, 1836. Married Charlotte Merrill Squires, 1846; participated in plural marriage. Migrated to the Salt Lake Valley, 1848. Ordained a member of the Quorum of the Twelve Apostles, 1849. Appointed to colonize Brigham City, Box Elder County, Utah Territory, 1853. Appointed president of the Quorum of the Twelve, 1889. Served as president of the Salt Lake temple. Served as fifth president of The Church of Jesus Christ of Latter-day Saints, 1898–1901. Died at Salt Lake City; buried at Brigham City. (4.28)

Snow, Minerva White (March 22, 1822–April 1, 1896). Born at Northbridge, Worcester County, Massachusetts; daughter of Achsah Wing and Alden White. Baptized, 1834. Married Erastus Snow as a plural wife, 1844; nine children. Migrated to the Salt Lake Valley, 1848. Served as counselor to Mary Isabella Horne in the Salt Lake City Fourteenth Ward Retrenchment Association. Died at Manti, Sanpete County, Utah. (4.28)

Southworth, Lucinda Kempton (May 3, 1831–March 10, 1911). Born in Kennebec County, Maine; daughter of Hannah Bradford and John Kempton. Baptized in Illinois, circa 1839. Married Henry Larkin Southworth, 1853; seven children. Migrated to the Salt Lake Valley, 1853. Settled in the Salt Lake City Fourteenth Ward. Appointed counselor to Phebe Woodruff in the Fourteenth Ward Relief Society presidency, 1856; also served on the visiting and appraiser committees. Moved to Provo, Utah County, Utah Territory, circa 1858. Died at Provo. (2.3, 4.28)

Spencer, James (April 23, 1784–after 1844). Born at Downham, Lancashire, England; son of Jane and Thomas Spencer. Immigrated to the United States aboard the *Sheffield,* 1841; arrived at Nauvoo, Hancock County, Illinois, circa 1841. Married Mary Mitchell, 1844. Performed baptisms for deceased parents and siblings at Nauvoo, 1844. (1.11)

Spencer, John Henry (August 29, 1835–August 20, 1891). Born at Waddington, Yorkshire, England; son of Mary Earnshaw and Richard Spencer. Immigrated to the United States aboard the *Sheffield,* 1841. Lived in Pottawattamie County, Iowa. Migrated to the Salt Lake Valley, 1852. Married first Jerusha Kibbee Elmer, 1858; participated in plural marriage. Married second Lucy Lodica Elmer, 1860. Settled at Payson, Utah County, Utah Territory. Appointed to settle in Thistle Valley, Sanpete County, Utah Territory, 1877. Served as bishop of the Indianola Ward in Indianola, Sanpete County. Died at Payson. (4.7)

Spencer, Lucy Lodica Elmer (July 3, 1843–December 14, 1890). Born in Lee County, Iowa Territory; daughter of Lucina (Lucinda) and Hiram Elmer. Migrated to the Salt Lake Valley, 1852. Married first Richard Spencer, 1858; widowed, 1858. Married second John Henry Spencer as a plural wife, 1860; ten children. Lived at Payson, Utah County, Utah Territory. Moved to Thistle Valley, Sanpete County, Utah Territory, 1877. Served as president of the Indianola Relief Society in Indianola, Sanpete County. Died at Lake Shore, Utah County; buried at Payson. (4.7)

Spencer, Sara Andrews (October 21, 1837–October 20, 1909). Born at Savona, Steuben County, New York; daughter of Elizabeth Loomis and Orra Andrews. Married Henry C. Spencer, 1864; three children. President of the Woman Franchise Association in Washington DC, 1871–1876. One of the seventy-three women who attempted to vote but were refused in 1871. Secretary of the National Woman Suffrage Association, 1874–1881. Secretary of the American Red Cross Auxiliary Association, 1887–1892. Died in New York; buried at Washington DC. (4.27)

Spofford, Jane H. Snow (1828–December 19, 1905). Born at Hampden, Penobscot County, Maine; daughter of Sophronia and Calvin Snow. Married Caleb Wheeler Spofford. Lived at Washington DC, where she and her husband were the proprietors of Riggs House hotel. Represented the District of Columbia Suffrage Association at national meetings. Appointed treasurer of the National Woman Suffrage Association, 1879. Died at Hampden. (4.27)

Staines, Priscilla Mogridge Lowry (March 11, 1823–January 4, 1899). Born at Widbrook, Wiltshire, England; daughter of Mary Crook and John Mogridge. Baptized, circa 1842. Immigrated to Nauvoo, Hancock County, Illinois, aboard the *Fanny* and the *Maid of Iowa,* 1844. Migrated to the Salt Lake Valley, circa 1855–1856. Married first Samuel Lowry, 1846; one child. Married second William Carter Staines, 1865. Served as president of the Salt Lake City Twelfth Ward Relief Society, 1868–1879. Elected vice president to Eliza R. Snow in the Home Industries Association, 1876. Appointed treasurer of the Central Purchasing Grain Committee, 1876. Served on the finance committee of the Deseret Hospital Association. Died at Salt Lake City. (3.13, 3.25, 4.11)

Stanford, Elizabeth Young (December 26, 1836–February 14, 1909). Born at Falkirk, Stirling, Scotland; daughter of Martha Martin and Thomas Young. Married Joseph Stanford, 1859; eleven children. Immigrated to the United States aboard the *Underwriter* and traveled to the Salt Lake Valley, 1861. Settled at Ogden, Weber County, Utah Territory. Served as treasurer of the Ogden City Relief Society, 1874–1875. Appointed counselor in the Weber County Silk Association, 1879. Served as counselor to Sarah Herrick in the Weber Stake Young Ladies' Mutual Improvement Association (Y.L.M.I.A.), 1884–1892; served as the Weber Stake Y.L.M.I.A. president, 1892–1905. Died at Ogden. (3.28)

Stanton, Elizabeth Cady (November 12, 1815–October 26, 1902). Born at Johnstown, Fulton County, New York; daughter of Margaret Livingston and Daniel Cady. Graduated from the Troy Female Seminary at Troy, Rensselaer County, New York, 1832. Married Henry Brewster Stanton, 1840; seven children. Participated in the first women's rights convention at Seneca Falls, Seneca County, New York, 1848. Served as president of the National Woman Suffrage Association, 1869–1890, and as president of the National American Woman Suffrage Association, 1890–1896. Died at New York City. (4.27)

Stevens, Abigail Elizabeth Holman (July 3, 1836–March 5, 1912). Born at Conneautville, Crawford County, Pennsylvania; daughter of Rebecca Whitcomb Greenleaf and Joshua Sawyer Holman. Baptized, 1844. Migrated to the Salt Lake Valley, 1850. Married Walter Stevens, 1854; ten children. Lived at Holden, Millard County, Utah Territory, and Fruitland, San Juan County, New Mexico Territory. Served as president of the Burnham Ward Relief Society in San Juan County. Died at Fruitland; buried at Kirtland, San Juan County. (4.21)

Tackipo, Mary (circa 1846–?). Born in what later became Utah Territory. Lived at Thistle Precinct, Sanpete County, Utah Territory. Married Tackipo; widowed, 1883. Participated in the Indianola Ward Relief Society in Indianola, Sanpete County. (4.7)

Taft, Harriet Ogden (April 12, 1809–October 7, 1888). Born at Cromney, Newcastle District, Upper Canada; daughter of Elizabeth (Betsy) Henderson and John Ogden. Married Seth Taft, 1828; four children. Baptized in Michigan, 1845. Migrated to the Salt Lake Valley, 1847. Appointed president of the Salt Lake City Ninth Ward Relief Society, circa 1856. Died at Salt Lake City. (4.28)

Talmage, James Edward (September 21, 1862–July 27, 1933). Born at Hungerford, Berkshire, England; son of Susannah Preater and James Joyce Talmage. Baptized, 1873. Immigrated to the United States; arrived in Utah Territory, 1876. Studied at Brigham Young Academy, Lehigh University, and Johns Hopkins University. Taught at Brigham Young Academy, 1884–1888. Married Merry May Booth, 1888. Served as president of Latter-day Saints' University, 1888–1892. Awarded a doctoral degree from the church board of education, 1889. Served as president of the University of Deseret, 1894–1897. Ordained a member of the Quorum of the Twelve Apostles, 1911. Awarded an honorary doctoral degree from Lehigh University, 1912. Awarded honorary law degrees from Brigham Young University and the University of Utah, 1922. Died at Salt Lake City. (4.28)

Tanner, Rebecca Estella Moore (November 13, 1844–January 20, 1929). Born at Montebello Township, Hancock County, Illinois; daughter of Clarissa Jane Drollinger and John Harvey Moore. Migrated to the Salt Lake Valley, 1852. Settled at Payson, Utah County, Utah Territory. Married David Dan Tanner, 1861; fourteen children. Lived in the Thistle Valley, Sanpete County, Utah Territory, circa 1879–1905. Served in the Indianola Relief Society presidency in Indianola, Sanpete County, circa 1881–1883. Died at Provo, Utah County; buried at Payson. (4.7)

Taylor, Anstis Elmina Shepard (September 12, 1830–December 6, 1904). Born at Middlefield, Otsego County, New York; daughter of Rozita Bailey and Daniel Shepard. Baptized, 1856. Married George Hamilton Taylor, 1856; seven children. Migrated to the Salt Lake Valley, 1859. Settled in the Salt Lake City Fourteenth Ward. Appointed secretary of the Fourteenth Ward Relief Society, 1867; superintendent of the Fourteenth Ward Young

Ladies' Mutual Improvement Association (Y.L.M.I.A.), 1874; and counselor to Mary Isabella Horne in the Salt Lake Stake Relief Society presidency, 1877. Served as the general president of the Y.L.M.I.A., 1880–1904. Became an ex officio vice president of the National Council of Women in connection with the Y.L.M.I.A., 1891. Died at Salt Lake City. (3.29, 4.3, 4.28)

Taylor, John (November 1, 1808–July 25, 1887). Born at Milnthorpe, Westmoreland, England; son of Agnes Taylor and James Taylor. Emigrated from England to Upper Canada, circa 1832. Married Leonora Cannon, 1833; participated in plural marriage. Baptized in Canada, 1836. Moved to Kirtland, Geauga County, Ohio, circa 1837, and to Far West, Caldwell County, Missouri, 1838. Ordained a member of the Quorum of the Twelve Apostles, 1838. Moved to Nauvoo, Hancock County, Illinois, circa 1841. Admitted to the Council of Fifty, 1844. Migrated to the Salt Lake Valley, 1847. Member of the Utah territorial legislature, 1857–1876. Presided over the church after the death of Brigham Young, 1877. Served as third president of The Church of Jesus Christ of Latter-day Saints, 1880–1887. Died at Kaysville, Davis County, Utah Territory. (1.2, 3.6, 3.26, 3.27, 3.30, 4.2, 4.4, 4.5, 4.11, 4.20, 4.28)

Taylor, Leonora Cannon (October 6, 1796–December 9, 1868). Born at Peel, Isle of Man; daughter of Leonora Callister and George Cannon. Immigrated to Canada, 1831. Married John Taylor, 1833; four children. Baptized in Canada, 1836. Moved to Kirtland, Geauga County, Ohio; to Far West, Caldwell County, Missouri; to Quincy, Adams County, Illinois; to Montrose, Lee County, Iowa Territory; and to Nauvoo, Hancock County, Illinois, 1838–1846. Joined the Female Relief Society of Nauvoo as a founding member, March 17, 1842. Traveled to the Salt Lake Valley, 1847. Lived in the Salt Lake City Fourteenth Ward; participated in the Fourteenth Ward Relief Society. Died at Salt Lake City. (1.2, 1.6, 2.3, 4.5, 4.28)

Taylor, Margaret (Maggie) Young (April 24, 1837–May 3, 1919). Born at Westport, Fairfield County, Connecticut; daughter of Margaret Holden and Ebenezer Russell Young. Baptized in New Jersey, 1852. Married John Taylor as a plural wife, 1856; nine children. Migrated to the Salt Lake Valley, 1858. Lived in the Salt Lake City Fourteenth Ward; served as secretary and counselor in the Fourteenth Ward Relief Society presidency. Served as secretary of the Salt Lake Stake Relief Society. Served as counselor to Anstis Elmina S. Taylor in the Young Ladies' Mutual Improvement Association general presidency, 1880–1887. Died at Salt Lake City. (4.4)

Taylor, Pleasant Green (February 8, 1827–May 16, 1917). Born at Bowling Green, Warren County, Kentucky; son of Elizabeth Patrick and William Taylor. Baptized, 1837. Married Clara Lake, 1847; participated in plural marriage. Traveled to the Salt Lake Valley, 1850. Settled at Harrisville, Weber County, Utah Territory, circa 1851. Served as bishop of the Harrisville Ward, 1877–1896. Died at Harrisville; buried at Ogden, Weber County. (3.28)

Taylor, Sophia Whitaker (April 21, 1825–February 27, 1887). Born at Blakedown, Worcestershire, England; daughter of Sophia Turner and Thomas Whitaker. Baptized in England, 1840. Immigrated to the United States, circa 1847. Married John Taylor as a plural wife, 1847; seven children. Migrated to the Salt Lake Valley, 1847. Settled in the Salt Lake City Fourteenth Ward. Participated in the Fourteenth Ward Relief Society, as early as 1856. Served on the finance committee for Deseret Hospital. Died at Salt Lake City. (2.3, 4.11)

Thatcher, Fanny Caroline Decker Young (January 25, 1849–January 21, 1892). Born at Salt Lake City; daughter of Lucy Ann Decker and Brigham Young. Married George W. Thatcher, 1867; seven children. Served as president of the Salt Lake City Eighteenth Ward Young Ladies' Mutual Improvement Association (Y.L.M.I.A.), circa 1879–1880; served as treasurer of the general board of the Y.L.M.I.A., 1880–1892. Died at Salt Lake City. (4.4, 4.15)

Thomas, Caroline Stockdale (April 22, 1848–April 5, 1931). Born at Plymouth, Devon, England; daughter of Jane Johnson and Michael Stockdale. Immigrated to the United States aboard the *Hudson* and traveled to the Salt Lake Valley, 1864. Married Richard Kendall Thomas, 1865; twelve children. Represented the Young Ladies' Mutual Improvement Association at the National Council of Women's first triennial meeting in Washington DC, 1891. Served on the Relief Society general board, 1902–1921. Died at Salt Lake City. (4.27)

Thompson, Mary. See "Richards, Mary Thompson," or "Thompson Taylor, Mary Jane."

Thompson Taylor, Mary Jane (June 14, 1838–August 4, 1901). Born at Far West, Caldwell County, Missouri; daughter of Mercy Rachel Fielding and Robert Blashell Thompson. Lived at Nauvoo, Hancock County, Illinois. Migrated to the Salt Lake Valley, 1847. Married David Taylor, 1859; one child. Lived in the Salt Lake City Sixteenth Ward. Appointed second counselor in the Sixteenth Ward Young Ladies' Retrenchment Society, 1870; appointed treasurer, 1874. Served as the first president of the Sixteenth Ward Primary Association, circa 1879–1881. Died at Salt Lake City. (3.30)

Thompson, Mercy Rachel Fielding (June 15, 1807–September 15, 1893). Born at Honeydon, Bedfordshire, England; daughter of Rachel Ibbotson and John Fielding. Immigrated to Upper Canada, 1832. Baptized, 1836. Moved to Kirtland, Geauga County, Ohio, 1837. Married Robert Blashell Thompson, 1837; one child. Moved to Far West, Caldwell County, Missouri, 1838; to Quincy, Adams County, Illinois, 1839; and to Commerce (later Nauvoo), Hancock County, Illinois, 1839. Widowed, 1841. Joined the Female Relief Society of Nauvoo, 1842. "Married or sealed" to Hyrum Smith as a plural wife, 1843. Migrated to the Salt Lake Valley, 1847. Served as treasurer of the Salt Lake City Sixteenth Ward Relief Society for twenty-one years. Served as a member of the Relief Society's Central Grain Committee. Died at Salt Lake City. (1.2, 3.25, 4.1)

Thorn, Maria Susannah Merrick (July 1, 1811–September 18, 1889). Born at Windsor Castle, Berkshire, England; daughter of Mary Vaux and James Merrick. Had four children with John Maddison, circa 1833–1846, but never married. Baptized, 1848. Immigrated to the United States aboard the *Ellen Maria* and traveled to the Salt Lake Valley, 1851. Married William Thorn as a plural wife, 1852; two children. Served as treasurer of the Salt Lake City Seventh Ward Relief Society. Died at Salt Lake City. (3.3)

Thorn, William (October 26, 1815–September 24, 1907). Born at Chalford, Oxfordshire, England; son of Margaret McGinty and Thomas Thorn. Married Sarah Lowe, 1842; participated in plural marriage. Baptized in England, 1849. Immigrated to the United States aboard the *George W. Bourne* and traveled to the Salt Lake Valley, 1851. Served as counselor in the Salt Lake City Seventh Ward bishopric, 1861–1870; appointed bishop of the Seventh Ward, 1870. Died at Salt Lake City. (3.3)

Thurber, Thirza Melvina Berry (December 23, 1836–May 9, 1900). Born at Dresden, Weakley County, Tennessee; daughter of Armelia Shanks and Jesse Woods Berry. Lived at Nauvoo, Hancock County, Illinois. Baptized, circa 1845. Migrated to the Salt Lake Valley, 1849. Married Albert King Thurber, 1851; eleven children. Settled at Spanish Fork, Utah County, Utah Territory; appointed treasurer of the Spanish Fork Relief Society, 1866. Moved to Richfield, Sevier County, Utah Territory, 1874. Served as a counselor in the Sevier Stake Relief Society presidency, 1879–1898. Died at Richfield. (2.5)

Thurston, Moses (September 13, 1817–August 5, 1873). Born at Belmont, Waldo County, Maine; son of Rebekah French and John Thurston. Baptized, 1842. Married Lucy Jane Leonard, 1846. Migrated to the Salt Lake Valley, 1847. Served as a counselor in the Salt Lake City Seventh Ward bishopric. Died at Salt Lake City. (3.3)

Tingey, Martha (Mattie) Jane Horne (October 15, 1857–March 11, 1938). Born at Salt Lake City; daughter of Mary Isabella Hales and Joseph Horne. Baptized, 1866. Appointed second counselor to Anstis Elmina S. Taylor in the Young Ladies' Mutual Improvement Association (Y.L.M.I.A.) general presidency, 1880. Married Joseph Stafford Tingey, 1884; seven children. Principal speaker on Utah Day at the World's Fair in Chicago, 1893. Served as the Y.L.M.I.A. delegate to National Council of Women triennial meetings in Washington DC, 1899, and Seattle, 1909. Served as general president of the Y.L.M.I.A., 1905–1929. Died at Salt Lake City. (4.4)

Udall, Eliza Luella (Ella) Stewart (May 21, 1855–May 28, 1937). Born at Salt Lake City; daughter of Margery Wilkerson and Levi Stewart. Baptized, 1863. Moved to Kanab, Kane County, Utah Territory, 1870. Married David King Udall, 1875; nine children. Moved to St. Johns, Apache County, Arizona Territory, 1880. Served as president of the St. Johns Stake Relief Society, 1887–1922. Served as matron of the temple at Mesa, Maricopa County, Arizona, 1927–1935. Died at St. Johns. (4.23)

Vance, Elizabeth Campbell (January 25, 1801–November 7, 1884). Born in Cocke County, Tennessee; daughter of Jane and Ezekiel Campbell. Married John Vance, 1837; three children. Baptized, circa 1845–1846. Migrated to the Salt Lake Valley, 1847. Participated in the Great Salt Lake City Relief Society, 1854. Served as president of the Salt Lake City Seventh Ward Relief Society, circa 1854–1861. Moved to St. George, Washington County, Utah Territory, 1861. Died at St. George; buried at Salt Lake City. (2.1, 3.3)

Van Schoonhoven, Mary Emma Greene (January 8, 1843–March 19, 1907). Born at Batavia, Genesee County, New York; daughter of Mary Eliza Nelson and John Portineus Greene. Migrated to the Salt Lake Valley, 1849. Married Gilbert Van Schoonhoven, circa 1859; four children. Participated in the Salt Lake City Seventh Ward Relief Society. Studied homeopathic medicine at the University of Michigan, circa 1891; practiced medicine in Salt Lake City. Died at Salt Lake City. (3.3, 4.11)

Walton, Jane McKechnie (July 16, 1846–July 24, 1891). Born at Edinburgh, Midlothian, Scotland; daughter of Jane Bee and John McKechnie. Immigrated to the United States aboard the *North Atlantic,* 1850. Migrated to the Salt Lake Valley, 1852. Married Charles Eugene Walton; three children. Lived at Bluff, San Juan County, Utah Territory; appointed president of the Bluff Ward Relief Society, circa 1880; served as president of the San Juan Stake Relief Society, 1883–1891. Died at Monticello, San Juan County. (4.21)

Ward, Martha Monks (September 14, 1839–May 8, 1899). Born near Bolton, Lancashire, England; daughter of Alice Fletcher and John Monks. Baptized, 1851. Married George P. Ward, 1860; ten children. Immigrated to New York aboard the *City of Paris,* 1861. Migrated to the Salt Lake Valley, 1861. Settled at Hyrum, Cache County, Utah Territory, 1862. Served as counselor to Anna Christine Liljenquist in the Hyrum Relief Society presidency. Moved to Salem, Fremont County, Idaho Territory, 1883; served as the first president of the Salem Relief Society. Died at Salem. (3.22)

Webb, Elizabeth Lydia Taft (December 6, 1827–February 22, 1909). Born at Cottrellville, St. Clair County, Michigan Territory; daughter of Harriet Ogden and Seth Taft. Baptized, 1844. Married Chauncey Griswold Webb, 1846; eleven children. Migrated to the Salt Lake Valley, 1848. Appointed counselor to Mary Isabella Horne in the Retrenchment Association, circa 1887. Served as a Salt Lake temple worker. Died at Salt Lake City. (4.28)

Wells, Daniel Hanmer (October 27, 1814–March 24, 1891). Born at Trenton, Oneida County, New York; son of Catherine Chapin and Daniel Wells. Married Eliza Rebecca Robison, 1837; participated in plural marriage. Lived at Nauvoo, Hancock County, Illinois; baptized at Nauvoo, 1846. Migrated to the Salt Lake Valley, 1848. Appointed to the Quorum of the Twelve Apostles and second counselor in the First Presidency, 1857. Presided over the European mission, 1864–1865, 1885–1887. Appointed counselor to the Quorum of the Twelve, 1877. Died at Salt Lake City. (3.26)

Wells, Emmeline Blanche Woodward Harris Whitney (February 29, 1828– April 25, 1921). Born at Petersham, Worcester County, Massachusetts; daughter of Diadama Hare and David Woodward. Baptized, 1842. Married first James Harvey Harris, 1843; one child. Moved to Nauvoo, Hancock County, Illinois, 1844. Separated from Harris, circa 1844. Married second Newel K. Whitney as a plural wife, 1845; two children. Migrated to the Salt Lake Valley, 1848. Widowed, 1850. Married third Daniel Hanmer Wells as a plural wife, 1852; three children. Appointed president of the Central Grain Committee, 1876. Edited the *Woman's Exponent,* 1877–1914. Appointed secretary of the Deseret Hospital Association, 1882. Appointed corresponding secretary of the Relief Society general board, 1888, and general secretary, 1892. Served as president of the Utah Woman Suffrage Association, 1893–1896; presided over a plenary session at the Chicago World's Fair, 1893. Served as fifth general president of the Relief Society, 1910–1921. Died at Salt Lake City. (3.25, 3.28, 3.30, 4.1, 4.3–4.5, 4.11, 4.14, 4.18, 4.19, 4.23, 4.27, 4.28)

Wells Cannon, Louise (Louie) Martha (August 27, 1862–May 16, 1887). Born at Salt Lake City; daughter of Emmeline Blanche Woodward and Daniel H. Wells. Sang in the Mormon Tabernacle Choir. Appointed secretary to Anstis Elmina S. Taylor in the Young Ladies' Mutual Improvement Association general presidency, 1880. Married John Quayle Cannon, 1886. Died at San Francisco; buried at Salt Lake City. (4.4)

West, Chauncey Walker (February 6, 1827–January 6, 1870). Born in Erie County, Pennsylvania; son of Sally Benedict and Alva West. Baptized, circa 1843. Married Mary Hoagland, 1846; participated in plural marriage. Migrated to the Salt Lake Valley, 1847. Served missions to New York, Southeast Asia, and India, 1852–1855, and to Europe, 1862. Settled at Ogden, Weber County, Utah Territory, 1855; served as bishop of the Ogden Third

Ward. Served as president of the European mission, circa 1862–1864. Died at San Francisco; buried at Ogden. (3.28)

West, Mary Ann Covington Stratton (March 31, 1815–October 5, 1908). Born at Bedford, Bedfordshire, England; daughter of Elizabeth Hodges and Berrill Covington. Baptized, circa 1840–1842. Married first Joseph Albert Stratton, 1846. Migrated to the Salt Lake Valley, 1847. Widowed, 1850. Married second Chauncey Walker West as a plural wife, 1852; two children. Settled at Ogden, Weber County, Utah Territory, 1855. Appointed treasurer of the Ogden Relief Society, 1867. Died at Ogden. (3.28)

West, Mary Hoagland (February 11, 1829–August 27, 1870). Born at Royal Oak, Oakland County, Michigan Territory; daughter of Margaret Quick and Abraham Hoagland. Moved to Nauvoo, Hancock County, Illinois, circa 1842. Baptized, 1846. Married Chauncey Walker West, 1846; five children. Migrated to the Salt Lake Valley, 1847. Settled at Ogden, Weber County, Utah Territory, 1855. Served as president of the Ogden Relief Society, 1867–1870. Elected president of the Ladies of Weber County Cooperative Mercantile Institution, 1869. Died at Ogden. (3.28)

Wheeler Olney, Phebe (Phoebe) Marietta Bartholomew (June 24, 1804–before 1873). Born at Waterbury, New Haven County, Connecticut; daughter of Phebe Richardson and Joseph Bartholomew. Married first Charles Wheeler, circa 1820. Widowed, by 1842. Lived at Nauvoo, Hancock County, Illinois, by 1842. Joined the Female Relief Society of Nauvoo as a founding member and appointed assistant secretary, March 17, 1842. Married second Oliver H. Olney, 1843. Died at Wadsworth, Stark County, Ohio. (1.2, 4.28)

Whitney, Elizabeth Ann Smith (December 26, 1800–February 15, 1882). Born at Derby, New Haven County, Connecticut; daughter of Polly Bradley and Gibson Smith. Married Newel K. Whitney, 1822; twelve children. Baptized, 1830. Moved to Carrollton, Greene County, Illinois, 1838; to Quincy, Adams County, Illinois, 1839; and to Commerce (later Nauvoo), Hancock County, Illinois, 1840. Joined the Female Relief Society of Nauvoo as a founding member; appointed counselor to Emma Smith, March 17, 1842. Migrated to the Salt Lake Valley, 1848. Served as second counselor to Eliza R. Snow in the general Relief Society presidency, 1880–1882. Died at Salt Lake City. (1.2, 1.3, 1.6, 3.27, 4.1, 4.4–4.6, 4.28)

Whitney, Helen Mar Kimball (August 22, 1828–November 15, 1896). Born at Mendon, Monroe County, New York; daughter of Vilate Murray and Heber C. Kimball. Baptized, 1836. Later identified herself as a plural wife of Joseph Smith, married circa May 1843. Married Horace Kimball Whitney, 1846; eleven children. Migrated to the Salt Lake Valley, 1848. Wrote two books on plural marriage and many articles for the *Woman's Exponent* and *Deseret News*. Died at Salt Lake City. (4.28)

Whitney, Newel Kimball (February 3 or 5, 1795–September 23, 1850). Born at Marlborough, Windham County, Vermont; son of Susanna Kimball and Samuel Whitney. Lived at Kirtland, Geauga County, Ohio, by 1822. Married Elizabeth Ann Smith, 1822; participated in plural marriage. Baptized, 1830. Appointed bishop at Kirtland, 1831. Moved to Carrollton, Greene County, Illinois; to Quincy, Adams County, Illinois; and to Commerce, Hancock County, Illinois. Appointed bishop of the Middle Ward at Commerce, 1839. Admitted to the Council of Fifty, 1844. Appointed presiding bishop of the church,

1847. Migrated to the Salt Lake Valley, 1848. Appointed bishop of the Salt Lake City Eighteenth Ward, 1849. Died at Salt Lake City. (1.2, 4.28)

Whitney, Orson Ferguson (July 1, 1855–May 16, 1931). Born at Salt Lake City; son of Helen Mar Kimball and Horace Kimball Whitney. Baptized, 1866. Married Zina Beal Smoot, 1879. Appointed bishop of the Salt Lake City Eighteenth Ward, 1878. Appointed to the Quorum of the Twelve Apostles, 1906. Died at Salt Lake City. (4.4)

Whittaker, Rachel Taylor (April 16, 1808–July 28, 1876). Born at Heywood, Bury, Lancashire, England; daughter of Alice Turner and James Taylor. Baptized, 1850. Married James Whittaker, 1829; seven children. Settled at Cedar City, Iron County, Utah Territory; appointed second counselor of the Cedar City Relief Society, 1856; served as president of the Cedar City Relief Society, 1868–1875. Died at Cedar City. (2.6)

Wilkey, Ann Gregory (November 5, 1831–August 27, 1908). Born at Beaulieu, Hampshire, England; daughter of Lucy Thorn and George Gregory. Married John Wilkey, 1852; seven children. Immigrated to the United States aboard the *Golconda* and traveled to the Salt Lake Valley, 1853. Settled at Nephi, Juab County, Utah Territory, 1854. Served in the Nephi Relief Society as treasurer and teacher, and as president for twelve years. Died at Nephi. (3.19)

Wilkins, George Washington (October 28, 1822–March 9, 1916). Born at Peterborough, Hillsborough County, New Hampshire; son of Mary Emmons and Abraham Wilkins. Baptized, 1842. Married Catherine Augusta Lovett, 1846; participated in plural marriage. Migrated to the Salt Lake Valley, 1849. Settled at Spanish Fork, Utah County, Utah Territory, 1855; served as a bishopric counselor and as bishop of the Spanish Fork Ward. Died at Spanish Fork. (2.5)

Wilkinson, Susan Hough Conrad (December 5, 1818–April 6, 1888). Born in Bucks County, Pennsylvania; daughter of Elisabeth Grove and John Conrad. Married William Bryant Wilkinson, 1837; eleven children. Baptized at Philadelphia, 1840. Migrated to the Salt Lake Valley, 1862. Appointed counselor to Mary Isabella Horne in the Salt Lake City Fourteenth Ward Relief Society presidency, 1867. Died at Salt Lake City. (4.28)

Willard, Frances Elizabeth Caroline (September 28, 1839–February 18, 1898). Born at Churchville, Monroe County, New York; daughter of Mary Thompson Hill and Josiah Flint Willard. Elected president of the National Woman's Christian Temperance Union, 1879. Helped organize the Prohibition Party, 1882. Elected president of the National Council of Women, 1888. Elected president of the World's Woman's Christian Temperance Union, 1891. Died at New York City. (4.27)

Williams, Zina Presendia Young. See "Card, Zina Presendia Young Williams."

Willie, James Grey (November 1, 1814–September 9, 1895). Born at Murrell Green, Hampshire, England; son of Mary Sutton and William Willie. Immigrated to the United States, circa 1836; lived in Connecticut. Baptized, 1842. Married Elizabeth Ann Pettit, 1846; participated in plural marriage. Migrated to the Salt Lake Valley, 1847. Served a mission to England, 1852–1856. Served as captain of the Willie handcart company, 1856. Served as bishop of the Salt Lake City Seventh Ward, 1856–1859. Settled at Mendon, Cache County, Utah Territory, 1859. Died at Mendon. (3.3)

Wilson, Lucy Benson (May 29, 1830–March 6, 1914). Born at Larima, Clinton County, Indiana; daughter of Cyntha Vail and Alva Benson. Baptized, 1841. Married John

Gill Wilson, 1852; nine children. Migrated to the Salt Lake Valley, 1852. Moved to Cache County, Utah Territory, 1862. Served as president of the first Primary organization in Hyrum, Cache County; as counselor to Anna Christine Liljenquist in the Hyrum Relief Society presidency; and as president of the Hyrum Relief Society. Died at Hyrum. (3.22)

Wood, Josephine Catherine Chatterly (September 10, 1853–February 10, 1909). Born at Cedar City, Iron County, Utah Territory; daughter of Catherine Clark and Joseph Chatterly. Baptized, 1861. Married Samuel Wood, 1871; ten children. Settled at Bluff, San Juan County, Utah Territory, 1882. Practiced medicine, midwifery, and obstetrics. Served as president of the Primary in Bluff for twenty-five years. Appointed second counselor to Jane McKechnie Walton in the San Juan Stake Relief Society presidency, 1888. Died at Monticello, San Juan County; buried at Bluff. (4.21)

Woodmansee, Emily Hill Mills (March 24, 1836–October 18, 1906). Born near Warminster, Wiltshire, England; daughter of Elizabeth Slade and Thomas Hill. Baptized, 1858. Immigrated to the United States aboard the *Thornton* and traveled to the Salt Lake Valley with the Willie handcart company, 1856. Married first William Gill Mills, 1857; one child; abandoned by husband, circa 1863. Married second Joseph Woodmansee, 1864; eight children. Died at Salt Lake City. (3.16, 4.15, 4.28)

Woodruff, Phebe (Phoebe) Whittemore Carter (March 8, 1807–November 10, 1885). Born at Scarborough, Cumberland County, Maine; daughter of Sarah Fabyan and Ezra Carter. Baptized, 1834. Moved to Kirtland, Geauga County, Ohio, circa 1835. Married Wilford Woodruff, 1837; nine children. Accompanied husband on a mission to Maine, circa 1837–1838. Joined the Female Relief Society of Nauvoo, Hancock County, Illinois, 1842. Accompanied husband on missions to England, 1845–1846, and the eastern states, circa 1848–1850. Migrated to the Salt Lake Valley, 1850. Appointed president of the Salt Lake City Fourteenth Ward Relief Society, 1856. Joined the Ladies' Cooperative Retrenchment Society, 1870; served as a board member of the General Retrenchment Society. Served on the Deseret Hospital Association board of directors, 1882–1885. Died at Salt Lake City. (1.2, 1.6, 2.3, 3.13, 3.16, 3.17, 4.1, 4.5, 4.11, 4.28)

Woodruff, Wilford (March 1, 1807–September 2, 1898). Born at Farmington, Hartford County, Connecticut; son of Beulah Thompson and Apheck Woodruff. Baptized in New York, 1833. Moved to Kirtland, Geauga County, Ohio, 1834. Ordained a seventy, 1836. Married Phebe Whittemore Carter, 1837; participated in plural marriage. Served missions to New England, 1837–1838. Ordained a member of the Quorum of the Twelve Apostles, 1839. Served a mission to Great Britain, 1839–1841. Admitted to the Council of Fifty, 1844. Presided over the British mission, 1844–1846. Migrated to the Salt Lake Valley, 1847. Served a mission to the eastern states, 1848–1850. Appointed assistant church historian, 1856; president of the St. George temple, 1877; president of the Quorum of the Twelve, 1880; and church historian and general church recorder, 1883. Served as the fourth president of The Church of Jesus Christ of Latter-day Saints, 1889–1898. Died at San Francisco. (4.11, 4.19, 4.20, 4.24, 4.25, 4.28)

Woodward, Maria Jane Johnston Johnson (October 28, 1824–February 14, 1911). Born at Wartrace Creek, Wilson County, Tennessee; daughter of Hannah Hall Buckley and Oliver Campbell Johnston. Baptized, circa 1838. Migrated to Nauvoo, Hancock County, Illinois. Appointed as a nurse by Joseph Smith; practiced nursing for over sixty years. Married first George Washington Johnson, 1844; later divorced; nine children. Migrated to the Salt Lake Valley, 1851. Married second James Woodward, 1863; two children. Moved to Huntington, Emery County, Utah Territory, circa 1885. Served as a counselor in the Huntington Relief Society presidency, 1889–1901. Died at Huntington. (4.25)

Woolley, Edwin Dilworth (June 27, 1807–October 14, 1881). Born at East Bradford Township, Chester County, Pennsylvania; son of Rachel Dilworth and John Woolley. Married Mary Wickersham, 1831; participated in plural marriage. Baptized, 1837. Migrated to the Salt Lake Valley, 1848. Served as bishop of the Salt Lake City Thirteenth Ward, circa 1853–1881. Died at Salt Lake City. (2.1, 3.7, 3.23)

Woolley, Mary Wickersham (November 4, 1808–March 29, 1859). Born at Newlin Township, Chester County, Pennsylvania; daughter of Amy Ward and Amos Wickersham. Married Edwin D. Woolley, 1831; eight children. Baptized, 1837. Moved to Commerce (later Nauvoo), Hancock County, Illinois, 1839. Joined the Female Relief Society of Nauvoo, 1842. Migrated to the Salt Lake Valley, 1848. Settled in the Salt Lake City Thirteenth Ward. Died at Salt Lake City. (1.2)

Works, Abigail Jerusha Marks (November 6, 1781–July 14, 1846). Born at Wilmington, Windham County, Vermont; daughter of Miriam Smith and Joseph Marks. Married Asa Works, circa 1800–1801; ten children. Lived at Williamstown, Orange County, Vermont; at Aurelius, Cayuga County, New York; and at Lockport, Will County, Illinois, circa 1810–1840. Moved to Nauvoo, Hancock County, Illinois, by 1842. Joined the Female Relief Society of Nauvoo, 1842. Died at Nauvoo. (1.2, 1.6)

Young, Brigham (June 1, 1801–August 29, 1877). Born at Whitingham, Windham County, Vermont; son of Abigail (Nabby) Howe and John Young. Married Miriam Angeline Works, 1824; participated in plural marriage. Baptized, 1832. Served missions to New York and Upper Canada, 1832–1833. Moved to Kirtland, Geauga County, Ohio, 1833. Ordained a member of the Quorum of the Twelve Apostles, 1835. Served a mission to New York and New England, 1835–1837. Served a mission to England, 1839–1841. Settled at Nauvoo, Hancock County, Illinois, 1841. Admitted to the Council of Fifty, 1844. Appointed to administer church affairs, 1844. Directed the migration of the Saints from Nauvoo to the Salt Lake Valley, 1846–1848. Appointed second president of The Church of Jesus Christ of Latter-day Saints, 1847. Governor of Utah Territory, 1850–1857. Died at Salt Lake City. (1.2, 1.13, 2.1, 2.3, 2.4, 3.1, 3.2, 3.4–3.7, 3.11–3.13, 3.16, 3.20, 3.23, 3.25, 3.26, 3.28–3.30, 4.5, 4.7, 4.14, 4.20, 4.24, 4.28)

Young, Celestia Armeda Snow (December 2, 1855–March 13, 1938). Born at Salt Lake City; daughter of Harriet Prichard Squires and Lorenzo Snow. Married Brigham Morris Young, 1875; ten children. Accompanied husband on a mission to the Sandwich Islands, 1883–1885. Lived at Salt Lake City; active in the Relief Society. Died at Salt Lake City. (4.13)

Young, Clarissa (Clara) Decker (July 22, 1828–January 5, 1889). Born at Freedom, Cattaraugus County, New York; daughter of Harriet Page Wheeler and Isaac Decker. Moved to Kirtland, Geauga County, Ohio, 1837; to Missouri, 1838; and to Nauvoo, Hancock County, Illinois, 1841. Married Brigham Young as a plural wife, 1844; five children. Traveled with the Brigham Young pioneer company; one of three women to enter the Salt Lake Valley on July 24, 1847. Died at Salt Lake City. (4.28)

Young, Emily Dow Partridge (February 28, 1824–December 9, 1899). Born at Painesville, Geauga County, Ohio; daughter of Lydia Clisbee and Edward Partridge. Baptized, 1832. Moved to Kirtland, Geauga County, 1831; to Jackson and Clay Counties, Missouri, 1833; to Caldwell County, Missouri, 1836; and to Commerce (later Nauvoo), Hancock County, Illinois, 1839. Joined the Female Relief Society of Nauvoo, 1842. Later identified herself as a plural wife of Joseph Smith, married on March 4, 1843. Married second Brigham Young as a plural wife, 1844; seven children. Migrated to the Salt Lake Valley, 1848. Served as a teacher in the Salt Lake City Thirteenth Ward Relief Society, 1868. Died at Salt Lake City. (1.2, 3.7)

Young Dunford Hagan, Eudora (Dora) Lovina (May 12, 1852–October 21, 1921). Born at Salt Lake City; daughter of Lucy Bigelow and Brigham Young. Served as counselor in the first Young Ladies' Department of the Ladies' Cooperative Retrenchment Association, 1870. Married first Moreland Dunford, 1871; two children. Divorced, 1874; moved to St. George, Washington County, Utah Territory. Elected president of the Young Ladies' Mutual Improvement Association in the Southern Stake Fourth Ward, 1877. Married second Albert Hagan; four children. Filed a legal complaint against church authorities and executors of her father's estate, charging them with defrauding heirs of their inheritance; excommunicated, 1880. Died at Salt Lake City. (3.18)

Young, Harriet Amelia Folsom (August 23, 1838–December 11, 1910). Born at Buffalo, Erie County, New York; daughter of Zerviah Eliza Clark and William Harrison Folsom. Moved to Nauvoo, Hancock County, Illinois, circa 1845; to Keokuk, Lee County, Iowa, 1847; and to Council Bluffs, Pottawattamie County, Iowa, circa 1855. Taught school at Omaha, Douglas County, Nebraska Territory. Migrated to the Salt Lake Valley, 1860. Lived at Salt Lake City. Married Brigham Young as a plural wife, 1863. Participated actively in the woman suffrage movement. Executive committee member for the Utah exhibit at the Centennial International Exhibition at Philadelphia, 1876. Died at Salt Lake City. (3.16, 3.17, 4.28)

Young, Harriet Elizabeth Cook (November 7, 1824–November 5, 1898). Born at Whitesboro, Oneida County, New York; daughter of Elizabeth Mosher and Archibald Cook. Baptized, 1842. Moved to Nauvoo, Hancock County, Illinois, 1843. Married Brigham Young as a plural wife, 1843; one child. Migrated to the Salt Lake Valley, 1848. Worked as a schoolmistress and bookkeeper. Died at Salt Lake City. (3.13, 3.16, 3.17)

Young, Harriet Page Wheeler Decker. See "Decker Young, Harriet Page Wheeler."

Young, John (May 22, 1791–April 27, 1870). Born at Hopkinton, Middlesex County, Massachusetts; son of Abigail (Nabby) Howe and John Young. Married Theodocia Kimball, 1813; participated in plural marriage. Baptized, 1833. Served a mission in Ohio, Pennsylvania, and New York, 1834–1836. Moved to Kirtland, Geauga County, Ohio, 1834; served as president of the Kirtland Stake. Migrated to the Salt Lake Valley, 1847. Served as president of the high priests quorum, 1849–1870. Appointed presiding patriarch of the church, 1853. Died at Salt Lake City. (2.5)

Young, Mary Ann Angell (June 8, 1803–June 27, 1882). Born at Seneca, Ontario County, New York; daughter of Phoebe Morton and James William Angell. Baptized, 1832. Moved to Kirtland, Geauga County, Ohio, circa 1833. Married Brigham Young, 1834; six children. Moved to Missouri; to Montrose, Lee County, Iowa; and to Nauvoo, Hancock County, Illinois, 1841. Migrated to the Salt Lake Valley, 1848. Died at Salt Lake City. (4.28)

Young, Phebe. See "Beatie, Phebe Young."

Young, Seymour Bicknell (October 3, 1837–December 15, 1924). Born at Kirtland, Geauga County, Ohio; son of Jane Adeline Bicknell and Joseph Young. Baptized, 1848. Migrated to the Salt Lake Valley, 1850. Served two missions to Great Britain, 1857–1858, 1870. Married Ann Elizabeth Riter, 1867; participated in plural marriage. Graduated from the University Medical College of New York, 1874. Appointed to the First Quorum of the Seventy, 1877, and as senior president of the Seventy, 1893. Died at Salt Lake City. (4.11)

Young, Zina Diantha Huntington Jacobs (January 31, 1821–August 28, 1901). Born at Watertown, Jefferson County, New York; daughter of Zina Baker and William Huntington. Baptized, 1835. Moved to Kirtland, Geauga County, Ohio, 1836; to Far West, Caldwell County, Missouri, 1838; to Quincy, Adams County, Illinois, 1839; and to Commerce (later Nauvoo), Hancock County, Illinois, 1839. Married first Henry Bailey Jacobs, 1841; later separated; two children. Later identified herself as a plural wife of Joseph Smith, married on October 27, 1841. Joined the Female Relief Society of Nauvoo, 1842. Married third Brigham Young as a plural wife; one child. Migrated to the Salt Lake Valley, 1848. Appointed treasurer of the Relief Society in Utah. Appointed president of the Deseret Silk Association, 1876. Served as vice president and later president of Deseret Hospital, 1880–1892. Appointed first counselor to Eliza R. Snow in the general Relief Society presidency, 1880. Appointed third general president of the Relief Society, 1888. Appointed first matron of the Salt Lake temple, 1893. Died at Salt Lake City. (1.2, 3.13, 3.15–3.17, 4.1, 4.3–4.6, 4.11, 4.18, 4.20, 4.23, 4.24, 4.26, 4.28)

Works Cited

This list of sources serves as a comprehensive guide to all sources cited in this volume (documentation supporting the biographical directory in the back of this volume may be found online at churchhistorianspress.org). In entries for manuscript sources, dates identify when the manuscript was created, which is not necessarily the time period the manuscript covers. Newspaper entries are listed under the newspaper titles used during the time period covered by this volume. Newspaper entries also provide beginning and ending years for the publication. Since newspapers often changed names or editors over time, such dates typically approximate the years the paper was active under a particular editor; when it is impractical to provide beginning and ending publication dates by an editor's tenure, dates may be determined by major events in the paper's history, such as a merger with another sizable newspaper.

Abbreviations for Frequently Cited Repositories

CHL   Church History Library, The Church of Jesus Christ of Latter-day Saints, Salt Lake City

FHL   Family History Library, The Church of Jesus Christ of Latter-day Saints, Salt Lake City

——————— ❧ ———————

Abraham (Book of). See *Pearl of Great Price.*

Acts, Resolutions and Memorials, Passed and Adopted during the Nineteenth Annual Session of the Legislative Assembly of the Territory of Utah. Salt Lake City: Joseph Bull, 1870.

Advocate of Moral Reform. New York City. 1835–1845.

Alexander, Ruth M. "'We Are Engaged as a Band of Sisters': Class and Domesticity in the Washingtonian Temperance Movement, 1840–1850." *Journal of American History* 75, no. 3 (Dec. 1988): 763–785.

Alexander, Thomas G. "An Experiment in Progressive Legislation: The Granting of Woman Suffrage in Utah in 1870." *Utah Historical Quarterly* 38, no. 1 (Winter 1970): 20–30.

———. *Things in Heaven and Earth: The Life and Times of Wilford Woodruff, a Mormon Prophet.* Salt Lake City: Signature Books, 1991.

Allen, James B., Ronald K. Esplin, and David J. Whittaker. *Men with a Mission, 1837–1841: The Quorum of the Twelve Apostles in the British Isles.* Salt Lake City: Deseret Book, 1992.

Allen, James B., and Glen M. Leonard. *The Story of the Latter-day Saints.* Salt Lake City: Deseret Book, 1976.

Allison, William Henry. *Inventory of Unpublished Material for American Religious History in*

Protestant Church Archives and Other Repositories. Washington DC: Carnegie Institution of Washington, 1910.

An American Dictionary of the English Language. . . . Edited by Noah Webster. New York: S. Converse, 1828.

An American Dictionary of the English Language; Exhibiting the Origin, Orthography, Pronunciation, and Definition of Words. Edited by Noah Webster. New York: Harper and Brothers, 1845.

The Anchor Bible Dictionary. 6 vols. Edited by David Noel Freedman. New York: Doubleday, 1992.

Anderson, Dawn Hall, and Marie Cornwall, eds. *Women Steadfast in Christ: Talks Selected from the 1991 Women's Conference Co-sponsored by Brigham Young University and the Relief Society.* Salt Lake City: Deseret Book, 1991.

Anderson, Lavina Fielding, ed. *Lucy's Book: A Critical Edition of Lucy Mack Smith's Family Memoir.* Salt Lake City: Signature Books, 2001.

Annual Report of the Territorial Superintendent of Common Schools for the Year 1868. Salt Lake City: George Q. Cannon, 1869.

Armitage, Susan, and Elizabeth Jameson, eds. *The Women's West.* Norman: University of Oklahoma Press, 1987.

Arrington, Chris Rigby. "The Finest of Fabrics: Mormon Women and the Silk Industry in Early Utah." *Utah Historical Quarterly* 46, no. 4 (Fall 1978): 376–396.

Arrington, Leonard J. *Brigham Young: American Moses.* New York: Alfred A. Knopf, 1985.

———. "The Deseret Telegraph—A Church-Owned Public Utility." *Journal of Economic History* 11 (Spring 1951): 117–139.

———. "The Economic Role of Pioneer Mormon Women." *Western Humanities Review* 9, no. 2 (Spring 1955): 145–164.

———. *Great Basin Kingdom: An Economic History of the Latter-day Saints, 1830–1900.* Cambridge, MA: Harvard University Press, 1958.

Arrington, Leonard J., and Melvin A. Larkin. "The Logan Tabernacle and Temple." *Utah Historical Quarterly* 41, no. 3 (Summer 1973): 301–314.

Autobiographical and Biographical Sketches of Burton, Peery, and Richards Families, n.d. Typescript. CHL.

Avery, Rachel Foster, ed. *Transactions of the National Council of Women of the United States, Assembled in Washington, D.C., February 22 to 25, 1891.* Philadelphia: Executive Board of the National Council of Women, 1891.

Bacon, Leonard. "Harriet A. Tucker." *Home Missionary* 49 (Apr. 1877): 280–282.

Bancroft, Hubert Howe. *History of Utah, 1540–1886.* Works of Hubert Howe Bancroft 26. San Francisco: History Company, 1889.

Baskin, Robert N. *Reminiscences of Early Utah with Reply to Certain Statements by O. F. Whitney.* Salt Lake City: Signature Books, 2006.

Baugh, Alexander L. *A Call to Arms: The 1838 Mormon Defense of Northern Missouri.* Dissertations in Latter-day Saint History. Provo, UT: Joseph Fielding Smith Institute for Latter-day Saint History; BYU Studies, 2000.

Beadle, J. H. *The Undeveloped West; or, Five Years in the Territories. . . .* Philadelphia: National, ca. 1873. Publisher's Dummy. Copy at CHL.

Beecher, Maureen Ursenbach, ed. *The Personal Writings of Eliza Roxcy Snow.* Life Writings of Frontier Women 5. Logan: Utah State University Press, 2000.

Beecher, Maureen Ursenbach, and Lavina Fielding Anderson, eds. *Sisters in Spirit: Mormon Women in Historical and Cultural Perspective.* Urbana: University of Illinois Press, 1987.

Beeton, Beverly. "A Feminist among the Mormons: Charlotte Ives Cobb Godbe Kirby." *Utah Historical Quarterly* 59, no. 1 (Winter 1991): 22–31.

———. "Woman Suffrage in Territorial Utah." *Utah Historical Quarterly* 46, no. 2 (Spring 1978): 100–120.

———. *Women Vote in the West: The Woman Suffrage Movement, 1869–1896.* American Legal and Constitutional History. New York: Garland, 1986.

Beltz, George Frederick. *Memorials of the Most Noble Order of the Garter, from Its Foundation to the Present Time. Including the History of the Order; Biographical Notices of the Knights in the Reigns of Edward III. and Richard II.; the Chronological Succession of the Members, and Many Curious Particulars Relating to English and French History from Hitherto Unpublished Documents.* London: William Pickering, 1841.

Bennett, John C. *The History of the Saints; or, An Exposé of Joe Smith and Mormonism.* Boston: Leland and Whiting, 1842.

Bennett, Richard E. *Mormons at the Missouri Winter Quarters, 1846–1852.* Norman: University of Oklahoma Press, 2004.

Bennion, Sherilyn Cox. "The *Woman's Exponent:* Forty-Two Years of Speaking for Women." *Utah Historical Quarterly* 44, no. 3 (Summer 1976): 222–239.

Bible. See *Holy Bible.*

A Bill in Aid of the Execution of the Laws in the Territory of Utah, and for Other Purposes. H.R. 696, 41st Cong., 2nd Sess. [1870].

Biographical Directory of the United States Congress, 1774–2005: The Continental Congress September 5, 1774, to October 21, 1788, and the Congress of the United States from the First through the One Hundred Eighth Congresses March 4, 1789, to January 3, 2005, Inclusive. Edited by Andrew R. Dodge and Betty K. Koed. Washington DC: Government Printing Office, 2005.

Bitton, Davis. "Zion's Rowdies: Growing Up on the Mormon Frontier." *Utah Historical Quarterly* 50, no. 2 (Spring 1982): 182–195.

Bitton, Davis, and Linda P. Wilcox. "Pestiferous Ironclads: The Grasshopper Problem in Pioneer Utah." *Utah Historical Quarterly* 46, no. 4 (Fall 1978): 336–355.

Black, Susan Easton, and Larry C. Porter, eds. *Lion of the Lord: Essays on the Life and Service of Brigham Young.* Salt Lake City: Deseret Book, 1995.

Bogdonoff, Nancy Dick. *Handwoven Textiles of Early New England: The Legacy of a Rural People, 1640–1880.* Harrisburg, PA: Stackpole Books, 1975.

The Book of Abraham. See *Pearl of Great Price.*

A Book of Commandments, for the Government of the Church of Christ, Organized according to Law, on the 6th of April, 1830. Zion [Independence], MO: W. W. Phelps, 1833. Also available in Robin Scott Jensen, Richard E. Turley Jr., and Riley M. Lorimer, eds., *Revelations and Translations, Volume 2: Published Revelations.* Vol. 2 of the Revelations and Translations series of *The Joseph Smith Papers,* edited by Dean C. Jessee, Ronald K. Esplin, and Richard Lyman Bushman (Salt Lake City: Church Historian's Press, 2011).

The Book of Common Prayer, and Administration of the Sacraments, and Other Rites and Ceremonies of the Church, according to the Use of the United Church of England and Ireland: Together with the Psalter or Psalms of David, Pointed as They Are to Be Sung or Said in Churches. Oxford: Clarendon, 1825.

The Book of Mormon: Another Testament of Jesus Christ. Salt Lake City: The Church of Jesus Christ of Latter-day Saints, 2013.

The Book of Moses (selections from). See *Pearl of Great Price.*

Bountiful Ward, Davis Stake. Bountiful Ward Relief Society Minutes and Records, 1868–1878. CHL.

Bowles, Samuel. *Across the Continent: A Summer's Journey to the Rocky Mountains, the Mormons, and the Pacific States, with Speaker Colfax.* Springfield, MA: Samuel Bowles; New York: Hurd and Houghton, 1865.

Box Elder Stake. Box Elder Stake Relief Society Minutes and Records, 1857–1944. CHL.

Bradley, Martha Sonntag. *ZCMI: American's First Department Store.* Salt Lake City: ZCMI, 1991.

Bradley, Martha Sonntag, and Mary Brown Firmage Woodward. *4 Zinas: A Story of Mothers and Daughters on the Mormon Frontier.* Salt Lake City: Signature Books, 2000.

Brekus, Catherine A. *Strangers and Pilgrims: Female Preaching in America, 1740–1845.* Gender and American Culture. Chapel Hill: University of North Carolina Press, 1998.

Briggs, Edmund C. "A Visit to Nauvoo in 1856." *Journal of History* 9, no. 4 (Oct. 1916): 446–462.

Brigham Young Office Files, 1832–1878. CHL.

Britsch, R. Lanier. *Unto the Islands of the Sea: A History of the Latter-day Saints in the Pacific.* Salt Lake City: Deseret Book, 1986.

Brooks, Juanita, ed. *On the Mormon Frontier: The Diary of Hosea Stout, 1844–1889.* 2 vols. Reprint. Salt Lake City: University of Utah Press, 2009.

Brown, Lisle G. "'Temple pro Tempore': The Salt Lake City Endowment House." *Journal of Mormon History* 34, no. 4 (Fall 2008): 1–68.

Brown, Samuel. "The Translator and the Ghostwriter: Joseph Smith and W. W. Phelps." *Journal of Mormon History* 34, no. 1 (Winter 2008): 26–62.

———. "William Phelps's Paracletes, an Early Witness to Joseph Smith's Divine Anthropology." *International Journal of Mormon Studies* 2 (Spring 2009): 62–82.

Buerger, David John. "The Development of the Mormon Temple Endowment Ceremony." *Dialogue: A Journal of Mormon Thought* 20, no. 4 (Winter 1987): 33–76.

Bunker, Edward. Autobiography, 1894. CHL.

Burgess, James. Journal, Oct. 1841–Dec. 1848. 2 vols. CHL.

Burgess-Olson, Vicky, ed. *Sister Saints.* [Provo, UT]: By the author, 1978.

Bushman, Claudia L. "Edward W. Tullidge and *The Women of Mormondom.*" *Dialogue: A Journal of Mormon Thought* 33, no. 4 (Winter 2000): 15–26.

———, ed. *Mormon Sisters: Women in Early Utah.* New ed. Logan: Utah State University Press, 1997.

Bushman, Richard Lyman. *Joseph Smith: Rough Stone Rolling.* With the assistance of Jed Woodworth. New York: Alfred A. Knopf, 2005.

Cache Valley Historical Society Papers, 1951–1962, 1983–2008. Special Collections and Archives, Merrill-Cazier Library, Utah State University, Logan.

Cannon, Abraham H. Diaries, 1879–1895. 20th Century Western and Mormon Manuscripts, L. Tom Perry Special Collections, Harold B. Lee Library, Brigham Young University, Provo, UT.

Cannon, George Q. Journal, 1855–1864, 1872–1901. CHL.

———. Letterbook, 1871–1879. CHL.

Cannon, Martha H. Collection, 1883–1912. CHL.

Cardston Ward, Alberta Stake. Cardston Ward Relief Society Minutes and Records, 1887–1911. CHL.

———. Cardston Ward Young Women's Mutual Improvement Association Minutes and Records, 1887–1917. CHL.

Careless, G. "Prayer." *Utah Musical Times* 1 (Sept. 1876): 104.

Carruth, LaJean Purcell, and Mark Lyman Staker. "John Taylor's June 27, 1854, Account of the Martyrdom." *BYU Studies* 50, no. 3 (2011): 25–62.

Carter, Kate B., comp. *Heart Throbs of the West: A Unique Volume Treating Definite Subjects of Western History.* 12 vols. Salt Lake City: Daughters of Utah Pioneers, 1939–1951.

Castle Dale Utah Stake. Castle Dale Utah Stake Relief Society Minutes and Records, 1882–1973. CHL.

Catalogue of Charities Conducted by Women, as Reported to the Women's Centennial Executive Committee of the United States. Philadelphia: Collins, Printer, 1876.

Cedar City Ward, Parowan Stake. Cedar City Ward Relief Society Minute Book, 1856–1875, 1892. CHL.

Challoner, Richard. *Considerations upon Christian Truths and Christian Duties; Digested into Meditations for Every Day in the Year.* Part 3. London: J. P. Coghlan, 1784.

Christian Women's Association. *A Handbook for Wives and Mothers of the Working Classes.* Glasgow: J. McGeachy, 1873.

Church History Department. Historical Department Office Journal, 1844–2012. 102 vols. CHL.

Clarkson, Thomas. *A Portraiture of Quakerism. Taken from a View of the Education and Discipline, Social Manners, Civil and Political Economy, Religious Principles and Character, of the Society of Friends.* 3 vols. New York: Samuel Stansbury, 1806.

Clayton, Ruth Vickers. "Clothing and the Temporal Kingdom: Mormon Clothing Practices, 1847 to 1887." PhD diss., Purdue University, 1987.

Clayton, William. Diary, 1847. CHL.

———. Journals, 1842–1845. CHL.

A Collection of Sacred Hymns, for the Church of the Latter Day Saints. Edited by Emma Smith. Kirtland, OH: F. G. Williams, 1835.

A Collection of Sacred Hymns, for the Church of Jesus Christ of Latter-day Saints, in Europe. Selected by Brigham Young, Parley P. Pratt, and John Taylor. Manchester: W. R. Thomas, 1840.

A Collection of Sacred Hymns for the Church of Jesus Christ of Latter Day Saints. Edited by Emma Smith. Nauvoo, IL: E. Robinson, 1841.

Compton, Todd. *In Sacred Loneliness: The Plural Wives of Joseph Smith.* Salt Lake City: Signature Books, 2001.

Congressional Record: Containing the Proceedings and Debates of the Forty-Eighth Congress, First Session. Washington DC: Government Printing Office, 1884.

Congressional Record: Containing the Proceedings and Debates of the Forty-Ninth Congress, First Session; Also, Special Session of the Senate. Washington DC: Government Printing Office, 1886.

Cook, Lyndon W., and Milton V. Backman Jr., eds. *Kirtland Elders' Quorum Record, 1836–1841.* Provo, UT: Grandin Book, 1985.

Cooperative Retrenchment Association. Cooperative Retrenchment Association Meeting Minutes, 1871–1874. CHL.

Coray, Martha Jane Knowlton. Notebook, n.d. CHL.

Cornwall, Marie, and Susan Howe, eds. *Women of Wisdom and Knowledge: Talks Selected from the BYU Women's Conferences.* Salt Lake City: Deseret Book, 1990.

Cott, Nancy F. *The Bonds of Womanhood: "Woman's Sphere" in New England, 1780–1835.* New Haven, CT: Yale University Press, 1997.

Coyner, J. M., comp. *Hand-Book on Mormonism.* Salt Lake City: Hand-Book Publishing, 1882.

Crawley, Peter. *A Descriptive Bibliography of the Mormon Church.* 3 vols. Provo, UT: Religious Studies Center, Brigham Young University, 1997–2012.

Crocheron, Augusta Joyce. *Representative Women of Deseret, a Book of Biographical Sketches, to Accompany the Picture Bearing the Same Title.* Salt Lake City: J. C. Graham, 1884.

Croly, Mrs. J. C. *The History of the Woman's Club Movement in America.* New York City: Henry G. Allen, 1898.

Davidson, Karen Lynn. *Our Latter-day Hymns: The Stories and the Messages.* Salt Lake City: Deseret Book, 1988.

Davidson, Karen Lynn, Richard L. Jensen, and David J. Whittaker, eds. *Histories, Volume 2: Assigned Historical Writings, 1831–1847.* Vol. 2 of the Histories series of *The Joseph Smith Papers,* edited by Dean C. Jessee, Ronald K. Esplin, and Richard Lyman Bushman. Salt Lake City: Church Historian's Press, 2012.

Davidson, Karen Lynn, David J. Whittaker, Mark Ashurst-McGee, and Richard L. Jensen, eds. *Histories, Volume 1: Joseph Smith Histories, 1832–1844.* Vol. 1 of the Histories series of *The Joseph Smith Papers,* edited by Dean C. Jessee, Ronald K. Esplin, and Richard Lyman Bushman. Salt Lake City: Church Historian's Press, 2012.

Davis Stake. Davis Stake Relief Society Minutes and Records, 1878–1915. CHL.

Daynes, Kathryn M. *More Wives Than One: Transformation of the Mormon Marriage System, 1840–1910.* Urbana: University of Illinois Press, 2001.

Dean, Joseph H. Journals, 1876–1944. CHL.

Derr, Jill Mulvay. *Mrs. Smith Goes to Washington: Eliza R. Snow Smith's Visit to Southern Utah.* Juanita Brooks Lecture Series. St. George, UT: Dixie State College, 2004.

———. "The Significance of 'O My Father' in the Personal Journey of Eliza R. Snow." *BYU Studies* 36, no. 1 (1996–1997): 85–126.

Derr, Jill Mulvay, Janath Russell Cannon, and Maureen Ursenbach Beecher. *Women of*

Covenant: The Story of Relief Society. Salt Lake City: Deseret Book; Provo, UT: Brigham Young University Press, 1992.

Derr, Jill Mulvay, and Karen Lynn Davidson, eds. *Eliza R. Snow: The Complete Poetry.* Provo, UT: Brigham Young University Press; Salt Lake City: University of Utah Press, 2009.

Derr, Jill Mulvay, and Matthew J. Grow. "Letters on Mormon Polygamy and Progeny: Eliza R. Snow and Martin Luther Holbrook, 1866–1869." *BYU Studies* 48, no. 2 (2009): 139–164.

Derr, Jill Mulvay, and Carol Cornwall Madsen. "Preserving the Record and Memory of the Female Relief Society of Nauvoo, 1842–92." *Journal of Mormon History* 35, no. 3 (Summer 2009): 88–117.

[The Deseret First Book by the Regents of the Deseret University]. Salt Lake City: Deseret University, 1868.

Deseret Hospital. Patient Accounts, 1886–1893. CHL.

Deseret News. Salt Lake City. 1850–.

Deseret Silk Association. Minutes, June 1875–Oct. 1878. CHL.

Deseret Sunday School Union Music Book, Containing a Large Collection of Choice Pieces for the Use of Sunday Schools. Salt Lake City: Deseret Sunday School Union, 1884.

Deseret Weekly. Salt Lake City. 1888–1898.

Dictionary of Canadian Biography. Vol. 14, *1911–1920.* Toronto: University of Toronto Press, 1998.

Directory of Ogden City, and North Utah Record. Ogden, UT: S. A. Kenner and Thos. Wallace, 1878.

Dirkmaat, Gerrit J., and LaJean Purcell Carruth. "The Prophets Have Spoken, but What Did They Say? Examining the Differences between George D. Watt's Original Shorthand Notes and the Sermons Published in the *Journal of Discourses.*" *BYU Studies* (forthcoming).

Doctrine and Covenants of the Church of the Latter Day Saints: Carefully Selected from the Revelations of God. Compiled by Joseph Smith, Oliver Cowdery, Sidney Rigdon, and Frederick G. Williams. Kirtland, OH: F. G. Williams, 1835. Also available in Robin Scott Jensen, Richard E. Turley Jr., and Riley M. Lorimer, eds., *Revelations and Translations, Volume 2: Published Revelations.* Vol. 2 of the Revelations and Translations series of *The Joseph Smith Papers,* edited by Dean C. Jessee, Ronald K. Esplin, and Richard Lyman Bushman (Salt Lake City: Church Historian's Press, 2011).

The Doctrine and Covenants of the Church of Jesus Christ of Latter Day Saints; Carefully Selected from the Revelations of God. Compiled by Joseph Smith. 2nd ed. Nauvoo, IL: John Taylor, 1844. Selections also available in Robin Scott Jensen, Richard E. Turley Jr., and Riley M. Lorimer, eds., *Revelations and Translations, Volume 2: Published Revelations.* Vol. 2 of the Revelations and Translations series of *The Joseph Smith Papers,* edited by Dean C. Jessee, Ronald K. Esplin, and Richard Lyman Bushman (Salt Lake City: Church Historian's Press, 2011).

The Doctrine and Covenants, of the Church of Jesus Christ of Latter-day Saints, Containing the Revelations Given to Joseph Smith, Jun., the Prophet, for the Building Up of the Kingdom of God in the Last Days. Salt Lake City: Deseret News, 1876.

The Doctrine and Covenants of the Church of Jesus Christ of Latter-day Saints: Containing Revelations Given to Joseph Smith, the Prophet, with Some Additions by His Successors in the Presidency of the Church. Salt Lake City: The Church of Jesus Christ of Latter-day Saints, 2013.

Domestic Economist and Advisor in Every Branch of the Family Establishment. London. Jan.– Mar. 1850.

Douglas, George and Ellen. Letter to Father and Mother, June 2, 1842. Typescript. CHL.

Doyle, Don H. "Rules of Order: Henry Martyn Robert and the Popularization of American Parliamentary Law." *American Quarterly* 32, no. 1 (Spring 1980): 3–18.

Driggs, Ken. "The Prosecutions Begin: Defining Cohabitation in 1885." *Dialogue: A Journal of Mormon Thought* 21, no. 1 (Spring 1988): 109–124.

Dublin, Thomas. "Women's Work and the Family Economy: Textiles and Palm Leaf Hatmaking in New England, 1830–1850." *Tocqueville Review* 5, no. 2 (1983): 297–316.

Dudden, Faye E. *Fighting Chance: The Struggle over Woman Suffrage and Black Suffrage in Reconstruction America.* New York: Oxford University Press, 2011.

East Bountiful Ward, Davis Stake. Manuscript History and Historical Reports, 1877–1897, CHL.

Ehat, Andrew F. "Joseph Smith's Introduction of Temple Ordinances and the 1844 Mormon Succession Question." Master's thesis, Brigham Young University, 1982.

1841 Scotland Census. Reels 1–151. General Register Office for Scotland. Edinburgh, Scotland.

Eighteenth Ward, Salt Lake Stake. Eighteenth Ward General Minutes, 1854–1976. CHL.

Eighth Ward, Liberty Stake. Eighth Ward Relief Society Minutes and Records, 1867–1969. CHL.

Ellsworth, George. "A Guide to the Manuscripts in the Bancroft Library Relating to the History of Utah." *Utah Historical Quarterly* 22, no. 3 (July 1954): 197–248.

———. "Hubert Howe Bancroft and the History of Utah." *Utah Historical Quarterly* 22, no. 2 (Apr. 1954): 99–124.

Embry, Jessie L. "Exiles for the Principle: LDS Polygamy in Canada." *Dialogue: A Journal of Mormon Thought* 18, no. 3 (Fall 1985): 108–116.

———. "Relief Society Grain Storage Program, 1876–1940." Master's thesis, Brigham Young University, 1974.

Encyclopedia of Mormonism. Edited by Daniel H. Ludlow. 5 vols. New York: Macmillan, 1992.

Falkner, Thomas M., Nancy Felson, and David Konstan, eds. *Contextualizing Classics: Ideology, Performance, Dialogue.* Lanham, MD: Rowman and Littlefield, 1999.

Farmington Ward, Davis Stake. Farmington Ward Relief Society Minutes and Records, 1868–1951. CHL.

Faulring, Scott H., Kent P. Jackson, and Robert J. Matthews, eds. *Joseph Smith's New Translation of the Bible: Original Manuscripts.* Provo, UT: Religious Studies Center, Brigham Young University, 2004.

Female Council of Health. Minutes, Aug. 14, 1852. CHL.

Fifteenth Ward, Riverside Stake. Relief Society Minutes and Records, 1868–1968. CHL.

Fifteenth Ward, Salt Lake Stake. Fifteenth Ward Relief Society Annual Message, 1873. CHL.

Fifth Ward, Temple View Stake. Fifth Ward Manuscript History and Historical Reports, 1849–1964. CHL.

Fillmore Ward, Millard Stake. Fillmore Ward Relief Society Minutes and Records, 1868–1947. CHL.

Firmage, Edwin Brown, and Richard Collin Mangrum. *Zion in the Courts: A Legal History of the Church of Jesus Christ of Latter-day Saints, 1830–1900.* Urbana: University of Illinois Press, 1988.

First Presidency. *Circular of the First Presidency of the Church of Jesus Christ of Latter-day Saints.* July 11, 1877. Copy at CHL.

———. First Presidency Circular Letters, 1855–2013. CHL.

———. First Presidency General Administration Files, 1923, 1932, 1937–1967. CHL.

———. Important to the People of the British Isles, [1911?]. CHL.

———. Joseph F. Smith Stake Correspondence, 1901–1918. CHL.

———. Letterpress Copybooks, 1877–1949. CHL.

Flake, Chad J., and Larry W. Draper, eds. *A Mormon Bibliography, 1830–1930: Books, Pamphlets, Periodicals, and Broadsides Relating to the First Century of Mormonism.* 2 vols. 2nd ed. Provo, UT: Religious Studies Center, Brigham Young University, 2004.

Flake, Kathleen. "The Development of Early Latter-day Saint Marriage Rites, 1831–53." *Journal of Mormon History* 41, no. 1 (Jan. 2015): 77–102.

———. "The Emotional and Priestly Logic of Plural Marriage." *Leonard J. Arrington Mormon History Lecture Series,* no. 15. Logan: Utah State University Press, 2010.

Flanders, Robert Bruce. *Nauvoo: Kingdom on the Mississippi.* Urbana: University of Illinois Press, 1965.

Ford, Thomas. *A History of Illinois, from Its Commencement as a State in 1818 to 1847. Containing a Full Account of the Black Hawk War, the Rise, Progress, and Fall of Mormonism, the Alton and Lovejoy Riots, and Other Important and Interesting Events.* Chicago: S. C. Griggs; New York: Ivison and Phinney, 1854.

Fourteenth Ward, Salt Lake Stake. Fourteenth Ward Relief Society Minutes and Records, 1864–1957. CHL.

Freeze, Lillie T. Papers, 1886–1928. CHL.

Gardner, Hamilton. "The Utah Territorial Militia." Unpublished typescript, [not after 1959]. Copy at CHL.

Garnsey, Caroline. "Ladies Magazines to 1850." *Bulletin of the New York Public Library* 58 (Feb. 1954): 74–88.

Gates, Susa Young. *History of the Young Ladies' Mutual Improvement Association of the Church of Jesus Christ of Latter-day Saints, from November 1869 to June 1910.* Salt Lake City: Deseret News, 1911.

———. Papers, 1852–1932. Utah State Historical Society, Salt Lake City.

———. Papers, ca. 1870–1933. CHL.

Geary, Edward A. *A History of Emery County.* Salt Lake City: Utah State Historical Society and Emery County Commission, 1996.

Ginzberg, Lori D. *Elizabeth Cady Stanton: An American Life.* New York: Hill and Wang, 2009.

———. *Women and the Work of Benevolence: Morality, Politics, and Class in the Nineteenth-Century United States.* New Haven, CT: Yale University Press, 1990.

Givens, Terryl L., and Matthew J. Grow. *Parley P. Pratt: The Apostle Paul of Mormonism.* New York: Oxford University Press, 2011.

Godfrey, Donald G., and Brigham Y. Card, eds. *The Diaries of Charles Ora Card: The Canadian Years, 1886–1903.* Salt Lake City: University of Utah Press, 1993.

Godfrey, Matthew C., Mark Ashurst-McGee, Grant Underwood, Robert J. Woodford, and William G. Hartley, eds. *Documents, Volume 2: July 1831–January 1833.* Vol. 2 of the Documents series of *The Joseph Smith Papers,* edited by Dean C. Jessee, Ronald K. Esplin, Richard Lyman Bushman, and Matthew J. Grow. Salt Lake City: Church Historian's Press, 2013.

Gordon, Sarah Barringer. "The Liberty of Self-Degradation: Polygamy, Woman Suffrage, and Consent in Nineteenth-Century America." *Journal of American History* 83, no. 3 (Dec. 1996): 815–847.

———. *The Mormon Question: Polygamy and Constitutional Conflict in Nineteenth-Century America.* Studies in Legal History. Chapel Hill and London: University of North Carolina Press, 2002.

Grow, Matthew J. *"Liberty to the Downtrodden": Thomas L. Kane, Romantic Reformer.* New Haven, CT: Yale University Press, 2009.

Gunnison Ward, Gunnison Stake. Gunnison Ward Manuscript History and Historical Reports, 1861–1949. CHL.

———. Gunnison Ward Relief Society Minutes and Records, 1872–1949. CHL.

Hales, Brian C. *Joseph Smith's Polygamy.* 3 vols. Salt Lake City: Greg Kofford Books, 2013.

Hamilton, C. Mark. *Nineteenth-Century Mormon Architecture and City Planning.* New York: Oxford University Press, 1995.

Hampshire, David, Martha Sonntag Bradley, and Allen Roberts. *A History of Summit County.* Utah Centennial County History Series. Salt Lake City: Utah State Historical Society, 1998.

Handbook of the Relief Society of the Church of Jesus Christ of Latter-day Saints. Salt Lake City: General Board of the Relief Society, 1931.

Harrisville Ward, Farr West Stake. General Minutes, 1850–1977. CHL.

Hartley, William G. *Another Kind of Gold: The Life of Albert King Thurber, a Utah Pioneer, Explorer and Community Builder.* Troy, ID: C. L. Dalton, 2011.

———. "Missouri's 1838 Extermination Order and the Mormons' Forced Removal to Illinois." *Mormon Historical Studies* 2, no. 1 (Spring 2001): 5–27.

———. "Mormons, Crickets, and Gulls: A New Look at an Old Story." *Utah Historical Quarterly* 38, no. 3 (Summer 1970): 224–239.

———. "The Priesthood Reorganization of 1877: Brigham Young's Last Achievement." *BYU Studies* 20, no. 1 (Fall 1979): 3–36.

Hawaii Honolulu Mission. Hawaii Honolulu Mission Manuscript History and Historical Reports, 1850–1967. CHL.

Hedges, Andrew H., and Richard Neitzel Holzapfel, eds. *Within These Prison Walls:*

Lorenzo Snow's Record Book, 1886–1897. Provo, UT: Religious Studies Center, Brigham Young University, 2010.

Hedges, Andrew H., and Alex D. Smith. "The Lady and the Governor: Emma Hale Smith's and Thomas Carlin's 1842 Correspondence." *Mormon Historical Studies* 9 (Fall 2008): 139–152.

Hedges, Andrew H., Alex D. Smith, and Richard Lloyd Anderson, eds. *Journals, Volume 2: December 1841–April 1843.* Vol. 2 of the Journals series of *The Joseph Smith Papers,* edited by Dean C. Jessee, Ronald K. Esplin, and Richard Lyman Bushman. Salt Lake City: Church Historian's Press, 2011.

Hedges, Andrew H., Alex D. Smith, and Brent M. Rogers, eds. *Journals, Volume 3: May 1843–June 1844.* Vol. 3 of the Journals series of *The Joseph Smith Papers,* edited by Ronald K. Esplin and Matthew J. Grow. Salt Lake City: Church Historian's Press, 2015.

Hicks, Michael. *Mormonism and Music: A History.* Urbana: University of Illinois Press, 1989.

Higbee, Janelle M. "'President Mrs. Kimball': A Rhetoric of Words and Works." Master's thesis, Brigham Young University, 1998.

Hill, Ivy Hooper Blood Hill, ed. *Jane Wilkie Hooper Blood Autobiography and Abridged Diary.* Logan, UT: J. P. Smith, 1966.

Historian's Office. General Church Minutes, 1839–1877. CHL.

———. Joseph Smith History, Draft Notes, ca. 1839–1856. CHL.

———. Joseph Smith History Documents, ca. 1839–1860. CHL.

———. Journal, 1844–1997. CHL.

———. Letterpress Copybooks, 1854–1879, 1885–1886. CHL.

———. Record of Members Collection, 1836–1970. CHL.

Historian's Office Catalogs and Inventories, 1846–1904. CHL.

The Historical Record, a Monthly Periodical, Devoted Exclusively to Historical, Biographical, Chronological and Statistical Matters. Salt Lake City. 1882–1890.

"History of Provo City." *Tullidge's Quarterly Magazine* 3, no. 3 (July 1884): 233–277.

History of Relief Society, 1824–1966. Salt Lake City: General Board of Relief Society, 1966.

"History of the Bountiful First Ward Relief Society Beginning 24 April 1857 to 5 February 1961." Unpublished typescript, 1961. Copy at CHL.

"History of the General Organization." *Contributor* 1, no. 1 (Oct. 1879): 21.

The Holy Bible, Containing the Old and New Testaments Translated out of the Original Tongues: And with the Former Translations Diligently Compared and Revised, by His Majesty's Special Command. Authorized King James Version with Explanatory Notes and Cross References to the Standard Works of the Church of Jesus Christ of Latter-day Saints. Salt Lake City: The Church of Jesus Christ of Latter-day Saints, 2013.

Horne, Joseph Smith. Autobiographical Sketch, ca. 1931. CHL.

Howe, Eber D. *Mormonism Unvailed; or, A Faithful Account of That Singular Imposition and Delusion, from Its Rise to the Present Time. With Sketches of the Characters of Its Propagators, and a Full Detail of the Manner in Which the Famous Golden Bible Was Brought before the World. To Which Are Added, Inquiries into the Probability That the Historical Part of the Said Bible Was Written by One Solomon Spalding, More Than*

Twenty Years Ago, and by Him Intended to Have Been Published as a Romance. Painesville, OH: By the author, 1834.

Howe, Julia Ward. "Battle Hymn of the Republic." *Atlantic Monthly* 9 (Feb. 1862): 10.

Hunter, Louis C. *Steamboats on the Western Rivers: An Economic and Technological History.* New York: Dover, 1993.

Huntington, William D. Cemetery Records, 1839–1845. CHL.

"The Husband-Wife Evidentiary Privilege in Criminal Proceedings." *Journal of Criminal Law and Criminology* 52, no. 1 (May–June 1961): 74–85.

Hymns: Church of Jesus Christ of Latter-day Saints. [Salt Lake City]: Church of Jesus Christ of Latter-day Saints, 1948.

Hyrum Ward, Hyrum Stake. Hyrum Ward Relief Society Minutes and Records, 1870–1901. CHL.

Indianola Ward, North Sanpete Stake. Indianola Ward Manuscript History and Historical Reports, 1860–1936. CHL.

Isom, Alice Parker. "Memoirs of Alice Parker Isom," ca. 1885. CHL.

Iverson, Joan. "The Mormon-Suffrage Relationship: Personal and Political Quandaries." *Frontiers: A Journal of Women Studies* 11, nos. 2–3 (1990): 8–16.

Jarvis, Zora Smith, comp. *Ancestry, Biography, and Family of George A. Smith.* Provo, UT: Brigham Young University Press, 1962.

Jefferson, Thomas. *A Manual of Parliamentary Practice: Composed Originally for the Use of the Senate of the United States.* Philadelphia: Hogan and Thompson, 1840.

Jensen, Richard L. "Forgotten Relief Societies, 1844–67." *Dialogue: A Journal of Mormon Thought* 16, no. 1 (Spring 1983): 105–125.

———. "Steaming Through: Arrangements for Mormon Emigration from Europe, 1869–1887." *Journal of Mormon History* 9 (1982): 3–23.

———. "Transplanted to Zion: The Impact of British Latter-day Saint Immigration upon Nauvoo." *BYU Studies* 31, no. 1 (Winter 1991): 77–87.

Jensen, Robin Scott, Richard E. Turley Jr., and Riley M. Lorimer, eds. *Revelations and Translations, Volume 2: Published Revelations.* Vol. 2 of the Revelations and Translations series of *The Joseph Smith Papers,* edited by Dean C. Jessee, Ronald K. Esplin, and Richard Lyman Bushman. Salt Lake City: Church Historian's Press, 2011.

Jenson, Andrew. *Encyclopedic History of the Church of Jesus Christ of Latter-day Saints.* Salt Lake City: Deseret News, 1941.

———. *Latter-day Saint Biographical Encyclopedia: A Compilation of Biographical Sketches of Prominent Men and Women in the Church of Jesus Christ of Latter-day Saints.* 4 vols. Salt Lake City: Andrew Jenson History Co., 1901–1936.

Jessee, Dean C. "The Reliability of Joseph Smith's History." *Journal of Mormon History* 3 (1976): 23–46.

———. "The Writing of Joseph Smith's History." *BYU Studies* 11, no. 4 (Summer 1971): 439–473.

Jessee, Dean C., Mark Ashurst-McGee, and Richard L. Jensen, eds. *Journals, Volume 1: 1832–1839.* Vol. 1 of the Journals series of *The Joseph Smith Papers,* edited by Dean C. Jessee, Ronald K. Esplin, and Richard Lyman Bushman. Salt Lake City: Church Historian's Press, 2008.

Jessee, Dean C., and David J. Whittaker. "The Last Months of Mormonism in Missouri: The Albert Perry Rockwood Journal." *BYU Studies* 28. no. 1 (Winter 1988): 5–41.

Johnson, Clark V., ed. *Mormon Redress Petitions: Documents of the 1833–1838 Missouri Conflict.* Religious Studies Center Monograph Series 16. Provo, UT: Religious Studies Center, Brigham Young University, 1992.

Jones, Sondra. "Saints or Sinners? The Evolving Perceptions of Mormon-Indian Relations in Utah Historiography." *Utah Historical Quarterly* 72, no. 1 (Winter 2004): 19–46.

The Joseph Smith Papers. http://www.josephsmithpapers.org.

Journal of Discourses. 26 vols. Liverpool: Various publishers, 1855–1886.

Jubilee History of Latter-day Saints Sunday Schools, 1849–1899. Salt Lake City: Deseret Sunday School Union, 1900.

Kane, Thomas L., and Elizabeth W. Collection, 1762–1892. L. Tom Perry Special Collections, Harold B. Lee Library, Brigham Young University, Provo, UT.

Kaysville Ward, North Davis Stake. Kaysville Ward Primary Association Minutes and Records, 1879–1940. CHL.

———. Kaysville Ward Relief Society Minutes and Records, 1878–1937. CHL.

Kelley, Mary. *Learning to Stand and Speak: Women, Education, and Public Life in America's Republic.* Chapel Hill: University of North Carolina Press, 2006.

Kimball, Presendia Lathrop Huntington. Reminiscences, 1881. CHL.

Kirtland Elders Quorum. "A Record of the First Quorumum of Elders Belonging to the Church of Christ: In Kirtland Geauga Co. Ohio," 1836–1838, 1840–1841. Community of Christ Library-Archives, Independence, MO.

Lapsansky, Emma Jones, and Anne A. Verplanck, eds. *Quaker Aesthetics: Reflections on a Quaker Ethic in American Design and Consumption.* Philadelphia: University of Pennsylvania Press, 2003.

Latter Day Saints' Messenger and Advocate. Kirtland, OH. Oct. 1834–Sept. 1837.

Latter-day Saints' Millennial Star. Liverpool. 1840–1970.

LDS Church News: News of the Church of Jesus Christ of Latter-day Saints. Salt Lake City. 1931–.

Lehi Ward, Alpine Stake. Lehi Ward Relief Society Minutes and Records, 1868–1892. CHL.

Leonard, Glen M. *Nauvoo: A Place of Peace, a People of Promise.* Salt Lake City: Deseret Book; Provo, UT: Brigham Young University Press, 2002.

Letters Pertaining to Freemasonry in Nauvoo, 1842. CHL.

Liberty Stake Relief Society Scrapbook Selections, 1915–1933. CHL.

Lightner, Mary E. Papers, 1865–1914. 20th Century Western and Mormon Manuscripts, L. Tom Perry Special Collections, Harold B. Lee Library, Brigham Young University, Provo, UT.

Lindquist, Jason. "'Unlocking the Door of the Gospel': The Concept of 'Keys' in Mormonism and Early American Culture." *Archive of Restoration Culture: Summer Fellows' Papers, 1997–1999.* Provo, UT: Joseph Fielding Smith Institute for Latter-day Saint History, 2000.

Little, Emma Priscilla Evans. Papers, 1870–1941. L. Tom Perry Special Collections, Harold B. Lee Library, Brigham Young University, Provo, UT.

Logan Utah Cache Stake. Logan Utah Cache Stake Relief Society Minutes and Records, 1868–1973. CHL.

London North Branch, London England North Stake. London North Branch Relief Society Minutes and Records, 1884–1973. CHL.

Lowe, Mary B. Statement, May 12, 1941. Typescript. CHL.

Lyman, Edward Leo, and Linda King Newell. *A History of Millard County.* Salt Lake City: Utah State Historical Society, 1999.

Lyman, Eliza Maria Partridge. Journal, 1846–1885. CHL.

Lyon, Thomas Edgar. "Evangelical Protestant Missionary Activities in Mormon Dominated Areas: 1865–1900." PhD diss., University of Utah, 1962.

MacKay, Michael Hubbard, Gerrit J. Dirkmaat, Grant Underwood, Robert J. Woodford, and William G. Hartley, eds. *Documents, Volume 1: July 1828–June 1831.* Vol. 1 of the Documents series of *The Joseph Smith Papers,* edited by Dean C. Jessee, Ronald K. Esplin, Richard Lyman Bushman, and Matthew J. Grow. Salt Lake City: Church Historian's Press, 2013.

MacKinnon, William P., ed. *At Sword's Point, Part 1: A Documentary History of the Utah War to 1858.* Kingdom in the West: The Mormons and the American Frontier 10. Norman, OK: Arthur H. Clark, 2008.

Madsen, Carol Cornwall. *An Advocate for Women: The Public Life of Emmeline B. Wells, 1870–1920.* Biographies in Latter-day Saint History. Provo, UT: Brigham Young University Press, 2006.

———, ed. *Battle for the Ballot: Essays on Woman Suffrage in Utah, 1870–1896.* Logan: Utah State University Press, 1997.

———. "Creating Female Community: Relief Society in Cache Valley, Utah, 1868–1900." *Journal of Mormon History* 21, no. 2 (Fall 1995): 126–154.

———. "'Remember the Women of Zion': A Study of the Editorial Content of the *Woman's Exponent,* A Mormon Woman's Journal." Master's thesis, University of Utah, 1977.

Madsen, Carol Cornwall, and Susan Staker Oman. *Sisters and Little Saints: One Hundred Years of Primary.* Salt Lake City: Deseret Book, 1979.

Manifesto of the Presidency and Apostles Issued December 12, 1889, Also the Official Declaration or Manifesto by President Wilford Woodruff Prohibiting Further Plural Marriages, and Its Adoption by the General Conference, October 6, 1890. Salt Lake City: Deseret News, [1890].

Massie, Michael A. "Reform Is Where You Find It: The Roots of Woman Suffrage in Wyoming." *Annals of Wyoming* 62 (Spring 1990): 2–21.

Maughan, Mary Ann Weston. Journal, 1817–1901. 3 vols. Typescript. Logan: Library of the Utah State Agricultural College, 1955.

Maxwell, John Gary. *Robert Newton Baskin and the Making of Modern Utah.* Norman: University of Oklahoma Press, 2013.

May, Dean. "A Demographic Portrait of the Mormons, 1830–1980." In *The New Mormon History: Revisionist Essays on the Past,* edited by D. Michael Quinn, 121–135. Salt Lake City: Signature Books, 1992.

McBride, Matthew. *A House for the Most High: The Story of the Original Nauvoo Temple.* Salt Lake City: Greg Kofford Books, 2006.

McElprang, Stella, comp. *"Castle Valley": A History of Emery County.* N.p.: Emery County Company of the Daughters of Utah Pioneers, 1949.

McGavin, E. Cecil, and Albert L. Zobell Jr. "Grain Storage among the Latter-day Saints." *Improvement Era* 44, no. 3 (Mar. 1941): 142–144, 180–186.

McKay, David. Letter to Mrs. James Hood, Mar. 16, 1916. Copy at CHL.

McMullin, Thomas A., and David Walker. *Biographical Directory of American Territorial Governors.* Westport, CT: Meckler, 1984.

Meeks, Priddy. Reminiscences, 1879. Typescript. CHL.

Melder, Keith E. *Beginnings of Sisterhood: The American Woman's Rights Movement, 1800–1850.* New York: Schocken Books, 1977.

Miller, David E. *Hole-in-the-Rock: An Epic in the Colonization of the Great American West.* Salt Lake City: University of Utah Press, 1966.

Missionary Department. Missionary Department Missionary Record Index, 1830–1971. CHL.

Moerman, Daniel E. *Native American Medicinal Plants: An Ethnobotanical Dictionary.* Portland: Timber Press, 2009.

Monroe, James M. Journal, 1841–1842, 1845. CHL.

Moore, Cornelius. *The Craftsman, and Freemason's Guide; Containing a Delineation of the Rituals of Freemasonry. . . .* Cincinnati: Jacob Ernst, 1854.

Moore, Thomas. *Letters and Journals of Lord Byron: With Notices of His Life.* 2 vols. London: John Murray, 1830.

Morgan Utah Stake. Morgan Utah Stake Relief Society Minutes and Records, 1878–1973. CHL.

"Morley's Settlement." *Nauvoo Journal* 11, no. 1 (Spring 1999): 153–155.

Mormonism: A Historical Encyclopedia. Edited by W. Paul Reeve and Ardis E. Parshall. Santa Barbara, CA: ABC-CLIO, 2010.

Mormon Pioneer Overland Travel, 1847–1868. Compiled by the Church of Jesus Christ of Latter-day Saints. http://history.lds.org/overlandtravels.

Mormon War Papers, 1838–1841. Missouri State Archives, Jefferson City.

"Mormon" Women's Protest. An Appeal for Freedom, Justice and Equal Rights. The Ladies of the Church of Jesus Christ of Latter-day Saints Protest against the Tyranny and Indecency of Federal Officials in Utah, and against Their Own Disfranchisement without Cause. Full Account of Proceedings at the Great Mass Meeting, Held in the Theatre, Salt Lake City Utah, Saturday, March 6, 1886. [Salt Lake City]: Deseret News Co., [1886].

Moses (selections from the Book of). See *Pearl of Great Price.*

Mott, Frank Luther. *A History of American Magazines.* Vol. 2, *1850–1865.* Cambridge, MA: Harvard University Press, 1957.

Nauvoo, IL. Records, 1841–1845. CHL.

Nauvoo, IL, Recorder. Marriage Record, 1842–1845. CHL.

Nauvoo City Council. "A Record of the Proceedings of the City Council of the City of Nauvoo Handcock County, State of Illinois, Commencing A.D. 1841," ca. 1841–1845. CHL.

Nauvoo High Council Minutes, 1839–1845. CHL.

Nauvoo Masonic Lodge Minute Book. / "Record of Na[u]voo Lodge under Dispensation," 1841–1846. CHL.

Nauvoo Neighbor. Nauvoo, IL. 1843–1845.

Neilson, Reid L., ed. *In the Whirlpool: The Pre-Manifesto Letters of President Wilford Woodruff to the William Atkin Family, 1885–1890.* With contributions by Thomas G. Alexander and Jan Shipps. Norman, OK: Arthur H. Clark, 2011.

Nephi Pratt Family Papers, 1867–1910. CHL.

Nephi Ward, Juab Stake. Nephi Ward Manuscript History and Historical Reports, 1847–1900. CHL.

———. Nephi Ward Relief Society Minutes and Records, 1868–1878. CHL.

Newell, Linda King, and Valeen Tippetts Avery. *Mormon Enigma: Emma Hale Smith.* 2nd ed. Urbana: University of Illinois Press, 1994.

Newman, Louise Michelle. *White Women's Rights: The Racial Origins of Feminism in the United States.* New York: Oxford University Press, 1999.

New York Herald. New York City. 1835–1924.

New York Times. New York City. 1851–.

Nugent, Walter. *Into the West: The Story of Its People.* New York: Alfred A. Knopf, 1999.

Ohio Star. Ravenna. 1830–1854.

Okker, Patricia. *Our Sister Editors: Sarah J. Hale and the Tradition of Nineteenth-Century American Women Editors.* Athens: University of Georgia Press, 1995.

Olsen, Andrew D. *The Price We Paid: The Extraordinary Story of the Willie and Martin Handcart Pioneers.* Salt Lake City: Deseret Book, 2006.

Orangeville Ward, Emery Stake. Orangeville Ward Relief Society Minutes and Records, 1882–1967. CHL.

The Oxford English Dictionary. Edited by James A. H. Murray, Henry Bradley, W. A. Craigie, and C. T. Onions. 12 vols. 1933. Reprint. Oxford: Oxford University Press, 1970.

The Oxford English Dictionary. Edited by J. A. Simpson and E. S. C. Weiner. 2nd ed. 20 vols. Oxford: Clarendon, 1989.

Paine, Judith. "The Women's Pavilion of 1876." *Feminist Art Journal* 4, no. 4 (Winter 1975–1976): 5–12.

Palmer, George Herbert, and Alice Freeman Palmer. *The Teacher: Essays and Addresses on Education.* Boston: Houghton Mifflin, 1908.

Palmer, Phoebe. *The Way of Holiness, with Notes by the Way; Being a Narrative of Experience Resulting from a Determination to Be a Bible Christian.* New York: Piercy and Reed, 1843.

Palmer, William Moroni. "A Sketch of the Life of Patience Delila Pierce Palmer," ca. 1927. CHL.

Parker, Ellen W. Letters, 1842–1851. CHL.

Parley P. Pratt Family Papers, 1846–1886. CHL.

Partridge, Edward, Jr. Journals, 1854–1899. CHL.

Partridge, George F., ed. "The Death of a Mormon Dictator: Letters of Massachusetts Mormons, 1843–1848." *New England Quarterly* 9 (Dec. 1936): 583–617.

Partridge, Sarah C. Journals, 1882–1885. CHL.

Paulsen, David L., and Martin Pulido. "'A Mother There': A Survey of Historical Teachings about Mother in Heaven." *BYU Studies* 50, no. 1 (2011): 70–97.

The Pearl of Great Price: A Selection from the Revelations, Translations, and Narrations of Joseph Smith, First Prophet, Seer, and Revelator to the Church of Jesus Christ of Latter-day Saints. Salt Lake City: The Church of Jesus Christ of Latter-day Saints, 2013.

Peterson, F. Ross. *A History of Cache County.* Salt Lake City: Utah State Historical Society, 1997.

Peterson, Paul H. "The Mormon Reformation of 1856–1857: The Rhetoric and the Reality." *Journal of Mormon History* 15 (1989): 59–87.

Pioneer Women of Faith and Fortitude. 4 vols. Salt Lake City: Daughters of Utah Pioneers, 1998.

Plewe, Brandon S., ed. *Mapping Mormonism: An Atlas of Latter-day Saint History.* Provo, UT: Brigham Young University Press, 2012.

The Poetical Works of Alexander Pope. 3 vols. London: William Pickering, 1835.

Poll, Richard D. "The Move South." *BYU Studies* 29, no. 4 (Fall 1989): 65–88.

Portnoy, Alisse Theodore. "'Female Petitioners Can Lawfully Be Heard': Negotiating Female Decorum, United States Politics, and Political Agency, 1829–1831." *Journal of the Early Republic* 23, no. 4 (Winter 2003): 573–610.

Pratt, Belinda Marden. *Defence of Polygamy, by a Lady of Utah, in a Letter to Her Sister in New Hampshire.* Salt Lake City: n.p., 1854.

Pratt, Eleanor J. McComb. Papers, ca. 1857. CHL.

Pratt, Parley P. *The Autobiography of Parley Parker Pratt, One of the Twelve Apostles of the Church of Jesus Christ of Latter-Day Saints, Embracing His Life, Ministry and Travels, with Extracts, in Prose and Verse, from His Miscellaneous Writings.* Edited by Parley P. Pratt Jr. New York: Russell Brothers, 1874.

———. Correspondence, 1842–1855. CHL.

———. *History of the Late Persecution Inflicted by the State of Missouri upon the Mormons, in Which Ten Thousand American Citizens Were Robbed, Plundered, and Driven from the State, and Many Others Imprisoned, Martyred, &c. for Their Religion, and All This by Military Force, by Order of the Executive. By P. P. Pratt, Minister of the Gospel. Written during Eight Months Imprisonment in That State.* Detroit: Dawson and Bates, 1839.

Presiding Bishopric. Presiding Bishopric Bishops Meeting Minutes, 1851–1884. CHL.

———. Presiding Bishopric Circular Letters, 1875–2013. CHL.

Price, William Bennett, ed. *The Register of the Parish Church of St. Leonard, Downham, 1605–1837.* Leyland, England: Lancashire Parish Register Society, 1979.

Primary Association. Primary Association General Board Minutes, 1889–1994. CHL.

Prince, Gregory A. *Power from on High: The Development of Mormon Priesthood.* Salt Lake City: Signature Books, 1995.

Proceedings of the First Three Republican National Conventions of 1856, 1860 and 1864. Minneapolis, MN: Charles W. Johnson, 1893.

Prophet. New York City. May 1844–May 1845.

Pyper, George D. Papers, 1834–1975. Special Collections, J. Willard Marriott Library, University of Utah, Salt Lake City.

Quincy Whig. Quincy, IL. 1838–1856.

Quist, John. "John E. Page: An Apostle of Uncertainty." *Journal of Mormon History* 12 (1985): 53–68.

"A Record of the Names of the Members of the Church of Jesus Christ of Latterday Saints, as Taken by the Lesser Priesthood, in the Spring of the Year 1842, and Continued, to Be Added as the Members Arrive in the City of Nauvoo, Hancock County; Illinois. Also the Deaths of Members, and Their Children, and Names of Children under 8 Years of Age," after 1844–after 1846. In Far West and Nauvoo Elders' Certificates, 1837–1838, 1840–1846. CHL.

Reeder, Jennifer. "Eliza R. Snow and the Prophet's Gold Watch: Time Keeper as Relic." *Journal of Mormon History* 31, no. 1 (Spring 2005): 119–141.

———. "'To Do Something Extraordinary': Mormon Women and the Creation of a Usable Past." PhD diss., George Mason University, 2013.

Relief Society. Narrative Reports, 1964–1971, 1973–1975. CHL.

———. Relief Society Annual Reports, 1913–1973. CHL.

———. Relief Society Stake Financial and Statistical Reports, 1882–1883. CHL.

Relief Society General Board Minutes, 1886–1911. CHL.

Relief Society Magazine. Salt Lake City, 1914–1970. Relief Society Record, 1880–1892. CHL.

"Relief Society Selects Centennial Seal by Jack Sears." *Improvement Era* 44, no. 9 (Sept. 1941): 542.

Relief Society Washing and Anointing Files, 1888, 1903, 1914–1916, 1922, 1946–1947. CHL.

Reorganized Church of Jesus Christ of Latter Day Saints v. Church of Christ of Independence, Missouri, et al. (C.C.W.D. Mo. 1894). Typescript. Testimonies and Depositions, 1892. CHL.

Revelations Collection, 1831–ca. 1844, 1847, 1861, ca. 1876. CHL.

Revolution. New York City. 1868–1972.

Rich, Sarah P. Autobiography, 1885. CHL.

Richards, Henry P. Papers, 1854–1900. CHL.

Richards, Jane S. Autobiographical Sketch, Mar. 30, 1881. CHL.

Richards Family Collection, 1837–1961. CHL.

Rives, John C. *Appendix to the Congressional Globe: Containing Speeches, Important State Papers, and the Laws of the Third Session Thirty-Seventh Congress.* Washington DC: Congressional Globe, 1863.

Robbins, Louise Barnum, ed. *History and Minutes of the National Council of Women of the United States, Organized in Washington, D. C., March 31, 1888.* Boston: E. B. Stillings, 1898.

Rogers, Aurelia Spencer. *Life Sketches of Orson Spencer and Others, and History of Primary Work.* Salt Lake City: George Q. Cannon and Sons, 1898.

Romney, Edyth Jenkins. Thomas Bullock Minutes (Loose Papers), 1848–1856. Brigham Young Office Files Transcriptions, 1974–1978. CHL.

Rowe, Nicholas. *The Tragedy of Jane Shore.* London: Bernard Lintot, 1736.

Rydberg, P. A. *Flora of the Rocky Mountains and Adjacent Plains.* New York: By the author, 1917.

Sacramento Daily Record-Union. Sacramento, CA. 1875–1903.

Sacramento Daily Union. Sacramento, CA. 1853–1875.

Sacred Hymns and Spiritual Songs, for the Church of Jesus Christ of Latter-day Saints, in Europe. Liverpool: F. D. Richards, 1851.

Sacred Hymns and Spiritual Songs. For the Church of Jesus Christ of Latter-day Saints. 12th ed. Liverpool: George Q. Cannon; London: L. D. Saints' Book Depot, 1863.

Sacred Hymns and Spiritual Songs. For the Church of Jesus Christ of Latter-day Saints. 13th ed. Liverpool: Albert Carrington; London: L. D. Saints' Book Depot, 1869.

Sacred Hymns and Spiritual Songs. For the Church of Jesus Christ of Latter-day Saints. 14th ed. Salt Lake City: George Q. Cannon, 1871.

Sacred Hymns and Spiritual Songs for the Church of Jesus Christ of Latter-day Saints. 15th ed. Liverpool: Albert Carrington, 1871.

Sadler, Richard W. "The Impact of Mining on Salt Lake City." *Utah Historical Quarterly* 47, no. 3 (Summer 1979): 236–253.

Saint Johns Arizona Stake. Saint Johns Arizona Stake Relief Society Minutes and Records, 1887–1973. CHL.

Saint Johns Ward, Saint Johns Stake. Saint Johns Ward Manuscript History and Historical Reports, 1880–1982. CHL.

Saints' Herald. Independence, MO. 1860–.

Salt Lake Daily Telegraph. Salt Lake City. 1868–1870.

Salt Lake Herald. Salt Lake City. 1870–1909.

Salt Lake Stake. Salt Lake Stake Relief Society Record Book, 1868–1903. CHL.

———. Salt Lake Stake Young Women's Mutual Improvement Association Minutes and Records, 1871–1973. 5 vols. CHL.

Salt Lake Tribune. Salt Lake City. 1871–.

Sangamo Journal. Springfield, IL. 1831–1847.

San Juan Stake. San Juan Stake Manuscript History and Historical Reports, 1833–1938. CHL.

———. San Juan Stake Relief Society Minutes and Records, 1885–1973. CHL.

———. San Juan Stake Relief Society Scrapbook, 1885–1968. CHL.

Savage, Hannah Adeline Hatch. *Record of Hannah Adeline Savage, Woodruff Arizona, and Journal.* Photoreproduction of original manuscript record and journal. Pinedale, AZ: Petersen, 1976.

Seventh Ward, Pioneer Stake. Seventh Ward Relief Society Minutes and Records, 1848–1922. CHL.

Seventh Ward, Salt Lake Stake. Seventh Ward Relief Society Records, 1858–1875. CHL.

Sewall, May Wright. *Genesis of the International Council of Women and the Story of Its Growth, 1888–1893.* Indianapolis, IN: n.p., 1914.

Shipp, Ellis R. Journal, 1871–1878. Photocopy. CHL.

Shirts, Morris A., and Kathryn H. Shirts. *A Trial Furnace: Southern Utah's Iron Mission.* Studies in Latter-day Saint History. Provo, UT: Brigham Young University Press, 2001.

Sixteenth Ward, Riverside Stake. Sixteenth Ward Relief Society Minutes and Records, 1868–1968. CHL.

Sixty-Eighth Annual Conference of the Church of Jesus Christ of Latter-day Saints, Held in the Tabernacle, Salt Lake City, April 6th, 7th, 8th and 10th, 1898, with a Full Report of the Discourses. Salt Lake City: Deseret News, 1898.

Sloan, E. L., comp. *The Salt Lake City Directory and Business Guide, for 1869.* Salt Lake City: By the author, 1869.

Smart, Donna Toland, ed. *Mormon Midwife: The 1846–1888 Diaries of Patty Bartlett Sessions.* Life Writings of Frontier Women 2. Logan: Utah State University Press, 1997.

Smith, Amanda Barnes. Autobiography, 1858. CHL.

———. Notebook, 1854–1866. CHL.

Smith, Andrew F. *The Saintly Scoundrel: The Life and Times of Dr. John Cook Bennett.* Urbana: University of Illinois Press, 1997.

Smith, Bathsheba W. Autobiography, ca. 1875–1906. CHL.

———. Collection, 1842–1948. CHL.

Smith, George A. Journal, Nov. 1872–June 1873. Typescript. CHL.

———. Journals, 1839–1875. George A. Smith, Papers, 1834–1877, CHL.

Smith, George A., Lorenzo Snow, Paul A. Schettler, and Eliza R. Snow. *Correspondence of Palestine Tourists; Comprising a Series of Letters by George A. Smith, Lorenzo Snow, Paul A. Schettler, and Eliza R. Snow, of Utah. Mostly Written While Traveling in Europe, Asia and Africa, in the Years 1872 and 1873.* Salt Lake City: Deseret News, 1875.

Smith, John L. Autobiography and Diaries, 1846–1895. CHL.

Smith, Joseph. Collection, 1827–1846. CHL.

———. "Copies of Letters, &c. &c.," 1839–1843. Joseph Smith Collection. CHL.

———. *General Smith's Views of the Powers and Policy of the Government of the United States.* Nauvoo, IL: John Taylor, 1844.

———, et al. History, 1838–1856. Vols. A-1–F-1 (original), A-2–E-2 (fair copy). CHL. The history for the period after August 5, 1838, was composed after the death of Joseph Smith.

———, et al. *History of the Church of Jesus Christ of Latter-day Saints.* Edited by B. H. Roberts. Salt Lake City: Deseret News, 1902–1912 (vols. 1–6), 1932 (vol. 7).

Smith, Joseph F. Affidavits about Celestial Marriage, 1869–1915. CHL.

———. Papers, 1854–1918. CHL.

Smith, Joseph Fielding, comp. *Life of Joseph F. Smith, Sixth President of the Church of Jesus Christ of Latter-day Saints.* Salt Lake City: Deseret News, 1938.

Smith, Lucy Mack. History, 1844–1845. 18 books. CHL. Also available in Lavina Fielding Anderson, ed., *Lucy's Book: A Critical Edition of Lucy Mack Smith's Family Memoir* (Salt Lake City: Signature Books, 2001) and on josephsmithpapers.org.

———. History, 1845. CHL. Also available on josephsmithpapers.org.

Smith, Lucy Meserve. "Historical Sketches of My Great Grandfathers," 1889. Lucy Meserve Smith, Papers, 1848–1892. Microfilm. CHL.

Smith, Mary Fielding. Collection, ca. 1832–1848. CHL.

Smith, Sherry L. *Reimagining Indians: Native Americans through Anglo Eyes, 1880–1940.* New York: Oxford University Press, 2000.

Smoot, Margaret T. Autobiographical Sketch, 1881. Photocopy. CHL.

Snow, Eliza R. Diaries, 1847–1849. Henry E. Huntington Library, San Marino, CA.

———. Journal, 1842–1882. CHL.

———. Letters, 1883–1884. CHL.

———. Papers, 1876. Special Collections, J. Willard Marriott Library, University of Utah, Salt Lake City.

———. *Poems: Religious, Historical, and Political.* 2 vols. Liverpool: F. D. Richards, 1856; Salt Lake City: Latter-day Saints' Printing and Publishing Establishment, 1877.

———. "Sketch of My Life," n.d. Bancroft Library, University of California, Berkeley.

———. *Time and Change: A Poem in Blank Verse. Also Two Odes, One for the Sons of Liberty, the Other for the Fourth of July. By Miss Eliza R. Snow.* Nauvoo, IL: E. Robinson, 1841.

———, et al. "Circular. To the Relief Societies, Retrenchment Associations, and the Women of Utah, Generally," [1875]. International Society Daughters of Utah Pioneers, Pioneer Memorial Museum, Salt Lake City.

Songs of Zion. N.p., [1853]. In John Freeman, Songbook, ca. 1849. CHL.

Sonne, Conway B. *Saints on the Seas: A Maritime History of Mormon Migration, 1830–1890.* Salt Lake City: University of Utah Press, 1983.

Spanish Fork Ward, Utah Stake. Spanish Fork Ward Manuscript History and Historical Reports, 1851–1900. CHL.

Spencer, Clarissa Young, and Mabel Harmer. *Brigham Young at Home.* Salt Lake City: Deseret Book, 1940.

Spurrier, Joseph H. *The Church of Jesus Christ of Latter-day Saints in the Hawaiian Islands.* Salt Lake City: Hawaii Honolulu Mission, 1978.

Staker, Mark L. "'A Comfort unto My Servant, Joseph': Emma Hale Smith (1804–1879)." In *Women of Faith in the Latter Days,* vol. 1, *1775–1820,* edited by Richard E. Turley Jr. and Brittany A. Chapman, 343–362. Salt Lake City: Deseret Book, 2011.

———. *Hearken, O Ye People: The Historical Setting of Joseph Smith's Ohio Revelations.* Salt Lake City: Greg Kofford Books, 2009.

Standard. Ogden, UT. 1888–1908.

Stanton, Elizabeth Cady. *Eighty Years and More (1815–1897): Reminiscences of Elizabeth Cady Stanton.* New York City: European Publishing, 1898.

Stanton, Elizabeth Cady, Susan B. Anthony, and Matilda Joslyn Gage, eds. *History of Woman Suffrage.* 3 vols. 1881–1886. Reprint. Rochester, NY: Susan B. Anthony, Charles Mann, 1887.

Stapley, Jonathan A., and Kristine Wright. "Female Ritual Healing in Mormonism." *Journal of Mormon History* 37, no. 1 (Winter 2011): 1–85.

———. "The Forms and the Power: The Development of Mormon Ritual Healing to 1847." *Journal of Mormon History* 35, no. 3 (Summer 2009): 42–87.

The Statutes at Large, Treaties, and Proclamations, of the United States of America. From December 5, 1859, to March 3, 1863. Arranged in Chronological Order and Carefully Collated with the Originals at Washington. With References to the Matter of Each Act and to the Subsequent Acts on the Same Subject. Vol. 12. Edited by George P. Sanger. Boston: Little, Brown, 1863.

Statutes of the United States of America, Passed at the First Session of the Forty-Seventh Congress, 1881–'82, and Recent Treaties and Executive Proclamations. Washington DC: Government Printing Office, 1882.

The Statutes at Large of the United States of America, from December, 1881, to March, 1883.

And Recent Treaties, Postal Conventions, and Executive Proclamations. Vol. 22. Washington DC: Government Printing Office, 1883.

Statutes of the United States of America, Passed at the First Session of the Forty-Ninth Congress, 1885–1886, and Recent Treaties and Executive Proclamations. Washington DC: Government Printing Office, 1886.

The Statutes at Large of the United States of America, from December, 1885, to March, 1887, and Recent Treaties, Postal Conventions, and Executive Proclamations. Vol. 24. Washington DC: Government Printing Office, 1887.

Stenhouse, Mrs. T. B. H. *"Tell It All": The Story of a Life's Experience in Mormonism.* Hartford, CT: A. D. Worthington, 1875.

Stowe, William W. *Going Abroad: European Travel in Nineteenth-Century American Culture.* Princeton, NJ: Princeton University Press, 1994.

Taylor, A. Elmina Shepard. Collection, 1844–1956. CHL.

Taylor, L. L., ed. *Past and Present of Appanoose County, Iowa: A Record of Settlement, Organization, Progress and Achievement.* 2 vols. Chicago: S. J. Clarke, 1913.

Third Ward, Liberty Stake. Primary Association Minutes and Records, 1879–1966. CHL.

Thirteenth Ward, Ensign Stake. Thirteenth Ward Relief Society Minutes and Records, 1868–1906. CHL.

Thirteenth Ward, Salt Lake Stake. Thirteenth Ward Relief Society Records, 1854–1857. CHL.

The Thirty Ninth Report of the American Home Missionary Society. Presented by the Executive Committee at the Anniversary Meeting, May 10, 1865. New York: John A. Gray and Green, 1865.

Thomas, E. A. "Female Suffrage in Wyoming." *Potter's American Monthly* 18 (May 1882): 492–495.

Thompson, Mercy Fielding. Autobiographical Sketch, 1880. CHL.

Thompson, Pamela Elizabeth Barlow. Papers, ca. 1875–1891. CHL.

Times and Seasons. Commerce/Nauvoo, IL. Nov. 1839–Feb. 1846.

Tullidge, Edward W. *Life of Brigham Young; or, Utah and Her Founders.* New York: Tullidge and Crandall, 1876.

————. *Tullidge's Histories, Containing the History of All the Northern, Eastern and Western Counties of Utah; Also the Counties of Southern Idaho, with a Biographical Appendix of Representative Men and Founders of the Cities and Counties; Also a Commercial Supplement, Historical.* Salt Lake City: Juvenile Instructor, 1889.

————. *The Women of Mormondom.* New York: Tullidge and Crandall, 1877.

Turley, Richard E., Jr., ed. *Selected Collections from the Archives of the Church of Jesus Christ of Latter-day Saints.* 2 vols. 74 DVDs. Provo, UT: Brigham Young University Press, 2002.

Turner, Raymond M., Janice E. Bowers, and Tony L. Burgess. *Sonoran Desert Plants: An Ecological Atlas.* Tucson: University of Arizona Press, 2005.

Tyler, Daniel. *A Concise History of the Mormon Battalion in the Mexican War, 1846–1847.* Salt Lake City: n.p., 1881.

Udall, David King, and Pearl Udall Nelson. *Arizona Pioneer Mormon: David King Udall, His Story and His Family, 1851–1938.* Tucson: Arizona Silhouettes, 1959.

Udall Family Correspondence Collection, 1859–1950. CHL.

U.S. and Canada Record Collection. FHL.

U.S. Bureau of the Census. Population Schedules. Microfilm. FHL.

Utah Department of Health. Vital Records and Statistics Death Certificates, 1904–1962.

Utah Department of Heritage and Arts, Cemeteries and Burials Database. http://utahdcc
.force.com/burials.

The Utah Directory, for 1883–84. Salt Lake City: J. C. Graham, 1883.

Utah Silk Association. Stock Certificate, Apr. 11, 1881. CHL.

Utah Territory Legislative Assembly. Utah Territory Legislative Assembly Papers, 1851–1872.
CHL.

Van Dyke, Blair G., and Lamar C. Berrett. "In the Footsteps of Orson Hyde: Subsequent
Dedications of the Holy Land." *BYU Studies* 47, no. 1 (2008): 57–93.

Van Wagenen, Lola. "In Their Own Behalf: The Politicization of Mormon Women and the
1870 Franchise." *Dialogue: A Journal of Mormon Thought* 24, no. 4 (Winter 1991): 31–43.

———. "Sister-Wives and Suffragists: Polygamy and the Politics of Woman Suffrage,
1870–1896." PhD diss., New York University, 1994. Also available as *Sister-Wives and
Suffragists: Polygamy and the Politics of Woman Suffrage, 1870–1896,* Dissertations in
Latter-day Saint History (Provo, UT: BYU Studies, 2003).

Van Wagoner, Richard S. *Sidney Rigdon: A Portrait of Religious Excess.* Salt Lake City:
Signature Books, 1994.

Walker, Francis A., comp. *Ninth Census–Volume I. The Statistics of the Population of the
United States, Embracing the Tables of Race, Nationality, Sex, Selected Ages, and
Occupations. To Which Are Added the Statistics of School Attendance and Illiteracy, of
Schools, Libraries, Newspapers and Periodicals, Churches, Pauperism and Crime, and of
Areas, Families, and Dwellings. Compiled, from the Original Returns of the Ninth Census,
(June 1, 1870,) under the Direction of the Secretary of the Interior.* Washington DC:
Government Printing Office, 1872.

Walker, Ronald W. "'Going to Meeting' in Salt Lake City's Thirteenth Ward, 1849–1881: A
Microanalysis." In *New Views of Mormon History: A Collection of Essays in Honor of
Leonard J. Arrington,* edited by Davis Bitton and Maureen Ursenbach Beecher, 138–161.
Salt Lake City: University of Utah Press, 1987.

———. "Lucy Mack Smith Speaks to the Nauvoo Saints." *BYU Studies* 32, nos. 1–2
(Winter and Spring 1992): 276–284.

———. "Rachel R. Grant: The Continuing Legacy of the Feminine Ideal." In *Supporting
Saints: Life Stories of Nineteenth-Century Mormons,* edited by Donald Q. Cannon and
David J. Whittaker, 17–42. Provo, UT: Religious Studies Center, Brigham Young
University, 1985.

———. "Toward a Reconstruction of Mormon and Indian Relations, 1847–1877." *BYU
Studies* 29, no. 4 (Fall 1989): 23–42.

———. *Wayward Saints: The Godbeites and Brigham Young.* Urbana: University of Illinois
Press, 1998.

Walker, Ronald W., and Doris R. Dant, eds. *Nearly Everything Imaginable: The Everyday
Life of Utah's Mormon Pioneers.* Studies in Latter-day Saint History. Provo, UT:
Brigham Young University Press, 1999.

Walker, Ronald W., Richard E. Turley Jr., and Glen M. Leonard. *Massacre at Mountain Meadows: An American Tragedy.* New York: Oxford University Press, 2008.

Warner, Elisha. *The History of Spanish Fork.* Spanish Fork, UT: Press Publishing, 1930.

Washington Post. Washington DC. 1877–1954.

Wasp. Nauvoo, IL. Apr. 1842–Apr. 1843.

Waspe, Ileen Ann. "The Status of Woman in the Philosophy of Mormonism from 1830 to 1845." Master's thesis, Brigham Young University, 1942.

Watson, Elden J. *Manuscript History of Brigham Young, 1846–1847.* Salt Lake City: By the author, 1971.

Watt, George D. Papers, ca. 1846–1865. CHL.

Weber Stake. Weber Stake Primary Association Minutes and Records, 1879–1968. CHL.

———. Weber Stake Relief Society Conference Minute Book, 1855–1899. CHL.

———. Weber Stake Relief Society Minutes and Records, 1867–1968. CHL.

Wells, Emmeline B., ed. *Charities and Philanthropies: Woman's Work in Utah.* Salt Lake City: George Q. Cannon and Sons, 1893.

———. Diaries, 1844–1920. 46 vols. L. Tom Perry Special Collections, Harold B. Lee Library, Brigham Young University, Provo, UT.

———. "The Grain Question." *Relief Society Bulletin* 1, no. 9 (Sept. 1914): 1–3.

Western Courier. Ravenna, OH. 1826–1833.

West Jordan Ward, West Jordan Utah South Stake. West Jordan Ward Relief Society Minutes and Records, 1868–1973. CHL.

Wheeler, Emily Anne Brooksby. "The Solitary Place Shall Be Glad for Them: Understanding and Treating Mormon Pioneer Gardens as Cultural Landscapes." Master's thesis, Utah State University, 2011.

Whitney, Orson F. *History of Utah.* 4 vols. Salt Lake City: George Q. Cannon and Sons, 1892–1904.

———. [Two poems:] *The Women of the Everlasting Covenant* and *The Land of Shinehah.* Salt Lake City: Deseret News, 1880.

Whittaker, David J. "The Bone in the Throat: Orson Pratt and the Public Announcement of Plural Marriage." *Western Historical Quarterly* 18, no. 3 (July 1987): 293–314.

Wilford Woodruff Stake Correspondence Files, 1887–1898. CHL.

Wilhelm, LeRoy C., and Mabel R. Wilhelm. *A History of the St. Johns Arizona Stake: A Triumph of Man and His Religion over the Perils of a Raw Frontier.* Orem, UT: Historical Publications, 1982.

Wilson, Brett. "Jane Shore and the Jacobites: Nicholas Rowe, the Pretender, and the National She-Tragedy." *ELH* 72 (Winter 2005): 823–843.

Wilson, Kami. "Substance versus Superficiality: Women's Prescribed Roles in Early Territorial Utah, 1850–70." *Journal of Mormon History* 32, no. 2 (Summer 2006): 139–172.

Woman's Exponent. Salt Lake City. 1872–1914.

Woman's Journal. Boston. 1870–1917.

Woman's Tribune. Beatrice, NE. 1883–1909.

Woodruff, Wilford. Journals, 1833–1898. Wilford Woodruff, Journals and Papers, 1828–

1898. CHL. Also available as *Wilford Woodruff's Journals, 1833–1898,* edited by Scott G. Kenney, 9 vols. (Midvale, UT: Signature Books, 1983–1985).

———. Journals and Papers, 1828–1898. CHL.

The Works of Thomas Goodwin, D.D., vol. 5. In *Nichol's Series of Standard Divines: Puritan Period,* edited by Rev. Thomas Smith. 12 vols. Edinburgh: James Nichol, 1863.

The Year of Jubilee. A Full Report of the Proceedings of the Fiftieth Annual Conference of the Church of Jesus Christ of Latter-day Saints, Held in the Large Tabernacle, Salt Lake City, Utah, April 6th, 7th and 8th, A. D. 1880. Salt Lake City: Deseret News, 1880.

Young, Ann Eliza. *Wife No. 19; or, The Story of a Life in Bondage, Being a Complete Exposé of Mormonism, and Revealing the Sorrows, Sacrifices and Sufferings of Women in Polygamy.* Hartford, CT: Dustin, Gilman, 1876.

Young, Brigham. Papers, 1832–1878. CHL.

Young, Emily Dow Partridge. Diary and Reminiscences, Feb. 1874–Nov. 1883. CHL.

Young, Zina D. H. Diary, 1844–1845. CHL. Also available as Maureen Ursenbach Beecher, ed., "'All Things Move in Order in the City': The Nauvoo Diary of Zina Diantha Huntington Jacobs," *BYU Studies* 19, no. 3 (Spring 1979): 285–320.

Young Ladies' Mutual Improvement Association. Certificate of Appointment to Carolina T. Thomas, ca. 1891. CHL.

Young Woman's Journal. Salt Lake City. 1889–1929.

Yount, Sylvia. "A 'New Century' for Women: Philadelphia's Centennial Exhibition and Domestic Reform." In *Philadelphia's Cultural Landscape: The Sartain Family Legacy,* edited by Katharine Martinez and Page Talbott, 149–160. Philadelphia: Temple University Press, 2000.

Zina Card Brown Family Collection, 1806–1972. CHL.

Zion's Cooperative Mercantile Institution. Zion's Cooperative Mercantile Institution Minutes, Oct. 1868–May 1973. CHL.

Acknowledgments

This volume is made possible through many individuals and institutions whose assistance and support span more than a decade. We give special thanks to administrators and officials of The Church of Jesus Christ of Latter-day Saints, Salt Lake City, for sponsoring the project, and to the management and staff of the Church History Library, Salt Lake City, where the majority of the documents in this volume are located.

In addition to the Church History Library, several other libraries and repositories have provided critical materials and assistance: Beinecke Rare Book and Manuscript Library, Yale University; Pioneer Memorial Museum, International Society Daughters of Utah Pioneers; Huntington Library; L. Tom Perry Special Collections, Harold B. Lee Library, Brigham Young University; Special Collections, J. Willard Marriott Library, University of Utah; and Special Collections and Archives, Merrill-Cazier Library, Utah State University.

We gratefully acknowledge two women whose foundational work provided the impetus for this project. The late Edyth Jenkins Romney, of what was then called the Church Historical Department, completed a transcript of the Nauvoo Relief Society minutes in 1979 that anchored the editors' initial work on this volume. Maureen Ursenbach Beecher, formerly of the Church Historical Department and Brigham Young University, generously shared with the editors her early 1980s research on Romney's transcript of the minutes.

This volume was initiated in 2001 at the Joseph Fielding Smith Institute for Latter-day Saint History at Brigham Young University, and we thank Ronald K. Esplin, then director, for his early support and encouragement. Marilyn R. Parks of the Smith Institute provided administrative assistance. Rebecca Boyce Hughes assisted with verification of initial transcripts. Kathryn M. Daynes of Brigham Young University and Cherry Bushman Silver reviewed early portions of the manuscript, and Sheree Maxwell Bench copyedited the first draft.

In 2005 the project moved to the Church History Department in Salt Lake City, where numerous employees, interns, missionaries, and volunteers have assisted in bringing the volume to completion. We express gratitude to Elder Marlin K. Jensen for his guidance of the project. Sharon E. Nielsen verified the transcript of the Nauvoo Relief Society Minute Book for the Joseph Smith Papers website, where the transcript was published on March 25, 2011. Rebekah Clark worked on the directory of biographies and helped to find and identify illustrations.

We acknowledge with appreciation the contributions of many other individuals from the Publications Division of the Church History Department. Gerrit J. Dirkmaat, Andrew H. Hedges, Robin S. Jensen, Michael Hubbard MacKay, and Alex D. Smith assisted with document verification, description, and annotation. Keaton T. Reed, Rachel Osborne, Amanda Owens, and Kimberly A. Dalton checked sources. Stephanie Steed checked sources and proofread the volume. Julia W. Ventura assisted with source citations in the biographical directory. Sharalyn D. Howcroft assisted with textual matters and permissions. Jeffrey G. Cannon helped identify illustrations and also assisted with permissions. Alison Palmer helped enter corrections into the typeset copy, helped edit the index, and typeset the index. Nathan N. Waite consulted on style and technology questions and helped edit the index. Caroline Bliss Larsen and Rachel I. Gessel helped edit the index. Kiersten Olson provided administrative assistance. We express special thanks to Riley M. Lorimer, who typeset the volume and assisted with design, editing, and managing the production process.

Additionally, we express gratitude to Christy Best for locating hard-to-find documents. We thank Ben E. Godfrey and Matthew McBride for leading the effort to design and create the website where the materials in this volume will be published. We express thanks to Welden C. Andersen for photographing the Nauvoo Relief Society Minute Book and to Jason D. Loscher and his associates for scanning or photographing many of the images in this volume. Thanks are also due to management and staff of Deseret Book Company, Salt Lake City, for their expertise in designing, printing, distributing, and marketing the volume. We particularly acknowledge Sheri L. Dew, Laurel Christensen Day, Lisa Roper, Amy Durham, Suzanne Brady, Richard Erickson, and David Kimball. We thank Debra Xavier for assisting with marketing. We are grateful to Margaret A. Hogan for her careful proofreading and to J. Naomi Linzer for creating the index in this volume.

A number of other people, many of them missionaries and volunteers at the Church History Library, contributed to the volume presented here, particularly in researching the individuals in the biographical directory: Everett Randolph Amis, Laura Anderson, Kathryn Esme Barnes, Joyce Bastian, Carolyn C. Beard, Marlene Breti, Cathy Chamberlain, Elizabeth Crane, Karen Lynn Davidson, Kelli Skinner Eyerly, Polly Flanders, Lauren Fuller, Deborah Gurtler, Patsy Hendrickson, Virlene Hirschi, Diane Jackson, John Stuart Jackson, James Aleksandr Jacobs, Beverly K. Jones, Hannah Jung, Viola Knecht, Keshia Lai, Allison McCord, Allison Morgan, Elizabeth Joy Mott, Andrea Nelson, Caroline Pedersen, Joy Reese, Brent Rogers, Marla Rogers, Shirley Larkins Romney, Karen Schvaneveldt, Paul Douglas Simpson, Jessica Snyder, Rita Somfai, Margaret J. Stair, Mark L. Staker, Rebecca Strein, Paula Stuart, Anissa Olson Taylor, Jean Taylor, Laura J. Tropple, Amy Amelia Anne Wallace, Maurine Carr Ward, LaKay Weber, Anita Wells, Brian Whitney, Judith Ann Wight, Nola Rae Wilkinson, and Kathleen Williams.

We extend special thanks to Ann Braude of Harvard Divinity School, Laurel Thatcher Ulrich of Harvard University, Kathleen Flake of the University of Virginia, Colleen McDannell of the University of Utah, and Jonathan A. Stapley, each of whom reviewed a draft of the entire volume and offered important comments and feedback.

Index

In addition to the documents themselves, introductory essays, annotation, and reference material have been indexed. Personal names are listed by their correct spellings, not by variant spellings that may be found in the documents, unless the correct spelling is unknown. Entries for married women are generally listed under the names used during the period covered by the volume. For example, Clarissa Ross Chase Young is indexed as "Chase Young, Clarissa Ross" because she was known by the married name Chase at the time she figures in this volume. Later married names were disregarded while alphabetizing this index; that is, "Chase Young, Clarissa Ross" appears before "Chase, Marianne." Any alternative names provided in parentheses were also ignored during alphabetization. Unidentified individuals, such as "Sister Davis," are included in this index. In addition to the biographical entries on pages 624–689 herein, short biographical summaries for about sixteen hundred individuals found in this volume are available at churchhistorianspress.org. The online directory also gives information about the possible identities of many people for whom identification is uncertain.

The abbreviation RS is used frequently in reference to the Relief Society. In subentry text, some Latter-day Saints, such as Eliza R. Snow (ERS), are referred to by initials. When found in an entry, "id." indicates an entry in the Biographical Directory for a person, "def." refers to a passage that defines the topic, and "illus." indicates a photograph or other illustration. Latter-day Saint wards in Salt Lake City are referred to in subentries by ward number without mention of the city name. The four time periods into which the volume is divided are referred to in this index by the following abbreviations:

Time Period	*Abbreviation*
Part 1: 1830, 1842–1845	Nauvoo RS
Part 2: 1854–1866	RS early Utah era
Part 3: 1867–1879	RS reestablishment era
Part 4: 1880–1892	RS general era

Dan, Mrs., 115
Dan, Sister, 120
Dana Rockwell, Elizabeth, 66
Dana, Ferra, 71
Dana, Margaret Kennedy Lusk, 63, 86
Daniel (biblical figure), 326
Daniels, Julia Beebe, 97
Daniels, Polly Larkcom, 74
Daniels, Sarah, 91
Daniels Winfield Taylor, Susan, 91
Darger, Martha Jackson Soper, 212
Daughters: mentors for BY's, xxxv, 353–354, 385–386; mothers' education of, 102, 127, 301, 411, 596; of Zion, xxvii–xxviii, 19, 35, 271, 353, 356, 371–372, 381–384, 386–388, 592–593
Davenport Kimball, Mary Marian, 123, 124
David, Martha Lloyd, 224
Davidson, Nancy H. Lytle, 85
Davis Watson, Annie, 470, 639 (id.)
Davis, Charles Augustus, 222, 639 (id.)
Davis Somerville Shepard Somerville, Eleanor Jane, 66
Davis, Emely, 131
Davis, Letitia Ann George, 222, 225–226, 639 (id.)
Davis, Mary, 81
Davis, Orpha Demill, 131
Davis, Ruth Kennan, 222, 224, 639 (id.)
Davis, Sally, 38, 41
Davis, Sarah, 47, 68
Davis, Sister, 387n416
Davis, Sophronia Fuller, 73
Davis Co., Utah Terr., 455
Davis Stake, Utah Terr.: Bountiful RS, 177, 182n18, 183, 474; Davis Stake RS quarterly conferences, 431, 461, 463–466, 474; Deseret Silk Association and, 455; Kaysville Ward RS, 454–456; Primary and, xxxv–xxxvi, 428–434, 429 (illus.), 458, 467, 474
Daynes, Joseph John, 591
Dayton, Permelia Bundy, 66
Dayton Bassett, Permelia Mindwell, 97
Deacons, xxv–xxvii, 31, 210n168, 285, 287n144, 288
Dean, Joseph Henry, 570–571
Debts as absolved, and fiftieth anniversary of church, 451
Decker, Delight Day, 190
Decker, Fanny Eliza Greene, 195
Decker Young, Harriet Page Wheeler, 53, 64, 639–640 (id.)
Defence of Polygamy (B. Pratt), 311, 480
Delany, Ann, 82
Delany, Eliza, 73
Delegations, overseas, 380–383. *See also* Proselytizing
Dell, S. M., 235
DeMill, Anna Knight, 80
Deming, Mary Ann, 89
Democratic Party, 524n287
Denmark, 439
Derby, Erastus H., 96
Derby, Ruhamah Burnham Knowlton, 48, 62, 68
Deseret, 184. *See also* Salt Lake City, Utah Terr.
Deseret Hospital, Salt Lake City: appointment of staff of, 506; articles of association of, 501; blessings and, 504–506; board of directors of, 499–500, 500 (illus.); choir performance during dedication of, 499; dedication of, 499–506; donations for, xxxv, 428, 498, 502, 506, 548; faith and, 504–506; harmony and, 501,

504; healing by men and, 440, 505, 568; healing by women and, 497; history of, 440, 497–498, 587, 609; Holy Ghost and, 502; hymns sung at dedication of, 499, 506; medical training and, 502; non-Mormons and, 497, 505; nursing and, 497; prayers at dedication of, 499, 505, 506; rules and regulations of, 502–503; statistics and, 548; Zion and, 505
Deseret News or *Deseret Evening News* (newspaper): Cullom Bill in, 305; Deseret Hospital dedication in, 497–506; editors of, 253; employment for women and, 253n51; "Female Relief Societies" editorial in, 253–255; "Female Relief Society" (ERS) in, 270–275; "Female Suffrage in Utah" editorial in, 333–337, 345n288; "Great Indignation Meeting" minutes in, 311–332; Ladies' Cooperative Retrenchment Society minutes in, 338–342; "Ladies Mass Meeting" in, 305–306; on parochial schools, 463n89; Quorum of the Twelve circular letter in, 451–453; RS reestablishment by BY in, 248–252, 270–271; JS sermon published in revised form in, 198–208, 448n43; ERS et al. correspondence on women suffrage in, 350–352; J. Taylor's preaching to women in, 410–412; BY's preaching to women in, 262–265, 294–304; YLMIA resolutions in, 355–357
Deseret Silk Association, 266n87, 455. *See also* Silk production (sericulture)
Deseret Sunday School Union: *Deseret Sunday School Union Music Book* and, 554, 556; history of, 428
Deuel, Eliza Avery Whiting, 91, 115
Deuel, Mary Whiting, 71, 106
Deuel, Mrs., 87
Devenport, Clarisa, 166
Devil (Satan): and attempts to dethrone God, 57–58, 205, 208; conflicts within the church and, 56–57, 93–94, 97, 130n289, 204; as evil one, 215; forgiveness versus, 78–79; guidance from JS against, 71; healing by women as not work of, 55, 203; men casting out, 202, 215n178; persecution of church and, 67, 155; resist evil and, 57, 205; speaking in tongues and, 59, 208; spiritual wife system and, 69, 93–94, 97, 130n289; unity versus, 56–57, 93–94, 97, 130n289, 204; women casting out, 53n150, 55, 201–203, 215, 448, 550. *See also* Evil spirits
DeVol, Delia Toby, 66
Dibble, Hannah Ann Dubois Smith, 53, 61, 96
Dickson, Mary Ann Stoddard, 73
Dickson, Nancy Stevens, 95
Dimick, Mary Ann Gates, 73
Dinwoody, Ellen Gore, 499
Discipline, church: disfellowshipment, 56n158, 78; excommunication, 30n97, 84n206, 130n289, 136, 142; institutional authority and, xxxi–xxxiii, 113, 272, 390, 392, 507, 515; manners and, 274, 407n467; officers' duties and, xxvii–xxviii, 54, 202, 285–289, 490, 550; pride and, 21, 263, 345, 355–356; vanity and, 356. *See also* Institutional authority; Institutional organization
Discourses. *See* Preaching
Disenfranchisement: in Greece, ancient, 335; mass meeting resolutions and, 319, 517–518, 521–525; plural marriage partners and, 305, 441, 517, 522n282, 524n288, 570; Utah women and, 319, 443, 447, 517–518, 522–524, 570, 584n468, 587n479, 593; women's rights movement and, 523–524

Hawley Wight, Mary, 89
Hawley, Sarah (Sally) Schrader, 72
Haws, Charlotte Harrington, 47, 48, 54
Hayes Dame, Lovina, 117
Hayes, Rutherford B., 444
Hayes, Sarah Ann Moore, 212
Hayle, Sarah, 64
Hayward, Ruth Hughes, 360
Hayward, Sister, 360
Head Whiting, Catharine Maggard, 53, 95
Head Oaks, Mary, 82
Head, Sarah, 47, 83
Head Bracken, Sarah, 82
Healing by men: blessings and, xxiv, 25; Deseret Hospital and, 440, 505, 568; faith and, 506; ordinances and, 540n329, 541n333; priesthood and, xxiv–xxv, 53n150, 55n156, 487n171; revelations and teachings of JS on, 55, 202
Healing by women: def., xxiii–xxiv; blessings and, xxiv, xxv, 55n156, 367, 477n146, 515n254, 533–534, 539, 541n333, 543, 552, 567; in Canada, 540; church conflict over, 55, 203; Deseret Hospital and, 440, 497; devil as cast out by women, 53n150, 55, 201–203, 215, 448, 550; faith and, xxiv–xxv, 55, 203, 208, 438, 448, 464n96, 487n171, 489, 506, 539, 540n328, 542, 567, 595; family life and, 19; Holy Ghost and, xxiii; Jesus Christ and, xxiv, xxv, 567; laying on of hands, xxiv–xxv, 52, 54–55, 59, 199, 203n109, 208, 489, 515, 542, 551, 606; migration to Utah Terr. and, xxiv; Nauvoo RS era and, 16, 85; ordinances and, xxix, 515–516, 539–540, 541n333; prayers for the sick, 203; priesthood and, xxiv–xxv, 540n329; RS general era and, xxiv–xxv, 464n96, 477, 489, 567; RS reestablishment era and, xxiv, 487, 516n255, 539n325; revelations and teachings of JS on, xxiii–xxiv, 54–55, 59, 199, 201–203, 208, 550; F. Richards's preaching on, 199, 438, 550–552; sealing and, 438; women's authority and, 53n150, 201, 438, 448, 539, 550–552. *See also* Anointing with oil; Washing; Women and priesthood
Health and illness: anointing with oil, 463, 489, 540n329; "Balm of Gilead" and, 460; of children, 261–263, 297–298, 459, 474, 487n171, 560; clothing requirements and, 264, 372; Deseret Hospital and, 440, 498–499; education and, 448; Female Council of Health, 179–180; home industries and, 363n350; meals and eating habits, xxxv, 242, 338, 340–342, 344, 349, 353, 412; medical training, 381, 387–388, 423, 440, 497, 530–531; medicinal plants, 363n350; midwifery, xxv, 179, 388n418, 440, 498n213, 502, 530–531, 532–534; Nauvoo climate and, 157, 274, 291; nursing and, 178, 387–388, 497, 502–503, 530, 533, 568; obedience and, 408; obstetrics, 387–388, 440, 497, 530, 533; smallpox, 298, 421, 423–424
Heap, Thomas, 125
Heaps, Mrs., 118
Heaven, law or order of, 6, 36, 270n99, 284, 284n133
Heavenly Father: "My Father in Heaven" (ERS) and, 172–175, 470, 474, 592; RS general era and, 569, 592–594; relocation and, 158, 615. *See also* God
Heavenly Mother, 16, 173–175
Helm Stewart, Elizabeth Howard, 81
Helsor, Martha Matilda Clinger, 85
Henderson, Brother, 104, 112
Henderson, Elizabeth Harris, 62

Henderson Tidwell, Elizabeth Jane, 95
Henderson Terry, Hannah Harris, 73
Henderson, Mary, 80, 88
Henderson Fleming Hobson, Nancy Simpson, 80
Hendricks (Hendryx) Albro, Catharine Lobdell, 64
Hendricks, Drusilla Dorris, 46, 86, 107, 110, 114, 117, 648 (id.)
Hendricks Bainbridge Gammel, Elizabeth, 81
Hendricks (Hendrix), Maria Louisa Lester, 89, 121
Hendrickson, Keziah Paddox, 64
Hennefer, Rebecca Ann Hays, 195, 196, 197, 648 (id.)
Herrick, Lester James, 405, 407, 410, 648 (id.)
Herrick, Sarah Ann Garner, 405, 406–407, 413, 422, 424, 545, 648 (id.)
Herriman, Clarissa Boynton, 97
Herriman, Fanny Ives Hampton, 91
Herr, Margaret String, 64, 68
Hess, Helena Julia Peterson, 458
Hess, John William, 431–432, 649 (id.)
Heywood, Serepta Maria Blodgett, 406, 425–427, 616, 649 (id.)
Hickerson, Sarah Woolsey Stephens, 91
Hierarchical system, xxiii, xxxi, 184–185, 204
Higbee McEwan, Amanda Melvina, 74
Higbee, Charlotte Woods Carter, 53
Higbee, Chauncey L., 67n175, 98n228
Higbee, Elias, 100n236, 520n74
Higbee, Francis M., 151n373
Higbee, Mrs., 41
Higbee, Sarah, 65, 86, 142, 144
Higbee, Sarah Ann Voorhees, 37
Higbee, Sarah Elizabeth Ward, 30, 649 (id.)
Higginbotham, Nancy Campbell (Cambel), 414n490
Higgins Chase, Almira, 91
Higgins, Sarah Blackman, 74
Hildreth, Louisa Merritt, 64
Hill, Agnes Hood, 122
Hill, Eliza, 63, 96
Hill, Margaret Fotheringham, 213
Hillman Coons, Sarah King, 37, 40–41, 142, 144, 649 (id.)
Hills, Elizabeth Ann Mansfield, 37
Hinson Ogle, Elizabeth Green, 91
Historian's Office, 24, 198–199, 305, 353, 354n313, 404, 409–410, 490–491
"History of Joseph Smith" (JS et al.) series, 42n122, 52n149, 185, 198–208, 215n178, 448
History of the Church (JS et al.), xix, 132, 137n312, 198–200
Hoagland, Abraham, 182, 209–210, 607, 649 (id.)
Hoagland Schwartz, Agnes Taylor Rich, 210, 212, 649–650 (id.)
Hoagland, Esther Ann Luce, 212
Hoagland, Margaret Quick, 212
Hoagland, Rebecca Merrill, 212
Hodge, Rebecca Rhoads, 74, 86, 109, 110, 118
Hodson, Maria Giller, 80
Holbrook, Eunice Dunning, 63, 86, 118, 280–281, 650 (id.)
Holden, Ruia Angeline Bliss, 88, 215, 217, 650 (id.)
Hole-in-the-Rock expedition, 553, 554
Holiness of women: Nauvoo RS era and, xxi, 70, 94; RS reestablishment era and, xxi–xxv, 149n364, 247, 355, 384

102, 111, 113, 118, 495, 597; overflow of members and, 42, 68, 77n195, 102–103, 127, 129, 152–153, 200; parliamentary procedure and, 33, 41, 133, 478, 566; prayers and, 28, 37, 42, 46, 49, 62, 65–66, 68, 72, 77, 87, 88, 91, 96, 102, 104, 106, 107, 108, 109, 111, 117, 118, 121, 123, 124, 125; schedule for, 26, 42; JS's attendance and, xviii–xix, xxi, xxiii–xxiv, 4, 25, 28, 30–31, 42–43, 52–59, 69–71, 75, 77n194, 78–79, 92–94, 127, 132, 139, 183, 272; wards and, 102, 103–125, 119n267

MEMBERSHIP

applications and qualifications for, xxvii n51, 10, 42, 53, 71–75, 77, 80–82, 85–86, 88–89, 91, 95–97, 115, 117, 122–125, 127, 129, 131, 149–150, 157, 549, 613; charter members and, 42, 145, 493, 597–598; committees for, 54, 92, 100–101, 149n364; and doubts about Nauvoo RS, 72, 134; duties and, xvii–xviii, xix, 4, 6n13, 10, 31–33, 36–37, 50, 54–57, 72, 77, 101–102, 127, 129–130, 550–551, 565; family life compared with, 104; immigrants and, 8, 45, 105, 119, 157–162; morality of, 7, 10, 12–14, 31, 36, 38–40, 43–44, 46–47, 53, 56, 69–70, 77, 92, 97–99, 127, 128–131, 151–152, 169, 274–275; self-care and, 229, 232

PREACHING

R. Cahoon and, 115–116; on evil spirits, xxii, 37, 39–40, 44–45, 47, 57, 66, 71, 76, 91, 93–94, 98, 205, 207; on repentance, 39, 78–79, 89, 128–129; revisions of JS's sermons, 42n122, 52n149, 185, 198–208, 215; by EHS, xxii, 7, 13, 18–20, 25; JS and, xviii–xix, xxi, xxiii, 4, 54–59, 78–79, 127; BY on suspension of organization and, 15, 168–171

PRESIDENT

def., xxvi–xxviii, xxxiii, xxxviii, 6–7, 13, 18–20, 621; elect lady title and, xxvi, 13, 18–20, 32, 271, 416, 495–496, 536; institutional organization and, xxvi–xxviii, 25, 31, 411, 471; ordination of, xxxiii, 6–7, 32, 471n123, 476, 549; precedents and, 7, 31, 42–43; term length for, 31. *See also* Smith Bidamon, Emma Hale (EHS)

Nauvoo Relief Society Minute Book: book for, xix, 22–24, 22 (illus.), 27 (illus.), 60 (illus.), 103 (illus.), 128 (illus.); Church History Library and, xix, 23–24; as constitution and model, xvii, xix, xix–xx, 4, 22, 24, 26, 31, 42–43, 198–199, 240, 266, 270, 380n427, 390, 490; dates and records in, 23–129, 96n225; as foundational document, xvii, xix, xxviii, 4; handwriting of individuals and, 23; possession of, xix, 24, 26, 198–199, 240, 270–271, 490; publications of, xix, 42n122, 52n149; record keeping and, xx, 25, 28n95, 492; reminiscences and, 26; title page of, 26, 27 (illus.), 28

Nauvoo temple, Ill.: blessings and, 54n155, 107; committee and, 43n126, 100, 115; construction and completion of, xxxvii, 5–9, 15, 32n105, 114, 164 (illus.), 166, 495; dedication ceremony for, 395n439; donations for, xxxvii, 8, 15, 32n105, 43n126, 100–102, 104, 106–107, 118, 163–167, 395n439, 416, 471n122, 495; family life and, 7; home industries and, 6, 24; marriage and, xxviii–xxxi, 348n296; ordinances and, xxviii–xxix, xxxi, 6–7, 9–10, 200, 202–203, 550, 613; plural marriage and, 348n296; reminiscences during RS fiftieth anniversary and, 32n105; revelations and teachings of JS and, xxviii, 9–10, 43n126, 100n235, 107n245, 550;

sealing and, 348n296; wards and, 102n238; Zion and daughters of Zion and, xxviii, 9, 43n126, 101

Nebraska, 587n481

Neibaur, Ellen Breakell, 89

Neilson, Sister, 556

Nelson, Jane Taylor, 63

Nelson Cotton, Martha, 73

Nelson, Mary S., 127

Nelson Kennedy, Rhoda, 73

Nephi (Book of Mormon figure), 181

Nephi Ward Relief Society, Utah Terr., xxiii, 358–364

Nesbit, William, 151n373

Netherlands, the (Holland), 610

Nevada, 437

Newberry, Mary Smith, 71, 74

Newcomb, Jemima Hunting, 83

Newell, (blank), 96

Newell Wilbur, Belinda Eddy, 115

Newell, Olive Comstock, 73

Newman Manwill, Losana Bentley, 64

New Mexico, 437

New York, and church, xvii, 3–4, 17, 19, 142, 163, 435, 586–587

New-York Messenger (Prophet) [newspaper], 130, 163, 165, 167

New York Times (newspaper), 333

New Zealand, 439, 610

Neyman Fisher, Jane Harper, 61, 89

Nicholson, N., 119

Nickerson, Huldah Chapman, 63

Nickerson, Mary Ann, 63, 85

Nickerson, Mrs., 118, 121

Nickerson, Sister, 107

Nickeson, Sister, 107, 125

Nicolson, Catherine, 80

Nielsen, Augusta Swenson, 534

Nielsen, George Gordon, 534

Nielsen, Jonas Ira, 534

Nielson, Jens, 554n367, 556, 661–662 (id.)

Nielson, Kirsten Jensen, 553, 556, 662 (id.)

Nixon, Eliza Hamson, 217

Nixon, Stephen, 217, 662 (id.)

Noah (biblical figure), 449

Noble, Mary Adeline Beman, 50

Noe, Sarah Jane, 48

Non-Mormons: charity donations from, 257, 261; charity from women's groups and, 6–8, 24, 34; Deseret Hospital and, 497, 505; economic self-sufficiency and, 240–241, 294; isolationism and, 237; leadership and, 257, 443; parochial schools and, 463, 568; political authority and, 433; RS's relationship with organizations and, 581, 588

Norris, Sarah Louisa Aber, 131

Norris, Sophronia Curtis, 47

North, Ariminta Howard, 80

Norway, 439

Nursing, 178, 387–388, 497, 502–503, 530, 533, 568

Nuttall, Leonard John, 471, 475, 499, 608, 662 (id.)

Nyman, Margaret J., 67n175

Nyman, Matilda J., 67n175

O

Oakes, Prudence Tremayne Barkdull, 62, 71, 90

Oakley Taylor, Mary Ann, 120

Treasurers (*continued*)

478n147, 556; RS reestablishment era and, 259n68, 260, 276–277, 277 (illus.), 280, 282, 288, 358, 616; reports from Relief Societies and, 492; Sandwich Islands RS and, 509n236. *See also* General treasurers; *and specific individuals*

Tryon, Rebecca Emma Conley, 89

Tullidge, Edward W.: *Life of Brigham Young*, 426–427; *The Women of Mormondom*, 8, 235–236, 247, 266n86, 331, 404, 418, 420, 424, 426–427

Turnbow, Deborah Ann Price Clements, 212

Turnbow, Maria Louisa Woodworth, 212

Turnbow, Sophronia Ellen Lenora, 212

Turner, Lucinda Morgan Howd, 64, 105

Turpin, Sarah Wooding Smith, 212

Tuttle Davenport, Catherine Vanever Geyer, 127

Twelfth Ward, Salt Lake City: history of, 257; Twelfth Ward RS and, 182n18, 190

Twentieth Ward Relief Society, Salt Lake City, 402–403

Twiggs, Martha Reed, 260

Twist, Jane Ann Chamberlain, 62

Tyler Pratt, Esther S. Annas, 89

Tyler, Ruth Welton, 66

U

Udall, David King, 560–561

Udall, Eliza Luella (Ella) Stewart, 439, 560–563, 682 (id.)

United States: American Indian and church land agreements and, 316; antipolygamy legislation opposition lobbying and, 443–444, 518; charity from non-Mormon women's groups and, 6–8, 24, 34; church land and property and, 168, 242, 305, 314, 316, 367n363, 443, 517, 570; and church, negative perception of, xxx, xxxiii, 14, 235–236, 390; *Congressional Record* and, 518, 524n287; Congress of, 443–444, 458, 518, 524, 525, 577–578; Cragin Bill and, 218, 243, 305, 318; Cullom Bill and, 243, 305–306, 309, 311–312, 320–321, 329, 334, 421; Democratic Party and, 524n287; economic self-sufficiency and, 237–238, 242; and elections, national, 350, 379n395, 458, 478–479; Fifteenth Amendment and, 333; kingdom of God and, 369; memorials in opposition to antipolygamy legislation and, 518, 525; Mexican-American War and Mormon Battalion and, 315–316, 324, 368–369, 611n536, 614; millennialism and, 238; morality and, 6; Mormon women's stereotypes and, xxxvi–xxxvii, 235–236, 243, 307, 323–324, 327, 336, 371, 375, 437, 441; opposition to church practices and, xxx, xxxvi–xxxvii, 177n2, 178, 186–187, 213–214, 218, 224n206, 226, 230n222, 233n227, 236, 237, 242–243, 445; patriotism and, 322, 367; plural marriage controversy and, xxx, xxxvi–xxxvii, 186, 235–236, 237, 242–243, 305, 317n237, 318n238; Poland Act and, 243–244, 312; political autonomy of church and, 237–238, 242–243, 444; poverty relief organizations and, 8n18; RS and culture of, 6–7, 24, 437; Republican Party and, 318, 320, 323, 333, 336n266, 367, 518, 524n287; JS's U.S. presidential candidacy and, 14; statehood for territories and, 437n5; Utah War and, 177n2, 186–187, 213, 214, 218, 224n206, 230, 236, 607; Wade Bill and, 243, 305; women's rights movement and, 237. *See also* Antipolygamy legislation; Antipolygamy legislation opposition;

Constitution, United States; Suffrage; Suffrage for women, and Utah Terr.; *and specific states and territories*

United States v. Reynolds (1878), 441

Unity: charity and, 8; church membership and, 443, 447; communication networks and, 437, 564; devil versus, 56–57, 93–94, 97, 130n289, 204; finances as threat against, 168; hierarchical system and, 184–185; institutional organization and, 437; Nauvoo RS minutes and, 5, 10, 14, 15n55, 91, 124, 129; ordinances and, 10; plural marriage as threat against, xxx, xxxiii, xxxvii, 7, 11–14, 15n55, 153, 165; political actions by women and, 7–9, 243; Quorum of the Twelve and, 5; RS early Utah era meetings and, 177, 184–185, 195n56, 196; RS general era and, 437, 443, 445–446, 447, 456n68, 529, 554–567, 589–591, 593; RS reestablishment era meetings and, 240–242, 245–247, 272–273, 410–412, 413, 417; teachings of JS and, 4, 10; ERS on, 273–274; succession as threat against, 165, 168, 170, 184; Utah Terr. settlement and, 184–185; visits to Relief Societies and, 564; women's practices and, xxxix; women's authority and, 7; Zion and, 10. *See also* Church conflicts; Conflicts; Opposition to church practices

University of Deseret (now University of Utah), 221n198, 299n186, 300n187, 301n188

Unmarried women, xxii n19, 254n57, 353, 542

Urie, Sarah Ann MacMillen Heyborne Farrell, 234

Utah Co., Utah Terr., 184, 197n70, 214

Utah Terr.: disenfranchisement of women and, 319, 443, 447, 517–518, 522–524, 570, 587n479, 593; governors of, 186–187, 280; history of, 178, 242–243; mining industry in, 240–241; parochial schools in, 463, 568; railroad and, xxxv, 238, 241, 262, 302, 399, 444, 562, 577nn444–445; suffrage for women in, 253n51, 333–337, 350, 365–366, 370n369, 379; telegraph and, 252, 300–303; Utah Silk Association and, 455n64, 469n116, 567n405. *See also specific cities and counties*

Utah Terr., and church: American Indians and, 179, 181–182, 188, 226–227, 614; antipolygamy legislation opposition and, 305–310, 319n239; centennial celebration fair and, 390; civil authority and, 184–186, 214, 218–219, 227, 229n221, 237; congressional delegates and, 444, 458, 577–578; Council of Health and, 179; demographic statistics and, 178; Female Council of Health and, 179; home industries and, 186; immigrants and, 178, 220–221, 228, 253n54, 439, 557–558; iron mining industry and, 227, 231; kingdom of God and, 184, 366–367, 426; Mountain Meadows Massacre and, 227, 229–230; order preservation and, 178; plural marriage and, 186, 214, 227, 237; priesthood and, 184, 186, 214; prosperity and, 316; purity and, 367–368; relocation to, 15–16, 177–178, 182–184, 209–210, 214, 217–218, 221n199, 228, 239, 268, 273, 315–316, 322–324, 326, 368–369, 391, 426, 430, 435, 606–608, 611, 613–615; relocation within, 187, 220–221, 454n59, 607; reminiscences and, 614–615; rural lives and, 378–379; separatism and, 184, 237–238, 445; smallpox and, 298, 421, 423–424; unity and, 184–185; Utah War and, 177n2, 186–187, 213, 214, 218, 224n206, 230, 236, 607; Zion and, 184–185, 237, 239–240, 381, 386, 557

Utah War, 177n2, 186–187, 213, 214, 218, 224n206, 230, 236, 607

Z